Fodor's 05

IRELAND

Where to Stay and Eat
for All Budgets

Must-See Sights
and Local Secrets

Ratings You Can Trust

Fodor's Travel Publications   New York, Toronto, London, Sydney, Auckland
www.fodors.com

FODOR'S IRELAND 2005

Editor: Robert I. C. Fisher

Editorial Production: Jacinta O'Halloran
Editorial Contributors: John Babb, Alannah Hopkin, Anto Howard, Catherine Morrison, Tom Swift
Maps: David Lindroth, *cartographer;* Rebecca Baer and Bob Blake, *map editors*
Design: Fabrizio La Rocca, *creative director;* Guido Caroti, *art director;* Moon Sun Kim, *cover designer;* Melanie Marin, *senior picture editor*
Production/Manufacturing: Robert B. Shields
Cover Photo (Dingle Peninsula): Nik Wheeler

ISBN 1–4000–1440–9

ISSN 0071-6464

SPECIAL SALES

Fodor's Travel Publications are available at special discounts for bulk purchases for sales promotions or premiums. Special editions, including personalized covers, excerpts of existing guides, and corporate imprints, can be created in large quantities for special needs. For more information, contact your local bookseller or write to Special Markets, Fodor's Travel Publications, 1745 Broadway, New York, New York 10019. Inquiries from Canada should be directed to your local Canadian bookseller or sent to Random House of Canada, Ltd., Marketing Department, 2775 Matheson Boulevard East, Mississauga, Ontario L4W 4P7. Inquiries from the United Kingdom should be sent to Fodor's Travel Publications, 20 Vauxhall Bridge Road, London SW1V 2SA, England.

AN IMPORTANT TIP & AN INVITATION

Although all prices, opening times, and other details in this book are based on information supplied to us at press time, changes occur all the time in the travel world, and Fodor's cannot accept responsibility for facts that become outdated or for inadvertent errors or omissions. So **always confirm information when it matters,** especially if you're making a detour to visit a specific place. Your experiences—positive and negative—matter to us. If we have missed or misstated something, **please write to us.** We follow up on all suggestions. Contact the Ireland editors at editors@fodors.com or c/o Fodor's at 1745 Broadway, New York, New York 10019.

PRINTED IN THE UNITED STATES OF AMERICA

10 9 8 7 6 5 4 3 2 1

DESTINATION: IRELAND

S it awhile in Dublin's Davy Byrne's pub, order a glass of stout and a bit of bread and cheese—as James Joyce once did—and pore over a map of Ireland. Beguiling place names fit for a Gaelic lullaby will fire your imagination—Ballyvourney, Labasheeda, Clonmacnoise, Lisdoonvara. In such rural towns as these you can start to divine the elusive nature of Irishness. Some say it has to do with the landscape whose greens shapeshift from pale emerald to deep forest to Éireann's own brilliant shade of Kelly. Others claim it is the civilized pace of local life and the fact that the Irish always take the time to smile at a stranger. Somehow, wherever you are, the "craic" or lively conversation seems to turn to Ireland's "Celtic Tiger" and booming economy, yet you'll be glad to hear—and see—that beneath the new affluence, that magical, Irish *thing* endures. You sense it as you ramble down a country lane at dusk, guided by the candlelight glow of a distant inn where, once inside, you are sure to find a cozy berth, a copy of the *Irish Times*, and a crowd so friendly, you'll be on first-name terms in minutes.

Tim Jarrell, Publisher

CONTENTS

ABOUT THIS BOOK

Once you've learned to find your way around the pages of *Fodor's Ireland 2005,* you'll be in great shape to find your way around your destination.

SELECTION

Our goal is to cover the best properties, sights, and activities in their category, as well as the most interesting communities to visit. We make a point of including local food-lovers' hot spots as well as neighborhood options, and we avoid all that's touristy unless it's really worth your time. It goes without saying that no property mentioned in the book has paid to be included.

RATINGS

Orange stars ★ denote sights and properties that our editors and writers consider Fodor's Choice, the very best in the area covered by the entire book. These, the best of the best, are listed in the Fodor's Choice section in the front of the book. Black stars ★ highlight the sights and properties we deem Highly Recommended, the don't-miss sights within any region. Use the index to find complete descriptions. In cities, sights pinpointed with numbered map bullets ❶ in the margins tend to be more important than those without bullets.

SPECIAL SPOTS

Pleasures & Pastimes focuses on types of experiences that reveal the spirit of the destination. Watch for Off the Beaten Path sights. If the munchies hit while you're exploring, look for Need a Break? suggestions.

TIME IT RIGHT

Check On the Calendar up front and chapters' Timing sections for weather and crowd overviews and best days and times to visit.

SEE IT ALL

Use Fodor's exclusive Great Itineraries as a model for your trip. (For a good overview of the entire destination, follow those that begin the book, or mix regional itineraries from several chapters.) In cities, Good Walks guide you to important sights in each neighborhood; ☞ indicates the starting points of walks and itineraries in the text and on the map.

BUDGET WELL

Hotel and restaurant price categories from ¢ to $$$$ are defined in the opening pages of each chapter—expect to find a balanced selection for every budget. For attractions, we always give standard adult admission fees; reductions are usually available for children, students, and senior citizens. AE, DC, MC, V following restaurant and hotel listings indicate whether American Express, Diners Club, MasterCard, or Visa are accepted.

BASIC INFO

Smart Travel Tips lists travel essentials for the entire area covered by the book; city- and region-specific basics end each chapter. To find the best way to get around, see individual modes of travel ("By Car," "By Train").

ON THE MAPS

Maps throughout the book show you what's where and help you find your way around. Black and orange numbered bullets ❶ ❶ in the text correlate to bullets on maps.

BACKGROUND	In general, we give background information within the chapters in the course of explaining sights as well as in Close-Up boxes and in Understanding Ireland at the end of the book. To get in the mood, review the suggestions in Books & Movies.
FIND IT FAST	Within the book, chapters are arranged in a roughly east-to-west-to north direction starting with Dublin. Chapters are divided into small regions, within which towns are covered in logical geographical order. Heads at the top of each page help you find what you need within a chapter.
DON'T FORGET	Restaurants are open for lunch and dinner daily unless we state otherwise; we mention dress only when there's a specific requirement and reservations only when they're essential or not accepted—it's always best to book ahead. If not noted otherwise, hotels have private baths, phone, TVs, and air-conditioning and operate on the European Plan (a.k.a. EP, meaning without meals), unless otherwise indicated (BP, breakfast plan with full breakfast; CP, Continental plan with Continental breakfast; FAP, full American plan, with all meals; MAP, modified American plan with breakfast and dinner). We always list facilities but not whether you'll be charged extra to use them, so when pricing accommodations, find out what's included.
SYMBOLS	

Many Listings

★ Fodor's Choice
★ Highly recommended
⊠ Physical address
✦ Directions
✐ Mailing address
☎ Telephone
🖶 Fax
⊕ On the Web
✉ E-mail
🖾 Admission fee
☉ Open/closed times
► Start of walk/itinerary
⊟ Credit cards

Outdoors

🏌 Golf
⛺ Camping

Hotels & Restaurants

🏨 Hotel
🛏 Number of rooms
✧ Facilities
🍽 Meal plans
✕ Restaurant
🖎 Reservations
🏛 Dress code
🚭 Smoking
🍷 BYOB
✕🏨 Hotel with restaurant that warrants a visit

Other

☢ Family-friendly
🛈 Contact information
⇨ See also
⊠ Branch address
☞ Take note

ON THE ROAD WITH FODOR'S

A trip takes you out of yourself. Concerns of life at home completely disappear, driven away by more immediate thoughts—about, say, what marvels will beguile the next day, or where you'll have dinner. That's where Fodor's comes in. We make sure that you know all your options, so that you don't miss something that's around the next bend just because you didn't know it was there. Because the best memories of your trip might well have nothing to do with what you came to Ireland to see, we guide you to sights large and small all over the region. You might set out to explore Georgian Dublin and shop on Grafton Street, but back at home you find yourself unable to forget the rugged coast, the languid days of golfing or fly-fishing, and the out-of-the-way pubs you discovered. With Fodor's at your side, serendipitous discoveries are never far away.

Our success in showing you every corner of the Emerald Isle is a credit to our extraordinary writers. Although there's no substitute for travel advice from a good friend who knows your style, our contributors are the next best thing—the kind of people you would poll for travel advice if you knew them.

For our coverage of Dublin, Anto Howard has checked every fact, burnished every metaphor to the fine gleam of ancient brogues, and has so lovingly described the towns and villages found in the Dublin Environs chapter that even their natives will leave for the pleasure of coming back. Six post-graduate years of living in New York City recently convinced Anto of the charms of his native Ireland and he duly returned to take up residence in Dublin. He has written and edited books and articles about such far-flung places as Costa Rica, Las Vegas, and Russia, and has contributed to such publications as *National Geographic Traveler* and *Esat Online*. Anto (christened Anthony—Dubliners have a habit of abbreviating perfectly

good names) is also a playwright, and his shows have been produced in Dublin and in New York.

Not even the most polished prose was an adequate substitute for the thrill of first-hand experience for journalist and playwright Tom Swift, so he hit the road and deliciously updated our chapters on the Midlands and the Southeast. Though a Dubliner born and bred, he's always had close links with both regions: as a child he was lucky enough to spend summers getting sunburned on the golden beaches of the "costa del Wexford" and also had the good fortune to spend other holidays in the (slightly rainier) environs of Coole, County Westmeath. When not traveling the highways and byways, Tom is associated with the award-winning Irish theater company The Performance Corporation. He is also a radio broadcaster and documentary producer, and lives—almost "beyond the Pale"—in Maynooth, County Kildare.

Alannah Hopkin grew up in London but spent most of her childhood summers on her uncle's farm near Kinsale, where she learned two of the most important things in life: how to ride a horse and how to sail a boat. After graduate studies in Irish literature, she worked as a writer in London—but ancestral voices were calling her home, and she spend more and more time in County Cork, where horses and boats were easier to find. After publishing her first novel, *A Joke Goes A Long Way in the Country,* she made the big leap, and moved to Kinsale for a trial six months—and is still there 20 years later. Another novel was followed by a book on the cult of St. Patrick and an acclaimed guide to the pleasures of County Cork. She has written on travel and the arts for the London *Sunday Times,* contributes regularly to the *Irish Examiner* and the *Irish Times,* and is writing a book on West Cork. She has worked on *Fodor's Ireland* since 1985, and this year she updated the Southwest and the West chapters. Just when she thinks she's seen everything her regions have to offer, she makes another discovery—and Fodor's is the clear winner.

Born and bred (if not buttered) in Belfast, Catherine Morrison is a true Belfastian through and through. A native of the beautiful but divided city, Catherine grew up there during the Troubles, and intends to stick around to see Belfast blossom in more peaceful times. Red of hair, but not of temperament, she spent a brief hiatus in Dublin studying literature and history but moved back home to start her journalistic career. While "Norn Iron," as it is pronounced by locals, is still coming to terms with its checkered past, its future looks bright. After all, you can now get a really good cappuccino in Belfast's city cen-ter—a must for this caffeine aficionado. Usually found with her nose in a book in one of Belfast's many parks, Catherine works as a reporter for the newspaper daily, the *Irish News,* and has contributed articles to other national newspapers. For this edition, Catherine blew the dust off the Northern Ireland and Northwest chapters, bringing both up to date.

Updater extraordinaire of our Essential Information chapter, John Babb honed his journalistic skills at the Canadian Broadcasting Corporation in Toronto before he moved to Warsaw, Poland, where he spent two years working as a business journalist. He has been laying low in Dublin for the last few years, studying Irish culture.

① Dublin

"All changed, changed utterly." Yeats could have talking about the last decade in Dublin, which has seen this once sleepy port city of a peripheral nation transformed into the thriving, trendsetting, triumphalist capital of Europe's fastest growing economy. Ireland, and Dublin in particular, are now importers of people. As the locals often say, "You can't walk up O'Connell Street without bumping into a new arrival to the city." What a change from a decade ago, when Dublin was the departure point for many Irish "taking the boat" to the U.K. and beyond. Spanish, Chinese, Middle Eastern, South American: this new cosmopolitan mix, when added to Dubliners' innate sense of how to have a good time, has given the city a vibrancy and adventurous vibe that is quite infectious. These new influences have also dramatically improved the dining and shopping landscapes in a city once famed for fake shamrocks and three types of potatoes on one dinner plate.

Despite all the change, a lot of what Joyce called his "dear, dirty Dublin's charm still gathers around the old rituals and traditions. Behind the hustle and bustle of the "Celtic Tiger" economy lies an intimate capital that's a graceful mix of elegant Georgian buildings, wrought-iron canals and bridges, an army of booksellers, and 800-odd pubs. Ireland chooses to exempt artists from taxes, designating them national resources of sorts, and filmmakers, painters, and writers are part of the local scenery, along with the "rale Dubs," or "jackeens"—the breezy natives.

On both sides of the River Liffey, within a comfortable walking space, are sights that nearly encompass the city's entire history. Let's not forget that Dublin has been, in sequence, a Celtic settlement, a Norse encampment, and the citadel-seat of the British colonizers. **Christ Church Cathedral** sits atop the hill where Dublin is said to have been founded over a thousand years ago. It looks down with solemn authority on the river as it meanders up toward the merely 400-year-old splendor of **Trinity College**—whose Old Library is home to the *Book of Kells*—and its enclosed, cobblestoned campus. The elegant and pricey shops of nearby **Grafton Street** will lead you down towards peaceful **St. Stephen's Green** and the wonderful **National Museum**. Any Whitman's Sampler of mustsees also includes **St. Patrick's Cathedral**, the **Gate Theatre**, the **James Joyce Cultural Centre**, and the **National Gallery of Art**, with its spectacular collections of old master paintings. And let's not forget the **Hugh Lane Dublin City Gallery**, aglow with Picassos in a grand Palladian town house, or the **Dublin Writers Museum**, or the antique shops of the **Liberties**, the hip scene-arenas of **Temple Bar**, and the hyper-elegant Georgian mansions that line **Merrion Square**.

But the real pleasures of Dublin are not measured in granite and mortar. They are afternoon tea at the **Shelbourne Hotel**, with scones slathered with Kerry Gold butter; a sneaky, early-evening pint in serene **Grogan's** on South William Street, with the sun demanding entrance through the smoke-stained windows and the collection of paintings (done by the clientele) looking down with envy from the walls; or your own cozy guest house with a breakfast "the likes of which you'll never see again" (as your landlady will perhaps promise). Add to these ageless pleasures Dublin's amazing economic and cultural renaissance and you'll find it a colossally entertaining city, all the more astonishing considering its relatively small size.

② Dublin Environs

Ireland's tumultuous history of conflict, myth, romance, and war are all deeply present in the beautiful landscape of the Pale, the area directly surrounding Dublin. County Meath is at the center of Irish Celtic mythology, and the ancient passage graves at **Newgrange** in the Boyne Valley and the Druidic stronghold of the **Hill of Tara** stand as solemn reminders of a vibrant, pre-Christian Ireland. How ironic then that this sacred native area, along with parts of Kildare and Wicklow to the south, were also those most strongly influenced by English rule. Stunningly beautiful ancestral homes of the dwindling members of the Anglo-Irish ascendancy dot the landscape, and lords and baronets down on their luck have turned hoteliers and welcome guests with adaptable grace. The Palladian masterpiece of **Castletown House** in Celbridge, County Kildare, and the studied grandeur of **Powerscourt House and Gardens** stand out as fine examples of the golden age of the "Big House."

From many of Dublin's wider streets you can turn south and enjoy the verdant, rolling hills of the Wicklow Mountains, tantalizingly close to the capital's southern edge. The county of Wicklow contains arguably the most peaceful place in Ireland, the evocative monastic settlement at **Glendalough.** Wicklow's scenic wooded valley is also home to abbeys, castles, great houses, and gardens. Further north lies the "wee county" of Louth and the dark and brooding Cooley Peninsula. It is here, by the coast of the Irish Sea and in the foothills of the Mourne Mountains that the greatest of Irish heroes, doomed Cuchculainn, fought his great battles and loved and lost the three women who dominated his emotional life.

Other delights await, including the 18th-century town of **Drogheda; Mellifont Abbey,** the first Cistercian monastery in Ireland; the high cross found at **Monasterboice; Mount Usher Gardens;** and the fabled estate of **Russborough.** Its Vermeers now hang in the National Gallery, but there are plenty of other treasures on view at this great Georgian-era house.

③ The Midlands

On you travels through the rest of Ireland you may often hear jokes about the "boring midlands." Write them all down, then consign them to the fire. The flat, fertile plain at the center of Ireland, broken up into small, fiercely tribal counties, is full of relatively undiscovered and uncrowded treasures such as historic towns, abbey ruins, grand houses, and a gamut of outdoor activities—including some of Europe's finest fishing. In fact, water is the life force in this area, with the River Shannon from the west feeding into countless dark-blue lakes like **Lough Derg.** A slow, carefree boat trip down the great river is the best way to appreciate the changing landscape and atmosphere of the region.

The unique, chocolate-brown landscape of Irish boglands is prevalent around the town of **Shannonbridge** in County Offaly. County Tipperary's rolling green flatlands and **Galtee Mountains** are known for champion greyhounds and the stud farms that have turned out winners for generations. The glories of the fading Anglo-Irish tradition are still visible in old stately homes like **Strokestown House, Birr Castle Gardens, Belvedere House Gardens;** the romantic, neo-Gothic toy castles of **Charleville Forest** and **Tullynally;** and at those landmarks of Irish Palladian elegance, **Emo Court** and **Bellamont Forest.** Early Christian Ireland found a spiritual home in parts of the Midlands, as witnessed by the beautifully melancholic monastic ruins of **Clonmacnoise.** These often forgotten counties at the center of Ireland also offer you the chance to get a little closer to the real pace and heartbeat of the natives. In other words, since they see less tourists, they'll probably be happier to see you.

(4) The Southeast

Topographically the "Sunny Southeast" is an invitation to invasion. Rich pastureland extends to a coastline of estuarial mudflats; low cliffs that fringe deep bays; and long, sandy beaches. First the Vikings and afterwards the Normans heeded the call and changed the history of Ireland forever. County Wexford was named by the Vikings after the consort of their one-eyed god Odin; it still bears the stamp of those fearless, seagoing settlers in its steep pathways and fine seafood of **Wexford Town.** Dubliners by the thousands are drawn to the busy, British-style seaside town of **Tramore** in Waterford. But there are much more tranquil and beautiful little fishing villages dotting the coast, like whisper-quiet **Fethard-on-Sea,** where you can watch fishermen set out in the morning and buy the best of their catch at their twilight return.

Kilkenny is one of Ireland's finest medieval cities, known for its artisans and dominated by mighty **Kilkenny Castle,** home of the once-great Butler family for more than 500 years. Stand in the 150-foot-long Long Gallery and gaze upon the faded portraits and frayed tapestries that whisper of days of yore. **Waterford City,** where the eponymous crystal is made at the confluence of three great rivers—the Nore, the Barrow, and the Suir—is home to thousand-year-old **Reginald's Tower,** a stern, unmoving monument to the part played by architecture and technology in the invasions of Ireland. There's some beautiful, rolling, "forty-shades-of-green" landscapes in Tipperary's Golden Vale, but everything else is put in the shade by the stunning **Rock of Cashel.** Seat of the kings of Munster for 700 years (it's where St. Patrick said his first mass in Ireland), the proud fortress on a hill was, along with Cahir Castle, one of the few places to resist Cromwell's hordes.

5 The Southwest

If you've ever seen a stereotypical postcard of Ireland—you know the type: thatched, whitewashed cottage, stone walls, a donkey meandering down Main Street—chances are the picture was taken somewhere in the Southwest. **Killarney, Kinsale, Bantry Bay;** even the names are evocative of everything Irish, and anyone who visits the counties of Cork, Kerry, and Limerick is guaranteed a visual and emotional taste of the (literally) emerald isle.

"The People's Republic of **Cork**" is what locals like to call this Rebel county, emphasizing their determination, Texas-style, to be different from the rest of the country. The county lends its name to Ireland's second-largest city, a port town that's full of canals and bridges and has a bustling mercantile center, as well as the country's best food market in the English Market. Cork was once home to writers Sean O'Faolain and Frank O'Connor, and is today a city of sport. Its team is always in the championship finals of hurling, that fast and furious ancient game that makes soccer look like kick the can. The city is also one of the few places where the 2,000-year-old game of road bowling is still played. If your taste runs to less athletic entertainment, head for the exquisite seaside village of **Kinsale,** long considered Ireland's culinary capital for its amazing density of quality restaurants and its annual Festival of Fine Food. The coastal road from Kinsale to wooded **Glengarriff** takes you through the rugged splendor of West Cork. The wild, tempestuous sea is the undoubted star of the trip, but the market town of **Skibbereen,** the crescent-shape fishing village of **Baltimore,** and the proud 18th-century majesty of **Bantry House** are all well worth a visit.

Kerry, too, has a nickname: "The Kingdom." Its natives will argue with all comers that it remains the most beautiful and inspirational county in Ireland. Two great peninsulas dominate the county's wild, rocky coast. The Iveragh Peninsula, known by everyone as **The Ring of Kerry,** is arguably Ireland's most popular tourist drive. Starting in Killarney, it winds around tiny roads, passing through tiny villages like **Sneem,** past the magisterial, world's-end, rock islands of the **Skelligs** (once seen, never forgotten), before ending in **Kenmare,** a market town nestled on the Kenmare River estuary. The **Dingle Peninsula** is dominated by the large, celebrity-popular (Julia Roberts has been spotted hiding out here) town of **Dingle.** On the peninsula itself, seabirds reel and wild donkeys graze among hedges awash in crimson velvet flowers; fields explode with deep yellow gorse, may-blossom, and honeysuckle against a dark-blue sky.

Frank McCourt's best-selling *Angela's Ashes* paints a grim picture of **Limerick City.** But Ireland's fourth-largest city, sitting proudly on the banks of the Shannon, although still beset with social problems, is home to the magnificent Hunt Museum and its famed collections of Celtic and medieval treasures. The surrounding countryside is not as wild and romantic as Cork or Kerry, but it does possess a couple of Ireland's most impressive stately homes open for accommodation; the Irish Gothic dottiness of **Glin Castle** and the Victorian Gothic splendor of **Adare Manor** (where Sir Paul McCartney and his Heather got hitched).

6 The West

Haunting might be the best word to describe the mysterious West, the most underpopulated part of Ireland, where you can sometimes go half a day across the beautiful, barren landscape without sight or sound of another human being. A journey through the counties of Clare, Galway, and Mayo will take you from the moonscape limestone of the **Burren** to the majestic **Cliffs of Moher** to the looming **Twelve Bens. Galway** is Ireland's fastest growing city and a buzzing university town that seems to host a different arts festival every second month. It is also the departure point for the sublime and spooky **Aran Islands,** celebrated by playwright J. M. Synge in *Riders to the Sea.* Here you'll hear lilting Irish spoken as a first language, just as it was a thousand years ago. Just to the west are the wild shores and dark, brooding mountains of **Connemara,** loved by painters, writers, and seekers of silence. Towns like **Clifden** and **Leenane** (situated on Ireland's only fjord) ring out with the sound of pipe, whistle, and fiddle, as nearly every pub houses hosts wild and impromptu traditional music sessions. It is another Gaeltacht (Irish-speaking area) and known for its ponies—descendants of the Andalusian horses that swam ashore from the Spanish fleet and bred with Celtic stock legendarily descended from Ice Age horses. The wildness of the west ends at Mayo, to the north, whose quiet, deep-green scenery has always appealed to discerning travelers.

Westport is a prosperous fishing town nestled on an inlet of Clew Bay, a wide expanse of sea dotted with islands and framed by mountains. Nearby beaches offer crystal-clear sand and azure Atlantic waters. On a clear day you can look out to **Achill Island,** with its wonderful cliff walks, acres of bog and wild heather, and empty beaches. Other must-dos include Lady Gregory's **Coole Park**; the picture-perfect village of **Kinvara**; the spectacular Gothic Revival house of **Kylemore Abbey**; and some of the grandest hotels in the land, including **Dromoland Castle** and **Ashford Castle,** the latter set near Cong, the pretty village where *The Quiet Man* was filmed.

7 The Northwest

The best-kept secret in Ireland, the enchanting Northwest is often overlooked by tourists because of its distance from Dublin. It's their loss. In a region full of self-sufficiency and confidence, where the greeting you receive is all the warmer because of the lack of visitors, you can observe rural Ireland at work and play amid some of the most stunning natural backdrops anywhere.

If Galway belongs to Synge, then Sligo will forever be Yeats Country. Ireland's greatest poet drew much of his inspiration from the fickle skies that change color with a whisper of wind, the incredible spectrum of reds and purples thrown up by the gorse- and heather-filled fields surrounded by dry stone walls, and the unforgiving Atlantic Ocean, that beats a relentless rhythm against ancient rocks at Rosses Point. Yeats even demanded to be buried here, "Under Ben Bulben," and not far from his mysterious Lake Isle of Innisfree. The county is overwhelmingly rural, but deceptively lively **Sligo Town** is a charming oasis of culture and good food.

County Donegal, in the far northwest, is ruggedly beautiful, with a rocky coast, turbulent surf, forlorn mountains, and windswept plateaus. It is full of legends about giants and witches, not to mention fairies known as *pishogues*. Irish is widely spoken here, and the music is famous; traditional groups, such as Clannad and De Dannaan, named after the prehistoric followers of the goddess Dana, are local heroes. When Enya, daughter of local musicians, hit the top of the charts in Europe and the United States with her Irish–New Age instrumentals, the roof flew off a pub in Gweedore, where spontaneous sessions for the music-loving community are regular happenings. Heading north, you'll find the waters of the astonishingly beautiful **Gartan Lough**, the 19th-century folly castle that lords over haunted **Glenveagh National Park**, and the **Inishowen Peninsula**, the most northerly point in Ireland.

8 Northern Ireland

The return of peace to Northern Ireland in the mid 1990s, after three decades of The Troubles, has at last opened up this relatively undiscovered country to the adventurous traveler. A new atmosphere is in the air—that wonderful, underrated scent of normalcy—and it seems to add an extra sheen to the whole region. From the countless new bars and restaurants of reborn **Belfast** north to the geological freak of the **Giant's Causeway**, through the wild Sperrin Mountains, inside the medieval walls of historic **Derry**, and down to serene Lough Erene, the whole province seems to have come back to life. The region is also known for the beauty of the Antrim Coast, a truly spectacular one-day drive from Carncastle to Bushmills. Inland lie the Celtic homelands of the **Glens of Antrim**, one of the fabled redoubts of the "wee folk"; the rich farmlands and lakelands of Fermanagh, where you'll experience the Irish farmer in all his stubborn splendor; the austere Mourne Mountains looking out over the Irish Sea; and many of the most beautiful 18th-century Anglo-Irish treasure houses, including **Florence Court**—its forest is reputedly haunted by the fairy world—and **Castle Coole, Castle Ward**, and **Mount Stewart**, which proudly flaunts its famous George Stubbs painting of the racehorse Hambletonian. People are as friendly and witty here as they are in the republic, but after all they've been through, they are truly happy to witness the sight of visitors coming to admire the beauty and history of Ulster.

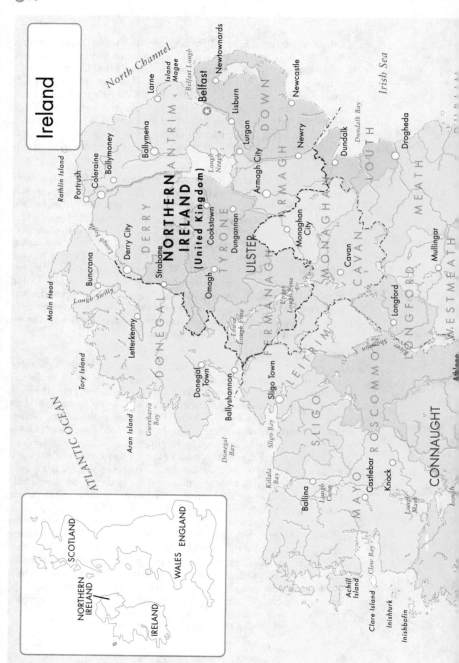

Ireland

North Channel
Irish Sea
ATLANTIC OCEAN

NORTHERN IRELAND
(United Kingdom)

ULSTER
CONNAUGHT

Rathlin Island
Tory Island
Aran Island
Malin Head
Achill Island
Clare Island
Inishturk
Inishbofin

Portrush
Coleraine
Ballymoney
Ballymena
Larne
Island Magee
Belfast Lough
Belfast
Newtownards
Lisburn
Lurgan
Newcastle
Newry
Dundalk
Dundalk Bay
Drogheda
Buncrana
Letterkenny
Derry City
Strabane
Cookstown
Dungannon
Armagh City
Monaghan City
Omagh
Cavan
Longford
Mullingar
Donegal Town
Ballyshannon
Sligo Town
Castlebar
Knock
Ballina
Lough Swilly
Gweebarra Bay
Donegal Bay
Killala Bay
Sligo Bay
Clew Bay
Lough Neagh
Upper Lough Erne
Lower Lough Erne
Lough Conn
Lough Mask

ANTRIM
DERRY
DONEGAL
TYRONE
FERMANAGH
ARMAGH
DOWN
MONAGHAN
CAVAN
LEITRIM
SLIGO
MAYO
ROSCOMMON
LONGFORD
WESTMEATH
MEATH
LOUTH

Shannon River

SCOTLAND
NORTHERN IRELAND
IRELAND
WALES
ENGLAND

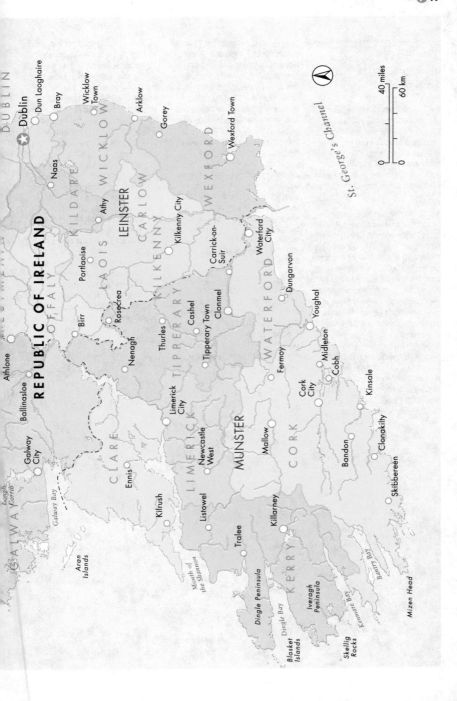

The East & the South
5 to 8 days

Dublin's literary charm and Georgian riches, and rugged County Wicklow and the historic Meath plains are all just a few hours' drive apart. In the south you'll find fishing towns and bustling markets, coastal panoramas, and stunning mountain-and-lake scenery.

DUBLIN

1 to 3 days. James Joyce's Dublin holds treasures for all sorts. Literary types: explore Trinity College, Beckett's stomping grounds, and its legendary *Book of Kells*. Visit key Joyce sights, the Dublin Writers Museum, and indulge in the *Dublin Literary Pub Crawl*. Joyce fanatics: arrive a week before Bloomsday (June 16) for Bloomstime celebrations. Literary or not, stroll around the city center and take in the elegant Georgian architecture around St. Stephen's Green, austere Dublin Castle, and the national treasures in the museums around Merrion Square and pedestrianized Grafton Street. Check out Temple Bar, Dublin's hip zone, and join locals in this city-of-1,000-pubs for a foamy pint in the late afternoon. Pay your respects by taking a tour of the ever-popular Guinness Brewery and Storehouse. Night options: catch a show at W. B. Yeats's old stomping grounds, the Abbey Theatre; see some Victorian music hall shows at the Olympia Theatre; or listen to traditional or alternative music at a pub or other venue. Spend as much time as you can muster in pubs—the real center of Dublin activity. Last-call arrives early, even here, so if you're still revved, go to Lesson Street and hit the nightclubs. For a dose of unmitigated Irish enthusiasm, join the roaring crowds at Croke Park and see some traditional Gaelic football and hurling.

BOYNE VALLEY & COUNTY WICKLOW

2 days. Rent a car or join an organized tour and head out to the Boyne Valley, a short trip north of the capital. Spend the morning walking among the Iron Age ruins of the rolling Hill of Tara. After a picnic lunch on top of the hill, drive through ancient Kells and then to Newgrange, one of Europe's most spectacular prehistoric tombs. One thousand years older than Stonehenge, the great white-quartz structure merits two or three hours. Spend the rest of your day driving through the low hills and valleys of County Meath and to the Georgian village of Slane. Dominating the town are elegant Slane Castle and 500-foot Slane Hill. Backtrack to Kells or continue on to Drogheda and spend the night. The following day, drive through the County Wicklow mountains. You might want to stop in one of the small, quiet towns along the Wicklow Way hiking trail and go for a short hike. Drive on to stately Powerscourt House, whose grounds are perhaps the finest in the country. On the way to Glendalough and the medieval monastery of the hermit St. Kevin, stop for a bite in Roundwood, Ireland's highest village.

WEST CORK & KERRY

2 days. Head southwest to Cork City, perfect for half a day of walking. Drive directly south to Kinsale, an old fishing town turned resort, with many good restaurants. A slow 3- or 4-hour drive along the coast and up through the small towns of West Cork takes you through the kind of landscape that inspired Ireland's nickname, the Emerald Isle. Spend the night in the market town of Skibbereen. Next morning, cross into County Kerry and head straight for Killarney, right at the center of a scattering of azure lakes and heather-clad mountains. It's a good base for exploring your pick of three great Atlantic-pounded peninsulas: the Beara Peninsula, the Ring of Kerry, and the Dingle Peninsula. All offer stunning ocean views, hilly landscapes, and welcoming towns with good B&Bs. The five-hour drive back to Dublin takes you through Limerick City and the lakes of the Midlands.

Irish Manors & Castles

5 to 7 days

If you have an interest in architecture, interior design, and history (including the sinister and macabre kind), consider a tour of Ireland's manors and castles. You might even decide to splurge and stay at one of the grand country-house hotels along the way. It's best to go between June and September, when most houses are open.

DUBLIN & ENVIRONS

2 to 3 days. Right in the center of Dublin are historic Dublin Castle and the elegant, 18th-century Royal Hospital Kilmainham. Walk along the inner-city stretch of the River Liffey for excellent views of two of architect James Gandon's Georgian masterpieces, the Custom House and the Four Courts. South of the river, Georgian domestic town architecture is at its best on Merrion Square and Fitzwilliam Street. On Day 2 go west of Dublin to Castletown House, one of Ireland's most magnificent Georgian structures, in Celbridge, County Kildare; it serves as the headquarters of the Irish Georgian Society. From here head south into County Wicklow to visit Russborough House near Blessington.

THE ROAD TO CORK

1 day. Leave early from Dublin, heading southwest to Cork. On the way, stop in Portarlington to visit the Emo Court and Gardens, another James Gandon design and one of the finest large country houses near Dublin open to the public. You'll pass the Rock of Cashel on your way to Cahir Castle. Continue to Cork City. If you have time, stop at the coastal bulwark Charles Fort, about half an hour south of the city. Spend the night in Cork.

AROUND KILLARNEY

2 to 3 days. From Cork City, a short detour off the main road to Killarney leads to ruined 15th-century Blarney Castle, where you can kiss the famed Blarney Stone. Nearby Blarney House was built in 1784 in Scottish baronial style. In Killarney National Park, Muckross House, a mid-Victorian manor, is worth seeing for its grounds full of flowers and outstanding rock garden. After a night in Killarney, head north to the Shannon estuary, on whose shore looms Glin Castle, ancestral home of the great Anglo-Norman FitzGeralds. Stop for tea or dinner at Adare Manor. Stay overnight in or near Limerick City or Ennis.

MAP KEY

Irish Manors & Castles

The East & the South

The West & the North

6 to 7 days

"To hell or to Connaught" was the choice given the native population by Cromwell, and indeed the harsh, barren landscape of parts of the west and north might appear cursed to the eye of an up-rooted farmer. But there's an appeal in the very wildness of counties Clare, Galway, Mayo, Sligo, and Donegal–their stunning, steep coastlines hammered and shaped for eons by the Atlantic. Here, in isolated communities, you'll hear locals speaking Irish as they go about their business. The arrival of peace has really opened the lush pastures of long-suffering Northern Ireland to travelers.

GALWAY & CLARE

2 days. A three-hour drive west from Dublin leads straight to the 710-foot-high Cliffs of Moher, perhaps the single most impressive sight in Ireland. Using the waterside village of Ballyvaughan as your base, spend a day exploring the lunar landscape of the harsh, limestone Burren. In spring it becomes a mighty rock garden of exotic colors. The next morning head north out of Ballyvaughan toward Galway City. On the way you'll pass 2-million-year-old Ailwee Cave and picture-perfect Kinvara. Galway City, spectacularly overlooking Galway Bay, is rapidly growing, vibrant, and packed with culture and history. If time allows, drive west to Ros an Mhil (Rossaveal) and take a boat to the fabled Aran Islands. Spend the night in Galway City.

NORTH & WEST TO DONEGAL

2 days. Northwest of Galway City is tiny Clifden, with some of the country's best Atlantic views. From here, head east through one of the most beautiful stretches of road in Connemara–through Kylemore Valley, home of Kylemore Abbey, a huge Gothic Revival castle. After seeing the castle and its grounds, head north through tiny Leenane (the setting of the hit Broadway play, *The Beauty Queen of Leenane*) and on to the most attractive town in County Mayo, Westport. It's the perfect spot to spend the night: the 18th-century planned town is on an inlet of Clew Bay, and some of the west coast's finest beaches are nearby. Your drive north leads through the heart of Yeats Country in Sligo. Just north of cozy Sligo Town is the stark outline of a great hill, Ben Bulben, in whose shadow poet Yeats wanted to be buried. South of town, follow the sign-posted Yeats Trail around woody, gorgeously scenic Lough Gill. Continuing north, you pass Yeats's simple grave in unassuming Drumcliff, a 3000 BC tomb in Creevykeel, and small Donegal Town. Head north through Letterkenny on the tight, meandering roads, into the windswept mountains and along the jagged coastline of northern Donegal. A trip on a fishing boat to one of the many islands off the coast is a must, as is a slow drive along the coast from the Gweedore Headland, covered with heather and gorse, to the former plantation village of Dunfanaghy (Dun Fionnachaid), heart of Donegal's Gaelic-speaking Gaeltacht region and a friendly place to spend the night.

NORTHERN IRELAND

2 days. Begin exploring the province in historic, divided Derry City (called Londonderry by Unionists), Northern Ireland's second city. A few hours is sufficient to take in the views from the old city walls and the fascinating murals of the Catholic Bogside district. Continue on to two of the region's main attractions, the 13th-century Norman fortress of Dunluce Castle and the Giant's Causeway, shaped from volcanic rock some 60 million years ago. Heading south, sticking to coastal roads for the best scenery, you'll soon pass through the Glens of Antrim, whose green hills roll down into the sea. Tucked away in the glens are a number of small, unpretentious towns with great hotels. Early in the morning, head straight to Northern Ireland's capital, Belfast. The old port city, gray and often wet, is a fascinating place, recovering from years of strife. A morning of driving through its streets will have to suffice before you head west through the rustic, pretty countryside to Lough Neagh, the largest lake in the British Isles. It's time to head back to Dublin, but if you're ahead of schedule, take the longer route that passes though the glorious Mountains of Mourne and around icy-blue Carlingford Lough.

MAP KEY

The West & the North

°C		°F
100		212
40		105
37		98.6
30		90
25		80
20		70
15		60
10		50
5		40
0		32
-5		20
-10		
-15		10
-20		0

In summer the weather is pleasant, the days are long (daylight lasts until after 10 in late June and July), and the countryside is green. But there are crowds in popular holiday spots, and prices for accommodations are at their peak. As British and Irish school vacations overlap from late June to mid-September, vacationers descend on popular coastal resorts in the south, west, and east. Unless you're determined to enjoy the short (July and August) swimming season, it's best to visit Ireland outside peak travel months. Fall and spring are good times to travel (late September can be dry and warm, although the weather can be unpredictable). Seasonal hotels and restaurants close from early or mid-November until mid-March or Easter. During this off-season, prices are lower than in summer, but your selection is limited, and many minor attractions close. St. Patrick's Week gives a focal point to a spring visit, but some Americans may find the saint's-day celebrations a little less enthusiastic than the ones back home. Dublin, however, has a weekend-long series of activities, including a parade and the Lord Mayor's Ball. If you're planning an Easter visit, don't forget that most theaters close from Thursday to Sunday of Holy Week (the week preceding Easter), and all bars and restaurants, except those serving hotel residents, close on Good Friday. Many hotels arrange Christmas packages. Mid-November to mid-February is either too cold or too wet for all but the keenest golfers, although some of the coastal links courses are playable.

Climate

🗂 Forecasts **Irish Meteorological Service** ☎ 01/806-4200 ⊕ www.meteireann.ie. **Marine Call** ☎ 0891/505-365 for marine forecasts. **Weathercall** ☎ 0891/500-427 for Northern Ireland forecasts. **Weather Channel Connection** ☎ 900/932-8437 95¢ a minute from a Touch-Tone phone ⊕ www.weather.com.

DUBLIN

Jan.	47F	8C	May	59F	15C	Sept.	63F	17C
	34	1		43	6		49	9
Feb.	47F	8C	June	65F	18C	Oct.	58F	14C
	36	2		49	9		43	6
Mar.	50F	10C	July	68F	20C	Nov.	50F	10C
	38	3		52	11		40	4
Apr.	56F	13C	Aug.	67F	20C	Dec.	47F	8C
	40	4		52	11		38	3

BELFAST

Jan.	43F	6C	May	59F	15C	Sept.	61F	16C
	36	2		43	6		49	9
Feb.	45F	7C	June	65F	18C	Oct.	56F	13C
	36	2		49	9		45	7
Mar.	49F	9C	July	65F	18C	Nov.	49F	9C
	38	3		52	11		40	4
Apr.	54F	12C	Aug.	65F	18C	Dec.	45F	7C
	50	4		52	11		38	3

Hundreds of festivals and events are held annually in Ireland. Here are some of the better known and better attended. If you plan to visit during one of them, book well in advance.

WINTER

December

The yearling, foal, and breeding stock sale at Goff's Bloodstock Sales, in Kill, County Kildare, shows how the rich buy and sell their prized horses. On December 26, St. Stephen's Day, the traditional Wren Boys in blackface and fancy dress wander the streets of some towns asking for money and singing (these days much of the money goes to charity); by far the most extravagant celebration takes place on Sandymount Green in Dublin.

SPRING

March

The Adare Jazz Festival in County Limerick fills the town's pubs with great jazz. The annual Arklow Music Festival includes orchestra, choir, solo singing, and drama competitions. Castleward Opera (⊕ www.castlewardopera.com) performs at Belfast's Grand Opera House. For three weeks on either side of St. Patrick's Day, the Celtic Spring Festival brings theatrical and rock music performances, and an Irish-language festival to Derry. Ireland's major St. Patrick's event is the Dublin Festival and Parade, (⊕ www.stpatricksday.ie) which includes a fireworks show and guest bands from the United States.

For 10 days, the Dublin Film Festival (⊕ www.dublinfilmfestival.com) presents films from Ireland and around the world, plus other events for cineasts. Dublin's Feis Ceoil is a festival of traditional Irish music. Bands of every stripe and size march in step and blow their horns in the annual Limerick International Band Festival, (⊕ www.ennisinformationagepark.ie/bandfest)which immediately follows the city's St. Patrick's Day celebrations.

April

The Antiques and Collectibles Fair brings dealers from all parts of Ireland to Dublin. With Easter arrives one of the biggest events of the racing calendar, the two-day Fairyhouse Easter Racing Festival, about 19 km (12 mi) north of Dublin.

May

Twenty-one days of concerts, competitions (including a marathon), and exhibitions take place during the Belfast Civic Festival; festivities kick off with the Lord Mayor's Show, a parade. Heritage properties and private gardens open to the public during the County Wicklow Garden Festival. The Fleadh Nua, the annual festival of traditional Irish music, song, and dance, takes place in Ennis, County Clare.

The Galway Early Music Festival (⊕ www.galwayearlymusic.com) fills Galway City with the sounds of pre-Baroque Irish and European music. Sixty-plus traditional music sessions take place over the first weekend in May at Kinvara's Cuckoo Fleadh. The Murphy's

International Mussel Fair in Bantry, County Cork, celebrates the peak of the harvest season for this delicacy. Theater, literary readings, and plenty of music fill the calendar of the Sligo Arts Festival, (⊕ www.sligofestival.com) which continues into early June.

SUMMER

June

Pick up some decorating tips while you're swooning over Schubert at the AIB Music Festival in Great Irish Homes, which puts on classical-music concerts in some of Ireland's finest country houses. Devoted Joyceans celebrate the fictional wanderings of *Ulysses*'s Leopold and Molly Bloom and Stephen Daedalus on June 16 (the day the novel was set, in 1904) in Dublin with Bloomsday; readings, dramatizations, and pilgrimages take place around the city. The Budweiser Irish Derby at the Curragh Racecourse, County Kildare, is the biggest race event of the year. Carlow celebrates the arts in its annual Éigse Carlow Arts Festival (⊕ www.eigsecarlow.com).

Ballycastle puts on its own lively three-day music and dance folk festival, the Fleadh Amhrán agus Rince. Cartoonists congregate in the Wicklow village of Rathdrum for the annual Guinness International Cartoon Festival. Listowel Writers' Week, one of Ireland's leading literary festivals, brings writers, poets, and lovers of literature together in this County Kerry town. The Weavers' Fair and Vintage Weekend comes to Ardara in County Donegal; the fair has as much to do with music, dance, and having fun as it does with selling homespun.

July

On July 12 Belfast and other towns throughout the north commemorate the 1690 Battle of the Boyne. The Coalisland International Music Festival (⊕ www.geocities.com/coalisland) attracts folk bands from all over Europe to County Tyrone. On the last Sunday in July, thousands of pilgrims climb the rocky slopes of Croagh Patrick (2,500 feet tall) in County Mayo to honor Saint Patrick. The Eagle Wing Festival at Groomsport in County Down celebrates 300 years of links with America; it has music, line dancing, lectures, and American food.

Galway is jam-packed for the two-week Galway Arts Festival, (⊕ www.galwayartsfestival.ie) which includes theater, film, music of all kinds, art exhibits, and a parade. Bachelors from throughout the country strut their stuff in Mullingar for the Guinness International Bachelor Festival. The Murphy's Irish Open Golf Championship is held on one of Ireland's premier links courses. The streets and pubs of Dublin's Temple Bar district resound day and night to jazz and blues during the Temple Bar Blues Festival.

Late July–early Aug.

Across the whole of County Derry, the country's best musicians take part in the Festival of Popular Irish Music. The Galway Races start the day after Galway's Arts Festival ends, for a week of revelry. Would-be beauty queens come to County Donegal from as far away as Australia and New Zealand to compete in the Mary of Dungloe International Festival.

August	Aeronautical enthusiasts can check out the Abbeyshrule Fly-in Festival and Air Show in County Longford. The Ballyshannon Folk and Traditional Music Festival (⊕ www.ballyshannonfolkfestival.com) in County Donegal is one of the best trad fests of the season. On the third Thursday, the Connemara Pony Show brings Ireland's finest yearlings and stallions to Clifden, County Galway. Kinvara, County Galway, hosts the Cruinniú na mBád (Festival of the Gathering of the Boats), in which brown-sailed hookers (a type of craft indigenous to the regions around Galway) are laden with turf and race across Galway Bay.
	The highlight of the traditional music calendar is the Fleadh Cheoil na hÉireann (pronounced flah kee'yole na herin), usually held during the last weekend in August or the first weekend in September. The granddaddy of all Irish music festivals, this extravaganza is held in varying towns across the country and recent venues have included Listowel and Clonmel. The latter, the seat of County Tipperary, hosted more than 250,000 people at the 2003 event. The weekend-long festival showcases some 4,000 traditional musicians in a dazzling array of céilithe, concerts, sessions, and street entertainments. For the complete scoop, log on to the official web site (⊕ www.clonmelfleadh.com) The International Story-telling Festival, a long weekend of simple entertainment for kids, takes place on Cape Clear Island, off the southwest coast near Baltimore. The Kerrygold Dublin Horse Show attracts a fashionable set to watch the best in Irish bloodstock. The Kilkenny Arts Week is a marvelous assemblage of classical music, art exhibits, and theater. If you're in the neighborhood of Ballycastle, County Antrim, don't miss Ireland's oldest fair, Oul' Lammas Fair, held every year since 1606 on the last Monday and Tuesday in August.
	The three-day Puck Fair (⊕ www.puckfair.ie), in Killorglin, County Kerry, retains vestiges of old pre-Christian fertility rites, like the garlanding with flowers of a large billy goat to signify his being crowned king. The world-famous Rose of Tralee International Festival (⊕ www.roseoftralee.ie) selects a "Rose of Tralee" from an international lineup of young women of Irish descent and packs this County Kerry town in the process. The competition coincides with the Tralee Races. Everyone's got the beat at the Waterford Spraoi, an international street-theater festival (⊕ www.spraoi.com).
FALL	
September	The Appalachian and Bluegrass Music Festival traces the roots of Appalachian music back to Ireland at the Ulster American Folk Park in Omagh, County Tyrone. Indulge in the "food of the gods" at the start of the oyster season at the Galway International Oyster Festival. The hugely popular Hurling and Gaelic Football Finals are played in Croke Park Stadium in Dublin.

Troupes from all over Europe compete at Waterford's Theatre Royal during the annual International Festival of Light Opera. Single people of all ages from throughout Ireland and beyond flock to County Clare for the Lisdoonvarna Matchmaking Festival in the hopes of finding a spouse—or at least a date. Opera Northern Ireland kicks off its autumn season in the Grand Opera House in Belfast.

October	At the Cork Film Festival, (⊕ www.corkfilmfest.org) new feature-length films and documentaries from Ireland and abroad share the bill with short films. The festival usually takes place during the second week of October. The Cork Jazz Festival (⊕ www.corkjazzfestival.com) draws jazz lovers late in the month. Runners fill the streets of Dublin in the Dublin City Marathon. The Dublin Theatre Festival puts on 10 visiting international productions, 10 Irish plays (most of them new), a children's festival, and a fringe of 60-plus plays. The Wexford Opera Festival (⊕ www.wexfordopera.com) brings in international stars to perform three rarely heard operas in a tiny Georgian theater.
November	The Belfast Festival at Queen's University (⊕ www.belfastfestival.com) is the city's preeminent arts festival, with hundreds of musical, film, theater, and ballet performances. The Irish Rugby Football season gets underway in Dublin with games between Ireland and nations *not* in the Six Nations group (Scotland, Wales, England, France, Italy, and Ireland). The three-day Millstreet Indoor International Horse Show brings equestrian enthusiasts to this County Cork town.

PLEASURES & PASTIMES

Those Tapping Feet *Ceol agus craic,* loosely translated as "music and merriment," are not simply recreations in Ireland. They are a way of life, part of the very fabric of the national identity. Ask most Irish men or women in exile what they miss most about home and, more than likely, those words "the craic" will be uttered. And the beat and rhythm that accompanies Irish fun is the "4/4" of the reel and the jig. Wherever you go you'll hear a musical air to accompany the scenery, and every town buzzes with its own blend of styles and sounds. The traditional music scene, far from becoming fossilized as a tourist fixture, has evolved with each generation, remaining lively and contemporary while still embracing the craft and skill of its past exponents. In its most exciting form, trad music is an impromptu affair, with a single guitar or fiddle player belting out a few tunes until other musicians—flute, whistle, uilleann pipes, concertina, and bodhrán drum—seem to arrive out of the pub's dark corners and are quickly drawn into the unstoppable force of the "session." Young traditional musicians are also unafraid to experiment with the music of other cultures, and it's not unusual to discover exciting mixtures of trad, folk, African rhythms, jazz improvisations, and even Appalachian mountain music. The deep-rooted musical tastes of the Irish are reflected in the live music scene in pubs, clubs, and theaters; a check of local event guides will turn up a wealth of live entertainment, from rock to folk to traditional, and it's often possible to go into a small venue and find a world-class artist in performance, whose talents are unsung outside a small circle of knowledgeable friends and fans.

Cuisine Irlandaise Ireland is in the throes of a food revolution. Many of the nation's chefs are young and widely traveled; they've absorbed the best influences of Europe, North America, and the Pacific Rim, and are producing a Pan-European, postmodern cuisine. This new Irish cuisine—sometimes referred to as *cuisine Irlandaise*—has moved beyond the heavy roast beef and Yorkshire pudding of the old Anglo-Irish country houses. Chefs are taking simple, traditional dishes—Clonakilty black pudding, Clare nettle soup, Galway oysters, Cong wild salmon—and sprucing them up with exotic, complicated preparations. The result: smart, unusual combinations of the best local, often organic, ingredients.

Regional cooking is a strength of Irish cuisine, and some of the best restaurants are tucked away in small fishing villages or remote locations. Hotel dining rooms vary in quality, but the best country-house hotels offer some of Europe's finest dining. Diehard traditionalists will still find many examples of old Celtic cooking in bars serving lunches of Irish stew, boiled bacon and cabbage, or steamed mussels. Guinness, the national drink, is a pitch-black malted stout. Pair it with raw oysters and Tabasco for a blissful marriage of opposites.

Homemade and Long Lasting

Let's be honest; prices in Ireland have risen sharply over the last few years and locals will never tire of telling you, in their own polite way, that the country is a "bleedin' rip off." You'll also spot plenty of "traditional Irish leprechauns" with a "made in China" sticker on the bottom. But if you look carefully and compare prices, Ireland has some of Europe's finest-quality goods. Stick to the traditional favorites, it's what the Irish do best: a Donegal tweed hat or a hand-knit Aran sweater, a Belfast linen tablecloth, or a piece of Waterford or Cavan crystal.

In Dublin look for antiques, books, and au courant European and Irish fashions. A new slew of young, native designers have invigorated the women's-wear scene, with Dublin shops like Costume and Platform stocking many of the more exciting items. The crowds in the capital can be overwhelming; regional cities offer a more serene shopping option. Cork City offers less variety but quite a few surprises, including the wonderfully eclectic English Market. Galway has its share of galleries and offbeat boutiques and is a great spot for book shopping, especially at the wonderful Kenny's Bookshop, with its specialist Irish and antiquarian sections. Most crafts shops sell a mix of goods from all over the country. Keep an eye open for signs indicating CRAFT WORKSHOPS, where independent craftspeople sell directly from their studios.

The best of the North's traditional products, many made according to time-honored methods, include exquisite linen and superior handmade woolen garments. The countrywomen of some Northern Ireland districts still craft handmade lace. Traditional music CDs and the unadorned blackthorn walking stick are two good choices at the other end of the price scale.

Gaelic Games

Gaelic football and hurling are played in most parts of the republic. Gaelic football is an extremely fast and rough form of football (closer to rugby than American football) that involves two teams of 15 that kick and run around a field with a round, soccerlike ball. The rules are complicated, but the skill and speed of the players make it exciting and impressive to watch, even if you don't quite understand what's going on. Hurling, considered by many to be the world's fastest field game, also involves two teams of 15 that use a three-foot-long wooden stick with a broad base to catch and hurl a leather-covered ball toward goalposts; a typical game produces several injuries. Gaelic games are organized by the Gaelic Athletic Association (GAA), and you can watch them free of charge at local GAA fields and sports centers around the republic. Interprovincial games and All-Ireland finals are played in July and August at the GAA stadiums in Cork and Dublin. Croke Park in Dublin is usually where the annual All-Ireland finals are held. Tickets for these matches can be hard to obtain, but the events are televised.

Where the Greens are Greener

There are more than 360 golf courses in Ireland—including Northern Ireland—from world-famous championship links courses to scenic 9-holers. About 50 of these courses have opened in the last two years. Choose between the challenging links of the Atlantic coast, the more subtle layouts on the eastern seaboard, and the mature parklands of the inland courses. Some of the best parkland courses are in the southeast, and there's also a championship links course at Rosslare. Mount Juliet, near Kilkenny, has been publicly acclaimed by Nick Faldo as one of Europe's best. Although the parkland courses of the Midlands may lack the spectacular challenge of the country's more famous scenic and coastal greens, they have a quiet charm all their own. Many of the southwest's 18-hole courses are world-famous, championship clubs amid wonderful scenery.

Home of the Wordsmith

"If only we had as many plumbers as we do bloody writers," a recent wag was heard to comment, disgusted with the difficulty in getting a man to sort out your pipes in modern Ireland. This tiny, peripatetic, long-colonized island on the outskirts of Europe has somehow managed to maneuver itself to the very heart of modern literature in the language of the invader itself, English. Ireland has produced no fewer than four Nobel prize winners—George Bernard Shaw, W. B. Yeats, Samuel Beckett, and Seamus Heaney. But the list of literary notables is a whole lot longer: Oscar Wilde, Sean O'Casey, Sean O'Faolain, Brian Friel, and Edna O'Brien. Indeed, the country's literary heritage is evident everywhere you go. In Dublin you'll find James Joyce's Liffey; Dean Swift's cathedral; Trinity College, alma mater of the 18th-century Anglo-Irish writers; and the Abbey Theatre, a potent symbol of Ireland's great playwrights. Yeats opens up the country of Sligo; the Aran Islands were the inspiration of J. M. Synge; and then there's Frank O'Connor's Cork; Castletownshend, home of Somerville and Ross; Oliver Goldsmith's Lissoy; and Frank McCourt's Limerick. If a landscape shapes a country's literature, then Irish writing developed its distinctive traits largely because of the country's physical isolation. Not even Julius Caesar wanted to conquer Ireland, and centuries later, it remained uninfluenced by the cultural excitement of the Renaissance. In the end, it produced a literature that conquered distant shores, partly through its grand dramatic tradition.

The Other Irish Church

"How do you walk the length of Ireland without passing a pub? You go into every one." The old joke shows just how prevalent and important the pub is to Irish culture. And visitors to the Emerald Isle quickly find their favorite, be it a trendy, "kicking" spot in Temple Bar, the sophisticated saloon called Horseshoe bar in the Shelbourne Hotel, or a tiny, whitewashed country hostelry. Irish Pub, a Dublin-based company, has shipped more than 1,000 of its five styles of "ready-to-pour" pubs—Victorian Dublin, Gaelic, Irish Brewery Pub, Irish Pub Shop, and Irish Country Cottage—to more than 35 countries around the world, at about $300,000 a pop. Back on their home turf, pubs are pillars of Irish social life—places to chat, listen, learn, and gossip about everything from horse racing to philosophy. Many pubs now serve food at lunchtime; most also serve tea and coffee during daylight hours. The revolutionary total smoking ban—introduced in 2004 to a great deal of national hand-wringing—means that a long night in a packed pub will no longer leave you waking up with your clothes reeking of nicotine aroma and your throat sour. A word about music in pubs: if it's in the main bar of a pub, you'll seldom have to pay a cover charge. If, however, you're really enjoying the *craic*, as it's called, it is good form to buy a pint for the performers. To dance to the music of a fully amplified band in a room adjacent to the bar, you may have to pay a cover.

Set Your Rod Ireland is well known as a game-angling resort: Atlantic salmon, brown trout, and sea trout abound in the rivers, lakes, and estuaries, and offshore is the deep-sea challenge. Coarse fishing (for all fish that are not trout or salmon) is also an option. In the Midlands, the River Shannon and its system of lakes attract anglers from around the world. Beam, rudd, tench, roach, perch, and hybrids are the main varieties; pike roam select waters. Monaghan, Cavan, Boyle, and the small lakes to the east and west of Lough Derg are the best coarse fishing areas, and you can find brown-trout lakes and rivers around Birr, Banagher, Mullingar, and Roscommon. For pike, you'll find the most fruitful areas around Cavan, Clones, Cootehill, Castleblaney, Kingscourt, Carrick-on-Shannon, Boyle, Belturbet, and Butlersbridge. The southwest has a plethora of sea-angling facilities, a wealth of salmon and trout rivers, and terrific surroundings—be they the black-slate cliffs of the coast or the vegetation of Killarney and the Ring of Kerry. You can shore-fish along the coast from Cobh in the east to Foynes in the west. Although the whole region has great lake- and river-fishing, most anglers head for Waterville or Killarney. Coarse anglers will find pike at Macroom and coarse-angling facilities at Mallow and Fermoy. Game-fishing for wild Atlantic salmon, wild brown trout, and sea trout is one of the main attractions of the west.

In the northwest there's so much space and so much water that it can feel as if you have the whole place to yourself. The best area for brown-trout angling is around Bundoran, including Lough Melvin. In western County Donegal, there are good opportunities for catching sea trout. Plenty of salmon and brown trout live in the rivers of southern County Donegal and northern County Sligo. You'll find more brown trout in the loughs near Dunfanaghy in northern County Donegal, near Bundoran on the border of Donegal and Sligo counties, and in the border area of Sligo and Leitrim counties. Pike and coarse anglers can cast their lines in the abundant County Leitrim lakes. With a 606-km (466-mi) coastline, part on the Atlantic and part on the Irish

Sea, as well as major lakes and an abundance of unpolluted rivers, the north is a great place for anglers. Set your rod for salmon on the Bann, Bush, and Foyle rivers and for brown trout in their tributaries. There are bigger lake trout in Loughs Neagh, Melvin, and Erne, although pike and other coarse (white) fish abound in the Erne. Turbot and plaice are taken off the north coast, where sea bass may be caught from the shore.

The Races

There's a horse race—with some of the planet's finest thoroughbreds—somewhere in Ireland almost every day of the year. The flat season runs from March to November; steeplechases are held throughout the year. Several courses—there are some 28 in all—are within easy reach of Dublin. The Curragh Racecourse, in Dublin's environs, hosts the Irish Derby and other international horse races. Fairyhouse in County Meath is the site of the Irish Grand National. Some of the best meetings are held in summer at smaller courses: Killarney in mid-July, Galway in late July–early August, Tramore in mid-August, Tralee in late August, and Listowel in late September. There are two horse racing tracks in Northern Ireland—the one at Downpatrick is particularly atmospheric.

Hiking Heaven

Wicklow's gentle, rolling hills are a terrific place to begin an Irish walking vacation. Devoted hikers come from all over the world to traverse the 137-km (85-mi) Wicklow Way, the first long-distance trail to open in Ireland and one of the best. The route begins in Marlay Park, just a few miles south of Dublin. It follows rough sheep tracks, forest firebreaks, and old bog roads, and much of it is above 1,600 feet.

Two trails cross the southeast, with its wooded hills, rich farmland, and rivers. The South Leinster Way begins in the County Carlow town of Kildavin and makes its way southwest over Mt. Leinster and the River Barrow, terminating in Carrick-on-Suir. The Munster Way leads through the Vee Gap in the Knockmealdown Mountains and on to Clogheen. The many forest park trails (at Killykeen, Lough Key, and Dun a Ri) and narrow country roads are great for touring the Midlands on foot. The impressive Slieve Bloom Way, east of Birr, runs through the Slieve Bloom Mountains on a 50-km (30-mi) circular route—it has deep glens, rock formations, waterfalls, and great mountain views.

The far southwest around Killarney and Dingle is classic hiking country, with a true feeling of wilderness—even though you're never more than 3 or 4 km (2 or 3 mi) from civilization. Two signposted, long-distance trails wind through the region: the 214-km (134-mi) Kerry Way begins in Killarney and loops around the Ring of Kerry, and the 153-km (95-mi) Dingle Way loops from Tralee around the Dingle Peninsula. Both routes consist of paths and "green (unsurfaced) roads," with some stretches linked by surfaced roads.

The 209-km (130-mi) Beara Way is mainly an off-road walk around West Cork's rugged Beara Peninsula.

The 168-km (104-mi) Blackwater Way follows the lower slopes of the Knockmealdown Mountains to the rich farms and woodlands of the Blackwater Valley. Sheep's Head Way encircles the Sheep's Head Peninsula and has glorious views of Bantry Bay along its 88-km (55-mi) route. There are other trails in Killarney National Park++CE: should this be a colon, i.e. are the rest of the walks in this sentence in the park? otherwise, reorganize?++; Gougane Barra, northeast of Ballylickey off R584 in County Cork; Farran, off N22 about 16 km (10 mi) west of Cork City in County Cork; the Ballyhoura Mountains on the Cork-Limerick border, off N20 at Ballyhea about 16 km (10 mi) north of Buttevant; and Currachase Forest Park, east of Askeaton off N69 in County Limerick.

The Burren Way runs from Lahinch Promenade to Ballyvaughan on the shores of Galway Bay, a distance of 35 km (22 mi). It takes you through the heart of the Burren's limestone landscape, with ever-changing views of the Aran Islands and the bay. The Western Way's County Galway section extends from Oughterard on Lough Corrib through the mountains of Connemara to Leenane on Killary Harbour, a distance of 50 km (30 mi). The 177-km (110-mi) County Mayo section, known as the Western Way (Mayo) and the Foxford Way, continues past Killary Harbour to Westport on Clew Bay, inland to Newport and across the boglands to the Ox Mountains east of Ballina. The Newport Bangor Trail runs for 48 km (30 mi) through the Nephin Mountain range in northwest Mayo. A 387-km (240-mi) route through Irish-speaking Connemara stretches along the shores of Galway Bay from Spiddle to Carraroe, Carna, Letterfrack, and Clonbur, on the northern shore of Lough Corrib.

In the northwest's mountain districts (such as the Blue Stacks, near Donegal Town) you can get in some satisfyingly rough walks with dramatic views. Long-distance footpaths are scattered across County Donegal, in County Leitrim, and around Lough Gill in County Sligo. Good shorter trails are also accessible within Glenveagh National Park. Northern Ireland is also magnificent walking country. Ask at tourist offices for details of local walking and cycling trails, 14 of which spring off the Ulster Way, an 896-km (560-mi) trek for serious hikers that runs around the ++CE: "north's"++six counties and links up with marked trails on the other side of the border.

FODOR'S CHOICE

The sights, restaurants, hotels, and other travel experiences on these pages are our editors' top picks—our Fodor's Choices. They're the best of their type in the area covered by the book—not to be missed and always worth your time. In the destination chapters that follow, you will find all the details.

PRINCELY LODGINGS

$$$$ **Ashford Castle,** Cong, Co. Mayo. Nearly bigger than the neighboring village of Cong, this famed mock-Gothic baronial showpiece was built in 1870 for the Guinness family and has been wowing visitors ever since—that is, if your guest list runs to Prince Rainier, John Travolta, and Jack Nicholson. Massive, flamboyantly turreted, it remains strong on luxury, charm, and good service, but light on authenticity.

$$$$ **Ballinalacken Castle,** Doolin, Co. Claire. Many guests regularly oversleep due to the quietness of this one hundred acre realm, replete with wildflower meadows, a low-slung Victorian lodge, and panoramic views of the Atlantic, the Aran Islands, and distant Connemara. Inside, chef Frank Sheedy will tempt you with nouvelle-yet-traditional delights.

$$$$ **Ballyvolane House,** near Fermoy, Co. Cork. With Georgian splendor in the terra-cotta, gilded, and black Italianate pillared hall and Regency coziness nonpareil in the daffodil yellow sitting room, Ballyvolane offers a setting as elegant as it is witty, as witness the tub in Roland's Room, in full view of all and on a wooden pedestal perched to give a garden view.

$$$$ **Castle Leslie,** Glaslough, Co. Monaghan. The most glorious hotel in Ireland, period. Hard to say which is more beautiful: the 1870 Gothic and Italianate structure or the reflection of it in the nearby lake. It's no wonder Paul McCartney and Heather Mills got married here.

$$$$ **Culloden Hotel.** Belfast, Co. Down. This imposingly 1876 grand vision in Belfast stone presides over the busy waters of Belfast Lough, is topped off with a storybook turret, and is done up in luxe Scottish Baronial style.

$$$$ **Dromoland Castle,** Newmarket-on-Fergus, Co. Clare. This massive, turreted, neo-Gothic castle bristles with towers and crenellations rising up over the forest and its picture-perfect lake looks like a storybook illustration from King Arthur and his knights. Inside, Dromoland really sets out to give you the full country-house treatment: oak paneling, ancestral portraits, plushly carpeted rooms, crystal chandeliers, Irish-Georgian antiques—all the creature comforts any duke would want.

$$$$ **Kildare Hotel and Country Club,** Straffan, Co. Kildare. A most indulgent place with an Arnold Palmer–designed golf course, clay target shooting, and game fishing, among other things.

$$$$ **Merchant's House,** Derry, Northern Ireland. The late Hurd Hatfield, star of the movie *The Picture of Dorian Gray.* enjoyed this grand B&B, a former Victorian merchant's family town home built to Georgian proportions, now replete with garnet-color walls, elaborate plasterwork, and a faintingly pink living room parlor.

$$$$ **Merrion,** Dublin. Four Georgian town houses, loads of marble, meandering gardens, and a spa.

$$$$ **Mount Juliet,** Thomastown, Co. Kilkenny. *Another* Georgian mansion on hundreds of acres? Yup. This one has a Jack Nicklaus–designed golf course and the usual estate sports: riding, archery, angling, and shooting.

$$$$ **Park Hotel,** Kenmare, Co. Kerry. The views from this stone château are of the Caha Mountains and terraced lawns that sweep down to the bay.

$$$$ **Slieve Donard Hotel,** Mountains of Mourne, Co. Down. A lavish redbrick monument to Victoriana, this turreted hotel stands like a palace on green lawns. Its traditional furnishings may make you feel as if you're stepping back to the town's turn-of-the-20th-century heyday as an elegant seaside resort.

$$$$ **St. Ernan's House,** Donegal Town. Imagine a handsome 19th-century country house on its own wooded, tidal island, and the term *unwind* takes on new meaning.

$$$–$$$$ **Hayfield Manor,** Cork, Co. Cork. This surprisingly soigné modern homage to the country-house style stars the Drawing Room—a symphony of gilded silk, with white marble fireplace, 19th-century chandelier, and chic armchairs.

$$$–$$$$ **Longueville House,** Mallow, Co. Cork. Come for the tranquility and the Irish-French dishes made with produce from the family farm, garden, and river.

$$–$$$$ **Ballynahinch Castle,** Recess, Co. Galway. A river's-edge hotel in rugged Connemara that's long been favored by statesmen and stars for its Persian rugs, leather chesterfields, and wooded acres.

$$$ **Abbeyglen Castle Hotel,** Clifden, Co. Galway. Creeper-covered, as if under a Sleeping Beauty spell, Abbeyglen sits framed by towering trees at the foot of the glorious Twelve Bens Mountains. If time hasn't completely stopped here, it has certainly slowed down—but that's just the way the relaxed guests want it. The gorgeous Victorian castle-manor, however, sometimes rocks with trad Irish music in its bar.

$$$ | Delphi Lodge, Leenane, Co. Galway. Surrounded by Mayo's highest mountains, this Georgian sporting lodge is in the heart of some gorgeous scenery, so it's little wonder that Prince Charles, a recent guest, brought his sketchbook with him.

$$$ | Dunbrody House, New Ross, Co. Wexford. An antiques-filled Georgian manor with pastoral views and a Continental restaurant.

$$$ | Moy House, Lalinch, Co. Claire. Built for Sir Augustine Fitzgerald, this enchanting, 18th-century Italianate-style lodge sits amid 15 private acres on an exhilarating, "Wuthering Heights"–like windswept cliff-top. With an alluring period decor, this peaceful haven makes you feel you are a guest in a privately-owned country house. Enjoy a drink at the "honesty bar" in the elegant drawing room and soak in the veranda view over Lahinch Bay. It all seems worlds away from the here and the now.

$$$ | Rosleague Manor, Letterfrack, Co. Galway. This pink, creeper-clad, two-story Georgian house overlooks an eye-knocking view: a gorgeous lawn backdropped by Ballinakill Bay and the dreamy mountains of Connemara. Inside, the clutter of walking sticks and shooting sticks beneath the grandfather clock in the hall sets the informal, country-house tone. The restaurant is superb.

$$–$$$ | Ash-Rowan Guest House, Belfast, Northern Ireland. In the former home of Thomas Andrews, designer of the *Titanic,* you can sit in the lounge and devour one of the many books scattered around the house.

$$–$$$ | Barberstown Castle, Straffan, Co. Kildare. What's a castle without a keep? The one here dates from the 13th century. Turf fires, period reproductions, and theme restaurants shed light on this structure's 750-odd years.

$$–$$$ | Gregan's Castle Hotel, Ballyvaughan, Co. Clare. Sharon Stone, Gabriel Byrne, and Edna O'Brien have all been guests at this quiet, meticulous, creeper-covered and highly romantic Victorian country house, set at the base of the aptly named Corkscrew Hill, and filled with stylish nooks and salons.

$$–$$$ | La Stampa, Dublin. Who said that velvet bedspreads from Paris wouldn't work in an Asian scheme? Certainly not the designers who dressed this boutique hotel.

$$–$$$ | Ross Lake House, Oughterard, Co. Galway. Well off the beaten path, this surprisingly stylish country hideaway was built by the land agent for Lord Iveagh at Ashford Castle and comes with a suavely furnished interior, 19th-century antiques, welcoming open fires, and a Regency-style dinner salon which showcases Connemara mountain lamb.

GREAT BUDGET HOTELS

$$	**Delphi Lodge,** Leenane, Co. Mayo. A lakeside Georgian sporting lodge surrounded by wildly beautiful mountain scenery.
$$	**Londonderry Arms Hotel,** Glens of Antrim, Co. Antrim. Once the property of Winston Churchill, this ivy-covered traditional inn on Carnlough Harbor was built as a coach stop in 1848. Enjoy the lovely seaside gardens, ivy-clad walls, gorgeous antiques, regional paintings and maps, and lots of fresh flowers.
$$	**Olde Railway Hotel,** Westport, Co. Mayo. When the English novelist William Makepeace Thackeray stayed here in 1842, he called it "one of the prettiest, comfortablist inns in Ireland." You can understand why once you see all the fishing trophies, Victorian plates, framed prints, and watercolors of this unusual, family-run inn.
$–$$	**Ariel Guest House,** Dublin. A Waterford-crystal chandelier is just one of the charms of this Victorian redbrick in leafy Ballsbridge. The friendly owner is another.
$–$$	**Crookedwood House,** Mullingar, Co. Westmeath. Rooms in this 200-year-old rectory are spacious and reasonably priced. Save your money to splurge on dinner in the restaurant; look for updated takes—and German twists—on salmon, pheasant, venison, and pork.
$–$$	**The Old Inn,** outside Belfast, Co. Down. This 1614 coach inn, reputedly Ireland's oldest, looks the part: it's pure 17th-century England, with a sculpted thatched roof, half doors, leaded-glass windows, and once hosted Swift, Tennyson, Thackery, Dickens, and Trollope, and the famous highwayman Dick Turpin.
$	**Carrigann,** Lissoonvarna, Co. Claire. Hikers love this small, friendly hotel, and hosts Mary and Gerard Howard keep a library of books on the Burren beside the turf fire in the sitting room. Choose between setting off with one of Mary's specially prepared walk sheets, join a guided group, or hire your own guide. On return, settle in for a fine slab of char-grilled sirloin steak.
$	**Dufferin Arms Coaching Inn,** near Downpatrick, Co. Down. Bar snugs, pub quizzes, four-poster beds, and a restaurant that hosts medieval feasts all make this 1803 inn next to Killyleagh Castle a lovely option.
$	**Hotel St. George,** Dublin. Georgian details fill this house at the top of O'Connell Street, an enviable location.
¢–$	**Ballymakeigh House,** Youghal, Co. Cork. It's a creeper-clad farmhouse amid lush dairy country—a true embodiment of the Ireland most people imagine.
¢–$	**Norman Villa,** Galway City. A tasteful Victorian town house characterized by a location that offers the best of all urban worlds.

¢   **Green Gate,** Ardvally, Co. Donegal. Its four rooms are in a thatched cottage overlooking Ardara, the Atlantic, and other spectacular Donegal scenes.

THE BEST RESTAURANTS

$$$$ **Ballymaloe House,** Shanagarry, Co. Cork. It's an elegant inn whose restaurant continues to revolutionize and refine Irish cooking and whose cooking school consistently turns out Ireland's top chefs.

$$$$ **Cromleach Lodge,** Castlebaldwin, Co. Sligo. Outstanding views *and* food. Expect quirky dishes with multidimensional flavors.

$$$$ **Patrick Guilbaud,** Dublin. Flawless food, impeccable service. Don't even think about skipping this place or its specialty, duck *à l'orange*. As for the plate of five chocolate desserts—life is short.

$$$$ **Rathsallagh House,** Dunlavin, Co. Wicklow. Think enthusiastic country-house cooking with an internationalist edge—produce from organic gardens, game in season, and seafood specialties.

$$$$ **Shanahans on the Green,** Dublin. A radiantly sumptuous and authentic Georgian townhouse now fires up a grill to offer carnivores the best steaks—all certified Irish Angus—in the land.

$$$$ **Shanks,** Bangor, Northern Ireland. Robbie Millar has a diver *hand-pick* scallops from the sea. The dishes here blend Asian spicing with European techniques and local ingredients; the results are piquant and exciting.

$$$$ **Thornton's,** Dublin. Newer-than-now nouvelle and grand ole Irish ingredients collide in the kitchen of famed chef Kevin Thornton— don't miss his moonshine sauce.

$$$–$$$$ **Chapter One,** Dublin. Set in the basement of the Dublin Writers Museum, and not far from the Abbey and Gate theaters, this is top spot thanks also to the culinary wizardry of chef Ross Lewis.

$$$–$$$$ **The Vintage,** Kinsale, Co. Cork. It's worth a jaunt to this seaside town just for the whole lobster in mustard-whiskey sauce.

$$$–$$$$ **Wineport Lodge,** Athlone, Co. Westmeath. The energetic, imaginative menu of this informal lakeside restaurant changes every eight weeks; braised lamb shank and roast venison are among the seasonal dishes.

$$$ **Halo,** Dublin. The chef is French, so your seared, cured salmon is both artful and delicious. The designer is Irish, and the space—soaring ceiling, dark wood, warm task lighting—is moody and mysterious, yet inviting.

$$–$$$ **Casino House,** Killbrittain, Co. Cork. Farmhouse-turned-restaurant where Irish country cooking has an elegant edge and flavors full of verve.

$$-$$$	**Deane's,** Belfast, Northern Ireland. Eclectic, Thai-influenced Michael Deane concocts innovative east–west dishes. Subtle spicing adds spirit-enhancing gusto to the meal.
$$-$$$	**Erriseask House,** Ballyconneely, Co. Galway. Think seasonal, market-fresh produce, meats, and seafood. And think contemporary, too.
$$-$$$	**Wine Vault,** Waterford City. An Elizabethan town house with a beguiling 350-label wine cellar and an intriguing Irish menu.
$$	**Cayenne,** Belfast, Northern Ireland. Culinary fireworks go off here, as you'll see if you order the duck and shitake pot stickers with sesame ginger sauce or the salt ëní chilli squid with chilli jam and aioli—and let's not forget the hot banana strudel. These are just a few of the creations of celebrity TV chefs Paul and Jeanne Rankin.

HALLOWED CHURCHES & MONASTERIES

Clonmacnoise, Co. Offaly. This isolated monastery at the confluence of two rivers was famous throughout Europe as a center for learning. It's also a royal burial ground.

Glendalough, Co. Wicklow. A monastery founded by a hermit in the 6th century, attacked by Vikings in the 9th and 10th centuries, and plundered by English soldiers in the 12th century—your typical Irish ruins.

Jerpoint Abbey, Co. Kilkenney. Cistercian church, tomb, and cloisters from the 12th century; the facade's decorative figures—human and otherwise—are beloved.

Kylemore Abbey, Kylemore Valley. It's hard to believe that this gray-stone Gothic-Revival pile was built as a residence in the 1860s rather than as the home for Benedictine nuns that it is today.

Rock of Cashel, Co. Tipperary. A cluster of ruins—cathedral, chapel, round tower—crowning a circular, mist-shrouded rock that rises from a plain.

St. Patrick's Cathedral, Dublin. The national cathedral of the Church of Ireland is old, massyGolf's Winner's Circle

Ballybunion Golf Club, Co. Kerry. On the Old Course, one of the country's classics, each and every hole is a pleasure.

The K Club, Co. Kildare. You'd have to be a non-golfer *and* a hermit not to have heard of this course, one of the country's most prestigious and demanding.

Mount Juliet Golf Course, Co. Kilkenney. A championship parkland course with a little something for every golfer.

Portmarnock Golf Club, Co. Dublin. One of the nation's "Big Four" golf clubs (along with Ballybunion, Royal County Down, and Royal Portrush), Portmarnock is a links course near Dublin.

Royal County Down, Northern Ireland. A lunar landscape makes this course as beautiful as it is difficult.

Royal Portrush, Co. Antrim, Northern Ireland. Portrush has hosted the British Open and is favored by Ireland's most renowned golfers.

HISTORIC SIGHTS & MUSEUMS

Chester Beatty Library, Dublin. Who knew that Ireland was home to one of the world's largest collections of Islamic and Far Eastern manuscripts and art?

Dublin Writers Museum, Dublin. Pay homage to Joyce, Shaw, Synge, Lady Gregory, Yeats, and Beckett in the exhibits on view in this regal 18th-century townhouse.

Hugh Lane Municipal Gallery of Modern Art, Dublin. The earl of Charlemont's "Palace Row" mansion is now home to top Impressionist works, masterpieces of Irish 20th-century art, and Francis Bacon's "studio."

Museum of Country Life, Turlough, Co. Mayo. The objects on display transport you back to a time when water came from wells and clothes were made by hand—often by the light of a winter's fire fueled by turf cut straight out of a bog.

National Gallery of Ireland, Dublin. Dutch masters, French Impressionists, and great Irish painters, too—all in a manageable collection.

Newgrange, Co. Meath. It's older than Stonehenge and built with 250,000 tons of stones. Come in the morning during winter solstice, when 20 minutes of light illuminate the interior.

Newman House, Dublin. The splendor of 18th-century Irish Neoclassism is on show in this princely set of townhouses, replete with Georgian stuccowork, Irish Rococo trim, and the hidden jewel of Iveagh Gardens.

Trinity College, Dublin. The university founded by Queen Elizabeth provided the greats—Beckett, Wilde, Stoker—with 40 acres of stomping grounds. It's also home to the masterfully illuminated *Book of Kells.*

Ulster Folk and Transport Museum, Belfast, Northern Ireland. On one side of the road is a living museum with reconstructed buildings and docents dressed in character. On the other side of the road is a collection of vehicles made in the region.

Waterford Treasures, Waterford City. A thousand years of history unfolds with an artful blend of audiovisuals and artifacts.

PURE IRELAND

Aghadoe, near Killarney. Even Queen Victoria was overwhelmed by the views from this town. At dusk the island-studded Lower Lake glows under an expansive sky.

The Aran Islands, Galway Bay. Immortalized in the books of J. M. Synge and Robert Flaherty's film, *Man of Aran,* the islands of Inishmore, Inishmaan, and Inisheer battle dramatically with sea and storm, and now welcome droves of visitors who fall under the spell of the islands' brooding beauty and spectacular views.

Ballyhack, Co. Waterford. Thatched cottages and an imposing 16th-century castle are highlights of a village surrounded by green hills.

Blasket Islands, off Dingle Peninsula, Co. Kerry. Slea Head's cliffs, above a beautiful and treacherous coastline, are a marvelous place from which to view these rugged, uninhabited islands.

The Burren, Co. Clare. A 300-square-km (116-square-mi) expanse that is one of Ireland's strangest landscapes, the Burren stretches off in all directions, as far as the eye can see, in a gray, rocky lunar landscape that becomes a wild rock garden in spring and remains a haven for an incredible diversity of animals.

Cliffs of Moher, Co. Clare. One of Ireland's most breathtaking natural sights, these majestic cliffs stretch for five miles—at some points, the only thing separating you from the sea, 700 feet below, is a patch of slippery heather.

Georgian Squares on a Sunday, Dublin. Tranquil, evergreen Merrion Square is full of great architecture and sculpture. The 27-acre St. Stephen's Green has flower gardens and expansive lawns.

Giant's Causeway, Co. Antrim, Northern Ireland. There are equal measures of legend and science surrounding this rock formation—a cluster of 37,000-odd volcanic basalt pillars.

Glens of Antrim, Northern Ireland. A beateous realm favored, it is said, by "the wee folk," this enchanted area is made up of nine wooded river valleys. Still haunted by the romantic, mystical Celtic legends, settled by farmers who still speak Gaelic language, the glens remain the final resting place of Ossian, the greatest of Celtic bards. Don't miss Glenariff Forest Park, called "Little Switzerland" by Thackeray.

Glenveagh National Park. It's County Donegal at its wildest and most dramatic: 24,000 acres of mountain, moorland, lakes, and woods.

Kenny's Bookshop, Galway City. Five floors of secondhand and antiquarian prints, maps, and books—many covering Ireland—as well as painting and sculpture by Irish artists.

Killary Harbour, Kylemore Valley. The dark, deep waters of this narrow fjord—which runs between County Mayo's Mweelrea Mountains and County Galway's Dorruagh Mountains—are as haunting as the reflections in them.

Kilmore Quay, Co. Wexford. A timeless town of whitewashed houses, fishermen, and the sea.

Kinvara, Co. Galway. This village is picture-perfect, thanks to its gorgeous bayside locale, great walks, and numerous pubs. North of the town is spectacularly sited Dunguaire Castle, noted for its medieval banquet evenings.

PUBS WE LOVE

Crown Liquor Saloon, Belfast, Northern Ireland. This ornate, snug pub is so true to its Victorian roots that it's still lit by gas lamps.

Grogans, Dublin. A William Street hangout packed with creative types.

Gus O'Connor's, Doolin, Co. Clare. Just one of the town's many pubs famed for their traditional Irish music evenings.

Monk's Pub, Ballyvaughan, Co. Clare. A waterfront watering hole where the bar food is almost as good as the Irish tunes and the folk music.

Stag's Head, Dublin. An old gathering place where students and theater folk mix.

Tigh Neachtain (Naughton's Pub), Galway City. Grab a spot in a snug and spend an evening listening to traditional music at this popular pub in the heart of the old town.

THE STATELIEST HOMES

Castle Ward, Co. Down. An architectural curiosity in that it was built inside and out in two distinct styles, Classical and Gothic (perhaps because Viscount Bangor and his wife never could agree on anything). Set overlooking the breathtaking Strangford Lough, there are delightful walks through the formal and informal gardens and woodland, as well as lakeside trails.

Castletown House, Co. Kildare. Renaissance Architect Andrea Palladio, would surely have approved of this large and grand Palladian country house. The interior is filled with 18th-century furniture and details.

Florence Court, Northern Ireland. An Irish-Palladian masterpiece, this Georgian-period estate presents the viewer with a bucolically baroque setting, as the Cuilcagh Mountains form a wonderful contrast to its shimmering white stone facade. The ancestral park is one of Northern Ireland's glories—dotted with noted heirloom trees (including the Florence Court weeping beech), it also has nooks and dells where, legend has it, you can hear the "song of the little people."

Mount Stewart, outside Belfast, Co. Down. The country seat of the Marquesses of Londonderry, Mount Stewart is famed for its Ards Peninsula gardens, family ghosts, and one of George Stubbs's most famous portraits, that of the celebrated racehorse Hambletonian.

Strokestown Park House, Co. Roscommon. Some wings date from the 17th century, others from the 18th and 19th centuries. The furnishings are all original; intriguing structural details and curiosities abound.

SMART TRAVEL TIPS

Half the fun of traveling is looking forward to your trip—but when you look forward, don't just daydream. There are plans to be made, things to learn about, and there's serious work to be done. After all, finding out about your destination before you leave home means you won't squander time organizing everyday minutiae once you've arrived. You'll be streetwise when you hit the ground and better prepared to explore the aspects of Ireland that drew you here in the first place. The organizations in this section can provide information to supplement this guide; contact them for up-to-the-minute details, and consult the A to Z sections that end each chapter for facts on the various topics as they relate to Ireland's many regions. Many trips begin by first touching base with the Irish Tourist Board; their office contacts are listed under Visitor Information, below. Happy landings!

ADDRESSES

We have tried to provide full addresses for hotels, restaurants, and sights, though many of Ireland's villages and towns are so tiny they barely have street names, much less house numbers. If in doubt, ask for directions. Outside of Dublin and Northern Ireland, postal codes aren't really used; what's more important here is the county, so be sure to include it when addressing an envelope.

AIR TRAVEL

From North America and the United Kingdom, Aer Lingus, the national flag carrier, has the most direct flights to Ireland. There are no direct flights from Australia or New Zealand. Regular service is available from most major airports in Ireland to many U.K. cities, including Leeds, Manchester, and Glasgow.

Flying into Ireland involves few hassles, although an increase in traffic in the last decade has caused a slight increase in flight delays and time spent waiting for baggage to clear customs. Flights within Ireland tend to be filled with business travelers. The lack of competition on internal routes coupled with the country's rela-

Addresses
Air Travel
Airports
Bike Travel
Boat & Ferry Travel
Business Hours
Bus Travel
Cameras & Photography
Car Rental
Car Travel
Children in Ireland
Computers on the Road
Consumer Protection
Cruise Travel
Customs & Duties
Disabilities & Accessibility
Discounts & Deals
Eating & Drinking
Electricity
Embassies
Emergencies
Gay & Lesbian Travel
Health
Holidays
Insurance
Language
Lodging
Mail & Shipping
Media
Money Matters
Packing
Passports & Visas
Rest Rooms
Safety
Senior-Citizen Travel
Shopping
Sports & the Outdoors
Students in Ireland
Taxes
Telephones
Time
Tipping
Tours & Packages
Train Travel
Travel Agencies
Visitor Information
Web Sites

tively small size make train and car travel more affordable and pleasurable options.

BOOKING

When you book, look for nonstop flights and remember that "direct" flights stop at least once. Try to avoid connecting flights, which require a change of plane. Two airlines may operate a connecting flight jointly, so ask whether your airline operates every segment of the trip; you may find that the carrier you prefer flies you only part of the way. To find more booking tips and to check prices and make on-line flight reservations, log on to www. fodors.com.

CARRIERS

Aer Lingus operates regularly scheduled flights to Shannon and Dublin from New York's JFK (John F. Kennedy Airport), Boston's Logan, Chicago's O'Hare, and LAX (Los Angeles International Airport). Delta has a daily departure from Atlanta that flies first to Shannon and then to Dublin. Continental flies daily direct to Dublin and Shannon, departing from Newark Liberty International Airport in New Jersey. With the exception of special offers, the prices of the four airlines tend to be similar.

London to Dublin is one of the world's busiest international air routes. Aer Lingus, British Airways, British Midland, and CityJet all have several daily flights. Ryanair—famous for its cheap, no-frills service—offers several daily flights from London Gatwick, Luton, and Stanstead airports. With such healthy competition, bargains abound. British Airways, British Midlands, and low-cost airline Easyjet offer regularly scheduled flights to Belfast from London Heathrow Airport.

Aer Lingus provides service within Ireland to Dublin, Cork, Galway, Kerry, and Shannon. Aer Arann Express flies from Dublin to Cork, Derry, Donegal, Galway, Knock, and Sligo. British Airways has daily service between Dublin and Derry.

🔃 To & from Ireland **Aer Arann Express** ☎ 353/ 1844-7700 in the Republic of Ireland, 0800/587-2324 in the U.K., 3531/814-1058 in the U.S., Canada, Australia, and New Zealand ⊕ www.aerarannexpress.

com. **Aer Lingus** ☎ 800/474-7424 in the U.S. and Canada, 0845/084-4444 in the U.K., 02/9244-2123 in Australia, 09/308-3351 in New Zealand ⊕ www. aerlingus.com. **British Airways** ☎ 800/147-9297 in the U.S. and Canada, 0845/773-3377 in the U.K., 02/ 8904-8800 in Australia, 0800/274-8477 in New Zealand ⊕ www.britishairways.com. **British Midlands** ☎ 0870/607-0555 in the U.K. ⊕ www.flybmi. com. **Continental** ☎ 800/231-0856 in the U.S. ⊕ www.continental.com. **Delta** ☎ 800/241-4141 in the U.S. and Canada ⊕ www.delta.com. **Ryanair** ☎ 0871/246-0000 in the U.K. ⊕ www.ryanair.com.

CHECK-IN & BOARDING

Always **find out your carrier's check-in policy.** Plan to arrive at the airport about two hours before your scheduled departure time for domestic flights and 2½ to 3 hours before international flights. You may need to arrive earlier if you're flying from one of the busier airports or during peak air-traffic times.

Checking in and boarding an outbound plane tends to be civilized. Security is professional but not overbearing, and airport staffers are usually helpful and patient. In the busy summer season lines can get long, and you should play it safe and arrive a couple hours before your flight.

To avoid delays at airport-security checkpoints, try not to wear any metal. Jewelry, belt and other buckles, steel-toe shoes, barrettes, and underwire bras are among the items that can set off detectors.

Assuming that not everyone with a ticket will show up, airlines routinely overbook planes. When everyone does, airlines ask for volunteers to give up their seats. In return, these volunteers usually get a several-hundred-dollar flight voucher, which can be used toward the purchase of another ticket, and are rebooked on the next flight out. If there are not enough volunteers, the airline must choose who will be denied boarding. The first to get bumped are passengers who checked in late and those flying on discounted tickets, so get to the gate and check in as early as possible, especially during peak periods.

Always **bring a government-issued photo I.D.** to the airport; even when it's not required, a passport is best.

CUTTING COSTS

The least expensive airplane tickets to Ireland are priced for round-trip travel and must usually be purchased in advance. Airlines generally allow you to change your return date for a fee; most low-fare tickets, however, are nonrefundable. It's smart to call a number of airlines and check the Internet; when you are quoted a good price, book it on the spot—the same fare may not be available the next day, or even the next hour. Always check different routings and look into using alternate airports. Also, price off-peak flights, which may be significantly less expensive than others. Travel agents, especially low-fare specialists (⇨ Discounts & Deals), are helpful.

Consolidators are another good source. They buy tickets for scheduled flights at reduced rates from the airlines, then sell them at prices that beat the best fare available directly from the airlines. (Many also offer reduced car-rental and hotel rates.) Sometimes you can even get your money back if you need to return the ticket. Carefully read the fine print detailing penalties for changes and cancellations, purchase the ticket with a credit card, and confirm your consolidator reservation with the airline.

Many airlines, singly or in collaboration, offer discount air passes that allow foreigners to travel economically in a particular country or region. These visitor passes usually must be reserved and purchased before you leave home. Information about passes often can be found on airlines' international Web pages, which tend to be aimed at travelers from outside the carrier's home country. Also, try typing the name of the pass into a search engine, or search for "pass" within the carrier's Web site.

Charter carriers, such as Sceptre Charters, offer flights to Dublin and Shannon from various U.S. cities. Air Canada Vacations and Regent Holidays fly from Canada. Note that in certain seasons, usually fall and winter, their charter deals include mandatory hotel and car-rental packages.

🛪 Charters **Air Transat** ☎ 1-877/872-6728 ⊕ www.airtransat.com. **Regent Holidays** ☎ 800/387-4860 in Canada. **Sceptre Charters** ☎ 800/221-0924 ⊕ www.sceptreireland.com.

🛪 Consolidators **AirlineConsolidator.com** ☎ 888/468-5385 ⊕ www.airlineconsolidator.com; for international tickets. **Best Fares** ☎ 800/880-1234 or 800/576-8255 ⊕ www.bestfares.com; $59.90 annual membership. **Cheap Tickets** ☎ 800/377-1000 or 800/652-4327 ⊕ www.cheaptickets.com. **Expedia** ☎ 800/397-3342 or 404/728-8787 ⊕ www.expedia.com. **Hotwire** ☎ 866/468-9473 or 920/330-9418 ⊕ www.hotwire.com. **Now Voyager Travel** ✉ 45 W. 21st St., Suite 5A New York, NY 10010 ☎ 212/459-1616 🖷 212/243-2711 ⊕ www.nowvoyagertravel.com. **Onetravel.com** ⊕ www.onetravel.com. **Orbitz** ☎ 888/656-4546 ⊕ www.orbitz.com. **Priceline.com** ⊕ www.priceline.com. **Travelocity** ☎ 888/709-5983, 877/282-2925 in Canada, 0870/876-3876 in the U.K. ⊕ www.travelocity.com.

🛪 Discount Passes **Boomerang Pass**, Qantas, ☎ 800/227-4500, 0845/774-7767 in the U.K., 131-313 in Australia, 0800/808-767 in New Zealand (outside Auckland), 03/578-900 in Auckland ⊕ www.qantas.com. **FlightPass**, EuropebyAir, ☎ 888/387-2479 ⊕ www.europebyair.com.

ENJOYING THE FLIGHT

State your seat preference when purchasing your ticket, and then repeat it when you confirm and when you check in. For more legroom, you can request one of the few emergency-aisle seats at check-in, if you're capable of moving obstacles comparable in weight to an airplane exit door (usually between 35 pounds and 60 pounds)—a Federal Aviation Administration requirement of passengers in these seats. Seats behind a bulkhead also offer more legroom, but they don't have underseat storage. Don't sit in the row in front of the emergency aisle or in front of a bulkhead, where seats may not recline.

Ask the airline whether a snack or meal is served on the flight. If you have dietary concerns, request special meals when booking. These can be vegetarian, low-cholesterol, or kosher, for example. It's a good idea to pack some healthful snacks and a small (plastic) bottle of water in your carry-on bag. On long flights, try to maintain a normal routine, to help fight jet lag. At night, get some sleep. By day, eat light meals, drink water (not alcohol), and **move around the cabin** to stretch your legs. For additional jet-lag tips consult *Fodor's FYI: Travel Fit & Healthy* (available at bookstores everywhere).

Smoking policies vary from carrier to carrier. Many airlines prohibit smoking on all of their flights; others allow smoking only on certain routes or certain departures. Ask your carrier about its policy.

FLYING TIMES
Flying time to Ireland is 6½ hours from New York, 7½ hours from Chicago, 10 hours from Los Angeles, 1 hour from London, and 27 hours from Sydney.

HOW TO COMPLAIN
If your baggage goes astray or your flight goes awry, complain right away. Most carriers require that you **file a claim immediately.** The Aviation Consumer Protection Division of the Department of Transportation publishes *Fly-Rights,* which discusses airlines and consumer issues and is available online. You can also find articles and information on mytravelrights.com, the Web site of the nonprofit Consumer Travel Rights Center.

▪ Airline Complaints Aviation Consumer Protection Division ✉ U.S. Department of Transportation, Office of Aviation Enforcement and Proceedings, C-75, Room 4107, 400 7th St. SW, Washington, DC 20590 🖷 202/366–2220 ⊕ airconsumer.ost.dot.gov. **Federal Aviation Administration Consumer Hotline** ✉ for inquiries: FAA, 800 Independence Ave. SW, Washington, DC 20591 🖷 800/322–7873 ⊕ www.faa.gov.

RECONFIRMING
Check the status of your flight before you leave for the airport. You can do this on your carrier's Web site, by linking to a flight-status checker (many Web booking services offer these), or by calling your carrier or travel agent. Always confirm international flights at least 72 hours ahead of the scheduled departure time.

AIRPORTS
The major gateways to Ireland are Dublin Airport (DUB) on the east coast, 10 km (6 mi) north of the city center, and Shannon Airport (SNN) on the west coast, 25 km (16 mi) west of Limerick. Two airports serve Belfast: Belfast International Airport

(BFS) at Aldergrove, 24 km (15 mi) from the city, handles local and U.K. flights, as well as all other international traffic; Belfast City Airport (BHD), 6½ km (4 mi) from the city, handles local and United Kingdom flights only. In addition, the City of Derry Airport (LDY) receives flights from Dublin, Manchester, Birmingham, and Glasgow in the United Kingdom.

▪ Airport Information Belfast City Airport 🕾 028/9045–7745 ⊕ www.belfastcityairport.com. **Belfast International Airport at Aldergrove** 🕾 028/9448–4848 ⊕ www.belfastairport.com. **City of Derry Airport** 🕾 028/7181–0784 ⊕ www.cityofderryairport.com. **Dublin Airport** 🕾 01/814–1111 ⊕ www.dublinairport.ie. **Shannon Airport** 🕾 061/712–000 ⊕ www.shannonairport.com.

DUTY-FREE SHOPPING
Duty-free shopping isn't available for people traveling between European Union (EU) countries, and you can no longer buy duty-free goods aboard many international Aer Lingus flights. If you like to shop and you're on one of these flights, stock up on goods at the airport before boarding. For duty-free allowances when entering Ireland from a non-EU country, *see* Customs & Duties.

BIKE TRAVEL
See "Sports & the Outdoors."

BIKES IN FLIGHT
Most airlines accommodate bikes as luggage, provided they are dismantled and boxed; check with individual airlines about packing requirements. Some airlines sell bike boxes, which are often free at bike shops, for about $20 (bike bags can be considerably more expensive). International travelers often can substitute a bike for a piece of checked luggage at no charge; otherwise, the cost is about $100. Most U.S. and Canadian airlines charge $40–$80 each way.

BOAT & FERRY TRAVEL
The ferry is a convenient way to travel between Ireland and elsewhere in Europe, particularly the United Kingdom. There are six main ferry ports to Ireland; four in the republic at Dublin Port, Dun Laoghaire, Rosslare, and Cork, and two in Northern Ireland at Belfast and Larne. The

cost of your trip can vary substantially, so spend time with a travel agent and compare prices carefully. Bear in mind, too, that flying can be cheaper, so look into all types of transportation before booking.

Irish Ferries operates the *Ulysses,* the world's largest car ferry, on its Dublin to Holyhead, Wales, route (3 hrs, 15 mins); there's also a swift service (1 hr, 50 mins) between these two ports. There are several trips daily. The company also runs between Rosslare and Pembroke, Wales (3 hrs, 45 mins), and has service to France. Stena Line sails several times a day between Dublin and Holyhead (3 hrs, 15 mins) and has swift service to Dun Laoghaire (1 hr, 40 mins). The company also runs a fast craft (1 hr, 45 mins) and a superferry (3 hrs, 15 mins) between Belfast and Stranraer, Scotland, as well as a fast craft (1 hr, 40 mins) and a superferry (3 hrs, 30 mins) between Rosslare and Fishguard, Wales. There are several trips daily on both routes.

SeaCat operates a service between Dublin and Liverpool (3 hrs, 45 mins); between Dublin and Belfast and the Isle of Man (2 hrs, 45 mins); and between Belfast and Troon, Scotland (2 hrs, 30 mins), and Heysham in northwestern England (3 hrs, 55 mins). Norse Merchant offers a Dublin and Belfast to Liverpool service (8 hrs). P&O Irish Sea vessels run between Larne and several U.K. destinations, including Troon, Scotland (4 hrs), a couple times a day. The company also sails from Dublin to Liverpool daily (7 hrs, 30 mins) or Mostyn (6 hrs) in England three times a week. Passengers with cars can also sail between Dublin (18 hrs) or Rosslare (20 hrs) and Cherbourg, France, three times a week. Swansea Cork Ferries travels between Swansea and Cork from mid-March to early November. The crossing takes 10 hours, but easy access by road to both ports makes this longer sea route a good choice for motorists.

A 10-minute car ferry crosses the River Suir between Ballyhack in County Wexford and Passage East (near Arthurstown) in County Waterford, introducing you to two pretty fishing villages. The ferry oper-

ates continuously during daylight hours and costs €4.45 per car, €1 for foot passengers. A boat from Tarbert in County Kerry leaves every hour on the half hour for Killimer in County Clare; return ferries leave Killimer every hour on the hour. The 30-minute journey across the Shannon Estuary costs €8.90 per car, €2.55 for foot passengers. The scenic Cork Harbor crossing allows those traveling from West Cork or Kinsale to Cobh and the east coast to bypass the city center. The five-minute car ferry runs from Glenbrook (near Ringaskiddy) in the west to Carrigaloe (near Cobh) in the east and operates continuously from 7:15 AM to 12:45 AM daily. It costs €3.80 per car, €0.75 for foot passengers.

There are regular services to the Aran Islands from Galway City, Rossaveal in County Galway, and Doolin in County Clare. Ferries also sail to Inishbofin off the Galway coast and Arranmore off the Donegal coast, and to Bere, Sherkin, and Cape Clear Islands off the coast of County Cork. The islands are all small enough to explore on foot, so the ferries are for foot passengers and bicycles only. Other islands—the Blaskets and the Skelligs in Kerry, Rathlin in Antrim, and Tory, off the Donegal coast—can be reached by private arrangements with local boatmen. Full details on ferries to the islands are available in a publication from the Irish Tourist Board (ITB, also known as Bord Fáilte).

FARES & SCHEDULES

You can get schedules and purchase tickets, with a credit card if you like, directly from the ferry lines. You can also pick up tickets at Dublin tourism offices and at any major travel agent in Ireland or the United Kingdom. Payment must be made in the currency of the country of the port of departure.

🚢 Boat & Ferry Information **Irish Ferries** ☎ 1890/313131 in Ireland, 08705/171717 in the U.K., 0143/944694 in France ⊕ www.irishferries.ie. **Norse Merchant** ☎ 01/819–2999 in Ireland, 0870/600–4321 in the U.K. ⊕ www.norsemerchant.com. **P&O Irish Sea** ☎ 1800/409049 in Ireland, 0870/2424777 in the U.K., 0803/013013 in France ⊕ www.poirishsea.com **SeaCat** ☎ 01/836–4019 in Ireland,

08705/523523 in Northern Ireland, 0151/236-2061 in the U.K., 0129/231-9103 in Scotland, 01624/645695 in the Isle of Man ⊕ www.seacat.co.uk. **Stena Line** ☎ 01/204-7777 in Ireland, 028/9074-7747 in Northern Ireland, 08705/707070 in the U.K. ⊕ www.stenaline.co.uk. **Swansea Cork Ferries** ☎ 021/427-1166 in Ireland, 01792/456116 in the U.K. ⊕ www.swansea-cork.ie.

BUSINESS HOURS

Business hours are 9–5, sometimes later in the larger towns. In smaller towns, stores often close from 1 to 2 for lunch. If a holiday falls on a weekend, most businesses are closed on Monday as well.

BANKS & OFFICES

Banks are open 10–4 weekdays. In small towns they may close from 12:30 to 1:30. They remain open until 5 one afternoon per week; the day varies, although it's usually Thursday. Post offices are open weekdays 9–5 and Saturday 9–1; some of the smaller branches close for lunch.

In Northern Ireland bank hours are weekdays 9:30–4:30. Post offices are open weekdays 9–5:30, Saturday 9–1. Some close for an hour at lunch.

GAS STATIONS

There are some 24-hour gas stations along the highways; otherwise, hours vary from morning rush hour to late evenings.

MUSEUMS & SIGHTS

Museums and sights are generally open Tuesday–Saturday 10–5 and Sunday 2–5.

PHARMACIES

Most pharmacies are open Monday–Saturday 9–5:30 or 6. Larger towns and cities often have 24-hour establishments.

SHOPS

Most shops are open Monday–Saturday 9–5:30 or 6. Once a week—normally Wednesday, Thursday, or Saturday—they close at 1 PM. These times do *not* apply to Dublin, where stores generally stay open later, and they can vary from region to region, so it's best to check locally. Larger malls usually stay open late once a week—generally until 9 on Thursday or Friday.

Shops in Belfast are open weekdays 9–5:30, with a late closing on Thursday,

usually at 9. Elsewhere in Northern Ireland, shops close for the afternoon once a week, usually Wednesday or Thursday; check locally. In addition, most smaller shops close for an hour or so at lunch.

BUS TRAVEL

In the Republic of Ireland, long-distance bus services are operated by Bus Éireann, which also provides local service in Cork, Galway, Limerick, and Waterford. There's really only one class, and prices are similar for all seats. Note, though, that outside of the peak season, services are limited; some routes (e.g., Killarney–Dingle) disappear altogether. There's often only one trip a day on express routes, and one a week to some remote villages. To ensure that a bus journey is feasible, buy a copy of Bus Éireann's timetable—€1.30 from any bus terminal—or check online. Many of the destination indicators are in Irish (Gaelic), so make sure you get on the right bus.

Numerous bus companies run between Britain and the Irish Republic, but be ready for long hours on the road and possible delays. All use either the Holyhead–Dublin or Fishguard/Pembroke–Rosslare ferry routes. National Express, a consortium of companies, has Supabus (as its vehicles are known) services from all major British cities to more than 90 Irish destinations. Slattery's, an Irish company, has services from London, Manchester, Liverpool, Oxford, Birmingham, Leeds, and North Wales to more than 100 Irish destinations.

In Northern Ireland, all buses are operated by the state-owned Ulsterbus. Service is generally good, with particularly useful links to those towns not served by train. Ulsterbus also offers tours. Buses to Belfast run from London and from Birmingham, making the Stranraer–Port of Belfast crossing. Contact National Express.

RESERVATIONS & PAYING

Check with the bus office to see if reservations are accepted for your route; if not, show up early to get a seat. Note: prepaid tickets don't apply to a particular bus time, just a route, so if one vehicle is full you can try another. You can buy tickets at

the main tourist offices, at the bus station, or on the bus (though it's cash only for the latter option).

You can save money by buying a multiday pass, some of which can be combined with rail service. There are also cost-cutting passes that will give access to travel in both Northern Ireland and the Republic of Ireland. A Freedom of Northern Ireland ticket costs £42 for seven days' unlimited bus and rail travel—a really good deal when you consider that a one-day ticket costs £12. In the republic, passes include the Irish Explorer Rail and Bus Pass, the Irish Rambler Card, the Irish Rover Card, and the Emerald Card. Contact Bus Éireann or Ulsterbus for details.

⚑ Bus Information Bus Éireann ☎ 01/836-6111 in the Republic of Ireland ⊕ www.buseireann.ie. **National Express** ☎ 08705/808-080 in the U.K. ⊕ www.nationalexpress.co.uk. **Slattery's** ☎ 020/ 7482-1604 in the U.K. **Ulsterbus** ☎ 028/9033-3000 in Northern Ireland ⊕ www.ulsterbus.co.uk.

CAMERAS & PHOTOGRAPHY

Nature has blessed Ireland with spectacular landscapes. In addition to cliffs, hills, and beaches, sunsets along the north and west coasts can be particularly dramatic because of the variable cloud cover and the clarity of light. Take a step outside at dusk during your visit wherever you may be and see if you can catch a sunset. The *Kodak Guide to Shooting Great Travel Pictures* (available at bookstores everywhere) is loaded with tips.

⚑ Photo Help Kodak Information Center ☎ 800/ 242-2424 ⊕ www.kodak.com.

EQUIPMENT PRECAUTIONS

Don't pack film or equipment in checked luggage, where it is much more susceptible to damage. X-ray machines used to view checked luggage are extremely powerful and therefore are likely to ruin your film. Try to ask for hand inspection of film, which becomes clouded after repeated exposure to airport X-ray machines, and keep videotapes and computer disks away from metal detectors. Always keep film, tape, and computer disks out of the sun. Carry an extra supply of batteries, and be prepared to turn on your camera,

camcorder, or laptop to prove to airport security personnel that the device is real.

FILM & DEVELOPING

Major brands of film are available throughout Ireland, although 24-hour developing is found only in cities. Advantix film and developing are available in larger centers. A roll of 36-exposure color film costs €6–€8. Many film processors are also able to make prints from digital cameras or transfer your digital photos to a CD.

VIDEOS

Videotape is widely available. The local tape standard is PAL, and a standard 180-minute cassette costs around €5.

CAR RENTAL

If you're renting a car in the Irish Republic and intend to visit Northern Ireland (or vice versa), make this clear when you get your car, and check that the rental insurance applies when you cross the border.

Renting a car in Ireland is far more expensive than organizing a rental before you leave home. Rates in Dublin for an economy car with a manual transmission and unlimited mileage are from €35 a day and €175 a week to €60 a day and €305 a week, depending on the season. This includes the republic's 12.5% tax on car rentals. Rates in Belfast begin at £30 a day and £160 a week and go up to around £35 a day and £200 a week, *not* including the 17.5% tax on car rentals in the North.

Both manual and automatic transmissions are readily available, though automatics cost extra. Typical economy car models include Toyota Corolla, Ford Mondeo, and Nissan Micra. Minivans, luxury cars (Mercedes or Alfa Romeos), and four-wheel-drive vehicles (say, a Jeep Cherokee) are also options, but the daily rates are high. Argus Rent A Car and Dan Dooley have convenient locations at Dublin, Shannon, Belfast, and Belfast City airports as well as at ferry ports.

⚑ Major Agencies Fax: 353 21 260 3773 **Alamo** ☎ 800/522-9696 in the U.S., 1800/301401 in Ireland, 01/260-3771 in Dublin ⊕ www.alamo.com. **Avis** ☎ 800/331-1084 in the U.S., 800/879-2847 in Canada, 0870/606-0100 in the U.K., 02/9353-9000 in Australia, 09/526-2847 in New Zealand, 1890/

405060 in Ireland, 01/605-7500 in Dublin ⊕ www. avis.com. **Budget** ☎ 800/527-0700 in the U.S., 0870/156-5656 in the U.K., 1850/575767 in Ireland ⊕ www.budget.com. **Dollar** ☎ 800/800-6000 in the U.S., 0800/085-4578 in the U.K., 01/670-7890 in Dublin ⊕ www.dollar.com. **Hertz** ☎ 800/654-3001 in the U.S., 800/263-0600 in Canada, 0870/844-8844 in the U.K., 02/9669-2444 in Australia, 09/256-8690 in New Zealand, 01/676-7476 in Ireland ⊕ www.hertz.com. **National Car Rental** ☎ 800/227-7368 in the U.S., 0870/600-6666 in the U.K., 01/844-4162 in Ireland, 12/603771 in Dublin ⊕ www.nationalcar.com.

CUTTING COSTS

For a good deal, book through a travel agent who will shop around. Also, price local car-rental companies—whose rates may be lower still, although their service and maintenance may not be as good as those of major rental agencies—and research rates on the Internet. Consolidators that specialize in air travel can offer good rates on cars as well (⇨ Air Travel). Remember to ask about required deposits, cancellation penalties, and drop-off charges if you're planning to pick up the car in one city and leave it in another. If you're traveling during a holiday period, also make sure that a confirmed reservation guarantees you a car.

Do look into wholesalers, companies that do not own fleets but rent in bulk from those that do and often offer better rates than traditional car-rental operations. Prices are best during off-peak periods. Rentals booked through wholesalers often must be paid for before you leave home.

🖬 Local Agencies **Argus** ☎ 01/490-4444 in Dublin, 048/9442-3444 in Belfast ⊕ www.argus-rentacar.com. **Dan Dooley** ☎ 800/331-9301 in the U.S., 0800/282189 in the U.K., 062/53103 in Ireland ⊕ www.dan-dooley.ie.

🖬 Wholesalers **Auto Europe** ☎ 207/842-2000 or 800/223-5555 🖷 207/842-2222 ⊕ www. autoeurope.com. **Destination Europe Resources** (DER) ✉ 9501 W. Devon Ave., Rosemont, IL 60018 ☎ 800/782-2424 🖷 800/282-7474 ⊕ www.der. com. **Europe by Car** ☎ 212/581-3040 or 800/223-1516 🖷 212/246-1458 ⊕ www.europebycar.com. **Kemwel** ☎ 877/820-0668 or 800/678-0678 🖷 207/842-2147 ⊕ www.kemwel.com.

INSURANCE

When driving a rented car you are generally responsible for any damage to or loss of the vehicle. Collision policies that car-rental companies sell for European rentals typically do not cover stolen vehicles. Before you rent—and purchase collision or theft coverage—see what coverage you already have under the terms of your personal auto-insurance policy and credit cards.

REQUIREMENTS & RESTRICTIONS

In Ireland your own driver's license is acceptable. An International Driver's Permit, which is recognized universally, is a good idea; it's available from the American or Canadian Automobile Association and, in the United Kingdom, from the Automobile Association or Royal Automobile Club.

Most rental companies require you to be over 23 to rent a car in Ireland (a few will rent to those over 21) and to have had a license for more than a year. Some companies refuse to rent to visitors over 70. Children under 12 years of age aren't allowed to ride in the front seat unless they're in a properly fitted child seat.

SURCHARGES

Before you pick up a car in one city and leave it in another, ask about drop-off charges or one-way service fees, which can be substantial. Also inquire about early-return policies; some rental agencies charge extra if you return the car before the time specified in your contract, while others give you a refund for the days not used. To avoid a hefty refueling fee, fill the tank just before you turn in the car, but be aware that gas stations near the rental outlet may overcharge. It's almost never a deal to buy the tank of gas that's in the car when you rent it; the understanding is that you'll return it empty, but some fuel usually remains.

Drivers between the ages of 21 and 25 and 70 and 75 will probably be subject to an insurance surcharge—if they're allowed to drive a rental car at all. An additional driver will add about €5 a day to your car rental, and a child seat costs about €19 for the rental and will require 24-hour advance notice.

CAR TRAVEL

Roads in the Irish Republic are generally good, though four-lane highways, or motorways, are the exception rather than the rule. In addition, many roads twist and wind their way up and down hills and through towns, which can slow you down. On small, rural roads, **watch out for cattle and sheep**; they may be just around the next bend. Reckless drivers are also a problem in the countryside, so remain cautious and alert. Ireland ranks third worst amongst the original 15 EU countries on road accident frequency and has the highest auto accident fatality rate in Europe.

Road signs in the republic are generally in both Irish (Gaelic) and English; in the northwest and Connemara, most are in Irish only, so get a good road map. On the new green signposts distances are in kilometers; on the old white signposts they're in miles. Knowing the name of the next town on your itinerary is more important than knowing the route number: neither the small local signposts nor the local people refer to roads by official numbers. Traffic signs are the same as in the rest of Europe, and roadway markings are standard.

There are no border checkpoints between the republic and Northern Ireland, where the road network is excellent and, outside Belfast, uncrowded. Road signs and traffic regulations conform to the British system.

All ferries on both principal routes to the Irish Republic take cars. Fishguard and Pembroke are relatively easy to reach by road. The car trip to Holyhead, on the other hand, is sometimes difficult: delays on the A55 North Wales coastal road aren't unusual. Car ferries to Belfast leave from the Scottish port of Stranraer and the English city of Liverpool; those to Larne leave from Stranraer and Cairnryan. Speed limits are generally 95 to 100 kph (roughly 60 to 70 mph) on the motorways, 90 kph (50 mph) on other roads, and 50 kph (30 mph) in towns.

EMERGENCY SERVICES

Membership in an emergency car service is a good idea if you're using your own vehicle in Ireland. The Automobile Association of Ireland is a sister organization of its English counterpart and is highly recommended. Note that the AA can only help you or your vehicle if you are a member of the association. If not, contact your car rental company for assistance. If involved in an accident you should note the details of the vehicle and the driver and witnesses and report the incident to a member of the Garda Síochána (the Irish Police) as soon as possible. Since traffic congestion is chronic in Dublin, emergency services are more likely to be dispatched quickly in order help you and to clear the road. If your car does break down, if at all possible try to stop it in a well-lit area near a public phone. If you are on a secondary or minor road, remain in your car with the doors locked after you call for assistance. If you break down on the motorway, you should pull onto the hard shoulder and stay out of your car with the passenger side door open and the other doors locked. This will allow you to jump into the car quickly if you sense any trouble. Make sure you check credentials of anyone who offers assistance—note the license-plate number and color of the assisting vehicle before you step out of the car.

🚗 **Automobile Association of Ireland** 🕾 01/617–9999 ⊕ www.aaireland.ie. **Police** 🕾 999.

GASOLINE

You'll find gas stations along most roads. Self-service is the norm in larger establishments. Major credit cards and traveler's checks are usually accepted. Prices are near the lower end for Europe, with unleaded gas priced around €0.90 a liter—more than three times what gasoline costs in the United States. Prices vary significantly from station to station, so it's worth driving around the block.

ROAD CONDITIONS

Most roads are paved and make for easy travel. Roads are classified as M, N, or R: those designated with an M for "motorway" are double-lane divided highways with paved shoulders; N, or national, routes are generally undivided highways with shoulders; and R, or regional, roads tend to be narrow and twisty.

Rush hour traffic in Dublin, Cork, Limerick, Belfast, and Galway can be intense. Rush hours in Dublin run 7 AM to 9:30 AM and 5 PM to 7 PM; special events such as football (soccer) games will also tie up traffic in and around the city.

ROAD MAPS
Road maps can be found at most gas stations and bookstores.

RULES OF THE ROAD
The Irish, like the British, **drive on the left-hand side of the road.** Safety belts must be worn by the driver and all passengers, and children under 12 must travel in the back unless riding in a car seat. It's compulsory for motorcyclists and their passengers to wear helmets.

Drunk-driving laws are strict. The legal limit is 80 mg of alcohol per 100 ml of blood. Ireland has a Breathalyzer test, which the police can administer anytime. If you refuse to take it, the odds are you'll be prosecuted anyway. As always, the best advice is **don't drink if you plan to drive.**

It is illegal to drive and talk on your mobile phone at the same time. If caught you face a stiff fine of €435. Speed cameras and radar are used throughout Ireland. Speeding carries on on-the-spot fine of €80 and if the Gardaí (police) charges you with excessive speeding you could be summoned to court. This carries a much higher fine and you will be summoned within six months (meaning you could be required to return to Ireland).

Note that a continuous white line down the center of the road prohibits passing. Barred markings on the road and flashing yellow beacons indicate a crossing, where pedestrians have right of way. At a junction of two roads of equal importance, the driver to the right has right of way. On a roundabout, vehicles approaching from the right have right of way. Also, remember there are no right turns permitted on a red light. If another motorist flashes their headlights at you they are not warning of a speed trap ahead, they are giving you right of way.

Despite the relatively light traffic, parking in towns can be a problem. Signs with the letter *P* indicate that parking is permitted; a stroke through the *P* warns you to stay away or you'll be liable for a fine of €19.05–€63.50; however, if youar car gets towed away, the fine is €190.45. In Dublin and Cork, parking lots are your best bet, but check the rate first in Dublin; they vary wildly.

In Northern Ireland there are plenty of parking lots in the towns (usually free except in Belfast), and you should use them. In Belfast, you can't park your car in some parts of the city center, more because of congestion than security problems.

CHILDREN IN IRELAND
Involve your youngsters as you outline your trip. When packing, include things to keep them busy en route. On sightseeing days try to schedule activities of special interest to your children. Although most attractions and bus and rail journeys offer a rate of half price or less for children, **look for "family tickets,"** which may be cheaper and usually cover two adults and up to four children. If you are renting a car, don't forget to arrange for a car seat when you reserve. For general advice about traveling with children, consult *Fodor's FYI: Travel with Your Baby* (available in bookstores everywhere).

FLYING
If your children are two or older, ask about children's airfares. As a general rule, infants under two not occupying a seat fly at greatly reduced fares or even for free. But if you want to guarantee a seat for an infant, you have to pay full fare. Consider flying during off-peak days and times; most airlines will grant an infant a seat without a ticket if there are available seats. When booking, confirm carry-on allowances if you're traveling with infants. In general, for babies charged 10% to 50% of the adult fare you are allowed one carry-on bag and a collapsible stroller; if the flight is full, the stroller may have to be checked or you may be limited to less.

Experts agree that it's a good idea to use safety seats aloft for children weighing less than 40 pounds. Airlines set their own policies: if you use a safety seat, U.S.

carriers usually require that the child be ticketed, even if he or she is young enough to ride free, because the seats must be strapped into regular seats. Do **check your airline's policy about using safety seats during takeoff and landing.** Safety seats are not allowed everywhere in the plane, so get your seat assignments as early as possible.

When reserving, request children's meals or a freestanding bassinet (not available at all airlines) if you need them. But note that bulkhead seats, where you must sit to use the bassinet, may lack an overhead bin or storage space on the floor.

FOOD

Most of the food in Ireland will feel familiar to children, from the traditional bacon-and-eggs breakfast to fish-and-chips. Pubs are your best bet if you want to be guaranteed children will recognize what they're eating. In the larger centers fast-food chains such as McDonald's, KFC, and Pizza Hut are common. Sausages and chips are popular with Irish children. "Chips" are what Americans call french fries (while potato chips are called crisps in Ireland). Hotel and pub restaurants often have children's menus and high chairs. Irish licensing laws allow children under 14 into pubs—although they may not consume alcohol on the premises until they're 18, and they're expected to leave by anywhere from 5:30 to 7 PM, depending on how busy the pub gets.

LODGING

Most hotels in Ireland allow children under a certain age to stay in their parents' rooms at no extra charge, but others charge for them as extra adults; be sure to **find out the cutoff age for children's discounts.** Family-friendly hotels at all levels will offer cots, cribs, and babysitting services, for an additional charge. Only more expensive hotels are likely to have swimming pools.

In Dublin there is a nice array of family friendly hotels. Across the country you would be wise to target a three- or four-star accommodation to insure better services. If your child is between the ages of

4 and 13, you should consider staying at one of the nine Quality Hotels across the country. They bill themselves as family-friendly hotels and during the first two weeks of July host Samba Soccer, a camp offering soccer and other team activities in a non-competitive environment—a great way for your child to make new friends on vacation.

🟥 **Quality Hotels** ☎ 1850/ 409-000 ⊕ www. choicehotelsireland.ie. **Samba Soccer** ☎ 1850/ 409-002 ⊕ www.sambasoccer.com.

SIGHTS & ATTRACTIONS

Places that are especially appealing to children are indicated by a rubber-duckie icon (🐤) in the margin. Ireland has a very young population and is experiencing a bit of a baby boom. Many hotels, restaurants, and tourist attractions are children-friendly. There are plenty of attractions in Dublin to amuse children, including castles, museums, and zoos. Listings of upcoming events are published in the *Irish Times* (€1.50) "The Ticket" supplement each Wednesday. In rainy weather, you may want to take in a show at the Lambert Puppet Theatre—it puts on a puppet show each Saturday and Sunday suitable for children from four years of age. Both the National Museum and Collins Barracks and the National Gallery have special classes for children. On a sunny day try Dublin Zoo, located on the city outskirts at Phoenix Park; the Airfield Trust (with its working educational farm in the center of the Dublin suburbs); or take a ride on the miniature railway at Marlay Park.

Outside Dublin, there is also a variety of sights for children to enjoy. Keep an eye on the weather; if you happen upon a good day, children can amuse themselves for hours at one of the many beaches. Theater productions for children can be found at playhouses around the country. In Belfast, children can learn about science in a hands-on way at the W5 Discovery Centre. As the name suggests, children are challenged to explore using all five senses. Out west in Tralee is the country's largest water park, the Aqua Dome. Over in Dingle, you can take a boat tour of the bay and hopefully spot the famed Fungi the

Dingle Dolphin riding the waters. Galway offers the Oceans Alive Visitor Centre while, over in Cork, Ireland's Prince August Toy Soldier Factory, in Macroom, makes for a truly fun outing. And don't forget: from coast to coast, there are magical medieval castles to delight children of *all* ages.

Local Information Airfield Trust ☎ 01/298-4301 ⊕ www.airfield.ie. **The Aqua Dome** ☎ 066/712-8899 ⊕ www.discoverkerry.com/aquadome. **Dublin Zoo** ☎ 01/474-8900 ⊕ www.dublinzoo.ie. **Fungi the Dingle Dolphin** ☎ 066/915-1967 ⊕ www.dinglemarine.com. *Irish Times* ⊕ www.ireland.com. **Lambert Puppet Theatre and Museum** ☎ 01/280-0974 ⊕ www.lambertpuppettheatre.com. **Marlay Park Miniature Railway** ☎ 01/668-0294. **National Gallery** ☎ 01/661-5133 ⊕ www.nationalgallery.ie. **National Museum** ☎ 01/677-7444 ⊕ www.museum.ie. **Oceans Alive Visitor Centre** ☎ 095/43473. **Prince August Toy Soldier Factory** ☎ 026/40222 ⊕ www.princeaugust.ie. **W5 The Discovery Centre** ☎ 028/9046-7700 ⊕ www.w5online.org.uk.

SUPPLIES & EQUIPMENT

Familiar brands of items and supplies for babies and children are available in every town and village; check the supermarket or family grocery store. A 400-gram (14.29-ounce) box of powdered baby formula will cost around €5.10 and 600 ml of premixed formula is about €7.60. Disposable diapers will cost between €5.10 and €6.35 for a package of 26.

TRANSPORTATION

Children under 16 years of age ride the train for half price and infants ride for free. You are allowed to bring your own car seats. Bassinets will not be provided for infants. Buses operate under the same system. Car seats are readily available at car-rental firms, but most require 24 hours' notice. Children under 12 years of age can't ride in the front seat unless in a car seat.

COMPUTERS ON THE ROAD

If you're traveling with a laptop, carry a spare battery and adapter. Most laptops will work at both 120V and 220V, but you will need an adapter so the plug will fit in the socket. In the countryside, a surge protector is a good idea.

Going online is becoming routine in Dublin, thanks, in part, to the wi-fi hotspots—which allow you to make a wireless connection from your laptop onto a network—popping up across the city. Nethouse has the most Internet cafés in the country, with nine locations in Dublin and one in Cork. There are also many independent Internet cafés across the country. Prices vary from the low end in Dublin of €2.60 per hour to €5.00 per hour in smaller cities. There are also new wi-fi hotspots in other major cities throughout the country, such as the Insomnia Coffee and Sandwich Bar chain in Galway. Dublin Airport and Dun Laoghaire Harbor have facilities to access wireless connection to the Internet. Hotels in Dublin that offer wi-fi access include the Conrad and the Four Seasons. A wi-fi connection will cost about €9 for an hour or €22 for unlimited access within a 24-hour period.

CONSUMER PROTECTION

Whether you're shopping for gifts or purchasing travel services, **pay with a major credit card** whenever possible, so you can cancel payment or get reimbursed if there's a problem (and you can provide documentation). If you're doing business with a particular company for the first time, contact your local Better Business Bureau and the attorney general's office in your state and (for U.S. businesses) the company's home state as well. Have any complaints been filed? Finally, if you're buying a package or tour, always consider travel insurance that includes default coverage (⇨ Insurance).

BBBs Council of Better Business Bureaus ✉ 4200 Wilson Blvd., Suite 800, Arlington, VA 22203 ☎ 703/276-0100 🖷 703/525-8277 ⊕ www.bbb.org.

CRUISE TRAVEL

Cruise travel in Ireland consists of sailing the inland waterways. The Shannon River system provides a great alternative to traveling overland. In some places bicycles can be rented so you can drop anchor and explore.

To learn how to plan, choose, and book a cruise-ship voyage, consult *Fodor's FYI:*

Plan & Enjoy Your Cruise (available in bookstores everywhere).

📕 Cruise Lines **Ireland Line Cruisers** ✉ Killaloe ☎ 061/375-011. **Leisure Afloat Ltd.** ✉ Shellumsrath House, Kilkenny ☎ 056/64395 ⊕ www. leisureafloat.com. **Riversdale Barge Holidays** ✉ Ballinamore ☎ 078/44122. **Shannon Castle Line** ✉ Williamstown Harbor, Whitegate ☎ 061/927-042. **Silver Line Cruisers** ✉ The Marina, Banagher ☎ 0509/51112 ⊕ www.silverlinecruisers.com. **Waveline Cruisers** ✉ Quigley's Marina, Killinure Point, Glassan ☎ 0902/85711 ⊕ www.waveline.ie.

CUSTOMS & DUTIES

When shopping abroad, keep receipts for all purchases. Upon reentering the country, **be ready to show customs officials what you've bought.** Pack purchases together in an easily accessible place. If you think a duty is incorrect, appeal the assessment. If you object to the way your clearance was handled, note the inspector's badge number. In either case, first ask to see a supervisor. If the problem isn't resolved, write to the appropriate authorities, beginning with the port director at your point of entry.

IN IRELAND

Duty-free allowances have been abolished for those traveling between countries in the EU. For goods purchased outside the EU, you may import duty-free: (1) 200 cigarettes or 100 cigarillos or 50 cigars or 250 grams of smoking tobacco; (2) 2 liters of wine, and either 1 liter of alcoholic drink over 22% volume or 2 liters of alcoholic drink under 22% volume (sparkling or fortified wine included); (3) 50 grams (60 ml) of perfume and ¼ liter of toilet water; and (4) other goods (including beer) to a value of €180.30 per person (€92.70 per person for travelers under 15 years of age). Goods that cannot be freely imported to the Irish Republic include firearms, ammunition, explosives, indecent or obscene books and pictures, oral smokeless tobacco products, meat and meat products, poultry and poultry products, plants and plant products (including shrubs, vegetables, fruit, bulbs, and seeds), and hay or straw even used as packing. Domestic cats and dogs from outside the United Kingdom and live animals from outside Northern Ireland must be quarantined for six months. No animals or pets of any kind may be brought into Northern Ireland without a six-month quarantine. Other items that may not be imported include fresh meats, plants and vegetables, controlled drugs, and firearms and ammunition.

📕 Customs and Excise ✉ Irish Life Building, 2nd floor, Middle Abbey St., Dublin 1 ☎ 01/878-8811 ⊕ www.revenue.ie. **HM Customs and Excise** ✉ Portcullis House, 21 Cowbridge Rd. E, Cardiff CF11 9SS ☎ 0845/010-9000 or 0208/929-0152, 0208/929-6731 or 0208/910-3602 complaints ⊕ www. hmce.gov.uk.

IN AUSTRALIA

Australian residents who are 18 or older may bring home A$400 worth of souvenirs and gifts (including jewelry), 250 cigarettes or 250 grams of cigars or other tobacco products, and 1,125 ml of alcohol (including wine, beer, and spirits). Residents under 18 may bring back A$200 worth of goods. Members of the same family traveling together may pool their allowances. Prohibited items include meat products. Seeds, plants, and fruits need to be declared upon arrival.

📕 Australian Customs Service ♐ Regional Director, Box 8, Sydney, NSW 2001 ☎ 02/9213-2000 or 1300/363263, 02/9364-7222 or 1800/020-504 quarantine-inquiry line ♐ 02/9213-4043 ⊕ www. customs.gov.au.

IN CANADA

Canadian residents who have been out of Canada for at least seven days may bring in C$750 worth of goods duty-free. If you've been away fewer than seven days but more than 48 hours, the duty-free allowance drops to C$200. If your trip lasts 24 to 48 hours, the allowance is C$50. You may not pool allowances with family members. Goods claimed under the C$750 exemption may follow you by mail; those claimed under the lesser exemptions must accompany you. Alcohol and tobacco products may be included in the seven-day and 48-hour exemptions but not in the 24-hour exemption. If you meet the age requirements of the province or territory through which you reenter Canada, you may bring in, duty-free, 1.5 liters of wine *or* 1.14 liters (40 imperial ounces) of liquor *or* 24 12-ounce cans or bottles of beer or ale. Also, if you meet the local age requirement for tobacco products, you may bring in, duty-free, 200 cigarettes and 50 cigars. Check ahead of time with the Canada Customs and Revenue Agency or the Department of Agriculture for policies regarding meat products, seeds, plants, and fruits.

You may send an unlimited number of gifts (only one gift per recipient, however) worth up to C$60 each duty-free to Canada. Label the package UNSOLICITED GIFT—VALUE UNDER $60. Alcohol and tobacco are excluded.

🔝 **Canada Customs and Revenue Agency** ✉ 2265 St. Laurent Blvd., Ottawa, Ontario K1G 4K3 ☎ 800/461-9999 in Canada, 204/983-3500, 506/636-5064 ⊕ www.ccra.gc.ca.

IN NEW ZEALAND

All homeward-bound residents may bring back NZ$700 worth of souvenirs and gifts; passengers may not pool their allowances, and children can claim only the concession on goods intended for their own use. For those 17 or older, the duty-free allowance also includes 4.5 liters of wine or beer; one 1,125-ml bottle of spirits; and either 200 cigarettes, 250 grams of tobacco, 50 cigars, *or* a combination of the three up to 250 grams. Meat products, seeds, plants, and fruits must be declared upon arrival to the Agricultural Services Department.

🔝 **New Zealand Customs** ✉ Head office: The Customhouse, 17–21 Whitmore St., Box 2218, Wellington ☎ 09/300-5399 or 0800/428-786 ⊕ www.customs.govt.nz.

IN THE U.K.

If you are a U.K. resident and your journey was wholly within the European Union, you probably won't have to pass through customs when you return to the United Kingdom. If you plan to bring back large quantities of alcohol or tobacco, check EU limits beforehand. In most cases, if you bring back more than 200 cigars, 3,200 cigarettes, 400 cigarillos, 10 liters of spirits, 110 liters of beer, 20 liters of forti-

fied wine, and/or 90 liters of wine, you have to declare the goods upon return. Prohibited items include unpasteurized milk, regardless of country of origin.

🔝 **HM Customs and Excise** ✉ Portcullis House, 21 Cowbridge Rd. E, Cardiff CF11 9SS ☎ 0845/010-9000 or 0208/929-0152 advice service, 0208/929-6731 or 0208/910-3602 complaints ⊕ www.hmce.gov.uk.

IN THE U.S.

U.S. residents who have been out of the country for at least 48 hours may bring home, for personal use, $800 worth of foreign goods duty-free, as long as they haven't used the $800 allowance or any part of it in the past 30 days. This exemption may include 1 liter of alcohol (for travelers 21 and older), 200 cigarettes, and 100 non-Cuban cigars. Family members from the same household who are traveling together may pool their $800 personal exemptions. For fewer than 48 hours, the duty-free allowance drops to $200, which may include 50 cigarettes, 10 non-Cuban cigars, and 150 ml of alcohol (or 150 ml of perfume containing alcohol). The $200 allowance cannot be combined with other individuals' exemptions, and if you exceed it, the full value of all the goods will be taxed. Antiques, which U. S. Customs and Border Protection defines as objects more than 100 years old, enter duty-free, as do original works of art done entirely by hand, including paintings, drawings, and sculptures. This doesn't apply to folk art or handicrafts, which are in general dutiable.

You may also send packages home duty-free, with a limit of one parcel per addressee per day (except alcohol or tobacco products or perfume worth more than $5). You can mail up to $200 worth of goods for personal use; label the package PERSONAL USE and attach a list of its contents and their retail value. If the package contains your used personal belongings, mark it AMERICAN GOODS RETURNED to avoid paying duties. You may send up to $100 worth of goods as a gift; mark the package UNSOLICITED GIFT. Mailed items do not affect your duty-free allowance on your return.

To avoid paying duty on foreign-made high-ticket items you already own and will take on your trip, register them with Customs before you leave the country. Consider filing a Certificate of Registration for laptops, cameras, watches, and other digital devices identified with serial numbers or other permanent markings; you can keep the certificate for other trips. Otherwise, bring a sales receipt or insurance form to show that you owned the item before you left the United States.

For more about duties, restricted items, and other information about international travel, check out U.S. Customs and Border Protection's online brochure, *Know Before You Go*.

U.S. Customs and Border Protection ✉ for inquiries and equipment registration, 1300 Pennsylvania Ave. NW, Washington, DC 20229 ⊕ www.cbp. gov ☎ 877/287-8667, 202/354-1000 ✉ for complaints, Customer Satisfaction Unit, 1300 Pennsylvania Ave. NW, Room 5.2C, Washington, DC 20229.

DISABILITIES & ACCESSIBILITY
Ireland has only recently begun to provide facilities such as ramps and accessible toilets for people with disabilities. Public transportation also lags behind. Visitors with disabilities will often find, however, that the helpfulness of the Irish makes up for the lack of amenities.

Local Resources Disability Action ✉ 2 Annadale Ave., Belfast ☎ 028/9029-7880 ⊕ www. disabilityaction.org. **Irish Wheelchair Association** ✉ Aras Cuchulainn, Blackheath Dr., Clontarf, Dublin ☎ 01/818-6400 ⊕ www.iwa.ie. **National Disability Authority** ✉ 25 Clyde Road, Ballsbridge, Dublin ☎ 01/608-0400 ⊕ www.nda.ie.

LODGING
In Dublin, the Conrad Dublin International has some of the best amenities for people using wheelchairs, including a ramped entrance, access to all floors, and bedrooms with adapted bathrooms. Jurys Christchurch Inn is also fully accessible to people using wheelchairs.

RESERVATIONS
When discussing accessibility with an operator or reservations agent, ask hard questions. Are there any stairs, inside *or* out? Are there grab bars next to the toilet *and* in the shower/tub? How wide is the doorway to the room? To the bathroom? For the most extensive facilities meeting the latest legal specifications, opt for newer accommodations. If you reserve through a toll-free number, consider also calling the hotel's local number to confirm the information from the central reservations office. Get confirmation in writing when you can.

TRANSPORTATION
Dublin Airport is accessible for people using wheelchairs. Assistance will be needed at other airports. The trains of the suburban rail system in Dublin (DART) have wheelchair access, but not all stations do. National rail system cars don't permit wheelchairs to move through the aisles, so accommodation is made in the vestibule area of the carriage, which is spacious and air-conditioned, though isolated. Few buses are equipped for wheelchairs, but several taxi companies operate wheelchair-accessible cars. Hand-controlled cars are no longer available for rent in Ireland due to the high cost of insurance.

Complaints Aviation Consumer Protection Division (⇨ Air Travel) for airline-related problems. **Departmental Office of Civil Rights** ✉ for general inquiries, U.S. Department of Transportation, S-30, 400 7th St. SW, Room 10215, Washington, DC 20590 ☎ 202/366-4648 ☎ 202/366-9371 ⊕ www.dot. gov/ost/docr/index.htm. **Disability Rights Section** ✉ NYAV, U.S. Department of Justice, Civil Rights Division, 950 Pennsylvania Ave. NW, Washington, DC 20530 ☎ ADA information line 202/514-0301, 800/ 514-0301, 202/514-0383 TTY, 800/514-0383 TTY ⊕ www.ada.gov. **U.S. Department of Transportation Hotline** ☎ for disability-related air-travel problems, 800/778-4838 or 800/455-9880 TTY.

TRAVEL AGENCIES
In the United States, the Americans with Disabilities Act requires that travel firms serve the needs of all travelers. Some agencies specialize in working with people with disabilities.

Travelers with Mobility Problems Access Adventures/B. Roberts Travel ✉ 206 Chestnut Ridge

Rd., Scottsville, NY 14624 ☎ 585/889-9096 ⊕ www.brobertstravel.com ✍ dltravel@prodigy. net, run by a former physical-rehabilitation counselor. **CareVacations** ✉ No. 5, 5110-50 Ave., Leduc, Alberta, Canada, T9E 6V4 ☎ 780/986-6404 or 877/ 478-7827 🖷 780/986-8332 ⊕ www.carevacations. com, for group tours and cruise vacations. **Flying Wheels Travel** ✉ 143 W. Bridge St., Box 382, Owatonna, MN 55060 ☎ 507/451-5005 🖷 507/451-1685 ⊕ www.flyingwheelstravel.com.

DISCOUNTS & DEALS

Be sure to take advantage of the Heritage Service Heritage Card, which gives you access to 65 Heritage sites for €19.05 (the family pass is €45.70). Cards are sold in Ireland at all Heritage Service sites.

Be a smart shopper and compare all your options before making decisions. A plane ticket bought with a promotional coupon from travel clubs, coupon books, and direct-mail offers or purchased on the Internet may not be cheaper than the least expensive fare from a discount ticket agency. And always keep in mind that what you get is just as important as what you save.

DISCOUNT RESERVATIONS

To save money, look into discount reservations services with Web sites and toll-free numbers, which use their buying power to get a better price on hotels, airline tickets (⇨ Air Travel), even car rentals. When booking a room, always **call the hotel's local toll-free number** (if one is available) rather than the central reservations number—you'll often get a better price. Always ask about special packages or corporate rates.

When shopping for the best deal on hotels and car rentals, look for guaranteed exchange rates, which protect you against a falling dollar. With your rate locked in, you won't pay more, even if the price goes up in the local currency.

🎫 Airline Tickets **Air 4 Less** ☎ 800/AIR4LESS; low-fare specialist.

🎫 Hotel Rooms **Accommodations Express** ☎ 800/444-7666 or 800/277-1064 ⊕ www.acex. net. **Hotels.com** ☎ 800/246-8357 ⊕ www.hotels. com. **Steigenberger Reservation Service** ☎ 800/

223-5652 ⊕ www.srs-worldhotels.com. **Turbotrip. com** ☎ 800/473-7829 ⊕ www.turbotrip.com.

PACKAGE DEALS

Don't confuse packages and guided tours. When you buy a package, you travel on your own, just as though you had planned the trip yourself. Fly/drive packages, which combine airfare and car rental, are often a good deal. In cities, ask the local visitor's bureau about hotel and local transportation packages that include tickets to major museum exhibits or other special events. If you **buy a rail/drive pass,** you may save on train tickets and car rentals. All Eurailpass holders get a discount on Eurostar fares through the Channel Tunnel and often receive reduced rates for buses, hotels, ferries, sightseeing cruises, and car rentals.

EATING & DRINKING

It wasn't so long ago that people shared jokes about Ireland's stodgy, overcooked, slightly gray food. But in the last decade there have been changes in all aspects of Irish life, including food and drink. The country is going through a culinary renaissance, and Dublin chefs are leading the charge. They're putting nouvelle spins on Irish favorites. And, spurred by a wave of new immigration, ethnic eateries of all types have sprung up in most major towns and cities. No longer, however, will you "enjoy" your favorite tipple in the blue haze of a smoke-filled pub. As of last year, smoking has been banned in all pubs and restaurants in the republic.

The restaurants we list are the cream of the crop in each price category. They're indicated in the text by ✕ . Establishments denoted by ✕🛏 stand out equally for their restaurants and their rooms.

CATEGORY	COST*
$$$$	over €29
$$$	€22-€29
$$	€15-€22
$	€8-€15
¢	under €8

*In Republic of Ireland: all prices are per person for a main course at dinner and are given in euros.

CATEGORY	COST*
$$$$	over £22
$$$	£18–£22
$$	£13–£18
$	£7–£13
¢	under £7

In Northern Ireland: all prices are per person for a main course at dinner and are given in pounds sterling.

MEALS & SPECIALTIES

A postmodern renaissance in Irish cuisine has lead to a pursuit for authenticity. Many of the finer restaurants in Dublin, Cork, and Galway now offer a couple of dishes that are variations on a traditional theme. *Coddle,* a boiled stew of bacon, sausage, and smoked meats, is an old Dublin favorite. A typical Irish breakfast includes fried eggs, rashers (bacon), black and white puddings (black pudding is made with pork, pork blood, cereals, and seasoning; white pudding is similar, but without the blood), sausage, tomatoes, beans, soda bread, and a pot of tea. Lunch might feature a hearty sandwich; dinners usually include meat and two vegetables. Some of the best food is found at family-run bed-and-breakfasts and in inexpensive cafés. Irish smoked salmon—usually served on brown soda bread with plenty of butter—is among the finest in the world, and many a wondrous dish has been created around the humble cockle and mussel, abundant in the clear Atlantic waters. Galway and the west are rapidly becoming famous for their oyster beds. Of course there's the omnipresent potato, too. The Irish have many words for the humble spud, and they've invented plenty of ways to serve it. The best of these is "boxty," a traditional pancake of once- and twice-cooked potatoes: it makes the perfect bed for a beef-and-Guinness stew, or the equally hearty lamb casserole. For more on the delights of the new (and old) Irish cuisine, see the introduction to the Where to Eat section in the Dublin chapter.

MEALTIMES

Breakfast is served from 7 to 10, lunch runs from 1 to 2:30, and dinners are usually mid-evening occasions.

Pubs are generally open Monday and Tuesday 10:30 AM–11:30 PM and Thursday–Saturday 10:30 AM–12:30 AM. The famous Holy Hour, which required city pubs to close from 2:30 to 3:30, was abolished in 1988, and afternoon opening is now at the discretion of the owner or manager; few bother to close. On Sunday, pubs are open 12:30 PM–12:30 AM or later on certain Sundays. All pubs close on Christmas Day and Good Friday, but hotel bars are open for guests.

Pubs in Northern Ireland are open 11:30 AM–11 PM Monday–Saturday and 12:30 PM–2:30 PM and 7 PM–10 PM on Sunday (note that Sunday openings are at the owner's or manager's discretion).

Unless otherwise noted, the restaurants listed in this guide are open daily for lunch and dinner.

PAYING

Traveler's checks and credit cards are widely accepted, although it's cash-only at smaller pubs and takeout restaurants.

RESERVATIONS & DRESS

Reservations are always a good idea; we mention them only when they're essential or not accepted. Book as far ahead as you can, and reconfirm as soon as you arrive. (Large parties should always call ahead to check the reservations policy.) We mention dress only when men are required to wear a jacket or a jacket and tie.

WINE, BEER & SPIRITS

All types of alcoholic beverages are available in Ireland. Beer and wine are sold in shops and supermarkets, and you can get drinks "to go" at some bars, although at inflated prices. Stout (Guinness, Murphy's, Beamish) is the Irish beer; whiskey comes in many brands, the most notable being Bushmills and Jameson, and is smoother and more blended than Scotch.

ELECTRICITY

The current in Ireland is 220 volts, 50 cycles alternating current (AC); wall outlets take plugs with three prongs. To use electric-powered equipment purchased in the U.S. or Canada, **bring a converter and adapter.** If your appliances are dual-volt-age, you'll need only an adapter. Don't use 110-volt outlets marked FOR SHAVERS ONLY for high-wattage appliances such as blow-dryers. Most laptops operate equally well on 110 and 220 volts and so require only an adapter.

EMBASSIES

🔢 Australia ✉ Fitzwilton House, Wilton Terr., Dublin 2 ☎ 01/676-1517

🔢 Canada ✉ 65 St. Stephen's Green, Southside Dublin 2 ☎ 01/478-1988 ✉ 35 The Hill, Groomsport Co. Down BT19 6JS ☎ 028/9127-2060.

🔢 New Zealand ✉ New Balance House, 118A Lisburn Rd., Glenavy, Co. Antrim BT29 4NY ☎ 028/9264-8098.

🔢 United Kingdom ✉ 29 Merrion Rd., Dublin 4 ☎ 01/205-3700.

🔢 United States ✉ 42 Elgin Rd., Ballsbridge, Dublin 4 ☎ 01/668-7122 ✉ Queen's House, 14 Queen St., Golden Mile, Belfast BT1 6EQ ☎ 028/9032-8239.

EMERGENCIES

The police force in the Republic of Ireland is called the Garda Síochána ("Guardians of the Peace," in English), usually referred to as the Gardaí (pronounced gar-dee). The force is unarmed and is headed by a government -appointed commissioner, who is answerable to the Minister for Justice, who in turn is accountable to the Dáil (the Irish legislature). Easily identified by their fluorescent yellow blazers during winter, or, if weather permits during the summer, by a dark blue shirt and peaked cap, the Gardaí are generally very helpful. They, and all other emergency forces, can be contacted through one phone number: 999. Wherever you are, this number will connect you with local police, ambulance, and fire services. You can expect a prompt response to your call. The Garda Síochána Web site provides contact information for local stations.

🔢 Ambulance, fire, police ☎ 999 An Garda Síochána ⊕ www.garda.ie.

GAY & LESBIAN TRAVEL

In 1993 the Republic of Ireland began to replace virulently homophobic laws (inherited from British rule and enforced up to the 1970s) with some of the most gay-pro-gressive statutes in the EU. Homosexual acts have been decriminalized, and hate crimes and discrimination in the workplace and public accommodation are now illegal.

This enlightened legal environment, however, doesn't readily translate into the same public lesbian and gay presence you find in the U.S. and cities on the European mainland. Outside the republic's major cities—Dublin, Cork, and Galway—signs of gay life can be difficult to find, and even in these cities you're likely to find them only in small pockets: a pub here, a café there. If you encounter any difficulties as a gay traveler, it's likely to be with lodging establishments. Proprietors at even some of the most upscale places may resist letting a room with one bed to same-sex couples; at other establishments, no one may so much as raise an eyebrow. Test the waters in advance: be explicit about what you want when you make your reservation.

🔢 Gay- & Lesbian-Friendly Travel Agencies **Different Roads Travel** ✉ 8383 Wilshire Blvd., Suite 520, Beverly Hills, CA 90211 ☎ 323/651-5557 or 800/429-8747 (Ext. 14 for both) 🖶 323/651-5454 ✎ lgernert@tzell.com. **Kennedy Travel** ✉ 130 W. 42nd St., Suite 401, New York, NY 10036 ☎ 212/840-8659, 800/237-7433 🖶 212/730-2269 ⊕ www.kennedytravel.com. **Now, Voyager** ✉ 4406 18th St., San Francisco, CA 94114 ☎ 415/626-1169 or 800/255-6951 🖶 415/626-8626 ⊕ www.nowvoyager.com. **Skylink Travel and Tour/Flying Dutchmen Travel** ✉ 1455 N. Dutton Ave., Suite A, Santa Rosa, CA 95401 ☎ 707/546-9888 or 800/225-5759 🖶 707/636-0951; serving lesbian travelers.

CORK

Ireland's second-largest city has the country's only lesbian and gay community center and a decade-old gay bar. The Cork Film Festival, held in October, incorporates the Irish Lesbian and Gay Film Festival. The Lesbian and Gay Line operates Wednesday 7 PM–9 PM and Saturday 3 PM–5 PM; it functions as a lesbian hot line Thursday 8 PM–10 PM. Loafers is Cork's main gay bar. The Other Place, a lesbian and gay community center, houses a bookstore and café and hosts Friday- and Saturday-night dances.

🔢 Cork Contacts **Cork Lesbian Line** ☎ 021/425-4710. **Gay Information Cork** ☎ 021/427-1087.

Loafers ⊠ 26 Douglas St. ☎ 021/311-612. **The Other Place** ⊠ 8 S. Main St. ☎ 021/278-470.

DUBLIN

By far, Dublin has more accessible lesbian and gay life than any other city in Ireland. Consult the *Gay Community News*, Ireland's free monthly lesbian and gay newspaper, and *In Dublin* for current information about what's going on in the community. The Gay Switchboard Dublin operates Sunday–Friday 8 PM–10 PM and Saturday 3:30 PM–6 PM. The George is the city's main gay bar, with a mainly male crowd, while Out on the Liffey draws both men and women.

🏳 Dublin Contacts **Gay Community News** (GCN) ☎ 01/671-9076 or 01/671-0939 ⊕ www.gcn.ie. **Gay Switchboard Dublin** ☎ 01/872-1055. **The George** ⊠ 89 S. Great George's St. ☎ 01/478-2983. *In Dublin* ⊠ 3-7 Camden Pl. ☎ 01/478-4322.

GALWAY

A young populace, a progressive university, and a few outstanding theater companies help make Ireland's bohemian left-coast city one of the country's most gay-friendly places. Zulu's Bar is Galway's first specifically gay bar. The Attic has gay nights on Friday and Sunday.

🏳 Galway Contacts **The Attic @ Liquid** ⊠ Salthill ☎ 091/522-715. **Galway Gay Helpline** ☎ 091/566-134 operates Tuesday and Thursday 8 PM–10 PM. **Galway Lesbian Helpline** ☎ 091/564-611 operates Wednesday 8 PM–10 PM. **Zulu's Bar** ⊠ Raven's Terr. ☎ 091/581-204.

HEALTH

Ireland is a very safe country for travel, with virtually no risk of health problems from food, drink, or insects. The weather, however, is another story; be sure to dress for the cold and rain or you may find yourself plagued by a constant chill.

HOLIDAYS

Irish national holidays in 2005 are as follows: January 1 (New Year's Day); March 17 (St. Patrick's Day); March 25 (Good Friday); March 28 (Easter Monday); May 3 (May Day); June 7 and August 2 (summer bank holidays); October 25 (autumn bank holiday); and December 25–26 (Christmas and St. Stephen's Day). If you plan to visit at Easter, remember that theaters and cinemas are closed for the last three days of the preceding week.

In Northern Ireland the following are holidays: March 17 (St. Patrick's Day); May 3 (May Day); May 31 (spring bank holiday); July 12 (Battle of the Boyne); and August 30 (summer bank holiday) and December 25–26 (Christmas and Boxing Day).

INSURANCE

The most useful travel-insurance plan is a comprehensive policy that includes coverage for trip cancellation and interruption, default, trip delay, and medical expenses (with a waiver for preexisting conditions).

Without insurance you'll lose all or most of your money if you cancel your trip, regardless of the reason. Default insurance covers you if your tour operator, airline, or cruise line goes out of business—the chances of which have been increasing. Trip-delay covers expenses that arise because of bad weather or mechanical delays. Study the fine print when comparing policies.

If you're traveling internationally, a key component of travel insurance is coverage for medical bills incurred if you get sick on the road. Such expenses aren't generally covered by Medicare or private policies. U.K. residents can buy a travel-insurance policy valid for most vacations taken during the year in which it's purchased (but check preexisting-condition coverage). British and Australian citizens need extra medical coverage when traveling overseas.

Always **buy travel policies directly from the insurance company**; if you buy them from a cruise line, airline, or tour operator that goes out of business you probably won't be covered for the agency or operator's default, a major risk. Before making any purchase, review your existing health and home-owner's policies to find what they cover away from home.

🏳 Travel Insurers In the U.S.: **Access America** ⊠ 2805 N. Parham Rd., Richmond, VA 23294 ☎ 800/284-8300 📠 804/673-1491 or 800/346-9265 ⊕ www.accessamerica.com. **Travel Guard International** ⊠ 1145 Clark St., Stevens Point, WI 54481 ☎ 715/345-0505 or 800/826-1300 📠 800/955-8785 ⊕ www.travelguard.com.

In the U.K.: Association of British Insurers
✉ 51 Gresham St., London EC2V 7HQ ☎ 020/
7600-3333 🖶 020/7696-8999 ⊕ www.abi.org.uk. In
Canada: **RBC Insurance** ✉ 6880 Financial Dr., Mississauga, Ontario L5N 7Y5 ☎ 800/668-4342 or 905/
816-2400 🖶 905/813-4704 ⊕ www.rbcinsurance.
com. In Australia: **Insurance Council of Australia**
✉ Insurance Enquiries and Complaints, Level 12,
Box 561, Collins St. W, Melbourne, VIC 8007 ☎ 1300/
780808 or 03/9629-4109 🖶 03/9621-2060 ⊕ www.
iecltd.com.au. In New Zealand: **Insurance Council of
New Zealand** ✉ Level 7, 111-115 Customhouse Quay,
Box 474, Wellington ☎ 04/472-5230 🖶 04/473-3011
⊕ www.icnz.org.nz.

LANGUAGE

Irish (also known as Gaelic)—a Celtic
language related to Scots Gaelic, Breton,
and Welsh—is the official national language. Though English is technically the
second language of the country, it is, in
fact, the everyday tongue of 95% of the
population. Nowadays just about all Irish
speakers are fluent in English. Irish-
speaking communities are found mainly
in sparsely populated rural areas along
the western seaboard, on some islands,
and in pockets in West Cork and County
Waterford. Irish-speaking areas are
known as Gaeltacht (pronounced *gale-
taukt*). Although most road signs in Ireland are given in English and Irish, within
Gaeltacht areas the signs are often in
Irish only. A good touring map will give
both Irish and English names to places
within the Gaeltacht. You really need
only know two Irish words: *fir* (men) and
mná (women)—useful vocabulary for a
trip to a public toilet.

LODGING

You should try to sample from Ireland's
vast range of accommodations. In Dublin
and other cities, boutique hotels combine
luxury with contemporary (and often
truly Irish) design. Manors and castles
offer a unique combination of luxury and
history. Less impressive, but equally
charming, are the provincial inns and
country hotels with simple but adequate
facilities. You'll meet a wide cross section
of Irish people by hopping from one B&B

to the next, or you can keep to yourself
for a week or two in a thatched cottage.
ITB-approved guest houses and B&Bs display a green shamrock outside and are
usually considered more reputable than
those without. Hotels and other accommodations in Northern Ireland are similar
to those in the Republic of Ireland.

The ITB has a grading system and publishes a list of "approved" hotels, guest
houses, B&Bs, farmhouses, hostels, and
campgrounds. For each accommodation,
the list gives a maximum charge that
can't be exceeded without special autho-
rization. Prices must be displayed in every
room; if the hotel oversteps its limit,
don't hesitate to complain to the hotel
manager and/or the ITB.

The lodgings we list are the cream of the
crop in each price category. We always
list the facilities that are available, but we
don't specify whether they cost extra;
when pricing accommodations, always
ask what's included and what costs extra.
Lodgings are assigned price categories
based on the range from their least-ex-
pensive standard double room at high
season (excluding holidays) to the most
expensive. Lodgings marked ✕ 🏠 are
lodgings whose restaurants warrant a
special trip.

Assume that hotels operate on the European Plan (EP, with no meals) unless we
specify that they use the Breakfast Plan
(BP, with a full breakfast), the Continental
Plan (CP, with a Continental breakfast),
the Full American Plan (FAP, all meals), or
the Modified American Plan (MAP, with
breakfast and dinner).

CATEGORY	COST*
$$$$	over €230
$$$	€180–€230
$$	€130–€180
$	€80–€130
¢	under €80

*Republic of Ireland: All prices are in euros and
are for two people in a double room, including
V.A.T. and a service charge (often applied in
larger hotels).*

CATEGORY	COST*
$$$$	over £160
$$$	£115–£160
$$	£80–£115
$	£50–£80
¢	under £50

Northern Ireland: All prices are in pounds sterling and are for two people in a double room, including V.A.T. and a service charge (often applied in larger hotels).

APARTMENT RENTALS

If you want a home base that's roomy enough for a family and comes with cooking facilities, consider a furnished rental. These can save you money, especially if you're traveling with a group. Home-exchange directories sometimes list rentals as well as exchanges.

International Agents **Hideaways International** ✉ 767 Islington St., Portsmouth, NH 03801 ☎ 603/430-4433 or 800/843-4433 🖷 603/430-4444 ⊕ www.hideaways.com, annual membership $145. **Interhome** ✉ 1990 N.E. 163rd St., Suite 110, North Miami Beach, FL 33162 ☎ 305/940-2299 or 800/882-6864 🖷 305/940-2911 ⊕ www.interhome. us.**Villas and Apartments Abroad** ✉ 183 Madison Ave., Suite 201, New York, NY 10016 ☎ 212/213-6435 or 800/433-3020 🖷 212/213-8252 ⊕ www. vaanyc.com.**Villas International** ✉ 4340 Redwood Hwy., Suite D309, San Rafael, CA 94903 ☎ 415/499-9490 or 800/221-2260 🖷 415/499-9491 ⊕ www.villasintl.com.

Local Agents **Days Serviced Apartments** ✉ 128 Lower Baggot St. Dublin 2 ☎ 01/ 639-1100 ⊕ www. www.apartments-dublin.com. **Board Failte** ✉ Baggot St. Bridge, Baggot St. Dublin 2 ☎ 01/602-4000 ⊕ www.failteireland.ie.

BED & BREAKFASTS

B&Bs are classified by the ITB as either town homes, country homes, or farmhouses. Many town and country B&Bs now have at least one bedroom with a bathroom, but don't expect this as a matter of course. B&Bs often charge an extra €0.60–€1.30 for a bath or shower. If this is in the family bathroom, you should ask about using it. The Irish farms that offer rooms by the week with partial or full board are more likely to be modern bungalows or undistinguished two-

story houses than creeper-clad Georgian mansions. Room and part board—breakfast and an evening meal—starts at €267 per week. Many travelers don't bother booking a B&B in advance. They are so plentiful in rural areas that it's often more fun to leave the decision open, allowing yourself a choice of final destinations for the night.

Reservation Services **Bed & Breakfast Association of Northern Ireland** ☎ 28/7082-3823. **Irish Farm Holidays** ✉ 2 Michael St., Limerick ☎ 61/400-700 ⊕ www.irishfarmholidays.com. **Northern Ireland Farm and Country Holidays Association** ✉ 63 Somerton Rd., Belfast ☎ 28/8284-1325 ⊕ www.nischa.com. **Town & Country Homes Association** ✉ Belleek Rd., Ballyshannon, Co. Donegal ☎ 71/982-2222 ⊕ www.townandcountry.ie.

CAMPING

An abundance of coastal campsites compensates for the shortage of inland ones. Rates start at about €5 per tent, €8 per caravan (RV) overnight.

Irish Caravan and Camping Council ✉ Box 4443, Dublin 2 ⊕ www.camping-ireland.ie.

COTTAGES AND GUEST HOUSES

Vacation cottages, which are usually in clusters, are rented by the week. Although often built in the traditional style, most have central heating and all the other modern conveniences. It's essential to reserve in advance. To qualify as a guest house, establishments must have at least five bedrooms. Some guest houses are above a bar or restaurant; others are part of a home. As a rule, they're cheaper (some include an optional evening meal) and offer fewer amenities than hotels. But often that's where the differences end. Most have high standards of cleanliness and hospitality. Some even have a bathroom, a TV, and a direct-dial phone in each room. An organization known as Premier Guesthouses is a good place to begin your search.

Reservations Services **Irish Cottage Holiday Homes Association** ✉ Bracken Court, Bracken Rd., Sandyford, Dublin 8 ☎ 01/205-2777 ⊕ www. irishcottageholidays.com. **Northern Ireland Self-Catering Holidays Association** ✉ 63 Somerton Rd.,

North Belfast Belfast BT15 4DD ☎ 28/9077-6174 ⊕ www.nischa.com. **Premier Guesthouses** ✉ Bracken Court, Bracken Rd., Sandyford, Dublin 8 ☎ 01/205-2826 ⊕ www.premierguesthouses.com.

CASTLES & MANORS

Some of the most magical experiences on an Irish vacation are stays at some of the country's spectacular castle-hotels, such as Dromoland (Newmarket-on-Fergus), Ashland (Cong), and Castle Leslie (Glaslough). For directories to help you get to know the wide array of manor house and castle accommodations, including a goodly number of private country estates and castles, contact Ireland's Blue Book of Country Houses & Restaurants or Hidden Ireland.

🗗 Reservations Services **Hidden Ireland** ☐ Box 31, Westport, Co. Mayo ☎ 98/66650 in Westport, 01/662-7166 in Dublin ⊕ www.hiddenireland.com. **Ireland's Blue Book** ✉ 8 Mount Street Crescent, Dublin South City Centre 2 ☎ 01/676-9914 ⊕ www.irelandsbluebook.com.

HOME EXCHANGES

If you would like to exchange your home for someone else's, join a home-exchange organization, which will send you its updated listings of available exchanges for a year and will include your own listing in at least one of them. It's up to you to make specific arrangements.

🗗 Exchange Clubs **HomeLink International** ☐ Box 47747, Tampa, FL 33647 ☎ 813/975-9825 or 800/638-3841 ☐ 813/910-8144 ⊕ www.homelink.org; $110 yearly for a listing, online access, and catalog; $70 without catalog. **Intervac U.S.** ✉ 30 Corte San Fernando, Tiburon, CA 94920 ☎ 800/756-4663 ☐ 415/435-7440 ⊕ www.intervacus.com; $125 yearly for a listing, online access, and a catalog; $65 without catalog.

HOSTELS

No matter what your age, you can save on lodging costs by staying at hostels. In some 4,500 locations in more than 70 countries around the world, Hostelling International (HI), the umbrella group for a number of national youth-hostel associations, offers single-sex, dorm-style beds and, at many hostels, rooms for couples and family accommodations. Membership in any HI national hostel association, open to travelers

of all ages, allows you to stay in HI-affiliated hostels at member rates; one-year membership is about $28 for adults (C$35 for a two-year minimum membership in Canada, £14 in the U.K., A$52 in Australia, and NZ$40 in New Zealand); hostels charge about $10–$30 per night. Members have priority if the hostel is full; they're also eligible for discounts around the world, even on rail and bus travel in some countries.

🗗 International Organizations **Independent Holiday Hostels of Ireland** ⊕ www.hostels-ireland.com. **Hostelling International–USA** ✉ 8401 Colesville Rd., Suite 600, Silver Spring, MD 20910 ☎ 301/495-1240 ☐ 301/495-6697 ⊕ www.hiusa.org. **Hostelling International–Canada** ✉ 205 Catherine St., Suite 400, Ottawa, Ontario K2P 1C3 ☎ 613/237-7884 or 800/663-5777 ☐ 613/237-7868 ⊕ www.hihostels.ca. **YHA England and Wales** ✉ Trevelyan House, Dimple Rd., Matlock, Derbyshire DE4 3YH, U.K. ☎ 0870/870-8808, 0870/770-8868, 0162/959-2600 ☐ 0870/770-6127 ⊕ www.yha.org.uk. **YHA Australia** ✉ 422 Kent St., Sydney, NSW 2001 ☎ 02/9261-1111 ☐ 02/9261-1969 ⊕ www.yha.com.au. **YHA New Zealand** ✉ Level 1, Moorhouse City, 166 Moorhouse Ave., Box 436, Christchurch ☎ 03/379-9970 or 0800/278-299 ☐ 03/365-4476 ⊕ www.yha.org.nz.

🗗 Irish Organizations **Independent Holiday Hostels** ✉ 57 Lower Gardiner St., Northside Dublin 1 ☎ 01/836-4700 ⊕ www.hostels-ireland.com. **Irish Youth Hostel Association (An Óige)** ✉ 67 Mountjoy St., North City Centre Dublin 7 ☎ 01/830-4555 ⊕ www.irelandyha.org. **Northern Ireland Hostelling International** ✉ 22-32 Donegal Rd., University Area Belfast BT12 5JN ☎ 28/9032-4733 ⊕ www.hini.org.uk.

HOTELS

Standard features in most hotels include private bath, air-conditioning, two twin beds (you can usually ask for a king-size instead), TV (often with VCR), free parking, and no-smoking rooms. There's usually no extra charge for these services. All hotels listed have private bath unless otherwise noted.

🗗 Information & Bookings **Ireland Hotels Federation** ✉ 13 Northbrook Rd., Ranelagh Dublin 6 ☎ 01/497-6459 ⊕ www.irelandhotels.com. **ITB** ⊕ www.tourismireland.com/info-accommodation. **Northern Ireland Hotels Federation** ✉ Midland

Building, Whitla St., Duncairn Belfast BT15 1JP ☎ 28/9035-1110 ⊕ www.nihf.co.uk.

🔳 Toll-Free Numbers **Best Western** ☎ 800/528-1234 ⊕ www.bestwestern.com. **Choice** ☎ 800/424-6423 ⊕ www.choicehotels.com. **Clarion** ☎ 800/424-6423 ⊕ www.choicehotels.com. **Comfort Inn** ☎ 800/424-6423 ⊕ www.choicehotels.com. **Four Seasons** ☎ 800/332-3442 ⊕ www.fourseasons.com. **Hilton** ☎ 800/445-8667 ⊕ www.hilton.com. **Holiday Inn** ☎ 800/465-4329 ⊕ www.ichotelsgroup.com. **Howard Johnson** ☎ 800/446-4656 ⊕ www.hojo.com. **Quality Inn** ☎ 800/424-6423 ⊕ www.choicehotels.com. **Radisson** ☎ 800/333-3333 ⊕ www.radisson.com. **Westin Hotels & Resorts** ☎ 800/228-3000 ⊕ www.starwood.com/westin.

MAIL & SHIPPING

Letters by standard post take a week to 10 days to reach the United States and Canada, 3 to 5 days to reach the United Kingdom.

OVERNIGHT SERVICES

If it absolutely has to get there the next day there are several overnight services available in Ireland. The most extensive and inexpensive service is the SDS service offered by the national postal carrier, An Post. Letters and packages can be sent from main post offices to any destination in Ireland. International deliveries can be made to more than 200 destinations. The EMS Courier offers next-day pre-noon delivery and it comes with a money-back guarantee for deliveries to Ireland and the U.K. Sending documents to North America will take two working days, parcels three. This courier is available from Dublin, Cork, Galway, Waterford, Limerick, and Shannon. Sending documents by EMS to U.K. cities and New York costs from €17 to €36. A 4.5-kg (2-pound) parcel will cost about €25 to send within Ireland, €62 to the U.K., and €95 to New York. Familiar global carriers such as DHL, Federal Express, and UPS also operate services in Ireland.

🔳 Local Contacts **DHL** ☎ 800/725-725 ⊕ www.dhl.ie **FedEx** ☎ 800/535-800 ⊕ www.fedex.com/ie **SDS Courier** ☎ 1890/367-737 ⊕ www.sds.ie **UPS** ☎ 800/575-757 ⊕ www.ups.com.

POSTAL RATES

Airmail rates to the United States and Canada from the Irish Republic are €0.60 for letters and postcards. Mail to all European countries goes by air automatically, so airmail stickers or envelopes are not required. Rates are €0.40 for letters and postcards.

Rates from Northern Ireland are 43p for letters and 37p for postcards (not over 10 grams). To the rest of the United Kingdom and the Irish Republic, rates are 26p for first-class letters and 20p for second-class.

RECEIVING MAIL

Mail can be held for collection at any post office free of charge for up to three months. It should be addressed to the recipient "c/o Poste Restante." In Dublin, use the General Post Office. The Irish postal service, known as An Post, has a Web site with a branch locator and loads of other postal information.

🔳 **An Post** ⊕ www.anpost.ie. **General Post Office** ✉ O'Connell St., Dublin 1 ☎ 01/705-8833.

MEDIA

NEWSPAPERS & MAGAZINES

In Ireland, there are three national daily broadsheet newspapers, the *Irish Times* and the *Irish Independent*—both Dublin based—and the *Irish Examiner,* which is published in Cork. The *Irish Times* is the most authoritative and esteemed of the three; the *Irish Independent* is the most popular; and the *Irish Examiner* is widely read in the southern counties. The British *Daily Star* and the *Sun* also have Irish editions.

The *Evening Herald* is the only nationwide evening newspaper. The *Evening Echo* is published by the Examiner group and sold in the Cork region. There are five Irish Sunday newspapers: the very popular and opinion-focused *Sunday Independent*; the more intellectual *Sunday Tribune*; the business-oriented *Sunday Business Post*; the popular tabloid, *Sunday World*; and *Ireland on Sunday*. Regional weekly newspapers are published in almost every county. In Northern Ireland, the main dailies are the *Belfast Telegraph* and the

Belfast Newsletter. The British broadsheet and tabloid dailies and Sunday newspapers are widely available throughout Ireland.

Most towns have their own daily or weekly newspapers. For instance, here is a list of just some of the papers published in the Southeast region alone: *Anglo Celt, Bray People, Carlow People, Corkman, Drogheda Independent, Enniscorthy Echo, Fingal Independent, Gorey Guardian, Kerryman, Mayo News, Meath Chronicle, Nenagh Guardian, New Ross Echo, Roscommon Herald, Sligo Champion, Tuam Herald, Westmeath Independent, Wexford Echo,* and *Wicklow People.*

There are several Irish glossy magazines to give you a taste of contemporary Ireland. *The Dubliner* is the monthly that will tell you about the latest trends, who's hip and who is not, the newest restaurants and the coolest finds. *In Dublin* is a popular source for what's happening in the entertainment and arts scenes. Magazines aimed at the women's market include the weekly *IT* (*Irish Tatler*) and *U,* both appear monthly. For women's fashion, try *Image*; for home styles in the country, buy *Image Interiors.* For a peek into the Irish music scene, see *Hotpress,* the long standing "insiders" guide to (mainly) music and movies. Other prominent titles include *The Phoenix* and *Magill,* both of which concentrate on news, current affairs, and political matters. Entertainment and cultural matters are also covered in two Dublin newspapers, *The Dublin Event Guide,* which features comprehensive listings of all entertainment events in the city, and *The Gay Community News,* which covers issues relating to the gay and lesbian community.

RADIO & TELEVISION

Radio Telefis Éireann (RTÉ) is Ireland's national television and radio network. There are two television channels—RTÉ 1, which concentrates on news and documentaries, and Network 2, which carries more feature films and light entertainment shows. TV3 is a private channel with a lot of American and British soaps and situation comedies. TG4 is an Irish-language channel (with English subtitles). The

British television channels (BBC 1, BBC 2, UTV, Channel 4) and many satellite channels—including SkyNews, SkyMovies, SkySports, CNN, MTV, and TV5 Europe—are also widely available.

There are two 24-hour national radio stations in Ireland—Radio 1 (mainly talk shows) and the popular music-dominated station 2FM. FM3 is a classical music station that is broadcast in the early mornings and evenings on the same wavelength as the daytime Irish-language radio station, Raidio Na Gaeltachta. There are more than 25 local commercial radio stations whose broadcasting standards vary from county to county. All the BBC radio channels are also available.

MONEY MATTERS

A modest hotel in Dublin costs about €130 a night for two; this figure can be reduced to under €90 by staying in a registered guest house or inn, and reduced to less than €45 by staying in a suburban B&B. Lunch, consisting of a good one-dish plate of bar food at a pub, costs around €8; a sandwich at the same pub costs about €3. In Dublin's better restaurants, dinner will run €25–€40 per person, excluding drinks and tip.

Theater and entertainment in most places are inexpensive—about €18 for a good seat, and double that for a big-name, pop-music concert. For the price of a few drinks and (in Dublin and Killarney) a small entrance fee of about €2, you can spend a memorable evening at a *seisun* (pronounced say-*shoon*) in a music pub. Entrance to most public galleries is free, but stately homes and similar attractions charge anywhere from €4 to a whopping €8 per person.

Just about everything is more expensive in Dublin, so add at least 10% to these sample prices: cup of coffee, €1; pint of beer, €3; soda, €1.20; and 2-km (1-mi) taxi ride, €5.10. Travelers from the United Kingdom will find value when visiting Ireland. Due to the exchange rate, Canadians, Australians, New Zealanders, and—to a lesser extent, Americans—will find Ireland a little pricey when they convert costs to their home currency.

Hotels and meals in Northern Ireland are less expensive than in the United Kingdom and the Republic of Ireland. Also, the lower level of taxation makes dutiable goods such as gasoline, alcoholic drinks, and tobacco cheaper.

Prices throughout this guide are given for adults. Substantially reduced fees are almost always available for children, students, and senior citizens. For information on taxes, *see* Taxes.

ATMS

ATMs are found in all major towns and are, by far, the easiest way to keep yourself stocked with euros along your trip. Most major banks are connected to Cirrus or PLUS systems; there is a four-digit maximum for your PIN.

CREDIT CARDS

Throughout this guide, the following abbreviations are used: **AE,** American Express; **DC,** Diners Club; **MC,** MasterCard; and **V,** Visa.

Note that when using your credit card, **check that the merchant is putting the transaction through in euros or pounds sterling.** If he or she puts it through in the currency of your home country—a transaction called a dynamic currency conversion—the exchange rate might be less favorable and the service charges higher than if you allow the credit card company to do the conversion for you.

🗐 Reporting Lost Cards **American Express** 🕿 0353/1205-5111. **Diners Club** 🕿 0353/661-1800. **MasterCard** 🕿 1800/557378. **Visa** 🕿 1800/558002.

CURRENCY

The Irish Republic is a member of the European Monetary Union (EMU). Euro notes come in denominations of €500, €200, €100, €50, €20, €10, and €5. The euro is divided into 100 cents, and coins are available as €2 and €1 and 50, 20, 10, 5, 2, and 1 cents.

The unit of currency in Northern Ireland is the pound sterling (£), divided into 100 pence (p). The bills (called notes) are 50, 20, 10, and 5 pounds. Coins are £2, £1, 50p, 20p, 10p, 5p, 2p, and 1p.

CURRENCY EXCHANGE

At this writing, one euro is equal to U.S. $1.23, CAN $1.64, U.K. 67p, AUS $1.64, and NZ $1.87. One pound sterling is equal to €1.49, U.S. $1.83, CAN $2.44, AUS $2.45, and NZ $2.79. Rates fluctuate regularly, though, particularly for the euro, so monitor them closely.

For the most favorable rates, **change money through banks.** Although ATM transaction fees may be higher abroad than at home, ATM rates are excellent because they're based on wholesale rates offered only by major banks. You won't do as well at exchange booths in airports or rail and bus stations, in hotels, in restaurants, or in stores. To avoid lines at airport exchange booths, get a bit of local currency before you leave home.

🗐 Exchange Services **International Currency Express** ✉ 427 N. Camden Dr., Suite F, Beverly Hills, CA 90210 🕿 888/278-6628 orders 🖷 310/278-6410 ⊕ www.foreignmoney.com. **Travel Ex Currency Services** 🕿 800/287-7362 orders and retail locations ⊕ www.travelex.com.

TRAVELER'S CHECKS

Do you need traveler's checks? It depends on where you're headed. If you're going to rural areas and small towns, go with cash; traveler's checks are best used in cities. Lost or stolen checks can usually be replaced within 24 hours. To ensure a speedy refund, buy your own traveler's checks—don't let someone else pay for them: irregularities like this can cause delays. The person who bought the checks should make the call to request a refund.

PACKING

In Ireland you can experience all four seasons in a day. There can be damp chilly stretches even in July and August, the warmest months of the year. Layers are the best way to go. Pack several long- and short-sleeve T-shirts (in winter, some should be thermal or silk), a sweatshirt, a lightweight sweater, a heavyweight sweater, and a hooded, waterproof windbreaker that's large enough to go over several layers if necessary. A portable umbrella is absolutely essential, and the smaller and lighter it is, the better, as you'll want it with you every second. You should bring at least two pairs of walking shoes; footwear can get soaked in minutes and then take hours to dry.

The Irish are generally informal about clothes. In the more expensive hotels and restaurants people dress formally for dinner, and a jacket and tie may be required in bars after 7 PM, but very few places operate a strict dress policy. Old or tattered blue jeans and running shoes are forbidden in certain bars and dance clubs.

If you're used to packing things or stowing dirty clothes in plastic shopping or drawstring bags, bring your own. About the only place you'll find them here is in the closets of better hotel rooms (for on-site dry cleaning and laundry). All Irish stores use only paper bags, and these often get soggy as soon as you step outside. Also, although salesclerks are good about wrapping crystal and pottery for travel, you can never be too careful with such items; bring along some bubble wrap.

In your carry-on luggage, pack an extra pair of eyeglasses or contact lenses and enough of any medication you take to last a few days longer than the entire trip. You may also ask your doctor to write a spare prescription using the drug's generic name, as brand names may vary from country to country. In luggage to be checked, **never pack prescription drugs, valuables, or undeveloped film.** And don't forget to carry with you the addresses of offices that handle refunds of lost traveler's checks. Check *Fodor's How to Pack* (available at online retailers and bookstores everywhere) for more tips.

To avoid customs and security delays, carry medications in their original packaging. Don't pack any sharp objects in your carry-on luggage, including knives of any size or material, scissors, nail clippers, and corkscrews, or anything else that might arouse suspicion. To avoid having your checked luggage chosen for hand inspection, don't cram bags full. The U.S. Transportation Security Administration suggests packing shoes on top and placing personal items you don't want touched in clear plastic bags.

CHECKING LUGGAGE

You're allowed to carry aboard one bag and one personal article, such as a purse or a laptop computer. Make sure what you carry on fits under your seat or in the overhead bin. Get to the gate early, so you can board as soon as possible, before the overhead bins fill up.

Baggage allowances vary by carrier, destination, and ticket class. On international flights, you're usually allowed to check two bags weighing up to 70 pounds (32 kilograms) each, although a few airlines allow checked bags of up to 88 pounds (40 kilograms) in first class. Some international carriers don't allow more than 66 pounds (30 kilograms) per bag in business class and 44 pounds (20 kilograms) in economy. On domestic flights, the limit is usually 50 to 70 pounds (23 to 32 kilograms) per bag. In general, carry-on bags shouldn't exceed 40 pounds (18 kilograms). Most airlines won't accept bags that weigh more than 100 pounds (45 kilograms) on domestic or international flights. Expect to pay a fee for baggage that exceeds weight limits. Check baggage restrictions with your carrier before you pack.

Airline liability for baggage is limited to $2,500 per person on flights within the United States. On international flights it amounts to $9.07 per pound or $20 per kilogram for checked baggage (roughly $640 per 70-pound bag), with a maximum of $634.90 per piece, and $400 per passenger for unchecked baggage. You can buy additional coverage at check-in for about $10 per $1,000 of coverage, but it often excludes a rather extensive list of items, shown on your airline ticket.

Before departure, itemize your bags' contents and their worth, and label the bags with your name, address, and phone number. (If you use your home address, cover it so potential thieves can't see it readily.) Include a label inside each bag and **pack a copy of your itinerary.** At check-in, make sure each bag is correctly tagged with the destination airport's three-letter code. Because some checked bags will be opened for hand inspection, the U.S. Transportation Security Administration recommends that you leave luggage unlocked or use the plastic locks offered at check-in. TSA screeners place an inspection notice inside searched bags, which are re-sealed with a special lock.

If your bag has been searched and contents are missing or damaged, file a claim with the TSA Consumer Response Center as soon as possible. If your bags arrive damaged or fail to arrive at all, file a written report with the airline before leaving the airport.

🚩 Complaints **U.S. Transportation Security Administration Contact Center** ☎ 866/289-9673 ⊕ www.tsa.gov.

PASSPORTS & VISAS
When traveling internationally, carry your passport even if you don't need one (it's always the best form of I.D.) and **make two photocopies of the data page** (one for someone at home and another for you, carried separately from your passport). If you lose your passport, promptly call the nearest embassy or consulate and the local police.

U.S. passport applications for children under age 14 require consent from both parents or legal guardians; both parents must appear together to sign the application. If only one parent appears, he or she must submit a written statement from the other parent authorizing passport issuance for the child. A parent with sole authority must present evidence of it when applying; acceptable documentation includes the child's certified birth certificate listing only the applying parent, a court order specifically permitting this parent's travel with the child, or a death certificate for the nonapplying parent. Application forms and instructions are available on the Web site of the U.S. State Department's Bureau of Consular Affairs (⊕ travel.state.gov).

ENTERING IRELAND
All U.S., Canadian, Australian, and New Zealand citizens, even infants, need a valid passport to enter Ireland for stays of up to 90 days. Citizens of the United Kingdom, when traveling on flights departing from Great Britain, do not need a

passport to enter Ireland. Passport requirements for Northern Ireland are the same as for the republic.

PASSPORT OFFICES
The best time to apply for a passport or to renew is in fall and winter. Before any trip, check your passport's expiration date, and, if necessary, renew it as soon as possible.

🚩 Australian Citizens **Passports Australia** Australian Department of Foreign Affairs and Trade ☎ 131-232 ⊕ www.passports.gov.au.

🚩 Canadian Citizens **Passport Office** ✉ to mail in applications: 200 Promenade du Portage, Hull, Québec J8X 4B7 ☎ 819/994-3500 or 800/567-6868 ⊕ www.ppt.gc.ca.

🚩 New Zealand Citizens **New Zealand Passports Office** ☎ 0800/22-5050 or 04/474-8100 ⊕ www.passports.govt.nz.

🚩 U.K. Citizens **U.K. Passport Service** ☎ 0870/521-0410 ⊕ www.passport.gov.uk.

🚩 U.S. Citizens **National Passport Information Center** ☎ 877/487-2778, 888/874-7793 TDD/TTY ⊕ travel.state.gov.

REST ROOMS
Public rest rooms are in short supply in Ireland. They will be easy enough to find in public places such as airports, train stations, and shopping malls, but if you don't find yourself in one of these locations your best bet is to look for the nearest pub (never more than a few minutes away in Ireland!) Pubs are increasingly putting up signs that rest rooms are for customers only—but this is difficult to enforce. If it is outside of shopping or pub hours your last option may be the nearest hotel. Most gas stations will have toilets available. Only toilets in hotels or shopping centers will be up to a polished North American standard. Although many toilets look well worn they are generally clean. Unfortunately, few toilets are heated and an open window is typically used for ventilation, making for uncomfortably cold rest rooms in the colder months.

SAFETY
Don't wear a money belt or a waist pack, both of which peg you as a tourist. Distribute your cash and any valuables (including your credit cards and passport) between a deep front pocket, an inside

jacket or vest pocket, and a hidden money pouch. Do not reach for the money pouch once you're in public.

The theft of car radios, mobile phones, cameras, video recorders, and other items of value from cars is common in Dublin and other major cities and towns. Never leave any valuable items on car seats or in the foot space between the back and front seats or in glove compartments. In fact, never leave anything whatsoever in sight in your car—even if you're leaving it for only a short time. You should also think twice about leaving valuables in your car while visiting tourist attractions anywhere in the country.

SENIOR-CITIZEN TRAVEL

To qualify for age-related discounts, mention your senior-citizen status up front when booking hotel reservations (not when checking out) and before you're seated in restaurants (not when paying the bill). Be sure to have identification on hand. When renting a car, ask about promotional car-rental discounts, which can be cheaper than senior-citizen rates.

Educational Programs Elderhostel ⊠ 11 Ave. de Lafayette, Boston, MA 02111-1746 ☎ 877/426–8056, 978/323–4141 international callers, 877/426–2167 TTY 🖷 877/426–2166 ⊕ www.elderhostel.org. **Interhostel** ⊠ University of New Hampshire, 6 Garrison Ave., Durham, NH 03824 ☎ 603/862–1147 or 800/733–9753 🖷 603/862–1113 ⊕ www.learn. unh.edu.

SHOPPING

Once a destination rich only in tales of leprechauns and fairies, Ireland has experienced an economic revival that has created a wealth of new shopping opportunities. From the souvenir shop selling the local woolen goods, linens, and crystal to internationally known retailers, the country has something for everyone's taste.

KEY DESTINATIONS

On a weekend, trying to navigate Grafton Street, Dublin's pedestrian shopping promenade, is not unlike being caught in rush-hour traffic. This is the heart of shopping in the country. Upscale department stores filled with designer labels can be found on the main strip, and fine boutiques await

discovery just off the beaten path, making Dublin a great shopping destination. Other major cities, such as Belfast, Cork, and Galway, also have a wide variety of stores, including a few large department stores. The west is the place for those chunky Aran sweaters and hand-knitted knitwear of all types. Donegal is famous for its tweed, of course, and for crystal you can choose between world-famous Waterford and slightly less expensive Cavan. Northern Ireland, especially Belfast, has a long tradition of producing fine Irish linens.

SMART SOUVENIRS

Top-quality antiques shops are concentrated around Dublin's Francis Street area, but it's still possible to pick up modestly priced pieces of 18th- and 19th-century silver, 19th-century pewter, and antique period furniture elsewhere—try Cork City, Castlecomer, Kilkenny, Galway City, and Limerick.

Irish lead crystal is justifiably world-famous. The best known of all, Waterford glass, is on sale all over Ireland in department stores and crafts shops. The demand is so great that substantial export orders can take weeks or even months to fill. Check out the lesser-known crystals— Cork, Dublin, Kinsale, Tipperary, Tyrone, and Galway—and the less formal, uncut glass from Jerpoint and Stoneyford. Locally made Parian china is a thin, fine, and pale product of very high quality and workmanship. Elaborate flower motifs and a basket-weave design are two distinctive features of this china, which has been a specialty of Belleek, on the Donegal-Fermanagh border, for more than 100 years.

Dublin and Cork City are the best spots for antique jewelry, but don't despair if the prices are beyond your resources. Beautiful reproductions of such Celtic treasures as the Tara brooch are on sale for a fraction of the cost. Other good buys include Claddagh friendship rings (Galway City is a particularly good place to shop for these) and beautiful pieces by modern silversmiths.

Made of plain, undyed wool, Aran sweaters are durable, soft, and often weatherproof and can be astonishingly warm. Not so long ago, these pullovers were worn by every County Donegal fisherman. Today there's a greater variety in patterns, but most of the sweaters still have that unmistakable Aran look. Aran sweaters were developed by the women of the Aran Isles to provide a working garment that was warm, comfortable, and weatherproof. The religious symbols and folk motifs woven into distinctive patterns once enabled local people to identify one another's families and localities. Even today, no two Arans are alike: if you want to buy a hand-knit, take your time and wait until you find one that really strikes your fancy. Cheaper and less durable Arans are referred to as "hand-loomed," which is another way of saying "machine-made." Other types of sweaters include classic, blue, fisherman's rib sweaters; homespun, hand-dyed hand-knits; picture sweaters; and sophisticated mohair garments.

A pure linen blouse, like an Aran sweater, can last a lifetime. Designs are classic, so they won't become dated. Linen handkerchiefs for men make useful gifts. Damask tablecloths and crocheted-linen place mats make ideal wedding gifts. Most Irish linen is made in Northern Ireland.

The best selection of traditional tweeds is still found in the specialist tweed shops of Counties Galway and Donegal. Weavers can also be found at work in Kerry, Dublin, Wicklow, Cork, and elsewhere in Connemara. Tweeds vary a good deal in type, from rugged-looking garments to clothes with jewel-like colors that have been popularized by Avoca Handweavers.

Irish whiskey has an altogether different taste from Scotch whisky, and a different spelling, too. Well-known brands include Powers, Paddy, Jameson, and Bushmills. There are also two excellent Irish liqueurs: Irish Mist, which contains whiskey and honey, and Bailey's Irish Cream, a concoction of whiskey and cream, sometimes drunk on ice as an aperitif.

Smoked salmon can vary greatly in taste and quality. Make sure it's wild salmon, not farmed; and if the label tells you what sort of wood it was smoked over, opt for oak chips. A cheaper but also delicious alternative is smoked trout. Or go for whole farmhouse cheeses like St. Killian's—a Camembert-like pasteurized cheese. More exotic and more expensive are the handmade farmhouse cheeses, each from an individual herd of cows. Milleens, Durrus, and Gubbeen are all excellent, though strong when ripe. A milder alternative is the Gouda-like Coolea cheese, found in most duty-free shops.

On the Aran Islands, sally rods are woven into attractive baskets (once used for potatoes or turf), and colorful woven belts, known as *crioses,* are hand-plaited from strands of wool. Handwoven woolen or mohair shawls or rugs provide an affordable touch of luxury. Musical instruments, traditionally made furniture, handmade beeswax candles, and dried flower arrangements are among Ireland's many other handicrafts.

SPORTS & THE OUTDOORS

BICYCLING

Ireland is a cyclist's paradise. The scenery is phenomenal; the roads are flat—with some gently rising hills—and uncrowded; repair and support services are good; and the distance from one village to the next is rarely more than 16 km (10 mi). Most ferries will transport bikes for free. If there's room, Irish buses and Irish Rail will transport them for a small fee. All that said, foul weather and rough roads in remote areas are all too common, so rain gear and spare parts are musts.

Most bike-rental shops offer 18- to 24-gear mountain bikes with index gears and rear carriers for about €15 per day or €65 per week. A refundable deposit of about €65 is often required. For a fee of €16 or so, you can rent a bike at one location and drop it off at another. Book well in advance for travel between May and September, as demand is high and availability is limited. Raleigh Ireland has dealers all over the country who do repairs and rentals.

If you enjoy bird life and sea vistas, try planning a coastal route, perhaps in the southeast. Between Arklow and Wexford it's predominantly flat, with expanses of sandy beaches. The Hook Peninsula between Wexford and Waterford has a network of small, quiet roads, many of them leading to tranquil fishing villages. If you travel from Waterford to Dungarvan via Dunmore East and Tramore, you'll see a variety of scenery combining cliff-top rides with stretches of beachfront.

In the Midlands, level terrain means a less strenuous ride. The twisting roads are generally in good condition, and there are pleasant picnic spots in the many state-owned forests just off the main roads. Bord Fáilte recommends two long tours: one in the Athlone-Mullingar-Roscommon area and another in the Cavan-Monaghan-Mullingar region. Avoid the major trunk roads that bisect the region.

The scenery is truly spectacular in the southwest around Glengarriff, Killarney, and Dingle. The length of the hills—rather than their steepness—is the challenge here, but without the hills there wouldn't be such great views. A less-strenuous option is the coast of West Cork between Kinsale and Glengarriff. The Beara Peninsula is popular for its varied coastal scenery and relative lack of vehicles. Traffic can be a problem in July and August on the Ring of Kerry, where there's a lack of alternative routes to the one main circuit.

Most airlines accommodate bikes as luggage, provided they're dismantled and boxed; check with individual airlines about packing requirements. Some airlines sell bike boxes, which are often free at bike shops, for about $15 (bike bags can be considerably more expensive). International travelers often can substitute a bike for a piece of checked luggage at no charge; otherwise, the cost is about $100. U.S. and Canadian airlines charge $40–$80 each way.

🚩 Bike Maps **Discovery Series** ✉ Ordnance Survey, Phoenix Park, Dublin 8 ☎ 01/820–6439 or 01/820–6443.

🚩 Bike Tours & Rentals **Irish Cycling Safaris** ✉ Belfield Bike Shop, Belfield House, University College, Dublin 4 ☎ 01/260–0749 ∰ www.cyclingsafaris.com. **Raleigh Ireland** ✉ Raleigh

House, Kylemore Rd., Dublin ☎ 01/626–1333. **VBT (Vermont Biking Tours)** ✉ 614 Monkton Rd., Bristol, VT 05443 ☎ 800/245–3868 ∰ www.vbt.com.

BOATING

In the west, you can still see Galway hookers—solid, heavy, broad-beamed sailing boats with distinctive, gaff-rigged, brownish-red sails—on the waters of Galway Bay. Enthusiasts maintain a small fleet and hold frequent races in July and August.

Because of Irish insurance laws, boat charter is still in its infancy in the Republic of Ireland, with only one company in business for bareboat charter. For the same reason, dinghy rentals are not widespread, and you will need to demonstrate your competence. Sailboards, on the other hand, are relatively easy to rent. Wet suits (also rentable) are essential for sailboarding except on the hottest days in July and August. Rental of sailboarding equipment, including wet suits, starts at about €13 an hour. Sailing dinghies, as well as sailboards, can be rented by the hour (from about €8) or by the day (from about €26). Dinghy- and sailboard-rental contacts are listed under the towns that provide them.

The average cost of a six-berth yacht between 28- and 35-foot-long ranges from €152 per person per week (low season) to €254 (high season). Contact Sail Ireland Charters for bareboat charters. For details of residential dinghy sailing courses, contact Glenans Irish Sailing Club. The club offers one- and two-week courses in sailing and board-sailing at its two centers. One is based on an otherwise uninhabited island in Clew Bay near Westport. The other is in Baltimore in West Cork.

In Northern Ireland, Ulster Cruising School offers yacht rentals from £285 per person per week (low season) to £345 (high season). Contact Sailing Holidays in Ireland for information on both the republic and Northern Ireland.

Cruising along Ireland's inland waterways is a great alternative to traveling overland and can provide a different perspective on the country. In some cases bicycles can be rented so you can drop anchor and explore. The Inland Waterways Association of Ireland is a gold mine of information on Ireland's extensive waterways network. The main backbone of the waterways is the River Shannon, which runs 250 km (160 mi) down the center of the country. 🎏 **Glenans Irish Sailing Club** ✉ 28 Merrion Sq., Dublin 2 ☎ 01/661-1481 ⊕ www.glenans-ireland. com. **Inland Waterways Association of Ireland** ☎ 086/254-7947 ⊕ www.iwai.ie **Sailing Holidays in Ireland** ⊕ www.sailingireland.com. **Sail Ireland Charters** ✉ Trident Hotel, Kinsale, Co. Cork ☎ 021/477-2927 ⊕ www.sailireland.com. **Ulster Cruising School** ✉ Carrickfergus Marina, The Marina 3 Quayside, Carrickfergus, Co. Antrim ☎ 028/9336-6668 ⊕ www.ulstercruising.com. **Waveline Cruisers** ☎ 090/648-5711 ⊕ www.waveline.ie.

FISHING

Salmon and sea trout restrictions limit your catch to one of either variety per day between January and May. The best period for sea trout is from June to late September. Permits are necessary for salmon and sea-trout fishing on privately owned waters or club waters. Besides the permit for the use of a certain stretch of water, those who wish to fish for salmon and sea trout by rod and line must also have a state license. In the Irish Republic, these licenses (€31.75 annually, or €12.70 for 21 days) are available in some tackle shops or from the Central Fisheries Board. No license is required for brown trout, rainbow trout, or coarse fish, including pike. Note that you must purchase share certificates if you intend to do coarse fishing or angling for brown trout in County Donegal; the rates are €3.80 for one day, €6.35 for 21 days, or €15.25 for a season. Contact the Northwestern Regional Fisheries Board for more information.

Northern Ireland's system of pricing and administrating fishing licenses and permits can seem anachronistic, unnecessarily complex, and bewildering. No license is needed for sea fishing. To catch freshwater fish, whether coarse or game, you need a rod license from the Fisheries Conservancy Board. You will need a license from the Foyle Fisheries Commission if you are fishing in the Derry area. Depending on the area, you may need a

local permit. The good news is that all fishing licenses and Department of Agriculture and Fisheries permits are available from the Northern Irish Tourist Board (NITB) Information Centre. A number of tourist information offices and tackle shops around the province stock fishing licenses and permits.

A license costs approximately £10 for eight days. You must also obtain a permit from the owner of the waters in which you plan to fish. Most of the waters in Northern Ireland are owned by the Department of Agriculture, which charges about £15 for a 15-day permit, and £3.50 for a 3-day permit. If you plan to fish outside the jurisdiction of the Department of Agriculture, you must obtain a permit from one of the local clubs. 🎏 **Central Fisheries Board** ✉ Balngowan House, Mobhi Boreen, Glasnevin, Dublin 9 ☎ 01/837-9206 ⊕ www.cfb.ie. **Department of Agriculture** ✉ Fisheries Division, Dundonald House, Upper Newtownards Rd., Belfast BT4 3SB ☎ 028/9052-4999 ⊕ www.dardni.gov.uk. **Fisheries Conservancy Board** ✉ FCB, 1 Mahon Rd., Portadown, BT62 3EE ☎ 028/3833-4666 ⊕ www.fcbni.org. **Foyle Fisheries Commission** ✉ 22 Victoria Rd., Derry BT47 2AB ☎ 028/7134-2100. **Northern Regional Fisheries Board** ✉ Ballyshannon, Co. Donegal ☎ 072/51435. **Northwestern Regional Fisheries Board** ✉ Ballina, Co. Mayo ☎ 096/22623. **Southern Regional Fisheries Board** ✉ Anglesea St., Clonmel, Co. Tipperary ☎ 052/80055. **South Western Regional Fisheries Board** ✉ 1 Nevilles Terr., Macroom, Co. Cork ☎ 026/41221.

SOCCER, GAELIC FOOTBALL,& HURLING

Soccer has increased in popularity over the last two decades with the dramatic successes of the Republic of Ireland team; most of the major towns and cities have a semiprofessional club in the National League that plays from August to May every year. For a truly Irish sports experience you should try to attend one of two Gaelic games, either Gaelic football or hurling; the first is played with a football, slightly smaller and rounder than a soccer ball, that is kicked or hand-passed, and the second with a wooden stick and a hard ball or sliotar, which is very much like a baseball. The speed and skill on display in both games can be breathtaking. An inter-county championship takes place from May through September.

🏈 **Football Association of Ireland** ✉ 80 Merrion Sq., Dublin 2 ☎ 01/676-6864 ⊕ www.fai.ie. **Gaelic Athletic Association** ✉ Croke Park, Dublin 4 ☎ 01/836-3222 ⊕ www.gaa.ie.

GOLF

What makes Irish golf so great—and in-creasingly popular—is quite simply the natural architecture. The wild, wonderful coastline seems to be made for links golf; unlike many international courses, these courses have few forests, ponds, or short roughs. Most famous of these links courses is the celebrated Ballybunion. For-tunately, links courses can be played year-round—an asset in a rainy country like Ireland. Pack plenty of sweaters and rain gear, and make sure you're in good shape: electric cars are only available at the most expensive courses. Golf clubs and bags can be rented almost anywhere. With the exception of the ancient Royal Belfast, all golf clubs in Ireland are happy to have visitors (and charge well for the privilege), and several tour operators have made golf excursions an art, so it's really easy to have the trip of a lifetime. For lots more information on the best golf courses in Ireland, see the Irish Greens chapter in this book.

🏌 Golf Information **Golfing Union of Ireland** ✉ 81 Eglington Rd., Donnybrook Dublin 1 ☎ 01/269-4111 ⊕ www.gui.ie.

🏌 Golf Tour Operators **Absolute Golf & Travel** ☎ 877/545-4653 ⊕ www.absolutely-golf.com. **Atlantic Golf Company** ✉ 800 Summer St., Suite 414, Stamford, CT 06901 ☎ 800/542-6224 ⊕ www.atlanticgolf.com. **Destination Golf** ✉ 416 West 13th St., Suite 313, New York, NY 10014 ☎ 800/441-9329 ⊕ www.destinations-golf.com. **Golf International** ✉ 14 E. 38th St., New York, NY 10016 ☎ 212/986-9176 or 800/833-1389 ⊕ www.golfinternational.com. **Irish Links Tours & Travel** ✉ 400 Main St., Suite 202, Stamford, CT 06901 ☎ 203/363-0970 or 800/824-6538 ⊕ www.irish-links.com. **Jerry Quinlan's Celtic Golf** ✉ 1129 Rte. 9 S, Cape May, NJ 08210 ☎ 609/465-0600 or 800/535-6148 ⊕ www.jqcelticgolf.com. **Owenoak International Golf Travel** ✉ 40 Richards Ave., Norwalk,

CT 06854 ☎ 203/854-9000 or 800/426-4498 ⊕ www.owenoak.com.

HIKING

Hikers from all over the world spend weeks on the almost 30 major and count-less minor trails covering the country. As with biking, the relatively flat landscape, stunning scenery, and nearness of towns to each other make hiking a relatively care-free activity. A tent is always a good idea, but you can certainly plan any walk so that you reach civilization every night. Pack for wind and rain, as there will al-ways be some. Good Ordnance Survey maps are also useful. They are available at leading map and book stores throughout Ireland; see the Ordnance Survey Ireland Web site for a list of where maps are sold.

The Irish Tourist Board (ITB) provides free information sheets on long-distance paths, set up throughout the country over the last few years with the consent of local landowners. You can also get route infor-mation from the Field Officer, Long Dis-tance Walking Routes Committee. Routes are indicated by trail markers and sign-posts. Most are between 30 and 60 km (18 and 37 mi) in length, with the exception of the Wicklow Way, the first to be opened and still one of the best. It's a 137-km (85-mi) trail that begins in the Dublin suburbs before winding its way through the Wick-low Mountains. Much of the route lies above 1,600 feet and follows rough sheep tracks, forest firebreaks, and old bog roads. Whether you're a novice or veteran hiker, Wicklow's gentle hills are a terrific place to begin an Irish walking vacation. Other popular hiking options include the Kerry Way, which starts and ends in Kil-larney, and the Donegal Walk across the center of wild rugged County Donegal.

In Northern Ireland, there is the challenge of the 790-km (491-mi) Ulster Way, a footpath that travels through spectacular coastal scenery. You can also try Way-marked Ways Northern Ireland, a network of eight walking routes—six more are being developed. (The 14 walks add up to about 600 km/373 mi.) The Countryside Access and Activity Network for Northern

Ireland (CAAN) distributes the brochure free; you can also get it from the Northern Ireland Tourist Board information center. Each route has a specific map guide to accompany it, and is available individually at tourist information centers (50p). The complete set of eight guides is available from CAAN for £5.50. Tougher walks in the hills are outlined in the informative handbook in the Irish Walks series, No. 4, *The North East*, by Richard Rogers, published by Gill & Macmillan, which is available in book and sporting goods stores in Northern Ireland; it gives precise details of 45 hill walks, complete with descriptions of the wildflowers you'll see along the way. For hikes in the Mountains of Mourne, you can obtain maps and details of suggested routes from the Mourne Countryside Centre. Walking Cycling Ireland members organize walking and cycling tours. Cross Country International and Destinations Ireland offer a wide range of walking trips.

🎐 **CAAN** ✉ House of Sport, Upper Malone Rd., Belfast, Co. Antrim ☎ 028/9038-3848 ⊕ www. countrysiderecreation.com. **Cross Country International** ☎ 800/828-8768 ⊕ www.walkingvacations. com. **Destinations Ireland** ✉ 416 W. 13th St., Suite 313, New York, NY 10014 ☎ 800/832-1848 ⊕ www. destinations-ireland.com. **Field Officer, Long Distance Walking Routes Committee** ✉ Irish Sports Council, 21 Fitzwilliam Sq., Dublin 2 ☎ 01/676-3837. **Ordinance Survey Ireland** ✉ Phoenix Park, Dublin 8 ☎ 01/802-5300 ⊕ www.osi.ie. **Walking Cycling Ireland** ⊕ www.kerna.ie/wci.

SURFING

Expect great surfing along the Atlantic shores of counties Donegal and Sligo. Head to Strandhill, Rossnowlagh, and Bundoran on the Sligo and southern County Donegal coasts or to Marble Strand and Rosapenna in northern County Donegal. These areas have excellent surfing conditions, although even at the height of summer only the most brave will venture in without a wet suit. Take note that in Ireland a surf shop can only rent surfing equipment to individuals taking lessons. Establishments recommended by the European Surf Federation and Irish Surfing Association have approved, qualified instructors, and are insured to give surfing instruction.

🎐 **Irish Surfing Association** ✉ Tigh-na-Mara, Rossnowlagh, Co. Donegal ☎ 096/49020.

STUDENTS IN IRELAND

To save money, **look into deals available through student-oriented travel agencies.** To qualify you'll need a bona fide student ID card. Members of international student groups are also eligible.

🎐 **I.D.s & Services STA Travel** ✉ 10 Downing St., New York, NY 10014 ☎ 212/627-3111, 800/777-0112 24-hr service center 📠 212/627-3387 ⊕ www.sta. com. **Travel Cuts** ✉ 187 College St., Toronto, Ontario M5T 1P7, Canada ☎ 800/592-2887 in the U.S., 416/979-2406 or 866/246-9762 in Canada 📠 416/979-8167 ⊕ www.travelcuts.com.

TAXES

VALUE-ADDED TAX

When leaving the Irish Republic, U.S. and Canadian visitors get a refund of the value-added tax (V.A.T.), which currently accounts for a hefty 20% of the purchase price of many goods and 13.5% of those that fall outside the luxury category. Apart from clothing, most items of interest to visitors, right down to ordinary toilet soap, are rated at 21%. V.A.T. is not refundable on accommodation, car rental, meals, or any other form of personal services received on vacation.

Many crafts outlets and department stores operate a system called Cashback, which enables U.S. and Canadian visitors to collect V.A.T. rebates in the currency of their choice at Dublin or Shannon Airport on departure. Some stores give you the rebate at the register; with others you claim your refund after you've returned home. Refunds forms must be picked up at the time of purchase, and they must be stamped by customs before you leave for home. If a store gives you a refund at the register, you'll also be given papers to have stamped by customs; you'll then put the papers in an envelope (also provided by the store) and mail it before you leave. Most major stores deduct V.A.T. at the time of sale if goods are to be shipped overseas; however, there's a shipping charge.

When leaving Northern Ireland, U.S. and Canadian visitors can also get a refund of the 17.5% V.A.T. by the over-the-counter and the direct-export methods. Most larger stores provide these services upon request and will handle the paperwork. For the over-the-counter method, you must spend more than £75 in one store. Ask the store for Form V.A.T. 407 (you must have identification—passports are best), to be given to customs when you leave the country. The refund will be forwarded to you in about eight weeks (minus a small service charge) either in the form of a sterling check or as a credit to your charge card. The direct-export method, where the goods are shipped directly to your home, is more cumbersome. V.A.T. Form 407/1/93 must be certified by customs, police, or a notary public when you get home and then sent back to the store, which will refund your money.

When making a purchase, **ask for a V.A.T. refund form** and find out whether the merchant gives refunds—not all stores do, nor are they required to. Have the form stamped like any customs form by customs officials when you leave the country or, if you're visiting several European Union countries, when you leave the EU. Be ready to show customs officials what you've bought (pack purchases together, in your carry-on luggage); budget extra time for this. After you're through passport control, take the form to a refund-service counter for an on-the-spot refund, or mail it to the address on the form (or the envelope with it) after you arrive home.

A service processes refunds for most shops. You receive the total refund stated on the form. Global Refund is a Europe-wide service with 210,000 affiliated stores and more than 700 refund counters—located at major airports and border crossings. Its refund form is called a Tax Free Check. The service issues refunds in the form of cash, check, or credit-card adjustment. If you don't have time to wait at the refund counter, you can mail in the form instead.

🚩 **V.A.T. Refunds Global Refund** ✉ 99 Main St., Suite 307, Nyack, NY 10960 ☎ 800/566-9828 🖨 845/348-1549 🌐 www.globalrefund.com.

TELEPHONES

Ireland's telephone system is up to the standards of the United Kingdom and the United States. Direct-dialing is common; local phone numbers have five to eight digits. You can make international calls from most phones, and some cell phones also work here, depending on the carrier.

Do not make calls from your hotel room unless it's absolutely necessary. Practically all hotels add 200% to 300% to the cost.

AREA & COUNTRY CODES

The country code for Ireland is 353; for Northern Ireland, which is part of the United Kingdom telephone system, it's 44. The local area code for Northern Ireland is 028. However, when dialing Northern Ireland from the republic you can simply dial 048 without using the U.K. country code. When dialing an Irish number from abroad, drop the initial 0 from the local area code. The country code is 1 for the United States and Canada, 61 for Australia, 64 for New Zealand, and 44 for the United Kingdom.

DIRECTORY & OPERATOR ASSISTANCE

If the operator has to connect your call, it will cost at least one-third more than direct dial.

🚩 Directory Information **Republic of Ireland** ☎ 11811 for directory inquiries in the republic and Northern Ireland, 11818 for U.K. and international numbers, 114 for operator assistance with international calls, 10 for operator assistance for calls in Ireland, Northern Ireland, and the U.K. **Northern Ireland and the U.K.** ☎ 192 for directory inquiries in Northern Ireland and the U.K., 153 for international directory inquiries, which includes the republic, 155 for the international operator, 100 for operator assistance for calls in the U.K. and Northern Ireland.

INTERNATIONAL CALLS

The international prefix from Ireland is 00. For calls to Great Britain (except Northern Ireland), dial 0044 before the exchange code, and drop the initial zero of the local code. For the United States and Canada dial 001, for Australia 0061, and for New Zealand 0064.

LOCAL CALLS

To make a local call just dial the number direct. Public phones take either coins (€0.25 for a call) or cards, but not both. At coin phones just pick up the receiver and deposit the money before you dial the number. At card phones pick up the receiver, wait until the display tells you to insert the card, then dial. In the republic, €0.25 will buy you a three-minute local call; around €1 is needed for a three-minute long-distance call within the republic. In Northern Ireland, a local call costs 10p.

LONG-DISTANCE CALLS

To make a long-distance call, dial the area code, then the number. The local code for Northern Ireland is 028, unless you're dialing from the republic, in which case you dial 048 or 4428, followed by the eight-digit number.

LONG-DISTANCE SERVICES

AT&T, MCI, and Sprint access codes make calling long-distance relatively convenient, but you may find the local access number blocked in many hotel rooms. First ask the hotel operator to connect you. If the hotel operator balks, ask for an international operator, or dial the international operator yourself. One way to improve your odds of getting connected to your long-distance carrier is to travel with more than one company's calling card (a hotel may block Sprint, for example, but not MCI). If all else fails, call from a pay phone.

🄵 Access Codes **AT&T Direct** ☎ 1800/550–000 from the Republic of Ireland, 0500/890–011 from Northern Ireland. **MCI WorldPhone** ☎ 1800/551–001 from the Republic of Ireland, 0800/890–222 from Northern Ireland using BT, 0500/890–222 using C&W. **Sprint International Access** ☎ 1800/552–001 from the Republic of Ireland, 0800/890–877 from Northern Ireland using BT, 0500/890–877 using C&W.

PHONE CARDS

"Callcards" are sold in post offices and newsagents. These come in denominations of 10, 20, and 50 units and range in price from about €2.55 for 10 calls to €20.30 for 100 calls.

PUBLIC PHONES

Public pay phones can be found in street booths and in restaurants, hotels, bars, and shops, some of which display a sign saying YOU CAN PHONE FROM HERE. There are at least three models of pay phones; read the instructions or ask for assistance.

TIME

Dublin is five hours ahead of New York and eight hours ahead of Los Angeles and Vancouver. It's 9 hours behind Auckland, and 10 hours behind Sydney and Melbourne.

TIPPING

In some hotels and restaurants a service charge of around 10%—rising to 15% in plush spots—is added to the bill. If in doubt, ask whether service is included. In places where it is included, tipping isn't necessary unless you have received particularly good service. If there's no service charge, add a minimum of 10% to the total. Tip taxi drivers about 10% of the fare displayed by the meter. Hackney cabs, who make the trip for a prearranged sum, don't expect tips. There are few porters and plenty of baggage trolleys at airports, so tipping is usually not an issue; if you use a porter, €1 is the minimum. Tip hotel porters at least €1 per suitcase. Hairdressers normally expect about 10% of the total spent. You don't tip in pubs, but for waiter service in a bar, a hotel lounge, or a Dublin lounge bar, leave about €1. It's not customary to tip for concierge service.

TOURS & PACKAGES

Because everything is prearranged on a prepackaged tour or independent vacation, you spend less time planning—and often get it all at a good price.

BOOKING WITH AN AGENT

Travel agents are excellent resources. But it's a good idea to collect brochures from several agencies, as some agents' suggestions may be influenced by relationships with tour and package firms that reward them for volume sales. If you have a special interest, find an agent with expertise in that area; the American Society of Travel Agents (ASTA; ⇨ Travel Agencies) has a database of specialists worldwide.

You can log on to the group's Web site to find an ASTA travel agent in your neighborhood. Make sure your travel agent knows the accommodations and other services of the place being recommended. Ask about the hotel's location, room size, beds, and whether it has a pool, room service, or programs for children, if you care about these. Has your agent been there in person or sent others whom you can contact? Do some homework on your own, too: local tourism boards can provide information about lesser-known and small-niche operators, some of which may sell only direct.

BUYER BEWARE

Each year consumers are stranded or lose their money when tour operators—even large ones with excellent reputations—go out of business. So check out the operator. Ask several travel agents about its reputation, and try to **book with a company that has a consumer-protection program.** (Look for information in the company's brochure.) In the United States, members of the United States Tour Operators Association are required to set aside funds ($1 million) to help eligible customers cover payments and travel arrangements in the event that the company defaults. It's also a good idea to choose a company that participates in the American Society of Travel Agents' Tour Operator Program; ASTA will act as mediator in any disputes between you and your tour operator.

Remember that the more your package or tour includes, the better you can predict the ultimate cost of your vacation. Make sure you know exactly what is covered, and beware of hidden costs. Are taxes, tips, and transfers included? Entertainment and excursions? These can add up.

🖪 Tour-Operator Recommendations **American Society of Travel Agents** (⇨ Travel Agencies). **National Tour Association** (NTA) ✉ 546 E. Main St., Lexington, KY 40508 ☎ 859/226-4444 or 800/682-8886 🖷 859/226-4404 ⊕ www.ntaonline.com. **United States Tour Operators Association** (USTOA) ✉ 275 Madison Ave., Suite 2014, New York, NY 10016 ☎ 212/599-6599 🖷 212/599-6744 ⊕ www.ustoa.com.

TRAIN TRAVEL

The republic's Irish Rail trains are generally reliable, reasonably priced, and comfortable. You can easily reach all the principal towns from Dublin, though services between provincial cities are roundabout. To get to Cork City from Wexford, for example, you have to go via Limerick Junction. It's often quicker, though perhaps less comfortable, to take a bus. Most mainline trains have one standard class. Round-trip tickets are usually cheapest.

Northern Ireland Railways has three main rail routes, all operating out of Belfast's Central Station. These are north to Derry, via Ballymena and Coleraine; east to Bangor along the shores of Belfast Lough; and south to Dublin and the Irish Republic. Note that Eurailpasses aren't valid in Northern Ireland.

You should plan to be at the train station at least 30 minutes before your train departs to ensure you will get a seat. It is not uncommon on busier routes to find that you have to stand since all seats have been sold and taken.

CUTTING COSTS

To save money, **look into rail passes.** But be aware that if you don't plan to cover many miles, you may come out ahead by buying individual tickets.Ireland (excluding Northern Ireland) is one of 17 countries in which you can **use Eurailpasses,** which provide unlimited first-class rail travel, in all of the participating countries, for the duration of the pass. If you plan to rack up the miles, get a standard pass. These are available for 15 days ($588), 21 days ($762), one month ($946), two months ($1,338), and three months ($1,654). In addition to standard Eurailpasses, **ask about special rail-pass plans.** Among these are the Eurail Youthpass (for those under age 26), the Eurail Saverpass (which gives a discount for two or more people traveling together), a Eurail Flexipass (which allows a certain number of travel days within a set period), the Euraildrive Pass and the Europass Drive (which combines travel by train and rental car). Whichever pass you choose, you must **purchase your pass before you leave** for Europe.

The Irish Explorer Rail & Bus Pass covers all the state-run and federal railways and bus lines throughout the republic. It does not apply to the North or to transportation within cities. An eight-day ticket for use on buses *and* trains during a 15-day period is €158. The Emerald Isle Card offers unlimited bus and train travel anywhere in Ireland and Northern Ireland, valid within cities as well. An 8-day pass gives you eight days of travel over a 15-day period; it costs roughly €182. A pass for 15 days of travel over a 30-day period costs about €316. Irish Rail International provides details on both passes.

In Northern Ireland, the **Freedom of Northern Ireland Pass** entitling you to seven days' unlimited travel on scheduled bus and rail services, April–October, is available from main Northern Ireland Railway stations. It costs £ 47 for adults (half price for children under 12 and senior citizens). Interrail tickets are also valid in Northern Ireland.

🚆 Information & Passes **CIE Tours International** ⌂ 100 Hanover Ave., Box 501, Cedar Knolls, NJ 07927 ☎ 800/243-8687 ⊕ www.cietours.com. **DER Travel Services** ✉ 9501 W. Devon Ave., Rosemont, IL 60018 ☎ 888/337-7350 ⊕ www.dertravel.com. **Rail Europe** ✉ 44 S Broadway, No. 11, White Plains, NY 10601 ☎ 800/438-7245 ⊕ www.raileurope.com ✉ 2087 Dundas E, Suite 105, Mississauga, Ontario L4X 2V7 ☎ 800/361-7245.

FARES & SCHEDULES

Train schedules are easy to obtain and available in a variety of formats. Irish Rail and Northern Ireland Rail have Web sites that produce a schedule in response to your input of an itinerary. Alternatively you can visit any train station to obtain a printed schedule or call either company's customer service line. Take special note of schedules when traveling on holiday weekends as they are usually changed. Both rail services print amended schedules well in advance.

Sample fares? A return ticket from Dublin to Cork will cost around € 51; Dublin to Belfast is approximately € 46.

🚆 Train Information **Irish Rail (Iarnrod Éireann)** ☎ 01/836-6222 ⊕ www.irishrail.ie is the rail division of CIE. **Northern Ireland Railways** ☎ 028/9089-9411 ⊕ www.translink.co.uk.

Belfast Central Station ✉ East Bridge St., Belfast BT1 3PB ☎ 028/ 9089-9400 ⊕ www.translink.co. uk. **Connolly Station** ✉ Amiens St., Dublin 1 ☎ 01/703-2358 ⊕ www.irishrail.ie. **Galway Station** ✉ Station Rd., Galway ☎ 091/ 562-730 ⊕ www. irishrail.ie. **Heuston Station** ✉ Dublin 8 ☎ 01/703-3299 ⊕ www.irishrail.ie. **Kent Station** ✉ Lower Glenmuir Rd., Cork ☎ 021/450-6766 ⊕ www.irishrail.ie.

PAYING

Tickets can be purchased online or at the train station. Cash, travelers' checks, and credit card payments are accepted. You must pay in the local currency. In Dublin, Connolly and Heuston stations have automated ticket machines that take either cash or credit-card payments, offering a convenient way to avoid long lines at ticket windows.

RESERVATIONS

Many travelers assume that rail passes guarantee them seats on the trains they wish to ride. Not so. You need to **book seats ahead even if you are using a rail pass.** Seat reservations are required on some European trains, particularly high-speed trains, and are a good idea on trains that may be crowded—particularly in summer on popular routes. You will also need a reservation if you purchase sleeping accommodations.

There is only one class of train travel in Ireland (with the exception of the Enterprise, the express train that travels from Dublin to Belfast, for which you can purchase a First Class or Standard Class ticket). In general, specific seat reservations can only be made for trains deemed to be busy (ask when buying your ticket if they are taking reservations for your route). For example, the train traveling from Dublin to Cork on a Friday evening is considered a peak time, thanks to all the students and business travelers heading home for the weekend. On such a route, you would just be able to buy a ticket, not a specific seat designation. At peak hours and for popular routes, it is advisable to arrive early at the station to purchase your ticket (or buy it online) or you may find yourself standing for a significant portion of your journey.

TRAVEL AGENCIES

A good travel agent puts your needs first. Look for an agency that has been in business at least five years, emphasizes customer service, and has someone on staff who specializes in your destination. In addition, **make sure the agency belongs to a professional trade organization.** The American Society of Travel Agents (ASTA)—the largest and most influential in the field with more than 20,000 members in some 140 countries—maintains and enforces a strict code of ethics and will step in to help mediate any agent-client disputes involving ASTA members if necessary. ASTA (whose motto is "Without a travel agent, you're on your own") also maintains a Web site that includes a directory of agents. (If a travel agency is also acting as your tour operator, *see* Buyer Beware *in* Tours & Packages.)

🚩 Local Agent Referrals **American Society of Travel Agents (ASTA)** ⊠ 1101 King St., Suite 200, Alexandria, VA 22314 ☎ 703/739-2782 or 800/965-2782 24-hr hotline ᕤ 703/684-8319 ⊕ www. astanet.com. **Association of British Travel Agents** ⊠ 68–71 Newman St., London W1T 3AH ☎ 020/7637-2444 ᕤ 020/7637-0713 ⊕ www.abta.com. **Association of Canadian Travel Agencies** ⊠ 130 Albert St., Suite 1705, Ottawa, Ontario K1P 5G4 ☎ 613/237-3657 ᕤ 613/237-7052 ⊕ www.acta.ca. **Australian Federation of Travel Agents** ⊠ Level 3, 309 Pitt St., Sydney, NSW 2000 ☎ 02/9264-3299 or 1300/363-416 ᕤ 02/9264-1085 ⊕ www.afta.com. au. **Travel Agents' Association of New Zealand** ⊠ Level 5, Tourism and Travel House, 79 Boulcott St., Box 1888, Wellington 6001 ☎ 04/499-0104 ᕤ 04/499-0786 ⊕ www.taanz.org.nz.

VISITOR INFORMATION

Learn more about foreign destinations by checking government-issued travel advisories and country information. For a broader picture, consider information from more than one country.

For information on travel in the Irish Republic, contact the **Irish Tourist Board** (ITB or Bord Fáilte; ⊕ www.ireland.travel.ie or www.tourismireland.com), known as Bord Fáilte (pronounced board *fal*-cha). Information on travel in the North is available from the **Northern Ireland Tourist Board** (NITB; ⊕ www.discovernorthernireland. com).

🚩 ITB **Ireland** ⊠ Baggot St. Bridge, Dublin 2 ☎ 01/602-4000, 669/792-083, 1850/230-330, toll-free* within Ireland. **U.K.** ⊠ Ireland House, 150 New Bond St., London W1Y 0AQ ☎ 020/7493-3201. **U.S.** ⊠ 345 Park Ave., New York, NY 10154 ☎ 212/418-0800 or 800/223-6470 ⊕ www.shamrock.org.
🚩 NITB **Northern Ireland** ⊠ 59 North St., Belfast BT1 1NB ☎ 028/9023-1221. **Canada** ⊠ 2 Bloor St. W, Suite 1501, Toronto, Ontario M4W 3E2 ☎ 416/925-6368. **U.K.** ⊠ 24 Haymarket, London SW1 4DG ☎ 020/7766-9920, 08701/555-250 info line. **U.S.** ⊠ 551 5th Ave., Suite 701, New York, NY 10176 ☎ 212/922-0101 or 800/326-0036.

🚩 Government Advisories **U.S. Department of State** ⊠ Overseas Citizens Services Office, 2100 Pennsylvania Ave. NW, 4th fl., Washington, DC 20520 ☎ 202/647-5225 interactive hotline or 888/407-4747 ⊕ www.travel.state.gov. **Consular Affairs Bureau of Canada** ☎ 800/267-6788 or 613/944-6788 ⊕ www.voyage.gc.ca. **U.K. Foreign and Commonwealth Office** ⊠ Travel Advice Unit, Consular Division, Old Admiralty Building, London SW1A 2PA ☎ 0870/606-0290 or 020/7008-1500 ⊕ www.fco. gov.uk/travel. **Australian Department of Foreign Affairs and Trade** ☎ 300/139-281 travel advice, 02/6261-1299 Consular Travel Advice Faxback Service ⊕ www.dfat.gov.au. **New Zealand Ministry of Foreign Affairs and Trade** ☎ 04/439-8000 ⊕ www. mft.govt.nz.

WEB SITES

Do check out the World Wide Web when planning your trip. You'll find everything from weather forecasts to virtual tours of famous cities. Be sure to visit Fodors.com (⊕ www.fodors.com), a complete travel-planning site. You can research prices and book plane tickets, hotel rooms, rental cars, vacation packages, and more. In addition, you can post your pressing questions in the Travel Talk section. Other planning tools include a currency converter and weather reports, and there are loads of links to travel resources.

For lots of entertaining bits—Irish and otherwise—visit ⊕ www.irishabroad.com. Its sister site, ⊕ www.irishsights.com, has links to Irish sites of all types. Some of the most popular sites are the Doras Directory (⊕ www.doras.ie) and Heritage Ireland (⊕ www.heritageireland.ie). ⊕ www. ireland-information.com is dedicated to providing as many free resources and as much free information about Ireland as possible on an array of topics from genealogy to shopping. For a central directory of links to all things Irish, log on to ⊕ www. finditireland.com. Comhaltas Ceoltóirí Eireann is an association that promotes the music, culture, and art of Ireland and its Web site ⊕ www.comhaltas.com has helpful news about the Irish traditional music scene. The site of ⊕ www.ireland-now.com can provide history legend and lore to enhance your visit to Ireland. Keep in mind that many of the leading newspapers of Ireland (⇨ Media) have Web sites,

which can be gold mines of timely information. For a weekly newsletter to keep Irish people abroad up to date on events at home, log on to ⊕ www.emigrant.ie.

Officially designated Heritage Towns are featured on ⊕ www.heritagetowns.com. For information on arts events of all kinds, try ⊕ www.art.ie, which is affiliated with and has links to the arts councils of both the Irish Republic and Northern Ireland. For more information on counties in the west of Ireland, try ⊕ www.trueireland. com or ⊕ www.irelandwest.ie. A handy regional site is ⊕ www.southeastireland. com. Portion's of the Bord Fáilte's eloquent magazine, *Ireland of the Welcomes,* are available online (⊕ www. irelandofthewelcomes.com).For an eloquent site devoted to some of Ireland's most historic buildings, see ⊕ www.irish-architecture.com, while ⊕ www. castlesireland.com and ⊕ www. celticcastles.com will please the castle lover. Green-thumbers will enjoy ⊕ www. gardensireland.com.

DUBLIN

1

RAISE A GLASS TO JAMES JOYCE
on a Literary Pub Crawl ⇨*p.131*

BE ILLUMINATED
by the medieval Book of Kells ⇨*p.28*

"ROCK 'N STROLL" YOUR WAY
through hip Temple Bar ⇨*p.131*

GO GLORIOUSLY GEORGIAN
on 18th century Merrion Square ⇨*p.33*

PLUCK A LUCKY FOUR-LEAF CLOVER
on St. Stephen's Green ⇨*p.27*

SNACK ON SPATCHCOCK QUAIL
at Bono's Tea Room celeb spot ⇨*p.70*

RECAPTURE ROCOCO TIMES
in the salons of Newman House ⇨*p.26*

GET SPIRITED (PUN INTENDED)
on a tour of the Guinness Brewery ⇨*p.50*

Updated by
Anto Howard

IN HIS INIMITABLE, irresistible way, James Joyce immortalized Dublin in *Ulysses, Dubliners,* and *A Portrait of the Artist as a Young Man,* filling these works with the people he knew speaking in their own words, and adding more than a few of his own. He has become one of Dublin's most famous exiles. Disappointed with the city's provincial outlook and small-town manners, he departed in 1902, at the age of 20 (his famed peers Sean O'Casey and Samuel Beckett soon followed). If, however, Joyce were to return to his genteel hometown today and take an extended, quasi-Homeric odyssey through the city (as he does so famously in *Ulysses*), would he even recognize Dublin as his "Dear Dirty Dumpling, foostherfather of fingalls and dotthergills"?

For instance, what would he make of Temple Bar—the city's erstwhile down-at-the-heels neighborhood, crammed with restaurants and stylish hotels in its present reborn state as Dublin's "Left Bank"? Or the old market area of Smithfield, whose Cinderella makeover has changed it into an impressive plaza and winter ice-skating venue? Or of the new Irishness, where every aspect of Celtic culture results in sold-out theaters: from Martin McDonagh's Broadway hit *The Beauty Queen of Leenane,* to *Riverdance,* the old Irish mass-jig recast as Las Vegas extravaganza? Plus, the returned Joyce might be stirred by the songs of U2, fired up by the films of Neil Jordan, and moved by the poems of Nobel laureate Seamus Heaney. In short, Irish is cool. As for Ireland's capital, elegant shops and hotels, galleries, art-house cinemas, coffeehouses, and a stunning variety of restaurants are springing up on almost every street in Dublin, transforming the genteel city that suffocated Joyce into a place almost as cosmopolitan as the Paris to which he fled.

Forget the Vikings and the English. Fast-forward to the new Dublin, where the army of invaders at the intersection of O'Connell Street and Temple Lane might be London lads on a wild bachelor spree, Europeans in search of a chic weekend, African and Asian immigrants seeking employment, and representatives from the United States of the "FBI"—foreign-born Irish. Thanks to "the Celtic Tiger"—the nickname given to the roaring Irish economy of the mid- to late-1990s—this most intimate of Western European capitals became a headline-making boomtown.

Dublin's popularity has provoked many of its citizens to protest that the rapid transformation of their heretofore tranquil city has changed its spirit and character. With the recent slowdown in the Irish economic miracle, these skeptics await the outcome of "Dublin: The Sequel"—can the "new Dublin" get beyond the rage stage and recover its rate of phenomenal growth or will it, like London, have to suffer recession and crisis to rediscover its soul?

Happily, enough of the old Dublin remains to enchant. The fundamentals—the Georgian elegance of Merrion Square, the Norman drama of Christ Church Cathedral, the foamy pint at an atmospheric pub—are still on hand to gratify. Fittingly, some of the more recent developments hark back to early times. Two multimedia shows in the downtown area testify that Norsemen were responsible for the city's original boom (various neighborhood names, such as Howth, Leixlip, and Dalkey, echo

It will take you about a week to cover almost all of the Dublin Exploring suggestions listed in this chapter, including the side trips. But in three or even two days, you can see many city-center sights and probably come away with a greater familiarity with the city than you could establish in a similar length of time in any of Europe's other capitals.

If you have 1 day

Touring the largest city in Ireland in the space of a day sounds like an impossible goal, but if you're determined you can do it in a single sunrise-to-sunset span. Think Dublin 101. South of the Liffey are graceful squares and fashionable terraces from Dublin's elegant Georgian heyday; interspersed with some of the city's leading sights, this area is perfect for an introductory tour of the city. You might begin at O'Connell Bridge—as Dublin has no central focal point, most natives have regarded it as the city's Piccadilly Circus or Times Square. Then head south down Westmoreland Street on your way to view one of Dublin's most spectacular buildings, James Gandon's 18th-century Parliament House, now the Bank of Ireland building. To fuel up for the walk ahead, first stop at Bewley's Oriental Café at 12 Westmoreland Street, an institution that has been supplying Dubliners with tea and scones since 1842. After you drink in the grand colonnade of the Bank of Ireland building, cross the street to the genteel, elegant campus of Trinity College—the oldest seat of Irish learning. Your first stop should be the Old Library, to see the staggering Long Room and Ireland's greatest art treasure, the *Book of Kells,* one of the world's most famous—and most beautiful—illuminated manuscripts.

Leave the campus and take a stroll along Grafton Street, Dublin's busiest shopping street and—"Who will buy my beautiful roses?"—open-air flower market. One of the city's favorite relaxation spots, the lovely St. Stephen's Green, is nearby. Head to the northeast corner of the park to find ground zero for the city's cultural institutions. Here, surrounding the four points of Leinster House (built by the earl of Kildare, Ireland's first patron of Palladianism), are the National Museum of Archaeology and History, replete with artifacts and exhibits dating from prehistoric times; the National Gallery of Ireland (don't miss the Irish collection and the Caravaggio *Taking of Christ*); the National Library; and the National Museum of Natural History. Depending on your interests, pick one to explore, and then make a quick detour westward to Merrion Square—one of Dublin's most famous Georgian landmarks.

For a lovely lunch, head back to St. Stephen's Green and the Victorian-era hotel, the Shelbourne, where the lobby salons glow with Waterford chandeliers and blazing fireplaces. From St. Stephen's Green walk west for 10 minutes to pay your respects to St. Paddy—St. Patrick's Cathedral. If, instead, the Dublin of artists and poets is more your speed, hop a double-decker bus and head north of the Liffey to the Dublin Writers Museum. End the day with a performance at the nearby Gate Theatre, another Georgian eye-knocker, or spend the evening exploring the cobbled streets, many cafés, and shops of Dublin's bohemian quarter, the compact Temple Bar area, back on the south bank of the Liffey.

Because you couldn't fit in a stop at the Guinness Brewery and Storehouse, top the evening off with a pint at the Stag's Head pub just across Dame Street.

If you have 3 days The above tour is the grand curtain-raiser for this itinerary. Dedicate your second day to the areas north and west of the city center. In the morning, cross the Liffey via O'Connell Bridge and walk up O'Connell Street, the city's widest thoroughfare, stopping to visit the General Post Office—the besieged headquarters of the 1916 rebels—on your way to the Dublin Writers Museum (if you didn't have a chance to visit on your first day) and the Hugh Lane Municipal Gallery of Modern Art. Be sure to join the thousands of Dubliners strolling down Henry, Moore, and Mary streets, the Northside's pedestrian shopping area. In the afternoon, head back to the Liffey for a quayside walk by Dublin's most imposing structure, the Custom House; then head west to the Guinness Brewery and Storehouse. Hop a bus or catch a cab back into the city for a blow-out dinner at the glamorous Tea Room in Temple Bar's Clarence Hotel. Spend the evening on a literary pub crawl to see where the likes of Beckett and Behan held court, perhaps joining a guided tour. On your third day tour the northern outskirts of Dublin from Glasnevin Cemetery and the National Botanic Gardens across to the sublime Marino Casino in Marino and the quaint fishing village of Howth. Back in the city, have tea at Bewley's and catch a musical performance at the Olympia Theatre or a play at the Abbey Theatre.

If you have 5 days Follow the two itineraries above and then head west to start your fourth day at Dublin's dawn—a multi-media history of Dublin can be seen at medieval Dublinia, across the street from ancient Christ Church Cathedral, whose underground crypt is Dublin's oldest structure. Head north, jumping across the Liffey to the Four Courts, James Gandon's Georgian masterpiece and the home of the Irish judiciary. Recross the river to the Southside and go west again to visit the Royal Hospital Kilmainham—which houses the Irish Museum of Modern Art—and Kilmainham Gaol, where the leaders of the Easter Uprising were executed. Return via Dublin Castle, residence of British power in Ireland for nearly 800 years, and now the home of the Chester Beatty Library, containing Chinese and Turkish exhibits. On your fifth and final day explore the southern outskirts of the city, accessible by DART train, including the suburban areas of Dalkey and Sandycove (where you can visit the James Joyce Martello Tower), and the busy ferry port of Dun Laoghaire. Before returning to the city center, take a stroll along the 5-km (3-mi) beach of Sandymount Strand—that is, if Irish skies are smiling.

---

their historic presence). Until 500 AD, Dublin was little more than a crossroads—albeit a critical one—of four of the main thoroughfares that traversed the country. It had two names: Baile Atha Cliath, meaning City of the Hurdles, which was bestowed by Celtic traders in the 2nd century AD and which you can still see on buses and billboards throughout the city; and Dubhlinn, or "dark pool," after a body of water (the murkiness of the water was caused by peat) believed to have been where Dublin Castle now stands.

In 837, Norsemen from Scandinavia carried out the first invasion of Dublin, only to be followed by new waves of warriors staking a claim to the city—from the 12th-century Anglo-Normans to Oliver Cromwell in 1651. Not until the 18th century did Dublin reach a golden age, when the patronage of wealthy nobles turned the city into one of Europe's most prepossessing capitals. Streets and squares, such as Merrion and Fitzwilliam squares, were constructed with neoclassic dignity and Palladian grace. If Dublin today is still redolent in parts of the elegance of the 18th century, it is due to the eminently refined Georgian style of art and architecture, which flowered in the city between 1714 and 1820 during the English reigns of the three Georges. To satisfy the taste for luxury of the rising class of titled, wealthy members of society, lemon-color chintz borders, gilded Derbyshire pier tables, and Adamesque wood paneling were installed in the salons of town houses. The arts also flourished: Handel, the German-born English composer, wrote much of his great oratorio *Messiah* here, where it was first performed in 1742. But the aura of "the glorious eighteenth" was short-lived; in 1800, the Act of Union brought Ireland and Britain together in a common United Kingdom, and political power moved from Dublin to London. Dublin quickly lost its cultural and social sparkle, as many members of the nobility moved to England's power capital, turning Ireland practically overnight into "the Cinderella of all nations," in historian Maurice Craig's words.

The 19th century proved to be a time of political turmoil and agitation, although Daniel O'Connell, the first Catholic lord mayor of Dublin (his statue dominates O'Connell Street), won early success with the introduction of Catholic Emancipation in 1829. During the late 1840s, Dublin escaped the worst effects of the famine, caused by potato blight, that ravaged much of southern and western Ireland. As an emerging Victorian middle class introduced an element of genteel snobbery to the city, Dublin began a rapid outward expansion to the enclaves of Ballsbridge, Rathgar, and Rathmines on the Southside, and Clontarf and Drumcondra on the Northside.

The city entered a period of cultural ferment in the first decade of the 20th century—an era whose political apotheosis occurred with the Easter Uprising of 1916. A war aimed at winning independence from Britain began in County Tipperary in 1919 and lasted for three years. During the Civil War, which followed the establishment of the Irish Free State in December 1921, two architectural gems, the Four Courts and the Custom House, came under fire and were severely damaged. Many sites in the capital had to be rebuilt during the 1920s. After the Civil War ended, Dublin entered a new era of political and cultural conservatism, which continued until the late 1970s. The major turning point in Dublin's fortunes occurred in 1972, when Ireland, emerging from 40 years of isolationism, joined the European Economic Community (EEC). In the 1980s, while the economy remained in the grasp of recession, Dublin and Ireland once again turned to the cultural sphere to announce themselves to the world. Irish musicians stormed the American and British barricades of rock and roll. Bob Geldof and the Boomtown Rats ("I Don't Like Mondays") and Chris de Burgh were among the most prominent of the musicians who found audiences far from their native shores, but it was U2 that climbed to the topmost heights of rock-and-roll stardom, forging a permanent place in international popular culture for Irish musicians. Sinéad O'Connor, the Cranberries, and the Corrs have since followed, with similarly talented performers running on the fast track.

If the 1980s saw the ascent of Irish rock stars, the 1990s and the first years of the 21st century were truly Ireland's boom years—a period of broadly improved economic fortunes, major capital investment, declining unemployment, and reversing patterns of immigration—set in motion to a great extent by the country's participation in the EEC (now the European Union, or EU). When Ireland overwhelmingly approved the new EU treaty in 1992, it was one of the poorest European nations; it qualified for EU grants of all kinds. Since then, money has, quite simply, *poured* into Ireland—nowhere more so than in Dublin. The International Financial Services Centre, gleaming behind the two-centuries-old Custom House, is one of the most overt signs of the success the city has had in attracting leading multinational corporations, particularly those in the telecommunications, software, and service industries. In 2000 the government announced that Ireland was the world's largest exporter of software. In the spring of 1998, the Irish overwhelmingly voted in favor of membership in the single European currency; since January 2002, Ireland's main currency has been the euro, the pound altogether withdrawn from circulation. The recent downturn in the global economy has slowed the Celtic Tiger to a crawling pace, and economists argue over the prospects for a country so dependent on exports.

Today, roughly a third of the Irish Republic's population of 3.9 million people lives in Dublin and its suburbs. This is a city of preponderantly young people—astonishingly so. Students from all over Ireland attend Trinity College and the city's dozen other universities and colleges. On weekends, their counterparts from Paris, London, and Rome fly in, swelling the city's youthful contingent, crowding its pubs and clubs to overflowing. After graduating, more and more young people are sticking around rather than emigrating to New York or London, filling the jobs set up by multinational corporations and contributing to the hubbub that's evident everywhere.

All this development has not been without growing pains; with London-level housing prices, increased crime, and major traffic problems, Dubliners are at last suffering the woes so familiar to city dwellers around the world. An influx of immigrants has caused resentment among some of the famously hospitable Irish. "Me darlin' Dublin's dead and gone" goes a traditional ballad, but the recent rebirth, although at times difficult and a little messy, has been a spectacular success.

And when is it best—or worst—to pay a call on the Irish capital? The summer offers a real lift, as the natives spill out of the dark pubs into the slew of new sidewalk cafés and open-air restaurants. The week around St. Patrick's Day (March 17th) is, naturally, a nonstop festival of parades, cultural happenings, and "hooleys" (long nights of partying) throughout the city. Christmas in Dublin seems to last a month, and the city's old-style illuminations match the genteel, warm mood of the locals. The downside quickly follows, however, for January and Febru-

For the Stout of Heart

It's been said that the pub is the poor man's university. If this is true, Dublin has more than 1,000 opportunities for higher education. Even if you only order an Evian, a visit to a Dublin pub (or two or three) is a must. The Irish public house is a national institution—down to the spectacle, at some pubs, of patrons standing at closing time for the playing of Ireland's national anthem." Samuel Beckett would often repair to a pub, believing a glass of Guinness stout was the best way to ward off depression. Indeed, Dublin is for the stout of heart—the city has one pub for every 450 of its 500,000 adults. There are actor's pubs, sports pubs, even pubs for failed literary types (Grogan's on South William Street). And any occasion—be it "ordinations, liquidations, cremations," as one storefront puts it—is the right occasion. Today, old-fashioned, traditional-look Irish pubs are being exported at a brisk rate around the world but, in Dublin, it's a different story altogether. Here, modern, European-style café-bars have made serious inroads on the capital's traditional drinking spots. The city center is now adorned with high-concept designer pubs with bright, arty facades and a pervasive scent of affluence. To be sure, in the City of 1,001 pubs, you're still certain of finding a good, old-fashioned watering hole. And if you do find yourself in a new spot, surrounded by the trappings of European chic, you'll soon discover that Dubliners still enjoy good *craic*—quintessentially Irish friendly chat and lively conversation—wherever they congregate. Wherever you go, remember that when you order a Guinness, the barman first pours it three-quarters of the way, then lets it settle, then tops it off and brings it over to the bar. The customer should then wait again until the top-up has settled, at which point the brew turns a deep black. The mark of a perfect pint? As you drink the glass down, the brew will leave thin rings to mark each mouthful.

The Gorgeous Eighteenth

If Dublin is extraordinary, it is the 18th century that made it so—at least in the minds of art lovers and connoisseurs. It was during the "gorgeous eighteenth" that dowdy Dublin was transformed between 1714 and 1820 by the Georgian style of art and architecture (so known because it was favored by the three English kings named George) into the architectural and decorative-arts extravaganza it is today. Where once Ladies of Quality and Distinction promenaded in their *coaches de cérémonie*—complete with four black horses, two postillions, and one 250-pound footman—you can now tour the lordly, lofty city and still find it a living record of the Age of Elegance. Of course, you have to know where to look: Georgian groupies first head to the great 18th-century urban set-pieces: Merrion, Fitzwilliam, Mountjoy, and Parnell Squares. Many like to saunter down Merrion Square East—the longest Georgian street in town—at dusk and watch how the setting sun magically draws fresh color from the claret-red brick of the houses. Elsewhere, fan-lighted doors (often lacquered in black, green, yellow, and red), "patent reveal" window trims, and vestibules and stairways done up in Rococo plasterwork delight and enchant. Many mansions of the Georgian age are still private but some of the greatest—like Newman House—are open to the public. No matter: by day, you can often peek at private ground-floor vestibules, while at night, when lamps come on, you can study some of the grand molded ceilings of second-floor salons.

Music & Merriment   Music fills Dublin's streets (especially Grafton Street) and its pubs, where *talk* of music is as popular as the tunes themselves. Many Dubliners are obsessed with music of every kind and will happily discuss anything from Elvis's earliest recordings (remember Jimmy's father in *The Commitments*?) to U2's latest incarnation. The city has been the stomping ground of so many big-league rock and pop musicians that Dublin Tourism has created a "Rock 'n Stroll" Trail, which covers 16 spots with musical associations, most of them in the city center and Temple Bar. It includes places like Bewley's Oriental Café, where Bob Geldof and the other members of the Boomtown Rats used to hang out, and the Bad Ass Café, where Sinéad O'Connor once worked. You're forgiven if you think some connections between the trail sites and the musicians seem hokey, but you're not if you don't seek out Dublin's lively, present-day music scene. Several small pubs and larger halls host live music, but the best places are midsize venues—such as the Olympia Theatre and the Temple Bar Music Centre—where you can hear well-established local acts *and* leading international artists (including world-renowned Irish musicians) playing everything from plugged-in Gaelic folk and folk-rock to jazz-funk and "dubcore," a term coined to describe the city's many noisy alternative bands. Traditional Irish music (or "Trad"), very much a child of rural Ireland, is alive and kicking in the urban sprawl of Dublin. Scores of city bars host impromptu "sessions" and professional gigs with fiddles, banjos, and the beat of the bodhran hand drum. The Cobblestone in lively Smithfield is one of the most famous and atmospheric venues.

ary are damp, hangover months. But only a fool comes to Dublin for the weather.

EXPLORING DUBLIN

In Dublin's fair city, "where the girls are so pretty"—thus goes the centuries-old ditty. Today, parts of the city—particularly the vast, uniform housing projects of the northern suburbs—may not be so fair or pretty. But even if you're not conscious of it while in the city center, Dublin has a most beautiful setting: it loops around the contours of Dublin Bay and spreads over a plain at the edge of the Dublin and Wicklow mountains, which rise softly to the south. From the famous Four Courts building in the heart of town, the sight of the city, the bay, and the mountains can take your breath away.

From north to south, Dublin stretches 16 km (10 mi). From its center, immediately adjacent to the port area and the River Liffey, the city spreads westward for an additional 10 km (6 mi), in total covering 28,000 acres. But its heart is far more compact than these numbers indicate. The River Liffey divides the capital into the Northside and the Southside, the two principal center-city areas, and almost all the major sights in either area are within an hour's walk from one another.

Coverage in this chapter is organized into eight sections exploring the main neighborhoods of Dublin city (plus two excursions into County Dublin—one to the southern suburbs, and one to the northern). The first section—North of the Liffey—covers major cultural sights, including the James Joyce Centre, Gate Theatre, Dublin Writers Museum, and the Hugh Lane Municipal Gallery of Modern Art. The next two sections—City Center and Dublin's Georgian Heart—focus on many of the Southside's major sights: Trinity College, St. Stephen's Green, Merrion Square, and Grafton Street. The fourth section—Temple Bar—takes you through this revived neighborhood, still the hottest, hippest zone in the capital. The Grand Canal and Ballsbridge, the fifth section, covers noteworthy sights along the canal, beginning in the northeast part of the city and ending in the southwest. It also covers the genteel suburb of Ballsbridge. The next section—Dublin West—picks up across Dame Street from Temple Bar and continues west to the Guinness Brewery and Storehouse, the city's most popular attraction. It also includes the rapidly developing Smithfield district, which locals are hailing as the future "Temple Bar of the Northside." The seventh section—The Liberties—takes you on a brief stroll through the old working-class but now increasingly fashionable area of Dublin, a historic but often overlooked part of the city. Finally, the Phoenix Park and Environs section covers the most western fringe of the Northside and the great public park itself. If you're planning to take in all the sights, you may wish to invest in the city's special tourist ticket, the **Dublin Pass**—for more information, see the entry in the A to Z section at the end of this chapter.

If you're visiting Dublin for more than two or three days, you'll have time to explore farther afield. There's plenty to see and do a short distance from the city center—in the suburbs of both north and south County Dublin. Worthwhile destinations in these parts of the county are covered in the Side Trips section.

Because of its compact size and traffic congestion (brought on in the last few years by an astronomical increase in the number of vehicles), the pace of *pedestrian* traffic—especially on the city center's busiest streets during rush hour—is astonishing. Watch out when you stop to consult your map or you're liable to be swept away by the ceaseless flow of the crowds.

Across the Liffey: The Northside

If you stand on O'Connell Bridge or the pedestrian-only Ha'penny span, you'll get excellent views up and down the River Liffey, known in Gaelic as the *abha na life,* transcribed phonetically as Anna Livia by James Joyce in *Finnegan's Wake*. Here, framed with embankments just like those along Paris's Seine, the river nears the end of its 128-km (80-mi) journey from the Wicklow Mountains into the Irish Sea. And near the bridges, you begin a pilgrimage into James Joyce country—north of the Liffey, in the center of town—and the captivating sights of Dublin's Northside, a mix of densely thronged shopping streets and refurbished, genteel homes.

Dublin
City Center

7 Eccles St.

Saint
Brendan's
Hospital

Belvedere
College

Parnell
Square

Four
Courts

New
Ormond
Hotel

St. James's Gate
Brewery

Mother's
Redcap
Market

Dublinia

National
College of
Art and Design

Iveagh
Market
Hall

St. Nicholas of
Myra's Church

Christ
Church
Cathedral

Dublin
Castle

Temple
Bar

City
Hall

Temple
Bar Sq.

Trinity
College

St. Patrick's
Cathedral

St. Patrick's
Park

Marsh's Library

ST. STEPHEN'S
GREEN

Iveagh
Garden

River Liffey

Grand Canal

Grand
Canal

0   330 yards

0   300 meters

KEY

ℹ️ *Tourist Information*

Tolka River

River Tolka Promenade

Ballybough Charleville Ave.

Royal Canal

North Strand Rd.

Portland Row

West Rd.

Church Rd.

E. Wall St.

East Rd.

Church Rd.

Killarney St.

Amiens St.

Seville Pl.

Bella Cohen's Brothel

Connolly Station

Lower Sheriff St.

Upper Sheriff St.

Inner Dock

Georges Dock

Commons Rd.

New Wapping St.

Mayor St.

Castleforbes Rd.

Busaras Bus Station

Custom House

Custom House Quay

Talbot Mem. Br.

George's Quay

North Wall Quay

Alexandra Basin

Tara St. Station

Gloucester St.

City Quay

River Liffey

East Link Toll Br.

Sir John Rogerson's Quay

Cardiff's la.

Hanover Quay

Pearse Station

Macken St.

Grand Canal Dock

Pearse St.

Grand Canal Quay

Ringsend Rd.

South Lotts Rd.

TO SOUTH WALL →

Sweny's Pharmacy

Fenian St.

Hogan Pl.

Lower Grand Canal St.

Lincoln Pl.

Westland Row

Lombard St.

Magennis Pl.

Upper Grand Canal St.

Clare St.

Bath Av.

Londonbridge Rd.

Church Av.

Merrion Sq. N.

Upper Merrion St.

Merrion St. West

Fitzwilliam La. Lower

Lower Fitzwilliam St.

Upper Mount St.

Merrion Sq. S.

Lower Mount St.

Shelbourne Rd.

Pembroke St.

Upper Fitzwilliam St.

Herbert St.

Herbert Pl.

Percy Pl.

North Umberland Rd.

Lansdowne Park

Lansdowne Rugby Ground

Newbridge Av.

Lower Baggot St.

Lad La.

Haddington Rd.

Lansdowne Rd.

Herbert Rd.

Wilton Terrace

Upper Baggot St.

Pembroke Rd.

Shelbourne Rd.

Mespil Rd.

Pembroke Lane

Pembroke Rd.

Beatt's Av.

Burleigh

Burlington Rd.

Waterloo Lane

Waterloo Rd.

Heytesbury Lane

Elgin Rd.

Wellington Rd.

Raglan Rd.

Raglan Lane

Pembroke Rd.

Sussex Rd.

Upper Leeson St.

Clyde Rd.

Clyde Lane

Serpentine

Wellington Lane

The Northside *absolutely* warrants a walk, for three reasons: major cultural institutions (the Gate Theatre, the James Joyce Centre, the Dublin Writers Museum, and the Hugh Lane Municipal Gallery of Modern Art), sites of historical significance with ties to Irish Republicanism, and vibrant busy streets.

During the 18th century, most of the upper echelons of Dublin society lived in the Georgian houses in the Northside—around Mountjoy Square—and shopped along Capel Street, which was lined with stores selling fine furniture and silver. But development of the Southside—Merrion Square in 1764, the Georgian Leinster House in 1745, and Fitzwilliam Square in 1825—permanently changed the Northside's fortunes. The city's fashionable social center crossed the Liffey, and although some of the Northside's illustrious inhabitants stuck it out, this area gradually became run-down. The Northside's fortunes have changed again, however. Once-derelict swaths of houses, especially on and near the Liffey, have been rehabilitated, and large shopping centers have opened on Mary and Jervis streets. The high-rise Docklands area, east of the Custom House, is the new hot place to live (a ferry taxi on the Liffey will soon connect it with Temple Bar, while a new swing bridge will connect City Quay to the Northside). A huge shopping mall and entertainment complex is planned for O'Connell Street, right where the defunct Carlton Cinema stands. Most impressive of all is the Spire, O'Connell Street's new 395-foot-high stainless-steel monument. Precisely because the exciting redevelopment that transformed Temple Bar is still in its early stages here—*because* it's a place on the cusp of transition—the Northside is an intriguing part of town.

Numbers in the text correspond to numbers in the margin and on the Dublin Northside map.

a good walk

Begin at O'Connell Bridge—a close look will reveal that it is wider than it is long—and head north up **O'Connell Street** ❶ ▶. Stop to admire the monument to Daniel O'Connell, "The Liberator," erected as a tribute to the great orator's achievement in securing Catholic Emancipation in 1829 (note the obvious scars from the fighting of 1916 on the figures). Towering over O'Connell and everything else in Dublin is **The Spire** ❷, the newly erected stainless-steel monument. Across from the Spire stands the **General Post Office** ❸, a major site in the Easter Uprising of 1916. Continuing north, follow O'Connell to the southeastern corner of Parnell Square. Heading counterclockwise around the square, you'll pass in turn the **Gate Theatre** ❹ and **Abbey Presbyterian Church** ❺ before coming to the **Dublin Writers Museum** ❻ and the **Hugh Lane Municipal Gallery of Modern Art.** ❼, both on the north side of the square and both housed in glorious neoclassic mansions; these are the two places where you should spend most of your time on the Northside. Either before you go in or after you come out, you might also want to visit the solemn yet serene **Garden of Remembrance** ❽. Before leaving Parnell Square, take a moment to admire the elaborate plasterwork in the chapel of the **Rotunda Hospital** ❾, toward the southwest corner of the square.

From here, you have two choices: to continue exploring the cultural sights northeast of Parnell Square and east of O'Connell Street, or to head to Moore, Henry, and Mary streets for a taste of middle-class Dublin that you won't get on the spiffier Southside. If you decide to shop with the locals, leave Parnell Square via the southwestern corner. Moore Street is your first left off Parnell Street and leads directly to Henry Street.

If you decide to continue your cultural explorations, jump two blocks northeast of Parnell Square to the **James Joyce Centre** ⑩, on North Great George's Street, and then head farther northeast to the once glamorous **Mountjoy Square** ⑪. About 1 km (½ mi) east of Mountjoy Square is Croke Park, a Gaelic football stadium and home of the Gaelic Athletic Association's **GAA Museum** ⑫. Return to Mountjoy Square and head north, stopping in at **St. Francis Xavier Church** ⑬ on Gardiner Street. Head south on Gardiner Street to Summerhill, turn right, and walk west along Summerhill. Make a left onto Marlborough Street (parallel to and between Gardiner and O'Connell streets) to visit the **Pro-Cathedral** ⑭. Continue down to the quays and jog a block east to the Georgian extravaganza that is the **Custom House** ⑮. East of the Custom House lies the newly developed Docklands, home to Dublin's high-earning high-rise dwellers.

TIMING   The Northside has fewer major attractions than the Southside and is less picturesque. As a result, you're unlikely to want to stroll leisurely here; zipping right through this walk, you could be done in less than two hours. But the two major cultural institutions—the Dublin Writers Museum and the Hugh Lane Municipal Gallery of Modern Art—easily deserve several hours each, so it's worth doing this walk only if you have time to devote to them. Also, a number of additional sights connected with James Joyce and *Ulysses*—covered in our Close-Up box, "Rejoice!: A Walk Through Joyce's Dublin"—are in the vicinity, so devoted Joyceans should consult this box before setting out on this walk.

What to See

❺ **Abbey Presbyterian Church.** Topped with a soaring spire, this church anchors the northeast corner of Parnell Square, an area that was the city's most fashionable address during the gilded days of the 18th-century Ascendancy. Popularly known as Findlater's Church—after Alex Findlater, the Dublin grocer who endowed it—the church was completed in 1864 with an interior that has a stark Presbyterian mood, despite stained-glass windows and ornate pews. For a bird's-eye view of the area, climb the small staircase that leads to the balcony. ⊠ *Parnell Sq., Northside* ☎ *01/837–8600* ☜ *Free* ⊗ *Hrs vary.*

⑮ **Custom House.** Seen at its best reflected in the waters of the Liffey during the short interval when the high tide is on the turn, the Custom House is the city's most spectacular Georgian building. Extending 375 feet on the north side of the river, this is the work of James Gandon, an English architect who arrived in Ireland in 1781, when construction commenced (it continued for 10 years). Crafted from gleaming Portland stone, the central portico is linked by arcades to the pavilions at either end. A statue of Commerce tops the copper dome, whose circumference, unfortunately, is on the puny side and out of proportion to the rest of the building. Stat-

Dublin Northside

KEY

▶ Start of walk

🛈 Tourist Information

Abbey Presbyterian Church **5**
Custom House **15**
Dublin Writers Museum **6**
GAA Museum **12**
Garden of Remembrance **8**

Gate Theatre **4**
General Post Office (GPO) **3**
Hugh Lane Municipal Gallery of Modern Art ...**7**
James Joyce Centre ...**10**
Mountjoy Square **11**
O'Connell Street **1**

Pro-Cathedral **14**
Rotunda Hospital **9**
St. Francis Xavier Church **13**
The Spire **2**

ues on the main facade are based on allegorical themes. Note the exquisitely carved lions and unicorns supporting the arms of Ireland at the far ends of the facade. After Republicans set fire to the building in 1921, it was completely restored and reconstructed to house government offices. A visitor center traces the building's history and significance, and the life of Gandon. ⊠ *Custom House Quay, Northside* ☎ *01/888–2538* ⊕ *www. visitdublin.com* ⊠ *€1* ⊙ *Mid-Mar.–Oct., weekdays 10–12:30, weekends 2–5; Nov.–mid-Mar., Wed.–Fri. 10–12:30, Sun. 2–5.*

★ ❻ **Dublin Writers Museum.** "If you would know Ireland—body and soul— you must read its poems and stories," wrote Yeats in 1891. Further investigation into the Irish way with words can be found at this unique museum, in a magnificently restored 18th-century town house on the north side of Parnell Square. The mansion, once the home of John Jameson, of the Irish whiskey family, centers on the Gallery of Writers, an enormous drawing room gorgeously decorated with paintings, Adamesque plasterwork, and a deep Edwardian lincrusta frieze. Rare manuscripts, diaries, posters, letters, limited and first editions, photographs, and other mementos commemorate the lives and works of the nation's greatest writers—and there are many of them, so leave plenty of time—including Joyce, Shaw, J. M. Synge, Lady Gregory, Yeats, Beckett, and others. On display are an 1804 edition of Swift's *Gulliver's Travels,* an 1899 first edition of Bram Stoker's *Dracula,* and an 1899 edition of Wilde's *Ballad of Reading Gaol.* There's a "Teller of Tales" exhibit showcasing Behan, O'Flaherty, and O'Faoláin. Readings are periodically held. The bookshop and café make this an ideal place to spend a rainy afternoon. If you lose track of time and stay until the closing hour, you might want to dine at Chapter One, a highly regarded restaurant in the basement, which would have had Joyce ecstatic over its currant-sprinkled scones. ⊠ *18 Parnell Sq. N, Northside* ☎ *01/872–2077* ⊕ *www. visitdublin.com* ⊠ *€6.25* ⊙ *June–Aug., weekdays 10–6, Sat. 10–5, Sun. 11–5; Sept.–May, Mon.–Sat. 10–5, Sun. 11–5.*

⓬ **GAA Museum.** In the bowels of Croke Park, the main stadium and headquarters of the GAA (Gaelic Athletic Association), this museum gives you a great introduction to native Irish sport. The four Gaelic games (football, hurling, camogie, and handball) are explained in detail, and if you're brave enough you can have a go yourself. High-tech displays take you through the history and highlights of the games. *National Awakening* is a really smart, interesting short film reflecting the key impact of the GAA on the emergence of the Irish nation and the forging of a new Irish identity. The exhilarating *A Day in September* captures the thrill and passion of All Ireland finals day—the annual denouement of the intercounty hurling and Gaelic football seasons—which is every bit as important to the locals as the Super Bowl is to sports fans in the U.S. Tours of the stadium, the fourth largest in Europe, are available. ⊠ *New Stand, Croke Park, North County Dublin* ☎ *01/855–8176* ⊕ *www.gaa.ie* ⊠ *Museum €5, museum and stadium tour €8.50* ⊙ *Mon.–Sat. 9:30–5, Sun. noon–5.*

❽ **Garden of Remembrance.** Opened 50 years after the Easter Uprising of 1916, the garden in Parnell Square commemorates those who died fighting for Ireland's freedom. At the garden's entrance is a large plaza; steps lead down

CloseUp
A PLAYWRIGHT ON EVERY CORNER

AS ANY VISIT TO THE DUBLIN WRITERS MUSEUM WILL PROVE, *this city packs more literary punch per square foot than practically any other spot on the planet—largely because of the ferment that took hold at the end of the 19th century, when two main cultural movements emerged. In 1893, Douglas Hyde, a Protestant who would become the first president of Ireland, founded the Gaelic League (Conradh na Gaelige), with a goal of preserving the Irish language and Gaelic traditions. The poet W. B. Yeats also played a pivotal role in the Irish literary renaissance. With funding from his patron Annie Horniman, Yeats and Lady Gregory founded the Abbey Theatre in 1903, to develop and produce a decidedly Irish repertoire. With this new venue, and the growing prominence of such playwrights as Sean O'Casey and J. M. Synge, Irish literature thrived. The Dublin Writers Museum gives a terrific introduction to this story and to the more than two dozen major writers Ireland subsequently produced. To go further back in literary history, head for Trinity College, where you can stroll through the hallowed campus where Samuel Beckett studied and where a theater now bears his name. If you're an Oscar Wilde fan, you may want to pay homage to him at 1 Merrion Square, where his parents lived. The CloseUp box "Rejoice!" guides you through some key sites connected with Joyce and his legendary novel, Ulysses. And if you want to stock up on anecdotes about the relationship between the pint and the pen, check out the Dublin Literary Pub Crawl, a guide available in Dublin bookstores, or take a guided tour of literary pubs.*

to the fountain area, graced with a sculpture by contemporary Irish artist Oisín Kelly, based on the mythological Children of Lír, who were turned into swans. The garden serves as an oasis of tranquility in the middle of the busy city. ⊠ *Parnell Sq., Northside* 🎫 *Free* ☉ *Daily 9–5.*

❹ Gate Theatre. The Gate has been one of Dublin's most important theaters since its founding in 1929 by Micháel MacLiammóir and Hilton Edwards, who also founded Galway City's An Taibhdhearc as the national Irish-language theater. The Gate stages many innovative productions by Irish as well as foreign playwrights—and plenty of foreign actors have performed here, including Orson Welles (his first paid performance) and James Mason (early in his career). Shows here begin as soon as you walk into the auditorium, which is a Georgian masterwork designed by Richard Johnston in 1784 as an assembly room for the Rotunda Hospital complex. ⊠ *Cavendish Row, Northside* 🕿 *01/874–4045* ☉ *Shows Mon.–Sat.*

❸ General Post Office. Known as the GPO, this is one of the great civic buildings of Dublin's Georgian era, but its fame is based on the role it played in the Easter Uprising. The building, with its impressive neoclassical facade, was designed by Francis Johnston and built by the British between

1814 and 1818 as a center of communications. This gave it great strategic importance—and was one of the reasons it was chosen by the insurgent forces in 1916 as a headquarters. Here, on Easter Monday, 1916, the Republican forces, about 2,000 in number and under the guidance of Pádrig Pearse and James Connolly, stormed the building and issued the Proclamation of the Irish Republic. After a week of shelling, the GPO lay in ruins; 13 rebels were ultimately executed, including Connolly, who was dying of gangrene from a leg shattered in the fighting and had to be propped up in a chair in front of the firing squad. Most of the original building was destroyed, though the facade survived—you can still see the scars of bullets on its pillars. Rebuilt and reopened in 1929, it became a working post office with an attractive two-story main concourse. A bronze sculpture depicting the dying Cuchulainn, a leader of the Red Branch Knights in Celtic mythology, sits in the front window. The 1916 Proclamation and the names of its signatories are inscribed on the green marble plinth. ⊠ *O'Connell St., Northside* ☎ *01/872–8888* ⊕ *www.anpost.ie* ✑ *Free* ☉ *Mon.–Sat. 8–8, Sun. 10:30–6.*

need a break? For a real Irish pub lunch, stop in at **John M. Keating** (⊠ 14 Mary St., Northside ☎ 01/873–1567), at the corner of Mary and Jervis streets; head upstairs, where you can sit at a low table, chat with the locals, and enjoy simple but high-quality carvery-board fare and one of the creamiest pints on the Northside. At the Jervis Street branch of Dublin's famous **Bewley's Oriental Café** (⊠ Jervis Shopping Centre, Jervis and Mary Sts., Northside ☎ 01/677–6761) the decor is not quite as elegant as that at the original Grafton Street café, but the coffee is almost as good as the people-watching.

★ ❼ **Hugh Lane Municipal Gallery of Modern Art.** Built as a town house for the earl of Charlemont in 1762, this residence was so grand its Parnell Square street was nicknamed "Palace Row" in its honor. Sir William Chambers, who also built the Marino Casino for Charlemont, designed the structure in the best Palladian manner. Its delicate and rigidly correct facade, extended by two demilune (half-moon) arcades, was fashioned from the "new" white Ardmulcan stone (now seasoned to gray). Charlemont was one of the cultural locomotives of 18th-century Dublin— his walls were hung with Titians and Hogarths, and he frequently dined with Oliver Goldsmith and Sir Joshua Reynolds—so he would undoubtedly be delighted that his home is now a gallery, named after Sir Hugh Lane, a nephew of Lady Gregory (Yeats's aristocratic patron). Lane collected both Impressionist paintings and 19th-century Irish and Anglo-Irish works. A complicated agreement with the National Gallery in London (reached after heated diplomatic dispute) stipulates that a portion of the 39 French paintings amassed by Lane shuttle between London and here. Time it right and you'll be able to see Pissarro's *Printemps,* Manet's *Eva Gonzales,* Morisot's *Jour d'Été,* and, the jewel of the collection, Renoir's *Les Parapluies.*

In something of a snub to the British art establishment, the late Francis Bacon's partner donated the entire contents of the artist's studio to the gallery. The studio of Britain's arguably premier 20th-century artist has been reconstructed here in all its gaudy glory as a permanent display. It gives you a unique opportunity to observe the bravura technique of the artist responsible for such masterpieces as *Study After Velázquez* and the tragic splash-and-crash *Triptych*. Also on display are Bacon's diary, books, and apparently everything else picked up off his floor.

Between the collection of Irish paintings in the National Gallery of Ireland and the superlative works on display here, you can quickly become familiar with Irish 20th-century art. Irish artists represented include Roderic O'Conor, well known for his views of the west of Ireland; William Leech, including his *Girl with a Tinsel Scarf* and *The Cigarette*; and the most famous of the group, Jack B. Yeats (W. B.'s brother). The museum has a dozen of his paintings, including *Ball Alley* and *There Is No Night*. There's also strikingly displayed stained-glass work by early-20th-century Irish master artisans Harry Clarke and Evie Hone. ✉ *Parnell Sq. N, Northside* ☎ *01/874–1903* ⊕ *www.hughlane.ie* ✉ *Gallery free; Bacon Studio €7, free Tues. 9:30–5* ⊙ *Tues.–Thurs. 9:30–6, Fri. and Sat. 9:30–5, Sun. 11–5.*

🔟 **James Joyce Centre.** Few may have read him, but everyone in Ireland has at least heard of James Joyce (1882–1941)—especially since a copy of his censored and suppressed *Ulysses* was one of the top status symbols of the early 20th century. Joyce is of course now acknowledged as one of the greatest modern authors, and his *Dubliners, Finnegan's Wake,* and *A Portrait of the Artist as a Young Man* can even be read as quirky "travel guides" to Dublin. Open to the public, this restored 18th-century Georgian town house, once the dancing academy of Professor Denis J. Maginni (which many will recognize from a reading of *Ulysses*), is a center for Joycean studies and events related to the author. It has an extensive library and archives, exhibition rooms, a bookstore, and a café. The collection includes letters from Beckett, Joyce's guitar and cane, and a celebrated edition of *Ulysses* illustrated by Matisse. The center is the main organizer of "Bloomstime," which marks the week leading up to the Bloomsday celebrations, which were bigger than ever in the centenary year of 2004. (Bloomsday, June 16, is the single day *Ulysses* chronicles, as Leopold Bloom winds his way around Dublin in 1904.) ✉ *35 N. Great George's St., Northside* ☎ *01/878–8547* ⊕ *www.jamesjoyce.ie* ✉ *€5, guided tour €10* ⊙ *Mon.–Sat., 9:30–5, Sun. 12:30–5.*

⓫ **Mountjoy Square.** Built over the course of the two decades leading up to 1818, this Northside square was once surrounded by elegant terraced houses. Today only the northern side remains intact. The houses on the once derelict southern side have been converted into apartments. Irishman Brian Boru, who led his soldiers to victory against the Vikings in the Battle of Clontarf in 1014, was said to have pitched camp before the confrontation on the site of Mountjoy Square. Playwright Sean O'-Casey lived here, at No. 35, and used the square as a setting for *The Shadow of a Gunman.*

▶ ❶ **O'Connell Street.** Dublin's most famous thoroughfare, which is 150 feet wide, was previously known as Sackville Street, but its name was changed in 1924, two years after the founding of the Irish Free State.

REJOICE! A WALK THROUGH JOYCE'S DUBLIN

J AMES JOYCE'S GENIUS for fashioning high art out of his day-to-day life brought him literary immortality and makes him, even today and possibly for all time, the world's most famous Dubliner. He set all his major works— Dubliners, A Portrait of the Artist as a Young Man, Ulysses, and Finnegan's Wake—in the city where he was born and spent the first 22 years of his life, and although he spent the next 36 years in self-imposed exile, he never wrote about anywhere else. Joyce knew and remembered Dublin in such detail that he bragged (and that's the word) that if the city were destroyed, it could be rebuilt in its entirety from his written works.

Joyceans flock to Dublin annually on June 16 to commemorate Bloomsday, the day in 1904 on which Leopold Bloom wanders through the city in Ulysses. Why this day? It had been an important one for Joyce— when he and his wife-to-be, Nora Barnacle, had their first date. Today Bloomsday has evolved into "Bloomstime," with events taking place in the days leading up to the 16th, then all day and well into the night. Even if you don't make it to Dublin on Bloomsday, you can still roam its streets, sniffing out Bloom's—and Joyce's—haunts.

Begin in the heart of the Northside, on **Prince's Street,** next to the GPO (General Post Office), where the office of the old and popular Freeman's Journal newspaper (published 1763–1924) was located before it was destroyed during the 1916 Easter Uprising. Bloom was a newspaper advertisement canvasser for the Journal. Head north up O'Connell Street down Parnell Square before turning right onto Dorset Street and then left onto Eccles Street. Leopold and Molly Bloom's fictional home stood at **7 Eccles Street,** north of Parnell Square. Head back to Dorset Street and go east. Take a right onto Gardiner Street and then a left onto Great Denmark Street and Belvedere College. Between 1893 and 1898, Joyce studied at **Belvedere College** (☎ 01/874–3974) under the Jesuits; it's housed in a splendid 18th-century mansion. The **James Joyce Centre** (☎ 01/878–8547 ⊕ www. jamesjoyce.ie), a few steps from Belvedere College on North Great George's Street, is the hub of Bloomsday celebrations. Go back to Gardiner Street and then south until you come to Railway Street on your left. The site of **Bella Cohen's Brothel** (✉ 82 Railway St., Northside) is in an area that in Joyce's day contained many houses of ill repute. A long walk back down O'Connell Street to the bridge and then a right will take you to Ormond Quay. On the western edge of the Northside, the **New Ormond Hotel** (✉ Upper Ormond Quay, Northside ☎ 01/872–1811) was an afternoon rendezvous spot for Bloom.

Across the Liffey, walk up Grafton Street to **Davy's Byrne Pub** (21 Duke St, 01/671— 1298). Here, Bloom comes to settle down for a glass of Burgundy and a Gorgonzola sandwich, meets his friend Nosey Flynn, and asks for a tip for the Ascot Gold Cup. Today, the pub has gone very upscale from its pre-World War II days but even Joyce would have cracked a smile at the sight of the shamrock-painted ceiling and the three murals of Joycean Dublin by Liam Proud. After a stop at Davy Byrne's proceed via Molesworth Street to the **National Library**—where Bloom has a near-meeting with Blazes Boylan, his wife's lover, and looks for a copy of an advertisement. Walk up Molesworth Street until you hit Trinity. Take a right and walk to Lincoln Place. No establishment mentioned by Joyce has changed less since his time than **Sweny's Pharmacy** (✉ Lincoln Pl., Southside), at the back of Trinity College, which still has its black-and-white exterior and an interior crammed with potions and vials.

After the devastation of the 1916 Easter Uprising, the Northside street had to be almost entirely reconstructed, a task that took until the end of the 1920s. At one time the main attraction of the street, Nelson's Pillar, a Doric column towering over the city center and a marvelous vantage point, was blown up in 1966, on the 50th anniversary of the Easter Uprising. The 356-foot-high Spire was built in its place in 2003, and today this gigantic, stainless-steel monument dominates the street. The large monument at the south end of the street is dedicated to Daniel O'-Connell (1775–1847), "The Liberator," and was erected in 1854 as a tribute to the orator's achievement in securing Catholic Emancipation in 1829. Seated winged figures represent the four Victories—Courage, Eloquence, Fidelity, and Patriotism—all exemplified by O'Connell. Ireland's four ancient provinces—Munster, Leinster, Ulster, and Connacht—are identified by their respective coats of arms. Look closely and you'll notice that O'Connell is wearing a glove on one hand, as he did for much of his adult life, a self-imposed penance for shooting a man in a duel. But even the great man himself is dwarfed by the newest addition to O'Connell Street, the silver Spire.

need a break?   Conway's (✉ Parnell St. near Upper O'Connell St., Northside ☎ 01/873–2687), founded in 1745, is reputed to be Dublin's second-oldest pub. Guinness-drinking men who like "a flutter on the gee gees" (to gamble on horse racing) mix with office workers on their lunch breaks availing themselves of the unpretentious pub grub. One of Dublin's oldest hotels, dating to 1817, the **Gresham** (✉ Upper O'Connell St., Northside ☎ 01/874–6881) was once the bastion of Dublin high society. Its high-ceilinged Georgian dining area is still a pleasant, old-fashioned spot for a morning coffee or afternoon tea.

⑭ Pro-Cathedral. Dublin's principal Catholic cathedral (also known as St. Mary's) is a great place to hear the best Irish male voices—a Palestrina choir, in which the great Irish tenor John McCormack began his career, sings in Latin here every Sunday morning at 11. The cathedral, built between 1816 and 1825, has a classical church design—on a suitably epic scale. The church's facade, with a six-Doric-pillared portico, is based on the Temple of Theseus in Athens; the interior is modeled after the Grecian-Doric style of St. Philippe du Roule in Paris. But the building was never granted full cathedral status, nor has the identity of its architect ever been discovered; the only clue to its creation is in the church ledger, which lists a "Mr. P." as the builder. ✉ *Marlborough St., Northside* ☎ *01/874–5441* ⊕ *www.procathedral.ie* ⊠ *Free* ☉ *Daily 8–6.*

⑨ Rotunda Hospital. The Rotunda, founded in 1745 as the first maternity hospital in Ireland and Britain, was designed on a grand scale by architect Richard Castle (1690–1751), with a three-story tower and a copper cupola. It's now most worth a visit for its chapel, with elaborate plasterwork, appropriately honoring motherhood, executed by Bartholomew Cramillion between 1757 and 1758. The Gate Theatre, in a lavish Georgian assembly room, is on the O'Connell Street side of this large complex. ✉ *Parnell St., Northside* ☎ *01/873–0700.*

⑬ **St. Francis Xavier Church.** One of the city's finest churches in the classical style, the Jesuit St. Francis Xavier's was begun in 1829, the year of Catholic Emancipation, and was completed three years later. The building is designed in the shape of a Latin cross, with a distinctive Ionic portico and an unusual coffered ceiling. The striking, faux-marble high altarpiece, decorated with lapis lazuli, came from Italy. The church appears in James Joyce's story "Grace." ⊠ *Upper Gardiner St., Northside* ☎ *01/836–3411* 🖼 *Free* ⊙ *Daily 7* AM–*8:30* PM.

② **The Spire.** Although it has been christened the "Stiletto in the Ghetto" by local wags, most people agree that this needlelike monument is the most exciting thing to happen to Dublin's skyline in decades. The Spire, also known as the Monument of Light, was originally planned as part of the city's millennium celebrations. But Ian Ritchie's spectacular 395-foot-high monument wasn't erected until the beginning of 2003. Seven times taller than the nearby General Post Office, the stainless-steel structure rises from the spot where Nelson's Pillar once stood. Approximately 10 feet in diameter at its base, the softly lighted monument narrows to only 1 foot at its apex—the upper part of the Spire sways gently when the wind blows. The monument's creators envisioned it serving as a beacon for the whole of the city, and it will certainly be the first thing you see as you drive into Dublin from the airport. ⊠ *O'Connell St., Northside.*

The City Center: From Trinity College to St. Stephen's Green

Dublin's center of gravity had traditionally been O'Connell Bridge, a diplomatic landmark in that it avoided locating the center to the north or south of the river—as strong local loyalties still prevailed among "Northsiders" and "Southsiders," and neither group would ever accept that the city's center lay elsewhere than on their own side. The economic boom, however, has seen diplomacy fall by the wayside—Dublin's heart now beats loudest southward across the Liffey, due in part to a large-scale refurbishment and pedestrianization of Grafton Street, which made this already upscale shopping address the main street on which to shop, stop, and be seen. At the foot of Grafton Street is the city's most famous and recognizable landmark, Trinity College; at the top of it is Dublin's most popular strolling retreat, St. Stephen's Green, a 27-acre landscaped park with flowers, lakes, bridges, and Dubliners enjoying their time-outs.

Numbers in the text correspond to numbers in the margin and on the Dublin Southside map.

a good walk

Showpiece of 18th-century Palladian architecture, fabled keep of the *Book of Kells,* and home to the spectacular Old Library, **Trinity College ⑯** ▶ makes an impressive start to this tour. After taking in the treasures on display here, explore Trinity's elegant quadrangles. If you want to see modern art, visit the collection housed in the Douglas Hyde Gallery, just inside the Nassau Street entrance to the college. When you come back out the front gate, you can either stop in at the **Bank of Ire-**

land ⑰, a Neoclassic masterpiece that was once the seat of the Irish Parliament, or make an immediate left and head south along **Grafton Street** ⑱, the pedestrian spine of the Southside. The **Dublin Tourism** ⑲ office, in a medieval former church, is just off Grafton Street, on the corner of Suffolk Street. If Grafton Street's shops whet your appetite for more browsing and shopping, turn right down Wicklow Street, then left onto South William Street to **Powerscourt Townhouse Centre** ⑳, where a faux-Georgian atrium (very dubiously set within one of Dublin's greatest 18th-century mansions) houses high-end shops and pleasant cafés. The **Dublin Civic Museum** ㉑ is next door to Powerscourt, across the alley on its south flank. If you're doing well on time and want to explore the shopping streets farther east, jog via the alley one block west to Drury Street, from which you can access the Victorian **George's Street Arcade** ㉒. Head back to Grafton Street, and stop in at Dublin institution Bewley's Oriental Café, a good place for a break. Grafton Street ends at the northwest corner of **St. Stephen's Green** ㉓, Dublin's most popular public garden, which absolutely demands a stroll-through. The Georgian **Newman House** ㉔ is on the south side of the green. Amble back across the green, exiting onto the northeast corner, at which stands the grand **Shelbourne** ㉕, a wonderful place for afternoon tea or a quick pint at one of its two pubs. The **Huguenot Cemetery** ㉖ is just down the street from the hotel, on the same side. If you want to see more art, head for the **RHA Gallagher Gallery** ㉗.

TIMING   To merely walk the streets of Dublin's compact city center would take only an hour, but it is so crammed with pleasures and treasures, you'll want to set aside at least a half a day to explore it. After all, Trinity College can easily take an hour or two. And who would ever want to rush up Grafton Street? Take a leisurely amble and then stroll through St. Stephen's Green for a fitting finale.

What to See

⑰ **Bank of Ireland.** Across the street from the west facade of Trinity College stands one of Dublin's most striking buildings, formerly the original home of Irish Parliament. Sir Edward Lovett Pearce designed the central section in 1729; three other architects would ultimately be involved in the rest of the building's construction. A pedimented portico fronted by six massive Corinthian columns dominates the grand facade, which follows the curve of Westmoreland Street as it meets College Green, once a Viking meeting place and burial ground. Two years after Parliament was abolished in 1801 under the Act of Union, which brought Ireland under the direct rule of Britain, the building was bought for €50,790 by the Bank of Ireland. Inside, stucco rosettes adorn the coffered ceiling in the pastel-hued, colonnaded, clerestoried main banking hall, at one time the Court of Requests, where citizens' petitions were heard. Just down the hall is the original House of Lords, with an oak-panel nave, a 1,233-drop Waterford glass chandelier, and tapestries depicting the Battle of the Boyne and the Siege of Derry; ask a guard to show you in. Visitors are welcome during normal banking hours; the Dublin historian and author Éamonn Mac Thomáis conducts brief guided tours every Tuesday at 10:30, 11:30, and 1:45. Accessed via Foster Place South, the small alley on the bank's east flank, the Bank of Ireland Arts Centre frequently mounts displays of contemporary Irish art and has a permanent exhibition, "Journey Through 200 Years." ⊠ *2 College Green, Southside* ☎ *01/677–6801 for bank, 01/671–1488 for Arts Centre* ⊕ *www.visitdublin.com* 🖾 *Bank free, Arts Centre €1* ⊙ *Bank Mon.–Wed. and Fri. 10–4, Thurs. 10–5; Arts Centre Tues.–Fri. 10–4, Sat. 2–5, Sun. 10–1.*

㉑ **Dublin Civic Museum.** Built between 1765 and 1771 as an exhibition hall for the Society of Artists, this building later was used as the City Assembly House, precursor of City Hall. The museum's esoteric collection includes Stone Age flints, Viking coins, old maps and prints of the city, and the sculpted head of British admiral Horatio Nelson, which used to top Nelson's Pillar, beside the General Post Office on O'Connell Street; the column was toppled by an IRA explosion in 1966 on the 50th anniversary of the Easter Uprising. The museum also holds temporary exhibitions relating to the city. ⊠ *58 S. William St., Southside* ☎ *01/679–4260* ⊕ *www.dublincitycouncil.ie* 🖾 *Free* ⊙ *Tues.–Sat. 10–6, Sun. 11–2.*

⑲ **Dublin Tourism.** Medieval St. Andrew's Church, deconsecrated and fallen into ruin, has been resurrected as the home of Dublin Tourism, a private organization that provides the most complete information on Dublin's sights, restaurants, and hotels; you can even rent a car here. The office has reservations facilities for all Dublin hotels, as well as guided tours, a plethora of brochures, and a gift shop. A pleasant café upstairs serves sandwiches and drinks. ⊠ *St. Andrew's Church, Suffolk St., Southside* ☎ *01/605–7700, 1850/230330 in Ireland* ⊕ *www.visitdublin.com* ⊙ *July–Sept., Mon.–Sat. 8:30–6, Sun. 11–5:30; Oct.–June, daily 9–6.*

㉒ **George's Street Arcade.** This Victorian covered market fills the block between Drury Street and South Great George's Street. Two dozen or so stalls sell books, prints, clothing (mostly secondhand), exotic foodstuffs, and trinkets. ⊠ *S. Great George's St., Southside* ⊙ *Mon.–Sat. 9–6.*

need a break? With its mahogany bar, mirrors, and plasterwork ceilings, the **Long Hall Pub** (⊠ 51 S. Great George's St., Southside ☎ 01/475–1590) is one of Dublin's most ornate traditional taverns. It's a good place to take a break with a sandwich and a pint of Guinness.

⑱ **Grafton Street.** It's no more than 200 yards long and about 20 feet wide, but brick-lined Grafton Street, open only to pedestrians, can claim to be the most humming street in the city, if not in all of Ireland. It's one of Dublin's vital spines: the most direct route between the front door of Trinity College and St. Stephen's Green, and the city's premier shopping street, with Dublin's most distinguished department store, Brown Thomas, as well as tried and trusted Marks & Spencer. Grafton Street and the smaller alleyways that radiate off it offer dozens of independent stores, a dozen or so colorful flower sellers, and some of the Southside's most popular watering holes. In summer, buskers from all over the world line both sides of the street, pouring out the sounds of drum, whistle, pipe, and string.

need a break? The granddaddy of the capital's cafés, **Bewley's Oriental Café** has been serving coffee and buns to Dubliners since it was founded by Quakers in 1842, and now has four locations. Bewley's trademark stained-glass windows were designed by Harry Clarke (1889–1931), Ireland's most distinguished early-20th-century artist in this medium. All the branches are fine places in which to observe Dubliners of all ages and occupations. The aroma of coffee is irresistible, and the dark interiors—marble-top tables, Bentwood chairs, and mahogany trim—evoke a more leisurely Dublin. The food is overpriced and not particularly good, but people-watching here over a cup of coffee or tea is a quintessential Dublin experience. (If you're interested in a more modern cup of coffee, check out the Metro Café, nearby at 43 South William Street—it's one of Dublin's best haunts for the caffeine-addicted and its staff is devoid of the devil-may-care, pseudo-existential inefficiency that seems to plague so many other Dublin cafés.) The Grafton Street branch of Bewley's stays open until 1 AM Sunday through Thursday and 4 AM Friday and Saturday; the Westmoreland Street branch closes daily at 9 PM. ⊠ *78 Grafton St., Southside* ☎ *01/677–6761 for all locations* ⊠ *12 Westmoreland St., Southside.*

㉖ Huguenot Cemetery. One of the last such burial grounds in Dublin, this cemetery was used in the late 17th century by French Protestants who had fled persecution in their native land. The cemetery gates are rarely open, but you can view the grounds from the street—it's on the northeast corner across from the square. ⊠ *27 St. Stephen's Green N, Southside.*

㉕ Shelbourne. The ebullient, redbrick, white-wood-trimmed facade of the Shelbourne has commanded "the best address in Dublin" from the north side of St. Stephen's Green since 1865. In 1921 the Irish Free State's constitution was drafted here, in a first-floor suite. The most financially painless way to soak up the hotel's old-fashioned luxury and genteel excitement is to step past the entrance—note the statues of Nubian princesses and attendant slaves—for afternoon tea (€17.15 per person, including sandwiches and cakes) in the green-wallpapered Lord Mayor's Lounge or for a drink in one of its two bars, the Shelbourne and the Horseshoe, both of which are thronged with businesspeople and politicos after the workday ends. Elizabeth Bowen wrote her novel *The Hotel* about this very place. ⊠ *27 St. Stephen's Green, Southside* ☎ *01/676–6471* ⊕ *www.shelbourne.ie.*

㉔ Newman House. One of the greatest glories of Georgian Dublin, Newman House is actually two imposing town houses joined together. The earlier of the two, No. 85 St. Stephen's Green (1738), was originally known as Clanwilliam House. Designed by Richard Castle, favored architect of Dublin's rich and famous, it features a winged Palladian window on the Wicklow granite facade. It has two landmarks of Irish Georgian style: the Apollo Room, decorated with stuccowork depicting the sun god and his muses; and the magnificent Saloon, "the supreme example of Dublin Baroque," according to scholars Jacqueline O'Brien and Desmond Guinness. The Saloon is crowned with an exuberant ceiling aswirl with cupids and gods, created by the Brothers Lafranchini, the finest *stuccadores* (plaster-workers) of 18th-century Dublin. Next door at No. 86 (1765), the staircase, on pastel walls, is one of the city's most beautiful Rococo examples—with floral swags and musical instruments picked out in cake-frosting white. Catholic University (described by James Joyce in *A Portrait of the Artist as a Young Man*) was established in this building in 1850, with Cardinal John Henry Newman as its first rector. To explore the houses you must join a guided tour. At the back of Newman House lies Iveagh Gardens, a delightful hideaway with statues and sunken gardens that remains one of Dublin's best-kept secrets (you can enter via Earlsfort Terrace and Harcourt Street). ⊠ *85–86 St. Stephen's Green, Southside* ☎ *01/716–7422* ⊕ *www. visitdublin.com* ⌲ *House and garden €5* ⊙ *Tours June–Aug., Tues.–Fri. at noon, 2, 3, and 4; Sat. at 2, 3, and 4; Sun. at 11, noon, and 1.*

㉔ Powerscourt Townhouse Centre. Lucky man, this Viscount Powerscourt. In the mid-18th century, not only did he build Ireland's most spectacular country house, in Enniskerry, County Wicklow (which bears the family name), but he also decided to rival that structure's grandeur with one of Dublin's largest stone mansions. Staffed with 22 servants and built of granite from the viscount's quarry in the Wicklow Hills, Powerscourt House was a major statement in the Palladian style. Designed by Robert Mack in 1771, it's a massive, Baroque-style edifice that towers over the little street it sits on (note the top story, framed by massive volutes, which was intended as an observatory). Inside, there are Rococo salons designed by James McCullagh, splendid examples of plasterwork in the Adamesque style and—surprise!—a shopping atrium, installed in and around the covered courtyard. The stores here include high-quality Irish crafts shops and numerous food stalls. The mall exit leads to the Carmelite Church of St. Teresa's and Johnson's Court. Beside the church, a pedestrian lane leads onto Grafton Street. ⊠ *59 S. William St., Southside* ☎ *01/679–4144* ⊙ *Mon.–Wed. and Fri. 10–6, Thurs. 10–8, Sat. 9–6, Sun. noon–6 (limited shops open Sun.).*

㉗ RHA Gallagher Gallery. The Royal Hibernian Academy, an old Dublin institution, is housed in a well-lighted building, one of the largest exhibition spaces in the city. The gallery holds adventurous exhibitions of the best in contemporary art, both from Ireland and abroad. ⊠ *15 Ely Pl., off St. Stephen's Green, Southside* ☎ *01/661–2558* ⊕ *www. royalhibernianacademy.com* ⌲ *Free* ⊙ *Mon.–Wed., Fri., and Sat. 11–5, Thurs. 11–8, Sun. 2–5.*

㉓ St. Stephen's Green. Dubliners call it simply Stephen's Green, and green it is (year-round)—a verdant, 27-acre Southside square that was used for the public punishment of criminals until 1664. After a long period of decline, it became a private park in 1814—the first time in its history that it was closed to the public. Its fortunes changed again in 1880, when Sir Arthur Guinness, later Lord Ardiluan (a member of the Guinness brewery family), paid for it to be laid out anew. Flower gardens, formal lawns, a Victorian bandstand, and an ornamental lake with lots of waterfowl are all within the park's borders, connected by paths guaranteeing that strolling here or just passing through will offer up unexpected delights (such as palm trees). Among the park's many statues are a memorial to Yeats and another to Joyce by Henry Moore, and the *Three*

Fodor'sChoice
★

Fates, a dramatic group of bronze female figures watching over human destiny. In the 18th century the walk on the north side of the green was referred to as the Beaux Walk because most of Dublin's gentlemen's clubs were in town houses here. Today it is dominated by the legendary Shelbourne Hotel. On the south side is the alluring Georgian-gorgeous Newman House. ⊠ *Free* ☉ *Daily sunrise–sunset.*

▶ **⑯** **Trinity College.** Founded in 1592 by Queen Elizabeth I to "civilize" (Her
Fodors Choice Majesty's word) Dublin, Trinity is Ireland's oldest and most famous col-
★ lege. The memorably atmospheric campus is a must; here you can track the shadows of some of the noted alumni, such as Jonathan Swift (1667–1745), Oscar Wilde (1854–1900), Bram Stoker (1847–1912), and Samuel Beckett (1906–89). Trinity College, Dublin (familiarly known as TCD), was founded on the site of the confiscated Priory of All Hallows. For centuries Trinity was the preserve of the Protestant Church. A free education was offered to Catholics—provided that they accepted the Protestant faith. As a legacy of this condition, until 1966 Catholics who wished to study at Trinity had to obtain a dispensation from their bishop or face excommunication.

Trinity's grounds cover 40 acres. Most of its buildings were constructed in the 18th and early 19th centuries. The extensive **West Front,** with a classical pedimented portico in the Corinthian style, faces College Green and is directly across from the Bank of Ireland; it was built between 1755 and 1759, and is possibly the work of Theodore Jacobsen, architect of London's Foundling Hospital. The design is repeated on the interior, so the view is the same from outside the gates and from the quadrangle inside. On the lawn in front of the inner facade stand statues of two alumni, orator Edmund Burke (1729–97) and dramatist Oliver Goldsmith (1730–74). Like the West Front, **Parliament Square** (commonly known as Front Square), the cobblestone quadrangle that lies just beyond this first patch of lawn, dates from the 18th century. On the right side of the square is Sir William Chambers's theater, or Examination Hall, dating from the mid-1780s, which contains the college's most splendid Adamesque interior, designed by Michael Stapleton. The hall houses an impressive organ retrieved from an 18th-century Spanish ship and a gilded oak chandelier from the old House of Commons; concerts are sometimes held here. The chapel, left of the quadrangle, has stucco ceilings and fine woodwork. The theater and the chapel were designed by Scotsman William Chambers in the late 18th century. The looming campanile, or bell tower, is the symbolic heart of the college; erected in 1853, it dominates the center of the square. To the left of the campanile is the Graduates Memorial Building, or GMB. Built in 1892, the slightly Gothic building now contains the offices of Philosophical and Historical societies, Trinity's ancient and fiercely competitive debating groups. At the back of the square stands old redbrick Rubrics, looking rather ordinary and out of place among the gray granite and cobblestones. Rubrics, now used as housing for students and faculty, dates from 1690, making it the oldest campus building still standing.

The **Old Library** houses Ireland's largest collection of books and manuscripts; its principal treasure is the *Book of Kells,* generally considered to be the most striking manuscript ever produced in the Anglo-Saxon world and one of the great masterpieces of early Christian art. The book, which dates to the 9th century, is a splendidly illuminated version of the Gospels. It was once thought to be lost—the Vikings looted the book in 1007 for its jeweled cover but ultimately left the manuscript behind. In the 12th century, Guardius Cambensis declared that the book was made by an angel's hand in answer to a prayer of St. Bridget; in the 20th century, scholars decided instead that the book originated on the island of Iona off Scotland's coast, where followers of St. Colomba lived until the island came under siege in the early to mid-9th century. They fled to Kells, County Meath, taking the book with them. The 680-page work was rebound in four volumes in 1953, two of which are usually displayed at a time, so you typically see no more than four original pages. (Some wags have taken to calling it the "Page of Kells.") However, such is the incredible workmanship of the *Book of Kells* that one folio alone is worth the entirety of many other painted manuscripts. On some pages, it has been determined that within a quarter inch, no fewer than 158 interlacements of a ribbon pattern of white lines on a black background can be discerned—little wonder some historians feel this book contains all the designs to be found in Celtic art. Note, too, the extraordinary colors, some of which were derived from shellfish, beetles' wings, and crushed pearls. The most famous page shows the "XPI" monogram (symbol of Christ), but if this page is not on display, you can still see a replica of it, and many of the other lavishly illustrated pages, in the adjacent exhibition—dedicated to the history, artistry, and conservation of the book—through which you must pass to see the originals.

Because of the fame and beauty of the *Book of Kells,* it is all too easy to overlook the other treasures in the library. They include the *Book of Armagh,* a 9th-century copy of the New Testament that also contains St. Patrick's Confession, and the legendary *Book of Durrow,* a 7th-century Gospel book from County Offaly. You may have to wait in line to enter the library if you don't get there early in the day.

The main library room, also known as the **Long Room,** is one of Dublin's most staggering sights. At 213 feet long and 42 feet wide, it contains in its 21 alcoves approximately 200,000 of the 3 million volumes in Trinity's collection. Originally the room had a flat plaster ceiling, but in 1859–60 the need for more shelving resulted in a decision to raise the level of the roof and add the barrel-vaulted ceiling and the gallery bookcases. Since the 1801 Copyright Act, the college has received a copy of every book published in Britain and Ireland, and a great number of these publications must be stored in other parts of the campus and beyond. Of note are the carved Royal Arms of Queen Elizabeth I above the library entrance—the only surviving relic of the original college buildings—and, lining the Long Room, a grand series of marble busts, of which the most famous is Roubiliac's depiction of Jonathan Swift. The Trinity College Library Shop sells books, clothing, jewelry, and postcards. ⊠ *Front Sq., Southside* ☎ *01/608–2308* ⊕ *www.tcd.ie* ✉ *€7.50* ⊙ *June–Sept., Mon.–Sat. 9:30–5, Sun. 9:30–4:30; Oct.–May, Mon.–Sat. 9:30–5, Sun. noon–4:30.*

Trinity College's stark, modern Arts and Social Sciences Building, with an entrance on Nassau Street, houses the **Douglas Hyde Gallery of Modern Art,** which concentrates on contemporary art exhibitions and has its own bookstore. Also in the building, down some steps from the gallery, is a snack bar with coffee, tea, sandwiches, and students willing to chat about life in the old college. ⊠ *Nassau St., Southside* ☏ *01/608–1116* ▧ *Free* ☉ *Mon.–Wed. and Fri. 11–6, Thurs. 11–7, Sat. 11–4:45.*

The **New Berkeley Library,** the main student library at Trinity, was built in 1967 and named after the philosopher and alumnus George Berkeley. The small open space in front of the library contains a spherical brass sculpture designed by Arnaldo Pomodoro. A very modern, sleek extension dominates the Nassau Street side of the campus. The library is not open to the public. ⊠ *Nassau St., Southside* ☏ *01/677–2941* ⊕ *www.tcd.ie* ☉ *Grounds daily 8 AM–10 PM.*

In the Thomas Davis Theatre in the arts building, the **"Dublin Experience,"** a 45-minute audiovisual presentation, explains the history of the city over the last 1,000 years. ⊠ *Nassau St., Southside* ☏ *01/608–1688* ▧ *€4.20* ☉ *Late May–early Oct., daily 10–5; shows every hr on the hr.*

Georgian Dublin: Museums and Marvels

If there's one travel poster that signifies "Dublin" more than any other, it's the one that depicts 50 or so Georgian doorways—door after colorful door, all graced with lovely fanlights upheld by columns. A building boom began in Dublin in the early 18th century as the Protestant Ascendancy constructed terraced town houses for themselves, and civic structures for their city, in the style that came to be known as Georgian, after the four successive British Georges who ruled from 1714 through 1830. The Georgian architectural rage owed much to architects like James Gandon and Richard Castle. They and others were influenced by Andrea Palladio (1508–80), whose *Four Books of Architecture* were published in the 1720s in London and helped to precipitate the revival of his style, which swept through England and its colonies. Never again would Dublin be so "smart," its visitors' book so full of aristocratic names, its Southside streets so filled with decorum and style. "Serene red and pink houses showed beautifully designed doorways, the one spot of variation in the uniformity of facade," as architectural historian James Reynolds puts it. Today, Dublin's Southside remains a veritable shop window of the Georgian style, though there are many period sights on the Northside (for instance, the august interiors of the Dublin Writers Museum and Belvedere College, or James Gandon's great civic structures, the Custom House and the Four Courts, found quayside).

But Georgian splendor is just the iced cake-frosting on this tour. For there are also four of the most fascinating and glamorous museums in Ireland, conveniently sitting cheek by jowl: the National Gallery of Ireland, the National Library, the National Museum of Natural History, and the National Museum of Archaeology and History. Priceless old master paintings, legendary Celtic treasures, mythic prehistoric "Irish elks," and George Bernard Shaw manuscripts—there is enough here to keep you interested for days.

Numbers in the text correspond to numbers in the margin and on the Dublin Southside map.

a good walk

When Dublin was transformed into a Georgian metropolis, people came from all over to admire the new pillared and corniced city. Today, walking through Fitzwilliam Square or Merrion Street Upper, you can still admire vistas of calm Georgian splendor. Begin your Palladian promenade at the northeast corner of St. Stephen's Green—here, in front of the men's clubs, was the Beaux Walk, a favorite 18th-century gathering place for fashionable Dubliners. Chances are you won't bump into a duke on his way to a Handel concert or an earl on his way to a costume ball, but then neither will you have to dodge pigs, which dotted the cityscape back then. Walk north on Merrion Street to **Merrion Square** ㉘ ▶—one of Dublin's most attractive squares. The east side of Merrion Square and its continuation, Fitzwilliam Street, form what is known as "the Georgian mile" (which actually measures less than a kilometer). On a clear day the Dublin Mountains are visible in the distance and the prospect has almost been preserved to give an impression of the spacious feel of 18th-century Dublin (excepting the unattractive, modern office block of the Electricity Supply Board). Walk down the south side of the square to one of Dublin's most fascinating historic house renovations, **No. 29 Lower Fitzwilliam Street** ㉙. Then cut back through the square to the refurbished **Government Buildings** ㉚ and **Leinster House** ㉛. Both are now occupied by government agencies and open on a very limited basis to the public, but their magisterial exteriors are well worth a study. Adjacent to these you'll find the charmingly 19th-century **National Museum of Natural History** ㉜—who can resist a gander at the skeletons of the prehistoric "Irish elk"? If you're more interested in gorgeous paintings, head directly across the square to the moderately sized **National Gallery of Ireland** ㉝, where you can feast your eyes on masterworks by Rubens, Caravaggio, Uccello, and Goya, then recharge and refuel with lunch at the museum's Fitzer's Wintergarden restaurant. The last leg—hopefully not literally—of this walk is up Kildare Street to the **National Library** ㉞. If you want to take a peek at the famously domed Reading Room, get a visitor's pass; or just be content to study the entrance hall's display of library treasures. Many visitors will bypass the library and go instead behind the back of Leinster House toward the looming domed rotunda entrance of the **National Museum of Archaeology and History** ㉟. Here, fabled Celtic treasures, including the Cross of Cong and the Gleninsheen Gorget, await you. If you're eager to find out a little about your own history, head a few blocks over to the **Heraldic Museum** ㊱—you might even uncover a family crest. A short walk west along Molesworth Street takes you to Dawson Street (the site of the annual and popular August Antiques Fair). **St. Ann's Church** ㊲, the reticent **Royal Irish Academy** ㊳, and private **Mansion House** ㊴—the mayor's residence—are all on the left side as you walk toward St. Stephen's Green. If you're interested in George Bernard Shaw you may want to take a 15-minute walk from the Green to the Shaw Birthplace—from the bottom of Dawson Street make a right and then a left around the green until you arrive at Harcourt Street. After a short walk south, make a right onto Harrington Street and a right again onto Synge Street and Shaw's house.

TIMING Dublin is so compact you could race through this walk in two hours, if you don't linger anywhere or set foot in one of the museums. But that is unthinkable—after all, the treasures at the National Gallery and the National Museum of Archaeology and History, and the green tranquility of Merrion Square are some of Dublin's most fabled attractions. In addition, many of Dublin's finest Georgian mansions line these streets (as do dozens of the city's most historic pubs). Take a full day to savor the sights here, then plan on returning to some of them at your greater leisure.

What to See

③⓪ Government Buildings. The swan song of British architecture in the capital, this enormous complex, a landmark of Edwardian Baroque, was the last neoclassical edifice to be erected by the British government. It was designed by Sir Aston Webb, who did many of the similarly grand buildings in London's Piccadilly Circus, to serve as the College of Science in the early 1900s. Following a major restoration, these buildings became the offices of the Department of the *taoiseach* (the prime minister, pronounced *tea*-shuck) and the *tánaiste* (the deputy prime minister, pronounced tawn-*ish*-ta). Fine examples of contemporary Irish furniture and carpets populate the offices. A stained-glass window, known as "My Four Green Fields," was made by Evie Hone for the 1939 New York World's Fair. It depicts the four ancient provinces of Ireland: Munster, Ulster, Leinster, and Connacht. The government offices are accessible only via 45-minute guided tours on Saturday, though they are dramatically illuminated every night. ⊠ *Upper Merrion St., Southside* ☎ *01/662–4888* ✆ *Free; pick up tickets from National Gallery on day of tour* ۞ *Tours Sat. 10:30–3:30.*

③⑥ Heraldic Museum. Looking for something original for your wall? If you're a Fitzgibbon from Limerick, a Cullen from Waterford, or a McSweeney from Cork, chances are that your family designed, begged, borrowed, or stole a coat of arms somewhere in its history. The Heraldic Museum has hundreds of family-crest flags, coins, stamps, and silver, all highlighting the uses and development of heraldry in Ireland. ⊠ *2 Kildare St., Southside* ☎ *01/661–4877* ✆ *Free* ۞ *Mon.–Wed. 10–8:30, Thurs. and Fri. 10–4:30, Sat. 10–12:30; guided tours by appointment.*

③① Leinster House. Commissioned by the Duke of Leinster and built in 1745, this residence—Dublin's Versailles—almost single-handedly ignited the Georgian style that dominated Dublin for 100 years. It was not only the largest private home in the city but Richard Castle's first structure in Ireland (Castle–or Casells, to use his original German spelling—was a follower of the 16th-century Venetian architect Palladio and designed some of the country's most important 18th-century country houses). Inside, the grand salons were ornamented with coffered ceilings, Rembrandts, and Van Dycks—fitting settings for the parties often given by the duke's wife (and celebrated beauty), Lady Emily Lennox. The building has two facades: the one facing Merrion Square is designed in the style of a country house; the other, on Kildare Street, resembles that of a town house. The latter facade—if you ignore the ground-floor level—-was a major inspiration for Irishman James Hoban's designs for the White House in Washington, D.C. Built in hard Ardbracan limestone, the exterior of the house makes a cold impression, and, in fact, the duke's heirs pronounced the house "melancholy" and fled. Today, the house is the seat of Dáil Éireann (the House of Representatives, pronounced dawl *e*-rin) and Seanad Éireann (the Senate, pronounced shanad *e*-rin), which together constitute the Irish Parliament. When the Dáil is not in session, tours can be arranged weekdays; when the Dáil is in session, tours are available only on Monday and Friday. The Dáil visitors' gallery is included in the tour, although it can be accessed on days when the Dáil is in session and tours are not available. To arrange a visit, contact the public relations office. ⊠ *Kildare St., Southside* ☎ *01/618–3000 for public-relations office* ⊕ *www.irlgov.ie* ✑ *Free.*

39 **Mansion House.** The mayor of Dublin resides at the Mansion House, which dates from 1710. It was built for Joshua Dawson, who later sold the property to the government on condition that "one loaf of double re-fined sugar of six pounds weight" be delivered to him every Christmas. In 1919 the Declaration of Irish Independence was adopted here. The house is not open to the public. ⊠ *Dawson St., Southside.*

▶ **28** **Merrion Square.** Created between 1762 and 1764, this tranquil square
Fodor'sChoice a few blocks east of St. Stephen's Green is lined on three sides by some
★ of Dublin's best-preserved Georgian town houses, many of which have brightly painted front doors crowned by intricate fanlights. Leinster House, the National Museum of Natural History, and the National Gallery line the west side of the square. It's on the other sides, however, that the Geor-gian terrace streetscape comes into its own—the finest houses are on the north border. Even when the flower gardens here are not in bloom, the vibrant, mostly evergreen grounds, dotted with sculpture and threaded with meandering paths, are worth a stroll. Several distin-guished Dubliners have lived on the square, including Oscar Wilde's par-ents, Sir William and "Speranza" Wilde (No. 1); Irish national leader Daniel O'Connell (No. 58); and authors W. B. Yeats (Nos. 52 and 82) and Sheridan LeFanu (No. 70). As you walk past the houses, read the plaques on the house facades, which identify former inhabitants. Until 50 years ago the square was a fashionable residential area, but today most of the houses are offices. At the south end of Merrion Square, on Upper Mount Street, stands the Church of Ireland St. Stephen's Church. Known locally as the "pepper canister" church because of its cupola, the structure was inspired in part by Wren's churches in London. ⊠ *Southside* ☉ *Daily sunrise–sunset.*

33 **National Gallery of Ireland.** Caravaggio's *The Taking of Christ* (1602),
Fodor'sChoice Reynolds's *First Earl of Bellamont* (1773), Vermeer's *Lady Writing a*
★ *Letter with Her Maid* (circa 1670) . . . you get the picture. The National Gallery of Ireland—the first in a series of major civic buildings on the west side of Merrion Square—is one of Europe's finest smaller art mu-seums, with more than 2,500 paintings and some 10,000 other works. Unlike Europe's largest art museums, the National Gallery can be thor-oughly covered in a morning or afternoon without inducing exhaustion. An 1854 Act of Parliament provided for the establishment of the mu-seum, which was helped along by William Dargan (1799–1867), who was responsible for building much of Ireland's rail network (he is hon-

THE AGE OF ELEGANCE

"**EXTRAORDINARY DUBLIN!**" *sigh art lovers and connoisseurs of the 18th century. It was during the "gorgeous eighteenth" that this duckling of a city was transformed into a preening swan, largely by the Georgian style of art and architecture that flowered between 1714 and 1820 during the reigns of the three English Georges.*

*Today Dublin remains in good part a sublimely Georgian city, thanks to enduring grace notes: the commodious and uniformly laid out streets, the genteel town squares, the redbrick mansions accented with demilune fan windows. The great 18th-century showpieces are **Merrion, Fitzwilliam, Mountjoy,** and **Parnell squares. Merrion Square East,** the longest Georgian street in town, reveals scenes of decorum, elegance, polish, and charm, all woven into a "tapestry of rosy brick and white enamel," to quote the 18th-century connoisseur Horace Walpole.*

Setting off the facades are fan-lighted doors (often lacquered in black, green, yellow, or red) and the celebrated "patent reveal" window trims—thin plaster linings painted white to catch the light. These half-moon fanlights—as iconic of the city as clock towers are of Zurich—are often in the Neoclassical style known as the Adamesque (which was inspired by the designs of the great English architect, Robert Adam).

Many facades appear severely plain, but don't be fooled: these town houses can be compared to bonbons whose sheaths of hard chocolate conceal deliciously creamy centers.

*Just behind their stately front doors are entry rooms and stairways aswirl with tinted rococo plasterwork, often the work of stuccadores (plasterworkers) from Italy (including the talented Lafranchini brothers). Magnificent **Newman House,***

*one of the finest of Georgian houses, is open to the public. **Belvedere College** (✉ 6 Great Denmark St., Northside ☎ 01/874–3974) is open by appointment only.*

*The Palladian style—as the Georgian style was then called—began to reign supreme in domestic architecture in 1745, when the Croesus-rich earl of Kildare returned from an Italian grand tour and built a gigantic Palladian palace called **Leinster House** in the seedy section of town.*

*"Where I go, fashion will follow," he declared, and indeed it did. By then, the Anglo-Irish elite had given the city London airs by building the **Parliament House** (now the Bank of Ireland), the **Royal Exchange** (now City Hall), the **Custom House,** and the **Four Courts** in the new style.*

But this phase of high fashion came to an end with the Act of Union: according to historian Maurice Craig, "On the last stroke of midnight, December 31, 1800, the gaily caparisoned horses turned into mice, the coaches into pumpkins, the silks and brocades into rags, and Ireland was once again the Cinderella among the nations."

*It was nearly 150 years before the spotlight shone once again on 18th-century Dublin. In recent decades, the conservation efforts of the **Irish Georgian Society** (✉ 74 Merrion Sq., Southside ☎ 01/676–7053 ⊕ www. irishgeorgiansociety.org) have done much to restore Dublin to its Georgian splendor. Thanks to its founders, the Hon. Desmond Guinness and his late wife, Mariga, many historic houses including that of George Bernard Shaw on Synge Street, have been saved and preserved.*

ored by a statue on the front lawn). The 1864 building was designed by Francis Fowke, who was also responsible for London's Victoria & Albert Museum.

A highlight of the museum is the major collection of paintings by Irish artists from the 17th through 20th centuries, including works by Roderic O'Conor (1860–1940), Sir William Orpen (1878–1931), and William Leech (1881–1968). The Yeats Museum section contains works by members of the Yeats family. Jack B. Yeats (1871–1957), the brother of writer W. B. Yeats, is by far the best-known Irish painter of the 20th century. Yeats painted portraits and landscapes in an abstract expressionist style not unlike that of the Bay Area Figurative painters of the 1950s and '60s. His *The Liffey Swim* (1923) is particularly worth seeing for its Dublin subject matter (the annual swim is still held, usually on the first weekend in September).

The collection also claims exceptional paintings from the 17th-century French, Dutch, Italian, and Spanish schools. Among the highlights are those mentioned above (the spectacular Caravaggio made headlines around the world in the late 1980s when it was found hanging undiscovered in a Jesuit house not far from the museum) and Rembrandt's *Rest on the Flight into Egypt* (1647), Poussin's *The Holy Family* (1649) and *Lamentation over the Dead Christ* (circa 1655–60), and Goya's *Portrait of Doña Antonia Zárate* (circa 1810). Don't miss the portrait of the *First Earl of Bellamont* (1773) by Reynolds; the earl was among the first to introduce the Georgian fashion to Ireland, and this portrait flaunts the extraordinary style of the man himself. The French Impressionists are represented with paintings by Monet, Sisley, and Pissarro. The British collection and the Irish National Portrait collection are displayed in the north wing of the gallery, while the Millennium Wing, a standout of postmodern architecture in Dublin, houses part of the permanent collection and also stages major international traveling exhibits. The amply stocked gift shop is a good place to pick up books on Irish artists. Free guided tours are available on Saturday at 3 and on Sunday at 2, 3, and 4. ⊠ *Merrion Sq. W, Southside* ☎ *01/661–5133* ⊕ *www. nationalgallery.ie* ✉ *Free; special exhibits €10* ☉ *Mon.–Wed., Fri., and Sat. 9:30–5:30, Thurs. 9:30–8:30, Sun. noon–5:30.*

> **need a break?**
>
> **Fitzer's** (⊠ Merrion Sq. W, Southside ☎ 01/661–4496), the National Gallery's self-service restaurant, is a find—one of the city's best spots for an inexpensive, top-rate lunch. The 16 to 20 daily menu items are prepared with an up-to-date take on European cuisine. It's open Monday–Saturday 10–5:30 (lunch is served noon–2:30) and Sunday 2–5.

㉞ **National Library.** Ireland is one of the few countries in the world where one can happily admit to being a writer. And few countries as geographically diminutive as Ireland have garnered as many recipients of the Nobel Prize for Literature. Along with works by W. B. Yeats (1923), George Bernard Shaw (1925), Samuel Beckett (1969), and Seamus Heaney (1995), the National Library contains first editions of every major

Irish writer, including books by Jonathan Swift, Oliver Goldsmith, and James Joyce (who used the library as the scene of the great literary debate in *Ulysses*). In addition, almost every book ever published in Ireland is kept here, along with an unequaled selection of old maps and an extensive collection of Irish newspapers and magazines—more than 5 million items in all. The main Reading Room opened in 1890 to house the collections of the Royal Dublin Society. Beneath its dramatic domed ceiling, countless authors have researched and written. The library also has a free genealogical consultancy service that can advise you on how to trace your Irish ancestors. ⊠ *Kildare St., Southside* ☎ *01/661–8811* ⊕ *www.nli.ie* ✉ *Free* ☉ *Mon.–Wed. 10–9, Thurs. and Fri. 10–5, Sat. 10–1.*

★ ③⑤ **National Museum of Archaeology and History.** Set just to the south of Leinster House, Ireland's National Museum of Archaeology and History houses a fabled collection of Irish artifacts dating from 7000 BC to the present. Organized around a grand rotunda, the museum is elaborately decorated, with mosaic floors, marble columns, balustrades, and fancy ironwork. It has the largest collection of Celtic antiquities in the world, including gold jewelry, carved stones, bronze tools, and weapons. The Treasury collection, including some of the museum's most renowned pieces, is open on a permanent basis. Among the priceless relics on display are the late Bronze Age gold collar known as the Gleninsheen Gorget; the 8th-century Ardagh Chalice, a two-handled silver cup with gold filigree ornamentation; the bronze-coated, iron St. Patrick's Bell, the oldest surviving example (5th–8th centuries) of Irish metalwork; the 8th-century Tara Brooch, an intricately decorated piece made of white bronze, amber, and glass; and the 12th-century bejeweled oak Cross of Cong, covered with silver and bronze panels. The Road to Independence Room is devoted to the 1916 Easter Uprising and the War of Independence (1919–21); displays here include uniforms, weapons, banners, and a piece of the flag that flew over the General Post Office during Easter Week, 1916. Upstairs, Viking Age Ireland is a permanent exhibit on the Norsemen, featuring a full-size Viking skeleton, swords, leather works recovered in Dublin and surrounding areas, and a replica of a small Viking boat. In contrast to the ebullient late-Victorian architecture of the main museum building, the design of the National Museum Annex is purely functional; it hosts temporary shows of Irish antiquities. The 18th-century Collins Barracks, near Phoenix Park (*see below*), houses the National Museum of Decorative Arts and History, a collection of glass, silver, furniture, and other decorative arts. ⊠ *Kildare St.; Annex, 7–9 Merrion Row, Southside* ☎ *01/677-7444* ⊕ *www.museum.ie* ✉ *Free* ☉ *Tues.–Sat. 10–5, Sun. 2–5.*

③② **National Museum of Natural History.** The famed explorer of the African interior, Dr. Stanley Livingstone (of "Dr. Livingstone, I presume?" fame), inaugurated this museum when it opened in 1857. It is little changed from Victorian times and remains a fascinating repository of mounted mammals, birds, and other flora and fauna. The Irish Room houses the most famous exhibits; skeletons of the extinct, prehistoric, giant "Irish elk." The World Animals Collection includes a 65-foot whale skeleton suspended

ANCESTOR-HUNTING

THE LATE PRESIDENTS KENNEDY and Reagan are only two among many thousands of Americans who have been drawn to Ireland in an attempt to track down their ancestors. This is such a popular activity that Ireland now has numerous facilities for those in search of their past. However, before you begin some genealogical Sherlock Holmesing, you'll need some detailed information. The memories of elderly relatives about the place from which they or their forebears emigrated, for example, is often a useful starting point. The county name is helpful, but the name of their village or town is even better. It can lead quickly to parish registers, often going back 200 years or more, which the local clergy will usually be very glad to let you see (keep in mind that many of these parish registers have been moved to regional town halls and government agencies). The National Library in Dublin is the best source of information on family names and family crests, and the consultancy service is free. Similarly, the Office of the Registrar General in Dublin's Custom House has details of many births, deaths, and marriages after 1864, and some marriages dating back to 1845 (a substantial part of the records here was destroyed, however, in the Troubles of 1921). The Public Record Office at the Four Courts and the Registry of the Deeds in Henrietta Street, both in Dublin, are two other potentially useful sources of information. The National Archives on Bishop Street is a great source of old census information. Of course, if your great-grandfather's name was Blarney Killakalarney, you should have an easy time sleuthing your family roots. But if your name is one of the more prominent surnames in Ireland (⇨ Irish Family Names map, in Chapter 10), it may take you longer to track down your ancestors among all the Ahernes and O'Briens.

---

from the roof. Don't miss the very beautiful Blaschka Collection, finely detailed glass models of marine creatures, the zoological accuracy of which has never been achieved again in glass. The museum is next door to the Government Buildings. ⊠ *Merrion Sq. W, Southside* ☎ *01/677-7444* ⊕ *www.museum.ie* ☒ *Free* ☉ *Tues.–Sat. 10–5, Sun. 2–5.*

㉙ **No. 29 Lower Fitzwilliam Street.** Everything in this carefully refurbished 1794 home, known simply as Number Twenty-Nine, is in keeping with the elegant lifestyle of the Dublin middle class between 1790 and 1820, the height of the Georgian period, when the house was owned by a wine merchant's widow. From the basement to the attic—in the kitchen, nursery, servant's quarters, and the formal living areas—the National Museum has re-created the period's style with authentic furniture, paintings, carpets, curtains, paint, wallpapers, and even bell pulls. ⊠ *29 Lower Fitzwilliam St., Southside* ☎ *01/702-6165* ⊕ *www.esb.ie/ education* ☒ *€3.50* ☉ *Tues.–Sat. 10–5, Sun. 2–5.*

㊳ **Royal Irish Academy.** The country's leading learned society houses important documents in its 18th-century library, including a large collection of ancient Irish manuscripts, such as the 11th- to 12th-century *Book of the Dun Cow,* and the library of the 18th-century poet Thomas

Moore. ⊠ *19 Dawson St., Southside* ☎ *01/676–2570* ⊕ *www.ria.ie* 🖃 *Free* ⊙ *Weekdays 9:30–5.*

③ **St. Ann's Church.** St. Ann's plain, neo-Romanesque granite exterior, built in 1868, belies the rich Georgian interior of the church, which Isaac Wills designed in 1720. Highlights of the interior include polished-wood balconies, ornate plasterwork, and shelving in the chancel dating from 1723—and still in use for distributing bread to the parish's poor. ⊠ *Dawson St., Southside* ☎ *01/676–7727* 🖃 *Free* ⊙ *Weekdays 10–4, Sun. for services.*

off the beaten path

SHAW BIRTHPLACE – "Author of many plays" is the simple accolade to George Bernard Shaw (1856–1950) on the plaque outside his birthplace. The Nobel laureate was born here to a once prosperous family fallen on harder times. Shaw lived in this modest, Victorian terrace house until he was 10 and remembered it as having a "loveless" feel. The painstaking restoration of the little rooms highlights the cramped, claustrophobic atmosphere. All the details of a family home—wallpaper, paint, fittings, curtains, furniture, utensils, pictures, rugs—remain, and it appears as if the family has just gone out for the afternoon. You can almost hear one of Mrs. Shaw's musical recitals in the tiny front parlor. The children's bedrooms are filled with photographs and original documents and letters that throw light on Shaw's career. ⊠ *33 Synge St., Southside* ☎ *01/475–0854* ⊕ *www.visitdublin.com* 🖃 *€6.25* ⊙ *May–Sept., Mon.–Sat. 10–1 and 2–5, Sun. 11–1 and 2–5.*

Temple Bar: The Changing Face

More than any other neighborhood in the city, Temple Bar represents the dramatic changes (good and bad) and ascending fortunes of Dublin that came about in the last decade of the 20th century. The area, which takes its name from one of the streets of its central spine, was targeted for redevelopment in 1991–92 after a long period of neglect, having survived widely rumored plans to turn it into a massive bus depot and/or a giant parking lot. Temple Bar took off *fast* into Dublin's version of New York's Soho, Paris's Bastille, London's Notting Hill—a thriving mix of high and alternative culture distinct from what you'll find in every other part of the city. Dotting the area's narrow cobblestone streets and pedestrian alleyways are new apartment buildings (inside they tend to be small and uninspired, though bearing sky-high rents), vintage-clothing stores, postage-stamp-size boutiques selling €250 sunglasses and other expensive gewgaws, art galleries, a hotel resuscitated by U2, hip restaurants, pubs, clubs, European-style cafés, and a smattering of cultural venues.

Temple Bar's regeneration was no doubt abetted by that one surefire real estate asset: location, location, location. The area is bordered by Dame Street to the south, the Liffey to the north, Fishamble Street to the west, and Westmoreland Street to the east. In fact, Temple Bar is situated so perfectly between everywhere else in Dublin that it's difficult to believe this neighborhood was once largely forsaken. It's now sometimes called the "playing ground of young Dublin," and for good reason: on weekend evenings and daily in the summer it teems with young people—not only from Dublin but from all over Europe—who fly into the city for the weekend, drawn by its pubs, clubs, and lively *craic* (good conversation and fun). Despite efforts to ban them, the area has become a favorite of young Englishmen on "stag weekends," 48-hour bachelor parties heavy on drinking and debauching. Some who have witnessed Temple Bar's rapid gentrification and commercialization complain that it's losing its artistic soul—*Harper's Bazaar* said it was in danger of becoming "a sort of pseudoplace," like London's Covent Garden Piazza or Paris's Les Halles. Over the next few years the more cautiously developed Smithfield area may replace Temple Bar at the cutting edge of Dublin culture, but for the moment there's no denying that this is one of the best places to get a handle on the city.

Numbers in the text correspond to numbers in the margin and on the Dublin Southside map.

a good walk

Start at O'Connell Bridge and walk down Aston Quay, taking in the terrific view west down the River Liffey. Alleys and narrow roads to your left lead into Temple Bar, but hold off turning in until you get to **Ha'penny Bridge** ⑩ ▶, a Liffey landmark. Turn left and walk through Merchant's Arch, the symbolic entry into the district (see if you can spot the surveillance cameras up on the walls), which leads you onto the area's long spine, named Temple Bar here but also called Fleet Street (to the east) and Essex Street (to the west). You're right at Temple Bar Square, one of the two largest plazas in the neighborhood. Just up on the right are two of the area's leading art galleries, the Temple Bar Gallery (at Lower Fownes Street) and, another block up, the Original Print Gallery and Black Church Print Studios. Walk west along Temple Bar and turn left onto Eustace Street. If you have children, you may want to go to **The Ark** ㊶, a children's cultural center. Across the street from the Ark, stop in at the district's Information Centre and pick up a handy *Temple Bar Guide*. Farther down Eustace Street is the **Irish Film Institute** ㊷, the area's leading cultural venue and a great place to catch classic or new indie films. In summer, the center organizes Saturday-night outdoor screenings on **Meeting House Square** ㊸, behind the Ark, accessed via Curved Street. The **National Photographic Archive** ㊹ and the nearby **Gallery of Photography** ㊺, Dublin's leading photography gallery, are also here. Walk a few steps west to the narrow cobbled Sycamore Street, and then turn left and walk to Dame Street, where you'll find the **Olympia Theatre** ㊻. Farther east along Dame Street, the ultramodern **Central Bank** ㊼ rises above the city.

TIMING   You can easily breeze through Temple Bar in an hour or so, but if you've got the time, plan to spend a morning or afternoon here, drifting in and out of the dozens of stores and galleries, relaxing at a café over a cup of coffee or at a pub over a pint, or, if you're looking for a change from sightseeing, maybe even catching a film.

What to See

🕐 ㊶ **The Ark.** If you're traveling with children and looking for something fun to do, stop by the Ark, Ireland's cultural center for children, housed in

DUBLIN NOW

A LOT OF VISITORS COME TO DUBLIN to experience that which never changes. Tradition is taken as seriously in the capital city as it is in the rest of this ancient isle. The castle-like churches, the hundred-year-old drinking holes, the intact Georgian Squares are all there to be seen and wondered at, their history written in every worn brick and lose roof tile.

But a wind of change has blown over the place in the last decade or so and it goes by that newspaper soundbite, the Celtic Tiger. So sudden and powerful has that change been that Dublin, "the dirty old town," Joyce's center of "paralysis," has rapidly become one of the most trendy, cutting-edge cities in Europe.

Outdoor cafés were once as rare in rainy Dublin as jobs. But now you can't swing the proverbial hip cat without knocking over a row of wicker chairs and a table topped with Pellegrino and crostini.

In fact, large quality awnings and powerful outdoor, gas heaters have made a lot of these spots habitable year round. The favorite topic of conversation in these cafés has been the road chaos caused by the massive LUAS works throughout the city center.

But now, at last, the new LUAS tram system is due to open in 2005, and design aficionados are dying to see the polished silver, bullet-like trains gliding past them through the streets.

For a long time during the 1990s Dublin nightlife was owned by dance music. Every club and pub thumped to the beat of drum-'n-bass or shook to the bang of heavy techno.

Things have slowed down a bit over the last few years, and now jazz and world music are becoming the sounds to get down to. Live music is also making a big comeback, with rock bands headlining nightly in small and large venues throughout the city.

St. Patrick's day was once a dirty word in Dublin, it evoked visions of hordes of drunken fools and a cheap, uninspired parade passing by in the rain, but for the last few years the whole week around March 17th has been turned into a firework-strewn, event-packed extravaganza with music, dancing, and, of course, a big parade at the center of it all.

You know the millennium has arrived in Dublin when you see the newly installed James Joyce Bridge, designed by world-renowned artist, engineer, and architect Dr. Santiago Calatravo. This gleaming modern structure stands in front of the house where Joyce set his most famous short-story, "The Dead."

a former Presbyterian church. Its theater opens onto Meeting House Square for outdoor performances in summer. A gallery and workshop space host ongoing activities. ✉ *Eustace St., Temple Bar* ☎ *01/670–7788* ⊕ *www.ark.ie* ▣ *Free* ☉ *Weekdays 9:30–5:30, weekends only if there is a show.*

47 **Central Bank.** Everyone in Dublin seems to have an opinion on the Central Bank. Designed by Sam Stephenson in 1978, the controversial, ultramodern glass-and-concrete building suspends huge concrete slabs around a central axis. It was originally a floor higher, but that had to be lopped off as it was hazardous to low-flying planes. Skateboarders and in-line skaters have taken over on the little plaza in front of the building. ⊠ *Dame St., Temple Bar* ☎ *01/671–6666* ⊕ *www.centralbank.ie* ⊙ *Weekdays 10–6.*

45 **Gallery of Photography.** Dublin's premier photography gallery has a permanent collection of early-20th-century Irish photography and also puts on monthly exhibits of work by contemporary Irish and international photographers. The gallery is an invaluable social record of Ireland. The bookstore is the best place in town to browse for photography books and pick up arty postcards. ⊠ *Meeting House Sq. S, Temple Bar* ☎ *01/671–4654* ⊕ *www.irish-photography.com* ⊠ *Free* ⊙ *Tues.–Sat. 11–6, Sun 1–6.*

▶ **40** **Ha'penny Bridge.** Every Dubliner has a story about meeting someone on this cast-iron Victorian bridge, a heavily trafficked footbridge that crosses the Liffey at a prime spot—Temple Bar is on the south side, and the bridge provides the fastest route to the thriving Mary and Henry Street shopping areas to the north. Until early in the 20th century, a half-penny toll was charged to cross it. Yeats was one among many Dubliners who found this too high a price to pay—more a matter of principle than of principal—and so made the detour via O'Connell Bridge. Congestion on the Ha'penny has been relieved with the opening of the Millennium Footbridge a few hundred yards up the river. A refurbishment, including new railings, a return to the original white color, and tasteful lighting at night, has given the bridge a new lease on life.

42 **Irish Film Institute (IFI).** The opening of the IFI in a former Quaker meetinghouse helped to launch the revitalization of Temple Bar. It has two comfortable art-house cinemas showing revivals and new independent films, the Irish Film Archive, a bookstore for cineastes, and a popular bar and restaurant-café, all of which make this one of the neighborhood's most vital cultural institutions and *the* place to be seen. On Saturday nights in summer, the center screens films outside on Meeting House Square. ⊠ *6 Eustace St., Temple Bar* ☎ *01/679–5744* ⊕ *www.fii.ie* ⊠ *Free* ⊙ *Weekdays 9:30 AM–midnight, weekends 11 AM–midnight.*

need a break? The trendy **Irish Film Institute Café** (⊠ 6 Eustace St., Temple Bar ☎ 01/679–5744) is a pleasant place for a lunchtime break. Sandwiches are large and healthful, with plenty of vegetarian choices, and the people-watching is unmatched.

43 **Meeting House Square.** The square, which is behind the Ark and accessed via Curved Street, takes its name from a nearby Quaker meetinghouse. Today it's something of a gathering place for Dublin's youth and artists. Numerous summer events—classic movies (Saturday nights), theater, games, and family programs—take place here. (Thankfully, seats are installed.) The square is also a favorite site for the continuously changing street sculpture that pops up all over Temple Bar (artists commissioned by the city sometimes create oddball pieces, such as half of a Volkswagen protruding from a wall). Year-round, the square is a great spot to sit, people-watch, and take in the sounds of the buskers who swarm to the place. There's also an organic food market here every Saturday morning.

④④ National Photographic Archive. Formerly housed in the National Library's main building, the National Photographic Archive now has a stylish home in Temple Bar. The collection comprises approximately 300,000 photographs, most of which are Irish, making up a priceless visual history of the nation. Although most of the photographs are historical, dating as far back as the mid-19th century, there's also a large number of contemporary pictures. Subject matter ranges from topographical views to studio portraits, from political events to early tourist photographs. You can also buy a print of your favorite photo. ☒ *Meeting House Sq., Temple Bar* ☎ *01/603–0371* ⊕ *www.nli.ie* ☒ *Free* ☉ *Weekdays 10–5, Sat. 10–2.*

★ ④⑥ Olympia Theatre. One of the best places in Europe to see musical acts, the Olympia is Dublin's second oldest and one of its busiest theaters. This classic Victorian music hall, built in 1879, has a gorgeous red wrought-iron facade. The Olympia's long-standing Friday and Saturday series, "Midnight at the Olympia," has brought numerous musical performers to Dublin, and the theater has also seen many notable actors strut across its stage, including Alec Guinness, Peggy Ashcroft, Noël Coward, and even Laurel and Hardy. Big-name performers like Van Morrison often choose the intimacy of the Olympia over larger venues. It's really a hot place to see some fine performances, so if you have a chance, by all means go. Conveniently, there are two pubs here—through doors directly off the back of the theater's orchestra section. ☒ *72 Dame St., Temple Bar* ☎ *01/677–7744.*

> **need a break?**
>
> The creamiest, frothiest coffees in all of Temple Bar can be had at the **Joy of Coffee/Image Gallery Café** (☒ 25 E. Essex St., Temple Bar ☎ 01/679–3393); the wall of windows floods light onto the small gallery where original photographs adorn the walls.

Town & Country: From the Grand Canal to Ballsbridge

At its completion in 1795, the 547-km (340-mi) Grand Canal was celebrated as the longest in Britain and Ireland. It connected Dublin to the River Shannon, and horse-drawn barges carried cargo (mainly turf) and passengers to the capital from all over the country. After the arrival of the railroad in the mid-19th century, the great waterway slowly fell into decline, until the last commercial traffic ceased in 1960. But the 6-km (4-mi) loop around the capital is ideal for a leisurely stroll.

The Grand Canal defines the southern border of the city center. Directly below the canal lies exclusive Ballsbridge, a leafy suburb whose northern reaches contain several of the city's best hotels and restaurants. Its major cultural attractions, however, are considerably farther south—a bit too far to reach on foot unless you're really an ambitious walker.

You can hop a cab or take the DART train to Sydney Parade, or Bus 7 or Bus 8 from Burgh Quay (on the south bank of the Liffey, just east of O'Connell Bridge).

Numbers in the text correspond to numbers in the margin and on the Dublin Southside map.

a good walk

Begin by walking east along the Pearse Street side of Trinity College until you arrive at the Ringsend Road Bridge. Raised on stilts above the canal is the **Waterways Visitors Centre** ㊽ ▶. Head south and then southwest along the bank until you reach the **Mount Street Bridge** ㊾. On the southeast side of the canal is Percy Place, a street with elegant, three-story terrace houses. On the northwest side, a small lane leads up to the famous **Scruffy Murphy's** ㊿ pub. At this point, take a detour along Northumberland Street and make a left onto Landsdowne Road. From here you can take the DART one stop to Sandymount Avenue, which leads east to the beach at Sandymount Strand.

Back at Scruffy Murphy's walk southwest along Herbert Place. You can get really close to the dark green water here as it spills over one of the many wood-and-iron locks (all still in working order) that service the canal. James Joyce lost his virginity to a prostitute on the next stretch of the Canal, around Lower Baggot Street Bridge, but these banks belong to the lonesome ghost of another writer, Patrick Kavanagh. A life-size **statue of Patrick Kavanagh** �51 sits here on a wooden bench, contemplative, arms folded, legs crossed. Less than 2 km (1 mi) past the statue, the canal narrows as it approaches Richmond Bridge. Just beyond the bridge is the **Irish Jewish Museum** �52. To finish your walk in style, retrace your steps to Richmond Street, make a left, and stroll past a few antiques stores until you arrive at **Bambrick's** �53, a public house in the best tradition of Dublin.

TIMING You could walk this section of the canal in half an hour if you hurried (and didn't make the detour to the Sandymount Strand), but a leisurely pace best suits a waterside walk, so give yourself a couple of hours to visit the Jewish Museum and explore the old streets off the canal.

What to See

�53 **Bambrick's.** This is a pub in the best Irish tradition: half-empty, frequented mostly by men over 50, and with a long, dark-wood bar and a staff whose sharp, grinning humor verges on rudeness. ⊠ *11 Richmond St. S, Grand Canal* ☎ *01/475–4402* ⊙ *Sun.–Thurs. 11 AM–11:30 PM, Fri.–Sat. 11 AM–12:30 AM.*

�52 **Irish Jewish Museum.** Roughly 5,000 European Jews fleeing the pogroms of Eastern Europe arrived in Ireland in the late 19th and early 20th centuries. Today the Jewish population hovers around 1,800. The museum, opened in 1985 by Israeli president Chaim Herzog (himself Dublin-educated), includes a restored synagogue and a display of photographs, letters, and personal memorabilia culled from Dublin's most prominent Jewish families. Exhibits trace the Jewish presence in Ireland back to 1067. In homage to Leopold Bloom, the Jewish protagonist of Joyce's *Ulysses,* every Jewish reference in the novel has been identified.

The museum is a 20-minute walk or so southwest from St. Stephen's Green. ⊠ *3–4 Walworth Rd., Grand Canal* ☎ *01/453–1797* 🎫 *Free* ◷ *May–Sept., Tues., Thurs., and Sun. 11–3:30; Oct.–Apr., Sun. 10:30–2:30.*

49 Mount Street Bridge. The bridge, which has a wooden lock on either side, is the perfect spot from which to watch these original gateways to the canal in operation. On the southwest corner of the bridge a small stone monument commemorates the battle of Mount Street Bridge in 1916 and the Irish Volunteers who died on this spot.

off the beaten path

SANDYMOUNT STRAND – The Sandymount Strand, a few blocks west of the Sydney Parade DART station, stretches for 5 km (3 mi) from Ringsend to Booterstown. It was cherished by James Joyce and his beloved, Nora Barnacle from Galway, and it figures as one of the settings in *Ulysses*. (The beach is "at the lacefringe of the tide," as Joyce put it.) When the tide recedes, the beach extends for 1½ km (1 mi) from the foreshore, but the tide sweeps in again very quickly. A sliver of a park lies between Strand Road and the beach, which is not suitable for swimming.

50 Scruffy Murphy's. Many a backroom deal by the country's political power brokers has been made in the back room of this classy wood-and-brass pub. It's the perfect spot for a pint and a snack. ⊠ *Lower Mount St., Grand Canal* ☎ *01/661–5006* ◷ *Sun.–Thurs. 11 AM–11:30 PM, Fri.–Sat. 11 AM–12:30 AM.*

51 Statue of Patrick Kavanagh. Patrick Kavanagh (1905–67)—Ireland's great rural poet who in 1942 published his best-known poem, *The Great Hunger,* about farming and poverty—spent the later years of his life sitting on a bench here writing about the canal, which flowed from his birthplace in the Midlands to the city where he would die. In one such poem he tells those who outlive him, "O commemorate me with no hero-courageous tomb, just a canal-bank seat for the passerby." Acknowledging Kavanagh's devotion to this spot, his friends commissioned a life-size bronze of the poet to be placed here. ⊠ *Canal bank along Wilton Terr., Grand Canal.*

▶ **48 Waterways Visitors Centre.** In this airy wood-and-glass building you can learn about the history of Irish rivers and canals through photos, videos, and models. ⊠ *Grand Canal Quay, Grand Canal* ☎ *01/677–7501* ⊕ *www.waterwaysireland.org* 🎫 *€2.50* ◷ *June–Sept., daily 9:30–5:30; Oct.–May, Wed.–Sun. 12:30–5:30.*

Dublin West: From City Hall and the Liberties to Old Jameson Distillery

A cornucopia of all things quintessentially Dublin, this area is studded with treasures and pleasures ranging from the opulent 18th-century salons of Dublin Castle to time-burnished St. Patrick's Cathedral, from the Liberties neighborhood—redoubt of the city's best antiques stores—to the Irish Museum of Modern Art (now housed at the strikingly renovated

Royal Hospital Kilmainham). You can time-travel from the 10th-century crypt at Christ Church Cathedral—the city's oldest surviving structure—to the modern plant of the Guinness Brewery and its storehouse museum. You can also cross the Liffey for a visit to Smithfield, the old market area being billed as the next hot location in the city. Bordered on the east by Church Street, on the west by Blackhall Place, to the north by King Street, and to the south by the Liffey, Smithfield is Dublin's old market area where flowers, fruit, vegetables, and even horses have been sold for generations. Chosen as a flagship for north inner-city renovation, the area has seen a major facelift in the last few years. The beautiful cobblestones of its streets have been removed, refinished, and replaced, and giant masts topped with gas lights send six-foot-high flames over Smithfield Square—now the venue for the occasional major rock concert (the square was where U2 were awarded the keys to Dublin city in 1999). Early morning is a special time in Smithfield, as the wholesale fruit and veg sellers still ply their trade in the wonderful 19th-century covered market. Traditional music bars like the Cobblestone, a favorite of the market traders, now sit side by side with modern hotels like Chief O'Neills and the award winning Old Jameson Distillery museum.

Keep in mind that Dublin is so compact that to separate out the following sights from those covered in the other city-center Southside walks is potentially to mislead by suggesting that this area is at some remove from the heart of the city center. In fact, this tour's starting point, City Hall, is just across the street from the Thomas Read pub, and Christ Church Cathedral is a very short walk farther west. The westernmost sights covered here—notably the Royal Hospital and Kilmainham Gaol—are, however, at some distance, so if you're not an enthusiastic walker, you may want to drive or catch a cab or a bus to them.

Numbers in the text correspond to numbers in the margin and on the Dublin West map.

a good walk

Begin with a brief visit to **City Hall** ㉞ ▶, and then walk up Cork Hill to the Castle Street entrance of **Dublin Castle** ㉟, whose highlights—the grand halls that show off Viceregal Dublin at its most splendid—are only visitable via a guided tour. In the castle you'll also find the **Chester Beatty Library** ㊱, a world-renowned collection of Asian art and manuscripts. Leave via the same gate, turn left, and walk west along Castle Street to the ancient, picturesque **Christ Church Cathedral** ㊲, situated on one of the city's few hills. At the southwest corner of the cathedral, connected via an utterly beguiling Victorian-era bridge, **Dublinia** ㊳ gives you a chance to experience life in medieval Dublin. Just down Nicholas Street is—*begorrah!*—**St. Patrick's Cathedral** ㊴. If you're eager to venture back to the 17th century or love old books, visit the quaint **Marsh's Library** ㊵, next door to St. Patrick's. In the shadow of St. Patrick's Cathedral, head from Patrick Close to Patrick Street. Look down the street toward the Liffey and take in the glorious view of Christ Church. Go west on Dean Street, where you'll find John Fallons Pub.

Take a right off Dean Street onto Francis Street—several quality antiques shops line both sides of the thoroughfare—and walk uphill to find yourself in the heart of **the Liberties,** a compact area of small, winding streets. A stroll through this neighborhood puts you in working-class Dublin, past and present, good and bad. The name derives from Dublin of the Middle Ages, when the area south and west of Christ Church Cathedral was outside the city walls and the jurisdiction of the city rulers. A certain amount of freedom, or "liberty," was enjoyed by those who settled here, which attracted people on the fringes of society, especially the poor. Halfway up Francis Street, on the right, behind hefty wrought-iron gates, is one of Dublin's most-overlooked treasures: **St. Nicholas of Myra's Church** ⓺ . Continue up Francis Street and take the next right onto Thomas Davis Street, named after a famous patriot and revolutionary (the Liberties area has long had a close association with Irish nationalism). The street is full of classic, two-story redbrick houses. The area, once the heart of "Darlin' Dublin" and the source of its distinctive accent, is rapidly becoming yuppified. Back at the top of Francis Street turn left onto Thomas Street. Across the road, on your right side, stands the wonderfully detailed exterior of St. Augustine and St. John, with its grandiose spire stretching above it. You'll notice churches all over the Liberties; the bishops thought it wise to build holy palaces in the poorest areas of the city as tall, shining beacons of comfort and hope. Farther up Thomas Street in another converted factory is the **National College of Art and Design** ⓺ .

From here you can stroll along the street—just follow your nose—straight up to James's Street and the **Guinness Brewery and Storehouse** ⓺ , where you can keep up your spirits in more ways than one. If you want to see more architecture and art, proceed farther west to the Irish Museum of Modern Art in the elegant 17th-century **Royal Hospital Kilmainham** ⓺ , and the historic prison house of **Kilmainham Gaol** ⓺ . If you don't elect to head this way, walk back down Thomas Street and make a left at Bridge Street, which you'll follow across the Liffey; north of the river the street becomes Church Street. On your right is **Four Courts** ⓺ , grand 18th-century seat of the High Courts of Justice. A little farther up on the left is **St. Michan's Church** ⓺ and the beginning of the Smithfield area. A quick jog to the west to Bow Street (via Mary's Lane) brings you to the **Old Jameson Distillery** ⓺ —here you can learn all there is to learn about Irish whiskey. End your walk with a thrilling ride up the glass elevator to the top of **The Chimney** ⓺ .

TIMING   Allow a few hours for this tour, especially if you want to include the Guinness Brewery and Storehouse and the Irish Museum of Modern Art at the Royal Hospital. Keep in mind that if you want to cover the easternmost sights—Dublin Castle, City Hall, Christ Church Cathedral, and environs—you can easily append them to a tour of Temple Bar.

What to See

⓺   **Chester Beatty Library.** After Sir Alfred Chester Beatty (1875–1968), a
FodorśChoice   Canadian mining millionaire, assembled one of the most significant
★   collections of Islamic and Far Eastern art in the Western world, he donated it to Ireland. Housed in the gorgeous clock tower building of Dublin Castle, and voted European Museum of the Year in 2002, the library is one of Dublin's real gems. Among the exhibits are clay tablets from Baby-

lon dating from 2700 BC, Japanese color wood-block prints, Chinese jade books, and Turkish and Persian paintings. The second floor, dedicated to the major religions, houses 250 manuscripts of the Koran from across the Muslim world, as well as one of the earliest Gospels. Life-size Buddhas from Burma and rhino cups from China are among the other curios on show. Guided tours of the library are available on Tuesday and Saturday at 2:30 PM. On sunny days the garden is one of the most tranquil places in central Dublin. The shop is full of unique and exotic souvenirs relating to the collection. ⊠ *Castle St., Dublin West* ☎ *01/407–0750* ⊕ *www.cbl.ie* ✉ *Free* ☉ *May–Sept., weekdays 10–5, Sat. 11–5, Sun. 1–5; Oct.–Apr., Tues.–Fri. 10–5, Sat. 11–5, Sun. 1–5.*

⟲ 🈲 **The Chimney.** Just in front of the Chief O'Neill Hotel stands one of the original brick chimneys, built in 1895, of the Old Jameson Distillery, which has been turned into a 185-foot-tall observation tower with the first 360-degree view of Dublin. The redbrick chimney now has a two-tier, glass-enclosed platform at the top. The trip aloft in the glass elevator is just as thrilling as the view from the platform. ⊠ *Smithfield Village, Dublin West* ☎ *01/817–3820* ⊕ *www.chiefoneills.com* ✉ *€5* ☉ *Mon.–Sat. 10–5:30, Sun. 11–5:30.*

★ 🈲 **Christ Church Cathedral.** You'd never know from the outside that the first Christianized Danish king built a wooden church at this site in 1038; because of the extensive 19th-century renovation of its stonework and trim, the cathedral looks more Victorian than Anglo-Norman. Construction on the present Christ Church—the flagship of the Church of Ireland and one of two Protestant cathedrals in Dublin (the other is St. Patrick's just to the south)—was begun in 1172 by Strongbow, a Norman baron and conqueror of Dublin for the English crown, and continued for 50 years. By 1875 the cathedral had deteriorated badly; a major renovation gave it much of the look it has today, including the addition of one of Dublin's most charming structures: a Bridge of Sighs–like affair that connects the cathedral to the old Synod Hall, which now holds the Viking multi-media exhibition, Dublinia. Remains from the 12th-century building include the north wall of the nave, the west bay of the choir, and the fine stonework of the transepts, with their pointed arches and supporting columns. Strongbow himself is buried in the cathedral beneath an impressive effigy. The vast, sturdy **crypt,** with its 12th- and 13th-century vaults, is Dublin's oldest surviving structure and the building's most notable feature. The Treasures of Christ Church exhibition includes manuscripts, various historic artifacts, and the tabernacle used when James II worshipped here. At 6 PM on Wednesday and Thursday you can enjoy the glories of a choral evensong. ⊠ *Christ Church Pl. and Winetavern St., Dublin West* ☎ *01/677–8099* ⊕ *www.cccdub.ie* ✉ *€5* ☉ *Weekdays 9:45–5, weekends 10–5.*

⚑ 🈲 **City Hall.** Facing the Liffey from Cork Hill at the top of Parliament Street, this grand Georgian municipal building (1769–79), once the Royal Exchange, marks the southwest corner of Temple Bar. Today it's the seat of the Dublin Corporation, the elected body that governs the city. Thomas Cooley designed the building with 12 columns that encircle the domed central rotunda, which has a fine mosaic floor and 12 frescoes depicting

Dublin West

KEY

▲ Start of walk

Dublin legends and ancient Irish historical scenes. The 20-foot-high sculpture to the right is of Daniel O'Connell, "The Liberator." He looks like he's about to begin the famous speech he gave here in 1800. The building houses a multimedia exhibition—with artifacts, kiosks, graphics, and audiovisual presentations—tracing the evolution of Ireland's 1,000-year-old capital. ⊠ *Dame St., Dublin West* ☎ *01/672–2204* ⊕ *www.dublincity.ie/cityhall/home.htm* 📷 *€4* ⊙ *Mon.–Sat. 10–5:15, Sun. 2–5.*

㊷ Dublin Castle. Neil Jordan's film *Michael Collins* captured Dublin Castle's near indomitable status well: seat and symbol of the British rule of Ireland for more than seven centuries, the castle figured largely in Ireland's turbulent history early in the 20th century. It's now mainly used for Irish and EU governmental purposes. The sprawling Great Courtyard is the reputed site of the Black Pool (Dubh Linn, pronounced *dove*-lin) from which Dublin got its name. In the Lower Castle Yard, the Record Tower, the earliest of several towers on the site, is the largest remaining relic of the original Norman buildings, built by King John between 1208 and 1220. The clock tower building now houses the Chester Beatty Library. Guided tours are available of the principal State Apartments (on the southern side of the Upper Castle Yard), formerly the residence of the English viceroys and now used by the president of Ireland to host visiting heads of state and EU ministers. The State Apartments are lavishly furnished with rich Donegal carpets and illuminated by Waterford glass chandeliers. The largest and most impressive of these chambers, St. Patrick's Hall, with its gilt pillars and painted ceiling, is used for the inauguration of Irish presidents. The Round Drawing Room, in Bermingham Tower, dates from 1411 and was rebuilt in 1777; numerous Irish leaders were imprisoned in the tower from the 16th century to the early 20th century. The blue oval Wedgwood Room contains Chippendale chairs and a marble fireplace. The Castle Vaults now hold an elegant little patisserie and bistro.

Carved oak panels and stained glass depicting viceroys' coats of arms grace the interior of the Church of the Holy Trinity (formerly called Chapel Royal), on the castle grounds. The church was designed in 1814 by Francis Johnston, who also designed the original General Post Office building on O'Connell Street. Once you're inside, look up—you'll see an elaborate array of fan vaults on the ceiling. More than 100 carved heads adorn the walls outside: St. Peter and Jonathan Swift preside over the north door, St. Patrick and Brian Boru over the east.

One-hour guided tours of the castle are available every half hour, but the rooms are closed when in official use, so call ahead. The easiest way into the castle is through the Cork Hill Gate, just west of City Hall. ⊠ *Castle St., Dublin West* ☎ *01/677–7129* ⊕ *www.dublincastle.ie* 📷 *State Apartments €4.50, including tour* ⊙ *Weekdays 10–5, weekends 2–5.*

㊺ ㊽ Dublinia. Ever wanted a chance to put your head in the stocks? Dublin's Medieval Trust has set up an entertaining and informative reconstruction of everyday life in medieval Dublin. The main exhibits use high-tech audiovisual and computer displays; you can also see a scale model of what Dublin was like around 1500, a medieval maze, a life-size reconstruction based on the 13th-century dockside at Wood Quay, and a fine view from the tower. For a more modern take on the city, check out the James Malton series of prints of 18th-century Dublin, hanging on the walls of the coffee shop. Dublinia is in the old Synod Hall (formerly a meeting place for bishops of the Church of Ireland), joined via a covered stonework Victorian bridge to Christ Church Cathedral. ⊠ *St. Michael's Hill, Dublin West* ☎ *01/679–4611* ⊕ *www.dublinia.ie* ▣ *Exhibit €5.75* ⊘ *Apr.–Sept., daily 10–5; Oct.–Mar., Mon.–Sat. 11–4, Sun. 10–4:30.*

66 Four Courts. The stately Corinthian portico and the circular central hall warrant a visit here, to the seat of the High Court of Justice of Ireland. The distinctive copper-covered dome topping a colonnaded rotunda makes this one of Dublin's most instantly recognizable buildings. The view from the rotunda is terrific. Built between 1786 and 1802, the Four Courts are James Gandon's second Dublin masterpiece—close on the heels of his Custom House, downstream on the same side of the River Liffey. In 1922, during the Irish Civil War, the Four Courts was almost totally destroyed by shelling—the adjoining Public Records Office was gutted, and many priceless legal documents, including innumerable family records, were destroyed. Restoration took 10 years. There is no tour of the building, but you are welcome to sit in while the courts are in session. ⊠ *Inns Quay, Dublin West* ☎ *01/872–5555* ⊕ *www.courts.ie* ⊘ *Daily 10–1 and 2:15–4.*

★ 63 Guinness Brewery and Storehouse. Ireland's all-dominating brewer—founded by Arthur Guinness in 1759 and at one time the largest stout-producing brewery in the world—spans a 60-acre spread west of Christ Church Cathedral. Not surprisingly, it's the most popular tourist destination in town—after all, the Irish national drink is Guinness stout, a dark brew made with roasted malt. The brewery itself is closed to the public, but the Guinness Storehouse is a spectacular attraction, designed to woo you with the wonders of the "dark stuff." In a 1904 cast-iron-and-brick warehouse, the museum display covers six floors built around a huge, central glass atrium. Beneath the glass floor of the lobby you can see Arthur Guinness's original lease on the site, for a whopping 9,000 years. The exhibition elucidates the brewing process and its history, with antique presses and vats, a look at bottle and can design through the ages, a history of the Guinness family, and a fascinating archive of Guinness advertisements. You might think it's all a bit much (it's only a drink, after all), and parts of the exhibit do feel a little over the top. The star attraction is undoubtedly the top-floor Gravity Bar, with 360-degree floor-to-ceiling glass walls that offer a nonpareil view out over the city at sunset while you sip your free pint. One of the bar's first clients was one William Jefferson Clinton. The Guinness Shop on the ground floor is full of funky lifestyle merchandise associated with the "dark stuff." ⊠ *St. James' Gate, Dublin West* ☎ *01/408–4800* ⊕ *www.guinness.com* ▣ *€13.50* ⊘ *June–July, daily 9:30–9; Sept–May, daily 9:30–5.*

65 Kilmainham Gaol. Leaders of many failed Irish rebellions spent their last days in this grim, forbidding structure, and it holds a special place in the myth and memory of the country. The 1916 commanders Pádrig Pearse and James Connolly were held here before being executed in the prison yard. Other famous inmates included the revolutionary Robert Emmet and Charles Stewart Parnell, a leading politician. You can only visit the prison as part of a guided tour, which leaves every hour on the hour. The cells are a chilling sight, and the guided tour and a 30-minute audiovisual presentation relate a graphic account of Ireland's political history over the past 200 years—from an Irish Nationalist viewpoint. A new exhibition displays items that haven't been seen together since Robert Emmet's failed rebellion of 1803. A small tearoom is on the premises. ⊠ *Inchicore Rd., Dublin West* 🕾 *01/453–5984* ⊕ *www. heritageireland.ie* 🖃 *€5* ⊙ *Apr.–Sept., daily 9:30–5; Oct.–Mar., Mon.–Sat. 9:30–4, Sun. 10–5.*

⑥⓪ Marsh's Library. When Ireland's first public library was founded and endowed in 1701 by Narcissus Marsh, the Archbishop of Dublin, it was made open to "All Graduates and Gentlemen." The two-story brick Georgian building has remained virtually the same since then. It houses a priceless collection of 250 manuscripts and 25,000 15th- to 18th-century books. Many of these rare volumes were locked inside cages, as are the readers who wish to peruse them. The cages were to discourage students who, often impecunious, may have been tempted to make the books their own. The library has been restored with great attention to its original architectural details, especially in the book stacks. The library is a short walk west from St. Stephen's Green and accessed through a charming little cottage garden. ⊠ *St. Patrick's Close off Patrick St., Dublin West* 🕾 *01/ 454–3511* ⊕ *www.marshlibrary.ie* 🖃 *€2.50* ⊙ *Mon. and Wed.–Fri. 10–12:45 and 2–5, Sat. 10:30–12:45.*

⑥② National College of Art and Design. The delicate welding of glass and iron onto the redbrick Victorian facade of this onetime factory makes this school worth a visit. Walk around the cobblestone central courtyard, where there's often the added bonus of viewing students working away in glass, clay, metal, and stone. ⊠ *Thomas St., The Liberties* 🕾 *01/671– 1377* ⊕ *www.ncad.ie* 🖃 *Free* ⊙ *Weekdays 9–7.*

⑥⑧ Old Jameson Distillery. Founded in 1791, this distillery produced one of Ireland's most famous whiskeys for nearly 200 years, until 1966, when local distilleries merged to form Irish Distillers and moved to a purpose-built, ultramodern distillery in Middleton, County Cork. Part of the complex was converted into the group's head office, and the distillery itself became a museum. There's a short audiovisual history of the industry, which had its origins 1,500 years ago in Middle Eastern perfume making. You can also tour the old distillery, and learn about the distilling of whiskey from grain to bottle, or view a reconstruction of a former warehouse, where the colorful nicknames of former barrel makers are recorded. The 40-minute tour includes a complimentary tasting (remember: Irish whiskey is best drunk without a mixer—try it straight or with water); four attendees are invited to taste different brands of Irish whiskey and compare them against bourbon and Scotch. If you have a large group and everyone wants to do this, phone in advance to arrange it. ⊠ *Bow St., Dublin West* 🕾 *01/807–2355* ⊕ *www.irish-whiskey-trail. com* 🖃 *€7.95* ⊙ *Daily 9:30–6; tours every ½ hr.*

★ ⑥④ Royal Hospital Kilmainham. This replica of Les Invalides in Paris is regarded as the most important 17th-century building in Ireland. Commissioned as a hospice for disabled and veteran soldiers by James Butler—the duke of Ormonde and viceroy to King Charles II—the building was completed in 1684, making it the first building erected in Dublin's golden age. It survived into the 1920s as a hospital, but after the founding of the Irish Free State in 1922, the building fell into disrepair. The entire edifice has since been restored to what it once was.

The structure's four galleries are arranged around a courtyard; there's also a grand dining hall—100 feet long by 50 feet wide. The architectural highlight is the hospital's Baroque chapel, distinguished by its extraordinary plasterwork ceiling and fine wood carvings. "There is nothing in Ireland from the 17th century that can come near this masterpiece," raved cultural historian John FitzMaurice Mills. The Royal Hospital also houses the **Irish Museum of Modern Art,** which concentrates on the work of contemporary Irish artists such as Richard Deacon, Richard Gorman, Dorothy Cross, Sean Scully, Matt Mullican, Louis Le Brocquy, and James Colman. The museum also displays works by some non-Irish 20th-century greats, including Picasso and Miró, and regularly hosts touring shows from major European museums. The Café Musée serves light fare such as soups and sandwiches. The hospital is a short ride by taxi or bus from the city center. ⊠ *Kilmainham La., Dublin West* ☎ *01/612–9900* ⊕ *www.modernart.ie* ☞ *Royal Hospital free; individual art shows may have separate charges; museum free, small charge for special exhibitions* ⊙ *Royal Hospital Tues.–Sat. 10–5:30, Sun. noon–5:30; tours every ½ hr. Museum Tues.–Sat. 10–5:30, Sun. noon–5:30; tours Wed. and Fri. at 2:30, Sat. at 11:30.*

67 **St. Michan's Church.** However macabre, St. Michan's main claim to fame is down in the vaults, where the totally dry atmosphere has preserved several corpses in a remarkable state of mummification. They lie in open caskets. Most of the resident deceased are thought to have been Dublin tradespeople (one was, they say, a religious crusader). Except for its 120-foot-high bell tower, this Anglican church is architecturally undistinguished. The church was built in 1685 on the site of an 11th-century Danish church (Michan was a Danish saint). Another reason to come is to see the 18th-century organ, which Handel supposedly played for the first performance of *Messiah*. Don't forget to check out the Stool of Repentance—the only one still in existence in the city. Parishioners judged to be "open and notoriously naughty livers" used it to do public penance. ⊠ *Lower Church St., Dublin West* ☎ *01/872–4154* ☞ *€3.50* ⊙ *Apr.–Oct., weekdays 10–12:45 and 2–4:45, Sat. 10–12:45, Sun. service at 10 AM; Nov.–Mar., weekdays 12:30–3:30, Sat. 10–12:45, Sun. service at 10 AM.*

61 **St. Nicholas of Myra's Church.** A grand neoclassical style characterizes this church, completed in 1834. The highly ornate chapel inside includes ceiling panels of the 12 apostles, and a pietà raised 20 feet above the marble altar, guarded on each side by angels sculpted by John Hogan while he was in Florence. The tiny nuptial chapel to the right has a small Harry Clarke stained-glass window. ⊠ *St. Nicholas St., The Liberties* ☞ *Free* ⊙ *Hrs vary.*

59 St. Patrick's Cathedral. The largest cathedral in Dublin and also the na-
Fodor'sChoice tional cathedral of the Church of Ireland, St. Patrick's is the second of
★ the capital's two Protestant cathedrals. (The other is Christ Church, and
the reason Dublin has two cathedrals is because St. Patrick's originally
stood outside the walls of Dublin, while its close neighbor was within
the walls and belonged to the see of Dublin.) Legend has it that in the
5th century, St. Patrick baptized many converts at a well on the site of
the cathedral. The original building, dedicated in 1192 and early English Gothic in style, was an unsuccessful attempt to assert supremacy
over Christ Church Cathedral. At 305 feet, this is the longest church in
the country, a fact Oliver Cromwell's troops—no friends to the Irish—
found useful as they made the church's nave into their stable in the 17th
century. They left the building in a terrible state; its current condition
is largely due to the benevolence of Sir Benjamin Guinness—of the
brewing family—who started financing major restoration work in 1860.

Make sure you see the gloriously heraldic Choir of St. Patrick's, hung with
colorful medieval banners, and find the tomb of the most famous of St.
Patrick's many illustrious deans, Jonathan Swift, immortal author of *Gulliver's Travels,* who held office from 1713 to 1745. Swift's tomb is in the
south aisle, not far from that of his beloved "Stella," Mrs. Esther Johnson. Swift's epitaph is inscribed over the robing-room door. Yeats—who
translated it thus: "Swift has sailed into his rest; Savage indignation there
cannot lacerate his breast"—declared it the greatest epitaph of all time.
Other memorials include the 17th-century Boyle Monument, with its numerous painted figures of family members, and the monument to Turlough
O'Carolan, the last of the Irish bards and one of the country's finest harp
players. Immediately north of the cathedral is a small park, with statues
of many of Dublin's literary figures and St. Patrick's Well. "Living Stones"
is the cathedral's permanent exhibition celebrating St. Patrick's place in
the life of the city. If you're a music lover, you're in for a treat; matins
(9:45 AM) and evensong (5:35 PM) are still sung on most days. ⊠ *Patrick
St., Dublin West* ☎ *01/453–9472* ⊕ *www.stpatrickscathedral.ie* ☒ *€4.20*
⊙ *May and Sept.–Oct., weekdays 9–6, Sat. 9–5, Sun. 10–11 and 12:45–3;
June–Aug., weekdays 9–6, Sat. 9–4, Sun. 9:30–3 and 4:15–5:15; Nov.–Apr.,
weekdays 9–6, Sat. 9–4, Sun. 10–11 and 12:45–3.*

"Take it aisy": Phoenix Park & Environs

Far and away Dublin's largest park, Phoenix Park (the name is an anglicization of the Irish *Fionn Uisce,* meaning clear water) is a vast,
green, arrowhead-shape oasis north of the Liffey, about a 20-minute walk
from the city center. Dubliners flock here to escape from the madding
crowds. It remains the city's main lung, escape valve, sports center
(cricket, soccer, Gaelic games, and polo), and the home of the noble creatures of the Dublin Zoo. A handful of other cultural sights near the park
are also worth visiting, but to combine a visit to any of them with any
of the other walks in this chapter would be a bit difficult. The Smithfield area and the Old Jameson Distillery, at the end of the Dublin West
walk, are the sights closest (the Guinness Brewery and Storehouse,
across the river, is also fairly close). So if you do make it to any of those,

think about whether you have enough time to append a visit to one or another of these sights. Otherwise, plan to make a special trip out here—walk if you're up to it, or take a car or cab.

Numbers in the text correspond to numbers in the margin and on the Dublin West map.

a good walk

Beginning at the Custom House, walk west along the quays on the north side of the Liffey until you come to Blackhall Place. Turn right and walk north on Blackhall Place and then make a left onto Arbour Hill; the **Arbour Hill Cemetery** ⑳ ► will be on your right. Directly across Arbour Hill is the **National Museum of Decorative Arts and History** ㉑, in the old Collins Barracks (the main entrance is on Benburb Street on the south side). On its west side Benburb becomes Parkgate Street, and it's just a short stroll farther down to the main entrance of **Phoenix Park** ㉒.

TIMING   Phoenix Park is *big*; exploring it on foot could easily take the better part of a day. If you're looking for a little exercise, head here: jogging, horseback riding, and bicycling are the ideal ways to explore the park more quickly than you can by simply strolling.

What to See

► ⑳   **Arbour Hill Cemetery.** All 14 Irishmen executed by the British following the 1916 Easter Uprising are buried here, including Pádrig Pearse, who led the rebellion; his younger brother Willie, who played a minor role in the uprising; and James Connolly, a socialist and labor leader wounded in the battle. Too weak from his wounds to stand, Connolly was tied to a chair and then shot. The burial ground is a simple but formal area, with the names of the dead leaders carved in stone beside an inscription of the proclamation they issued during the uprising. ⊠ *Arbour Hill, Dublin West* ⊑ *Free* ☉ *Mon.–Sat. 9–4:30, Sun. 9:30–noon.*

★ ㉑   **National Museum of Decorative Arts and History.** Connoisseurs of the decorative arts have always had a special fondness for Irish style, whose glories range from Bronze Age Celtic jewels to the moderne 20th-century furniture of Eileen Gray. Here, in one gigantic treasure chest, is the full panoply of the National Museum's collection of glass, silver, furniture, and other decorative arts. The setting is spectacular: the huge Collins Barracks, named for the assassinated Irish Republican leader Michael Collins (1890–1922). Built in the early 18th century, designed by Captain Thomas Burgh, these erstwhile "Royal Barracks" were stylishly renovated to become a showcase for the museum, which opened in September 1997. The displays are far ranging, covering everything from one of the greatest collections of Irish silver in the world to Irish period furniture—you'll see that the country's take on Chippendale was far earthier than the English mode—to "The Way We Wore: 250 Years of Irish Clothing and Jewelry." Headlining the collections are some extraordinary objects, including the Fonthill Vase, the William Smith O'Brien Gold Cup, and the Lord Chancellorís Mace. ⊠ *Benburb St., Dublin West* ☎ *01/677-7444* ⊕ *www.museum.ie* ⊑ *Free* ☉ *Tues.–Sat. 10–5, Sun. 2–5.*

☾ ㉒   **Phoenix Park.** Europe's largest public park, which extends about 5 km (3 mi) along the Liffey's north bank, encompasses 1,752 acres of verdant green lawns, woods, lakes, and playing fields. Sunday is the best time to visit: games of cricket, football (soccer), polo, baseball, hurling (a combination of lacrosse, baseball, and field hockey), and Irish football are likely to be in progress. Old-fashioned gas lamps line both sides of Chesterfield Avenue, the main road that bisects the park for 4 km (2½ mi), which was named for Lord Chesterfield, a lord lieutenant of Ireland, who laid out the road in the 1740s. To the right as you enter the park is the People's Garden, a colorful flower garden designed in 1864.

Among the park's major monuments are the Phoenix Column, erected by Lord Chesterfield in 1747, and the 198-foot obelisk, built in 1817 to commemorate the Duke of Wellington, the Irish general who defeated Napoleon for the British. (Wellington was born in Dublin but, true to the anti-Irish prejudice so prevalent in 19th-century England, balked at the suggestion that he was Irish: "If a man is born in a stable, it doesn't mean he is a horse," he is reputed to have said.) A tall white cross marks the spot where Pope John Paul II addressed more than a million people during his 1979 visit to Ireland. Wild deer can be seen grazing in the many open spaces of the park, especially near here.

You're guaranteed to see wildlife at the **Dublin Zoo** (☎ 01/677–1425 ⊕ www.dublinzoo.ie), the third-oldest public zoo in the world, founded in 1830, and just a short walk beyond the People's Garden. The place looks a little dilapidated, but a five-year renovation is scheduled for completion in 2006. Animals from tropical climes are kept in unbarred enclosures, and Arctic species swim in the lakes close to the reptile house. Interestingly, the zoo is one of the few places in the world where lions will breed in captivity. Some 700 lions have been bred here since the 1850s, one of whom became familiar to movie fans the world over when MGM used him for its trademark. (As they will tell you at the zoo, he is in fact yawning in that familiar shot: an American lion had to be hired to roar and the "voice" was dubbed.) The African Plains section houses the zoo's larger species; the Nakuru Safari is a new 25-minute tour of this area. Pets Corner and City Farm has goats, guinea pigs, and lambs. In summer the Lakeside Café serves ice cream and drinks. Admission to the Dublin Zoo is €12.50. Hours are March through September, Monday through Saturday, 9:30 to 6, and Sunday, 10:30 to 6; from October through February, Monday through Saturday, 9:30 to 5, and Sunday, 10:30 to 5. ⊠ *Dublin West.*

Both the president of Ireland and the U.S. ambassador have official residences in the park (the president's is known as Aras an Uachtarain), but neither building is open to the public. Also within the park is a **visitor center** (☎ 01/677–0095 ⊕ www.heritageireland.ie), in the 17th-century fortified Ashtown Castle; it has information about the park's history, flora, and fauna. Admission to the center is €2.75. Hours are mid-March through September, daily 10 to 6; October, daily 10 to 5; November to mid-Marchy, weekends, from 10 to 5. ⊠ *Dublin West.*

need a break?

Ryan's Pub (⊠ 28 Parkgate St., Dublin West ☎ 01/677–6097), one of Dublin's last remaining genuine late-Victorian-era pubs, has changed little since its last remodeling—in 1896. It's right near the entrance to Phoenix Park.

WHERE TO EAT

By Anto
Howard

"Come in! Come in! Your dinners' poured out!" goes the old North Dublin joke, but, in truth, its description of Irish food as being best when hidden in soup wasn't so far off the mark for years. "Irish cuisine" used to be nothing more than a convenient way of grouping potatoes and stout under the same heading. The days, however, when critics bemoaned the *pot*luck of the Irish are thankfully gone. Today, be prepared to have your preconceptions overturned, and, on occasion, to be enthralled and very happily sated in the process. No longer does a pub-crawl turn up a better meal than one in a fancy restaurant. Dubliners now forgo heading to the "local" to down a pint after work because they've made reservations at the newest eateries and hippest showplaces (of course, the pubs and the pints come later in the evening). Happily, if these chowhounds are intent on enjoying the fruits of Ireland's gastronomic revolution, Dublin's best chefs have been leading the charge.

Month after month, these euro-toques continue to come up with new and glorious ways to abuse your waistline. Skewered John Dory wrapped in nori and served with a daring mint and pea risotto? Sautéed rabbit loin with Clonakilty black pudding? Or a dazzling dessert like lavender jelly with Cooleeney Camembert sauce? As these dishes reveal, Dublin's top cooks are determined to take advantage of the fact that Ireland has some of the best "raw materials" in the world. Given that it is a small island on which one is never farther than an hour and a half drive from the coast, it is not only its seaside restaurants that can claim to serve fish on the same day that it is landed. In addition, the freshest Limerick hams, tastiest Cork *crubins* (pigs' trotters), and most succulent Galway Bay oysters arrive in the city every day. But since young Dubliners love to travel the world, they have also demanded Indian curries, Thai chilies, and pan-Asian fireworks. Ethnic restaurants, as a result, have blossomed—so you can indulge your passion for superb French or Italian food one day, then enjoy fusion the next. This interest in far-flung food has heralded a new wave of internationally trained professionals who have stamped their own *blás* (Irish for "gloss") on traditional ingredients.

In 2004, the craze for minimalist, fusion eateries (usually with one-word names like "Dish" or "Citron") at last has started to die down and the old cream of the Irish dining scene has gently risen back to the top. Patrick Guilbaud, Chapter One, One Pico, and other high-end places prove the simple adage: great chefs make great restaurants. Many of these top eateries have started offering affordable fixed lunch menus, which are great bargains for the cash-conscious epicurean. A recent welcome phenomenon has been the arrival of little, family-run Italian joints with great food, no fuss, and real coffee, all at a good price. Bar Italia on the quays and the fantastically bustling Dunne and Crescenzi near Trinity are two of the best. To the usual array of ethnic choices—including Chinese, Japanese, and Indian—Dublin is adding even more exotica, including Montys of Kathmandu, a Nepalese spot in Temple Bar, and the Philippino Bahay Kubo.

The Irish dine later than Americans. They stay up later, too, and reservations are usually for tables not booked before 6:30 or 7 PM and up to around 11 PM. Lunch is generally served from 12:30 to 2:30. Pubs often serve food through the day—until 8:30 or 9 PM. Most pubs are family-friendly and welcome children until 7 PM. The Irish are an informal bunch, so smart casual dress is typical. The more formal restaurants, however, do expect you to wear a jacket and tie (noted below). And remember: Shorts and sneakers are out here.

Prices

A word of warning: forget about singing, you will pay for your supper in Dublin. High overhead and staffing costs have pushed up prices, especially in upscale places. The good news is that although Dublin doesn't have Starbucks, there are scores of inexpensive cafés serving excellent coffee, and often good sandwiches. Other eateries, borrowing trends from all around the world, serve inexpensive pizzas, focaccia, pitas, tacos, and wraps (which are fast gaining popularity over the sandwich). It's worthwhile to see if the restaurant of your choice offers an early-bird and/or pre- or post-theater menu, with significantly lower set prices at specific times, usually up to 7:30 PM and after the show. Value Added Tax (V. A.T.)—a 13.5% tax on food and a government excise tax on drinks—will automatically be added to your bill. Before paying, check to see whether a service charge has been included on your bill, which is often the case. If so, you can pay the entire bill with a credit card; if not, it's usual to leave a tip in cash (10% to 15%) if paying the main bill by credit card.

	WHAT IT COSTS in euros				
	$$$$	**$$$**	**$$**	**$**	**¢**
AT DINNER	over €29	€22–€29	€15–€22	€8–€15	under €8

Prices are per person for a main course at dinner.

North of the Liffey

Contemporary

$$$–$$$$
FodorsChoice
★

✕ **Chapter One.** If you spot the maitre d' strolling between tables and handing out tickets, you know you're at the hugely popular pre-theater special at Chapter One. Yes, they actually go pick up your tickets from the nearby Abbey or Gate theaters, and you can return after your show for dessert. The place gets its name from its location, downstairs in the vaulted, stone-wall basement of the Dublin Writers Museum; the natural stone and wood setting gives it a cozy cavelike feel. This contemporary French eatery is currently the culinary king of the Northside, thanks to chef-proprietor Ross Lewis's way with roasted venison with mustard and herb lentils, pancetta, chestnut dumplings, and roasted beetroot. Yeats himself would have loved the chivet of rabbit with bruised celery, lardons, organic carrots, and Dauphine potatoes, while Synge probably would have fancied the Dublin version of Proust's madeleine: rich bread-and-butter pudding, a favorite of working-class Irish mothers for generations, here turned into an outrageously filling work of art. ✉ *18–19*

Parnell Sq., Northside ☎ *01/873–2266* ⊕ *www.chapteronerestaurant. com* ⚱ *Reservations essential* ⊟ *AE, DC, MC, V* ⊘ *Closed Sun. and Mon. No lunch Sat.*

$$$–$$$$ ✕ **23.** Where now the glories of Babylon? It's a long time since O'Connell Street was the social center of Dublin and the Gresham Hotel was *the* place to be seen dining. But recent years have seen something of a comeback for the famous old hotel, and the ultra-modern 23 is a big part of that revival. The decor leaves some cold, but the blend of droplights, tubular tables, and contemporary art against the backdrop of a dramatic glass wall would certainly delight the readers of *Wallpaper.* The brasserie-style cooking makes use of local ingredients in seafood, duck, chicken, steak, and vegetarian dishes. The pavlova trio, crammed with raspberries, blueberries, and strawberries, is a firm favorite, and a short but varied wine list has been well thought out. The breakfast—buffet-style or from a menu that includes eggs and a full Irish breakfast—attracts early-rising tourists and locals. ⊠ *Gresham Hotel, 23 Upper O'Connell St., Northside* ☎ *01/817–6116* ⚱ *Reservations essential* ⊟ *AE, DC, MC, V* ⊘ *Closed Sun. No lunch.*

$$$ ✕ **Halo.** Judges from the nearby Four Courts rest their wigs on empty seats while the fashion crowd sits over multicolored drinks at this chic restaurant in the even more chic Morrison Hotel. With a soaring ceiling and minimalist decor, the dramatic two-story dining room, devised by fashion designer John Rocha, looks moody and mysterious by night, and a little forbidding by day. French and fusion are the two Fs favored by chef Jean-Michel Poulot, with seafood comprising his star dishes. Seared, cured salmon on creamed spinach with *pomme vapour* (mashed potatoes) with tomato and coriander is one of the ever-changing specialties. The baked oysters starter is imaginatively combined with good old green cabbage and lemon and chive sabayon. Desserts are miniature works of art on enormous china platters. ⊠ *Morrison Hotel, Ormond Quay, Northside* ☎ *01/887–2421* ⊕ *www.morrisonhotel.ie* ⊟ *AE, DC, MC, V.*

$–$$ ✕ **Harbour Master.** You just have to look out the window to understand why this big, airy restaurant and bar in the Irish Financial Services Centre north of the Liffey is so popular: It overlooks the serene and calming canal basin. At lunch the place is packed with stockbrokers and lawyers; dinner is more subdued. You can dine bistro-style at the cavernous bar, but it's better to head for the more spacious—and relaxing—dining area. Try the blackened salmon on a basil polenta mash, served with sautéed chorizo and poppy-seed yogurt dressing. ⊠ *Custom House Docks, Northside* ☎ *01/670–1688* ⊟ *AE, DC, MC, V.*

$ ✕ **The Vaults.** Come eat under the train station! Not exactly the best sales pitch you've ever heard—yet this wonderful, long-neglected space beneath Connolly Station was imaginatively revamped in 2002 to create one of the city's most fashionable dining spots. Cavernous arches, smooth Portland stone floors, striking furniture, and dramatic lighting create the background for a mostly young business set. Each of the vaults is decorated in its own style, ranging from hyper-modern to turn-of-the-century elegant. Cocktails are a specialty, although it's worth a visit for the food alone. The Italian chef makes everything from scratch, in-

ON THE MENU

T IS ONLY A DECADE SINCE *"ethnic" food in Dublin meant sitting at home in front of the TV with a very uninspired Chinese dish of sweet-and-sour chicken.* A flood of foreign restaurants has resuscitated the often staid and boring Dublin dining scene and forced native chefs to rethink their menus and reinvent old favorites.

The abundant high-quality produce the country is famous for is finally receiving the care and attention of world-class chefs in the capital city's restaurants. Salmon is mixed with smoked haddock for fish cakes served with anchovy and parsley butter; black pudding is butter-fried and covered in an apple compote; and Irish beef is spiced and topped with a tangy avocado salsa.

Even the humble potato is being shaped and transformed into potato cakes and boxty (potato-and-flour pancake), and colcannon—a traditional Irish dish with bacon and cabbage—is getting a nouvelle spin.

Being an agricultural country with a maritime climate, Ireland benefits from a copious supply of freshly grown and readily available produce and seafood. Excellent Irish beef, pork, ham, and lamb appear on almost every menu.

Keep an eye out, too, for seasonal specials, such as wild and farmed quail and pheasant. Rich seafood harvests mean you'll find fresh and smoked salmon, oysters, mussels, and shellfish in many guises—all vying with tender cuts of meat and an appetizing selection of quality vegetables.

Excellent dairy products are also essential to Irish cuisine. Dollops of fresh cream with home-baked desserts promise some exciting conclusions to these feasts—though you could also opt to finish a meal with a selection of native cheeses.

Leave room for the mature cheddars and luscious blue cheeses, the slightly sweet Dubliner, St. Tola goat's cheese from Clare, and Carrigburne Brie from Wexford—only a few of the many fine artisan cheeses produced around the country.

While you're in Dublin, do indulge at least once in the traditional Irish breakfast, which is often served all day. It includes rashers (bacon), sausages, black and white pudding (types of sausage), mushrooms, tomatoes, and a fried egg— with lots of traditional homemade brown and soda breads and the famous Irish creamery butter. You'll need a pot or two of tea to wash this down. Known as an "Ulster Fry" in Northern Ireland, this breakfast is often the biggest—and best— meal of the day.

cluding the pizza dough. A wide-ranging menu covers light snack options alongside more substantial dishes like the house pizza, a blend of tomato, mozzarella, prawns, red onion, and herbs. Be sure to leave room for the excellent homemade ice cream. Note that dinner is served only until 8. ⊠ *Harbourmaster Pl., Northside* ☎ *01/605–4700* ⊕ *www. thevaults.ie* ⌂ *Reservations essential* ▤ *AE, DC, MC, V.*

Irish

¢ ✕ **Soup Dragon.** This tiny café and take-out soup shop serves an astonishing array of fresh soups daily. Soups come in three sizes, and you can get vegetarian soup or soups with meat- or fish-based broth. Best bets include red pepper, tomato, and goat cheese soup; fragrant Thai chicken soup; and hearty mussel, potato, and leek soup. The friendly staff makes fine coffee and delicious smoothies. The cost of soup includes bread and a piece of fruit for dessert—an excellent value. ⊠ *168 Capel St., Northside* ☎ *01/872–3277* ⊟ *No credit cards* ⊘ *Closed Sun. No dinner.*

Italian

$–$$ ✕ **Il Vignardo.** Sometimes when it comes to dining, the where is more important than the what. Il Vignardo serves some of Dublin's tastiest cheap and cheerful pizzas and pasta, but it's the unique decor that elevates this place a little above the rest. The dramatically vaulted ceilings, painted with creeping vines and branches, burst into bloom as they rise from Tuscan columns and evoke thoughts of Italian vineyards and sunshine. Outside, the sheltered courtyard garden, a real oasis in a city center setting, is perfect for summer dining or just a little aperitif. The extra-hot Mexican special is a great pizza, while the penne entrecote is the best of the pastas. If you want to spend a little extra, try the veal il Vignardo, sliced and cooked in a white wine cream sauce. But who can resist the lasagna, served up with minced Irish beef? ⊠ *Hotel Isaccs, Store St., Northside* ☎ *01/855–3099* ⊟ *AE, DC, MC, V.*

Mediterranean

$–$$ ✕ **101 Talbot.** Sardi's it's not, but the 101 has that certain buzz that only comes from restaurants popular with the artistic and literary set. Conveniently close to the Abbey and Gate theaters, so there's no danger of missing a curtain call, this comfortable upstairs restaurant showcases an ever-changing exhibition of local artists' work. The creative contemporary food—with Mediterranean and Middle Eastern influences—uses fresh local ingredients. Try the roast pork fillet marinated in orange, ginger, and soy, served with fried noodles. The cashew and red-pepper *rissole* (turnover) with chili and ginger jam, served with wild and basmati rice, also impresses. Healthful options and several vegetarian choices make this a highly versatile restaurant. ⊠ *101 Talbot St., Northside* ☎ *01/874–5011* ☙ *Reservations essential* ⊟ *AE, DC, MC, V* ⊘ *Closed Sun. and Mon.*

City Center

American

★ $$$$ ✕ **Shanahans on the Green.** The management describes this as an "American-style steak house" and if they mean big steaks—Texas-big—they deliver. Happily, quantity doesn't necessarily diminish quality and Shanahans arguably serves the best beef in the country, all certified Irish Angus, of course. In point of fact, the only things "American" here are those humongous portions and the basement bar, the Oval Office, full of Americana and presidential paperwork. The building itself is an Irish Georgian glory, designed by Richard Cassels, Dublin's leading 18th-century architect. Glowing with gilded chandeliers and graced with a few marble fireplaces, this restored townhouse offers a sleekly elegant setting in which to chow down on some of the tenderest beef this side of Kobe (they cook it in a special high-temperature oven, searing the outside to keep the inside good and juicy). If steak doesn't float your boat, they also do a mean oven-braised John Dory with parsnip cream and confit of baby fennel. Oreo-cookie-crust cheesecake is the perfect way to finish off the feast but many will consider the decor—think sash windows, gilt mirrors, and plush carpets—rich enough. ⊠ *119 St. Stephen's Green, City Center* ☎ *01/407–0939* ⊕ *www.shanahans.ie* ⌕ *Reservations essential* ☐ *AE, DC, MC, V* ⊙ *No lunch Mon.–Thurs. and weekends.*

Café

¢   ✕ **Busyfeet & Coco Café.** This bustling, quirky café emphasizes good, wholesome food. Organic ingredients play a prominent role on a menu that's laden with delicious salads and sandwiches. Try the grilled goat cheese salad served with walnut-and-raisin toast and sun-dried-tomato tapenade on a bed of arugula. The delicious homemade-hummus sandwich—served on poppy-seed bread, and topped with roasted red and yellow peppers, red onions, and zucchini—is a must. ⊠ *41–42 S. William St., City Center* ☎ *01/671–9514* ☐ *No credit cards.*

Fodor'sChoice ★

Continental

★ $$$$ ✕ **Locks.** Situated near poet Patrick Kavanagh's favorite spot on the Grand Canal where "here by a lock Niagariously roars," a genuinely warm welcome awaits you at this adorabaly soigné country house–style restaurant. The dining room is all "Irish mother," meaning cozy and old-fashioned, with banquette seating, open fires, and starched table linens. Hearty portions are served on antique ironstone plates. The mouth-watering menu combines the best of peasant French fare with a modern Irish touch. Classic starters include Locks's special potato skins—dished up with prawns, tomato, and spinach and served with a fabulous hollandaise sauce—and excellent smoked salmon. The roast rack of lamb with ratatouille, pomme puree, and a rosemary jus is nonpareil in the city. ⊠ *1 Windsor Terr., Portobello, City Center* ☎ *01/ 454–3391* ⌕ *Reservations essential* ☐ *AE, DC, MC, V* ⊙ *Closed Sun. No lunch Sat.*

French

★ $$$$ ✕ **Thornton's.** If there has been something of a revolution in Irish cooking in the last decade then Kevin Thornton has been the movement's Lenin, and his permanently full restaurant is the Kremlin. Forget the stretched metaphors; if you're passionate about food, this place is a must. Thornton's cooking style is light, and his dishes are small masterpieces of structural engineering, piled almost dangerously high in towers of food. A highlight is the braised suckling pig served with trotter and loin in a *poitin* (Irish moonshine made from potatoes) sauce. Desserts range from banana ice cream to warm chocolate tartlet with raspberries. Sheridans of Dublin supplies the enormous selection of cheeses. The dining room is simple and elegant—there's little to distract you from the exquisite food. ⊠ *Fitzwilliam Hotel, St. Stephen's Green, City Center* ☎ *01/478–7000* ⊕ *www.fitzwilliam-hotel.com* ⌕ *Reservations essential* ☐ *AE, DC, MC, V* ⊙ *Closed Sun. and Mon.*

Where to Eat in Dublin

Killarney St.

Amiens St.

9 Connolly Station

Seville Pl.

Church Rd.

Lower Sheriff St.

Inner Dock

Upper Sheriff St.

0   1/4 mi

0   1/4 km

10 Georges Dock

Commons St.

New Wapping St.

Mayor St.

'ouse Quay
albot Mem.
r.

North Wall Quay

City Quay

River Liffey

ucester St.

Sir John Rogerson's Quay

Cardiff's La.

Lombard St. E.
Magennis Pl.

Westland Row

Pearse Station

Pearse St.

Hanover Quay

Grand Canal Dock

Macken St.

Grand Canal Quay

TO SOUTH WALL →

Ringsend Rd.

Fenian St.

Hogan Pl.

Lower Grand Canal St.

Merrion Sq. N.

Merrion Square

Lower Mount St.

Upper Grand Canal St.

South Lotts Rd.

Merrion Sq. S.

illiam La.

Lower Fitzwilliam St.
Upper Fitzwilliam St.

Upper Mount St.

Bath Av

Lower

54 James's Pl. **55**

Herbert St.

Percy Pl.

Northumberland Rd.

Upper Baggot St.

Herbert Pl.

Haddington Rd.

56 →

Lansdowne Park

Wilton Terrace

Upper Baggot St.

Lansdowne Rd.

Mespil Rd.

Pembroke Rd.

rleigh

Pembroke Lane

59 **60**

57

58

Burlington Rd.
Waterloo Lane
Waterloo Rd.
Heytesbury Lane
Wellington Lane
Raglan Rd.
Raglan Lane
Elgin Rd.
Pembroke Rd.

¢ ✕ **Lemon Crêpe and Coffee Co.** Avoid this place on Fat Tuesday (known as Pancake Tuesday in Ireland) because there will be a line halfway down the street. On any other day this tiny place has the best crepes in town, and hungry Dubliners know it. The space is compact, white, and minimalist. A few sidewalk tables—complete with an outdoor heater—make this a great spot for a tasty snack while you watch Dublin saunter by. Ham, cheese, bacon, and spinach are a few of the savory filling choices. Favorite sweet fillings include banana, Nutella, cream, and the old classic, lemon juice and sugar. Take-out service is swift. ⊠ *66 S. William St., City Center* ☏ *01/672–9044* 🖃 *No credit cards.*

Indian

$–$$ ✕ **Jaipur.** Call to mind all the stereotypes of bad, production-line Indian restaurants. Then consign them to the flames, for Jaipur is something different altogether. A spacious room with a sweeping staircase and contemporary furnishings reflects Jaipur's modern, cutting-edge approach to Indian cuisine. Mixed with traditional dishes, such as chicken tikka masala, are more unusual preparations, such as *rara gosdh* (lamb slowly cooked with black-eyed peas). The delightful *karwari* is a sweet and sour butterfish in a tamarind-flavored broth redolent of coastal-south-Indian spices. Dishes can be toned down or spiced up to suit your palate, and service is courteous and prompt. Another plus: the wine list is well thought out. ⊠ *41 S. Great George's St., City Center* ☏ *01/677–0999* 🍴 *Reservations essential* 🖃 *AE, MC, V.*

$–$$ ✕ **Khyber Tandoori.** The Khyber Tandoori doorman, dressed in traditional colorful costume complete with a dashing white turban, has become something of a living landmark in modern Dublin. A short walk from St. Stephen's Green, this gem of a restaurant specializes in Pakistani cuisine but also serves a broad selection of Indian dishes. Try the *shami* (Syrian) kebabs—dainty, spiced patties of minced lamb and lentils—or *kabuli chicken tikka shashlik* (marinated, diced chicken with onions and red and green peppers), which comes bright red and sizzling on an iron platter. Settle in and admire the richly embroidered wall hangings and the great gusts of steam coming from the tandoori oven in the glassed-in area. ⊠ *44–45 S. William St., City Center* ☏ *01/670–4855* 🖃 *AE, DC, MC, V* ☺ *No lunch Sun.*

Italian

$$–$$$ ✕ **Il Primo.** Eccentric, gregarious Dieter Bergman likes to run his little two-story Italian restaurant like an intimate dinner party. So don't be surprised if he joins you at your table for a chat. Old wooden tables and chairs give the two small dining rooms a casual feel, and the friendly, if cramped, surroundings attract a devoted clientele. The *gnocchi di patate*, potato dumplings with tomato, spinach, and ricotta, is typical of the hearty fare. For the more adventurous the *scaloppina di vitello*—veal with a Madeira cream sauce served with mash, prosciutto, and parmesan shavings—is a must. The wine list is, to quote a local phrase, as long as your arm. ⊠ *Montague St. off Harcourt St., City Center* ☏ *01/478–3373* 🖃 *AE, DC, MC, V* ☺ *No lunch weekends.*

¢–$ ✕ **Dunne and Crescenzi.** Nothing succeeds like success. So popular is this classy little Italian joint just off Nassau Street that they've expanded into the premises two doors down. Pity the poor little coffee shop in between

FodorśChoice
★

trying to compete with the unpretentious brilliance of this brother-and-sister restaurant and deli. The menu couldn't be simpler: *paninis* (sandwiches), antipasti, a single pasta special, and desserts. But the all-Italian kitchen staff work wonders with high-quality imported ingredients. The antipasto *misto,* an assortment of thinly sliced Parma ham, three types of salami, sun-dried tomatoes, cheeses, peppers in olive oil, and artichoke hearts makes a great light lunch. A couple of long tables make it perfect for a group, and the hundreds of bottles of wine on shelves cover every inch of the walls. ⊠ *14 S. Fredrick St., City Center* ☎ *01/677–3815* ⊟ *AE, MC, V.*

¢–$ ✕ **The Steps of Rome.** Discerning natives flock to this place for a cheap lunch, or a good take-out. Just a few steps from Grafton Street, this Italian eatery is also popular for a late-night bite. Slices of delicious, thin-crust pizza, with all the traditional toppings, are the main attraction. The *fungi* (mushroom) pizza is particularly good. The few tables are usually full, but it's worth waiting around for the classic Italian pasta dishes. Some diners just opt for the fresh salads with focaccia. Follow it all with cheesecake or tiramisu, and good strong espresso. ⊠ *1 Chatham Ct., City Center* ☎ *01/670–5630* ⊟ *No credit cards.*

Japanese

$–$$ ✕ **Yamamori.** Dublin's young and mobile folk went noodle-mad a few years ago and Yamamori jumped to the top of the list for these ramen addicts. The open plan and family-style tables have kept it popular with the buzz crowd. The meals-in-a-bowl are a splendid slurping experience, and although you'll be supplied with a small Chinese-style soup spoon, the best approach is with chopsticks. The *yasai yaki soba,* Chinese-style noodles with Asian vegetables and egg, garnished with menma and spring onions is a favorite example. You can also get sushi and sashimi, plus delicious chicken teriyaki. ⊠ *71–72 S. Great George's St., City Center* ☎ *01/475–5001* ⊟ *AE, MC, V.*

$ ✕ **Wagamama.** Canteen food wasn't like this at your school. Modeled on a Japanese canteen, Wagamama, with its long wooden tables and benches and high ceilings with exposed metal piping, ensures a unique communal dining experience. It attracts a young, loud crowd and is constantly busy. Formal courses aren't acknowledged—food is served as soon as it's ready, and appetizers and main courses arrive together. *Edamame*—steamed and salted green soybeans in the pod—are a delicious starter and great fun to pop open and eat. Choose from filling bowls of *cha han* (fried rice with chicken, prawns, and vegetables) or chili beef ramen, and wash it down with fresh fruit or vegetable juice. There's also a fine selection of beers and sakes for the less abstentious. ⊠ *S. King St., City Center* ☎ *01/478–2152* ⊟ *AE, DC, MC, V.*

Pan-Asian

$–$$ ✕ **Mao.** Everything is Asian-fusion at this bustling café, from the little Andy Warhol pastiche of Chairman Mao on the washroom door to the eclectic mix of dishes on the menu, which combine Thai, Vietnamese, and other Southeast Asian elements. Top choices include the Malaysian chicken, chili squid, and the *nasi goreng* (Indonesian fried rice with chicken and shrimp). Go early to be sure of a seat. ⊠ *2 Chatham Row, City Center* ☎ *01/670–4899* ⚎ *Reservations not accepted* ⊟ *MC, V.*

Vegetarian

¢ ✕**Nude.** One-word titles for restaurants and cafés were all the rage in Dublin about five years ago. Many of them have fallen by the wayside, but Nude, a sleek, eco-friendly fast-food café, has been such a success that owner Norman Hewson—brother of U2's Bono—has opened another branch for takeout only on Upper Leeson Street. The canteen-style tables set the extremely casual atmosphere—don't be surprised if your neighbor strikes up a conversation. You order at the counter and someone delivers to your table in double-quick time. The menu is mostly vegetarian, and everything on it is made with organic and free-range ingredients. Choose from homemade soups and vegetable wraps (hummus and peppers is a classic), smoothies, and fresh-squeezed juices. ✉ *21 Suffolk St., City Center* ☎ *01/677–4804* ▭ *DC, MC, V* ⊙ *Closed weekends. No dinner.*

Southside

Contemporary

$$–$$$ ✕**Dish.** "Genetically modified" are two dirty words you never hear within the confines of Gerard Foote's trendy Southside eatery. Organic beef, lamb, and vegetables, fresh daily fish, and true free-range chickens—Dish's reputation has been built on the quality of its local ingredients as much as the considerable skill of its chef. The large white room with sanded floorboards and long narrow mirrors impresses with its simple, uncluttered space. Dishes range from grilled Clonakilty black pudding (sausage with dried pig's blood) with roasted red pepper and borlotti beans to roasted monkfish with bacon, Savoy cabbage, beetroot, and cream. It's popular for Sunday brunch, and the weekday lunch is an excellent value. ✉ *146 Upper Leeson St., Southside* ☎ *01/664–2135* ⊕ *www.tribeca.ie* ⌖ *Reservations essential* ▭ *AE, DC, MC, V.*

★ $–$$$ ✕**La Stampa.** "Like eating on stage at the Met in the middle of Act Two" is how one wag described the sheer opulence of the jaw-dropping dining room at this classic French brasserie. Roman urns, little bronze cupids, busts of emperors, huge Regency mirrors, elaborate candelabras, and a large stained-glass skylight create a gloriously over-the-top Neoclassical ambience under the intricately plastered high ceilings. Such an operatic setting gives every meal a sense of fun and occasion. The food is in danger of being upstaged, but try the beautiful rack of organic lamb with braised beans, tomatoes, and rosemary jus; roasted scallops with artichoke mash and tomato vinaigrette; or giant prawns served with garlic or mango mayonnaise. Expect brisk but friendly service. ✉ *35 Dawson St., Southside* ☎ *01/677–8611* ▭ *AE, DC, MC, V.*

Continental

★ $$–$$$ ✕**Brownes Brasserie.** "Dress to Impress" would seem to be the motto of this established brasserie; as soon as you walk up the granite steps into the small drawing room, the eclectic, luxurious decor almost assaults you. Italian-style friezes, jewel-color walls covered in gilded mirrors, velvet-draped tall windows, and crystal chandeliers all vie for your attention. In a sort of culinary fantasy, the food matches the decor in richness and variety. Favorites include char-grilled brochette of swordfish served on a bed of garlic potato with garlic puree and salsa verde, and escalopes of veal marinated in Parma ham and garlic, served with globe artichokes, linguine, and saffron cream. The lavender-scented crème brûlée is a lovely finish to a meal. ⊠ *22 St. Stephen's Green, Southside* ☎ *01/638–3939* ⊕ *www.brownesdublin.com* ⌂ *Reservations essential* ▤ *AE, DC, MC, V* ⊘ *No lunch Sat.*

French

$$$$
Fodor's Choice
★

✕ **Patrick Guilbaud.** The words "Dublin's finest restaurant" often share the same breath as the name of this do-be-impressed place on the ground floor of the Merrion Hotel. The menu is described as French, but the genius at Guilbaud's lies in his occasional daring use of traditional Irish ingredients—so often abused and taken for granted—to create the unexpected. With the eponymous chef in charge, you can always expect superb cooking. His best dishes are simple—and flawless: Châlons duck à l'orange, Connemara lobster in season, and braised pig's trotters. Follow that, if you can, with the *assiette au chocolat* (a tray of five hot and cold chocolate desserts). The ambience is just as delicious—if you're into modern art, that is. There are no Georgian Gainsboroughs to be found here. Instead, you'll think you've wandered into Manhattan's Soho, thanks to the marvelously lofty dining room and minimalist art hanging on the walls (the Roderick O'Connor and Louis LeBrocquys are all from the owner's private collection). Nearly as impressive is the 70-page wine list, the view of the Merrion's manicured gardens, and the lunch special for under 30 euros. Soaring white vaults and empty white walls won't make you feel warm and cozy but you can always go somewhere else for that. What you won't find anywhere else is Guilbaud. ⊠ *21 Upper Merrion St., Southside* ☎ *01/676–4192* ⊕ *www.merrionhotel.com/* ⌂ *Reservations essential* ▤ *AE, DC, MC, V* ⊘ *Closed Sun. and Mon.*

Irish

$$–$$$$

✕ **Dobbins.** Don't be deceived by the sawdust on the floor and the simple furnishings: the combination of cozy booth seating, friendly service, and classic bistro food makes Dobbins popular with businesspeople. In contrast to the intimate darkness of the main dining room, the little conservatory with sliding roof is great on a warm summer evening. Owner John O'Byrne presides over an impressive cellar with hundreds of wines from around the world. Tempura of prawns is a popular starter; boned brace of quail with black pudding and foie gras stuffing is a typical entrée. There's valet parking, and the staff is expert at summoning taxis. ⊠ *15 Stephens La., off Mount St., Southside* ☎ *01/676–4679* ⌂ *Reservations essential* ▤ *AE, DC, MC, V* ⊘ *Closed Sun. and Mon. No lunch Sat.*

$$–$$$

✕ **One Pico.** Grown women have been known to swoon when chef/owner Eamonn O'Reilly walks into the dining room of his little restaurant tucked away in a quiet lane only a few minutes from Stephen's Green. Eamonn cuts quite a dash, but it's his sophisticated, daring, contemporary cuisine that tends to seduce visitors to One Pico. Try the incredible parsley and garlic soup with poached quail egg to start. Dishes such as corn-fed chicken on kale-and-bacon mashed potatoes demonstrate a savvy use of native ingredients. Follow this with the baked chèvre cheesecake garnished with praline chocolate and orange confit. As is usual with Dublin's

PUB FOOD

MOST PUBS SERVE FOOD at lunchtime, many throughout the day and into the early evening. This is an inexpensive way to eat out, and the quality of the food is often quite good.

Davy Byrne's. James Joyce immortalized this pub in Ulysses. Nowadays it's more akin to a cocktail bar than a Dublin pub, but it's good for fresh and smoked salmon, salads, fresh oysters, and a hot daily special. ⊠ 21 Duke St., Southside ☎ 01/671–1298 ▤ AE, MC, V.

The Odeon. The converted main building of Harcourt Street's old railway station houses this large, modern bar. Both the lunch and dinner menus include fresh panini, beef-and-Guinness stew, chicken wings, and homemade sausages. Sunday brunch is served between noon and 5. ⊠ 57 Harcourt St., Southside ☎ 01/478–2088 ▤ AE, MC, V.

The Old Stand. This pub, one of the oldest in Dublin, is conveniently close to Grafton Street, and serves grilled food, including steaks. ⊠ 37 Exchequer St., Southside ☎ 01/677–7220 ▤ AE, MC, V.

Stag's Head. The most beautiful pub in Dublin, period. Built in 1895, it is a Victorian-era mahogany masterpiece. Serving one of Dublin's best pub lunches, this place is a favorite among Trinity students. ⊠ 1 Dame Ct., Southside ☎ 01/679–3701 ▤ No credit cards.

Zanzibar. This spectacular, immense bar on the Northside looks as though it might be more at home in downtown Marrakech. Laze away an afternoon in one of the wicker chairs and enjoy hearty pastas, burgers, salads, and cocktails. ⊠ 34–35 Lower Ormond Quay, Northside ☎ 01/878–7212 ▤ AE, MC, V.

luxe eateries, the fixed-price lunch menu offers great value. ⊠ 5–6 Molesworth Pl., off Schoolhouse La., Southside ☎ 01/676–0300 ⚐ Reservations essential ▤ AE, DC, MC, V ☉ Closed Sun.

¢–$ ✕ **Kilkenny Kitchen.** Take a break from shopping and sightseeing at this big self-service restaurant on the upper floor of the Kilkenny Shop. Homemade soup, casseroles, cold meats, and salads are arranged on a long buffet, along with lots of tasty breads and cakes. Try to get a table by the window overlooking the playing fields of Trinity College. Lunchtime is busy, but Kilkenny is very pleasant for morning coffee or afternoon tea. ⊠ 5–6 Nassau St., Southside ☎ 01/677–7066 ▤ AE, DC, MC, V.

Italian

¢–$ ✕ **Milano.** The big open kitchen at this bright cheerful place turns out tasty flashy pizzas, with such combinations as tomato and mozzarella, ham and eggs, Cajun with prawns and Tabasco, spinach and egg, and ham and anchovies. There are also simple salads such as tomato and mozzarella with dough balls, and some baked pasta dishes. This is a good place to dine late, with last orders at midnight. Three other branches have opened: one in Temple Bar, another on Bachelor's Walk, and the third in the Irish Financial Services Centre. ⊠ 38 Dawson St., Southside ☎ 01/670–7744 ▤ AE, DC, MC, V.

Mediterranean/French

$$-$$$ ✕ **Bruno's.** Experienced French-born restaurateur Bruno Berta has a hit on his hands with his French-Mediterranean bistro under Mitchell's wine shop across the road from the side door of the Shelbourne Hotel. The design is all sleek lines and track lighting, and a chanteuse often entertains diners from a quiet corner. Caramelized cauliflower soup with blue cheese and walnut wonton is a starter that hints at the rich, adventurous nature of the cuisine to come. Confit of pork belly with red cabbage, apple, and tarragon sauce is a truly hearty entrée. Pan-fried John Dory with Jerusalem artichoke, baby fennel, and tarragon nut butter is a little—only a little—lighter on the stomach. Keep room for the bitter-lemon-pudding dessert. The new Lotus Lounge is Bruno's stylish cocktail bar. ⊠ *21 Kildare St., Southside* ☎ *01/662–3856* ▭ *AE, DC, MC, V* ✆ *Closed Sun.*

Pan-Asian

$$-$$$ ✕ **Chai-Yo.** Be educated while you eat! There is always something thrilling about getting close-up and watching a master at work. The Japanese teppan-yaki area at this classy pan-Asian restaurant on bustling Baggot Street, where the chef cooks your food right on your tabletop, is a feast for the eye as well as the palate. Choose from a selection of scallops, sea bass, steak, teriyaki chicken, and prawns, and watch as a beautiful grilled dish is whipped up before your eyes. The white walls and dark lacquered furnishings give Chai-Yo a serene ambience, enhanced by the delicate glassware and fine, green-washed-porcelain plates. The menu picks the best from Chinese, Thai, and Japanese dishes. The deep-fried crispy quail eggs are a tasty starter, and the king scallops in Thai chili oil with scallion and onion is the place's most popular main course. ⊠ *100 Lower Baggot St., Southside* ☎ *01/662–2767* ▭ *AE, DC, MC, V* ✆ *No lunch Sun.*

$-$$$ ✕ **Diep le Shaker.** Comfortable high-back chairs, pristine table linen, and elegant stemware make this big, flamboyant Thai restaurant a lovely, and posh, place to dine. It's a place where half the reason for going is to see and be seen. Try the steamed scallops and ginger, or lobster in garlic pepper and Thai herbs. Don't be surprised to see people ordering champagne with their meals—there's a permanent party vibe here, which attracts Ireland's wealthy in droves. It's slightly off the beaten track, on a narrow lane off Pembroke Street. ⊠ *55 Pembroke La., Southside* ☎ *01/661–1829* ▭ *AE, DC, MC, V* ✆ *Closed Sun.*

Temple Bar

American–Casual

$-$$ ✕ **Elephant & Castle.** The Elephant was long established in Temple Bar before the Tiger (Celtic, that is) changed the neighborhood forever. Large windows are great for people-watching in the city's trendiest area, but "nothing fancy" would be a good motto for the traditional American food. Charcoal-grilled burgers, salads, omelets, sandwiches, and pasta comprise the much-thumbed menu. Sunday brunch is always packed. The portions are some of the most generous in Dublin. When the service is good, the turnover tends to be quick, although you may be inclined to linger. New Yorkers take note: yes, this is a cousin of the restaurant of the same name in Greenwich Village. ✉ *18 Temple Bar, Temple Bar* ☎ *01/ 679–3121* ♙ *Reservations not accepted* ▤ *AE, DC, MC, V.*

¢–$$ ✕ **Bad Ass Café.** If you want to make a Dublin native wince, mention with excitement that Sinéad O'Connor used to wait tables at this lively café in a converted warehouse between the Central Bank and Ha'penny Bridge. (A "Rock 'n Stroll" tour plaque notes O'Connor's past here.) Old-fashioned cash shuttles whiz around the ceiling of the barnlike space, with bare floors and primary colors inside and out. You can indulge in some great people-watching behind the wall of glass here. The food—mainly pizzas and burgers—is unexceptional, but the Bad Ass can be a lot of fun and appetites of all ages love it. ✉ *9–11 Crown Alley, Temple Bar* ☎ *01/671–2596* ▤ *AE, MC, V.*

Cajun–Creole

$–$$ ✕ **Tante Zoe's.** The Deep South comes to Dublin with this dark, bustling restaurant, a firm favorite with vacationers and large parties. Images from the heyday of the antebellum South, bamboo, and dark wood set a broody, atmospheric scene for colorful Creole cooking. Seafood fans shouldn't miss the cajun popcorn—a mountain of spicy baby shrimp coated in bread crumbs and served with a creamy tomato mayonnaise. Spicy blackened chicken with savory rice is another favorite. Desserts are reliably good, particularly the Mississippi mud pie. ✉ *1 Crow St., Temple Bar* ☎ *01/ 679–4407* ♙ *Reservations essential* ▤ *AE, DC, MC, V.*

Contemporary

★ $$$$ ✕ **The Tea Room.** Situated in the Clarence Hotel, you can sit around all day and hope that Bono and the boys of U2—they own the joint after all—might turn up for a quick snack. Other stars of stage and screen often stay at the hotel and stop in at the Tea Room. Mimimalistically hued in golden oak, eggshell white, and light yellows, the high-ceilinged room is a perfect stage for off-duty celebs. The contrast between this high-vaulted cocoon and busy Essex Street—whose madding crowds can be glimpsed through the double-height windows—is nowhere else as dramatic. Drama is also found on the newer-than-now nouvelle menu. You can opt for either adventurous specials—Spatchcock Quail, with pea pureé, truffled wild mushroom, and pistachio vinaigrette, anyone?—or such consistently good, typically mouth-watering delights as the pan-fried fois gras with caramelized onion tatin, "wicked apple" cider, and muscat raisins or the risotto of Carlingford mussels and courgettes. Obviously, the menu is as chic as the customers. ✉ *Clarence Hotel, 6–8 Wellington Quay, Temple Bar* ☎ *01/407–0813* ⊕ *www.theclarence.ie* ♙ *Reservations essential* ▤ *AE, DC, MC, V.*

$$–$$$$ ✕ **Mermaid Café.** Hope you don't mind sharing your dinner conversation with the people next to you. The Mermaid has the simple, crowded feel of a very up-market canteen, with large tables set close together and casual, but classy, service. One of the chef/owners dabbles in fine art, and his tastes in this area are reflected in his artistic and decorative style of bistro cooking. It's not cheap, but the food is reliable. Lunch is an exceptional value—piquant crab cakes, huge hearty seafood casseroles, ribeye steak, or radicchio and melted goat cheese. Attention to detail and a thoughtful wine list make this modest restaurant with tall windows look-ing onto busy Dame Street one of the most popular eateries in Temple Bar. ⊠ *69 Dame St., Temple Bar* ☎ *01/670–8236* ⊟ *MC, V.*

★ **$$–$$$** ✕ **Eden.** One of Dublin's hippest places, Eden is where arty and media types are likely to gather to talk about.well, themselves. It has an open kitchen and a high wall of glass through which you can observe one of Temple Bar's main squares. Patio-style doors lead to an outdoor eating area—a major plus in a city with relatively few alfresco dining spots. On weekend nights in summer you can enjoy an outdoor movie in Meeting House Square while you eat. Seasonal menus are in vogue here, but standout dishes include duck leg confit with lentils, and mus-tard-crusted braised hock of ham served with *champ* (creamy, buttery mashed potatoes with scallions). Desserts include rhubarb crème brûlée and homemade ice creams and sorbets. ⊠ *Meeting House Sq., Temple Bar* ☎ *01/670–5372* ⊕ *www.edenrestaurant.ie* ⌢ *Reservations essen-tial* ⊟ *AE, DC, MC, V.*

French

★ **$$$–$$$$** ✕ **Les Frères Jacques.** A lot of restaurants call themselves French, but this elegant eatery next to the Olympia Theatre positively reeks of Gallic panache. Old prints of Paris and Deauville hang on the green-papered walls, and the French waiters, dressed in white Irish linen and black bow ties, exude a European charm without being excessively formal. Expect traditional French cooking that nods to the seasons. Seafood is a major attraction, and lobster (fished right from the tank—a "plus" that peo-ple with delicate sensibilities will find a definite minus) is typically roasted and flambéed with Irish whiskey. Others prefer the roast lamb tian with aubergine, courgette and thyme. Also recommended are the seasonal game specialties. A piano player performs Friday and Satur-day evenings and on the occasional weeknight. ⊠ *74 Dame St., Tem-ple Bar* ☎ *01/679–4555* ⌢ *Reservations essential* ⊟ *AE, MC, V* ☺ *Closed Sun. No lunch Sat.*

Italian

$–$$$ ✕ **Osteria Romano.** Learn Italian for free! Simply book a table and eaves-drop on the people next to you at this cheerful eatery where members of Dublin's Italian community congregate in the evenings to enjoy au-thentic Roman cuisine and lament the Irish weather. Specialties include *melanzane parmigiani,* a delicious dish of baked eggplant and cheese, and the excellent cream-based pastas, such as spaghetti Alfredo and car-bonara. Beware of finishing the meal with too many flaming *sambucas* (anise-flavored, semisweet Italian liqueurs). The best table, by the win-dow, overlooks the street. ⊠ *5 Crow St., Temple Bar* ☎ *01/670–8662* ⊟ *AE, DC, MC, V.*

¢–$ ✕ **Milano.** Like the original Milano eatery on the Southside, in Dublin's Georgian Heart, this branch turns out flashy pizzas, salads, and pasta dishes. ⊠ *19 Essex St. E, Temple Bar* ☎ *01/670–3384* ⊟ *AE, DC, MC, V.*

Nepalese

$–$$ ✕ **Montys of Kathmandu.** Montys proudly declares itself the "only Nepalese restaurant in Dublin." Was there ever any doubt? The bland decor is nothing to write home about, but the food at this little eatery in the middle of hyper-modern Temple Bar is as authentic as it is unique. *Poleko* squid—lightly spiced and barbecued in a tandoori oven and served in a sizzler; or lamb *Choila*—lamb with fresh chilies, ginger, garlic, herbs, and a dash of red wine—are the more adventurous starters. For a main course try *Mo Mo*, dumplings served with Mo Mo chutney, a favorite street dish in Kathmandu. The wine cellar is surprisingly varied. ⊠ *28 Eustace St., Temple Bar* ☎ *01/670–4911* ▭ *AE, DC, MC, V* ⊘ *No lunch Sun.*

The Grand Canal & Ballsbridge

Contemporary

$$$–$$$$ ✕ **Seasons.** The Four Seasons group prides itself on luxury service and attention to detail, and you should expect no less at the Dublin branch of the hotel's restaurant, with its large, slightly overwhelming, silver-service dining room. But this place is relatively new and has taken a little while to find its feet in and out of the kitchen. Highly dramatic dishes creatively incorporate Irish, often organic, ingredients. A starter of roasted scallops, cauliflower purée, and raisin-and-caper dressing might be followed by roasted loin and braised shank of lamb with sauce *paloise* (hollandaise flavored with mint). Sommelier Simon Keegan is one of the best in the country. Sunday brunch has become a ritual for many well-to-do Dublin families. ⊠ *Four Seasons Hotel, Simmonscourt Rd., Ballsbridge* ☎ *01/665–4642* ⌣ *Reservations essential* ▭ *AE, DC, MC, V.*

★ $$$ ✕ **O'Connells.** When it comes to cooking, pedigree can count. Owner Tom O'Connell is a brother to Ireland's favorite celebrity chef, Darina Allen, famed for her "slow food" Ballymaloe Cookery School in Cork. Tom follows the family blueprint by showcasing locally produced meats and game which can be traced back to its source (in many cases, an individual farm). Add to this a focus on fresh Irish produce and baked goods cooked in a unique wood-fired oven and you have the makings of a feast that is deliriously, quintessentially Irish. Spiced beef is prepared according to an old Cork recipe, salmon fillet is "hot smoked" by the restaurant itself, while Ashe's Annascaul Black Pudding is handmade on the Dingle peninsula. You can also try the spit-roasted duck or the monkfish with a lemon and garlic sauce, and an omelet made from organic eggs from free-range chickens, peppers, zucchini, and a sweet chili sauce. A tremendous selection of fresh breads is on display in the open kitchen, which turns into a buffet for breakfast and lunch. The cheese board is a who's-who of Irish farmhouse cheeses, including the Ferguson family's tangy Gubbeen. Serving as a cool backdrop, O'Connell's vast modern space is beautifully fitted out with sleek timber paneling and floor-to-ceiling windows. ⊠ *Merrion Rd., Ballsbridge* ☎ *01/647–3304* ⊕ *www.oconnellsballsbridge.com* ▭ *AE, DC, MC, V.*

French

$ ✕ **French Paradox.** Like the people of the south of France that inspired the place, relaxed but stylish would best describe decor and dining at this little restaurant set over a wine shop. French Paradox has found a real niche in the Dublin scene. Wine buffs, Francophiles, and gourmets flock here for the hearty traditional fare and Mediterranean environment. Share the *assiette le fond de barrique,* a selection of charcuterie, pâté, and cheese, or perhaps indulge in a smoked-duck salad or a selection from the foie gras menu. Select a nice bottle from the ground-floor wine shop (mostly French labels) and sip it in situ for a mere €8 corkage fee. Seating is limited. ⊠ *53 Shelbourne Rd., Ballsbridge* ☎ *01/660–4068* ⚑ *Reservations essential* ☰ *AE, MC, V* ⊙ *Closed Sun.*

Philippine

$–$$ ✕ **Bahay Kubo.** Don't always believe what you read. The very basic English translations on the menu fail miserably to capture the excitement and diversity of the dishes at Ireland's only Philippine restaurant. Persevere and you'll find a fine selection of authentic Philippine cooking with touches of Chinese and Malaysian cuisines. Chicken, beef, and prawns all feature heavily, with red-curry chicken in coconut milk the most popular choice with regulars. Desserts have been brought in frozen, so it's best to stick to starters and entrées and finish up with a coffee. The starched white linen and pale-wood flooring give the place an open and light feel. ⊠ *14 Bath Ave., Ballsbridge* ☎ *01/660–5572* ⚑ *Reservations essential* ☰ *AE, MC, V* ⊙ *Closed Mon. No lunch Sat.–Wed.*

Dublin West

Irish

¢   ✕ **Burdock's.** Old man Burdock has moved on and the place hasn't been the same since. But the hordes still join the inevitable queue at Dublin's famous takeout fish-and-chips shop, right next door to the Lord Edward pub. You can eat in the gardens of St. Patrick's Cathedral, a 5-minute walk away. ⊠ *2 Werburgh St., Dublin West* ☎ *01/454–0306* ☰ *No credit cards.*

Italian

¢–$ ✕ **Bar Italia.** We hope you're not shy about being seen eating, because the front of tiny Bar Italia is a sheer wall of glass that looks out onto the Liffey and the Civic Offices at Wood Quay. If the weather is good, snag one of the tables on the patio and grin at the office workers trudging back to work after lunch. The menu is short and simple, but everything on it is guaranteed to be fresh and cooked like your mother back in Naples would have done. The minestrone soup is, without question, the best in Ireland, and the melt-on-your-tongue gnocchi is served in a few different sauces. People travel miles to have their coffee here and the house wines never let you down. ⊠ *Essex Quay, Dublin West* ☎ *01/679–5128* ☰ *No credit cards.*

The Liberties

Café

¢   ✕ **Gallic Kitchen.** Canny Dubliners make regular pilgrimages to Sarah Webb's bakery, where some of the best pastries in town are available daily. There's no seating in this powerhouse patisserie, but long counters allow space for perching your coffee and tucking into the finest sweet and savory treats. Pop in for morning coffee and pear tart; for lunch try quiche or salmon roulade with homemade salsa; and take afternoon tea with a scrumptious scone. Expect queues at lunchtime, and be sure to buy in bulk for the tastiest take-out picnic in town. ✉ *49 Francis St., The Liberties* ☎ *01/454–4912* ☰ *No credit cards* ⊘ *Closed Sun. No dinner.*

Russian

$$–$$$ ✕ **Old Dublin.** The Russians understand the wonder of the potato, so it's no surprise that this brasserie-style restaurant near St. Patrick's Cathedral has been a Dublin success. It specializes in Russian and Scandinavian food, and in the evening, glowing fires warm the cozy-but-elegant low-ceiling rooms, and candles light the tables. Blini, borscht, chicken Kiev, and beef Stroganoff figure on the menu, along with a few Irish staples such as roasted lamb and fresh baked salmon. One fine surprise on the menu is planked sirloin Hussar, a steak baked between two oak planks, and served on an oak platter with salad and sweet pickle. ✉ *90–91 St. Francis St., Dublin West* ☎ *01/454–2028* ☰ *AE, DC, MC, V* ⊘ *Closed Sun. No lunch Mon., Tues., and Sat.*

Phoenix Park & Environs

Eclectic

$–$$$ ✕ **Nancy Hands.** It's a fine line to walk; re-create tradition without coming across like a theme bar. Nancy Hands just about pulls it off. A galleylike room juxtaposes old wood, raw brick, and antiques with contemporary art to create a convivial, cozy dining area. The bar food is good, but the upstairs restaurant operates on a more serious level. Specialties include Flanagan's Twist—a mousseline of scallop and crab encased in fresh salmon—and a Mediterranean skewer laden with succulent chicken and beef. The menu includes Thai- and Japanese-style dishes, too. Numerous wines are served by the glass, and the selection of spirits is one of the most impressive in the country. ✉ *30–32 Parkgate St., Dublin West* ☎ *01/677–0149* ⟁ *Reservations essential* ☰ *AE, DC, MC, V.*

WHERE TO STAY

Lost in a soft swell of handsewn linen and fine cotton quilts, you awaken. Your eyes adjust to the morning sunshine streaming in the great half-moon windows as it plays on your room's glittering chandelier, the dawn's-early-gold plasterwork, and Queen Anne chairs. The light draws you to the window and, still blinking, you look onto a perfect Georgian square, surrounded by Neoclassical town houses every bit as exquisite as the one you are in. It's early morning, the traffic is sparse, and, for a moment, you could be back in the "gorgeous eighteenth," those magical hundred years that saw Dublin transformed from ugly duckling to the envy of Europe.

At this moment, it is quite possible to feel that the 18th century lives on in Dublin. If you're lucky enough to stay at one of the classy hotels and elegant B&Bs located in former Georgian town houses on both sides of the Liffey, you'll quickly realize that entering one of these little domestic palaces really is a trip back in time. But this does not mean the 20th century has not arrived. "An absolute avalanche of new hotels" is how the *Irish Times* characterized Dublin's recent hotel boom. New lodgings have sprung up all over the city, including the much-talked-about Westin at College Green, and a few in Ballsbridge, an inner "suburb" that's a 20-minute walk from the city center.

Dublin has a decent selection of inexpensive accommodations, including many moderately priced hotels with basic but agreeable rooms. Many B&Bs, long the mainstay of the economy end of the market, have upgraded their facilities and now provide rooms with private bathrooms or showers, as well as cable color televisions and direct-dial telephones. The bigger hotels are all equipped with in-room data ports. If you've rented a car and you're not staying at a hotel with secure parking facilities, it's worth considering a location out of the city center, such as Dalkey or Killiney, where the surroundings are more pleasant and you won't have to worry about parking on city streets.

Prices

Demand for rooms means that rates are high at the best hotels by the standards of any major European or North American city (and factoring in the exchange rate means a hotel room can take a substantial bite out of your budget). The recent slump in tourism, however, has caused a few hotels to cut prices considerably. Service charges range from 15% in expensive hotels to zero in moderate and inexpensive ones. Be sure to inquire when you make reservations.

As a general rule of thumb, lodgings on the north side of the Liffey River tend to be more affordable than those on the south. B&Bs charge as little as €46 a night per person, but they tend to be in suburban areas—generally a 15-minute bus ride from the center of the city. This is not in itself a great drawback, and savings can be significant. Many hotels have a weekend, or "B&B," rate that's often 30% to 40% cheaper than the ordinary rate; some hotels also have a midweek special that provides discounts of up to 35%. These rates are available throughout the year but are harder to get in high season. Ask about them when booking a room (they are available only on a prebooked basis), especially if you plan a brief or weekend stay.

WHAT IT COSTS in euros				
$$$$	**$$$**	**$$**	**$**	**¢**
FOR 2 PEOPLE over €230	€180–€230	€130–€180	€80–€130	under €80

Prices are for two people in a standard double room in high season, including V.A.T. and a service charge (often applied in larger hotels), but with no meals (EP) or, if indicated, BP (Breakfast Plan).

North of the Liffey

In Town

$$$$ **The Morrison.** How do you make a Dublin hotel instantly trendy? Simple; get the country's top fashion guru to design the interiors. John Rocha had the last word on everything at this uber-modern trend-setting hotel, down to the toiletries and staff uniforms. The flamboyant, over-the-top public areas contrast with the very unfussy, almost Scan-

CloseUp

MORE BANG FOR YOUR BUCK

YOU GET WHAT YOU PAY FOR. *For decades Dublin was synonymous with cheap but unexciting accommodation. The Celtic Tiger has transformed expectations for visitors to Dublin. When it comes to their hotels, it is indeed the best of times and the worst of times. Choice and quality have expanded exponentially, but so have prices. So it's more important than ever to get the best deal for your dollar. The Merrion is one of the most expensive hotels in the city, but its location between Merrion Square and St. Stephen's Green is perfect, the parking is free, and the rooms are the biggest in town. As an added bonus, staying here secures you the right to brag that you've slept in the former home of the Duke of Wellington himself. If location is a priority but you don't want to spend a fortune, try the moderately priced, redbrick Central Hotel, which lives up to its name: it's 100 yards from the front gate of Trinity College. The rooms are small but stylish,*

and you have easy access to the wonderful Library Bar, the most serene drinking spot in Dublin. To stay just off the ever-trendy Grafton Street for less than €150 is a real treat, and the Grafton Guesthouse also throws in beautifully furnished rooms in a Victorian town house. Or, in Victorian-era Ballsbridge, head to the charming Hibernian, decorated in best smoking-room Edwardian style. A pleasant outdoor courtyard, en suite showers, a peat fire, and a delicious all-you-can-eat breakfast—does that sound like a hostel to you? Well, it is—Globetrotters Tourist Hostel is the pick of its kind in the city, and it even has a cute B&B next door. Perhaps because the Hotel Saint George is on the Northside, its prices do not reflect its opulence. Add in the free parking and oversize rooms and you know you've found a real bargain.

dinavian bedrooms. Some visitors complain that the place leaves them a little cold, others that the Morrison is as good as a London's boutique hotel but it is almost five times the size. Halfway between the Ha'penny and Capel Street bridges, the Morrison is no more than a 10-minute walk from Trinity College. The Halo restaurant has an Asian fusion theme. ⊠ *Ormond Quay, Northside, 1* ☎ *01/887–2400* 🖷 *01/878–3185* 🌐 *www.morrisonhotel.ie* 🛏 *88 rooms with bath, 7 suites* ⚘ *2 restaurants, room service, in-room data ports, minibars, cable TV, in-room VCRs, 2 bars, dry cleaning, laundry service, concierge, business services, meeting rooms, free parking, no-smoking rooms* 🗀 *AE, DC, MC, V* ⋈ *EP.*

$$$–$$$$ 🏨 **Clarion Hotel IFSC.** Built with business guests in mind, this high-rise hotel has been a surprise hit with tourists. Smack in the middle of the International Financial Services Centre, the Clarion—with an office-block-like exterior—is indistinguishable from many of the financial institutions that surround it. The public spaces are bright and cheery, if a little uninspired, but the bedrooms—big by Dublin standards—are all straight lines and contemporary light-oak furnishings. Shades of blue and taupe do create a calm environment (the hotel claims its environment is guided by eastern philosophy, no less), but for true serenity try to get a room at the front with great views out over the Liffey. Because the hotel mainly caters to business travelers, weekend bargains are a definite possibility—make sure you ask. ☒ *IFSC, Northside, 1* 🕾 *01/433–8800* 🖨 *01/ 433–8811* ⊕ *www.clarionhotelifsc.com* 🖙 *147 rooms, 13 suites* △ *Restaurant, room service, in-room data ports, minibars, cable TV, indoor pool, health club, massage, bar, dry cleaning, laundry service, free parking, no-smoking rooms* 🖃 *AE, DC, MC, V* ⦿I *EP.*

$$$ 🏨 **Royal Dublin Hotel.** No, the queen never stayed here and O'Connell Street is not what it once was, but there are plans to bring new life to this Old Lady. One of the big pluses of this renovated, beige-plush and chandelier-lit hotel is its perfect location at the top of the thoroughfare, near the Northside's major attractions (while a 10-minute walk south deposits you at Trinity College). The public spaces are subtly lit and decorated in slightly loud glass and brass. Rooms are spacious, and the hotel has built a solid reputation for extra-friendly service. The Georgian Room and Raffles bar try to put on posh English airs (think crisp linens), but the casual warmth of the staff undoes the stuffiness. ☒ *O'Connell St., Northside, 1* 🕾 *01/873–3666* 🖨 *01/873–3120* ⊕ *www.royaldublin. com* 🖙 *117 rooms, 3 suites* △ *Restaurant, room service, in-room data ports, minibars, cable TV, in-room VCRs, bar, dry cleaning, laundry service, no-smoking rooms* 🖃 *AE, MC, V* ⦿I *EP.*

★ **$–$$** 🏨 **Charleville Lodge.** If Dublin's city center is a Georgian wonder, a short commute out to the historic Phibsborough area of Dublin's Northside will transport you to the elegantly Victorian 19th century. Here, in a row of beautifully restored terraced houses, you can enjoy quality time in Charleville Lodge's dramatically lit residents' lounge, all twinkling chandeliers, plush wing armchairs, and working fireplace. An antiquarian's delight, this grand salon is a great spot to chat with other travelers who have dared to stray off the beaten path. Upstairs, guest rooms are brightly colored, wide, and refreshingly high. As for the commute, the No. 10 bus takes but five minutes and it's even a great walk in good weather. All in all, this hostelry offers a touch of luxury at great value. ☒ *268–272 N. Circular Rd., Northside, 7* 🕾 *01/838–6633* 🖨 *01/838– 5854* ⊕ *www.charlevillelodge.ie* 🖙 *30 rooms with bath* △ *Free parking, no-smoking rooms; no a/c* 🖃 *MC, V* ⦿I *BP.*

★ **$** 🏨 **Hotel Saint George.** At last, a silk purse for the price of a couple of sow's ears. A splendid period staircase, original plasterwork, Neoclassical portal, and beautiful marble fireplaces are delightful surprises at this Northside Georgian guesthouse. Bedrooms have little period patina, but are large, with high ceilings and pastel color schemes. The Saint George is close to the airport and numerous cultural highlights; the Abbey and Gate theaters, the Dublin Writers Museum, and the Hugh Lane Municipal Gallery of Modern Art are all within walking distance. ☒ *7 Parnell Sq. E, Northside, 1* 🕾 *01/874–5611* 🖨 *01/874–5582* ⊕ *www.hotel-st-george.ie* 🖙 *50 rooms* △ *Free parking, no-smoking rooms; no a/c* 🖃 *MC, V* ⦿I *BP.*

¢–$ 🏨 **Clifden Guesthouse.** The Gardiner Street area deservedly gets some bad press, as it is home to a host of cheap, poor-quality guest houses. But there's a few diamonds in the rough, and the Clifden, although still certainly a bargain, is a cut above the rest. The Georgian building has been stylishly refurbished, and the rooms are huge, with simple furnishings and wonderfully tall, period windows. O'Connell Street is only a 5-minute walk away. As an added bonus, you can park here for free even after you have checked out. ☒ *32 Gardiner Pl., Northside, 1* ☎ *01/874–6364* 🖷 *01/874–6122* ⊕ *www.clifdenhouse.com* ⟿ *14 rooms* ♻ *Free parking, no-smoking rooms; no a/c* ⊟ *MC, V* ⦿ *BP.*

¢–$ ▦ **Globetrotters Tourist Hostel.** Globetrotters is a giant step up from many Dublin hostels, with a pleasant outdoor courtyard; clean, locking dorm rooms with en suite showers; a turf fire; comfortable bunk beds (with lamps for late-night reading); and a delicious all-you-can-eat breakfast. Plus, you're within walking distance of the city center, one block from the bus station, and two blocks from the train station. The owners also run Town House, a cute B&B in the same building. ☒ *46 Lower Gardiner St., Northside, 1* ☎ *01/873–5893* 🖷 *01/878–8787* ⊕ *www.townhouse.ie* ⟿ *94 dorm beds with shared bath, 38 double rooms* ♻ *Restaurant, no-smoking rooms; no a/c, no room TVs* ⊟ *MC, V* ⦿ *BP.*

¢ ▦ **Marian Guest House.** A veritable Everest of fine Irish meats, the Marian's mighty full Irish breakfast, with black pudding and smoked bacon, is reason enough to stay at this family-run guest house (the whole family can speak Irish, by the way). The place only has six rooms, so you get lots of attention and pampering. Rooms are fairly basic, but clean and pleasant. ☒ *21 Upper Gardiner St., Northside, 1* ☎ *01/874–6364* ⟿ *6 rooms* ♻ *Free parking; no a/c* ⊟ *MC, V* ⦿ *BP.*

Dublin Airport

$$$–$$$$ ▦ **Holiday Inn Dublin Airport.** Seen one seen 'em all. The saying is fairly accurate when talking about airport hotels, and this Holiday Inn is no exception. But the low-rise redbrick structure with a plain exterior has one big plus; rooms big enough to make you forget about the cookie-cutter decor. The Bistro Restaurant serves fish, meat, and vegetarian dishes; Sampans serves Chinese cuisine and is open for dinner only. There's live music in the bar on weekends. Guests have access to a nearby health club. ☒ *Dublin Airport, North County Dublin* ☎ *01/808–0500* 🖷 *01/844–6002* ⊕ *www.ichotelsgroup.com* ⟿ *247 rooms* ♻ *2 restaurants, room service, in-room data ports, bar, free parking, no-smoking rooms* ⊟ *AE, DC, MC, V* ⦿ *EP.*

$$–$$$$ ▦ **Great Southern Hotel.** You could sleepwalk to your plane from the Great Southern. Situated near the main terminal, and next to the main road into the city center is this modern five-story hotel that's part of one of Ireland's most respected chains. Rooms are spacious and comfortable, if unexciting, but the service is exceptional. Double glazing insures the roar of a 747 doesn't interrupt any beauty sleep. Twelve of the rooms are designated "Lady Executive." ☒ *Dublin Airport, North County Dublin* ☎ *01/844–6000* 🖷 *01/844–6001* ⊕ *www.gsh.ie* ⟿ *229 rooms* ♻ *Restaurant, room service, in-room data ports, bar, free parking* ⊟ *AE, DC, MC, V* ⦿ *EP.*

$–$$ ▦ **Skylon.** Location, location . . . and spacious rooms; the three reasons for choosing the Skylon. On the main road into Dublin city center from the airport stands this modern five-story hotel with a concrete-and-glass facade and generous-size rooms, plainly decorated in cool, sea-bright

colors. Double beds and a pair of easy chairs are almost the only furniture in the rooms. A glass-fronted lobby with a large bar and the Rendezvous Room restaurant dominate the public areas. The cooking is
adequate but uninspired, with dishes such as grilled steak, poached
cod, and omelets. ✉ *Upper Drumcondra Rd., North County Dublin*
☎ *01/837–9121* 🖨 *01/837–2778* ⊕ *www.skylon.org* ↩ *88 rooms*
⚒ *Restaurant, bar, free parking* ⊟ *AE, DC, MC, V* ⍾ *EP.*

City Center

★ **$$$$** ⬚ **Shelbourne.** Paris has the Ritz, New York has the Plaza, and Dublin
has the Shelbourne. Grand dame of Stephen's Green (natives always drop
the "St."), its broad, ornamented, pink-and-white, mid-Victorian facade
graces the north side of the square. This used to be famed as the Dublin
home of the nation's literati, the Anglo-Irish marquesses (who, rumor
had it, could no longer foot the bill for living in their Dublin town houses
year-round), and the touring Boston Brahmins. Authors from Thackeray to Elizabeth Bowen have roundly sung its praises in their books;
the Constitution of the Irish Free State was framed within its venerable
walls. Today, Waterford chandeliers, gleaming old master daubs on the
wall, and Irish Chippendale chairs still invite you to linger in the cream-
and-crystal lobby. There is little history left in the guest rooms, but you
can't have everything. Most are now your basic white box, nicely
adorned with fine, carefully selected furniture and colorfully luxurious
drapes. If you opt for some of the older suites, you can rest your cell
phone on some splendid antiques. Rooms in front overlook the Green
(one of Dublin's squares more blighted than most by modern development), but rooms in the back, without a view, are quieter. The Lord
Mayor's Lounge, off the lobby, is a perfect rendezvous spot and offers
a lovely afternoon tea—a real Dublin tradition. The city's grandest Edwardian dining saloon is now the hotel's posh and ambitious restaurant, No. 27 The Green, which offers menus that merge the best of Irish
and French cuisines. ✉ *27 St. Stephen's Green, Southside, 2* ☎ *01/663–*
4500, 800/543–4300 in the U.S. 🖨 *01/661–6006* ⊕ *www.shelbourne.*
ie ↩ *181 rooms, 9 suites* ⚒ *2 restaurants, room service, in-room data*
ports, indoor pool, health club, hot tub, sauna, 2 bars, free parking, no-
smoking rooms ⊟ *AE, DC, MC, V* ⍾ *EP.*

$$$$ ⬚ **Westbury.** Just off Grafton Street, the shopping mecca of Dublin, this
luxurious, chandelier-filled, modern hotel is a favorite with the platinum
credit-card set. You can join elegantly dressed Dubliners for afternoon
tea in the spacious mezzanine-level main lobby, furnished with a grand
piano and a great view out onto the busy streets. Alas, the utilitarian
rooms—painted in pastels—don't share the lobby's elegance. More
inviting are the suites, which combine European stylings with tasteful
Japanese screens and prints. The flowery Russell Room serves formal
lunches and dinners; the downstairs Sandbank, a seafood restaurant and
bar, looks like a turn-of-the-20th-century establishment. ✉ *Grafton*
St., Southside, 2 ☎ *01/679–1122* 🖨 *01/679–7078* ⊕ *www.jurysdoyle.*
com ↩ *204 rooms, 8 suites* ⚒ *2 restaurants, room service, in-room data*
ports, minibars, cable TV, in-room VCRs, bar, dry cleaning, laundry ser-
vice, free parking, no-smoking rooms ⊟ *AE, DC, MC, V* ⍾ *EP.*

$$$$ ⛫ **Westin Dublin.** If you've ever dreamed of spending the night in a bank, here's your chance. Reconstructed from three 19th-century landmark buildings (including a former bank) across the road from Trinity College, the Westin is all about location. The public spaces recreate a little of the splendor of yesteryear: marble pillars, tall mahogany doorways, blazing fireplaces, and period detailing on the walls and ceilings. The bedrooms, on the other hand, are functional and small, with the crisp, white Indian linen and custom-made beds the only luxurious touches. The rooms that overlook Trinity College are a little more expensive, but the chance to watch the students in a leisurely game of cricket on a summer weekend makes all the difference. The restaurant and Mint Bar are in the original vaults of the bank. ⊠ *College Green, Southside, 2* ☎ *01/645–1000* 🖷 *01/645–1234* ⊕ *www.westin.com* ⇌ *141 rooms, 22 suites* ⌕ *Restaurant, room service, in-room data ports, minibars, cable TV, 2 bars, dry cleaning, laundry service, concierge, business services, meeting rooms, free parking, no-smoking rooms* ⊟ *AE, DC, MC, V* ¶⊙¶ *EP.*

$$$ ⛫ **Drury Court Hotel.** The cozy, parquet-floor rathskeller dining room is the most charming thing about this small, good value hotel. Public areas are purely functional but subtle greens, golds, and burgundies add a certain warmth to the rooms. The location is ideal, a two-minute walk from Grafton Street and just around corner from some of the city's best restaurants. Lunch is served in the casual Digges Lane Bar, frequented by many new-money, young Dubliners. ⊠ *28–30 Lower Stephens St., Southside, 2* ☎ *01/475–1988* 🖷 *01/478–5730* ⊕ *www.drurycourthotel.com* ⇌ *30 rooms, 2 suites* ⌕ *Restaurant, room service, bar, dry cleaning, laundry service, meeting room* ⊟ *AE, DC, MC, V* ¶⊙¶ *EP.*

$$$
FodorśChoice
★
⛫ **La Stampa.** Definitely a good thing in a very pretty, small package, this intimate town-house hotel, above the ever-popular and spectacular La Stampa restaurant and 50 yards from Trinity College, is the classiest new arrival on the Dublin scene. Each suite is individually decorated with an Asian theme—lots of wood, simple color schemes, and velvet bedspreads imported from Paris add to the luxury. For the price, there are few better spots in town. ⊠ *35 Dawson St., Southside, 2* ☎ *01/677–4444* 🖷 *01/677–4411* ⊕ *www.lastampa.ie* ⇌ *21 suites* ⌕ *Restaurant, room service, minibars, cable TV, in-room VCRs, dry cleaning, laundry service, free parking, no-smoking rooms* ⊟ *AE, DC, MC, V* ¶⊙¶ *EP.*

★ **$$–$$$** ⛫ **Central Hotel.** Every modern city needs its little oases of sanctuary and the Central's book-and-armchair-filled Library bar—warmed by its Victorian fireplace—nicely fits the bill. Established in 1887, this grand, old-style redbrick spot is in the heart of the city center, steps from Grafton Street, Temple Bar, and Dublin Castle. Recently renovated rooms are snug but you'll hardly notice the dimensions thanks to the high ceilings and the cossetingly elegant and stylish furnishings—flocked bedspreads, racing paintings, and 19th-century bric-a-brac make some of these rooms *World of Interiors*–worthy. Aristocratically stately, the hotel dining room delights with its pastel-green walls, bookcases, and gilt-framed pictures. Much less soigné and a good deal more lively is Molly

Malone's Tavern, adjacent to the hotel, with plenty of regulars who come for the atmosphere and the live, traditional Irish music on Friday and Saturday nights. ✉ *1–5 Exchequer St., Southside, 2* ☎ *01/679–7302* 🖨 *01/679–7303* 🌐 *www.centralhotel.ie* 🛏 *67 rooms, 3 suites* ⚓ *Restaurant, room service, in-room data ports, 2 bars, dry cleaning, laundry service, concierge, business services, meeting rooms* ▭ *AE, DC, MC, V* 🍽 *EP.*

$–$$ 🏨 **Georgian House Hotel.** The name says it all. The owners of this hotel took three classic Georgian houses near St. Stephen's Green, added a modern extension, and opened one of Dublin's best value hotels. So you get an 18th-century-Dublin experience—high ceilings, original fireplaces, antique gilded mirrors—at guest-house prices. Within the hotel, McGuires is a cozy, unpretentious little pub. ✉ *18 Lower Bagott St., Southside, 2* ☎ *01/661–8832* 🖨 *01/661–8834* 🛏 *70 rooms* ⚓ *Restaurant, bar, free parking; no a/c* ▭ *AE, MC, V* 🍽 *BP.*

$–$$ 🏨 **Grafton Guesthouse.** A stone's throw from the famous shopping street that gave it its name, this Victorian Gothic–style building has been tastefully transformed into one of central Dublin's best bargains. The rooms are a little cramped, but they are brightly decorated with cheerful pine furnishings, and the small size of the place ensures warm, friendly service. ✉ *26–27 S. Great George's St., Southside, 2* ☎ *01/679–2041* 🖨 *01/677–9715* 🛏 *15 rooms* ⚓ *No-smoking rooms; no a/c* ▭ *AE, MC, V* 🍽 *BP.*

Southside

$$$$ 🏨 **Conrad Dublin International.** Ask for, no, insist on a room on the top three floors. The best thing about the seven-story, redbrick and smoked glass Conrad are the spectacular views out over the city. Located just off St. Stephen's Green, the Conrad firmly aims for international business travelers. Gleaming light-color marble graces the large formal lobby. Rooms are rather cramped but are nicely outfitted with natural-wood furnishings, painted in sand colors and pastel greens, and have Spanish marble in the bathrooms. A note to light sleepers: the air-conditioning/heating system can be noisy. The hotel has two restaurants: the informal Plurabelle and the plusher Alexandra Room. ✉ *Earlsfort Terr., Southside, 2* ☎ *01/676–5555* 🖨 *01/676–5424* 🌐 *www.conradhotels. com* 🛏 *182 rooms, 9 suites* ⚓ *2 restaurants, room service, in-room data ports, in-room safes, minibars, cable TV, in-room VCRs, gym, bar, concierge, business services, meeting rooms, free parking, no-smoking floor* ▭ *AE, DC, MC, V* 🍽 *EP.*

$$$$ 🏨 **Merrion.** Arthur Wellesley, the Duke of Wellington and hero of Waterloo, once famously commented when queried about his Irish birth: "Just because a man is born in a stable doesn't make him a horse." His "stable," directly across from Government Buildings between Stephen's Green and Merrion Square, is one of the four exactingly restored Georgian town houses that make up this luxurious hotel. Some of the stately guest rooms are appointed in classic Georgian style—from the crisp linen sheets to the Carrara-marble bathrooms. Some are vaulted with delicate Adamesque plasterwork ceilings, and others are graced with magnificent, original marble fireplaces. The decor is almost too spiffy—the

Fodor'sChoice
★

Where to Stay in Dublin

"spirit" of the 18th century has been channeled here, not its detailed re-creation. Rooms in the old house are more expensive than those in the new extension. You know this place must be special, because leading Dublin restaurateur Patrick Guilbaud has moved his eponymous and fabulous restaurant here. ⊠ *Upper Merrion St., Southside, 2* 🕾 *01/603–0600* 🖷 *01/603–0700* ⊕ *www.merrionhotel.com* ⇌ *120 rooms, 25 suites* ⚒ *2 restaurants, room service, in-room data ports, in-room safes, minibars, cable TV, in-room VCRs, indoor pool, health club, hair salon, massage, steam room, 2 bars, dry cleaning, laundry service, concierge, business services, meeting rooms, free parking, no-smoking floor* ⊟ *AE, DC, MC, V* ⭘ *EP.*

$$$–$$$$ 🖭 **Davenport.** The gorgeous, bright-yellow neoclassical facade of this hotel behind Trinity College was built in the 1860s to front a church designed by famous architect Alfred Jones. Victorian Bourgeois meets Modern in the tasteful deep colors and functional furnishings that decorate reasonably spacious rooms and larger suites, many of which are named after architects who built some of Dublin's major buildings. The hotel restaurant, Lanyon's, serves breakfast, lunch, and dinner amid traditional Georgian surroundings. In the comfortable President's Bar, see how many heads of state you can identify in the photos covering the walls. ⊠ *Merrion Sq., Southside, 2* 🕾 *01/661–6800, 800/327–0200 in the U.S.* 🖷 *01/661–5663* ⊕ *www.ocallaghanhotels.ie* ⇌ *113 rooms, 2 suites* ⚒ *Restaurant, room service, in-room data ports, minibars, cable TV, in-room VCRs, bar, dry cleaning, laundry service, concierge, business services, meeting rooms, free parking, no-smoking rooms* ⊟ *AE, DC, MC, V* ⭘ *EP.*

★ $$–$$$$ 🖭 **Number 31.** Sam Stephenson, Dublin's most famous and highly controversial modernist architect, strikingly renovated two Georgian mews strikingly in the early 1960s as a private home. They are now connected via a small garden to the grand own house they once served. Together they form a marvelous guest house a short walk from St. Stephen's Green, which give you a choice of bedroom styles; Georgian elegance or cool modern. Owners Deirdre and Noel Comer serve made-to-order breakfasts at refectory tables in the balcony dining room. The white-tile sunken living room, with its black leather sectional sofa and modern artwork that includes a David Hockney print, may make you think you're in California. If that essay in *Wallpaper*-modern doesn't send you, you'll be happy enough ensconced in one of the period-style guest rooms, one of which—No. 21—has a ceiling so lofty and corniced even a royal would feel at home. ⊠ *31 Leeson Close, Southside, 2* 🕾 *01/676–5011* 🖷 *01/676–2929* ⊕ *www.number31.ie* ⇌ *18 rooms* ⚒ *Dry cleaning, laundry service, free parking, no-smoking rooms; no a/c* ⊟ *AE, MC, V* ⭘ *EP.*

$$$ 🖭 **Clarion Stephen's Hall Hotel & Suites.** Get a top-floor suite and lord it over the whole Southside in this all-suites hotel situated in a tastefully modernized Georgian town house just off St. Stephen's Green. The suites, considerably larger than the average hotel room, include one or two bedrooms, a separate sitting room, a fully equipped kitchen, and bath. The modern, motel-functional furniture is nondescript, but top-floor suites have spectacular city views, and ground-floor suites have private entrances. The Romanza restaurant serves breakfast, lunch, and dinner with an Italian flavor. ⊠ *14–17 Lower Leeson St., Southside, 2* ☎ *01/661–0585* 🖷 *01/661–0606* ⊕ *www.premgroup. ie* ⤴ *34 suites* ⌂ *Restaurant, room service, kitchens, cable TV, 2 bars, meeting rooms, free parking, no-smoking rooms* ▤ *AE, DC, MC, V* ⍉ *EP.*

$–$$ ▦ **Kilronan House.** A good guest house should cheer you up when you come home at the end of a long day's touring. This large, late-19th-century terraced house with an elegant white facade will bring a smile to your face every time. Just a five-minute walk from St. Stephen's Green, Kilronan flaunts richly patterned wallpaper and carpets in its guest rooms, while orthopedic beds (rather rare in Dublin hotels, let alone guest houses) help to guarantee a restful night's sleep. ⊠ *70 Adelaide Rd., Southside, 2* ☎ *01/475–5266* 🖷 *01/478–2841* ⊕ *www.dublinn. com* ⤴ *12 rooms* ⌂ *Free parking, no-smoking room; no a/c* ▤ *MC, V* ⍉ *EP.*

Temple Bar

$$$$ ▦ **The Clarence.** If coolness is contagious you definitely want a room at Temple Bar's most prestigious hotel. You might well bump into celebrity friends of co-owners Bono and the Edge of U2. Dating to 1852, the grand old hotel was given a total, no-expense-spared overhaul by its new owners in the early 1990s. The unique shapes and Arts and Crafts style of the old hotel were maintained in the Octagon Bar and the Tea Room Restaurant. Guest rooms are decorated in a mishmash of earth tones accented with deep purple, gold, cardinal red, and royal blue. With the exception of those in the penthouse suite, rooms are small. The laissez-faire service seems to take its cue from the minimalist style, so if you like to be pampered, stay elsewhere. ⊠ *6–8 Wellington Quay, Temple Bar, 2* ☎ *01/407–0800* 🖷 *01/407–0820* ⊕ *www.theclarence.ie* ⤴ *47 rooms, 3 suites* ⌂ *Restaurant, in-room data ports, minibars, cable TV, bar, dry cleaning, laundry service, meeting rooms, free parking, no-smoking rooms* ▤ *AE, DC, MC, V* ⍉ *EP.*

$$–$$$ ▦ **Paramount.** This medium-size hotel in the heart of trendy Temple Bar has opted to maintain its classy Victorian facade. The foyer continues this theme of solid elegance, with incredibly comfortable leather couches, bleached-blond-oak floors, and burgundy curtains. Dark woods and subtle colors decorate the bedrooms—very 1930s (if not Bogie and Bacall). If you're fond of a tipple, try the hotel's art-deco Turks Head Bar and Chop House. ⊠ *Parliament St. and Essex Gate, Temple Bar, 2* ☎ *01/ 417–9900* 🖷 *01/417–9904* ⊕ *www.paramounthotel.ie* ⤴ *70 rooms* ⌂ *Restaurant, in-room data ports, cable TV, bar, laundry service, no-smoking rooms* ▤ *AE, DC, MC, V* ⍉ *EP.*

$$–$$$ ▦ **Parliament.** As with many Dublin hotels, the interiors of the Parliament do not quite live up to the fabulous facade of one of Dublin's finest Edwardian buildings. Inside, the atmosphere is very much functional, if tidy, and appeals to mainly a business clientele—drawn by the location near the Central Bank and Trinity College. But rooms are a good size, with a simple, slightly monotonous beige and off-white color scheme. The Senate restaurant and Forum bar keep up the democratic theme with reliable selections. ⊠ *Lord Edward St., Temple Bar, 2* ☎ *01/670–8777* 🖷 *01/670–8787* ⊕ *www.regencyhotels.com* ⤻ *63 rooms* ⟂ *Restaurant, cable TV, bar, no-smoking rooms* ⊟ *AE, DC, MC, V* ⦿ *EP.*

$$–$$$ 🔲 **Temple Bar.** Dublin doesn't usually do Art Deco, so the 1920s-style lobby of the Temple Bar—with its old-fashioned cast-iron fireplace, natural-wood furniture, and legions of exotic plants—is a refreshing change. Off the lobby are a small cocktail bar and the bright, airy, glass-roof Terrace restaurant, great spots to hang out and enjoy a pre-theatre martini. Mahogany wood and autumn green and rust colors characterize the guest rooms, nearly all of which have big double beds (which can leave them a little cramped). The Boomerang nightclub on the premises is open to both guests and the public. The hotel is in a former bank building, around the corner from Trinity College. ⊠ *Fleet St., Temple Bar, 2* ☎*01/677–3333* 🖷*01/677–3088* ⊕*www.towerhotelgroup.ie/templebar* ⤻ *129 rooms* ⟂ *Restaurant, cable TV, 2 bars, nightclub, parking (fee)* ⊟ *AE, DC, MC, V* ⦿ *EP.*

The Grand Canal & Ballsbridge

$$$$ 🔲 **Berkeley Court.** A beauty-and-the-beast combination, the Berkeley Court is a somewhat ugly, glass-and-concrete building designed in a modern, blocklike style surrounded by serene and verdant grounds. The interior may be the most quietly elegant in any of Dublin's large modern hotels. The vast white and plushly carpeted lobby, with its huge central chandelier, has roomy sofas and antique planters. Golds, yellows, and greens decorate the large guest rooms, filled with antiques or period reproductions; bathrooms are tiled in marble. The Berkeley Room has table d'hôte and à la carte menus; the more informal Conservatory Grill, with large windows, serves grilled food and snacks. ⊠ *Lansdowne Rd., Ballsbridge, 4* ☎ *01/660–1711, 800/550–0000 in the U.S.* 🖷 *01/661–7238* ⊕ *www.jurysdoyle.com* ⤻ *158 rooms, 24 suites* ⟂ *2 restaurants, room service, in-room data ports, cable TV, gym, hair salon, some hot tubs, bar, shops, dry cleaning, laundry service, business services, meeting rooms, free parking, no-smoking rooms* ⊟ *AE, DC, MC, V* ⦿ *EP.*

$$$$ 🔲 **Burlington.** In high contrast to the hotel's impersonal, 1972 glass-and-concrete facade, the staff at Ireland's largest hotel is famously friendly and attentive. Public rooms, especially the large bar, have mahogany counters and hanging plants that enhance the conservatory-style setting and take the edge off the uninspired building. The generous-size rooms—recently refurbished in a modern minimalist design, with neutral tones—have large picture windows. At night, Annabel's nightclub and the seasonal Irish cabaret are both lively (sometimes too lively!) spots. The Burlington has no sports and health facilities, but the Doyle hotel group, which runs it, has an arrangement that allows you to use the RiverView Sports Club in nearby Clonskeagh for €6.35 a visit. ⊠ *Upper Leeson St., Ballsbridge, 4* ☎ *01/660–5222* 🖷 *01/660–8496* ⊕ *www.jurysdoyle.com* ⤻ *506 rooms* ⟂ *2 restaurants, room service, in-room data ports, cable TV, 3 bars, cabaret (May–Oct.), nightclub, shops, dry cleaning, laundry service,* *business services, meeting rooms, free parking, no-smoking rooms* ▭ *AE, DC, MC, V* ❙❖❙ *EP.*

$$$$ ▦ **Four Seasons.** Much controversy surrounds the brash postmodern—critics would say faux-Victorian-Georgian hybrid—architecture of this hotel, set in its own 4-acre gardens. The six-floor building mixes pre-20th-century design with modern glass and concrete. The impressive landscaping aims to makes the hotel seem like an oasis; a big effort has been made to ensure that a bit of greenery can be seen from most rooms. Guest rooms are spacious, with large windows that allow light to flood in. A selection of landscapes on the hotel walls lends the place a warm touch. The lower-level spa is one of the finest in the country, with a naturally lit lap pool. ✉ *Simmonscourt Rd., Ballsbridge, 4* ☏ *01/665–4000* 🖷 *01/665–4099* ⊕ *www.fourseasons.com* ↩ *192 rooms, 67 suites* ⚑ *Restaurant, room service, in-room data ports, coffee shop, cable TV, indoor pool, hot tub, bar, shop, dry cleaning, laundry service, business services, meeting rooms, free parking, no-smoking rooms* ▭ *AE, DC, MC, V* ❙❖❙ *EP.*

$$$$ ▦ **Herbert Park Hotel.** For maximum pleasure secure a room overlooking the park of the same name adjacent to this hotel, which is also beside the Dodder River. Two of the suites even have large balconies with views of the park or the leafy suburbs. Relaxing shades of blue and cream predominate in the spacious rooms; all have individually controlled air-conditioning, a large desk, and two telephone lines. The hotel's large, light-filled lobby has floor-to-ceiling windows and a slanted glass roof. The spacious bar, terrace lounge, and restaurant are Japanese-inspired-minimalist in style. You can dine on the restaurant terrace in warm weather. ✉ *Merrion Rd., Ballsbridge, 4* ☏ *01/667–2200* 🖷 *01/667–2595* ⊕ *www. herbertparkhotel.ie* ↩ *150 rooms, 3 suites* ⚑ *Restaurant, cable TV, gym, bar, business services, free parking, no-smoking rooms* ▭ *AE, DC, MC, V* ❙❖❙ *EP.*

$$$$ ▦ **Jurys Ballsbridge and the Towers.** Farmers and their families up in "the big smoke" for a shopping weekend have always favored the laid back atmosphere of Jurys. These adjoining seven-story hotels, also popular with businesspeople, have more atmosphere than most comparable modern hotels. The Towers has an edge over its older, larger, less-expensive companion, Jurys Ballsbridge. Rooms in the Towers are decorated in blue and gold with built-in, natural-wood furniture; the large beds and armchairs are great for lounging about in. Jurys Ballsbridge, on the other hand, has large, plainly decorated rooms with light walls and brown drapes; furnishings are functional and uninspired. ✉ *Pembroke Rd. (Jurys Ballsbridge) and Lansdowne Rd. (the Towers), Ballsbridge, 4* ☏ *01/660–5000* 🖷 *01/679–7078* ⊕ *www.jurysdoyle.com* ↩ *Jurys Ballsbridge: 300 rooms, 3 suites. The Towers: 100 rooms, 5 suites* ⚑ *2 restaurants, coffee shop, some kitchenettes, indoor-outdoor pool, hot tub, bar, cabaret (May–Oct.), shop, dry cleaning, laundry service, business services, meeting rooms, free parking* ▭ *AE, DC, MC, V* ❙❖❙ *EP.*

★ **$$$–$$$$**   ▦ **Hibernian.** "Charming" and "Irish" are sometime thought of as synonyms and this adorable and cute hotel proves it. Set in an Edwardian extravaganza of a building—the early-20th-century edifice was originally a nurses' home designed by Albert E. Murray (one of the architects of the Rotunda Hospital)—the Hibernian has the feel of a secluded country house in the middle of the city. One of the city's most distinctive and intimate hotels, it cheerfully welcomes you with its ruddy red-and-amber brick facade. Inside, guest rooms may be small but they are exquisitely decorated, some in best smoking-room-Edwardian manner, other with country-house pastels, all with deep-pile carpets and luxurious furniture. The public rooms, in cheerful chintz and stripes, include a period-style library and a sun lounge—both comfortable spaces to relax before or after a dinner in the hotel's intimate restaurant, the Patrick Kavanagh Room—an oh-so-genteel vision of neoclassical yellow walls, bayed windows, and flounced curtains. ⊠ *Eastmoreland Pl. off Upper Baggot St., Ballsbridge, 4* ☎ *01/668–7666 or 800/414243* 📠 *01/660–2655* ⊕ *www.hibernianhotel.com* ⇗ *40 rooms* ⚓ *Restaurant, bar, parking (fee)* ⊟ *AE, DC, MC, V* ⑩ *EP.*

$$–$$$ 🏨 **Mount Herbert Hotel.** The Loughran family's sprawling accommodation includes a number of large, Victorian-era houses. The hotel overlooks some of Ballsbridge's fine rear gardens and is just near the main rugby stadium; the nearby DART will have you in the city center in seven minutes. The simple rooms are painted in light shades and contain little besides beds. The lounge is a good place to relax. The restaurant, which overlooks the English-style back garden (floodlighted at night) and children's play area, serves three meals a day; at dinner you can dine on steaks and stews. ⊠ *7 Herbert Rd., Ballsbridge, 4* ☎ *01/668–4321* 📠 *01/660–7077* ⊕ *www.mountherberthotel.ie* ⇗ *200 rooms* ⚓ *Restaurant, cable TV, sauna, bar, shop, business services, meeting rooms, free parking, no-smoking rooms; no a/c* ⊟ *AE, DC, MC, V* ⑩ *EP.*

$$ 🏨 **Lansdowne Manor.** To stay at luxurious Lansdowne Manor is to dip
Fodor's Choice your toe into Victorian Dublin, with all its redbrick propriety and im-
★ maculately finished rooms. Situated in the heart of "Embassy Row," this supremely comfortable guesthouse, located in two adjoining early Victorian mansions, has gone out of its way to re-create the original feel and look of the houses. Everything from the period chandeliers to the dark-wood wardrobes has been chosen with care to evoke the atmosphere of 19th-century France, apparently a period that obsessed the original owners. Every one of the large, high-ceilinged bedrooms has a period drawing to complete the picture. ⊠ *46-48 Lansdowne Rd., Ballsbridge, 4* ☎ *01/668–8848* 📠 *01/668–8873* ⇗ *13 rooms, 9 suites* ⚓ *Bar, free parking; no a/c* ⊟ *AE, DC, MC, V* ⑩ *EP.*

$$ 🏨 **McEniff Grand Canal Hotel.** It's definitely worth the small extra cost to get one of the spacious Grand Canal rooms with wraparound balconies offering cracking views of Dublin City, Dublin Port, Lansdowne Road Stadium, and residential Georgian Dublin. On big rugby and soccer match days you can sit back and watch the green-clad hordes flowing past below. "Go on Ireland!" is the standard salute. The redbrick-and-glass exterior has the look of the ubiquitous modern Dublin apartments, but the interiors are very contemporary, with clean lines and vibrant colors throughout. The hotel is built on the site of the once famous Kitty O'Shea's bar and a new Kitty's is now an integral and very lively part of the set up. ✉ *Grand Canal St., Ballsbridge, 4* ☎ *01/646–1000* 🖷 *01/646–1001* ⊕ *www.grandcanalhotel.com* ⇌ *142 rooms* ♿ *Restaurant, bar, in-room data port, free parking; no a/c* ▤ *AE, DC, MC, V* ⦿⦿ *EP.*

★ **$–$$** 🖾 **Ariel Guest House.** The homemade preserves and oven-warm scones are reason enough to stay at this redbrick 1850 Victorian guest house in one of Dublin's poshest tree-lined suburbs. It is just a few steps from a DART stop and a 15-minute walk from St. Stephen's Green. Restored rooms in the main house are lovingly decorated with Georgian antiques, Victoriana, and period wallpaper and drapes. The 13 rooms at the back of the house are more spartan, but all are immaculate. A Waterford-crystal chandelier hangs over the comfortable leather and mahogany furniture in the gracious, fireplace-warmed drawing room. Owner Michael O'Brien is an extraordinarily helpful and gracious host. ✉ *52 Lansdowne Rd., Ballsbridge, 4* ☎ *01/668–5512* 🖷 *01/668–5845* ⇌ *40 rooms* ♿ *Free parking; no a/c* ▤ *MC, V* ⦿⦿ *BP.*

Dublin West

$$–$$$ 🖾 **Chief O'Neill's.** This strikingly modern hotel is at the center of the rejuvenation of the old fruit market area north or the Liffey known as Smithfield Village, a district named after a 19th-century Corkman who became chief of police in Chicago and happened to be potty about Irish music. The top floors have delightful rooftop gardens with views of the city on both sides of the Liffey. Smallish, high-tech rooms all have in-room data ports and look thoroughly up-to-date, thanks to their glass-tile walls, hot-and-cool Miami Beach colors, '60s-mod and minimalist furnishings (chrome, anyone?), and feng shui–inspired bathrooms. The café-bar has live traditional music and contemporary Irish food, and Asian cuisine is available in Kelly & Ping, a bright, airy restaurant off Duck Lane, a shopping arcade that's part of the hotel complex. ✉ *Smithfield Village, Dublin West, 7* ☎ *01/817–3838* 🖷 *01/817–3839* ⊕ *www.chiefoneills. com* ⇌ *70 rooms, 3 suites* ♿ *Restaurant, room service, in-room data ports, minibars, cable TV, in-room VCRs, gym, bar, shops, dry cleaning, laundry service, free parking, no-smoking rooms* ▤ *AE, DC, MC, V* ⦿⦿ *EP.*

$ 🖾 **Jurys Christchurch Inn.** Expect few frills at this functional budget hotel, part of a Jurys minichain that offers a low, fixed room rate for up to three adults or two adults and two children. (The branch at Custom House Quay operates according to the same plan.) The biggest plus is the pleasant location, facing Christ Church Cathedral and within walking distance of most city-center attractions. The rather spartan rooms are decorated in pastel colors and have utilitarian furniture. ✉ *Christ Church Pl., Dublin West, 8* ☎ *01/454–0000* 🖷 *01/454–0012* ⊕ *www. jurysdoyle.com* ⇌ *182 rooms* ♿ *Restaurant, bar, parking (fee), no-smoking rooms* ▤ *AE, DC, MC, V* ⦿⦿ *EP.*

¢ 🖾 **Avalon House.** Many young, independent travelers rate this cleverly restored redbrick Victorian building, a 5-minute walk southwest from Grafton Street and 5 to 10 minutes from some of the city's best music venues, the most appealing of Dublin's hostels. Avalon House has a mix of dormitories, rooms without bath, and rooms with bath. The dorm rooms and en suite quads all have loft areas that offer more privacy than you'd typically find in a multibed room. The Avalon Café serves food until 10 PM but is open as a common room after hours. ⊠ *55 Aungier St., Dublin West, 2* ☎ *01/475–0001* 🖷 *01/475–0303* ⊕ *www.avalon-house.ie* ⟲ *40 4-bed rooms, 35 with bath; 26 twin rooms, 4 with bath; 4 single rooms with shared bath; 5 12-bed dorms, 1 10-bed dorm, and 1 26-bed dorm, all with shared bath* ⚬ *Café, bar; no a/c, no room TVs* ▤ *AE, MC, V* ⦿ *EP.*

¢ ▦ **Bewleys at Newlands Cross.** Cheap and cheerful would best sum up this four-story hotel on the southwest outskirts of the city. It is ideal if you're planning to head out of the city early (especially to points in the southwest and west) and don't want to deal with morning traffic. The hotel is emulating the formula popularized by Jurys Inns, in which rooms—here each has a double bed, a single bed, and a sofa bed—are a flat rate for up to three adults or two adults and two children. ⊠ *Newlands Cross, at Naas Rd., Dublin West, 22* ☎ *01/464–0140* 🖷 *01/464–0900* ⊕ *www.bewleyshotels.com* ⟲ *256 rooms* ⚬ *Café, free parking, no-smoking rooms; no a/c* ▤ *AE, MC, V* ⦿ *EP.*

NIGHTLIFE & THE ARTS

Long before Stephen Daedalus's excursions into "nighttown" in James Joyce's *A Portrait of the Artist as a Young Man,* Dublin was proud of its lively after-hours scene, particularly its thriving pubs. But the Celtic Tiger economy, the envy of all Europe, turned Dublin into one of the most happening destinations on the whole continent. Some of the old watering holes were replaced with huge, London-style "superbars" which, with the ubiquitous DJ in the corner, walk the fine line between pub and club. So in the last few years most nights the city's nightspots overflow with young cell phone–toting Dubliners and Europeans who descend on the capital for weekend getaways. The city's 900-plus pubs are its main source of entertainment; many public houses in the city center have live music—from rock to jazz to traditional Irish.

Theater has always been taken seriously in the city that was home to O'Casey, Synge, Yeats, and Beckett. Today Dublin has eight major theaters that reproduce the Irish "classics," and also present newer fare from the likes of Martin Macdonagh and Conon Macpherson. At long last, the Gaiety Theatre has given long-overlooked opera a home in Dublin. There are some 20 cinema screens in the city center, plus a number of large, multiscreen cinema complexes in the suburbs, which show current releases made in Ireland and abroad.

The visual arts have always been the poor cousin in the Dublin cultural family. In recent years small galleries have sprung up all over the city, and the development of Temple Bar Galleries has encouraged a new generation of painters, photographers, and sculptors.

Check the following newspapers for informative listings: the *Irish Times* publishes a daily guide to what's happening in Dublin and the rest of the country, and has complete film and theater schedules. The *Evening Herald* lists theaters, cinemas, and pubs with live entertainment. The *Big Issue* is a weekly guide to film, theater, and musical events around the city. The *Event Guide,* a weekly free paper that lists music, cinema, theater, art shows, and dance clubs, is available in pubs and cafés around the city. In peak season, consult the free Bord Fáilte (Irish Tourist Board) leaflet "Events of the Week." The **Temple Bar Web site** (⊕ www.temple-bar.ie) provides information about events in the Temple Bar area.

Nightlife

Dubliners have always enjoyed a night out, but in the last decade or so they have turned the pleasure into a work of art. The city has undergone a major nightlife revolution and now, for better or worse, it bears more than a passing resemblance to Europe's nightclub hotspot, London. The streets of the city center, previously hushed after the pubs closed, are the scene of what appears to be a never-ending party—you're as likely to find crowds at 2 AM on a Wednesday as you are at the same time on a Saturday. Loud, brash dance clubs, where style and swagger rule, have replaced the old-fashioned discos, once the only option for late-night entertainment. In Dublin's clubs the dominant sound is electronic dance music, and the crowd that flocks to them every night of the week is of the trendy, under-30 generation. Leeson Street—just off St. Stephen's Green, south of the Liffey, and known as "the strip"—is a main nightclub area that revs up at pub closing time and lasts until 4 AM. It has lost its gloss since a number of lap-dancing establishments have opened. The dress code at Leeson Street's dance clubs is informal, but jeans and sneakers are not welcome. Most of these clubs are licensed only to sell wine, and the prices can be exorbitant (up to €26 for a mediocre bottle); the upside is that most don't charge to get in.

There are plenty of alternatives to the electronic dance scene, including nightclubs where the dominant sounds range from soul to salsa—such as the weekend nightclub at the Gaiety Theatre and the totally Latin Sugar Club. While jazz isn't a big part of the nightlife here, a few regular venues do draw the best of local and international talent. And if you're looking for something more mellow, the city doesn't disappoint: there are brasseries, bistros, cafés, and all manner of other late-night eateries where you can sit, sip, and chat until 2 AM or later.

In another trend, some of Dublin's classic pubs—arguably some of the finest watering holes in the world—have been reinvented and are now popular spots, with modern interiors and designer drinks, to attract a younger, upwardly mobile crowd. Beware Dublin Tourism's "Official Dublin Pub Guide," which has a tendency to recommend many of these bland spots. Despite the changes, however, the traditional pub has steadfastly clung to its role as the primary center of Dublin's social life. The city has nearly 1,000 pubs ("licensed tabernacles," writer Flann O'Brien calls them). And although the vision of elderly men enjoying a chin wag over a creamy pint of stout has become something of a rarity, there are still plenty of places where you can enjoy a quiet drink and a chat. Last drinks are called at 11:30 PM Monday to Wednesday, 12:30 AM Thursday to Saturday, and 11 PM on Sunday.

Some city-center pubs have extended opening hours and don't serve last drinks until 1:45 AM.

A word of warning: although most pubs and clubs are extremely safe, the lads can get lively—public drunkenness is very much a part of Dublin's nightlife. Whereas this is for the most part seen as the Irish form of unwinding after a long week (or, well, day), it can sometimes lead to regrettable incidents (fighting, for instance). In an effort to keep potential trouble at bay, bouncers and security guards maintain a visible presence in all clubs and many pubs around the city. At the end of the night, the city center is full of young people trying to get home, which makes for extremely long lines at taxi stands and late-night bus stops, especially on weekends. The combination of drunkenness and impatience can sometimes lead to trouble, so act cautiously. If you will need late-night transportation, try to arrange it with your hotel before you go out.

Irish Cabaret, Music & Dancing

CITY CENTER **Harcourt Hotel** (⊠ Harcourt St., Southside ☎ 01/478–3677) is where some of the best traditional musicians gather for wild jam sessions.

BALLSBRIDGE **Burlington Hotel** (⊠ Upper Leeson St., Ballsbridge ☎ 01/660–5222) has a high-class lounge featuring a well-performed Irish cabaret—with dancing, music, and song.

Jurys Hotel (⊠ Pembroke Rd., Ballsbridge ☎ 01/660–5000) stages a traditional Irish cabaret.

DUBLIN WEST **Castle Inn** (⊠ Christ Church Pl., Dublin West ☎ 01/475–1122) is really just a huge pub that has traditional Irish music and dancing with dinner in a medieval-style banquet hall.

Jazz

JJ Smyth's (⊠ 12 Aungier St., Southside ☎ 01/475–2565) is an old-time jazz venue where Louis Stewart, the granddaddy of Irish jazz, is a regular visitor.

Jurys Ballsbridge (⊠ Pembroke Rd., Ballsbridge ☎ 01/660–5000) attracts the country's top jazz musicians and voices to its lively Sunday-evening sessions.

Mother Redcap's Tavern (⊠ Back La., Dublin West ☎ 01/453–8306) is home to fabulous big-band jazz and swing every Monday night.

Nightclubs

NORTH OF THE LIFFEY **Spirit** (⊠ 57 Middle Abbey St., Northside ☎ 01/677–9999), currently the cutting-edge club in Dublin, attracts a party-time, young crowd which is serious about two things: dancing and more dancing. Spirit likes to call itself a "holistic venue" and its three floors are loosely designed around the themes of Mind, Body, and Soul. Mind is the basement level full of scented candles, chill-out couches, and ambient sounds; Body is the main dance floor with full-on dance tracks; while Soul is more funky.

CITY CENTER **Lillie's Bordello** (⊠ Grafton St., Southside ☎ 01/679–9204) is a popular spot for a trendy professional crowd, as well as for rock and film stars.

The Pod (✉ Harcourt St., Southside ☎ 01/478–0166), also known as the "Place of Dance," qualifies as Dublin's most renowned dance club, especially among the younger set. Whether you get in depends as much on what you're wearing as on your age.

Red Box (✉ Old Harcourt St. Station, Harcourt St., Southside ☎ 01/478–0166), adjacent to the Pod and the Chocolate Bar, can pack in more than 1,000 people and surround them with state-of-the-art sound and light. It regularly hosts Irish and international rock acts, and celebrity DJs from Europe and the United States. It has full bar facilities.

Renards (✉ St. Fredrick St., Southside ☎ 01/677–5876) is where you'll find thirtysomethings who like to let their hair down. The music can be a bit predictable, but you might just bump into Bono.

Rí Ra (✉ Dame Ct., Southside ☎ 01/677–4835) is part of the hugely popular Globe bar. The name means "uproar" in Irish, and on most nights the place does go a little wild. It's one of the best spots in Dublin for fun, no-frills dancing. Upstairs is more low-key.

Sugar Club (✉ Lower Lesson St., Southside ☎ 01/678–7188) is a refreshing mix of cocktail bar, nightclub, and performance venue. The place is known for its smooth Latin sounds and plush surroundings.

TEMPLE BAR **Temple Bar Music Centre** (✉ Curved St., Temple Bar ☎ 01/670–9202) claims to provide a different sound every night, including house, tribute bands, guitar-driven rock, and Latin music.

Viper Room (✉ 5 Aston Quay, Temple Bar ☎ 01/672–5566), decorated in rich reds and purples, is a delightfully decadent late-night club that plays funk, chart, and rhythm and blues. Downstairs there's live jazz and salsa.

Pubs

Cynics may say that Dublin can only look good through the bottom of a pint glass, but in reality it's impossible to think of Dublin without also thinking of its 1,000 or so public houses. These are what gives Dublin so much of its character, and they're largely to blame for the fierce loyalty Dublin inspires among locals and visitors. Some wag once asked if it was possible to cross Dublin without passing a single pub along the way. The answer has been a consistent, emphatic "no."

NORTH OF THE **The Flowing Tide** (✉ Lower Abbey St., Northside ☎ 01/874–0842), di-
LIFFEY rectly across from the Abbey Theatre, draws a lively pre- and post-theater crowd. No TVs, quality pub talk, and a great pint of Guinness make it a worthwhile visit.

GUBU (✉ Capel St., Northside ☎ 01/874–0710), run by the hugely successful owners of the Globe, is a mixed gay and straight bar. The music is loud and dance-driven, and the downstairs pool table is an added bonus.

Lobo (✉ Morrison Hotel, Upper Ormond Quay Northside ☎ 01/878–2999)is a stylish late-night bar where cocktails are the drink of choice for the well-to-do Dublin set which gathers on the long, lounging sofas.

Cassidy's (⊠42 Lower Camden St., Southside ☎01/475–1429), is a quality neighborhood pub with a pint of stout so good that former president Bill Clinton dropped in for one during a visit to Dublin.

Cellar Bar (⊠ 24 Upper Merrion St., Southside ☎ 01/603–0600), at the Merrion Hotel, is in a stylish 18th-century wine vault with bare brick walls and vaulted ceilings. It tends to draw a well-heeled crowd.

Davy Byrne's (⊠ 21 Duke St., Southside ☎ 01/671–1298) is a pilgrimage stop for Joyceans. In *Ulysses,* Leopold Bloom stops in here for a glass of burgundy and a Gorgonzola-cheese sandwich. He then leaves the pub and walks to Dawson Street, where he helps a blind man cross the road. Unfortunately, the pub is greatly changed from Joyce's day, but it still serves some fine pub grub.

Dockers (⊠ 5 Sir John Rogerson's Quay, Southside ☎ 01/677–1692), a trendy quayside spot east of the city center, is just around the corner from Windmill Lane Studios—where U2 and other noted bands record. At night the area is a little dicey, so it's best to visit during the day.

Doheny & Nesbitt (⊠ 5 Lower Baggot St., Southside ☎ 01/676–2945), a traditional spot with snugs, dark wooden furnishings, and smoke-darkened ceilings, has hardly changed over the decades.

Doyle's (⊠ 9 College St., Southside ☎ 01/671–0616), a small, cozy pub, is a favorite with journalists from the *Irish Times* office, just across the street.

George (⊠89 S. Great George's St., Southside ☎01/478–2983), Dublin's two-floor main gay pub, draws an almost entirely male crowd; its nightclub stays open until 2:30 AM except Tuesday. The "alternative bingo night," with star drag act Miss Shirley Temple Bar, is a riot of risqué fun.

Globe (⊠ 11 S. Great George's St., Southside ☎ 01/671–1220), one of the hippest café-bars in town, draws arty, trendy Dubliners who sip espresso drinks by day and pack the place at night. There's live jazz on Sunday.

Fodor's Choice **Grogans** (⊠ 15 S. William St., Southside ☎ 01/677–9320), also known
★   as the Castle Lounge, is a small place packed with creative folk. Owner Tommy Grogan is known as a patron of local artists, and his walls are covered with their work.

Hogan's (⊠ 35 Great St. George's St., Southside ☎01/677–5904), a huge space on two levels, gets jammed most nights, but the old place maintains its style through it all.

Horseshoe Bar (⊠ Shelbourne, 27 St. Stephen's Green, Southside ☎ 01/676–6471) is a popular meeting place for Dublin's businesspeople and politicians, though around the semicircular bar there's comparatively little space for drinkers.

Kehoe's (⊠ 9 S. Anne St., Southside ☎ 01/677–8312) is popular with Trinity students and academics. The tiny back room is cozy, and the upstairs is basically the owner's living room, opened to the public.

Kitty O'Shea's (✉ Upper Grand Canal St., Southside ☎ 01/660–9965) has Pre-Raphaelite–style stained glass, and lots of sports paraphernalia on the walls, and is popular with sports fans of all types. Its sister pubs are in Brussels and Paris; this is the original.

Lesson Lounge (✉ 148 Upper Lesson St., Southside ☎ 01/660–3816) has the look of a classic old Dublin "boozer," with one notable exception: it has a television. The Lesson is known as a place to watch televised sports of all kinds, and it's always pleasant and inclusive.

Library Bar (✉ Central Hotel, 1–5 Exchequer St., Southside, 2 ☎ 01/679–7302) is the place to go when you're ready to get away from all the madness. The book-lined shelves, big armchairs and sofas, and blazing fire make this first-floor hideaway one of the most serene nighttime spots in Dublin.

Long Hall Pub (✉ 51 S. Great George's St., Southside ☎ 01/475–159), one of Dublin's most ornate traditional taverns, has Victorian lamps, a mahogany bar, mirrors, chandeliers, and plasterwork ceilings, all more than 100 years old. The pub serves sandwiches and an excellent pint of Guinness.

McDaid's (✉ 3 Harry St., Southside ☎ 01/679–4395) attracted boisterous Brendan Behan and other leading writers in the 1950s; its wild literary reputation still lingers, although the bar has been discreetly modernized and is altogether quieter.

Mulligan's (✉ 8 Poolbeg St., Southside ☎ 01/677–5582) is synonymous in Dublin with a truly inspirational pint of Guinness. Until a few years ago no women were admitted. Today journalists, locals, and students of both genders flock here for the perfect pint.

Neary's (✉ 1 Chatham St., Southside ☎ 01/677–7371), with an exotic, Victorian-style interior, was once the haunt of music-hall artists and a certain literary set, including Brendan Behan. Join the actors from the adjacent Gaiety Theatre for a good pub lunch.

O'Donoghue's (✉ 15 Merrion Row, Southside ☎ 01/676–2807), a cheerful smoky hangout, has impromptu musical performances that often spill out onto the street.

The Old Stand (✉ 37 Exchequer St., Southside ☎ 01/677–7220), one of the oldest pubs in the city, is named after the Old Stand stadium at Lansdowne Road, home to Irish rugby and football. The pub is renowned for great pints and fine steaks.

Solas (✉ 31 Wexford St., Southside ☎ 01/470–0583) offers not only some of Dublin's top DJs but also a wide selection of imported beers. The result: a young, hip crowd that likes to dance.

Fodor'sChoice
★
Stag's Head (✉ 1 Dame Ct., Southside ☎ 01/679–3701) dates from 1770 and was rebuilt in 1895. Theater people from the nearby Olympia, journalists, and Trinity students gather around the unusual Connemara red marble bar. The interior is a Victorian beaut.

Dublin
Pubs

Toner's (✉ 139 Lower Baggot St., Southside ☎ 01/676–3090), though billed as a Victorian bar, actually goes back 200 years, with an original flagstone floor to prove its antiquity, as well as wooden drawers running up to the ceiling—a relic of the days when bars doubled as grocery shops. Oliver St. John Gogarty, who was the model for Buck Mulligan in James Joyce's *Ulysses,* accompanied W. B. Yeats here, in what was purportedly the latter's only visit to a pub.

TEMPLE BAR **Front Lounge** (✉ 33 Parliament St., Temple Bar ☎ 01/679–3988), a modern pub, caters to a mixed crowd of young professionals, both gay and straight.

Oliver St. John Gogarty (✉ 57 Fleet St., Temple Bar ☎ 01/671–1822) is a lively bar that attracts all ages and nationalities; it overflows with patrons in summer. On most nights there is traditional Irish music upstairs.

Palace Bar (✉ 21 Fleet St., Temple Bar ☎ 01/677–9290), scarcely changed since the 1940s, is tiled and rather barren looking, but is popular with journalists and writers (the *Irish Times* is nearby.) The walls are lined with cartoons drawn by the illustrators who used to spend time here.

The Porterhouse (✉ 16–18 Parliament St., Temple Bar ☎ 01/679–8847) is one of the few bars in Ireland to brew its own beer. The Plain Porter has won the best stout at the "Brewing Oscars," beating out the mighty Guinness. The tasteful interior is all dark woods and soft lighting.

BALLSBRIDGE **Dubliner Pub** (✉ Jurys Hotel, Pembroke Rd., Ballsbridge ☎ 01/660–5000), an old-fashioned Irish pub, is a busy meeting place during lunch and after work.

O'Brien's (✉ Sussex Terr., Ballsbridge ☎ 01/668–2594), beside the Doyle Burlington Hotel, is a little antique gem of a pub, scarcely changed since the 1950s, with traditional snugs.

DUBLIN WEST **Brazen Head** (✉ Bridge St., Dublin West ☎ 01/677–9549), Dublin's oldest pub (the site has been licensed since 1198), has stone walls and open fires—it has hardly changed over the years. The pub is renowned for traditional-music performances and lively sing-along sessions on Sunday evenings. On the south side of the Liffey quays, it's a little difficult to find—turn down Lower Bridge Street and make a right into the old lane.

Chief O'Neill's (✉ Smithfield Village, Dublin West ☎ 01/817–3838), a Dublin hotel, has a large bar-café that's open and airy; it often hosts traditional Irish sessions.

Cobblestone (✉ N. King St., Dublin West ☎ 01/872–1799) is a glorious house of ale in the best Dublin tradition, popular with Smithfield Market workers. Its chatty imbibers and live traditional music are attracting a wider, younger crowd from all over town.

Mother Redcap's Tavern (✉ Back La., Dublin West ☎ 01/453–8306) is an authentic re-creation of a 17th-century Dublin tavern, with stone walls from an old flour mill, beams, and old prints of the city.

Out on the Liffey (✉ 27 Ormond Quay, Dublin West ☎ 01/872–2480) is Dublin's second-oldest gay pub; it draws a mixed gay and straight crowd of both men and women.

Ryan's Pub (✉ 28 Parkgate St., Dublin West ☎ 01/677–6097) is one of Dublin's last genuine, late-Victorian-era pubs, and has changed little since its last (1896) remodeling.

The Arts

Art Galleries

NORTH OF THE LIFFEY

The Bridge, a restored 18th-century Georgian house on the river, has an impressive, open-plan gallery. An internal bridge leads from the gallery shop to the big space at the back with exhibits of established and rising Irish artists in all media. ✉ *6 Upper Ormond Quay, Northside* ☎ *01/872–9702* ☉ *Mon.–Sat. 10–6, Sun. 2–5.*

CITY CENTER

Green on Red Galleries, a rather unprepossessing gallery near the back of Trinity College, is one of Dublin's best. The constantly changing exhibitions showcase the work of some of the country's—and Britain's—most promising up-and-coming artists. ✉ *26–28 Lombard St. E, Southside* ☎ *01/671–3414* ☉ *Weekdays 11–6, Sat. 11–5.*

Kerlin Gallery, perhaps Dublin's most important commercial gallery, exhibits the work of many of Ireland's important contemporary artists, including such internationally recognized figures as New York–based Sean Scully, Kathy Prendergast, Paul Seawright, and Stephen McKenna. This large space is behind Grafton Street. ✉ *Anne's La., S. Anne St., Southside* ☎ *01/670–9093* ☉ *Weekdays 10–5:45, Sat. 11–4:30.*

Rubicon Gallery, a second-floor gallery overlooking St. Stephen's Green, holds yearly exhibitions in all media. ✉ *10 St. Stephen's Green, Southside* ☎ *01/670–8055* ☉ *Mon.–Sat. 11–5:30.*

Solomon Gallery, although not exactly a risk-taker, has slowly developed a reputation as one of Dublin's leading fine-art galleries. ✉ *Powerscourt Townhouse Centre, S. William St., Southside* ☎ *01/679–4237* ☉ *Mon.–Sat. 10–5:30.*

TEMPLE BAR

Artselect is a newer gallery that offers a delightful melting pot of fine art, graphics, photography, and, unusually, three-dimensional pieces, including bronze, ceramic, and glasswork. A number of artists will be exhibited at any time, making it a great place to browse. ✉ *Meeting House Sq., Temple Bar* ☎ *01/635–1046* ☉ *Mon.-Sat. 10–6.*

National Photographic Archive is a trove of over 300,000 Irish photographs from the late 19th and early 20th centuries up to the present day. The Archive also hosts exhibits of work from contemporary Irish photographers—north and south. ✉ *Meeting House Sq., Temple Bar* ☎ *01/603–0200* ☉ *Weekdays 10–5, Sat. 10–2.*

Original Print Gallery, in an ultramodern building by the same prominent Dublin architect who designed Temple Bar Gallery, specializes in handmade limited editions of prints by Irish artists. Also in the building, the **Black Church Print Studio** (☎ 01/677–3629) exhibits prints. ✉ 4

Temple Bar, Temple Bar ☎ *01/677–3657* ⊙ *Tues.–Fri. 10:30–5:30, Sat. 11–5, Sun. 2–6.*

Temple Bar Gallery, with its unique, shop front–style windows, is the flagship of the Temple Bar redevelopment project. Expect to see the work of emerging Irish photographers, painters, sculptors, and other artists. Shows are on monthly rotating schedules. ⊠ *5–9 Temple Bar, Temple Bar* ☎ *01/671–0073* ⊙ *Mon.–Sat. 11–6, Sun. 2–6.*

DUBLIN WEST **5th** is the gallery in which every Irish artist wants to be shown. The location is spectacular: on the fifth floor of the impressive Guinness Storehouse. Regularly changing exhibits include painting and sculpture, but the emphasis is on innovative installation and Web art from all over the world. ⊠ *St. James Gate, Dublin West* ☎ *01/408–4800* ⊙ *Daily 9–5:30.*

Classical Music & Opera

CITY CENTER **The Bank of Ireland Arts Center** (⊠ Foster Pl. S, Southside ☎ 01/671–1488) is great at lunchtime, when classical music and opera recitals take place.

National Concert Hall (⊠ Earlsfort Terr., Southside ☎ 01/475–1666 ⊕ www.nch.ie), just off St. Stephen's Green, is Dublin's main theater for classical music of all kinds, from symphonies to chamber groups. The slightly austere, neoclassical building was transformed in 1981 into one of Europe's finest medium-sized concert halls. It houses the cream of Irish classical musicians, the National Symphony Orchestra of Ireland. A host of guest international conductors and performers—Maxim Vengerov, Radu Lupu, and Pinchas Zukerman are just a few of the soloists scheduled to appear in 2004–05—keep the standard very high, and performances continue throughout the year. The concert year picks up speed in mid-September and sails through to June but July and August also get many dazzling troupes.

Opera Ireland (⊠ John Player House, 276–288 S. Circular Rd., Southside ☎ 01/453–5519 ⊕ www.operaireland.com) performs at the Gaiety Theatre; call to find out what's on and when.

St. Stephen's Church (⊠ Merrion Sq., Southside ☎ 01/288–0663) stages a regular program of choral and orchestral events under its glorious "pepper canister" cupola.

TEMPLE BAR **Opera Theatre Company** (⊠ Temple Bar Music Centre, Curved St., Temple Bar ☎ 01/679–4962) is Ireland's only touring opera company. It performs at venues in Dublin and throughout the country.

DUBLIN WEST **Royal Hospital Kilmainham** (⊠ Military Rd., Dublin West ☎ 01/671–8666 ⊕ www.rhk.ie) presents frequent classical concerts in its magnificent 17th-century interior.

Film

NORTH OF THE LIFFEY **Savoy Cinema** (⊠ O'Connell St., Northside ☎ 01/874–6000), just across from the General Post Office, is a four-screen theater with the largest screen in the country.

UGC Multiplex (⊠ Parnell Center, Parnell St., Northside ☏ 01/872–8400), a 17-screen theater just off O'Connell Street, is the city center's only multiplex movie house; it shows the latest commercial features.

TEMPLE BAR **Irish Film Institute** (⊠ 6 Eustace St., Temple Bar ☏ 01/677–8788) shows classic and new independent films.

CITY CENTER **Screen Cinema** (⊠ 2 Townsend St., Southside ☏ 01/671–4988), between Trinity College and O'Connell Street Bridge, is a popular three-screen art-house cinema.

Rock & Contemporary Music

NORTH OF THE LIFFEY **The Ambassador** (⊠ 1 Parnell Sq., Northside ☏ 01/889–9403) was once a cinema attached to the Gate Theatre. The plush interior and seats have been removed, and the stripped-down venue now houses visiting bands and "school-disco" nights with music from the '70s and '80s.

The Point (⊠ Eastlink Br., Northside ☏ 01/836–3633 ⊕ www.thepoint. ie), a 6,000-capacity arena about 1 km (½ mi) east of the Custom House on the Liffey, is Dublin's premier venue for internationally renowned acts. Call or send a self-addressed envelope to receive a list of upcoming shows; tickets can be difficult to obtain, so book early.

CITY CENTER **International Bar** (⊠ Wicklow St., Southside ☏ 01/677–9250) has a long-established, tiny, get-close-to-the-band venue upstairs. It hosts theater in the afternoons.

Whelan's (⊠ 25 Wexford St., Southside ☏ 01/478–0766), just off the southeastern corner of St. Stephen's Green, is one of the city's best—and most popular—music venues. Well-known performers play everything from rock to folk to traditional music. The same owners run The Village bar and venue next door.

TEMPLE BAR **Olympia Theatre** (⊠ 72 Dame St., Temple Bar ☏ 01/677–7744) puts on "Midnight from the Olympia" shows every Friday and Saturday from midnight to 2 AM, with everything from rock to country.

Temple Bar Music Centre (⊠ Curved St., Temple Bar ☏ 01/670–0533) is a music venue, rehearsal space, television studio, and pub rolled into one. It buzzes with activity every day of the week. Live acts range from rock bands to world music to singer-songwriters.

DUBLIN WEST **Vicar Street** (⊠ 58–59 Thomas St., Dublin West ☏ 01/454–5533), just across from Christ Church Cathedral, is a venue for intimate concerts. It often plays host to folk music, jazz, and comedy, as well as rock performances.

Theater

NORTH OF THE LIFFEY **Abbey Theatre** (⊠ Lower Abbey St., Northside ☏ 01/878–7222 ⊕ www. abbeytheatre.ie) is the fabled home of Ireland's national theater company. In 1904 W. B. Yeats and his patron, Lady Gregory, opened the theater, which became a major center for the Irish literary renaissance—the place that first staged works by J. M. Synge and Sean O'-Casey, among many others. The year 2004 celebrated the 100th anniversary of this landmark theater. One, however, shouldn't arrive here expecting 19th-century grandeur: the original structure burned down in 1951. Unfortuntately, an ugly concrete boxlike auditorium was built in its place—but what it may lack in visuals it makes up for in space and acoustics. Some say the repertory is overly reverential and mainstream, but last year that was only proper, and such chestnuts as Dion Boucicault's *The Shaughran* wound up being applauded by many. Happily, the Abbey's sister theater at the same address, the Peacock, offers more experimental drama. But the Abbey will always be relevant since much of the theatergoing public still looks to it as a barometer of Irish culture.

Gate Theatre (⊠ Cavendish Row, Parnell Sq., Northside ☎ 01/874–4045 ⊕ www.gate-theatre.ie), an intimate 371-seat theater in a jewel-like Georgian assembly hall, produces the classics and contemporary plays by leading Irish writers.

CITY CENTER **Andrew's Lane Theatre** (⊠ 9–11 Andrew's La., Southside ☎ 01/679–5720) presents experimental productions.

Gaiety Theatre (⊠ S. King St., Southside ☎ 01/677–1717) is the home of Opera Ireland when it's not showing musical comedy, drama, and revues. On weekends this elegant theater is taken over by a nightclub with live music and cabaret.

Samuel Beckett Centre (⊠ Trinity College, Southside ☎ 01/608–2266) is home to Trinity's drama department, as well as visiting European groups. Dance is often performed here by visiting troupes.

TEMPLE BAR **New Project Arts Centre** (⊠ 39 E. Essex St., Temple Bar ☎ 01/671–2321) is a theater and performance space in the center of Temple Bar. Fringe and mainstream theater, contemporary music, and experimental art have all found a home here.

Olympia Theatre (⊠ 72 Dame St., Temple Bar ☎ 01/677–7744) is Dublin's oldest and premier multipurpose theatrical venue. In addition to its high-profile musical performances, it has seasons of comedy, vaudeville, and ballet.

DUBLIN WEST **Tivoli** (⊠ 135–138 Francis St., Dublin West ☎ 01/454–4472) brings culture to the heart of old working-class Dublin, the Liberties. Comedy-based shows and the occasional Shakespeare play are favored.

SPORTS & THE OUTDOORS

Health clubs have really caught on in Dublin and seem to be sprouting up in every corner of the city. But Dublin has no dearth of opportunities for getting out and moving about. It's true you'll have to travel to the suburbs north and south to enjoy most of them, but it's well worth it for the chance to explore a beach, horseback-ride through a forest, or bike through Phoenix Park.

Beaches

The main beach for swimming on the south side of Dublin is at **Killiney** (⊠ 13 km [8 mi] south of the city center, South County Dublin), a

3-km-long (2-mi-long) shingle (pebbly) beach. The DART train station is right by the beach; get off at Killiney. **Malahide,** a charming village on the Northside DART line, has a clean and easily accessible beach, though the current can be strong. To the north of Dublin city is **North Bull Island,** created over years by the action of the tides. The fine sand here stretches for almost 3 km (2 mi). Bus 130 from Lower Abbey Street stops by the walkway to the beach. Near Dublin city center, **Sandymount Strand** is a long expanse of fine sand where the tide goes out nearly 3 km (2 mi), but it's not suitable for swimming or bathing because the tide races in so fast. The strand can be reached easily by the DART train.

Bicycling

It's not a good idea to ride bicycles in the city center—traffic is heavy, and most roads don't have shoulders, much less bike lanes. Phoenix Park and some suburbs (especially Ballsbridge, Clontarf, and Sandymount), however, are pleasant once you're off the main roads. There's plenty of challenging terrain immediately south of the city, in the Dublin and Wicklow mountains. Don't forget to secure your bicycle if you leave it unattended. You can rent bicycles for about €57 a week; an equivalent amount will be charged for deposit. Nearly 20 companies in the Dublin region rent bicycles; Tourist Information Offices (TIOs) have a full list. **McDonald's** (⊠ 38 Wexford St., Southside ☎ 01/475–2586) is a central bike-repair and -rental shop. **Mike's Bike Shop** (⊠ Dun Laoghaire Shopping Center, Dun Laoghaire ☎ 01/280–0417) is a long-established bike outfit in the southern suburbs of Dublin. **Tracks Cycles** (⊠ 8 Botanic Rd., ☎ 01/873–2455) has a reputation for being trustworthy in repairs, sales, and rentals of all types of bikes.

Bowling

Bowling is a popular sport in Dublin. Two kinds are played locally. The sedate, exclusive, outdoor variety known as crown green bowling is played at a number of locations in the suburbs. Dublin also has six indoor 10-pin bowling centers. **Bray Leisure Bowl** (⊠ Quinsboro Rd., Bray ☎ 01/286–4455), an indoor bowling center, serves the area near the Wicklow border. **Herbert Park** (⊠ Ballsbridge ☎ 01/660–1875) has a splendid, baby-soft bowling green. **Kenilworth Bowling Club** (⊠ Grosvenor Sq., Rathmines ☎ 01/497–2305) welcomes paying visitors, and lessons are available. The green is half the size of a soccer pitch, and smooth as a carpet. **Leisureplex Coolock** (⊠ Malahide Rd., North County Dublin ☎ 01/848–5722 ⊠ Village Green Center, Tallaght ☎ 01/459–9411) is popular with bowlers from both sides of the city, as it has plenty of lanes and is easy to reach.

Metro Bowl (⊠ 149 N. Strand Rd., North County Dublin ☎ 01/855–0400) tends to attract the more serious bowlers. **Stillorgan Bowl** (⊠ Stillorgan Rd., Stillorgan ☎ 01/288–1656), opened in 1963, is the oldest 10-pin center in Ireland. **Superdome** (⊠ Palmerston Shopping Centre, Palmerston ☎ 01/626–0700) draws big crowds of teenage and family bowlers.

Football

Soccer—called football in Europe—is very popular in Ireland, largely due to the euphoria resulting from the national team's successes since the late 1980s. However, the places where you can watch it aren't ideal—they tend to be small and out-of-date. **Lansdowne Road Stadium** (⊠ 62 Lansdowne Rd., Ballsbridge ☎ 01/668–4601), a vast rugby stadium, is the main center for international matches. A huge redevelopment of the stadium has recently been approved by the government and is due to start in a couple of years.

League of Ireland matches take place throughout the city on Friday evenings or Sunday afternoons from March to November. For details, contact the **Football Association of Ireland** (⊠ 80 Merrion Sq. S, Southside ☎ 01/676–6864).

Gaelic Games

The traditional games of Ireland, Gaelic football and hurling, attract a huge following, with roaring crowds cheering on their county teams. Games are held at Croke Park, the stunning, high-tech national stadium for Gaelic games, just north of the city center. For details of matches, contact the **Gaelic Athletic Association** (GAA; ⊠ Croke Park, North County Dublin ☎ 01/836–3222 ⊕ www.gaa.ie).

Golf

Think idyllic. The Dublin region is a great place for golfers—it has 32 18-hole courses, 16 9-hole courses, and several more 18-hole courses on the way. Below are only some of the major 18-hole courses around Dublin. **Deer Park** (⊠ Deer Park Hotel, Howth, North County Dublin ☎ 01/832–6039) is a top-quality parkland golf course. It has 48 holes, and the longest 18-hole course is 6,830 yards. **Edmonstown** (⊠ Rathfarnham, South County Dublin ☎ 01/493–2461), a beautiful golf course, serves an upscale clientele. The championship 18-hole course is 6,011 yards long. Expert instruction is available. **Elm Park** (⊠ Donnybrook, South County Dublin ☎ 01/269–3438) welcomes visiting golfers and beginners. **Foxrock** (⊠ Torquay Rd., Foxrock, South County Dublin ☎ 01/289–3992) is a tough 9-hole golf course with a gorgeous location in the Southside suburbs.

The 18-hole, 6,010-yard **Hermitage** (⊠ Lucan, North County Dublin ☎ 01/626–4781) is one of the city's more difficult golf courses. **Newlands** (⊠ Clondalkin, South County Dublin ☎ 01/459–2903) attracts golfers from the Southside. The 18-hole course is 6,100 yards. The golf course at **Sutton** (⊠ Sutton, South County Dublin ☎ 01/832–3013) has only 9 holes, but they're top-quality and the course is as exclusive and as pricey as everything else in this wealthy suburb. **Woodbrook** (⊠ Bray, South County Dublin ☎ 01/282–4799) is worth the trip out of the city for a day of golf by the sea. The very long 18-hole course is 6,836 yards.

At **Golf D2** (⊠ Cow St., Temple Bar ☎ 01/672–6181) you can practice even if it's raining. You strike a real ball with a real club against a huge screen, which tracks the virtual course of your shot. It's a cool idea, and it works. You can play 34 of the world's most famous courses, including St. Andrews and Pebble Beach. It costs €19.05 for a half hour, and you must book ahead.

Health Clubs

Not far from the Ballsbridge hotels, **Equinox Leisure** (✉ St. John's Rd. E, near Sydney Parade DART station, Ballsbridge ☎ 01/269–5764) has a full gym and nightly fitness classes of all levels. The **Iveagh Fitness Club** (✉ Christ Church St., Dublin West ☎ 01/454–6555) is next to Christ Church Cathedral, in a complex of beautiful old redbrick buildings. It has a pool, sauna, and full weight room. Just off Grafton Street, the **Jackie Skelly Fitness Centre** (✉ 41–42 Clarendon St., Southside ☎ 01/677–0040) is perfect if you're staying in a city-center hotel without a gym. In Rathgar village, the **Orwell Club** (✉ 75 Orwell Rd., Rathgar, South County Dublin ☎ 01/492–3146) is not far from many of the Southside hotels. The city-center **Riverside Fitness Centre** (✉ Eden Quay, Northside ☎ 01/878–7303) even has baby-sitting facilities for young children.

Horse Racing

Horse racing—from flat to hurdle to steeplechase—is one of the great sporting loves of the Irish. The sport is closely followed and betting is popular, but the social side of attending races is equally important to Dubliners. The main course in Dublin is **Leopardstown** (✉ Leopardstown Rd., Southside ☎ 01/289–3607 ⊕ www.leopardstown.com), an ultramodern course that in February hosts the Hennessey Gold Cup, Ireland's most prestigious steeplechase. Summertime is devoted to flat racing, and the rest of the year to racing over fences. You can also nip in for a quick meal at the restaurant.

The **Curragh** (☎ 045/441–205 ⊕ www.curragh.ie), southwest of Dublin off M7, hosts the five Classics, the most important flat races of the season, from May to September. There are numerous bars here and two restaurants. **Fairyhouse** (✉ Co. Meath ☎ 01/825–6167) hosts the Grand National, the most popular steeplechase of the season, every Easter Monday. **Punchestown** (☎ 045/897–704), outside Naas, County Kildare, is the home of the ever-popular Punchestown National Hunt Festival in April.

Rugby

For details about rugby in Ireland, contact the **Irish Rugby Football Union** (☎ 01/647–3800 ⊕ www.irishrugby.ie). International rugby matches run during the winter and spring at the vast **Lansdowne Road Stadium** (✉ 62 Lansdowne Rd., Ballsbridge ☎ 01/668–4601). Local matches are also played every weekend during that time.

Running

Traffic in Dublin, heavy from early morning until late at night, is getting worse, so if you jog here, expect to dodge vehicles and stop for lights. (Remember *always* to look to your right *and* your left before crossing a street.) If you're staying in Temple Bar or on the western end of the city and you can run 9 km (5½ mi), head to Phoenix Park, easily the nicest place in Dublin for a jog. If you're on the Southside, Merrion Square, St. Stephen's Green, and Trinity College are all good places for short jogs, though be prepared to dodge pedestrians; if you're looking for a longer route, ask your hotel to direct you to the Grand Canal, which has a pleasant path you can run along as far east as the Grand Canal Street Bridge.

Swimming

Swimming in Ireland will never be the same since the opening of the spectacular **National Aquatic Centre** (✉ Sungborough Rd., Blanchardstown, 15 North County Dublin ☎ 01/646–4325) in Blanchardstown, just 10 km (6 mi) outside the city to the northwest. Wave pools, bubble pools, a pirate ship, and a dark hole flume are a few of the added attractions to the Olympic-size pool. The private pool at **Dundrum Family Recreation Center** (✉ Meadowbrook, Dundrum, South County Dublin ☎ 01/298–4654) is open to the public for a small fee. There are usually two lanes open for lap swimming, and the showers and changing rooms are clean. For a hardy dip, there's year-round sea swimming at the **Forty Foot Bathing Pool,** a traditional sea-bathing area—in use for more than a century (and popular with older nude men)—in Sandycove. It is deep and nicely sheltered from the wind. Steps lead down into the water. **St. Vincent's** (✉ Navan Rd., North County Dublin ☎ 01/838–4906) is a public pool in the northern suburbs of the city. Two lanes are available for laps in the morning, at lunchtime, and in the late evening. Changing rooms have good showers, but you have to take your clothes into the pool area.

Terenure College (✉ Templeogue Rd., Terenure, South County Dublin ☎ 01/490–7071) is a high school with a pool that's open to the public when school's not in session and competitions aren't taking place. The modern changing rooms have lockers with locks, and there are usually a couple of lanes open for lap swimming. One of the best of Dublin's 12 public pools is **Townsend Street** (✉ Townsend St., Southside ☎ 01/672–9121). Six lanes are available for laps every evening from 5 to 7. Lockers and showers are provided. **Williams Park** (✉ Williams Rd., Rathmines, South County Dublin ☎ 01/496–1275) is a quality public pool in the southern suburbs. Five lanes are available for early-morning laps on Tuesday and Thursday. Showers are provided, and you bring your clothes poolside in a basket.

Tennis

Tennis is one of Dublin's most popular participant sports, and some public parks have excellent tennis facilities. For information about playing tennis in Dublin, contact **Tennis Ireland** (✉ 22 Argyle Sq., South County Dublin ☎ 01/668–1841).

Bushy Park (✉ Terenure, South County Dublin ☎ 01/490–0320) has well-maintained public tennis courts. The 12 asphalt courts are available for €1.50 an hour and are open daily from 10 to dusk. Thanks to its excellent facilities, **Herbert Park** (✉ Ballsbridge ☎ 01/668–4364) attracts some serious tennis players to its public courts. The 12 asphalt courts cost €2.50 an hour and are open daily from 8 to dusk. **Kilternan Tennis Centre** (✉ Kilternan Golf and Country Club Hotel, Kilternan, South County Dublin ☎ 01/295–3729) has everything a tennis player could want—lessons, serving machines, racket stringing—at a price. Four indoor and four outdoor floodlighted Savannah-grass courts are available for €14 an hour. It's open daily 9 to 10. **St. Anne's Park** (✉ Dollymount Strand, North County Dublin ☎ 01/833–8898) has 12 quality asphalt courts within sniffing distance of the ocean. The courts cost €3 an hour and are open from 10 until an hour before dusk every day. **West Wood Lawn Tennis Club** (✉ Leopardstown Racecourse, Foxrock, South County Dublin ☎ 01/289–2911) is popular with young, serious players. Lessons are offered for €5 an hour on the 11 indoor and 4 outdoor courts. It's open daily 8 to 10.

SHOPPING

The only known specimens of leprechauns or shillelaghs in Ireland are those in souvenir-shop windows, and shamrocks mainly bloom around the borders of Irish linen handkerchiefs and tablecloths. But today you'll find much more than kitschy designs. There's a tremendous variety of stores in Dublin, many of which are quite sophisticated—as a walk through Dublin's central shopping area, from O'Connell to Grafton Street, will prove. Department stores stock internationally known fashion-designer goods and housewares, and small (and often pricey) boutiques sell Irish crafts and other merchandise. Don't expect too many bargains here. And be prepared, if you're shopping in central Dublin, to push through crowds—especially in the afternoons and on weekends. Most large shops and department stores are open Monday to Saturday 9 to 6. Although nearly all department stores are closed on Sunday, some smaller specialty shops stay open. Those with later closing hours are noted below. You're particularly likely to find sales in January, February, July, and August.

Shopping Streets

Each of Dublin's dozen or so main shopping streets has a different character. Visit them all to appreciate the wide selection of items for sale here. The main commercial streets north of the river have both chain and department stores that tend to be less expensive (and less design-conscious) than their counterparts in the city center on the other side of the Liffey.

North of the Liffey

Henry Street, where cash-conscious Dubliners shop, runs westward from O'Connell Street. Arnotts department store is the anchor here; smaller, specialty stores sell CDs, footwear, and clothing. Henry Street's continuation, Mary Street, has a branch of Marks & Spencer and the Jervis Shopping Centre.

O'Connell Street, the city's main thoroughfare, more downscale than Southside city streets (such as Grafton Street), is still worth a walk. One of Dublin's largest department stores, Clery's, is here, across from the GPO. On the same side of the street as the post office is Eason's, a large book, magazine, and stationery store.

City Center

Dawson Street, just east of Grafton Street between Nassau Street to the north and St. Stephen's Green to the south, is the city's primary bookstore avenue. Waterstone's and Hodges Figgis face each other from opposite sides of the street.

Francis Street and surrounding areas, such as the Coombe, have plenty of shops where you can browse. It's all part of the Liberties, the oldest part of the city and the hub of Dublin's antiques trade. If you're looking for something in particular, dealers will gladly recommend the appropriate store to you.

Grafton Street, Dublin's bustling pedestrian-only main shopping street, has two upscale department stores: Marks & Spencer and Brown Thomas. The rest of the street is taken up by shops, many of them branches of international chains, such as the Body Shop and Bally, and many British chains. This is also the spot to buy fresh flowers, available at reasonable prices from outdoor stands. On the smaller streets off Grafton Street—especially Duke Street, South Anne Street, and Chatham Street—are worthwhile crafts, clothing, and designer housewares shops.

Nassau Street, Dublin's main tourist-oriented thoroughfare, has some of the best-known stores selling Irish goods, but you won't find many locals shopping here. Still, if you're looking for classic Irish gifts to take home, you should be sure at least to browse along here.

Temple Bar, Dublin's hippest neighborhood, is dotted with small, precious boutiques—mainly intimate, quirky shops that traffic in a small selection of *très* trendy goods, from vintage clothes to some of the most avant-garde Irish garb anywhere in the city.

Shopping Centers

North of the Liffey

Ilac Center (⊠ Henry St., Northside) was Dublin's first large, modern shopping center, with two department stores, hundreds of specialty shops, and several restaurants. The stores are not as exclusive as those at some of the other centers, but there's plenty of free parking.

Jervis Shopping Centre (⊠ Jervis and Mary Sts., Northside ☎ 01/878–1323) is a slightly high-end center housing some of the major British chain stores. It has a compact design and plenty of parking.

City Center

Powerscourt Townhouse Centre (⊠ 59 S. William St., Southside), the former town home of Lord Powerscourt, built in 1771, has an interior courtyard that has been refurbished and roofed over; a pianist often plays on the dais at ground-floor level. Coffee shops and restaurants share space with a mix of stores selling antiques and crafts. You can also buy original Irish fashions here by young designers, such as Gráinne Walsh.

Royal Hibernian Way (⊠ Off Dawson St. between S. Anne and Duke Sts., Southside ☎ 01/679–5919) is on the former site of the two-centuries-old Royal Hibernian Hotel, a coaching inn that was demolished in 1983.

WHEN IN DUBLIN, WEAR WHAT THE LOCALS MAKE

THE SUCCESS OF SHOPS *like Costume and Platform has at last given young Irish designers the confidence to produce more original and impressive work. One of Costume's most popular designers,* **Helen James,** *graduated from NCAD textile design in 1992. She went straight to New York, where she worked for Donna Karan, Club Monaco, and Victoria's Secret, among others. She returned to Ireland in 2002 and developed her line of unique, hand-printed textile accessories. Many people say there is a delicate Japanese feel to her work.*

Footwear has long been an area overlooked by Irish designers, but Irishwoman **Eileen Shields** *has been living and working in New York since 1988 and, for almost ten years, designed footwear for Donna Karan. Eileen has just gone out on her own and her premiere*

collection is all about clean, bold lines. Materials include antique kid, fine suede, python, and soft patent leather. Textures are often strongly contrasting, while colors are sensual and sophisticated. You can get the shoes online at www. eileenshields.com, or in her new store which will open in late 2004 on Scarlett Row in the city center.

The Tucker family has been a key player in Irish fashion for 40 years, and daughter **Leigh Tucker** *has quickly established herself as one of Dublin's classiest young designers. Fine tailoring is her trademark— the finish on her evening wear is nonpareil—and beaded French lace and draped jersey are her favorite materials. Her newest line can be found in boutiques across Ireland and at Costume in Dublin.*

The pricey, stylish shops—about 20 or 30, many selling fashionable clothes—are small in scale and include a branch of Leonidas, the Belgian chocolate firm.

St. Stephen's Green Centre (✉ Northwest corner of St. Stephen's Green, Southside ☎ 01/478–0888), Dublin's largest and most ambitious shopping complex, resembles a giant greenhouse, with Victorian-style ironwork. On three floors overlooked by a vast clock, the 100 mostly small shops sell crafts, fashions, and household goods.

Tower Design Centre (✉ Pearse St., Southside ☎ 01/677–5655), east of the heart of the city center (near the Waterways Visitors Centre), has more than 35 separate crafts shops in a converted 1862 sugar-refinery tower. On the ground floor are workshops devoted to heraldry and Irish pewter; the other six floors have stores that sell hand-painted silks, ceramics, hand-knit items, jewelry, and fine-art cards and prints.

Westbury Mall (✉ Westbury Hotel, off Grafton St., Southside) is an upmarket shopping mall where you can buy designer jewelry, antique rugs, and decorative goods.

Department Stores

Arnotts (✉ Henry St., Northside ☎ 01/872–1111 ✉ Grafton St., Southside ☎ 01/872–1111), on three floors, stocks a wide selection of clothing, household, and sporting goods. The smaller Grafton Street branch sells new fashion and footwear.

A-Wear (✉ Grafton St., Southside ☎ 01/671–7200 ✉ Henry St., Northside ☎ 01/872–4644) specializes in fashion for men and women. Many of the items are seasonal and closely follow ever-changing trends. Leading Irish designers, including John Rocha, supply A-Wear with a steady stream of clothing.

Brown Thomas (✉ Grafton St., Southside ☎ 01/679–5666), Dublin's most exclusive department store, stocks the leading designer names (including many Irish designers) in clothing and cosmetics, plus lots of stylish accessories. There's also a good selection of crystal.

Clery's (✉ O'Connell St., Northside ☎ 01/878–6000), once the city's most fashionable department store, is still worth a visit. You'll find all kinds of merchandise—from fashion to home appliances—on its four floors. Note that goods sold here reflect a distinctly modest, traditional sense of style.

Dunnes Stores (✉ St. Stephen's Green Centre, Southside ☎ 01/478–0188 ✉ Henry St., Northside ☎ 01/872–6833 ✉ Ilac Center, Mary St., Northside ☎ 01/873–0211) is Ireland's largest chain of department stores. All of the branches stock fashion, household, and grocery items, and have a reputation for value and variety.

Eason's (✉ O'Connell St., Northside ☎ 01/873–3811 ✉ Ilac Center, Mary St., Northside ☎ 01/872–1322) is known primarily for its large selection of books, magazines, and stationery; the larger O'Connell Street branch sells tapes, CDs, records, videos, and other audiovisual goodies.

Marks & Spencer (✉ Grafton St., Southside ☎ 01/679–7855 ✉ Henry St., Northside ☎ 01/872–8833), perennial competitor to Brown Thomas, stocks everything from fashion (including lingerie) to tasty unusual groceries. The Grafton Street branch even has its own bureau de change, which doesn't charge commission.

Roches Stores (✉ Henry St., Northside ☎ 01/873–0044), once Dublin's home of "sensible" clothes, has recently undergone a radical face-lift, with top European brands like Zara drawing crowds of fashion- and price-conscious shoppers.

Outdoor Markets

Liberty Market, on the north end of Meath Street in the Liberties section of Southside, sells bric-a-brac Friday and Saturday from 10 to 6 and Sunday from noon to 5:30. Listening to the banter between buyers and sellers can be lots of fun.

Meeting House Square Market, held Saturday mornings at the heart of Temple Bar, is a good place to buy homemade foodstuffs: breads, chocolate, and organic veggies.

Moore Street, on the Northside behind the Ilac Center, is open Monday through Saturday from 9 to 6. Stalls, which line both sides of the street, sell fruits and vegetables; this is also a good place to buy shoes and boots. Moore Street vendors are known for their sharp wit, so expect the traditional Dublin repartee when you're shopping.

Specialty Shops

Antiques

Dublin is one of Europe's best cities in which to buy antiques, largely due to a long and proud tradition of restoration and high-quality craftsmanship. The Liberties, Dublin's oldest district, is, fittingly, the hub of the antiques trade, and is chockablock with shops and traders. Bachelor's Walk, along the quays, also has some decent shops. It's quite a seller's market, but bargains are still possible.

Antiques and collectibles fairs take place at **Newman House** (✉ 85–86 St. Stephen's Green, Southside ☎ 01/670–8295) every second Sunday throughout the year.

Conlon Antiques (✉ 21 Clanbrassil St., Dublin West ☎ 01/453–7323) sells a diverse selection of antiques, from sideboards to fanlights.
Ha'penny Bridge Galleries (✉ 15 Bachelor's Walk, Northside ☎ 01/872–3950) has four floors of curios, with a particularly large selection of bronzes, silver, and china.
O'Sullivan Antiques (✉ 43–44 Francis St., Dublin West ☎ 01/454–1143 or 01/453–9659) specializes in 18th- and 19th-century furniture and has a high-profile clientele, including Mia Farrow and Liam Neeson.

Books

You won't have any difficulty weighing down your suitcase with books. Ireland, after all, produced four Nobel literature laureates in just under 75 years. If you're at all interested in modern and contemporary literature, be sure to leave yourself time to browse through the bookstores, as you're likely to find books available here you can't find back home. Best of all, thanks to an enlightened national social policy, there's no tax on books, so if you only buy books, you don't have to worry about getting V.A.T. slips.

Books Upstairs (✉ 36 College Green, Southside ☎ 01/679–6687) carries an excellent selection of special-interest books, including gay and feminist literature, psychology, and self-help books.
Cathach Books (✉ 10 Duke St., Southside ☎ 01/671–8676) sells first editions of Irish literature and many other books of Irish interest, plus old maps of Dublin and Ireland.
Dublin Bookshop (✉ 24 Grafton St., Southside ☎ 01/677–5568) is an esteemed, family-owned store that sells mass-market books.
Eason's/Hanna's (✉ 29 Nassau St., Southside ☎ 01/677–1255) sells secondhand and mass-market paperbacks and hardcovers, and has a good selection of works on travel and Ireland.

Flying Pig Bookshop (✉ 17 Crow St., Temple Bar ☎ 01/679–5099) stocks Ireland's largest selection of secondhand science fiction and fantasy books.

Greene's (✉ Clare St., Southside ☎ 01/676–2544) carries an extensive range of secondhand volumes and new educational and mass market books.

Hodges Figgis (✉ 56–58 Dawson St., Southside ☎ 01/677–4754), Dublin's leading independent bookstore, stocks 1½ million books on three floors. There's a pleasant café on the first floor.

Hughes & Hughes (✉ St. Stephen's Green Centre, Southside ☎ 01/478–3060) has strong travel and Irish-interest sections. There's also a store at Dublin Airport.

Waterstone's (✉ 7 Dawson St., Southside ☎ 01/679–1415), a large two-story branch of the British chain, features a fine selection of Irish and international books.

Winding Stair (✉ 40 Ormond Quay, Northside ☎ 01/873–3292) is a charming new- and used-book store overlooking the Liffey. The little upstairs café is the perfect spot for an afternoon of reading.

China, Crystal, Ceramics & Jewelry

Ireland is *the* place to buy Waterford crystal, which is available in a wide selection of products, including relatively inexpensive items. Other lines are now gaining recognition, such as Cavan, Galway, and Tipperary crystal.

Blarney Woollen Mills (✉ 21–23 Nassau St., Southside ☎ 01/671–0068) is one of the best places for Belleek china, Waterford and Galway crystal, and Irish linen.

China Showrooms (✉ 32–33 Lower Abbey St., Northside ☎ 01/878–6211), which has been operating since 1942, carries all the top brand names in fine china, including Aynsley, Royal Doulton, and Belleek. It also stocks Waterford, Tyrone, and Tipperary hand-cut crystal.

Crafts Centre of Ireland (✉ St. Stephen's Green Centre, Southside ☎ 01/475–4526) carries an impressive inventory of Ireland's most famous contemporary designers, including Michael Kennedy and Diane McCormick (ceramics), Glen Lucas (wood turning), and Jerpoint Glass (glassworks).

Crannóg (✉ Crown Alley, Temple Bar ☎ 01/671–0805) specializes in ceramics and contemporary Irish jewelry, especially silver pendants and rings.

Designyard (✉ E. Essex St., Temple Bar ☎ 01/677–8453) carries beautifully designed Irish and international tableware, lighting, small furniture, and jewelry.

House of Ireland (✉ 37–38 Nassau St., Southside ☎ 01/671–6133) has an extensive selection of crystal, jewelry, tweeds, sweaters, and other upscale goods.

Kilkenny Shop (✉ 5–6 Nassau St., Southside ☎ 01/677–7066) specializes in contemporary Irish-made ceramics, pottery, and silver jewelry, and regularly holds exhibits of exciting new work by Irish craftspeople.

McDowell (✉ 3 Upper O'Connell St., Northside ☎ 01/874–4961), a jewelry shop popular with Dubliners, has been in business for more than 100 years.

Tierneys (✉ St. Stephen's Green Centre, Southside ☎ 01/478–2873) carries a good selection of crystal and china. Claddagh rings (composed of two hands clasped around a heart with a crown above it), pendants, and brooches are popular.

Weir & Sons (✉ 96 Grafton St., Southside ☎ 01/677–9678), Dublin's most prestigious jeweler, sells not only jewelry and watches, but also china, glass, lamps, silver, and leather.

Clothing Stores

Costume (✉ 10 Castel Market, Southside ☎ 01/679–4188) is a classy boutique where Dubliners with fashion sense and money like to shop for colorful, stylish clothes. Local designers include Leigh, Helen James, and Antonia Campbell-Hughes; Temperley and Preen are among the international designers featured.

Platform (✉ 50 S. William St., Southside ☎ 01/677–7380), with its modern, sleek clothing, is run by the unique Joan Woods, who always seems to have her little dog in tow. You enter the narrow, cozy shop through a set of beautiful stone arches. Scandinavian and Dutch labels are sold alongside Ireland's Tim Ryan and hats by Philip Tracy.

Smock (✉ West Essex St., Temple Bar ☎ 01/613–9000) is a tiny designer shop with great, left-field taste. International labels include Pearson, Veronique, and A.F. Vandevoft. They also carry a beautiful line in fine jewelry.

Urban Outfitters (✉ 4 Cecilia St., Temple Bar ☎ 01/670–6202) is a U.S. chain shop that has become hugely popular with the locals. The music is almost as loud as the clothes, but this is a great place to shop with teenagers and young adults. Besides all the major street labels, they have a wide range of accessories.

Museum Stores

National Gallery of Ireland Shop (✉ Merrion Sq. W, Southside ☎ 01/678–5450) has a terrific selection of books on Irish art, plus posters, postcards, note-cards, and lots of lovely bibelots.

National Museum of Archaeology and History Shop (✉ Kildare St., Southside ☎ 01/677–7444 Ext. 327) carries jewelry based on ancient Celtic artifacts in the museum collection, contemporary Irish pottery, a large selection of books, and other gift items.

Trinity College Library Shop (✉ Old Library, Trinity College, Southside ☎ 01/608–2308) sells Irish-theme books, *Book of Kells* souvenirs, clothing, jewelry, and lovely Irish-made items.

Music

Celtic Note (✉ 12 Nassau St., Southside ☎ 01/670–4157) is aimed at the tourist market, with lots of compilations and greatest-hits formats.

Claddagh Records (✉ 2 Cecilia St., Temple Bar ☎ 01/679–3664) has a good selection of traditional and folk music.

Gael Linn (✉ 26 Merrion Sq., Southside ☎ 01/676–7283) specializes in traditional Irish-music and Irish-language recordings; it's where the aficionados go.

HMV (✉ 65 Grafton St., Southside ☎ 01/679–5334 ✉ 18 Henry St., Northside ☎ 01/872–2095) is one of the larger record shops in town.

McCullogh Piggott (⌧ 25 Suffolk St., Southside ☎ 01/677–3138) is the best place in town to buy instruments, sheet music, scores, and books about music.

Tower Records (⌧ 6–8 Wicklow St., Southside ☎ 01/671–3250) is the best-stocked international chain.

Sweaters & Tweeds

Don't think Irish woolens are limited to Aran sweaters and tweed jackets. You can choose souvenirs from a wide selection of hats, gloves, scarves, blankets, and other goods here. If you're traveling outside of Dublin, you may want to wait to make purchases elsewhere, but if Dublin is it, you still have plenty of good shops from which to choose. The tweed sold in Dublin comes from two main sources: Donegal and Connemara. Labels inside the garments guarantee their authenticity. The following are the largest retailers of traditional Irish woolen goods in the city.

An Táin (⌧ 13 Temple Bar Sq. N, Temple Bar ☎ 01/679–0523) carries hyperstylish handmade Irish sweaters, jackets, and accessories.

Blarney Woollen Mills (⌧ 21–23 Nassau St., Southside ☎ 01/671–0068) stocks a good selection of tweed, linen, and wool sweaters in all price ranges.

Cleo Ltd (⌧ 18 Kildare St., Southside ☎ 01/676–1421) sells hand-knit sweaters and accessories made only from natural fibers; it also carries its own designs.

Dublin Woollen Mills (⌧ Metal Bridge Corner, Northside ☎ 01/677–5014) at Ha'penny Bridge has a good selection of hand-knit and other woolen sweaters at competitive prices.

Kevin and Howlin (⌧ 31 Nassau St., Southside ☎ 01/677–0257) specializes in handwoven tweed men's jackets, suits, and hats, and also sells tweed fabric.

Monaghan's (⌧ Grafton Arcade, 15–17 Grafton St., Southside ☎ 01/677–0823) specializes in cashmere.

Vintage

Flip (⌧ 4 Upper Fownes St., Temple Bar ☎ 01/671–4299), one of the original stores in Temple Bar, sells vintage and retro clothing from the '50s, '60s, and '70s.

Harlequin (⌧ Castle Market, Southside ☎ 01/671-0202) isn't cheap, but the owner/buyer has great taste in classic men's and women's wear.

Jenny Vander (⌧ Georges Street Arcade, Southside ☎ 01/677–0406) is the most famous name in Irish vintage and retro clothing. Just browsing through her collection is a pleasure.

SIDE TRIPS

Dubliners are undeniably lucky. Few populaces enjoy such glorious—and easily accessible—options for day trips. Just outside the city lie some of the region's most unique sights, including the James Joyce Martello Tower, Marino Casino, and Malahide Castle. Beyond the southern neighborhood of Ballsbridge, sights are too spread out to cover on foot, and it's necessary to use either a car or public transportation (the bus or DART). If you have a car, then head to Rathfarnham, directly south of the city. Alternatively, head east and follow the coast road south to Dun Laoghaire and points even farther south. Traveling to and from each of the suburbs will take up most of a day, so you need to pick and choose the excursions you prefer.

South County Dublin

Dublin's southern suburbs are home to its more affluent and well-heeled citizens. As is usually the case, the wealthy folk have chosen some of the most scenic parts of the city, with the beautiful coastline to the east and Wicklow and its mountains to the south.

Numbers in the text correspond to numbers in the margin and on the South County Dublin map.

Rathfarnham

❶ *Bus 47A from Hawkins Street in the city center goes to both parks in Rathfarnham. Or drive, leaving the city center via Nicholas Street just west of Christ Church Cathedral and following it south through Terenure.*

Two parks lie in the suburb of Rathfarnham, due south of the city at the edge of the Dublin Mountains. The 18th-century house in **St. Enda's National Historic Park** has been turned into the **Pearse Museum**, commemorating Pádrig Pearse, leader of Dublin's 1916 Easter Uprising. In the early 20th century, the house was an Irish-language boys' school, which Pearse and his brother Willie founded. The museum preserves Pearse-family memorabilia, documents, and photographs. A lake and nature trails are also on the park's 50-acre grounds, and guides are available for tours of the park or simply for information. ✉ *Grange Rd., South County Dublin* ☎ *01/493–4208* ⊕ *www.heritageireland.ie* 🎟 *Free* ☉ *Park daily 8:30–dusk. Museum May–Aug., daily 10–1 and 2–5:30; Sept.–Oct. and Feb.–Apr., daily 10–1 and 2–5; Nov.–Jan., daily 10–1 and 2–4.*

☾ **Marlay Park** marks the start of the Wicklow Way, a popular walking route that crosses the Wicklow Mountains for 137 km (85 mi), through some of the most rugged landscapes in Ireland. In addition to its woodlands and nature walks, the 214-acre park has a cobbled courtyard, home to brightly plumaged peacocks. Surrounding the courtyard are crafts workshops, where you're welcome to observe bookbinding, jewelry making, and furniture making in process. Every Saturday from 3 to 5, kids can take a free ride on the model steam railway. To get here, leave St. Enda's Park via Grange Road and walk up the hill for about 1 km (½ mi), turning left at the T junction and continuing another ½ km (¼ mi). ✉ *Grange Rd., South County Dublin* ☎ *01/493–4059* 🎟 *Free* ☉ *Feb. and Mar., daily 10–6; Apr. and Sept., daily 10–8; May–Aug., daily 10–9; Oct., daily 10–7; Nov.–Jan., daily 10–5.*

NIGHTLIFE **Johnnie Fox's** (✉ Glencullen, South County Dublin ☎ 01/295–5647), 12 km (7½ mi) from the city center and 1½ km (1 mi) from Rathfarnam, sits 1,000 feet up in the Dublin Mountains, making it the highest licensed premises in Ireland. You approach it by a winding and steeply

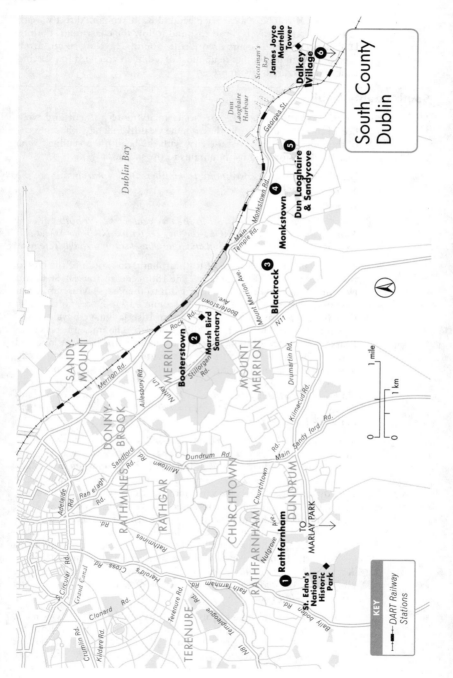

South County Dublin

Dublin Bay

Scotsman's Bay

James Joyce Martello Tower
Dalkey Village **6**

Dun Laoghaire Harbour

Georges St.

Dun Laoghaire & Sandycove **5**

Monkstown **4**

Main Temple Rd.

Monkstown Rd.

Blackrock **3**

Mount Merrion Ave.

N11

Booterstown Ave.

Rock Rd.

Booterstown **2**
Marsh Bird Sanctuary

Stillorgan Rd.

MERRION

Nutley Ln.

Merrion Rd.

Ailesbury Rd.

SANDY-MOUNT

MOUNT MERRION

Drumartin Rd.

Kilmacud Rd.

Main Sandyford Rd.

DUNDRUM

Dundrum Rd.

DONNYBROOK

Sandford Rd.

Milltown Rd.

RATHMINES

Ranelagh Rd.

Adelaide Rd.

RATHGAR

Rathmines Rd.

CHURCHTOWN

Churchtown Rd.

RATHFARNHAM

Nutgrove Ave.

Rathfarnham Rd.

Harold's Cross Rd.

TERENURE

Terenure Rd.

Templeogue Rd.

S. Circular Rd.

Grand Canal

Clonard Rd.

Crumlin Rd.

Kildare Rd.

N81

Rathfarnham **1**
St. Edna's National Historic Park

Ballyboden Rd.

TO MARLAY PARK →

1 mile

1 km

0

0

KEY

▬▬▬ DART Railway Stations

climbing route that turns off the main Dublin–Enniskerry road at Stepaside. Refusing to bow to the whims of modernization, the owners have steadfastly maintained its traditional character—oak tables, rough-stone floor flags strewn with sawdust, and ancient bric-a-brac, including copper kettles, crockery, old prints, and guns—and appears very much as it did in the early 19th century, when Daniel O'Connell used it as a safe house for his seditious meetings. You can get lunch and dinner here; the specialty is seafood, and it alone is worth the journey. In the evenings expect to hear traditional Irish music.

Booterstown

2 *Take the DART local train from either Tara Street or Pearce Street. Or take R118 from the corner of Lower Merrion Street and Merrion Square.*

Booterstown stretches along Dublin Bay south of Sandymount. The **Booterstown Marsh Bird Sanctuary** is the largest wildlife preserve in the Dublin area. Curlews, herons, kingfishers, and other fairly rare migratory species come to nest here; information boards along the road describe the birds. Also on this main road is Glena, the house where Athlone-born John McCormack, one of the best and most popular tenors in the first quarter of the 20th century, died on September 16, 1945. ⊠ *Between the DART line and Rock Rd.* ☎ *01/454–1786.*

Blackrock

3 *3 km (2 mi) south of Booterstown on Rock Rd. Take the DART line from the city center to Blackrock.*

Fine sea views, swimming, a weekend market, and a major shopping center draw Dubliners down to Blackrock, a bedroom community where James Joyce's parents lived with their large brood for most of 1892. Above the Blackrock DART station, at **Idrone Terrace**—lined with restored, old-fashioned lamps—you can take in a lovely view across the bay to Howth Peninsula.

SHOPPING   The **Blackrock** (☎01/283–1660) is one of the most customer-friendly shopping centers around. It's built on two levels, looking onto an inner courtyard, with the giant Superquinn Foodstore, cafés, and restaurants, as well as shops selling clothes, electronics, and crafts. Blackrock can be reached conveniently on the DART train line; it has its own stop.

Monkstown

4 *3 km (2 mi) south of Blackrock on R119. Take the DART train from the city center to the Monkstown/Seapoint station.*

One of Dublin's most exclusive suburbs, Monkstown is known for its two architectural curiosities. John Semple, the architect of Monkstown's **Anglican parish church**, built in 1833, was inspired by two entirely different styles, the Gothic and the Moorish, which he joined into an unlikely hybrid of towers and turrets. The church, which is in the town's main square, is only open during Sunday services. The well-preserved ruins of **Monkstown Castle** lie about 1 km (½ mi) south of the suburb; it's a 15th-century edifice with a keep, a gatehouse, and a long wall section, all surrounded by greenery. The **Lambert Puppet Theatre** (⊠ Clifton

La., South County Dublin ☎ 01/280–0974), which stages regular puppet shows every Saturday and Sunday, houses a puppetry museum which can only be viewed after a show.

Comhaltas Ceoltóiri Éireann (✉ 35 Belgrave Sq., South County Dublin ☎ 01/ 280–0295) is the place to go for a boisterous summer evening of Irish music and dancing.

Dun Laoghaire & Sandycove

❺ *2½ km (1½ mi) southeast of Monkstown along R119, the Monkstown Crescent.*

After the British monarch King George IV disembarked for a brief visit in 1821, Dun Laoghaire (pronounced dun *lear*-ee) was renamed Kingstown, but it reverted to its original Irish name 99 years later. Its Irish name refers to Laoghaire, the High King of Tara who in the 5th century permitted St. Patrick to begin converting Ireland to Christianity. The town was once a Protestant stronghold of the old ruling elite; in some of the neo-Georgian squares and terraces behind George's Street, the main thoroughfare, a little of the community's former elegance can still be seen.

Dun Laoghaire has long been known for its great harbor, enclosed by two piers, each 2½ km (1½ mi) long. The harbor was constructed between 1817 and 1859 using granite quarried from nearby Dalkey Hill; the west pier has a rougher surface and is less favored for walking than the east pier, which has a bandstand where musicians play in summer. The workaday business here includes passenger-ship and freight-services sailings to Holyhead in north Wales, 3½ hours away. Dun Laoghaire is also a yachting center, with the members-only Royal Irish, National, and Royal St. George yacht clubs, all founded in the 19th century, lining the harbor area. A 15-minute walk south of Dun Laoghaire along the coast road brings you to the village of Sandycove, with a lovely little beach and the famous Martello Tower.

The **National Maritime Museum,** west of the harbor and across from the Gresham Royal Marine Hotel and the People's Park, is in the former Mariners' church. Its nave makes a strangely ideal setting for exhibits like the longboat captured during an aborted French invasion at Bantry, County Cork, in 1796. A particularly memorable exhibit is the old optic from the Baily Lighthouse on Howth Head, across Dublin Bay; the herringbone patterns of glass reflected light across the bay until several decades ago. ✉ *Haigh Terr., South County Dublin* ☎ *01/280–0969* 🎟 *€1.90* ☉ *May–Sept., Tues.–Sun. 1–5.*

From the harbor area, Marine Parade leads alongside Scotsmans Bay for 1¼ km (¾ mi), as far as Sandycove and the **Forty Foot Bathing Pool,** a traditional bathing area that attracts mostly nude older men. Women were once banned from here, but now hardy swimmers of both genders are free to brave its cold waters.

★   Built in 1804, when Napoléon's invasion seemed imminent, the **James Joyce Martello Tower** was demilitarized in the 1860s along with most of the rest of the 34 Martello towers that ring Ireland's coast (the name

"Martello" derives from the small tower fort on Mortello Point in Corsica, which inspired the English to create their own version). Martello towers were first built in Italy to protect the coastline against the possibility of a French naval invasion. In Ireland, they were built by the British to protect Irish shores from the same threat and were remarkable for their squat and solid construction, rotating cannon at the top, and—most importantly—their proximity to one another, so that each one is within visible range of the one next to it. In 1904, this tower was rented to Oliver St. John Gogarty, a medical student who was known for his poetry and ready wit, for £8 a year. He wanted to create a nurturing environment for writers and would-be literati. Joyce spent a week here in September 1904 and described it in the first chapter of *Ulysses,* using his friend as a model for the character Buck Mulligan. The tower now houses the **Joyce Museum,** founded in 1962 thanks to Sylvia Beach, the Paris-based first publisher of *Ulysses.* The exhibition hall contains first editions of most of Joyce's works. Joycean memorabilia include his waistcoat, embroidered by his grandmother, and a tie that he gave to Samuel Beckett (who was Joyce's onetime secretary). The gunpowder magazine stores the Joyce Tower Library, including a death mask of Joyce taken on January 13, 1941. The tower stands a few steps away from the Forty Foot Bathing Pool. ✉ *Sandycove* ☎ *01/280–9265* ⊕ *www.visitdublin.com* ✉ *€6.25* ⊙ *Feb.–Oct., Mon.–Sat. 10–1 and 2–5, Sun. 2–6; Nov.–Jan. by appointment.*

WHERE TO STAY
& EAT
$$–$$$ ✗ **Brasserie Na Mara.** Chef Derek Breen serves Irish dishes with a modern twist in this brasserie. *Na mara* means "of the sea" in Gaelic, and although he kept the name when he took over, he jettisoned the exclusive emphasis on seafood. Fish, is nonetheless one specialty, and baked monkfish tops the list. For serious carnivores the rack of lamb with sautéed spinach, herb potatoes, and garlic jus is a cleverly jazzed-up Irish standard. The building has an unusual history: the first railway in Ireland, opened in 1834, was built from Westland Row (now Pearse Station) in Dublin to Dun Laoghaire. Much of the original station's entrance and ticketing area has been converted into this restaurant—now tall Georgian windows overlook the busy Dun Laoghaire ferry-port. Reservations are essential on weekends. ✉ *Dun Laoghaire Harbour, Dun Laoghaire, South County Dublin* ☎ *01/280–6767* ⊟ *AE, DC, MC, V* ⊙ *No lunch Sat. No dinner Sun.*

$$ ✗ **Caviston's.** Stephen Caviston and his family have been dispensing fine food for years from their fish counter and delicatessen in Sandycove, and their name is synonymous with quality produce served in a stylish formula. The fish restaurant next door to the deli is an intimate place, with a few cozy tables and the friendliest service you could ask for. Typical entrées include panfried scallops served in the shell with a thermidor sauce, and steamed Dover sole with mustard sauce. You can also get a halved lobster with a simple butter sauce for an exceptionally good price. Other than seafood, organic vegetables, regional cheeses, and local meats fill out the mouth-watering menu. ✉ *58–59 Glasthule Rd., Sandycove, South County Dublin* ☎ *01/280–9120* ⊟ *MC, V* ⊙ *Closed Sun., Mon., and late Dec.–early Jan. No dinner.*

$$ ✕ **The Forty Foot.** From the wall of windows that dominates this ultra-modern, two-story bar and restaurant you can look out onto the sea and the famous 40-foot-wide rocky cove (and bathing spot) that gave the place its name. The brightness and large open spaces give the Forty Foot a very casual feel, and it is popular with a young, business crowd. The long, New York–style bar is the perfect spot to have a drink while waiting to be seated. The menu changes regularly, but usually offers the very popular starter tian of salmon and crab in a cream sauce with tomato and oil dressing. European influences can be found in most of the main courses, including chicken stuffed with chorizo, and fillet of pork wrapped in pancetta. ⊠ *Pavilion Centre, Dun Laoghaire, South County Dublin* ☎ *01/284–2982* 🖃 *MC, V.*

Dalkey Village

6 *From the James Joyce Martello Tower in Sandycove, it's an easy walk or quick drive 1 km (½ mi) south to Dalkey. Or take the DART line from the city center to Dalkey.*

Along Castle Street, the town's main thoroughfare, are the substantial stone remains—resembling small, turreted castles—of two 15th- and 16th-century fortified houses. From the mainland's Vico Road, beyond Coliemore Harbour, are astounding bay views as far as Bray in County Wicklow. On Dalkey Hill stands **Torca Cottage,** home of the Nobel prize–winning writer George Bernard Shaw from 1866 to 1874. You can return to Dalkey Village by Sorrento Road. The cottage is closed to the public. The **Heritage Centre** attached to Dalkey Castle has exhibits on local history, including a script written by playwright and local resident Hugh Leonard. ⊠ *Castle St., South County Dublin* ☎ *01/285–8366* 🖃 *Free* ⊙ *Apr.–Oct., weekdays 9:30–5:50, weekends 11–5; Nov.–Mar., weekends 11–5.*

In summer, small boats make the 15-minute crossing from Coliemore Harbour to **Dalkey Island,** covered with long grass, uninhabited except for a herd of goats, and graced with its own Martello tower—and an excellent bird sanctuary. The 8th-century ruins of St. Begnet's church sit right beside the bird sanctuary.

WHERE TO STAY
★ **$$$$** 🖼 **Fitzpatrick Castle Dublin.** Like a storybook vision out of an Irish Disneyland, this 18th-century stone "castle" comes complete with gorgeous lime-green dressed-stone walls, white machicolations, and fairytale turrets. Add in its sweeping views over Dun Laoghaire and Dublin Bay and you can see why the Fitzpatrick is well worth the 15-km (9-mi) drive from the Dublin city center. Not a castle per se, but a stately home built to look like one, this popular landmark now has an interior renovated to within its eye teeth, but happily its modern hallways and public spaces sport some antiques. Some will opt for a room and the four-poster beds in the 18th-century wing; others will like the cool calm of the rooms in the substantial modern addition. In all cases, bathrooms are large. The hotel is convenient to golfing, horseback riding, and fishing, and the fitness facilities include a heated pool. The views from Killiney Hill, behind the hotel, are spectacular, and the seaside resort village of Dalkey and Killiney Beach are both

within walking distance. ⊠ *Killiney, South County Dublin* ☎ *01/ 230–5400* 🖶 *01/230–5466* ⊕ *www.fitzpatrickhotels.com* ⇌ *113 rooms with bath* ☖ *Restaurant, in-room data ports, cable TV, indoor pool, health club, bar, meeting rooms, free parking* ▤ *AE, DC, MC, V* ⵊ◎ⵊ *BP, EP.*

North County Dublin

Dublin's northern suburbs remain largely residential, but there are a few places worth the trip, such as the architectural gem Marino Casino. As with most suburban areas, walking may not be the best way to get around. It's good, but not essential, to have a car. Buses and trains serve most of these areas—the only drawback is that to get from one suburb to another by public transportation, you have to backtrack through the city center. Even if you're traveling by car, visiting all these sights will take a full day, so plan your trip carefully before setting off.

Numbers in the text correspond to numbers in the margin and on the North South County Dublin map.

Glasnevin

❼ *Drive from the north city center by Lower Dorset Street, as far as the bridge over the Royal Canal. Turn left, go up Whitworth Road, by the side of the canal, for 1 km (½ mi); at its end, turn right onto Prospect Road and then left onto the Finglas road, N2. You can also take Bus 40 or Bus 40A from Parnell Street, next to Parnell Square, in the northern city center.*

Glasnevin Cemetery, on the right-hand side of the Finglas road, is the best-known burial ground in Dublin. It's the site of the graves of many distinguished Irish leaders, including Eamon De Valera, a founding father of modern Ireland and a former Irish *taoiseach* (prime minister) and president, and Michael Collins, the celebrated hero of the Irish War of Independence. Other notables interred here include the late-19th-century poet Gerard Manley Hopkins and Sir Roger Casement, an Irish rebel hanged for treason by the British in 1916. The large column to the right of the main entrance is the tomb of "The Liberator" Daniel O'Connell, perhaps Ireland's greatest historical figure, renowned for his nonviolent struggle for Catholic rights and emancipation, achieved in 1829. The cemetery is freely accessible 24 hours.

The **National Botanic Gardens,** on the northeastern flank of Glasnevin Cemetery and the south banks of the Tolka River, date from 1795 and have more than 20,000 varieties of plants, a rose garden, and a vegetable garden. The main attraction is the beautifully restored Curvilinear Range—400-foot-long greenhouses designed and built by a Dublin ironmaster, Richard Turner, between 1843 and 1869. The Great Palm House, with its striking double dome, was built in 1884 and houses orchids, palms, and tropical ferns. ⊠ *Glasnevin Rd., North County Dublin* ☎ *01/837–4388* 🖾 *Free* ☉ *Apr.–Sept., Mon.–Sat. 9–6, Sun. 11–6; Oct.–Mar., Mon.–Sun. 10–4:30.*

North County Dublin

KEY
DART Railway
Stations

0 — 1 km
0 — 1 mile

9 North Bull Island

10 Howth

11 Malahide

8 Marino Casino

7 Glasnevin
National Botanic Gardens
Glasnevin Cemetery

KILBARRACK
RAHENY
KILLESTER
CLONTARF
BEAUMONT
SANTRY
BALLYMUN
WHITEHALL
DRUMCONDRA
GLASNEVIN

Kilbarrack Rd.
Sutton Strand
James Larkin Rd.
Watermill Rd.
Howth Rd.
Sybil Hill Rd.
Vernon Ave.
St. Anne's Park
Tonlegee Rd.
Malahide Rd.
Oscar Traynor Rd.
Collins Ave.
Beaumont Rd.
Griffith Ave.
Swords Rd.
N1
Collins Ave.
Grace Park Rd.
Ballymun Rd.
Glasnevin Ave.
Griffith Ave.
Mobhi Rd.
Drumcondra Rd.
River Tolka
Royal Canal
Ballymun Rd.
Dorset St.
Royal Canal

Marino Casino

★ ❽ *Take the Malahide road from Dublin's north city center for 4 km (2½ mi). Or take Bus 20A or Bus 24 to the Casino from Cathal Brugha Street in the north city center.*

One of Dublin's most exquisite, yet also most underrated, architectural landmarks, the Marino Casino (the name has nothing to do with gambling—it means "little house by the sea," and the building overlooks Dublin Harbour) is a small-scale, Palladian-style Greek temple, built between 1762 and 1771 from a plan by Sir William Chambers. Often compared to the Petit Trianon at Versailles, it was commissioned by the great Irish grandee Lord Charlemont as a summerhouse. Although the grand mansion on Charlemont's estate was tragically demolished in 1921, this sublime casino was saved and lovingly restored (Sir William's original plans survived). Inside, highlights are the china-closet boudoir, the huge golden sunset in the ceiling of the main drawing room, and the signs of the zodiac in the ceiling of the bijou library. When you realize that the structure has, in fact, 16 rooms—there are bedrooms upstairs—Sir William's sleight-of-hand is readily apparent: from its exterior, the structure seems to contain only one room. The tricks don't stop there: the freestanding columns on the facade are hollow so they can drain rainwater, and the elegant marble urns on the roof are chimneys. Last but not least, note the four stone lions on the outside terrace—they were carved by Joseph Wilson, who created the British royal coronation coach in London. All in all, this remains, to quote scholar Desmond Guinness, "one of the most exquisite buildings in Europe." It makes a good stop on the way to Malahide, Howth, or North Bull Island. ✉ *Malahide Rd., Marino, North County Dublin* ☎ *01/833–1618* ⊕ *www.heritageireland.ie* ✑ *€2.75* ☺ *Feb., Mar., and Nov., Sun. and Thurs. noon–4; Apr., Sun. and Thurs. noon–5; May and Oct., daily 10–5; June–Sept., daily 10–6.*

North Bull Island

❾ *From Dublin's north city center, take the Clontarf road for 4 km (2½ mi) to the causeway.*

A 5-km-long (3-mi-long) island created in the 19th century by the action of the tides, North Bull Island is one of Dublin's wilder places—it's a nature conservancy with vast beach and dunes. The island is linked to the mainland via a wooden causeway that leads to Bull Wall, a 1½-km (1-mi) walkway that stretches as far as the North Bull Lighthouse. The island is also accessible via a second, northerly causeway, which takes you to Dollymount Strand. (The two routes of entry don't meet at any point on the island.) You can reach this causeway from the mainland via James Larkin Road. The small **visitor center** here largely explains the island's bird life. ✉ *Off the northerly causeway, North County Dublin* ☎ *01/833–8341* ✑ *Free* ☺ *Mar.–Oct., Mon.–Wed. 10:15–1 and 1:30–4, Thurs. 10:15–1 and 1:30–3:45, Fri. 10:15–1 and 1:30–2:30, weekends 10–1 and 1:30–5:30; Nov.–Feb., Mon.–Wed. 10:15–1 and 1:30–4, Thurs. 10:15–1 and 1:30–3:45, Fri. 10:15–1 and 1:30–2:30, weekends 10–1 and 1:30–4:30.*

On the mainland directly across from North Bull Island is **St. Anne's Park,** a public green with extensive rose gardens (including many prize hybrids blooms) and woodland walks. ☒ *James Larkin Rd. and Mt. Prospect Ave., North County Dublin.*

Howth

🔟 *From Dublin, take the DART train, or Bus 31B from Lower Abbey Street in the city center. Or, by car, take the Howth road from the north city center for 16 km (10 mi).*

A fishing village at the foot of a long peninsula, Howth (derived from the Norse *hoved,* meaning head; it rhymes with "both") was an island inhabited as long ago as 3250 BC. Between 1813 and 1833, Howth was the Irish terminus for the sea crossing to Holyhead in north Wales, but it was then superseded by the newly built harbor at Kingstown (now Dun Laoghaire). Today, its harbor, which supports a large fishing fleet, includes a marina. Both arms of the harbor pier form extensive walks. Separated from Howth Harbour by a channel nearly 1½ km (1 mi) wide is **Ireland's Eye,** with an old stone church on the site of a 6th-century monastery, and an early-19th-century Martello tower. In calm summer weather, local boatmen make the crossing to the island from the East pier in Howth Harbour. Contact head boatman Frank Doyle (☎ 01/831–4200 or 087/267–8211) for times and details.

At the King Sitric restaurant on the East Pier, a 2½-km (1½-mi) cliff walk begins, leading to the white **Baily Lighthouse,** built in 1814. In some places, the cliff path narrows and drops close to the water, but the views out over the Irish Sea are terrific. Some of the best views in the whole Dublin area await from the parking lot above the lighthouse, looking out over the entire bay as far south as Dun Laoghaire, Bray, and the north Wicklow coast. You can also see quite a bit of Dublin.

Until 1959, a tram service ran from the railway station in Howth over Howth Summit and back down to the station. One of the open-top Hill of Howth trams that plied this route is now the star at the **National Transport Museum,** a short, 800-yard walk from Howth's DART station. Volunteers spent several years restoring the tram, which stands alongside other unusual vehicles, including horse-drawn bakery vans. ☎ 01/848–0831 or 01/847–5623 ⊠ €3 ☉ *June–Aug., daily 10–5; Sept.–May, weekends 2–5.*

The **Howth Castle Gardens,** next door to the Transport Museum and accessible from the Deer Park Hotel, were laid out in the early 18th century. The many rare varieties in its fine rhododendron garden are in full flower April through June; there are also high beech hedges. The rambling castle, built in 1654 and considerably altered in the following centuries, is not open to the public, but you can access the ruins of a tall, square, 16th-century castle and a Neolithic dolmen. ☒ *Deer Park Hotel, North County Dublin* ☎ 01/832–2624 ⊠ Free ☉ *Daily 8–dusk.*

WHERE TO EAT ✕ **King Sitric.** Sitric was an 11th-century Norse king of Dublin who seemed
$$$$ to be very fond of Howth. Joan and Aidan MacManus's well-known

seafood restaurant down by the harbor attracts many contemporary visitors to the old town. It is in a Georgian house, with the yacht marina and port on one side and sea views from which you can watch the boats land the very fish that might be tomorrow's special. The upstairs seafood bar is great for informal lunches in summer. A house specialty is black sole meunière, grilled and finished with a nut-brown butter sauce, but lobster, caught just yards away in Balscadden Bay, is the big treat—it's best at its simplest, in butter sauce. Crab is equally fresh, dressed with mayonnaise or Mornay sauce. Game and other meat dishes are also on offer, and Aidan is something of a collector when it comes to fine wines. ⊠ *East Pier, North County Dublin* ☎ *01/832–5235* ▤ *AE, DC, MC, V* ☉ *Closed Sun. No lunch Sat.*

★ **$$–$$$$** ✕ **Abbey Tavern.** The stone walls, flagged floors, blazing turf fires, and old gaslights of the 16th-century building—built as a seminary for monks—that accent this old-world tavern certainly give your evening an enchanting medieval ambiance. The upstairs restaurant serves traditional Irish and Continental cuisine, and specializes in fish dishes. Sole Abbey (filleted and stuffed with prawns, mushrooms, and herbs) is a house specialty, and fresh Dublin Bay prawns can be cooked to order. The Irish classics of homemade brown bread and corned beef and cabbage are as good as anywhere in the country, but chef Lemercier also offers more adventurous dishes, such as baked goat cheese in sesame crust. Traditional Irish music is performed in a different part of the building. The restaurant is a five-minute walk from the DART station; call for directions. ⊠ *Abbey St., North County Dublin,* ☎ *01/839–0307* ⌁ *Reservations essential* ▤ *AE, DC, MC, V* ☉ *No dinner Sun.*

Malahide

⓫ *By car, drive from the north city center on R107 for 14½ km (9 mi). Or catch the hourly train from Connolly Station. Or board Bus 42 to Malahide, which leaves every 15 minutes from Beresford Place behind the Custom House.*

★ ♺ Malahide is chiefly known for its glorious **Malahide Castle,** a picture-book castle occupied by the Anglo-Irish and aristocratic Talbot family from 1185 until 1976, when it was sold to the Dublin County Council. The great expanse of parkland, designed by Lord Talbot de Malahide between 1948 and 1973, around the castle has over 5,000 different species of trees and shrubs, all clearly labeled. The castle itself combines styles and crosses centuries; the earliest section, the three-story tower house, dates from the 12th century. Hung with many family portraits (including pictures depicting descendants of the 14 ill-fated Talbot cousins who breakfasted here before riding out to the Battle of the Boyne in 1690, never to return), the medieval great hall is the only one in Ireland that is preserved in its original form. Authentic 18th-century pieces furnish the other rooms. Within the castle, the **Fry Model Railway Museum** houses rare, handmade models of the Irish railway. Children can enjoy one of the world's largest miniature railway displays, which covers an area of 2,500 square feet. The castle's self-service restaurant serves good homemade food all day. ⊠ *10 km (6 mi) north of Howth on the Coast Rd., North County Dublin* ☎ *01/*

846–2184 ⊕ *www.malahide.ie* ⊠ *€6.25* ⊙ *Apr.–Oct., Mon.–Sat. 10–5, Sun. 11–6; Nov.–May, Mon.–Sat. 10–5, Sun. 11–5.*

★ ☺ One of the greatest stately homes of Ireland, **Newbridge House**, in nearby Donabate, was built between 1740 and 1760 for Charles Cobbe, Archbishop of Dublin. A showpiece in the Georgian and Regency styles, the house is less a museum than a home because the Cobbe family still resides here, part of a novel scheme the municipal government allowed when they took over the house in 1985. The sober exterior and even more sober entrance hall—all Portland stone and Welsh slate—don't prepare you for the splendor of Newbridge's Red Drawing Room, perhaps Ireland's most sumptuous 18th-century salon. Cobbe's son, Thomas, and his wife, Lady Betty Beresford, sister of the marquess of Waterford, had amassed a great collection of paintings and needed a hall to show them off, so they built a back wing of the house to incorporate this enormous room built for entertaining and impressing. That it does, thanks to its crimson walls, fluted Corinthian columns, dozens of old masters, and a glamorous Rococo-style plaster ceiling designed by the Dublin stuccodore Richard Williams. Elsewhere in the house are fascinating family heirlooms: the kitchens still have their original utensils; crafts workshops and some examples of old-style transportation, such as coaches, are in the courtyard; and there is even a Museum of Curiosities, complete with the mummified ear of an Egyptian bull and relics of Lady Betty's medical practice (her chilblain plaster became famous). Some fine paintings are left, but the greatest were sold centuries ago in order to build proper houses for the estate servants. Beyond the house's walled garden are 366 acres of parkland and a restored 18th-century animal farm. Tara's Palace, a dollhouse that was made to raise funds for children's charities, is also here; it has 25 rooms, all fully furnished in miniature. The exterior of the dollhouse is based on the facades of three great Irish houses—Carton, Castletown, and Leinster. The coffee shop is renowned for the quality and selection of its homemade goods. You can travel from Malahide to Donabate by train, which takes about 10 minutes. From the Donabate train station, it's a 15-minute walk to the Newbridge House grounds. ⊠ *Donabate, 8 km (5 mi) north of Malahide, signposted from N1, North County Dublin* ☎ *01/843–6534* ⊠ *€6.20* ⊙ *Apr.–Sept., Tues.–Sat. 10–5, Sun. 2–6; Oct.–Mar., weekends 2–5.*

WHERE TO EAT ✕ **Bon Appetit.** The striking floral decor creates a cozy traditional air at
$$$–$$$$ this stylish basement restaurant, an impression heightened by the staff of black-jacketed waiters and the collection of paintings daubed by local artists. Owner/chef Patsy McGuirk's Continental menu includes such entrées as warm salad of Dublin Bay king prawns with pine nuts, prawn oil, and shavings of Parmesan, or the delicious sole McGuirk— filleted, stuffed with prawns and turbot, and baked with white wine and cream. ⊠ *9 James's Terr., North County Dublin* ☎ *01/845–0314* ⊟ *AE, DC, MC, V* ⊙ *Closed Sun. No lunch Sat.*

DUBLIN A TO Z

To research prices, get advice from other travelers, and book travel arrangements, visit www.fodors.com.

AIR TRAVEL

There are daily services to Dublin from all major London airports. Flights to Dublin also leave from Birmingham, Bristol, East Midlands, Liverpool, Luton, Manchester, Leeds/Bradford, Newcastle, Edinburgh, and Glasgow. Prices vary a great deal between companies and at different seasons. There are also numerous flights from Europe and North America.

From the United Kingdom, six airlines serve destinations in Ireland: Aer Lingus, British Airways, British Midland, City Jet, Go, and Ryanair. Aer Lingus operates 12 flights from Heathrow and Gatwick Airports. British Airways has a regular schedule out of Heathrow. British Midland operates 10 flights to Dublin from Heathrow. City Jet flies from the very central London City Airport. Go flies from Edinburgh. Ryanair operates several no-frills, low-price flights from Luton, Stanstead and other airports throughout the United Kingdom—Ryanair is known for being the cheapest, but this means cutting back on comfort and services.

Major European carriers, such as Air France, Alitalia, Lufthansa, Sabena, and SAS, run direct services to Dublin from most European capital cities and major regional airports, especially those in Germany.

Three airlines have regularly scheduled flights from the United States to Dublin. Aer Lingus flies direct from New York, Boston, Los Angeles, Baltimore, Washington, and Chicago to Dublin. Continental flies from New York (Newark Liberty International Airport) to Dublin. Delta flies from Atlanta to Dublin via New York.

Within Ireland, Aer Lingus operates flights from Dublin to Belfast, Cork, Derry, Kerry, Shannon, Galway, Knock in County Mayo, Donegal, and Sligo. Ryanair flies to Belfast, and Aer Arann fly to Cork, Kerry, Sligo, Knock, Galway, and Donegal.

🛄 Carriers **Aer Arann** ☎ 01/814-5240. **Aer Lingus** ☎ 01/844-4747. **British Airways** ☎ 800/626-747. **British Midland** ☎ 01/283-8833. **City Jet** ☎ 01/844-5566. **Continental** ☎ 1890/925-252. **Delta** ☎ 01/844-4166 or 01/676-8080. **Go** ☎ 1890/923-922. **Ryanair** ☎ 01/844-4411.

AIRPORTS

Dublin Airport, 10 km (6 mi) north of the city center, serves international and domestic flights.

🛄 Airport Information **Dublin Airport** ☎ 01/844-4900.

TRANSFERS Dublin Bus operates a shuttle service between Dublin Airport and the city center, with departures outside the arrivals gateway; you pay the driver inside the bus. The single fare is €5. Service runs from 5:45 AM to 11:30 PM, at intervals of about 20 minutes (after 8 PM buses run every hour), to as far as Dublin's main bus station (Busaras), behind the Custom House on the Northside. Journey time from the airport to the city center is normally 30 minutes, but it may be longer in heavy traffic. If you have time, you can save money by taking a regular bus for €2. Airlink runs an express coach to Heuston and Connolly stations and Busaras every 20 minutes from 5:45 AM to 11:30 PM. A taxi is a quicker alternative than the bus to get from the airport to Dublin center. A line of taxis waits by the arrivals gateway; the fare for the 30-minute journey to any of the main city-center hotels is about €17 to €19 plus tip (tips don't have to be large but they are increasingly expected). Ask about the fare before leaving the airport.

🚹 **Airlink** ☎ 01/872-0000 **Busaras** ☎ 01/830-2222. **Dublin Bus** ☎ 01/873-4222.

BOAT & FERRY TRAVEL

Irish Ferries runs a regular car and passenger service directly into Dublin port from Holyhead in Wales. Stena Sealink docks in Dun Laoghaire port and has service to Holyhead (3½ hours) and a high speed service, known as "HSS," which takes about 1 hour and 40 minutes. P & O sails from Dublin to Liverpool. Prices and departure times vary according to season, so call to confirm. In summer, reservations are strongly recommended. Dozens of taxis wait to take you into town from both ports, or you can take DART or a bus to the city center.

🚹 **Boat & Ferry Lines Irish Ferries** ✉ Merrion Row, Southside ☎ 01/661-0511. **P & O** ✉ Terminal 3, Dublin Port City Centre ☎ 01/407-3434. **Stena Sealink** ✉ Ferryport, Dun Laoghaire, South County Dublin ☎ 01/204-7777.

BUSINESS HOURS

Banks are open weekdays 10–4 and remain open on Thursday until 5. All stay open at lunchtime. Most branches have ATMs that accept bank cards and MasterCard and Visa credit cards. Museums are normally open Tuesday–Saturday and Sunday afternoon. Stores are open Monday–Saturday 9–5:30 or 9–6, except on Thursday, when they're open until 8. Smaller city-center specialty stores are open on Sunday as well, usually 10–6. Most department stores are closed on Sunday. Most pubs open Monday–Saturday at 10:30 AM and 12:30 PM on Sunday. They must stop serving at 11:30 PM Monday–Wednesday, 12:30 AM Thursday–Saturday, and 11 PM on Sunday, but take another hour to empty out. A number of bars in the city center have permission to serve until 2 AM on weekend nights.

BUS TRAVEL

Busaras, just behind the Custom House on the Northside, is Dublin's main station for buses to and from the city. In town, there's an extensive network of buses, most of which are green double-deckers. Some bus services run on cross-city routes, including the smaller "Imp" buses, but most buses start in the city center. Buses to the north of the city begin in the Lower Abbey Street–Parnell Street area, while those to the west begin in Middle Abbey Street and in the Aston Quay area. Routes to the southern suburbs begin at Eden Quay and in the College Street area. Several buses link the DART stations, and another regular bus route connects the two main provincial railway stations,

Connolly and Heuston. If the destination board indicates AN LÁR, that means that the bus is going to the city center. Museumlink is a shuttle service that links up the National Museum of Natural History, National Museum of Archaeology and History, and the National Museum of Decorative Arts and History. You can catch it outside any of the three museums.

FARES & SCHEDULES Timetables (€3.20) are available from Dublin Bus, staffed weekdays 9–5:30, Saturday 9–1. Fares begin at 85 cents and are paid to the driver, who will accept inexact fares, but you'll have to go to the central office in Dublin to pick up your change as marked on your ticket. Change transactions and the city's heavy traffic can slow service considerably. Most bus lines run to 11:30 at night, but some late-night buses run Monday to Saturday until 3 AM on all major routes; the fare is €4–€6.

🚌 **Busaras** ☎ 01/830-2222. **Dublin Bus** ✉ 59 Upper O'Connell St., Northside ☎ 01/873-4222 ⊕ www.dublinbus.ie.

CAR RENTAL
Renting a car in Dublin is very expensive, with high rates and a 12½% local tax. Gasoline is also expensive by U.S. standards, at around €1 a liter. Peak-period car-rental rates begin at around €260 a week for the smallest stick models, like a Ford Fiesta. Dublin has many car-rental companies, and it pays to shop around and to avoid "cowboy" outfits without proper licenses.

A dozen car-rental companies have desks at Dublin Airport; all the main national and international firms also have branches in the city center. Some reliable agencies are listed below.

🚗 **Agencies Avis** ✉ 1 Hanover St. E, Southside ☎ 01/677-5204 ✉ Dublin Airport, North County Dublin ☎ 01/844-5204. **Budget** ✉ 151 Lower Drumcondra Rd., North County Dublin ☎ 01/837-9802 ✉ Dublin Airport, North County Dublin ☎ 01/844-5919. **Dan Dooley** ✉ 42-43 Westland Row, Southside ☎ 01/677-2723 ✉ Dublin Airport, North County Dublin ☎ 01/844-5156. **Hertz** ✉ Leeson St. Bridge, Southside ☎ 01/660-2255 ✉ Dublin Airport, North County Dublin ☎ 01/844-5466. **Murray's Rent-a-Car** ✉ Baggot St. Bridge, Southside ☎ 01/668-1777 ✉ Dublin Airport, North County Dublin ☎ 01/844-4179.

CAR TRAVEL
Traffic in Ireland has increased exponentially in the last few years, and nowhere has the impact been felt more than in Dublin, where the city's complicated one-way streets are congested not only during the morning and evening rush hours but often during much of the day. If possible, avoid driving a car except to get in and out of the city (and be sure to ask your hotel or guest house for clear directions to get you out of town).

DUBLIN PASS
Like many tourist capitals around the world, Dublin now features a special pass to help travelers save on admission prices. In conjunction with Dublin Tourism, the Dublin Pass is issued for one, two, three, or six days, and allows free (or, rather, reduced, since the cards do cost something) admission to 30 sights, including the Guinness Brewery, the Dublin

Zoo, the Dublin Writers Museum, and Christ Church Cathedral. Prices are €29 for one day; €49 for two days; €59 for three days; and €89 for six days; children's prices are much lower. You can buy your card on-line and have it waiting for your at one of Dublin's tourist information offices when you arrive. Another plus: you can jump to the head of any line at participating museums and sights.

🔃 **Dublin Tourism** ✉ Suffolk St., off Grafton St., Southside ☎ 01/605-7700 in Dublin, 1850/230-330 in rest of Ireland ⊕ www.visitdublin.com/thedublinpass.

EMBASSIES

Embassies are open weekdays 9–1 and 2–5.

🔃 **Australia** ✉ Fitzwilton House, Wilton Terr., Southside ☎ 01/676-1517. **Canada** ✉ 65 St. Stephen's Green, Southside ☎ 01/478-1988. **United Kingdom** ✉ 29 Merrion Rd., Southside ☎ 01/205-3700. **United States** ✉ 42 Elgin Rd., Southside ☎ 01/668-8777.

EMERGENCIES

Call the Eastern Help Board for the names of doctors in the area. The Dublin Dental Hospital has emergency facilities and lists of dentists who provide emergency care. Hamilton Long, a Dublin pharmacy, is open Monday–Wednesday and Saturday 8:30–6, Thursday 8:30–8, and Friday 8:30–7. Temple Bar Pharmacy is open Monday–Wednesday, Friday, and Saturday 9–7, Thursday 9–8.

🔃 Doctors & Dentists **Dublin Dental Hospital** ✉ 20 Lincoln Pl., Southside ☎ 01/662-0766. **Eastern Help Board** ☎ 01/679-0700.

🔃 Emergency Services **Ambulance, fire, police (gardai)** ☎ 999.

🔃 Hospitals **Beaumont** ✉ Beaumont Rd., North County Dublin ☎ 01/837-7755. **Mater** ✉ Eccles St., Northside ☎ 01/830-1122. **St. James's** ✉ 1 James St., Dublin West ☎ 01/453-7941. **St. Vincent's** ✉ Elm Park, South County Dublin ☎ 01/269-4533.

🔃 Late-Night Pharmacies **Hamilton Long** ✉ 5 Upper O'Connell St., Northside ☎ 01/874-8456. **Temple Bar Pharmacy** ✉ 20 E. Essex St., Temple Bar ☎ 01/670-9751.

INTERNET CAFÉS

In the city center are a number of Internet cafés, which charge between €3 and €6 an hour. Some of the cheapest places are on Thomas Street, as it's not smack in the center of town. Central Cybercafe is popular with students. Planet Cyber Café is the city's best, with top-notch computers and a good coffee bar.

🔃 **Central Cybercafe** ✉ 6 Grafton St., Southside ☎ 01/677-0541. **Planet Cyber Café** ✉ 23 S. Great George's St., Southside ☎ 01/679-0583.

MAIL & SHIPPING

Post offices are open weekdays 9–1 and 2–5:30, Saturday 9–12:30. Main post offices are open Saturday afternoons, too (look for green signs that say "An Post"). The General Post Office (GPO) on O'Connell Street, which has foreign exchange and general delivery facilities, is open Monday–Saturday 8–8, Sunday 10:30–6:30.

SIGHTSEEING TOURS

BUS TOURS Dublin Bus has three- and four-hour tours of the city center that include Trinity College, the Royal Hospital Kilmainham, and Phoenix Park. The one-hour City Tour, with hourly departures, allows you to hop on and off at any of the main sights. Tickets are available from the driver or Dublin Bus. There's also a continuous guided open-top bus tour (€12.50), run by Dublin Bus, that allows you to hop on and off the bus as often as you wish and visit some 15 sights along its route. The company also conducts a north-city coastal tour, going to Howth, and a south-city tour, traveling as far as Enniskerry.

Gray Line Tours runs city-center tours that cover the same sights as the Dublin Bus itineraries. Bus Éireann organizes day tours out of Busaras, the main bus station, to country destinations such as Glendalough.
🚩 Bus Éireann ☎ 01/836-6111. **Dublin Bus** ☎ 01/873-4222. **Gray Line Tours** ☎ 01/670-8822.

CARRIAGE TOURS Horse-drawn-carriage tours are available around Dublin and in Phoenix Park. For tours of the park, contact the Department of the Arts, Culture and the Gaeltacht. Carriages can be hired at the Grafton Street corner of St. Stephen's Green, without prior reservations.
🚩 Department of the Arts, Culture and the Gaeltacht ☎ 01/661-3111.

PUB & MUSICAL TOURS Dublin Tourism has a booklet to its self-guided "Rock 'n Stroll" Trail, which covers 16 sights with associations to such performers as Bob Geldof, Christy Moore, Sinéad O'Connor, and U2. Most of the sights are in the city center and Temple Bar. The Traditional Musical Pub Crawl begins at Oliver St. John Gogarty and moves on to other famous Temple Bar pubs. Led by two professional musicians who perform songs and tell the story of Irish music, the tour is given May–October, daily at 7:30 PM; the cost is €9. Discover Dublin runs the Musical Bus every Friday and Saturday night, with musicians on board leading you on a pub crawl of Dublin's best rock and roll pubs. It costs €22. The award-winning Viking Splash Tour is a big hit with kids. The amphibious ex–U.S. military vehicle takes your on a tour of the city center before launching onto the water down by the IFSC. Kids get a Viking helmet to wear and love terrifying native pedestrians with the "Viking Roar." An adult ticket is €13.50.

Colm Quilligan arranges highly enjoyable evening tours of the literary pubs of Dublin, where "brain cells are replaced as quickly as they are drowned." The *Dublin Literary Pub Crawl* is a 122-page guide to those Dublin pubs with the greatest literary associations; it's widely available in the city's bookstores.
🚩 Colm Quilligan ☎ 01/454-0228. **Music Bus** ☎ 01/475-3313. **Oliver St. John Gogarty** ✉ 57 Fleet St., Temple Bar ☎ 01/671-1822. **Traditional Musical Pub Crawl** ✉ Discover Dublin, 20 Lower Stephens St., Southside ☎ 01/478-0191. **Viking Splash** ☎ 01/707-6000.

TRAIN TOURS Guided tours of Dublin using the DART system are organized by Views Unlimited.
🚩 Views Unlimited ✉ 8 Prince of Wales Terr., Bray, South County Dublin ☎ 01/286-0164 or 01/285-6121.

WALKING TOURS Historical Walking Tours of Dublin, run by Trinity College history graduate students, are excellent two-hour introductions to the city. The Bord Fáilte–approved tours take place from May to September, starting at the front gate of Trinity College, daily at 11 AM and 3 PM, with an extra tour on weekends at noon; tours are also available October–April, Friday–Sunday at noon. The cost is €10.

A Georgian/Literary Walking Tour leaves from the Grafton Street branch of Bewley's Oriental Café June–September, daily at 11; each tour lasts approximately two hours and costs €9. Trinity Tours organizes walks of the Trinity College campus on weekends from March 17 (St. Patrick's Day) through mid-May and from mid-May to September daily. The half-hour tour costs €7.60 and includes the *Book of Kells* exhibit; tours start at the college's main gate every 40 minutes from 10:15 AM. There are generally 9 tours a day. The Zozimus Experience is an enjoyable walking tour of Dublin's medieval past, with a particular focus on the seedy, including great escapes, murders, and mythical happenings. Tours, which are led by a guide in costume, are by arrangement only and start at the main gate of Dublin Castle at 6:45 PM; the cost is €10 per person. (Prepare yourself for a surprise.)

🖪 **Georgian/Literary Walking Tour** ☎ 01/496-0641. **Historical Walking Tours of Dublin** ☎ 01/878-0227. **Trinity Tours** ☎ 01/608-2320. **Zozimus Experience** ☎ 01/661-8646.

SAFETY

What crime there is in Dublin is often drug-related. Side streets off O'-Connell Street can be dangerous, especially at night. When you park your car, *do not* leave any valuables inside, even under a raincoat on the back seat or in the trunk; be especially careful parking around the Guinness Brewery and the Old Jameson Distillery.

TAXIS

Official licensed taxis, metered and designated by roof signs, do not cruise. There are taxi stands beside the central bus station, and at train stations, O'Connell Bridge, St. Stephen's Green, College Green, and near major hotels; the Dublin telephone directory has a complete list. The initial charge is €2.75, with an additional charge of about €2 per kilometer thereafter. The fare is displayed on a meter (make sure it's on). You may, instead, want to phone a taxi company and ask for a cab to meet you at your hotel, but this may cost up to €2.55 extra. Many taxis run all night, but the demand, especially on weekends (and particularly near clubs on the Leeson Street strip and elsewhere, which stay open until 4 AM or later), can make for long lines at taxi stands. Hackney cabs, which also operate in the city, have neither roof signs nor meters and will sometimes respond to hotels' requests for a cab. Negotiate the fare before your journey begins. Although the taxi fleet in Dublin is large, the cabs are nonstandard and some cars are neither spacious nor in pristine condition. Cab Charge has a reliable track record. Metro is one of the city's biggest but also the busiest. VIP Taxis usually has a car available for a longer trip.

🖪 **Taxi Companies Cab Charge** ☎ 01/677-2222. **Metro** ☎ 01/668-3333. **VIP Taxis** ☎ 01/478-3333.

TRAIN AND TRAM TRAVEL

Connolly Station provides train service to and from the east coast, Belfast, the north (with stops in Malahide, Skerries, and Drogheda), the northwest, and some destinations to the south, such as Wicklow and Arklow. Heuston Station is the place for trains to and from the south and west; trains run from here to Kildare Town, west of Dublin, via Celbridge, Sallins, and Newbridge. Pearse Station is for Bray and connections via Dun Laoghaire to the Liverpool-Holyhead ferries. Contact the Irish Rail Travel Centre for information.

An electric railway system, the Dublin Area Rapid Transit (DART), connects Dublin with Howth to the north and Bray to the south on a fast, efficient line. There are 25 stations on the route, which is the best means of getting to seaside destinations, such as Howth, Blackrock, Du Laoghaire, Dalkey, Killiney, and Bray.

The brand new LUAS tram service is due to open in late 2004, linking inland Dublin suburbs north and south to the city center. One line will carry the super sleek silver trams from Tallaght in the southwest to the Abbey Street station, located north of the Liffey, and on down to the city center's Connolly Station. This line will get you from Royal Hospital Killmainham and carry you across the Liffey, through Smithfield, and down to the Abbey Street hub. The other line runs from the Sandyford residential suburb in the south sector of the city north to St. Stephen's Green—this line is useful for ferrying the tourist between the city district of Ballsbridge to St. Stephen's Green in the city center. Together, these lines cross the city center north and south, and so the LUAS will be ideal for short hops across those areas.

FARES & SCHEDULES   DART service starts at 6:30 AM and runs until 11:30 PM; at peak periods, 8–9:30 AM and 5–7 PM, trains arrive every five minutes. At other times of the day, the intervals between trains are 15 to 25 minutes. Call ahead to check precise departure times (they do vary, especially on bank holidays). Tickets can be bought at stations, but it's also possible to buy weekly rail tickets, as well as weekly or monthly "rail-and-bus" tickets, from the Irish Rail Travel Centre. Individual fares begin at €1 and range up to €4. You'll pay a heavy penalty for traveling the DART without a ticket. LUAS prices are expected to be similar to those of DART.

▓ Train Information **Connolly Station** ✉ Amiens St., Northside. **DART** ☎ 01/836-6222 ⊕ www.irishrail.ie/dart. **Heuston Station** ✉ End of Victoria Quay, Dublin West. **Irish Rail Travel Centre** ✉ 35 Lower Abbey St., Northside ☎ 01/836-6222 ⊕ www.irishrail.ie. **Pearse Station** ✉ Westland Row, Southside.

TRAVEL AGENCIES

▓ Local Agents **American Express** ✉ 116 Grafton St., Southside ☎ 01/677-2874. **Thomas Cook** ✉ 118 Grafton St., Southside ☎ 01/677-1721.

VISITOR INFORMATION

Bord Fáilte, the Irish Tourist Board, has its own visitor information offices in the entrance hall of its headquarters at Baggot Street Bridge; it's open weekdays 9:15–5:15. A suburban tourist office in Tallaght is open March–December, daily 9:30–5.

The main Dublin Tourism center is located in the former (and still spectacular) St. Andrew's Church on Suffolk Street and is open July–September, Monday–Saturday 8:30–6, Sunday 11–5:30, and October–June, daily 9–6. On site are many service counters, souvenir stands, and even an sandwich bar. The Dublin Airport branch is open daily 8 AM–10 PM; the branch at the Ferryport, Dun Laoghaire, is open daily 10–9.

The Temple Bar Information Centre produces the easy-to-use, annually updated *Temple Bar Guide*, which provides complete listings of the area's stores, pubs, restaurants, clubs, galleries, and other cultural venues.

🖪 Tourist Information **Bord Fáilte** ✉ Baggot St. Bridge, Southside ☎ 01/602–4000 in Dublin, 1850/230–330 in the rest of Ireland ✉ The Square, Tallaght ☎ 1850/230–330 ⊕ www.ireland.travel.ie. **Dublin Tourism** ✉ Suffolk St., off Grafton St., Southside ☎ 01/605–7700 in Dublin, 1850/230–330 in rest of Ireland ⊕ www.visitdublin.com. **Temple Bar Information Centre** ✉ 18 Eustace St., Temple Bar ☎ 01/671–5717.

DUBLIN ENVIRONS

2

LISTEN FOR ANCIENT ECHOES
at the windswept Hill of Tara ⇨*p.143*

OPT FOR OPULENCE
at palatial Russborough House ⇨*p.165*

SIZE UP SUGAR LOAF MOUNTAIN
from the gardens at Powerscourt ⇨*p.157*

IMAGINE YOURSELF THE SQUIRE
of gracious Castletown House ⇨*p.163*

DIVE INTO THE "SEAFOOD SYMPHONY"
at the Hungry Monk eatery ⇨*p.156*

LET YOUR SPIRITS SOAR
to the towers of sacred Glendalough ⇨*p.158*

HIKE INTO PRE-HISTORY
at the Neolithic site of Newgrange ⇨*p.145*

Updated by
Anto Howard

LIKE AN OPEN-AIR MUSEUM layered with legendary Celtic sites, grand gardens, and elegant Palladian country estates, the small counties immediately north, south, and west of Dublin—historically known as the Pale—seem expressly designed for the sightseer. Due to its location on the Irish Sea facing Europe, the area has always been the first in which conquerors have established themselves and over which they exercised the most influence. The traces of each new wave remain: the Celts chose Tara as the center of their kingdom, the Danes traveled down the Rivers Boyne and Liffey to establish many of today's towns, and the region's great Protestant-built houses of the 18th century remind us that the Pale was the starting point and administrative center for the long, violent English colonization of the whole island.

The Dublin environs include three basic geographical regions: County Wicklow's coast and mountains, the Boyne Valley, and County Kildare. Lying tantalizingly close to the south of Dublin is the mountainous county of Wicklow, which contains some of the most *et-in-Arcadia-ego* scenery in the Emerald Isle. Here, the gently rounded Wicklow Mountains—to some tastes Ireland's finest—contain the evocative monastic settlement at Glendalough, many later abbeys and churches, and many of the most noted attractions for the art lover: the great 18th-century estates of the Anglo-Irish aristocracy. These lords and ladies, always prone to a certain inferiority complex, were determined not to be outdone by the extravagant efforts of their English compatriots. The result was a string of spectacular stately-home extravaganzas, such as Castletown, Powerscourt, and Russborough. Once you see their astonishingly elegant decoration, you may thank the lord for vanity. A quick change of pace is nearby—an impressive eastern coastline that stretches from Counties Wicklow to Louth, punctuated by delightful harbor towns and fishing villages. The coast is virtually unspoiled for its entire length.

North of Dublin lies the Boyne Valley, with its abundant ruins of Celtic Ireland extending from Counties Meath to Louth. Some of the country's most evocative Neolithic ruins—including the famous passage graves at Newgrange—are nestled into this landscape, where layer upon layer of history penetrates down into earlier, unknowable ages. It was west of Drogheda—a fascinating town settled by the Vikings in the early 10th century—that the Tuatha De Danann, onetime residents of Ireland, went underground when defeated by the invading Milesians and became, it is said, "the good people" (or fairies) of Irish legend. In pagan times this area was the home of Ireland's high kings, and the center of religious life. All roads led to Tara, the fabled Hill of Kings, the royal seat and the place where the national assembly was held. Today, time seems to stand still there—and you should do so, too, for it is almost sacrilegious to introduce a note of urgency.

Southwest of Dublin are the flat pastoral plains of County Kildare; the plains stretch between the western Midlands and the foothills of the Dublin and Wicklow mountains—both names actually refer to one mountain range, but each marks its county's claim to the land. Kildare is the flattest part of Ireland, a playing field for the breeding, training, and racing of some of the world's premier thoroughbreds.

Numbers in the text correspond to numbers in the margin and on the Dublin Environs map.

If you have
3 days

Travel south from Dublin along N11 to that opuluent Irish Xanadu that is the **Powerscourt House, Gardens, & Waterfall** ⑲ ▶. Follow the road up to **Roundwood** ⑳, the highest village in Ireland. Move on to the time-stained monastic settlement of **Glendalough** ㉑. Follow R752 south to Rathnew and proceed to **Avoca** ㉕, home of Ireland's oldest mill. End your day in 🏨 **Wicklow Town** ㉓, north of Avoca on R754; or, if you want to remain Dublin based, return to the capital via N11.

Begin your second day with a visit to one of Ireland's greatest stately mansions, **Castletown House** ㉗ near Celbridge, easily reached via N4 and R403. Continue south and turn left at Clane until you reach **Naas** ㉙. From here head southeast along R410 and go the short distance to **Russborough House** ㉚, an 18th-century estate with one of Ireland's finest private art collections. Or, continue west toward **Kildare Town** ㉝, an elegant, prosperous town surrounded by the broad, flat plains of **the Curragh** ㉜. The National Stud Farm and Japanese Gardens, just outside Kildare Town, are area highlights. (If you spent your first night in Wicklow, return to Glendalough and proceed toward Kildare via the Wicklow Gap, a maze of winding roads that take you through the villages of Granabeg, Hollywood, and Kilcullen.) Spend your second night in 🏨 **Straffan** ㉘ or back in 🏨 **Dublin.**

On your third day, head north of Dublin to Counties Meath and Louth via N3, which will take you to the **Hill of Tara** ②, the important Celtic site. Travel back another 2,000 years with a visit to **Newgrange** ⑤. On your way north to **Monasterboice** ⑩, with its fine high cross, visit the small Georgian village of **Slane** ⑥. Make a stop along N51 at **King William's Glen** ⑦, site of the Battle of the Boyne in 1690.

If you have
5 days

Driving south from Dublin, stop in the coastal town of **Bray** ⑱ ▶, a Victorian seaside resort, before heading toward the splendor of the Georgian **Powerscourt House, Gardens, and Waterfall** ⑲; sky-kissing **Roundwood** ⑳; and the great monastic site of 🏨 **Glendalough** ㉑. On your second day, take in the sylvan **Mount Usher Gardens** ㉒ and, for a taste of more recent history, follow N11 a few miles south to Rathnew and drive inland on R752 until you reach **Avondale House and Forest Park** ㉔, the home of the 19th-century Irish leader Charles Stewart Parnell. Overnight in 🏨 **Wicklow Town** ㉓. On your third morning, visit the seaside resort of **Arklow** ㉖, entry to the idyllic Vale of Avoca, then head back north to Country Kildare and the pomp and ceremony of fabulous **Russborough House** ㉚, then top the day out with a visit to **Castletown House** ㉗, an 18th-century Palladian-style extravaganza. Overnight in nearby 🏨 **Straffan** ㉘. On your fourth morning, head north above Dublin to the Celtic and prehistoric sights of County Meath. Be sure to visit the 12th-century remains of **Mellifont Abbey** ⊙, near **Slane** ⊙, and the town of **Kells** ⊙, a former monastic community. Stay overnight on your fourth night in historic ⊡ **Drogheda** ⊙. On your fifth day, travel north to **Dundalk** ⊙, the border town of **Omeath** ⊙, and **Inniskeen** ⊙, home of poet Patrick Kavanagh. Spend the night in Drogheda, returning to Dublin the morning next day via the ancient town of **Louth** ⊙.

Exploring Dublin Environs

This chapter is organized into three sections, each of which makes a reasonable day trip. Keep in mind that it's easy to lose an hour or so making detours, chatting with locals, and otherwise enjoying the unexpected. The itineraries below cover the area's highlights; if you have fewer than three days, use parts of each day's suggested itinerary to plan your excursion. A car is essential for visiting most sights—and don't plan on visiting both the north and south of Dublin during the same day. You can also reach some points of interest by public transport: bus tours from Dublin cover County Wicklow as far as Glendalough in the southwest and the Boyne Valley to the north; suburban bus services reach into the foothills of the Dublin Mountains; and Bus Éireann services take in the outlying towns. Some popular sights have direct connections to Dublin, including Enniskerry and Powerscourt Estate, which can be reached by taking the No. 44 bus from the Dublin quays area.

About the Restaurants & Hotels

Dining out in the area is essentially a casual affair, but the innovations and experimentation of Dublin's top restaurateurs are influencing the cooking—and the prices—at the finer establishments outside the capital. As in the southwest, chefs here have a deep respect for fresh, locally grown and locally raised produce. You'll find everything from Continental-style meals to hearty ploughman's lunches.

In Counties Wicklow and Kildare there are excellent accommodations, even if the choice may not be vast. If you have only a night or two outside Dublin, try to stay at least one night in one of the area's country-house or manor-house hotels, where some of Ireland's finest hosts welcome you into sometimes glorious, sometimes rustic, but almost invariably comfortable homes. Old-style hotels in Counties Meath and Louth are showing signs of improvement and are becoming more popular. Bed-and-breakfasts, as elsewhere in Ireland, are always a delightful option. Accommodations throughout the region can book up in July and August, so be sure to reserve far ahead if you're visiting during this time. On the chart below, hotel prices are listed for room rates that include no meals (EP, European Plan) or, if indicated, CP (with Continental breakfast) or BP (Breakfast Plan, with full breakfast). Higher prices prevail for board plans such as MAP (Modified American Plan, with breakfast and dinner); inquire when booking.Assume that all hotel rooms have air-conditioning, in-room phones, TVs, and private bathrooms unless otherwise noted.

WHAT IT COSTS In euros					
	$$$$	**$$$**	**$$**	**$**	**¢**
RESTAURANTS	over €29	€22–€29	€15–€22	€8–€15	under €8
HOTELS	over €230	€180–€230	€130–€180	€80–€130	under €80

Restaurant prices are per person for a main course at dinner; note that if a restaurant offers only prix-fixe meals, it has been given the price category that reflects the full set-price. Hotel prices are for two people in a standard double room in high season, including V.A.T. and a service charge (often applied in larger hotels).

Timing

The wild mountains of Wicklow and the flat pasturelands of Kildare are at their best in spring and summer. However, the rainfall is often higher in March and April. If you're planning to tour the towns and historic sites, consider touring the area in fall or winter in order to avoid the crush. Bring warm clothing and boots, and, in winter, be prepared for light snow on the hills.

THE BOYNE VALLEY

For every wistful schoolboy in Ireland the River Boyne is a name that resonates with history and adventure. It was on the banks of that river in 1014 that the Celtic chieftain Brian Boru defeated the Danish in a decisive battle that returned the east of Ireland to native rule. It was also by this river that Protestant William of Orange defeated the Catholic armies of exiled James II of England in 1690. In fact this whole area, only 48 km (30 mi) north of cosmopolitan Dublin, is soaked in stories and legends that predate the pyramids. You can't throw a stick in the valley without hitting some trace of Irish history. The great prehistoric, pagan, and Celtic monuments of the wide arc of fertile land known as the Boyne Valley invariably evoke a grand sense of wonder. You don't have to be an archaeologist to be awed by Newgrange and Knowth—set beside the River Boyne—or the Hill of Tara, Mellifont Abbey, and the high cross of Monasterboice. One way to approach exploring this area is to start at the town of Trim, the locale closest to Dublin, and work your way north. Keep in mind that Omeath and the scenic Cooley Peninsula at the end of this section are on the border of Northern Ireland. (If you make it this far north, consult Chapter 8, particularly the coverage of the Mountains of Mourne, which are just across Carlingford Lough.)

Trim

❶ *51 km (32 mi) northwest of Dublin via N3 to R154.*

The heritage town of Trim, on the River Boyne, contains some of the finest medieval ruins in Ireland. In 1359, on the instructions of King Edward III, the town was walled and its fortifications strengthened. In the 15th century several parliaments were held here. Oliver Cromwell massacred most of its inhabitants when he captured the town in 1649.

Trim Castle, the largest Anglo-Norman fortress in Ireland, dominates present-day Trim from its 2½-acre site, which slopes down to the river's placid waters. Built by Hugh de Lacy in 1173, the castle was soon destroyed and then rebuilt from 1190 to 1220. The ruins include an enormous keep with 70-foot-high turrets flanked by rectangular towers. The outer castle wall is almost 500 yards long, and five D-shape towers survive. The admission price includes a house tour. ⊠ *Trim* ☎ *046/943–8619* ⊕ *www.heritageireland.ie* 🎫 *Keep and grounds €3.50, grounds only €1.50* ⊙ *May–Oct., daily 10–6.*

Facing the river is the **Royal Mint,** a ruin that illustrates Trim's political importance in the Middle Ages. It produced coins with colorful names like "Irelands' and "Patricks" right into 15th century. The **Yellow Steeple** overlooks Trim from a ridge opposite the castle. The structure was built in 1368 and is a remnant of the Augustinian abbey of St. Mary's, founded in the 13th century, which itself was the site of a great medieval pilgrimage to a statue of the Blessed Virgin. Much of the tower was destroyed in 1649 to prevent its falling into Cromwell's hands, and today only the striking, 125-foot-high east wall remains. The Church of Ireland **St. Patrick's Cathedral** (⊠ Loman St.) dates from the early 19th century, but the square tower belongs to an earlier structure built in 1449.

In the old town hall, the "The Power and the Glory" audiovisual display of the **Visitor Center** tells the story of the arrival of the Normans and of medieval Trim. ⊠ *Castle St.* ☎ *046/943–7227* ⊕ *www.meathtourism. ie* 🎫 *€3.20* ⊙ *Mon.–Wed. and Sat.10–5, Fri. 10-6, Sun. noon–5:30.*

If your ancestors are from County Meath, take advantage of the family-history tracing service at the **Meath Heritage and Genealogy Center.** ⊠ *Castle St.* ☎ *046/943–6633* 🎫 *Free* ⊙ *Weekdays 9–1 and 1:30–5.*

At **Newtown,** 1¼ km (¾ mi) east of Trim on the banks of the River Boyne, are the ruins of what was the largest cathedral in Ireland, built beginning in 1210 by Simon de Rochfort, the first Anglo-Norman bishop of Meath. At **Laracor,** 3 km (2 mi) south of Trim on R158, a wall to the left of the rectory is where Jonathan Swift (1667–1745), the satirical writer, poet, and author of *Gulliver's Travels,* was rector from 1699 until 1714, when he was made dean of St. Patrick's Cathedral in Dublin. Nearby are the walls of the cottage where Esther Johnson, the "Stella" who inspired much of Swift's writings, once lived. One of the most pleasant villages of south County Meath, **Summerhill,** 8 km (5 mi) southeast of Laracor along R158, has a large square and a village green with a 15th-century cross. **Cnoc an Linsigh,** an attractive area south of Summerhill with forest walks and picnic sites, is ideal for a half day of meandering. Many of the lanes that crisscross this part of County Meath provide delightful driving between high hedgerows and afford occasional views of the lush, pastoral countryside.

off the beaten path

RATHCAIRN – This town is the only Gaeltacht (Irish-speaking) region in the province of Leinster. Thanks to a 1930s social experiment, a number of Connemara Irish-speaking families were transported to this fertile part of County Meath. They flourished, and Rathcairn is proud to be the only expanding Gaeltacht area. Spend a few hours in the

2

"Elegance & Prodigality"

Of all the artistic delights that beckon both north and south of Dublin, few enchant as much as the imposing country estates of County Wicklow. France has its châteaux of the Loire Valley, England the treasure houses of Kent and Sussex, Germany its castles of the Rhine, but the grand houses of the Pale rank highly in the galaxy of stately style. Here, during the "glorious eighteenth," great Anglo-Irish estates were built by English "princes of Elegance and Prodigality." Only an hour or two from Dublin, these estates—Russborough, Powerscourt, and Castletown are but three of the most famous—were profoundly influenced by the country villas of the great Italian architect Andrea Palladio, who erected the estates of the Venetian aristocracy along the Brenta Canal, only a short distance from the city on the lagoon. As in other parts of Ireland, the ancestral homes of the dwindling members of the Anglo-Irish ascendancy dot the landscape in the Pale. Today, lords and baronets down on their luck have turned into hoteliers who welcome guests to castle holidays with adaptable grace.

Ireland's Ancient Heart

The Boyne Valley, which straddles the county of Louth and runs through the flat heartland of Meath, holds 10% of all prehistoric monuments in Ireland. Foremost among these is Neolithic Newgrange, passage graves built in the 4th millennium BC. The Hill of Tara, one of the focal points for the ancient High Kings of Ireland, was where disputes between clans were settled, new laws were passed, and, eventually, the arrival of Christianity was proclaimed from the summit by St. Patrick. The advent of Christianity led to the construction of County Wicklow's Glendalough monastery, founded by one of St. Patrick's followers, St. Kevin. Later, in the 12th century, the first Cistercian house in Ireland, the monastery of Mellifont, was founded. North of Mellifont are the ruins of Monasterboice, another monastic site, where one of the finest high crosses in Ireland stands in the shadow of a 9th-century round tower.

Calling All Hike-a-holics

Whether you're a novice or veteran hiker, Wicklow's gentle, rolling hills are a terrific place to begin an Irish walking vacation. Devoted hikers come from all over the world to traverse the 137-km/85-mi Wicklow Way, the first long-distance trail to open in Ireland and one of the best. Much of the route lies above 1,600 feet and follows rough sheep tracks, forest firebreaks, and old bog roads (rain gear, windproof clothing, and sturdy footwear are essential). The trail is picked up in the outskirts of Dublin suburbs, then ascends into the Wicklow mountain foothillls, before passing glens, farms, and historic sights like Rathgall, home to the Kings of Leinster, and the Mill of Purgatory—a venerated "wardrobe" in Aghowle Church—before finishing up in Clonegal. Consider participating in one of the walking festivals held at Easter, in May, and in autumn. If your feet are less than bionic, you might opt for biking, another excellent way to see the area.

Dublin Environs

NORTHERN IRELAND

17 Omeath

Carlingford Lough

Kilkeel

16 Greenore

15 Carlingford

Cooley Peninsula Drive

13 Dundalk

14

Inniskeen

Carrickmacross

Rathnetty

12 Louth

Dundalk Bay

CAVAN

Bailieborough

Kingscourt

LOUTH

11 Ardee

Dunleer

Clogherhead

10 Collon

Monasterboice

Baltray

Virginia

Lough Ramor

Crossakiel

Kells **4**

Mellifont Abbey **9**

King William's Glen **7** **8**

Slane **6**

5 **Newgrange**

Drogheda

NORTHERN IRELAND

IRELAND

Navan **3**

Duleek

Balbriggan

Irish Sea

Delvin

Rathcairn

Athboy

Hill of Tara **2**

Kilmessan

Garristown

Skerries

Rush

Trim **1**

Laracor

Newtown

Swords

Malahide

Kinnegad

Summerhill

Kilcock

6 miles

9 km

Enfield

Maynooth

Leixlip

Lucan

Dublin

Howth

Castletown House **27**

Straffan **28**

Edenderry

Prosperous

Liffey

Dun Laoghaire

Dalkey

Robertstown

Hill of Allen

Newbridge

Naas **29**

Blessington

Bray **18**

Killruddery

Enniskerry

Monasterevin

Russborough House **30**

31

Poulaphouca Reservoir **19**

Powerscourt House, Gardens & Waterfall

Newtownmountkennedy

33 **32**

Kildare Town

The Curragh

National Stud Farm and Japanese Gardens

KILDARE

Dunlavin

Roundwood **20**

Mount Usher Gardens

Ashford

WICKLOW

Stradbally

Athy

Ardscull

Ballytore

Irish Pewter Mill

Moone High Cross

Castledermot

Glendalough **21**

Laragh

22

Rathnew

Glenealy

23

Wicklow Town

Wicklow Head

WICKLOW MOUNTAINS

Rathdrum

Brittas Bay

24 **Avondale House & Forest Park**

25 **Avoca**

Carlow

Tullow

Tinahely

Aughrim

Woodenbridge

26 **Arklow**

Castlecomer

CARLOW

Shillelagh

KEY

Rail Lines

Start of itinerary

sleepy town and the surrounding land, where, charmingly, everything is conducted in Irish. To get here from Trim, follow R154 12 km (7½ mi) northwest; you'll enter the town a few miles before you hit Athboy.

Where to Stay & Eat

¢ ✕▦ **Brogan's.** Despite the old-world feel of the place, bedrooms at this family-run guest house on High Street in the heart of Trim are modern, spacious, and very comfortable. Made with the freshest local produce, the food at the pub-restaurant ($) on the ground floor is better than typical pub fare. The joint of lamb is a treat. The outdoor beer garden is always a jovial gathering point for locals in the summer. ✉ *High St., Co. Meath* ☎ *046/943–1237* 🖷 *046/943–7648* ➽ *14 rooms* ♿ *Restaurant, bar; no a/c* ➡ *AE, MC, V* ❍| *BP.*

¢ ▦ **Tigh Catháin.** The "House of O'Catháin" is a Tudor-style country cottage about 1 km (½ mi) outside of town on the Longwood road. Owner Marie Keane has artfully decorated the three large bedrooms in different color schemes based on the natural colors of the region. But the real wonders here are the lovely gardens out back and in front, perfect for lounging around in the sun. Family rooms include a double and two single beds. ✉ *High St., Co. Meath* ☎ *046/943–1996* ➽ *3 rooms* ❍| *BP.*

Hill of Tara

❷ *14½ km (9 mi) east of Trim, 33 km (20½ mi) northwest of Dublin on N3.*

In the legends and the popular imagination of the Irish this ancient site has taken on mythic proportions. As with much of the glorification of the Celtic past, it was the 19th-century revival led by Yeats and Lady Gregory that was responsible for the near-religious veneration of this Celtic site, which is set at the meeting point of the five ancient roads of Ireland and known in popular folklore as the seat of the High Kings of Ireland. The 19th-century ballad by Thomas Moore, "The Harp That Once Through Tara's Halls," was also a major factor in the long over-romanticized view of Tara. Today, its ancestral banqueting hall and great buildings (one was the former palace of the Ard Rí, or High King) have all vanished but for a few columns. Still, the site is awe-inspiring. From the top of the Hill—it rises more than 300 feet above sea level—you can see across the flat central plain of Ireland, with the mountains of east Galway rising nearly 160 km (100 mi) away. In the mid-19th century, the nationalist leader Daniel O'Connell staged a mass rally here that supposedly drew more than a million people—nearly a third of Ireland's current population. On site, first pay a call on the Interpretative Center housed in an old Church of Ireland church on the hillside. Here, you'll learn the story of Tara and its legends. Without this background it will be difficult to identify many of the earthworks at Tara. Or just call upon your imagination to evoke the millennia-old spirit of the place and picture it in its prime, when the tribes were gathered for some great pagan ceremony.

Systematic excavation by 20th-century archaeologists has led to the conclusion that the largest remains are those of an Iron Age fort that had multiple ring forts, some of which were ruined in the 19th century by religious zealots from England who believed they would find the Ark of the Covenant here. The "Mound of the Hostages," a Neolithic passage grave, most likely gave the place its sacred air. During the hill's reign as a royal seat, which lasted to the 11th century, a great *feis* (national assembly) was held here every three years, during which laws were passed and tribal disputes settled. But Tara's decline was predicted one eventful Easter Eve in the 5th century on a night when, according to the Druid religion, no fires could be lit. Suddenly on a hillside some miles away, flames were spotted. "If that fire is not quenched now," said a Druid leader, "it will burn forever and will consume Tara." The fire seen by the court at Tara was lit by St. Patrick (circa 5th century) at Slane, to celebrate the Christian rites of the Paschal. Tara's influence waned with the arrival of Christianity; the last king to live here was Malachy II, who died in 1022. But like with so many other prominent sites of the Irish pre-Christian era, Christianity remade Tara in its own image. Today a modern statue of St. Patrick stands here, as does a pillar stone that may have been the coronation stone (it was reputed to call out in approval when a king was crowned). In the graveyard of the adjacent Anglican church is a pillar with the worn image of a pagan god and a Bronze Age stone standing on end. ⊠ *Hill of Tara* ☎ *046/902–5903* ⊕ *www.heritageireland.ie* ☜ *€2* ☉ *May–Oct., daily 10–6.*

Navan

❸ *10 km (6 mi) northwest of the Hill of Tara on N3, 48 km (30 mi) north of Dublin on N3.*

Navan, at the crucial juncture of the Rivers Blackwater and Boyne, is a busy market and mining town with evidence of prehistoric settlements. It took off in the 12th century, when Hugh de Lacy, lord of Trim, had the place walled and fortified, making it a defensive stronghold of the English Pale in eastern Ireland. It is now the administrative center of Meath. At **St. Mary's Church,** built in 1839, you'll find a late-18th-century wood carving of the Crucifixion, the work of a local artist, Edward Smyth—who at the time was the greatest sculptor Ireland had produced since the Middle Ages. On Fridays, the **Fair Green,** beside the church, hosts a bustling outdoor market. ⊠ *Trimgate St.* ☜ *Free* ☉ *Daily 8–8.*

The best views of town and the surrounding area are from the top of the **Motte of Navan,** a grassy mound said to be the tomb of Odhbha, the deserted wife of a Celtic king who, the story goes, went on to die of a broken heart. It's more likely that the 50-foot-high mound was formed naturally. In the twelfth century, D'Angulo, the Norman baron, adapted it into a motte and bailey (a type of medieval Norman castle), but there are no structural remains here from this period.

Kells

❹ *16 km (10 mi) northwest of Navan on N3.*

In the 9th century, a group of monks from Iona in Scotland took refuge at Kells (Ceanannus Mór) after being expelled by the Danes. St. Columba had founded a monastery here 300 years earlier, and although some historians think the indigenous monks wrote and illustrated the *Book of*

Kells—the Latin version of the four Gospels and one of Ireland's greatest medieval treasures—most scholars now believe that the Scottish monks brought it with them. Reputed to have been fished out of a watery bog at Kells, the legendary manuscript was removed for safekeeping during the Cromwellian wars to Trinity College, Dublin, where it remains. A large exhibit is now devoted to it in the college's Old Library, where a few of the original pages at a time are on view. A copy of the *Book of Kells* is on display in the Church of Ireland **St. Columba's** in Kells; it's open until 5 on weekdays and until 1 on Saturdays. Four elaborately carved high crosses stand in the church graveyard; you'll find the stump of a fifth in the marketplace—during the 1798 uprising against British rule it was used as a gallows.

Similar in appearance to St. Kevin's Church at Glendalough and Cormac's Chapel at Cashel, **St. Colmcille's House** is a small, two-story, 7th-century church measuring about 24 feet square and nearly 40 feet high, with a steeply pitched stone roof. The nearly 100-foot-high **round tower,** adjacent to St. Colmcille's House, dates prior to 1076 and is in almost perfect condition. Its top story has five windows, each facing an ancient entrance to the medieval town.

Where to Stay

¢ ▥ **Lennoxbrook.** This fine, 200-year-old-plus farmhouse is run by Pauline Mullan, whose children are the fifth generation of the family to occupy the home. A casual, friendly mood prevails throughout the house. Upstairs, finely patterned wallpaper and period furniture decorate the rooms. Lamb is a typical dinner entrée. The house, 5 km (3 mi) north of Kells on N3, is also convenient to Newgrange. The prehistoric forts, passage graves, and other remains dating from 2000 BC on the Loughcrew Hills are a 15-minute drive away. ⌧ *Co. Meath* ☎ *046/924–5902* ➥ *4 rooms* ⌂ *Dining room* ▭ *MC, V* ⏣ *BP, FAP.*

Newgrange

5 *11 km (7 mi) east of Navan on N51, 24 km (15 mi) east of Kells.*

Fodor'sChoice
★

Expect to see no less than one of the most spectacular prehistoric tombs in Europe when you come to Newgrange. Built in the 4th millennium BC—which makes it roughly 1,000 years older than Stonehenge—Newgrange was constructed with some 250,000 tons of stones, much of which came from the Wicklow Mountains, 80 km (50 mi) to the south. How the people who built this tumulus transported the stones here remains a mystery. The mound above the tomb measures more than 330 feet across and reaches a height of 36 feet at the front. White quartz stones were used for the retaining wall, and egg-shape gray stones were studded at intervals. The passage grave may have been the world's earliest observatory. It was so carefully constructed that, for five days on and around the winter solstice, the rays of the rising sun still hit a roof box above the lintel at the entrance to the grave. The rays then shine for about 20 minutes down the main interior passageway to illuminate the burial chamber. The site was restored in 1962 after years of neglect and quarrying. A visit to the passage grave during the winter solstice is considered to be the most memo-

rable experience of all, in part due to the luck needed to witness the illu-
mination. You'll have to get on the nine-year waiting list to reserve one
of the 24 places available on each of the five mornings (December 19–23).
And even if you have a place, there's no guarantee that clouds won't be
obscuring the sun. But if you visit the interior of this Bronze Age tomb
you can see the effect artificially re-created. The geometric designs on some
stones at the center of the burial chamber continue to baffle experts.

The prehistoric sites of nearby Dowth and Knowth have been under excavation since 1962, and although Dowth is still closed to the public,
Knowth is open at last. The great tumulus at Knowth is comparable in
size and shape to Newgrange, standing at 40 feet and having a diameter of approximately 214 feet. Some 150 giant stones, many of them
beautifully decorated, surrounded the mound. However, the mound itself is different in its composition from that of Newgrange, consisting
of layers of stones, turf, and clay. More than 1,600 boulders, each
weighing from one to several tons, were used in the construction. The
earliest tombs and carved stones date from the Stone Age (3000 BC), although the site was in use until the early 14th century. In the early Christian era (4th–8th centuries AD) it was the seat of the High Kings of Ireland.
Much of the site is still under excavation, and you can often watch archaeologists at work here. Access to Newgrange and Knowth is solely
via **Brú na Bóinne** ("Palace of the Boyne"), the Boyne Valley visitor center. Arrive early if possible, because Newgrange often sells out. ⊠ *Off
N2, signposted from Slane, Donore* ☎ *041/988-0300* ⊕ *www.
heritageireland.ie* 🎟 *Newgrange and interpretive center €5.50; Knowth
and interpretive center €4.25; Newgrange, Knowth, and interpretive center €9.75* ☉ *Newgrange May, daily 9:30–6:30; June–mid-Sept., daily
9:30–7; mid-Sept.–Feb., daily 10–4:30; Mar. and Apr., daily 10–5.
Knowth June–mid-Sept., daily 9–7; May and mid-Sept.–end of Sept., daily
9–6:30; Mar., Apr., and Oct., daily 9:30–5:30; Nov.–Feb., daily 9:30–5.*

Slane

❻ *2½ km (1½ mi) north of Newgrange, 46 km (29 mi) northwest of
Dublin on N2.*

Slane Castle is the draw at this small, Georgian village, built in the 18th
century around a crossroads on the north side of the River Boyne. The
16th-century building known as the **Hermitage** was constructed on the
site where St. Erc, a local man who was converted to Christianity by St.
Patrick, led a hermit's existence. All that remains of his original monastery
is the faint trace of the circular ditch, but the ruins of the later church
includes a nave and a chancel with a tower in between.

The stately 18th-century **Slane Castle** is beautifully situated overlooking a natural amphitheater. In 1981 the castle's owner, Anglo-Irish Lord
Henry Mountcharles, staged the first of what have been some of Ireland's largest outdoor rock concerts; U2, still only one album old, had
second billing to Thin Lizzy that year. Most of rock's greatest names
have performed here since, including Bob Dylan, Bruce Springsteen, David
Bowie, and the Rolling Stones—REM's show holds the record for at-
tendance, with 70,000. In 2001, after a decade of renovation following

a devastating fire, the castle reopened to the public for tours. The tour includes the main hall, with its delicate plasterwork and beautiful stained glass, the dazzling red, neo-Gothic ballroom completed in 1821 for the visit of King George IV, and other rooms. The stunning parklands were laid out by Capability Brown, the famous 18th-century landscape gardener. For a tidy sum you and your friends can rent the entire castle for the weekend. ☎ *041/988–4400* ⊕ *www.slanecastle.ie* ✉ *€7* ⊙ *Late May–early Sept., Mon.–Thurs. noon–5.*

North of Slane town is the 500-foot-high **Slane Hill,** where St. Patrick proclaimed the arrival of Christianity in 433 by lighting the Paschal Fire. From the top, you have sweeping views of the Boyne Valley. On a clear day, the panorama stretches from Trim to Drogheda, a vista extending 40 km (25 mi).

A two-hour tour of farmer Willie Redhouse's fully functioning arable and livestock **Newgrange Farm** includes feeding the ducks, bottle-feeding the lambs, a tour of the aviaries with their exotic birds, and a donkey ride for the kids. Demonstrations of sheepdog work, threshing, and horseshoeing are given. Every Sunday at 3 PM the "Sheep Derby" takes place, with teddy bears tied to the animals in the place of jockeys. Visiting children are made "owners" of individual sheep for the duration of the race. The farm lies 3 km (2 mi) east of Slane on N51. ☎ *041/982–4119* ✉ *€6* ⊙ *Easter–Aug., daily 10–5.*

Where to Stay & Eat

$ ✕🏨 **Conyngham Arms Hotel.** Built in the mid-19th century, the Conyngham Arms, at the crossroads in Slane, maintains its village-inn look. Four-poster beds in the guest rooms let you imagine what it's like to sleep like the aristocracy. The Gamekeeper's Lodge Bistro ($$) serves simple but delightful fresh meat and fish dishes. Try the salmon in season. ✉ *Co. Meath* ☎ *041/988–4444* 🖨 *041/982–4205* ⇌ *14 rooms* ⚬ *Restaurant, bar; no a/c* ⊟ *AE, MC, V* ⑩ *BP, FAP, MAP.*

King William's Glen

❼ *7½ km (4½ mi) east of Slane on N51.*

On the northern bank of the River Boyne, King William's Glen is where a portion of King William of Orange's Protestant army hid before the Battle of the Boyne in 1690. They won by surprising the Catholic troops of James II, who were on the southern side, but many of the Protestant-Catholic conflicts in present-day Northern Ireland can be traced to the immediate aftermath of this battle. The site is marked with an orange-and-green sign; part of the site is also incorporated in the nearby, early 19th-century **Townley Hall Estate,** which has forest walks and a nature trail (the house is not open to the public).

Drogheda

❽ *6½ km (4 mi) east of King William's Glen on N51, 45 km (28 mi) north of Dublin on N1.*

Drogheda (pronounced draw-*hee*-da) is one of the most enjoyable and historic towns on the east coast of Ireland—and a setting for one of the most tragic events in Irish history (*see* the Bloody Cromwell Close-Up box). It was colonized in 911 by the Danish Vikings; two centuries later, the town was taken over by Hugh de Lacy, the Anglo-Norman lord of Trim, who was responsible for fortifying the towns along the River Boyne. At first, two separate towns existed, one on the northern bank, the other on the southern bank. In 1412, already heavily walled and fortified, Drogheda was unified, making it the largest English town in Ireland. Today, large 18th-century warehouses line the northern bank of the Boyne. In the center of town, around West Street, is the historic heart of Drogheda. Towering over the river is the long **railway viaduct**. Built around 1850 as part of the railway line from Dublin to Belfast, it is still used and is a splendid example of Victorian engineering. Because of its height above the river, the viaduct remains Drogheda's most prominent landmark.

The bank building on the corner of West and Shop streets, called the **Tholsel**, is an 18th-century square granite edifice with a cupola. The 13th-century **St. Laurence's Gate,** one of the two surviving entrances from Drogheda's original 11 gates in its town walls, has two four-story drum towers and is one of the most perfect examples in Ireland of a medieval town gate. **Butler's Gate,** near the Millmount Museum, predates St. Laurence's Gate by 50 years or more.

The Gothic Revival, Roman Catholic **St. Peter's Church** (⊠ West St.) houses the preserved head of St. Oliver Plunkett. Primate of all Ireland, he was martyred in 1681 at Tyburn in London; his head was pulled from the execution flames. A severe, 18th-century church within an enclosed courtyard, the Anglican **St. Peter's** (⊠ Fair St.) is rarely open except for Sunday services. It's worth a peek for its setting and the fine views over the town from the churchyard.

Perhaps the main attraction in Drogheda lies across the river from the town center. The **Millmount Museum and Martello Tower,** off the Dublin road (N1) south of Drogheda, shares space in a renovated British Army barracks with crafts workshops, including a pottery- and picture-gallery and studio. It was on the hill at Millmount that the townsfolk made their last stand against the bloodthirsty Roundheads of Cromwell. Perhaps in defiance of Cromwell's attempt to obliterate the town from the map, the museum contains relics of eight centuries of Drogheda's commercial and industrial past, including painted banners of the old trade guilds, a circular willow and leather coracle (the traditional fishing boat on the River Boyne), and many instruments and utensils from domestic and factory use. Most moving are the mementos of the infamous 1649 massacre of 3,000 people by Cromwell. The exhibit inside the Martello Tower adjacent to the museum focuses on the military history of Drogheda. ⊠ *Millmount* ☎ *041/983–3097* ✆ *Museum €3, tower €2.50* ☉ *Mon.–Sat. 10–5:30, Sun. 2:30–5:30.*

Across the Meath border in County Dublin, 18 km (11 mi) south of Drogheda, is **Ardgillan Demesne,** one of the prettiest parks along the coast. Its 194 acres consist of rolling pastures, mixed woodland, and gardens overlooking the Bay of Drogheda, with splendid views of the coast-

BLOODY CROMWELL!

I N MUCH OF THE *English-speaking world Oliver Cromwell is regarded as something of a hero, a deeply religious self-made man, master general, and leader of the victorious parliamentary side in the English Civil Wars.*

But in Ireland, Cromwell's name is usually followed by a spit and a curse. In 1649 Old Ironsides arrived in Ireland to subdue a Royalist and Catholic rebellion once and for all. His methods were simple: burn every building, and kill every person that stood in his way.

"To Hell or to Connaught" (the latter being the most westerly of Ireland's four provinces) was the dire choice he offered the native population as he drove them ever westward and off the more fertile lands of the east and south. When he approached the walled town of Drogheda, the gates were closed to him.

Led by the Anglo-Irish Sir Arthur Aston, the native Catholic population bravely defended their town against Cromwell's relentless siege, twice driving back the advancing army. On the third attempt the town fell, and the order went out that no mercy was to be shown.

It is estimated that up to 3,500 men, women, and children were slaughtered. One group hid in the steeple of St. Peter's Church, so Cromwell burned it down with them all inside. Sir Arthur was beaten to death with his own wooden leg.

While the massacre at Drogheda frightened many Irish towns into submission (and thereby prevented other battles), the bloody stain on Cromwell's reputation was permanent.

line. The castle here, built in 1738 for a landowning family, rises two stories. Ground-floor rooms are decorated in Georgian and Victorian styles; first-floor rooms house a permanent display of 17th-century maps, and host an annual program of exhibitions. ⊠ *Balbriggan* ☎ *01/849–2212* ⊕ *www.fingalcoco.ie* 🎫 *€3.80* ☉ *Apr.–June and Sept., Tues.–Sun. 11–6; Oct.–Mar., Tues.–Sun. 11–4:30; July–Aug., daily 11–dusk.*

Where to Stay & Eat

¢–$ ✕ **Monk's.** This little café on the river is always full of locals looking for healthful food at a decent price. Monk's specializes in delicious, somewhat off-center sandwiches, including a wonderful goat-cheese bruschetta and a spicy Mexican chicken sandwich. The hot breakfasts are a treat, chunky French toast and fruit being the most popular dish. ⊠ *North Quay* ☎ *041/984–5630* 🖃 *MC, V.*

$$ ✕🛏 **Boyne Valley Hotel and Country Club.** A 1-km (½-mi) drive leads to this 19th-century mansion on 16 acres that was once owned by a Drogheda brewing family. The newer wing of this owner-run hotel has double rooms, all with contemporary furnishings and bright color schemes full of pinks and pastels. The public spaces have been restored in period fashion, with neoclassical pillars, intricate plasterwork, and crystal chandeliers. A large conservatory houses a bar and overlooks the

grounds, while a spacious hall is decorated with antiques and comfy chairs. The Cellar Restaurant specializes in fresh fish. ⊠ *Dublin Rd., Co. Louth* ☎ *041/983–7737* 🖨 *041/983–9188* ⊕ *www.boyne-valley-hotel. ie* ➡ *71 rooms* ⚲ *Restaurant, 18-hole golf course, 2 tennis courts, indoor pool, health club, bar* ⊟ *AE, DC, MC, V* ⦿ *BP.*

Mellifont Abbey

❾ *8 km (5 mi) west of Drogheda on R168, 11 km (7 mi) north of Newgrange on N2.*

On the eastern bank of the River Mattock, which creates a natural border between Counties Meath and Louth, lie the remains of Mellifont Abbey, the first Cistercian monastery in Ireland. Founded in 1142 by St. Malachy, archbishop of Armagh, it was inspired by the formal structure around a central courtyard of St. Bernard of Clairvaux's monastery, which St. Malachy had visited. Among the substantial ruins are the two-story chapter house, built in 12th-century English-Norman style and once a daily meeting place for the monks; it now houses a collection of medieval glazed tiles. Four walls of the 13th-century octagonal lavabo, or washing place, still stand, as do some arches from the Romanesque cloister. At its peak Mellifont presided over almost 40 other Cistercian monasteries throughout Ireland, but all were suppressed by Henry VIII in 1539 after his break with the Catholic Church. Adjacent to the car park is a small **architectural museum** depicting the history of the abbey and the craftsmanship that went into its construction. ⊠ *Near Collon* ☎ *041/982–6459* 🎟 *€2* ⊙ *May–mid-June and mid-Sept.–Oct., daily 10–5; mid-June–mid-Sept., daily 9:30–6:30.*

Where to Eat

$$–$$$ ✕ **Forge Gallery Restaurant.** For generations the local forge was the burning heart of any rural Irish community and this well-established restaurant is still something of a beacon to locals and visitors for miles around. Warm rose and plum tones and antique furnishings decorate this two-story eatery in a converted forge, and an old fireplace fills the place with a comforting warmth and light. The cuisine mixes French Provençal with a strong hint of traditional Irish cooking. Two popular specialties are salmon and crab in phyllo pastry, and prawns and scallops in a cream-and-garlic sauce. Make sure you try one of the seasonal homemade soups. Paintings by local artists hang in the reception area and are for sale. Reservations are essential on weekends. ⊠ *North of Slane on N2, Collon* ☎ *041/982– 6272* ⊟ *AE, DC, MC, V* ⊙ *Closed Sun., Mon., and second wk of Jan.*

Monasterboice

❿ *8 km (5 mi) northeast of Mellifont Abbey on N1, 8 km (5 mi) north of Drogheda.*

Ireland has more carved-stone high crosses than any other European country, and an outstanding collection is in the small, secluded village of Monasterboice, a former monastic settlement. Dating to AD 923, the **Muireadach Cross** stands nearly 20 feet high and is considered to be the best-preserved example of a high cross in Ireland. Its elaborate panels depict biblical scenes, including Cain slaying Abel, David and Goliath, and a centerpiece of the Last Judgment. (Figurative scenes are not a characteristic of earlier high crosses, such as those found in Ahenny, County Clare.) The **West Cross** stands a couple of feet taller than Muiredach's, making it one of the tallest in Ireland. Its engravings are less impressive—many of them have been worn away by centuries of Irish wind and rain. From the adjacent, 110-foot-high **round tower**, the extent of the former monastic settlement at Monasterboice is apparent. The key to the tower door is kept at the nearby gate lodge.

Ardee

⓫ *14½ km (9 mi) northwest of Monasterboice on N2.*

In this market town, formerly at the northern edge of the Pale (originally the Pale referred to the area of eastern Ireland ruled directly by the Normans), stand two 13th-century castles: Ardee Castle and Hatch's Castle. The town of Ardee (Baile Átha Fhirdia or Ferdia's Ford), interestingly, was named after the ford where the mythical folk hero Cuchulainn fought his foster brother Ferdia. There's a statue depicting this battle at the start of the riverside walk. **Ardee Castle** (the one with square corners) was founded by Roger de Peppard in 1207, but much of the present building dates to the 15th century and after. The castle faces north—built to protect the Anglo-Irish Pale from the untamed Celtic tribes of Ulster. It was converted into a courthouse in the 19th century. **Hatch's Castle** (with rounded corners) is a private residence and not open to the public. Built in the 13th century, it was given by Cromwell as a gift to the loyal Hatch family. If you look closely you can see it still flaunts two 18th-century cannons at its entrance. **St. Mary's Church of Ireland** on Main Street incorporates part of a 13th-century Carmelite church burned by Edward the Bruce in 1316, including the holy water font. The current building was constructed in the 19th century.

Where to Eat

★ $$–$$$ ✕ **Rolf's Bistro.** When the husband and wife team of Paul and Bernadette Svender (Rolf is Paul's father's name) opened their new restaurant in Ardee they knew what they wanted: an informal atmosphere with high quality food. They renovated an old house in the middle of town, retaining much of its cozy charm with the help of discreet lighting, old pine floors, and a luxurious antique sofa in the waiting area. The menu reflects chef Paul's Scandinavian background, with Swedish caviar and beef Lindstrom (minced meat with capers and beetroot) a popular starter and main course. The steamed mussels served with chili sauce and aioli bread are refreshingly spicy. ✉ *52 Market St.* ☎ *041/685–7949* ▭ *MC, V.*

$$ ✕ **Gables House and Restaurant.** At this family-run spot off N2, not far from the Dundalk junction, expect a French-influenced cooking style, generous portions, and a fine catch of the day—often monkfish, halibut, or sole. The restaurant has lush, traditional-style furnishings: antique mahogany furniture, deep-burgundy velvet curtains, and oil paintings by local artists. Polished tables, silver cutlery, linen napkins, lace coasters, and gleaming leaded-crystal glasses add an elegant touch. For dessert, satisfy your sugar craving with the Gables Medley: cheese-

cake, profiteroles, and homemade ice cream. ⊠ *Dundalk Rd.* ☎ *041/ 685–3789* ☰ *MC, V.*

Louth

⑫ *11½ km (7 mi) north of Ardee on R171.*

Louth warrants a visit, if only for the splendidly preserved oratory here. St. Patrick, Ireland's patron saint, was reputed to have built his first church (which is no longer here) in this hilltop village in the 5th century. He also made St. Mochta (d. 534) the first bishop of Louth. Standing at the center of the village is the excellently preserved **St. Mochta's House,** an oratory dating from the 11th century, which has a steeply pitched stone roof that can be reached by a stairway. The house is freely accessible— but watch out for cattle (and their droppings) in the surrounding field.

Inniskeen

⑬ *6½ km (4 mi) north of Louth.*

On the road to Dundalk and just over the Louth county boundary in Monaghan lies Inniskeen, a small farming town that doubles as a social hearth for the area's far-flung community. Patrick Kavanagh (1906–69), the area's most famous poet, is commemorated at the **Inniskeen Folk Museum,** housed in a converted church next to a round tower. Born and raised here, Kavanagh immortalized the town in his early poem "Inniskeen Road"—where as a child he spied on young lovers and their "wink and elbow language of delight"—before becoming one of Ireland's leading poets. He was brought back to the village for burial. ☎ *042/937–8109* ☞ *Donations accepted* ☉ *May–Sept., Sun. 3–6, or by appointment.*

Dundalk

⑭ *14½ km (9 mi) east of Inniskeen, 80 km (50 mi) north of Dublin on N1.*

Dundalk is a thriving, if uninspiring, frontier town—only 9½ km (6 mi) from the Northern Ireland border—with some fine historic buildings. It's the main town of County Louth (Ireland's smallest county), and it dates from the early Christian period, around the 7th century. The area near the town is closely connected with Cuchulainn (pronounced *coo*-chu-lain)—"a greater hero than Hercules or Achilles," as Frank McCourt, in *Angela's Ashes,* recalls his father claiming. Cuchulainn, the warrior of the old Irish epic *Táin Bó Cuailnge* (Cattle Raid of Cooley), was the hero of ancient Ulster—which then included the Dundalk area—and defended her borders and interests against newcomers.

On Mill Street, the **bell tower** of a Franciscan monastery with Gothic windows dates from the 13th century. The **St. Patrick's Cathedral** was built between 1835 and 1847, when the Gothic Revival was at its height. With its buttresses and mosaics lining the chancel and the side chapel walls, the cathedral was modeled on the 15th-century King's College Chapel at Cambridge, England. The fine exterior was built in Newry granite, and the high altar and pulpit are of carved Caen stone. ⊠ *Town center* ☉ *Daily 8–6.*

The Market House, the Town Hall, and the Courthouse are examples of the town's 19th-century heritage; the **Courthouse** is the most impressive of the three, built in the 1820s in a severe Greek Revival style, with Doric columns supporting the portico. It stands north of St. Patrick's Cathedral.

The **Dundalk County Museum** is dedicated to preserving the history of the dying local industries, such as beer brewing, cigarette manufacturing, shoe and boot making, and railway engineering. Other exhibits deal with the history of Louth from 7500 BC to the present. ⊠ *Joycelyn St.* ☎ *042/932–7056* ⊕ *www.louthcoco.ie* 🖾 *€3.80* ⊙ *Tues.–Sat. 10:30–5:30, Sun. 2–6.*

Where to Stay & Eat

★ **$–$$** ✕**Cube.** It might be situated right across the road from St. Patrick's Cathedral but there's nothing traditional about Cube. The funky colored walls and leather armchairs in the bar prepare you for the leather banquettes and dramatic floor lighting of the stylish dining room. The menu is equally eclectic, and attempts an exotic twist to many "blue-collar" dishes; wild boar bangers and mash and oversized chips with mushy peas and battered cod are two examples. There's always plenty of seafood on offer, including poached oysters, bouillabaisse, and langoustine ravioli; they even do a sushi starter. Cube also has rack of lamb (fresh from the surrounding hills) and a number of steak options. ⊠ *5 Roden Pl.* ☎ *042/932–9898* 🖃 *MC, V.*

$$–$$$$ ✕🏨**Ballymascanlon House Hotel.** On 130 acres on the scenic Cooley Peninsula just north of Dundalk, you'll find this converted Victorian mansion with a reputation for comfort and good cuisine. Reproduction period pieces fill the large guest rooms, which overlook the spacious gardens or old stable yard. The restaurant ($$$) serves a set menu of Irish and French cuisine; it specializes in fresh seafood, such as lobster in season. Vegetarian plates are also available. ⊠ *Dundalk, Co. Louth* ☎ *042/935–8200* 🖨 *042/937–1598* ⊕ *www.ballymascanlon.com* 📞 *90 rooms* ⚂ *Restaurant, 18-hole golf course, 2 tennis courts, indoor pool, health club, 2 bars* 🖃 *AE, DC, MC, V* ¶◯¶ *BP.*

¢–$ 🏨**Balrobin House.** This Georgian house was the home of Sir Lionel Harty and his wife Lady Lucy, who in the late 19th century would wine and dine Ireland's elite in its lush surroundings. A marble fireplace, a walled garden, and antique gates are among the many original features of the house. The rooms maintain a period look with high, plasterwork ceilings and ornate furnishings. ⊠ *Kilkerley, Co. Louth* ☎ *042/937–7701* 📞 *4 rooms* 🖃 *MC, V* ¶◯¶ *BP.*

Cooley Peninsula Drive

⓯ *Beginning in Dundalk, 80 km (50 mi) north of Dublin.*

A soft, misty rain falling on the ancient, mysterious Cooley Peninsula is a quintessential Irish scene. If you have a car and three or four free hours, go for a scenic drive around the peninsula and indulge in some of the finest views of the east coast of Ireland. A 64-km (40-mi) round-trip beginning and ending in Dundalk will take you by the Carlingford Lough on the north side of the peninsula, with the Mountains of

Mourne rising in the distance. The area is steeped in Celtic mythology, especially with the daring feats of the doomed hero Cuchulainn. You could do worse for a travel guide than a modern translation of the *Táin Bó Cuailnge* epic itself. From Gyles Quay, a small coastal village with a clean, safe beach, you can take in excellent views southward along the County Louth coast to Clogher Head. A coast road winds east around the Cooley Peninsula to Greenore, a town built in Victorian times as a ferry terminal. If you feel like getting out of your car, the Táin Trail is a 25-mi meandering hike up through the Windy Gap and Clermont Cairn, and then down through Ravensdale Forest and back to the R174 road. This trail begins in Carlingford and passes through such towns as Omeath before ending in Ravensdale—so you'll find plenty of places to stay along the way. Shorter walks are also marked.

Carlingford

16 *21 km (13 mi) east of Dundalk, 6½ km (4 mi) south of Omeath on R173.*

The small, medieval fishing town of Carlingford appeals for its natural scenery, as well as its striking whitewashed, thatched cottages. The mountains of the Cooley Peninsula back right up to the town, the Carlingford Lough lies at its feet, and the Mountains of Mourne rise only 5 km (3 mi) away across the lough. Some remnants from the area's medieval days include a tower from the town wall and one of its gates, which later became the town hall. The 15th-century **Mint Tower House,** in an alley off Market Square, is notable for its mullioned, limestone windows. **Taaffe's Castle,** a 16th-century fortified town house on the quay, has classic Norman defensive features. A massive, 13th-century fortress that rises up over the entrance to Carlingford Lough, **King John's Castle** has an unusual trait: its west gateway is only wide enough to admit one horseman. It was built in the 1190s and named for the English king who paid a brief visit in 1210. The highlight of the **Holy Trinity Heritage Centre,** in a beautifully restored medieval church, is a mural depicting the village at the height of the Middle Ages. An audiovisual display focuses on village history and the efforts to preserve Carlingford's medieval heritage. ⊠ *Churchyard Rd.* ☎ *042/937–3888* 🎫 *€2* ⊗ *Weekdays 10–12:30 and 2–4:30.*

Omeath

17 *6½ km (4 mi) northwest of Carlingford on R173.*

This northernmost town on Cooley Peninsula is blessed with a stunning landscape and the distinction of having outdoor pictures of the Stations of the Cross that Catholics pray before in a solemn procession every Good Friday. Omeath was the last main Gaeltacht (Irish-speaking) village in this part of Ireland (most extant Gaeltacht villages are in the southwest and the west). There's a narrow road that climbs the mountains behind Omeath. As you ascend, the views become ever more spectacular, stretching over the Mountains of Mourne in the north and as far south as Skerries, 32 km (20 mi) north of Dublin. This narrow road leads back to Dundalk.

On the eastern side of the Omeath, on the outside of a shrine, are the open-air **Stations of the Cross**—14 pictures of the key moments during Christ's last days—at the monastery of the Rosminian Fathers. Jaunting cars (horse-drawn carts) take visitors to the site from the quayside. Daily from June to September, stalls at the **quay** sell all kinds of shellfish, including oysters and mussels, from the nearby lough. In July and August, a ferry service runs until 6 PM from here to Warrenpoint, across the lough in Northern Ireland; the trip takes five minutes.

COUNTY WICKLOW

Make your way to the fourth or fifth story of almost any building in Dublin that faces south and you'll see off in the distance—amazingly, not *that* far off in the distance—the green, smooth hills of the Dublin and Wicklow mountains. On a clear day the mountains are even visible from some streets in and around the city center. If your idea of solace is green hills, and your visit to Ireland is otherwise limited to Dublin, County Wicklow—or Cill Mhantain (pronounced kill *wan-*tan), as it is known in Irish—should be on your itinerary. Not that the secret isn't out; rugged and mountainous with dark, wooded forests, central Wicklow, known as the "garden of Ireland," is a popular picnic area among Dubliners. It has some of Ireland's grandest 18th-century mansions, and cradles one of the country's earliest Christian retreats: Glendalough. Nestled in a valley of dense woods and placid lakes, Glendalough and environs can seem (at least during the off-season) practically untouched since their heyday 1,000 years ago. The granite mountains that have protected Glendalough all these years run into the sea along the east coast, which has several popular sandy beaches. Journey from Dublin down to Arklow, sticking to the east side of the Wicklow Mountains. A quick note about getting here: it takes stamina to extract yourself from the unmarked maze of the Dublin exurbs (your best bet is to take N11, which becomes M11, and then again N11). Once you've accomplished that feat, this gorgeous, mysterious terrain awaits.

Bray

▶ ⑱ *22 km (14 mi) south of Dublin on N11, 8 km (5 mi) east of Enniskerry on R755.*

One of Ireland's oldest seaside resorts, Bray is a trim village known for its dilapidated summer cottages and sand-and-shingle beach, which stretches for 2 km (1 mi). When the trains first arrived from Dublin in 1854, Bray became the number one spot for urban vacationers and subsequently took on the appearance of an English oceanfront town. Some Dubliners still flock to the faded glory of Bray's boardwalk to push baby carriages and soak up the sun. It's the terminus of the DART train from Dublin, so it's easy to get here without a car. Uncrowded trails for hiking and mountain-biking crisscross the mountains bordering Bray to the south. One of the best is a well-marked path leading from the beach to the 10-foot-tall cross that crowns the spiny peak of Bray Head, a rocky outcrop that rises 791 feet from the sea. The semi-difficult, one-hour climb affords stunning views of Wicklow Town and Dublin Bay.

The **Heritage Centre,** opposite the Royal Hotel, in the old courthouse, houses on its lower level a re-created castle dungeon with a 1,000-years-of-Bray exhibition. Upstairs is a huge model railway and a display about modern Bray. ⊠ *Lower Main St.* ☎ *01/286–6796* 🖃 *€3.80* ☉ *June–Sept., weekdays 9–5, Sat. 10–4, Sun. noon–5; Oct.–May, weekdays 9:30–4:30, Sat. 10–4:30.*

One Martello Terrace (☎ 01/286–8407), at the harbor, is Bray's most famous address. James Joyce (1882–1941) lived here between 1887 and 1891 and used the house as the setting for the Christmas dinner in *A Portrait of the Artist as a Young Man.* Today the house is owned by an Irish Teachta Dála (member of Parliament, informally known as a "TD"). The phone number listed above rings at her constituency office; someone there should be able to help scholars and devotees arrange a visit. (Call on Thursday between 10 AM and 1 PM.) Although the residence has been renovated, the dining room portrayed in Joyce's novel maintains the spirit of his time.

☺ **National Sealife** is an aquarium and museum dedicated to the creatures of the sea, with an emphasis on those that occupy the waters around Ireland. Besides massive sea tanks that contain all manner of swimming things, there's a major conservation project with captive breeding of sea horses. **FinZone** is an undersea adventure trail perfect for kids, with puzzles to solve. Touch-screen computers and video games give the whole thing a high-tech feel. In winter, call to confirm opening times before visiting. ⊠ *Strand Rd.* ☎ *01/286–6939* ⊕ *www.sealife.ie* 🖃 *€8.50* ☉ *Daily 10–5.*

The 17th-century formal gardens at **Killruddery House** are precisely arranged, with fine beech hedges, Victorian statuary, and a parterre of lavender and roses. The Brabazon family, the earls of Meath, have lived here since 1618. In 1820 they hired William Morris to remodel the house as a revival Elizabethan mansion. The estate also has a Crystal Palace conservatory modeled on those at the botanic gardens in Dublin. ⊠ *Off the Bray–Greystones Rd., 3 km (2 mi) south of Bray, Killruddery* ☎ *01/286–2777* 🖃 *House and gardens €8, gardens only €5* ☉ *Gardens May–Sept., daily 1–5; house May–June and Sept., daily 1–5; by appointment at other times.*

Where to Eat

$$–$$$ ✕ **Hungry Monk.** The cloisters and refectory style decor is definitely
Fodor'sChoice tongue in cheek at this upbeat, fun bistro in sleepy Greystones, an old-
★ fashioned seaside resort a couple miles south of Bray. Owner Pat Keown is a great host and his laughter and love of good food and fine wine are catching. Dinner is served by candlelight and the menu specializes in uncluttered seafood dishes in summer and wild game on those cold winter nights. The "Seafood Symphony" is a particular favorite. Sunday lunches are famous for the length of time they go on (often into the early evening) and for the lively atmosphere. ⊠ *1 Church Rd., Greystones* ☎ *01/287–5759* ⊟ *AE, DC, MC, V* ☉ *Closed Mon. and Tues.*

¢–$ ✕ **Summerville Country Cooking.** This restaurant's ceilings are high, the space is airy and bright, and the food—ranging from shepherd's pie to vegetarian quiche—tastes absolutely delicious. In summer, take advantage of the sun-drenched garden terrace. ⊠ *1 Trafalgar Rd., Greystones* ☎ *01/287–4228* ▤ *V.*

Powerscourt House, Gardens & Waterfall

★ ᛚ ☛ ⑲   *25 km (16 mi) south of Dublin on R117, 22 km (14 mi) north of Glendalough on R755.*

Within the shadow of famous Sugar Loaf mountain, Enniskerry is one of the prettiest villages in Ireland. It is built around a sloping central triangular square with a backdrop of the wooded Wicklow Mountains. From Dublin you can get to Enniskerry directly by taking the No. 44 bus from the Dublin quays area.

The main reason to visit the area around Enniskerry is the **Powerscourt Estate.** The grounds were granted to Sir Richard Wingfield, the first viscount of Powerscourt, by King James I of England in 1609. Richard Castle (1690–1751), the architect of Russborough House, designed Powerscourt House in a grand Palladian style, and it was constructed between 1731 and 1743. The original ballroom on the first floor—once "the grandest room in any Irish house," according to historian Desmond Guinness—still gives a sense of the house's former life.

Powerscourt Gardens, considered among the finest in Europe, were laid out from 1745 to 1767 following the completion of the house—and were radically redesigned in the Victorian style, from 1843 to 1875. The redesign was the work of the eccentric, boozy Daniel Robertson, who liked to be tootled around the gardens-in-progress in a wheelbarrow while nipping at his bottle of sherry. The Villa Butera in Sicily inspired him to set these gardens with sweeping terraces, antique sculptures, and a circular pond and fountain flanked by winged horses. There's a celebrated view of the Italianate patterned ramps, lawns, and pond across the beautiful, heavily wooded Dargle Valley, which stair-steps to the horizon and the noble profile of Sugar Loaf mountain. The grounds include many specimen trees (plants grown for exhibition), an avenue of monkey puzzle trees, a parterre of brightly colored summer flowers, and a Japanese garden. The kitchen gardens, with their modest rows of flowers, are a striking antidote to the classical formality of the main sections. A self-serve restaurant, crafts center, garden center, and a children's play area are also on the grounds. ⊠ *Enniskerry* ☎ *01/204–6000* ⊕ *www.powerscourt.ie* ⊠ *House €2.50, gardens €6* ☾ *Mar.–Oct., daily 9:30–5:30; Nov.–Feb., daily 9:30–dusk.*

One of the most inspiring sights to the writers and artists of the Romantic generation, the 400-foot **Powerscourt Waterfall,** 5 km (3 mi) south of the gardens, is the highest in the British Isles. ⊠ *Enniskerry* ⊠ *€4* ☾ *June–Aug., daily 9:30–7; Sept.–May, daily 10:30–dusk.*

Where to Eat

$ ✕ **Poppies Country Cooking.** This cozy café—with a pine-paneled ceiling, farmhouse furniture, and paintings of poppies on the walls—is a great place for breakfast, lunch, or late-afternoon tea. Expect potato cakes,

Fodor's Choice ★

shepherd's pie, lasagna, vegetarian quiche, house salads, and soup. But the most popular dishes are Poppies chicken (a casserole-like concoction) and homity pie (pot pie with potatoes, onion, garlic, and cream cheese). For dessert try the apple pie or the rhubarb crumble, which is so good that the Irish rugby team stops by for it after practice. ⊠ *The Square, Enniskerry* ☎ *01/282–8869* ⊟ *MC, V* ⊘ *No dinner.*

Roundwood

★ ❷ *18 km (11 mi) south of Enniskerry on R755.*

At 800 feet above sea level, Roundwood is the highest village in Ireland. It's also surrounded by spectacular mountain scenery. The Sunday-afternoon market in the village hall, where cakes, jams, and other homemade goods are sold, livens up what is otherwise a sleepy place. From the broad main street, by the Roundwood Inn, a minor road leads west for 8 km (5 mi) to two lakes, Lough Dan and Lough Tay, lying deep between forested mountains like Norwegian fjords.

Where to Eat

★ **$$–$$$** ✕ **Roundwood Inn.** Travel back to the 17th-century at this inn evocatively furnished in a traditional style, with wooden floors, dark furniture, and diamond-shape windows. It's best known for its good, reasonably priced bar food—eaten at sturdy tables beside an open fire. The restaurant offers a combination of Continental and Irish cuisines, reflecting the traditions of the German proprietor, Jurgen Schwalm, and his Irish wife, Aine. The separate bar and lounge also serve an excellent menu that includes a succulent seafood platter of salmon, oysters, lobster, and shrimp. ⊠ *Main St., Roundwood village center* ☎ *01/281–8107* ⊰ *Reservations essential* ⊟ *AE, MC, V* ⊘ *Closed Mon.–Tues. No dinner Sun.*

Glendalough

❷ *9½ km (6 mi) southwest of Roundwood, 54 km (33 mi) south of Dublin*
Fodor'sChoice *on R117 and R755.*
★

Nestled in a lush, quiet valley deep in the rugged Wicklow Mountains, among two lakes, evergreen and deciduous trees, and acres of windswept heather, Glendalough is one of Ireland's premier monastic sites. It flourished as a monastic center from the 6th century until 1398, when English soldiers plundered the site, leaving the ruins that you see today. (The monastery survived earlier 9th- and 10th-century Viking attacks.) The monastery was founded by St. Kevin (Coemghein, or "fair begotten" in Irish [d. 618]), a descendant of the royal house of Leinster, who renounced the world and came here to live as a hermit before opening the monastery in 550. Note that in high season, hordes of visitors to Glendalough make it difficult to appreciate the quiet solitude that brought St. Kevin to this valley. The visitor center is a good place to orient yourself and pick up a useful pamphlet. Many of the ruins are clumped together beyond the visitor center, but some of the oldest surround the Upper Lake, where signed paths direct you through spectacular scenery absent of crowds. Most ruins are open all day and are freely accessible.

Probably the oldest building on the site, presumed to date from St. Kevin's time, is the **Teampaill na Skellig** (Church of the Oratory), on the south shore of the Upper Lake. A little to the east is **St. Kevin's Bed,** a tiny cave in the rock face, about 30 feet above the level of the lake, where St. Kevin lived his hermit's existence. It's not easily accessible; you approach the cave by boat, but climbing the cliff to the cave can be dangerous. At the southeast corner of the Upper Lake is the 11th-century **Reefert Church,** with the ruins of a nave and a chancel. The saint also lived in the adjoining, ruined beehive hut with five crosses, which marked the original boundary of the monastery. You get a superb view of the valley from here.

The ruins by the edge of the Lower Lake are the most important of those at Glendalough. The **gateway,** beside the Glendalough Hotel, is the only surviving entrance to an ancient monastic site anywhere in Ireland. An extensive **graveyard** lies within, with hundreds of elaborately decorated crosses, as well as a perfectly preserved six-story **round tower.** Built in the 11th or 12th century, it stands 100 feet high, with an entrance 25 feet above ground level.

The largest building at Glendalough is the substantially intact 7th- to 9th-century **cathedral,** where you'll find the nave (small for a large church, only 30 feet wide by 50 feet long), chancel, and ornamental oolite limestone window, which may have been imported from England. South of the cathedral is the 11-foot-high Celtic **St. Kevin's Cross.** Made of granite, it is the best-preserved such cross on the site. **St. Kevin's Church** is an early barrel-vaulted oratory with a high-pitched stone roof.

A note about getting here directly from Dublin: you can take the St. Kevin's bus service. If you're driving from Dublin, consider taking the scenic route along R155, which includes awesome, austere mountaintop passes. Don't drive this route if you're in a hurry, and don't look for a lot of signage—just concentrate on the glorious views. ☎ *0404/45325* ⊕ *www. heritageireland.ie* ✏ *€2.75* ☺ *Mid-Mar.–mid-Oct., daily 9:30–6; mid-Oct.–mid-Mar., daily 9:30–5; last admission 45 mins before closing.*

Where to Stay & Eat

$$ ✕⊡ **Glendalough Hotel.** Purists object to the proximity of this old-fashioned, early 19th-century hotel to the ruins at Glendalough, but to others it's a convenience. Some of the bedrooms, decorated in pastel colors, overlook the monastery and the wooded mountain scenery; others face the grounds. The burble of running water from the Glendassan River audibly enhances the experience. The restaurant ($$–$$$) also has views of the lawn. The Irish menu is simple, but portions are hearty and the pub is the only one for miles around. ⊠ *Co. Wicklow* ☎ *0404/45135* 🖷 *0404/ 45142* ⊕ *www.glendaloughhotel.com* ➥ *40 rooms* ⚒ *Restaurant, fishing, bar; no a/c* ⊟ *AE, DC, MC, V* ☺ *Closed Dec. and Jan.* ❍ *BP.*

Mount Usher Gardens

★ ㉒ *13 km (8 mi) east of Glendalough, 14½ km (9 mi) southeast of Roundwood on R764.*

Settled into more than 20 acres on the banks of the River Vartry, the gardens here were first laid out in 1868 by textile magnate Edward

Walpole. Succeeding generations of the Walpole family further planted and maintained the grounds, which today have more than 5,000 species. The gardener has made the most of the riverside locale by planting eucalypti, azaleas, camellias, and rhododendrons. The river is visible from nearly everyplace in the gardens; miniature suspension bridges bounce and sway underfoot as you cross the river. Near the entrance, you'll find a cluster of crafts shops (including a pottery workshop) as well as a bookstore and self-service restaurant. The twin villages of Ashford and Rathnew are to the south and east, and Newtownmountkennedy is to the north. ⊠ *Ashford* ☎ *0404/40205* ⊕ *www.dublingardens.com* 🎫 *€6* ☉ *Mid-Mar.–Oct., daily 10:30–5:30.*

Where to Stay & Eat

★ **$$$–$$$$** ✕🏠 **Tinakilly House.** William and Bee Power have beautifully restored this Victorian-Italianate mansion, built in the 1870s by Captain Robert Halpin. The lobby has mementos of Captain Halpin and his nautical exploits, including paintings and ship models; Victorian antiques fill the house. Some bedrooms have four-poster beds, sitting areas, and views of the Wicklow landscape, the Irish Sea, or the lovely gardens on the 7-acre grounds. In the dining room ($$$), expect to be served French-influenced Irish cuisine, with fresh vegetables from the garden. Brown and fruit breads are baked daily. ⊠ *Rathnew, Co. Wicklow* ☎ *0404/69274* 🖨 *0404/67806* ⊕ *www.tinakilly.ie* 🛏 *52 rooms, 5 suites* 🍴 *Restaurant, tennis court, some hot tubs, bar; no a/c* ▤ *AE, DC, MC, V* ⊩*BP.*

Wicklow Town

㉓ *26 km (16 mi) east of Glendalough on R763, 51 km (32 mi) south of Dublin on N11.*

At the entrance to the attractive, tree-lined Main Street of Wicklow Town—its name, from the Danish *wyking alo,* means "Viking meadow"—sprawl the extensive ruins of a 13th-century Franciscan friary. The **friary** was closed down during the 16th-century dissolution of the monasteries, but its ruins are a reminder of Wicklow's stormy past, which began with the unwelcome reception given to St. Patrick on his arrival in AD 432. Inquire at the nearby **priest's house** (⊠ Main St. ☎ 0404/67196) to see the ruins. The streets of Wicklow ran with blood during the 1798 rebellion when Billy Byrne, member of a wealthy local Catholic family, led rebels from south and central Wicklow against the forces of the Crown. Byrne was eventually captured and executed at Gallow's Hill just outside town. There is a memorial to him in the middle of Market Square.

The old town jail, just above Market Square, has been converted into a museum and **Heritage Centre,** where it's possible to trace your genealogical roots in the area. Computer displays and life-size models tell the gruesome history of the jail, from the 1798 rebellion to the late 19th century. ⊠ *Market Sq.* ☎ *0404/61599* ⊕ *www.wicklow.ie* 🎫 *€5.70* ☉ *Apr.–Dec., daily 10–5.*

The **harbor** is Wicklow Town's most appealing area. Take Harbour Road down to the pier; a bridge across the River Vartry leads to a second, smaller pier, at the northern end of the harbor. From this end, follow the shingle beach, which stretches for 5 km (3 mi); behind the beach is the broad lough, a lagoon noted for its wildfowl. Immediately south of the harbor, perched on a promontory that has good views of the Wicklow coastline, is the ruin of the **Black Castle.** This structure was built in 1169 by Maurice Fitzgerald, an Anglo-Norman lord who arrived with the English invasion of Ireland. The ruins (freely accessible) extend over a large area; with some difficulty, you can climb down to the water's edge.

Between one bank of the River Vartry and the road to Dublin stands the Protestant **St. Lavinius Church,** which incorporates various unusual details: a Romanesque door, 12th-century stonework, fine pews, and an atmospheric graveyard. The church is topped off by a copper, onion-shape cupola, added as an afterthought in 1771. ⊠ *Free* ⊘ *Daily 10–6.*

Where to Stay & Eat

$ ✕ **Pizza del Forno.** Take advantage of this great spot for people-watching on Main Street. The place has red-and-white-check tablecloths, low lighting, and a pizza oven blazing away. The inexpensive pizzas, pasta, steaks, and vegetarian dishes appeal to a wide array of appetites. ⊠ *Main St.* ☎ *0404/67075* ⊟ *AE, MC, V* ⊘ *Closed Christmas–mid-Feb.*

$$$ ⊞ **Wicklow Head Lighthouse.** This 95-foot-high stone tower—first built in 1781—once supported an eight-sided lantern, and has been renovated by the Irish Landmark Trust as a lodging. It sleeps four to six people in two delightfully quirky octagonal bedrooms and one double sofa bed in the sitting room. The kitchen–dining room at the top has stunning views out over the coast. Don't forget anything in the car; it's a long way down. You rent the entire lighthouse, and you must book for at least two nights. The old lighthouse is just south of town on Wicklow Head, right next to the new, automated one. ⊠ *Wicklow Head, Co. Wicklow* ☎ *01/670–4733* 🖷 *01/670–4887* ⊕ *www.irishlandmark.com* ⊃ *2 rooms sleep up to 8 people* ⊟ *MC, V* ⦶ *EP.*

$$ ⊞ **Old Rectory Country House.** Once a rectory, this charming 19th-century Greek Revival country house—only open in summer—now serves as a B&B. Black-and-white marble fireplaces, bright colors, original oil paintings, and antique and contemporary furniture fill the house. The light, spacious guest rooms are decorated in white and pastel shades, and have antique Victorian and country-house pieces. The Old Rectory is perched on a hillside just off the main road from Dublin on the approach to Wicklow Town. ⊠ *Wicklow Town, Co. Wicklow* ☎ *0404/67048* 🖷 *0404/69181* ⊃ *8 rooms* ⊟ *AE, MC, V* ⊘ *Closed Sept.–May* ⦶ *BP.*

Avondale House & Forest Park

㉔ *17 km (10½ mi) southwest of Wicklow Town on R752.*

Outside the quaint village of Rathdrum, on the west bank of the Avondale River, is the 523-acre **Avondale Forest Park.** Part of a then-burgeoning movement to preserve and expand the Irish forest, it was, in 1904, the first forest in Ireland to be taken over by the state. There's a fine 5½-km (3½-mi) walk along the river, as well as pine and exotic-tree trails. **Avondale House,** on the grounds of the park, resonates with Irish history. The house was the birthplace and lifelong home of Charles Stewart Parnell (1846–91), the "Uncrowned King of Ireland," the country's leading politician of the 19th century and a wildly popular campaigner for democracy and land reform. His career came to a halt after he fell in love with a married woman, Kitty O'Shea—her husband started divorce proceedings and news of the affair ruined Parnell's political career. He died a year later. (Joyce dramatized the controversy, in *A Portrait of the Artist as a Young Man*, in a keenly contested argument during the Daedalus family dinner.) Parnell's house, built in 1779, has been flawlessly restored—except for the reception and dining rooms on the ground floor, which are filled with Parnell memorabilia, including some of his love letters to Kitty O'Shea and political cartoons portraying Parnell's efforts to secure home rule for Ireland. ☎ *0404/46111* ⊕ *www.coillte.ie* ✎ *House €5, parking €5* ۞ *Mar.–Oct., daily 11–6.*

Avoca

㉕ *6½ km (4 mi) south of Avondale Forest Park on R754.*

Heavily forested hills surround the small, lovely hamlet of Avoca, at the confluence of the Rivers Avonbeg and Avonmore. Beneath a riverside tree here, the Irish Romantic poet Thomas Moore (1779–1852) composed his 1807 poem, "The Meeting of the Waters." There are some pleasant forest walks nearby, with scenic views of the valley. The oldest hand-weaving mill in Ireland, dating to 1723, **Avoca Handweavers** offers a short tour of the still-operating mill. The store sells a wide selection of its superb fabrics and woven and knit apparel, some of which is difficult to find elsewhere. ☎ *0402/35105* ✎ *Free* ۞ *Mill: mid-Mar.–Oct., daily 8–4:30; Nov.–mid-Mar., weekdays 8–4:30. Shop: mid-Mar.–Oct., daily 9:30–6; Nov.–mid-Mar., daily 9:30–5:30.*

Arklow

㉖ *11 km (7 mi) southeast of Avoca on R754.*

An ideal point to access the rolling hills and forest walks of the intensely pastoral Vale of Avoca, the small beach town of Arklow is wrapped around an old port. The **Maritime Museum**, in the public library building near the railway station, traces Arklow's distinguished seafaring tradition. Exhibits include old photographs, historic boats, and the shipping diaries of long-dead captains. To get here, take a left at St. Peter's Church as you're heading out of town in the direction of Gorey and Wexford. ✉ *St. Mary's Rd.* ☎ *0402/32868* ✎ *€7* ۞ *May–Sept., Mon.–Sat. 10–1 and 2–5; Oct.–Apr., weekdays 10–1 and 2–5.*

☻ Immediately north of Arklow is **Brittas Bay,** an expanse of white sand, quiet coves, and rolling dunes—perfect for adventurous kids. In summer it's popular with vacationing Dubliners.

Shopping

If you love bread or have a sweet tooth, stop in at **Stone Oven Bakery** (✉ 65 Lower Main St. ☎ 0402/39418) at the bottom of the hill. The German-born baker, Egon Friedrich, prepares sourdough breads and delicious sweet treats, including hazelnut-chocolate triangles. You can also get simple cheese-and-bread sandwiches to go—or you can eat in the tiny, slightly haphazard café.

COUNTY KILDARE & WEST WICKLOW

Horse racing is a passion in Ireland—just about every little town has at least one betting shop—and County Kildare is the country's horse capital. Nestled between the basins of the River Liffey to the north and the River Barrow to the east, its gently sloping hills and grass-filled plains are perfect for breeding and racing thoroughbreds. For some visitors, the fabled National Stud Farm just outside Kildare Town provides a fascinating glimpse into the world of horse breeding. The Japanese Gardens, adjacent to the National Stud, are among Europe's finest, while Castletown House, in Celbridge to the north, is one of Ireland's foremost Georgian treasures. You may want to pick up this leg from Glendalough—the spectacular drive across the Wicklow Gap, from Glendalough to Hollywood, makes for a glorious entrance into Kildare. One last note: consult Chapter 4, the Southeast, if you make it as far south as Castledermot, because Carlow and environs are only 10 km (6 mi) farther south.

Castletown House

27
24 km (15 mi) southwest of Dublin via N7 to R403, 6½ km (4 mi) south
Fodor'sChoice *of Maynooth.*
★

In the early 18th century, a revival of the architectural style of Andrea Palladio (1508–80) swept through England. Architects there built dozens of houses reinterpreting that style. The rage took hold of Ireland's Anglo-Irish aristocracy as well. Arguably the largest and finest example of an Irish Palladian–style house is Castletown, begun in 1722 for William Conolly (1662–1729), the speaker of the Irish House of Commons and at the time the country's wealthiest man. Conolly hired the Italian architect Alessandro Galilei, who designed the facade of the main block; in 1724, the young Irish architect Sir Edward Lovett Pearce completed the design of the house by adding the colonnades and side pavilions. Conolly's death brought construction to a halt; it wasn't until his great-nephew, Thomas Conolly, and his wife, Lady Louisa (née Lennox), took up residence in 1758 that work on the house picked up again. Today Castletown is the largest house built as a private residence in this part of Ireland. (The American poet Robert Lowell lived here for a time in the 1960s.) The house was rescued in 1967 by Desmond Guinness of the brewing family, who was president of the Irish Georgian Society. Now the Irish state owns the property. It's also the headquarters of the Irish Georgian Society and contains many pieces from the original furniture collection.

Within the house, the hall plasterwork was done by the Lafranchini brothers, Swiss-Italian craftsmen who worked in Dublin in the mid-18th century. The ground-floor Print Room is the only 18th-century example in Ireland of this elegant fad—like oversize postage stamps in a giant album, black-and-white prints were glued to the walls by fashionable young women. Upstairs at the rear of the house, the Long Gallery, almost 80 feet by 23 feet, is the most notable of the public rooms—it's decorated in Pompeian style and has three Venetian Murano glass chandeliers. ⊠ *Celbridge* ☎ *01/628–8252* ⊕ *www.heritageireland.ie* ☒ *€4* ☾ *Apr.–Sept., weekdays 10–6, weekends 1–6; Oct., weekdays 10–5, Sun. 1–5; Nov., Sun. 1–5.*

In Maynooth, a tiny Georgian town slightly to the west of Castletown House, you'll find **St. Patrick's College.** What was once a center for the training of Catholic priests is now one of Ireland's most important lay universities. The visitor center chronicles the college's history and that of the Catholic Church in Ireland. Stroll through the university gardens—the Path of Saints or the Path of Sinners. At the entrance to St. Patrick's College are the ruins of **Maynooth Castle,** the ancient seat of the Fitzgerald family. The Fitzgeralds' fortunes changed for the worse when they led the rebellion of 1536 (it failed). The castle keep, which dates from the 13th century, and the great hall are still in decent condition. Mrs. Saults at 9 Parson Street has the key. ☎ *01/628–5222* ⊕ *www.may.ie* ☒ *Free* ☾ *St. Patrick's May–Sept., Mon.–Sat. 11–5, Sun. 2–6; guided tours every hr.*

Where to Stay & Eat

$$$$ ✕🏠 **Moyglare Manor.** Owner Nora Devlin has exuberantly decorated this majestic Georgian manor house with her renowned antiques collection. Velvet chairs, oil paintings, and thickly draped windows furnish the drawing room, and the grand bedrooms have four-poster canopy beds, roomy wardrobes, marble fireplaces, and comfortable, chintz-covered armchairs. Lamp-shaded wall sconces add a romantic touch to the formal dining room, where a traditional French five-course set menu is served. The manor, which occupies 16 pastoral acres dotted with sheep and cows, is 29 km (18 mi) west of Dublin. ⊠ *Maynooth, Co. Kildare* ☎ *01/628–6351* 🖨 *01/628–5405* ⊕ *www.moyglaremanor.ie* ☞ *17 rooms* ♨ *Restaurant, 2 bars* ☰ *AE, DC, MC, V* ⦿ *BP, MAP.*

Straffan

🟤 *5 km (3 mi) southwest of Castletown House on R403, 25½ km (16 mi) southwest of Dublin.*

Its attractive location on the banks of the River Liffey, its unique butterfly farm, and the Kildare Hotel and Country Club—where Arnold Palmer designed the K Club, one of Ireland's most renowned 18-hole golf courses—are what make Straffan so appealing. The only one of its kind in Ireland, the **Straffan Butterfly Farm** has a tropical house with exotic plants, butterflies, and moths. Mounted and framed butterflies are for sale. ☎ *01/627–1109* ☒ *€7* ☾ *June–Sept., daily noon–5:30.*

The **Steam Museum** covers the history of Irish steam engines, handsome machines used both in industry and agriculture—churning butter, threshing corn. There's also a fun collection of model locomotives. Engineers are present on "live steam days;" phone in advance to confirm. ⊠ *Lodge Park* ☎ *01/627–3155* ☒ *Live steam days €7, other times €6* ☾ *Easter–May and Sept., Sun. 2–6; June–Aug., Tues.–Sun. 2–6.*

Where to Stay & Eat

$$$$ ✕⊡ **Kildare Hotel and Country Club.** Manicured gardens and the renowned
Fodor'sChoice Arnold Palmer–designed K Club golf course surround this mansard-roofed
★ country mansion. The spacious, comfortable guest rooms are each
uniquely decorated with antiques, and all have large windows that
overlook either the Liffey or the golf course. (The rooms in the old house
are best.) The hotel also has a leasing agreement with several privately
owned cottages on the property. Chef Michel Flamme serves an
unashamedly French menu—albeit with the hint of an Irish flavor—at
the Byerly Turk Restaurant (named after a famous racehorse). ⊠ *Co.
Kildare* ☎ *01/601–7200* 🖷 *01/601–7299* ⊕ *www.kclub.ie* ⇆ *69 rooms,
26 apartments* ♨ *2 restaurants, 18-hole golf course, 4 tennis courts, indoor pool, hair salon, fishing, horseback riding, squash, 3 bars* ▤ *AE,
DC, MC, V* ⦿ *BP, MAP.*

$$$ ✕⊡ **Barberstown Castle.** With a 13th-century castle keep at one end, an
Fodor'sChoice Elizabethan central section, and a large Georgian country house at the
★ other, Barberstown represents 750 years of Irish history. Turf fires blaze
in ornate fireplaces in the three sumptuously decorated lounges. Repro-
duction pieces fill the bedrooms, some of which have four-poster beds.
The Georgian-style restaurant serves creatively prepared French food, also
on tap for special parties in the banqueting room of the castle keep. ⊠ *Co.
Kildare* ☎ *01/628–8157* 🖷 *01/627–7027* ⊕ *www.barberstowncastle.
ie* ⇆ *22 rooms* ♨ *Restaurant, bar* ▤ *AE, DC, MC, V* ⦿ *BP, MAP.*

Naas

㉙ *13 km (8 mi) south of Straffan on R407, 30 km (19 mi) southwest of
Dublin on N7.*

The seat of County Kildare and a thriving market town in the heartland
of Irish thoroughbred country, Naas (pronounced nace) is full of pubs
with high stools where short men (trainee jockeys) discuss the merits of
their various stables. Naas has its own small racecourse, but **Punchestown
Racecourse** (⊠ 3 km [2 mi] south of Naas on R411 ☎ 045/897–704) has
a wonderful setting amid rolling plains, with the Wicklow Mountains a
spectacular backdrop. Horse races are held regularly here, but the most
popular event is the Punchestown National Hunt Festival in April.

Russborough House

★ **㉚** *16 km (10 mi) southeast of Naas on R410.*

Another shockingly grand Palladian house in the middle of nowhere,
this extravagance was paid for by beer: in 1741, a year after Joseph Lee-
son inherited a vast fortune from his father, a successful Dublin brewer,
he commissioned Richard Castle (who also designed Powerscourt) to
built him a palatial home. Castle, spending another man's money, spared
no expense; the result is a confident, majestic, slighly over-the-top house,
now home to one of the greatest collections of Old Master paintings in
Ireland. One of the highlights of the western part of County Wicklow,
Russborough House is among the finest of the many Palladian-style houses
built by the Anglo-Irish ascendancy during the first half of the 18th cen-

tury—Castletown House, Emo Court, and Castle Coole are the other stars in this constellation. Castle worked on Russborough until his death, after which his associate Francis Bindon took over. They pulled out all the stops to create a grand house with a silver-gray Wicklow granite facade that extends for more than 700 feet—the longest house frontage in Ireland—and encompasses a seven-bay central block, off which radiate two semicircular loggias connecting the flanking wings.

Baroque exuberance reigns in the house's main rooms, especially in the lavishly ornamented plasterwork ceilings executed by the Lafranchini brothers, who also worked at Castletown House. Their decorative flair adorns the Music Room and Library, but even these pale compared to the the plasterwork done by an unknown artisan in the Staircase Hall— an extravaganza of whipped-cream moldings, cornucopias, and rococo scrolls ("the ravings of a maniac," according to Sibthorpe, who guessed that only an Irishman would have had the blarney to pull this off). After a long succession of owners, Russborough was bought in 1952 by Sir Alfred Beit, the nephew of the German cofounder (with Cecil Rhodes) of the De Beers diamond operation and art collector extraordinaire. He and his wife often hosted the beau monde, who enjoyed waking up to the Old Master paintings that lined the walls here. In 1988, after two major robberies, the finest works in the Beits' art collection were donated to the National Gallery of Ireland in Dublin, including their great Vermeer, *Lady Writing a Letter with Her Maid*. However, works by Gainsborough, Guardi, Murillo, Reynolds, and Rubens remain, as well as bronzes, silver, and porcelain, all exhibited in grand period rooms refurbished in the 1950s by the legendary decorator, Lady Colefax. The views from Russborough's windows take in the foothills of the Wicklow Mountains and a small lake in front of the house; the extensive woodlands on the estate are open for exploration. ⊠ *Off N81, Blessington* ☎ *045/865–239* ⛨ *€6, upstairs bedrooms €3.50* ⊘ *May–Sept., daily 10:30–5:30; Apr. and Oct., Sun. 10:30–5:30.*

Poulaphouca Reservoir

③ *3 km (2 mi) southeast of Russborough House, 33 km (21 mi) northwest of Glendalough on R758 via R756.*

Known locally as the Blessington Lakes, Poulaphouca (pronounced pool-a-*fook*-a) Reservoir is a large, meandering, artificial lake minutes from Russborough House that provides Dublin's water supply. You can drive around the entire perimeter of the reservoir on minor roads; on its southern end lies Hollywood Glen, a particularly beautiful natural spot. On the western shore of the lakes, the small market town of **Blessington,** with its wide main street lined on both sides by tall trees and Georgian buildings, is one of the most charming villages in the area. It was founded in the late 17th century, and was a stop on the Dublin–Waterford mail-coach service in the mid-19th century. Until 1932, a steam train ran from here to Dublin. Beyond the southern tip of the Poulaphouca Reservoir, 13 km (8 mi) south of Blessington on N81, look for a small sign for the **Piper's Stones,** a Bronze Age stone circle that was probably used in a ritual connected with worship of the sun. It's just a short walk from the road. You can take in splendid views of the Blessington Lakes from the top of **Church Mountain,** which you reach via a vigorous walk through Woodenboley Wood, at the southern tip of Hollywood Glen. Follow the main forest track for about 20 minutes and then take the narrow path that heads up the side of the forest to the mountaintop for about another half an hour.

Where to Stay & Eat

$$$$ ✕🖭 **Rathsallagh House.** At the end of a long drive that winds through
Fodor'sChoice a golf course and set in 530 acres of parkland is Rathsallagh House, which
★ came into being when low-slung, ivy-covered Queen Anne stables were converted into a farmhouse in 1798. Enveloping couches and chairs, fresh flower arrangements, large windows, fireplaces, and lots of lamps furnish the two drawing rooms. Large rooms have enchanting, pastoral names like Buttercup and Over Arch and The Yellow Room, with its claw-foot bath set in an alcove. Try to get a room overlooking the walled garden, where the scent of wildflowers wafts in through the beautiful French doors. Kay's outstanding haute-Irish dinner menu changes daily. Specialties include paupiette of herb-filled salmon with onion and chive beurre blanc. ⊠ *Dunlavin, Co. Wicklow* ☎ *045/403–112* 🖷 *045/403–343* ⊕ *www.rathsallagh.com* ⇆ *31 rooms* ⌂ *Restaurant, 18-hole golf course, tennis court, indoor pool, massage, sauna, croquet, bar, meeting rooms* ➾ *AE, DC, MC, V* ⏀ *BP, MAP.*

The Curragh

❸❷ *8 km (5 mi) southwest of Naas on M7, 25½ km (16 mi) west of Poulaphouca Reservoir.*

The broad plain of the Curragh, bisected by the main N7 road, is the biggest area of common land in Ireland, encompassing about 31 square km (12 square mi) and devoted mainly to grazing. This is Ireland's major racing center, home of the **Curragh Racecourse** (⊠ N7 ☎ 045/441–205 ⊕ www.curragh.ie); the Irish Derby and other international horse races are run here.

The **Curragh Main Barracks,** a large camp where the Irish Army trains, has a small museum with a collection of small firearms and military paraphernalia from modern Irish history. One of its prize relics is an armored car used by Michael Collins, the famed head of the Irish Army. In December 1921 Collins signed the Anglo-Irish Treaty, designating a six-county North to remain in British hands in exchange for complete independence for Ireland's remaining 26 counties. The car can be seen with permission from the commanding officer. ☎ *045/445–161 ask for the command adjutant* ✉ *Free.*

Kildare Town

❸❸ *5 km (3 mi) west of the Curragh on M7, 51 km (32 mi) southwest of Dublin via N7 and M7.*

Horse breeding is the cornerstone of County Kildare's thriving economy, and Kildare Town is the place to come if you're crazy about horses.

Right off Kildare's main market square, the **Silken Thomas** (☎ 045/522–232) pub re-creates an old-world atmosphere with open fires, dark wood, and leaded lights; it's a good place to stop for lunch before exploring the sights here.

The Church of Ireland **St. Brigid's Cathedral** is where the eponymous saint founded a religious settlement in the 5th century. The present cathedral, with its stocky tower, is a restored 13th-century structure. It was partially rebuilt around 1686, but restoration work wasn't completed for another 200 years. The stained-glass west window of the cathedral depicts three of Ireland's greatest saints: Brigid, Patrick, and Columba. In pre-Christian times druids gathered around a sacred oak that stood on the grounds and from which Kildare (*Cill Dara*), or the "Church of the Oak," gets its name. Also on the grounds is a restored fire pit reclaimed from the time of Brigid, when a fire was kept burning—by a chaste woman—in a female-only fire temple. Interestingly, Brigid started the place for women, but it was she who asked monks to move here as well. ⊠ *Off Market Sq.* ☎ *No phone* ⊙ *Daily 10–6.*

The 108-foot-high **round tower,** in the graveyard of St. Brigid's Cathedral, is the second highest in Ireland (the highest is in Kilmacduagh in County Galway). It dates from the 12th century. Extraordinary views across much of the Midlands await you if you're energetic enough to climb the stairs to the top. ☎ *045/521–229* ▨ *€2.55* ⊙ *May–Sept., daily 10–1 and 2–5.*

If you're a horse aficionado, or even just curious, check out the **National Stud Farm,** a main center of Ireland's racing industry. The Stud was founded in 1900 by brewing heir Colonel William Hall-Walker, and transferred to the Irish state in 1945. It's here that breeding stallions are groomed, exercised, tested, and bred. Spring and early summer, when mares have foals, are the best times to visit. Besides being crazy about horses, Walker may just have been crazy, or at least a little eccentric—he believed in astrology, so foals had their charts done. Those with unfavorable results were sold right away. He even built the stallion boxes with lantern roofs that allow the moon and stars to work their magic on the occupants. The **National Stud Horse Museum,** also on the grounds, recounts the history of horses in Ireland. Its most outstanding exhibit is the skeleton of Arkle, the Irish racehorse that won major victories in Ireland and England during the late 1960s. The museum also contains medieval evidence of horses, such as bones from 13th-century Dublin, and some early examples of equestrian equipment. ⊠ *½ km (⅓ mi) south of Kildare Town* ☎ *045/521–617* ⊕ *www.irish-national-stud.ie* ▨ *€8.50 (includes entry to Japanese Gardens)* ⊙ *Mid-Feb.–mid-Nov., daily 9:30–6.*

★ Adjacent to the National Stud Farm, the **Japanese Gardens** were created between 1906 and 1910 by the Stud's founder, Colonel Hall-Walker, and laid out by a Japanese gardener, Tassa Eida, and his son Minoru. The gardens are recognized as among the finest Asian gardens in the world, although they're more of an East–West hybrid than authentically Japanese. The Scots pine trees, for instance, are an appropriate stand-in for traditional Japanese pines, which signify long life and happiness. The gardens symbolically chart the human progression from birth to death, although the focus is on the male journey. A series of landmarks runs along a meandering path: the Tunnel of Ignorance (No. 3) represents a child's lack of understanding; the Engagement and Marriage bridges (Nos. 8 and 9) span a small stream; and from the Hill of Ambition (No. 13), you can look back over your joys and sorrows. It ends with the Gateway to Eternity (No. 20), beyond which lies a Zen Buddhist meditation sand garden. This is a worthwhile destination any time of the year, though it's particularly glorious in spring and fall. ⊠ *About 2½ km (1½ mi) south of Kildare Town, clearly signposted off market square* ☎ *045/521– 617* ⊕ *www.irish-national-stud.ie* ⊠ *€8.50 (includes entry to National Stud)* ☉ *Mid-Feb.–mid-Nov., daily 9:30–6.*

Where to Stay & Eat

$$ ✕⊡ **The Red House Inn.** Boutique hotels are a rarity outside Dublin, but as soon as this well-known Kildare restaurant added 12 rooms a few years ago it became an instant success. Owner/manager Brian Fallon has used the beautiful conservatory and landscaped garden at the back to create a serene, meditative atmosphere aimed at the weary traveler. The Victorian-style rooms are richly decked out in wines and deep-greens, with tapestry curtains, heavy throws on the canopy beds, and dark-wood, antique furniture. The brasserie-style restaurant ($$-$$$), with great views out over the garden and courtyard, mixes Modern Irish and French styles. Try the roasted tomato and asparagus salad with pancetta, followed by tagiatelle pasta with sauté of wild mushroom and a cepe cream sauce. The wine cellar is very impressive. ⊠ *Newbridge, Co. Kildare* ☎ *045/ 431–657* ☎ *045/431–934* ⊕ *www.redhouse.ie* ↩ *12 rooms* ⚐ *Restaurant, bar, meeting rooms; no a/c* ⊟ *AE, DC, MC, V* ⦿| *BP.*

DUBLIN ENVIRONS A TO Z

To research prices, get advice from other travelers, and book travel arrangements, visit www.fodors.com.

BUS TRAVEL

Bus services link Dublin with the main and smaller towns in the area. All buses for the region depart from Dublin's Busaras, the central bus station, at Store Street. For bus inquiries, contact Bus Éireann. You can reach Enniskerry and the Powerscourt Estate by taking Dublin Bus No. 44 from the Dublin quays area.

St. Kevin's, a private bus service, runs daily from Dublin (outside the Royal College of Surgeons on St. Stephen's Green) to Glendalough, stopping off at Bray, Roundwood, and Laragh en route. Buses leave Dublin daily at 11:30 AM and 6 PM (7 PM on Sunday); buses leave Glendalough weekdays at 7:15 AM and 4:15 PM (9:45 AM and 4:15 PM on Saturday, 9:45 AM and 5:30 PM on Sunday). One-way fare is €9; a round-trip ticket costs €15.

🚹 Bus Information **Bus Éireann** ☎01/836-6111 ⊕www.buseireann.ie. **Dublin Bus** ☎01/ 873-4222 ⊕www.dublinbus.ie. **St. Kevin's** ☎01/281-8119 ⊕www.glendaloughbus.com.

CAR TRAVEL

The easiest and best way to tour Dublin's environs is by car, because many sights are not served by public transportation, and what service there is, especially to outlying areas, is infrequent. (⇨ If you need to rent a car, *see* Car Rental *in* Dublin A to Z *in* Chapter 1.) To visit destinations in the Boyne Valley, follow N3, along the east side of Phoenix Park, out of the city and make Trim and Tara your first stops. Alternatively, leave Dublin via N1/M1 toward Belfast. Try to avoid the road during weekday rush hours (8 AM–10 AM and 5 PM–7 PM); stay on it as far as Drogheda and start touring from there.

To reach destinations in County Kildare, follow the quays along the south side of the River Liffey (they are one-way westbound) to St. John's Road West (N7); in a matter of minutes, you're heading for open countryside. Avoid traveling this route during the evening peak rush hours, especially on Friday, when Dubliners are themselves making their weekend getaways.

To reach destinations in County Wicklow, N11/M11 is the fastest and most clearly marked route. The two more scenic routes to Glendalough are R115 to R759 to R755, or R177 to R755.

EMERGENCIES

🚩 Ambulance, fire, police 🕿 999.

TOURS

Bus Éireann runs guided bus tours to many of the historic and scenic locations throughout the Dublin environs daily during the summer. Visits include trips to Glendalough in Wicklow; Boyne Valley and Newgrange in County Louth; and the Hill of Tara, Trim, and Navan in County Meath. All tours depart from Busaras Station, Dublin; information is available by phone Monday–Saturday 8:30–7, Sunday 10–7. Gray Line, a privately owned touring company, also runs many guided bus tours throughout the Dublin environs between May and September. Wild Coach Tours has half- and full-day trips to Glendalough, Powerscourt House and Garden, and Malahide Castle in small Mercedes coaches. Prices start at €20.

Wicklow Trail Rides takes experienced adult horseback riders on weeklong rides through the Wicklow Mountains (May–September), with overnight stays in country homes and guest houses. Instructional holidays for children and adults at the riding center are also available.

The Wicklow Way is Ireland's most popular walking route, a 137-km (85-mi) trek through the Dublin and Wicklow mountains. The walk begins in Marlay Park, just south of Dublin city center, where there is a selection of trails. County Wicklow sponsors three annual walking festivals. The two-day Rathdrum Easter Walking Festival includes hill walks of varying lengths over Easter weekend. The first weekend of May, the Wicklow Mountains May Walking Festival is centered on Blessington. The Wicklow Mountains Autumn Walking Festival is based in the Glenmalure area.

🚩 Bus Tours **Bus Éireann** 🕿 01/836-6111 ⊕ www.buseireann.ie/site/home. **Gray Line** 🕿 01/661-9666. **Wild Coach Tours** 🕿 01/280-1899 ⊕ www.discoverdublin.ie.

🚶 Walking Tours & Events **Rathdrum Easter Walking Festival** ☎ 0404/46262. **Wicklow Mountains Autumn Walking Festival** ☎ 0404/66058. **Wicklow Mountains May Walking Festival** ☎ 0404/66058. **Wicklow Way Information** ☎ 01/493-4059.

TRAIN TRAVEL

Irish Rail (Iarnród Éireann) trains run the length of the east coast, from Dundalk to the north in County Louth to Arklow along the coast in County Wicklow. Trains make many stops along the way; there are stations in Drogheda, Dublin (the main stations are Connolly Station and Pearse Station), Bray, Greystones, Wicklow, and Rathdrum. From Heuston Station, the Arrow, a commuter train service, runs westward to Celbridge, Naas, Newbridge, and Kildare Town. Contact Irish Rail for schedule and fare information.

🚆 Train Information **Connolly Station** ✉ Amiens St., Northside, Dublin. **Heuston Station** ✉ Victoria Quay and St. John's Road W, Dublin West, Dublin. **Irish Rail** ☎ 01/836-6222. **Pearse Station** ✉ Westland Row, Southside, Dublin.

VISITOR INFORMATION

For information on travel in the Dublin environs and for help in making lodging reservations, contact one of the following Tourist Information Offices (TIOs) year-round: Dublin Tourism and Bord Fáilte, Dundalk, Mullingar, Trim, or Wicklow Town. Mullingar is the head office of tourism for Counties Louth, Meath, and Kildare; it can give you contact information for temporary TIOs in these areas. During summer temporary TIOs are open throughout the environs, in towns such as Arklow in County Wicklow, Drogheda and Dundalk in County Louth, and Kildare Town in County Kildare.

🛈 Tourist Information **Arklow** ✉ The Coach House ☎ 0402/32484. **Bord Fáilte** ☎ 1850/230-330 in Ireland, 800/223-6470 in the U.S. and Canada, 800/039-7000 in the U.K., 02/9299-6177 in Australia, 09/379-8720 in New Zealand. **Drogheda** ✉ Bus Éireann Depot ☎ 041/983-7070. **Dublin Tourism** ✉ Suffolk St. ☎ 01/605-7700 or 01/602-4129. **Dundalk** ✉ Jocelyn St. ☎ 042/933-5484. **Kildare** ✉ Market House ☎ 045/521-240. **Mullingar** ✉ Market House, Market Sq. ☎ 044/48761. **Trim** ✉ Old Town Hall, Castle St. ☎ 046/943-7227. **Wicklow Town** ✉ Rialto Houae, Fitzwilliam Sq. ☎ 0404/69117.

THE MIDLANDS

3

LET THE *RIVER QUEEN* CARRY YOU
on a cruise down the Shannon ⇨*p.201*

GO FOR THE GREEN
at the beautiful Birr Golf Club ⇨*p.204*

LIFT YOUR SPIRITS
at St. Ciaran's Clonmacnoise ⇨*p.199*

WHISPER "I DO"
at baronial Castle Leslie where
Sir Paul wed his Heather ⇨*p.193*

DALLY IN THE MAGICAL PARKLAND
of elegant Bellamont Forest ⇨*p.191*

EXPLORE BOG COUNTRY
on the Bord na Móna Rail Tour ⇨*p.201*

SAVOR THE PERFECT PINT
at 1775-era Morrissey's Store ⇨*p.178*

TREE-HUG ONE OF THE GREAT YEWS
towering over Tullynally Gardens ⇨*p.187*

Updated by
Tom Swift

IRISH SCHOOLCHILDREN WERE ONCE TAUGHT to think of their country as a saucer, with mountains around the edge and a dip in the middle. The dip is the Midlands—or the Lakelands, as it is sometimes referred to—and this often-overlooked region comprises nine counties: Cavan, Laois (pronounced leash), Westmeath, Longford, Offaly, Roscommon, Monaghan, Leitrim, and Tipperary. Ask people from the rest of Ireland what the purpose of the Midlands is and they will jest that the region exists simply to hold the other parts of the island together.

Indeed, the Midlands is sometimes looked upon with disdain by the Irish people, who consider it dull and mundane (the worst of offenses in Ireland). The perception is at least partially true, the flat plains of the Midlands being the kind of place you rush through on the way to somewhere else; with no major city in the region (Dublin lies to the east, Galway and Limerick to the west, and Cork to the south), it remains a quiet and geographically unspectacular place. Night owls should probably head elsewhere—the wildest thing in these parts is the wind.

But that is precisely why many travelers consider the Midlands a gem in the making. For when it comes to studying how Ireland gets on with its daily life, there are few better places. Here, a town's main hotel is usually one of the prime social centers and can be a good place from which to participate in local life. If you miss out witnessing a wedding reception, First Communion supper, or meeting of the Lion's Club, you can get to know the locals just with a walk along a village's main street. Happily so, since there are plenty of folks who have nothing to do but be pleasant. Hereabouts, the pace of life is slower, every neighbor's face is familiar, and there are plenty of minor roads linking the more scenic areas—if you're in no particular hurry, these are the ones to take. And if you spend enough time in the region, you might even get to recognize the difference between a Cavan twang and a Tipperary brogue.

But don't think this region is missing out on any number of cultural highlights. Among them are Clonmacnoise, Ireland's most important monastic ruins; historic towns with age-old industries, such as lace making and crystal making; the gorgeous gardens of Birr Castle; and some of Ireland's finest Anglo-Irish houses—Strokestown Park House, Castle Leslie, and Emo Court. As for scenic pleasures, this region of the country has more than its fair share of Ireland's 800 bodies of water. Speckling this lush countryside, these lakes were often formed by glacial action some 10,000 years ago. Many are quite small, especially in Cavan and Monaghan, and anglers can expect to often have a lake to themselves. Because of all the water, much of the landscape lies under blanket bog, a unique ecosystem that's worth exploring. The River Shannon, one of the longest rivers in Europe and the longest in the British Isles, bisects the Midlands from north to south, piercing a series of loughs (lakes): Lough Allen, Lough Ree, and Lough Derg. The Royal Canal and the Grand Canal cross the Midlands from east to west, ending in the Shannon north and south of Lough Ree.

The main roads, from Dublin to the south and the west, cross the area. These roads ultimately came to eclipse the Shannon and the canals as important transportation arteries. The Laois Heritage Trail, a day-long drive, leads to some of the region's less frequented villages, where visitors still have some novelty value. Wilderness hiking and horseback-riding trails run through the Slieve Bloom Mountains, on the Laois-Offaly border, to pretty villages and across bogland and woodlands, often with sweeping views of unspoiled countryside. Attractive hill and lake scenery can be found in the forest parks of Killykeen and Lough Key. The towns themselves—including Nenagh, Roscommon, Athlone, Boyle, Mullingar, Tullamore, Longford, and Cavan—are not among Ireland's most distinctive, but more than a few of them are now considered by trendy Dublin toilers to be worth the lengthy commute. After all, if Charlotte Brönte spent her honeymoon here and Anthony Trollope settled in one of the region's villages to write two of his novels, it sure is good enough for them

Exploring the Midlands

This chapter is organized into three Midlands sections: the eastern, the northern, and the western. The first two areas can easily be covered in an extended visit to the Midlands, as they chart a course almost due north from the initial starting point in Abbeyleix, County Laois. The third section includes sights west of those in the first two, which means they can easily be visited if you're flying into Shannon and beginning your explorations of Ireland in the western half of the country. In fact, because the Midlands border virtually every major county of Ireland, there are three places in this chapter where you should be alert to nearby locales covered in other chapters: the easternmost sights in the Midlands (Emo Court and Coolbanagher) are within a few miles of the westernmost sites in the Dublin environs; the westernmost sights in the Midlands (Boyle and Lough Key Forest Park) are just across the border from County Sligo; and the northernmost sights and towns of the Midlands are just across the border from Northern Ireland.

About the Restaurants & Hotels

The Midland town of Birr is known as the "belly button of Ireland" because of its central location, not because this region focuses on your stomach or the delicacies of haute cuisine. Most restaurants hereabouts are simple eateries, ranging in price from inexpensive ($) to moderate ($$), and are often attached to family-run hotels. Nevertheless, there are restaurants that will entice you right in off the street, especially those offering beef—Mullingar, in the center of the Midlands, is the beef capital of Ireland—and fish specialties, as the many lakes and rivers of the region provide an abundance of fresh salmon and trout. Delightfully, since no place is more than an hour and a half from the sea, expect to find lots of fresh ocean fish. If you ever find your dinner a bit anemic, you can always look forward to a spectacular breakfast, as long as you don't mind the damage the fried sausages, bacon, and pudding will do to your waistline. If you're in need of even more fuel by lunch, head for one of the meat-carveries that are a prominent feature of many village pubs. Assume that all hotel rooms have air-conditioning, in-room phones, TVs, and private bathrooms unless otherwise noted.

Numbers in the text correspond to numbers in the margin and on the Midlands map.

If you have
3 days

Heading east from Shannon Airport, turn off the N7 Limerick–Dublin road for ⬚ **Birr** ⓴ ▶, a quiet Georgian town built around its magnificent castle and gardens. Then take the Bord na Mona Bog Rail Tour, near Shannonbridge, a good introduction to the flora and fauna of Ireland's many bogs. While you're in the area, stop at **Clonmacnoise** ⓲, Ireland's most important monastic settlement, and return to Birr for the night. The next day head for **Strokestown** ⓯ and its namesake house, where a museum documents the causes and effects of the 1845–49 Great Famine. If you have time, drive east to **Longford** ⑨ and visit the nearby Carrigglas Manor, a romantic 1837 Tudor-Gothic house that has Jane Austen associations. Head to ⬚ **Boyle** ⓮, a good place to stay overnight. If the weather is good on Day 3, take some fresh air in Lough Key Forest Park, or just take time to explore this old-fashioned town. From here you'll be well positioned to explore western and northwestern Ireland.

If you have
5 days

Heading from Dublin or from points east in Wicklow and Kildare, start at **Portarlington** ③ ▶, making sure to visit the nearby Emo Court and Gardens, a large-scale country house designed by James Gandon, the architect responsible for much of Georgian Dublin. Move north to the Charleville Forest Castle outside **Tullamore** ④, then to **Kilbeggan** ⑤, where you can learn about whiskey-making at Locke's Distillery; if you have time, stop at the beautiful Belvedere House Gardens to the north. Stay in or around ⬚ **Mullingar** ⑥ for the night. On the morning of your second day, briefly explore Mullingar, and then head north on scenic R394 to **Castlepollard** ⑦ and the massive Tullynally Castle and Gardens. Crystal aficionados should stop in **Cavan** ⑩, while nature buffs can easily spend the afternoon exploring the nearby water-laced Killykeen Forest Park. Spend the night in ⬚ **Cootehill** ⑪, an old-fashioned, friendly County Cavan town popular with anglers. On Day 3 you can either jump across the border to explore the southernmost sights in Northern Ireland or head southwest to the border town of ⬚ **Clones** ⑬, a lace-making center. On your fourth day, return to Cavan and pick up the road to **Longford** ⑨. To the west lies **Strokestown** ⓯ and its namesake house. ⬚ **Athlone** ⑰ is a convenient place to spend the night—from here you're well positioned for an early-morning visit to **Clonmacnoise** ⓲, the most important early Christian monastic site in Ireland. Take in the Bord na Mona Bog Rail Tour near Shannonbridge on your way to **Banagher** ⑲, where you can either take a two-hour Shannon cruise (a great trip in good weather) or drive around **Lough Derg** ㉑. You can choose to end up in either ⬚ **Birr** ⓴, **Roscrea** ㉒, or ⬚ **Nenagh** ㉓; from any of these towns you're not far from Shannon Airport and points to the west and southwest.

Accommodations run from modest spots hidden behind doors with emerald-cut stained glass to opulent country-house hotels, such as Castle Leslie, where Sir Paul and Heather McCartney got hitched in 2002. But in most Midland towns, the choice is usually between a small-town hotel offering a reasonable standard of basic comfort and a scenic country-house bed-and-breakfast. In summer, reserve far ahead for boating resorts on the Shannon and its loughs. In winter, ask the concierge if he has electric blankets handy—a lifesaver if you've been out on a wet and windy evening. On the chart below, hotel prices are listed for room rates that include no meals (EP, European Plan) or, if indicated, CP (with Continental breakfast) or BP (Breakfast Plan, with full breakfast). Higher prices prevail for board plans such as MAP (Modified American Plan, with breakfast and dinner); inquire when booking.

WHAT IT COSTS In euros				
$$$$	**$$$**	**$$**	**$**	**¢**
RESTAURANTS over €29	€22–€29	€15–€22	€8–€15	under €8
HOTELS over €230	€180–€230	€130–€180	€80–€130	under €80

Restaurant prices are per person for a main course at dinner; note that if a restaurant offers only prix-fixe meals, it has been given the price category that reflects the full set-price. Hotel prices are for two people in a standard double room in high season, including V.A.T. and a service charge (often applied in larger hotels).

Timing

The Midlands are a good year-round choice because, unlike those in the more popular destinations in western and southwestern Ireland, the restaurants, accommodations, and major attractions stay open all year. The area is usually quiet, except at the boating resorts on the Shannon and its loughs, which are heavily booked by Irish vacationers in July and August.

THE EASTERN MIDLANDS

The eastern fringe of the Midlands is about an hour's drive from Dublin, and a visit to the area could easily be grafted onto a trip to the Dublin environs. In spite of its proximity to the capital, or perhaps because of it, this area is a bit removed from the regular tourist trail, and is a source of constant surprises. Unspoiled Georgian villages, ruined castles, and quaint "towns-that-time-forgot" dot the landscape. There are also plenty of opportunities for hill walking, horse riding, and other outdoor pursuits. Stately-home buffs are in for a treat, as Emo Court and Gardens, Charleveille Forest Castle, Belvedere House Gardens, and Tullynally Castle await them. The Eastern Midlands fan out from the central point of Mullingar. With richer farmland than is found in the northern area of the Midlands, the eastern region tends toward agriculture. But the Dublin commuter culture means that you're as likely to be delayed on a back road by a badly parked BMW as by a slow-moving tractor on its way home from the dairy. A good tour begins at Abbeyleix and

3

Green Mansions

Thrill seekers beware: The Midlands is sometimes referred to as the biggest farm in the world. But within all that lush green acreage, green-thumbers will also find an abundance of elegant gardens, many of them designed and planted 250 years ago. Most of these green oases are found in the grounds of the famed stately homes that dot the region. Many of the Anglo-Irish gentry were enthusiastic botanists and went to great lengths to find rare plant specimens from far-flung parts of the world. The earls of Rosse have been planting exotic plants from as far away as South America since the 17th century in the demesne of their castle in Birr. The adventurer/botanist archetype is very much alive in the person of Thomas Pakenham, the current earl of Longford, and author of *Meetings with Remarkable Trees*. He has traveled the globe searching for exotic plants. The gardens in his home at Pakenham Hall in County Westmeath continue to evolve from their 18th-century origins. A new addition is an "Oriental" garden featuring rare magnolias and lilies he collected as seed in China and other Asian countries. Elsewhere, efforts are underway to preserve ancient gardening techniques and designs. The gardeners at Strokestown House in County Roscommon have restored a 6-acre walled garden and now tend it with methods used in the 1700s; among its charming features are a Georgian peach house and an old vinery. But you can visit modern gardens, too. The best example is Heywood Gardens in County Laois, which were completed in 1912. These formal gardens, featuring wonderful water terraces, were designed by the famous architect Sir Edwin Lutyens (who also created the War Memorial Park in Dublin). What typifies all the gardens in this part of Ireland is a lush serenity and the profusion of growth which is synonymous with the Irish landscape.

Water, Water, Everywhere

Delightfully, the Irish Midlands region is littered with thousands of lakes and rivers as well as an extensive canal system. Historically, these waterways were the lifeblood of Ireland's commercial life. In the 18th century, the construction of the Royal and Grand canals allowed the transport of food, livestock, and, of course, Guinness brew, from Dublin to the west. Nowadays, whether it is water sports, fishing, or nature-watching you seek, Ireland's heartland is full of water-borne opportunities for the tourist. The Shannon, flowing majestically through the center of the region, is the longest river in Ireland and Britain and one of Europe's great waterways. Along the course of the river lie two major lakes, Lough Ree (north of Athlone) and Lough Derg (north of Limerick city). The best way to see the Shannon is by river cruiser. These boats are for hire at riverside towns like Carrick-on-Shannon in County Leitrim and Ballina in County Offaly. These "self-drive" boats accommodate up to 12 people and allow amateur mariners to take a relaxing meander along the river, with opportunities for fishing, swimming, and "refueling stops" at pretty shoreside villages like Terryglass, County Tipperary, where cozy pubs and excellent restaurants are the order of the day. Other activities, like water-skiing and canoeing, are also popular along the Shannon. You can also navigate the Shannon-Erne Waterway, a recently reopened canal which links the majestic expanse of Upper and Lower Lough

Erne in Northern Ireland to the Shannon. The link has created Europe's longest (750-km) navigable leisure waterway. Or if you just want to take in the riverscape at leisure, opt for a cruise on the Viking which sets sail from Athlone. The northern Midlands are known as Ireland's Lakelands, thanks to thousands of pristine lakes and rivers dotting the landscape. The area is a paradise for anglers. The loughs of Cavan and Monaghan are also famed for their huge and rather fearsome pike fish.

moves northwest to Castlepollard and environs, stopping just short of Longford, the jumping-off point for the northern Midlands.

Abbeyleix

❶ *99 km (61 mi) southwest of Dublin.*

One of the most elegant small towns in Ireland, Abbeyleix has retained its charming Georgian ambience and is noted for its broad main street, lined with well-appointed, stone-cut buildings and original shop fronts in the traditionally ornate Irish style. The entire tree-lined village was built in the 18th century on the orders of the Viscount de Vesci to house servants and tradesmen working on his nearby estate. Many town houses and vernacular buildings date from the 1850s but more recent buildings, including the Market House, erected in 1906, and the Hibernian Bank, from 1900, contribute greatly to the town's tranquil and refined character. Don't miss **Morrissey's Pub and Grocery Store** (⊠ Main St. ☎ 0502/31281), which has been a working public house since 1775. One of Ireland's best loved drinking emporiums, it has a dark, wood-paneled interior furnished with antique bar fittings. Customers can warm themselves by an ancient potbellied stove. The pub also serves as a shop, which means you can purchase groceries while enjoying the obligatory pint of Guinness.

The **Heritage House,** a former Patrician Brothers School, has informative displays on the de Vesci family and the history of Abbeyleix. ⊠ *Top of town* ☎ *0502/31653* ⊕ *www.laois.local.ie* ⊠ *€2* ⊙ *May–Sept., weekdays 9–5, weekends 9–1; Oct.–Apr., weekdays 9–5.*

Ballinakill, a pretty Georgian village about 5 km (3 mi) south of Abbeyleix, contains the **Heywood Gardens,** designed by the English architect Sir Edward Lutyens in the early 20th century within an existing 18th-century park. The Lutyenses' house burned down, but the gardens, regarded as among the architect's finest, are still worth visiting (even as they undergo restoration). A formal lawn flanked by traditional herbaceous borders leads to a sunken Italian garden. ⊠ *Ballinakill* ☎ *0502/33563* ⊕ *www.heritageireland.ie* ⊠ *Free* ⊙ *Daily 9–dusk.*

Where to Stay & Eat

$-$$ ✕▥ **Preston House.** This ivy-clad Georgian building on the main Cork–Dublin road was a schoolhouse until the 1960s. Now it is a popular lunch and coffee stop by day, renowned for good home cooking. By night the restaurant ($–$$; closed Sunday and Monday) takes on a

The
Midlands

NORTHERN
IRELAND

IRELAND

KEY

▶ *Start of itinerary*

0   20 miles
0   30 km

more formal aspect. Owner Allison Dowling offers a menu featuring hearty, heartwarming dishes such as honey roast duck with plum and port sauce and sautéed venison with cream potatoes and red currants. The spacious guest rooms, furnished with solid Victorian antiques, have views of the long back gardens and fields beyond. ⊠ *Main St., Co. Laois* 🖩📠 *0502/31432* ✑ *4 rooms* ♺ *Restaurant, some pets allowed; no smoking, no a/c* ☱ *MC, V* ⫶♋⫶ *BP.*

¢ 🖾 **Foxrock Inn.** A friendly red setter by the name of Grouse greets new arrivals at this modest but friendly guest house in the picturesque heart of the County Laois countryside. The main attractions of this inn, set in the tiny village of Clough, are the genuinely warm welcome, the peace and quiet, and the owners, Sean and Mary Hyland. This enthusiastic young couple can bring you up to date on the 200-year history of the inn and adjacent pub, advise you on hiking in the Slieve Bloom Mountains, and organize golf and angling packages. Rooms are plain but clean and comfortable. Simple, home-cooked dinners and packed lunches are available. Clough is located 8 km (5 mi) west of Abbeyleix (signposted off the R434 road to Borris-in-Ossory). ⊠ *Clough, Ballacolla, Co. Laois* 🖩📠 *0502/38637* ⊕ *www.foxrockinn.com* ✑ *5 rooms* ♺ *Dining room; no a/c, no room TVs, no room phones* ☱ *V* ⫶♋⫶ *BP.*

Shopping

The Rathdowney Designer Outlet (⊠ Rathdowney ☎ 0505/48900 ⊕ www.rathdowneyretailoutlet.ie) would not look out of place in Midwestern America and offers the usual mix of top labels at easy-on-the-pocket prices. The extraordinary thing about this huge indoor mall is its location. The investors behind this venture adopted a "build it and they will come" approach. It is (as the Irish would say) in the "back of beyond," on the outskirts of a sleepy country town in County Laois. It's perfect for the addicted label hunter and also has attractions for non-shoppers curious to sample a surreal slice of pure Americana in rural Ireland. To get here from Abbeyleix, follow R433 west for 19 km (12 mi).

Portlaoise

❷ *14 km (9 mi) north of Abbeyleix.*

Near the heart of County Laois, the rich farmland south and west of Portlaoise, an hour by train or car from Dublin, is one of Ireland's undiscovered gems. Golf, fishing, hiking, and horseback riding are traditional sports hereabouts, and the development of the Grand Canal for recreational purposes is adding to the area's attractions. Explore the pretty villages and romantic, ivy-covered ruins by car, or follow one of the many hiking trails.

Portlaoise's name is derived from the Gaelic for "Fort of Laois" and refers to the town's strife-filled history. In terms of its architecture, it is rather eclectic—it feels as if bits of other towns were picked up and dropped randomly on the site. Once best known for having Ireland's highest-security prison, which still looms over the town and housed the IRA's most notorious members during the 1970s and '80s, the town is undergoing a renaissance. The main street, which once formed part of the main Dublin-

Cork road, is now largely given over to pedestrians; pubs and restaurants are beginning to flourish; and a thriving Dunamaise Arts Centre adds that extra dash of culture to the proceedings. In addition to being a good base from which to explore the surrounding countryside, Portlaoise is a good place to stay to avoid the heavy traffic that can clog the main N7 Dublin road. At the Tourist Information Office in Portlaoise you can pick up a map of the **Laois Heritage Trail** (⊕ www.laoistourism. ie/HeritageTrail1.htm), a signposted, day-long drive on quiet back roads that takes in 13 heritage sites, ranging from Abbeyleix to Emo Court; the circular trail starts in Borris-in-Ossary on N7.

The famous **Rock of Dunamase** is a dramatic 150-foot-high limestone outcrop which dominates the landscape east of Portlaoise. For this reason, it was used as a military stronghold. As far back as AD 140 its occupants kept watch against marauders and it was fought over in turn by the Vikings, Normans, Irish, and English. Today it is crowned by the ruins of a 12th-century castle, once home to Dermot Mac Murrough, king of Leinster, who precipitated the Norman invasion when he invited the famed and feared Norman leader Strongbow to Ireland to marry his daughter, whose dowry included the Rock. Some of the castle's thick walls still stand. The main reason for visiting the Rock today is to take the short walk to its summit to enjoy the view of the Slieve Bloom Mountains to the north and the Wicklow Mountains to the south. ⊠ *5 km (3 mi) east of Portlaoise on the N80 Stradbally road.*

Where to Stay & Eat

$–$$ ✕ **Kingfisher.** Set in the town center, this is a particularly lively and stylish spot. The high-ceiling room was once a banking hall, but now its softly lighted walls glow with warm terra-cotta tones, the perfect complement to the spicy-but-not-too Punjabi cuisine. *Pappadams* (crunchy lentil-flour bread) and condiments appear before you order, and the friendly staff in traditional dress will guide you expertly through the long menu. Dishes vary from mild and creamy *kormas* (curried meat dishes) to fresh cod with a mild blend of spices and lemon juice to chicken "cooked with angry green chilies." ⊠ *Old AIB Bank, Main St.* ☎ *0502/62500* ▤ *AE, MC, V* ☉ *No lunch Sat.–Tues.*

$–$$ ✕ **The Lemon Tree.** Although set on Portlaoise's main street, this spot is its best kept culinary secret. It combines an informal atmosphere with modern-but-cozy surroundings. Owner Kevin Hennessy used to be front-of-house supremo at swanky Dublin eatery Shanahans on the Green and has now managed to import the style without the snobbishness. Starters might include duck confit with hoisin sauce while many enjoy the prime Irish Angus sirloin for the main course. ⊠ *Main St.* ☎ *0502/62200* ▤ *MC, V* ☉ *No lunch.*

$$–$$$$ ▦ **The Heritage.** Imagine a hotel so imposing that it does not need a street address and you're getting close to the ambitious scale of The Heritage. A six-pillar classic portico dominates the massive facade, which single-handedly transformed the town center from run-down to swanky. The best of modern Irish design—handmade rugs and specially crafted wood paneling—decorates the public rooms. Guest rooms are spacious and restful, with plain, warm-color walls and custom-made Victorian-style furniture. Three restaurants, ranging from the elegantly traditional Fitz-Maurice to the casual Coffee Bean, offer a culinary cornucopia. A shuttle service is provided to the 18-hole golf course, designed by Seve Ballesteros. A blast of modern glitz in back-road Ireland, The Heritage may be just the change of pace you're looking for. ⊠ *Co. Laois* ☎ *0502/78588* 🖷 *0502/78577* ⊕ *www.theheritagehotel.com* ⌨ *110 rooms, 10 suites* ♿ *2 restaurants, coffee shop, in-room data ports, cable TV, golf privileges, indoor pool, health club, massage, sauna, steam room, 3 bars, nightclub; no a/c* ▤ *AE, DC, MC, V* ⦿ *BP.*

★ **$** ▥ **Ivyleigh House.** Owners Dinah and Jerry Campion say they like to give their guests "the best of everything" and that maxim is certainly in evidence the minute you step inside this elegant Georgian town house next to the Portlaoise railway station. Open fires, antiques, and sumptuously cozy sofas await you in the beige-on-brown, wood-accented sitting room. Upstairs, luxurious drapes grace the sash windows of the spacious bedrooms, most done in dramatic hues like pink and emerald. A virtual avalanche of plump cushions scattered on your antique bed reinforces the tone of rest and relaxation. Guests find it hard to decide from all the goodies in the yumptious breakfast menu. Suffice to say the bread is home-baked, the food is locally produced, and no one can resist the Cashel blue-cheese cakes with mushrooms and tomatoes. Room TVs are available by request. ⊠ *Bank Pl., Co. Laois* ☎ *0502/22081* 🖷 *0502/63343* ⊕ *www.ivyleigh.com* ⌨ *6 rooms* ♿ *No a/c, no room TVs, no smoking* ▤ *MC, V* ⦿ *BP.*

Nightlife & the Arts

Also known as Turley's bar, the canalside **Anchor Inn** (⊠ Grand Canal, near Stradbally, Vicarstown ☎ 0502/25189), 10 km (6 mi) east of Portlaoise on N80, is popular for its lively Monday-night traditional-music sessions, which start around 9. Sessions take place more frequently in the summer. The lively **Dunamaise Arts Centre** (⊠ Main St. ☎ 0502/63355 ⊕ www.dunamaisetheatre.com), formerly the town jail, built into the back of the 18th-century stone courthouse, has a 238-seat theater, an art gallery, and a friendly coffee shop (open 8:30–5:30). You may catch a professional production on tour or a local amateur show. The art exhibits, usually by contemporary Irish artists, are of a high standard. It's on a corner between a multistory car park and the Heritage Hotel.

Sports & the Outdoors

The **Heritage Golf & Heritage Club** (⊠ Killenard ☎ 0502/45994), just off the main Dublin-Cork road, is an 18-hole, par-72 course. This parkland championship course was co-designed by Seve Ballesteros and features challenging doglegs, as well as five lakes and a number of streams, to keep those fond of dodging water traps happy.

Portarlington

▶ ❸ *13 km (8 mi) northeast of Portlaoise.*

Built on the River Barrow in the late 17th century, Portarlington was originally an English settlement. Later, a Huguenot colony developed here, and French surnames are still common in the area. Some good examples of Georgian architecture can be seen in the town. A quintessential landmark of Irish Palladian elegance lies just 7 km (4½ mi) south ★ of Portarlington: **Emo Court and Gardens,** one of the finest large-scale country houses near Dublin open to the public. If you elect to skip over much of the Midlands, at least try to tack on a visit to Emo, especially if you're in County Kildare or Wicklow. To come upon the house from the main drive, an avenue lined with magisterial Wellingtonia trees, is to experience one of Ireland's great treasure-house views. Begun in 1790 by James Gandon, architect of the Custom House and the Four Courts in Dublin, Emo (the name derives from the Italian version of the original Irish name Imoe) is thought to be Gandon's only domestic work matching the grand scale of his Dublin civic buildings. Construction continued on and off for 70 years, as family money troubles followed the untimely death of Emo's first patron and owner, the first earl of Portarlington.

In 1996 Emo's English-born owner, Mr. Cholmeley-Harrison, donated the house to the Irish nation. The ground-floor rooms have been beautifully restored and decorated. Among the highlights are the entrance hall, with trompe l'oeil paintings in the apses on each side, and the library, which has a carved Italian-marble mantle with putti frolicking among grapevines. But the showstopper, and one of the finest rooms in Ireland, is the domed rotunda—the work of one of Gandon's successors, the Irish architect William Caldbeck—inspired by the Roman Pantheon. Marble pilasters with gilded Corinthian capitals support the rotunda's blue-and-white coffered dome. Emo's 55 acres of grounds include a 20-acre lake, lawns planted with yew trees, a small garden (the Clocker) with Japanese maples, and a larger one (the Grapery) with rare trees and shrubs. ⊠ *Emo* ☎ *0502/26573* ⊕ *www.heritageireland.ie* ▢ *Gardens free, house €2.75* ⊙ *Gardens daily 9–dusk; house mid-June–mid-Sept., Tues.–Sun. 10–5 (last tour at 4:30).*

★ **Coolbanagher Church,** the familiar name for the exquisite Church of St. John the Evangelist, was, like Emo Court and Gardens, designed by James Gandon. On view inside are Gandon's original 1795 plans; there's also an elaborately sculpted 15th-century font from an earlier church that stood nearby. Adjacent to the church is Gandon's mausoleum for Lord Portarlington, his patron at Emo. The church is open daily from spring through autumn; at other times, ask around in the tiny village for a key, or at the rectory, a 10-minute drive away. ⊠ *8½ km (5 mi) south of Portarlington on R419* ☎ *0502/24143 rectory* ▢ *Free* ⊙ *May–Oct., daily 9–6.*

Where to Stay

★ **$$** ▦ **Roundwood House.** This imposing and gorgeous Palladian villa, built in the 1730s, nestles at the foot of the Slieve Bloom Mountains amid 18 acres of mature woodland and pasture. Antique family portraits of the builders, the Sharps—a prominent Quaker family whose riches derive from the mid-1600s woolen industry—adorn the walls of the curio-filled drawing room. The bedrooms in the main house are elegant, airy, and painted in dramatic greens, yellows, and blues. If you prefer a cozier option, there are several rooms in the adjacent 17th-century Old House, or on the grounds in the picturesque Coach House and Forge.

Tiniest of all is The Cottage, a stone charmer whose original tenants may have been Hansel and Gretel, at least according to hosts Frank and Rose-marie Kennan, who often share your table at dinner. The house is located three miles from Mountrath on the scenic road to Kinnitty. ⊠ *Mountrath, Co. Laois* ☎ *0502/32120* 🖷 *0502/32711* ⊕ *www. hidden-ireland.com/roundwood.html* 🗫 *10 rooms* ⚵ *Dining room; no a/c, no room phones, no room TVs* 🞸 *AE, DC, MC, V* |◎| *BP.*

¢ 🏠 **Eskermore House.** Though this 1745 farmhouse has been modernized, it still has roses growing over the front door, a chiming grandfather clock, and an organ in the sitting room for musically gifted guests. Located 8 km (5 mi) north of Portarlington on R402, this is a good base for hiking in the Slieve Bloom Mountains. The guest rooms are simply but comfortably furnished and face south over a beech-tree-lined avenue and semi-wild gardens; room TVs are available on request. The sitting room has an open turf fire, a piano, and cable TV. Host Ann Mooney will prepare a wholesome dinner with advance notice. ⊠ *Mount Lucas, Edenderry, Co. Offaly* ☎ *0506/53079* ⊕ *www.eskermore.com* 🗫 *3 rooms* ⚵ *Some pets allowed; no a/c, no room phones* 🞸 *MC, V* |◎| *BP.*

Tullamore

❹ *27 km (17 mi) northwest of Portarlington.*

Tullamore, the county seat of Offaly, flourished thanks to its position on the Grand Canal. One relic of its former splendor is found on the southwestern edge of town, where, if you take the road heading to Birr from the center of Tullamore, you'll find a storybook vision in splen-

★ did Tin Soldier Fortress style: **Charleville Forest Castle.** Perhaps the finest neo-Gothic 19th-century castle in Ireland, its Flag Tower and turrets rise above its demesne of 30 acres of woodland walks and gardens. The Georgian-Gothic Revival castellated house was built as a symbol (in fact, the floor plan is even modeled on the Union Jack) of English might triumphant over French force—the French revolutionary forces, to be exact, who had become a little too cozy with the Irish locals. Commissioned by Baron Tullamore and dating from 1812, the castle is a rural example of the work of architect Francis Johnston, responsible for many of Dublin's stately Georgian buildings. The interiors are somewhat the worse for wear—most are gigantic chambers with a few sticks of furniture—but the William Morris–designed dining room still has its original stenciled wallpaper. Guided tours of the interior are available. Descended through the Bury family, fortunes depleted, and without heirs, the castle became an orphan in the 1960s but has been slowly restored. The surrounding forest is said to be the haunting grounds of the ancient Druids. ⊠ *1½ km (1 mi) outside Tullamore on N52 to Birr* ☎ *0506/21279* ⊕ *www. charlevillecastle.com* 🎟 *€5* ⊗ *May, weekends 2–5; June–Sept., Wed.–Sun. 2–5; Oct.–Apr., groups of 4 or more by appointment.*

Sports & the Outdoors

BOATING Exploring the inland waterways steering your own boat is a leisurely way to discover the unspoiled scenery, hidden villages, and abundant wildlife of Ireland's interior. You can rent a river cruiser for a floating holiday from **Celtic Canal Cruisers Ltd** (⊠ 24th Lock ☎ 0506/21861).

GOLF **Esker Hills Golf & Country Club** (⊠ 5 km [3 mi] north of Tullamore on N80 ☏0506/55999) is a challenging 18-hole, par-71 championship course with natural lakes and woodlands.

Kilbeggan

⑤ *11 km (7 mi) north of Tullamore.*

It's the whiskey (the Irish spell their traditional tipple with an "e") that brings most people to the unassuming little town of Kilbeggan. The town is the home of **Locke's Distillery,** which was established in 1757 to produce a traditional Irish malt whiskey. It closed down in 1954 and was reopened in 1987 by Cooley Distillery, which now makes its whiskey in County Louth but brings it here to be matured in casks. The distillery has been restored as a museum of industrial archaeology illustrating the process of Irish pot-whiskey distillation and the social history of the workers. "Irish" is a straight pot-still whiskey, and has a characteristic flavor which distinguishes it from Scotch, bourbon, or rye. Irish is not drunk until it has matured for at least seven years in wooden casks. Also, it is best quaffed without a mixer, so try it straight or with water. ☏ *0506/ 32134* ⊕ *www.lockesdistillerymuseum.com* ☐ *€4* ⊘ *Apr.–Oct., daily 9–6; Nov.–Mar., daily 10–4.*

Mullingar

⑥ *24 km (15 mi) northeast of Kilbeggan.*

Irish farmers describe a good young cow as "beef to the ankle, like a Mullingar heifer." Set in an area of rich farmland, Mullingar is known as Ireland's beef capital. It's also County Westmeath's major town—a busy commercial and cattle-trading center on the Royal Canal, midway between two large, attractive lakes, Lough Owel and Lough Ennel. Buildings here date mostly from the 19th century. While best used as a base to tour the surrounding countryside, Mullingar has some interesting sights. The town's largest structure is the Renaissance-style Catholic **Cathedral of Christ the King,** completed in 1939. Note the facade's finely carved stonework and the mosaics of St. Patrick and St. Anne by the Russian artist Boris Anrep in the spacious interior. ⊠ *Mary St.* ☏ *044/ 48391* ⊘ *Daily 9–5:30.*

Mullingar Bronze and Pewter Centre offers free tours of its workshop, where the age-old craft of pewter making is still practiced. Sculptured bronze figures are also being made here (by Genesis Fine Art). You can purchase pewter and bronze in the showroom. There's also a coffee shop on the premises. ⊠ *Great Down, The Downs* ☏ *044/44948* ☐ *Free* ⊘ *Weekdays 9:30–5:30, Sat. 10–5:30.*

★ ℃ **Belvedere House Gardens** occupies a beautiful spot: the northeast shore of Lough Ennel. Access to this stately mid-18th-century hunting lodge with extensive gardens is through the servants' entrance—so you can see what life behind the scenes was like back then. Cries and whispers haunt this estate. Built in 1740 by architect Richard Cassels for Robert Rochfort, first earl of Belvedere, it became a byword for debauchery and dissipation thanks to the hijinks of Rochfort's wife, the "very handsome" Mary Molesworth. After falling passionately in love with Rochfort's younger brother (and bearing him a child), she was locked up in another family house for decades. Robert regaled guests with the "scandal" while offering sumptuous dinners at this house under its great 18th-century plasterwork ceilings. He spent much of his family fortune dotting the estate with garden "follies," including the Jealous Wall, a gigantic mock-castle ruin that served to cover up a view of the adjoining estate, owned by another brother, also hated. Today, the interiors are a quirky mix of Georgian stateliness and Victorian charm. The noted bow and Palladian windows have great parkland views sloping down to the lake and its islands. You can tour the 160 acres of the estate and woodland trails on the Belvedere tram. Also on the estate are a coffee shop, an animal sanctuary, and a children's play area. ⊠ *4 km (2½ mi) south of Mullingar on N52* ☎ *044/40861* ⊕ *www.belvedere-house.ie* ✉ *House and parkland €6, tram €1.30* ☉ *May–Sept, daily 10:30–6, Oct.–Apr, daily 10:30–4:30.*

Where to Stay & Eat

★ $$$–$$$$ ╳⊡ **Crookedwood House.** Set beside a 15th-century church and overlooking Lough Derravaragh, this former rectory is now home to one of the best restaurants in the Midland. Chef/owner Noel Kenny has conjured up an exciting, German-inspired take on modern Irish cuisine. Venison goulash, anyone? In winter, try the Hunter's Plate—a selection of pheasant, wild duck, and pigeon. Also irresistible is the trio of salmon, sole, and scallops with lobster sauce. The unusual combination of honey-roasted pork steak and salmon is wrapped in phyllo pastry and baked with grapes. The restaurant's decor—rough white walls and oak beams—won't do too much for the digestive juices. But the guest rooms upstairs are tranquil and some are even accented with 19th-century style pieces. The house is 13 km (8 mi) north of Mullingar on the R394 Castlepollard road. ⊠ *Co. Westmeath* ☎ *044/72165* 🖷 *044/72166* ⊕ *www. crookedwoodhouse.com* ⊲ *18 rooms* ⋄ *Restaurant, cable TV* ⊟ *AE, MC, V* ⎟⊙⎟ *BP* ☉ *No dinner Sun.–Mon.*

$$$$ ╳⊡ **Temple Country House and Spa.** If you're hoping to recharge your batteries, this is just the place. It's a lovely family-run Victorian farmhouse, surrounded by 100 acres of parkland, and boasts all you could want in terms of relaxation therapy. B&B rates are available, but guests are encouraged to go for the (very pricey—more than €400) 24-hour package which includes yoga and an hour-long spa treatment, plus a delicious, freshly prepared breakfast, lunch, and dinner from Bernadette Fagan's kitchen. Temple Country House and Spa is along N6, almost equidistant from Mullingar, Tullamore, and Athlone. ⊠ *Horseleap, Moate, Co. Westmeath* ☎ *0506/35118* 🖷 *0506/35008* ⊕ *www.templespa.ie/* ⊲ *8 rooms* ⋄ *Massage, sauna, spa, steam room, bicycles, no-smoking rooms; no a/c, no room TVs* ⊟ *AE, MC, V* ☉ *Closed Christmas wk* ⎟⊙⎟ *AI.*

$$$–$$$$ ⊡ **Bloomfield House Hotel.** A rambling two-story former convent with a castellated roof on the shores of Lough Ennel has been converted into a comfortable hotel with an excellent fitness center. The style here is cheerful—modern furniture decked out in warm shades of plaid. The rooms are spacious, and all have peaceful country views. The Brinsley Restau-

rant has tall Georgian-style windows overlooking the lake, and specializes in local fish and game. The hotel lies 3 km (2 mi) south of Mullingar on N52. ✉ *Tullamore Rd., Co. Westmeath* ☎ *044/40894* 🖷 *044/ 43767* ⊕ *www.bloomfieldhouse.com* ⇒ *65 rooms* ⚐ *Restaurant, cable TV, indoor pool, gym, hot tub, sauna, steam room, bar, meeting rooms; no a/c* ▭ *AE, DC, MC, V* ⭍ *BP.*

Sports & the Outdoors

GOLF **Delvin Castle Golf Club** (✉ Delvin ☎ 044/64315) is an 18-hole course in a mature parkland setting. It has beautiful views across north Westmeath.

Castlepollard

❼ *21 km (13 mi) north of Mullingar.*

★ A pretty village of multi-hued 18th- and 19th-century houses laid out around a large, triangular green, Castlepollard is also home to **Tullynally Castle and Gardens,** the largest castle in Ireland that still functions as a family home. This is not just any family, but the Pakenhams, that famous Irish tribe that has given us Elizabeth Longford (whose biography of Queen Victoria is in most libraries) and Antonia Fraser, wife of Harold Pinter and best-selling biographer of Mary, Queen of Scots, among others. In fact, Tullynally—the name, literally translated, means "Hill of the Swans"—has been the home of 10 generations of this family, which also married into the earldom of Longford. Lady Fraser's brother Thomas, an historian, is the current earl but does not use the title. After all this, it is a bit of a letdown to learn the house itself is private, but don't be too broken up about it. Most of the rooms are vast and barren, a result of the 18th-century "Gothicization" of a former Georgian house into a faux-castle. Where the house really comes into its own is as a stage set for the surrounding park, since the gray-stone structure is so long and has so many towers it looks like a miniature town from a distance. The total circumference of the building's masonry adds up to nearly ½ km (¼ mi) and includes a motley agglomeration of towers, turrets, and battlements that date from the first early fortified building, circa 1655, up through the mid-19th century, when additions in the Gothic Revival style went up one after another. Two wings designed by Sir Richard Morrison in 1840 that joined the main block to the stable court had dramatically different purposes: one was given over entirely to luxurious quarters for the dowager countess; the other housed 40 *indoor* servants.

Today, more attention is given to the beautiful parkland, in part because Thomas Pakenham is a tree-hugger extraordinaire. Author of several books, his most famous is *Meetings with Remarkable Trees* (1996), an exceptional art book that includes many of his magnificent photographs. The estate's rolling parkland was laid out in 1760, much along the lines you see today, with fine rhododendrons, numerous trees, and two ornamental lakes. A garden walk through the grounds in front of the castle leads to a spacious flower garden, a pond, a grotto, and walled gardens. The kitchen garden here is one of the largest in Ireland, with a row of old Irish yew trees. Don't miss the forest path, which takes you around the perimeter of the parkland and affords excellent views back to the romantic castle. ⊠ 1½ km (1 mi) west of Castlepollard on the R395 road to Granard ☎ 044/61159 ⊕ www.tullynallycastle.com ☑ €5 ☉ May–Aug., daily 2–6.

Fore

❽ 5 km (3 mi) east of Castlepollard.

Irish myth permeates this village known for its "seven wonders," and it's worth a fun walk to discover "the water that runs uphill" or "the stone raised by St. Fechin." The monk founded a monastery here in the 7th century, and the village is now known not only for its legend, but also for its medieval church and the remains (supposedly the largest in Ireland) of a Benedictine abbey. The spectacular remains of **Fore Abbey** dominate the simple village—its structure is massive and its imposing square towers and loophole windows make it resemble a castle rather than an abbey. Elsewhere in town, St. Fechin's Church, dating from the 10th century, has a massive, cross-inscribed lintel stone.

THE NORTHERN MIDLANDS

Our Northern Midlands coverage starts in Longford and works its way north, leaving the ancient kingdom of Leinster for Ulster's two most southerly counties, Cavan and Monaghan. The land in the north of County Cavan is known as "drumlin country," after the thousands of small, round hills consisting of boulder clay left behind by the glacial retreat 10,000 years ago. The boulder clay also filled in many of the pre-glacial river alleys, causing the rivers to change course, resulting in the creation of many shallow lakes, which provide superb fishing and angling. Little wonder this region is also rightly heralded as the Northern Lakelands.

Longford

❾ 37 km (23 mi) west of Castlepollard, 124 km (77 mi) northwest of Dublin.

Longford, the seat of County Longford and a typical little market-town community, is rich in literary associations, though after Oliver Goldsmith, the names of the county's writers' pantheon may draw a blank from all but the most dedicated Irish literature enthusiast. In fact, it is Jane Austen—that most British of writers—who may intrigue you into visiting **Carrigglas Manor**. The romantic Tudor-Gothic house, built in 1837 by Thomas Lefroy, offers a glimpse into gracious country living in 19th-century surroundings. Lefroy's descendants, who still live here, note that as a young man in England he was romantically involved with the novelist. Why they never married is a mystery, but it is believed that Austen based the character of Mr. Darcy in *Pride and Prejudice* on Mr. Lefroy. The house still has high-quality plasterwork and many of its original mid-19th-century furnishings. A magnificent stable yard, part of an earlier house on the site, was designed in 1790 by James Gandon, architect of Dublin's Custom House and Four Courts. Go into the stable yard and gardens to enter the small costume museum, which displays mostly 18th-century apparel found in the house. There's also an outdoor tea room in the plush period gardens. ⊠ *5 km (3 mi) northeast of Longford on the R194 road to Granard* ☏ *043/45165* ⊕ *www.carrigglas. com* ⊡ *Stable yard, gallery, and shop free; gardens and museum* €9 ⊘ *Stable yard, gardens, and museum daily 11–3; house by appointment only, May–Sept., Mon., Tues., Fri., and Sat. 2–6.*

Where to Stay & Eat

★ **$–$$** ▦ **Viewmount House.** Beautiful old lime trees and sweeping lawns provide the perfect setting for this sweet and exquisite Georgian home. Once owned by the earl of Longford and used as an estate office, it has recently been restored to its former charm by James and Beryl Kearney. The bedrooms are full of character and have impressive period wallpapers and antique mahogany wardrobes and beds. Breakfast is served in a vaulted room, cheerily painted in robin's blue. The four acres of grounds which surround the house are a gardener's paradise with an old orchard, a formal garden, and a Japanese garden replete with full-size pagoda. The house is 2 km (1 mi) outside the town, just off the old Dublin road (R393). ⊠ *Dublin Rd., County Longford* ☏ *043/41919* ⊟ *043/42906* ⊕ *www.viewmounthouse.com* ⊸ *5 rooms, 1 suite* ⚘ *No a/c, no room TVs* ▭ *AE, MC, V* ⊙⫿ *BP.*

Cavan

⑩ *53 km (33 mi) northeast of Longford, 114 km (71 mi) northwest of Dublin.*

A small, quiet, undistinguished town serving the local farming community, Cavan is also, increasingly, known for its crystal factory. There are two central streets. With its pubs and shops, Main Street is like many other streets in similar Irish towns. Farnham Street has Georgian houses, churches, and a courthouse. **Cavan Crystal** is an up-and-coming rival to Waterford in the cut-lead-crystal line; the company offers guided factory tours and access to its factory shop. This is a good opportunity to watch skilled craftspeople at work if you can't make it to Waterford. A major building attached to the factory houses a visitor center, glass museum, restaurant, and coffee shop. ⊠ *Dublin Rd.* ☏ *049/433–1800* ⊕ *www.cavancrystaldesign.com* ⊡ *Free* ⊘ *Guided tours weekdays at 9:30, 10:30, and 11:30.*

off the beaten path
KILLYKEEN FOREST PARK – This park is part of the beautiful, mazelike network of lakes called Lough Oughter. Within the park's 600 acres are a number of signposted walks and nature trails, stables offering horseback riding, and boats and bicycles for rent. Twenty-eight fully outfitted two- and three-bedroom cottages are available for weeklong, weekend, or midweek stays. Rates vary according to the season; call for details. ⊠ *11 km (7 mi) north of Cavan* ☏ *049/433–2541* ⊕ *www.coillte.ie* ⊡ *Free, parking €1.90* ⊘ *Daily 9–5.*

Where to Stay & Eat

$$$$ ✕▦ **Slieve Russell Hotel and Country Club.** Outdoors types, especially golfers, prick up their ears when they hear of the facilities on offer at this palatial modern country hotel on 300 acres. Apart from two golf courses, it also has an excellent health club as well as freshwater and trout fishing. From the outside, this hotel looks like a rather wan 20th-century redo of a stately home. No matter. One comes here for modern-day luxuries and de-stressing activities, not the grace notes of yesteryear. The bright and sprightly bedrooms have chunky, art deco–style furniture. White linen and wrought-iron chandeliers decorate the formal Conall Cearnach restaurant, where the extensive menu includes traditionally prepared seafood dishes such as black sole on the bone or salmon hollandaise. The Brackley Buttery restaurant ($–$$$) is more informal. The hotel, which is 26 km (16 mi) west of Cavan, is a convenient and luxurious place to break a journey between Dublin and Sligo. ⊠ *Ballyconnell, Co. Cavan* ☎ *049/952–6444* 🖷 *049/952–6474* ⊕ *www.quinn-group.com* 🛏 *209 rooms, 10 suites* ⚭ *2 restaurants, in-room data ports, cable TV, some minibars, 9- and 18-hole golf courses, 4 tennis courts, 2 indoor pools, health club, hot tub, sauna, fishing, horseback riding, Ping-Pong, 2 bars, meeting rooms; no a/c* ☰ *AE, DC, MC, V* ⫟◯⫙ *BP.*

$–$$$ ✕🏠 **Cabra Castle.** With its crenellations and Gothic windows, this enormous gray-stone castle, built in 1699, is the centerpiece of a 1,000-acre estate, most of which now belongs to the Dun a Ri National Park. For the full effect, ask for a "castle room," furnished with especially elaborate Victorian antiques. The Victorian-Gothic theme is carried through in the bar and the restaurant (fixed-price Continental menu) with varying degrees of success. Don't miss the castle gallery, which has hand-painted ceilings and leaded-glass windows. ⊠ *65 km (40 mi) south of Cavan, Kingscourt, Co. Cavan* ☎ *042/966–7030* 🖷 *042/ 966–7039* ⊕ *www.cabracastle.com* 🛏 *80 rooms* ⚭ *Restaurant, cable TV, 9-hole golf course, fishing, horseback riding, bar, meeting rooms, some pets allowed; no a/c* ☰ *AE, MC, V* ⫟◯⫙ *BP.*

★ ¢–$ ✕🏠 **MacNean House & Bistro.** The village of Blacklion was certainly never known as a culinary hotspot—that is, until Ireland's best known TV chef, Neven Maguire, set up shop in his home town. His style is contemporary Continental—scallops wrapped in Parma ham or crab ravioli in a lobster cream sauce are two winners—while he also offers several inspired takes on traditional Irish dishes, such as a delicious lamb in an herb crust. Desserts are Neven's specialty—try the hazelnut nougat glacé. The guest bedrooms are simply furnished in a modern Irish style and, given the remoteness of Blacklion, you might want to book a room when reserving a table, to avoid a post-dinner, late-night drive. The 65-km (40-mi) detour makes sense if you are heading from Dublin northwest to Sligo or Donegal. ⊠ *Blacklion, Co. Cavan* ☎ *071/985–3022* 🖷 *071/9853404* 🛏 *4 rooms* ⚭ *Restaurant; no a/c* ☰ *MC, V* ⫟◯⫙ *BP.*

Cootehill

⓫ *26 km (16 mi) northeast of Cavan.*

One of the most underestimated small towns in Ireland, Cootehill commands a lovely outpost on a wooded hillside in the heart of County Cavan. Its wide streets, with intriguing old shops, are always busy without being congested. Most who come here are anglers from Europe, the United Kingdom, and the rest of Ireland. Only pedestrians are allowed through the gates of the Bellamont Forest park. After about a mile of woodland, ★ a gorgeous trail leads to **Bellamont Forest,** designed in 1728 by Edward Lovett Pearce, architect of Dublin's Bank of Ireland. Considered by some to be Ireland's loveliest 18th-century house, it was built for the Coote family in 1729 by Sir Edward Lovett Pearce, who was greatly inspired by the Palladian villas he saw on his Italian Grand Tour. He was also related by marriage to the house's most infamous owner, the earl of Bellamont, Charles Coote. A notorious seducer of women (leading to his nickname, the "Hibernian Seducer"), he was shot in the groin by Lord Townshend—giving rise to much speculation about his future extracurricular activities—then gloriously painted by Sir Joshua Reynolds in pink silks and ostrich plumes (the life-size canvas is now in the National Gallery of Ireland). Famously, he gave his inaugural speech as quartermaster-general of Ireland in *French*, continually referred to his County Cavan neighbors as "Hottentots," and wound up marrying the daughter of the super-rich duke of Leinster (providing for his three illegitimate daughters—as well as his three legitimate daughters—in his will). Small but perfectly proportioned, his house has remained virtually unaltered since it was built. It's now a private home, but is occasionally opened to the public. If you're interested, inquire locally or at the Tourist Information Office (TIO) in Cavan. Walk up the main street of Cootehill to "the top of the town" (past the White Horse hotel), and you'll see the entrance to Bellamont Forest opposite St. Michael's Church. The parkland is quintessentially Irish and allows some views of the private Bellamont Forest mansion.

Where to Stay

$ ✕▨ **The White Horse.** This typical market-town hotel serves as a lively gathering place for the community, and is particularly popular with visiting anglers. Some rooms in the rambling Victorian building are a bit small; all are plainly decorated. The quieter rooms are in the back. The restaurant ($–$$$), a softly lighted room with mahogany furniture, is popular with locals, who head here for generous portions and simply cooked Irish dishes. ✉ *Market St., Co. Cavan* ☎ *049/555–2124* 🖷 *049/555–2407* ☞ *30 rooms, 25 with bath* ♿ *Restaurant, 2 bars; no a/c.* ☰ *MC, V* ⦿ *BP.*

¢ ▨ **Riverside House.** It's the "Céad Míle Failte" (Irish for "a hundred thousand welcomes") that keeps them coming back, according to Una Smith, owner of this quaint farmhouse overlooking the River Analee. In the main, serious anglers and those seeking a little bit of peace and pastoral solitude favor this off-the-beaten-track retreat. All rooms have peaceful views and are individually decorated with modest antiques and family hand-me-downs. Dinner can be served by arrangement. Bring your boots if you want to explore around this working dairy farm. The lodging is signposted 1 km (½ mi) outside town off R188. ✉ *Co. Cavan* ☎ *049/555–2150* 🖷 *049/555–2150* ⊕ *www.irishfarmholidays. com* ☞ *6 rooms, 5 with bath* ♿ *Dining room, boating, fishing; no room phones* ☰ *MC* ⦿ *BP.*

THE GREAT HUNGER

I N HIS EPIC POEM The Great Hunger, generally regarded as one of the masterpieces of Irish literature, poet Patrick Kavanagh (1904–67) summed up his native Monaghan as a place whose peasant populace remained "locked in a stable with pigs and cows forever."

The intellectual and sexual paralysis reflected in the work is undoubtedly a thing of the past, but the unremitting barrenness of Kavanagh's vision is still evident in the county's unvarying landscape. Given the acerbic nature of the poem, it's rather ironic that Kavanagh-centered tourism is big business in the region.

Kavanagh worked on the family farm in his youth: though closed to the public, the farmhouse, a plain building dating from 1791, is signposted off the R179 Carrickmacross road.

Kavanagh's bittersweet relationship with Monaghan led to self-imposed exile in Dublin. A lover of controversy in his lifetime, Kavanagh in death remains a source of conflict and debate: in 1998, 31 years after he died, a monument at his grave in memory of his widow, Katherine, was extensively damaged and anonymously replaced by an old wooden cross and stepping stones removed from the garden of his family home at Mucker, a short distance from the village in which he was reared.

Today, the Patrick Kavanagh Center in Inniskeen (☎ 042/937-8560, ⊕ www.patrickkavanaghcountry.com) hosts poetry competitions and writer's weekends.

Monaghan

🕛 24 km (15 mi) north of Cootehill.

This former British garrison town is built around a central square known as the Diamond. On the square, the town's old Market House, elegantly constructed of limestone in 1792, is now the tourist office. The **County Museum** houses an eclectic collection of over 70,000 objects, which help to tell the story of the county. Exhibits include everything from the remains of a Giant Irish Red Deer (an extinct species that roamed the area 9,000 years ago) to one of the first televisions to arrive in the county. The most important artifact in the museum is the Cross of Clogher, a religious relic thought to date from the 14th century. ⊠ Hill St., Co. Monaghan ☎ 047/82928 ⊕ www.monaghan.ie ☉ June–Sept., Tues.–Sat. 11–5; Oct.–May, Tues.–Sat. 11–1 and 2–5.

off the beaten path

ROSSMORE FOREST PARK – For fresh air in pleasant surroundings, head to this park with 691 acres of low hills, small lakes, and pleasant forest walks through rhododendron groves. Nature trails are signposted. The park is just outside Monaghan, on the R189 Newbliss road.

Where to Stay & Eat

$$$$
Fodor'sChoice
★

✕▥ Castle Leslie. From Sir Winston Churchill to Sir Paul McCartney (who wed his fair Heather here in 2002), they came, they saw, and they were completely conquered. You will be too. Half baronial palace, half charming home, this *ne plus ultra* of Irish hotels has been pleasing guests since 1870, when Sir John Leslie built this family seat on the shores of Glaslough lake. Mixing in "Free Range Gothic" with "Late Rothschild" and "Jacobean Bloody," he and his son came up with a grand granite castle eminence, complete with a colonnaded loggia said to have been copied from Michelangelo's cloister at Santa Maria degli Angeli in Rome. Step inside and you'll see that while there are many magnificent historic houses doing double duty as hotels, few are as atmospheric as this. Grand reception rooms are full of lush delights—heavily carved and deeply cushioned furniture, velvet curtains, Wordsworth's harp, lovely 19th-century paintings (Sir John was a noted Pre-Raphaelite painter), Persian rugs, a Della Robbia fireplace, and the feeling of wraparound comfort that only this kind of companionable Victorian splendor can give. Better yet are the many mementos of this noted family, which is said to have descended from Attila the Hun, and also funded the education of the duke of Wellington (his death mask is displayed here), married into the Jennie Jerome family, and sprouted a bumper crop of writers and biographers (when Jonathan Swift stayed here, he wrote in the guest book: "Glaslough with rows of books upon its shelves/written by the Leslies about themselves"). You can almost hear the spirits of Uncle Shane or Aunt Alice rattling the doorknobs of the exquisite bedrooms, all adorned with important antiques and period color schemes: the Mauve Room welcomed the duke and duchess of Connaught and many other titled honeymooners ("Hence the loo beyond the bathroom is called 'The Throne Room' in honor of all the royalty who have rained," according to the hotel's delightful Web site); the Chinese Room is a symphony in regal Regency reds; the Red Room is filled with Renaissance-style treasures brought back from Perugia; Norman's Room, with brooding Jacobean bed and framed photos, honors Uncle Norman ("top cadet of his class at Sandhurst Military College"); while others will fancy Sir John's magisterially green velvet bedroom. For dinner, head downstairs to the sumptuous dining room, lined with 19th-century paintings, to dine on fine Irish fare served by candlelight by waitresses in Victorian dress; noisettes of Irish lamb with sweet potato and rosemary gratin is one particular treat. Outside, a 1,000-acre park beckons, with fishing and golfing to fill the hours, but many will simply repair to the castle's venerable drawing room with a glass of sherry to dream the afternoon away as Lord or Lady of the Manor. ✉ *11 km (7 mi) northeast of Monaghan, Glaslough, Co. Monaghan* ☎ *047/88109* 🖷 *047/88256* ⊕ *www.castleleslie.com* ⇆ *14 rooms* ♿ *Dining room, boating, fishing; no a/c, no room phones, no room TVs, no kids, no smoking* ▭ *MC, V* ⊙| *BP.*

Clones

⑬ *24 km (15 mi) southwest of Monaghan.*

Although in terms of its population Clones is a relatively unimportant Midlands town, culturally it has had an impact far beyond its size. Among the more famous citizens of the town are Barry McGuigan, former world featherweight boxing champion and one of the most popular sports figures ever to emerge in Ireland; Thomas Bracken, the man who penned New Zealand's national anthem; and, currently the area's most celebrated citizen, novelist Patrick McCabe, whose novels perfectly capture the vaguely time-locked quality of life in the town. McCabe's novel *The Butcher Boy* put Clones on the map internationally, particularly when Neil Jordan, Ireland's preeminent movie director, made a film based on the book in and around the town. As he was quoted saying, "If I ever want to quantify anything, I measure it against Clones. There is nothing you will ever encounter in life you haven't seen in some form in Clones."

Nowadays Clones (pronounced clo-*nez*), a small, agricultural market town 1 km (½ mi) from the Northern Ireland border, is one of two lace-making centers in County Monaghan (the other is Carrickmacross). It also has some ruins worth seeing. In early Christian times, Clones was the site of a monastery founded by St. Tighearnach, who died here in AD 458. An **Augustinian abbey** replaced the monastery in the 12th century, and its remains can still be seen near the 75-foot-tall round tower on Abbey Street. A 10th-century Celtic **high cross**, with carved panels depicting scriptural scenes, stands in Clones's central diamond. In an attempt to earn some income in the 19th century, the wives of local rectors took up lace-making. Crochet work and small raised dots are two hallmarks of Clones lace. A varied selection of Clones lace is on display around town and can be purchased at the **Clones Lace Centre.** ⊠ *Cara St.* ☎ *047/52125* ☉ *Mon. and Wed.–Sat. 10–6.*

off the beaten path

ANNAGHMAKERRIG – This small forest park with a lake is the site of Annaghmakerrig House, home of the Shakespearean stage director Sir Tyrone Guthrie until his death in 1971. He left it to the nation as a residential center for writers, artists, and musicians. It's not officially open to the public, but if you have a special interest in the arts or in its previous owner, do ask to be shown around. You can wander through and picnic on its grounds. ⊠ *13 km (8 mi) southeast of Clones* ☎ *047/54003* ⊕ *www.tyroneguthrie.ie.*

Where to Stay

★ **$$$–$$$$** 🏠 **Hilton Park.** Standing majestically at the center of 500 acres of parkland, lakes, and woods, the colonnaded facade of this ancestral home makes a lasting impression on visitors. Johnny and Lucy Madden are the eighth generation of the family to live here, and their house is furnished with family heirlooms (including an Erard concert grand piano which Chopin reputedly played). Bedrooms—some with four-poster beds—have beautiful views of the lakes and parkland. Dinners (for guests only) are prepared from organic vegetables from the garden, fish from the lakes, and local produce. Guests can play free of charge on Clones Golf Club, which forms part of the estate. To find Hilton Park, look for large black gates adorned with silver falcons 5 km (3 mi) outside Clones on the R183 Ballyhaise road. ⊠ *Co. Monaghan* ☎ *047/56007* 🖷 *047/56033* ⊕ *www. hiltonpark.ie* 🛏 *6 rooms* ⚭ *Dining room, 18-hole golf course, lake, boat-*

ing, fishing, croquet; no a/c, no room phones, no room TVs, no kids under 8, no smoking ⊟ *MC, V* ⊘ *Closed Oct.–Mar.* ⫮⊙⫮ *BP.*

THE WESTERN MIDLANDS

This section covers the area's western fringe, picking up in the town of Boyle in County Roscommon. It skirts Lough Key, Lough Ree, Lough Derg, and the River Shannon. Depending on how you travel south, you may journey through the hilly landscape of County Leitrim, dappled with lakes and beloved of anglers for its fish-filled waters. This region is almost uninhabited (though it has a light sprinkling of villages and is the home of one of Ireland's leading writers, John McGahern). Much of the land is bog. The towns are small and undistinguished, except Birr and Strokestown, both designed to complement the "big houses" that share their names. The historic highlight in this region is the ancient site of Clonmacnoise, an important monastery of early Christian Ireland. The route then takes you southward, to northern County Tipperary.

Boyle

🄔 *190 km (118 mi) northwest of Dublin.*

An old-fashioned town on the Boyle River midway between Lough Gara and Lough Key, Boyle makes a good starting point for visits to the nearby Curlew Mountains. **King House,** a massive edifice in the center of town, was built about 1730 by the King family, which moved 50 years later to larger quarters at Rockingham in what is now Lough Key Forest Park; that house burned down in 1957. The King family came from Staffordshire, England, and aggressively worked to establish themselves as local nobility. Edward King, an ancestor of the Kings who settled here, drowned in the Irish Sea in 1636; he was the subject of Milton's poem "Lycidas." From 1788 to 1922 the house was used as a barracks for the Connaught Rangers, known as the fiercest regiment of the British Army (Wellington called them the "Devil's Own"), notorious for their savagery in putting down the Irish. After extensive renovations, the house is now open to the public, with exhibits on the Connaught Rangers and the Kings of Connaught, many done with waxwork figures in full period costume. A coffee shop serves traditional Irish breakfasts and hearty lunches, both with plenty of homemade baked goods on the menu. ☎ *071/966–3242* ⊕ *www.roscommoncoco.ie/kinghouse.htm* ⊠ *€4* ⊘ *Apr.–mid-Oct., daily 10–6 (last tour at 5).*

The ruins of the **Cistercian abbey** reflect its long history. The church was founded in the late 12th century, when the Romanesque style still prevailed, but as construction went on, the Gothic style arrived in Ireland, evident in the arches on the north side. A 17th-century gatehouse, through which you enter the abbey, has a small exhibition. ⊠ *On N4* ☎ *071/966–2604* ⊠ *Free* ⊘ *Apr.–Oct., daily 9:30–6:30.*

Where to Stay

$ ⫼⫮ **Royal Hotel.** The Royal's 250-year history of serving the town means it is a veritable local institution. The chief reason to stay here, apart from good angling nearby, is to experience the slower pace of life of an old-fashioned Irish small town. Rooms vary in shape and size and are plainly but adequately furnished and well equipped. The restaurant overlooks a pretty stretch of river and serves both Chinese and Continental food. ⊠ *Bridge St., Co. Roscommon* ☏ *071/966–2016* 🖷 *079/ 62016* 🖘 *16 rooms* ⚒ *Restaurant, coffee shop, in-room data ports, cable TV, bar; no a/c* ⊟ *AE, DC, MC, V* ❍⫯ *BP.*

The Outdoors

Boyle is a good starting point for bicycling over the lake-dotted landscape that extends north into neighboring County Leitrim and west into County Sligo. The 40-km (25-mi) scenic Arigna Drive from Boyle to Cootehall winds through unspoiled countryside on the shores of Lough Key and Lough Arrow on narrow, quiet roads that are ideal for cycling. **Brendan Sheerin** (⊠ Main St. ☏ 079/62010) rents bicycles.

Strokestown

⓯ *28 km (17 mi) south of Boyle.*

Strokestown has the widest main street in Ireland—laid out to rival the Ringstrasse in Vienna—and the curious, Anglo-Irish Strokestown Park House. The town's main street leads to three Gothic arches that mark ★ the entrance to the grounds of the vast **Strokestown Park House**, occupied by the Pakenham Mahon family from 1660 to 1979. The house once sat on 27,000 acres and was the second-largest estate in County Roscommon, after the King family's Rockingham. To some degree, the complicated architectural history mirrors the histories of other Anglo-Irish houses. The oldest parts of the house date from 1696; Palladian wings were added in the 1730s to the original block; and the house was extended again in the early 19th century. Its contents are a rich trove specific to the site, as they were never liquidated in the auctions that plagued so many other stately houses. The interior is full of curiosities, such as the gallery above the kitchen, which allowed the lady of the house to supervise domestic affairs from a safe distance. Menus were dropped from the balcony on Monday mornings with instructions to the cook for the week's meals. The 4-acre walled pleasure garden has the longest herbaceous border in Britain and Ireland. The **Irish Famine Museum,** in the stable yards, documents in detail the disastrous famine (1845–49) and the subsequent mass emigration. ☏ *071/963–3013* ⊕ *www. strokestownpark.ie* 🖾 *House €5; house, museum, and garden €12* ☉ *Apr.–Oct., daily 9:30–5:30; Nov.–Mar., groups by appointment.*

Roscommon

⓰ *19 km (12 mi) south of Strokestown.*

Sheep- and cattle-raising are the main occupations here in the capital of County Roscommon, a pleasant little town with many solid stone buildings, including the Bank of Ireland, in the former courthouse. The former county jail, a large stone building in the town center, has been transformed into a shopping mall—an unlikely venture that has to be seen to be believed. On the southern slopes of a hill in the lower part of town sit the remains of **Roscommon Abbey,** founded in the 12th century. In the abbey's principal ruin, a church, are eight sculpted figures that represent gallowglasses (medieval Irish professional soldiers) and stand at the base of the choir. The ruins are freely accessible. To the north of Roscommon town are the weathered remains of **Roscommon Castle,** a large Norman stronghold first built in the 13th century.

Where to Stay

$ **Castlecoote House.** A colorful history attends this grand house which stands in the crook of a bend in the River Suck. It was built in the 17th century on the remains of a medieval castle, then won in a poker game by the Gunning family, and partially gutted in a fire during the 1980s. Owner Kevin Finnerty has meticulously restored the house to its authentic Georgian splendor and installed under-floor heating (a luxury previous owners never dreamt of as they huddled round the hearth for warmth). The bedrooms are luxurious, with four-poster beds, while the main salon— all crystal chandeliers, pale emerald walls, and white trimmed doorways— is pure elegance in the 18th-century Irish fashion. Dinner must be booked by noon. To get there, drive 5 km (3 mi) on the R366 from Roscommon to Castlecoote. The limestone entrance gate, which is unmarked, is next to Castlecoote Stores. ⊠ *Castlecoote, County Roscommon* ☎ *01/853–3680* 🖷 *01/833–0666* ⊕ *www.castlecootehouse.com* 🛏 *5 rooms* ⚂ *Tennis, croquet, fishing; no a/c, no room phones, no room TVs, no kids under 12, no smoking* ▭ *MC, V* ❶ *BP.*

Athlone

17 *29 km (18 mi) southeast of Roscommon, 127 km (79 mi) west of Dublin, 121 km (75 mi) east of Limerick.*

The mighty Shannon flows majestically through the heart of Athlone, yet for years it seemed as if the town was happy to turn its back on one of Europe's great waterways. That trend has now been well and truly reversed and with it has come a real buzz of regeneration. The area around Athlone Castle has transformed into a veritable "Left Bank" and on both sides of the Shannon, new restaurants and stylishly modern buildings are beginning to spring up along streets lined with 200-year-old buildings. Once upon a time, tourists were few and far between in what was cuttingly termed the "dead center" of Ireland—but this renaissance has made Athlone an increasingly attractive destination. Beside the River Shannon, at the southern end of Lough Ree, stands **Athlone Castle,** built in the 13th century. After their defeat at the Battle of the Boyne in 1691, the Irish retreated to Athlone and made the river their first line of defense. The castle, a fine example of a Norman stronghold, houses a small museum of artifacts relating to Athlone's eventful past. Admission includes access to an interpretive center depicting the siege of Athlone in 1691, the flora and fauna of the Shannon, and the life of the tenor John McCormack (1884–1945), an Athlone native and perhaps the finest lyric tenor Ireland has produced. ⊠ *Town Bridge* ☎ *090/649–2912* 🖆 *€5* ⊙ *May–Sept., daily 10–5; Oct.–Apr. by appointment.*

CloseUp

GOLDSMITH COUNTRY

ALL THAT GLITTERS *may not be Goldsmith but that hasn't prevented the Irish tourist board from promoting the Northern Lakelands to the burgeoning literary tourism market as "Goldsmith Country." Yes, this is the region that gave birth to the writer Oliver Goldsmith (1730–44), celebrated for his farcical drama* She Stoops to Conquer *and his classic novel* The Vicar of Wakefield. *Goldsmith, however, left his homeland as a teenager and returned rarely. He is thought to have drawn on memories of his native Longford for his most renowned poem, "The Deserted Village." At Goldsmith's childhood home in Lissoy in County Longford, only the bare walls of the family house, remain standing. At Pallas, near Ballymahon in County Longford, his birthplace, there's a statue in his memory but little else. The plot of* She Stoops to Conquer *involves a misunderstanding in which a traveler mistakes a private house for an inn. This actually happened to Goldsmith at Ardagh House, now a college, in the center of the village of Ardagh (just off N55) in County Longford. In the same play the character Tony Lumpkin sings a song about a pub called the Three Jolly Pigeons; today the pub of the same name, on the Ballymahon road (N55) north of Athlone, is the headquarters of the Oliver Goldsmith Summer School. Every year on the first weekend in June, leading academics from around the world speak on Goldsmith at this pub and other venues, and there are readings by the best of Ireland's contemporary poets and evening traditional-music sessions in this tiny, atmospheric, traditional country pub. Call 0902/85162 for more information.*

Where to Stay & Eat

$$–$$$ ✕ **Le Château.** A former Presbyterian church in Athlone's colorful Old Quarter now houses this romantic restaurant. The furniture may be ecclesiastical, but the decoration strikes a nautical note appropriate to the quayside location. The raised floors of the upstairs section resemble the deck of a galleon; the church theme is present in the original windows. Candlelighted tables are set with fine old bone china. Owner/chef Stephen Linehan's menu may include medallions of veal with smoked bacon and garlic or roast peppered monkfish with fresh herb sauce. For dessert try the lemon tart or, in summer, fresh strawberry vol-au-vents with homemade ice cream. ⊠ *St. Peter's Port, The Docks* ☎ *090/649–4517* ▭ *AE, DC, MC, V.*

★ **$$$–$$$$** ✕▣ **Wineport Lodge.** Once a wooden boathouse and current headquarters of Lough Ree Yacht Club, this lakeside restaurant-with-rooms is now billed as Ireland's first "wine hotel." Stylishly modern—all orange cedarwood and plate-glass window—and set against parkland groves of trees, the striking light-filled wood-and-glass building seems like it was airlifted from Sweden. Inside, guests make a beeline to the restaurant, where chef Feargal O'Donnell draws praise for his imaginative cooking and the way he matches food to the extensive wine menu. Mouthwatering offerings like maple roast chicken with cumin-spiced couscous or mustard-crusted rack of lamb with wild mushroom ratatouille are standard fare, but bar food ($) is also available from 4 PM to 6 PM. The guest rooms are minimalist but filled with stylish touches like leopard-skin prints. Once you've wined and dined, treat yourself to one of the alluring spa treatments Bliss Dublin provides to guests. Glasson lies 5 km (3 mi) north of Athlone on the shores of Lough Ree. ⊠ *Glasson, Co. Westmeath* ☎ *090/648–5466* 🖷 *090/648–5471* ⊕ *www. wineport.ie* ⇆ *10 rooms* ⚬ *Restaurant, minibars, in-room data ports, fishing, bar* �: *AE, DC, MC, V* ⏺⏻ *BP.*

★ **$$–$$$$** ✕🏠 **Hodson Bay Hotel.** A grand vision standing on the shores of Lough Ree, this four-story mansion—once an 18th-century family home—has its own marina and is adjacent to Athlone's golf course. All guest rooms are coordinated in deep pastel shades with art deco–style wooden furniture. The hotel has babysitting facilities and in summer it runs a kid's camp on the hotel grounds. Basic meals are served all day in the Waterfront bar; the romantic, candlelighted tables of L'Escale restaurant ($$–$$$) overlook the lake. To get to the hotel from Athlone (the hotel is 4 km [2½ mi] outside of town), take the Athlone bypass–ring road to the N61 Roscommon road, from which the hotel is clearly signposted. ⊠ *Roscommon Rd., Co. Westmeath* ☎ *090/648–0500* 🖷 *090/648–0520* ⊕ *www.hodsonbayhotel.com* ⇆ *133 rooms, 7 suites* ⚬ *2 restaurants, cable TV, 18-hole golf course, 2 tennis courts, indoor pool, health club, massage, fishing, horseback riding, bar, meeting rooms; no a/c* �: *AE, DC, MC, V* ⏺⏻ *BP.*

Sports & the Outdoors

BICYCLING A combination of unfrequented back roads and lakeside scenery makes this attractive biking country. Rent bikes from **M. R. Hardiman** (⊠ Irishtown ☎ 090/647–8669).

BOATING A boat trip reveals the importance of Athlone's strategic location on the River Shannon as well as the beauty of the region. *The Viking* (⊠ The Strand ☎ 090/647–9277) is a riverboat that travels up the Shannon to nearby Lough Ree. The cost is €6.35; sailings take place daily from July through September at 11, 2:30, and 4. A river cruiser for a floating holiday can be rented by the week from **Athlone Cruisers Ltd** (⊠ Jolly Mariner Marina ☎ 090/647–2892).

GOLF **Athlone Golf Club** (⊠ Hodson Bay ☎ 090/649–2073) is a lakeside 18-hole parkland course. **Glasson Golf & Country Club** (⊠ Glasson ☎ 0902/85120), an 18-hole parkland course, is bordered on three sides by Lough Ree and the River Shannon. **Mount Temple Golf Club** (⊠ Campfield Lodge, Moate ☎ 090/648–1545) is an 18-hole parkland course 8 km (5 mi) east of Athlone.

Clonmacnoise

★ ⓲ 20 km (12 mi) south of Athlone, 93 km (58 mi) east of Galway.

Many ancient sites dot the River Shannon, but Clonmacnoise is early Christian Ireland's foremost monastic settlement and, like Chartres, a royal site. The monastery was founded by St. Ciaran between 543 and

549 at a location that was not as remote as it now appears to be: near the intersection of what were then two of Ireland's most vital routes—the Shannon River, running north–south, and the Eiscir Riada, running east–west. Like Glendalough, Celtic Ireland's other great monastic site, Clonmacnoise benefited from its isolation; surrounded by bog, it is accessible only via one road or via the Shannon. Thanks to this location, it almost survived everything thrown at it, including raids by feuding Irish tribes, Vikings, and Normans. But when the English garrison arrived from Athlone in 1552, they ruthlessly reduced the site to ruin. Still, with a little imagination, you can picture life here in medieval times, when the nobles of Europe sent their sons to be educated by the local monks.

The monastery was founded on an esker (natural gravel ridge) overlooking the Shannon and a marshy area known as the Callows, which today is protected habitat for the corncrake, a wading bird. Numerous buildings and ruins remain. The small **cathedral** dates as far back as the 10th century but has additions from the 15th century. It was the burial place of kings of Connaught and of Tara, and of Rory O'Conor, the last high king of Ireland, buried here in 1198. The two round towers include **O'Rourke's Tower,** which was struck by lightning and subsequently rebuilt in the 12th century. There are eight **smaller churches,** the littlest of which is thought to be the burial place of St. Ciaran. The only church of this group not built within the monastery walls is Nun's Church, about 1 km (½ mi) to the east. The high crosses have been moved into the visitor center to protect them from the elements (copies stand in their original places); the best preserved of these is the Cross of the Scriptures, also known as Flann's Cross. Some of the treasures and manuscripts originating from Clonmacnoise are now housed in Dublin; most are at the National Museum, although the 12th-century *Book of the Dun Cow* is at the Royal Irish Academy Library.

Clonmacnoise has always been a prestigious burial place. Among the ancient stones are many other graves dating from the 17th to the mid-20th century, when a new graveyard was consecrated on adjoining land. The whole place is time-burnished, though in mid-summer it can be difficult to avoid the throngs of tourists. ☒ *Near Shannonbridge* ☎ *090/ 967–4195* ⊕ *www.heritageireland.ie* ☑ *€5* ☉ *Nov.–mid Mar., daily 10–5:30; mid-Mar.–mid-May, daily 10–6; mid-May–early Sept., daily 9–7; mid-Sept.–Oct. daily 10–6. Last admission 45 mins. before closing.*

Banagher

⑲ *31 km (19 mi) south of Clonmacnoise.*

A small but lively village on the shores of the River Shannon, Banagher has a marina that makes the town a popular base for water-sports enthusiasts. Anthony Trollope (1815–82), who came to Ireland as a post office surveyor in 1841, lived here while he wrote his first book, *The Macdermots of Ballycloran.* Charlotte Brontë (1816–55) spent her honeymoon here. **Flynn's** (☒ Main St. ☎ 0509/51312), in the center of town, is worth visiting to appreciate its light and spacious Victorian-style design. The lunch menu includes generously filled sandwiches, salad platters, a roast meat of the day, and chicken, fish, or burgers with chips.

BORD NA MÓNA BOG RAIL TOUR

FROM A DISTANCE, *an Irish peat bog looks like a flat, treeless piece of waterlogged land. But a close-up view shows a much more exciting landscape.*

Bogs support an extraordinary amount of wildlife, including larks and snipe, pale-blue dragonflies, and Greenland white-fronted geese. Amid the pools and lakes of the peat bog, amazing jewel-like wildflowers thrive, from purple bell heather to yellow bog asphodel, all alongside grasses, lichens, and mosses.

As you pass through the small town of Shannonbridge, 10 km (6 mi) south of Clonmacnoise, on either side of the road are vast stretches of chocolate-brown boglands and isolated industrial plants for processing the area's natural resource.

Bord na Mona, the same government agency that makes commercial use of other boglands, has jurisdiction over the area.

To take a closer look at the bog, join the **Bord na Móna Bog Rail Tour** *(⊠ Near Shannonbridge, Uisce Dubh ☎ 0905/ 74114 ⊕ www.bnm.ie ⊠ €5.50 ⊙ Tour Apr.–Oct., daily 10–5 on the hr) which leaves from Uisce Dubh.*

A small, green-and-yellow diesel locomotive pulls one coach across the bog while the driver provides commentary on a landscape unchanged for millennia.

There are more than 1,200 km (745 mi) of narrow-gauge bog railway, and the section on the tour, known as the Clonmacnoise and South Offaly Railway, is the only part accessible to the public.

If you happen to be in Banagher on a Thursday or a Sunday in summer, consider taking a two-hour **Shannon cruise** on *The River Queen,* an enclosed launch that seats 54 passengers and has a full bar on board. *Silver Line Cruisers Ltd.* ⊠ *The Marina* ☎ *0509/51112* ⊠ *€9* ⊙ *Cruises June–mid-Sept., Thurs. at 3, Sun. at 2:30 and 4:30, weather permitting.*

Paddling a canoe is a nice alternative to a river cruise. **Shannon Adventure Canoeing and Camping Holidays** rents Canadian-class canoes which allow you to explore the Shannon and other waterways on your own terms. ⊠ *The Marina* ☎ *0509/51411* ⊕ *www.iol.ie/~advcanoe/index. html* ⊙ *May–Oct.*

Birr

▶ **⑳**   *12 km (7 mi) southeast of Banagher, 130 km (81 mi) west of Dublin.*

This heritage town is a quiet, sleepy place with tree-lined malls and modest Georgian houses. The settlement's roots go back to the 6th century, but it wasn't until the mid-18th century, when a Georgian building boom took hold, that Birr was given its modern-day appearance.

Fodor'sChoice   All roads in Birr lead to the gates of **Birr Castle Demesne,** a gorgeous Gothic
★   Revival castle (built around an earlier 17th-century castle that was

damaged by fire in 1823) that is still the home of the earls of Rosse. It's not open to the common man, but you can visit the surrounding 150 acres of gardens. The present earl and countess of Rosse continue the family tradition of making botanical expeditions all over the world for specimens of rare trees, plants, and shrubs. The formal gardens contain the tallest (32 feet) box hedges in the world and vine-sheltered hornbeam allées. In spring, check out the wonderful display of flowering magnolias, cherries, crab apples, and naturalized narcissi; in autumn, the maples, chestnuts, and weeping beeches blaze red and gold. The grounds are laid out around a lake and along the banks of two adjacent rivers; above one of these stands the castle. The grounds also contain **Ireland's Historic Science Centre,** an exhibition on astronomy, photography, botany, and engineering housed in the stable block. The giant (72-inch-long) reflecting telescope, built in 1845, remained the largest in the world for 75 years. The recently-opened **National Birds of Prey Centre** is another attraction on the castle grounds. A tour allows you to get up close and personal with eagles, hawks, and other fearsome birds. Falconry experts display this ancient art for visitors. Allow at least two hours to see everything. ⊠ *Rosse Row* ☎ *0509/20336* ⊕ *www.birrcastleireland. com* ▨ *Castle and grounds €8.50, joint admission for Birds of Prey Centre and Castle €12* ⊗ *Nov.–Mar., daily 10–4; Apr.–Oct., daily 9–6.*

Where to Stay & Eat

$–$$ ✕ **The Thatch Bar.** It's worth venturing 2 km (1 mi) south of Birr, just off the N62 Roscrea road, into this thatched country pub and restaurant, which together serve a good selection of imaginative, freshly cooked Irish food. Inexpensive meals are available at the bar at lunchtime and early evening (until 7:30), although in the evening the restaurant offers a choice of a five-course dinner menu or an à la carte menu. Local pigeon and rabbit terrines, sirloin steak with mushrooms in garlic, or roast loin of pork with a rhubarb compote might appear on the menu. ⊠ *Crinkle* ☎ *0509/20682* ▤ *DC, MC, V* ⊗ *Closed Mon. Oct.–Apr. and Sun.–Tues. May–Sept.*

$$$$ ✕▥ **Kinnitty Castle.** Venture over to the foot of the Slieve Bloom Mountains, 16 km (10 mi) east of Birr, to this exuberant, turreted, Gothic Revival edifice, rebuilt in 1927 of ashlar granite. Everything is on a grand scale—large four-poster beds and intricately carved chairs fill the bedrooms, and heavy old beams are incorporated into the bathrooms in the old house. Accommodations in the new wing are smaller. The dining room has enormously tall windows and a dark wood floor. Typical main courses are panfried loin of lamb with its own sweetbreads or ragout of lobster, finished with sevruga caviar. ⊠ *Kinnitty, Co. Offaly* ☎ *0509/ 37318* ▤ *0509/37284* ⊕ *www.kinnittycastle.com* ↩ *37 rooms* ♿ *Restaurant, tennis court, fishing, horseback riding, bar, meeting rooms; no a/c, no room TVs* ▤ *AE, DC, MC, V* ⦿ *BP.*

$ ✕▥ **Dooly's.** There are no pretensions about this friendly country hotel which has retained a charmingly old-style atmosphere. Floral patterns, open fires, and a relaxed welcome all form part of the decor. It's located in Birr's central square, and just a five-minute walk from the castle. The bustling bar and coffee shop are popular with locals. For a more formal dining experience you could try the Emmet Restaurant ($–$$), where fish dishes like baked sea bass in phyllo pastry and honey-glazed cod steak are specialties. ✉ *Emmet Sq., Co. Offaly* ☎ *0509/20032* 🖶 *0509/21332* ⊕ *www.doolyshotel.com* ➲ *18 rooms* ⚲ *Restaurant, coffee shop, cable TV, fishing, horseback riding, bar, meeting rooms; no a/c* ✉ *AE, DC, MC, V* ◎| *BP.*

¢ ✕◫ **The Maltings.** Sheltering beneath the eaves of Birr Castle on a riverbank, this converted stone-cut storehouse is a good option for families and offers special rates for children. The spacious rooms have small windows, country pine furniture, and simple matching floral drapes and spreads. The cheerful, low-ceiling restaurant ($–$$) overlooks the river and serves good value in plain Irish cooking. ✉ *Castle St., Co. Offaly* 🖶🖶 *0509/21345* ➲ *13 rooms* ⚲ *Restaurant; no a/c* ✉ *MC, V* ◎| *BP.*

Lough Derg

㉑ *16 km (10 mi) west of Birr on R489.*

Between Portland and Portumna, the River Shannon widens into 32,000 acres of unpolluted water, known as Lough Derg, a popular center for water sports, including water-skiing, yachting, and motor-cruising. Anglers flock here as well for pike and coarse fishing. Excellent woodland walks wind around the shore of the lake. (Be sure not to confuse this Lough Derg with the lake of the same name in County Donegal.) The well-signposted, scenic **Lough Derg Drive**, approximately 90 km-long (56 mi), encircles the lake, passing through a number of pretty waterside villages, from Portumna in the north to Killaloe in the south. **Terryglass**, on the eastern shore of Lough Derg and well signposted on R439 from Birr, is particularly popular with water-sports enthusiasts and anglers, as well as regular vacationers seeking an away-from-it-all destination; replete with grand church, tree-tunnel street, and cute cottages, it is considered one of the prettiest villages in Ireland.

Where to Stay

$ ◫ **Kylenoe.** Virginia Moeran is famed for breeding racehorses, including top stallion Vinnie Roe (the only horse ever to win the Irish St. Leger three times in a row), owned by Irish movie director Jim Sheridan. But she and her family also find time to welcome guests to their 200-year-old stone house, which stands on 150 acres of farm and woodland close to Lough Derg. Relax in front of the log fire, explore the countryside on foot or horseback, or enjoy water sports. Rooms are spacious, with modest antique furnishings and family heirlooms. Children are welcome. Virginia Moeran's breakfasts have won awards, and she also cooks dinner (for guests only), which must be booked by 2:30 PM, from fresh local produce. To get here follow the lakeside road from Terryglass in the Ballinderry direction. ✉ *Nenagh, Terryglass, Co. Tipperary* ☎ *067/22015* 🖶 *067/22275* ➲ *4 rooms, 2 with bath* ⚲ *Dining room, some pets allowed; no a/c, no room phones, no smoking* ✉ *MC, V* ◎| *BP.*

Sports & the Outdoors

BOATING **Shannon Sailing** (✉ New Marina Complex, Dromineer ☎ 067/24499) organizes cruises of scenic Lough Derg by water bus and also hires out cruisers and sailboards. **Lough Derg Powerboat School** (✉ Sallybay House,

Ballina ☎ 061/375–474 ⊕ www.boatschool.ie) runs powerboat and motor-cruiser training courses. Courses vary in length from half a day to four days.

GOLF   Discerning golfers love the 18-hole parkland course at **Birr Golf Club.** (✉ The Glens ☎ 0509/20082). It's one of the best parkland courses in the country. Even though it is miles from the sea, the undulating fairways and dry sod make it reminiscent of a links course.

HIKING   Birr is in the heart of an excellent hiking area. The Offaly Way and the Grand Canal Way are marked trails to the north of town; to the east is the 50-km (31-mi) Slieve Bloom Trail, a circular route that winds through some infrequently visited areas with spectacular views and rich plant and wildlife. Pick up brochures and maps locally, or consult the expert, **Christine Byrne** (✉ Ardmore House, Kinnitty ☎ 0509/37009 ⊕ www.kinnitty.net), who organizes guided walks for all levels.

Roscrea

❷ *19 km (12 mi) south of Birr.*

Every corner you turn in this charming town will offer reminders of its rich and sometimes turbulent past. Ancient castles, towers, and churches dot the town's skyline, proof of a heritage that goes back to the 7th century. Roscrea is on the main N7 road between Dublin and Cork, making it ideal as a stopover en route to the south. The road cuts right through the remains of a monastery founded by St. Cronan. It also passes the west facade of a 12th-century Romanesque church that now forms an entrance gate to a modern Catholic church. Above the structure's round-headed doorway is a hood molding enclosing the figure of a bishop, probably St. Cronan. In the very center of town is **Roscrea Castle,** a Norman fortress dating from 1314, given by King Richard II to the duke of Ormond. Inside are vaulted rooms graced with tapestries and 16th-century furniture. A ticket to it also gains entry to the adjacent **Damer House,** a superb example of an early-18th-century town house on the grand scale. It was built in 1725 within the curtain walls of the castle, at a time when homes were often constructed beside or attached to the strongholds they replaced. The house has a plain, symmetrical facade and a magnificent carved-pine staircase inside; on display are exhibits about local history. To get here, start with your back to St. Cronan's monastery, turn left, and then right onto Castle Street. ✉ *Castle St.* ☎ *0505/21850* ⊕ *www. heritageireland.ie* 🎫 *€3.10* ☉ *May–Sept., daily 9:30–6; Oct.–Apr., weekends 10–5.*

Sports & the Outdoors

Three marked trails—measuring 9 km (5½ mi), 3 km (2 mi), and 1½ km (1 mi)—run through the 450-acre, organic **Fairymount Farm** (✉ Ballingarry ☎ 067/2139 ⊕ www.fairymountfarm.com), with woodlands, horses, and sheep. Points of interest are explained in a booklet you can pick up here. The trails can also be followed on horseback (the farm's rangers can help you arrange this), and you can fish for pike or perch in the farm's 25-acre lake. Access to the farm costs €5.

Nenagh

㉓ *35 km (22 mi) west of Roscrea, 35 km (22 mi) east of Limerick.*

Originally a Norman settlement, Nenagh grew into a market town in the 19th century. Standing right in the center of Nenagh, the **Castle Keep** is all that remains of the original town. Once one of five round towers linked by a curtain wall, and measuring 53 feet across the base, it rises to 100 feet, with 19th-century crenellations at the top. The gatehouse and governor's house of Nenagh's old county jail now form the **Nenagh Heritage Centre,** which has permanent displays of rural life before mechanization, as well as temporary painting and photography exhibits. ⊠ *Kickham St.* ☎ *067/44587* ⌨ *€3* ☽ *Easter–Oct., weekdays 9:30–5, Sun. 2:30–5; Nov.–Easter, weekdays 9:30–5.*

Where to Stay & Eat

\$ ✕ **Country Choice.** Food lovers from all over Ireland seek out this well-stocked delicatessen or come to sample the home-cooked fare in the simple coffee shop at the back of the store. Owner Peter Ward is an expert on Irish cheeses, and local varieties like Baylough farmhouse cheddar are particularly popular with customers. Other specialties include a soup of broccoli and Cashel Blue (an Irish blue cheese), as well as slow-cooked meat dishes like lamb ragout or beef in Guinness casserole. Home-baked bread and pastries are made with local flour. ⊠ *25 Kenyon St.* ☎ *067/32596* ▭ *No credit cards* ☽ *Closed Sun. No dinner.*

\$\$ ✕▣ **Waterman's Lodge.** Escape to this rural lodge, whose quiet setting overlooking the Shannon makes it a perfect hideaway for stressed-out city types. Open fires, piles of books, high ceilings, and timber floors create a relaxing country-house mood. Rooms have brass or cast-iron beds and modest antiques. The Courtyard Restaurant is renowned for its imaginative treatment of seasonal local produce. Try the roast rack of lamb with a parsley crust and lamb jus. ⊠ *26 km (16 mi) north of Nenagh, Ballina, Killaloe, Co. Clare* ☎ *061/376–333* ▤ *061/375–445* ⊕ *www.watermanslodge.ie* ⤴ *10 rooms* ♻ *Restaurant, in-room data ports, fishing, horseback riding; no a/c* ▭ *AE, DC, MC, V* ☽ *Closed Christmas wk* ¶ *BP.*

\$ ▣ **Ashley Park House.** The plantation–style verandas which adorn the front of this distinctly Irish Georgian home lend an intriguing and eccentric feel to this enchanting place. This tone is echoed by the charmingly offbeat welcome extended to guests by manager Sean Mounsey. This genial tweed-clad gent will want to show you every antique-crammed nook of the building and to recount its history—if you have time. The house has a walled garden, with extensive woodland walks, and overlooks Lough Ourna, a small lake bristling with ducks, herons, and other wildlife. You can borrow a rowboat if you wish to get closer to the birds. Dinners created from fresh local produce may include the trout you'll hopefully catch in the lake. Book early for one of the large rooms with lake views. ⊠ *Ardcroney, Co. Tipperary* ☎▤ *067/38223* ⤴ *5 rooms* ♻ *Boating, fishing, some pets allowed; no a/c, no room phones, no TV in some rooms* ▭ *No credit cards* ¶ *BP.*

THE MIDLANDS A TO Z

To research prices, get advice from other travelers, and book travel arrangements, visit www.fodors.com.

AIRPORTS

Dublin Airport is the principal international airport that serves the Midlands; car-rental facilities are available here. Sligo Airport has daily flights from Dublin on Aer Lingus.

🖪 Airport Information **Aer Lingus** ☎ 01/844-4747. **Dublin Airport** ☎ 01/844-4900. **Sligo Airport** ☎ 071/68280.

BUS TRAVEL

Bus Éireann runs an express bus from Dublin to Mullingar in 1½ hours, with a round-trip fare of €12.05. Buses depart three times daily. A regular-speed bus, leaving twice daily, makes the trip in two hours. Express buses also make stops at Longford (2¼ hours), Carrick-on-Shannon (3 hours), Boyle (3¼ hours), and Sligo (4¼ hours). There's also a daily bus from Mullingar to Athlone and an express service connecting Galway, Athlone, Longford, Cavan, Clones, Monaghan, and Sligo. Details of all bus services are available from the Bus Éireann depots listed below.

🖪 Bus Information **Athlone Railway Station** ☎ 0902/72651. **Bus Éireann** ☎ 01/836-6111 in Dublin ⊕ www.buseireann.ie. **Cavan Bus Office** ☎ 049/433-1353. **Longford Railway Station** ☎ 043/45208. **Monaghan Bus Office** ☎ 047/82377. **Sligo Railway Station** ☎ 071/69888.

CAR RENTAL

🖪 Agencies **Gerry Mullin** ⊠ North Rd., Monaghan ☎ 047/81396. **Hamill's Rent-a-Car** ⊠ Dublin Rd., Mullingar ☎ 044/44500. **O'Reilly & Sons/Euromobil** ⊠ Dublin Rd., Longford ☎ 043/46496.

CAR TRAVEL

A car is necessary to really explore the region. Mullingar, Longford, and Boyle are on the main N4 route between Dublin and Sligo. It takes one hour to drive the 55 km (34 mi) from Dublin to Mullingar and two hours from Mullingar to Sligo (150 km [93 mi]). To get from Mullingar to southwestern Ireland, you can take N52 to Nenagh, where it meets N7, and follow that into Limerick. R390 from Mullingar leads you west to Athlone, where it connects with N6 to Galway. The 120-km (75-mi) drive takes about 2½ hours.

If you're driving in the north of Counties Cavan and Monaghan, be sure to avoid "unapproved" roads crossing the border into Northern Ireland. The approved routes into Northern Ireland connect the towns of Monaghan and Aughnacloy, Castlefinn and Castlederg, Swalinbar and Enniskillen, Clones and Newtownbutler, and Monaghan and Rosslea. If you're driving a rental car, make sure it has been cleared for cross-border journeys.

ROAD
CONDITIONS
Most of the winding roads in the Midlands are uncongested, although you may encounter an occasional animal or agricultural machine cross-

ing the road. In Mullingar, the cattle-trading town, roads can become badly crowded.

EMERGENCIES

The general emergency number in the area is 999. For medical service, contact the General Hospital in Mullingar.

🔲 Emergency services **Ambulance, fire, police** ☎ 999. **General Hospital** ✉ Mullingar ☎ 044/40221.

🔲 Pharmacy **Weir's Chemist** ✉ Market Sq., Mullingar ☎ 044/48462.

TRAIN TRAVEL

A direct-rail service links Mullingar to Dublin (Connolly Station), with three trains every day making the 1½-hour journey. It costs €13 one-way and €18.50 round-trip. Contact Irish Rail for information. Trains from Mullingar, departing twice daily weekdays and Sunday, stop at Longford (35 minutes), Carrick-on-Shannon (1 hour), Boyle (1¼ hours), and Sligo (2 hours).

🔲 Train Information **Irish Rail** ☎ 01/836-6222 ⊕ www.irishrail.ie.

VISITOR INFORMATION

Five Midlands Tourist Information Offices (TIOs) are open all year: Carrick-on-Shannon, Cavan, Monaghan, Mullingar, and Portlaoise. The Mullingar TIO has information on Counties Westmeath, Offaly, Monaghan, Cavan, and Laois. Another six Midlands TIOs are open seasonally: Athlone (April–October), Birr (May–September), Clonmacnoise (April–October), Longford (June–September), Tipperary (May–October), and Tullamore (mid-June–mid-September). For inquiries about Boyle and Roscommon, consult the Sligo TIO. For off-season inquiries about Tipperary, contact the Waterford City TIO.

🔲 Tourist Information **Athlone** ✉ Church St., Co. Westmeath ☎ 0902/94630. **Birr** ✉ Rosse Row, Co. Offaly ☎ 0509/20110. **Carrick-on-Shannon** ✉ The Marina, Co. Leitrim ☎ 078/20170. **Cavan** ✉ Farnham St., Co. Cavan ☎ 049/433-1942 ⊕ www.irelandnorthwest.travel.ie. **Clonmacnoise** ✉ near Clonmacnoise ruins, Co. Offaly ☎ 0905/74134. **Longford** ✉ Main St., Co. Longford ☎ 043/46566. **Monaghan** ✉ Market House, Co. Monaghan ☎ 047/81122 ⊕ www.irelandnorthwest.travel.ie. **Mullingar** ✉ Dublin Rd., Co. Westmeath ☎ 044/48650 🖶 044/40413 ⊕ www.ecoast-midlands.travel.ie. **Portlaoise** ✉ James Fintan Lawlor Ave., Co. Laois ☎ 0502/63989 ⊕ www.laoistourism.ie. **Sligo Town TIO** ✉ Temple and Charles Sts., Co. Sligo ☎ 071/61201 ⊕ www.irelandnorthwest.ie. **Tipperary** ✉ Excel Centre, Co. Tipperary ☎ 062/51457. **Tullamore** ✉ Bury Quay, Co. Offaly ☎ 0506/52617. **Waterford City TIO** ✉ 41 The Quay, Co. Waterford ☎ 051/875823 ⊕ www.southeastireland.com.

THE SOUTHEAST

4

Updated by
Tom Swift

THE IRISH LIKE TO PUT LABELS ON AREAS, and "Ireland's Sunny Southeast" is the tag they've applied to Counties Wexford, Carlow, Kilkenny, Tipperary, and Waterford. The moniker is by no means merely fanciful: the weather station on the coast at Rosslare reports that this region receives more hours of sunshine than any other part of the country. The southeast has the driest weather in Ireland, with as little as 40 inches of rainfall per year—compared to an average of 80 inches on parts of the west coast. This is saying something in a country where seldom do more than three days pass without some rain, which can vary from the finest light drizzle (a soft day, thank goodness!) to a full-blown downpour. Little wonder the outdoors-loving Irish have made the southeast's coast a popular vacation destination. The whole area is rich with natural beauty: not the rugged and wild wonders found to the north and west, but an inland landscape of fertile river valleys and lush, undulating pastureland, with a coast that alternates between long, sandy beaches and rocky bays backed by low cliffs. Although the region is blessed with idyllic country sights and charming fishing villages, you'll find you needn't travel far to find the bright lights—the cities of Kilkenny, Waterford, and Wexford.

The landscape of the region is diverse, the appeal universal: whitesand beaches and fishing villages with thatched cottages along the coast, Kilkenny's Georgian cobbled streets and Tudor stone houses, Tipperary's verdant, picturesque Golden Vale. Anglers appreciate the variety of fishing and scenery along the Rivers Barrow, Nore, and Suir, and especially in the Blackwater Valley area. There are plenty of intrinsically Irish things here, one being Waterford's famed handcut crystal. The region doesn't lack for culture, either: fans flock to Wexford for the Opera Festival, which draws top talent from around the world.

The southeast's coastal and inland areas have long, interesting histories. The kings of Munster had their ceremonial center on the Rock of Cashel, a vast, cathedral-topped rock rising above the plain. Legend has it that St. Patrick converted the High King of Ireland to Christianity here. In the 7th century Cashel became an important monastic settlement and bishopric, and there were also thriving early Christian monasteries at Kilkenny, Ardmore, and Lismore. But the quiet life of Christian Ireland was disrupted from the 9th century onward by a series of Viking invasions. The Vikings liked what they found here—a pleasant climate; rich, easily cultivated land; and a series of sheltered harbors— so they stayed and founded the towns of Wexford and Waterford. (Waterford's name comes from the Norse Vadrefjord, Wexford's from Waesfjord.) Less than two centuries later, the same cities were conquered by Anglo-Norman barons and turned into walled strongholds. The Anglo-Normans and the Irish chieftains soon started to intermarry, but the process of integration came to a halt in 1366 with the Statutes of Kilkenny, based on English fears that if such intermingling continued they would lose whatever control over Ireland they had. The next great crisis was Oliver Cromwell's Irish campaign of 1650, which, in attempting to crush Catholic opposition to the English parliament, brought widespread woe.

History-rich Carlow Town, the cities of Kilkenny and Waterford, and Wexford Town have retained traces of their successive waves of invaders—Celt, Viking, and Norman. The most beautiful of these destinations is Kilkenny City, an important ecclesiastic and political center until the 17th century and now a lively market town. Its streets still hold remnants from medieval times—most notably St. Canice's Cathedral—and a magnificent 12th-century castle that received a sumptuous Victorian makeover. Wexford's narrow streets are built on one side of a wide estuary, and it has a delightful maritime air. Waterford, although less immediately attractive than Wexford, is also built at the confluence of two of the region's rivers, the Suir and the Barrow. It offers a rich selection of Viking and Norman remains, some attractive Georgian buildings, and the famed Waterford Glass Factory, which is open to visitors.

Deeper into the countryside, rustic charms beckon. The road between Rosslare and Ballyhack passes through quiet, atypical, flat countryside dotted with thatched cottages. Beyond Tramore, level, sandy beaches give way to rocky Helvick Head and the foothills of the Knockmealdown Mountains at Dungarvan. Among the inland riverside towns, Carrick-on-Suir and Clonmel each have a quiet charm worth exploring. In the far southwest of County Waterford, near the Cork border, Ardmore presents early Christian ruins on an exposed headland, while in the wooded splendor of the Blackwater Valley, the tiny cathedral town of Lismore has a hauntingly beautiful fairy-tale castle.

Exploring the Southeast

The southeast is a large region, stretching from the town of Carlow near the border of County Wicklow in the north to Ardmore near the border of County Cork in the south. A car is not essential for getting around here but it certainly helps: the frequency of public transport can be patchy if you plan on leaving the major towns and cities. Apart from June, July, and August, when the Irish head here for vacations, the region is relatively free of traffic, making it ideal for leisurely exploration. Wexford, Waterford, and Kilkenny have compact town centers best explored on foot, and they make good touring bases.

About the Restaurants & Hotels

This region of Ireland holds some real dining treasures, often in the smallest and most informal places. Seafood—especially Wexford mussels, crab, and locally caught salmon—appears on most menus, along with local lamb, beef, and game in season. Food is usually prepared in a simple, country-house style, but be ready for some pleasant surprises, as there are a number of ambitious Irish chefs at work in the area in both restaurants and hotels. The coast is popular with Irish families during the summer months, so if you are planning to come then, it is advisable to book your hotel room in advance, especially at places right on the water. On the chart below, hotel prices are listed for room rates that include no meals (EP, European Plan) or, if indicated, CP (with Continental break-

4

Numbers in the text correspond to numbers in the margin and on the Southeast, Kilkenny City, Wexford Town, and Waterford City maps.

If you have
3 days

Bewitched by both the Gothic and Victorian styles, 🖼 **Kilkenny City** ④–⑩ ► offers a great start to your southeast express tour. After checking out its Georgian streets and 900-year-old Norman citadel, enjoy your first overnight there, then head west through Urlingford for the medieval drama of the Rock of 🖼 **Cashel** ㊷ and the castle of **Cahir** ㊵. Overnight in Cashel, then spend your third day heading south to the postcard-beautiful village of **Lismore** ㊴, presided over by the duke of Devonshire's great castle and gardens, then end up with dinner in 🖼 **Dungarvan** ㊳ at one of Ireland's best restaurants, The Tannery, and perhaps a sunset over Dungarvan Bay.

If you have
5 days

Start in the north of the region, approaching it through **Carlow Town** ① ►. Cross the River Barrow at **Leighlinbridge** ②, noted for its time-hallowed Lord Bagenal Inn, and drive down to **Graiguenamanagh** ⑫, a hilly riverside village with an abbey. Continue on through **Thomastown** ⑪, a stone-built village on the River Nore that is home to Jerpoint Abbey, to the enchantments of time-stained 🖼 **Kilkenny City** ④–⑩. The second morning you can explore the medieval city center with its castle and cathedral on foot. Drive on through Urlingford to the Rock of Cashel in **Cashel** ㊷. If you continue to 🖼 **Cahir** ㊵ at the foot of the Galtee Mountains, you can visit a Norman castle.

On Day 3, drive up through the scenic Vee Gap and detour to visit Mount Melleray Abbey. Continue to **Lismore** ㊴, which has one of Ireland's prettiest castles. Then head for the coast and the main road south, which leads to 🖼 **Dungarvan** ㊴— a cheerful little fishing town noted for The Tannery restaurant. On the fourth day drive through the pretty market town **Clonmel** ㊸, and follow the River Suir through **Carrick-on-Suir** ㊹—home to the gorgeous Ormonde Castle—to the port of **Waterford City** ㉓–㉟. Head east to the thatched-cottage village of **Ballyhack** ㉔; signposts from here mark the way to the John F. Kennedy Arboretum, which is near the cottage at Dunganstown where the president's great-grandfather was born. Then you can pick up the main road to 🖼 **Wexford Town** ⑯–㉑.

On Day 5, if you are heading north, take the N11 Dublin road via **Enniscorthy** ⑬, a historic town dominated by a Norman castle, then head back north up to Kilkenny. Or, if you are heading south with time to spare, drive the small coastal road through **Kilmore Quay** ㉒, past thatched cottages and narrow lanes, to Ballyhack, where you can take a car ferry across the harbor back to Waterford and the road south.

fast) or BP (Breakfast Plan, with full breakfast). Higher prices prevail for board plans such as MAP (Modified American Plan, with breakfast and dinner); inquire when booking. Assume that all hotel rooms have air-conditioning, in-room phones, TVs, and private bathrooms unless otherwise noted.

WHAT IT COSTS In euros				
	$$$$	**$$$**	**$$**	**$**	**¢**
RESTAURANTS	over €29	€22–€29	€15–€22	€8–€15	under €8
HOTELS	over €230	€180–€230	€130–€180	€80–€130	under €80

Restaurant prices are per person for a main course at dinner; note that if a restaurant offers only prix-fixe meals, it has been given the price category that reflects the full set-price. Hotel prices are for two people in a standard double room in high season, including VAT and a service charge (often applied in larger hotels).

Timing

Off-season is a good time to visit the southeast. Most restaurants and accommodations stay open between November and March, months when many places in the more touristy western regions are closed. Avoid late December through at least mid-January, though, when many restaurateurs take their own holidays, and some lodgings and restaurants use the time to refurbish for the following season. Drier weather in the southeast also makes it a good choice if you're visiting in spring or autumn. Remember that in July and August, the Irish themselves descend on the coastal resorts, so if you plan to head for the beaches of the southeast in summer, be prepared for crowds.

KILKENNY TO WEXFORD

Notably rich in historical and maritime attractions, this region has many sights to help make a visit here memorable. From Carlow Town's small county seat you travel through the farmlands of the Barrow Valley to Kilkenny City, which, from an architectural point of view, is among the most pleasing towns of inland Ireland. Thanks to the country gentry who made their headquarters here in the 18th century, the historic city center of Kilkenny is endowed with fine Georgian town houses. From Thomastown, just outside Kilkenny, another cross-country drive follows the River Nore to New Ross, where it meets the River Barrow and proceeds to John F. Kennedy's ancestral home and the arboretum planted in his memory. You can then journey to the old Viking port of Wexford Town, which hosts a celebrated opera festival that presents rare works in the restored 18th-century Theatre Royal.

Carlow Town

▶ ❶ *83 km (52 mi) south of Dublin on N9.*

Carlow Town was established on the banks of the River Barrow by the Anglo-Normans in the 12th century. Its position on the border of the English Pale—the area around Dublin that was dominated by the English from Elizabethan times onward—made it an important strategic center and hence the scene of many bloody battles and sieges. Today Carlow is a lively market town about an hour and a half by car from central Dublin. The presence of the large Institute of Technology here gives the town a lively buzz. It also has a thriving indigenous arts-and-crafts community. The ruins of the 13th-century **Carlow Castle**, a strate-

Hurling: Fast & Ferocious

Get chatting with the locals in almost any pub across the southeast, mention the sport of hurling, and an enthusiastic and often passionate conversation is bound to ensue. The region is the heartland of this ancient sport whose followers have an almost religious obsession with the game. It's a kind of aerial field hockey with players wielding curved sticks. Its history comes from Ireland's Celtic ancestors, but it bears about the same relation to field hockey as ice hockey does to roller-skating. It is no accident that prowess on the hurling field is regarded as a supreme qualification for election to public office. A man who succeeds at hurling is eminently capable of dealing with anything which fate and the spite of other politicians can throw at him. Hurling is also an extremely skilful sport. A player must have excellent hand-eye coordination combined with an ability to run at high speeds while balancing a small golf-ball-size ball on his camán (hurling stick). Fans will also proudly tell you it's also the world's fastest team sport. Ireland's other chief sporting pastimes, including soccer and hurling's cousin, Gaelic football, take a back seat in this part of the country. Stars like Kilkenny's D. J. Carey, rather than professional soccer players, are sporting icons for local kids. Counties Tipperary, Wexford, and Waterford are among the top teams in the region, but Kilkenny (nicknamed "The Cats") is currently the undisputed top team in the country. It has won three out of the last five All-Ireland hurling championships and is considered the best in the game.

There's an intense rivalry between the counties, especially between old foes Tipperary and Kilkenny. When it gets down to club level, passions run even higher. Almost every parish in the region has a hurling club, and a quick enquiry with locals will usually be enough to find out when the next game is on. Even for the uninitiated, hurling is a great spectator sport. Sporty types wishing to give it a go, be warned; it's fast, furious, and entails more than a hint of danger, as players flail the air to capture the bullet-fast sliotar (hurling ball).

Passion on the High C's

Held in October, the 18-day-long annual Wexford Opera Festival is the biggest social and artistic event not just in the town but in the entire southeast of the country. From mid-September until the final curtain comes down, Wexford becomes home to a colorful cast of international singers, designers, and musicians, as the town prepares for the annual staging of three obscure grand opera productions at the tiny Theatre Royal. The festival has a huge international cachet, and the actual productions are expensive, full-dress affairs. The selection of operas runs toward the recherché, rare, and exotic and the choice is usually the envy of opera maestros around the world. In 2004, the operas presented were Saverio Mercadante's La Vestale (which Verdi had in mind when he created Aida), Josef Bohuslav Foerster's Eva, and Walter Braunfels' Prinzessin Brambilla (whose composer earned Hitler's special enmity). Current prices are €75 a ticket, but the extensive fringe events and concerts are usually around €15, and sometimes far more fun. Best thing about the festival for non-opera buffs, though, is the excitement in the air: Art exhibitions, street music, parades, and window-dressing contests are held every year, and local bars compete in a Singing Pubs competition. Now the bad news: Nearly every single bed within a large radius of Wexford is booked during the festival weeks, and usually for months before the actual event kicks off.

Strongbow's Legacy

The southeast was the location of the most significant turning point in Ireland's recorded history. In 1169 the Normans (who had conquered England a hundred years before) landed at Bannow Bay in County Wexford. It was the beginning of what Irish patriots commonly describe as "800 years of English oppression." The English were invited into Ireland by the former king of Leinster, Dermot MacMurrough, who hoped to regain his crown with the help of the Norman earl, Richard FitzGilbert de Clare, famously known as "Strongbow." To seal their pact, Dermot's daughter Aoife married Strongbow. It was symbolic of the way that the Normans, once they had conquered the country, integrated into Irish life. It wasn't long before the Normans were described as being "more Irish than the Irish themselves."

To this day, reminders of the Norman influence on Ireland remain strongest in the southeast. Norman surnames are the most obvious indicator of the region's history, as names like Butler, Fitzgerald, Roche, and Fitzmaurice are all commonplace hereabouts. The architectural legacy of the Normans is also easy to spot in this part of Ireland. The streetscapes of Kilkenny, Wexford, and Waterford cities owe their origins to the Normans. Travel the rural side roads of the region and it won't be long before you come across the ruins of a Norman castle, or "keep." These vary in size and condition and many are in a semi-collapsed condition due to the common practice of pilfering the stonework to build other houses. Some are used to house animals or hay, while the best preserved are those which were integrated into later medieval or Georgian structures.

gically important fortification on the southeastern corner of the Pale, afford imposing views of the River Barrow. This castle withstood a siege by Cromwell's troops in 1650, only to be destroyed accidentally in 1814 when a Dr. Philip Middleton attempted to renovate the castle for use as a mental asylum. While setting off explosives to reduce the thickness of the walls, he managed to demolish all but the west-side curtain wall and its two flanking towers.

The Gothic-style, Roman Catholic **Cathedral of the Assumption,** completed in 1883, is notable for its stained-glass windows and a magnificently sculpted marble monument of its builder, Bishop James Doyle (1786–1834), a champion of Catholic emancipation. The monument was carved by the Irish sculptor John Hogan (1800–58). ⊠ *College St.* ☎ *059/913–1227* ✉ *Free* ⊙ *Daily 7:30–7:30.*

One of the most poignant sites in Carlow town is the **Croppies Grave** (⊠ 98 St. off Maryborough St.), a small memorial garden where the bodies of 640 United Irishmen—called "Croppies" because they cropped their hair to mark their allegiance to a free, independent Ireland—were buried in a mass grave, following the Battle of Carlow during the 1798 rebellion against English rule. Two of the trees planted by a widowed mother of three young men slain in the battle still stand; the third fell in a storm, and its two halves are inscribed with a testimonial to the courage of the Croppies.

The famous **Browne's Hill Dolmen,** a stone monument dating from 2500 BC with a capstone weighing in at 100 tons, is one of the largest dolmens in Europe. The Stone Age megalithic tomb is thought to mark the burial place of a local king. The dolmen is reached via a pathway from the parking lot. ⊠ *Hacketstown Rd., 3 km (2 mi) east of Carlow Town on R726* ⛶ *Free.*

Where to Stay

$ ⊡ **Barrowville Town House.** Comfort, good food, and a refined atmosphere typify this elegant Regency-style house. Rooms vary in size, but all are handsomely decorated, and a grand piano and a welcoming fireplace adorn the drawing room. Irish breakfast, which includes smoked salmon and an Irish-cheese board, is served in a large conservatory overlooking the garden, under a grapevine that enjoys rude good health (despite the temperamental Irish weather). The guest house is minutes from the center of Carlow Town. ⊠ *Kilkenny Rd., Co. Carlow* ☎ *059/914–3324* 🖷 *059/914–1953* ⊕ *www.barrowvillehouse.com* ⟿ *7 rooms* ⌂ *Croquet; no a/c* ▤ *AE, MC, V* ⍩ *BP.*

Nightlife & the Arts

Started in 1979 as a weekend event to bring together the visual and performing arts, literature, and the Irish language, **Éigse,** Carlow's annual festival, takes over the town in June for 10 days. Drama, classical and pop music, and street entertainment vie with impressive visual-arts exhibitions—including works by international artists—around town. Irish music and dance play a prominent part in the celebrations. For information, contact the **Éigse Festival Office** (☎ 059/9140491).

Sports & the Outdoors

GAELIC FOOTBALL & HURLING — Gaelic football and hurling are played at **Dr. Cullen Park GAA** (☎ 01/836–3222 Gaelic Athletic Association in Dublin).

GOLF — **Carlow Golf Club** (⊠ Deerpark ☎ 059/913–1695), 3 km (2 mi) north of town on the Dublin road, is in a wild deer park; the 18-hole course remains open all year.

Leighlinbridge

❷ *10 km (6 mi) south of Carlow Town on N9.*

Shure, Ireland 'tis a land of sweet vistas, and one of the most romantic is found here on the east bank of Leighlinbridge: romantic, Norman-
★ era **Black Castle,** poetically mirrored in the waters of the River Barrow and framed by the bulk of a grandly medieval bridge. With five stone arches spanning the river since 1320, this is reputed to be one of the oldest functioning bridges in Europe and makes a magnificent repoussoir for the castle. Built in 1181 as one of the earliest Norman fortresses in Ireland, it has been the scene of countless battles and sieges. Its hulking, 400-year-old main tower still stands by an ageless towpath, all but daring you to set up your easel and canvas.

The
Southeast

Rathdowney

LAOIS

Silvermines

Templemore

Templetuohy

Johnstown

Borrisoleigh

Urlingford

Freshford   D

Milestone

Thurles

Holycross Abbey

N8

Cappamore

Cahirconlish

Cappawhite

Ballingarry

Killenaule

Bennet

Herbertstown

N74

Rock of Cashel ◆ **Cashel**

42

TIPPERARY

Callan

S

Fethard

N24

41 **Tipperary Town**

Bansha

R688

SLIEVENAMON MOUNTAIN

Windgap

Knocklong

Glen of Aherlow

Cahir

40

N24

43 **Clonmel**

Ah

R697

Kilfinane

Ballylanders

GALTEE MOUNTAINS

Mitchelstown Caves

44

LIMERICK

N8

Burncourt

The Nire Valley

Carrick-on-Suir

Portl

Mitchelstown

Ballyporeen

IR655

Clogheen

Ballymacarbry

N2

Kildorrery

Shanballymore

Knockmealdown Mountains

Mount Melleray Abbey

Kilmacthomas

Lemybrien

Fermoy

Ballyduff

R666

R669

Cappoquin

R672

Bunme

R675

Rathcormac

R. Blackwater

39

Lismore

N72

WATERFORD

Stradball

Conna

N72

Tallow

38

Clonea

Dungarvan

Watergrasshill

Ballyknock

R634

Ring

N8

R627

CORK

Youghal

N25

Cork

Midleton

Ardmore

Cobh

Ballycotton

Castlecomer
Ballyragget
R430
N78
Old Leighlin ③ ② Leighlinbridge
Kilkenny City
④ - ⑩
See detail map
nmore ◆ Cave
bridge
neyford
nocktopher
ny
KILKENNY
Mullinavat
N10
N24
w
R675
N9
R700
R705
R703
⑫ Graiguenamanagh
R729
Thomastown
⑪
◆ Jerpoint Abbey
Inistioge
St. Mullins
Clonroche
New Ross
N25
R733
John F. Kennedy
◆ Arboretum
Dunganstown
Wellington Bridge
Cheekpoint
Passage East
⑭ Ballyhack
R733
Duncannon
Carrick
Fethard-on-Sea
Hook Peninsula
Churchtown
Waterford City
㉕ - ㉟
See detail map
⑰ Tramore ⑯ Dunmore East
R685 *R684*
Harbour
Annestown
R726
Carlow Town ①
Tullow
Kildavin
N9
Muine Bheag (Bagenalstown)
CARLOW
Borris
R430
WICKLOW
Woodenbridge
Arklow
Shillelagh
Gorey
Bunclody
Ferns
R725
R741
R742
⑬ Enniscorthy
R744
R. Slaney
Oilgate
Blackwater
Curracloe
Irish National Heritage Park ◆
WEXFORD
N79
N11
N25
Piercetown
Wellington Bridge
Duncormick
R736
Tomhaggard
Lady's Island
⑳ Kilmore Quay
Forlorn Pt.
Saltee Islands
Wexford Town
⑭ - ㉑
See detail map
Wexford Harbour
Rosslare ㉒
Rosslare Harbour
St. George's Channel
TO WALES, FRANCE
R739

Celtic Sea

Waterford

NORTHERN IRELAND

IRELAND

KEY
⊢⊢⊢ *Rail Lines*
⛴ *Ferry*
⚑ *Start of itinerary*

0   20 miles
0   30 km

Where to Eat

$$$ ✕ **Lord Bagenal Inn.** This famous old pub beside the River Barrow was built in the early 1800s and is full of cozy nooks and fireplaces. It even has a small playroom for children (open until 8 PM). Besides being a wine buff (the cellar here is award-winning), owner James Kehoe is something of an art connoisseur, as you can see from the modern Irish artworks that line the walls. As for the kitchen, it specializes in fish dishes like fresh turbot with asparagus in beurre blanc. The inn has 12 rooms ($) if you want to stay overnight in Leighlinbridge. ⊠ *Main St., Co. Carlow* ☎ *059/972–1668* ⊕ *www.lordbagenal.com* ▭ *DC, V.*

Old Leighlin

❸ *5¾ km (3 mi) west of Leighlinbridge, signposted to the right off N9.*

Home to one of Ireland's undiscovered gems of late medieval architecture, the tiny village of Old Leighlin first found fame as the site of a monastery, founded in the 7th century by St. Laserian, that once accommodated 1,500 monks. It hosted the church synod in 630 at which the Celtic Church first accepted the Roman date for the celebration of Easter (the date was officially accepted at the Synod of Whitby in 664); this decision marked the beginning of a move away from old Brehon Law and the de-liberalization of the Church. This old monastery was rebuilt in the 12th century as **St. Laserian's Cathedral.** Sitting among green fields, with a castellated tower and Irish-Gothic windows, it evokes a stirring sense of Wordsworthian forlornness. Enlarged in the 16th century, its interior is noted for its 11th-century font, a 200-year-old grand wind organ, and a fine wooden vaulted ceiling. Guided tours are available. ☎ *059/972–1411* ⊕ *www.cashel.anglican.org/laserians.shtm* ▱ *Free* ☉ *July–Aug., weekdays 10–5.*

Glasses of ale have been served up for centuries at **Carey's,** the village pub, which has been in the same family since 1542.

Kilkenny City

24 km (15 mi) southwest of Leighlinbridge on N10, 121 km (75 mi) southwest of Dublin.

Dubbed "Ireland's Medieval Capital" by its tourist board, and also called "the Oasis of Ireland" for its many pubs and watering holes, Kilkenny is one of the country's most alluring destinations. It demands to be explored by foot or bicycle, thanks to its easily circumnavigated town center, a 900-year-old Norman citadel that is now a lovely place filled with Georgian streets and Tudor stone houses. The city (population 20,000) is impressively preserved and attractively situated on the River Nore, which forms the moat of the magnificently restored Kilkenny Castle. In the 6th century, St. Canice (aka "the builder of churches") established a large monastic school here. The town's name reflects Canice's central role: Kil Cainneach means "Church of Canice." Kilkenny did not take on its medieval look for another 400 years, when the Anglo-Normans fortified the city with a castle, gates, and a brawny wall.

The city center is small, and despite the large number of historic sights and picturesque streets—in particular, Butter Slip and High Street—can easily be covered in less than three hours. One of the most pleasant cities south of Dublin (and one of its most sports-minded—during June and July, practically the only topic of conversation is the fate of the city's team at the All-Ireland Hurling Championship), Kilkenny City has become in recent years something of a haven for artists and craft workers seeking an escape from Dublin. At such venues as the Kilkenny Design Centre, you'll find an array of crafts, especially ceramics and sweaters, for sale. The city also has more than 60 pubs, many of them on Parliament and High streets, which also support a lively music scene. Many of the town's pubs and shops have old-fashioned, highly individualized, brightly painted facades, created as part of the town's 1980s revival of this Victorian tradition. So after taking in Kilkenny Castle and the Riverfront Canal Walk—an overgrown pathway that meanders along the castle grounds—mosey down High and Kieran streets. These parallel avenues, considered the historic center of Kilkenny, are connected by a series of horse-cart-wide lanes and are fronted with some of the city's best-preserved pubs and Victorian flats. Be sure to look up over the existing modern storefronts to catch a glimpse of how the city looked in years past, as many of the buildings still have second-floor facades preserving historic decorative styles. High and Kieran streets eventually merge into Parliament Street—the main commercial street—which stretches down to Irishtown.

Kilkenny holds a special place in the history of Anglo-Irish relations. The infamous 1366 Statutes of Kilkenny, intended to strengthen English authority in Ireland by keeping the heirs of the Anglo-Norman invaders from assimilating into the Irish way of life, was an attempt at apartheid. Intermarriage became a crime punishable by death. Anglo-Norman settlers could lose their estates for speaking Irish, for giving their children Irish names, or for dressing in Irish clothes. The native Irish were forced to live outside town walls in shantytowns. Ironically, the process of Irish and Anglo-Norman assimilation was well under way when the statutes went into effect; perhaps if this intermingling had been allowed to evolve naturally, Anglo-Irish relations in the 20th century might have been more harmonious.

By the early 17th century, Irish Catholics began to chafe under such repression; they tried to bring about reforms with the Confederation of Kilkenny, which governed Ireland from 1642 to 1648, with Kilkenny as the capital. Pope Innocent X sent money and arms. Cromwell responded in 1650 by overrunning the town and sacking the cathedral, which he then used as a stable for his horses. This marked the end of Kilkenny's "Golden Age"; however, the succeeding centuries were not uneventful. In 1798 the city was placed under martial law due to a revolt by the United Irishmen; in 1904 King Edward VII paid a visit; and in 1923, at the height of Ireland's civil war, forces opposed to a government peace deal with the British briefly occupied Kilkenny Castle.

❹ In spite of Cromwell's defacements, **St. Canice's Cathedral** is still one of the finest cathedrals in Ireland; it's the country's second-largest medieval church, after St. Patrick's Cathedral in Dublin. The bulk of the 13th-century structure (restored in 1866) was built in the early-English style. Within the massive walls is an exuberant Gothic interior, given a somber grandeur by the extensive use of a locally quarried black marble. Many of the memorials and tombstone effigies represent distinguished descendants of the Normans, some depicted in full suits of armor. Look for a female effigy in the south aisle wearing the old Irish, or Kinsale cloak; a 12th-century black-marble font at the southwest end of the nave; and St. Ciaran's Chair in the north transept, also made of black marble, with 13th-century sculptures on the arms. The biggest attraction on the grounds is the 102-foot-high round tower, which was built in 847 by King O'Carroll of Ossory and is all that remains of the monastic development reputedly begun in the 6th century, around which the town rose. If you have the energy, climb the tower's 167 steps for the tremendous 360-degree view from the top as well as the thrill of mounting 102 steps on makeshift wooden stairs. Next door is St. Canice's Library, containing some 3,000 16th- and 17th-century volumes. ⊠ *Dean St.* ☎ *056/ 776–4971* 🖃 *Cathedral €3, tower €2* ⊙ *Cathedral Easter–Sept., Mon.–Sat. 9–1 and 2–6, Sun. 2–6; Oct.–Easter, Mon.–Sat. 10–1 and 2–4, Sun. 2–4; tower access depends on weather.*

FROM STAKE TO STEAK

KYTELER'S INN IS FAMOUS for having been owned by the notorious Dame Alice Kyteler—a beautiful enchantress from the Middle Ages who went through four wealthy husbands quicker than you can say "poison." Her behavior aroused suspicion in the superstitious Kilkenny farm folk, and she was charged with witchcraft and finally convicted of sacrificing animals to an evil demon she referred to as "Art."

The story picks up speed when the bishop of Ossory, Richard de Ledrede, paid a Lenten visit to the priory. Following an inquisition into a Kilkenny sect of heretics, Dame Le Kyteler and her former brother-in-law, one Roger Outlawe, were ordered to appear before the bishop to answer charges of witchcraft. Outlawe was supported by Arnold de Paor, lord of Kells, who arrested the bishop and had him imprisoned in Kilkenny Castle for 17 days. This, in turn, caused great scandal among the townsfolk and on his release the bishop managed to successfully prosecute the "heretics."

Dame Alice wound up being tossed into the dungeons of Kilkenny Castle, but thanks to her quick tongue—and the fact that her guards were beaten senseless (on order of Ireland's chancellor)—she managed to flee to England. The only problem is that she forgot to take her maid, Petronella de Meath, who promptly became Ireland's first heretic to be burned at the stake in 1324.

Kyteler's Inn (⊠ Kieran St. ☎ 056/772–1064 ⊕ www.kytelers.com) is now a popular pub-restaurant serving excellent bar food as well as traditional meals and good-quality steaks. Head down to the cellar for some pub grub and a chance to vent your hurrahs—or curses—at an effigy of Dame Alice.

★ ❺ With a stained-glass, carved-stone interior that seems right out of the musical *Camelot*, the 13th-century **Black Abbey** is one of the most evocative and beautiful of Irish medieval structures. Note the famous 1340 five-gabled Rosary Window, an entire wall agleam with ruby and sapphire glass, depicting the life of Christ. Home to a Dominican order of monks since 1225, the abbey was restored as a church by this order (whose black capes gave the abbey its name). Nearby is the Black Freren Gate (14th century), the last remaining gateway to the medieval city of yore. ⊠ *South of St. Canice's Cathedral* ☎ *056/7721279* ☒ *Free* ⊙ *Daily 9–1 and 2–6.*

❻ Set with splendidly sturdy stonework, **Rothe House** is an example of a typical merchant-class house of the Tudor period. Built by John Rothe between 1594 and 1610, it is owned by the Kilkenny Archaeological Society and houses a motley collection of Bronze Age artifacts, ogham stones, and period costumes. There's also a genealogical research facility that can help you trace your ancestors. ⊠ *Parliament St.* ☎ *056/7722893* ☒ *€3* ⊙ *Mar.–Oct., Mon.–Sat. 10:30–5, Sun. 3–5; Nov.–Feb., Mon.–Sat. 1–5.*

❼ **Kyteler's Inn,** the oldest in town, is notorious as the place where Dame Alice Le Kyteler, a member of a wealthy banking family and an alleged witch and "brothel keeper," was accused in 1324 of poisoning her four husbands. So, at least said the enemies of this apparently very merry widow. The restaurant retains its medieval aura, thanks to its 14th-century stonework and exposed beams down in the cellar, built up around Kieran's Well, which predates the house itself. Food and drink in this popular pub are as simple and plentiful as they would have been in Dame Alice's day—but without her extra ingredients (see the Close-Up box "From Stake to Steak" for more info). ⊠ *Kieran St.* ☎ *056/772–1064.*

❽ The **Tholsel,** or town hall, which was built in 1761 on Parliament Street, stands near the site of the medieval Market Cross. With its distinctive clock tower and grand entrance portico, this limestone-marble building stands on the site of the execution of poor Petronilla, the "witch" burnt at the stake in the 14th century in lieu of her mistress, Dame Alice Kyteler. The building itself burned down in 1985, but has since been completely rebuilt to its former glory and now houses the city's municipal archives. Adjacent to the Thosel is **Alice's Castle,** a town jail rather grandly fitted out in 18th-century architectural ornamentation.

❾ The **Tourist Information Office (TIO)** is housed in the Shee Alms House (off the east side of High Street). The building was erected in 1582 by Sir Richard Shee as a hospital for the poor and functioned as such until 1895. ⊠ *Rose Inn St.* ☎ *056/775–1500* ⊕ *www.southeastireland.com* ✆ *Apr.–Oct., Mon.–Sat. 9–6; Nov.–Mar., Mon.–Sat. 9–5.*

★ ❿ A bewitching marriage of Gothic and Victorian styles, **Kilkenny Castle** dominates the south end of town. From the outside, amid its rolling lawns beside the River Nore on 50 acres of landscaped parkland (look for the garden shaped in the form of a gigantic Celtic cross), the gray-stone castle conjures up fairy-tale images of knights and damsels, thanks to its battlements, spired towers, and numerous chimneys. It was first built in 1172 and served for more than 500 years, beginning in 1391, as the seat of one of the more powerful clans in Irish history, the Butler family, later designated earls and dukes of Ormonde. In 1967, the sixth marquess of Ormonde handed over the building to the state for the rather pathetic sum of £75. Around 1820, William Robert, son of the first marquess of Ormond, overhauled the castle to make it a wonderland in the Victorian Feudal Revival style. In 1859, John Pollen was called in to redo the most impressive interior, the 150-foot-long, aptly named Long Gallery, a refined, airy hall. Its dazzling green walls are hung with a vast collection of family portraits and frayed tapestries, while above looms a marvelous skylighted, decorated ceiling, replete with oak beams carved with Celtic lacework and adorned with brilliantly painted animal heads. The main staircase was also redone at this time to become a showpiece of Ruskinian 19th-century Gothic. These and other salons can be seen on a guided tour, but you can fast-forward to the 20th century by heading to the castle's Butler Gallery, home to a superb collection of Irish modern art, including examples by Nathaniel Hone, Jack B. Yeats, Sir John Lavery, Louis Le Brocquy, and James Turrell. ⊠ *The Parade* ☎ *056/772–1450* ⊕ *www. heritageireland.ie* ▨ *Castle tour €5, grounds and Butler Gallery free* ✆ *Apr. and May, daily 10:30–5; June–Sept., daily 10–7; Oct.–Mar., Mon.–Sat. 10:30–12:45 and 2–5, Sun. 10:30–12:45 and 2–5.*

Where to Stay & Eat

$–$$$ ✕ **Ristorante Rinuccini.** A warm glow emanates from this excellent Italian restaurant as you descend the steps into its dining room in the basement of a Georgian town house. Owner-chef Antonio Cavaliere is intensely involved in preparing the luscious pasta dishes—such as tortellini stuffed with ricotta cheese and spinach, served in a Gorgonzola sauce—as well as specialties such as organic Irish veal and fresh seafood from Kilmore Quay. A splendid all-Italian wine list complements the menu, and there's a host of delicious homemade desserts. Conveniently set across from Kilknenny Castle, this is of the best Italian options in town. ⊠ *1 The Parade* ☎ *056/7761575* ⊕ *www.rinuccini.com* ✍ *Reservations essential* ☲ *AE, DC, MC, V.*

$–$$ ✕ **Café Sol.** There's always a lively buzz about this small eatery, with its tropical-colored decor and chirpy staff. The emphasis is on contemporary Mediterranean-influenced cuisine. During the day, light meals and sandwiches are on offer; by night, the restaurant takes on a more formal aspect. ⊠ *William St.* ☎ *056/776–4987* ☲ *MC, V* ☉ *Closed Sun.*

$$–$$$ ✕▣ **Langton's.** When it comes to restaurants and pubs, this is Kilkenny Central. A landmark since the 1940s, Langton's is a labyrinth of interconnected bars and eateries. Most of the seating areas, with open fires, have different personalities—from the leather-upholstered gentlemen's club in the Horseshoe Bar to an attempt at art deco in the spacious dining room ($$–$$$). Up front is one of Ireland's most famous "eating pubs," low-ceilinged and often crammed to the rafters with punters. For more tranquil environs, head out back, where you can chow down in a neo-Gothic garden framed by a stretch of the old city walls. The main restaurant has a great reputation and offers well-prepared traditional dishes, including (of course) Irish stew. Upstairs, creams and browns decorate the art deco–style guest rooms, which have king-size beds, and bathrooms with chic massaging showers. ⊠ *69 John St., Co. Kilkenny* ☎ *056/776–5133* ⎙ *056/776–3693* ⇝ *28 rooms, 2 suites; no a/c* ☲ *AE, DC, MC, V* ⑩ *BP.*

$–$$ ✕▣ **Zuni Townhouse and Restaurant.** One of Kilkenny's hippest hotels, Zuni is particularly popular with a younger set in search of the city's legendary nightlife. Relaxed and welcoming; room decor is minimalist with walls painted in strong modern colors. This spot also has one of the city's up-and-coming restaurants, where the food, like the decor, is contemporary and light. The signature is the Asian-influence, as seen in such dishes as spice-crusted cod with a mango and mint dressing. ⊠ *26 Patrick St., Co. Kilkenny* ☎ *056/772–3999* ⎙ *056/775–6400* ⊕ *www.zuni.ie* ⇝ *12 rooms, 1 suite* ⚭ *Restaurant, bar; no a/c* ☲ *AE, DC, MC, V* ⑩ *BP.*

★ **$$–$$$** ▣ **Butler House.** The 18th-century former town house of the dowager duchess of Ormonde, this elegant Georgian house—still an integral part of the Kilkenny Castle complex—will charm you with its ivy-covered, three-bayed facade and walled garden. Inside, the reception salon has a magnificent plastered ceiling and marble fireplaces. Upstairs, any dowager might look askance—a gradual renovation of the guest rooms is ongoing, so the decor ranges from muted 70's minimalist to bright modern. The rooms vary in size, with some big as a palace and others on the snug side. If you can, treat yourself to one of the huge, high-ceiling bedrooms overlooking the garden and castle. Breakfast is served in the adjoining Kilkenny Design Centre. ⊠ *16 Patrick St., Co. Kilkenny* ☎ *056/65707* 🖷 *056/65626* ⊕ *www.butler.ie* ⇲ *12 rooms, 1 suite* ⚬ *Meeting rooms; no a/c* 🖃 *AE, DC, MC, V* 🍽 *BP.*

Nightlife & the Arts

Kilkenny is the famed host for **The Cat Laughs Festival** (☎ 056/776–3837 ⊕ www.thecatlaughs.com)—Ireland's most popular comedy event and, indeed, one of Europe's top "giggle-fests." The festival is held each year on the first weekend in June (a big bank holiday in Ireland) and attracts the cream of Irish and international talent. Audiences and performers alike seem to revel in the intimate atmosphere at the festival where most gigs are held in the backrooms of local pubs. Previous big name visitors from the states include Bill Murray and George Wendt, the wisecracking bar-fly "Norm" from *Cheers.*

If you're craving a pint, there are plenty of pubs to choose from along Parliament and High streets. **John Cleere's** (⊠ 22 Parliament St. ☎ 056/776–2573) is the best pub in town for a mix of live traditional music, poetry readings, and theatrical plays. **The Pumphouse** (⊠ 26 Parliament St. ☎ 056/776–3924) has traditional music during the week and live rock and pop on weekends. **Tynan's Bridge House** (⊠ 2 Horseleap Slip ☎ 056/21291) is set on one of Kilkenny's famous "slips" which was first used as an exercise run for dray horses. Inside, you can see the pub is more than 200 years old from all the gas lamps, silver tankards, and historic teapots on display. The **Widow McGraths** (⊠ 29 Parliament St. ☎ 056/775–2520) celebrates the Fourth of July with a barbecue in its beer garden. It's also a good spot for live music.

The Watergate Theatre (⊠ Parliament St. ☎ 056/61674) hosts opera, plays, concerts, comedy, and other entertainment at reasonable prices.

Sports & the Outdoors

BICYCLING Bikes for exploring the quiet countryside around Kilkenny can be rented through **J. J. Wall** (⊠ 88 Maudlin St. ☎ 056/772–1236).

GAELIC FOOTBALL & HURLING The 1366 Statutes of Kilkenny expressly forbade the ancient Irish game of hurling. No matter: today, Kilkenny is considered one of the great hurling counties. Like its neighbor and archenemy, Wexford, Kilkenny has a long history of success in hurling, and as the annual All-Ireland Hurling Championships draws to its final stages during June and July, interest in the county's team runs to fever pitch. Catch the home team at matches held at **Kilkenny GAA Grounds** (⊠ Nowlan Park ☎ 056/777–0008).

Shopping

Kilkenny is a byword for attractive, original crafts that combine traditional arts with modern design elements. You can see glass being blown at the **Jerpoint Glass Studio** (⊠ Stoneyford ☎ 056/772–4350), where the glass is heavy, modern, uncut, and hand-finished. The studio's factory shop is a good place to pick up a bargain. The town's leading outlet, the **Kilkenny Design Centre** (⊠ Kilkenny Castle ☎ 056/772–2118), in the old stable yard opposite the castle, sells ceramics, jewelry, sweaters, and handwoven textiles. **Murphy's Jewellers** (⊠ 85 High St. ☎ 056/772–1127) specializes in heraldic jewelry.

★ **Nicholas Mosse Pottery** (⊠ Bennettsbridge ☎ 056/772–7505) is the best-known name in Irish ceramics. Nicholas first set up his potter's wheel in an old flour mill in this quiet village (set 10 mi south of Kilkenny) in 1975. Since then, the business has boomed and the rustic floral-pattern pottery created here is instantly recognizable for its "spongeware" designs. A visit here allows you to see the pottery being made, and the adjoining factory shop often has good bargains. **Rudolf Heltzel** (⊠ 10 Patrick St. ☎ 056/772–1497) is known for its striking, modern designs of gold and silver jewelry. **Stoneware Jackson Pottery** (⊠ Bennettsbridge ☎ 056/772–7175) makes distinctive, hand-thrown tableware and lamps. The **Sweater Shop** (⊠ 81 High St. ☎ 056/776–3405) carries great sweaters.

Thomastown

⑪ *14½ km (9 mi) south of Kilkenny on R700 and N9.*

Thomastown, originally the seat of the kings of Ossory (an ancient Irish kingdom), is a pretty, stone-built village on the River Nore. It takes its name from Thomas FitzAnthony of Leinster, who circled the town with a wall in the 13th century. Fragments of this medieval wall remain, as do the partly ruined 13th-century church of St. Mary and Mullins Castle, adjacent to the town bridge. Landmarked by its rearing and massive 15th-century tower, **Jerpoint Abbey**, near Thomastown, is one of the most notable Cistercian ruins in Ireland, dating from about 1160. The church, tombs, and the restored cloisters are a must for lovers of the Irish Romanesque. The vast cloister is decorated with carvings of affecting human figures and fantastical mythical creatures, including knights and knaves (one with a stomach ache) and the assorted dragon or two. Dissolved in 1540, Jerpoint was taken over, as was so much around these parts, by the earls of Ormonde. The one part of the abbey that remains alive, so to speak, is its hallowed cemetery—the natives are still buried here. Guided tours of the impressive complex are available from mid-June to mid-September (last admission is 45 minutes before closing). ⊠ *2 km (1 mi) south of Thomastown on N9* ☎ *056/24623* ⊕ *www.heritageireland.ie* ☒ *€2.75* ☉ *Mar.–May and Oct.–mid-Nov., daily 10–5; June–Sept., daily 9:30–6:30.*

Fodor'sChoice ★ (text beside "Jerpoint Abbey" paragraph)

Where to Stay & Eat

$$$$
Fodor'sChoice
★
✕▣ **Mount Juliet.** Once part of the nearby medieval Jerpoint Abbey estate, later owned by the earls of Carrick, and then famous as the seat of a horse-racing stud, Mount Juliet has long been an address of note in County Kilkenny. Today, this 1,500-acre kingdom is still lorded over by its three-story Georgian mansion, which the second earl of Carrick built along the banks of the River Nore and named in honor of his wife, Lady Juliana. Now a Conrad hotel, this estate still gives you the full princely treatment, thanks to a spa, famous golf course, and an array of restaurants that tempt one never to leave the grounds. The imposing mansion, whose elegant sash windows and mansard roof are creeper-covered in the best stately-house manner, was subjected to full-blast renovation

treatment in 1968. Begone, creaky floors and time-stained walls (and yesteryear's charm?); hello, large accommodations decorated with vibrant hues and fine fabrics, and suites with super-king-size beds and original fireplaces. Rooms are also available in a separate building, the Hunters Yard, plus there are 11 modern two-room lodges, including the Rose Garden suites, each of which comes with two bedrooms, a kitchen, and very luxe decor. For many, the Jack Nicklaus–designed golf course—which has hosted the Irish Open on three occasions—is *the* reason to head here. More sedate types will enjoy a sherry in the Tetrarch Bar (named for the greatest horse to come out of this estate's stud), a light lunch in Kendalls—a wood-trimmed casual bistro in the Yard complex—or fine Irish haute cuisine in the Lady Helen McAlmont Restaurant, its tables adorned with crystal, silverware, and fine linen, and its windows with a grand vista over the Nore Valley. ⊠ *Co. Kilkenny* ☎ *056/777–3000* 🖷 *056/777–3009* ⊕ *www.mountjuliet.com* ⌇ *48 rooms, 11 lodges* ⌂ *2 restaurants, 18-hole golf course, tennis court, indoor pool, sauna, spa, fishing, archery, croquet, horseback riding, 3 bars; no a/c* ▭ *AE, DC, MC, V.*

★ **$** 🏠 **Ballyduff House.** Relaxation, long walks, and a warm welcome can be found at this picturesque 18th-century manor house, set in rolling countryside overlooking the River Nore. The house has been used as a film location on more than one occasion (including for the 1995 film *Circle of Friends*). Three large period bedrooms (one is a heavenly, super-stylish vision in multiple hues of green) are decorated with Georgian furniture and ornate wallpaper and afford wonderful views of the river. You're welcome to walk around the gardens and partake in trout and salmon fishing. Mount Juliet Golf Course is less than a five-minute drive away. ⊠ *Co. Kilkenny* ☎🖷 *056/775–8488* ⌇ *3 rooms* ⌂ *Fishing; no a/c* ▭ *No credit cards* ❑ *BP* ⊘ *Closed Nov.–Feb.*

Sports & the Outdoors

GOLF Visitors are welcome at the 18-hole **Mount Juliet Golf Course** (⊠ Mount Juliet Estate ☎ 056/772–4455), a championship parkland course. The course was designed by Jack Nicklaus and includes practice greens and a driving range.

Graiguenamanagh

⑫ *15 km (9 mi) northeast of Thomastown on R703.*

The village of Graiguenamanagh (pronounced *gray*-gun-a-manna) sits on the banks of the River Barrow at the foot of Brandon Hill. This is good walking country; ask for directions to the summit of **Brandon Hill** (1,694-ft-high), a 7-km (4½-mi) hike. In the 13th century the early English–style church of **Duiske Abbey** was the largest Cistercian church in Ireland. The choir, the transept, and a section of the nave of the original abbey church are now part of a Catholic church. Purists will be disappointed by the modernization, carried out between 1974 and 1980, although medieval building techniques were used. ☎ *059/972-4238* ⊘ *Daily 9:30–7.*

Where to Stay & Eat

★ **$** ✕🏠 **Waterside.** Delightfully, this beautifully restored 19th-century stone corn mill is right on the River Barrow. The mill's original pitch-pine beams have been retained in the guest rooms, which are simply and brightly decorated in reds and yellows. The restaurant ($$), which occupies the ground floor also has exposed beams and decorated windows; it serves Continental cuisine and has a good wine list. Hill-walking trips, including transport and packed lunches, can be arranged for small groups. ⊠ *The Quay, Co. Kilkenny* ☎ *059/972–4246* 🖷 *059/972–4733* ⊕ *www. watersideguesthouse.com* ⇥ *10 rooms* ⚿ *Restaurant, fishing; no a/c* ▭ *AE, MC, V* ⦿◻ *BP.*

Enniscorthy

⓭ *32 km (20 mi) northeast of New Ross on N79.*

Enniscorthy, on the sloping banks of the River Slaney and on the main road between Dublin and Wexford, to the south of the popular resort of Gorey, is a thriving market town, rich in history. The town is dominated by **Enniscorthy Castle**, built in the first quarter of the 13th century by the Prendergast family. The imposing Norman castle was the site of fierce battles against Oliver Cromwell in the 17th century and during the Uprising of 1798. Its square-towered keep now houses the County Wexford Museum, which contains thousands of historic items, including military memorabilia from the 1798 and 1916 uprisings. ⊠ *Castle Hill* ☎ *054/35926* ▦ *€4.50* ⊙ *May–Sept., Mon.–Sat. 10–6, Sun. 2–5:30.*

The **National 1798 Center** tells the tale of the United Irishmen and the ill-fated 1798 rebellion. ⊠ *Arnold's Cross* ☎ *054/37596* ▦ *€6* ⊙ *Mid-Mar.–Nov., Mon.–Sat. 9:30–5, Sun. 11–5; Dec.–mid-Mar., weekdays 9:30–4, weekends 11–4.*

St. Aidan's Cathedral stands on a commanding site overlooking the Slaney. This Gothic Revival structure was built in the mid-19th century under the direction of Augustus Welby Pugin, the architect of the Houses of Parliament in London. ⊠ *Cathedral St.* ☎ *054/35777* ▦ *Free* ⊙ *Daily 10–6.*

Where to Stay

$$ ⌂ **Salville House.** Local legend has it that this fine Victorian farmhouse was once the home of a couple of "disreputable" ladies who danced at the Folies Bergères in Paris. Things are much more respectable nowadays: Gordon and Jane Parker have created a hilltop haven where food and relaxation are the order of the day. Gordon's inspired contemporary cuisine has a growing group of fans. Guests dine around a large mahogany table and are invited to bring their own wine. The bedrooms are spacious, with plenty of books on the shelves and a great view of the River Slaney. In summer, a grass tennis court in front of the house adds to its charm. To get there, look out for the signpost, 2 km (1 mi) out of Enniscorthy on the Wexford road. ⊠ *Wexford Road* ☎ *054/35252* 🖷 *054/ 35252* ⊕ *www.salvillehouse.com* ⇥ *5 rooms* ⚿ *Tennis court (in summer); no a/c, no room phones, no room TVs* ▭ *No credit cards* ⦿◻ *BP.*

Shopping

Carley's Bridge Pottery (⊠ Carley's Bridge ☎ 054/33512), established in 1654, specializes in large terra-cotta pots. **Kiltrea Bridge Pottery** (⊠ Kiltrea, Caime ☎ 054/35107) stocks garden pots, plant pots, and country kitchen crocks.

Wexford Town

24 km (15 mi) south of Enniscorthy on N11, 142 km (88 mi) south of Dublin.

From its appearance today, you would barely realize that Wexford is an ancient place—in fact, it was defined on maps by the Greek cartographer Ptolemy as long ago as the 2nd century AD. Its Irish name is Loch Garman, but the Vikings called it Waesfjord—the harbor of the mud flats—which became Wexford in English. Wexford became an English garrison town after it was taken by Oliver Cromwell in 1649. (The Anglo-Norman conquest of Ireland began in County Wexford in 1169, so the British presence has deep roots, and Wexford has been an English-speaking county for centuries.)

The River Slaney empties into the sea at Wexford Town. The harbor has silted up since the days when Viking longboats docked here; nowadays only a few small trawlers fish from here. Wexford Town's compact center is on the south bank of the Slaney. Running parallel to the quays on the riverfront is the main street (the name changes several times)—the major shopping street of the town, with a pleasant mix of old-fashioned bakeries, butcher shops, stylish boutiques, and a share of Wexford's many pubs. It can be explored on foot in an hour or two. Allow at least half a day in the area if you also intend to visit the Heritage Park at nearby Ferrycarrig, and a full day if you want to take in Johnstown Castle Gardens and its agricultural museum, or walk in the nature reserve at nearby Curracloe Beach. The town is at its best in late October and early November, when the Wexford Opera Festival creates a carnival atmosphere.

Rising above the town's rooftops are the graceful spires of two elegant examples of 19th-century Gothic architecture. These **twin churches** have identical exteriors, their foundation stones were laid on the same day, and their spires each reach a height of 230 feet. The **Church of the Assumption** is on Bride Street. The **Church of the Immaculate Conception** is on Rowe Street.

⑭ The **Tourist Information Office** (TIO; ✉ Crescent Quay ☎ 053/23111) is a good place from which to start exploring Wexford Town on foot and to find out about guided walking tours organized by local historians.

⑮ Standing in the center of Crescent Quay, a large bronze **statue of Commodore John Barry** (1745–1803) commemorates the man who came to be known as the father of the American Navy. Born in 1745 in nearby Ballysampson, Barry settled in Philadelphia at age 15, became a brilliant naval fighter during the War of Independence (thus avenging his Irish ancestors), and trained many young naval officers who went on to achieve fame.

⑯ The **Franciscan Church** has a ceiling worth noting for its fine, locally crafted stuccowork. ✉ *School St.* ☎ *053/22758* 🏷 *Free* 🕐 *Daily 8:30–6:30.*

Wexford
Town

⓱ The **Wexford Bull Ring** (⊠ Quay St., back toward the quays) was once the scene of bull baiting, a grotesque medieval sport that was popular among the Norman nobility. Also in this arena, in 1649, Cromwell's soldiers massacred 300 panic-stricken townspeople who had gathered here to pray as the army stormed their town. The legacy of this bloodless leader has remained a dark folk memory for centuries and is only now beginning to fade; a new housing development at the old Cromwell's Fort is one of the ritzier developments in town.

⓲ The red sandstone **Westgate Tower** (⊠ Westgate) was the largest of five fortified gateways in the Norman and Viking town walls, and it is the only one remaining. The early-13th-century tower has been sensitively restored. Keep an eye out as you wander this part of town for other preserved segments of the old town walls.

⓳ The ruins of the 12th-century **Selskar Abbey** (⊠ Selskar St., south of Westgate Tower) still stand. Here the first treaty between the Irish and the Normans was signed in 1169.

⓴ The **Wexford Wildfowl Reserve,** on the north bank of the Slaney, is a short walk across the bridge from the main part of town. One-third of the world's Greenland white-fronted geese—as many as 10,000—spend their winters on the mud flats, known locally as slobs, which also draw ducks, swans, and other waterfowl. Observation hides are provided for bird-watchers, and an audiovisual show and exhibitions are available at the visitor center. ⊠ *North Slob, Wexford Harbor* ☎ *053/23129* ⓢ *Free* ⊙ *Mid-Apr.–Sept., daily 9–6; Oct.–mid-Apr., daily 10–5.*

★ ☾ **㉑** The **Irish National Heritage Park,** a 35-acre, open-air living history museum beside the River Slaney, is one of Ireland's most successful and enjoyable family attractions. In about an hour and a half, a guide takes you through 9,000 years of Irish history—from the first evidence of humans on this island, at around 7000 BC, to the Norman settlements of the mid-12th century. Full-scale replicas of typical dwelling places illustrate the changes in beliefs and lifestyles. Highlights of the tour include a prehistoric homestead, a *crannóg* (lake dwelling), an early Christian *rath* (fortified farmstead), a Christian monastery, a horizontal water mill, a Viking longhouse, and a Norman castle. There are also examples of pre-Christian burial sites and a stone circle. Most of the exhibits are "inhabited" by students in appropriate historic dress who will answer questions. The riverside site includes several nature trails. ⊠ *5 km (3 mi) north of Wexford Town on N11, Ferrycarrig* ☎ *053/20733* ⊕ *www.inhp.com* ⓢ *Mar.–Oct. €7, Nov.–Feb. €5.50* ⊙ *Mar.–Oct., daily 9:30–6:30; Nov.–Feb., daily 9:30–5:30.*

Fodor'sChoice
★

Only Walt Disney might have bettered the storybook look of the massive, Victorian-Gothic, gray-stone castle at **Johnstown Castle Gardens,** 5 mi (3 mi) southwest of Wexford following the N25 (direction Rosslare). A magical Gothic Revival extravaganza, this turreted, battlemented, and machicolated edifice, which bristles in silver-grey ashlar, was built for the Grogan-Morgan family between 1810 and 1855. They're not around to see how magnificently their parklands—with splendid towering trees, lakes, and ornamental gardens—have framed the grand castle. Unfortunately, you can't tour the house (it houses a national agricultural college) other than its entrance hall, but the stunning, well-maintained grounds are open to the public. The centerpiece is the 5-acre lake, one side of which has a terrace, replete with statues, from which to take in the panorama of the mirrored castle. Because there is such a variety of trees framing the view—Japanese cedars, Atlantic blue cedars, golden Lawson cypresses—there's color through much of the calendar. Nearby are the Devil's Gate walled garden—a woodland garden set around the ruins of the medieval castle of Rathlannon—and the **National Museum of Agriculture and Rural Life.** The latter, housed in the quadrangular stable yards, shows what life was once like in rural Ireland. It also contains a 5,000-square-foot exhibition on the potato and the Great Famine (1845–49). ⊠ *Signposted just off the N25, 6 km (4 mi) southwest of Wexford Town* ☎ *053/42888* ⊕ *www.johnstowncastle.com* ⊠ *Gardens May–Sept. €2, Oct.–Apr. free. Museum €5* ☉ *Gardens daily 9:30–5:30; museum Apr., May, and Sept.–Nov., weekdays 9–12:30 and 1:30–5, weekends 2–5; June–Aug., weekdays 9–5, weekends 11–5; Dec.–Mar., weekdays 9–12:30 and 1:30–5.*

off the beaten path

CURRACLOE BEACH – This was the location used for the Normandy landing in Steven Spielberg's film *Saving Private Ryan*. It's a popular swimming place in summer and is home to many migratory birds in winter. It's 9 km (5½ mi) long, with a 1-km (½-mi) nature trail in the seashore sand dunes. ⊠ *11 km (7 mi) northeast of Wexford Town on R742.*

Where to Stay & Eat

$$ ✕ **La Riva.** Right in the center of town, this is a cozy waterfront restaurant with an emphasis on modern Mediterranean cuisine. Lots of people opt for two or three starters, in order to try as many as possible of owner-chef Warren Gillen's unusual combos—such as panfried rabbit loin with Parma ham and goat-cheese ravioli. Don't miss the warm coffee-poached pear served with a chocolate brownie and Bailey's custard. The extensive menu makes use of organic ingredients, and a wide selection of fresh seafood is available. ⊠ *Crescent Quay* ☎ *053/24330* ▭ *MC, V.*

$–$$ ✕ **Heavens Above.** Owners John and Nuala Barron have received ample praise for the unusual wine policy at this wood-paneled loft restaurant (above a ground-floor pub). Diners can accompany their meal with a bottle bought from the adjoining wine shop—with no corkage charge. The food has also been acclaimed, as you'll understand with your first bite of their Slaney salmon fillet en paupiette with black pepper and lime butter. ⊠ *112 S. Main St.* ☎ *053/21273* ▭ *MC, V.*

$–$$ ✕ **Oak Tavern.** The pub-restaurant in this old-fashioned, family-run inn on the River Slaney is a good place to stop for a bite on your way into Wexford Town. In cold weather, you can warm yourself beside the log fires that blaze in the lounge; in fair weather, you can relax on the riverside terrace. The menu includes steaks, local salmon, and other seafood options. The tavern is about 2 km (1 mi) from town, and is not far from the gates of the Irish National Heritage Park on the N11 Dublin road. ⊠ *Enniscorthy Rd., Ferrycarrig* ☎ *053/20922* ▭ *AE, MC, V.*

$$ ✕⊞ **Ferrycarrig.** Regular visitors to Wexford Town love this hotel, which overlooks the Slaney Estuary 3 km (2 mi) from town on the N11. Even with its very modern architecture, the hotel blends well into its peaceful, riverside location—for example, trees have been placed just offshore to encourage birds to perch there. All the bedrooms have wonderful views of the river, and some also have balconies. Choose between dining in the casual Boathouse Bistro or the more formal Tides Restaurant, which serves Continental cuisine. ⊠ *Ferrycarrig Bridge, Co. Wexford* ☎ *053/20999* 🖶 *053/20982* ⊕ *www.griffingroup.ie* 📞 *103 rooms* ♨ *2 restaurants, indoor pool, health club, fishing, bar; no a/c* ⊟ *AE, DC, MC, V* ⍾◎⍾ *BP.*

$ ⊞ **Darral House.** A handsome Georgian townhouse, Darral Houe offers a good base for exploring Wexford Town and is within five minutes walk of the town center. Constructed at the turn of the 19th century, it has recently been renovated: Guest rooms are tastefully decorated in harmony with the history of the house. The owner, Kathleen Nolan, is well known for her excellent "Full Irish"—the classic Irish breakfast. ⊠ *Spawell Rd., Co. Wexford* ☎ *053/24264* 🖶 *053/24284* ⊕ *www.wexford-bedandbreakfast.com* 📞 *4 rooms* ♨ *Free parking; no a/c, no room phones* ⊟ *MC, V* ⍾◎⍾ *BP.*

$ ⊞ **McMenamin's Town House.** Early breakfast by arrangement and exceptional comfort—for the price range—make this four-story Victorian villa an ideal stopover en route to or from the Rosslare ferries. The bedrooms are spacious, warm, and immaculate, with large pieces of highly polished Victorian furniture and antique beds, including a mahogany half-tester. There are about eight choices at breakfast, including fresh fish of the day and hot porridge. Make sure you taste Kay and Seamus McMenamin's homemade whiskey marmalade. Book months in advance if you want a room here during the Opera Festival, held in October and early November. ⊠ *3 Auburn Terr., Redmond Rd., Co. Wexford* ☎🖶 *053/46442* ⊕ *www.wexford-bedandbreakfast.com* 📞 *5 rooms* ♨ *No a/c, no room phones* ⊟ *MC, V* ⍾◎⍾ *BP* ⊙ *Closed last 2 wks of Dec.*

Nightlife & the Arts

Touring companies and local productions can be seen in Wexford at the **Theatre Royal** (⊠ 27 High St. ☎ 053/22400). The **Wexford Opera Festival** (☎ 053/22144 box office ⊕ www.wexfordopera.com), held during the last two weeks of October and the beginning of November, is the town's leading cultural event. The festival, which has been going strong for half a century, features seldom-performed operas sung by top talent from all over the world. Along with an ever-expanding fringe element, the festival supplies a feast of concerts and recitals that start at 11 AM and continue until midnight. For the full aria, see this chapter's Pleasures & Pastimes write-up, "Passion on the High C's."

As the saying goes, if you can find a street without at least one bar on it, you're not still in Wexford. **Centenary Stores** (⊠ Charlotte St. ☎ 053/24424) is a Victorian-style pub, popular with a young crowd. Lunch is available Monday through Saturday, and there's traditional music every Sunday morning. The **Sky and the Ground** (⊠ 112 S. Main St. ☎ 053/21273) is one of the best pubs in town for good food (served daily) and fine traditional music sessions (Monday through Thursday). Dating to the 13th century, the **Thomas Moore Tavern** (✉ Cornmarket ☎ 053/24348) is Wexford's oldest pub, named after the renowned Irish poet whose parents lived here. The pub has its original medieval walls and fine old beams along the ceiling. It's the perfect place for a quiet drink by the fire.

Sports & the Outdoors

BICYCLING If you'd like to explore the long, sandy coast of this area at a leisurely pace, rent a bike at **Hayes Cycles** (✉ 108 S. Main St. ☎ 053/22462).

GAELIC FOOTBALL & HURLING Gaelic football and hurling can be seen at the **Wexford Park GAA** (✉ Clonard Rd. ☎ 01/836–3222 for the GAA of Ireland in Dublin).

Shopping

Barker's (✉ 36 S. Main St. ☎ 053/23159) stocks Waterford crystal, local pottery, and crafts. **Martins Jewelers** (✉ 14 S. Main St. ☎ 053/22635) sells handmade Celtic jewelry and Waterford crystal. **Simone Walsh** (✉ 85 S. Main St. ☎ 053/23567) features Irish art and design and original paintings. **Westgate Design** (✉ 22 N. Main St. ☎ 053/23787) carries a good selection of Irish crafts, pottery, candles, and jewelry; there's also a restaurant here. **The Wool Shop** (✉ 39–40 S. Main St. ☎ 053/22247) is a good place to buy souvenirs, knitting yarn, and handmade Aran sweaters.

ALONG THE COAST TO WATERFORD

This journey takes you along mainly minor roads through the prettiest parts of the coast in Counties Wexford and Waterford, pausing midway to explore Waterford city—home of the dazzling cut glass—on foot. Along the way expect to see long golden beaches, quaint fishing villages like Kilmore Quay and Ballyhack, some of the country's best nature reserves, and Tramore, Ireland's most unredeemable family waterside resort. If you're coming from the Continent or England, chances are you'll end up on a ferry bound for Rosslare Harbour, one of Ireland's busiest ferry ports.

Rosslare

②② *16 km (10 mi) southeast of Wexford Town on R470.*

Sometimes called Ireland's sunniest spot, the village of Rosslare is a seaside getaway with an attractive beach. Vacationers generally head here to hike, golf, sun, and swim. **Rosslare Harbor,** 8 km (5 mi) south of the village, is the terminus for car ferries from Fishguard and Pembroke in Wales (a 4-hour trip) and from Cherbourg and Roscoff in France (a 22-hour trip). Indeed, taking the ferry is the only reason you should find yourself in this otherwise dull little town. The two ferry companies, Irish Ferries and Stena Sealink (contact information in Southeast A to Z, *below*), serving Rosslare Harbour have small information kiosks in the ultramodern terminal, which also has a tourist office (☎ 053/33622), lockers, a sprawling waiting room, and a café. You can purchase ferry tickets at the terminal, but try to reserve a space in advance through the companies' Cork or Dublin office to avoid the frequent sellouts, particularly in summer and any time the Irish soccer team is playing in a major tournament abroad. Reservations are also a must if you're traveling by car because onboard parking space is at a premium. The Rosslare Harbour rail depot (☎ 053/33162), adjacent to the ferry terminal, is served by frequent trains to Dublin's Connolly Station and Cork (change at Limerick Junction). Bus Éireann's Rosslare Harbour depot also adjoins the rail station.

Where to Stay & Eat

★ **\$\$**   ✕⊠ **Kelly's.** Nestling in a beautiful beachfront location, this hotel has been a favorite with generations of Irish vacationers. Comfortable, rustic furnishings fill the guest rooms. Rooms facing the front have lovely sea views. Waterford-glass chandeliers hang in the Ivy Room restaurant, where the menu includes fresh local produce served in classic French style. You can also dine in La Marine, a casual, bistro-style restaurant that does a fine job of cooking up Mediterranean-style Irish produce. The resort has extensive recreational facilities. In July and August there's a one-week minimum stay. ⊠ *Co. Wexford* ☎ *053/32114* 🖷 *053/ 32222* ⊕ *www.kellys.ie* ⇆ *106 rooms* ⚭ *2 restaurants, 18-hole golf course, 4 tennis courts, indoor pool, wading pool, gym, hair salon, hot tub, outdoor hot tub, sauna, steam room, bicycles, croquet, playground; no a/c* ⊟ *AE, MC, V* ⟊ *AI* ⊗ *Closed Dec.–Feb.*

Nightlife & the Arts

Portholes bar (⊠ Rosslare Harbor ☎ 053/33110), at the Hotel Rosslare, is a popular spot for live music on weekends.

Sports & the Outdoors

Rosslare Golf Club (⊠ Rosslare Strand ☎ 053/32203) is a 27-hole, par-72 championship links. A mixture of links and parkland can be found at the 27-hole **St. Helen's Bay** (⊠ Kilrane ☎ 053/33234).

Kilmore Quay

㉓ *22 km (14 mi) south of Rosslare on R739.*

Fodor'sChoice
★

A quiet, old-fashioned seaside village of thatched and whitewashed cottages noted for its fishing industry, Kilmore Quay is also popular with recreational anglers and bird-watchers. From the harbor there is a pleasant view to the east over the flat coast that stretches for miles. **Kehoe's Pub** (⊠ Kilmore Quay ☎ 053/29830) is the hub of village activity; its collection of maritime artifacts is as interesting as that of many museums. During two weeks in July (generally mid-month), the village hosts a lively **seafood festival** (☎ 053/29922) with a parade, seafood barbecues, and other events.

★ The **Kilmore Quay Maritime Museum** is onboard the lightship *Guillemot*. Built in 1923, this is the last Irish lightship to be preserved complete with cabins and engine room, and it contains models and artifacts relating to the maritime history of the area. ⊠ *Kilmore Quay* ☎ *053/21572* 🖭 *€5* ⊗ *June–Aug., daily noon–6; Sept. and Apr., weekends noon–6.*

🜂 The **Saltee Islands,** Ireland's largest bird sanctuary, are a popular offshore day trip from Kilmore Quay. In late spring and early summer, several million seabirds nest among the dunes and on the rocky scarp on the south of the islands. Even if you are not an ornithologist, it's worth making the trip at these times to observe the sheer numbers of gulls, kittiwakes, puffins, guillemots, cormorants, and petrels. From mid-May to mid-September, look for boats at the village waterfront or on the marina to take you to the islands, weather permitting.

Where to Stay & Eat

$–$$ ✕ **Silver Fox.** This busy family-run seafood restaurant is considered one of the best in the area. Chef and co-owner Nicky Cullen prepares up to a dozen seafood options, including a popular grilled lemon sole, topped with a creamy sauce of fresh prawns, scallops, mushrooms, and onions—plus a sprinkling of cheese. He also cooks a few non-seafood options: stuffed garlic mushrooms and deep-fried St. Killian (a local Camembert-like) cheese among them. Simplicity and freshness define the food here. ⊠ *Kilmore Quay* ☎ *053/29888* ⌔ *Reservations essential* ☰ *AE, MC, V* ⊙ *Closed mid-Jan.–mid-Feb. No lunch Mon.–Sat.*

¢ ☷ **Quay House.** A perfect base for those interested in boating or fishing, this whitewashed guest house is only a three-minute walk from the pier. The homey interior has Douglas fir pine floors throughout and country pine bedroom furniture. Guests—generally outdoor types—are encouraged to socialize in the lounge and the dining room, although many avail themselves of the great waterside walks and boating options (a room for drying and storing diving equipment is available). ⊠ *Kilmore Quay, Co. Wexford* ☎ *053/29988* ☒ *053/29808* ⊕ *www.kilmorequay.net* ⇥ *10 rooms* ⌂ *Restaurant, fishing; no a/c* ☰ *AE, MC, V* ⦿| *BP.*

Shopping

Country Crafts (⊠ Kilmore Quay ☎ 053/29885), which overlooks the harbor of Kilmore Quay, sells Irish-made crafts, antique pine furniture, and paintings by local artists.

---

en route On leaving Kilmore Quay, make your way north to R736, and then head west through Duncormick and on to Wellington Bridge. Past the bridge, head toward Fethard-on-Sea on the **Ring of Hook** drive. This is a strange and atypical part of Ireland, where the land is exceptionally flat and the narrow roads run straight.

Ballyhack

㉔ *34 km (21 mi) west of Kilmore Quay.*

Fodor'sChoice
★ On the upper reaches of Waterford Harbor, the pretty village of Ballyhack, with its square castle keep, wooden buildings, thatched cottages, and green, hilly background, is admired by painters and photographers. A small car ferry makes the five-minute crossing to Passage East and Waterford. The gray-stone keep of **Ballyhack Castle** dates from the 16th century. It was once owned by the Knights Templars of St. John of Jerusalem, who held the ferry rights by royal charter; traditionally, they were required to keep a boat at Ballyhack to transport injured knights to the King's Leper Hospital at Waterford. The first two floors have been renovated and house local-history exhibits. Guided tours are available by appointment, and the last admission is 45 minutes before closing.

☎ 051/389–468 ⊕ www.heritageireland.ie ☜ €1.50 ☉ Mid-June–mid-Sept., weekdays 10–1 and 2–6, weekends 10–6.

Twelve kilometers (8 miles) to the north of Ballyhack lies the **John F. Kennedy Arboretum,** with more than 600 acres of forest, nature trails, and gardens, plus an ornamental lake. The grounds contain some 4,500 species of trees and shrubs, and serve as a resource center for botanists and foresters. Go to the top of the park to get fine panoramic views. The arboretum is clearly signposted from New Ross on R733, which follows the banks of the Barrow southward for about 5 km (3 mi). The cottage where the president's great-grandfather was born is in Dunganstown; Kennedy relatives still live in the house. About 2 km (1 mi) down the road at Slieve Coillte you'll see the entrance to the arboretum. ☒ Dunganstown ☎ 051/388–171 ⊕ www.heritageireland.ie ☜ €2.75 ☉ May–Aug., daily 10–8; Apr. and Sept., daily 10–6:30; Oct.–Mar., daily 10–5.

Where to Stay & Eat

$$$$
Fodor'sChoice
★

×☒ **Dunbrody Country House.** A rural jewel, this sprawling two-story 1830s Georgian manor house used to be the digs of the seventh marquess of Donegall, Dermot Chichester, who must be smiling down at the current chatelaines, Kevin and Catherine Dundon. Under their magic touch, the gardens are soul-restoring, the manse's public salons are a soigné symphony of mix-and-match tangerine-hue fabrics and stuffed arm chairs, the views over the Barrow estuary remain grand, and the guest rooms charm with a judiciously luxe combination of period antiques and fine reproductions. Gourmands come here to stuff themselves cross-eyed in the ruby-red Harvest Room, because master chef Kevin's Barbary duck in burnt orange sauce, medallions of beef in Rhône wine jus, and chocolate "selection of indulgences" make most meals here memorable, sip-to-sup. In fact, you may learn how to cook these delights yourself; Kevin runs a cooking school on the premises (with classes conveniently scheduled for weekends sessions). After dinner, with a goblet of Irish mist in hand, catch a dramatic sunset fading over the Hook Peninsula. No need to rush the next morn: the famous breakfasts are served until noon. ☒ Arthurstown, New Ross, Co. Wexford ☎ 051/389–600 ☒ 051/389–601 ⊕ www.dunbrodyhouse.com ⇆ 15 rooms, 7 suites ⌂ Restaurant, horseback riding, bar; no a/c ☰ AE, DC, MC, V ⦿ BP.

Waterford City

10 km (6 mi) west of Ballyhack by ferry and road (R683), 62 km (39 mi) southwest of Wexford Town, 158 km (98 mi) southwest of Dublin.

The largest town in the southeast and Ireland's oldest city, Waterford was founded by the Vikings in the 9th century and was taken over by Strongbow, the Norman invader, with much bloodshed in 1170. The city resisted Cromwell's 1649 attacks—his phrase "by Hook or by Crooke" refers to his two siege routes here, one via Hook Head, the other via Crooke Village on the estuary—but fell the following year. It did not prosper again until 1783, when George and William Penrose set out to create "plain and cut flint glass, useful and ornamental," and thereby set in motion a glass-manufacturing industry without equal.

Waterford has better-preserved city walls than anywhere else in Ireland but Derry. Initially, the slightly run-down commercial center doesn't look promising. You'll need to park your car and proceed on foot to discover the heritage that the city has made admirable efforts over the past decade to preserve, in particular the grand 18th-century Georgian buildings that Waterford architect John Roberts (1714–1796) built, including the town's Protestant and Catholic cathedrals. The compact town center can be visited in a couple of hours. Allow at least another hour if you intend to take the Waterford crystal factory tour. The **city quays**— at the corner of Custom House Parade and Peter Street—are a good place to begin a tour of Waterford City. (The TIO is also down here, at the Granary on Merchant's Quay.) The city quays stretch for nearly 2 km (1 mi) along the River Suir and were described in the 18th century as the best in Europe.

㉕ **Reginald's Tower,** a waterside circular tower on the east end of Waterford's quays, marks the apex of a triangle containing the old walled city of Waterford. Built by the Vikings for the city's defense in 1003, it has 80-foot-high, 10-foot-thick walls; an interior stairway leads to the top. The tower served in turn as the residence for a succession of Anglo-Norman kings (including Henry II, John, and Richard II), a mint for silver coins, a prison, and an arsenal. It is said that Strongbow's marriage to Eva, the daughter of Dermot MacMurrough, took place here in the late 12th century, thus uniting the Norman invaders with the native Irish. It has been restored to its original medieval appearance and furnished with appropriate 11th- to 15th-century artifacts. ⊠ *The Quay* ☎ *051/ 304–220* ▱ *€2* ⊙ *June–Aug., daily, 9:30–9; May and Sept., daily 9:30–9; Oct.–Apr., daily 10–5.*

㉖ One of Waterford's finer Georgian buildings, **City Hall,** on the Mall, dates from 1783 and was designed by John Roberts, a native of the city. Nearby are some good examples of domestic Georgian architecture—tall, well-proportioned houses with typically Irish semicircular fanlights above the doors. The arms of Waterford hang over City Hall's own entrance, which leads into a spacious foyer that originally was a town meeting place and merchants' exchange. The building contains two lovely theaters, an old Waterford dinner service, and an enormous 1802 Waterford glass chandelier, which hangs in the Council Chamber (a copy of the chandelier hangs in Independence Hall in Philadelphia). The Victorian horseshoe-shape Theatre Royal is the venue for the annual Festival of Light Opera in September. ⊠ *The Mall* ☎ *051/309–900* ▱ *Free* ⊙ *Weekdays 9–5.*

㉗ The **Bishop's Palace** is among the most imposing of the remaining Georgian town houses. Only the foyer is open to the public. ⊠ *Alongside City Hall on the Mall* ▱ *Free* ⊙ *Weekdays 9–5.*

Off Colbeck Street along Spring Garden Alley, you'll see one of the remaining portions of the **old city wall;** there are sections all around the town center.

★ ㉘ Lovers of Georgian decorative arts will want to visit the late-18th-century Church of Ireland **Christ Church Cathedral,** designed by local architect John Roberts and the only neoclassical Georgian Cathedral in

Waterford City

River Suir

PEOPLE'S PARK

Court House

Fire Station

Bailey's New St.

Greyfriar's St.

Henrietta St.

Colbeck St.

City Wall

Olaf St.

High St.

Peter St.

Michael St.

Broad St.

Barronstrand St.

George's St.

Great George's St.

Meagher's Quay

Tourist Information Office

Granville Hotel

Arts Centre

O'Connell St.

Barker St.

Thomas St.

The Glen

Merchants Quay

Bridge St.

Summer Hill

Morgan St.

Ballybricken

Mayors Walk

Govt. Office

Green

Patrick St.

Alexander St.

New St.

Browne's Lane

City Wall

Health Centre

Castle St.

Spring Garden Alley

Parnell St.

Catherine St.

Beau St.

The Mall

William St.

Johns R.

Rose Lane

Adelphi Quay

The Quay

Custom House Parade

1/8 mile

200 meters

Bishop's Palace 27
Blackfriars Abbey 31
Christ Church
Cathedral 28
City Hall 26
French Church 29
Holy Trinity
Cathedral 32

Reginald's Tower 25
St. Olaf's Church 30
Victorian
Clock Tower 33
Waterford Glass
Factory 35
Waterford Treasures ..34

Ireland. Inside, all is cup-of-tea elegance—yellow walls, white stucco trim in designs of florets and laurels, grand Corinthian columns—and you can see why architectural historian Mark Girouard called this "the finest 18th-century ecclesiastical building in Ireland." It stands on the site of a great Norman Gothic cathedral. The then Bishop Cheneix, it is oft told, wouldn't consider knocking that great edifice down—never, that is, until it was arranged for a little stone vaulting to fall in his path. Medievalists will be sad, but those who prize Age-of-Enlightenment high style will rejoice. ⊠ *Henrietta St.* ☎ *051/858–958* ⊕ *www. christchurchwaterford.org* 🖃 *€3* ⊗ *Easter–Sept., daily 10–1 and 2–5.*

㉙ Roofless ruins are all that remain of **French Church** (⊠ Greyfriar's St.), a 13th-century Franciscan abbey. The church, also known as Greyfriars, was given to a group of Huguenot refugees (hence the "French") in 1695. A splendid east window remains amid the ruins. The key is available at Reginald's Tower.

㉚ **St. Olaf's Church** (⊠ St. Olaf's St.) was built, as the name implies, by the Vikings in the mid-11th century. All that remains of the old church is its original door, which has been incorporated into the wall of the existing building (a meeting hall).

㉛ The ruined tower of **Blackfriars Abbey** (⊠ High St.) belonged to a Dominican abbey founded in 1226 and returned to the crown in 1541 after the dissolution of the monasteries. It was used as a courthouse until Cromwellian forces destroyed it in the 17th century.

㉜ The Roman Catholic **Holy Trinity Cathedral** has a simple facade and a richly (some would say garishly) decorated interior with high, vaulted ceilings and ornate Corinthian pillars. It was designed in Neoclassical style by John Roberts, who also designed Christ Church Cathedral and City Hall. Surprisingly, it was built in the late 18th century—when Catholicism was barely tolerated—on land granted by the Protestant city fathers. ⊠ *Barronstrand St. between High St. and the clock tower on the quays* ☎ *051/875–166* 🖃 *Free* ⊗ *Daily 8:30–5:30.*

㉝ The **Victorian Clock Tower** (⊠ Merchant's Quay) was built in 1864 with public donations. Although it has no great architectural merit, it serves as a reminder of the days when Waterford was a thriving, bustling port.

㉞ **Waterford Treasures,** above the southeast's main TIO, uses interactive audiovisual technology to guide you through 1,000 years in the history of Waterford. Entertaining and educational, the exhibition displays Waterford's rich inheritance of rare and beautiful artifacts—from the Charter Roll of 1372, a list of all charters granted to Waterford up to that time, written in Latin on vellum, to the sword of King Edward IV to 18th-century crystal. A restaurant and a shop are also on the premises. ⊠ *The Granary, Merchant's Quay* ☎ *051/304–500* 🖃 *€6* ⊗ *Sept.–May, daily 10–5; June–Aug., daily 9:30–9.*

FodorśChoice
★

㉟ The city's most popular attraction is the **Waterford Glass Factory,** about 2 km (1 mi) from the TIO, where the world-famous crystal is created. The factory opened in 1783, crafting elegant and ornate stemware, chandeliers, and other pieces. Over the years, its clientele and product line di-

CloseUp

ROLLS-ROYCE OF CRYSTAL

SILICA SAND + **POTASH** + *litharge* = Waterford crystal: it reads like cold science, but something magical happens when the craftsmen of Waterford produce arguably the top crystal in the world (although France's Baccarat might have something to say about that).

When the Waterford Glass Factory opened in 1783, it provided English royalty and nobility with a regular supply of ornate handcrafted stemware, chandeliers, and decorative knickknacks. Since then Waterford crystal has graced the tables of heads of states the world over, and Waterford's earlier pieces have become priceless heirlooms.

The best Waterford glass was produced from the late 18th century to the early 19th century. This early work, examples of which can be found in museums and public buildings all over the country, is characterized by a unique, slightly opaque cast that is absent from the modern product.

Crystal glass is not cheap: each piece is individually fashioned by almost two dozen pairs of hands before it passes final inspection and receives the discreet Waterford trademark.

If you're in Waterford, put a tour of the factory at the top of your itinerary. There you can see master craftspeople at work, fashioning the molten glass, blowing it into bulbous shapes, and then cutting and carving to give each piece those wonderful light-catching facets that cast multicolored reflections. You probably won't need any protective eye gear, but considering all the razzle-dazzle, sunglasses might come in handy.

versified, and today the United States is the biggest market. The tour of the factory takes you through the specialized crafts of blowing, cutting, and polishing glass—all carried out against a noisy background of glowing furnaces and ceaseless bustle. An extensive selection of crystal is on view (and for sale) in the showroom. Tours are offered on weekends (often booked solid weeks in advance during summer), but on weekdays you are allowed to go at a more relaxed pace, which is infinitely preferable. To reserve a place in a 60-minute tour, which includes an optional 18-minute audiovisual show, call the factory or the tourist office. To get here, take the N25 Waterford–Cork road south from the quay, or ask at the tourist office about the regular bus service. ⊠ *Cork Rd., Kilbarry* ☎ *051/ 332–500* ⊕ *www.waterfordcrystalvisitorcentre.com* ⊠ *€7.50* ⊙ *Jan.–Feb. and Nov.–Dec., daily 9–5; Mar.–Oct., daily, 8:30–6.*

If the weather is favorable, consider taking a **cruise** along Waterford's harbor and the wide, picturesque estuary of the River Suir. You can enjoy lunch, afternoon tea, or dinner aboard a luxury river cruiser or simply take in the sights. The boat departs from the quay opposite the TIO, where you can purchase tickets. ☎ *051/421–723 Galley Cruises* ⊕ *www.rivercruises.ie* ⊙ *Cruises Apr.–Oct., daily at 12:30, 3, and 7, weather permitting.*

Where to Stay & Eat

$$–$$$$ ✕ **Chez Ks Steak & Seafood Restaurant.** Bright mosaic-adorned walls, an open kitchen, and a lively atmosphere make this one of Waterford's most popular restaurants. Grilled food is the specialty and you can watch your steak or seafood item being prepared in the open kitchen. Customize your meal with a choice of trimmings, sauces, and side dishes, while choosing from such house favorites as steak fillet with pepper sauce, and Irish sea bass with lemon beurre blanc. ⊠ *20–22 William St.* ☎ *051/844–180* ⌕ *Reservations essential* ☰ DC, MC, V.

★ **$$–$$$** ✕ **Dwyers of Mary Street.** Walls painted in shades of gray and wine, and beech dressers displaying antique and modern glass soften and warm the interior of the old Royal Irish Constabulary barracks, which is where you'll find this French-influenced restaurant. The menu changes every four weeks; a typical meal might consist of a tartlet of Jerusalem artichokes and roast scallops, followed by a venison loin roast, carved on a bed of celeriac and served with a port-and-orange sauce. ⊠ *8 Mary St.* ☎ *051/877–478* ⊕ *www.dwyersrestaurant.com* ⌕ *Reservations essential* ☰ AE, DC, MC, V ⊘ *Closed Sun. No lunch.*

$$–$$$ ✕ **Goose's Barbecue & Wine House.** The rustic dining room complements the ranch-style cooking that's served at this unusual restaurant in the historic quarter of the city. Exposed brick, robust furniture, and bright walls make convivial surroundings for a meat-heavy menu. Locals return again and again for the house specialties—saucy sausages, hickory-smoked spareribs, and cajun chicken wings—which are cooked in an open kitchen. Balance your meal with a giant baked potato, healthy helping of greens from the self-service salad bar, and a bottle of wine from an interesting list. Efficient table service, good desserts, and hearty food guarantee a satisfying night out. ⊠ *19 Henrietta St.* ☎ *051/858–426* ⌕ *Reservations essential* ☰ MC, V ⊘ *Closed Sun. and Mon.*

$–$$ ✕ **The Wine Vault.** You'd never know it but underneath this modern building lies the cellar of an Elizabethan town house, thought to have been built by Peter Rice, the mayor of Waterford back in 1426. Famed for forging links between Waterford and the Spanish shrine of Santiago de Compostela, Rice was also a wealthy wine merchant and for centuries this fortified town house held stocks of Bordeaux, Port, Madeira, Claret, and Hock. Today, fittingly, you can sit down at the polished wooden tables of the restored bonded warehouse to enjoy the creations of chef Fergal Phelan, who likes to buy wines to match food. His results—glazed monkfish served on a ragout of butter beans and red peppers, or chargrilled balsamic chicken with lime and baby potatoes—are intriguing and make this informal bistro one of Waterford's longtime favorites. On your way out, be sure to peruse the vintages, hailing from Australia to Alsace, on sale in the basement wine shop. ⊠ *High St.* ☎ *051/853–444* ⊕ *www.waterfordwinevault.com* ☰ AE, MC, V ⊘ *Closed Sun.*

Fodor's Choice ★

$$$$ ✕🖾 **Waterford Castle.** Not only does this fairy-tale castle come with an 800-year-old history, it sits in the middle of a 310-acre island, and allows lucky guests to be bed-and-boarded in the grandest Irish style. Back in Norman times, the Kfyeralds built a keep here and over the centuries—as their name became Fitzgeralds, "Kings of Ireland in all but name"—they added two Elizabethan-style wings in the 17th century, fitting them

Fodor's Choice ★

out with rooftop gargoyles brought from Castle Irwell in Manchester. Today, the air of exclusivity lingers as the private ferry picks you up on the shores of the River Suir, and heightens with one step inside the Great Hall, a magnificent faux-baronial room in Portland stone and hung with medieval tapestries. Nearby is the Munster Dining Room, whose luxe— oak paneling, darkened with age, and ancestral portraits spotlit in gilt frames—compliments one of the most stylish menus around. Most guest rooms are exquisitely done in real "country-house" style, some with canopied beds, chintz armchairs, and dark mahogany furniture. To top it all off, a prize-winning 18-hole golf course adjoins the castle. Obviously, the last great Fitzgerald to occupy the house, Mary Frances (whose son, Edward Fitzgerald, translated the *Rubaiyat of Omar Khayyam* into English) would be happy to see her former domaine so lovingly cared for. ⊠ *The Island, Ballinakill, Co. Waterford* ☎ *051/878– 203* 🖷 *051/879–316* ⊕ *www.waterfordcastle.com* ⤴ *14 rooms, 5 suites* ⚐ *Restaurant, 18-hole golf course, 2 tennis courts, fishing, croquet; no a/c* ⊟ *AE, DC, MC, V* ⦿⃝ *BP.*

$–$$
Fodor'sChoice
★
✕⊡ **O'Gradys Restaurant & Guesthouse.** Excellent cooking and a friendly welcome typify this beautifully restored lodge house on the outskirts of the city. Low-key furnishings and a good art collection dominate the family-friendly restaurant ($–$$; reservations essential) run by husband-and-wife team Cornelius and Sue. The freshest local ingredients are given a modern Irish treatment, with seafood taking center stage. Expect delights like rock oysters gratiné, lobster in various tempting guises, and baked paupiettes of lemon sole with a lemongrass vinaigrette. There are nine simple, comfortable guest rooms. ⊠ *Cork Rd., Co. Waterford* ☎ *051/378–851* ⤴ *9 rooms, 1 apartment* ⚐ *Restaurant, no a/c* ⊟ *AE, DC, MC, V* ⦿⃝ *BP.*

$$–$$$
⊡ **Tower Hotel.** Located opposite Reginald's Tower and overlooking the river Suir, this modern hotel is one of the city's busiest. It's touted as a family-friendly hotel, and there's a kid's club June through August with activities ranging from face painting to disco dancing to storytelling. Creams, beiges, and solid wood furniture create the soothing palette. ⊠ *The Mall, Co. Waterford* ☎ *051/875–801* 🖷 *051/870–129* ⊕ *www.towerhotelwaterford.com* ⤴ *140 rooms* ⚐ *2 restaurants, indoor pool, gym, hot tub, sauna, bar, children's programs (ages 2–7); no a/c* ⊟ *AE, DC, MC, V.*

$$
⊡ **Dooley's Hotel.** The welcome at this family-run hotel is what makes it popular. Dooley's is also just minutes walk from all the main attractions and is perfect for families. The rooms are simple, bright, and decorated in vibrant colors. The service is excellent and the traditional-style bar is popular with locals. The New Ship restaurant serves Continental dishes and has an early-bird menu. ⊠ *30 The Quay, Co. Waterford* ☎ *051/873–531* 🖷 *051/870–262* ⊕ *www.dooleys-hotel.ie* ⤴ *115 rooms* ⚐ *Restaurant, bar; no a/c* ⊟ *AE, DC, MC, V* ⦿⃝ *BP.*

$
⊡ **Foxmount Farm & Country House.** For a pleasant change of pace, you can stay on a working dairy farm in the peaceful countryside. This elegant 17th-century creeper-clad farmhouse on extensive grounds has an informal style, with welcoming log fires and intriguing antiques. It's about 5 km (3 mi) outside town on the road to the Passage East ferry. Your host, Margaret Kent, is renowned for her evening meals (for residents only). She uses the farm's produce, and fruit and herbs from her own

garden. You're invited to bring your own wine and enjoy a glass or two around the hearth after dinner. ⊠ *Passage East Rd., Co. Waterford* 🕾 *051/ 874–308* 🖷 *051/854–906* ⊕ *www.tipp.ie/foxmount.htm* ↝ *5 rooms* ♿ *Dining room, tennis court; no a/c, no room TVs* ⊟ *No credit cards* ¶◎ *BP* ☉ *Closed Nov.–mid-Mar.*

Nightlife & the Arts

The **Spraoi Festival** (🕾 051/841–808 ⊕ www.spraoi.com) is billed as the "biggest street carnival in Ireland"—with street theater, live music, and fireworks. This free outdoor festival, which appeals to children and adults alike, takes place annually during the August bank holiday, the first weekend of the month). The **Waterford International Festival of Light Opera** (🕾 051/874–402 ⊕ www.waterfordfestival.com), the only competitive event of its kind, is a great draw for amateur musical societies from Ireland and Great Britain. The festival runs for 17 nights every September at the Theatre Royal (⊠ City Hall, The Mall 🕾 051/874–402). The **Waterford Show** tells the story of Waterford's culture and heritage through music, song, and dance. The show begins at 9 PM on Tuesday, Thursday, and Saturday at City Hall from May through September. The admission cost of €11 includes a preshow drink and a glass of wine during the show. Book at Waterford Glass Factory or the Tourist Information Office (🕾 051/875–788).

You can see a wide selection of work by contemporary artists at the **Dyehouse Gallery and Waterford Pottery** (⊠ Dyehouse La. 🕾 051/844–770 ⊕ www.dyehouse-gallery.co), one of Ireland's only modern purpose-built galleries. The building is an attraction in itself and has won numerous awards for its architectural design. The **Forum** (⊠ The Glen 🕾 051/871–111 ⊕ www.forumwaterford.com) is a large entertainment venue that houses a 300-seat theater. Here you can watch local productions or those of traveling theater companies. Two music venues host big names as well as local acts performing all kinds of music. Culture buffs shouldn't miss the **Garter Lane Arts Centre** (⊠ 22A O'Connell St. 🕾 051/855–038), which hosts concerts, exhibits, and theater productions. The five-screen **Waterford Cineplex** (⊠ Patrick St. 🕾 051/874–595) shows current releases.

Geoffs (⊠ 9 John St. 🕾 051/874–787) is a dimly lighted pub frequented by students on weekends. A mixed crowd gathers during the week. Big flagstones cover the floors, and seating is on old wooden benches. A wide selection of food is served all day, every day.

If it's Georgian style you're after, head for the historic facade of **The Kings** (⊠ 8 Lombard St. 🕾 051/874–495), which dates from 1776 and has been a landmark around the Waterford docks ever since. Housed in an 800-year-old building, the **Old Ground** (⊠ 10 The Glen 🕾 051/852–283) is a popular pub with locals. Lunch is served daily, and traditional-music sessions are held every Friday night. The circa-1700 **T & H Doolan's Bar** (⊠ 32 George's St. 🕾 051/872–764), reputed to be one of the oldest pubs in Ireland, hosts traditional Irish music most summer nights and Monday through Wednesday year-round. Known to the natives as Meade's Under the Bridge, **Jack Meades** (⊠ Cheekpoint Rd., Halfway House Ballycanavan 🕾 051/873–187) is snug under a time-stained stone bridge, a coach stop used over the centuries on the road from Waterford to Passage East. There's a pub menu from May through September, and singalong sessions are held throughout the year on the weekends. In winter the fireplaces roar, illuminating the wood beams and bric-a-brac.

Sports & the Outdoors

GAELIC FOOTBALL & HURLING
Gaelic football and hurling can be seen at the **Waterford GAA Grounds** (⊠ Walsh Park ☎ 01/836–3222 for the GAA in Dublin).

GOLF
Faithlegg Golf Club (⊠ Faithlegg House, Checkpoint ☎ 051/382–241) is an 18-hole, par-72 course set in mature landscape on the banks of the River Suir. **Waterford Castle Golf Club** (⊠ The Island, Ballinakill ☎ 051/871–633) is an 18-hole, par-72 course that claims to be Ireland's only true island course.

Shopping

City Square Shopping Centre (⊠ City Sq. ☎ 051/853–528) has more than 40 shops, ranging from small Irish fashion boutiques to large international department stores. Fashion shows and other forms of entertainment take place on the stage area in the center of the mall. **Joseph Knox** (⊠ 3 Barronstrand St. ☎ 051/875–307) displays the best selection of crystal in Waterford City. **Kellys** (⊠ 75–76 The Quay ☎ 051/873–557) has excellent Irish souvenirs, including traditional musical instruments, dolls, Irish linen, jewelry, Waterford crystal, and CDs. While in Waterford, definitely pay a visit to the famed **Waterford Glass Factory** (⊠ Cork Rd., Kilbarry ☎ 051/332–500). The showroom displays an extensive selection of Waterford crystal and Wedgwood china.

Dunmore East

36 *16 km (10 mi) southeast of Waterford City via R683 and R684.*

Dunmore East is a quaint, one-street fishing village of thatched cottages and an attractive lighthouse at the head of Waterford Harbor. Note the many colorful but noisy kittiwakes that nest in the steep cliffs overlooking the harbor. Many small beaches and cliff walks are nearby, and you get a wonderful view of the estuary from the hill behind the village.

Where to Eat

$$–$$$ ✕ **Ship Restaurant.** Chef Billy Fitzpatrick emphasizes fresh, local seafood at this simply furnished restaurant on the ground floor of a 19th-century house overlooking the bay. The cuisine mixes French and Irish influences. Start with an arrangement of seafood with ratatouille enhanced by gazpacho sauce. Entrées include grilled or panfried black sole, and roulade of Dover sole filled with saffron mousse. ☎ *051/383–141* ▭ *AE, DC, MC, V.*

Tramore

37 *11 km (7 mi) south of Waterford City on R675, 4 km (2½ mi) west of Dunmore East.*

Tramore's 5-km-long (3-mi-long) **beach** is a popular escape for families from Waterford and other parts of the southeast, as the many vacation homes and camper parks indicate. This is Ireland's biggest seaside resort and a dream-come-true for young children, but it's not to everybody's taste. A 50-acre amusement park, a miniature railway, and vacation-home developments overshadow part of the seafront. (The upper half of town is more quiet and reserved.) At the western end of the beach, the sand gives way to rocky cliffs guarded by the Metal Man, a giant cast-iron figure which stands atop a great pillar. It's said that if a young woman hops on one foot around the base of the pillar three times, she will be married within a year. This custom, which is still observed in a lighthearted way, can be traced back to a stone that stood on the spot centuries ago and was used in ancient Celtic fertility rites.

Where to Stay

$ 🏠 **Annestown House.** Romantically perched above the sea, this large, white Victorian has a private path down to Annestown Cove, one of many secluded coves along the breathtakingly beautiful "Copper Coast" between Tramore and Dungarvan. The house has been in the family of John Galloway since 1820. John and his wife, Pippa, welcome guests into a home full of nooks and crannies, lots of books, and a large billiard table. Bedrooms are generally large and full of character, with wonderful sea views at the front of the house. Dinner is served at 7:45; book by noon. ⊠ *Annestown, Co. Waterford* ☎ *051/396–160* 🖷 *051/396–474* ⊕ *www.annestown.com* 🛏 *5 rooms* ♿ *Dining room, tennis court, billiards, croquet; no a/c, no room TVs* ⊟ *AE, MC, V* ⦿ *BP* ⊘ *Closed Nov.–mid-Mar.*

Dungarvan

38 *42 km (26 mi) southwest of Tramore on R675.*

With their covering of soft grasses, the lowlands of Wexford and eastern Waterford gradually give way to heath and moorland; the wetter climate of the hillier western Waterford countryside creates and maintains the bog. The mountains responsible for this change in climate rise up behind Dungarvan, the largest coastal town in County Waterford. This bustling fishing and resort spot sits at the mouth of River Colligan, which empties into Dungarvan Bay here. It's a popular base for climbers and hikers. In **Ring (An Rinne),** a Gaeltacht area on Dungarvan Bay, the Irish language is still in daily use—this is unusual in the south and east of the country. At Colaiste na Rinne, a language college, courses in Irish have been taught since 1909. ⊠ *7 km (4¼ mi) southeast of Dungarvan, off N674F.*

Where to Stay & Eat

★ $$ ✕ **The Tannery.** Pity those poor Dubliners. Many of their restaurants are stuck in the nouvelle trenches, but out here in the boonies that Knockmealdown mountain air must do something to clear the brain and allow chefs to focus and purify. Perhaps this is why this place is besieged on weekends, when crowds head here to taste the creations of culinary wizard Paul Flynn. Little wonder foodies—Sir Andrew Lloyd Webber, to name one—are raving. One bite of the fillet steak set atop a little pie filled with chopped kidney and potato, then topped with that high-fashion veg— mushy peas—will seduce all. The roast guinea fowl garnished with potato dauphinoise and a sauce thickened with Parmesan will delight. Gastro-pub fare like breast of wood pigeon on toasted brioche with creamed onions and truffle oil will make many clamor for seconds. The decor is nothing to fly to Ireland for, as it is your standard-issue mega-sized white-on-white Soho loft room. But you won't mind when you dig into one of Flynn's dessert "puds," including his take on the famous Ivy Restaurant (London, don't you know?) hot chocolate pudding with Kirsch cherries. Top it all off with a fine liqueur and a bite of Knockanore cheese. Incidentally, it is much easier to snag a table during weekdays. ⊠ *10 Quay St.* ⊕ *www.tannery.ie* ☎ *058/45420* ⊟ *AE, DC, MC, V* ⊘ *Closed Mon., 1st wk of Sept., and 2 wks in Jan. No dinner Sun.*

$–$$ ▣ **The Gold Coast Golf Hotel.** Overlooking Dungarvan Bay, this hotel is one of the newest parts of a family-run and family-friendly property, including 21 self-catering holiday cottages (built around the 37-bedroom hotel) and 10 golf villas on the edge of a woodland course on a links setting. Rooms are bright, comfortable, and spacious. Guests can use the facilities of the Gold Coast's sister hotel, the Clonea Strand, just 2½ km (1½ mi) away, which include a games room, a leisure complex, and Clonea's 3-km-long (2-mi-long) sandy beach. ⊠ *Co. Waterford* ☎ *058/42249 or 058/42416* 🖷 *058/43378* ⊕ *www.clonea.com* 🛏 *37 rooms, 21 cottages, 10 villas* ⚒ *Restaurant, 18-hole golf course, tennis court, indoor pool, gym, fishing, bar, playground* ⊟ *AE, DC, MC, V* ⊺ *BP.*

Nightlife & the Arts

Several miles away from Dungarvan, a *ceilí* (Irish dance) is held nightly in summer at **Colaiste na Rinne** (⊠ Ring ☎ 058/46104).

IN & AROUND COUNTY TIPPERARY

"It's a long way to Tipperary . . .": so run the words of that famed song sung all over the world since World War I. Actually, Tipperary is *not* so far to go, considering that, as Ireland's biggest inland county, it's within easy striking distance of Waterford and Cork. Moving in from the coastline, you can travel through some of Ireland's most lush pasture-lands and to some of its most romantic sights, such as Lismore Castle. The Nire Valley, in the mountains between Dungarvan and Clonmel, is a popular area for hiking and pursuing other outdoor pleasures. The Blackwater Valley is renowned for its beauty, peacefulness, and excellent fishing. Some of the finest racehorses in the world are raised in the fields of Tipperary, which is also the county where you'll find the Rock of Cashel—the greatest group of monastic ruins in all Ireland.

Lismore

39 *40 km (25 mi) northwest of Ardmore on N72 and R671.*

Fodor'sChoice
★

Popular with both anglers and romantics, the enchanting little town of Lismore is built on the banks of the Blackwater, a river famous for its trout and salmon. From the 7th to the 12th century it was an important monastic center, founded by St. Carthac (or Carthage), and it had one of the most renowned universities of its time. The village has two cathedrals; a Roman Catholic one from the late 19th century and the

Church of Ireland St. Carthage's, which dates from 1633 and incorporates fragments of an earlier church. Glamour arrived in the form of the dukes of Devonshire, who built their Irish seat here (their main house is Chatsworth in England); in the 1940s, Fred Astaire, whose sister, Adele, had married Lord Charles Cavendish, younger son of the ninth duke, would bend the elbow at the town's Madden's Pub. There were darker interludes to the town's history: Lismore was hard hit by the Great Famine of 1845 and its Famine Graveyard bears poignant witness.

★ As you cross the bridge entering Lismore, take in the dramatic view of the magnificent **Lismore Castle,** a vast, turreted gray-stone building atop a rock that overhangs River Blackwater. There has been a castle here since the 12th century, but the present structure, built by the sixth duke of Devonshire, dates from the mid-19th century. Today, the house remains the Irish estate of the current duke and duchess and is not open to the public (although you can call it your own for a very posh rental fee). But the upper and lower gardens, which consist of woodland walks, including an unusual yew walk said to be more than 800 years old (Edmund Spencer is said to have written parts of *The Faerie Queen* there), are open during certain months of the year. Comprising seven acres set with 17th-century defensive walls, the gardens have an impressive display of magnolias, camellias, and shrubs, and are adorned with examples of contemporary sculpture. ☎ *058/54424* ⊕ *http://lismorecas-tle.com* ✉ *€5* ☉ *Apr., May, Sept., and Oct., daily 1:45–4:45; June–Aug., daily 11–4:45.*

Almost the definitive example in these Islands of an Estate town, Lismore has, in recent years taken the firm decision to project a pride of place linked with a deep sense of history. The **Lismore Heritage Center,** housed in the former town courthouse, lies at the core of the town and exhibits focus on the town's Celtic origins and its links to many famous people from Sir Walter Raleigh to Prince Charles to Fred Astaire. An award-winning video presentation on the history of the town from its monastic 7th century origins up to the present day is shown. ⊠ *The Old Courthouse* ☎ *058/54975* ⊕ *www.lismore-ireland.com/heritage/* ✉ *€4* ☉ *June–Aug, Mon.–Sat., 9;30–6, Sun. 9:30–5:30,; Apr.–May and Sept.–Oct., Mon.–Sat., 9:30–5:30, Sun., 10–5:30.*

Mount Melleray Abbey was the first post-Reformation monastery, founded in 1832 by the Cistercian Order in what was then a barren mountainside wilderness. Over the years the order has transformed the site into more than 600 acres of fertile farmland. The monks maintain strict vows of silence, but you are welcome to join in services throughout the day and are permitted into most areas of the abbey. It is also possible to stay in the guest lodge by prior arrangement. If you are heading into the Knockmealdown Mountains from Lismore, you can easily stop on the way at the abbey for a visit. ⊠ *South of the Vee Gap, signposted off R669, 13 km (8 mi) from Lismore, Cappoquin* ☎ *058/54404* ✉ *Free* ☉ *Daily 7:45 AM–8 PM.*

Leaving Lismore, heading east on N72 for 6½ km (4 mi) toward Cappoquin, a well-known coarse-angling center, you can pick up R669 north into the **Knockmealdown Mountains.** Your route is signposted as the Vee Gap road, the Vee Gap being its summit, from where you'll have superb views of the Tipperary plain, the Galtee Mountains in the northwest, and a peak called Slievenamon in the northeast. If the day is clear, you should be able to see the Rock of Cashel, ancient seat of the kings of Munster, some 32 km (20 mi) away. Just before you enter the Vee Gap, look for a 6-foot-high mound of stones on the left side of the road. It marks the grave of Colonel Grubb, a local landowner who liked the view so much that he arranged to be buried here standing up so that he could look out over the scene for all eternity.

Where to Stay & Eat

★ **$$-$$$** ✕🖭 **Richmond House.** It's been 300 years since the Earl of Cork and Burlington built this handsome country house, and it still retains an aura of courtly elegance. Today, happily, owners Claire and Paul Deevy give it a relaxed and welcoming touch. The public rooms, with log fires and traditional rust-and-cream decor, are reminiscent of a classic country hotel, although one graced with silver plate, a tapestry, and a stuffed owl. The pièce de résistance here, however, is the restaurant ($$$$), where Paul and his small staff wow critics and diners (many of whom are not guests at the hotel) alike. Famous for his warm asparagus wrapped in smoked salmon, he prides himself on using local game in season and fish from Helvic, Dunmore, and Ardmore, then adding his personal flair. Triumphs include wild Blackwater salmon with Thai spices, a spring roll with smoked duck breast, and rabbit with black pudding. Reservations are essential for the restaurant. ⊠ *Cappoquin, Co. Waterford* ☎ *058/ 54278* 🖶 *058/54988* ⊕ *www.richmondhouse.net* ⇆ *9 rooms* ⚬ *Restaurant, fishing, horseback riding, bar; no a/c* ☰ *AE, DC, MC, V* ⏱ *BP* ⊙ *Closed late Dec.–mid-Jan.*

Cahir

⓵ *37 km (23 mi) north of Lismore, at crossroads of R668, N24, and N8.*

A pleasant Georgian square lies at the heart of this easy-going town, but **Cahir Castle** remains the unavoidable focal point. Perched on a rocky island on the River Suir, it is one of Ireland's largest and best-preserved castles, retaining its dramatic keep, tower, and much of its original defensive structure. An audiovisual show and guided tour are available upon request. ☎ *052/41011* ⊕ *www.heritageireland.ie* 🎟 *€2.75* ⊙ *Mid-Mar.–mid-June and mid-Sept.–mid-Oct., daily 9:30–5:30; mid-June–mid-Sept., daily 9–7:30; mid-Oct.–mid-Mar., daily 9:30–4:30; last admission 45 mins before closing.*

If there is little storybook allure to the brute mass of Cahir Castle, we are very much in fairy-tale realms with a visit to the first earl of Glengall's 1812 **Swiss Cottage,** a dreamy relic from the days when Romanticism conquered 19th-century Ireland. A mile south of town on a particularly picturesque stretch of the River Suir, this "cottage orné" was probably designed by John Nash, one of the Regency's most fashionable architects. Half thatched-roof cottage, half mansion, bordered by verandas constructed of branched trees, it was a veritable theater set that allowed the lordly couple to fantasize about being "simple folk" (down

FodorsChoice ★

to the fact that secret doorways were constructed to allow family retainers to bring drinks and food without being noticed). Inside, some of the earliest Dufour wallpapers printed in Paris charm the eye. The Cottage is signposted from the R670 along the Cahir to Ardfinnan road, or you can hike from Cahir Castle on a footpath along the enchanting river. In peak season, crowds can be fierce. ☎ 052/41144 ⊕ *www.heritageireland.ie* 🎟 €6 ⊘ *Mid-Mar.–Mar. 31, Tues.–Sun. 10–1, 2–4:30; Apr., Tues.–Sun. 10–1, 2–5; May–Sept., daily 10–6; Oct.–Nov., Tues.–Sun. 10–1, 2–4:30.*

Where to Stay

¢ 🏰 **Bansha Castle.** Venture into the heart of quiet, wooded country backed by the Glen of Aherlow, about 8 km (5 mi) from Cahir on the N24 Tipperary road, to this 18th-century stone house with a Norman-style round tower. Large rooms, all with great views, are simply furnished with plain carpets and mahogany reproduction pieces, but walls are decorated in strong, vibrant colors. The drawing room has marble fireplaces, polished wooden floors, and floral patterned furniture. Locally grown organic produce is used in the good home cooking. Outdoor activities, such as walking, golfing, salmon and trout fishing, and horseback riding, are nearby. ⊠ *Bansha, Co. Tipperary* ☎ *062/54187* 🖷 *062/54294* ➥ *6 rooms, 5 with bath* ⚘ *Dining room; no a/c, no room TVs* ▭ *No credit cards* ⦿⃝ *BP.*

Tipperary Town

❹❶ *22 km (14 mi) northwest of Cahir on N24.*

Tipperary Town, a dairy-farming center at the head of a fertile plain known as the Golden Vale, is a good starting point for climbing and walking in the hills around the Glen of Aherlow; but the small country town, on the River Ara, is worth visiting in its own right. In New Tipperary, a neighborhood built by local tenants during Ireland's Land War (1890–91), old buildings, like Dalton's Heritage House, have been restored; you can visit the Heritage House by calling the offices of Clann na hEireann. You can also visit the old Butter Market on Dillon Street; the Churchwell at the junction of Church, Emmet, and Dillon streets; and the grave of the grandfather of Robert Emmett—one of the most famous Irish patriots—in the graveyard at St. Mary's Church. A statue of Charles Kickham, whose 19th-century novel *The Homes of Tipperary* chronicled the devastation of this county through forced emigration, has a place of honor in the center of town. Adjacent to Bridewell Jail on St. Michael's Street is St. Michael's Church, with its stained-glass window depicting a soldier killed during World War I. The **headquarters of Clann na hEireann** (⊠ 45 Main St. ☎ 062/33188) researches the origins and history of surnames throughout Ireland, and promotes clan gatherings.

Cashel

❹❷ *17 km (11 mi) northeast of Tipperary Town on N74.*

Cashel is a market town on the busy Cork–Dublin road, with a lengthy history as a center of royal and religious power. From roughly AD 370 until 1101, it was the seat of the kings of Munster, and it was probably at one time a center of Druidic worship. Here, according to legend, St. Patrick arrived in about AD 432 and baptized King Aengus, who became Ireland's first Christian ruler. One of the many legends associated with this event is that St. Patrick plucked a shamrock to explain the mystery of the Trinity, thus giving a new emblem to Christian Ireland.

Fodor's Choice ★   The awe-inspiring, oft-mist-shrouded **Rock of Cashel** is one of Ireland's most visited sites. The rock itself, a short walk north of town, rises as a giant, circular mound 200 feet above the surrounding plain; it's crowned by a tall cluster of gray monastic remains. Legend has it that St. Patrick baptized King Aengus here and that the devil, flying over Ireland in a hurry, took a bite out of the Slieve Bloom Mountains to clear his path (the gap, known as the Devil's Bit, can be seen to the north of the rock) and spat it out in the Golden Vale.

The shell of **St. Patrick's Cathedral** is the largest structure on the summit. The original 13th-century cathedral, built in a flamboyant variation on Romanesque style, was destroyed by fire in 1495. The restored building was desecrated during the 16th century in an ugly incident in which hundreds of townspeople who had sought sanctuary in the cathedral were burned to death when Cromwell's forces surrounded the building with turf and set the structure afire. A series of sculptures in the north transept represents the apostles, other saints, and the Beasts of the Apocalypse. Look for the octagonal staircase turret that ascends beside the Central Tower to a series of defensive passages built into the thick walls. From the top of the Central Tower, you'll have a wonderful view of the surrounding plains and mountains. Another passage gives access to the round tower, a well-preserved, 92-foot-high building.

The entrance to **Cormac's Chapel,** the best-preserved building on top of the Rock, is behind the south transept of the cathedral. The chapel was built in 1127 by Cormac Macarthy, king of Desmond and bishop of Cashel (combination bishop-kings were not unusual in the early Irish church). Note the high corbeled roof, modeled on the traditional covering of early saints' cells (as at Glendalough and Dingle); the typically Romanesque, twisted columns around the altar; and the unique carvings around the south entrance.

The **museum** across from the entrance to the Rock provides a 15-minute audiovisual display, as well as enthusiastic young guides who will ensure that you don't miss the many interesting features of the buildings on top of the Rock of Cashel. The best approach to the rock is along the Bishop's Walk, a 10-minute hike that begins outside the drawing room of the Cashel Palace hotel on Main Street. ⊠ *Rock of Cashel* ☎ *062/61437* ⊕ *www.heritageireland.ie* ☜ *€5* ☉ *Mid-Mar.–mid-June, daily 9–5:30; mid-June–mid-Sept., daily 9–7; mid-Sept.–mid-Mar., daily 9–4:30.*

In the same building as the TIO, the **Cashel of the Kings Heritage Center** explains the historic relationship between the town and the Rock and includes a scale model of Cashel as it looked during the 1600s. ⊠ *City Hall, Main St.* ☎ *062/62511* ☜ *Free* ☉ *Daily 9:30–5:50.*

The **G. P. A. Bolton Library,** on the grounds of the St. John the Baptist Church of Ireland Cathedral, has a particularly fine collection of rare books, manuscripts, and maps, some of which date from the beginning of the age of printing in Europe. ✉ *John St.* ☎ *062/61944* 🎫 *€2* ☉ *Daily 10–4.*

Where to Stay & Eat

★ **$$–$$$$** ✕ **Chez Hans.** Food-lovers travel from miles around to enjoy the exceptional food at this restaurant, housed in a converted Victorian church at the foot of the Rock of Cashel. The dark wood decor and tapestries provide a wonderfully elegant background for the white-linen tables. Chef Jason Matthia prepares contemporary cuisine with a hint of nouvelle and does wonders with fresh Irish ingredients—especially seafood. You can order salmon, hake, or mussels, served in a light chive velouté. Another specialty is diced lamb with ratatouille and couscous. ✉ *Rockside* ☎ *062/61177* ♨ *Reservations essential* ▤ *MC, V* ☉ *Closed Sun. and Mon. and late Jan.–early Feb. No lunch.*

★ **$$$–$$$$** ✕▥ **Cashel Palace.** Once a bishop's palace, this Queen Anne–style mansion seems regal enough to welcome Elizabeth herself. Built in 1730 for archbishop Theophilus Bolton, it was designed by Sir Edward Lovett Pearce, who also created the Old Parliament House in Dublin. Fittingly, the exterior is very grand—this was described as a bona fide "palace" even in the 18th century—and is gorgeously offset by the parkland, replete with fountains and centuries-old trees. Inside, red-pine paneling, barley-sugar staircases, Corinthian columns, and a surfeit of cossetting antiques all create an air of Georgian volupté. Guest rooms on the second floor are cozier, though not small. The Bishop's Buttery restaurant ($$–$$$) relies on game in season, local lamb and beef, and fresh fish creatively prepared, and also serves simple, light meals all day. Don't miss the lovely gardens at the rear of the house, where you can see the descendants of the original hop plants used by Richard Guinis to brew the first "Wine of Ireland." Guinis went on, with his son, Arthur, to found the Guinness Brewery in Dublin. ✉ *Main St., Co. Tipperary* ☎ *062/ 62707* 🖨 *062/61521* 🌐 *www.cashel-palace.ie* ⬅ *23 rooms* ♨ *2 restaurants, fishing, bar; no a/c* ▤ *AE, DC, MC, V* ⦿ *BP.*

$$ ▥ **Dundrum House Hotel.** Nestled beside the River Multeen, 12 km (7½ mi) outside busy Cashel, is this imposing, four-story Georgian house. Sixteen high-ceiling bedrooms take up the main house; the rest are in a three-story wing built during the house's previous incarnation as a convent. Although highly renovated, many of the older rooms have accent pieces of early Victorian furniture. A big plus: lovely views of the surrounding parkland. The old convent chapel, stained-glass windows intact, is now a cocktail bar. Elaborate plaster ceilings, attractive period furniture, and open fires make the spacious dining room and lounge inviting. ✉ *Dundrum, Co. Tipperary* ☎ *062/71116* 🖨 *062/71366* 🌐 *www. dundrumhousehotel.com* ⬅ *85 rooms* ♨ *2 restaurants, 18-hole golf course, pool, sauna, steam room, fishing, 3 bars; no a/c* ▤ *AE, DC, MC, V* ⦿ *BP.*

Nightlife & the Arts

You can enjoy folksinging, storytelling, and dancing from mid-June through September, Tuesday through Saturday, at the **Bru Boru Heritage**

Center (☎ 062/61122) at the foot of the Rock of Cashel. Entertainment usually begins at 9 PM and costs €15, €40 with dinner.

Sports & the Outdoors

GAELIC FOOTBALL & HURLING
About 20 km (12 mi) north of Cashel, **Semple GAA Stadium** (✉ Thurles ☎ 0504/22702) is where major hurling and Gaelic football championships in the southeast take place, as well as many exciting minor contests.

GOLF
The natural features of the mature Georgian estate at Dundrum House Hotel have been incorporated into an 18-hole, par-72 course for the **County Tipperary Golf and Country Club** (✉ Dundrum House Hotel, Dundrum ☎ 062/71717).

Clonmel

🔸 *24 km (15 mi) southeast of Cashel on R688.*

As the county seat of Tipperary, Clonmel is set on the prettiest part of the River Suir, with wooded islands and riverside walks. This is one of Ireland's largest and most prosperous inland towns. There has been a settlement here since Viking days; in the 14th century the town was walled and fortified as a stronghold of the Butler family. At one end of town is the West Gate, built in 1831 on the site of the medieval one. Among other notable buildings are the Main Guard, built in 1695 to house the courts of the Palatinate, a separate jurisdiction ruled by the Butlers; and the Franciscan friary and St. Mary's Church of Ireland, both of which incorporate remains of earlier churches and some interesting tombs and monuments.

Where to Stay & Eat

$–$$ ✕ **Mulcahy's of Clonmel.** In this superb series of interconnecting bars and restaurant areas you'll find a wide selection of food, from the East Lane Café's à la carte menu to the daily carvery lunch to the Kitchen Grill menu of good pub grub, like deep-fried scampi. Mulcahy's has 10 modern bedrooms over the pub. ✉ *47 Gladstone St.* ☎ *052/22825* 🖃 *AE, DC, MC, V.*

$$–$$$ ✕🖾 **Hotel Minella.** The bedrooms of this granite-face Georgian manor hotel have fine views of the river Suir or the nearby Comeragh Mountains. Three of the eight suites have four-poster beds and private steam rooms; the remaining five have hot tubs. Comfortable Victorian furnishings fill the main house, and hunting prints line the walls. The oak-paneled restaurant ($–$$$) is noted for its well-prepared traditional Irish cuisine. ✉ *Coleville Rd., Co. Tipperary* ☎ *052/22388* 🖨 *052/24381* ⊕ *www.hotelminella.ie* 🛏 *62 rooms, 8 suites, 10 apartments* ⅄ *Restaurant, health club, fishing, bar; no a/c* 🖃 *AE, DC, MC, V* ⅋ *BP.*

Sports & the Outdoors

GAELIC FOOTBALL & HURLING
Gaelic football and hurling are played at the **Clonmel GAA Grounds** (✉ Western Rd. ☎ 052/23873).

Carrick-on-Suir

🔸 *20 km (12 mi) east of Clonmel on N24.*

Carrick-on-Suir lies partly in County Tipperary and partly in County Waterford. The beautifully restored **Ormonde Castle** is the town's main attraction. The castle, dating from 1450, is fronted by the 16th-century Ormonde Manor House, an interesting and well-preserved Tudor mansion. The town is one of several claiming to be the birthplace of Anne Boleyn, and the house is said to have been built in order to host her daughter, Queen Elizabeth I, who never visited here. The castle contains some good early stuccowork, especially in the 100-foot Long Room, and many arms and busts of old Bess. ☎*051/640–787* ⊕*www.heritageireland. ie* ☒ *€2.55* ☼ *Mid-June–Sept., daily 9:30–6:30.*

Shopping
Tipperary Crystal Factory Shop (☒ Ballynoran ☎ 051/641–188), a factory outlet, has its showroom in a replica of a thatched cottage.

THE SOUTHEAST A TO Z

To research prices, get advice from other travelers, and book travel arrangements, visit www.fodors.com.

AIR TRAVEL
Aer Arann flies once daily in both directions between Waterford City and London's Luton Airport.

🔢 Carrier **Aer Arann** ☎ 1890/462–726 ⊕ www.aerarannexpress.ie.

AIRPORT
Waterford Regional Airport is on the Waterford–Ballymacaw road in Killowen. Waterford City is less than 10 km (6 mi) from the airport. A hackney cab from the airport into Waterford City costs approximately €15.

🔢 Airport Information **Waterford Regional Airport** ☎ 051/875–589.

BOAT & FERRY TRAVEL
The region's primary ferry terminal is just south of Wexford Town at Rosslare. Irish Ferries connects Rosslare to Pembroke, Wales, and France's Cherbourg and Roscoff. Stena Sealink sails directly between Rosslare Ferryport and Fishguard, Wales.

🔢 Boat & Ferry Information **Irish Ferries** ☎ 053/33158. **Stena Sealink** ☎ 053/33115.

BUS TRAVEL
Bus Éireann makes the Waterford–Dublin journey 10 times a day for about €10 one-way. There are six buses daily between Waterford City and Limerick, and four between Waterford City and Rosslare. The Cork–Waterford bus runs 13 times a day. In Waterford City, the terminal is Waterford Bus Station.

🔢 Bus Information **Bus Éireann** ☎ 01/836–6111 in Dublin, 051/879–000 in Waterford.

CAR RENTAL
The major car-rental companies have offices at Rosslare Ferryport, and in most large towns rental information is available through the local tourism office. Typical car-rental prices start at about €55 per day (€32 per day for seven days) with unlimited mileage, and they usually include insurance and all taxes. Budget has offices in Rosslare Harbor and at Waterford Airport. Hertz has offices in Rosslare Harbor.

🖅 Agencies **Budget** ✉ The Ferryport, Rosslare Harbor ☎ 053/33318 ✉ Waterford Airport ☎ 051/421-670. **Hertz** ✉ The Ferryport, Rosslare Harbor ☎ 053/33238.

CAR TRAVEL
Waterford City, the regional capital, is easily accessible from all parts of Ireland. From Dublin, take N7 southwest, change to N9 in Naas, and continue along this highway through Carlow Town and Thomastown until it terminates in Waterford. N25 travels east–west through Waterford City, connecting it with Cork in the west and Wexford Town in the east. From Limerick and Tipperary Town, N24 stretches southeast until it, too, ends in Waterford City.

ROAD CONDITIONS For the most part, the main roads in the southeast are of good quality and are free of congestion. Side roads are generally narrow and twisting, and you should keep an eye out for farm machinery and animals on country roads.

EMERGENCIES
🖅 Emergency Services **Ambulance, fire, police** ☎ 112 or 999.
🖅 Hospital **Waterford Regional Hospital** ✉ Ardkeen ☎ 051/848-000.

TOURS
Irish City Tours in Kilkenny operates open-top coach tours from the castle gate Easter through September, daily 10:30–5.

Burtchaell Tours in Waterford City leads a Waterford walk at noon and 2 PM daily from March through September. Tours depart from the Granville Hotel. Walking tours of Kilkenny are arranged by Tynan Tours from the Kilkenny TIO; tours take place daily April through October, and Tuesday through Saturday, November to March. Walking tours of historic Wexford Town can be prebooked for groups by contacting Seamus P. Molloy of Wexford Town Walking Tours.
🖅 Bus Tour **Irish City Tours** ☎ 01/458-0054.
🖅 Walking Tours **Burtchaell Tours** ☎ 051/873-711. **Tynan Tours** ☎ 087/265-1745. **Wexford Town Walking Tours** ☎ 053/22663.

TRAIN TRAVEL
Waterford City is linked by Irish Rail service to Dublin. Trains run from Plunkett Station in Waterford City to Dublin four times daily, making stops at Thomastown, Kilkenny, Bagenalstown, and Carlow Town. The daily train between Waterford City and Limerick makes stops at Carrick-on-Suir, Clonmel, Cahir, and Tipperary Town. The train between Rosslare and Waterford City runs twice daily.
🖅 Train Information **Irish Rail** ☎ 01/836-6222 in Dublin, 051/873-401 in Waterford ⊕ www.irishrail.ie.

VISITOR INFORMATION
Ten Tourist Information Offices (TIOs) in the southeast are open all year. They are Carlow Town, Carrick-on-Suir, Clonmel, Dungarvan, Enniscorthy, Gorey, Kilkenny, Lismore, Waterford City, and Wexford Town. Another seven TIOs are open seasonally: Ardmore (June–mid-September); Cahir (May–September); Cashel (April–September); New Ross

(May–September); Rosslare (April–September); Tipperary Town (May–October); Tramore (June–August).

🛈 Tourist Information **Ardmore** ✉ Co. Waterford ☎ 024/94444. **Cahir** ✉ Castle Car Park, Co. Tipperary ☎ 052/41453. **Carlow Town** ✉ College St., Co. Carlow ☎ 059/913–1554. **Carrick-on-Suir** ✉ Heritage Centre, Main St., Co. Tipperary ☎ 051/640–200. **Cashel** ✉ Cashel Heritage Centre, Co. Tipperary ☎ 062/62511. **Clonmel** ✉ Community Office, 8 Sarsfield St., Co. Tipperary ☎ 052/22960. **Dungarvan** ✉ The Courthouse, Co. Waterford ☎ 058/41741. **Enniscorthy** ✉ Wexford Museum, The Castle, Castle Hill, Co. Wexford ☎ 054/34699. **Gorey** ✉ Markethouse, Main St., Co. Wexford ☎ 055/21248. **Kilkenny** ✉ Shee Alms House, Rose Inn St., Co. Kilkenny ☎ 056/775–1500. **Lismore** ✉ Heritage Centre, Co. Waterford ☎ 058/54975. **New Ross** ✉ Harbour Centre, The Quay, Co. Wexford ☎ 051/421–857. **Rosslare** ✉ Rosslare Ferry Terminal, Kilrane, Rosslare Harbor, Co. Wexford ☎ 053/33232. **Tipperary Town** ✉ 3 Mitchel St., Co. Tipperary ☎ 062/51457. **Tramore** ✉ Town Centre, Co. Waterford ☎ 051/381–572. **Waterford City** ✉ 41 The Quay, Co. Waterford ☎ 051/875–823 ⊕ www.southeastireland.com. **Wexford Town** ✉ Crescent Quay, Co. Wexford ☎ 053/23111.

THE SOUTHWEST

5

KISS THE BLARNEY STONE
and leave with a special gift ➪*p.280*

COUNT UP YOUR BLESSINGS
at the sites of *Angela's Ashes* ➪*p.331*

VOLUNTEER AS A "WHISKEY TASTER"
at the Old Midleton Distillery ➪*p.285*

SAIL THE SEAWRAPPED REALM
of the iconic Skellig Islands ➪*p.306*

RAVE TO THE KNIGHT OF GLIN
over his art-filled castle ➪*p.327*

TEACH YOUR TONGUE GOOD TASTE
at a food festival in Kinsale ➪*p.288*

INHALE FRAGRANT·ESSENCES
on the garden isle of Illnacullin ➪*p.299*

STEEL YOURSELF FOR YOUR FIRST VIEW
of the bay from Bantry House ➪*p.297*

CHOOSE TO EAT OR TO COOK
at Darina Allen's Ballymaloe House ➪*p.284*

Updated by
Alannah
Hopkin

CORK, KERRY, LIMERICK, AND CLARE—these southwest Ireland county names have an undeniable Irish lilt. Just as evocative is the scenery in each county: from Kinsale along the coast west to Mizen Head in the far southwest corner to the glorious mountains and lakes of Killarney. Thanks to its accomplished chefs and the bounty of farms, fields, lakes, and coast, County Cork has become a little paradise of fresh, rustic Irish cuisine. You'll also find a mild climate, Irish-speaking areas, and Ireland's second- and third-largest cities—Cork and Limerick. But the most notable attractions are the miles and miles of pretty country lanes meandering through rich but sparsely populated farmland. To be in a hurry here is to be ill-mannered. It was probably a Kerryman who first remarked that when God made time, he made plenty of it.

As you look over fuchsia-laden hedges at thriving dairy farms or stop at a wayside restaurant to sample seafood or locally raised meat, it's difficult to imagine that some 150 years ago this area was decimated by famine. Thousands perished in fields and workhouses, and thousands more took "coffin ships" from Cobh in Cork Harbor to the New World. Between 1845 and 1849 Ireland's population decreased by more than a million, or roughly 30% (according to the 1841 census, the Irish population was then 8,175,124). Many small southwest villages were wiped out. The region was battered again in the War for Independence and the Civil War that was fought with intensity in and around "Rebel Cork" between 1919 and 1921. Economic recovery didn't pick up until the late 1960s, and tourist development did not surge until the mid-'90s.

The Irish economic boom coincided with a marketing push to increase visitor numbers. The result has been a mixed blessing. The southwest's main routes are no longer traffic-free, but the roads themselves are better. There's a greater choice of accommodations, with improved facilities, but many of the newer hotels and bed-and-breakfasts are bland. Even the traditional, warm Irish welcome is less ubiquitous, given the increased pace of everyday life. Furthermore, much of the development threatened the environment, although the southwest is making a concerted effort to attract more visitors while keeping beaches and rivers clean and scenery unspoiled.

South of Cork City, the region's main business and shopping community, the resort town of Kinsale is the gateway to a rocky, attractive coastline containing Roaring Water Bay, with its main islands, and Bantry Bay, a magnificent natural harbor. The region's southwest coast is formed by three peninsulas: the Beara, the Iveragh, and the Dingle; the road known as the Ring of Kerry makes a complete circuit of the Iveragh Peninsula. Killarney's blue lakes and sandstone mountains, inland from the peninsulas, have a unique and romantic splendor, immortalized in the 19th century in the writings of William Thackeray and Sir Walter Scott. Around the Shannon Estuary you enter "castle country," an area rich with ruined castles and abbeys, the result of Elizabeth I's 16th-century attempt to subdue the old Irish province of Munster. Limerick City, too, bears the scars of history, from a different confrontation with the English—the Siege of Limerick, which took place in 1691. Its other "scars"—described so memorably in Frank McCourt's best-seller *Angela's Ashes*—lure travelers, who discover that modern Limerick is a compact, vibrant city, with a lively riverfront bar, café, and arts scene. Although the southwest has several sumptuous country-house hotels, it's basically an easygoing, unpretentious region, where informality and simplicity prevail. As in the rest of Ireland, social life revolves around the pub, and a visit to any neighborhood favorite is the best way to find out what's going on.

Exploring the Southwest

This chapter is organized into seven sections: Cork City, which includes a side trip to Blarney Castle, home of the Blarney Stone; East Cork and the Blackwater Valley, covering Youghal and Ballymaloe; Kinsale to Glengarriff, including Mizen Head, Cape Clear, and other points in the far southwest; the Ring of Kerry; In and Around Killarney; the Dingle Peninsula; and North Kerry and Shannonside. The first section is Cork City, and there's an assumption that you'll approach from points east and make a clockwise sweep of the area. The chapter ends on the northern fringe, crossing over the border from County Kerry into County Limerick and then briefly dipping into the southeastern reaches of County Clare in the area immediately around Shannon Airport. If you fly into Shannon, you can simply reverse the entire sequence.

Among the southwest's most notable attractions are Killarney's lakes, which require a day or more of your time; you simply must explore these wonders partly on foot to enjoy them fully. Killarney also makes a good base for discovering the Ring of Kerry and the Dingle Peninsula. The main cities in the area—Cork, Tralee, and Limerick—have their own quiet charm, but they can't compete with the magnificent scenery farther west. Kinsale is a favorite starting point for a leisurely drive through the coast west to Bantry, which can take one day or three, depending on your appetite for unscheduled stops and impromptu exploration. Two national parks, Glengarriff near the sea and Gougane Barra in the mountains, are also worth visiting.

About the Restaurants & Hotels

The southwest, especially County Cork, rivals Dublin as Ireland's food-culture epicenter. Cork has astonishing resources: waters full of a wide array of fish, acre after acre of potato fields, cows galore, wild mushrooms and berries—not to mention inventive chefs who transform this bounty into feasts. In tiny Shanagarry, Darina Allen trains hundreds of chefs every year at the Ballymaloe Cookery School. Outstanding restaurants and the Festival of Fine Food in October draw crowds to Kinsale, where high-quality cuisine is the order of the day. Whether trained at home or abroad, area chefs put a premium on fresh, local (often organically grown) produce.

Mussels and scallops are farmed in the waters off the coast of Cork and Kerry, while the rivers teem with wild salmon. Small smokeries process salmon, trout, mussels, and mackerel over either oak or beech wood chips, with mouthwatering results. Most restaurants in the region bake their own bread daily, often producing both yeast breads and Irish soda

5

Numbers in the text correspond to numbers in the margin and on the South-west, Cork City, and Killarney and Environs maps.

**If you have
3 days**

Base yourself in ⊞ **Killarney** �40 ☞ for both nights, and reserve one day to explore Killarney's dreamy lakes and mountains. Visit the **Gap of Dunloe** �47 on a tour and walk or ride horseback through the gap itself, crossing the lake beyond by rowboat. The next day head for the Ring of Kerry via King Puck's **Killorglin** �39 and enjoy the cliffs as well as the subtropical vegetation, which exists thanks to the Gulf Stream. On the third day, follow the Pass of Keimaneigh to **Bantry** ⓷① to pay a call on Bantry House—one of Ireland's loveliest country houses—and savor its spectacular perch amid terraced gardens over the bay. The cliff-top road between Bantry and Glengarriff (N71) affords sea views along the 24-km-long (15-mi) Bantry Bay inlet. The stretch between **Glengarriff** ⓷② and Killarney, known as the tunnel road, is a famous scenic route, much loved by Thackeray and Sir Walter Scott. It comes into Killarney past the **Ladies' View** ⓸⑧, which has changed little since it impressed Queen Victoria's ladies-in-waiting. From hereabouts you can take the ferry out to have a grand finale on the garden island of Ilnacullin.

**If you have
5 days**

For a gastronomic tour, begin in ⊞ **Cork City** ❶–⓱ ☞ with a trip to the English Market. Stay overnight and sample the classic French cuisine at Fleming's. The next day head out to world-famous Ballymaloe House in ⊞ **Shanagarry** ②①, where the emphasis is on local produce and fish from nearby Ballycotton. If you plan carefully, you may be able to fit in a one-day cooking class at the nearby Ballymaloe Cookery School and Gardens. On your third day, drive northwest to ⊞ **Mallow** ②④ and the stately-home hotel of Longueville House. Proprietor William O'Callaghan's President's restaurant earns raves as one of the finest in Ireland. From here, on your fourth day, head to another culinary hot spot, the town of ⊞ **Kenmare** ③③, where the Park Hotel's terraced lawns sweep down to Kenmare Bay; stroll in the gardens before dinner. On your fifth day drive back toward the foodie waterfront village of ⊞ **Kinsale** ②⑥, for a meal in one of its many acclaimed restaurants. Return to Cork City the next day.

**If you have
7 days**

Start with the knightly magic of **Bunratty Castle & Folk Park** ⑥①☞, the nearest attraction to Shannon Airport. Continue on to **Glin Castle** ⑤⑧—containing one of the most enchanting collections of Irish decorative arts—and its nearby neighbor, ⊞ **Adare** ⑤⑨, one of Ireland's prettiest villages, where you can enjoy an idyllic overnight stay. The second day, head south about 75 km (50 mi) to **Blarney** ⑱ to, well, kiss the stone (and shop for crafts). Proceed to ⊞ **Cork City** ❶–⓱ for the night. The third day head east to Cobh, where the Queenstown Heritage Centre documents Irish emigration. Cross the harbor by ferry and visit ⊞ **Kinsale** ②⑥, a historic and fashionable port town. The fourth day, drive through West Cork around Bantry Bay and into **Glengarriff** ③②, a beauty spot where you can take a boat to the fabled garden estate on Ilnacullin. Continue on to ⊞ **Kenmare** ③③ and ⊞ **Killarney** ④⓪ via the Windy Gap. Spend the fourth night here and make an early start on your fifth day, either visiting the **Gap of Dunloe** ⓸⑦ or touring **Muckross House** ④③. In the afternoon, leave for the Ring of Kerry, driving past ⬚ **Sneem** ㉞, with its multicolored village homes, to ⬚ **Waterville** ㉟. On your sixth day, marvel at **The Skelligs** ㊱, three tiny rock islands that are among Ireland's most magisterial natural wonders. From Cahirciveen you can see the Dingle Peninsula and the stretch of road that takes you to ⬚ **Dingle Town** ㊿ for your overnight. Cliffs and early Christian remains are just a short ride outside town, beyond **Slea Head** ㊾. On your seventh day, drive across the Connor Pass and up to ⬚ **Tralee** ㊺. Return to Limerick City and Shannon Airport on the Adare road (N21) or take N69 to Tarbert and the ferry into County Clare to reach Galway.

---

bread, which uses buttermilk and bicarbonate of soda in place of yeast. Kerry is famous for its delicately flavored mountain lamb, while local beef ensures a wide selection of tender steak cuts. Organic pork from heirloom breeds of pigs might remind you how tasty pork can be. And while in the southwest, make a point of trying some local farmhouse cheeses; look out for Milleens, Coolea, Durrus, Coomkeen, Gubbeen, or the superb hard cheeses, Desmond and Gabriel, made by West Cork Natural Cheeses.

While the smaller country restaurants ooze ambience, service can be a little slow, especially in the peak season of July and August. The food is freshly prepared and usually worth waiting for, so meanwhile sample some of that home-baked bread, and maybe a glass of local stout or your usual aperitif, or maybe chat to the people at the next table to pass the time. It's all part of the Irish experience. If you want to dress up for dinner, as some people do, feel free. By and large, however, informality rules. Restaurants outside main cities tend to be seasonal, and choices are limited between November and mid-March. To sample the region's best cuisine, consult the gastronomic tour below.

The southwest has a number of sumptuous country-house hotels, and although some appear grand, their main aim is to provide a relaxed stay in beautiful surroundings. There are more modest establishments, too, and many are in spectacular seaside locations. A good pair of walking boots and a sensible raincoat are more useful here than a fancy wardrobe. Keep in mind that facilities may be minimal—only expensive hotels have fitness centers, for instance. The staffs at many places can, however, organize golf, deep-sea-fishing, freshwater-angling, and horseback-riding expeditions as well as recommend hiking routes.

Most B&Bs have introduced private bathrooms; rooms at such properties in larger towns may also have TVs and direct-dial phones. Accommodations in West Cork, Killarney, and Dingle are seasonal; between November and March, many places close down, but outside these months—especially from July to mid-October—hotels are busy, so book well in advance. On the chart below, hotel prices are listed for room rates that include no meals (EP, European Plan) or, if indicated, CP (with Continental breakfast) or BP (Breakfast Plan, with full breakfast). Higher prices prevail for board plans such as MAP (Modified American Plan, with breakfast and dinner); inquire when booking. Assume that all hotel rooms have air-conditioning, in-room phones, TVs, and private bathrooms unless otherwise indicated.

	WHAT IT COSTS In euros				
	$$$$	**$$$**	**$$**	**$**	**¢**
RESTAURANTS	over €29	€22–€29	€15–€22	€8–€15	under €8
HOTELS	over €230	€180–€230	€130–€180	€80–€130	under €80

Restaurant prices are per person for a main course at dinner; note that if a restaurant offers only prix-fixe meals, it has been given the price category that reflects the full set-price. Hotel prices are for two people in a standard double room in high season, including V.A.T. and a service charge (often applied in larger hotels).

Timing

The weather is most likely to be warm and sunny in July and August, though there's never a guarantee against rain. July and August are the busiest months, with Irish, British, and Continental tourists heading for the area in large numbers. Visiting in high season means the bars and restaurants of the area will be lively but also crowded. The best times to visit are the "shoulder seasons"—May through June and September through October—when the weather is mild, most accommodations and attractions are open, and crowds are scarce. You may feel chilled from the dampness and the rain, but it rarely gets truly cold. Regardless of when you visit, pack clothing that layers well and a good windbreaker or rain slicker—preferably one that you can readily fold and put in a handbag or knapsack with your collapsible umbrella.

CORK CITY

► ❶–⓱ *254 km (158 mi) south of Dublin, 105 km (65 mi) south of Limerick City.*

The major metropolis of the south, Cork is Ireland's second-largest city (population 175,000), but put this in perspective—roughly half of Ireland's 3.6 million people live in and around Dublin, a city 10 times the size. Though small relative to the capital, Cork is a spirited, lively place, with a formidable pub scene, a lively traditional music scene, a respected and progressive university, attractive art galleries, and offbeat cafés. Preparations are well under way for 2005, when Cork will be designated European City of Culture, and the buzz had already started at this writing, with a striking but controversial redesign of the city center (Patrick's Street and Grand Parade) by Barcelona-based architect Beth Galli.

The city received its first charter in 1185 from Prince John of Norman England, and it takes its name from the Irish word *corcaigh,* meaning "marshy place." The original 6th-century settlement was spread over 13 small islands in the River Lee. Major development occurred during the 17th and 18th centuries with the expansion of the butter trade, and many attractive Georgian-design buildings with wide bowfront windows were constructed during this time. As late as 1770, Cork's present-day main streets—Grand Parade, Patrick Street, and the South Mall—were submerged under the Lee. Around 1800, when the Lee was partially dammed, the river divided into two streams that now flow through the city, leaving the main business and commercial center on an island, not unlike Paris's Île de la Cité. As a result, the city features a number of bridges and quays, which, although initially confusing, add greatly to the port's unique character.

"Rebel Cork" emerged as a center of the Nationalist Fenian movement in the 19th century. The city suffered great damage during the War of Independence in 1919–21, when much of its center was burned down. Cork is now regaining some of its former glory as a result of sensitive commercial development and an ongoing program of inner-city renewal. In late summer and early autumn, the city hosts some of Ireland's premier festivals, including October's huge Cork Jazz Festival, which draws about 50,000 visitors from around the world, and the Cork Film Festival, also in October.

Exploring Cork City

"Cork is the loveliest city in the world. Anyone who does not agree with me either was not born there or is prejudiced." Whether or not Cork merits this accolade of native poet and writer Robert Gibbings, the city does have plenty to recommend it, including several noteworthy historic sites. These, though spread out, are still best visited on foot. Patrick Street is the city center's main thoroughfare.

a good walk

Start your walk on Grand Parade, the geographical center of the city—where you'll find the Tourist Information Office (TIO). **Bishop Lucey Park ❶ ▶**, a green space opposite the TIO, leads to the **Triskel Arts Centre ❷**, where you can see exhibitions and films and find out about arts events around town. From here, take Washington Street to the corner of Grattan Street and the 19th-century **Court House ❸**. Backtrack to North Main Street and take it to the **Cork Vision Centre ❹**, in a once derelict 18th-century church; it has a scale model of the city that is most helpful to visitors. Continue down North Main Street to the River Lee. Cross Shandon Bridge and make the serious hike up to **St. Mary's Pro-Cathedral.** Halfway up the hill on the right is Shandon, a maze of tiny terraced houses, in the midst of which is **St. Anne's Church ❺**, and Cork's old butter market, the Firkin Crane.

Take Upper Street back to the river and the modern Christy Ring Bridge, which leads to **Cork Opera House ❻** and **Crawford Municipal Art Gallery ❼**. Beside the gallery is **Paul Street ❽**, with boutiques, bookstores, and cafés. Take one of the narrow left-hand lanes to **Patrick Street ❾**, Cork's main, pedestrian-only shopping street. Following it to your left, you'll come upon **Patrick's Bridge ❿**, where you'll have a view of the city's steep north side. Take Winthrop Street, off Patrick, to Oliver Plunkett Street, and admire the neoclassic **General Post Office ⓫**; browse, if you wish, at the shops nearby. Return, via Oliver Plunkett Street, to the Grande Parade, with the **English Market ⓬**, a covered food bazaar, on your right. A left will take you to a pedestrian footbridge across the river; go right, following the quays westward, until you reach Bishop Street and the 19th-century Gothic **St. Finbarre's Cathedral ⓭**.

5

Medieval Evenings

Now it may be that you're the kind of traveler who wouldn't wish to cover any ground that your parents might have trod before you, but a visit to a medieval banquet in a genuine Irish castle does still exert a powerful tug. A popular tourist attraction throughout the country almost since Irish tourism began, the experience ranks up there with climbing the Empire State Building or having your photo taken beside a beefeater guardsman in front of the Tower of London, a been-there-got-the-T-shirt kind of thing. Despite their distinctly hokey reputation, these showcase events have progressed beyond the leprechaun and blarney stage of yesteryear into something in tandem with today's more demanding and hip tourist. As well as plentiful food—chicken, beef, lamb, and all the trimmings—served by, yes, red-haired colleens in traditional garb, it provides four hours of often unexpected entertainment that includes medieval and Gaelic songs, poems, and theatrical presentations, replete with Irish harp and fiddle music, choral accompaniments, and *Camelot*-ian minstrel halls. Don't expect anything too highbrow or authentic and you'll be pleasantly surprised. While many head first for the show at Bunratty Castle, a few miles from Shannon Airport, there are even more evocative medieval banquets presented at Knappogue Castle, located just a few miles from Bunratty. For a taste of ancient evenings, these can't be beat.

Accent on Style

A wide variety of creative types have chosen to live in the southwest of Ireland, attracted by the relaxed pace of life and accessible property prices. The result is an increasing number of studios and workshops producing good quality handmade crafts and original works of art. Locally-made ceramics, knitwear, glass, jewelry, wood turning, and photography can be found in the region's craft shops, but it is also worth stopping to investigate signposts on the road directing you to the studios themselves. Blarney, Midleton, Kinsale, Schull, Kenmare, Killarney, and Dingle all have an interesting variety of craft shops and art galleries selling locally produced work. This can range from traditional sweaters to high fashion linen shirts, from handmade candles to black and white photographs. In general, the more interesting crafts are found outside the region's main cities (Cork, Limerick, and Tralee), so you'll want to head to smaller towns where overheads are lower, the scenery is better, and visitors have time to browse. The successful potter Louis Mulclahy, for example, has his studio close to the magnificent beach at Ballyferriter on the Dingle Peninsula. Many of West Cork's small villages—Schull, Ballydehob, Baltimore and Adrigole—have art galleries open from Easter to September.

One of the most successful ventures is the Stephen Pearce Pottery at Shanagarry in East Cork, not far from the famous Ballymaloe Restaurant. The clean, modern lines and chunky traditional feel of Pearse's pottery has made it a modern classic. He is the biggest and longest established of local producers who have banded together to create a signposted craft trail, "East Cork Creates" (☎ 021/461–3432 ⊕ www.eastcork.com), which welcomes visitors to their workshops in the area between Youghal and Midleton. The trail leads you to 15 enterprises that include one-woman operations like Shanagarry Knitwear–Simply Irish (which, this being Ireland, is actually just outside Youghal) and Roz Hague, who produces elegant hand-loomed knitwear with hand-crochet trim in cottons and silks along with a chunky line of brightly-colored children's wear. The Craft and Kitchen Shop at Ballymaloe House, also in Shanagarry, has an excellent range of Irish-made crafts, with an emphasis on local work. There is a strong tradition of pottery in the area, due to ready supplies of clay. Youghal Pottery and Craft Centre is midway between the town and the bypass. Also on this trail is Sean Sciobal Pottery at Cloyne and at Ballycotton, as well as the handmade stoneware studio of Dwyer Ceramic Design Pottery in Midleton. In Midleton, the Courtyard Craft and Exhibition Centre, at 8 Main Street, holds regular exhibits of local crafts and visual art. Israeli silversmith Shmulik Yolzari (yes, he married an Irishwoman, but would you also guess he plays the uillean pipes?), an ingenious designer who combines silver with ebony, has his studio-shop Silverstone Dimensions in the same complex. And if you are near Midleton on a Saturday morning, don't miss the Farmer's Market (Hospital Road, near Supervalu, 9 AM–1 PM), one of the best in the country. Elsewhere, Medulla Furniture is a one-woman show run by Ethna Bohane, maker of small items—clocks, lamps, magazine racks, candleholders—that make great gifts. Her waterside showroom is at Whitegate, on the road to Roches Point. Yet another studio trail can be followed on the Beara Peninsula, whose rugged scenery and splendid isolation has attracted some of Ireland's leading visual artists, including Cormac Boydell, Sarah Walker, and John McConnell. Their leaflet is available locally (⊕ www.millcovegallery.com).

To extend your walk by about 3 km (2 mi), turn left upon leaving the cathedral and take the small road downhill on the right. Go left where it meets the river and cross the bridge to Lancaster Quay. Follow the street, which turns into Western Road, and make a left—you'll reach the architecturally noteworthy campus of **University College Cork** ⑭. Across Western Road is the **Mardyke** ⑮, a riverside walk that leads to the well-tended **Fitzgerald's Park** ⑯ and the Cork Public Museum. Turn left out of the museum and take Daly Bridge, which leads to Sunday's Well, a hilly residential area with the castlelike **Cork City Gaol** ⑰. Return to the city center along Sunday's Well Road and North Mall, where you'll pass several restored Georgian houses.

TIMING You could easily complete the first part of this walk, from the TIO to St. Finbarre's Cathedral, in a morning or an afternoon, depending on how much you plan to shop along the way. To really see everything, however, allow a full day, with a break for lunch at the Farmgate Café in the English Market. Also note that the Crawford Gallery and the English Market are closed on Sunday.

What to See

▶ ❶ **Bishop Lucey Park.** This tiny green park in the heart of the city was opened in 1985 in celebration of the 800th anniversary of Cork's Norman charter. During its excavation, workers unearthed portions of the city's original fortified walls, now preserved just inside the arched entrance. Sculptures by contemporary Cork artists are scattered throughout the park. ⊠ *Grand Parade, Washington Village* ⊠ *Free.*

⑰ Cork City Gaol. This castlelike building contains an austere, 19th-century prison. Life-size figures occupy the cells, and sound effects illustrate the appalling conditions that prevailed here from the early 19th century through the founding of the Free State, after the 1916 Uprising. A **Radio Museum** in the Governor's House tells the history of broadcasting in Cork. ⊠ *Sunday's Well Rd., Sunday's Well* ☎ *021/430–5022* ⊕ *www.corkcitygaol.com* ▭ *€5* ⊘ *Nov.–Feb., daily 10–4; March–Oct., daily 9:30–5.*

⑥ Cork Opera House. It's an unattractive concrete hulk that went up in 1965 to replace an ornate and much-loved opera house that was ruined in a fire. Later attempts to integrate the opera house with its neighbor, the Crawford Municipal Art Gallery, have softened the grim facade. The piazza outside has sidewalk cafés and street performers. ⊠ *Lavitt's Quay, City Center South* ☎ *021/427–0022* ⊕ *www.corkoperahouse.ie.*

④ Cork Vision Centre. This historical society, which is in an area that was once the bustling heart of medieval Cork, provides an excellent introduction to the city's geography and history. The highlight is a detailed 1:500 scale model of Cork, showing how it has grown and changed over the ages. ⊠ *N. Main St., Washington Village* ☎ *021/427–9925* ⊕ *www.corkvisioncentre.com* ▭ *Suggested donation. Guided tours of city model on request €1.50* ⊘ *Tues.–Sat. 10–5.*

③ Court House. A landmark in the very center of Cork, this magnificent classical building has an imposing Corinthian portico and is still used as the district's main courthouse. The exterior has been cleaned and fully restored and looks every bit as good as it did when it was built in 1835. ⊠ *Washington St., Washington Village* ☎ *021/427–2706* ⊘ *Weekdays 9–5.*

⑦ Crawford Municipal Art Gallery. The large redbrick building was built in 1724 as the customs house and is now home to Ireland's leading provincial art gallery. An imaginative expansion has added an extra 10,000 square feet of gallery space—for visiting exhibitions and adventurous shows of modern Irish artists. The permanent collection includes landscape paintings depicting Cork in the 18th and 19th centuries. Take special note of works by Irish painters William Leech (1881–1968), Daniel Maclise (1806–70), James Barry (1741–1806), and Nathaniel Grogan (1740–1807). The café, run by the Allen family of Ballymaloe, is a good place for a light lunch or a homemade sweet. ⊠ *Emmet Pl., City Center South* ☎ *021/427–3377* ⊕ *www.crawfordartgallery.com* ▭ *Free* ⊘ *Weekdays 9–5, Sat. 9–1.*

★ ⑫ English Market. Food lovers: head for one of the misleadingly small entrances to this large market in an elaborate, brick-and-cast-iron Victorian building. (Its official name is the Princes Street Market, and it's also known locally as the Covered Market.) Among the 140 stalls, keep an eye out for the Alternative Bread Co., which produces more than 40 varieties of handmade bread every day. Iago, Sean Calder-Potts's deli, has fresh pasta, lots of cheeses, and charcuterie. The Olive Stall sells olive oil, olive-oil soap, and olives from Greece, Spain, France, and Italy. Kay

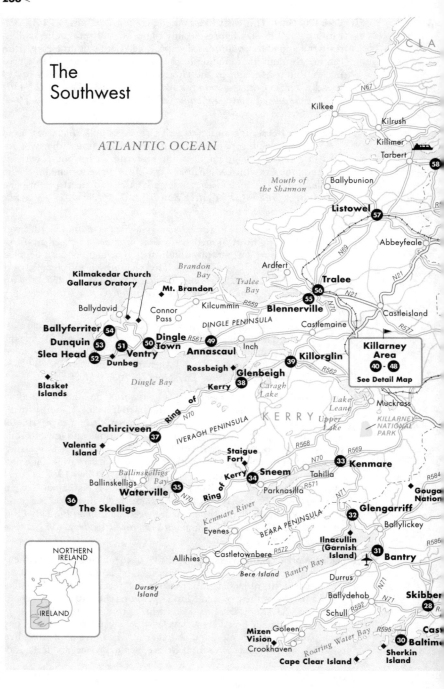

The
Southwest

ATLANTIC OCEAN

CLA

Kilkee
Kilrush
Killimer
Tarbert
58

*Mouth of
the Shannon*

Ballybunion

Listowel 57

Abbeyfeale

R

N67

N69

N21

Ardfert

Kilmakedar Church
Gallarus Oratory

*Brandon
Bay*

*Tralee
Bay*

◆ Mt. Brandon

Ballydavid

Connor
Pass

Kilcummin

R559

Tralee
56

Blennerville
55

Castleisland

N21

R577

Ballyferriter 54

Dunquin 53

Slea Head 52

51

Ventry

◆ Dunbeg

50

Dingle
Town

R561

DINGLE PENINSULA

Castlemaine

Killarney
Area

49

Annascaul

Inch

40 - **48**

See Detail Map

Killorglin

R562

◆
**Blasket
Islands**

Dingle Bay

Rossbeigh

Glenbeigh

38

Kerry

*Caragh
Lake*

39

*Lake
Leane*

Muckross

*Upper
Lake*

KILLARNEY
NATIONAL
PARK

Ring

of

N70

Cahirciveen

37

IVERAGH PENINSULA

K E R R Y

**Valentia
Island** ◆

R568

R569

33 **Kenmare**

R584

*Ballinskelligs
Bay*

**Staigue
Fort**

Kerry

34

Sneem

Tahilla

N70

Ballinskelligs

Waterville

35

Ring

of

N70

Parknasilla

R571

N71

◆ **Gouga
Nation**

36

The Skelligs

Kenmare River

Glengarriff

32

Ballylickey

R586

Eyenes

BEARA PENINSULA

Allihies

Castletownbere

R572

Durrus

Bere Island

**Ilnacullin
(Garnish
Island)**

31 **Bantry**

Bantry Bay

NORTHERN
IRELAND

IRELAND

*Dursey
Island*

Ballydehob

Schull

R592

N71

Skibber

28

R.

**Mizen
Vision**

Goleen

Crookhaven

R595

Roaring Water Bay

Cape Clear Island ◆

Cast

30 **Baltim**

**Sherkin
Island** ◆

Tuamgraney
Ennis
Quin
63 **Craggaunowen Project**
Nenagh
Killaloe
62 **Knappogue Castle**
Thurles
Bunratty Castle & Folk Park
TIPPERARY
Shannon ✈ N18
61
◆ **Plassey**
N75
River Shannon
Limerick City **60**
Foynes
Askeaton
N20
Cashel
R518
LIMERICK
N24
✈
59 **Adare**
Rathkeale
Croom
Holycross
N74
Ballingarry
Tipperary
N24
Newcastle West
N20
Kilmallock
Cahir
Milford
Kilfinnane
N8
Cloggheen
Mitchelstown
WATERFORD
Castletownroche
N72
25
23 River Blackwater
Lismore
N72
Kanturk
24
Fermoy
Dungarvan
N72
Mallow
CORK
N20
Rathcormac
Cork City
1 · **17**
See Detail Map
Youghal
Blarney **18**
R579
R611
Midleton **22**
N25
20
Macroom
N22
Cork Harbour **19**
R629
21 **Shanagarry**
N71
✈
N27
Cloyne
N28
Dunmanway
N71
Bandon
Cobh
Ballycotton
Cork Harbour
KEY
Kilbrittain
26 **Kinsale**
R600
↤↦ *Rail Lines*
Timoleague **27**
Charles Fort
⛴ *Ferry*
Clonakilty
Courtmacsherry
▶ *Start of itinerary*
Rosscarbery
Glandore
nion Hall
nshend
Celtic Sea
0   20 miles
0   30 km

Cork City

KEY
▲ Start of walk

1/4 mile
400 meters

MONTENOTTE

TO TIROLI

SUNDAY'S WELL

WESTERN ROAD

WASHINGTON VILLAGE

SHANDON

CITY CENTRE NORTH

CITY CENTRE SOUTH

SOUTH DOCKLANDS

Bus Station

Tourist ♦ Information Office

Bishop Lucey Park 1
Cork City Gaol 17
Cork Opera House 6
Cork Vision Centre 4
Court House 3
Crawford Municipal Art Gallery 7
English Market 12

Fitzgerald's Park/ Cork Public Museum ...16
General Post Office 11
Mardyke 15
Patrick Street 9
Patrick's Bridge 10
Paul Street 8

St. Anne's Church 5
St. Finbarre's Cathedral 13
Triskel Arts Centre 2
University College Cork (UCC) 14

O'Connell's Fish Stall, in the legendary fresh-fish alley, purveys local smoked salmon. O'Reilly's Tripe and Drisheen is the last existing retailer of a Cork specialty, tripe (cow's stomach) and *drisheen* (blood sausage). Upstairs is the Farmgate, an excellent café. ⊠ *Entrances on Grand Parade and Princes St., City Center South* ⊕ *www.corkcity.ie* ⊙ *Mon.–Sat. 9–5:30.*

16 **Fitzgerald's Park.** This small, well-tended park is beside the River Lee's north channel in the west of the city. The park contains the **Cork Public Museum,** a Georgian mansion that houses a well-planned exhibit about Cork's history since ancient times, with a strong emphasis on the city's Republican history. ⊠ *Western Rd., Western Road* ☎ *021/427–0679* ⊕ *www.corkcity.ie* ⊠ *Free* ⊙ *Museum weekdays 11–1 and 2:15–5, Sun. 3–5.*

11 **General Post Office.** This Neoclassical building with an elegant colonnaded facade was once Cork's opera house. It dominates a street otherwise occupied by boutiques, jewelry stores, and antiques shops. ⊠ *Oliver Plunkett St., City Center South* ☎ *021/427–2000* ⊙ *Weekdays 9–5:30, Sat. 9–5.*

> **need a break?**
>
> The friendly, old **Long Valley** (⊠ Winthrop St., City Center South ☎ 021/427–2144), popular with artists, writers, students, and eccentrics, serves tea, coffee, pints, and sandwiches. The dark, mismatched interior is like a time warp taking you back to early-20th-century Cork. Some of the booths are built from wood salvaged from wrecked ocean liners—ask to be told the story. The generously filled sandwiches, made to order from home-cooked meat and thickly cut bread, also seem to belong to another age.

15 **Mardyke.** This popular riverside walk links the city center with Fitzgerald's Park. Beside it is a field where cricket, very much a minority sport in Ireland, is played on summer weekends. ⊠ *Western Rd., Western Road.*

9 **Patrick Street.** Extending from Grand Parade in the south to Patrick's Bridge in the north, Panna (as it's known locally) is Cork's main shopping thoroughfare. It has been designed as a pedestrian-priority area with wide walks and special street lights. A mainstream mix of department stores, boutiques, pharmacies, and bookshops line the way. If you look above some of the plate-glass storefronts, you'll see examples of the bowfront Georgian windows that are emblematic of old Cork. The street saw some of the city's worst fighting during the War of Independence. ⊠ *City Center South.*

10 **Patrick's Bridge.** From here you can look along the curve of Patrick Street and north across the River Lee to St. Patrick's Hill, with its tall Georgian houses. The hill is so steep that steps are cut into the pavement. Tall ships that served the butter trade used to load up beside the bridge at Merchant's Quay before heading downstream to the sea. The design of the large, redbrick shopping center on the site evokes the warehouses of old. ⊠ *Patrick St., City Center South* ⊕ *www.corkcity.ie.*

CloseUp

REBEL CITY IN A REBEL COUNTY

F COUNTY CORK IS THE *"Rebel County"*—a label it wears proudly—Cork City can claim to be the heart of that tradition of stout resistance.

Since its formation the city has gallantly resisted domination, in turn defying the Vikings, Oliver Cromwell, and King Billy's Protestant army.

More recently, Cork was a beehive of IRA activity (Michael Collins, the IRA's greatest tactician and leader, was a Corkman) and a constant thorn in the side of the crown forces.

In the 1920s the infamous Black and Tans were unleashed with great ferocity on troublesome Cork City. They quickly murdered Thomas MacCurtain, the mayor.

His successor, Terence MacSwiney, was arrested and died on hunger strike with his comrade Joseph Murphy in Brixton prison, London. The two men refused food for 76 days, one of the longest hunger strikes in history, and their names loom large in the Republican cause, especially in the southwest.

In the bloody civil war that followed victory in the War of Independence, Cork remained staunch IRA country and in general opposed the new state and its army.

Michael Collins was killed by a sniper as he drove through Béal na mBláth (pronounced baale-na-mlaw), not far from the city.

8 Paul Street. A narrow street between the River Lee and Patrick Street and parallel to both, Paul Street is the backbone of the trendy shopping area that now occupies Cork's old French Quarter. The area was first settled by Huguenots fleeing religious persecution in France. Musicians and other street performers often entertain passersby in the Paul Street Piazza. The shops here offer the best in modern Irish design—from local fashions to handblown glass—and antiques, particularly in the alley north of the piazza. ⊠ *City Center South.*

5 St. Anne's Church. The church's pepper-pot Shandon steeple, which has a four-sided clock and is topped with a golden, salmon-shape weather vane, is visible from throughout the city and is the chief reason why St. Anne's is so frequently visited. The Bells of Shandon were immortalized in an atrocious but popular 19th-century ballad of that name. Your reward for climbing the 120-foot-tall tower is the chance to ring the bells, with the assistance of sheet tune cards, out over Cork. Beside the church, Firkin Crane, Cork's 18th-century butter market, houses two small performing spaces. Adjacent is the Shandon Craft Market. ⊠ *Church St., Shandon* ⊕ *www.corkcity.ie* 🖂 *€1.50 church, €2 church and bell tower* ☉ *May–Oct., Mon.–Sat. 9:30–5; Nov.–Apr., Mon.–Sat. 10–3:30.*

off the beaten path

ST. MARY'S PRO-CATHEDRAL – It's worth hiking up to St. Mary's, which dates from 1808, only if you're interested in tracing your Cork ancestors. Its presbytery has records of births and marriages dating from 1784. ☒ *Cathedral Walk, Shandon* ⊕ *www.corkcathedral.com* 🖃 *Free* ☉ *Daily 9–6.*

⑬ St. Finbarre's Cathedral. This was once the entrance to medieval Cork. According to tradition, St. Finbarre established a monastery on this site around AD 650 and is credited as being the founder of Cork. The present, compact, three-spire Gothic cathedral, which was completed in 1879, belongs to the Church of Ireland and houses a 3,000-pipe organ. ☒ *Bishop St., Washington Village* ☎ *021/496–3387* ⊕ *www.cathedral. cork.anglican.org* 🖃 *Free* ☉ *Oct.–Mar., Mon.–Sat. 10–12:45 and 2–5; Apr.–Sept., Mon.–Sat. 10–5:30.*

❷ Triskel Arts Centre. An excellent place to get the pulse of artsy goings-on in town, Triskel Arts Centre occupies a converted pair of town houses, also home to a coffee shop and a small auditorium that hosts films and plays. Often on display are exhibitions devoted to contemporary art and crafts. ☒ *Tobin St., Washington Village* ☎ *021/427–2022* ⊕ *www. triskelartscentre.com* 🖃 *Free* ☉ *Weekdays 11–6, Sat. 11–5.*

⑭ University College Cork. The Doric, porticoed gates of UCC stand about 2 km (1 mi) from the center of the city. The college, which has a student body of roughly 10,000, is a constituent of the National University of Ireland. The main quadrangle is a fine example of 19th-century university architecture in the Tudor-Gothic style, reminiscent of many Oxford and Cambridge colleges. Several ancient ogham stones are on display, as are occasional exhibitions of archival material from the old library. The Honan Collegiate Chapel, east of the quadrangle, was built in 1916 and modeled on the 12th-century, Hiberno-Romanesque style, best exemplified by the remains of Cormac's Chapel at Cashel. The UCC chapel's stained-glass windows, as well as its collection of art and crafts, altar furnishings, and textiles in the Celtic Revival style, are noteworthy. Three large, modern buildings have been successfully integrated with the old, including the Boole Library, named for noted alumnus, mathematician George Boole (1815–64), whose algebra laid the foundation for modern computing. Both indoors and out the campus is enhanced by works from the campus's outstanding collection of contemporary Irish art. The Lewis Glucksman Gallery opened in late 2004, in a striking new building located in a wooded gully beside the college's entrance gates. Besides displaying works from the college's collection, it will host cutting-edge contemporary art exhibits. ☒ *Western Road* ☎ *021/490–3000* ⊕ *www.ucc.ie* 🖃 *Free* ☉ *Weekdays 9–5, but call to confirm hrs Easter wk, July–Aug., and mid-Dec.–mid-Jan.*

Where to Eat & Stay

$$$–$$$$ ✕ **Ivory Tower.** Seamus O'Connell, the adventurous young owner-chef, famous in Ireland through his television series, Soul Food, describes his approach as "trans-ethnic fusion." He has cooked in Mexico and Japan, so his accomplished menu has such brilliantly eclectic dishes as wild duck with vanilla, sherry, and jalapeños; pheasant tamale; and wild sea trout smoked to order over oak, with whiskey and scallion sauce. Imaginative presentation, including a surprise taster to set the mood, compensates for the bare wooden floors and somewhat stark decor of the first-floor corner dining room. ☒ *35 Princes St., Washington Village* ☎ *021/427–4665* ▤ *AE, DC, MC, V* ☺ *Closed Mon. and Tues.*

$$$ ╳ **Les Gourmandises.** With a Breton sommelier, Soizic, working the front of the house, and her U.K.-and-Dublin-trained Irish husband, Pat, in the kitchen, you can expect a genuinely interesting eating experience. The restaurant is in a small but high-ceilinged room. Natural light pours in from an overhead skylight, brightening the quarry-tile floor and red velvet chairs that are arrayed around the tables. Crisp white linen and fresh flowers are typical of Soizic's attention to detail. Pat's training with Marco Pierre White, John Burton Race, and Patrick Guilbaud shows in his mastery of robust modern French repertoire. Roasted fillet of cod is served with braised lentils, thyme and balsamic dressing, while roast guinea fowl comes with buttered cabbage and Madeira sauce. Desserts include coffee crème brulée with a Swiss meringue and chocolate madeleine. Good-value set menus are also available. ☒ *17 Cook St., City Center South* ☎ *021/425–1959* ▤ *MC, V* ☺ *Closed last wk of Feb., last 2 wks of June, and first wk of Sept.*

$$–$$$$ ╳ **Lovett's.** Since 1977 the Lovett family has been setting high culinary standards in the formal, portrait-lined dining room of a Georgian house 5 km (3 mi) south of Cork City. The extensive wine list emphasizes vineyards whose owners have Irish roots, but who left for Bordeaux and other wine-making regions in the 18th century. Try the hot black-and-white pudding terrine with onion and raisin confit, followed perhaps by black sole on the bone with citrus butter. The brasserie is less formal. ☒ *Churchyard La., off Well Rd., Douglas* ☎ *021/429–4909* ▤ *AE, DC, MC, V* ☺ *Closed Sun., Mon., first wk of Aug., and Christmas wk. No lunch.*

$$–$$$ ╳ **Café Paradiso.** The Mediterranean-style food is so tasty that even dedicated meat eaters forget that it's vegetarian. Australian owner-chef Denis Cotter, who has published two acclaimed cookbooks, garners raves for his risottos with seasonal vegetables, his *gougère-choux* pastries with savory fillings, and his homemade desserts. The simple café-style dining room is busy and colorful, with enthusiastic young waiters who love to recite the daily specials. The food is creatively arranged on massive platters or bowls, which add sense of occasion. The restaurant is near the university and across from Jurys hotel. ☒ *16 Lancaster Quay, Western Road* ☎ *021/427–7939* ▤ *AE, MC, V* ☺ *Closed Sun., Mon., and last 2 wks of Aug.*

$$–$$$ ╳ **Jacques.** Hidden away in a tiny side street is one of Cork's favorite restaurants. Its windowless interior with its warm terra-cotta walls and curved art deco–style bar is carefully lit to provide a calming ambience that makes you forget the world outside. Sisters Jacque and Eithne Barry have run the place for 25 years, and know their business. Food is always sourced locally, so is as fresh as it comes. Eithne's cooking lets the flavor shine through, whether in a starter of fresh crab and baby spinach salad, or a main course of traditional roast duck with potato and apri-

cot stuffing and red cabbage. For dessert try the fruited bread and butter pudding, or indulge in a chocolate and hazelnut torte. There is a special-value early dinner menu from 6 PM, and on Sundays a light menu is served from 4:30 PM. ⊠ *Phoenix St., off Oliver Plunkett St. near GPO City Center South* ☎ *021/427–7387* ▭ *MC, V* ⊗ *Closed Sun. lunch.*

$–$$$ ✕**Jacobs on the Mall.** Mercy Fenton's imaginative cooking is one attraction; the other is the location—an erstwhile Victorian-style Turkish bath. The dining room has a high ceiling, an enormous skylight, cast-iron pillars, modern art, and a tall banquette room divider. Starters include duck liver parfait with plum chutney and oysters with ginger and lime relish. For a main course, try seared John Dory with coconut rice or roast haunch of venison with celeriac and parsnip pureé and beetroot confit. Look for such desserts as date and butterscotch pudding with bourbon cream. ⊠ *30A South Mall, City Center South* ☎ *021/425–1530* ▭ *AE, DC, MC, V* ⊗ *Closed Sun.*

$–$$ ✕**Isaac's.** Cross Patrick's Bridge to the River Lee's north side and turn right to reach this large, atmospheric brasserie in a converted 18th-century warehouse. Modern art, jazz, high ceilings, and well-spaced tables covered in oilcloth set an eclectic tone. The East-meets-Mediterranean menu includes many tempting dishes, such as warm salads with Clonakilty black pudding, and king prawns in spicy tomato sauce. ⊠ *MacCurtain St., City Center North* ☎ *021/450–3805* ▭ *AE, DC, MC, V* ⊗ *No lunch Sun.*

$–$$ ✕**Proby's Bistro.** Proby's striking modern building, in a riverside location near St. Finbarre's Cathedral, sets the tone for stylish modern cooking that gives a Mediterranean treatment to fresh local produce. Patio tables and sun umbrellas optimistically placed on the terrace reinforce the Continental feel, and the interior dining room has an open fire and bold modern furnishings that complement the light, flavorful food. West Cork black pudding with grainy mustard and mashed potatoes is a favorite starter, while honey-glazed roast duck is a popular daily special. A pianist plays in the evening. ⊠ *Proby's Quay, Crosses Green, Washington Village* ☎ *021/431–6531* ▭ *AE, MC, V* ⊗ *Closed Sun.*

$ ✕**Café-Bar-Deli.** The portions are generous, and the ingredients are fresh. Share a selection of freshly baked breads with olive oil while you choose from the tempting, imaginative salads, pizzas, and pasta dishes listed on the place-mat menu. This minimalist café is a smaller, more intimate annex of the fashionable Bodega Bar—a stylish, noisy establishment housed in a vast limestone building that was once a wine warehouse—that serves the same menu until 5 PM. ⊠ *Cornmarket St., City Center South* ☎ *021/427–2878* ▭ *MC, V* ⊗ *Closed Mon. and Tues. No lunch.*

$ ✕**Farmgate Café.** One of the best—and busiest—informal lunch spots in town is on a terraced gallery above the fountain at the Princes Street entrance to the covered English Market. One side of the gallery opens onto the market and is self-service; the other side is glassed in and has table service (reservations advised). Tripe and drisheen is one dish that is always on the menu; daily specials include less challenging but no less traditional dishes, such as corned beef with *colcannon* (potatoes and cabbage mashed with butter and seasonings) and loin of smoked bacon with *champ* (potatoes mashed with scallions or leeks). ☒ *English Market, City Center South* ☏ 021/427–8134 ▭ *DC, MC, V* ⊘ *Closed Sun. No dinner.*

★ **$$$–$$$$** ✕▦ **Hayfield Manor.** The Manor, a surprisingly soigné modern homage to the country-house style, is beside the UCC campus, five minutes' drive from the city center. Ruddy with red brick and classy white-sash windows, its exterior hints at the comfy luxe within. Beyond a splendid, carved-wood double staircase, you'll find the Drawing Room—a symphony of gilded silk, with white marble fireplace, 19th-century chandelier, and chic armchairs—and the wood-paneled library, which overlooks a walled patio and garden. Rooms are spacious and ever-so-eleganty furnished in a version of the Louis XV style. The Victorian-style bar serves lunch, and then bar food until 7 PM, when the Manor Room restaurant opens for dinner. ☒ *College Rd., Western Road, Co. Cork* ☏ 021/431–5900 🖷 021/431–6839 ⊕ *www.hayfieldmanor.ie* ⇆ *53 rooms* ⟡ *Restaurant, in-room data ports, cable TV, indoor pool, health club, bar, meeting rooms* ▭ *AE, DC, MC, V* ⦿| *BP.*

$$$–$$$$ ✕▦ **Kingsley Hotel.** The riverside location is a boon, being close to open countryside yet just a 10-minute walk from the city center. The Kingsley overlooks a rowing club on a pretty section of the River Lee, beside the Lee Fields, a big meadow whose paths are popular with joggers. The lobby and lounge of this spanking new establishment are paneled with dark wood and furnished with upright velvet armchairs, like an old-style gentleman's club. Guest rooms have large bathrooms, super-king-size beds, mahogany furniture, workstations, and CD players. Otters, the more formal restaurant, serves imaginative local seafood and seasonal game dishes, while a lighter menu is served in the bar and library. The health center has a 20-meter pool and an outdoor hot tub. ☒ *Victoria Cross, Western Road, Co. Cork* ☏ 021/480–0500 🖷 021/480–0527 ⊕ *www.kingsleyhotel.com* ⇆ *69 rooms* ⟡ *Restaurant, in-room data ports, in-room fax, some minibars, cable TV, indoor pool, health club, bar* ▭ *AE, DC, MC, V* ⦿| *BP.*

$–$$$ ✕▦ **Hotel Isaac's.** A stylish renovation transformed an old, city center warehouse into a busy restaurant and hotel complex. Rooms are bright and cheerful, with polished wood floors and rustic pine furniture. The restaurant and some of the rooms overlook a tiny courtyard garden with a waterfall cascading down one side. The dining room also operates as Greene's restaurant, where they serve seafood—king prawns with chili sauce, oysters poached in Guinness, brill, swordfish, and hake—as well as other intriguing concoctions, such as veal with apricot stuffing, Asian vegetables, and ginger soufflé. ☒ *48 MacCurtain St., City Center North, Co. Cork* ☏ 021/450–0011 🖷 021/450–6355 ⊕ *www.isaacs.ie* ⇆ *47 rooms* ⟡ *Restaurant, cafeteria, in-room data ports, cable TV, Ping-Pong* ▭ *AE, MC, V* ⦿| *BP.*

★ **$$** ✕▦ **The Ambassador.** It is not the fanciest hotel in Cork, nor the hippest, but it has the most character and the best view—which you pay for by a steep ten-minute walk up from the town center. It's worth visiting the bar here just to enjoy the panoramic view of Cork City's docks, river, railway line, church steeples, and distant surrounding hills. An imposing redbrick and cut-limestone Victorian-era nursing home now converted into a comfortable hotel (affiliated with the Best Western group), the Ambassador is near the army barracks in a hilly area made famous by Frank O'Connor's short stories, an area now favored by style-conscious academics and bohos. Architecture buffs may question some features, such as the modern, double-glazed windows, but overall the interior retains its Victorian charm and spaciousness. The corridors are so wide one could drive a car down them, but patterned carpet runners help dispel any remaining institutional atmosphere. The Embassy Bar has dark wood paneling and a large bay window overlooking the city, while the cocktail lounge, with book-filled shelves and Chesterfield sofas by an open fire, is a quieter venue. Guest rooms are massive, with large bathrooms, patterned wallpapers, small sitting areas, and matching floral curtains and drapes. There are three floors of bedrooms and the higher you go, the better the view—some rooms even have splendid walk-out balconies at no extra charge. ⊠ *Military Hill, St. Luke's, City Center North* ☎ *021/455–1996* 🖷 *021/455–1997* ⊕ *www.ambassadorhotel.ie* ↪ *60 rooms* ⚫ *Two bars, restaurant, cable TV, in-room data ports, meeting rooms, health club; no a/c* ▤ *AE, DC, MC, V.*

$–$$ 🎫 **Lancaster Lodge.** Free city-center parking, a great location next to the lively Jurys Hotel, and value for money are the main reasons to stay at this modern, four-story inn. Rooms look out over the car park or across a narrow, fast-flowing branch of the River Lee, to the main road, but in compensation they're spacious and stylish, with pale wood furniture and large bathrooms. A hearty breakfast from an extensive menu—served in your room or in the bright, contemporary dining room—is another plus. ⊠ *Lancaster Quay, Western Road, Co. Cork* ☎ *021/425–1125* 🖷 *021/425–1126* ⊕ *www.lancasterlodge.com* ↪ *37 rooms, 2 suites* ⚫ *Dining room, in-room data ports, cable TV, free parking; no a/c* ▤ *AE, DC, MC, V* 🍽 *BP.*

$ 🎫 **Brookfield Hotel.** Next door to the campus of University College Cork, this budget hotel sits in ten acres of private parkland with mature trees and is surrounded by blocks of redbrick, Georgian-style student accommodations, which double as a self-catering holiday village outside term time. This pleasant, quiet location, complete with secure car parking, is less than a mile from the city center. The hotel shares its main door with the pool and gym (a bonus in this price range), with a staircase leading up to reception, and three floors of guest rooms. Rooms are a mite boxy, with blond wood desks, plain walls and carpets, patterned spreads, and dark-hue drapes, but are redeemed by the pretty views of green lawns and pine trees from the windows. ⊠ *Brookfield Holiday Village, College Rd., Western Rd.* ☎ *021/480–4700* 🖷 *021/480–4793* ⊕ *www.brookfieldcork.ie* ↪ *24 rooms* ⚫ *Restaurant, cable TV, indoor pool, health club, bar, tennis court; no a/c* ▤ *AE, DC, MC, V* ⊙ *Closed Dec 23–Jan. 2.*

$ ✕🎫 **Flemings.** On a hillside overlooking the river, this stately Georgian house is set in extensive grounds that include a kitchen garden which supplies the restaurant. The grounds could be tidier, but owner-chef Michael Fleming is more interested in cooking. Classical French food is his forte, and is served, appropriately, in a dining room decorated in the French Empire style with plush Louis XV–style chairs, gilt-framed portraits, and crystal chandeliers. Local ingredients are important; a starter

CORK, CAPITAL OF CULTURE

THE BIGGEST THING *happening in Europe in 2005 is happening in Cork"—so say the organizers of the "Cork 2005" festival (⊕ www. cork2005.ie). This year the title of European Capital of Culture, which has been held by Glasgow, Stockholm, Madrid, Avignon, and Genoa, among others, is coming to Cork. It is the smallest city ever to have held this designation, and also has one of the smallest budgets (€13 million—and growing), but such facts only make the organizers, led by the dynamic John Kennedy—previously tour manager for U2—vow to try harder. As it turns out, the definition of "culture" being adopted is as wide and democratic as possible. Indeed, one plan in development is a football tournament between teams from previously designated cities. The many events of the festival are in good part the result of a public appeal to the people of Cork for project proposals. More than 2000 schemes were submitted.*

Cork City Council has responded by pulling out all stops on completing an ambitious capital investment program of over €196 million. The city's main artery, Patrick Street, has had a €12 million redesign by Barcelona-based architect Beth Gallo. A new pedestrian bridge links north and south sectors of the city, and Blackrock Castle—a long neglected landmark on the seaward approach to Cork Harbour—will reopen as a visitor center and restaurant. University College Cork's exciting new Lewis Glucksmann Gallery comes online in time to play a major role, hosting "Forty Shades of Green." This is an exhibition of visual arts and crafts that attempts to redefine the legacy of the schmaltzy Emerald Isle image popularized in the economically lean years of the 1950s and '60s. It will also show pages created for An Leabhar Mór, or "The Great Book of Gaelic"—a

collaboration between 100 Gaelic-language poets and 100 artists. "The Rebel Crowned, " an exhibition at the Crawford Municipal Art Gallery, will feature silver and gold manufactured in Cork between 1605 and 2005.

Departing from Roches Point, a rowing race from the ocean to Cork City will be the focal point of a weeklong maritime festival, starting on the first weekend in June. European Quartet Week will bring some of the world's finest musicians to Cork, including the Tokyo, Vogler, and Debussy Quartets. Highlights of an exciting dance program include Jean-Pierre Perreault from Canada and the Sol Pico company from Barcelona. From May to September, Cork will become a living theater, as local company Corcadorca—renowned for their outdoor productions—collaborates with its European counterparts from Scotland, France, and Poland to present a series of spectacular creations using the city as stage. "Access All Beckett," by the Paris-based Gare St Lazare Players, will present a series of Samuel Beckett's prose work in locations around the city in interesting venues.

Throughout the year, Eighteen Turns—the pavilion designed by architect Daniel Libeskind (whose World Trade Center project is beginning in New York)—commissioned by the Serpentine Gallery in London, will be present in Cork, and used as an events venue. The city's regular festivals—choral, jazz, film—will be bigger and better than usual. For example, Cork International Film Festival in October will include a screening of the "One Hundred Greatest Shorts." For updates and details on "Cork 2005" see the festival Web site.

of pan-fried foie gras is accompanied by black pudding from West Cork and glazed apple. Grilled monkfish from Michael's home town, Court-macsherry, is served with a basil oil dressing and red wine sauce. The quiet, large guest rooms have high ceilings and elegant brocade fabrics. Ask about the special-value "dine and stay" package. ⊠ *Silver Grange House, Tivoli, Co. Cork* ☎ *021/482–1621* 🖷 *021/482–1178* 🖙 *4 rooms* ⌂ *Restaurant, cable TV, bar; no a/c* ⊟ *AE, DC, MC, V* ⎮◯⎮ *BP.*

$ 🏠 **Seven North Mall.** Discerning visitors favor Angela Hegarty's home, a substantial, 250-year-old, terraced house on a tree-lined mall overlooking the River Lee. Common-area furnishings are quietly elegant, and modest antiques are used to good advantage in the guest rooms. From here it's only a short walk to theaters, art galleries, shops, and restaurants. A limited amount of off-road parking is available. ⊠ *7 North Mall, Shandon, Co. Cork* ☎ *021/439–7191* 🖷 *021/430–0811* ⊕ *www.sevennorthmall.com* 🖙 *5 rooms* ⌂ *Cable TV; no a/c* ⊟ *MC, V* ⎮◯⎮ *BP* ⊙ *Closed 2 wks at Christmas.*

Nightlife & the Arts

See the *Examiner* or the *Evening Echo* for details about movies, theater, and live music performances.

Galleries

The **Fenton Gallery** (⊠ Wandesford Quay, Washington Village ☎ 021/431–5294 ⊕ www.artireland.net) shows work by important Irish artists. The **Lavit Gallery** (⊠ 5 Father Mathew St., off South Mall, City Center South ☎ 021/427–7749 ⊕ www.the lavitgallery.com) sells work by members of the Cork Arts Society and other Irish artists. Offbeat exhibits can be found at the **Triskel Arts Centre** (⊠ Tobin St., off S. Main St., Washington Village ☎ 021/427–2022 ⊕ www.trsikelartscentre.com). The **Vangard Gallery** (⊠ Carey's La., Paul St., City Center South ☎ 021/427–8718) exhibits leading contemporary Irish artists.

Performing Arts & Film

Cork Opera House (⊠ Lavitt's Quay, City Center South ☎ 021/427–0022) is the city's major hall for touring productions and variety acts. Smaller theatrical productions are staged at the **Everyman Palace** (⊠ MacCurtain St., City Center North ☎ 021/450–1673), which has an ornate Victorian interior. **The Kino** (⊠ Washington St., Washington Village ☎ 021/427–1571) is Cork's only art-house cinema. Three films are usually showing, from 2:30 onward.

Pubs & Nightclubs

La Bodega (⊠ Cornmarket St., City Center South ☎ 021/427–2878), a converted wine warehouse, is the hip meeting spot for Cork's thirtysomethings. Traditional music sessions can happen anytime at **An Bodhrán** (⊠ 42 Oliver Plunkett St., City Center South ☎ 021/437–1392). You'll hear Cajun, folk, or Irish music from Sunday to Wednesday at the **Corner House** (⊠ 7 Coburg St., City Center North ☎ 021/450–0655). Night owls flock to **Half Moon** (⊠ Half Moon St., City Center South ☎ 021/427–0022), the Cork Opera House's late-night music club. It showcases local, up-and-coming jazz and blues bands most weekends starting at 11 PM.

Loafers (⊠ 26 Douglas St., South Docklands ☎ 021/431–1612) is a friendly gay bar with a beer garden. **The Lobby** (⊠ Union Quay, South Docklands ☎ 021/431–1113) has nightly music sessions: traditional and acoustic in the bar, folk and rock upstairs. **Long Valley** (⊠ Winthrop St., South City Center ☎ 021/427–2144) is a Cork institution, famous for its doorstep sandwiches (made with very thick slices of bread and lots of fillings) that are impossible to eat tidily, and its conversation, which is always lively. The bar at the **Metropole Hotel** (⊠ MacCurtain St., City Center North ☎ 021/450–8122) is one of Cork's best jazz spots. The **Pavilion** (⊠ Carey's La., City Center South ☎ 021/427–6228) has late-night disco every night but Tuesday.

Shopping

Department Stores

Brown Thomas (⊠ 18 Patrick St., City Center South ☎ 021/427–6771), Ireland's high-end department store, carries items by Irish and international designers. The ground floor has an excellent cosmetics hall and a good selection of menswear and Irish crystal. Refuel at the coffee shop, which sells healthful open sandwiches and homemade soups. **Dunnes Stores** (⊠ Merchant's Quay, City Center South ☎ 021/427–4200) began in Cork as a family-owned drapery store and became the place where all of Ireland buys its socks, underwear, and much more. The British retail giant **Marks and Spencer** (⊠ 6–8 Patrick St., Merchant's Quay, City Center South ☎ 021/427–5555) is as popular for its foods (great for picnics) and housewares as for its clothing basics. For inexpensive rain gear, T-shirts, underwear, and any other garments you forgot to pack, head for **Penney's** (⊠ 27 Patrick St., City Center South ☎ 021/427–1935). **Roches Stores** (⊠ Patrick St., City Center South ☎ 021/427–7727), Cork's largest department store, is a family-owned business that occupies a beautiful landmark building with a central glass dome.

Mall

The **Merchant's Quay Shopping Centre** (⊠ Merchant's Quay, City Center South ☎ 021/427–5466) is a large downtown mall.

Specialty Shops

ANTIQUES **Irene's** (⊠ 22 Marlboro St., City Center South ☎ 021/427–0642) sells antique jewelry. **Mills Antiques** (⊠ 3 Paul's La., City Center South ☎ 021/427–3528) carries Irish, English, and European paintings, prints, silver, porcelain, and small furniture. **Pinnacle** (⊠ 44A MacCurtain St., City Center North ☎ 021/450–1319) stocks antique glass, porcelain, paintings, and prints. **Victoria's** (⊠ 2 Oliver Plunkett St., City Center South ☎ 021/427–2752) carries interesting jewelry and Victoriana.

BOOKS **Connolly's Bookshop** (⊠ Paul Street Piazza, City Center South ☎ 021/427–5366) has an extensive stock of new and secondhand books, with a good selection of Irish-interest titles. **Mainly Murder Bookstore** (⊠ 2A Paul St., City Center South ☎ 021/427–2413) is a must for lovers of crime fiction. **Mercier Bookshop** (⊠ 18 Academy St., City Center South ☎ 021/427–5040), off Patrick Street, sells new books and publishes a list of Irish and local-interest titles. **Vibes & Scribes** (⊠ 3 Bridge St., City

Center North ☎ 021/450–5370 ⊕ www.vibesandscribes.com) attracts a loyal following of avid readers, with three floors of new, secondhand, and discount books as well as CDs and videos. **Waterstones** (⊠ Patrick St., City Center South ☎021/427–6522) is the biggest bookshop in town, with a great choice of new fiction and nonfiction as well as a wide selection of locally published books.

CLOTHING   **Cocoon** (⊠ 6 Emmet Pl., City Center South ☎ 021/427–3393), a little shop in a hexagonal tower, has a ravishing selection of sexy Italian boots and shoes alongside unusual jewelry and accessories. Fashion lovers vibe with the array of evening and business attire at the **Dressing Room** (⊠ 8 Emmet Pl., City Center South ☎ 021/427–0117), a tiny but tony boutique opposite the entrance to the Cork Opera House. For funky, retro styles and vintage clothes, check out **Hale Bopp** (⊠ 22 Paul St., City Center South ☎ 021/425–4876). **Monica John** (⊠ French Church St., City Center South ☎ 021/427–1399) sells locally designed high-fashion ladies' wear as well as some imported lines. **Quills** (⊠ 107 Patrick St., City Center South ☎ 021/427–1717) has a good selection of Irish-made apparel for women and men. **Samui** (⊠ 17 Drawbridge St., City Center South ☎ 021/427–8080) stocks dramatic—often quirky, but always flattering—clothes from Ireland, France, Germany, and the U.K. For casual weatherproof clothing, try the **Tack Room** (⊠ Unit 3, Academy St., City Center South ☎ 021/427–2704).

JEWELRY   **Marlboro Gold Arts Ltd** (⊠ 33 Marlboro St., City Center South ☎ 021/427–7052) has imaginative, modern jewelry.

MUSIC   This **HMV** (⊠ Patrick St. ☎ 021/427–4433) has a good selection of Irish traditional music in its classical and jazz sections. The best place for recordings of Irish music is **Living Tradition** (⊠ 40 MacCurtain St., City Center North ☎ 021/450–2040). **Vibes & Scribes** (⊠ 3 Bridge St., City Center North ☎021/450–5370) has a good selection of bargain and secondhand tapes, CDs, DVDs, and videotapes. The **Vinyl Room** (⊠ 79 Grand Parade, City Center South ☎ 021/427–3379) specializes in dance, house, and hip-hop. Chart hits are the main business of the **Virgin Megastore** (⊠ Queen's Old Castle, City Center South ☎ 021/427–9299), but you'll find some traditional Irish music for sale in the small classical and jazz sections.

SPORTING GOODS   The **Golf Addict** (⊠ 6 Emmet Pl., City Center South ☎ 021/427–3393) stocks everything the serious golfer could need, as well as a range of nonessential golf paraphernalia and gifts. The **Great Outdoors** (⊠ 23 Paul St., City Center South ☎ 021/427–6382) caters to most outdoor sports needs. **Matthews** (⊠ Academy St., City Center South ☎ 021/427–7633) has a wide selection of sporting gear.

Side Trips From Cork City

Blarney, northwest of Cork City on R617, and Cork Harbour, east of the city on N25 (follow signposts to Waterford), make perfect day trips. Blarney's attractions are Blarney Castle and the famous Blarney Stone. Cork Harbour's draws include Fota Island, with an arboretum, a wildlife park, and Fota House—a renovated hunting lodge and estate—and the fishing port of Cobh.

Blarney

(18) *10 km (6 mi) northwest of Cork City.*

"On Galway sands they kiss your hands, they kiss your lips at Carney, but by the Lee they drink strong tea, and kiss the stone at Blarney." This famous rhyme celebrates one of Ireland's most noted icons—the Blarney Stone, which is the main reason most people journey to this small community built around a village green.

In the center of Blarney is **Blarney Castle**, or what remains of it: the ruined central keep is all that's left of this mid-15th-century stronghold. The castle contains the famed Blarney Stone; kissing the stone, it's said, endows the kisser with the fabled "gift of gab." It's 127 steep steps to the battlements. To kiss the stone, you must lie down on the battlements, hold on to a guardrail, and lean your head way back. It's good fun and not at all dangerous. Expect a line from mid-June to early September; while you wait, you can admire the views of the wooded River Lee valley and chuckle over how the word "blarney" came to mean what it does. As the story goes, Queen Elizabeth I wanted Cormac MacCarthy, Lord of Blarney, to will his castle to the crown, but he refused her requests with eloquent excuses and soothing compliments. Exhausted by his comments, the queen reportedly exclaimed, "This is all Blarney. What he says he rarely means."

You can take pleasant walks around the castle grounds; Rock Close contains oddly shaped limestone rocks landscaped in the 18th century and a grove of ancient yew trees that is said to have been the site of Druid worship. Two hundred yards from the castle is Blarney Castle House, which was built in 1784 in the style of a Scottish baronial mansion. The three-story, gray-stone building has picture-book turrets and fancy, stepped gables. Inside are Elizabethan and Victorian antiques, a fine stairwell, and family portraits. ☎ *021/438-5252* ⊕ *www.blarneycastle.ie* ✉ *Blarney Castle: €7. Blarney Castle House: €5* ☉ *Blarney Castle: May and Sept., Mon.–Sat. 9–6:30, Sun. 9–5:30; June–Aug., Mon.–Sat. 9–7, Sun. 9–5:30; Oct.–Apr., Mon.–Sat. 9–sundown, Sun. 9–5:30. Blarney Castle House: June–mid-Sept., Mon.–Sat. noon–5.*

WHERE TO
STAY & EAT
$–$$$

✕ **Blair's Inn.** Surrounded by woods just five minutes from Blarney, Blair's Inn—noted for its exuberant window-box displays—is the perfect retreat from Blarney's tour-bus crowds. This is a real "local," complete with genial owner-hosts, John and Anne, as well as a busy restaurant. In summer, enjoy the beer garden; in winter, warm wood fires flicker in the cozy interior. Freshly prepared local produce is served in generous portions: best bets include Irish stew with lamb, carrots, and potatoes, as well as corned beef and a memorable gratin of prawns, crab and salmon, served piping hot. There's live entertainment every Sunday at 9 PM as well as on Monday from May to October. ✉ *Cloghroe* ☎ *021/438–1470* ⊟ *MC, V.*

¢–$

▦ **Maranatha Country House.** This gray-stone Victorian manor surrounded by pretty gardens and 27 woodland acres makes an excellent base for exploring Blarney, Cork City, and even Killarney, an hour and a half away. The guest rooms in Olwen and Douglas Venn's impeccably run family home are individually decorated with antiques (Olwen has a passion for

French inlaid furniture) and striking textiles. The Regal Suite has a four-poster bed swathed in pink, green, and white sprigged fabric that matches the ruched drapes, as well as a sunken bath with a hot tub. Breakfast is served in the conservatory, which overlooks rolling lawns and majestic trees. To get here drive through Blarney village on the R617 for 3 km (2 mi) to the village of Tower. ⊠ *Tower* ☎ *021/438–5102* ⊕ *www. maranathacountryhouse.com* ⌨ *6 rooms* ⚡ *No a/c, no room TVs, no smoking* ▣ *MC, V* ⑩ *BP* ⊘ *Closed Dec.–mid-Mar.*

SHOPPING   Blarney has lots of crafts shops south and west of the village green, a two-minute walk from the castle. **Blarney Woolen Mills** (☎ 021/438–5280 ⊕ www.blarney.ie) has the largest stock and the highest turnover of Blarney's crafts shops. It sells everything from Irish-made high fashion to Aran hand-knit items to leprechaun key rings.

Cork Harbour

19 *16 km (10 mi) east of Cork City.*

☾ The 70-acre **Fota Island Wildlife Park** is 12 km (7 mi) east of Cork via N25, R624, and the main Cobh road. It's an important breeding center for cheetahs and wallabies, and also is home to monkeys, zebras, giraffes, ostriches, flamingos, emus, and kangaroos. ☎ *021/481–2678* ⊕ *www.fotawildlife.ie* ⌨ *€8* ⊘ *Mid-Mar.–Oct., Mon.–Sat. 10–6, Sun. 11–6; Nov.–St. Patrick's Day, Sat. 10–3, Sun. 11–3.*

Next to the Fota Island Wildlife Park is **Fota House,** the Smith-Barry ancestral estate: its name is derived from the Irish Fód te, which means "warm soil," a tribute to the unique tidal estuary microclimate here and the reason why one of Ireland's most exotic botanical gardens was established here. The original lodge house was built in the mid-18th century for the Smith-Barry family, which owned vast tracts of land in South Cork, including the whole of Fota Island. The next generation of the powerful family employed the renowned architects Richard and William Vitruvius Morrison to convert the structure into an impressive Regency–style house that has now been painstakingly restored. The symmetrical facade is relatively unadorned and stands in contrast to the resplendent Adamesque plasterwork of the formal reception rooms (somewhat denuded of furniture). The servants' quarters are almost as big as the house proper. Fota's glories continue in the gardens, which include an arboretum, a Victorian fernery, an Italian garden, an orangerie, and a special display of magnolias. You can relax over cake and scones in the tearoom after shopping in the crafts store. ☎ *021/481–5543* ⊕ *www.fotahouse.com* ⌨ *€5* ⊘ *Apr.–Sept., Mon.–Sat. 10–5:30, Sun. 11–5:30; Oct.–Mar., daily 11–4.*

Many of the people who left Ireland on immigrant ships for the New World departed from **Cobh,** a pretty fishing port and seaside resort 24 km (15 mi) southeast of Cork City on R624. The **Queenstown Story at Cobh Heritage Center,** in the old Cobh railway station, re-creates the experience of the million emigrants who left from here between 1750 and the mid-20th century. It also tells the stories of great transatlantic liners, including the *Titanic,* whose last port of call was Cobh, and the *Lusitania,* which was sunk by a German submarine off this coast on May

7, 1915. Many of the *Lusitania's* 1,198 victims are buried in Cobh, which has a memorial to them on the local quay. ☎ *021/481–3591* ⊕ *www. cobhheritage.com* ✉ *€5* ⊙ *Oct.–Apr., daily 10–5; May–Sept., daily 10–6.*

The best view of Cobh is from **St. Colman's Cathedral,** an exuberant neo-Gothic granite church designed by the eminent British architect E. W. Pugin in 1869, and completed in 1919. Inside, granite niches portray scenes of the Roman Catholic Church's history in Ireland, beginning with the arrival of St. Patrick. ☎ *021/481–3222* ⊕ *www.cloyne. irl.com* ✉ *Free.*

ART GALLERIES Philip Gray served as a diver in the Irish navy, and left to paint, which he does extremely well. The sea in all its guises is his subject. **The Philip Gray Gallery of Fine Art** (✉ Slipway Two, Cork Dockyard, Rushbrooke, Cobh ☎ 021/481–4170 ⊕ www.philipgray.com) is on a slipway of a dockyard in Cork Harbour.

SPORTS & THE Explore the sheltered, island-studded waters of Cork Harbour by rent-
OUTDOORS ing a sailing dinghy from **International Sailing Center** (✉ 5 E. Beach, Cobh ☎ 021/481–1237).

EAST CORK & THE BLACKWATER VALLEY

Although most visitors to Cork head west out of the city for the coastal areas between Cork and Glengarriff, the east and the north of the county are also worth exploring. East Cork, Youghal in particular, is popular with Irish tourists, who love the long sandy beaches here. North Cork's main attraction is the Blackwater River, which crosses the county from east to west. It's famous for its trout and salmon fishing and its scenery.

Youghal

 48 km (30 mi) east of Cork City on N25, 74 km (46 mi) south of Waterford.

Youghal (pronounced yawl), an ancient walled seaport with a fine natural harbor, has a long sandy beach, making it popular with summer day-trippers. The opening of a new section of the main N25 enabling through traffic to bypass the town has restored its quiet charm, though renovation of the center is still ongoing. The town is at the mouth of the Blackwater River, on the border between Counties Cork and Waterford. It was included in a 40,000-acre land grant given to Sir Walter Raleigh by Elizabeth I in the late 16th century. According to local legend, Sir Walter Raleigh planted the first potatoes in Ireland here, a claim disputed by residents of several other locations (and by all accounts he spent little time here). The town is in the throes of some major investment, aimed at updating its appeal. Rising above it all is Main Street's clock tower, which dates from 1776 and was built as a jail. Steps beside the tower lead to a well-preserved stretch of the old town walls. From here there's a magnificent panorama of the town and the estuary.

The **Youghal Heritage Centre** relates the town's history through an audiovisual presentation. If this whets your appetite, trained guides are available to show you the town; a walking tour takes about 90 minutes. ☒ *Market Sq.* ☎ *024/20170* ⊕ *www.youghal.ie* ☑ *€2, tour €5* ⊗ *June–mid-Sept., daily 9:30–7; mid-Sept.–May, weekdays 9:30–5:30.*

The **Moby Dick Lounge Bar** (☒ Market Sq. ☎ 024/92756) contains memorabilia of the filming here of John Huston's version of Melville's *Moby-Dick*, in which Youghal masqueraded as New Bedford, Massachusetts.

St. Mary's Collegiate Church dates from the 13th century and contains many interesting monuments, including the tomb of Richard Boyle (1566–1643), who succeeded Sir Walter Raleigh as Mayor of Youghal and became the first earl of Cork. The brightly painted monument commemorates his three wives and 16 children and is similar to the monument in St. Patrick's Cathedral in Dublin which Sir Richard ordered because he was not sure whether he would die in Dublin or Youghal. ☒ *Emmet Pl.* ☎ *024/92350* ☑ *Free* ⊗ *Key available from adjacent lodge.*

Where to Stay & Eat

$$–$$$ ✕⌂ **Aherne's.** In the Fitzgibbon family since 1923, Aherne's has a highly regarded seafood restaurant-bar ($$–$$$) with a magnetic appeal—it even draws food lovers from Cork City (less than an hour's drive away). Popular main courses include hot buttered lobster, grilled salmon with fresh fennel, and plaice (flounder) stuffed with oysters in a red-wine sauce. The inexpensive bar food includes seafood pie topped with mashed potatoes. The 12 bedrooms, which occupy their own modern wing, are furnished with Victorian and Georgian antiques. ☒ *163 N. Main St., Co. Cork* ☎ *024/92424* 🖷 *024/93633* ⊕ *www.ahernes.com* ⇨ *13 rooms* ⌂ *Restaurant, cable TV, fishing, bar* ⊟ *AE, DC, MC, V* ⌾ *BP.*

$ ✕⌂ **Ballymakeigh House.** Consider this the Irish farmhouse of your
Fodor's Choice   dreams, the kind of place where you can easily end up staying a day or
★   two longer than planned. From the conservatory behind the creeper-clad house—with its cozy, impeccably kept guest rooms—you can breakfast on one of Margaret Browne's fresh strawberry muffins while watching the cows amble out to pasture after milking time. Reserve by 5 PM for her legendary six-course dinners, often made with herbs and edible flowers straight from the garden. The house is signposted off N25, 9½ km (6 mi) west of Youghal. ☒ *Killeagh, Co. Cork* ☎ *024/95184* 🖷 *024/95370* ⊕ *www.ballymakeighhouse.com* ⇨ *6 rooms* ⌂ *Cable TV, tennis court, bicycles, Ping-Pong; no a/c* ⊟ *MC, V* ⌾ *BP* ⊗ *Closed Nov.–Mar.*

Shanagarry

㉑   *27 km (17 mi) southwest of Youghal via N25 and R632.*

There are two reasons to come to Shanagarry, a farming village known chiefly for its Quaker connections: Ballymaloe House, one of Ireland's first country-house hotels, and Ballymaloe Cookery School and Gardens, a top destination for chefs-in-training.

The most famous Shanagarry Quaker was William Penn (1644–1718), the founder of the Pennsylvania colony, who grew up in **Shanagarry House,** still a private residence in the center of the village. The entry gates are across from Shanagarry Castle, now owned and being restored by the potter and entrepreneur Stephen Pearce. The house's most famous tenant since William Penn was Marlon Brando, who stayed here in the summer of 1995 while filming *Divine Rapture* in nearby Ballycotton.

A standard-bearer for the New Irish cuisine, **Ballymaloe Cookery School and Gardens** attracts students of the culinary arts from all over Ireland and, increasingly, points beyond. Run by Darina Allen, one of Ireland's best-known chefs, its cooking classes and programs range from one day to 12 weeks, and you'll find graduates in the kitchens of many Irish restaurants. Darina tends formal herb, fruit, and vegetable gardens as well as a knee-high Celtic maze. The property's free-range hens delight children. A meal or a snack at the Garden Café, serving the famous Ballymaloe-style food as well as pizzas from a wood-burning oven, should add greatly to your visit. ⊠ *Kinoith House* ☎ *021/464–6785* ⊕ *www.cookingisfun. ie* ⌨ *Gardens €5* ☉ *May–Sept., daily 9–6.*

Where to Stay & Eat

$$$–$$$$
Fodor'sChoice
★

✕🖼 **Ballymaloe House.** Originally a farmhouse and family home, albeit on a grand scale, Ballymaloe is one of Ireland's best known country houses. It still functions partly as a working farm, and is surrounded by pleasant, fertile countryside. Each guest room is prettily decorated with wit and imagination, using every corner of the often unusual shapes in the main house, originally a Norman castle. New, more spacious rooms downstairs have direct access to the pool and tennis court, and to views of the river and the garden's abundant bird life. The three generations of the Allen family involved in the business, and their loyal staff, have the knack of making a guest feel like a cosseted member of the family. The house is closed to visitors outside mealtimes to ensure privacy for guests. Myrtle Allen, who led the revival in traditional Irish cooking, presides over the dining room ($$$$), which houses the family's notable Irish art collection. Chef Rory O'Connell presents a six-course, haute Irish menu that relies on fresh fish from nearby Ballycotton, local lamb and beef, and homegrown herbs and vegetables—testament to Myrtle's practice of supporting small, local food purveyors, a philosophy that she pioneered over 40 years ago. ⊠ *Co. Cork* ☎ *021/465–2531* 🖨 *021/ 465–2021* ⊕ *www.ballymaloe.ie* ⛵ *33 rooms* ⚲ *Restaurant, tennis court, 9-hole golf course, pool, bar, some pets allowed; no a/c, no TV in some rooms* 🟰 *AE, DC, MC, V* 🍽 *BP.*

$–$$

✕🖼 **Barnabrow House.** Owners John and Geraldine O'Brien stylishly combined the old and the new when they renovated the interior of this rambling 17th-century house. Specially made modern wood furniture from Africa sits beside Victorian antiques and against intensely colored walls. The results are romantic and relaxed and are helped by the stunning views across the countryside to Ballycotton Bay. The garden is lovely, and wildflowers are encouraged. The O'Briens pride themselves on the informal, relaxed atmosphere, which includes a cockerel that announces the break of day (you have been warned). Main house rooms have high ceilings and canopy beds; courtyard rooms are cozier and have low, beamed ceilings. The Trinity Rooms restaurant ($–$$$; closed to non-residents

Monday through Wednesday) resembles a medieval banqueting hall, with a high beamed ceiling and church windows, and is painted wine-red. It serves imaginative dishes made with local produce, including fish from nearby Ballycotton. ⊠ *Cloyne* 🖼🖼 *021/465–2534* ⊕ *www. barnabrowhouse.com* ⤳ *21 rooms* ⚄ *Restaurant, bar, some pets allowed; no a/c, no room TVs, no smoking* ▭ *DC, MC, V* ⵏ◉⵱ *BP.*

Shopping

The ceramicist Stephen Pearce makes tablewares and bowls in four signature styles that are available in many Irish crafts shops. He sells a wide selection at his own **Stephen Pearce Emporium** (⊠ near Cloyne 🖼 021/ 464–6262), where he also stocks an interesting range of Irish-made crafts.

Midleton

❷❷ *15 km (9 mi) northwest of Shanagarry on R629, 12 km (8 mi) east of Cork City on N25.*

Midleton is famous for its school, Midleton College, founded in 1696, and its distillery, founded in 1825 and modernized in 1975, which manufactures spirits—including Irish whiskey—for distribution worldwide. A pleasant market town set at the head of the Owenacurra estuary, near the northeast corner of Cork Harbour, it has many gray-stone buildings dating mainly from the early 19th century.

The **Jameson Heritage Centre** has tours of the Old Midleton Distillery, to show you how Irish whiskey—*uisce beatha* (pronounced ishkeh bah-ha), "the water of life"—was made in the old days. The old stone buildings are excellent examples of 19th-century industrial architecture, the impressively large old waterwheel still operates, and the pot still—a copper dome that can hold 32,000 imperial gallons of whiskey—is the world's largest. Early in the tour, requests are made for a volunteer "whiskey taster"—so be alert if this option appeals. Tours end with a complimentary glass of Jameson's Irish whiskey (or a soft drink). A crafts center and café are also on the premises. 🖼 *021/461-3594* ⊕ *www. whiskeytours.ie* 🖼 €7.95 ⊙ *Mar.–Oct., daily 9–4:30; Nov.–Feb., tours only, weekdays at 12:30 and 3, weekends at 2 and 4.*

Fermoy

❷❸ *35 km (22 mi) north of Cork City on N8, 43 km (27 mi) west of Youghal on R634 (Tallow Rd.), which adjoins N72.*

An army town dating mainly from the mid-19th century, Fermoy is a major crossroads on the Dublin–Cork road (N8); the east–west road that passes through town (N72) is an attractive 98-km (61-mi) alternative route to Killarney. The bridge that spans the Blackwater is flanked by two weirs dating from 1689. From mid-April to early July you can watch salmon working their way back to their spawning grounds. A few miles upstream on the same river is Castlehyde, a fine Georgian house which is now the home of the lord of Irish dance, Michael Flatley. It is easy to see why he was so charmed by the quiet, lush country that surrounds this famous salmon river.

Where to Stay & Eat

$$ ✕🏠 **Ballyvolane House.** With Georgian splendor in the terrra-cotta, gilded,
Fodor's Choice and black Italianate pillared hall (complete with Bluthner baby grand)
★ and Regency coziness nonpareil in the daffodil yellow sitting room (fit-
tingly hung with a bouquet of prints and engravings), Ballyvolane offers
a setting as elegant as it is charming. Although this 1728 stone house looks
imposing, life here unfolds with country-house informality. That is be-
cause this house *is* a home to two generations of the Greene family, with
the owners' son, Justin, and his wife, Jenny, now acting as hosts. Expect
to find old fishing gear and walking sticks lying about and the family
dog greeting your return. The spacious bedrooms are beautifully deco-
rated with a rich assortment of antiques and heirlooms, but also display
an unpredictable sense of humor—the tub in Roland's Room, in full view
of all (on a wooden pedestal perched to give a garden view), always raises
a smile. The guest rooms look out onto wonderful gardens, including a
bluebell wood (early June) and a fairy-tale walled flower garden, with a
100-acre dairy farm beyond. Dinner is served at a large table in the for-
mal dining room ($$$$), with family silver set on white linens (both din-
ner and rooms must be booked at least 24 hours in advance). The village
of Castlelyons is signposted off N8 in Rathcormac, just south of Fermoy.
✉ *Castlelyons, Co. Cork* ☎ *025/36349* 🖷 *025/36781* ⊕ *www.
ballyvolanehouse.ie* ⮐ *6 rooms* ⌂ *Dining room, fishing; no a/c, no
room phones, no smoking* ▭ *AE, MC, V* ⦿*| BP.*

Mallow

㉔ *30 km (18 mi) west of Fermoy on N72.*

Mallow, an angling center and market town, was, in the 18th century,
a popular spa. Mallow lies at the intersection of the Cork–Limerick and
Waterford–Killarney roads, within an hour's drive of all four towns. At
the bottom of Mallow's Main Street, you'll find the **Clock House,** a half-
timber building dating from 1855. It shares the site with the Rakes of
Mallow Club, the headquarters of the notorious 18th-century gam-
blers, drinkers, and fortune hunters remembered in the song "The Rakes
of Mallow." Not much remains today of Mallow's glory, but the old
Spa Well can still be seen in the town center, and there are several in-
teresting facades with overhanging bay windows on Main Street, dat-
ing from the 18th and early 19th centuries. The English novelist Anthony
Trollope lived at No. 139 for a time, and he rode with the Duhallow
Hunt, enhancing the fame of the local pack. The ruins of the late-16th-
century **Mallow Castle** are at the bottom of the main street, freely accessible
behind ornamental gates. The castle was burned by the Jacobites in 1689,
and its stables were later converted into a house, which is still in use as
a private home. From here you can view the white fallow deer that are
unique to Mallow and were presented by Elizabeth I.

| off the beaten path | | **ANNE'S GROVE GARDENS –** These gardens were inspired by the ideas of William Robinson, a 19th-century gardener who favored naturalistic planting. Exotic foliage borders the paths winding down to the Blackwater; magnificent spring magnolias and primulas and |

summer hydrangeas are among the plants on view in the rolling countryside. ✉ *12 km (7 mi) east of Mallow, Castletownroche* ☏ *022/26145* ⊕ *www.annesgrovegardens.com* ☝ *€5* ⊙ *Mid-Mar.–Sept., Mon.–Sat. 10–5, Sun. 1–6.*

Where to Stay & Eat

$$$–$$$$ ✕🏠 **Longueville House.** Perched over the Blackwater Valley—the Irish
Fodor'sChoice Rhine—this imposing Georgian white-stone mansion graces one of the
★ most beautiful of all Irish river valleys (with one of its vista framed, no less, by oak trees planted in the formation of the English and French battle lines at Waterloo). Built about 1720 by the Longfields—who changed their names to Longueville to favor the French side of the family and distance themselves from any Cromwellian associations—this family seat is framed by limestone quoins around a classically symmetrical facade. Inside, Georgian grace notes continue, with a few 18th-century plaster ceilings, Adamesque fireplaces, and a glowing dining salon lined with ancestral portraits. In the Presidents' Restaurant ($$$$), chef William O'Callaghan, son of founding proprietors Michael and Jane O'-Callaghan, serves an outstanding and elegant Irish-French–style menu prepared in large measure with produce from the house's farm, garden, and river. The Victorian era delightfully intrudes with a glass-and-iron conservatory, used as a private dining room, and designed by Richard Turner, whose other ironwork creations include the greenhouses at Kew. This is not a place for jeans and sneakers: the surroundings will make you want to dress up for dinner. The bedrooms are roomy and elegant, with a peaceful air and color-coordinated in restful pastel shades. The super-king-size beds each have a padded velvet ottoman at the foot, while embossed wallpaper and velvet drapes are complemented by a few carefully chosen Victorian and Edwardian antiques. Little wonder this is favored as a posh forgetaway by lucky travelers. ✉ *Co. Cork* ☏ *022/47156* 🖷 *022/47459* ⊕ *www.longuevillehouse.ie* ⇌ *20 rooms* ⚭ *Restaurant, cable TV, fishing, bar, meeting rooms; no a/c* ▭ *AE, DC, MC, V* ⲟⲓ *BP* ⊙ *Closed late Dec.–mid–Mar.*

Sports
Mallow Golf Club (✉ Ballyellis, Co. Cork ☏ 022/21145) is an 18-hole, par-72 parkland course with excellent views of the Blackwater Valley.

Kanturk

㉕ *15 km (9 mi) west of Mallow on N72 and R579.*

Kanturk is at the confluence of two rivers, the Allow and the Dalua. It's more of a village than a town, but its interesting Victorian shop fronts bear witness to its past importance as a market town. The freely accessible **Kanturk Castle** (✉ 2 km [1 mi] outside town on the R579 Banteer road) was built by a local MacCarthy chieftain in 1601, but its completion was prevented by English neighbors who complained that it was too large for an Irishman. Ornate stone fireplaces and mullioned windows in the five-story shell give some idea of the scope of MacCarthy's ambitions.

Where to Stay & Eat

★ **$$$-$$$$** ✕⊡ **Assolas Country House.** A Queen Anne mansion covered in creepers; a section of the Owenbeg River; a pair of swans floating gracefully on the water; otters playing at dusk; and small wooden boats and rubber boots there for the taking—all in all, this peaceable kingdom, while slightly off the beaten track, makes for an excellent base for touring and allows you to savor the peace of the deep, deep countryside. Combining prettiness and elegance with historical charm, the 1740 manor house is a rare Irish example of Queen Anne style, with a symmetrical center block and rounded bays at either end, topped by a mansarded roof and pediment with a circular Palladian window. Picturesquely, the house is surrounded by a grove of mature trees, fronted by a rolling lawn, and threaded by the Owenbeg River. Add to this attentive hosts, the Burke family, who have presided over Assolas since the 1960s and brought more than a few antique heirlooms with them. Hosts Joe and Hazel Bourke are the second generation; Joe had the great fortune to marry Hazel, a talented chef, who revels in preparing delicious dinners from produce organically grown in their walled garden, and sourced from local farmers and fishermen. Dinner ($$$$) begins in front of the blazing log fire in the drawing room, where you peruse the menu over aperitifs. Family silver and white linen are on the tables in the red Queen Anne dining room, but the fare may be less traditional—-an Ardrahan cheese soufflé, or prawns with fresh tomato and herb salsa to start, perhaps followed by roast duck with pickled pear. Top it all off with gooseberry crumble and a night of pure peace. ✛ *Signposted off N72 west of Mallow (in Killarney direction)* ⊠ *Co. Cork* ☎ *029/50015* 🖶 *029/50795* 🌐 *www.assolas.com* ↗ *9 rooms* ⚭ *Restaurant, tennis court, boating, fishing; no a/c, no room TVs* ▤ *MC, V* ⊺◎⊺ *BP* ⊗ *Closed Nov.–Mar.*

KINSALE TO GLENGARRIFF

The historic old port—and now booming seaside town—of Kinsale is the perfect place to begin the 136-km (85-mi) trip, via Bantry Bay and through a variety of seascapes, to the lush vegetation of Glengarriff. If you tackle this scenic West Cork coastal route nonstop, the drive takes less than two hours, but the whole point of this journey is to linger in places that tickle your fancy. Must-dos include the famed 18th-century manse of Bantry House and the romantic island gardens of Ilnacullin.

Kinsale

㉖ *29 km (18 mi) southwest of Cork City on R600.*

Foodies flock to Kinsale—long considered Ireland's culinary capital—for its annual Autumn Flavours Festival in October. In the town center, at the tip of the wide, fjordlike harbor that opens out from the River Bandon, upscale shops and eateries with brightly painted facades line small streets. Houses with slate roofs and unusual slate fronts have Spanish influences that can be traced back to the Battle of Kinsale in 1601, when the Irish and Spanish joined forces to fight the English—and lost. The defeat was a serious one for the Irish aristocracy, and they soon took off for Europe, leaving their lands to English settlers. Kinsale went on to become an important fishing port as well as a British army and naval base. Kinsale has two yacht marinas, and skippers with deep-sea angling boats offer day charters. The Kinsale Yacht Club hosts racing and cruising events during the sailing season, which runs from March to October for hardy souls and from June to August for everyone else. This town is also where you'll find Ireland's only bareboat charter company.

The **Desmond Castle and the International Museum of Wine** are in a 15th-century fortified town house—originally a custom house—that has a dark history. It was used as a prison for French and American seamen in the 1700s, and was subsequently a jail and then a workhouse. Now it contains displays that tell the story of the wine trade and its importance to the Irish diaspora to France, America, Australia, and New Zealand. ⊠ *Cork St.* ☎ *021/477–4855* ⊕ *www.heritageireland.ie* ⊠ *€2.75* ☉ *Mid–Apr. to mid–June, Tues.–Sun. 10–6; mid-June–mid-Oct., daily 10–6* ☉ *Closed mid-Oct. to mid-Apr.*

Memorabilia from the wreck of the *Lusitania* are among the best artifacts in the **Kinsale Museum,** which is in a 17th-century, Dutch-style courthouse. The 1915 inquest into that ship's sinking took place in the courtroom, briefly making it the focus of the world's attention; it has been preserved as a memorial. Because the staff consists of volunteers, it's best to call to confirm opening times. ⊠ *Old Courthouse, Market Pl.* ☎ *021/477–2044* ⊠ *€2.50* ☉ *Mon.–Sat. 11–5, Sun. 3–5.*

★ The British built **Charles Fort** on the east side of the Bandon River estuary in the late 17th century, after their defeat of the Spanish and Irish forces. One of Europe's best-preserved "star forts" encloses some 12 clifftop acres and is similar to Fort Ticonderoga in New York State. If the sun is shining, take the footpath signposted Scilly Walk; it winds along the harbor's edge under tall trees and then through the village of Summer Cove. ⊠ *3 km (2 mi) east of town* ☎ *021/477–2263* ⊕ *www. heritageireland.ie* ⊠ *€3.50* ☉ *Mid-Mar.–Oct., daily 10–6; Nov.–mid-Mar., weekends 10–5.*

The **Spaniard Inn** (⊠ Scilly ☎ 021/477–2436) looks over the town and harbor from a hairpin bend on the road to Charles Fort. Inside, sawdust-covered floors and a big open fire make this onetime fishermen's bar a cozy spot in winter. In summer, you can take a pint to the veranda and watch the world go by on land and sea.

Where to Stay & Eat

★ $$$–$$$$ ✕ **The Vintage.** The cozy, beamed interior of this informal, cottage-style restaurant is enhanced by Swiss owner Raoul de Gendre's art collection. Tables are beautifully set, with specially designed glassware and white linen cloths. European dishes with Irish influences fill the à la carte menu; consider trying the whole lobster with mustard-whiskey sauce. Appetizers include caviar and fresh duck foie gras. The wine list has more than 150 wines, primarily from Europe. ⊠ *50 Main St.* ☎ *021/477–2502* ▭ *AE, DC, MC, V* ☉ *Closed Jan.–mid-Mar. No lunch.*

$$–$$$ ✕ **Man Friday.** Yes, the name refers to Kinsale's alleged connection with the original Robinson Crusoe, Alexander Selkirk, for the town was reputedly his last port of call before shipwreck. Set about 1 km (½ mi) outside town, next to the Spaniard Inn, on a hilltop overlooking the harbor, the restaurant focuses on steaks and seafood, prepared in an unpretentious Continental style. A rustic downhill walkway leads to a series of interconnected rooms and a terrace where diners enjoy drinks in fine weather. The generous portions and the warm atmosphere make it the sort of place you'll want to revisit. ⊠ *Scilly* ☎ *021/477–2260* ▤ *AE, DC, MC, V* ⊘ *Closed Sun. No lunch.*

★ $$–$$$ ✕ **Crackpots.** A grocery shop was transformed into Carole Norman's "ceramic café," a simple but elegant eatery with warm yellow walls, an open fire, and cozy dining areas. The most popular tables are in the front "shop window" area. Behind the restaurant is Carole's pottery workshop; if you like your dinner plate, you can buy it. The eclectic menu has plenty of light dishes in the lower price range, with vegetarian dishes a strong point. Choices range from spinach and ricotta cheese filo baked with red pepper sauce to Moroccan meatballs with couscous to Thai-style prawns with fragrant rice. There's always a steak option, too. ⊠ *3 Cork St.* ☎ *021/477–2847* ▤ *MC, V* ⊘ *Closed Mon.–Wed. in Nov.–Mar.*

$$–$$$ ✕ **Fishy Fishy Café.** Behind an impressive display of fresh seafood, chef Martin Shanahan's team concocts the specials that make this a place of pilgrimage for fish-lovers. People stand in line for a table at peak times (1–2:30). Martin, who learned his craft in San Francisco, brings California pizzazz to his dishes. Look for langoustines with lemon, garlic and sweet chili sauce; a fresh crab open sandwich; and seafood salad with a tangy herb dressing. ⊠ *Guardwell (opposite St. Multose Church)* ☎ *021/477–4453* ⌦ *Reservations not accepted* ▤ *No credit cards* ⊘ *Closed Sun. Oct.–Mar. No dinner.*

$$–$$$ ✕ **Max's Wine Bar.** Low, beamed ceilings and polished antique tables of different shapes and sizes lend this town house considerable charm. Lunches are light; it's a good place if you're keen on salads. At dinner, owner-chef Olivier Queva's classical French background is evident in his treatment of the daily catch and in his clever ways with such unusual cuts of meat as oxtail and trotters. The wine list is long and includes a good selection of French and New World wines, ranging in price from €16 to €84. ⊠ *Main St.* ☎ *021/477–2443* ▤ *MC, V* ⊘ *Closed Nov.–mid-Mar.*

$$–$$ ✕ **The Bulman.** Kinsale has other pub-restaurants, but none with such an idyllic waterside location. In summer drinks are taken outside, either at tables or on the big stone quay which looks back to the town and out to the unspoiled outer harbor. At lunch, simple pub grub—mussels steamed in white wine or a meaty burger and chips—is served at the bar. In the evening, the first-floor restaurant has tables with splendid views of the sun setting over the harbor. The menu includes steaks, freshly made pasta, Thai chicken curry, and local salmon. ⊠ *Summercove* ☎ *021/477–2131* ▤ *MC, V* ⊘ *No lunch Sun.*

$$$ ✕▥ **Blue Haven.** A restaurant and small hotel occupy this attractive, yellow-stucco, blue-trim town house. Rooms in the main house, though small, are cheerful and have paintings by local artists; newer rooms in

an adjacent building have dark-oak furniture, antique canopy beds, and more spacious baths. Inexpensive bar food is served until 9:30 PM in the lounge, the patio, and the conservatory, all of which have swagged curtains and nautical brass. Some nights a pianist entertains, and there is always a pleasant buzz, as the bar is a popular local haunt. The quiet, pastel-color seafood restaurant overlooks a garden and fountain, and is renowned for its seafood. ⊠ *3 Pearse St., Co. Cork* ☎ *021/477–2209* 🖷 *021/477–4268* ⊕ *www.bluehavenkinsale.com* ⤳ *17 rooms* ⌖ *Restaurant, cable TV, fishing, bar; no a/c* ⊟ *AE, DC, MC, V* ⦿ *BP.*

$–$$ ✕🖾 **The White House.** One of Kinsale's oldest inns has maintained the tradition of a warm Irish welcome. Bedrooms vary in size, but all have fully tiled bathrooms and pastel color schemes. A bar menu is served both in the bar and in the quieter side room called Chelsea's Bistro; the boiled bacon and cabbage—served with enormous potatoes—and the fish of the day are good bets. Ask about the two- and three-day dinner-and-lodging specials. ⊠ *Pearse St. and the Glen, Co. Cork* ☎ *021/ 477–2125* 🖷 *021/477–2045* ⊕ *www.whitehouse-kinsale.ie* ⤳ *12 rooms* ⌖ *Restaurant, cable TV, bar; no a/c* ⊟ *AE, DC, MC, V* ⦿ *BP.*

$$$–$$$$ 🖾 **Innishannon House.** A pretty country house built in 1720 in the Petit Château style on the banks of the Bandon, Innishannon retains plenty of casual character. Bar and dining room are hung with contemporary Irish art, and have a busy local trade. Guest rooms vary greatly in shape and size, as do the windows, but have a variety of interesting antiques and strong color schemes. The hotel is surrounded by gardens and woods, with an attractive stretch of the Bandon River running through it, bordering the grounds. It is in a quiet, rural location just off N7, about 6 km (4 mi) from Kinsale; it's quite perfect both as a retreat and as a base for touring the area. ⊠ *Innishannon, Co. Cork* ☎ *021/477–5121* 🖷 *021/477–5609* ⊕ *www.innishannon-hotel.ie* ⤳ *12 rooms* ⌖ *Restaurant, cable TV, boating, fishing, bar, meeting rooms; no a/c* ⊟ *AE, DC, MC, V* ⦿ *BP.*

★ **$$$–$$$$** 🖾 **Perryville House.** Pretty in pink and white stone trim, offset by a black wrought-iron veranda, and boasting a perch overlooking the inner harbor, Perryville House is in an adorable nook of town where homes often flower with hanging baskets and window boxes. The main salon hits all the right notes—emerald green walls, gilt-framed portrait, white fireplace—and one gets the impression of being in a private home. Front bedrooms have sea views, but rooms at the rear are quieter—key in July and August, when the town gets busy. All guest rooms are imaginatively furnished with Victorian antiques and have large beds and such extras as robes and fresh flowers. The lodging has a wine license, so you can buy by the glass or the bottle. ⊠ *Long Quay, Co. Cork* ☎ *021/477– 2731* 🖷 *021/477–2298* ⊕ *www.perryvillehouse.com* ⤳ *27 rooms* ⌖ *Cable TV; no a/c, no kids under 13, no smoking* ⊟ *AE, DC, MC, V* ⦿ *BP* ⦿ *Closed Nov.–Mar.*

★ **$$–$$$$** 🖾 **Old Bank House.** Owners Michael and Marie Riese manage this Georgian town house with flair and loving attention to detail. The large, high-ceilinged rooms have fresh-flower arrangements, original Irish art, and tall double-glazed windows. The whole look is not, however, period Georgian but vacation casual, with throw-pillows and plants setting a most informal note. The higher the room, the better the view, and there is an elevator for your convenience. Michael was previously a full-time chef—no wonder his breakfasts are so memorable. ⊠ *Pearse St., Co. Cork* ☎ *021/477–4075* 🖷 *021/477–4296* ⊕ *www.oldbankhousekinsale.com* ⇥ *17 rooms* ⚫ *Cable TV; no a/c* ⊟ *AE, MC, V* ⑩ *BP.*

¢ 🖾 **Kilcaw House.** Low room rates and off-street parking make this attractive, newly-built country guest house a good choice. On busy weekends, when the town buzz continues into the small hours, Kilcaw's location—2 km (1 mi) outside town on the Cork side of the R600—guarantees peace and quiet. An open fire in the lobby, polished pine floors, and striking colors add character to the farmhouse-style building. Rooms are well equipped, spacious, and uncluttered, with country pine furniture and throw rugs on wooden floors. ⊠ *Pewter Hole Cross (on R600), Co. Cork* ☎ *021/477–4155* 🖷 *021/477–4755* ⊕ *www.kilcawhouse.com* ⇥ *7 rooms* ⚫ *Cable TV; no a/c* ⊟ *AE, MC, V* ⑩ *BP.*

Nightlife

The **Boom Boom Room** (⊠ Guardwell ☎ 021/477–2382) has late-night dancing for the over-25s. The **Shanakee** (⊠ Market St. ☎ 021/477–4472) is renowned for live music—both rock and Irish traditional. Check out the **Spaniard Inn** (⊠ Scilly ☎ 021/477–2436) for rock and folk groups. There is a traditional Irish session on Wednesdays from 10 PM year round.

Sports & the Outdoors

BICYCLES Rent a bike from **D&C Cycles** (⊠ 18 Main St. ☎ 021/477–4884) to explore the picturesque hinterland of Kinsale.

FISHING For deep-sea angling off the Old Head of Kinsale contact **William Van Dyk** (☎ 021/477–8944) or **Arthur Long** (☎ 021/477–8969), both of whom operate out of **Castlepark Marina** (⊠ Castlepark, Co. Cork). For bareboat charters or skippered cruises—of a day or longer—contact **Sail Ireland Charters** (⊠ Trident Hotel, Kinsale, Co. Cork ☎ 021/477–2927 ⊕ www.sailireland.com).

WATER SPORTS & TENNIS The **Oysterhaven Holiday and Activity Center** (⊠ Sign-posted off R600, Oysterhaven ☎ 021/477–0738) is in a sheltered inlet 10 km (6 mi) east of Kinsale. Rental of sailboarding equipment and wet suits starts at €20 per hour. Topaz dinghies rent for €30 per hour. If Irish weather permits, you can also book a tennis court here for €10 an hour.

Shopping

Boland's Craft Shop (⊠ Pearse St. ☎ 021/477–2161) sells some unusual items, including sweaters, designer rain gear, and linen shirts exclusive to this shop. **Giles Norman Photography Gallery** (⊠ 44 Main St. ☎ 021/477–4373) sells black-and-white photographs of Irish scenes. **Granny's Bottom Drawer** (⊠ 53 Main St. ☎ 021/477–4839) has fine linen and lace in classic and contemporary styles. The **Keane on Ceramics** (⊠ Pier Rd. ☎ 021/477–2085) gallery represents the best of Ireland's ceramics artists. **Kingfisher Crafts** (⊠ 41 Main St. ☎ 021/477–4434) sells unusual, Irish-made decorative items,

You can spend quite a bit of time browsing through the excellent selection of Irish poetry and books on local history at the **Kinsale Book-**

shop (⊠ 8 Main St. ☎ 021/477–4244 ⊕ www.kinsalebookshop.ie). **Kinsale Crystal** (⊠ Market St. ☎ 021/477–4463) is a studio that sells 100% Irish, handblown, hand-cut crystal. Ceramics artist **Sara Flynn** (⊠ 42 Main St. ☎ 021/477–7201 ⊕ www.saraflynnceramics.com) has a studio and gallery in a cleverly converted old town house. Her porcelain forms are simultaneously simple and elegant. **The Trading House** (⊠ 54 Main St. ☎ 021/477–7497) has exclusive housewares from France, Spain, and Scandinavia alongside Irish and French antiques. **Victoria Murphy** (⊠ Market Quay ☎ 021/477–4317) sells small antiques and antique jewelry.

Timoleague

❷ *19 km (12 mi) west of Kinsale on R600.*

The romantic silhouette of its ruined abbey dominates the view when you're approaching Timoleague, a village of multicolored houses on the Argideen River estuary. The town marks the eastern end of the Seven Heads Peninsula, which stretches around to Clonakilty. A mid-13th-century **Franciscan abbey** at the water's edge is Timoleague's most striking monument. (Walk around the back to find the entrance gate.) It was sacked by the English in 1642 but, like many other ruins of its kind, was used as a burial place until the late 20th century. A tower and walls with Gothic-arched windows still stand, and you can trace the ground plan of the old friary—chapel, refectory, cloisters, and wine cellar (at one time the friars were well-known wine importers). The **Timoleague Castle Gardens** are right in the village. Although the castle is now a ruin adjoining a modest early-20th-century gray-stone house, the original gardens have survived. Palm trees and other frost-tender plants flourish in the mature shrubbery. There are two large, old-fashioned walled gardens, one for flowers and one for fruits and vegetables. ☎ *023/46116* ⌨ *€3* ☉ *Easter weekend and June–Aug., daily noon–6.*

You can glimpse **Courtmacsherry,** the postcard village of multicolored cottages, just across the water. It has a sandy beach that makes it a favorite for vacationers. To reach it follow the signposts from Timoleague. Farther on, you'll find that many storefronts in **Clonakilty,** a small market town 9½ km (6 mi) west of Timoleague on R600/N71, have charmingly traditional, hand-painted signs and wooden facades. **Inchydoney,** 3 km (2 mi) outside Clonakilty, is one of the area's finest sandy beaches. It's a great place for shell collectors.

off the beaten path

BIRTHPLACE OF MICHAEL COLLINS – The birthplace of Michael Collins (1890–1922) is signposted 9 km (6 mi) west of Timoleague off N71 (past the village of Lissavaird). You can see the ground plan of the simple homestead where the controversial founder of the modern Irish Army was born. There's also a bronze memorial (freely accessible), and another memorial in the nearest village, Woodfield, opposite the pub where Collins is said to have had his last drink on the day he was shot in an ambush.

Where to Stay & Eat

$$–$$$ ✕ **Casino House.** Stop midway between Kinsale and Timoleague, on
FodorsChoice coastal route R600, for a meal at this farmhouse, which has been ren-
★ ovated in a cool, minimalist style and converted to a restaurant. The
two small but airy and well-lit dining rooms—one blue and one green—
have private sitting rooms for predinner drinks next to an open fire, a
treat which sets the tone of gentle pampering that typifies the highly
professional co-owner Kerrin Relja's hospitality. Menu highlights from
talented Croatian owner-chef Michael Relja include garlic prawn salad
with lobster risotto, a fine roast loin of lamb served with Roman gnoc-
chi, and, as one of the top seasonal desserts, summer fruits with
sabayon. ⊠ *Coolmaine, Kilbrittain* ☎ *023/49944* ▤ *MC, V* ☺ *Closed
mid-Jan.–mid-Mar. Apr.–Dec. dinner only, Mon.–Sat., closed Wed.,
lunch only Sun.*

$$$$ ▦ **The Lodge & Spa at Inchydoney Island.** With its dream location above
a long beach, this modern hotel is a refuge for overworked city folk. Although the island is connected to the mainland by a causeway, it still
feels remote. Earth tones, plump sofas, and terrific natural light—reflected
off the Atlantic—are soothing. Public-area palettes continue in the guest
rooms, which have plush robes, soft slippers, and posh soaps. Although
staffers are pleasant, service can be laid-back. If this causes you stress,
unwind in the thalassotherapy spa, where treatments draw on the benefits of seawater, or head out on a golf, fishing, or horseback-riding excursion. ⊠ *Inchydoney Island, 5 km (3 mi) south of Clonakilty* ☎ *023/
33143* 🖷 *023/35229* ⊕ *www.inchydoneyisland.com* ⊱ *64 rooms*
⌂ *Restaurant, room service, IDD phones, in-room data ports, in-room
safes, minibars, cable TV, indoor saltwater pool, health club, beach, Ping-
Pong, bar* ▤ *AE, DC, MC, V* ▮◎▮ *BP.*

Shopping

The hand-crafted gifts and housewares at **Clonakilty Craft Centre** (⊠ Strand
Rd., Clonakilty ☎ 023/35802) showcase contemporary Irish design. **De-
laney's** (⊠ Clonakilty ☎ 023/48361) is full of small antiques as well as
antiquarian and secondhand books. **Edward Twomey** (⊠ 16 Pearse St.,
Clonakilty ☎ 023/33365) is a traditional butcher's shop famed for its
Clonakilty Black Pudding, a breakfast product that's prominently featured on the shop's nifty T-shirts—the ultimate West Cork souvenirs.
Spiller's Lane Gallery (⊠ Spiller's La., Clonakilty ☎ 023/38416), in a converted grain store at a pretty mews, sells Irish-made jewelry, cutlery, pottery, and paintings.

Skibbereen

 35 km (22 mi) west of Timoleague.

Skibbereen is the main market town in this neck of southwest Cork, and
a good base for nearby sights. If you really want to see the place at its
liveliest, come on a Wednesday when the cattle market is in full swing
and the sound of men spitting and back-slapping fills the air. In addition, the Friday country market and the plethora of pubs punctuated by
bustling shops and coffeehouses keep the place jumping year-round. A
thoughtful renovation of a stone gasworks building has created an at-

tractive, architecturally appropriate home for the **Skibbereen Heritage Center.** An elaborate audiovisual exhibit on the Great Famine presents dramatized firsthand accounts of what it was like to live in this community when it was hit hard by hunger. Other attractions include displays on area marine life, walking tours, access to local census information, and a varying schedule of special programs. ☒ *Upper Bridge St.* ☎ *028/40900* 🖭 *€4* ☉ *Mid-Mar.–late May and mid-Sept.–mid-Oct., Tues.–Sat. 10–6; late May–mid-Sept., daily 10–6; mid-Oct.–mid-Mar. by appointment.*

The **Mizen Vision Visitor Centre,** which occupies a lighthouse at the tip of the Mizen Head (follow the R591 through Goleen to the end of the road), is the Irish mainland's most southerly point. The lighthouse itself is on a rock at the tip of the headland; to reach it, you must cross a dramatic 99-step suspension footbridge. The lighthouse was completed in 1910; the Engine Room and Keepers' House have been restored by the local community. The exhilaration of massive Atlantic seas swirling 164 feet below the footbridge and the great coastal views guarantee a memorable outing. ☒ *Harbour Rd., Goleen* ☎ *028/35115* ⊕ *www.mizenhead.net* 🖭 *€5* ☉ *Mid-Mar.–May and Oct., daily 10:30–5; June–Sept., daily 10–6; Nov.–mid-Mar., weekends 11–4.*

Where to Stay & Eat

★ **$$$$** ✕ **Island Cottage.** Set on Heir Island, this unlikely venture is a pilgrimage spot for food lovers, who praise the high standard of cooking and the location. Hosts John Desmond and Ellmary Fenton know what they are talking about, he having worked at the Paris Ritz, Taillevent, and as an instructor at the famed La Varenne cooking school, while she hails from Paris's Hôtel de Crillon. But true to themselves and Ireland, their five-course meals focus on local produce, some of it picked in the wild on the island. Expect good, honest, unfussily prepared food—the best of new Irish Traditional. The restaurant is country-casual and tables seat 10, so be prepared to share; it adds to the fun of an unusual outing. Cape Clear turbot with sea spinach is typical; for dessert, try the terrine of vanilla ice cream with meringue in blackberry sauce. And if you get inspired, remember the couple offers "the world's smallest cooking school" here. Advance booking for the restaurant and courses is necessary; call for details about the four-minute ferry ride to the island from Cunnamore, which is about 15 km (9 mi) west of Skibbereen (follow signs on the road to Ballydehob). ☒ *Heir Island* ☎ *028/38102* ⊕ *www.islandcottage.com* ▭ *No credit cards* ☉ *Closed mid-Sept.–mid-May and Mon.–Tues. June–Sept. No lunch.*

$$$ ✕ **Annie's.** A meal at this mildly eccentric cottage, in an offbeat village 16 km (10 mi) west of Skibbereen, is a true West Cork experience. Annie Barrie and her chef husband, Dano, have been running the place for more than 20 years. When you arrive, chances are that Annie will send you across the road to Levi's Pub, where you'll wait for your table, peruse the menu, and eventually give Annie your order. Dano's simple, well-judged cooking lends the restaurant considerable magic. Dishes are made from outstanding farmhouse cheeses, locally reared cattle, and the freshest seafood. ☒ *Main St., Ballydehob* ☎ *028/37292* ▭ *MC, V* ☉ *Closed Sun. and Mon. and Oct. and Nov.*

$-$$ ✕▢ **West Cork Hotel.** On the River Ilen, this Victorian-period hotel is a local institution, having been in the Murphy family since 1900. It is well noted for its restaurant (those generous portions of food!) and its lively nighttime bar. Guest rooms are comfortable and well-equipped, with specially-made bird's eye maple furniture, padded headboards, Regency-striped armchairs, and color-coordinated drapes and spreads. The restaurant ($–$$$) spotlights traditionally grilled steaks and lamb cutlets but also serves monkfish, scallops, and duck prepared in a contemporary Irish style. ⊠ *Bridge St., Co. Cork* ☎ *028/21277* 🖷 *028/22333* ⊕ *www.westcorkhotel.com* �'*30 rooms* ⌂ *Restaurant, cable TV, fishing, bar, some pets allowed; no a/c* ▭ *AE, DC, MC, V* ◯ *BP.*

The Arts

The **West Cork Arts Center** (⊠ North St., Skibbereen ☎ 028/22090) has regular exhibits of work by local artists and an on-site crafts shop.

Castletownshend

㉙ *8 km (5 mi) southeast of Skibbereen.*

This town has an unusual number of large, gracious stone houses, most of them dating from the mid-18th century, when it was an important trading center. The main street runs steeply downhill to the 17th-century castle (built by the noted regional family of the Townshends) and the sea. The sleepy town awakens in July and August, when its sheltered harbor bustles. Sparkling views await from cliff-top St. Barrahane's Church, which has a medieval oak altarpiece and three stained-glass windows by early-20th-century Irish artist Harry Clarke.

Where to Eat

★ **$$-$$$$** ✕ **Mary Ann's.** Writer Edna O'Brien calls this her favorite pub in the world. Low-beamed, and one of Ireland's oldest, Mary Ann's attracts wealthy visitors from the U.K. and from other parts of Ireland, who mingle happily with the few locals left in the village in the front bar room, the quieter back room, or the large garden beyond. Energetic owner-manager Fergus O'Mahony is a brilliant host, and is always on the spot, supervising operations and contributing to the *craic* (lively conversation). Upstairs, the 28-seat restaurant nearly always buzzes, so reservations are a good idea. Try the trademark baked avocado stuffed with crab meat, the massively generous platter of Castlehaven Bay shellfish and seafood, or the succulent T-bone steak. ⊠ *Main St.* ☎ *028/36146* ▭ *MC, V* ◯ *Nov.–Mar. no food Mon.*

Baltimore

㉚ *13 km (8 mi) southwest of Skibbereen on R595.*

The beautiful, crescent-shape fishing village of Baltimore is a popular sailing center and attracts its share of vacationing families from Ireland and abroad, especially in summer. The village was sacked in 1631 by a band of Algerian sailors; as a result, watchtowers were installed at the harbor mouth. **Sherkin Island** (☎ 028/20125 for ferry information) is 1 km (½ mi) off the coast, only a 10-minute ferry ride away. On the island, you'll find the ruins of Dún Na Long Castle and Sherkin Abbey, both built around 1470 by the O'Driscolls, a seafaring clan known as the "scourge of the Irish seas." The island's population today is 90, and there are several safe, sandy beaches and abundant wildlife. Simply walking on Sherkin's almost-traffic-free roads and taking in the scenery is memorable.

The rugged, dramatic **Cape Clear Island** (☎ 028/39119 for ferry information ⊕ www.oilean-chleire.ie) is part of the West Cork Gaeltacht, or Irish-speaking area. The ferry to the 2- by 5-km (1- by 3-mi) island, which is 6 km (4 mi) offshore, takes about an hour from Baltimore. It's exciting to watch the skipper thread his way through the rocks and islets of Roaring Water Bay. You'll get excellent views of the Fastnet Rock Lighthouse, which is the focus of a biennial yachting race. Sparsely populated (about 150 residents), the island has little road traffic, a few bars, a youth hostel, and a few simple B&Bs. Bird-watchers should relish their time here—Cape Clear is the southernmost point of Irish territory, and its observatory, the country's oldest, has racked up all kinds of sightings of rare songbird migrants. Whales, dolphins, and large flocks of oceangoing birds can be seen offshore in the summer. In late August, the island hosts the International Story-telling Festival, a long weekend of simple entertainment for adults and kids; beware, it gets packed.

Where to Stay & Eat

¢ ✕🔲 **Rolf's Holiday Hostel.** Oozing a memorable, offbeat charm, with its chunky stone buildings, stone-built garden terrace, semi-wild garden, and stunning coastal views, this family-run establishment is just outside Baltimore, surrounded by wild gorse and above Roaring Water Bay. More like a Continental pension than a true hostel, its stone outbuildings (originally farmyard structures) house the communal kitchen and some of the unpretentious, cheery guest rooms. Café Art, the contemporary yet rustic restaurant ($–$$), offers local produce, steaks, and seafood. The menu prepared by chef Johannes Haffner includes continental treats—beef stroganoff cooked with vodka, for example, and Flemish apple tart—along with innovative contemporary dishes like mussels steamed with lemon grass and ginger. ✉ *Baltimore Hill* ☎ *028/20289* ⊕ *www.rolfsholidays.com* 🛏 *12 rooms, 1 12-bed dorm room* ⌂ *Restaurant, kitchen, laundry facilities; no a/c, no room phones, no room TVs* ▭ *MC, V.*

The Outdoors

Baltimore Sailing School (✉ The Pier ☎ 028/20141 ⊕ www.baltimoresailingschool.com) offers five-day sailing courses for adults and teenagers, in National 18 dinghies, costing €275.

Bantry

❸❶ *25 km (16 mi) northwest of Skibbereen on N71.*

As you enter Bantry—an unprepossessing town at the head of Bantry Bay (topped out with a large market square and long plaza which attracts artisans, craftspeople, and musicians in summer)—on the right-hand side of the road you'll see the porticoed entrance to **Bantry House.** One of Ireland's most enchanting manors, it is famed for its picture-perfect perch: on a steep hillock above the south shore of Bantry Bay, it is

Fodor'sChoice
★

surrounded by a series of stepped gardens and parterres that comprise "the stairway to the sky." Spreading out below the Georgian mansion lies the bay and, in the far distance, the spectacular range of the Caha Mountains—one of the great vistas of Ireland. Built in the early 1700s and altered and expanded later that century, the house was the ancestral seat of the White family, who was famed for its part in helping to repel two invading fleets, the Irish Nationalists and then the French. The house as it looks today is largely the vision of Richard White, the second earl of Bantry, who traveled extensively through Europe and brought a lot of it back with him: fabulous Aubusson tapestries—said to have been commissioned by Louis XV—adorn the Rose Drawing Room, while state portraits of King George III and Queen Charlotte glitter in floridly Rococo gilt frames in the hyper-theatrical, Wedgwood-blue-and-gold dining room. Not for nothing has this house been called "the Wallace Collection of Ireland."

Outside, the drama continues in the stepped garden terraces, set with marble statues, framed by stone balustrades, and showcasing such delights as an embroidered parterre of dwarf box. This Italianate exercise in horticulture pays off with a grand Cinerama view of the entire Bantry Bay. The estate is occupied by the descendants of the original family and you can sense the ancestral style of the current owners, Egerton and Brigitte Shelswell-White, from the lived-in charm of the reception rooms. Next to Bantry House is the **Bantry 1796 French Armada Exhibition Center,** a small but worthwhile museum illustrating the abortive attempt by Irish Nationalist Wolfe Tone and his French ally General Hoche to land 14,000 troops in Bantry Bay to effect an uprising. During summer the house hosts concerts in the grand library room, notably the West Cork Chamber Music Festival (held during the first week of July). ✛ *Bantry House is on the right hand side of the N71 as you enter the town from the easterly Cork City direction* ☎ *027/50047* ⊕ *www.bantryhouse.ie* ▨ *House, museum, and gardens €10; museum and gardens €4* ☉ *Mar.–Oct., daily 9–6.*

Where to Stay & Eat

$$–$$$ ✕▨ **Blair's Cove House.** In the converted stables of a Georgian mansion, gleaming silverware, pink tablecloths, and a large crystal chandelier are set off against stone walls and exposed beams. A covered, heated terrace overlooks a fountain and a rose-filled courtyard. The owners are French, and the cuisine ($$$$) is a mixture of French and Irish. Starters are displayed on a self-service buffet; a popular main course is steak or local lamb cooked on the open wood-fired grill. Stone outbuildings have been converted into well-equipped guest rooms furnished with country antiques and morning views of the still-blue waters of Dunmanus Bay (which are breathtaking). ⊠ *Blair's Cove, Durrus* ☎ *027/61041* ⊕ *www.irelandsbluebook.com* ◛ *3 rooms* ♨ *Cable TV, some pets allowed; no a/c* ▤ *DC, MC, V* ⏶ *BP* ☉ *Restaurant closed Sun. and Mon. and Nov.–mid-Mar. Accommodation closed Nov.–Feb.*

★ **$$$** ▨ **Sea View House.** Among private, wooded grounds overlooking Bantry Bay, you'll find this large, three-story, 19th-century country house. Owner-manager Kathleen O'Sullivan keeps an eagle eye on what was, until 1980, her private home and today remains an oasis of calm, nestled in its own gardens well away from the main road. Antique furniture, plump sofas, polished brass, and ornate curtains provide comfort and elegance. Some bedrooms have sea views and small sofas in bay windows; others have views of the wooded gardens. In the dining room, polished tables are set with crocheted mats and linen napkins; service is friendly and informal. ⊠ *Ballylickey, Co. Cork* ☎ *027/50073* 🖶 *027/ 51555* ⊕ *www.seaviewhousehotel.com* ↩ *25 rooms* ♿ *Restaurant, cable TV, fishing, bar; no a/c* ▭ *AE, DC, MC, V* ⍾ *BP* ⊘ *Closed mid-Nov.–mid-Mar.*

Sports

Bantry Park Golf Club (⊠ Donemark, Co. Cork ☎ 027/50579) is an 18-hole, par-71 course that overlooks Bantry Bay.

Shopping

One of the southwest's larger independents, **Bantry Bookstore** (⊠ New St. ☎ 027/50064) has six rooms full of new, antiquarian, and second-hand books. **Manning's Emporium** (⊠ Ballylickey ☎ 027/51049) is a showcase for locally made farmhouse cheeses, pâtés, and salamis—an excellent place to put together a picnic or just to browse.

Glengarriff

㉜ *14 km (8 mi) northwest of Bantry on N71, 21 km (13 mi) south of Kenmare.*

One of the jewels of Bantry Bay is Glengarriff, the "rugged glen" much loved by Thackeray and Sir Walter Scott. The descent into wooded, sheltered Glengarriff reveals yet another landscape: thanks to the Gulf Stream, it's mild enough down here for subtropical plants to thrive. Trails along the shore are covered with rhododendrons and offer beautiful views of the nearby inlets, loughs, and lounging seals. You're very much on the beaten path, however, with crafts shops, tour buses, and boatmen soliciting your business by the roadside. Many are heading this way because

★ of that Irish Eden, Ilnacullin. Set on Garnish Island, **Ilnacullin**, about 10 minutes offshore from Glengariff and beyond islets populated by comical-looking basking seals, you'll find one of the country's horticultural wonders. In 1910, a Belfast businessman, John Annan Bryce, purchased this rocky isle, and, with the help of famed English architect Howard Peto and Scottish plantsman Murdo Mackenzie, transformed it into a botanical Disneyland. The main showpiece is a wisteria-covered "Casita"—a rather strange-looking half-shed, half-mansion Peto cooked up—which is over a sunken Italian garden. A touch of Japan is supplied by the bonsai specimens lining the terrace. In fact, Ilnacullin has a little bit of everything, from a Grecian temple to a Martello tower (from which the British watched for attempted landings by Napoleonic forces) to a Happy Valley, all bedded with extraordinary shrubs, trees, and many unusual subtropical flowers. You get to Ilnacullin by taking a Blue Pool ferry which departs for the island from Glengarriff. George Bernard Shaw found Ilnacullin peaceful enough to allow him to begin his *St. Joan* here; maybe you'll find Garnish inspiring too. ☎ *027/63040* ⊕ *www.heritageireland.*

ie 🖼 *Gardens: €3.50. Boat ride: €7.50 round-trip* ☉ *July and Aug.,
Mon.–Sat. 9:30–6:30, Sun. 11–7; Apr.–June and Sept., Mon.–Sat. 10–6:30,
Sun. 1–7; Mar. and Oct., Mon.–Sat. 10–4:30, Sun. 1–5.*

Glengarriff is the gateway to the **Ring of Beara,** a 137-km (85-mi) scenic
drive that circles the Beara Peninsula on R572. The least famous of the
southwest's three peninsulas is also the least frequented—and, some would
say, the most ruggedly beautiful. One of the main attractions is the Beara
Way, a 196-km (120-mi) marked walking route that takes one to many
prehistoric archaeological sites. Just beyond the busy fishing port of Castletownbere are the freely accessible ruins of Dunboy Castle and House.
Dursey Island, at the peninsula's tip, is a bird-watcher's paradise that
you reach by cable car. From Dursey Island, head for tiny Allihies, the
former site of a huge copper mine, which now houses studios (open
May–September) for some of Ireland's leading artists. This is also great
hiking country—known for some of the most scenic stretches of the Beara
Way. Continue along a breathtaking coastal road to Eyeries—a village
overlooking Coulagh Bay—and then up the south side of the Kenmare
River to Kenmare. If you have time left over after exploring the Ring
of Beara, you might want to backtrack to R584 and visit **Gougane Barra
National Park** (⊕ www.coillte.ie/tourism_and_recreation/guagan.htm),
where the hermit St. Finbarr had his mountain retreat. It's the source
of the River Lee, and it has nature trails.

Where to Stay

¢ 🏨 **Old Presbytery.** This spacious waterside house, amid four acres of gardens, was formerly the home of the parish priest and is a typical example
of the solid comfort in which the clergy used to live. It's about 1 km (½
mi) from Castletownbere, on a narrow peninsula, discreetly distanced
from the sometimes noisy activity of this busy fishing port. Rooms are
comfortable and individually furnished, with pleasant sea views. Breakfast is served in the conservatory, which overlooks a private cove. This
is an excellent base for touring Beara. Hosts David and Mary Wrigley
will arrange dinner at one of the restaurants nearby. ⊠ *Brandy Hall,
Castletownbere* ☎ *027/70424* 🖷 *027/70420* ⊕ *www.midnet.ie/
oldpresbytery/index.htm* ⏏ *5 rooms* ♿ *Cable TV; no a/c* ▭ *MC, V* 🍽 *BP*
☉ *Closed Oct.–Mar.*

THE RING OF KERRY

Along the perimeter of the Iveragh Peninsula, the dramatic Ring of
Kerry is probably Ireland's single most popular tourist route. Stunning
mountain and coastal views are around almost every turn. The only drawback: on a sunny day, it seems like half the nation's visitors are traveling along this two-lane road, packed into buses, riding bikes, or
backpacking. The route is narrow and curvy, and the local sheep think
nothing of using it for a nap; take it slowly. Tour buses tend to start in
Killarney and ply the Ring counterclockwise, so consider jumping ahead
and starting in Killorglin or following the route clockwise, starting in
Kenmare (although this means you risk meeting tour buses head-on on
narrow roads). Either way, bear in mind that most of the buses leave

Killarney between 9 and 10 AM. The trip covers 176 km (110 mi) on N70 (and briefly R562) if you start and finish in Killarney; the journey will be 40 km (25 mi) shorter if you only venture between Kenmare and Killorglin. Because rain blocks views across the water to the Beara Peninsula in the east and the Dingle Peninsula in the west, hope for sunshine. It makes all the difference. To do the ring full justice, you'll need a minimum of two days on bike, more if you're traveling by bus. The Ring can be explored in as little as a day, either by car or on guided tour, but most of the Ring's best sites are found on spontaneous detours and winding back roads—the sort of pleasant traps that take time to fall into.

Kenmare

33 *21 km (13 mi) north of Glengarriff on N71, 34 km (21 mi) south of Killarney.*

A lively touring base, this market town is set at the head of the sheltered Kenmare River estuary. It is currently a matter of lively debate as to whether Kenmare, and not Kinsale, is the culinary capital of Ireland. Kenmare offers an amazing number of stylish little restaurants for a town its size, and also boasts two of Ireland's most highly reputed hotels, The Park and the Sheen Falls. The shopping is pretty good too, with Irish high fashion, crafts, and original art vying for your attention. The town was founded in 1670 by Sir William Petty (Oliver Cromwell's surveyor general, a multitasking entrepreneur), and most of its buildings date from the 19th century, when it was part of the enormous Lansdowne Estate—itself assembled by Petty. The **Kenmare Heritage Centre** explains the town's history and can outline a walking route to Kenmare's places of interest. ⊠ *The Square* ☎ *064/41233* 🎫 *Free* ⊙ *Easter–Sept., Mon.–Sat. 9:30–5:30.*

Where to Stay & Eat

$$ ✕ **Lime Tree.** An open fire, stone walls, and a minstrel's gallery on a large balcony above the main room lend considerable character to this restaurant in a former schoolhouse. Try one of the imaginative vegetarian options—mille-feuille of goat's cheese with spicy crumble—or go for local free-range duck or Kerry lamb oven-roasted with sweet mint pesto. Leave room for a warm dessert, such as blackberry and pear fruit crumble. ⊠ *Shelburne St.* ☎ *064/41225* 🖬 *MC, V* ⊙ *Closed Nov.–Mar.*

$–$$ ✕ **An Leath Phingin.** The name means "The Half Penny." It's a stylish little place with stone walls and modern pine tables, and it specializes, oddly enough, in northern Italian cuisine. The explanation lies in owner-chef Con Guerin's links with Bologna, where he learned the art of making fresh pasta. The combination of Irish and Italian dishes is reflected in a starter of baked aubergine with olive oil, tomato, local goat's cheese, and basil, or a 12-inch *quattro formaggi* pizza with four Irish cheeses—Milleens, Cashel Blue, local goat's, and Gubeen. ⊠ *35 Main St.* ☎ *064/41559* 🖬 *AE, MC, V* ⊙ *Closed Tues. and Wed., Dec. and Jan. No lunch.*

$–$$ ✕ **Packies.** Owner-chef Maura O'Connell Foley established Kenmare's original first-class restaurant, the Lime Tree, but has since opted for a quieter life at this smaller, cozier venue. Stone walls, fireplace, and floors are warmed up by colorful local paintings, and the buzz of expectation among the closely packed diners. The contemporary Irish menu may feature crab cakes with tartar sauce, or rack of lamb with rosemary and garlic gravy. Leave room for desserts, which include homemade praline ice cream and a memorable sticky toffee pudding. ⊠ *Henry St.* ☎ *064/41508* ⊟ *AE, MC, V* ⊘ *Closed Sun. and Mon. and Christmas to Feb. No lunch.*

$$$$ ✕⊡ **Park Hotel.** One of Ireland's premier country-house hotels, this
Fodor'sChoice 1897 stolid and vast stone château has spectacular views of the Caha
★ Mountains. No one can fault its setting: an 11-acre parkland, where every tree seems manicured and where magnificent terraced lawns sweep down to the bay. A welcoming fire is always burning in the lobby—a cute and traditional setting, replete with tall grandfather clock. Beyond lies a drawing room aglow with ivory flocked wallpapers and any number of comfy chairs. Each of the spacious bedrooms is unique, though most have late-Victorian pieces; suites have walnut or mahogany beds, wardrobes, and chests of drawers. Be sure to eat at the restaurant ($$$–$$$$)—an elegant room with lovely views of rolling lawns— which serves justly famed modern Irish cuisine. From the trio of nibbles that appears with your aperitif to the theatrical Irish coffee ritual that ends your meal, service and attention to detail are outstanding. To pamper both your body and soul, repair to the deluxe spa, set on a wooded knoll adjoining the hotel, and sign up for one of its individualized "Lifestyle" programs, which incorporate outdoor activities, including tai chi, meditation walks, mountain biking, golf, horseback riding, and walks on the Kerry Way. ⊠ *Shelburne Rd., Co. Kerry* ☎ *064/41200* 🖶*064/41402* ⊕*www.parkkenmare.com* ⇝*35 rooms, 9 suites* ♿*Restaurant, in-room data ports, cable TV, 18-hole golf course, pool, spa, tennis court, fishing, bicycles, croquet, Ping-Pong, bar, library, some pets allowed; no a/c* ⊟ *AE, DC, MC, V* ⦿l *BP* ⊘ *Closed Jan. 2–mid-Apr.*

$$$$ ✕⊡ **Sheen Falls Lodge.** Once the Irish country seat of the Marquis of
★ Lansdowne, the magnificence of this bright yellow, slate-roof stone manor is only matched by its setting: 300 secluded acres of lawns, gardens, and forest between Kenmare Bay and the falls of the River Sheen. The water is close enough that, as the sun sets over the MacGillicuddy Reeks, you'll undoubtedly be thinking about aquatic activities, like boating and fishing, for the morrow. In the meanwhile, all you need to do is choose between La Cascade restaurant ($$$$), which overlooks the falls and headlines modern Irish cuisine, or Oscar's Bistro ($–$$$) for its Mediterranean fare. Then you can enjoy a glass of Bushmills in one of the public salons, painted in warm, terra-cotta tones, or the mahogany-paneled library with more than 1,000 books, mainly on Ireland. Guest rooms—all modern-traditional, in bright yellows and tranquil beiges—have bay or river views. You can hire one of the hotel's vintage cars, which include a Bentley and a Rolls, for picnics, trips into town, and other excursions. ⊠ *Sheen Falls, Co. Kerry* ☎ *064/41600* 🖶 *064/ 41386* ⊕ *www.sheenfallslodge.ie* ⇝ *55 rooms, 11 suites* ♿ *2 restaurants, cable TV, tennis court, indoor pool, health club, sauna, steam room, spa, fishing, bicycles, billiards, croquet, horseback riding, 2 bars, library* ⊟ *AE, DC, MC, V* ⊘ *Closed Jan.*

$$ ⊡ **Sallyport House.** Across the bridge on the way into Kenmare, this 1932 family home has been enlarged to serve as a comfortable B&B. The spotless rooms, all with harbor or mountain views, are furnished with a variety of Victorian and Edwardian antiques. Owner Janey Arthur has placed family heirlooms everywhere; if you're interested in old Irish furniture, ask for a tour. A varied breakfast menu—which might include apples from Sallyport's own orchard—is served in a sunny room overlooking the garden. ⊠ *Glengarriff Rd., Co. Kerry* ☎ *064/42066* ⊟ *064/42067* ⊕ *www.sallyporthouse.com* ⊸ *5 rooms* ⚲ *Cable TV; no a/c* ⊟ *No credit cards* ⏐⊖⏐ *BP* ⊗ *Closed Nov.–Mar.*

$ 🖼 **Sea Shore Farm.** Mary Patricia O'Sullivan offers a warm but professional welcome to her spacious farmhouse on Kenmare Bay. Weather permitting, there are views across the sea to the hills on the Beara Peninsula, and although the place is very close to Kenmare, you can walk across her farmland to the deserted seashore and enjoy its plentiful bird and wildlife. You can also walk—or run—the mile into town along a scenic back road. Rooms are furnished with ornate heirlooms and have good-size bathrooms and placid views. Breakfast includes a choice of pancakes, kippers, or smoked salmon as well as the usual fry. ⊠ *Tubrid, Co. Kerry* ☎☎ *064/41270* ⊸ *6 rooms* ⚲ *No smoking, no a/c* ⊟ *MC, V* ⏐⊖⏐ *BP* ⊗ *Closed mid Nov.–Feb.*

Nightlife

Try **O Donnabhain** (⊠ Henry St. ☎ 064/41361) for traditional Irish tunes.

The Outdoors

☾ **Seafari** (⊠ Kenmare Pier ☎ 064/83171 ⊕ www.seafariireland.com) has two-hour, fun, eco-nature and seal-watching cruises, with complimentary tea and coffee for adults, and lollipops for the kids. Cruises cost €20 per adult, with special family rates.

Shopping

Avoca Handweavers (⊠ Moll's Gap, on the N71 road to Killarney ☎ 064/34720) sells wool clothing and mohair rugs and throws in remarkable palettes and a variety of weaves. **Black Abbey Crafts** (⊠ 28 Main St. ☎ 064/42115) specializes in fine Irish-made crafts. **Brenmar Jon** (⊠ 25 Henry St. ☎ 064/41138 ⊕ www.brenmar-jon.com) sells sophisticated knitwear. **Cleo's** (⊠ 2 Shelbourne St. ☎ 064/41410) stocks Irish-made woolens and linens that have striking designs, often drawn from Ireland's past.

Jam (⊠ 6 Henry St. ☎ 064/41591 ⊕ www.jam-kenmare.com) is a busy café that sells deli items and baked goods. **Kenmare Art Gallery** (⊠ Bridge St. ☎ 064/42999 ⊕ www.kenmareartgallery.com) has a good selection of works by contemporary artists, all of whom live locally but show internationally. **Noel & Holland** (⊠ 3 Bridge St. ☎ 064/42464) stocks secondhand books, including Irish-interest and children's titles. At **PFK** (⊠ 18 Henry St. ☎ 064/42590), Paul Kelly makes striking, modern jewelry in gold and silver.

Sneem

🟤 *27 km (17 mi) southwest of Kenmare on N70.*

The pretty village of Sneem (from the Irish for "knot") is settled around an English-style green on the Ardsheelaun River estuary, and its streets are filled with houses washed in different colors. Beside the parish church are the "pyramids," as they're known locally. These 12-foot-tall, traditional stone structures with stained-glass insets look as though they've been here forever. In fact, the sculpture park was completed in 1990 to the design of the Kerry-born artist James Scanlon, who has won international awards for his work in stained glass.

The approximately 2,500-year-old, stone **Staigue Fort,** signposted 4 km (2 mi) inland at Castlecove, is almost circular and about 75 feet in diameter with a single south-side entrance. From the Iron Age (from 500 BC to the 5th century AD) and early Christian times (6th century AD), such "forts" were, in fact, the fortified homesteads for several families of one clan and their cattle. The walls at Staigue Fort are almost 13 feet wide at the base and 7 feet wide at the top; they still stand 18 feet high on the north and west sides. Within them, stairs lead to narrow platforms on which the lookouts stood. (Private land must be crossed to reach the fort, and a "compensation for trespass" of €1 is often requested by the landowner.)

Where to Stay

$$$$ 🏨 **Parknasilla Great Southern.** "Parkansilla." For many travelers in
Fodor'sChoice decades past, this word alone conjured up an Irish Xanadu—a tower-
★ ing, awe-inspiring, faux-baronial pile, stunningly set by the waters of the Kerry coast, with the sort of grand, slightly stuffy, early-20th-century sensibility that welcomed visitors with a porter in a frock coat and striped gray pants. So it's little wonder everyone from Charles de Gaulle to Princess Grace headed here; George Bernard Shaw found it so accommodating he wrote much of *Saint Joan* here. Although some rooms are a bit plain, most are tastefully decorated in soft pinks and blues. Continental cuisine is served in the Pygmalion restaurant, and you can down your sherry in the Doolittle Bar. The sheltered coastal location—3 km (2 mi) south of Sneem—and excellent sporting facilities make this hotel an ideal retreat and an incomparable little world in County Kerry. ⊠ *Parknasilla, Co. Kerry* ☎ *064/45122* 🖷 *064/45323* ⊕ *www.gshotels. com* ⌷ *84 rooms* ⚶ *Restaurant, cable TV, some minibars, 12-hole golf course, tennis court, indoor pool, sauna, boating, fishing, horseback riding, bar, some pets allowed; no a/c* ▤ *AE, DC, MC, V* ⦿I *BP.*

★ **$** 🏨 **Tahilla Cove Country House.** An idyllic location—with its own stone jetty in a sheltered private cove—gives this place its particular charm. The house itself is modern and much added to over the years, and has the appeal of a modest but comfortable private home. No doubt it won't be difficult to enjoy the plump chintz armchairs and open log fire in the large sitting room, or to laze on the terrace overlooking 14 acres of subtropical gardens and the cove. Rooms vary in size and are comfortably furnished, and all but two have sea views. ⊠ *Tahilla Cove, Co. Kerry* ☎ *064/45204* 🖷 *064/45104* ⊕ *www.tahillacove.com* ⌷ *9 rooms* ⚶ *Restaurant, cable TV, fishing, bar, some pets allowed; no a/c* ▤ *AE, DC, MC, V* ⦿I *BP* ⊘ *Closed mid-Oct.–Mar.*

⬭ en route   **Derrynane House** was the home of Daniel O'Connell (1775–1847), "The Liberator," who campaigned for Catholic Emancipation (the granting of full rights of citizenship to Catholics), which became a reality in 1828. The house, with its lovely garden and 320-acre estate, now forms Derrynane National Park. The south and east wings of the house (which O'Connell himself remodeled) are open to visitors and contain much of the furniture and other items associated with O'Connell. ⊠ *Near Caherdaniel, 30 km (18 mi) west of Sneem off N70* ☎ *066/947–5113* ⊠ *€2.50* ☉ *Nov.–Mar., weekends 1–5; Apr. and Oct., Tues.–Sun. 1–5; May–Sept., Mon.–Sat. 9–6, Sun. 11–7.*

Waterville

③⑤ *35 km (22 mi) west of Sneem.*

Waterville is famous for its game-fishing, its 18-hole championship golf course (adopted as a warm-up spot for the British Open by Tiger Woods, who was a big hit with the locals), and for the fact that Charlie Chaplin and Charles de Gaulle spent summers here. Besides all that, the village, like many others on the Ring of Kerry, has a few restaurants and pubs, but little else. There's excellent salmon and trout fishing at nearby Lough Currane. Outside Waterville and 1 km (½ mi) before Ballinskelligs, an Irish-speaking fishing village, is the **Cill Rialaig**, an artistic retreat. Here, a cluster of derelict stone cottages in a deserted village were given new life as artists' studios. Cill Rialaig attracts both Irish and international artists for residencies, and their work, and ceramics, metalwork, jewelry, and other handmade crafts, are exhibited and sold at the attractively designed, beehive-shaped store. There's also a coffee shop. ⊠ *R566* ☎ *066/947–9277* ⊠ *Free* ☉ *Daily 11–5.*

Where to Stay & Eat

$ ✕☒ **Smuggler's Inn.** Lucille and Harry Hunt's small cliff-top pub is on a 2-km-long (1-mi-long) sandy beach, and has an immensely popular restaurant with fine, fresh seafood. It's an ideal spot for a leisurely dinner ($$–$$$$) or a quick pint and sandwich. Bedrooms are individually decorated with chintz spreads and curtains; in seven of them expect great sea views. ⊠ *Cliff Rd., Co. Kerry* ☎ *066/947–4330* 🖷 *066/947–4422* ⊕ *www.welcome.to/thesmugglersinn.com* ➪ *17 rooms* ♻ *Cable TV, fishing; no a/c* ⊟ *AE, DC, MC, V* ⏀❙ *BP* ☉ *Closed Nov.–Feb.*

$$$ ☒ **Butler Arms.** Charlie Chaplin loved it here. The vast building—with white, castellated corner towers—is a familiar landmark on the Ring. It has been in the same family for four generations, and the clientele returns year after year for the excellent fishing and golf facilities nearby and the proximity of long, sandy, windswept beaches. Many regulars like the smallish rooms in the old part of the hotel, which are neither smart nor chic. More spacious rooms, with streamlined decor and sensational sea views, can be had in a newer wing, and there are 12 junior suites. The rambling old lounges with open turf fires are comfortable places to relax and read or converse. ⊠ *Waterville, Co. Kerry* ☎ *066/947–4144* 🖷 *066/947–4520* ⊕ *www.butlerarms.com* ➪ *32 rooms* ♻ *Restaurant, in-room data ports, cable TV, tennis court, fishing, horseback riding; no a/c* ⊟ *AE, DC, MC, V* ⏀❙ *BP* ☉ *Closed Nov.–Mar.*

Nightlife

Head to the **Inny Tavern** (⊠ Inny Bridge, Waterville ☎ 066/947–4512) for live Irish music.

Sports

Waterville Golf Links (⊠ Co. Kerry ☎ 066/947–4102), an 18-hole, par-72 course, is one of the toughest and most scenic in Ireland or Britain.

The Skelligs

36 *21 km (13 mi) northwest of Waterville.*

In the far northwestern corner of the Ring, Valentia Island lies across Portmagee Channel. Some of the romance of visiting an island has been lost since Valentia was connected to the mainland by a bridge in 1971.

Fodor'sChoice ★ Visible from Valentia on a clear day are the **Skelligs,** one of the most dazzling, spectacular sights in Ireland. Sculpted as if by the hand of God, Little Skellig, Great Skellig, and the Washerwoman's Rock are iconic visions of what islands are all about. Distinctively conical-shaped, surrounded by blue swirling seas, these rock islands seem to symbolize world's end. The largest rock, the Great Skellig, or Skellig Michael, rises 700 feet from the Atlantic. It has the remains of a settlement of early Christian monks, reached by climbing 600 increasingly precipitous steps. In spite of a thousand years of battering by Atlantic storms, the church, oratory, and beehive-shape living cells are surprisingly well preserved.

To see the Skelligs up close (landing is prohibited without a special permit), you can take a 1½-hour guided cruise that is perfect for adventurers who pack plenty of Dramamine. During the journey, you'll pass Little Skellig, the breeding ground of more than 22,000 pairs of gannets. Puffin Island, to the north, has a large population of shearwaters, storm petrel, and puffins. But the masterpiece is the phenomenal Skelig Michael, home to that amazing 16th-century village of monastic beehive dwellings, and offering vertigo-inducing views. Note that the waters are choppy at the best of times, and trips are made when the weather permits. The cruises are conducted by the **Skellig Experience,** located where the bridge joins Valentia Island. This center contains exhibits on local bird life, the history of the lighthouse and keepers, and the life and work of the early Christian monks. There's also a 15-minute audiovisual show that allows you to "tour" the Skelligs without leaving dry land. But if you are up for it, don't you *dare* miss the boat ride out to the rocks. Be warned: the pinnacles of this ancient Christian (possibly pagan) center of worship will haunt you for days. ⊠ *Valentia Island* ☎ *066/947–6306* ⊕ *www. skelligexperience.com* ☞ *€32 museum and cruise; €6 museum only* ☉ *Apr.–June and Sept., daily 9:30–5; July and Aug., daily 9:30–7.*

Cahirciveen

37 *18 km (11 mi) north of Waterville on N70.*

Cahirciveen (pronounced cah-her-sigh-*veen*), at the foot of Bentee Mountain, is the gateway to the western side of the Ring of Kerry and the main market town for southern Kerry. Following the tradition in this part of the world, the modest, terraced houses are each painted in different colors (sometimes two or three)—the brighter the better. The **O'Connell Memorial Church,** a large, elaborate, neo-Gothic structure that dominates the main street, was built in 1888 of Newry granite and black limestone to honor the local hero Daniel O'Connell. It's the only church in Ireland named after a layman. The **Cahirciveen Heritage Centre** is in the converted former barracks of the Royal Irish Constabulary, an imposing, castlelike structure built after the Fenian Rising of 1867 to suppress further revolts. The center has well-designed displays depicting scenes from times of famine in the locality, the life of Daniel O'Connell, and the restoration of this fine building from a blackened ruin. ⊠ *Barracks* ☎ *066/947–2777* ⊕ *www.kerry-insight. com* 🎫 *€3.50* ⊙ *June–Sept., Mon.–Sat. 10–6, Sun. 2–6; Mar.–May and Oct., weekdays 9:30–5:30.*

Glenbeigh

38 *27 km (17 mi) northeast of Cahirciveen on N70.*

The road from Cahirciveen to Glenbeigh is one of the Ring's highlights. To the north is Dingle Bay and the jagged peaks of the Dingle Peninsula, which will, in all probability, be shrouded in mist. If they aren't, the gods have indeed blessed your journey. The road runs close to the water here, and beyond the small village of Kells it climbs high above the bay, hugging the steep side of Drung Hill before descending to Glenbeigh. Note how different the stark character of this stretch of the Ring is from the gentle, woody Kenmare Bay side.

On a boggy plateau by the sea, the block-long town of Glenbeigh is a popular holiday base, with excellent hiking in the Glenbeigh Horseshoe, as the surrounding mountains are known, and exceptionally good trout fishing in Lough Coomasaharn. The area south of Glenbeigh and west of Carrantouhill Mountain, around the shores of the Caragh River and the village of Glencar, is known as the Kerry Highlands. The scenery is wild and rough but strangely appealing. A series of circular walks have been signposted, and parts of the Kerry Way pass through here. The area attracts serious climbers who intend to scale Carrantouhill, Ireland's highest peak (3,408 feet).

☙ Worth a quick look, the **Kerry Bog Village Museum** is a cluster of reconstructed, fully furnished cottages that vividly portray the daily life of the region's working class in the early 1800s. ⊠ *Beside Red Fox Bar* ☎ *066/976–9184* 🎫 *€3.50* ⊙ *Mar.–Nov., daily 8:30–7; Jan. and Feb. by request.*

A signpost to the right outside Glenbeigh points to **Caragh Lake,** a tempting excursion south to a beautiful expanse of water set among gorse- and heather-covered hills and majestic mountains. The road ☙ hugs the shoreline much of the way. North of Glenbeigh, the beach at **Rossbeigh** consists of about 3 km (2 mi) of soft, sandy coast backed by high dunes. It faces Inch Strand, a similar formation across the water on the Dingle Peninsula.

Where to Stay & Eat

$$$–$$$$ ✕🗵 **Caragh Lodge.** Seven acres of gardens filled with azaleas, camellias, and magnolias surround this mid-19th-century fishing lodge by Caragh Lake. Two large rooms in the main house are furnished with Victorian and Georgian antiques. Rooms in the courtyard and the garden annexes are smaller, and another block has six larger rooms and one suite. Comfortable sitting rooms overlook the lake, as does the dining room. Owner Mary Gaunt supervises the quiet, relaxing dining room ($$–$$$; nonguests should book in advance). The food is Irish, with produce from the gardens, homemade bread, and local meats and seafood. ⊠ *Caragh Lake, Killorglin, Co. Kerry* 🕾 *066/976–9115* 🖷 *066/976–9316* ⊕ *www. caraghlodge.com* 🔁 *14 rooms* ♨ *Restaurant, tennis court, sauna, boating, fishing; no a/c, no room TVs* ▤ *AE, DC, MC, V* ⭑◯⫾ *BP* ⊗ *Closed mid-Oct.–mid-Apr. No lunch.*

$$$$ 🗵 **Ard na Sidhe.** "Sidhe" (pronounced sheen) means "Hill of the Fairies,"
Fodor'sChoice   and this secluded, gabled Edwardian mansion certainly looks like it be-
★   longs in a fairy tale. Its picture-perfect, ivy-covered stone walls are punctuated by casement windows set in gorgeous stone mullions, while the neatly manicured lakeside gardens contrast with the surrounding wilderness. The storybook mansion, built by Lady Gordon in 1913, has attractive, large rooms furnished with coordinated carpets and spreads, and floral drapes on bay windows; rooms in the main building are the nicest. Antiques and fireplaces dot the traditionally furnished lobby and lounges, but most of the furnishings are reproduction quality. Still, the setting and the house itself are incomparable. ⊠ *Caragh Lake, Co. Kerry* 🕾 *066/976–9105* 🖷 *066/976–9282* ⊕ *www.iol.ie/khl* 🔁 *20 rooms* ♨ *Restaurant, boating, fishing, bar; no a/c, no room TVs* ▤ *AE, DC, MC, V* ⭑◯⫾ *BP* ⊗ *Closed Oct.–Apr.*

$–$$ 🗵 **Glencar House.** A hunting lodge—built in 1670 by the earl of Lansdowne—on the Caragh River is now an unpretentious guest house with huge elk antlers over its fireplace and taxidermy hung at every turn. The large rooms have country pine furniture and breathtaking views of Killarney's famous mountains, MacGillicuddy's Reeks. The house is a 20-minute drive from Killarney, Waterville and Kenmare, and is a popular base for golfers. (From Killarney, turn off the N72 Killorglin road for Beaufort, and follow signs for Glencar.) When asked if the hotel had installed air-conditioning, the concierge replied "No, we have real air!" ⊠ *Glencar, Co. Kerry* 🕾 *066/976–0102* 🖷 *066/976–0167* ⊕ *www. glencarhouse.com* 🔁 *18 rooms* ♨ *Restaurant, cable TV, tennis court, fishing, Ping-Pong, bar; no a/c* ▤ *AE, MC, V* ⭑◯⫾ *BP.*

¢ 🗵 **Blackstones House.** Padraig and Breda Breen's farmhouse is a rambling old building on Caragh River in Lickeen Wood, where a gentle stretch of rapids leads to a salmon pool. With four golf courses within 20 minutes' drive, and fishing and hiking on the doorstep, the conversion to guest house was a good move. All rooms have a river view and are simply furnished with country pine bedsteads and pink, blue, and yellow floral drapes and spreads against plain walls and carpets. Breda provides a simple evening meal on request. ⊠ *Glencar* 🕾 *066/976–0164* 🖷 *066/976–0164* ⊕ *www. iol.ie/~blstones* 🔁 *9 rooms* ♨ *Dining room, fishing, bicycles; no a/c, no room phones, no TV in some rooms* ▤ *MC, V* ⭑◯⫾ *BP* ⊗ *Closed Nov.–Mar.*

Sports

Dooks Golf Club (☎ 066/976–8205) is a challenging traditional links course on the shore of Dingle Bay.

Killorglin

39 *14 km (9 mi) east of Glenbeigh, 22 km (14 mi) west of Killarney.*

The hilltop town of Killorglin is the scene of the Puck Fair, three days of merrymaking during the second weekend in August. A large billy goat with beribboned horns, installed on a high pedestal, presides over the fair. The origins of the tradition of King Puck are lost in time. Though some horse, sheep, and cattle dealing still occurs at the fair, the main attractions these days are free outdoor concerts and extended drinking hours. The crowd is predominantly young and invariably noisy, so avoid Killorglin at fair time if you've come for peace and quiet. On the other hand, if you intend to join in the festivities, be sure to book accommodations well in advance.

Where to Eat

$–$$$$ ✕ **Nick's Seafood and Steak.** Owner Nick Foley comes from the family that established Killarney's famous eatery, Foley's, and has made a name for himself as a chef. The old stone town house has a bar-cum-dining room at street level and a quieter dining room on the floor above. Foley is known for his generous portions, his wide choice of local seafood, and his steaks. In winter, sample the haunch of Kerry venison in red-wine and juniper sauce. ✉ *Main St.* ☎ *066/976–1219* ▭ *AE, DC, MC, V* ☉ *Closed Nov. and Mon.–Tues. Dec.–Easter.*

IN & AROUND KILLARNEY

One of southwest Ireland's most attractive locales, Killarney is also the most heavily visited town in the region (its proximity to the Ring of Kerry and to Shannon Airport helps to ensure this). Light rain is typical of the area, but because of the topography, it seldom lasts long. And the clouds' approach over the lakes and the subsequent showers can actually add to the spectacle of the scenery. The rain is often followed within minutes by brilliant sunshine and, yes, even a rainbow.

Exploring Killarney & Environs

▶ **40**–**48** *Killarney: 87 km (54 mi) west of Cork City on N22, 19 km (12 mi) south-east of Killorglin, 24 km (15 mi) north of Glengarriff.*

Such great writers as Sir Walter Scott and William Thackeray struggled to find the superlatives to describe Killarney's heather-clad peaks, subtropical vegetation, and deep-blue waters dotted with wooded isles. Indeed, the lakes and the mountains have left a lasting impression on a long stream of people, beginning in the 18th century with the English travelers Arthur Young and Bishop Berkeley. Visitors in search of the natural beauty so beloved by the Romantic movement began to flock to the southwest. By the mid-19th century, Killarney's scenery was considered as exhilarating and awe-inspiring as anything in Switzerland. The influx of affluent visitors that followed the 1854 arrival of the railway transformed the lives of Kerry's impoverished natives and set in motion the commercialization that continues today.

The air here smells of damp woods and heather moors. The red fruits of the Mediterranean strawberry tree (*Arbutus unedo*) are at their height in October and November, which is also about the time when the bracken turns rust, contrasting with the evergreens. In late April and early May, the purple flowers of the rhododendron *ponticum* put on a spectacular display. This Turkish import has adapted so well to the climate that its vigorous growth threatens native oak woods, and many of the purple plants are being dug up by volunteers in an effort to control their spread.

Much of the area is part of Killarney National Park, which has more than 24,000 acres and is famous for such native habitats and species as oak holly woods, yew woods, and red deer. Signposted self-guiding trails within the park introduce these habitats. At the park's heart is Muckross Demesne; the entrance is 4 km (2½ mi) from Killarney on N71. The National Park Visitor Centre is at Muckross House. Cars aren't allowed in Muckross Demesne; you can either walk, rent a bicycle, or take a traditional jaunting car—that is, a pony and a trap.

40 You may want to limit time spent in **Killarney** itself if discos, Irish cabarets, and singing pubs—the last a local specialty with a strong Irish-American flavor—aren't your thing. The nightlife is at its liveliest from May to September; the Irish and Europeans pack the town in July and August. Peak season for Americans follows in September and October. At other times, particularly from November to mid-March, when many of the hotels are closed, the town is quiet to the point of being eerie. Given the choice, go to Killarney in April, May, or early October.

41 **Aghadoe** (⊠ 5 km [3 mi] west of Killarney on the R562 Beaufort–Killorglin road) is an outstanding place to get a feel for what Killarney is all about: lake and mountain scenery. Stand beside Aghadoe's 12th-century ruined church and round tower, and watch the shadows creep gloriously across Lower Lake, with Innisfallen Island in the distance and the Gap of Dunloe to the west.

42 You reach **Torc Waterfall** (⊠ Killarney National Park, N71 [Muckross Rd.], 8 km [5 mi] south of Killarney) by a footpath that begins in the parking lot outside the gates of the Muckross Demesne. After your first view of the roaring cascade, which will appear after about 10 minutes' walk, it's worth the climb up a long flight of stone steps to the second, less-frequented clearing.

★ **43** **Muckross House**, a 19th-century, Elizabethan-style manor, now houses the Kerry Folklife Centre, where bookbinders, potters, and weavers demonstrate their crafts. Upstairs, elegantly furnished rooms portray the lifestyle of the landed gentry in the 1800s; downstairs in the basement you can experience the conditions of servants employed in the house. Inside you'll also find the Killarney National Park Visitor Centre. The informal grounds are noted for their rhododendrons and azaleas, the water garden, and the outstanding limestone rock garden. In the park beside the house, the Muckross Traditional Farms comprise reconstructed farm buildings and outhouses, a blacksmith's forge, a carpenter's workshop, and a selection of farm animals. It's a reminder of the way things were done on the farm before electricity and the mechanization of farming. Meet and chat with the farmers and their wives as they go about their work. The visitor center has a shop and a restaurant. ⊠ *Killarney National Park, Muckross Demesne, Muckross Rd. (N71), 6½ km (4 mi) south of Killarney* ☎ *064/31440* ⊕ *www.muckross-house.ie* ☜ *Visitor center free, farms or house €5.50, farms and house €8.25* ☉ *House Sept.–June, daily 9–5:30. Visitor center Nov.–mid-Mar., on request; mid-Mar.–June, Sept., and Oct., daily 9–6; July and Aug., daily 9–7. Farms mid-Mar.–Apr., weekends 2–6; May, daily 1–6; June–Sept., daily 10–7; Oct., daily 2–6.*

44 The 15th-century Franciscan **Muckross Friary** is amazingly complete, although roofless. The monks were driven out by Oliver Cromwell's army in 1652. An ancient yew tree rises above the cloisters and breaks out over the abbey walls. Three flights of stone steps allow access to the upper floors and living quarters, where you can visit the cloisters and what was once the dormitory, kitchen, and refectory. ⊠ *Killarney National Park, Muckross Demesne, Muckross Rd. (N71), 4 km (2½ mi) south of Killarney* ☜ *Free* ☉ *Mid-June–early Sept., daily 10–5.*

⑤ Ross Castle, a fully restored 14th-century stronghold, was the last place in the province of Munster to fall to Oliver Cromwell's forces in 1652. A later dwelling has 16th- and 17th-century furniture. ⊠ *Knockreer Estate, off Muckross Rd. (N71), 2 km (1 mi) south of Killarney* ☎ *064/ 35851* ☑ *€3.80* ☉ *Apr. and Oct., daily 10–5; May and Sept., daily 9–6; June–Aug., daily 9–6:30.*

㊻ The romantic ruins on **Innisfallen Island** date from the 6th or 7th century. Between 950 and 1350 the *Annals of Innisfallen* were compiled here by monks. (The book survives in the Bodleian Library in Oxford.) To get to the island, which is on Lough Leane, you can rent a rowboat at Ross Castle (€4 per hour), or you can join a cruise (€8) in a covered, heated launch.

★ ☾ **㊼** Massive, glacial rocks form the side of the **Gap of Dunloe,** a narrow mountain pass that stretches for 6½ km (4 mi) between MacGillicuddy's Reeks and the Purple Mountains. The rocks create strange echoes: give a shout to test it out. Five small lakes are strung out beside the road. Cars are banned from the gap, but in summer the first 3 km (2 mi) are busy with horse and foot traffic, much of which turns back at the halfway point.

At the entrance to the Gap of Dunloe, **Kate Kearney's Cottage** (⊠ 19 km [12 mi] west of Killarney ☎ 064/44116) is a good place to rent a jaunting car or pony. Kate was a famous beauty who sold illegal *poteen* (moonshine) from her home, contributing greatly, one suspects, to travelers' enthusiasm for the scenery. Appropriately enough, Kearney's is now a pub and a good place to pause for an Irish coffee.

The gap's southern end is marked by **Lord Brandon's Cottage,** a tea shop serving soup and sandwiches. From here, a path leads to the edge of Upper Lake, where you can journey onward by rowboat. It's an old tradition for the boatman to carry a bugle and illustrate the echoes. The boat passes under Brickeen Bridge and into Middle Lake, where 30 islands are steeped in legends, many of which your boatman is likely to recount. Look out for caves on the left-hand side on this narrow stretch of water. ⊠ *7 km (4½ mi) west of Killarney* ☉ *Easter–Sept., 10 AM–dusk.*

★ **㊽** If the weather is fine, head southwest 19 km (12 mi) out of Killarney on N71 to **Ladies' View,** a famed panorama of the three lakes and the surrounding mountains. The name goes back to 1905, when Queen Victoria was a guest at Muckross House. Upon seeing the view, her ladies-in-waiting were said to have been dumbfounded by its beauty.

Where to Stay & Eat

$$$–$$$$ ✕ **Gaby's Seafood.** Expect the best seafood in Killarney from Belgian owner-chef Gert Maes. Inside the rustic exterior is a little bar beside an open fire; steps lead up to the main dining area. Try the seafood platter (seven or eight kinds of fish in a cream-and-wine sauce) or lobster Gaby (shelled, simmered in a cream-and-cognac sauce, and served back in the shell). ⊠ *27 High St.* ☎ *064/32519* ═ *AE, DC, MC, V* ☉ *Closed Sun. and mid-Feb.–mid-Mar. No lunch.*

★ **$$–$$$** ✕ **Old Presbytery.** This beautiful Georgian house is across the road from Killarney's cathedral and was once a residence for the clergy. Its interior has been transformed into a spacious, two-floor restaurant. Proceed past the bar area, with its open fire and leather sofas, into a room with wooden floors, brocade-upholstered chairs, and candlelit tables. Chef Simon Regan's imaginative menu is served by a friendly, efficient staff. Try the baked monkfish with aubergine caviar and sauce Provençale or the grilled beef fillet with horseradish and red onion soufflé. ⊠ *Cathedral Pl.* ☎ *064/30555* ⊕ *www.oldpresbytery.com* ▭ *AE, DC, MC, V* ⊗ *Closed Tues. and Jan. 7–Feb. 1. No lunch.*

¢–$ ✕ **Panis Angelicus.** Daylight streams in through the large plate-glass shop windows of this stylish, contemporary café, and mellow jazz plays softly in the background. Add black-tile floors, original art on dark red walls, and the smell of freshly ground coffee, and you have the ideal place to take a break. There are home-baked breads and cakes as well as a good selection of sandwiches, and the hot Irish potato cake with garlic butter and green salad is delicious. Dinner menus feature pasta specials, seafood salad, and other light bites. ⊠ *15 New St.* ☎ *064/39648* ▭ *MC, V* ⊗ *No dinner Oct.–Apr.*

$$$$ ✕▦ **Aghadoe Heights.** The lake views from here are unforgettable, and the 8 acres of grounds ensure absolute peace. The interior is an agreeable combination of antique and modern styles but the building itself is modern—not the most atmospheric of styles. Most bedrooms have mountain vistas, and all are large, with good-size bathrooms, floral fabrics, lace-covered cushions, and natural wood furniture. Fredericks, the rooftop restaurant ($$$$; jacket and tie required), is romantic with silver candelabras, white linen, and upholstered chairs. Chef Robin Suter prepares a seasonal French menu. Main courses include both classics—black sole grilled or meunière—and more unusual dishes, such as medallions of veal with crab soufflé. ⊠ *Aghadoe Heights, 4 km (2½ mi) outside Killarney (on the Tralee side, signposted off N22), Co. Kerry* ☎ *064/31766* ☒ *064/31345* ⊕ *www.aghadoeheights.com* ⇒ *66 rooms, 3 suites* ♨ *Restaurant, in-room data ports, minibars, cable TV, tennis court, indoor pool, health club, sauna, fishing, bar, meeting rooms* ▭ *AE, DC, MC, V* ⦿ *BP* ⊗ *Closed Jan.–March.*

$$$$ ✕▦ **Killarney Park.** When Irish hoteliers visit Killarney, this is where they stay. Owners Joe and Margaret Scally ensure the personal touch, while Margaret's family has run hotels in Killarney for generations. So it was easy for them to add elegance and atmosphere to this traditional-style building. The lobby is done in a Victorian country-house style, with a sweeping staircase. Sofas and armchairs are invitingly grouped around open fires, and there's a fine library in which to lounge. Guest rooms are spacious, and individually designed, with fresh flowers, sumptuous drapes, brass lampstands, and graceful, often French or Italian antiques. The staff is famed for its warmth and dedication. The large, opulent restaurant ($$$–$$$$), with its massive central chandelier, serves classic Continental cuisine with Irish influences. Simpler meals are served in the Garden Bar. ⊠ *Kenmare Pl., Co. Kerry* ☎ *064/35555* ☒ *064/35266* ⊕ *www.killarneyparkhotel.ie* ⇒ *25 rooms, 5 suites* ♨ *Restaurant, in-room safes, minibars, cable TV, indoor pool, health club, hot tub, outdoor hot tub, bicycles, billiards, bar, library, meeting rooms, some pets allowed* ▭ *AE, DC, MC, V* ⦿ *BP* ⊗ *Closed Dec. 23–26.*

$ ✕▦ **Foley's Townhouse and Restaurant.** Rooms in this 19th-century row of interconnected town houses have Victorian antiques and rustic, pine furniture. Windows are double-glazed, so the rooms are quieter than you would expect for a hotel right in the center of Killarney. In the restaurant ($$–$$$$) chef-owner Carol Hartnett makes use of local ingredients, including superior Irish cream and butter. Roulade of trout stuffed with prawn mousse and grilled T-bone steak with garlic butter are typical dishes. The wine list has more than 200 selections, and a pianist entertains in summer. ✉ *23 High St., Co. Kerry* ☎ *064/31217* 🖷 *064/34683* ⊕ *www.foleystownhouse.com* ⤸ *32 rooms* ⟐ *Restaurant, in-room data ports, cable TV* ⊟ *AE, DC, MC, V* ⦿ *BP* ⊗ *Closed mid-Nov.–Feb.*

$ ✕▦ **Mills Inn.** If you wince at tour-bus crowds, consider this coaching inn in Ballyvourney, a village 15 minutes outside Killarney and on the main Cork–Killarney road. The inn is beside the rapid-flowing River Sullane, and its grounds have old castle ruins as well as a stable yard and gardens. Its bar, established in 1755, is popular with Irish-speaking locals and has music on Wednesday and Sunday nights. Rooms are well insulated from bar and traffic noise and have mahogany four-poster beds and a cream-and-gold color scheme. The restaurant ($$–$$$) serves generous portions of local beef and seafood; at the bar you'll get simple fare, such as Irish stew. ✉ *Ballyvourney, Macroom, Co. Cork* ☎ *026/45237* 🖷 *026/45454* ⊕ *www.millsinn.ie* ⤸ *12 rooms* ⟐ *Restaurant, cable TV, 2 bars; no a/c* ⊟ *MC, V* ⦿ *BP.*

$ ▦ **Fuchsia House.** Tom and Mary Treacy come from a long line of Killarney hoteliers, which explains their professional approach. The house is located in a strip of newly-built, depressingly standardized B&Bs that have sprung up between the town and Muckross Park, but this one is different. It was built in 1992 in a gracious Edwardian style, with square bay windows beneath high gables and a redbrick ground floor, promising a spacious, comfortable interior. Tea and homemade cake are served to guests on arrival in the drawing room; guests can also enjoy a large conservatory which overlooks the garden (Tom is a keen gardener). Bedrooms are luxuriously furnished with coordinating fabrics, and better equipped than many hotels. The home-baked goodies on offer have made Mary's breakfasts legendary. ✉ *Muckross Rd.,* ☎ *064/33743* 🖷 *064/ 36588* ⊕ *www.fuchsiahouse.com* ⤸ *9 rooms* ⟐ *No a/c, no smoking* ⊟ *MC, V* ⊗ *Closed mid Nov.–Feb.*

$$ ▦ **Earls Court House.** In a quiet suburb within walking distance of Killarney's center, this comfortable guest house is furnished with interesting antiques collected by Emer Moynihan, who likes to greet her guests with tea or coffee and scones. Bedrooms are spacious, with large bathrooms and a mix of antique and reproduction Victorian furniture. Breakfast is served at mahogany tables in a large, sunny, wooden-floored room; menu choices include pancakes and kippers. The house has a wine license. ✉ *Woodlawn Junction, Muckross Rd. (N71), Co. Kerry* ☎ *064/ 34009* 🖷 *064/34366* ⊕ *www.killarney-earlscourt.ie* ⤸ *11 rooms* ⟐ *Dining room, in-room data ports; no a/c* ⊟ *MC, V* ⦿ *BP* ⊗ *Closed Dec.–Jan.*

¢ ▦ **Lime Court.** On the Muckross Road between Killarney and the national park—yet only a five-minute walk from the town center—this modern guest house has two large bay windows in front. Rooms are in an extension at the back and away from the road. Antiques and large potted plants decorate the reception area; a baby grand piano anchors the spacious lounge. Although guest rooms are plain, they're comfortable and light; all overlook green fields and have small sitting areas. ✉ *Muckross Rd. (N71), Co. Kerry* ☎ *064/34547* 🖷 *064/34121* ⊕ *www.limecourt.com* ⇆ *16 rooms* ☒ *Cable TV; no a/c* ☰ *MC, V* ¶❉ *BP.*

Nightlife & the Arts

Bars where a professional leads the songs and encourages audience participation and solos are popular in Killarney. Try the **Laurels** (✉ Main St. ☎ 064/31149). **Buckley's Bar** (✉ College St. ☎ 064/31037) in the Arbutus Hotel has traditional Irish entertainment nightly from June to September. **Gleneagles** (✉ Muckross Rd. ☎ 064/31870) is the place for big-name cabaret—from Sharon Shannon to the Wolfe Tones. It also has a late-night disco. **McSorleys Nite Club** (✉ College St. ☎ 064/39770) is a lively late-night venue for the over-25s.

Sports & the Outdoors

BICYCLING A bicycle is the perfect way to enjoy Killarney's mild air, whether within the confines of Muckross Park or farther afield in the Kerry Highlands. Rent by the day or week from **O'Sullivan's Cycles** (✉ Bishop's La., off New St. ☎ 064/31282).

FISHING Salmon and brown trout populate Killarney's lakes and rivers. To improve your technique contact **Angler's Paradise** (✉ Loreto Rd., Muckross ☎ 064/33818), where the Michael O'Brien International Fishing School organizes game, coarse, and deep-sea fishing trips by day or by night. **O'Neill's** (✉ Plunkett St. ☎ 064/31970) provides fishing tackle, bait, and licenses.

GOLF **Beaufort Golf Course** (✉ Churchtown, Beaufort ☎ 064/44440) has an 18-hole, par-71 course surrounded by magnificent scenery, and unlike most other Irish golf clubs, it has buggy-, trolley-, and club-rental facilities. For many, the two courses at the legendary **Killarney Golf and Fishing Club** (✉ Mahony's Point ☎ 064/31034) are the chief reason for coming to Killarney.

HIKING The **Kerry Way**, a long-distance walking route, passes through the Killarney National Park on its way to Glenbeigh. You can get a detailed leaflet about the route from the tourist information office. For the less adventurous, four safe and well-signposted nature trails of varying lengths are in the national park. Try the 4-km (2½-mi) Arthur Young's Walk, which passes through old yew and oak woods frequented by Sika deer. You can reach the **Mangerton walking trail,** a small tarred road leading to a scenic trail that circles Mangerton Lake, by turning left off N71 midway between Muckross Friary and Muckross House (follow the signposts). The summit of **Mangerton Mountain** (2,756 feet) can be reached on foot in about two hours—less if you rent a pony. It's perfect if you want a fine, long hike with good views of woodland scenery. **Torc Mountain** (1,764 feet) can be reached off Route N71; it's a satisfying 1½-hour climb, with lake views. Don't attempt mountain climbing in the area in misty weather; visibility can quickly drop to zero.

Shopping

Bricín Craft Shop (⊠ 26 High St. ☎ 064/34902) has interesting handicrafts, including candles, ceramics, and woolens. **Christy's Design Store** (⊠ 3 New St. ☎ 064/35406) stocks contemporary Irish pottery, ironwork, woodwork, crystal, and jewelry. Visit the **Frank Lewis Gallery** (⊠ 6 Bridewell La., beside General Post Office ☎ 064/34843) for original paintings and sculptures. If you have Irish roots, you can learn all about your name and buy an item with its heraldic crest—from key rings to crystal to sweaters—at **House of Names** (⊠ Kenmare Pl. ☎ 064/ 36320 ⊕ www.iol.ie/shopping/houseofnames).

The **Killarney Bookshop** (⊠ 32 Main St. ☎ 064/34108) has local-interest books as well as fiction, biography, and travel titles. **MacBee's** (⊠ New St. ☎ 064/33622) is a modern boutique stocking the best of Irish high fashion. **Quills Woolen Market** (⊠ Market Cross ☎ 064/32277) has the town's biggest selection of Irish knitwear. It also carries tweeds, linens, and Celtic jewelry. **The Woodpotters** (⊠ 24 High St. ☎ 064/31217) sells unusual gifts and such housewares as picture frames, potpourri, and wicker trays.

THE DINGLE PENINSULA

The brazenly scenic Dingle Peninsula stretches for some 48 km (30 mi) between Tralee (pronounced tra-*lee*) in the east and Slea Head in the west. Rugged mountains and cliffs are interspersed with softly molded glacial valleys and lakes. Long sandy beaches and Atlantic-pounded cliffs unravel along the coast. Drystone walls enclose small, irregular fields, and exceptional prehistoric and early Christian remains dot the countryside. As you drive over its high mountain passes, the Dingle may conjure up images of the Alps or Rockies, and the lushly forested mountains along the shore look like they belong on a South Pacific island. Unfortunately, Dingle is notorious for its heavy rainfall and impenetrable sea mists, which can strike at any time of year. If they do, sit them out in Dingle Town or the village of Dunquin and enjoy the friendly bars, cafés, and crafts shops. West of Dingle Town, the peninsula, like parts of County Kerry, is Gaeltacht: English is considered a second language.

You can cover the peninsula in a long day trip of about 160 km (99 mi). If mist or continuous rain is forecast, postpone your trip until visibility improves. From Killarney, Killorglin, or Tralee, head for Castlemaine, and take the coast road (R561 and R559) to Dingle Town. You'll pass through the sheltered seaside resort of Inch, 19 km (12 mi) west of Castlemaine and 45 km (28 mi) northwest of Killarney, where the head of Dingle Bay is cut off by two sand spits that enclose Castlemaine Harbour. Inch has a 6½-km (4-mi) beach backed by dunes that are home to a large colony of natterjack toads.

Annascaul

 7 km (4½ mi) west of Inch.

An important livestock center until the 1930s, this village—near the junction of the Castlemaine and Tralee roads—has a wide road as cattle trading was once carried out in the streets. The town also has many pubs. Photographers will be tempted to snap **Dan Foley's** (☎ 066/915–7252) flamboyantly painted pub. Wander in for a pint; the legendary Dan Foley, who was a magician, a farmer, and an expert on local history, is no longer with us, but tales about him are still told in Annascaul.

The South Pole Inn (☎ 066/915–7388) was set up by local Tom Crean when he returned from Walter Scott's Antarctic expedition.

Dingle Town

50 *18 km (11 mi) west of Annascaul, 67 km (42 mi) west of Killarney, 45 km (28 mi) west of Killorglin on R561.*

Backed by mountains and facing a sheltered harbor, Dingle, the chief town of its eponymous peninsula, has a year-round population of 1,400 that more than doubles in summer. Although many expect Dingle to be a quaint and undeveloped Gaeltacht village, it has many crafts shops, seafood restaurants, and pubs. Still, you can explore its main thoroughfares—the Mall, Main and Strand streets, and the Wood—in less than an hour. Celebrity hawks, take note: off-season Dingle is favored as a hideaway by the likes of Julia Roberts, Paul Simon, and Dolly Parton. These and others have their visits commemorated on Green Street's "path of stars."

Dingle's pubs are well known for their music, but among them **O'Flaherty's** (✉ Bridge St., at the entrance to town ☎ 066/915–1983), a simple, stone-floored bar, is something special and a hot spot for traditional musicians. Spontaneous sessions occur most nights in July and August, less frequently at other times. Even without music, this pub is a good place to compare notes with fellow travelers.

Since 1985, Dingle's central attraction, apart from its music scene, has been a winsome bottle-nosed dolphin who has taken up residence in the harbor. The Dingle dolphin, or **Fungi**, as he has been named, will play for hours with swimmers (a wet suit is essential) and scuba divers, and he follows local boats in and out of the harbor. It is impossible to predict whether he will stay, but boatmen have become so confident of a sighting that they offer trippers their money back if Fungie does not appear. Boat trips (€8) leave the pier hourly in July and August between 11 and 6, weather permitting. At other times, call **Jimmy Flannery Sr.** (☎ 066/915–1967).

Where to Stay & Eat

$$–$$$ ✕ **Beginish.** Owner-chef Pat Moore double-checks every detail of her elegant but informal town house restaurant—from the wild flower nosegay on each table to the provenance of the local produce on the menu. Tables are glass-topped, with dark blue table mats and beige linen napkins; yellow walls hung with contemporary and beige window blinds complete the relaxed, airy, uncluttered look. Eastern and Mediterranean influences give variety to Ms. Moore's contemporary Irish cuisine. Starters may include Provençal-style *soupe de poisson* (fish soup), crab salad with avocado salsa and chili mayonnaise, or grilled goat's cheese with shallot jam and green salad. Local lobster in a brandy, herb, and cream sauce is a house specialty. ⊠ *Green St.* ☎ *066/915–1588* ▭ *MC, V* ⊘ *Closed Mon. and mid-Dec.–mid-Feb. No lunch.*

★ **$$** ✕ **Chart House.** Host Jim McCarthy is often found in the early evening leaning over the red half-door of the low, cabin-like stone building. The exterior gives little hint of the spacious, cleverly lit dining room within, nor of the beautiful pair of windows at the back that frame lovely views of Dingle Harbor's trawler fleet. Nautical artifacts, including an antique compass, complement the rusty-red walls and matching tablecloths. Have a drink at the smart little bar while studying the night's menu. The atmosphere is pleasantly informal, but both food and service are polished and professional. The signature starter is a phyllo parcel of Annascaul black pudding with chutney. Move on to roast cod fillet with a basil mash, or roast guinea fowl, served with a simple but perfectly judged port-wine jus. Finish the meal with a selection of Irish cheeses, served with a glass of port, or a homemade apple and clove tartlet with ginger nut crumble and a glass of calvados. ⊠ *The Mall* ☎ *066/915–2255* ▭ *MC, V* ⊘ *Closed Tues. and Jan.–mid-Feb. No lunch.*

$–$$ ✕ **Fenton's.** Step beyond the yellow door of this town house to find a cozy, cottage-style restaurant with quarry-tile floors, a stone fireplace, and local art (for sale) on the soft blue walls. Rush-seat ladder-back chairs are drawn up to wood-top candlelit tables. The bistro-style menu is unfussy, allowing for quick turnovers during Dingle's hectic high season. Some dishes, such as the cassoulet of mussels in garlic cream sauce, are available in starter or main-course portions. Lamb and beef come from the Fenton family farm. Sirloin steak may be served with caramelized onions and a red-wine sauce, or try local black sole on the bone with fresh herb butter. ⊠ *Green St.* ☎ *066/915–1209* ▭ *AE, DC, MC, V* ⊘ *Closed mid-Nov.–mid-Mar.*

$$$$ ✕▥ **Dingle Skellig.** Rambling and modern as this building may be, its center is occupied by a beehive-like shape that's intended to echo local *clocháns* (prehistoric beehive huts). The octagonal reception area has wood cladding, contemporary stained-glass doors, and original paintings. Modern, pale-wood furniture and bold fabrics adorn the spacious rooms, which are in separate wings, most of which have sea views. The bar is a busy local meeting place where anything can—and does—happen. Floor-to-ceiling windows in the Coastguard restaurant look out over Dingle Bay. As you'd expect, the specialty is seafood. ⊠ *Co. Kerry* ☎ *066/915–0200* 🖷 *066/915–1501* ⊕ *www.dingleskellig.com* ⇋ *110 rooms* ⚐ *Restaurant, cable TV, indoor pool, gym, health club, hot tub, spa, steam room, bar, meeting rooms* ▭ *AE, DC, MC, V* ⊚❘ *BP.*

$$$$ ▥ **Emlagh House.** You'll be right on the waters' edge in this spacious, mansard-roofed, yellow-painted family home. Although most accommodations in Dingle are cottagelike, the Kavanagh family chose the more spacious Georgian style: Emlagh looks like a historic mansion, but actually dates from the late 20th century. The marble-floored lobby, with its exquisite mahogany side table and large vase of fresh flowers, sets a tone of quiet, unostentatious luxury. Relax on the goosedown–filled velvet sofas in front of the drawing room's open fire while sipping a drink from the honor bar. Bedrooms are large, with sitting areas in the bay windows. Each one is color-themed to a local wildflower, with plush carpets, Regency-striped drapes, and Victorian antiques. There are over 185 pieces of original Irish art in the house from the family's private collection. For rainy days, there's a piano in the drawing room, history books and Internet access in the library, and CD players in the bedrooms. Dine on simply prepared local seafood and meat in the small restaurant. Enjoy the short walk into town as dessert. ☒ *Dingle Harbour,* ☎ *066/915–2345* 🖶 *066/915–2369* ⊕ *www.emlaghhouse. com* ⟿ *10 rooms* ♿ *In-room data-ports, cable TV* ▭ *AE, DC, MC, V* ⊘ *Nov.–Feb.*

$$ 🎦 **Greenmount House.** Wonderful views of the town and harbor await at this modern B&B, a short walk uphill from the town center (turn right at the traffic circle at the entrance to Dingle and right again when you come to the first T-junction). It looks just like many modern bungalows, but the interior has been cleverly redesigned by a local architect, with bright color schemes enlivening the traditional chintzy look. There are six suites in a connecting wing, each with a sitting room and balcony. Rooms in the original house, though smaller, are impeccable and comfortable, with pine beds and floral fabrics. Mary Curran is known for her baking, so an outstanding breakfast is served in the conservatory, which connects the two buildings. ☒ *Upper John St., Co. Kerry* ☎ *066/915–1414* 🖶 *066/915–1974* ⊕ *www.greenmounthouse.com* ⟿ *9 rooms* ♿ *Cable TV, lobby lounge; no a/c* ▭ *MC, V* ⊙¦ *BP* ⊘ *Closed Dec. 10–27.*

$$ 🎦 **Pax House.** You can stand on the outdoor terrace of this modern bungalow and watch the boats return with their catch while the sun sets slowly in the west. Rooms are simple but well equipped. Breakfast is a generous affair, with fresh seafood on the menu and a selection of Irish cheeses on the buffet. Pax House is 1 km (½ mi) from the town center. ☒ *Upper John St., Co. Kerry* ☎ *066/915–1518* 🖶 *066/915–2461* ⊕ *www.pax-house.com* ⟿ *12 rooms* ♿ *Cable TV, lobby lounge; no a/c* ▭ *MC, V* ⊙¦ *BP* ⊘ *Closed Nov.–Mar.*

$ 🎦 **Alpine House.** The landmark Alpine is neither spanking-new nor old-world. One of Dingle's original guest houses—dating from 1963—is a plain, family-run, three-story establishment located in spacious grounds on the edge of town that has many admirers; book well in advance. Pine pieces furnish bright, cheerful, well-equipped rooms. The location, at the entrance to town with views over Dingle Bay, is superb: it's quiet, yet the harbor, pubs, and restaurants are only a two-minute walk away. ☒ *Mail Rd., Co. Kerry* ☎ *066/915–1250* 🖶 *066/915–1966* ⊕ *www. alpineguesthouse.com* ⟿ *10 rooms* ♿ *Cable TV, free parking; no a/c, no smoking* ▭ *AE, MC, V* ⊙¦ *BP.*

Nightlife

Nearly every bar on the Dingle Peninsula, particularly in the town of Dingle, offers live music nightly in July and August. **O'Flaherty's** (☒ Bridge St., at the entrance to town ☎ 066/915–1983) is a gathering place for traditional musicians—you can hear impromptu music sessions most nights in July and August. For sing-along and dancing, try **An Reált— The Star Bar** (☒ The Pier ☎ No phone).

The Outdoors

You're likely to remember a bike ride around Slea Head for a long time. You can rent bicycles at **Dingle Bicycle Hire** (⌧ The Tracks ☎ 066/915–2166).

Shopping

Don't miss Dingle's café-bookshop, **An Cafe Liteartha** (⌧ Bothar An Dadhgaide ☎ 066/915–2204), which locals insist is one of the world's first (it has been here since the 1970s). Regardless, you'll find friendly conversation as well as new and secondhand books. You can watch **Brian de Staic** (⌧ Green St. ☎ 066/915–1298 ⊕ www.briandestaic.com) and his team make modern, Celtic-inspired jewelry in his studio, which is also a shop. **Leác a Ré** (⌧ Strand St. ☎ 066/915–1138) sells handmade Irish crafts. Lisbeth Mulcahy at the **Weaver's Shop** (⌧ Green St. ☎ 066/915–1688) sells outstanding handwoven, vegetable-dyed woolen wraps, mufflers, and fabric for making skirts.

Ventry

⑤ *8 km (5 mi) west of Dingle Town on R561.*

The next town after Dingle along the coast, Ventry has a small outcrop of pubs and small grocery stores (useful, since west of Dingle Town you'll find few shops of any kind), and a long sandy beach with safe swimming and ponies for rent. Between Ventry and Dunquin are several interesting archaeological sites on the spectacular cliff-top road along Slea Head.

Continuing west along the coast road beyond **Dunbeg,** you'll see signs for PREHISTORIC BEEHIVE HUTS, called clocháns (pronounced cluck-awns) in Irish. Built of drystone on the southern slopes of Mt. Eagle, these cells were used by hermit monks in the early Christian period; some 414 exist between Slea Head and Dunquin. Some local farmers, on whose land these monuments stand, charge a "trespass fee" of €1 to €2.

Slea Head

㊾ *16 km (10 mi) west of Dingle Town on R561, 8 km (5 mi) west of Ventry.*

From the top of the towering cliffs of Slea Head at the southwest extremity of the Dingle peninsula, the view of the Blasket Islands and the Atlantic Ocean is guaranteed to stop you in your tracks. Alas, Slea Head has become so popular that tour buses, barely able to negotiate the narrow road, are causing traffic jams, particularly in July and August. Coumenole, the long sandy strand below, looks beautiful and sheltered, but swimming here is dangerous. This treacherous stretch of coast has claimed many lives in shipwrecks—most recently in 1982, when a large cargo boat, the *Ranga,* foundered on the rocks and sank. In 1588, four ships of the Spanish Armada were driven through the Blasket Sound; two made it to shelter, and two sank. One of these, the *Santa Maria de la Rosa,* is being excavated by divers during summer.

THE SILENCE STRIKES YOU AT ONCE

THE GREAT BLASKET, which measures roughly 2 miles by half a mile, has no traffic, no pub, no hotel, and no electricity. Yet this island is probably one of the most memorable places in Ireland to visit.

These days it takes only 20 minutes from Dunquin Pier to make the 2-mi crossing of the Blasket Sound, but even on a calm day the swell can be considerable. In summer the island is inaccessible on about one day in five; in winter, it can be cut off for weeks. Until 1954 a small community of hardy fisherfolk and subsistence farmers eked out a poor living here.

Today, visitors are usually attracted by the literary heritage of the island—the Irish-language writings of Tomás O Criomhthain, Muiris Ó Suilleabhain, and Peig Sayers—but what makes people return is something else: a rare quality of light and an intense peace and quiet in beautiful, unspoiled surroundings.

The inadequacy of the existing piers limits visitors to the island to a maximum of about 400 per day, a figure which is reached only rarely, with the average under 200. Most visitors stay for three or four hours, walking, sketching or taking photographs.

The pier leads straight to a bank of springy maritime grass, typical of the island paths, which makes you want to tear off your walking boots and run about barefoot, like the island children of old.

The silence strikes you at once. The sea birds, stone chats, and swallows sound louder than on the mainland; sheep graze silently on the steep hillside.

The simple domestic ruins are very touching; you do not need to know the history to work out what happened to their owners (most departed for other locales,

with many settling in Springfield, Massachusetts).

When the last boat of day trippers leaves, the foreshore teems with rabbits, and seals bask on the white strand. At the time of writing, camping is permitted, but it may well be banned in the near future. You can book a bed in the small hostel and self-cater, or eat an evening meal in the island café before sitting outside to watch the stars.

Many visitors, including John Milington Synge, have warned that there is something addictive about the Great Blasket. "I have a jealousy for that Island," he wrote after his 1907 sojourn, " . . . like the jealousy of men in love."

The Blasket Island Boatman (☎ 066/915–6455) makes the 20-minute crossing from Dunquin Pier to the island daily from May to September, weather permitting, costing €20 round-trip. Peig Sayers ferry (☎ 066/915–1344) sails from Dingle Town to the island and takes about 30 minutes, costing €30 for a round-trip ticket.

Visitors may want to call in advance if the weather looks bad to see if these ferries are running. As for accommodations on the island, you'll have to settle for a bed, costing €18, at the hostel (☎ 086/852–2321 or 086/848–6687). Before you go, get a copy of Maurice O'Sullivan's Twenty Years A-Growing, which gives a fascinating account of a simple way of life that has only recently disappeared on the Blaskets.

—Alannah Hopkin

The largest of the **Blasket Islands** visible from Slea Head, the Great Blasket was inhabited until 1953. The Blasket islanders were great storytellers and were encouraged by Irish linguists to write their memoirs. *The Islandman,* by Tomás O Crohán, gives a vivid picture of a hard way of life. "Their likes will not be seen again," O Crohán poignantly observed. The Blasket Centre explains the heritage of these islanders and celebrates their use of the Irish language with videos and exhibitions. ✉ *Dunquin* ☎ *066/915–6371* ⊕ *www.heritageireland. ie* ✆ *€3.10* ۞ *Easter–June and Sept., daily 10–6; July and Aug., daily 10–7.*

Dunquin

❺❸ *13 km (8 mi) west of Ventry on R559, 5 km (3 mi) north of Slea Head.*

Once the mainland harbor for the Blasket islanders, Dunquin is at the center of the Gaeltacht, and attracts many students of Irish language and folklore. David Lean shot *Ryan's Daughter* hereabouts in 1969. The movie gave the area its first major boost in tourism, though it was lambasted by critics—"Gush made respectable by millions of dollars tastefully wasted," lamented Pauline Kael—sending Lean into a dry spell he didn't come out of until 1984's *A Passage to India.* **Kruger's Pub** (☎ 066/915–6127), Dunquin's social center, has long been frequented by artists and writers, including Brendan Behan; it's also the only eatery for miles.

Dunquin's **pier** (signposted from the main road) is surrounded by cliffs of colored Silurian rock, more than 400 million years old and rich in fossils. Down at the pier you'll see *curraghs* (open fishing boats traditionally made of animal hide stretched over wooden laths and tarred) stored upside down, usually covered in canvas. Three or four men walk the curraghs out to the sea, holding them over their heads. Similar boats are used in the Aran Islands, and when properly handled they're extraordinarily seaworthy. In good weather **Blasket Island Boatmen** (✉ Dunquin Pier ☎ 066/915–6455 ⊕ www.greatblasketisland. com) vessels ferry you from Dunquin Pier to the Great Blasket Island, a 20-minute trip. Landing is by transfer to rubber dinghy, and the island is steep and rocky, so you need to be fit and agile. Still, the unique experience offered by the deserted village and old cliff paths of the island makes it well worth the effort. The cost of the boat ride is €20 round-trip. Boats run from 10 to 4, weather permitting, between Easter and September.

en route **Clogher Strand,** a dramatic, windswept stretch of rocks and sand, is not a safe spot to swim, but it's a good place to watch the ocean dramatically pound the rocks when a storm is approaching or a gale is blowing. Overlooking the beach is **Louis Mulcahy's pottery studio.** One of Ireland's leading ceramic artists, Mulcahy produces large pots and urns that are both decorative and functional. You can watch the work in progress and buy items at workshop prices. ✉ *Clogher Strand* ☎ *066/915–6229* ۞ *Daily 9:30–6.*

Ballyferriter

 5 km (3 mi) northeast of Dunquin, 14 km (9 mi) west of Dingle on R559.

Like the other towns at this end of the Dingle Peninsula, Ballyferriter is a Gaeltacht village and mainly a spot for vacationers with RVs, many of them German or Dutch. The area around here is great for walking. A top sight in Ballyferriter itself is one of Ireland's best-preserved, early Christian churches, **Gallarus Oratory.** It dates from the 7th or 8th century and ingeniously makes use of corbeling—successive levels of stone projecting inward from both side walls until they meet at the top to form an unmortared roof. The structure is still watertight after more than 1,000 years. ⊠ *8 km (5 mi) northeast of Ballyferriter on R559* 🖼 *€2.50.*

Kilmakedar Church is one of the finest surviving examples of Romanesque architecture. Although the Christian settlement dates from the 7th century, the present structure was built in the 12th century. Native builders integrated foreign influences with their own traditions, keeping the blank arcades and round-headed windows but using stone roofs, sloping doorway jambs, and weirdly sculpted heads. Ogham stones and other interestingly carved, possibly pre-Christian stones are on display in the churchyard. ⊠ *8 km (5 mi) northeast of Ballyferriter on R559* 🖼 *Free.*

> off the beaten path

CONNOR PASS – This mountain route, which passes from south to north over the center of the peninsula, offers magnificent views of Brandon Bay, Tralee Bay, and the beaches of North Kerry. The road is narrow, and the drops on the hairpin bends are precipitous. Be sure to nominate a confident driver who isn't scared of heights—such a soul is especially important in misty weather. It was from Brandon Bay that Brendan the Navigator (AD 487–577) is believed to have set off on his voyages in a specially constructed curragh. On his third trip he may have reached Newfoundland or Labrador, then Florida. Brendan was an inspiration to many voyagers, including Christopher Columbus.

The summit of Mt. Brandon (3,127 feet) is on the left as you cross the Connor Pass (from south to north). It's accessible only to hikers. Don't attempt the climb in misty weather. The easiest way to make the trek is to follow the old pilgrims' path, Saint's Road; it starts at Kilmakedar Church and rises to the summit from Ballybrack, which is the end of the road for cars. At the summit, you'll reach the ruins of an early Christian settlement. You can also approach the top from a path that starts just beyond Cloghane (signposted left on descending the Connor Pass); the latter climb is longer and more strenuous.

Blennerville

 60 km (37 mi) east of Ballyferriter, 5 km (3 mi) west of Tralee on R560.

The five-story **windmill** with black and white sails is the main attraction in Blennerville, a village on the western edge of Tralee. The surrounding buildings have been turned into a visitor center, with crafts workshops and an exhibition recalling the town's past as County Kerry's main point of emigration during the Great Famine (1845–49). ☎ 066/712–1064 ☒ €5 ⊘ Apr.–Oct., daily 9–6. A popular **steam railway** shuttles along the 3 km (1½ mi) of tracks between Blennerville and Tralee, with departures from each terminus every half hour from May through September. ☎ 066/712–7444 ☒ €5.

Tralee

⑤ *5 km (3 mi) northeast of Blennerville, 50 km (31 mi) northeast of Dingle on R559.*

County Kerry's capital and its largest town, Tralee (population 21,000) has long been associated with the popular Irish song "The Rose of Tralee," the inspiration for the annual Rose of Tralee International Festival. The last week of August, Irish communities worldwide send young women to join native Irish competitors; one of them is chosen as the Rose of Tralee. Visitors, musicians, and entertainers pack the town then. A two-day horse-race meeting—with seven races a day—runs at the same time, which contributes to the crowds. Tralee is also the home of Siamsa Tíre—the National Folk Theatre of Ireland—which stages dances and plays based on Irish folklore.

Kerry County Museum, Tralee's major cultural attraction, traces the history of Kerry's people since 5000 BC, using dioramas and an entertaining audiovisual show. You can also walk through a life-size reconstruction of a Tralee street in the Middle Ages. ☒ *Ashe Memorial Hall, Denny St.* ☎ *066/712-7777* ⊕ *www.kerrycountymuseum.com* ☒ *€8* ⊘ *Jan.–March, Tues.–Fri. 10–4:30; April and May, Tues.–Sat. 9:30–5:30; June–Aug., daily 9:30–5:30; Sept.–Dec., Tues–Sat., 9:30–5.*

Ireland's biggest water complex, **AquaDome,** includes sky-high water slides, a wave pool, raging rapids, water cannons, and other thrills. Adults can seek refuge in the Sauna Dome. ☒ *Dingle Rd.* ☎ *066/712-8899* ⊕ *www. discoverkerry.com/aquadome* ☒ *€8* ⊘ *Mid-May–Aug., daily 10–10; Sept.–mid-May, weekdays 2–10, weekends 11–8.*

Where to Stay &Eat

$$–$$$ ✕ **Restaurant David Norris.** A modest terrace of modern buildings on the edge of the town park is home to this pleasant first-floor restaurant. You are greeted in a small reception area with sofa and stool, and offered a drink at the small bar while you peruse the owner-chef's menu of the day. Pale wood furniture in a crisp art deco style is complemented by a dusky pink and cream decor, with linen cloths and fresh flowers on the well-spaced tables. The menu is built around seasonal local produce, and everything is made on the premises, including bread, pasta, and ice cream. Roast fillet of Kerry beef may be served with black pepper mash, fried mushrooms, and caramelized onions and garlic. Seafood is always well-represented, and there is always a vegetarian option. For extra value for money, try the "early-bird menu" served until 7:30. ☒ *Ivy House, Ivy Terrace* ☎ *066/718-5654* ▭ *AE, MC, V* ⊘ *Closed Sun., Mon., and 1 wk in Nov. and 2 wks in late Jan.–early Feb. No lunch.*

$$–$$$ ✕▭ **Meadowlands.** Located in a quiet suburb on the road to Listowel, 10 minutes' walk from Tralee's city center, this lively new luxury hotel is turreted in the French château style and done up in exuberant, sumptuously stylish decors. Touches of nouvelle country-house style are everywhere, from the grand barrel-vaulted reception area to the two-story bar, which has a balcony library. A light bar menu is offered here, but for the full treatment, repair to the restaurant, a cozy bedazzlement of stonework, timber beams, and stone pillars. The hotel's owner runs a fleet of fishing boats in Dingle, so seafood is a major draw, with seared west coast scallops with lime and butter sauce and panfried Annascaul black pudding, or a kilo of steamed Atlantic mussels being two top choices. Large and exceptionally comfortable in an unfussy way, with dark-wood, Victorian-style furniture and plaster cornices on the ceiling, the guest rooms are decorated in sumptuous hues or tranquil beiges. The hotel is popular with golfers, who generally find the small extra fee for upgrading to an even larger room with two double beds well worth it. A festive, friendly, and stylish place, Meadowlands turns up the charm on weekends, when the bar hosts live music. ⊠ *Oakpark Co. Kerry* ☎ *066/718–0444* 🖷 *066/718–0694* ⊕ *www.meadowlands-hotel.com* 🛏 *58 rooms* ⚘ *Restaurant, cable TV, bar, parking (fee)* ☰ *AE, DC, MC, V.*

$$ 🏨 **Barrow Country House.** The location—on Barrow Harbor and next to the Arnold Palmer–designed Tralee Golf Club—makes this tastefully converted period house popular with golfers. The drawing room, furnished in the Regency style, and the breakfast room have vistas that look across a tranquil stretch of water to the mountains of the Dingle Peninsula. Rooms are spacious and well equipped, more like those in a hotel than those in a B&B. A helicopter service is provided for golfers keen to sample Killarney, Ballybunion, and Waterville. (To get to the hotel, leave Tralee on R551, turning left on the R558 after Oyster Tavern. Follow signs to Churchill.) ⊠ *West Barrow, Ardfert Co. Kerry* ☎ *066/713–6437* 🖷 *066/713–6402* ⊕ *www.barrowhouse.com* 🛏 *16 rooms* ⚘ *Fishing, helipad; no a/c* ☰ *AE, MC, V* ⍾ *BP* ⊘ *Closed Dec. 20–Feb. 14.*

$$ 🏨 **Abbeygate.** Built on the site of Tralee's old marketplace, in a quiet spot behind the main shopping street, Abbeygate is an attractive modern hotel. Rooms have country-style wood furniture and large, tiled bathrooms. The Old Market Place Pub, a rambling, imaginatively designed bar, seats 500 people and is built in the traditional style, with wooden floors and open fireplaces. There's bar food at lunch and music and dancing nightly from June to September and at least three nights a week at other times. ⊠ *Maine St., Co. Kerry* ☎ *066/712–9888* 🖷 *066/712–9821* ⊕ *www.abbeygate-hotel.com* 🛏 *100 rooms* ⚘ *Restaurant, cable TV, 2 bars, meeting rooms; no a/c* ☰ *AE, DC, MC, V* ⍾ *BP.*

¢ 🏨 **Westward Court.** This modern building in Tralee's town center offers basic, backpacker-style accommodation in rooms sleeping two or four people. The place is basic but well-run, with good facilities for budget travelers. The small rooms are painted a cheerful yellow, with yellow-and-blue-check comforters, and a tiny chip-board desk separating the beds. Windows are double-glazed against late-night noise. Continental breakfast is included in the room price, as is use of a self-catering kitchen; there's also a pay-launderette. There is no bar on the premises, but over a dozen within a short walk. The residents' lounge often has an open turf fire in the brick fireplace, and is a good place to swap notes with other travelers. ⊠ *Mary St.* ☎ *066/718–0081* 🖷 *066/718–0082* ⊕ *www.io.ie/kerry-insight/westward* 🗩 *43 rooms* ♨ *Restaurant, parking (free); no a/c, no room phones, no room TVs* ▤ *MC, V.*

Nightlife & the Arts

Ballad sessions are more popular here than traditional Irish music. **Horan's Hotel** (⊠ Clash St. ☎ 066/712–1933) has dance music and cabaret acts nightly during July and August and on weekends only during the off-season. Try to catch the **National Folk Theater of Ireland** (Siamsa Tíre). Language is no barrier to this colorful entertainment, which re-creates traditional rural life through music, mime, and dance. ⊠ *Godfrey Pl.* ☎ *066/712–3055* ⊙ *Shows July and Aug., Mon.–Sat. at 8:30 PM; May, June, and Sept., Tues. and Thurs. at 8:30 PM.*

Sports & the Outdoors

BICYCLES You can rent bicycles from **Tralee Bicycle Supplies** (⊠ Strand St. ☎ 066/712–2018).

GOLF Tralee is the heart of great golfing country. The **Ballybunion Golf Club** (Old Course; ⊠ Ballybunion ☎ 068/27146) is universally regarded as one of golf's holiest grounds. The **Tralee Golf Club** (⊠ West Barrow, Ardfert ☎ 066/713–6379) is a seaside links, designed by Arnold Palmer, with cliffs, craters, and dunes.

NORTH KERRY & SHANNONSIDE

Until several decades ago, Shannon meant little more to most people—if it meant anything at all—than the name of the longest river in Ireland and Great Britain, running for 273 km (170 mi) from County Cavan to Limerick City in County Clare. But mention Shannon nowadays and people think immediately of the airport, which has become western Ireland's principal gateway. In turn, what also comes to mind are many of the glorious sights of North Kerry and Shannonside: a slew of castles, including Bunratty, Glin, and Knappogue; Adare, sometimes called "Ireland's Prettiest Village," and the neighboring Adare Manor, a grand country-house hotel; and Limerick City, which attracts visitors tracing the memories so movingly captured in Frank McCourt's international bestseller *Angela's Ashes*. You could begin a tour of the area in Listowel, in northwest County Kerry, and then jump across the Kerry–Limerick border to Glin, on the south side of the Shannon River estuary. Limerick City and those parts of County Clare on the north side of the Shannon round out the tour.

Listowel

❺⑦ *27 km (16 mi) northeast of Tralee on N69.*

The small, sleepy market town of Listowel comes alive for its annual horse race during the third week of September. You reach the town from the west by driving along a plain at the base of Stack's Mountain.

Where to Stay & Eat

$ ✕🍽 **Allo's Bar and Bistro.** Just off Listowel's main square, this cheerful, welcoming bar, which dates from 1859, serves the best local foods. Chef

Armel Whyte and his partner, Helen Mullane, are known for their lively combinations of traditional and contemporary Irish cooking ($–$$$). The spacious bedrooms are furnished with baroque-style mirrors, designer lampshades, cherubs, and oil paintings, and have four-poster beds and large, Connemara marble bathrooms. If you like Irish whiskey, Armel will be pleased to introduce you to his collection; be warned, one vintage malt costs €60 a shot. ⊠ *41 Church St.* ☎☎ *068/22880* 🛏 *3 rooms* ⟁ *Restaurant, bar; no a/c* ⊟ *AE, MC, V* ⦿ *BP* ⊘ *Bar and bistro closed Sun. and Mon.*

Glin

❺⑧ *6½ km (4 mi) east of Tarbert on N69, 51 km (32 mi) north of Tralee on N69.*

Fodor'sChoice
★

If you're into Irish decorative arts of the 17th and 18th centuries, you'll want to make a beeline for **Glin Castle**, a fantastical neo-Gothic crenellated structure, set on the banks of the Shannon, which has been home to the FitzGerald family for centuries. The present knight of Glin—the family's ancestral title (and we do mean ancestral—the current knight is the 29th)—Desmond FitzGerald, a Harvard-educated art historian, is an expert on Irish style and an outspoken arts advocate, so it's fitting that the house now has an exceptional collection of Irish 18th-century mahogany and walnut furniture. The rich, red dining room is set with baronial Jacobean-style furniture, the Morning Room is lined with family curios, and the main Hall is set with Corinthian columns and a dazzling Dublin-style Georgian plaster ceiling. Everywhere you look are exceptional antiques, most with the vibrant, virile Irish touch. It wasn't always so. The family has seen more than its fair share of decapitations, bankruptcies, and other hair-raising tales (one knight was tied to a cannon by Cromwell's forces and threatened with being blown apart; another was drawn and quartered during the Middle Ages). The family was, in fact, of English origin but became "more Irish than Irish" by marrying into the Gaelic chieftainry families. Their latest house was built in 1785, then largely expanded between 1820 and 1836 into a full-fledged Irish Gothic mansion by the 25th knight, who added castellations and pepper-pot towers, which look like gigantic chess pieces. Inside, many marvel at the splendid "flying" staircase, the full-length family portraits, the equine paintings of Lady Rachel FitzGerald, and the famous mahogany furniture. Outside, clipped yews, walled gardens, an "antique" temple, and a neo-Gothic henhouse cast their own spell. To really pitch in, you can become overnight guests of the family—your room rates help keep the knightly splendor of this desmesne intact. ☎ *068/34173* ⊕ *www.glincastle.com* ⊠ *€7* ⊘ *May and June, daily 10–noon and 2–4; other times by appointment.*

---

off the beaten path

FLYING BOAT MUSEUM – Nine kilometers (5½ mi) east of Glin on N69, Foynes was the landing place for transatlantic air traffic in the 1930s and 1940s. This museum in the terminal of the original Shannon Airport celebrates Foynes's aviation history; it's a must for aviation buffs. ☎ *069/65416* ⊠ *€5* ⊘ *Apr.–Oct., daily 10–5.*

Where to Stay & Eat

$$$$ ✕⊞ **Glin Castle.** Experience top-of-the-scale Irish castle living at the
Fodor'sChoice knight of Glin's imposing ancestral home, which has been in the FitzGer-
★ ald family for 700 years. The large, castellated building is surrounded
by formal gardens and parkland in the midst of 500 acres of woodland
and has views of the Shannon Estuary. The palatial rooms showcase Glin's
famous collection of 18th-century Irish furniture, and are superbly comfortable. The guest rooms are magnificent exercises in country-house
style, with four-poster beds, export china–adorned walls, and furnishings that are the height of historic Irish chic. Traditional cuisine is served
in the red dining room ($$$$), beneath portraits of FitzGerald ancestors. On the menu you'll find locally produced meat and poultry, freshly
caught fish, and produce from the walled garden. Nonresidents are
welcome for dinner but must reserve in advance. ⊠ *Co. Limerick*
☎ *068/34112* ⊟ *068/34364* ⊕ *www.glincastle.com* ⇔ *15 rooms*
⚘ *Dining room, cable TV, tennis court, boating, fishing, croquet, horseback riding, meeting rooms, some pets allowed; no a/c, no kids under
10* ⊟ *AE, DC, MC, V* ⊧◯⊧ *BP* ⊘ *Closed Nov.–Mar.*

Adare

59 *19 km (12 mi) southwest of Limerick City on N21, 82 km (51 mi) north-*
Fodor'sChoice *east of Tralee on N21, 40 km (25 mi) east of Glin.*
★

A once-upon-a-timefied village with several thatched cottages amid
wooded surroundings on the banks of the River Maigue, Adare is rich
in ruins. On foot, you can find the remains of two 13th-century abbeys,
a 15th-century friary, and the keep of a 13th-century Desmond castle.
Providing that time-burnished allure that has helped make Adare famous
as one of Ireland's prettiest villages, the many stone-built cottages, often
adorned with colorful, flower-filled window boxes, have a centuries-old
look. They were, in fact, built in the mid-19th century by the third earl
of Dunraven, a popular landlord, for the tenants on his estate. Some
now house boutiques selling Irish crafts and antiques, along with a fine
restaurant called the Wild Geese. Adare Manor, an imposing Tudor–Gothic
Revival mansion, which was once the grand house of the Dunraven peer-
age, is now a celebrated hotel. **Adare Heritage Center** has an exhibit with
a 15-minute audiovisual display that details the history of the village
since 1223. There's also a restaurant and three retail outlets: one sells
sweaters, another crafts, and the third heraldry items. Guided walking
tours of the village (€5) are offered from July to September. ⊠ *Main
St.* ☎ *061/396666* ⊟ *€7.50* ⊘ *Jan.–Mar., daily 10–5; Apr. and May,
daily 9:30–5:30; June–Sept., daily 9–6:30; Dec., daily 9:30–4:30.*

Where to Stay & Eat

★ **$$$–$$$$** ✕ **The Wild Geese.** There is a charming, old-world atmosphere in the se-
ries of small dining rooms in this low-ceilinged thatched cottage, one
of the prettiest in a village famed for its fairy-tale looks. Co-owner and
chef David Foley uses the best local produce to create imaginative and
seriously good dishes. Try roast rack of lamb with tempura vegetables
or roast breast of duck with an onion tartlet and mushroom-flavored
rice. Lobster—grilled with snow peas and shallots and topped with a

chive mayonnaise—is a popular summer option. The house dessert platter for two lets you sample all desserts, including the fantastic homemade ice cream. The restaurant is opposite the Dunraven Arms. ⊠ *Rose Cottage* ☎ *061/396-451* 🖃 *AE, DC, MC, V* 😌 *Closed Sun., Mon., and 3 wks in Jan.*

$$$$ ✕🖾 **Dunraven Arms.** Adare's landmark coach-stop inn, established in 1792, makes a popular first port of call if you're arriving at Shannon Airport, 40 km (25 mi) northwest—Charles Lindbergh, in fact, stayed in Room 6 while he advised on the airport's design. He might still cotton to the tranquil, antiques-adorned, but somewhat over-restored and generic look of this place. Paintings and prints of horseback riders decorate the pale yellow walls of the cozy bar and lounges; the county hunt still meets here regularly, continuing a centuries-old tradition. The comfortable bedrooms (and there are lots of them) are tastefully furnished with antiques, and have large, luxurious bathrooms. Junior suites in the newer wing have antique four-poster beds. The elegant Maigue restaurant ($$–$$$$) specializes in modern Irish cuisine; in winter local game, including pheasant, is a popular option. You can dine informally in the bright, airy bar overlooking the rose garden. Service is impeccable, yet the staff also manages to find time to have a friendly chat, knowing the difference this can make. ⊠ *Main St., Co. Limerick* ☎ *061/396-633* 🖃 *061/ 396-541* ⊕ *www.dunravenhotel.com* ⇌ *76 rooms, 20 suites* ⚒ *Restaurant, in-room data ports, cable TV, indoor pool, health club, fishing, horseback riding, bar, meeting rooms; no a/c* 🖃 *AE, DC, MC, V* 🍽 *BP.*

★ $$ ✕🖾 **Mustard Seed at Echo Lodge.** Dan Mullane's spacious Victorian country-house hotel and restaurant ($$$$) has flamboyantly decorated themed guest rooms—black-and-white, carnival, Chinese, and so on—and commands a view over the countryside. Chef Tony Schwartz uses only the best local produce, plus herbs and vegetables from his organic garden. Shark is an unusual seafood option in summer; more typical is the honey-glazed lamb shank with a cassoulet of beans and homegrown baby vegetables. His basil-flavored potato cakes are renowned. Fruits from the garden are used in such desserts as hot crunchy apple-and-black-currant crumble with calvados, cream, and caramel sauce. The hotel is 13 km (8 mi) southwest of Adare in Ballingarry. ⊠ *Ballingarry, Co. Limerick* ☎ *069/68508* 🖃 *069/68511* ⊕ *www.mustardseed.ie* ⇌ *14 rooms, 3 suites* ⚒ *Restaurant, bar, library; no a/c* 🖃 *AE, MC, V* 🍽 *BP.*

$–$$ ✕🖾 **Fitzgeralds Woodlands House Hotel and Spa.** In the energetic, capable hands of the Fitzgerald family, what was once a small B&B has evolved into a thriving modern hotel. It's on 44 acres of landscaped grounds at the Limerick side of the village. Rooms are spacious, individually decorated in various modern styles, and well maintained. Expect to see locals in Timmy Mac's bar. The Brennan Rooms ($$) serves a traditional Irish table d'hôte menu: lamb, pork, and beef. More adventurous cooking takes place in the bistro-style restaurant in Timmy Mac's ($), which serves locally grown organic food. ⊠ *Knockanes, Co. Limerick* ☎ *061/ 605-100* 🖃 *061/396-073* ⊕ *www.woodlands-hotel.ie* ⇌ *84 rooms, 8 suites* ⚒ *2 restaurants, cable TV, indoor pool, health club, massage, spa, fishing, horseback riding, bar, meeting rooms; no a/c* 🖃 *AE, DC, MC, V* 🍽 *BP.*

★ **$$$–$$$$** ☒ **Adare Manor.** Play king or queen for a day at this spectacular (and, interestingly, American-owned) Victorian Gothic mansion, once the abode of the earls of Dunraven. The castellated mansion is enormous and set amid French-style gardens. Inside is a wonderland of vast stone arches and heavy wood carvings. Center stage is taken by the decorated ceiling in the baronial central hall and the 36-foot-high, 100-foot-long Minstrels' Gallery, wainscoted in oak. As for decor, a period air is retained but several of the color schemes are as bright as today and, thus, much of the time-burnished ambience is lost. The eight "staterooms" in the original house are the most sumptuous, with huge marble bathrooms and stone-mullioned windows. Most rooms have super-king-size beds; all have heavy drapes and carpets and overlook the 840 acres of grounds. Adare's golf course, designed by Robert Trent Jones Sr., is one of Ireland's best. (Note that breakfast is a hefty €23 extra here; plan accordingly.) ☒ *Co. Limerick* ☎ *061/396–566* 🖷 *061/39–6124* ⊕ *www. adaremanor.ie* ⇱ *63 rooms* ☖ *Restaurant, cable TV, 18-hole golf course, indoor pool, sauna, fishing, horseback riding, 2 bars, meeting rooms; no a/c* ▭ *AE, DC, MC, V.*

Sports

GOLF **Adare Manor Golf Course** (☎ 061/396204) is an 18-hole, par-69 parkland course.

Shopping

Adare Gallery (☒ Main St. ☎ 061/396898) sells Irish-made jewelry, porcelain, and woodwork, as well as original paintings. **Carol's Antiques** (☒ Main St. ☎ 061/396–977) has antique furniture, silver, china, and art objects from one of Adare's tiny cottages. At **George Stacpoole** (☒ Main St. ☎ 061/396–409) you'll find antiques and books.

Limerick City

⬤ *19 km (12 mi) northeast of Adare, 198 km (123 mi) southwest of Dublin.*

Before you ask, there's *no* direct connection between Limerick City and the facetious five-line verse form known as a limerick, which was first popularized by the English writer Edward Lear in his 1846 *Book of Nonsense*. The city, at the head of the Shannon estuary and at the intersection of a number of major crossroads, is an industrial port and the republic's fourth-largest city (population 75,000). If you fly into or out of Shannon Airport, and have a few hours to spare, do take a look around. The area around the cathedral and the castle is dominated by mid-18th-century buildings with fine Georgian proportions. What's more, the city has undergone considerable revitalization since the days recounted in Frank McCourt's childhood memoir, *Angela's Ashes*. Still and all, Limerick retains a somewhat infamous reputation with locals and visitors alike as one of the dullest places for travelers to find themselves.

Limerick was originally a 9th-century Danish settlement; Richard I granted the city's charter in 1197. In 1691, after the Battle of the Boyne, the Irish retreated to the walled city, where they were besieged by William of Orange, who made three unsuccessful attempts to storm the

THE CITY OF ANGELA

HE ALCOHOLIC PA. *The starving, shivering brood of children. The sheep's head for Christmas. The rags for diapers. The little white coffin. And the long-suffering, abused ma.* These are some of the elements that rivet the reader of Angela's Ashes (1996), Frank McCourt's memoir of his impoverished childhood in Limerick—a rags-to-riches story, with the riches always being more spiritual than material. Called by Newsweek "the publishing event of the decade," and compared by some to the Grapes of Wrath *in its power, pain, and joy*, Angela's Ashes has sold a few million hardcover copies, won the Pulitzer, and gone Hollywood. The book seems to speak to the Irish in everyone's soul, if best-seller lists from Japan to Germany are any indication. Not surprisingly, the city of Limerick—the rain-sodden setting of this 1930s–'40s hard-luck saga—has become a pilgrimage place for readers eager to partake of the tearfulness of it all. Busloads of McCarthys and O'Dwyers now clamber over the sites described in the book, ending up at South's pub to raise a pint in Frank's honor and to count their blessings.

In the memoir narrated from a child's perspective, Limerick looms as "a gray place with a river that kills." Many children, including McCourt's twin brothers, succumb to tuberculosis, with the rest condemned to run an obstacle course—in shoes with flapping soles—of flea-ridden bedcovers, cane-wielding teachers, doomsday-spouting priests, and fathers who drink their paycheck, beat their wives, and tell their sons to search the skies for the Angel of the Seventh Step, bringer of new babies. Yes, Limerick has its historic sights, but now the down-and-out addresses of McCourt's childhood draw as much attention from visitors. As it turns out, the slums described so

unflinchingly in the book have long been torn down; in fact, Limerick is flush with new money, renovated 19th-century Georgian row houses, prosperous shopping malls, and restaurants with fancy names. An exhibit featuring a replica of the rooms where the McCourt family lived and memorabilia of the film has been built in the coach house behind 2 Pery Square, a refurbished Georgian row house overlooking People's Park.

Even the dread River Shannon has undergone a makeover—swans, not refuse, now navigate its flowing stream. Nevertheless, plenty of Angela's Ashes sites remain: Leamy's National School on Hartstonge Street, where "Hoppy" O'Halloran and other schoolmasters beat any charges who couldn't add 19 to 47; the St. Vincent de Paul Society, where Angela went begging for furniture and other assistance; People's Park, where Frank took his younger brothers to make them forget their empty stomachs; plus many other emotional landmarks.

Like the Irish shanachie—storyteller—still spouting tales at many a local pub, Frank McCourt has dug deep into the communal wellspring of Irish memory. The fact that his story has nothing to do with leprechauns and Celtic queens and everything to do with a family history that most families would wish to hide, let alone hang out in the sun to dry, says a good deal about the new Ireland and its people's wish for closure. McCourt's childhood experiences may not have been the happiest, but they are surely worth reading about, remembering, and revisiting, as so many travelers are now making a point of doing.

city but then raised the siege and marched away. A year later, another of William's armies overtook Limerick for two months, and the Irish opened negotiations. The resulting Treaty of Limerick—which guaranteed religious tolerance—was never ratified, and 11,000 men of the Limerick garrison joined the French Army rather than fight in a Protestant "Irish" army.

In the Old Customs House on the banks of the Shannon in the city center, the **Hunt Museum** has the finest collection of Celtic and medieval treasures outside the National Museum in Dublin. Ancient Irish metalwork, European objets d'art, and a selection of 20th-century European and Irish paintings—including works by Jack B. Yeats—are on view. A café overlooks the river. ⊠ *Rutland St.* ☎ *061/312–833* ⊕ *www.huntmuseum. com* ▦ *€6* ☾ *Mon.–Sat. 10–5, Sun. 2–5.*

Limerick is a predominantly Catholic city, but the Protestant **St. Mary's Cathedral** is the city's oldest religious building. Once a 12th-century palace—pilasters and a rounded Romanesque entrance were part of the original structure—it dates mostly from the 15th century (the black-oak carvings on misericords in the choir stalls are from this period). ⊠ *Bridge St.* ☎ *061/416–238* ☾ *Daily 9–5.*

The office of the **Limerick Regional Archives** (⊠ Michael St. ☎ 061/415–125 ⊕ www.limerickancestry.com) is in the granary, built in 1774. For a small fee, the archives provides a genealogical research service.

☾ First built by the Normans in the early 1200s, **King John's Castle** still bears traces on its north side of a 1691 bombardment. If you climb the drum towers (the oldest section), you'll have a good view of the town and the Shannon. Inside, a 22-minute audiovisual show illustrates the history of Limerick and Ireland; an archaeology center has three excavated, pre-Norman houses; and two exhibition centers display scale models of Limerick from its founding in AD 922. ⊠ *Castle St.* ☎ *061/411–201* ⊕ *www. shannonheritage.com/KingJohnsCastle* ▦ *€7* ☾ *Daily 9:30–5.*

☾ The **Georgian House and Garden** will show you how people lived in Limerick's 18th-century heyday. A tall, narrow row house has been meticulously restored and filled with furnishings from the period, and the garden has been planted in a manner true to the time. The coach house at the rear of the house gives on to a Limerick lane and contains displays relating to the filming of *Angela's Ashes*, including a life-size reconstruction of the McCourt family home. ⊠ *Tontine Buildings, 2 Pery Sq.* ☎ *061/ 314–130* ⊕ *www.shannon-dev.ie* ▦ *€5* ☾ *Weekdays 10–4, weekends by appointment.*

On **O'Connell Street**, you'll find the main shopping area, which mainly consists of modest chain stores. However, the street lies one block inland from (east of) the Arthur's Quay Shopping Centre, a mall, which, along with the futuristic tourist information center, is one of the first fruits of a civic campaign to develop the Shannonside quays. **Cruises Street**, an inviting pedestrian thoroughfare, has chic shops and occasional street entertainers. It's on the opposite side of O'Connell Street from the Arthur's Quay Shopping Centre.

Plassey, 5–10 minutes from Limerick on the ring road (signposted Dublin N7), is the setting for the University of Limerick, which has a small, but very attractive, campus notable for its rolling lawns and several striking architectural features.

Where to Stay & Eat

$$-$$$ ✕ **Brulées Restaurant.** The dining rooms in this redbrick Georgian town house, on a corner just a block from the River Shannon, are elegantly furnished in a simple, classical style. Chef and co-owner Teresa Murphy uses only the finest local ingredients, and gives a contemporary touch to Irish fare. Try the beef fillet with black-pudding mash or the grilled liver and bacon with grain mustard and mushroom cream. And, yes, the menu does include a classic crème brûlée among the tempting desserts. ⊠ *8 Lower Mallow St.* ☎ *061/319–931* ☰ *AE, DC, MC, V* ⊘ *Closed Sun. No lunch Mon. and Sat.*

$$-$$$ ✕ **Freddy's Bistro.** On a quiet lane between busy O'Connell and Henry streets, this informal two-story restaurant fills a charming 18th-century coach house. Old brick walls are complemented by a warm color scheme that glows in candlelight. Steak with brandy, bacon, and mushroom sauce and monkfish with basil and lemon pesto are popular main courses. For dessert try the hot, sticky, toffee pudding. ⊠ *Theatre La., off Lower Glentworth St.* ☎ *061/418–749* ☰ *MC, V* ⊘ *No lunch. Closed Sun. and Mon.*

$$ ✕ **Green Onion Café.** The Irish-French chef team of Marie Munnelly and Geoff Gloux produces a witty, stylish menu at this hip eatery across from the Hunt Museum. The large room, which used to comprise the town hall, is split into two levels, which are, in turn, divided into intimate spaces through a judicious use of booths. Typical dishes include smoked Irish cheese (Gubbeen) and spinach tartlet, pork fillet coated in pistachio nuts with herb butter, jerk chicken with jalapeño salsa, and salmon with basil beurre blanc. For dessert, try the prune-and-toffee pudding with roasted nutty butterscotch. ⊠ *Old Town Hall Building, Rutland St.* ☎ *061/400–710* ☰ *AE, DC, MC, V* ⊘ *Closed Sun.*

¢-$ ✕ **Mortell's.** For fish-and-chips, this is *the* place. It's a simple café, but it serves only the freshest local seafood. You can also get full Irish breakfasts and baked goods. Mortell's has been in the family for more than 40 years, and everything, from the doughnuts to the brown bread to the mayo, is made on the premises. It's in the main shopping area. ⊠ *49 Roches St.* ☎ *061/415–457* ☰ *AE, DC, MC, V* ⊘ *Closed Sun. No dinner.*

$$-$$$ ✕▥ **Castletroy Park.** This large, redbrick-and-stone hotel, which grandly crowns a hill on the outskirts of town, is close to the university campus, and has splendid views of the Clate hills. The lobby, with its polished woods and Asian rugs, leads to a conservatory–cum–coffee shop overlooking an Italian-style courtyard. Guest rooms, scented with potpourri, have solid wood furniture, muted floral drapes and spreads, and rag-rolled walls. The fitness center is one of the best in the region. You can mix with the locals in the Merry Pedlar Pub and Bistro or enjoy a formal meal in MacLaughlin's restaurant ($$). ⊠ *Dublin Rd., Co. Limerick* ☎ *061/335–566* ☒ *061/331–117* ⊕ *www.castletroy-park.ie* ⇘ *101 rooms, 6 suites* ⚹ *2 restaurants, in-room data ports, cable TV, indoor pool, health club, bar, meeting rooms* ☰ *AE, DC, MC, V* ⊧⊙⊧ *BP.*

$ ⌂ **Jurys Inn.** Clean, airy, and in good shape, unlike some of Limerick's other inner-city lodgings, this big, well-run hotel is part of the Jurys budget chain. Rooms are a good size and have light-wood furnishings. The hotel overlooks an urban stretch of the Shannon being converted from industrial to leisure use and is a short step from the main shopping and business district. ⊠ *Lower Mallow St., Mount Kennett Pl., Co. Limerick* ☎ *061/207–000* 🖷 *061/400–966* ⊕ *www.jurysdoyle.com* 🛏 *151 rooms* ♿ *Restaurant, cable TV, bar; no a/c* ⊟ *AE, DC, MC, V* ⦿⦿ *BP.*

$ ⌂ **Sarsfield Bridge Hotel.** This modern budget accommodation has a great location beside the Sarsfield Bridge, midway between old Limerick and the shopping area. The popular, ground-floor Pier One bar-restaurant has leather sofas overlooking the river. Rooms above are built in a square around an enclosed courtyard; those on the inside have no views but are truly quiet. Red velvet armchairs are the only touches of luxury in otherwise plain, small rooms, but overall, the hotel offers good value for the money. ⊠ *Sarsfield Bridge* ☎ *061/317–179* 🖷 *061/317–182* ⊕ *www.tsbh.ie* 🛏 *55 rooms* ♿ *Restaurant, cable TV; no a/c* ⊟ *AE, MC, V.*

Nightlife & the Arts

ART GALLERIES The **Belltable Arts Center** (⊠ 69 O'Connell St. ☎ 061/319–866) has exhibition space and a small auditorium for touring productions. The **Limerick City Gallery** (⊠ Pery Sq. ☎ 061/310–633) owns a small permanent collection of Irish art and mounts exhibits of contemporary art.

PUBS, CABARET **Dolan's Pub** (⊠ 3–4 Dock Rd. ☎ 061/314–483) is a lively waterfront spot
& DISCOS with traditional Irish music every night, and dancing classes from September to May. Dolan's Warehouse, under the same management and in the same location, is a live music venue with top national and international acts. **Hogan's** (⊠ 20–24 Old Clare St. ☎ 061/411–279) has a traditional music session every Monday, Wednesday, and Saturday. The riverside **Locke Bar** (⊠ 3 George's Quay ☎ 061/413–733) is one of Limerick's oldest bars, dating from 1724, and has Irish music Sunday, Monday, and Tuesday nights. It's also a great place for outdoor drinking in summer. There's traditional music at **Nancy Blake's Pub** (⊠ 19 Denmark St. ☎ 061/416–443) year-round Sunday–Wednesday from 9 PM. **William G. South's Pub** (⊠ The Crescent ☎ 061/318–850) is an old-fashioned pub that's typical of the age of Frank McCourt's *Angela's Ashes*. There's no music, but do drop by for bar food (1:30 to 3 PM, Mon.–Sat.) or a drink.

Shopping

DEPARTMENT Limerick has a branch of **Brown Thomas** (⊠ O'Connell St. ☎ 061/472–
STORES 222), Ireland's upscale department store. **Dunnes Stores** (⊠ 130 Sarsfield St. ☎ 061/412–666) is, perhaps, Ireland's favorite department store chain. **Penneys** (⊠ 137 O'Connell St. ☎ 061/227–244) sells inexpensive clothing; it's a great place for low-price rain gear. **Roches Stores** (⊠ O'Connell St. ☎ 061/415–622) is a large, mid-range department store.

MALLS The shops in **Arthur's Quay Shopping Centre** (⊠ Arthur's Quay ☎ 061/419888) mainly sell clothing and accessories. The **Crescent Shipping Center** (⊠ Dooradoyle ☎ 061/228560), Limerick's biggest, swankiest mall, with branches of most High Street fashion chains, is a five-minute bus or car ride from the city center.

SPECIALTY SHOPS   The **Celtic Bookshop** (✉ 2 Rutland St. ☎ 061/401–155) specializes in books of Irish interest. **Davern & Bell** (✉ 22 Thomas St. ☎ 061/481—967) is a gallery of contemporary Irish crafts, mainly ceramics. **Deoidín** (✉ 6 Sarsfield St. ☎ 061/318–011) has an interesting selection of crafts, jewelry, and gifts. **Lane Antiques** (✉ 45 Catherine St. ☎ 061/339–307) sells collectibles, antiquarian books, prints, and paintings.

Bunratty Castle & Folk Park

★ ☺ ☛ ❻ *18 km (10 mi) west of Limerick City on N18 (road to Shannon Airport).*

Bunratty Castle and Folk Park are two of those rare attractions that appeal to all ages and manage to be both educational and fun. Built in 1460, the castle—a stolid, massive affair with four square keep towers—has been fully restored and decorated with 15th- to 17th-century furniture and furnishings. It gives wonderful insight into the life of those times. As you pass under the walls of Bunratty, look for the three "murder holes" that allowed defenders to pour boiling oil on attackers below.

The castle is the site of medieval banquets, which are held nightly at 5:45 and 8:45; the cost is €48.50. You're welcomed by Irish colleens in 15th-century dress, who bear the traditional bread of friendship. Then you're led off to a reception, where you'll quaff mead made from fermented honey, apple juice, clover, and heather. Before sitting down at long tables in the candlelit great hall, you'll don a bib. You'll need it, because you eat the four-course meal medieval-style—with your fingers. Serving "wenches" take time out to sing a few ballads or pluck harp strings. The banquets may not be authentic, but they're fun; they're also popular, so book as far in advance as possible.

On the castle grounds the quaint Bunratty Folk Park re-creates a 19th-century village street and has examples of traditional rural housing. Exhibits include a working blacksmith's forge; demonstrations of flour milling, bread making, candle making, thatching, and other skills; and a variety of farm animals. An adjacent museum of agricultural machinery can't compete with the furry and feathered live exhibits. If you can't get a reservation for the medieval banquet at the castle, a *ceilí* (known as the Traditional Irish Night; held nightly May to September at 5:45 and 9 for €40) at the folk park is the next-best thing. The program features traditional Irish dance and song and a meal of Irish stew, soda bread, and apple pie. No visit to Bunratty is complete without a drink in **Durty Nelly's** (☎ 061/364072), an old-world (but touristy) pub beside the folk park entrance. Its fanciful decor has inspired imitations around the world. ☎ *061/361–511* ⊕ *www.shannonheritage.com* 🎫 *€10.50* ☉ *Sept.–May, daily 9:30–5:30 (last entry 4:15); June–Aug., daily 9:30–7 (last entry 6).*

Knappogue Castle

★ ☺ ❻ *21 km (13 mi) north of Bunratty.*

With a name that means "hill of the kiss," Knappogue is one of Ireland's most beautiful medieval tower-house castles. A 15th-century MacNamara stronghold, Knappogue Castle was renovated in the Victorian era and fitted with storybook details. Restored by a wealthy American family, the castle has now been retro-ed in 15th-century style to host fun and fabulous "medieval-style" banquets. You are first greeted at the main door by the Ladies of the castle who escort you to the Dalcassian Hall, where you enjoy a goblet of Mead (honey wine), listen to Harp and Fiddle, then proceed to the banqueting hall for a four-course meal, great Irish choral music, and a theatrical set-piece in which the Butler and the Earl argue the virtues of Gallantry. Outside, the walled garden is something out of a medieval Book of Hours illustration. As an added allure, the castle looks spectacular when floodlit. Who can resist? ⊠ *5 km (3 mi) southeast of Quin on R649* ☎ *061/368–103* ⊕ *www.shannonheritage. com* ⊠ *€7.95* ⊗ *May–Sept., daily 9:30–4:30.*

Craggaunowen Project

⑥ *6 km (4 mi) northeast of Knappogue Castle.*

★ ⟳ It's a strange experience to walk across the little wooden bridge above reeds rippling in the lake into Ireland's Celtic past as a jumbo jet passes overhead on its way into Shannon Airport—1,500 years of history compressed into an instant. But if you love all things Celtic, you'll have to visit the **Craggaunowen Project.** The romantic centerpiece is Craggaunowen Castle, a 16th-century tower house restored with furnishings from the period. Huddling beneath its battlements are two replicas of early Celtic-style dwellings. On an island in the lake, reached by a narrow footbridge, is a clay-and-wattle *crannóg,* a fortified lake dwelling; it resembles what might have been built in the 6th or 7th century, when Celtic influence still predominated in Ireland. The reconstruction of a small ring fort shows how an ordinary soldier would have lived in the 5th or 6th century, at the time Christianity was being established here. Characters from the past explain their Iron Age (500 BC–AD 450) lifestyle; show you around their small holding, stocked with animals; and demonstrate crafts skills from bygone ages. ⊠ *Signposted off road to Sixmilebridge about 10 km (6 mi) east of Quin, Kilmurry, Sixmilebridge* ☎ *061/367–178* ⊕ *www. shannonheritage.com* ⊠ *€10* ⊗ *May–Oct., daily 10–6.*

THE SOUTHWEST A TO Z

To research prices, get advice from other travelers, and book travel arrangements, visit www.fodors.com.

AIR TRAVEL

AIRPORTS   The southwest has two international airports: Cork on the southwest coast, and Shannon in the west. Cork Airport, 5 km (3 mi) south of Cork City on the Kinsale road, is used primarily for flights to and from the United Kingdom. Regular 30-minute internal flights are scheduled between Shannon and Dublin, Shannon and Cork, and Cork and Dublin. Shannon Airport, 26 km (16 mi) west of Limerick City, is the point of arrival for many transatlantic flights; it also serves some flights from the United Kingdom and Europe. Kerry County Airport at Farranfore, 16 km (10 mi) from Killarney, mainly services small planes but is gradually increasing its commercial traffic, with at least one daily flight from London.

⚡ Airport Information **Cork Airport** ☎ 021/431-3131. **Kerry County Airport** ☎ 066/976-4644. **Shannon Airport** ☎ 061/471-444.

TRANSFERS   Bus service runs between Cork Airport and the Cork City Bus Terminal every 30 minutes, on the hour and the half hour. The ride takes about 10 minutes and costs about €3. Bus Éireann runs a regular bus service from Shannon Airport to Limerick City between 8 AM and midnight. The ride takes about 40 minutes and costs €5.

You'll find taxis outside the main terminal building at Shannon and Cork airports. The ride from Shannon Airport to Limerick City costs about €30; from Cork Airport to Cork City costs about €10.

⚡ Shuttles **Bus Éireann** ☎ 061/474-311. **Cork City Bus Terminal** ✉ Parnell Pl. ☎ 021/450-6066.

BOAT & FERRY TRAVEL

From the United Kingdom, the southwest has two ports of entry: Rosslare (in County Wexford) and Cork City. Stena Sealink sails directly between Rosslare Ferryport and Fishguard, Wales. Pembroke, Wales, and France's Cherbourg and Roscoff can be reached on Irish Ferries. Swansea–Cork Ferries, which can also be accessed from the United Kingdom, operates a 10-hour crossing between the two ports on a comfortable, well-equipped boat. Supabus will get you to the Swansea ferry from anywhere in the United Kingdom.

⚡ Boat & Ferry Information **Irish Ferries** ☎ 053/33158. **Stena Sealink** ☎ 053/33115. **Swansea-Cork Ferries** ☎ 1792/456-116.

BUS TRAVEL

Bus Éireann operates express services from Dublin to Limerick City, Cork City, and Tralee. Most towns in the region are served by the provincial Bus Éireann network. The main bus terminals in the region are at Cork, Limerick, and Tralee. An Irish company, Slattery's, runs a bus service from London to Cork and Tralee. The journey to Cork via Rosslare is by bus and ferry, and, at about 14 hours, arduous.

FARES &   The provincial bus service, cheaper and more flexible than the train, cov-
SCHEDULES   ers all the region's main centers. Express services are available between Cork City and Limerick City (twice a day); Cork and Tralee (once a day, high season only); and Killarney, Tralee, Limerick, and Shannon (once a day, twice in peak season).

If you plan to travel extensively by bus, a copy of the Bus Éireann timetable (€1.50 from bus terminals) is essential. As a general rule, the smaller the town, and the more remote, the less frequent its bus service. For example, Kinsale, a well-developed resort 29 km (18 mi) from Cork, is served by at least five buses a day, both arriving and departing, while some of the smaller villages on the remote Dingle Peninsula have bus service only on Friday. Consult with hotel concierges, tourist board staffers, or the bus line web site for the full scoop on bus schedules.

⚡ Bus Information **Bus Éireann** ☎ 01/836-6111 in Dublin, 061/313-333 in Limerick, 021/450-8188 in Cork, 066/712-3566 in Tralee ⊕ www.buseireann.ie. **Cork Bus Station**

⊠ Parnell Pl. ☎ 021/450-8188. **Limerick Bus Station** ⊠ Colbert Station ☎ 061/313-333. **Slattery's** ⊠ London U.K. ☎ 020/7482-1604, add the prefix 00-44 if dialing from Ireland. **Tralee Bus Station** ⊠ Casement Station ☎ 066/712-3566.

CAR RENTAL

All the major car-rental companies have desks at Shannon and Cork airports.

🖪 Agencies **Alamo** ⊠ Cork Airport ☎ 021/432-0755 ⊕ www.carhire.ie. **Avis** ⊠ Cork Airport ☎ 021/428-1111 ⊕ www.avis.com ⊠ Killarney ☎ 064/36655 ⊠ Shannon Airport ☎ 061/471-094. **Budget** ⊠ Cork Airport ☎ 021/431-4000 ⊕ www.budget.ie ⊠ Killarney ☎ 064/34341 ⊠ Shannon Airport ☎ 061/471-361. **Dan Dooley** ⊠ Shannon Airport ☎ 061/471-098 ⊕ www.dan-dooley.com. **Enterprise** ⊠ Cork Airport ☎ 021/497-5133. **Hertz** ⊠ Cork Airport ☎ 021/496-5849 ⊠ Shannon Airport ☎ 061/471-369. **Murray's Europcar** ⊠ Cork Airport ☎ 021/491-7300 ⊕ www.europcar.ie ⊠ Shannon Airport ☎ 061/701-200. **Sixt Irish Car Rentals** ⊠ Shannon Airport ☎ 061/328-328, Cork: 021/431-8644 ⊕ www.irishcarrentals.ie ⊠ Ennis Rd., Limerick ☎ 061/206-000.

CAR TRAVEL

The main driving route from Dublin is N7, which goes 192 km (120 mi) directly to Limerick City; from Dublin, pick up N8 in Portlaoise and drive 257 km (160 mi) to Cork City. The journey time between Dublin and Limerick runs just under three hours; between Dublin and Cork it takes about three hours. From Rosslare Harbour by car, take N25 208 km (129 mi) to Cork; allow 3½ hours for the journey. You can pick up N24 in Waterford for the 211-km (131-mi) drive to Limerick City, which also takes about 3½ hours.

A car is the ideal way to explore this region, packed as it is with scenic routes, attractive but remote towns, and a host of out-of-the-way restaurants and hotels that deserve a detour. Getting around the southwest is every bit as enjoyable as arriving, provided you set out in the right frame of mind—a relaxed one. There's no point in imposing a rigid timetable on your journey when you're visiting one of the last places in western Europe where you are as likely to be held up by a donkey cart, a herd of cows, or a flock of sheep as by road construction or heavy trucks.

ROAD CONDITIONS Roads are generally small, with two lanes (one in each direction). You will find a few miles of four-lane highway on the outskirts of Cork City, Limerick City, and Killarney, but much of your time will be spent on roads so narrow and twisty that it is not advisable to exceed 64 kph (40 mph).

EMERGENCIES

🖪 **Ambulance, fire, police** ☎ 999. **Mid-Western Health Board** ⊠ 31-33 Catherine St., Limerick ☎ 061/316-655. **Southern Health Board** ⊠ Dennehy's Cross, Cork ☎ 021/454-5011.

🖪 Pharmacies **Phelan's** ⊠ 9 Patrick St., Cork ☎ 021/427-2511. **P. O'Donoghue** ⊠ Main St., Killarney ☎ 064/31813. **Roberts** ⊠ 105 O'Connell St., Limerick City ☎ 061/414-414.

TOURS

BOAT TOURS Cork Harbour opens to the sea some 8 km (5 mi) from Cobh at Roches Point. One-hour harbor tours from Marine Transport are a splendid way to take in Cobh's glorious watery environs. They're conducted daily from May to September at 10, 11, noon, 1:30, and 2:30; the cost is €5.50. ⚓ **Marine Transport** ✉ Kennedy Pier ☎ 021/481-1485.

BUS TOURS   Bus Éireann, part of the state-run public-transport network, offers a range of day and half-day guided tours from June to September. You can book them at the bus stations in Cork or Limerick or at any tourist office. A full-day tour costs about €22, half-day €12. Bus Éireann also offers open-top bus tours of Cork City on Tuesday and Saturday in July and August for €5.10.

Dero's Tours, Corcoran's Tours, and Killarney & Kerry Tours will organize full-day and half-day trips by coach or taxi around Killarney and the Ring of Kerry.
⚓ **Fees & Schedules Bus Éireann** ☎ 01/836-6111 in Dublin, 061/313-333 in Limerick, 021/450-8188 in Cork, 066/712-3566 in Tralee ⊕ www.buseireann.ie. **Corcoran's Tours** ✉ 10 College St., Killarney ☎ 064/36666. **Dero's Tours** ✉ 22 Main St., Killarney ☎ 064/31251 ⊕ www.derostours.com. **Killarney & Kerry Tours** ✉ Innisfallen, 15 Main St., Killarney ☎ 064/33880.

SPECIAL-   Gerry Coughlan of Arrangements Unlimited can prearrange special-in-
INTEREST TOURS   terest group tours of the region. Half-day and full-day tours are individually planned for groups of 10 or more to satisfy each visitor's needs. Country House Tours organizes self-driven or chauffeur-driven group tours with accommodations in private country houses and castles. It also conducts special-interest tours, including gardens, architecture, ghosts, and golf. Into the Wilderness organizes guided walking, climbing, and cycling tours in the Kerry Highlands and Killarney National Park.

Shannon Castle Tours will escort you to an "Irish Night" in Bunratty Folk Park or take you to a medieval banquet at Bunratty or Knappogue Castle; although the banquets aren't authentic, they are boisterous occasions and full of goodwill.

Destination Killarney is the foremost Killarney tour operator. Besides offering full-day and half-day tours of Killarney and Kerry by coach or taxi, the group will prearrange your visit, lining up accommodations, entertainment, special-interest tours, and sporting activities in one package. A full-day (10:30–5) tour costs from €15 to €18 per person, excluding lunch and refreshments. The Killarney Local Circuit tour is an excellent half-day 10:30–12:30 orientation. The memorable Gap of Dunloe tour at €20 includes a coach and boat trip. Add €15 for a horseback ride through the gap. More conventional day trips can also be made to the Ring of Kerry, the Loo Valley, and Glengarriff; the city of Cork and Blarney Castle; Dingle and Slea Head; and Caragh Lake and Rossbeigh.

Jaunting cars (pony and trap) that carry up to four people can be rented at a stand outside the Killarney tourist office. They can also be found at the entrance to Muckross Estate and at the Gap of Dunloe. A ride costs between €16 and €32, negotiable with the driver, depending on duration (one to two hours) and route. Tangney Tours is the leading jaunting-car company and will also organize tours by coach or water bus, as well as entertainment.

🎫 Fees & Schedules **Arrangements Unlimited** ✉ 1 Woolhara Park, Douglas, Cork City, Co. Cork ☎ 021/429-3873 📠 021/429-2488 ⊕ www.arrangements.ie. **Country House Tours** ✉ 71 Waterloo Rd., Dublin 4 ☎ 01/668-6463 📠 01/668-6578 ⊕ www.tourismresources.ie. **Destination Killarney** ✉ Scott's Gardens, Killarney, Co. Kerry ☎📠 064/32638 ⊕ www.gleneagle-hotel.com. **Shannon Castle Tours** ✉ Bunratty Folk Park, Bunratty, Co. Clare ☎ 061/360-788 ⊕ www.shannonheritage.ie. **Tangney Tours** ✉ Kinvara House, Muckross Rd., Killarney, Co. Kerry ☎ 064/33358.

WALKING TOURS   SouthWest Walks Ireland has a variety of packages for all levels of walkers. Trips include accommodation, baggage transfer, and evening meals for self-guided or escorted groups. Go Ireland specializes in active vacations, included walking and cycling excursions along the Kerry Way or the Dingle Peninsula. Michael Martin's Titanic Trail, a 90-minute guided walking tour of Cobh, takes its name from the *Titanic*, but in fact covers the whole of Cobh's fascinating history, ranging from coffin ships to ocean liners via naval fire power and tall ships. Trips are held daily at 11 AM starting from outside the Commodore Hotel; the cost is €7.50. Martin can also customize a walk or tour by minibus.

Richard Clancy, an expert on the legends and history of Killarney, offers a two-hour guided walk in Killarney National Park daily at 11 AM (other times by arrangement). Trips leave from the Shell gas station on Lower New Street. The cost is €7. Limerick City Tours provides inexpensive walking tours of Limerick from June to September (and by arrangement other months). St. Mary's Action Centre has walking tours of Limerick's historic centers and of locations highlighted in Frank McCourt's *Angela's Ashes*. They're conducted daily at 11 and 2:30.

🎫 **Go Ireland** ✉ Killorglin ☎ 066/976-2094 ⊕ www.goactivities.com. **Limerick City Tours** ✉ Noel Curtin, Rhebogue ☎ 061/311935. **Richard Clancy** ☎ 064/33471 ⊕ www.kerrygems.ie/killarneywalks. **St. Mary's Action Centre** ✉ 44 Nicholas St., Limerick ☎ 061/318-106 ⊕ www.iol.ie/~smidp. **SouthWest Walks Ireland** ✉ 6 Church St., Tralee ☎ 066/712-8733 ⊕ www.southwestwalksireland.com. **Titanic Trail** ✉ Cobh ☎ 021/481-5211 ⊕ www.titanic-trail.com.

TRAIN TRAVEL

From Dublin Heuston Station the region is served by three direct rail links, to Limerick City, Tralee, and Cork City. Journey time from Dublin to Limerick is 2½ hours; to Cork, 2¾; to Tralee, 3¼.

The rail network, which covers only the inner ring of the region, is mainly useful for moving from one touring base to another. Except during the peak season of July and August, only four trains a day run between Cork (or Limerick) and Tralee. More frequent service is offered between Cork City and Limerick City, but the ride involves changing at Limerick Junction—as does the journey from Limerick to Tralee—to wait for a connecting train. Be sure to ascertain the delay involved in the connection. The journey from Cork to Tralee takes about 2 hours; from Cork to Limerick, about 1¼ hours; from Limerick to Tralee, about 3 hours.

A suburban rail service from Kent Station has stops at Fota Island and Cobh and offers better Cork Harbour views than the road.

f Train Information **Dublin Heuston Station** ☎ 01/836-6222. **Inquiries** ☎ 061/315-555 in Limerick, 021/450-6766 in Cork, 066/712-3522 in Tralee. **Kent Station** ☎ 021/450-6766 for timetable.

VISITOR INFORMATION

Bord Fáilte provides a free information service; its tourist information offices (TIOs) also sell a selection of tourist literature. For a small fee it will book accommodations anywhere in Ireland.

Seasonal TIOs in Bantry, Cahirciveen, and Clonakilty are open from May to October; offices in Dingle and Kinsale are open from March to November; the TIO in Kenmare is open April to October, and the one in Youghal is open May to mid-September. All of the seasonal TIOs are generally open Monday–Saturday 9–6; in July and August they are also open Sunday 9–6. Year-round TIOs can be found in Blarney, Clonakilty, Cork City, Dingle, Killarney, Limerick, Shannon, Skibbereen, and Tralee and are open Monday–Saturday 9–6; in July and August they are also open Sunday 9–6.

f Tourist Information **Adare** ✉ Heritage Centre ☎ 061-396-255 ⊕ www.shannon-dev.ie. **Bantry** ✉ Co. Cork ☎ 027/50229 ⊕ www.corkkerry.ie. **Blarney** ✉ Co. Cork ☎ 021/438-1624 ⊕ www.corkkerry.ie. **Cahirciveen** ✉ The Old Barracks, Co. Kerry ☎ 066/947-2589 ⊕ www.corkkerry.ie. **Clonakilty** ✉ Co. Cork ☎ 023/33226 ⊕ www.corkkerry.ie. **Cork City** ✉ Grand Parade, Co. Cork ☎ 021/425-5100 ⊟ 021/425-5199 ⊕ www.corkkerry.ie. **Dingle** ✉ The Quay, Co. Kerry ☎ 066/915-1188. **Kenmare** ✉ Co. Kerry ☎ 064/41233. **Killarney** ✉ Aras Fáilte, Beech Rd., Co. Kerry ☎ 064/31633 ⊟ 064/34506 ⊕ www.corkkerry.ie. **Kinsale** ✉ Pier Rd., Co. Cork ☎ 021/477-2234, 021/477-4417 off-season ⊟ 021/477-4438. **Limerick** ✉ Arthur's Quay, Co. Limerick ☎ 061/317-522 ⊕ www.shannon-dev.ie. **Shannon Airport** ✉ Co. Clare ☎ 061/471-664 ⊕ www.shannon-dev.ie. **Skibbereen** ✉ North St., Co. Cork ☎ 028/21766. **Tralee** ✉ Ashe Memorial Hall, Denny St., Co. Kerry ☎ 066/712-1288 ⊕ www.shannon-dev.ie. **Youghal** ✉ Co. Cork ☎ 024/92390.

THE WEST

6

Updated by
Alannah
Hopkin

WHILE MOST OF IRELAND IS CHARGING HEADFIRST into the 21st century, the west seems bent on retaining an unspoiled and rugged way of life. With the most westerly seaboard in Europe, the region remains a place apart, full of nature's magnificence: the majestic Cliffs of Moher, the rocky expanse of the Burren (whose gray rocks hide a profusion of wild plants), Connemara's rugged combination of coastline, mountain, moorland, and lakes, and the Aran Islands, which do constant battle with the stormy Atlantic. But there are also characterful small country towns, such as Lisdoonvarna, Clifden, and Westport, which abound in good restaurants and pubs to visit, and Galway, the city that loves to celebrate.

Within Ireland, the west refers to the region that lies west of the River Shannon; most of this area falls within the old Irish province of Connaught. The coast of this region lies at the far western extremity of Europe, facing its nearest North American neighbors across 3,200 km (2,000 mi) of Atlantic ocean. Although the east, the southwest, and the north were influenced by either Norman, Scots, or English settlers, the west largely escaped systematic resettlement and, with the exception of the walled town of Galway, remained purely Irish in language, social organization, and general outlook far longer than the rest of the country. The land in the west, predominantly mountains and bogs, did not immediately tempt the conquering barons. Oliver Cromwell was among those who found the place thoroughly unattractive, and he gave the Irish chieftains who would not conform to English rule the choice of going "to Hell or Connaught."

It wasn't until the late 18th century, when better transport improved communications, that the west started to experience the so-called foreign influences that had already Europeanized the rest of the country. The west was, in effect, propelled from the 16th century into the 19th. Virtually every significant building in the region dates either from before the 17th century or from the late 18th century onward. As in the southwest, the population of the west was decimated by the Great Famine (1845–49) and by the waves of emigration that persisted until the 1950s. Towns as communities were unknown in pre-Christian Irish society, and even today, more than 150 years after the famine, many residents still live on small farms rather than in towns and villages. Especially during the wet, wintry months, you can still walk out of your country house, hotel, or bed-and-breakfast in the morning and smell the nearby turf fires.

Today, the west is, for many, the most typically Irish part of the country. Particularly in western County Galway, the region has the highest concentration of Gaeltacht (Irish-speaking) communities in all of Ireland, with roughly 40,000 native Irish speakers making their homes here. The country's first Irish-language TV station broadcasts from the tiny village of Spiddle, on the north shore of Galway Bay in the heart of the Gaeltacht. Throughout this area, you'll see plenty of signs printed in Irish only. Who would suspect that Gaillimh is Irish for Galway? But wherever you go in the west, you'll not only see, but more importantly *hear,* the most vital way in which traditional Irish culture survives here—musicians play in pubs all over the west, and they are acknowledged to be the best in the Republic.

A major factor in the region's economic development has been the lure of its spectacular scenery to visitors. So far, the typical development that comes with the cultivation of tourism in the west has been mercifully low-key. Yes, residents of the west have encouraged the revival of such cottage industries as knitting, weaving, and woodworking. But there is also a strong environmental lobby, campaigning for land preservation. The 5,000-acre Connemara National Park is the result of a successful lobby for peatland protection, and Ireland's last remaining peat-burning electricity generating station—at Bellacorick in County Mayo—has closed. The campaign on behalf of an environment which echoes traditional vernacular buildings has been less successful so far, although awareness is increasing. If you spot a traditional thatched cottage in the landscape, nine times out of ten it will be a vacation or weekend home. In some places, such as Kilkee or Achill Island, the building of clusters of such holiday homes, which remain empty for much of the year, has made locals wary of such projects. Galway City's suburbs have spread in all directions, and throughout the region the landscape is marked by newly built bungalows and houses. The visitor may criticize the often flamboyant modern architecture of these homes, and see them as a scar on the wilderness, but he or she should also remember that these are the kind of homes that people now aspire to, for many still associate the traditional cottage with poverty and deprivation. With increasing prosperity, the west of Ireland is undoubtedly losing some of its traditional visual charm. But while this is regrettable in terms of unspoiled views, for the people who live in the area, it is a boon.

It's nothing new that the west's greatest virtue for visitors—apart from its glorious scenery and vibrant capital city of Galway—is its people. No matter how many times you get out of the car for a photo-op (and you should expect to *fly* through rolls of film here), the stories that you'll most likely tell when you show your friends and family those pictures are going to be about the *seisún,* or sessions (informal performances of traditional music) you stumbled upon in a small pub; the tiny, far-from-the-madding-crowds lake near Connemara that you made your own; and the great *craic* ("crack," or good conversation and fun) you're likely to discover wherever you go.

Exploring the West

This chapter is organized into five parts, covering the territory from south to north. The first section, the Burren and Beyond—West Clare to South Galway—picks up minutes from Shannon Airport and is not far from Ennis, the gateway to coastal County Clare. The second section shows you the best of buzzing, bustling Galway City, and the third takes you out to the three Aran Islands, standing guard at the mouth of Galway Bay. The fourth section, covering Connemara and County Mayo, brings you north of Galway Bay and west of Galway City into fabled Connemara, and its spectacularly situated "capital," Clifden, and beyond to the highlights of County Mayo: monumental Croagh Patrick, the pretty town of Westport, and breathtaking Achill Island. The fifth section gives a brief overview of some of the highlights along the North Mayo coast. Allow at least four days for exploring the region, seven days if you aim

Numbers in the text correspond to numbers in the margin and on the West and Galway City maps.

If you have 5 days

Even if you are not overnighting, drop in on the stately splendor of Dromoland Castle hotel in **Newmarket-on-Fergus** ❶ ⌐, then make a bee-line for for the natural wonders of the famed **Cliffs of Moher** ❺. Next stop should be the heart of **the Burren** ❽, one of Ireland's fiercest landscapes. Both **Doolin** ❻ and the spa town of 🖼 **Lisdoonvarna** ❼ are within the Burren and famous for their traditional music. Spend the night in Lisdoonvarna, or in one of the picture-perfect villages of 🖼 **Kinvara** ⑫ and 🖼 **Ballyvaughan** ❾, both on Galway Bay. On your second day, head for 🖼 **Galway City** ⑬–㉖, the chic and cosmopolitan arts and student hub. Spend the morning exploring its historic market-town center on foot. In the afternoon, take a cruise up the River Corrib or drive along the north shore of Galway Bay to Salthill and beyond into the Gaeltacht.

On your third day, you can kick around Galway, take the ferry out to the sublime **Aran Islands** ㉗–㉙ for the day, or make the quick trip south to Lady Gregory's estate at **Coole Park** ❿ and Yeats's house at **Thoor Ballylee** ⑪. Spend the night in Galway or at one of the country houses outside town. Another option for your third day is to head out through the moorlands of Connemara and the angling center of **Oughterard** ㉚ to **Ballynahinch** ㉝ or Roundstone for lunch. Then go on to the Alpine-like coastal village of 🖼 **Clifden** ㉞. Spend the night here or in a country house, hotel, or B&B in or around 🖼 **Cashel** ㉜ or 🖼 **Letterfrack** ㉟, where you'll find a national park replete with historic peat fields.

If you've spent your third night in Galway, or if you have stayed the night in or near Clifden, follow the alternative day-three itinerary above, but don't linger too long in Clifden. Push on, first to Connemara National Park and then to Kylemore Abbey—one of the most spectacular houses in Ireland—in the **Kylemore Valley** ㊱. Continue through tiny but world-famous **Leenane** ㊲ to Georgian-era 🖼 **Westport** ㊳, the prettiest village in County Mayo and a good place to spend the night. On the way, you won't be able to miss the distinctive conical shape of Croagh Patrick. On your fifth day, walk up Croagh Patrick or stroll around Clew Bay and see how many islands you can count. If the weather cooperates, venture out to **Achill Island** ㊴. At the end of the day, continue north to Sligo or head for a Midlands destination.

If you have 7 days

The five-day itinerary can easily be expanded into a seven-day trip, with the following modifications: spend two days exploring the extraordinary 🖼 **Aran Islands** ㉗–㉙ and opting for an overnight stay. At the end of the week, spend two nights in 🖼 **Westport** ㊳ to incorporate a visit to the Museum of Country Life in **Turlough** ㊶. Or, from Westport, head north and spend a full day and night on 🖼 **Achill Island** ㊴ with a final day touring the dramatic coastline (watch out for those blowholes!) of the **North Mayo Coast.**

to visit the Aran Islands and Achill Island. Although distances between sights are not great, you may want to take scenic—and slower—national secondary routes. Covering 80 km to 112 km (50 mi to 70 mi) per day on these roads is a comfortable target.

About the Restaurants & Hotels

Because the west has a brief high season—from mid-June to early September—and a quiet off-season, it doesn't have as broad a choice of small, owner-operated restaurants as do other parts of Ireland. Often the best place to eat is a hotel—Sheedy's Restaurant and Country Inn in Lisdoonvarna, for example, which has one of the best chefs in County Clare, or Rosleague Manor in Letterfrack. The dominant style of cuisine in the west is an unfussy, traditional approach that allows the natural flavors of fresh local delights—locally reared lamb and beef, and freshly landed seafood—to shine through. Look out for wild salmon or sea trout, and Connemara mountain lamb, three regional delicacies that are well worth the premium. Most of the chefs working in the region have traveled widely, and on many menus you will find a whiff of Asia—Thailand especially—along with the expected classic French repertoire. A handful of restaurants, including Kirwan's Lane Creative Cuisine and K. C. Blake's in Galway, showcase adventurous contemporary Irish cooking with a bold fusion element. But many of the best things to eat in these parts are extremely simple, which makes a bar-food lunch a tempting option. It is hard to beat a platter of freshly sliced smoked salmon with half a lemon squeezed over it, home-baked brown bread with butter, and a glass of dry white wine. Oysters, too, (the local one is the European oyster, *ostrea edulis*) are often ordered in their shells and slipped directly into the mouth; followed by a bite of soda bread and butter and a sip of black stout, it's a combination made in heaven, many say. Home-baked brown bread, whether soda (made with buttermilk) or yeast, is one of the great pleasures of the region, and another is the home-baking—porter cake, fruit scones, breakfast muffins—which is on offer at many of the region's B&Bs and inns.

Some of Ireland's finest country-house and castle hotels, distinguished old hotels, and inexpensive B&Bs are in the west. Ashford and Dromoland castles shine as the stars of the region, but less over-the-top places, such as Ballynahinch Castle and Cashel House—both in Connemara—offer similar comfort on a smaller, more intimate scale. One of the great attractions of staying in the west, however much you pay for the night, is the restful environment of many of these hotels and guest houses, which often sit in the middle of a large private estate beside a lake or river, overlooking the sea or a hilly valley. Most of the moderately priced hotels are relatively new, and thus more modern than charming, but these newer hotels often have facilities—tennis courts and indoor pools—that are scarce at B&Bs and older hotels. Accommodations are busy in July and August, and the best places are also filled in May, June, and September, particularly on weekends, so reserve well in advance. On the chart below, hotel prices are listed for room rates that include no meals (EP, European Plan) or, if indicated, CP (with Continental breakfast) or BP (Breakfast Plan, with full breakfast). Higher prices prevail for board plans such as MAP (Modified American Plan, with breakfast and dinner); in-

The Wooly Wild West

Shopper alert: Irish tweeds, hand-knit woolen sweaters, Aran jerseys, hand-made ceramics, wood turning, original paintings, photographs, and jewelry abound in these regions, often at surprisingly affordable prices. Many items are made by artists and craftspeople who have moved to the area and offer a chance to buy direct from their studio workshops. Other craftspeople showcase their work in places like the famed Design Concourse Ireland in Galway City, and the Doolin Crafts Gallery near the Cliffs of Moher. A traditional hand-knitted Aran sweater (or "gansey") in chunky, off-white wool that has been worn by generations of fishermen as protection against the weather is hard to resist, and may well become a family heirloom (Auntie Jacinta probably owns one knitted by her great-aunt circa 1970 and still going strong). But the less expensive, lighter-weight, hand-loomed sweaters (knitted on a mechanical loom, not with needles) are less than half the price, and more practical for most lifestyles. They come in a tempting array of colors and styles (check out Connemara Handcrafts in Letterfrack or O'Reilly/Turpin in Westport, among others). Don't buy the first one you see; take a good look around, visiting any number of craft shops—it's part of the fun, and you'll probably end up with woolen hiking socks, a woolen hat, and a mohair rug as well. Tweed comes in traditional mode (try Millar's Connemara Tweeds in Clifden) or modern designer variants (Design Ireland Plus in Galway or Joyce's of Maam Cross). In Galway, the traditional Claddagh ring comes in all price ranges, while affordable modern silver jewelry using Connemara marble and other local stones is also worth investigating. While all towns in the area have a few craft shops, be prepared to stop anywhere on the road where you see a sign, because you never know what you'll find: musical instruments, handmade beeswax candles, batik, watercolor paintings, modern lead crystal, or stoneware.

When Ireland Celebrates

For both visitors and locals, festivals provide both free entertainment and a chance to meet people from all backgrounds who share a common interest. Some festivals are traditional events, now tarted up with entertaining side shows: Kinvara's Criuinniú na mBád on the third Thursday in August centers around turf-laden "hookers" (heavy wooden sailing boats) racing across Galway Bay, while on the third weekend in August the Connemara Pony Show in Clifden attracts a nationwide equine entry, and creates a terrific buzz. The Ballinasloe International October Fair and Festival during the first week in October has its origins in an annual horse-trading event that dates back almost 300 years, and attracts numerous side entertainers, including traditional Irish musicians. In contrast, the Galway Arts Festival, in the middle two weeks of July, hosts an international array of the best of contemporary theatre, film, rock, jazz, traditional music, poetry readings, comedy acts, visual arts exhibitions, and an open-air parade by the street theatre company Macnas, one of several local troupes to gain international recognition. This is followed immediately by the Galway Races, the "only place" for Irish socialites to be seen in late July. These thoroughbred horse races now feature a new sport: the game of Spot the Celebrity (usually arriving by helicopter). Throughout the year Galway's Town Hall Theatre hosts local and touring productions of high caliber, including some by the Druid Theatre Company, which performs regularly in Dublin and London. Both Galway and neighboring Clarinbridge have Oyster Festivals in September, celebrating the local product with oyster-opening competitions and lots of free entertainment. Westport's Arts Festival takes place the last week of September, and like Clifden's mid-September Community Arts Week, has many fans, who enjoy the quieter ambience, and the way that famous visitors—usually writers and musicians—mingle informally with the people.

The Great Outdoors

While the West's rugged scenery has always been popular with outdoor types, the biggest growth area in recent years has been in provision of facilities for walkers and hikers. The last decade has seen the completion of various "way-marked" (signposted) walking routes. Better, there are also several new tour operators specializing in customized walking holidays, providing accommodation and a guide, or annotated walking maps (see Tour Operators in A to Z at end of this chapter). If you like challenging hills and relatively rough terrain, the West is excellent hiking country. The unusual, almost lunar landscape of the Burren in County Clare is less demanding than the terrain in Connemara. Here, and in the area north of Connemara in South County Mayo, the countryside is sparsely populated and subject to sudden changes in weather, usually a shower of rain. There are four signposted trails in the area, but it is always advisable to buy a good map locally before setting out. The **Burren Way** runs from Lahinch to Ballyvaughan on the shores of Galway Bay, a distance of 35 km (22 mi). The most spectacular part of the trail runs along the top of the Cliffs of Moher from Doolin to the coast near Lisdoonvarna, a distance of about 5 km (3 mi). The trails continue through the heart of the Burren's grey, rocky limestone landscape, with ever-changing views offshore of the Aran Islands and Galway Bay. The **Western Way's County Galway section** extends from Oughterard on Lough Corrib through the mountains of Connemara to Leenane on Killary Harbour, a distance of 50 km (30 mi). Its 177-km (110 mi) County Mayo section, known as the Western Way (Mayo), continues past Killary Harbor to Westport on Clew Bay to the Ox Mountains east of Ballina; this trail includes some of the finest mountain and coastal scenery in Ireland. A new, 387-km (240-mi) hiking route through Irish-speaking Connemara stretches along the shores of Galway Bay from Spiddle to Carraroe, Carna, Lettterfrack, and Clonbur.

quire when booking. Assume that all hotel rooms have air-conditioning, in-room phones, TVs, and private bathrooms unless otherwise indicated.

WHAT IT COSTS In euros				
$$$$	**$$$**	**$$**	**$**	**¢**
RESTAURANTS over €29	€22–€29	€15–€22	€8–€15	under €8
HOTELS over €230	€180–€230	€130–€180	€80–€130	under €80

Restaurant prices are per person for a main course at dinner; note that if a restaurant offers only prix-fixe meals, it has been given the price category that reflects the full set-price. Hotel prices are for two people in a standard double room in high season, including V.A.T. and a service charge (often applied in larger hotels).

Timing

"Soft weather," as the Irish call on-again, off-again rainy days, is almost always a possibility in the west, but the months of May and October are generally drier than the rest of the year. The Burren is at its best in May, when the wildflowers are in season. April, May, and October are good times for an off-peak visit. In July and August, expect to rub elbows with Irish families taking their holidays; these are also the best months to hear traditional music. It doesn't take many people to overwhelm Galway City's narrow streets, so if you don't love crowds, steer clear in late July, when the Arts Festival and the Galway Races take place back to back. The best time to visit the Aran Islands is May and early June, while the unusual, Burren-like flora is at its best and before the bulk of the approximately 200,000 annual visitors arrives. Many restaurants and accommodations in Connemara and the Burren are seasonal and close from October to Easter, although thanks to a steady rise in demand, the season is definitely extending slightly each year. If you visit the west between November and March your choice of places to stay and to eat will be limited, but you do get to feel as though you have the place to yourself. A word of warning, though: in winter, the weather in the west can be harsh, with gales and rain sweeping in day after day from the Atlantic.

THE BURREN & BEYOND

County Clare claims two of Ireland's unique natural sights: the awesome Cliffs of Moher and the stark, mournful landscape of the Burren, which hugs the coast from Black Head in the north to Doolin and the Cliffs of Moher in the south. Yet western County Clare is widely beloved among native Irish for a natural phenomenon significantly less unique than these: its beaches. Though just another Irish beach town to some, Kilkee, to name just one, is a favorite summer getaway. So whether you're looking for inimitable scenery or just a lovely beach to plunk down on for a few hours and relax in the sun (if you're lucky!), this section will introduce you to the natural wonders of the west.

This journey begins at Newmarket-on-Fergus, within minutes of Shannon Airport, a good jumping-off point for a trip through the west if you've just arrived in Ireland and are planning to head for Galway. This route also follows directly from the end of Chapter 5, which concludes 10 km (6 mi) down the road, at Bunratty Castle and Folk Park (and the Knappogue Castle and Craggaunowen Project, also nearby), so be sure to take a moment to glance at those sights to decide whether to include them as you get under way. This area is also the connecting link between County Limerick (and other points in the southwest) and Galway City. If you're approaching it from the southwest and you're not going into Limerick City, it's easy to begin exploring the region from Killimer, reached via the ferry from Tarbert.

The West

TO BANGOR
Céide Fields
Cross-molina
Ballina
TO KILLALA

Glen of Nephin
NEPHIN BEG RANGE
Lough Conn
Foxford
Charlestown

Achill Island
Keel
Achill Sound
R319
Mulrany
Lough Feeagh
N59
Pontoon
River Moy
Swinford
N5

MAYO
Ballyvary
N5
Knock
N17

Clare Island
Clew Bay
Newport
Turlough
Castlebar

Louisburg
R335
N60
Westport
Claremorris

Inishturk
Croagh Patrick
Sheffry Hills
Partry Mountains
N59
Lough Mask
Ballinrobe
N60

Inishbofin Island
Mweelrea Mtns.
Killary Harbour
Renvyle
Kylemore Valley
Delphi
R336
Cong
Tuam

Kylemore Abbey
Letterfrack
Connemara Nat'l Park
Maumturk Mountains
Leenane
GALWAY

Clifden
N59
Recess
N59
Lough Corrib
TO CRAUGHWELL
N84
N17

Ballynahinch
Cashel
R341
Maam Cross
Oughterard
Athenry
N6

Ballyconneely
Roundstone
R340
R336
Rosscahill
N59

Bertraghboy Bay
Ros an Mhil (Rossaveal)
Galway City
13 - 26
See detail map
Oranmore

ATLANTIC OCEAN
R336
Spiddle
Barna
Salthill
Clarinbridge
Kilcolgan

Galway Bay
Kinvara
Thoor Ballylee

Inishmore
Dún Aengus Fort
Kilronan
Inishmaan
Aran Islands
Ailwee Cave
The Burren
Coole Park

NORTHERN IRELAND
IRELAND
Conor Fort
Inisheer
Doolin
Ballyvaughan
Lisdoonvarna
Gort
Lough Cutra
R477
N67
R480
R460

The Cliffs of Moher
Burren Centre
CLARE

Lahinch
Kilfenora
Corofin
Ennistymon
N18

Mal Bay
Milltown Malbay
R476
Ennis
N85
R474
N67
Clarecastle

Newmarket-on-Fergus

0 10 miles
0 15 km

Kilkee
Shannon
N68

Kilrush
Kilkee
Killimer R473
Kilrush
R487
Loop Head
Mouth of Shannon
Glin
N69
Tarbert

KEY
Start of itinerary

Newmarket-on-Fergus

▶ ❶ *13 km (8 mi) north of Shannon Airport on N18.*

A small town in County Clare, Newmarket-on-Fergus is chiefly remarkable as the town nearest the famed hotel of Dromoland Castle, formerly the home of Lord Inchiquin, chief of the O'Brien clan.

Where to Stay & Eat

$$$$
Fodor'sChoice
★

✕▦ **Dromoland Castle.** This massive, turreted, neo-Gothic castle—the
ancestral home of the O'Briens, the descendants of Brian Boru, High
King of Ireland—certainly looks the part. Dating from the 19th century
(it replaced the 16th-century original) and now one of Ireland's grandest and best loved hotels, it bristles with towers and crenellations rising
up over the forest and its picture-perfect lake like a storybook illustration from King Arthur and his knights. Inside, Dromoland really sets
out to give you the full country-house treatment: oak paneling, ancestral portraits, plushly carpeted rooms, crystal chandeliers, Irish-Georgian antiques—all the creature comforts any duke would want. But the
warmth of the long-serving staff, and the pervading aroma of woodsmoke
help to create an easygoing, relaxing ambience. Bedrooms (suites, in fact)
in the main wing are the biggest and most elaborate, with massive four-
poster beds, ruched drapes on the tall windows, custom fabrics, and genuine Heppelwhite armoires. Rooms in the discreetly added newer wings
are more hotel-like, with Regency-style furniture, but all have exceptionally luxurious bathrooms. The neo-Gothic, oak-wainscoted Earl of
Thomond Restaurant is magnificent, with beautifully presented tables
decked with crystal and Irish linen, a harpist providing gentle background
music, period wallpapers, Japanese vases, and spectacular chandeliers.
Classic French cuisine is served with appropriate ceremony—poached
lobster with steamed greens, perhaps for the main course, or roast Clare
lamb with salsa vert. The Green Room Bar and the Fig Tree restaurant
offer more casual dining. For activities, the estate offers a full golf
course, tennis, fishing, a spa, and those idyllic woodlands and gardens—perfect for jogging, cycling, or a blissful stroll. ⊠ *Five km (3 mi)
west of Newmarket-on-Fergus, signposted from N18, Co. Clare* ☎ *061/
368–144* 🖷 *061/363–355* ⊕ *www.dromoland.ie* ➹ *100 rooms* ♨ *2
restaurants, 18-hole golf course, 2 tennis courts, spa, fishing, bicycles,
bar; no a/c* ▤ *AE, DC, MC, V.*

$
✕▦ **Hunter's Lodge.** A good first or last stop for those arriving at Shannon, this unpretentious village pub with rooms is only 12 km (7 mi) from
the airport. The village itself is still basking in the pleasure of no longer
being on the main road, since it was bypassed by a new highway in 2003.
The resulting cheerful little community will suit those who like to get
to know "the real people" when arriving in a new country. Downstairs
is a plush, upmarket version of an Irish pub, with dark mahogany furniture and brass trim in the bar, where locals congregate around a roaring open fire. Select pieces of old oak furniture fill the attractive,
well-equipped guest rooms, and scatter rugs decorate the timber floors.
The restaurant ($–$$), known for its cheerful service, has an uncom-
plicated menu of old familiars like surf n' turf (steak and salmon), burg-

ers béarnaise, pasta Alfredo, and, the most popular of all, salmon *en croute* (wrapped in pastry with a seafood sauce). ⊠ *The Square, Co. Clare* ☎ *061/368–577* ⊟ *061/368–057* ⇄ *6 rooms* ⚴ *Restaurant, bar, free parking; no a/c* ⊟ *AE, DC, MC, V* ⏐⚬⏐ *BP.*

Sports & the Outdoors

Dromoland Golf Course (☎ 061/368–144) is one of the most scenic in the country, set in a 700-acre estate of rich woodland on the grounds of Dromoland Castle. The 18-hole, par-71 course has a natural lake that leaves little room for error on a number of holes.

Ennis

❷ *9½ km (6 mi) north of Newmarket-on-Fergus on N18, 37 km (23 mi) northwest of Limerick, 142 km (88 mi) north of Tralee.*

A major crossroads and a convenient stop between the west and the southwest, Ennis is the main town of County Clare. The pleasant market town has an attractively renovated, pedestrian-friendly center, bisected by the fast-flowing River Fergus. Ennis has always fostered traditional arts, especially fiddle-playing and step-dancing (a kind of square dance). The **Fleadh Nua** (pronounced fla-*nooa*) festival at the end of May attracts both performers and students of Irish music and serves as the venue for the National Dancing Championships.

Two **statues** in Ennis bear witness to the role its citizens have played in Irish democracy. On a tall limestone column above a massive pediment in the town center stands a **statue of Daniel O'Connell** (1775–1847), "The Liberator," a member of Parliament for County Clare between 1828 and 1831 who was instrumental in bringing about Catholic Emancipation. Outside the courthouse (in the town park, beside the River Fergus, on the west side of Ennis) stands a larger-than-life bronze **statue of Eamon De Valera** (1882–1975), who successfully contested the election here in 1917, thus launching a long political career. He was the dominant figure in Irish politics during the 20th century, serving as prime minister for most of the years from 1937 until 1959, when he resigned as leader of Fianna Fáil, the party he founded, and went on to serve as president of Ireland until 1973. Although De Valera was born in the United States, his maternal forebears were from County Clare.

Where to Stay & Eat

$$ ✕⊞ **Lynch West County.** You will meet both leisure and business travelers from all walks of life at this popular stopping point on the Limerick–Galway road (N18), a lively modern hostelry affiliated with Best Western. It's a five-minute walk from Ennis's town center. Rooms are ample; most overlook the car park but at least are quiet. Service is helpful and friendly, despite the hotel's relatively large size. In July and August there's nightly Irish cabaret-style entertainment in the large bar, Boru's Porterhouse, which also serves bar food. The Grill Room is a more intimate venue ($$) serving an à la carte menu of traditional Irish fare, while the Pine Room ($) offers a value-for-money four-course set menu. ⊠ *Clare Rd., Co. Clare* ☎ *065/682–3000* ⊟ *065/682–3759* ⊕ *www.*

lynchotels.com ⟿ *152 rooms* ⌂ *3 restaurants, coffee shop, bar, indoor pool, health club; no a/c* ⊟ *AE, DC, MC, V* ⦿| *BP.*

$$ ⊞ **Temple Gate.** Before its conversion, this lodging was a Gothic-style convent, and remnants of its previous existence (including the chapel, which is now a banquet hall) give character to this bright, modern hotel in the town center. Coordinated drapes and bedspreads in warm, earthy colors decorate the compact, well-equipped rooms, which have unusual views of pretty corners of Ennis's historic center. Preacher's Bar is popular with locals, while the guest lounge is a country house–style library. The entrance is via a cobblestoned courtyard adorned with Victorian street lamps. ⊠ *The Square, Co. Clare* ☎ *065/682–3300* 🖷 *065/692–3322* ⊕ *www.templegatehotel.com* ⟿ *70 rooms* ⌂ *Restaurant, in-room data ports, bar, library; no a/c* ⊟ *AE, DC, MC, V* ⦿| *BP.*

Nightlife & the Arts

Although Ennis is not as fashionable as, say, Galway, it is one of the west's traditional-music hot spots. You're likely to hear sessions at the following pubs, but keep in mind that sessions don't necessarily take place every night and that the scene is constantly changing. Phone ahead to check whether a session is happening.

Cruise's (⊠ Abbey St. ☎ 065/684–1800). **Fawl's** (⊠ The Railway Bar, 69 O'Connell St. ☎065/682–4463). **Kerins'** (⊠Lifford ☎065/682–0582). **Knox's** (⊠ Abbey St. ☎ 065/682–9264). **Poet's Corner Bar** (⊠ Old Ground Hotel, Main St. ☎ 065/682–8155). **Preachers** (⊠ The Temple Gate Hotel, The Square ☎ 065/682–3300).

Sports & the Outdoors

BICYCLING You can follow the scenic Burren Cycleway (69 km [43 mi]) to the famous Cliffs of Moher on a bike rented from **Tierney Cycles & Fishing** (⊠ 17 Abbey St. ☎ 065/682–9433 ⊕ www.ennisrentabike.com).

Shopping

Stop in at the **Antique Loft** (⊠Clarecastle ☎065/684–1969) for collectibles and pine and mahogany antiques. The **Belleek Shop** (⊠ 36 Abbey St. ☎ 065/682–9607) carries Belleek china, Waterford crystal, and Donegal Parian china, as well as Lladró, Hummel, and other collectible china. **Carraig Donn** (⊠ 29 O'Connell St. ☎ 065/682–8188) sells its own line of knitwear. **Clare Craft and Design** (⊠ 20 Parnell St. ☎ 065/682–4723) exhibits and sells art, pottery, and crafts produced by local artists. **The Rock Shop** (⊠ 2 O'Connell St. ☎ 065/682–2636) displays polished gemstones, fossils, and other rocks alongside jewelry and small sculptures in stone and marble. At the factory outlet **Shannon Crystal** (⊠ Sandfield Center, Galway Rd. ☎ 065/682–1250), craftspeople display the art of hand-cutting lead crystal.

Corofin

❸ *14 km (10 mi) northwest of Ennis via N18.*

Corofin? It's not a town, it's a tiny village of perhaps 200 people, just a line of houses, and some lovely, unspoiled country pubs—but perhaps that is all you are looking for today. Corofin's **Clare Heritage and**

Genealogical Center has a genealogical service and advice for do-it-your-selfers researching their Irish roots. Displays on west-Ireland 19th-century history cover culture, traditions, emigration, and famine, and also expose some grim statistics. In 1841, for example, the population of County Clare was 286,394. Fifty years later, famine and emigration had reduced this number to 112,334, and the population continued to decline, reaching an all-time low of 73,597 in 1956. (It is now heading back to the 90,000 mark.) ⊠ *Main St.* ☎ *065/683–7955* ⊕ *www. clareroots.com* 🖾 *€3* ☉ *Apr.–Oct., weekdays 9:30–5:30; Nov.–Mar. by appointment.*

A 15th-century castle on the edge of Corofin houses the **Clare Archaeology Centre,** which has an exhibition on the antiquities of the Burren. Twenty-five monuments stand within a 1½-km (1-mi) radius of the castle; these date from the Bronze Age to the 19th century, and all are described at the center. ⊠ *Dysert O'Dea Castle* ☎ *065/683–7722* 🖾 *€4* ☉ *Daily 10–6.*

Lahinch

❹ *30 km (18 mi) west of Ennis on N85.*

Lahinch, a busy resort village beside a long, sandy beach backed by dunes, is best known for its links golf courses and—believe it or not—its surfing. In 1972 the European Surfing Finals were held here, putting Lahinch on the world surfing map, where it has stayed ever since. Tom and Rosemary Buckley's **Lahinch Surf Shop** (⊠ The Promenade ☎ 065/708–1543) is the main center for County Clare surfers. But the center ring here is occupied by golf—with three world-class courses and a dazzling bayview backdrop, Lahinch is often called the "St. Andrews of Ireland."

Where to Stay & Eat

$$$ ✕🖾 **Moy House.** Built for Sir Augustine Fitzgerald, this enchanting,
Fodor'sChoice 18th-century Italianate-style lodge sits amid 15 private acres on an ex-
★ hilarating, "Wuthering Heights"–like windswept cliff-top that's a three-minute drive from Lahinch. It's a world away from the bustling seaside resort—a peaceful haven, where you are made to feel like you are a guest in a privately-owned country house. The decor is most alluring, with period velvet sofas, marble fireplaces, and gilt-framed paintings. Upstairs, brocade curtains and Oriental rugs complement the guest rooms' Georgian and Victorian polished mahogany antiques. Some rooms have open fires, some have free-standing cast-iron bathtubs, six have stunning sea views, and two overlook the pretty, sheltered garden. Once you settle in, enjoy a drink at the "honesty bar" in the elegant drawing room (help yourself, and write it down), one of many touches that make the place so relaxing. In bad weather, curl up with a book in the peaceful library on the lower floor. Guests are given the run of the kitchen should they need to rustle up a snack in the night. The cozy dining room (guests only) serves an imaginative four-course dinner of contemporary cuisine. The real dessert is the vista from the veranda over Lahinch Bay. ⊠ *Milltown Malbay Rd., Co. Clare* ☎ *065/708–2800* 🖨 *065/708–2500* ⊕ *www.*

moyhouse.com ⤴ 9 rooms ᚼ Dining room, in-room data ports; no a/c ▭ AE, MC, V ⊘ Closed 1st 2 wks of Jan. ⌑ BP.

$–$$$ ✕⌑ **Berry Lodge.** Just south of Milltown Malbay, 8 km (5 mi) south of Lahinch (near the turn-off for Spanish Point) and way out in the country but within view of the sea, this is a good choice for people who relish peace and quiet, birdsong, and simple home comforts. The traditional two-story, white-painted, slate-roofed house dates from 1775, and has been in Rita Meade's family for three generations. At an age when most of us would be putting our feet up, Rita not only runs the guesthouse and restaurant but hosts a popular local radio show on cooking. The country-pine pieces in her crisply clean rooms are genuine antiques, beds are covered in patchwork quilts, and the sprigged curtains have pretty tiebacks. Floors are genuine old pine, fireplaces are originals, and the rooms are dotted with local craft work. You eat in a large room with a sofa and armchairs at one end, and a tall dresser laden with family treasures (reservations essential; telephone to confirm restaurant is open from September to June, when opening is subject to demand—otherwise open daily July and August). Cooking is simple and unfussy, the fresh local ingredients first-rate. A typical main course might be slow-roasted spiced duckling with red onion marmalade and a Guinness, honey, and orange sauce. ✉ Annagh, Milltown Malbay ☎ 065/708-7022 📠 065/ 708-7011 ⊕ www.berrylodge.com ⤴ 5 rooms ᚼ No a/c, no room phones ▭ MC, V ⊘ Closed Jan.–mid-Feb.

$$ ⌑ **The Greenbrier Inn.** A well-designed modern building, this inn was designed as a guesthouse and both the guest rooms and the large lounge–dining room overlook Lahinch's famous golf links, Liscannor Bay, and the Atlantic Ocean. Set 250 yards from the beach, with ample parking, this is a practical, good-value choice for golfers and for those who like things traditional-modern and uncomplicated. The location and the views are the strong points here. Rooms are a good size, and have double-glazed windows with great views; some have small balconies. ✉ Ennistymon Rd., Co. Clare ☎ 065/708–1242 📠 065/708–1247 ⊕ www. greenbrierinn.com ⤴ 14 rooms ▭ MC, V ⊘ Closed early Jan.–early Mar. ⌑ BP.

Nightlife & the Arts

For traditional music try the **19th Bar** (✉ Main St. ☎ 065/708–1440). **O'Looney's** (✉ The Promenade ☎ 065/708–1414) is known as Lahinch's surfers' pub; there's music every night in summer and on Saturday nights in winter.

Sports & the Outdoors

Doonbeg Golf Club (✉ On main N67 between Lahinch and Kilkee, Doonbeg ☎ 065/905–5246), an 18-hole links course designed by Greg Norman, winds along 2½ km (1½ mi) of crescent-shape beach; the ocean is visible from almost every hole. The 6,613-yard, 18-hole, par-72 championship course at **Lahinch Golf Club** (✉ The Seafront ☎ 065/708–1003), which opened in 1892, has challenging links that follow the natural contours of the dunes. The 18-hole, par-72 **Castle Course** (✉ The Seafront ☎ 065/708–1003) is ideal for a carefree round of seaside golf, with shorter holes than the championship course at Lahinch Golf Club.

Shopping

The small **Design Lodge** (✉ Main St. ☎ 065/708–1744) carries Irish-made goods, including sweaters, linen, tweed, and other gift items.

The Cliffs of Moher

★ ❺ *10 km (6 mi) northwest of Lahinch on R478.*

One of Ireland's most breathtaking natural sights, the majestic Cliffs of Moher rise vertically out of the sea in a wall that stretches over a long, 8-km (5-mi) swath and in places reaches a height of 710 feet. Stratified deposits of five different rock layers are visible in the cliff face. This was considered a venerated place in the Celtic era and a favorite hunting retreat by Brian Boru, the High King of Ireland. Numerous seabirds, including a large colony of puffins, make their homes in the shelves of rock on the cliffs. On a clear day you can see the Aran Islands and the mountains of Connemara to the north, as well as the lighthouse on Loop Head and the mountains of Kerry to the south. Built in 1835 by Cornelius O'Brien—of Bunratty Castle fame and a descendant of the Kings of Thomond—**O'Brien's Tower** is a defiant, broody sentinel built at the cliffs' highest point and was built to encourage tourism (yes, there were even tourists back then). Cornelius also erected here a wall of Moher flagstones (noted for their imprints of prehistoric eels). His tower is located near the village of Liscannor. The **Visitor Centre,** a good refuge from passing rain squalls, has a gift shop and tearoom. Its parking area is a favorite spot of performers; in high season, there's likely to be free entertainment—step dancers, fiddle players, or even a one-man band. ☎ *065/708–1565* ⊕ *www.shannonheritage.com* ✇ *Free, parking €2.50* ☉ *Cliffs daily, 24 hrs; Visitor Centre daily 9:30–5:30; O'Brien's Tower Mar.–Oct., daily 9:30–5:30, weather permitting.*

Doolin

❻ *6 km (4 mi) north of the Cliffs of Moher on R479.*

A tiny village consisting almost entirely of B&Bs, hostels, pubs, and restaurants, Doolin is widely reputed to have three of the best pubs in Ireland for traditional music. But with the worldwide surge of interest in Irish music during the last decade, the village is more of a magnet for European musicians than it is for young, or even established, Irish artists. On **Doolin Pier,** about 1½ km (1 mi) outside the village, fisherfolk sell their fresh catch right off the boat—lobster, crayfish, salmon, and mackerel.

Doolin Ferries (☎ 065/707–4455) makes the 30-minute trip from Doolin Pier to Inisheer, the smallest of the Aran Islands, from spring until early fall (weather permitting). There are at least three round-trip sailings a day, and up to eight in July and August, but inquire on the day you plan to embark, as schedules vary according to weather and demand. Sometimes more than one ferry company operates out of Doolin; your return ticket will only be valid with the company that took you out, so when boarding the outbound ferry, be sure to check the return schedule.

Where to Stay & Eat

Because Doolin is known as a center of traditional music, it gets quite crowded with foreign visitors. If you're having trouble finding a room or you want to stay somewhere other than a B&B, you may want to follow the lead of many Irish vacationers, who tend to stay in nearby Lisdoonvarna, which is just 5 km (3 mi) away and has a wider selection of lodgings.

★ **$$–$$$**   ✕▣ **Ballinalacken Castle.** One hundred acres of wildflower meadows surround this restored, low-slung Victorian lodge, which was built beside the 16th-century ruins of an O'Brien castle—hence its name. It's one of the most memorably sited of Ireland's coastal inns, with panoramic views of the Atlantic, the Aran Islands, and distant Connemara: the sense of spaciousness is exhilarating, and manager Marian Sheedy reports that many guests regularly oversleep due to the quietness. The public rooms display a mix of comfy old armchairs and antique, baronial-style Irish oak, amid floral wallpaper and rampant aspidistras. Guest rooms in the older house have massive four-poster beds, marble fireplaces, and high ceilings. Some large, sunny rooms have bay windows to frame that stunning view; nice but plainer rooms, with antique-style decor, in the new wing are equally sought after. Chef Frank Sheedy, who has cooked in some of Ireland's best restaurants, serves an imaginative and sophisticated Continental menu ($$$$)—you'll want to finish off your feast of roast loin of Burren lamb with a platter of Cashel blue, Cooney, and smoked Gubeen cheeses. Book in advance or you may not get a table. Ballinalacken is about 1 km (½ mi) outside Doolin on the Lisdoonvarna road. ⊠ *Coast Rd., Co. Clare* ☎ *065/707–4025* 🖶 *065/707–4025* ⊕ *www.ballinalackencastle.com* ⤙ *19 rooms, 2 suites* ⚖ *Restaurant, bar; no a/c* ▤ *AE, DC, MC, V* ⊘ *Closed Nov.–mid-Apr.* ⏀ *BP.*

$–$$ ✕▣ **Aran View House.** This extensively modernized 1736 house on 100 acres of farmland offers magnificent views in nearly every direction: the Aran Islands to the west, the Cliffs of Moher to the south, and the gray limestone rocks of the Burren to the north. The interior is decorated with antique touches, such as four-poster beds and Georgian reproduction furniture. You can savor the view from the restaurant's bay windows while enjoying the Continental cuisine ($$–$$$$), featuring top seafood, with an atmosphere nicely enhanced by Regency chairs and dusky pink napery. It's on the coast road in the Fanore direction, about a 10-minute walk north from Doolin village. ⊠ *Coast Rd., Co. Clare* ☎ *065/707–4061* 🖶 *065/707–4540* ⊕ *www.aranview.com* ⤙ *19 rooms* ⚖ *Restaurant, bar; no a/c* ▤ *AE, DC, MC, V* ⊘ *Closed Nov.–mid-Apr.* ⏀ *BP.*

★ **$**   ✕▣ **Cullinan's Seafood Restaurant and Guesthouse.** The small restaurant ($$–$$$) here, in the back of a modest traditional farmhouse, is famed for its fresh, simply prepared seafood, but vegetarian and meat dishes are also served. Local ingredients—Inagh goat cheese, Burren smoked salmon, Doolin crabmeat, and Aran scallops—form the basis of a light, imaginative menu. A €25 early-bird set menu is served from 6 to 7. The floor-to-ceiling windows on two sides of the restaurant overlook the Aille River. The cottage-style rooms have simple pine furniture, fresh cotton-covered comforters, pleasant country views, and room TVs on request. ⊠ *Coast Rd., Co. Clare* ☎ *065/707–4183* 🖶 *065/707–4239* ⊕ *www.*

cullinansdoolin.com ⊸ 6 rooms ⚘ *Restaurant; no a/c* ⊟ *MC, V* ☉ *Guesthouse closed Christmas wk, restaurant closed Oct.–Easter* ⑩ *BP.*

Nightlife & the Arts

Doolin's three pubs are famous for their traditional-music sessions. They all serve simple bar food from midday until 9 (Irish stew is a good bet) and are designed to hold big crowds, which means you should expect minimal comfort: hard benches or bar stools if you're lucky, and spit-and-sawdust flooring. The theory is that the music will be so good, you won't notice anything else. Interesting music-related memorabilia hang on the walls. **Gus O'Connor's** (⊠ Fisher St. ☎ 065/707–4168) sits midway between the village center and the pier and has tables outside near a stream. **McDermott's** (⊠ Lisdoonvarna Rd. ☎ 065/707–4700) is popular with locals. Autumn through spring it's sometimes closed during the daytime. **McGann's** (⊠ Lisdoonvarna Rd. ☎ 065/707–4133), across the road from McDermott's, is the smallest of Doolin's three famous pubs and has been run by the same family for 70 years.

Sports & the Outdoors

Cycle along the coast on a bike rented from **Patrick Moloney, Doolin Hostel** (⊠ Coast Rd. ☎ 065/707–4006).

Shopping

★ **Doolin Crafts Gallery** (⊠ Coast Rd. ☎ 065/707–4309), beside the cemetery and the church, carries only Irish-made goods: sweaters, modern lead crystal, linen, lace, and tweed. A jeweler's workshop and a resident batik-maker are also on the premises. Don't miss the 1-acre garden, which has more than 600 plants from all over the world. The garden and the Flagship Restaurant are open daily from Easter through September.

Lisdoonvarna

❼ *5 km (3 mi) east of Doolin on R478.*

One of only three spa towns in Ireland (the others are Enniscrone, in western County Sligo, and Ballybunion, in County Kerry), Lisdoonvarna has several sulfurous and iron-bearing springs with radioactive properties, all containing iodine. In the late 19th century the town grew to accommodate visitors who wanted to "take the waters"; today, a major refurbishment of the spa facilities is underway. The buildings reflect a mishmash of mock architectural styles: Scottish baronial, Swiss chalet, Spanish hacienda, and American motel. Depending on your taste, it's either lovably kitschy or just plain tacky. It is a popular weekend spot for Dubliners and other Irish vacationers, who stay at the big hotels (not those below) and many of these roustabouts like to party well into the night. It's also the traditional vacation spot for the west's bachelor farmers, who used to congregate here at harvest time in late September with the vague intention of finding wives. (Irish farmers are notoriously shy with women; many don't marry until their mid- or late fifties, if ever.) This tradition is now formalized in the Matchmaking Festival, held during late September. Middle-aged singles (and some in their sixties, seventies, and eighties) dance to the strains of country-and-western bands, and a talent contest is held to name the most eligible bachelor. If you're curious about health cures, the **Lisdoonvarna Spa and Bath House** is worth a visit. Iron and magnesia elements make the drinking water taste terrible (as does most spa water), but the bathing water is pleasant, if enervating. Electric sulfur baths, massage, wax baths, a sauna, and a solarium are available at the spa complex, which is on the edge of town in an attractive parkland setting. ✉ *Town Park* ☎ *065/707–4023* 💳 *Complex free, sulfur baths €6.50 (book in advance)* ☼ *Early June–early Oct., daily 10–6, subject to refurbishment: check in advance by phone.*

Where to Stay & Eat

★ $–$$ ✕🏨 **Sheedy's Restaurant and Country Inn.** A 17th-century farmhouse just a short walk from the town center and the spa wells has been converted into this small, friendly hotel. It's been in the hands of the Sheedy family since 1855. Proprietor John Sheedy, who was chef de cuisine at Ashford Castle until moving back home, makes creative use of local produce in contemporary French-Irish fare ($$–$$$), and has turned Sheedy's into a much-lauded gastronomic destination. The green-grey dining room with plain, candlelit tables provides a suitably sophisticated background for John's unusual and confident cooking. Try his fresh prawn soup, or a starter of warm salad of roasted monkfish with smoked bacon, mushrooms, and champagne dressing. His menu also features classic dishes like slow-roasted crispy duck with potato stuffing and apple sauce. The guest rooms are spacious and well-designed, with hip touches like power showers and CD players. All have relaxing views of the hilly surrounding countryside. ✉ *Spa Rd., Co. Clare* ☎ *065/707–4026* 📠 *065/707–4555* ⊕ *www.sheedyscountryhouse.com* ⟋ *11 rooms* ⌂ *Restaurant, bar; no a/c* ▤ *MC, V* ☼ *Closed Oct.–mid-Mar.* ⦿ *BP.*

★ $ ✕🏨 **Carrigann.** Hikers love this small, friendly hotel, ensconced in trim, pretty gardens, and just a two-minute walk from the village center. You get exceptional comfort here for the price. Hosts Mary and Gerard Howard keep a library of books on the Burren beside the turf fire in the sitting room, and are themselves generous sources of information. Choose between setting off with one of Mary's specially prepared walk sheets, join a guided group (most weekends–see hotel Web site), or hire your own guide. On return, if your gear is wet it will be taken off to a drying room by one of the friendly staff. Guest rooms are large, quiet, and comfortable, with dark, polished, Victorian-style furniture, quilted cream spreads, and plain *eau de nil*–green carpets. Gerard also runs his own butcher shop, guaranteeing top-quality beef and lamb on the dinner menu ($$–$$$). The dining room is pleasantly unfussy, with cream linen cloths and napkins, fresh flowers on the tables, and comfortable cream-upholstered chairs. Try a starter of pan-seared sea scallops with black pudding on potato blini with whole-grain mustard sauce, or a more conventional platter of local smoked salmon, trout, mackerel, and eel with a dill dressing. Menus usually showcase char-grilled sirloin steak, while a simpler bar-food menu is also available. ✉ *Carrigann Rd., Co. Clare* ☎ *065/707–4036* 📠 *065/707–4567* ⊕ *www.gateway-to-the-burren.com* ⟋ *20 rooms* ⌂ *Restaurant, fishing; no a/c* ▤ *MC, V* ☼ *Closed Nov.–Feb.* ⦿ *BP.*

Nightlife & the Arts

Country music and ballad singing are popular in the bars of Lisdoonvarna. For traditional music try the **Roadside Tavern** (⊠ Doolin Rd.
☎ 065/707–4084).

Shopping

To see an audiovisual presentation on smoking Atlantic salmon, plus
live demonstrations of the oak-smoking process, visit the **Burren Smoke-
house Ltd** (⊠ Ballyvaughan Rd. ☎ 065/707–4432). Neatly packaged whole
sides of salmon, organic treats, and unusual crafts are for sale.

The Burren

★ ❽ *Extending throughout western County Clare from the Cliffs of Moher
in the south to Black Head in the north, as far southeast as Corofin.*

As you travel north toward Ballyvaughan, the landscape becomes rock-
ier and stranger. Instead of the seemingly ubiquitous Irish green, gray
becomes the prevailing color. You're now in the heart of the Burren, a
300-square-km (116-square-mi) expanse that is one of Ireland's strangest
landscapes. The Burren is aptly named: it's an Anglicization of the Irish
word *bhoireann* (a rocky place). Stretching off in all directions, as far
as the eye can see, are vast, irregular slabs of fissured limestone, known
as karst, with deep cracks between them. From a distance, it looks like
a lunar landscape, so dry that nothing could possibly grow on it. But
in spring (especially from mid-May to mid-June), the Burren becomes
a wild rock garden as an astonishing variety of wildflowers blooms between the cracks in the rocks, among them at least 23 native species of
orchid. The Burren also supports an incredible diversity of wildlife, including frogs, newts, lizards, badgers, stoats, sparrow hawks, kestrels,
and dozens of other birds and animals. The wildflowers and other
plants are given life from the spectacular caves, streams, and potholes
that lie beneath the rough, scarred pavements. With the advent of spring,
turloughs (seasonal lakes that disappear in dry weather) appear on the
plateau's surface. Botanists are particularly intrigued by the cohabita-
tion of Arctic and Mediterranean plants, many so tiny (and so rare, so
please do not pick any) you can't see them from your car window; make
a point of exploring some of this rocky terrain on foot. Numerous signposted walks run through both coastal and inland areas. For a private
guided tour, contact Mary Angela Keane (☎ 065/707–4003 ✍ €35 per
hour), or Shane Connolly of Burren Hill Walks (☎ 065/707–7168
✍ €15 per person). May and June are peak months for flora, but a tour
is worthwhile at any time of year.

The tiny **Burren Centre** has a modest audiovisual display and other exhibits that explain the Burren's geology, flora, and archaeology. Also here
are a café and a crafts shop with good maps and locally published
guides. ⊠ *8 km (5 mi) southeast of Lisdoonvarna on R476, Kilfenora*
☎ *065/708–8030* ⊕ *www.theburrencentre.ie* ✍ *€5* ⊙ *Mid-Mar.–May,
Sept., and Oct., daily 10–5; June–Aug., daily 9:30–6.*

Beside the Burren Centre in Kilfenora, the ruins of a small 12th-century
church, once the **Cathedral of St. Fachtna,** have been partially restored

as a parish church. There are some interesting carvings in the roofless choir, including an unusual, life-size human skeleton. In a field about 165 feet west of the ruins is an elaborately sculpted high cross that is worth examining, even though parts of it are badly weathered.

Nightlife & the Arts

Vaughan's Pub (✉ Main St., Kilfenora ☎ 065/708–8004) is known for its traditional-music sessions.

Ballyvaughan

❾ *16 km (10 mi) north of Lisdoonvarna on N67.*

A pretty little waterside village and a good base for exploring the Burren, Ballyvaughan attracts walkers and artists who enjoy the views of Galway Bay and access to the Burren. **Aillwee Cave** is the only such chamber in the region accessible to those who aren't spelunkers. This vast 2-million-year-old cave is illuminated for about 3,300 feet and contains an underground river and waterfall. ✉ *5 km (3 mi) south of Ballyvaughan on R480* ☎ *065/707–7036* ⊕ *www.aillweecave.ie* ✆ *€8* ⊙ *Jan.–June and Sept.–Dec., daily 10–6 (last tour at 5:30); July and Aug., daily 10–7 (last tour at 6:30).*

Where to Stay & Eat

¢–$ ✗ **Trí na Chéile.** A shop front in the center of Ballyvaughan leads into an attractive room fitted with skylights, a high wooden Dutch ceiling, and an old-style varnished flag floor. Real ladder-back súgan chairs (with rush seats) bring Irish style to simple oilcloth-covered tables. The friendly staff brings out the honest fare, a mix of old familiars—pasta dishes, warm salads, the ubiquitous seafood chowder—and Irish specials. Irish stew with creamed potatoes is a favorite, as are Irish bacon and colcannon (cabbage and potato), and salmon with potato gratin. This spot is open from noon until "late"; reservations are advised in July and August. ✉ *Main St.* ☎ *065/707–7103* ▤ *MC, V* ⊙ *Closed Nov.–Feb.*

★ $$–$$$ ✗▥ **Gregan's Castle Hotel.** Sharon Stone, Gabriel Byrne, and Edna O'Brien have all been guests at this quiet, meticulous, creeper-covered and highly romantic Victorian country house, set at the base of the aptly named Corkscrew Hill (on N67, midway between Ballyvaughan and Lisdoonvarna). The Haden family obviously knows a thing or two about hospitality. They certainly know how to decorate in the loveliest fashion—the Corkscrew Bar is a cozy corner hung with copper pots, the guest bedrooms are lined with wallpaper patterns based on William Morris designs and stocked with Georgian and Victorian antiques, while the dining room allures in brilliant red. The house is surrounded by gardens and overlooks Galway Bay and the gray mountains of the Burren. The spacious ground-floor rooms have private patio gardens but lack the splendid views of the rooms upstairs. Ask about special deals for three-day stays. The restaurant ($$$–$$$$; jacket and tie required) serves updated French cuisine. ✉ *Base of Corkscrew Hill, Co. Clare* ☎ *065/707–7005* 🖷 *065/707–7111* ⊕ *www.gregans.ie* ✆ *18 rooms, 4 suites* ⚘ *Restaurant, fishing, bicycles, croquet, bar; no room TVs, no a/c* ▤ *AE, MC, V* ⊙ *Closed Nov.–Mar.* ⦿ *BP.*

$ ╳🖼 **Hyland's Hotel.** A turf fire greets you in the lobby of the hotel, a cheerful, welcoming spot with a reputation for friendliness and good entertainment. This unpretentious yellow-and-red coaching inn, in the heart of the Burren, dates from the early 18th century, and has been much extended and added-to. Rooms vary in size and shape, but all have pine furniture and color-coordinated drapes and spreads. Ask for a room overlooking the Burren. The restaurant ($$), cheerfully decorated with country pine and red tablecloths, specializes in simply prepared local produce. The bar hosts live music most nights from June to mid-September, and Irish storytelling once a week. Ask about special weekend rates. ✉ *Main St., Co. Clare* ☎ *065/707–7037* 🖷 *065/707–7131* ⌨ *30 rooms* ♿ *Restaurant, bar; no a/c* ▤ *AE, DC, MC, V* ⍾ *BP.*

$ 🖼 **Drumcreehy House.** The pretty gabled facade with dormer windows is traditional in style, but, in fact, Bernadette Moloney and her German husband, Armin Grefkes, designed and built this house specifically as a B&B. It is just across the road from the sea, about 1 mi north of the village, just beyond the Whitethorn Craft Shop. The interior has character and style, thanks to a mix of imposing 19th-century German antiques, stripped pine floors, and comfortable sofas and armchairs. Rooms are spacious and well-aired, with small sitting areas overlooking the peaceful countryside. Each room is individually styled on a wildflower theme, with plain walls, color-coordinated quilts and curtains, brass bed-heads, and attractive small antiques. A light, bar-food style menu is served in the lounge, where you can also take a glass of wine; from April to October you can reserve for a more formal evening meal. The multichoice breakfast offers an unusually wide choice, including French toast, kippers, or creamed mushrooms on toast. Your hosts are knowledgeable and enthusiastic about the area, and have a good supply of books and maps. ☎ *065/707–7377* 🖷 *065/707–7379* ⊕ *www.drumcreehyhouse.com* ⌨ *12 rooms* ♿ *No a/c, no smoking* ▤ *MC, V.*

Nightlife & the Arts

FodorśChoice The friendly **Monk's Pub** (✉ Main St. ☎ 065/707–7059), near the wa-
★ terfront, hosts great sessions of traditional and folk music. The bar food is excellent.

Coole Park

❿ *24 km (15 mi) northeast of Corofin on N18.*

Coole Park, north of the little town of Gort, was once the home of Lady Augusta Gregory (1859–1932), patron of W. B. Yeats and cofounder with the poet of Dublin's Abbey Theatre. Yeats visited here often, as did almost all the other writers who contributed to the Irish literary revival in the first half of the 20th century, including George Bernard Shaw (1856–1950) and Sean O'Casey (1880–1964). Douglas Hyde (1860–1949), the first president of Ireland, was also a visitor. The house fell derelict after Lady Gregory's death and was demolished in 1941; the grounds are now a national forest and wildlife park. Picnic tables make this a lovely alfresco lunch spot. The only reminder of its literary past is the Autograph Tree, a copper beech on which many of Lady Gregory's famous guests carved their initials. There is also a visitor center with displays on Lady Gregory and Yeats. ⊠ *Galway Rd.* ☎ *091/631–804* 🖃 *Park free, visitor center* €3 ⊗ *Park daily 10–dusk; visitor center Apr.–mid-June, Tues.–Sun. 10–5; mid-June–Aug., daily 9:30–6:30; Sept., daily 10–5.*

Thoor Ballylee

⓫ *5 km (3 mi) north of Coole Park, signposted from N66.*

Thoor Ballylee is a sight Yeats fans won't want to miss. (It's one of the few major Yeats-related sights in the west that's not in County Sligo.) In his fifties and newly married, Yeats bought this 14th-century Norman "thoor," or tower, as a ruin in 1916 for £35 (about €44). The tower stands beside a whitewashed, thatched-roof cottage with a tranquil stream running alongside it. Its proximity to Lady Gregory's house at Coole Park made this a desirable location, though it required significant work on Yeats's part to make the ruin livable. He stayed here intermittently until 1929 and penned some of his more mystical works here, including *The Tower* and *The Winding Stair*. It's now fully restored and some rooms showcase the poet's original furnishings. The audiovisual display is a useful introduction to Yeats and his times. High up the tower's parapet you can get some great views of Coole's Seven Woods. ⊠ *N66, 3 mi north of Gort* ☎ *091/631–436* 🖃 €5 ⊗ *Easter–Sept., Mon.–Sat. 10–6.*

Kinvara

★ **⓬** *13½ km (8 mi) east of Ballyvaughan, 15 km (9 mi) northwest of Gort on N67, 25 km (15½ mi) south of Galway City.*

The picture-perfect village of Kinvara is a growing holiday base, thanks to its gorgeous bayside locale, great walking and sea angling, and numerous pubs. It's well worth a visit, whether you're coming from Ballyvaughan or Gort. Kinvara is best known for its long-standing early August sailing event, Cruinniú na mBád (Festival of the Gathering of the Boats), in which traditional brown-sailed Galway hookers laden with turf race across the bay. Hookers were used until the early part of this century to carry turf, provisions, and cattle across Galway Bay and out to the Aran Islands. A sculpture in Galway's Eyre Square honors their local significance.

★ On a rock north of Kinvara Bay, the 16th-century **Dunguaire Castle** spectacularly commands all the approaches to Galway Bay. It is said to stand on the site of a 7th-century castle built by the King of Connaught. Built in 1520 by the O'Hynes clan, the tiny, storybook castle takes its name from the fabled King of Connaught, Guaire. In 1929 it was purchased by Oliver St. John Gogarty, the noted surgeon, man of letters, and model for Buck Mulligan, a character in James Joyce's *Ulysses*. To his outpost came many of the leading figures of the 19th-century Celtic revival in Irish literature. Today Dunguaire is used for a "Middle-Ages" style banquet that honors local writers and others with ties to the west, including Lady Gregory, W. B. Yeats, Sean O'Casey, and Pádraic O'-Conaire. ⊠ *West Village* ☎ *091/637–108* ⊕ *www.shannonheritage.*

com ⌘ *Castle €5, banquet €47.50* ⊘ *May–Sept., daily 9:30–5; banquet at 5:30 and 8:30.*

Where to Stay & Eat

★ **$–$$$** ✕ **Moran's Oyster Cottage.** Signposted off the main road on the south side of Clarinbridge, this waterside thatched cottage, the home of the Moran family since 1760, houses a simply furnished restaurant at the back that serves only seafood: Gigas oysters, chowder, smoked salmon, seafood cocktail, lobster with boiled potatoes and garlic butter, and fresh crab salad. It's *the* place to sample the local oysters, grown on a nearby bed owned by the Moran family, who have had the pub for six generations. Hope for good weather, so that you can eat outside overlooking the weir and watch the swans float by. The front bar has been preserved in the "old style," which means it is small and cramped, but very interesting if you want to get an idea of what most pubs around here were like 50 years ago. ⊠ *The Weir, Kilcolgan* ☎ *091/796–113* 🖶 *091/796–503* ⊟ *AE, MC, V.*

$ ✕▥ **Merriman Inn.** Don't let its traditional looks deceive you: this whitewashed, thatched inn on the shores of Galway Bay is, in fact, a midsize hotel, decorated with locally made, well-designed furniture, and original crafts, paintings, and sculpture. Guest rooms are medium-sized with smallish, cottage-style windows at head height, and modern pine furniture; small paintings of local scenes provide the principal color. If you're lucky you could get a room with a breathtaking view of Galway Bay; less than half have one, so if it matters, ask when booking. The Quilty Room is a large, airy restaurant ($–$$$) hung with interesting landscape and still-life paintings by an artist named Quilty. Its menu is French-influenced—try the outstanding tournedos of salmon pan-seared with a confit of fennel and a sharp, spicy jus. ⊠ *Main St., Co. Galway* ☎ *091/ 638–222* 🖶 *091/637–686* ⊕ *www.merrimanhotel.com* ⇩ *32 rooms* ⌂ *Restaurant, bar; no a/c* ⊟ *AE, DC, MC, V* ⊘ *Closed Jan.–mid-Mar.* ¶○| *BP.*

¢–$ ▥ **Burren View Farm.** A million-dollar view awaits you at this modest, yellow, two-story B&B on the edge of Galway Bay, 5 km (3 mi) west of Kinvara. Set on a working sheep and cattle farm, it is relatively isolated amid stone-walled fields dotted with sheep. The breakfast room, sun lounge, and front bedrooms look out across a wide sea inlet to the gray expanse of the Burren. Rooms are plain and homey but clean and well maintained. Wholesome evening meals, Irish or Continental style, are cooked on request, and food is also available in the local pub, a 5-minute walk away. ⊠ *Doorus, Co. Galway* ☎ *091/637–142* ⊕ *www. homepagetennis/~burrenviewfarm* ⇩ *5 rooms, 2 with bath* ⌂ *Dining room, tennis court, fishing; no a/c, no room phones, no room TVs* ⊘ *Closed Nov.–Mar.* ¶○| *BP.*

Nightlife & the Arts

The first weekend in May, Kinvara hosts the annual **Cuckoo Fleadh** (⊠ Main St. ☎ 091/637–145), a traditional-music festival. Traditional music is played most nights at the **Winkles Hotel bar** (⊠ The Square ☎ 91/ 637–137), where Sharon Shannon got her start in the music business.

GALWAY CITY

25 km (15½ mi) north of Kinvara, 219 km (136 mi) west of Dublin, 105 km (65 mi) north of Limerick.

Galway is often said to be a state of mind as much as it is a specific place. The largest city in the west today (population 60,000) and the ancient capital of the province of Connaught, Galway is also one of the fastest-growing cities in Europe. It's an astonishing fact, and you have to wonder where this city can possibly grow. For despite Galway's size, its commercially busy ring road, and its ever-spreading suburbs, its heart is *tiny*—a warren of streets so compact that if you spend more than a few hours here, you'll soon be strolling along with the sort of easy familiarity you'd feel in your hometown.

For many Irish people, Galway is a favorite weekend getaway: known as the city of festivals, it's the liveliest place in the Republic. It's also a university town: University College Galway (or UCG as it's locally known) is a center for Gaelic culture (Galway marks the eastern gateway to the west's large Gaeltacht). A fair share of UCG's 9,000 students pursue their studies in the Irish language. Galway is, in fact, permeated by youth culture. On festival weekends, you'll see as many pierced and tattooed teenagers and twentysomethings here as you'd find at a rock concert. (If you're looking for the quiet, quaint side of Ireland depicted on travel posters, have a quick look at Galway and push on to Clifden or Westport, where you can still savor the atmosphere of a small old-world town.) But its students aren't its only avant-garde, as Galway has long attracted writers, artists, and musicians. The latter whip up brand-new jigs while they keep the traditional-music pubs lively year-round. And the city's two small but internationally acclaimed theater companies draw a steady stream of theater people.

Although you're not conscious of it when you're in the center of town, Galway is spectacularly situated, on the north shore of Galway Bay, where the River Corrib flows from Lough Corrib to the sea. The seaside suburb of Salthill, on the south-facing shore of Galway Bay, has spectacular vistas across the vividly blue bay to Black Head on the opposite shore.

Galway's founders were Anglo-Normans who arrived in the mid-13th century and fortified their settlement against "the native Irish," as local chieftains were called. Galway became known as "the City of the Tribes" because of the dominant role in public and commercial life of the 14 families that founded it. Their names are still common in Galway and elsewhere in Ireland: Athy, Blake, Bodkin, Browne, D'Arcy, Dean, Font, French, Kirwan, Joyce, Lynch, Morris, Martin, and Skerret. The city's medieval heritage, a fusion of Gaelic and Norman influences, is apparent in the intimate two- and three-story stucco buildings, the winding streets, the narrow passageways, and the cobblestones underfoot.

Galway's growth and popularity mean that at its busiest moments, pedestrians jam-pack its narrow, one-way streets, while cars are gridlocked. If there's a city that doesn't sleep in Ireland, this is it. In fact, if you want to be guaranteed a quiet night's sleep, either ask for a room in the back of your center-city hotel or simply stay outside of town.

Exploring Galway City

Most of the city's sights, aside from the cathedral and the university campus, can be found in a narrow sector of the medieval town center that runs from Eyre Square in a southwesterly direction to the River Corrib. Eyre Square is easily recognizable, as it is the only green space in central Galway. It only takes five minutes to walk straight down Galway's main shopping street, the continuation of the north side of Eyre Square, to the River Corrib, where it ends (note that the name of this street changes several times). Not only is the city center compact, it is also largely pedestrian-friendly, so the best way to explore it is on foot. Even the farthest point, the university campus, is less than a 15-minute walk from Eyre Square. A walk (or drive, for that matter) to Galway's seaside suburb, Salthill, 3 km (2 mi) west of Galway, and its long seaside promenade, is a favorite local occupation, traditionally undertaken on a Sunday afternoon.

a good walk

Orient yourself at **Eyre Square** ⑬ ⌐, part of which is occupied by Kennedy Park. Before you really get going, you may want to stop in at the **Tourist Information Office** ⑭ on Forster Street, off the east corner of the square. At the top (north side) of Eyre Square, turn left down Williamsgate Street. This is the spine of old Galway. Its name changes four times before the street reaches the River Corrib: it's successively called William Street, Shop Street, High Street, and Quay Street. If you have postcards to mail, you may want to stop at the General Post Office, on the left side of Eglinton Street, the first right off Williamsgate Street. At the corner of William and Shop streets, **Lynch's Castle** ⑮ is one of Galway's oldest buildings. Continue down Shop Street to the pedestrian way just beyond Abbeygate Street; here **Lynch Memorial Window** ⑯ and **Collegiate Church of St. Nicholas** ⑰ are adjacent to one another. James Joyce fans might want to make a brief detour across Lombard and Market streets to Bowling Green, site of the **Nora Barnacle House** ⑱.

It's a minute's walk from the church to **Tigh Neachtain** ⑲ ("Naughton's" in English, but pronounced *knock*-tons), a pub popular with locals, that stands at the corner of Cross Street and Quay/High Street. This corner is the very heart of old Galway's main historic and commercial district: nearly all the city's best restaurants, bars, boutiques, art galleries, crafts shops, antiques stores, and bookstores line the narrow, winding streets and alleys in this vicinity. Nothing is more than a five-minute walk from anything else. If this area is bursting at the seams, you may want to head one block to the east of Shop/High Street, between Abbeygate and Cross streets, to quieter Middle Street, which has worthwhile stores and restaurants, as well as the national Irish-language theater.

The **Spanish Arch** ⑳ and the **Galway City Museum** ㉑ are adjacent, right on the river's east bank, across from the Jurys Galway Inn parking lot. Just beyond Jurys but before crossing the Wolfe Tone Bridge, turn right onto the pedestrian path that parallels the river. Follow it past the

William O'Brien Bridge to the **Salmon Weir Bridge** ㉒ (you'll need to jog off the path onto Abbeygate Street just short of the bridge to gain access to it). As you cross the bridge, look ahead to the **Cathedral of Our Lady Assumed into Heaven and St. Nicholas** ㉓, known locally simply as "the cathedral." A five-minute walk northwest along University Road brings you to **University College Galway** ㉔. For a pretty stroll back to the center of town, turn right onto Canal Road and follow it back to the intersection of Dominick Street, Fairhill, and Raven Terrace. From here it's a brief stroll to Claddagh Quay, which will take you out to the **Claddagh** ㉕ district. If you've come this far, you may want to continue on to **Salthill** ㉖; otherwise, head back to the center of town.

TIMING You could easily complete this walk in a morning or afternoon (minus the walk out to Salthill), although if you browse in stores, chat with locals, or stop off for a pint or a cup of tea, you could stretch it out into a *very* leisurely all-day excursion. You may want to plan your day so you hit only what most interests you, leaving time to explore along the bay, get out to Salthill, or take a bay cruise.

What to See

㉓ **Cathedral of Our Lady Assumed into Heaven and St. Nicholas.** On Nun's Island, which forms the west bank of the River Corrib beside the Salmon Weir Bridge, stands Galway's largest Catholic church, dedicated by Cardinal Cushing of Boston in 1965. The cathedral was built on the site of the old Galway jail; a white cross embedded in the pavement of the adjacent parking lot marks the site of the cemetery that stood beside the prison. ▨ *Free* ☉ *Freely accessible.*

㉕ **Claddagh.** On the west bank of the Corrib estuary, this district was once an Irish-speaking fishing village outside the walls of the old town. The name is an Anglicization of the Irish *cladach,* which means "marshy ground." It retained a strong, separate identity until the 1930s, when its traditional thatched cottages were replaced by a conventional housing plan and its unique character and traditions were largely lost. One thing has survived: the Claddagh ring, composed of two hands clasped around a heart with a crown above it (symbolizing love, friendship, and loyalty), is still used by many Irish people as a wedding ring. Traditionally, the ring, which is often passed down from mother to daughter, is worn with the heart facing into you if you're married or otherwise unavailable and with the heart facing outward (indicating your heart is open) if you're still looking for Mr. or Ms. Right. Reproductions in gold or silver are favorite Galway souvenirs.

⑰ **Collegiate Church of St. Nicholas.** Built by the Anglo-Normans in 1320 and enlarged in 1486 and again in the 16th century, the church contains many fine carvings and gargoyles dating from the late Middle Ages, and it is one of the best-preserved medieval churches in Ireland. Legend has it that Columbus prayed here on his last stop before setting off on his voyage to the New World. On Saturday mornings, a street market, held in the pedestrian way beside the church, attracts two dozen or so vendors and hundreds of shoppers. ⊠ *Lombard St., Center* ▨ *Free* ☉ *Daily 8–dusk.*

Galway City

► ⓭ **Eyre Square.** The largest open space in central Galway and the heart of the city, on the east side of the River Corrib, Eyre Square encompasses a hodgepodge of monuments and concrete and grassy areas. In the center is **Kennedy Park,** a patch of lawn named in honor of John F. Kennedy, who spoke here when he visited the city in June 1963. At the north end of the park, a 20-foot-high steel sculpture standing in the pool of a fountain represents the brown sails seen on Galway hookers, the area's traditional sailing boats. Seated beside this sculpture is the genial stone figure of Pádraic O'Conaire, a pioneer of the Irish-language revival at the turn of the last century who was born in Galway in 1882 (his birthplace, fronting the docks, is marked with a plaque). When he died in a Dublin hospital in 1928, his only possessions were his pipe (a replica of which he holds here), his tobacco, and an apple. Now the entrance to Kennedy Park, the **Browne Doorway** was taken in 1905 from the Browne family's town house on Upper Abbeygate Street; it has the 17th-century coats of arms of both the Browne and Lynch families, called a "marriage stone" because when the families were joined in marriage their coats of arms were, too. Keep an eye out for similar if less elaborate versions of the entranceway as you walk around the old part of town. The **bronze cannons** were presented at the end of the Crimean War (1853–56) to the Connaught Rangers, a legendary regiment of the British Army made up of men recruited from the west of Ireland.

㉑ **Galway City Museum.** The city's civic museum, next door to the Spanish Arch, contains materials relating to local history: old photographs, antiquities (the oldest is a stone axe head carbon-dated to 3500 BC), and other historical gewgaws. ⊠ *The Long Walk, Spanish Arch* ☎ *091/567–641* 🖱 *€1.50* ⊙ *Daily 10–1 and 2:15–5:15.*

⓰ **Lynch Memorial Window.** Embedded in a stone wall above a built-up Gothic doorway off Market Street, the window marks the spot where, according to legend, James Lynch FitzStephen, mayor of Galway in the early 16th century, condemned his son to death after he confessed to murdering a Spanish sailor who had romanced his girlfriend. When no one could be found to carry out the execution, Judge Lynch hanged his son himself, ensuring that justice prevailed, before retiring into seclusion. ⊠ *Market St., Center.*

⓯ **Lynch's Castle.** Now a branch of the Allied Irish Banks, this is the finest remaining example in Galway of a 16th-century fortified house—fortified because neighboring Irish tribes persistently raided the village, whose commercial life excluded them. The decorative details on its stone lintels are of a type usually found only in southern Spain. Like the Spanish Arch, it serves as a reminder of the close trading links that once existed between Galway and Spain. ⊠ *Shop St., Center.*

⓲ **Nora Barnacle House.** On June 16, 1904, James Joyce (1882–1941) had his first date with Nora Barnacle, who would later become his wife. He subsequently chose to set *Ulysses* on this day, now known universally as Bloomsday—"a recognition of the determining effect upon his life of his attachment to her," as Joyce's biographer Richard Ellman has said. Nora, the daughter of a poor baker, was born here. Today it has a modest collection of photographs, letters, and memorabilia, and a small gift

CloseUp

LITTLE EYE-OPENERS

WHILE GALWAY *contains many grandiose monuments, it also holds many obscure yet fascinating relics—things that are only glimpsed on foot by visitors whose eyes aren't too fogged from the previous night's late session.*

Footscrapers: In the 18th century, many areas of the city were unpaved and very mucky in wet weather. Gadgets called footscrapers became popular outside the front doors of prosperous houses, enabling guests to divest themselves of the street ooze before entering. The best examples of these cast-iron contraptions are on either side of the main door of the Great Southern Hotel in Eyre Square.

Jostle stones: These small conical stones were placed at corners of narrow lanes and gateways to prevent carriage drivers from cutting corners too closely and breaking their wheels. One still remains

outside Eason's bookshop on Church Lane.

Mermaids: Galway has more carvings of these sea nymphs than anyplace else in Ireland, and some fine examples can be seen in the windows of Collegiate Church of St. Nicholas on Lombard Street. Local historian Jim Higgins's book Irish Mermaids *documents the many myths surrounding these creatures, including one that dubbed the sighting of a mermaid as a warning of a crime committed and a portent of severe bad luck.*

Marriage stones: Over many doorways are stone plaques bearing two interlinked coats of arms. The plaques commemorate marriages between leading Galway families.

Water troughs: One flower-filled example of these stone creations remains—at the entrance to the Fairgreen car park in Forster Street.

---

shop. ✉ *4 Bowling Green, Center* ☎ *091/564–743* 🎫 *€3* 🕐 *Mid-May–mid-Sept., Mon.–Sat. 10–5; mid-Sept.–mid-May by appointment.*

★ ㉒ **Salmon Weir Bridge.** The bridge itself is nothing special, but in season—from mid-April to early July—shoals of salmon are visible from its deck as they lie in the clear river water before making their way upstream to the spawning grounds of Lough Corrib. ✉ *West end of St. Vincent's Ave., Center.*

㉖ **Salthill.** A lively, hugely popular seaside resort, Salthill is beloved for its seaside promenade—the traditional place "to sit and watch the moon rise over Claddagh, and see the sun go down on Galway Bay," as Bing Crosby used to croon in the most famous song about the city. The main attraction of the village, set 3 km (2 mi) west of Galway, is the long sandy beach along the edge of Galway Bay and the promenade above it. The building of big new hotels along the seafront has nevertheless left plenty of room for the traditional amusement arcades (full of slot machines), seasonal cafés, and a fairground.

⑳ **Spanish Arch.** Built in 1584 to protect the quays where Spanish ships unloaded cargoes of wines and brandies, the arch now stands in the parking lot opposite Jurys Galway Inn. It's easily (and often) mistaken for a pile of weathered stones, yet it's another reminder of Galway's—and Ireland's—past links with Spain. ⊠ *The Long Walk, Spanish Arch.*

⑲ Tigh Neachtain (Naughton's Pub). You can hear traditional music every
Fodor'sChoice night at this popular pub, which stands at a busy little crossroads in the
★ heart of the old town. Grab a spot at one of its old-fashioned partitioned snugs at lunchtime for an inexpensive selection of imaginative bar food. It's a good place to mingle with local actors, writers, artists, musicians, and students, although it can become sardine-can crowded. ⊠ *17 Cross St., Spanish Arch* ☎ *091/566–172.*

⑭ Tourist Information Office (TIO). Just off Eyre Square, east of the bus and train station and the Great Southern Hotel, this is the place to make reservations for events around town and find out about the latest happenings. ⊠ *Forster Pl., Center* ☎ *091/537–700* ⊕ *www.irelandwest.ie* ⊗ *Weekdays 9–6, Sat. 9–1.*

㉔ University College Galway (UCG). Opened in 1846 to promote the development of local industry and agriculture, the UCG today is a center for Irish-language and Celtic studies. The Tudor Gothic–style quadrangle, completed in 1848, is worth a visit, though much of the rest of the campus is architecturally undistinguished. The library here has an important archive of Celtic-language materials, and in July and August the university hosts courses in Irish studies for overseas students. The campus is across the River Corrib, in the northwestern corner of the city. ⊠ *Newcastle Rd., University.*

Where to Stay & Eat

★ $–$$$$ ✕ **McDonagh's Seafood House.** This longtime Galway landmark is partly a fish-and-chips bar and partly a "real" fish restaurant. If you haven't yet tried fish-and-chips, this is the place to start: cod, whiting, mackerel, haddock, or hake is deep-fried in a light batter while you watch. The fish is served with a heap of freshly cooked chips (french fries). Or try Galway oysters au naturel or a bowl of mussels steamed in wine and garlic. The McDonaghs are one of Galway's most entrepreneurial families, in charge of several hotels in addition to this spot. ⊠ *22 Quay St., Spanish Arch* ☎*091/565–001* ▭*DC, MC, V* ⊗*No lunch Sun. Oct.–Apr.*

$$–$$$ ✕ **Kirwan's Lane Creative Cuisine.** Look for Mike O'Grady's stylish modern restaurant in a revamped alley at the river end of Quay Street. Blue-stained wooden tables, narrow floor-to-ceiling windows, and a quarry-tile floor set the stage for an informal, bistro-style menu. Fresh prawn cocktail is served with sauce Marie-Rose and a passion-fruit mayonnaise; confit of duck leg comes with braised red cabbage, star anise, and balsamic oil. Main courses have similarly unpredictable twists—rack of lamb is accompanied by sweet potato mash, basil oil, and apricots, and monkfish tails are dressed with a simple lemon and coriander dressing. ⊠ *Kirwan's La., Spanish Arch* ☎ *091/568–266* ▭ *AE, DC, MC, V* ⊗ *Closed Sun.*

$$–$$$ ✕ **Malt House.** Hidden away in an alley off High Street in the center of old Galway, Barry and Therese Cunningham's cozy pub-restaurant has long been popular with both locals and visitors. In a city where the dining scene is trend-driven and youth-oriented, this is an oasis of calm and tradition, where nothing ever changes much, and you wouldn't want it to—just like your favorite armchair. You can either eat in the bar itself or just off the bar in the restaurant, a square room with beamed ceilings, chintz curtains, and white, rough-cast walls. Fresh prawns panfried in garlic butter are popular; the sirloin steak with green-peppercorn sauce and the rack of lamb with a parsley crust should please landlubbers. ⊠ *Old Malte Arcade, High St., Center* ☎ *091/563–993* 🖃 *AE, DC, MC, V* ⊘ *Closed Sun. Oct.–Apr.*

$$–$$$ ✕ **Nimmo's.** Good food and a great ambience, due partly to the friendly, enthusiastic staff, makes this bustling bistro one of Galway's most popular restaurants. The central location in an old stone building overlooking the Corrib River adds to the pleasure. The long, spacious, second-floor room has original paintings on the walls and well-spaced tables set with white linen. The menu is short but well balanced, and while presentation is flamboyant, the food also tastes good. Try the salmon and chive terrine wrapped in smoked almonds, or rack of lamb with roasted red peppers and spring-onion mashed potatoes. There is a separate wine bar downstairs. ⊠ *The Long Walk, Spanish Arch* ☎ *091/562–353* 🖃 *AE, DC, MC, V* ⊘ *Closed Sun. No lunch.*

$–$$ ✕ **K. C. Blake's.** K. C. stands for Casey, as in owner-chef John Casey, a larger-than-life character, who turned a medieval stone town house once associated with the Blake family—one of the families that founded Galway—into an ultramodern eatery. The hard-edged, minimalist decor, which features sleek black walls, provides a strong contrast with the old stone building. Dishes range from traditional beef-and-Guinness stew to funky starter combinations like black pudding croquettes with pear and cranberry sauce. ⊠ *10 Quay St., Spanish Arch* ☎ *091/561–826* 🖃 *AE, MC, V.*

★ $$$$ ✕▣ **St. Cleran's.** Once home to famed director John Huston, this graystone, veddy, veddy proper Georgian mansion has been dramatically restored by its present owner, entertainer Merv Griffin, into a super-luxe inn. Subtle it is not, and some people are overwhelmed by the deep-pile carpets and ubiquitous crystal chandeliers; others find the furnishings delightful and revel in all the top-quality antiques. You can also expect superb views of the rolling countryside, and excellent opportunities for country sports. The elegant, formal restaurant (reservations essential) has a highly renowned Japanese chef, who cooks mainly in the classic French style with just the odd Japanese touch—tempura of tiger prawns with wasabi mayonnaise may be featured alongside a French classic like honey-roasted duck breast with orange-Cointreau sauce. It's 35 km (22 mi) east of Galway on the N6 Dublin road. ⊠ *Craughwell, Loughrea, Co. Galway* ☎ *091/846–555* 🖷 *091/846–752* ⊕ *www.merv.com* ⤙ *12 rooms* ₺ *Restaurant, miniature golf, fishing, horseback riding, bar; no a/c* 🖃 *AE, MC, V* �ⓞ *BP.*

$$–$$$$ ✕▣ **Glenlo Abbey.** Built as a private home in 1740, the Abbey is just 5 km (2 ½ mi) from Galway (on the N59 Clifden road), but feels like the heart of the country. Its rather grand name comes from a vast church built beside the house for the owner's ailing wife who, sadly, died before it was consecrated. Today, it is a lavender-hued catering hall and showpiece for this 138-acre estate. Replete with views over Lough Corrib and its own golf course, Glenlo Abbey is a bit of a white(-stone) elephant. The interiors strive to make this behemoth into an enticing place—the lobby resembles a gentlemen's club, with parquet floors, Chesterfield sofas, and leather-bound books—but don't quite succeed. Upstairs, official and correct Georgian-style furniture, brass lamps, and king-size beds fill the spacious bedrooms. Warming everything up, happily, is the genuinely friendly service, providing a delightfully unstuffy atmosphere, best seen in the Pullman Restaurant ($–$$). This is set in two *Orient Express* carriages installed on the grounds (and used in the famous Agatha Christie film of that name), offering a fun dining experience, complete with background click-clacks and train whistles. For more dignified surroundings, repair to the classical River Room restaurant. Chandeliers hang from high, stuccoed ceilings and tall windows framed by peach-colored curtains overlook the river. The food, beautifully served, includes delights like marinated venison on a bed of braised red cabbage. ☒ *Bushy Park, Co. Galway* ☎ *091/526–666* 🖷 *091/527–800* ⊕ *www.glenlo.com* ↝ *38 rooms, 6 suites* ⚹ *2 restaurants, in-room data ports, cable TV, 9-hole golf course, tennis court, sauna, fishing, bar* ▤ *AE, DC, MC, V.*

$$$$ ⊞ **Galway Great Southern.** Built in 1845 right on Eyre Square, to coincide with the arrival of the railway, this is still the smartest address in town, and a popular gathering spot. Tastefully muted, color-coordinated schemes and Georgian-style tables and chairs decorate all the guest rooms. The deluxe rooms in the original building have tall ceilings and windows and are particularly elegant, though those at the front directly above the bar can be noisy late into the night. Rooms in the back, on the fifth floor, have views of the docks and Galway Bay. The rooftop spa includes an open-air hot tub. French-Irish cuisine is served at the formal, pleasantly old-fashioned Oyster Room. ☒ *Eyre Square, Center, Co. Galway* ☎ *091/564–041* 🖷 *091/566–704* ⊕ *www.gsh.ie* ↝ *112 rooms, 3 suites* ⚹ *Restaurant, spa, hot tub, sauna, 2 bars; no a/c* ▤ *AE, DC, MC, V* ⑩ *BP.*

★ $$$ ⊞ **Ardilaun House.** This lovely 19th-century house sits at the end of a tree-lined avenue in a quiet suburb, midway between the city center and the Salthill promenade. Open fires, fresh flower arrangements, and Regency-style furniture characterize the quiet public rooms overlooking the gardens. The individually designed bedrooms have pastel schemes and Irish-made mahogany furniture with brass trim. For views of the bay, book an even-numbered room on the top floor. Other rooms, which are just as pleasant, overlook the flower garden and a fountain. ☒ *Taylor's Hill, Salthill, Co. Galway* ☎ *091/521–433* 🖷 *091/521–546* ⊕ *www.ardilaunhousehotel.ie* ↝ *81 rooms, 7 suites* ⚹ *Restaurant, in-room data ports, indoor pool, health club, 2 bars; no a/c* ▤ *AE, DC, MC, V* ⑩ *BP.*

$$$ ⊞ **Galway Bay.** It's big and modern, but it's also comfortable, with a panoramic view of Galway Bay. The facade of this giant at the quiet end of Salthill is divided into small-scale sections with peaked gables. The beach and the 1-km (½-mi) promenade, popular with joggers, are right across the road. More than two-thirds of the rooms have a sea view;

the rest overlook a quiet residential area. The spacious, color-coordinated rooms have large windows and all-modern facilities, from mini-bars to in-room data ports. Advantages of staying 3 km (2 mi) outside town include hassle-free parking and quiet nights. ⊠ *The Promenade, Salthill, Co. Galway* ☎ *091/520–520* 🖷 *091/520–530* ⊕ *www.galwaybayhotel.net* 🛏 *148 rooms, 2 suites* ♨ *Restaurant, coffee shop, in-room data ports, cable TV, indoor pool, health club, sauna, steam room, fishing, bar; no a/c* ⊟ *AE, DC, MC, V* ⊺⊙⊺ *BP.*

$$ 🖾 **Cregg Castle.** Half country-manor, half fortified keep, this 17th-century castle, on a 165-acre wildlife preserve, remains pleasantly informal thanks to its warm and laid-back hosts. The Brodericks all play musical instruments; traditional-music sessions often take place around the huge log-and-turf fire in the Great Hall. Bedrooms, which vary in shape and size, are decorated mainly with sturdy Victorian bygones. Breakfast is served until noon around an antique dining table that seats 18 people. It's about 15 km (9 mi) north of Galway on N17 (turn left for Corrandulla just beyond Claregalway). ⊠ *Tuam Rd., Corrandulla, Co. Galway* ☎🖷 *091/791–434* ⊕ *www.creggcastle.com* 🛏 *8 rooms, 7 with bath* ⊟ *AE, MC, V* ⊗ *Closed Nov.–Feb.* ⊺⊙⊺ *BP.*

¢–$$ 🖾 **Jurys Galway Inn.** Expect good-quality budget accommodation at this four-story hotel beside the historic Spanish Arch and the river. Each room is big enough for three adults, or two adults and two children, and the fixed-price policy applies to all options. The light, airy rooms have modern pine fittings, plain carpets and walls, double-glazed windows, and fully equipped bathrooms. Those overlooking the river are quieter than those in front. The atmosphere runs toward anonymous-international, but the inn is central—at the foot of Galway's busy Quay Street, right on the bank of the Corrib—and the level of comfort is high for the price range. ⊠ *Quay St., Spanish Arch, Co. Galway* ☎ *091/566–444* 🖷 *091/568–415* ⊕ *www.bookajurysinn.com* 🛏 *128 rooms* ♨ *Restaurant, bar, parking (fee); no a/c* ⊟ *AE, DC, MC, V* ⊺⊙⊺ *EP.*

$ 🖾 **Adare Guest House.** Just a five-minute walk from the city center, this family-run guest house, managed by the son of the original owners, makes a handy base for exploring Galway. There's ample space to park your car, and there's none of the nighttime noise of the city center. Rooms are relatively spacious for the price, extremely well equipped, and plainly decorated in browns and creams. The multichoice breakfast is served in a sunny room, with country pine furniture and floors, that overlooks a flower-filled patio. ⊠ *9 Father Griffin Pl., Spanish Arch, Co. Galway* ☎ *091/582–638* 🖷 *091/583–693* ⊕ *www.adarebedandbreakfast.com* 🛏 *11 rooms* ♨ *Dining room; no a/c* ⊟ *AE, MC, V* ⊺⊙⊺ *BP.*

★ ¢–$ 🖾 **Norman Villa.** Dee and Mark Keogh's imposing Victorian town house is away from the bustle but within easy walking distance of both the city center and the seaside promenade of Salthill. From the outside it looks plain, but the interior is a visual treat, evidence of the owners' wit and imagination. Brightly painted walls, Victorian brass beds with Irish-linen sheets, varnished floorboards, wooden shutters, and fun, contemporary paintings side by side with antique artifacts characterize this lively, pleasant B&B. Best of all: the suite in a converted coach-house at the end of the tiny garden. ⊠ *86 Lower Salthill, Salthill, Co. Gal-*

way 🏨🏤 *091/521–131* ⊕ *www.normanvilla.com* 🛏 *6 rooms* ♿ *Free parking; no a/c* ▭ *MC, V* ⊘ *Closed last 2 wks of Jan.* ⦿ *BP.*

Nightlife & the Arts

Because of its small size and concentration of pubs and restaurants, Galway can seem even livelier at 11 PM than it does at 11 AM. On weekends, when there are lots of students and other revelers in town, Eyre Square and environs can be rowdy after pub-closing time. On the plus side, if you've been staying out in the country and you're ready for a little nightlife, you're certain to find plenty of it here.

Clubs & Pubs

The best spot for traditional music is the area between Eyre Square and the Spanish Arch. There's a big post-nightclub (open until 1 or 2) scene here—there are some clubs in town, but most everyone heads to Salthill, the small suburban community 3 km (2 mi) west of Galway. The main road, Upper Salthill, is lined with clubs.

CLUBS **Cuba** (✉ Prospect Hill, Center ☎ 091/565–991), in the heart of Galway City, with three floors, draws diners and salsa lovers for Cuban cocktails and cigars to the beat of Latin music from DJs and live bands. Busy with students from the university, **GPO** (✉ Eglinton St., Center ☎ 091/563–073) is perhaps the most popular dance club in the city center. Try **Liquid** (✉ The Promenade, Salthill ☎ 091/722–715) for nightly independent and techno music. **McSwiggan's** (✉ 3 Eyre St., Wood Quay, Center ☎ 091/568–917) is a huge Galway City place, with everything from church pews to ancient carriage lamps contributing to its eclectic character. **Roisin Dubh** (✉ Dominick St., Spanish Arch ☎ 091/586–540) is a serious venue for emerging rock and traditional bands; it often showcases big, if still-struggling, talents. For late-night sounds heard from the comfort of your own table, try **Sevn'th Heav'n Restaurant** (✉ Courthouse La., off Quay St., Spanish Arch ☎ 091/563–838), where blues and folk sounds pour forth from 11:30 PM onward. **Warwick** (✉ O'-Connor's Warwick Hotel, Lower Salthill, Salthill ☎ 091/521–244) has a DJ on Friday nights and a band on Saturdays, both playing rock and pop oldies. Admission is €4 to €10.

PUBS **Aras na Gael** (✉ 45 Lower Dominick St., Spanish Arch ☎ 091/526–509) is one of the few pubs in the city center where Irish is spoken. Up-and-coming young musicians play at the cozy **Cottage Bar** (✉ 76 Lower Salthill, Salthill ☎ 091/526–754), which has good acoustics. Master of the tin whistle Seán Ryan plays every Sunday at **Crane's** (✉ 2 Sea Rd. ☎ 091/587–419). You will usually find a session after about 9 PM at **King's Head** (✉ 15 High St., Center ☎ 091/566–630). **Paddy's** (✉ Prospect Hill, Center ☎ 091/567–843) is a good place for a pint near the bus and train station. **Taaffe's** (✉ 19 Shop St., Center ☎ 091/564–066), in the midst of the shopping district, is very busy on afternoons. **Tigh Neachtain** (✉ 17 Cross St., Spanish Arch ☎ 091/568–820) is *the* place for traditional music in Galway City, and each visit will be an experience.

A YEAR-ROUND FLEADH

GALWAY IS THE CENTER of Ireland's traditional-music universe, a city where you can hear this music all through the year, whether or not there's a fleadh, or traditional-music festival, going on. Galway City and its environs have given rise to some of the most durable names in Irish music: De Danann, Arcady, singers Dolores and Seán Keane, and the mercurial accordion genius Mairtín O'Connor. Seán Ryan, acknowledged master of the tin whistle, has been playing every Sunday at **Crane's** since the 1980s. The hottest sessions these days take place at the **Cottage Bar** in Lower Salthill, where up-and-coming young musicians are drawn by the cozy surroundings and the fine acoustics. In the city itself, there's still plenty of music to be found at old reliables such as **Tigh Neachtain, Taaffe's,** and **Aras na Gael.** South of Galway, the fishing village of Kinvara hosts the annual **Cuckoo Fleadh,** a small but growing festival that takes place in May. Resident musicians like De Danann alumni Jackie Daly and Charlie Piggott play regularly at **Winkles Hotel,** where, in 1989, a very young and relatively unknown accordion player got together with a few friends for a casual recording session. The resulting album, Sharon Shannon, became the most successful Irish traditional-music recording ever released. Down the road, the market town of Ennis has come into its own, attracting a growing cadre of musicians: the Custys, Siobhán and Tommy Peoples, Josephine Marsh, P. J. King, flute player Kevin Crawford, and accordion whiz kid Murt Ryan, from Tipperary. Sessions take place at an ever-changing roster of pubs, including **Knox's** and, most notably, **Cruise's.** In May, Ennis hosts the **Fleadh Nua** festival—with concerts, competitions, workshops, and ceilís (Irish dancing and song).

Theater

An Taibhdhearc (✉ Middle St., Center ☎ 091/562–024), pronounced "on *tie*-vark," was founded in 1928 by Hilton Edwards and Mícheál Macliammóir as the national Irish-language theater. It continues to produce first-class shows, mainly of Irish works in both the English and the Irish languages.

The **Druid Theatre company** (✉ Chapel La., Center ☎ 091/568–617) is esteemed for its adventurous and accomplished productions, mainly of 20th-century Irish and European plays. The players perform at the Royal Court's small stage in London. When they're home, they usually appear at the Town Hall, and they host many productions during the Galway Arts Festival in late July.

Macnas (✉ Fisheries Field, Salmon Weir Bridge, Center ☎ 091/561–462) is an internationally renowned, Galway-based troupe of performance artists who have raised street theater to new levels. Their participation in the Galway Arts Festival's annual parade is always much anticipated.

Visual Arts & Galleries

Art Euro Gallery (✉ The Bridge Mills, O'Brien's Bridge, Spanish Arch ☎ 091/562–884) has a collection of free-blown glass and unusual handmade ceramics by Irish and other European artists. High-quality paintings and sculpture by local artists can be found at **Kenny's Bookshop** (⊠ High St., Center ☎ 091/562–739). The art gallery at **University College Galway** (⊠ Newcastle Rd., University ☎ 091/524–411) has a number of exhibits each year.

Sports & the Outdoors

Bicycling

Set off to explore the Galway area, especially its coast, by renting a bike from **Mountain Trail Bike Shop** (⊠The Cornstore, Middle St., Center ☎091/569–888).

Fishing

Galway City is the gateway to Connemara, and Connemara is the place to fish. You can get fishing licenses, tackle, and bait, and arrange to hire a traditional fly-fishing guide or book a sea-angling trip, at **Freeny's Sports** (⊠ 19–23 High St., Center ☎ 091/562–609). **Murt's** (⊠ 7 Daly's Pl., Woodquay ☎ 091/561–018) can handle your fishing needs.

Golf

Galway Bay Golf and Country Club (⊠ Renville, Oranmore ☎ 091/790–500) is an 18-hole, par-72 parkland course, designed by Christy O'Connor Jr., on the shores of Galway Bay. The **Galway Golf Club** (⊠ Blackrock, Salthill ☎ 091/522–033) is an 18-hole, par-71 course with excellent views of Galway Bay, the Burren, and the Aran Islands. Some of the fairways run close to the ocean.

River Cruising

A **Corrib Cruise** (☎ 091/592–447) from Wood Quay, behind the Town Hall Theatre at the Rowing Club, is a lovely way to spend a fine afternoon; it lasts 1½ hours and travels 8 km (5 mi) up the River Corrib and about 6 km (4 mi) around Lough Corrib. The trip costs €8, and boats depart daily at 2:30 and 4:30 from May through September, with an additional departure at 12:30 July through August. You can also rent the boat for an evening.

Shopping

Bookstores

Charlie Byrne's Bookshop (⊠ The Cornstore, Middle St., Center ☎ 091/561–766) sells a large, varied selection of used books and remainders. Lovers of all things Irish, poetic, and historical will make a bee-line to **Kenny's Bookshop** (⊠ High St., Center ☎ 091/562–739 ⊕ www.kennys.ie), five floors—and counting—-of books on Irish topics, mainly secondhand and antiquarian, as well as prints, maps, and a small art gallery. A Galway institution, Kenny's is presided over by octogenarian Maureen Kenny, who has a smile for everyone. She and her late husband started the business in one room, back in 1940. Over the years, the tradition has grown up of photographing visiting writers—current photos range from Allen Ginsberg to Annie Proulx. Book-lovers should allow at least an hour to explore all the nooks and crannies. Every inch of the space, whether windowsills or turf baskets, is used to display books.

FodorsChoice
★

Maps, prints, engravings and rare editions sit alongside the latest Irish fiction, history, and poetry, many of the latter signed by their authors. Irish poetry is a special feature here, lovingly tended in its own room by Des Kenny, and Irish fiction and history are also strong points. A warehouse at Liosbaun Industrial Estate holds most of the quarter of a million out-of-print and rare books that make up Kennys stock, all of which is inventoried on Kenny's fantastic web site.

Clothing, Crafts, & Gifts

★ Don't miss **Design Concourse Ireland** (✉ Kirwan's La., Center ☎ 091/566-016), a spectacular one-stop shop for the best in Irish handcrafted design. Ceramics, small pieces of furniture, contemporary basketware, hand-made jewelry, wood turnings, hand-blown glass—in fact, just about anything for the home that can be hand-made—will be found in this two-story treasure trove. **Design Ireland Plus** (✉ The Cornstore, Middle St., Center ☎ 091/567-716 ✉ The Grainstore, Lower Abbeygate St., Center ☎ 091/566-620) carries an excellent range of contemporary Irish-made crafts and clothing. **Faller's Sweater Shop** (✉ 25 High St., Center ☎ 091/564-833 ✉ 35 Eyre Sq., Center ☎ 091/561-255) has the choicest selection of Irish-made sweaters, competitively priced. **Galway Irish Crystal** (✉ Dublin Rd., Merlin Park ☎ 091/757-311 ⊕ www.galwaycrystal. ie), a factory outlet on the city's ring road, has hand-cut Irish glass, an informative heritage center on Galway lore, a crystal workshop you can visit, and a restaurant with a view of Galway Bay.

Meadows & Byrne (✉ Castle St., Center ☎ 091/567-776) sells the best in modern household items. **O'Máille's** (✉ 16 High St., Center ☎ 091/562-696) carries Aran sweaters, handwoven tweeds, and classically tailored clothing. Browse in **Treasure Chest** (✉ William St., Center ☎ 091/563-862) for china, crystal, gifts, and classic clothing.

Jewelry

Dating from 1750, **Thomas Dillon's** (✉ 1 Quay St., Spanish Arch ☎ 091/566-365 ⊕ www.claddaghring.ie) claims to be the original maker of Galway's famous Claddagh ring. In the back of the shop there's a small but interesting display of antique Claddagh rings and old Galway memorabilia.

Malls

Slightly off the beaten path, the **Cornstore** (✉ Middle St., Center) has stylish shops selling contemporary goods; the stores tend to be less crowded than their competitors on the main streets. On the southwest side of Eyre Square and imaginatively designed to incorporate parts of the old town walls, the **Eyre Square Shopping Centre** is a good spot to pick up moderately priced clothing and household goods.

Music

Back2Music (✉ 30 Upper Abbeygate St., Center ☎ 091/565-272) specializes in traditional Irish musical instruments, including the handheld drum, the *bodhrán* (pronounced bau-*rawn*). **Mulligan** (✉ 5 Middle St. Court, Center ☎ 091/564-961) carries thousands of CDs, records, and cassettes, with a large collection of traditional Irish music.

Vintage Goods

Twice as Nice (⊠ 5 Quay St., Spanish Arch ☎ 091/566–332) sells a mix of new and vintage men's and women's clothing, linens, lace, and jewelry at reasonable prices.

THE ARAN ISLANDS

No one knows for certain when the Aran Islands—Inishmore, Inishmaan, and Inisheer—were first inhabited, but judging from the number of Bronze Age and Iron Age forts found here (especially on Inishmore), 3000 BC is a safe guess. Why wandering nomads in deerskin jerkins would be attracted to these barren islets remains a greater mystery, not the least because fresh water and farmable land were (and still are) scarce commodities. Remote western outposts of the ancient province of Connaught (though they are not the country's westernmost points; that honor belongs to the Blasket Islands), these three islands were once as barren as the limestone pavements of the Burren, of which they are a continuation. Today, the land is parceled into small, human-made fields surrounded by stone walls: centuries of erosion, generations of backbreaking labor, sheep, horses, and their attendant tons of manure have finally transformed this rocky wasteland into reasonably productive cropland.

During the 1800s, the islands, wracked by famine and mass emigration, were virtually forgotten by mainland Ireland. At the turn of the 20th century, however, the books of J. M. Synge (1871–1909)—who learned Irish on Inishmaan and wrote about its people in his famous play *Riders to the Sea*—prompted Gaelic revivalists to study and document this isolated bastion of Irish culture. Liam O'Flaherty became one of the most famous sons of Inishmore through his novels, such as *Famine*. And in 1934, American director Robert Flaherty filmed his classic documentary *Man of Aran* on Inishmore, recording the islanders' dramatic battles with sea and storm, and bringing the islands into the world spotlight (the film is shown in the Community Hall in Kilronan, Inishmore, every afternoon during July, August, and early September).

While traditional Irish culture fights a rear-guard battle on the mainland, the islanders continue to preserve as best as they can a culture going back generations. Still, the Irish-speaking inhabitants enjoy a daily air service to Galway (subsidized by the government), motorized curraghs, cable TVs, and all the usual modern home conveniences. Yet they have retained a distinctness from mainlanders, preferring simple home decor, very plain food, and tightly knit communities, like the hardy fisher and farming folk from whom they are descended. Crime is virtually unknown in these parts; at your B&B, you'll likely find no locks on the guest-room doors, and the front-door latch will be left open. Many islanders have sampled life in Dublin or cities abroad but have returned to raise families, keeping the population stable at around 1,500. Tourists now flock here, to see the ancient sights and savor the spectacular views: the uninterrupted expanse of the Atlantic on the western horizon; the Connemara coast and its Twelve Bens to the northeast; and County Clare's Burren and the Cliffs of Moher to the southeast.

To appreciate the fierce loneliness of the islands you must spend the night on one. Because all the islands, especially Inishmore, crawl with day-trippers, it is difficult to let their rugged beauty sink into your soul until 10 PM, when the sky is dark and the pubs fill with the acrid smell of peat smoke and Guinness. Once the day-trippers clear out, the islands' stunningly fierce and brooding beauty is disturbed only by the "baa" of the sheep and the incessant rush of the wind. The only hotel on the islands is on Inisheer, but there's no shortage of small guest houses and B&Bs, mostly in simple family homes. The best way to book is through the Galway City TIO. Each island has at least one wine-licensed restaurant serving plain home cooking. Most B&Bs will provide a packed lunch and an evening meal (called high tea) on request.

Inishmore

★ ⓘ *24 km (15 mi) south of Ros an Mhil (Rossaveal), 48 km (30 mi) west of Galway Docks.*

With a population of 900, Inishmore (Inis Mór) is the largest of the islands and the closest to the Connemara coast. It's also the most commercialized, its appeal slightly diminished by road traffic. In summer, ferries arriving at Kilronan, Inishmore's main village and port, are met by minibuses and pony-and-cart drivers, all eager to show visitors "the sights." More than 8 km (5 mi) long and about 3 km (2 mi) wide at most points, with an area of 7,640 acres, the island is just a little too large to explore comfortably on foot in a day. The best way to see it is really by bicycle; bring your own or rent one from one of the vendors operating near the quay. The **Aran Heritage Centre** explains the history and culture of the islanders, who for many years lived in virtual isolation from the mainland. ⊠ *Kilronan* ☎ *099/61355* ⌨ *€3* ⊗ *Apr.–Oct., daily 10–7.*

Even if you only have a few hours to explore Inishmore, rent a bike (next to the pier) and head straight for **Dún Aengus,** one of the finest prehistoric monuments in Europe, dating from about 2000 BC. Spectacularly set on the edge of a 300-foot-tall cliff overlooking a sheer drop, the fort has defenses consisting of three rows of concentric circles. Whom the builders were defending themselves against is a matter of conjecture. From the innermost rampart there's a great view of the island and the Connemara coast. In order to protect this fragile monument from erosion, you should approach it only through the visitor center, which gives access to a 1-km (½-mi) uphill walk over uneven terrain—wear sturdy footwear. ⊠ *7 km (4 mi) west of Kilronan, Kilmurvey* ☎ *099/61010* ⊕ *www.heritageireland.ie* ⌨ *€1.25* ⊗ *Mar.–Oct., daily 10–6; Nov.–Feb., daily 11:30–3:30.*

Where to Stay

★ ¢–$ ▦ **Kilmurvey House.** This rambling 200-year-old stone farmhouse is the first choice of many visitors to the island. It's at the foot of Dún Aengus fort, just three minutes' walk from the beach, and about 6½ km (4 mi) from the quay and the airport (accessible by minibus). The old stone house has been cleverly extended to provide extra guest rooms. The neatly-kept front garden leads to a large, high-ceilinged hall and wide stairs, giving a pleasant sense of space. The walls are hung with portraits of the house's previous owners, the warrior clan of O'Flahertys—one of whom was Oscar Wilde's godfather—and whose descendants include the famed writers Liam and Robert. Rooms are spacious and comfortable, with wonderful sea views. Dinners are cooked about five nights a week by the warm, chatty owner, Treasa Joyce, and are not to be missed. Vegetables and herbs come from the back garden, the floury potatoes are island-grown, and wild Atlantic salmon is a popular main course. ✉ *Kilronan, Co. Galway* ☎ *099/61218* 🖷 *099/61397* ⊕ *www. kilmurveyhouse.com* 🔄 *12 rooms* ♻ *Dining room; no a/c, no room TVs, no smoking in guest rooms* ☰ *MC, V* ⊘ *Closed Nov.–Mar.* †◎† *BP.*

¢ ▦ **Ard Einne Guesthouse.** Almost every window at this B&B on Inishmore looks out to the sea, making it the perfect place to de-stress. The rambling 80-year-old house, with its distinctive dormer windows, is close to both the beach and the town; many guests base themselves here for two or three nights, to make a thorough exploration of the island. The public rooms and guest rooms are relaxed, with modern decor including light-color linens and walls paneled with blond wood. Simple evening meals ($) are prepared by your host, Clodagh Ní Ghoill, who will discuss the four-course set menu in advance. ✉ *Kilronan, Co. Galway* ☎ *099/ 61126* 🖷 *099/61388* ⊕ *www.ardeinne.com* 🔄 *14 rooms* ♻ *Dining room, fishing; no a/c, no room phones, no room TVs* ☰ *MC, V* ⊘ *Closed mid-Dec.–Jan.* †◎† *BP.*

Nightlife

The place to go for traditional music is the **American Bar** (✉ Kilronan ☎ 099/61130). **Joe Mac's** (✉ Kilronan ☎ 099/61248), right off the pier, is a good place for a pint while waiting for the ferry home. **Joe Watty's** (✉ Main Rd., Kilronan ☎ 099/61155) is a good bet for traditional music virtually every night in summer.

Sports & the Outdoors

Bicycles can be rented from May through October for €10 per day from **Aran Bike Hire** (☎ 099/61132), at the ferry landing at Inishmore Pier.

Inishmaan

28 *3 km (2 mi) east of Inishmore.*

The middle island in both size and location, Inishmaan (Inis Meáin) has a population of about 300 and can be comfortably explored on foot. In fact, you have no alternative if you want to reach the island's major antiquities: **Conor Fort,** a smaller version of Dún Aengus; the ruins of two **early Christian churches;** and a chamber tomb known as the **Bed of Diarmuid and Grainne,** dating from about 2000 BC. You can also take wonderful cliff walks above secluded coves. It's on Inishmaan that the traditional Aran lifestyle is most evident. Until the mid-1930s, Aran women dressed in thick, red-woolen skirts to keep out the Atlantic gales, while the men wore collarless jackets, baggy trousers made of homespun tweed with *pampooties* (hide shoes without heels, suitable for walking on rocks), and wide, hand-plaited belts called *críos* (pronounced krish).

Most islanders still don hand-knitted Aran sweaters, though nowadays they wear them with jeans and sneakers.

Shopping

Inis Meáin Knitting (⊠ Carrown Lisheen ☎ 099/73009) is a young company producing quality knitwear in luxury fibers for the international market—including Liberty of London, Barneys New York, and Bergdorf Goodman—while providing much-needed local employment. The factory showroom has an extensive selection of garments at discount prices. To get here from the pier, walk five minutes due west.

Inisheer

㉙ *4 km (2½ mi) east of Inishmaan, 8 km (5 mi) northwest of Doolin.*

The smallest and flattest of the islands, Inisheer (Inis Oírr) can be explored on foot in an afternoon, though if the weather is fine you may be tempted to linger on the long, sandy beach between the quay and the airfield. Only one stretch of road, about 500 yards long, links the airfield and the sole village. In summer, Inisheer's population of 300 is augmented by high school students from all over Ireland attending the Gaeltacht, or Irish-language, school.

It's worth making a circuit of the island to get a sense of its utter tranquility. A maze of footpaths runs between the high stone walls that divide the fields, which are so small that they can support only one cow each, or two to three sheep. Those that are not cultivated or grazed turn into natural wildflower meadows between June and August, overrun with harebells, scabious, red clover, oxeye daisies, saxifrage, and tall grasses. It seems almost a crime to walk here—but how can you resist taking a rest in the corner of a sweet-smelling meadow on a sunny afternoon, sheltered by high stone walls with no sound but the larks above and the wind as it sifts through the stones? "The back of the island," as Inisheer's uninhabited side facing the Atlantic is called, has no beaches, but people swim off the rocks.

The **Church of Kevin,** signposted to the southeast of the quay, is a small, early Christian church that gets buried in sand by storms every winter. Each year the islanders dig it out of the sand for the celebration of St. Kevin's Day on June 14. A pleasant walk through the village takes you up to **O'Brien's Castle,** a ruined 15th-century tower on top of a rocky hill—the only hill on the island.

Where to Stay

¢ ▥ **Hotel Inisheer.** A pleasant, modern low-rise in the middle of the island's only village, a few minutes' walk from the quay and the airstrip, this simple, whitewashed building with a slate roof and half-slated walls has bright, plainly furnished rooms. The 5 newer rooms are slightly larger than the other 10. The restaurant (open to nonguests) is the best bet on the island, although some of the food is imported frozen. ⊠ *Lurgan Village, Co. Galway* ☎ *099/75020* 🖶 *099/75099* ⃗ *15 rooms* ☼ *Restaurant, bicycles, bar; no a/c, no room phones, no room TVs* ⊟ *AE, DC, MC, V* ☼ *Closed Oct.–Mar.* ⑩ *BP.*

CONNEMARA & COUNTY MAYO

Bordered by the long expanse of Lough Corrib on the east and the jagged coast of the Atlantic on the west is the rugged, desolate region of western County Galway known as Connemara. Like the American West, it's an area of spectacular, almost myth-making geography—of glacial lakes; gorgeous, silent mountains; lonely roads; and hushed, uninhabited boglands. The Twelve Bens, "the central glory of Connemara," as author Brendan Lehane has called them, together with the Maamturk Mountains to their north, lord proudly over the area's sepia boglands. More surprisingly, stands of Scotch pine, Norwegian spruce, Douglas fir, and Japanese Sitka grow in Connemara's valleys and up hillsides—the result of a concerted national project that has thus far reforested 9% of Ireland. In the midst of this wilderness there are few people, since Connemara's population is sparse even by Irish standards. Especially in the off-season, you're far more likely to come across sheep strolling its roads than another car.

Two main routes—one inland, the other coastal—lead through Connemara. To take the inland route described below, leave Galway City on the well-signposted outer-ring road and follow signs for N59—Moycullen, Oughterard, and Clifden. If you choose to go the coastal route, you'll travel due west from Galway City to Rossaveal on R336 through Salthill, Barna, and Spiddle—all in the heart of the west's strong Gaeltacht, home to roughly 40,000 Irish speakers. Although this is one of the most impressive and unspoiled coastal roads in Ireland, it has been scarred by modern one-story concrete homes—a sort of faux–Spanish hacienda style favored by locals. (Most of the traditional thatched houses in the west are now used as vacation homes.) You can continue north on R336 from Rossaveal to Maam Cross and then head for coastal points west, or pick up R340 and putter along the coast.

Oughterard

30 *27 km (17 mi) northwest of Galway City on N59.*

Bustling Oughterard (pronounced *ook*-ter-ard) is the main village on the western shores of Lough Corrib and one of Ireland's leading angling resorts. The prettiest part of the village is on the far (Clifden) side, beyond the busy commercial center, beside a wooded section of the River Corrib. The lough is signposted to the right in the village center, less than 1½ km (1 mi) up the road. From mid-June to early September, local boatmen offer trips on the lough, which has several islands. It's also possible to take a boat trip to the village of Cong, at the north shore of the lough. Midway between Oughterard and Cong, Inchagoill Island (the Island of the Stranger), a popular destination for a half-day trip, has several early-Christian church remains. The cost of boat rides is negotiable; expect to pay about €10 per person.

Where to Stay

★ **$$–$$$** ✕📷 **Ross Lake House.** Well off the beaten path, this surprisingly stylish country hideaway sits near a stream and is surrounded by five acres of colorful gardens. Built by James Edward Jackson, land agent for Lord Iveagh at Ashford Castle, the white-trim Georgian house, managed by the enthusiastic Henry and Elaine Reid, has a suavely furnished interior, with 19th-century antiques and welcoming open fires. Guest rooms in the converted stables are simpler and a little smaller than those in the house, but all have peaceful garden views. A table d'hôte dinner menu, set in a salon with Regency-striped wallpapers, offers good-quality, plain country-house cooking featuring local delicacies, including the much-sought after Connemara mountain lamb. The house is 5 km (3 mi) from Oughterard. ⊠ *Rosscahill, Co. Galway* 🖭🖭 *091/550–109* ⊕ *www. rosslakehotel.com* ⇥ *13 rooms* ⚭ *Restaurant, tennis court, fishing, horseback riding, bar; no a/c* ⊟ *AE, DC, MC, V* ⊗ *Closed Nov.–mid-Mar.* �OI *BP.*

Nightlife
For good traditional music try **Faherty's** (⊠ Main St. 🖭 091/552–194).

---

en route As you continue northwest from Oughterard on N59, you'll soon pass a string of small lakes on your left; their shining blue waters reflecting the blue sky are a typical Connemara sight on a sunny day. About 16 km (10 mi) northwest of Oughterard, the continuation of the coast road (R336) meets N59 at Maam Cross in the shadow of Leckavrea Mountain. Once an important meeting place for the people of north and south Connemara, it's still the location of a large monthly cattle fair. Walkers will find wonderful views of Connemara by heading for any of the local peaks visible from the road. Beyond Maam Cross, some of the best scenery in Connemara awaits on the road to Recess, 16 km (10 mi) west of Maam Cross on N59. At many points on this drive, a short walk away from either side of the main road will lead you to the shores of one of the area's many small loughs. Stop and linger if the sun is out—even intermittently—for the light filtering through the clouds gives splendor to the distant, dark-gray mountains and creates patterns on the brown-green moorland below. In June and July, it stays light until 11 PM or so, and it's worth taking a late-evening stroll to see the sun's reluctance to set. In Recess, **Joyce's** (🖭 095/34604) is a craft shop owned by a family that is famed for its traditional Connemara tweeds. The emporium has a good selection of tweed, and also carries a enticing selection of contemporary ceramics, handwoven shawls, books of Irish interest, original paintings, and small sculptures.

Cong

㉛ *23 km (14 mi) northeast of Maam Cross on N59.*

On a narrow isthmus between Lough Corrib and Lough Mask on the County Mayo border, the pretty, old-fashioned village of Cong, near Maam Cross, is dotted with ivy-covered thatched cottages, dilapidated farmhouses, and one immensely posh hotel, Ashford Castle. Cong is surrounded by many stone circles and burial mounds, but its most notable ruins are those of the **Augustine Abbey** (⊠ Abbey St.), dating from the early 13th century and still exhibiting some finely carved details. It can be seen overlooking a river near fabulous Ashford Castle, now a hotel.

Cong's 15 minutes of fame came in 1952, when John Ford filmed *The Quiet Man,* one of his most popular films, here; John Wayne plays a prizefighter who goes home to Ireland to court the fiery Maureen O'Hara. (Film critic Pauline Kael called the movie "fearfully Irish and green and hearty.") The **Quiet Man Heritage Cottage,** in the village center, is an exact replica of the cottage used in the film, with reproductions of the furniture and costumes, a few original artifacts, and pictures of actors Barry Fitzgerald and Maureen O'Hara on location. ⊠ *Cong Village Center* ☎ *094/954–6089* ▣ *€3.75* ☉ *Mar.–Nov., daily 10–6.*

Where to Stay

★ **$$$$** ⊞ **Ashford Castle.** Nearly bigger than the neighboring village of Cong, this famed mock-Gothic baronial showpiece was built in 1870 for the Guinness family and has been wowing visitors ever since—that is, if your guest list runs to Prince Rainier, John Travolta, and Jack Nicholson. Massive, flamboyantly turreted, built of stone with towers and bridges, crenellations and mullioned windows, Ashford is the very picture of a romantic Irish castle. As a world apart from the normal hubbub of Irish life, it remains strong on luxury, charm, and good service, but—some pundits would say—light on authenticity as time-stained charm has given way to too many creature comforts. Still, this is the reason why Pierce Brosnan took over the whole castle for two days for his wedding to Keely Shaye Smith, and it remains a popular destination with honeymooners from all over the world. The 82 bedrooms include presidential and executive suites—and for once the name isn't just hopeful, as presidents of both the United States (Reagan, on his trip back to his ancestral homelands) and France have stayed here. Inside, large paintings in gilt frames hang from the castle's carved stone walls above polished wood paneling, illuminated by crystal chandeliers. Deluxe rooms have generous sitting areas, heavily carved antique furniture, open fireplaces and extra-large bathrooms. Standard bedrooms in the discreetly added new wing are smaller, with marble bathroom fittings and Victorian-style antiques and, while they have everything you would expect from five-star accommodation, they lack the scale and baronial flamboyance of the rest of the castle. The suites in the original castle building are vast, with double-height windows, furnished with Georgian antiques, and blissfully comfortable. The Prince of Wales Cocktail Bar (named for the one who visited in the 1890s) is the venue for elegant pre-dinner drinks. The cuisine, by distinguished Swiss chef, Stefan Matz, is stylish and unfussy, showcasing fresh local ingredients. The hotel makes the most of its superb location at the head of Lough Corrib and the surrounding formal lawns and gardens are possibly the most neatly manicured outdoor space in Ireland. Accordingly, fly fishing is a popular outdoor sport, and the river bank has recently been landscaped to facilitate anglers—typical of the no-expense-spared Ashford approach—while there has also been massive investment in the hotel's spa facilities. ⊠ *Co. Mayo* ☎ *094/954–6003* 🖷 *094/954–6260* ⊕ *www.ashford.ie* ⌁ *72 rooms, 11 suites* ♿ *2 restaurants, in-room data ports, cable TV, 9-hole golf course,*

2 tennis courts, health club, boating, fishing, bicycles, horseback riding, 2 bars; no a/c ☰ AE, DC, MC, V.

Cashel

㉜ *8 km (5 mi) south of Recess on R340, 49½ km (31 mi) west of Cong.*

Cashel is a quiet, extremely sheltered angling center at the head of Bertraghboy Bay. General de Gaulle is among the many people who have sought seclusion here. A word of caution: stray sheep, bolting Connemara ponies, cyclists, and reckless local drivers are all regular hazards on the narrow mountain roads hereabouts.

Where to Stay & Eat

$$$$ ✕⊡ **Cashel House.** Forty acres of woodlands at the head of Cashel Bay—with exotic shrubs flowering and Connemara ponies grazing out back—seclude this large, white country house. Inside, curios, intricately carved tables, Biedermeier bureaus, gilt mirrors, Georgian bookcases, ormolu clocks, and too many new sofas and armchairs are scattered around the public rooms; more antiques turn up in the bedrooms, which have king-size beds (canopied in the 13 minisuites). Front rooms have views of the sea. The table d'hôte menu in the dining room lists more choices than most country houses and is strong on fresh local seafood. ⊠ *Cashel Bay, Co. Galway* ☏ *095/31001* 🖷 *095/31077* ⊕ *www. cashel-house-hotel.com* 🛏*19 rooms, 13 suites* ⚲ *Restaurant, tennis court, beach, boating, fishing, bicycles, horseback riding, in-room data ports; no a/c* ☰ *AE, DC, MC, V* ⊘ *Closed mid-Jan.–earlyFeb.* ❙⊙❙ *BP.*

★ $$$ ⊡ **Zetland Country House.** On a hill overlooking secluded Cashel Bay, John and Mona Prendergast's mid-Victorian country retreat offers an idyllic experience of quiet, elegant country living. Once a 19th-century sporting lodge favored by the earl and countess of Zetland, the rambling white house is surrounded by large old trees, wooded grounds, and flowering shrubs. A dining room with massive antique sideboards adorned with family silver overlooks the bay, as does the large and blissfully serene sitting room. The main drawing room is a picture of Georgian grace, replete with chandelier, marble fireplace, and glowing-yellow walls. Upstairs, guest bedrooms are large, and many have sea views, but those with garden views are also attractive. Fine Georgian and Victorian antiques of polished mahogany decorate the comfortable quarters. ⊠ *Cashel Bay, Co. Galway* ☏ *095/31111* 🖷 *095/31117* ⊕ *www.zetland.com* 🛏 *19 rooms* ⚲ *Restaurant, tennis court, fishing, bar; no a/c* ☰ *AE, DC, MC, V* ⊘ *Closed Nov.–mid-Apr.* ❙⊙❙ *BP.*

Sports & the Outdoors

Cashel Equestrian Center (⊠ Cashel House, Cashel Bay ☏ 095/31001) offers scenic treks and the chance to ride a Connemara pony on its home ground.

Ballynahinch

㉝ *10 km (6 mi) west of Cashel on R341.*

Forested country runs along the shores of Ballynahinch Lake, which nowadays is accessible to the general public. Woodland in this part of Ireland indicates the proximity of a "big house" whose owner can afford to plant trees for pleasure and prevent their being cut down for fuel. Surely enough, soon after the woodland hereabouts begins, you will come to the gate lodge of the noted country-house hotel, Ballynahinch Castle. This being Connemara, with its Irish settlement pattern, there is no village as such, just an area named Ballynahinch.

Where to Stay

$$$–$$$$
Fodor'sChoice
★

☒ **Ballynahinch Castle.** Built in the late 18th century on the Owenmore River amid 40 walkable wooded acres, this huge, rambling, castellated, and gorgeous country house was the home of Richard Martin (1754–1834), known as "Humanity Dick," the founder of the Royal Society for the Prevention of Cruelty to Animals. Set in the midst of 300 of the most beautiful acres of Connemara, this has long been a favored forgetaway for the famous, from the O'Flaherty Chieftains to Grace O'-Malley—the Pirate Queen of Connemara—to H.R.H. the Maharajah Ranjitsinji, "Prince of Cricketeers." Comfort without ostentation is the hallmark here, and because many guests are here for the fishing, the bar and restaurant are pleasantly informal. The tiled lobby with Persian rugs has two inviting leather chesterfields in front of an open fire. The biggest bedrooms, all most stylishly decorated, in the ground-floor wing, have four-poster beds and floor-to-ceiling windows opening onto lawns that run down the river. Rooms in the old house are equally comfortable and quiet. The Owenmore restaurant enjoys a panoramic riverside perch and high style cuisine. The castle is signposted off N59 between Recess and Clifden. ☒ *Ballynahinch, Recess, Co. Galway* ☎ *095/31006* ☐ *095/ 31085* ⊕ *www.ballynahinch-castle.com* ☞ *30 rooms, 10 suites* ☾ *Restaurant, tennis court, fishing, bar; no a/c* ☰ *AE, DC, MC, V* ☾ *Closed last wk of Dec. and Feb.* ¶⊙| *BP.*

off the
beaten
path

ROUNDSTONE MUSICAL INSTRUMENTS – From Ballynahinch, take N59 to the small seaside town of Roundstone, where you'll find this delightful music shop and museum. Artisans here have been handcrafting bodhráns (Irish drums) here for dozens of years. The workshop is in an old Franciscan monastery with a beautiful bell tower. Besides the bodhráns, you can buy traditional CDs, books, and coffee—and you can also expect a good chat. If you wish, you can have your drum hand-painted with your family crest, a Celtic design, or your initials while you wait. ☒ *I.D.A. Craftcenter, Roundstone* ☎ *095/35808* ⊕ *www.bodhran.com* ☾ *May, June, Sept., and Oct., daily 9:30–6; July and Aug., daily 9–7; Nov.–Apr., Mon.–Sat. 9:30–6.*

Clifden

★ *23 km (14 mi) west of Recess, 79 km (49 mi) northwest of Galway City on N59.*

With roughly 1,100 residents, Clifden would be called a village by most, but in these parts it's looked on as something of a metropolis. It is far and away the prettiest town in Connemara, as well as its unrivaled "capital." Clifden's first attraction is its location—perched high above Clifden Bay on a forested plateau, its back to the spectacular Twelve Ben Mountains. The tapering spires of the town's two churches add to its alpine feel. A selection of small restaurants, lively bars with music most summer nights, pleasant accommodations, and excellent walks make the town a popular base. It's quiet out of season, but in July and August crowds flock here, especially for August's world-famous Connemara Pony Show. In fact, Clifden's popularity, which has led to a chaotic one-way traffic system and loud techno music blasting out of certain bars, means that if you're over 25 and value your peace and quiet, you'd best choose a base outside town.

A 2-km (1-mi) walk along the beach road through the grounds of the ruined **Clifden Castle** is the best way to explore the seashore. The castle was built in 1815 by John D'Arcy, the town's founder, who laid out the town's wide main street on a long ridge with a parallel street below it. D'Arcy was High Sheriff of Galway, and his greatest wish was to establish a center of law and order in what he saw as the lawless wilderness of Connemara. Before the founding of Clifden, the interior of Connemara was largely uninhabited, with most of its population clinging to the seashore. Take the aptly named **Sky Road** to really appreciate Clifden's breathtaking scenery. Signposted at the west end of town, this high, narrow circuit of about 5 km (3 mi) heads west to Kingstown, skirting Clifden Bay's precipitous shores.

Where to Stay & Eat

$–$$ ✕ **Mitchell's Seafood.** A town-center shop has been cleverly converted into a stylish, two-story eatery. On the first floor, beyond the plate-glass windows, there's a welcoming open fire, and you can eat at the bar or at one of the polished wood tables. Exposed stone walls and wooden floors are alluring accents on the quieter second level. Braised whole sea bass with fennel butter typifies the simple treatment given to seafood. The all-day menu also features lighter options like homemade spicy fishcakes and fresh crab salad. There are several meat options, including traditional Irish stew of Connemara lamb and fresh vegetables. ⊠ *Market St.* ☎ *095/21867* ⊟ *MC, V* ⊘ *Closed Nov.–Feb.*

$$$ ✕ **O'Grady's Seafood.** A Clifden institution, this intimate, town-center restaurant serves fresh local ingredients, primarily seafood, in a style that's more modish than you might expect in the wilds of Connemara. Aiming for imaginatively flavored food in a relaxed informal atmosphere, O'Grady pleases with its mussels with garlic, sweet chilies, and spring onions in coconut milk, or its roast duckling with red cabbage, rosti and redcurrant sauce. The bright, minimalist decor provides a perfect backdrop for work by local artists, most of which is for sale. ⊠ *Market St.* ☎ *095/21450* ⊟ *MC, V* ⊘ *Closed Sun. and Nov.–Apr. No lunch.*

★ $$$ ✕▨ **Rock Glen Manor House.** You will probably be "greeted" by Gregory, a tiny Connemara pony who likes to stand at the gate savoring the breeze. Enter this realm and you'll see riding boots and tennis rackets in the hall—clearly, John and Evangeline Roche's beautifully converted 1815 shooting lodge feels more like a private home than a top-class hotel. A turf fire warms the large, sumptuous drawing room—an eye-knocking symphony in red chicly fitted out with houndstooth-check armchairs and gilt-framed mirrors (plus a lovely array of magazines, books, and board games). Fluffy mohair or chintz spreads cover the beds in the sweetly furnished guest rooms. In the Victorian-style restaurant ($$–$$$), you can expect such winners as roasted rack of lamb with an herb crust and duxelles. To get here from Clifden, cross the bridge at the west end of town and walk less than 1 km (½ mi) down the R341 Roundstone road. ☒ *Co. Galway* ☎ *095/21035* 🖷 *095/21737* ⊕ *www. connemara.net/rockglen-hotel* ➳ *26 rooms* ⚥ *Restaurant, tennis court, fishing, horseback riding, bar; no a/c* ⊟ *AE, MC, V* ⊘ *Closed Nov.–mid-Feb. No lunch* ⊙ *BP.*

★ **$$$** ⊞ **Abbeyglen Castle Hotel.** Creeper-covered, as if under a Sleeping Beauty spell, Abbeyglen sits framed by towering trees at the foot of the glorious Twelve Bens Mountains. If time hasn't completely stopped here, it has certainly slowed down—but that's just the way the relaxed guests want it. Surrounded by gardens with waterfalls and streams, the Victorian castle-manor was built in 1832 by John D'Arcy, the founder of Clifton and builder of Clifden Castle. Inside, each guest room is uniquely decorated with heavy, ornate, dark-wood furniture and rich colors befitting a castle. Although it's in a very quiet and seemingly secluded location, the hotel becomes busy during complimentary afternoon tea, and has a busy nightlife scene, with live traditional music in its bar and big-name touring acts in its function room. This makes it a particularly popular weekend destination with Irish city-dwellers. ☒ *Sky Rd., Co. Galway* ☎ *095/22832* 🖷 *095/21797* ⊕ *www.abbeyglen.ie* ➳ *38 rooms* ⚥ *Restaurant, tennis court, pool, sauna, fishing, bar; no a/c* ⊟ *AE, DC, MC, V* ⊘ *Closed last 3 wks of Jan.* ⊙ *BP.*

$$ ⊞ **Quay House.** A roaring turf fire in the sitting room greets you at this three-story Georgian house, Clifden's oldest building (1820). It's a short walk from the busy town center, and an oasis of calm beside the harbor quay. Rooms are unusually spacious, and those in the main house are imaginatively decorated with deep-color walls and witty bygones; all but one have sea views. There are also seven studio rooms with balconies overlooking the harbor. Proprietors Julia and Patrick Foyle have tucked in homey touches, such as books and model boats. ☒ *The Quay, Connemara, Co. Galway* ☎ *095/21369* 🖷 *095/21608* ⊕ *www. thequayhouse.com* ➳ *14 rooms* ⚥ *Some kitchenettes, fishing; no a/c* ⊟ *MC, V* ⊘ *Closed Nov.–mid-Mar., except by arrangement* ⊙ *EP.*

Nightlife

Abbeyglen Castle Hotel (☒ Sky Rd. ☎ 095/21201) hosts musical sessions in the bar most nights from June to September and occasional visits by big-name acts.

Sports & the Outdoors

BICYCLING Explore Connemara by renting a bike from **John Mannion & Son** (☒ Railway View ☎ 095/21160).

GOLF On a dramatic stretch of Atlantic coastline, the 18-hole, par-72 course at the **Connemara Golf Club** (☒ South of Clifden, Ballyconneely ☎ 095/23502) measures 7,174 yards.

Shopping

The Connemara Hamper (☒ Market St. ☎ 095/21054), a small but well-stocked specialist food shop, is an ideal place to pick up picnic fare, with its excellent Irish farmhouse cheeses, pâtés, smoked Connemara salmon, and Irish handmade chocolates. **Millar's Connemara Tweeds** (⊠ Main St. ☎ 095/21038), an arts-and-crafts gallery, carries a good selection of traditional tweeds and hand knits. The **Station House Courtyard** (⊠ Old Railway Station, Bridge St. ☎ 095/21699) is a cobbled courtyard with crafts studios and designer-wear outlets.

Letterfrack

㉟ *14 km (9 mi) north of Clifden on N59.*

The 5,000-acre **Connemara National Park** lies southeast of the village of Letterfrack. Its visitor center covers the area's history and ecology, particularly the origins and growth of peat—and presents the depressing statistic that more than 80% of Ireland's peat, 5,000 years in the making, has been destroyed in the last 90 years. You can also get details on the many excellent walks and beaches in the area. The misleadingly-named "park" is, in fact, just rocky or wooded wilderness territory, albeit with some helpful trails marked out to aid your exploration. It includes part of the famous **Twelve Bens** mountain range, which are for experienced hill walkers only. An easier hike is the spectacular **Pollrark River Gorge** and **Glanmore Valley.** Ask for advice on a hike suited to your abilities and interests at the visitor center. ☎ 095/41054 ⌛ *Park free, visitor center €2.50* ☉ *Park freely accessible; visitor center Apr., May, and Sept.–mid-Oct., daily 10–5:30; June, daily 10–6:30; July and Aug., daily 9:30–6:30.*

Where to Stay & Eat

★ **$$$** ✕▦ **Renvyle House.** A lake at its front door, the Atlantic Ocean at its back door, and the mountains of Connemara as a backdrop form the enthralling setting for this hotel 8 km (5 mi) north of Letterfrack. Once the legendary retreat of that noted Irish man of letters, Oliver St. John Gogarty of Dublin (on whom James Joyce modeled Buck Mulligan in *Ulysses*)—and, as such, a focal point for the Irish literary renaissance of the early 20th century—Renvyle is rustic and informal; it has exposed beams and brickwork, and numerous open turf fires. The main salon, called The Long Room, is one of the most eminently civilized rooms in Ireland—all tranquil beige, endless chairs, and pretty pictures. The comfortable guest rooms, elegantly decorated in a floral style, all have breathtaking views. The softly lighted restaurant's table d'hôte menu is based on traditional Irish fare ($$$$). ⊠ *Renvyle, Co. Galway* ☎ *095/ 43511* ◱ *095/43515* ⊕ *www.renvyle.com* ⇱ *56 rooms* ⌂ *Restaurant, 9-hole golf course, 2 tennis courts, pool, fishing, horseback riding, bar; no a/c* ▤ *AE, DC, MC, V* ☉ *Closed Jan.–mid-Feb.* �◎ *BP.*

★ **$$$** ✕▦ **Rosleague Manor.** This pink, creeper-clad, two-story Georgian house occupies 30 lovely acres overlooking an eye-knocking view: a gorgeous lawn backdropped by Ballinakill Bay and the dreamy mountains of Connemara. Inside, the clutter of walking sticks and shooting sticks beneath the grandfather clock in the hall sets the informal, country-house tone. Well-used antiques, four-poster or large brass bedsteads, and drapes that match the William Morris wallpaper decorate the solidly comfortable and impeccably kept bedrooms. The best rooms are at the front on the first floor, overlooking the bay. At dinner in the superb restaurant ($$–$$$$), baked monkfish with crispy capers and balsamic vinegar is a typical entrée. ✉ *Rosleague Bay, Co. Galway* ☎ *095/41101* 🖷 *095/ 41168* ⊕ *www.rosleague.com* 🛏 *20 rooms* ☆ *Restaurant, tennis court, sauna, horseback riding, bar; no a/c* ☐ *AE, MC, V* ⊘ *Closed Nov.–mid-Mar.* ❍❘ *BP.*

Nightlife

For traditional music, try the **Bards' Den** (✉ Main St. ☎ 095/41042).

Shopping

Connemara Handcrafts (✉ Village center ☎ 095/41058), on the N59, carries an extensive selection of crafts and women's fashions made by the stellar Avoca Handweavers; there's also a quaint coffee shop.

Kylemore Valley

36 *Runs for 6½ km (4 mi) between Letterfrack and the intersection of N59 and R344.*

One of the more conventionally beautiful stretches of road in Connemara passes through Kylemore Valley, which is between the Twelve Bens to the south and the naturally forested Dorruagh Mountains to the north. Kylemore (the name is derived from Coill Mór, Irish for "big wood") looks "as though some colossal giant had slashed it out with a couple of strokes from his mammoth sword," as artist and author John Fitz-Maurice Mills has written. **Kylemore Abbey,** one of the most photographed castles in all of Ireland, is visible across a reedy lake with a backdrop of wooded hillside. The vast Gothic Revival, turreted, gray-stone castle was built as a private home between 1861 and 1868 by Mitchell Henry, a member of Parliament for County Galway, and his wife, Margaret, who had fallen in love with the spot during a carriage ride while on their honeymoon. The Henrys spared no expense—the final bill for their house is said to have come to £1.5 million—and employed mostly local laborers, thereby abetting the famine relief effort (this area was among the worst hit in all of Ireland). Adjacent to the house is a spectacular Neo-Gothic church, which, sadly, became the burial place for Margaret, who died after contracting "Nile fever" on a trip to Egypt. In 1920, nuns from the Irish Abbey of the Nuns of St. Benedict, who fled their abbey in Belgium during World War I, eventually sought refuge in Kylemore, which had been through a number of owners and decades of decline after the Henrys died. Still in residence, the Benedictine nuns run a girls' boarding school here. Three reception rooms and the main hall are open to the public, as are a crafts center and a simple cafeteria. There's also a 6-acre walled Victorian garden; a shuttle bus from the abbey departs every 15 minutes during opening hours for the garden. An exhibition and video explaining the history of the house can be viewed year-round at the abbey, and the grounds are freely accessible most of the year. Ask at the excellent crafts shop for directions to the **Gothic Chapel** (a five-minute walk from the abbey), a tiny replica of Norwich Cathedral built by the Henrys. (Norwich was built by the English Benedictines, in a felicitous anticipation of Kylemore's fate.)

Fodor'sChoice
★

✉ *About ¼ km (½ mi) back from the Kylemore Valley road* ☎ *095/ 41146* ⊕ *www.kylemoreabbey.com* ✉ *Chapel and grounds free; exhibition and garden €7, including shuttle bus to garden* ⊙ *Crafts shop, grounds, and cafeteria mid-Mar.–Nov., daily 10–6; exhibition and garden Easter–Nov., daily 9–5:30.*

Fodor'sChoice
★
Beyond Kylemore, N59 travels for some miles along **Killary Harbour,** a narrow fjord (the only one in Ireland) that runs for 16 km (10 mi) between County Mayo's Mweelrea Mountains to the north and County Galway's Dorruagh Mountains to the south. The dark, deep water of the fjord reflects the magnificent steep-sided hills that border it, creating a haunting scene of natural grandeur. The harbor has an extremely safe anchorage, 13 fathoms (78 feet) deep for almost its entire length and sheltered from storms by mountain walls. The rafts floating in Killary Harbour belong to fish-farming consortia that artificially raise salmon and trout in cages beneath the water. This is a matter of some controversy all over the west. Although some people welcome the employment opportunities, others bemoan the visual blight of the rafts. From mid-April through mid-October **Sea Cruise Connemara** (✉ Nancy's Point, 2 km [1 mi] west of Leenane on the N59 Clifden road ☎ 091/566–736) runs 1½-hour trips around Killary Harbour in an enclosed catamaran launch with seating for 120 passengers, plus a bar and restaurant.

Leenane

③⑦ *18 km (11 mi) east of Letterfrack on N59.*

Nestled idyllically at the foot of the Maamturk Mountains and overlooking the tranquil waters of Killary Harbour, Leenane is a tiny village noted for its role as the setting for the film *The Field,* which starred Richard Harris. Its name appears in Martin McDonagh's *Leenane Trilogy,* an unflattering view of rural Irish life featuring a cast of tragicomic grotesques. Although the play was an international hit for Galway's Druid Theatre Company, it brought a renown that the people of Leenane presumably could have done without. Leenane's **Cultural Centre,** in the center of the small town, focuses on the traditional industry of North Connemara and West Mayo. More than 20 breeds of sheep graze around the house, and there are demonstrations of carding, spinning, weaving, and the dyeing of wool with natural plant dyes. ☎ *095/42323* ⊕ *www. leenane-connemara.com* ✉ *€3* ⊙ *Apr.–June, Sept., and Oct., daily 9:30–7; July and Aug., daily 9–7.*

Where to Stay

$$$–$$$$ ✕▦ **Delphi Mountain Resort & Spa.** Built entirely from natural materials, chiefly local stone and storm-felled timber, and topped off with a grass roof, this spectacular resort and spa blends exquisitely into its stunning surroundings. The design may feel futuristic but the curving corridors are meant to recall traditional Irish ring forts. While natural stone is used at every opportunity, indoors as well as out, the result is surprisingly comfortable; it doesn't hurt that there's a massive turf fire, whose aroma penetrates the whole hotel, lighting in the reception area from early morning. Guest rooms continue the organic theme with nat-

ural fabrics and modern wood furnishings; all have either a balcony or patio, and are decorated with contemporary paintings and ceramics. Large windows in the bar and restaurant enable you to make the most of the views of unspoiled hills all around. The Canadian chef, Jeff McCourt, is committed to using organic produce in short, strongly seasonal menus prepared in a contemporary Irish style. While a wide range of body-pampering therapies are offered in the spa, there is no gym: the idea is that you use the great outdoors as your gym, and staff will advise on suitable activities. The mountain air itself is a tonic, and, what's more, it's free. ⊠ *Co. Galway* ☎ *095/42208* 🖷 *095/42303* ⊕ *www.delphiescape. com* ⌁ *8 suites, 14 rooms with bath* ⚭ *Restaurant, spa, fishing, cycling, hiking, horseback riding, bar* ▤ *AE, MC, V* ⊙ *Closed mid-Dec.–mid-Jan.*

$$$ 🖭 **Delphi Lodge.** In the heart of what is arguably Mayo's most spectac-
Fodor'sChoice ular mountain and lake scenery, 5 km (3 mi) east of Leenane off N59,
★ this attractive Georgian sporting lodge heavily stocked with fishing paraphernalia has a lovely lakeside setting. Owners Peter and Jane Mantle are gracious hosts and valuable storehouses of information and stories. Fishing is the main attraction, but guests also come for the peace and quiet, or like England's Prince Charles, a recent visitor, to sketch the scenery. Pine furniture, floral curtains, and wonderfully comfortable beds fill the bright, spacious bedrooms, some with lake views. Don't expect a TV: because of the surrounding mountains, there is no reception. Guests dine together at a long oak table; there's an excellent wine list and a self-service bar. There are also cottages, which require a three-day minimum stay. ⊠ *Co. Galway* ☎ *095/42222* 🖷 *095/42296* ⊕ *www. delphilodge.ie* ⌁ *12 rooms, 5 cottages* ⚭ *Dining room, fishing, billiards, lounge, library; no a/c, no room TVs* ▤ *AE, MC, V* ⊙ *Closed mid-Dec.–mid-Jan.* ⊙l *BP.*

en route You have two options for traveling onward to Westport. The first is to take the direct route on N59. The second is to detour through the **Doolough Valley** between the Mweelrea Mountains (to the west) and the Sheeffry Hills (to the east) and on to Westport via Louisburgh (on the southern shore of Clew Bay). The latter route adds about 24 km (15 mi) to the trip, but devotees of this part of the west claim that it will take you through the region's most impressive, unspoiled stretch of scenery. If you opt for the longer route, turn left onto R335 1½ km (1 mi) beyond Leenane. Just after this turn, you'll hear the powerful rush of the Aasleagh Falls. You can park over the bridge, stroll along the river's shore, and soak in the splendor of the surrounding mountains.

Look out as you travel north for the great bulk of 2,500-foot-high **Croagh Patrick**; its size and conical shape make it one of the west's most distinctive landmarks. On clear days a small white building is visible at its summit (it stands on a ½-acre plateau), as is the wide path that ascends to it. The latter is the Pilgrim's Path. Each year about 25,000 people, many of them barefoot, follow the path to pray to St. Patrick in the oratory on its peak. St. Patrick spent the 40 days and nights of Lent here during the period in which he was converting

Ireland to Christianity. The traditional date for the pilgrimage is the last Sunday in July; in the past, the walk was made at night, with pilgrims carrying burning torches, but that practice has been discontinued. The climb involves a gentle uphill slope, but you need to be fit and agile to complete the last half-hour, over scree (small loose rocks with no trail). This is why most climbers carry a stick or staff (traditionally made of ash, and called an ash plant) which helps you to stop sliding backwards. These can sometimes be bought in the car park. The hike can be made in about three hours (round-trip) on any fine day and is well worth the effort for the magnificent views of the islands of Clew Bay, the Sheeffry Hills to the south (with the Bens visible behind them), and the peaks of Mayo to the north. The climb starts at Murrisk, a village about 8 km (5 mi) before Westport on the R335 Louisburgh road.

Westport

★ ⑧ *32 km (20 mi) north of Leenane on R335.*

By far the most attractive town in County Mayo, Westport is on an inlet of Clew Bay, a wide expanse of sea dotted with islands and framed by mountain ranges. One of the most gentrified and Anglo-Irish heritage towns in Ireland, its Georgian origins are clearly defined by the broad streets skirting the gently flowing river and, particularly, by the lime-fringed central avenue called the Mall. Built as an O'Malley stronghold, the entire town received a face lift when the Brownes, who came from Sussex in the reign of Elizabeth I, constructed Westport House and much of the modern town, which was laid out by architect James Wyatt when he was employed to finish the grand estate of Westport House. Today, Westport's streets radiate from its central **Octagon**, where an old-fashioned farmers' market is held on Thursday mornings; look for work clothes, harnesses, tools, and children's toys for sale. Traditional shops—of ironmongers, drapers, and the like—dot the streets that lead to the Octagon, while a riverside mall is lined with tall lime trees. At Westport's Quay, about 2 km (1 mi) outside town, a large warehouse has been attractively restored as holiday apartments, and there are some good bars and decent restaurants.

The showpiece of the town remains **Westport House and Country Park,** a stately home built on the site of an earlier castle (believed to have been the home of the 16th-century warrior queen, Grace O'Malley) and most famed for its setting right on the shores of a beautiful lake. The house was begun in 1730 to the designs of Richard Castle, added to in 1778, and completed in 1788 by architect James Wyatt for the Marquess of Sligo of the Browne family. The rectangular, three-story house is furnished with late-Georgian and Victorian pieces. Family portraits by Opie and Reynolds, a huge collection of old Irish silver and old Waterford glass, plus an opulent group of paintings—including *The Holy Family* by Rubens—are on display. A word of caution: Westport isn't your usual staid country house. The old dungeons now house video games and the grounds have given way to a small amusement park for children and a children's zoo. In fact, the lake is now littered with swan-shaped "pedaloes," boats that may be fun for families but help destroy the perfect Georgian grace of the setting. If these elements don't sound like a draw, arrive early when it's less likely to be busy. The Farmyard area has garden-plant sales, an indoor soft-play area, a gift shop, and a coffee shop. ⊠ *Off N59 south of Westport turnoff, clearly signposted from the Octagon* ☎ *098/25430* 🏠 *House €10, family day-ticket for all attractions €40* ☉ *House May and Sept., weekends 2–5. Grounds and house June and Aug. 22–31, daily 2–6; July–Aug. 21, Mon.–Sat. 11:30–6, Sun. 2–6.*

Clew Bay is said to have 365 islands, one for every day of the year. The biggest and most interesting to visit is **Clare Island,** at the mouth of the bay. In fine weather the rocky, hilly island, which is 8 km (5 mi) long and 5 km (3 mi) wide, affords beautiful views south toward Connemara, east across Clew Bay, and north to Achill Island. About 150 people live on the island today, but before the 1845–47 famine it had a population of about 1,700. A 15th-century tower overlooking the harbor was once the stronghold of Granuaile, the pirate queen, who ruled the area until her death in 1603. She is buried on the island, in its 12th-century Cistercian abbey. Today most visitors seek out the island for its unusual peace and quiet, golden beaches, and unspoiled landscape. Ferries depart from Roonagh Pier, near Louisburgh, a scenic 19-km (12-mi) drive from Westport on R335 past several long sandy beaches. The crossing takes about 15 minutes. Dolphins often accompany the boats on the trip, and there are large populations of seals under the island's cliffs. Birdwatchers, hikers, cyclists, and sea anglers may want to stay for longer than a day trip; inquire at the Westport TIO or call the **Clare Island Development Office** (☎ 098/25087) for information about accommodations on the island. ☎ *098/25045 O'Malley's Ferries, 098/25212 for the Pirate Queen boat* 🚢 *Ferry €15 round-trip* ☉ *Sailings usually twice daily, May–mid-Sept., weather permitting.*

Where to Stay & Eat

★ **$$–$$$** ✕ **Quay Cottage.** Fishing nets, glass floats, lobster pots, and greenery hang from the high-pitched, exposed-beam roof of this tiny waterside cottage at the entrance to Westport House. It is both an informal wine bar and a shellfish restaurant. Rush-seat chairs, polished oak tables, and an open fire in the evenings add to the comfortable, none-too-formal atmosphere. Try the chowder special (a thick vegetable and mussel soup), garlic-butter crab claws, or a half-pound steak fillet, and be sure to sample the homemade brown bread and ice cream. ⊠ *The Quay* ☎ *098/26412* ▱ *AE, MC, V* ☉ *Closed Jan.*

$$$$ ✕▥ **Newport House.** This handsome, riverside Georgian house dominates the village of Newport, 12 km (7 mi) north of Westport on N59. Kieran and Thelma Thompson's grand and elegant private home has spacious public rooms furnished with gilt-framed family portraits, Regency mirrors and chairs, handwoven Donegal carpeting, and crystal chandeliers. A sweeping staircase leads to the bedrooms, which are decorated with pretty chintz drapes and a mix of Victorian antiques and old furniture. Most bedrooms have sitting areas and good views of the gardens. Home-smoked salmon and fresh local seafood are specialties on the traditional four-course set dinner menu; the ice cream is also homemade. ⊠ *Newport, Co. Mayo* ☎ *098/41222* 🖶 *098/41613* ⊕ *www.newporthouse. ie* ⌨ *19 rooms* ⚿ *Restaurant, fishing, bar; no a/c, no room TVs* ☰ *AE, DC, MC, V* ⊘ *Closed Oct.–mid-Mar.* ⭤ *BP.*

★ **$$** ✕⊞ **Olde Railway Hotel.** When the English novelist William Makepeace Thackeray stayed here in 1842, he called it "one of the prettiest, comfortablist inns in Ireland." You can understand why. Fishing trophies, Victorian plates, framed prints, and watercolors brighten up the lobby and lounge of this unusual, family-run inn. A fascinating mix of Victorian and older antiques decorates the sunny bedrooms, which have double-glazed Georgian sash windows. Delightfully, the rooms overlook either the Carrowbeg River or the pretty gardens. The pretty glass-paned Conservatory Restaurant ($$$$) serves fresh local produce and game specialties and the bar has an excellent, good-value menu. ⊠ *The Mall, Co. Mayo* ☎ *098/25166* 🖶 *098/25090* ⊕ *www.anu.ie/railwayhotel* ⌨ *25 rooms* ⚿ *Restaurant, cable TV, fishing, bar; no a/c* ☰ *AE, MC, V* ⭤ *BP.*

Nightlife

A good spot to try for traditional music and good pub grub is the **Towers Pub and Restaurant** (⊠ The Quay ☎ 098/26534). In summer, there are outdoor tables set up here beside the bay. In Westport's town center try **Matt Molloy's** (⊠ Bridge St. ☎ 098/26655); Matt Malloy is not only the owner but also a member of the musical group the Chieftains. Traditional music is, naturally, the main attraction.

Sports & the Outdoors

BICYCLING   Enjoy the spectacular scenery of Clew Bay at a leisurely pace on a rented bike from **J. P. Breheny & Sons** (⊠ Castlebar St. ☎ 098/25020).

FISHING   Fishing tackle, bait, and licenses can be obtained at **Hewetson Bros** (⊠ Bridge St. ☎ 098/26018). To book a place for the day on a deep-sea-fishing boat operating out of Westport's Clew Bay, contact **Francis Clarke or Austin Gill** (☎ 098/25481).

GOLF   The Fred Hawtree–designed **Westport Golf Club** (⊠ Carrowholly ☎ 098/28262), beneath Croagh Patrick, overlooks Clew Bay. The 18-hole, par-73 course has twice been the venue for the Irish Amateur Championship.

Shopping

Carraig Donn (⊠ Bridge St. ☎ 098/26287) carries its own line of knitwear and a good selection of crystal, jewelry, and ceramics. **McCormack's** (⊠ Bridge St. ☎ 098/25619) has a traditional butcher shop downstairs, but upstairs it's an attractive gallery and café with work by local artists for sale. **O'Reilly/Turpin** (⊠ Bridge St. ☎ 098/28151) sells the best of contemporary Irish design in knitwear, ceramics, and other decorative items. **Satch Kiely** (⊠ Westport Quay ☎ 098/25775) carries fine antique furniture and decorative pieces. **Treasure Trove** (⊠ Bridge St. ☎ 098/25118) has a good stock of antiques and curios, including linen and local memorabilia. **Westport Crystal** (⊠ The Quay ☎ 098/27780) is a factory outlet that sells exclusive stemware and giftware.

Achill Island

39 *16 km (10 mi) west of Mulrany, 58 km (36 mi) northwest of Westport.*

Heaven on earth in good weather, when its splendid scenery can be fully appreciated, Achill Island is a destination you'll probably want to head for—but only if you're able to *see* its cliff walks and sandy beaches. At 147 square km (57 square mi) and only 20 feet from the mainland, this mass of bogs and wild heather is the largest island off Ireland's coast. A short causeway leads from the mainland to Achill Sound, the first village on the island. The main road runs through rhododendron plantations to Keel, which has a 3-km (2-mi) beach with spectacular cathedral-like rock formations in the cliffs at its east end. There's a longer scenic route signposted ATLANTIC DRIVE. Dugoort, on the north shore of the island, is a small village with a beautiful golden strand. Nearby is the cottage used by Heinrich Böll, the German writer and Nobel prize winner whose *Irish Diary,* written in the 1950s, has introduced many people to this part of Ireland. The cottage is now part of a center for German-Irish cultural exchanges. On Achill's north coast above Dugoort, 2,204-ft-high Slievemore is the island's highest summit. Until ten years ago, the people of Achill made a very poor living. Tourism has improved things, as has the establishment of cottage industries (mainly knitting) and shark fishing, which is popular from April through July. Alas, Achill's popularity has led to a rash of new, not always appropriate, development, most noticeably clusters (or "villages") of bleak concrete vacation cottages that stand empty for 10 months out of 12.

Where to Stay

$–$$ ✕☲ **Gray's Guest House.** Vi McDowell's establishment occupies a series of houses that have been ingeniously joined together, occupying a whole street of the tiny village of Dugort. She has many regular visitors—some of whom have been coming here since it opened in 1970—and you'll be sure to find one curled up with a book beside the blazing fire in a comfortable old armchair, or another seeking out a sunny spot in one of several conservatories. Due to the age and unusual physical shapes of the houses, guest rooms and bathrooms vary considerably in shape and size. The emphasis is on old-fashioned comfort rather than style— something you will be thankful for if the weather confines you indoors. Children are welcome and have an indoor playroom and a safe outdoor play area. The restaurant is open to non-residents, and serves a traditional set menu. ⊠ *Dugort (about ten mi north of Achill Sound and the causeway, on the coast road)* ☎ *098/43244* 🖷 *098/43315* 🖙 *15 rooms* ♻ *Restaurant, some room phones, table tennis, croquet, fishing, some pets allowed; no a/c* ▭ *No credit cards* ☉ *Closed Christmas wk.*

Sports & the Outdoors

Tour the cliffs of Achill on a bike from **O'Malley's Island Sports** (⊠ Keel ☎ 098/43125).

en route The shortest route to Ballina (N59 via Bangor and Crossmolina) runs for about 24 km (15 mi) across desolate, almost uninhabited bog, some of which has had its turf cut down to rock level by successive generations searching for fuel. If you intend to visit the Mullet Peninsula, take this route. If you are heading directly for Ballina, take the longer but more interesting route by backtracking to Newport and continuing through Castlebar, Pontoon, and Foxford.

Castlebar

40 *40 k (26 mi) east of Achill Island, 18 km (11 mi) east of Westport on N5.*

The administrative capital of Mayo, Castlebar is a tidy little town with an attractive, tree-bordered green. Hatred of landlords ran high in the area, due to the ruthless, battering-ram evictions ordered by the earl of Lucan during the mid-19th-century famine. The disappearance in the 1960s of his high-living successor, the seventh earl, after the violent death in London of his children's nanny, is said to have given today's tenants a perfect pretext for withholding their rents. In 1879 Michael Davitt founded the Land League, which fought for land reform, in the **Imperial Hotel** (⊠ The Green ☎ 094/902–1961); it's worth a visit to take in the splendor of the decor in the Gothic-style dining room, which was used for many historic meetings in the 19th century. At the **Linen Hall Arts Centre** (⊠ Linenhall St. ☎ 094/902–3733), exhibitions and performances are often scheduled.

Turlough

41 *6½ km (4 mi) east of Castlebar on N5.*

Before the opening of the Museum of Country Life, Turlough was chiefly visited for its round tower (freely accessible), which marks the site of an early monastery, traditionally associated with Saint Patrick, and the nearby ruins of a 17th-century church. Nowadays, it is one of many Irish villages whose empty streets bear witness to dramatic changes in the rural way of life. Once a thriving hub, with a village school, two pubs, and a busy shop, Turlough now has a population of about 300, one pub with a small shop attached, and no school. Rather than working on the land, most of the locals commute to jobs in nearby Castlebar. To understand the forces that have led to such dramatic changes in Turlough, pay a visit to the **Museum of Country Life**, which focuses on rural Ireland between 1860 and 1960—a way of life that remained unchanged for many years, then suddenly came to an end within living memory. At this highly acclaimed museum, the only branch of the National Museum of Ireland outside Dublin, you're invited to imagine yourself back in a vanished world, before the internal combustion engine, rural electrification, indoor plumbing, television, and increased education transformed people's lives and expectations. For many, this is a journey into a strange place, where water had to be carried from a well, turf had to be brought home from the bog, fires had to be lighted daily for heat and cooking, and clothes had to be made painstakingly by hand in the long winter evenings. Among the displayed items are authentic furniture and utensils; hunting, fishing, and agricultural implements; clothing; and objects relating to games, pastimes, religion, and education.

FodorsChoice
★

The museum experience starts in Turlough Park House, built in the High Victorian Gothic style in 1865 and set in pretty lakeside gardens. Just three rooms have been restored to illustrate the way the landowners lived. A sensational modern four-story, curved building houses the main exhibit. Cleverly placed windows allow panoramic views of the surrounding park and the distant round tower, allowing you to reflect on the reality beyond the museum's walls. Temporary exhibitions, such as one called "Romanticism and Reality," help illustrate the divide between the dreamy image of old rural life and its actual hardships. The shop sells museum-branded and handcrafted gift items as well as a good selection of books on related topics. A café with indoor and outdoor tables is in the stable yard, and you can take scenic lakeside walks in the park. Craft demonstrations and workshops take place on Wednesday and Sunday afternoons. ⊠ *Turlough Park* ☎ *01/648–6453 in Dublin* ⊕ *www.museum.ie* ☜ *Free* ☉ *Tues.–Sat. 10–5, Sun. 2–5.*

en route

As you travel from Turlough northeast to Ballina, you have a choice of two routes. The longer and more scenic is via the tiny, wooded village of Pontoon, skirting the western shore of Lough Conn and passing through the rough bogland of the Glen of Nephin, beneath the dramatic heather-clad slopes of Nephin Mountain (2,653 feet). The shorter route follows N5 and N58 to Foxford, a pretty village with several crafts and antiques shops. A good place for a break is the **Foxford Woolen Mills Visitor Center,** where you can explore the crafts shop and grab a bite at the restaurant. The "Foxford Experience" tells the story of the wool mill, famous for its tweeds and blankets, from the time of the famine in the mid-19th century—when it was founded by the Sisters of Charity to combat poverty—to the present day. ⊠ *Lower Main St., Foxford* ☎ *094/925–6756* ☜ *€8* ☉ *Nov.–Apr., Mon.–Sat. 10–6, Sun. 2–6; May–Oct., Mon.–Sat. 10–6, Sun. noon–6; tour every 20 mins.*

Ballina

42 *34 km (22 mi) northeast of Turlough.*

Ballina's chief attraction is fishing for salmon and trout in the River Moy and nearby Lough Conn. With a population of 7,500, this is the largest town in County Mayo. To some eyes, Ballina's town center may appear rundown, but its unspoiled, old-fashioned shops and pubs contain many treasures. Try the bar food (Mon.–Sat. 11 AM–6 PM) at **Gaughan's** (⊠ O'Rahilly St. ☎ 096/21151), where the classic wooden interior dates from the mid-19th century.

Where to Stay & Eat

$$ ✕⊡ **Enniscoe House.** Magnificent and magical, this pink-hued, square Georgian mansion is dramatically sited on the shores of Lough Conn under towering Mount Nephin. However, there is nothing intimidating about its interior, even though its well-worn grandeur is steeped in history. Susan Kellett is a descendant of the original family who arrived here in the 1660s, and will give you the story behind the many ances-

FodorsChoice ★

tral portraits staring at you from the calico-flocked library walls. Your jaw may drop at the sight of the magisterial main salon—a vast room done in stately-house ivories and beiges, swathed in period wallpapers and draperies, set with 18th-century breakfronts, gilded French side tables, Chippendale mahogany chairs, gilt-framed paintings, and enough cozy corners to please even a Jane Austen. A maze of quirky corridors and staircases leads to the guest rooms, which are both charming and characterful, with candy-striped wallpapers, floral drapes on tall sash windows, and massive beds (some four-posters are so high you need a step ladder to get in). The beauty continues outside, as the demesne's 150 acres are crisscrossed with walks and have more than 3 km (2 mi) of peaceful lakeshore. All paths lead to the five acres of Victorian gardens, now under restoration. Here you'll find historic farm buildings converted into offices housing independent organizations, including a Mayo genealogy center, an antiques shop, and a tearoom. Meals ($$$$; reserve ahead) include fruits and vegetables grown in the organic garden. There are also four self-catering apartments. The house lies 4½ km (3 mi) south of Crossmolina and 20 km (12½ mi) west of Ballina. All in all, this is a hotel that remains a fabulous destination in itself. Go! ⊠ *Castlehill, near Crossmolina, Co. Mayo* ☎ *096/31112* 🖷 *096/31773* ⊕ *www.enniscoe.com* 🛏 *6 rooms* ♨ *Restaurant, fishing; no a/c, no room TVs* ☰ *AE, MC, V* ☉ *Closed mid-Oct.–Mar.* ⅥⓄⅠ *BP.*

$$ 🏨 **Downhill House Hotel.** Anglers and outdoorsy types flock to this hotel on 40 wooded acres beside a gushing tributary of the River Moy (just off the N59 Sligo road). The late-Victorian main house has been pretty well consumed by the bustling modern hotel, but it's a comfortable base with good all-weather leisure facilities. Rooms are decorated with Georgian-style furniture and tastefully coordinated quilts and drapes. Those in the newer wing tend to be smaller than the ones in the main house, but the former have good views of the river across the garden. There's music in the bar on weekends and midweek in July and August. Ask about weekend specials. ⊠ *Downhill Rd., Co. Mayo* ☎ *096/21033* 🖷 *096/21338* ⊕ *www.downhillhotel.ie* 🛏 *50 rooms* ♨ *Restaurant, 3 tennis courts, indoor pool, gym, hot tub, sauna, steam room, fishing, squash, 2 bars; no a/c* ☰ *AE, DC, MC, V* ⅥⓄⅠ *BP.*

Sports & the Outdoors

BICYCLING Head for the coast north of Ballina on a bike from **Gerry's Cycle Center** (⊠ 6 Lord Edward St. ☎ 096/70455).

FISHING Fishing bait, tackle, and licenses can be obtained from **John Walkin** (⊠ Tone St. ☎ 096/22442).

GOLF **Ballina Golf Club** (⊠ Bonniconlon Rd. ☎ 096/21718) is an 18-hole parkland course, built in 1924, 1½ km (1 mi) from the town center; you can rent golf clubs here. The 18-hole **Carne Golf Links** (⊠ Belmullet ☎ 097/82292), at Belmullet Golf Club, 72 km (45 mi) west of Ballina, is one of Ireland's renowned links courses.

Shopping

McGrath's Foodland Delicatessen (⊠ O'Rahilly St. ☎ 096/21198) is an old-fashioned grocery, handy for picnic ingredients.

The North Mayo Coast

Starts 12 km (7½ mi north of Ballina at Killala.

The north Mayo coast, a dramatic, windswept stretch of cliffs, runs from Killala, the gateway to the coast, to Erris Head on the Mullet peninsula in the far west of the county. The sparsely inhabited landscape beneath an ever-changing sky consists of small farms and open moorland. The small roads and stunning views are attractive to cyclists, but be warned: the wind howls in across the Atlantic directly from Iceland, the nearest landmass. Although there are no signposted trails on this coast, there are plenty of cliff footpaths and small roads for walkers to explore. Don't miss the blowholes on Downpatrick Head—great gaps in the rocks through which plumes of water spew in rough weather. **Killala,** 12 km (7½ mi) north of Ballina, is a pleasant little seaside town overlooking Killala Bay. This was the scene of the unsuccessful French invasion of Ireland, led by Wolfe Tone in 1798. The history of this tiny bishopric goes back much further, though, as evidenced by its round, 12th-century tower.

★ ❸ Nowadays, the chief reason for visiting this coast is to see the **Céide Fields.** Widely recognized as one of Europe's most significant megalithic sites, the fields consist of rows and patterns of stones that have been preserved under a 5,000-year-old bog. These stones are the remnants of dwelling places and stone-walled fields built by a peaceful, well-organized farming community. A striking glass-and-steel pyramid houses the visitor center, where displays and an audiovisual show bring this strange landscape to life. Admission includes an optional guided walk through an excavated section of the stones; wet-weather gear is provided when necessary. ⊠ *R314, 5 km (3 mi) west of Ballycastle* ☎ *096/43325* ⊕ *www. heritageireland.ie* 🎫 *€3.50* ⊗ *Mid-Mar.–May and Oct., daily 10–5; June–Sept., daily 9:30–6:30; Nov., daily 10–4:30; Dec.–mid-Mar. by advance booking only.*

Shopping

Hackett & Turpin (⊠ Carrowteige, Ballina ☎ 097/88925) is a factory outlet for Irish sweaters. From R314 beyond the Céide Fields, follow signs for Benwee Head.

THE WEST A TO Z

To research prices, get advice from other travelers, and book travel arrangements, visit www.fodors.com.

AIR TRAVEL

Aer Lingus has daily flights from London's Heathrow Airport to Galway and Knock via Dublin; the trip takes about two hours. Ryanair flies to Knock twice daily from London's Stanstead Airport; flying time is 80 minutes. Aer Arann flies to Knock from Manchester daily.

Aer Arann has four flights daily on weekdays and two flights on weekends to the Aran Islands from Connemara Airport in Inverin. During July and August planes leave every half hour. The flights call at all three

Aran Islands. The journey takes about six minutes and costs about €44 round-trip, or about €74 including one night's B&B. For about €32 you can fly one-way and travel one-way by boat from Rossaveal. Ask about other special offers at the time of booking.

🚆 Carriers **Aer Arann** ☎ 091/593-034. **Aer Lingus** ☎ 01/844-4747. **Ryanair** ☎ 01/844-4411.

AIRPORTS

The west's most convenient international airport is Shannon, 25 km (16 mi) east of Ennis in the southwest. Galway Airport, near Galway City, is used mainly for internal flights, with steadily increasing U.K. traffic. Knock International Airport, at Charlestown—near Knock, in County Mayo—is also used for internal flights and has direct daily services to London's Stansted and to Manchester. A small airport for internal traffic only is at Knockrowen, Castlebar, in County Mayo. Flying time from Dublin is 25 to 30 minutes to all airports. No scheduled flights run from the United States to Galway or Knock; use Shannon Airport. Connemara Airport at Inverin, which is 29 km (18 mi) west of Galway on R336, services the Aran Islands.

🚆 Airport Information **Connemara Airport** ☎ 091/593-034. **Galway Airport** ☎ 091/752-874. **Knock International Airport** ☎ 094/936-7222. **Shannon Airport** ☎ 061/471-444.

TRANSFERS From Shannon Airport you can pick up a rental car to drive into the west, or you can take a bus to Limerick, from which there are bus connections into the west. Galway Airport is 6½ km (4 mi) from Galway City. No regular bus service is available from the airport to Galway, but most flight arrivals are taken to Galway Rail Station in the city center by an airline courtesy coach. Inquire when you book. A taxi from the airport to the city center costs about €10. If you're flying to Knock International Airport, you can pick up your rental car at the airport. Otherwise, inquire at the time of booking about transport to your final destination. No regular bus service is available from the airport. Connemara Airport is accessible by shuttle bus.

BOAT & FERRY TRAVEL

A ferry leaves Tarbert for Killimer every hour on the half hour and takes 20 minutes. The ferry runs every day of the year except Christmas and costs €16 one-way, €32 round-trip. (Ferries return from Killimer every hour on the hour.)

There are several options for traveling to the Aran Islands. Aran Ferries runs a boat to the islands from Rossaveal, 32 km (20 mi) west of Galway City, which makes the crossing in 20 minutes and costs about €28 round-trip, including the shuttle bus from Galway. If you are heading for Inisheer, the smallest island, the shortest crossing is from Doolin in County Clare. Aran Ferries offers service from Doolin Pier, with up to 12 sailings daily, from June through the end of September. The crossing takes about 20 minutes and costs €20 round-trip.

Island Ferries, which has a booking office in the TIO (Travel Information Office) in Galway City, has a one-hour crossing from Rossaveal for

€25 round-trip, with up to five sailings a day in summer, weather permitting. Bicycles are transported free off-season, but there may be a charge in July and August: inquire when booking. Discounts are available for families, students, and groups of four or more. If you want to stay a night or two on the islands, ask about accommodations when booking your ferry, as there are some very competitive deals. Between June and September, O'Brien Ferries sails for the Aran Islands from Galway Docks, a five-minute walk from Eyre Square. The ferries run three times a week in June and September (usually Tuesday, Thursday, and Saturday), daily in July and August. The crossing takes 90 minutes and costs €20 round-trip.

For travel between the Aran Islands, frequent inter-island ferries (run by Aran Ferries, Island Ferries, and O'Brien Ferries) are available in summer, but tickets are nontransferable, so ask the captain of your ferry about the inter-island schedule if you plan to visit more than one island; otherwise, your trip can become expensive. You can purchase ferry tickets on the island or at the TIO in Galway.

🚢 Boat & Ferry Information **Aran Ferries** ⊠ Travel Information Office, Forster St., Eyre Sq., Galway City ☎ 091/568-903 or 091/537-700. **Island Ferries** ⊠ Victoria Place, Eyre Sq., Galway City ☎ 091/565-352. **O'Brien Ferries** ⊠ New Docks, Galway City ☎ 091/567-676. **Tarbert-Killimer Ferry** ☎ 065/905-3124.

BUS TRAVEL

Bus Éireann runs several expressway buses into the region from Dublin, Cork City, and Limerick City to Ennis, Galway City, Westport, and Ballina, the principal depots in the region. Expect bus rides to last about one hour longer than the time it would take you to travel the distance by car. In July and August, the provincial bus service is augmented by daily services to most resort towns. Outside these months, many coastal towns receive only one or two buses per week. Bus routes are often slow and circuitous, and service can be erratic. A copy of the Bus Éireann timetable (€0.95 from any station) is essential. Citylink operates frequent buses, with up to 14 departures daily, between Galway City and Dublin and Dublin Airport. The trip costs €10 one-way, €15 round-trip.

🚌 Bus Depots **Ballina Station** ☎ 096/71800. **Ennis Station** ☎ 065/682-4177. **Galway City Station** (Ceannt Station) ☎ 091/562-000. **Westport Station** ☎ 098/25711.

🚌 Bus Lines **Bus Éireann** ☎ 01/836-6111 in Dublin, 061/313-333 in Limerick, 021/508-188 in Cork ⊕ www.buseireann.ie. **Citylink** ⊠ Unit 1, Forster Ct., Galway City ☎ 091/564-163 ⊕ www.citylink.ie.

CAR RENTAL

If you haven't already booked a rental car at Shannon Airport, try the following rental agencies.

🚗 Agencies **Avis** ⊠ Galway Airport ☎ 091/568-886. **Budget** ⊠ Eyre Sq., Galway City ☎ 091/566-376. **Casey's Auto Rentals** ⊠ Turlough Rd., Castlebar ☎ 094/902-4618. **Diplomat Rent A Car** ⊠ Knock International Airport, Charlestown ☎ 094/936-7252. **Enterprise** ⊠ Oldenway Business Park, Ballybrit Galway City ☎ 091/771-200. **Euro Mobil** ⊠ Tuam Rd., Galway City ☎ 091/753-037. **Hertz Rent A Car** ⊠ Galway Airport ☎ 091/752-502. **Johnson & Perrot** ⊠ Headford Rd., Galway City ☎ 091/568-886. **National** ⊠ Galway Airport ☎ 091/771-929.

CAR TRAVEL

A car is the best means of traveling within the west. The 219-km (136-mi) Dublin–Galway trip takes about three hours. From Cork City take N20 through Mallow and N21 to Limerick City, picking up the N18 Ennis–Galway road in Limerick. The 209-km (130-mi) drive from Cork to Galway takes about three hours. From Killarney the shortest and most pleasant route to cover the 193 km (120 mi) to Galway (three hours) is to take N22 to Tralee, then N69 through Listowel to Tarbert and the ferry across the Shannon Estuary to Killimer in County Clare. From there, join N68 in Kilrush, and then pick up N18 in Ennis.

ROAD CONDITIONS   The west has good, wide main roads (National Primary Routes) and better-than-average local roads (National Secondary Routes), both known as "N" routes. If you stray off the beaten track on the smaller Regional ("R") or unnumbered routes, particularly in Connemara and County Mayo, you may encounter some hazardous mountain roads. Narrow, steep, and twisty, they are also frequented by untended sheep, cows, and ponies grazing "the long acre" (as the strip of grass beside the road is called) or simply straying in search of greener pastures. If you find a sheep in your path, just sound the horn, and it should scramble away. A good maxim for these roads is: "you never know what's around the next corner." Bear this in mind, and adjust your speed accordingly. Hikers and cyclists constitute an additional hazard on narrow roads.

Within the Connemara Irish-speaking area, signs are in Irish only. The main signs to recognize are Gaillimh (Galway), Ros an Mhil (Rossaveal), An Teach Doite (Maam Cross), and Sraith Salach (Recess).

ROAD MAPS   A good map, available through newsagents and TIOs (Travel Information Offices), gives Irish and English names where needed.

EMERGENCIES

For a doctor or dentist in County Clare, contact the Mid-Western Health Board (in County Limerick); in Counties Galway and Mayo, contact the Western Health Board.

🗊 Doctors & Dentists **Mid-Western Health Board** ✉ Catherine St., Limerick ☎ 061/316-655. **Western Health Board** ✉ Merlin Park, Galway City ☎ 091/751-131.

🗊 Emergency Services **Ambulance, fire, police** ☎ 999.

🗊 Pharmacies **Matt O'Flaherty** ✉ 39 Eyre Sq., Galway City ☎ 091/562-927. **O'Donnell's** ✉ Bridge St., Westport ☎ 098/25163.

TOURS

Galway City's TIO (Travel Information Office) has details of walking tours of Galway, which are organized by request. All TIOs in the west provide lists of suggested cycle tours.

The only full- and half-day guided bus tours in the region start from Galway. Bus Éireann coordinates two full-day tours, one covering Connemara and the other the Burren (each €15.25). Tours run from early June to mid-October only, with the widest choice available between mid-July and mid-August. Book in advance at the Galway City TIO, Ceannt Railway Station on Eyre Square, or the Salthill TIO, which also serve as departure points.

Lally Tours runs a day tour through Connemara and County Mayo and another to the Burren. It also operates a vintage double-decker bus, departing from Eyre Square, which runs hourly tours of Galway City from 10:30 AM until 4:30 PM from mid-March to October; tickets cost €10.

O'Neachtain Day Tours operates full-day tours of Connemara and the Burren. Tickets, €16.50 each, can be purchased from the Galway City TIO; tours depart across the street.

Burren Walking Holidays organizes two- and three-night guided walking tours of the Burren on weekends between mid-March and September. Walks are graded according to ability, and are mostly on "green roads" (grassy pathways) with great views over the Atlantic. In early summer there are a series of special themed weekends on wildflowers, environmental heritage, and farming traditions. Contact Mary Howard at the Carrigann Hotel in Lisdoonvarna, Co. Clare.

Croagh Patrick Walking Holidays offer week-long walking holidays between April and September, based in B&B accommodations in the countryside near Westport on Clew Bay. Prices include pickup from Shannon Airport, all transfers to and from walks, and the services of an experienced guide. Contact Gerry Greensmyth in Belclare, Westport, Co. Mayo.
🎫 Tours **Burren Walking Holidays** ⊠ Carrigann Hotel, Lidsoonvarna, Co. Clare ☎ 065/707-4036 ⊕ www.gateway-to-the-burren.com. **Bus Éireann** ☎ 091/562-000. **Ceannt Railway Station** ☎ 091/562-000. **Ceannt Railway Station** ☎ 091/562-000. **Lally Tours** ☎ 091/562-905. **Croagh Patrick Walking Holidays** ⊠ Belclare, Westport, Co. Mayo ☎ 098/26090 ⊕ www.walkingguideireland.com. **O'Neachtain Day Tours** ☎ 091/553-188 ⊕ www.oneachtaintours.com. **Salthill TIO** ☎ 091/520-500.

TRAIN TRAVEL

The region's main rail stations are in Galway City, Westport, and Ballina. For County Clare, travel from Cork City, Killarney, or Dublin's Heuston Station to Limerick City and continue the journey by bus. Trains for Galway, Westport, and Ballina leave from Dublin's Heuston Station. The journey time to Galway is three hours; to Ballina, 3¾ hours; and to Westport, 3½ hours.

Rail service within the region is limited. The major destinations of Galway City and Westport/Ballina are on different branch lines. Connections can only be made between Galway and the other two cities by traveling inland for about an hour to Athlone.
🚆 Train Information **Ballina Station** ☎ 096/71818. **Galway Station** ☎ 091/564-222. **Heuston Station** ☎ 01/836-6222. **Limerick City Station** ☎ 061/315-555. **Westport Station** ☎ 098/25253.

TRANSPORTATION AROUND THE WEST

A car is essential in the west, especially from September through June. Although the main cities of the area are easily reached from the rest of Ireland by rail or bus, transport within the region is sparse and badly coordinated. If a rental car is out of the question, your best option is to make Galway your base and take day tours (available mid-June through September) west to Connemara and south to the Burren, and a day or overnight trip to the Aran Islands. It *is* possible to explore the region by local and intercity bus services, but you will need plenty of time.

VISITOR INFORMATION

Bord Fáilte provides free information service, tourist literature, and an accommodations booking service at its TIOs (Travel Information Offices). The following offices are open all year, generally weekdays 9–6, daily during the high season: Aran Islands (Inishmore), Ennis, Galway City, Oughterard, and Westport.

Other TIOs, which operate seasonally, generally weekdays 9–6 and Saturday 9–1, are open as follows: Achill (June–August), Ballina (April–October), Castlebar (May–mid-September), Clifden (March–October), Cliffs of Moher (April–October), Kilkee (May–August), Kilrush (June–August), Salthill (May–September), Thoor Ballylee (April–mid-October).

🖪 Tourist Information The areas covered in this chapter comes under two different regional headquarters of tourism: Shannon ⊕ www.shannonregiontourism.ie and West of Ireland ⊕ www.irelandwest.ie. The following come under Shannon: Cliffs of Moher, Ennis, and Kilrush. All the rest are Ireland West. **Achill** ⊠ Co. Mayo ☎ 098/45384. **Aran Islands (Inishmore)** ⊠ Co. Galway ☎ 099/61263 🖷 099/61420. **Ballina** ⊠ Cathedral Rd., Co. Mayo ☎ 096/70848. **Castlebar** ⊠ Linenhall St., Co. Mayo ☎ 094/902-1207. **Clifden** ⊠ Galway Rd., Co. Galway ☎ 095/21163. **Cliffs of Moher** ⊠ Co. Clare ☎ 065/708-1171. **Ennis** ⊠ Arthur's Row, Town Center, Co. Clare ☎ 065/682-8366 ⊕ www.shannon-dev.ie/tourism. **Galway City** ⊠ Forster St., Eyre Sq., Co. Galway ☎ 091/537-700 ⊕ www.irelandwest.ie. **Kilkee** ⊠ O'Connell Sq., Co. Clare ☎ 065/905-6112. **Kilrush** ⊠ The Square, Co. Clare ☎ 065/905-1577. **Oughterard** ⊠ Main St., Co. Galway ☎ 091/552-808. **Salthill** ⊠ The Promenade, Co. Galway ☎ 091/520-500. **Thoor Ballylee** ⊠ Near Gort, Co. Clare ☎ 091/631-436. **Westport** ⊠ The Mall, Co. Mayo ☎ 098/25711 🖷 098/26709.

THE NORTHWEST

7

TAKE A POETRY BREAK
alongside Yeats' grave under
Ben Bulben mountain ⇨*p.422*

GET YOURSELF FITTED OUT
with an Aran sweater in Ardara ⇨*p.431*

WALK BEHIND GARBO'S SPIRIT
through Glenveagh Castle ⇨*p.440*

IMMERSE YOURSELF IN IRISH ART
at Sligo town's Model Arts Centre ⇨*p.415*

DRINK FLOWER-POWERED WINE
made in Glencolumbkille ⇨*p.430*

STAND ATOP A 40,000-TON CAIRN
on the summit of Knocknarea ⇨*p.419*

Updated by
Catherine
Morrison

GLANCE AT A MAP OF IRELAND THAT HAS scenic roads printed in green, and chances are your eye will be drawn to the far-flung peninsulas of northwest Ireland. At virtually every bend in the roads weaving through counties Donegal, Leitrim, and Sligo, there's something to justify all those green markings. On an island where there's no shortage of majestic scenery, the northwest claims its full share. Cool, clean waters from the roaring Atlantic have shaped the terrain into long peninsulas—creating a raw, sensual landscape that makes it seem as if the earth is still under construction.

But what you see *this moment* may not be what you will see an hour from now. Clouds and rain linger over mountains, glens, cliffs, beaches, and bogs, to be chased minutes later by sunshine and rainbows. The air, the light, and the colors of the countryside change as though with a turn of a kaleidoscope. Skies brighten, then darken, calling forth a spectrum of subtle reds and purples from the unkempt gorse and heather, and then just as quickly painting the grassy meadows greener than any green you've ever seen. The writer William Butler Yeats and his brother Jack Butler Yeats, a painter, immortalized this splendidly lush and rugged countryside in their work.

Northwest Ireland covers the most northerly part of Ireland's Atlantic coastline, running from Sligo in the south along Donegal's remote, windswept peninsulas to Malin Head in the far north. These maritime landscapes are said to have given their colors to the most famous local product, handwoven tweed, which reflects the browns of the peaty heathland and the purples of the heather. Donegal, a sparsely populated rural county of small farms and fishing boats, shares its inland border with Northern Ireland; the border is partly formed by the River Foyle. Inland from Sligo is Leitrim, a county best known for its numerous lakes and loughs, some of which join up with the River Shannon, on the easterly border of this region.

County Donegal was part of the near-indomitable ancient kingdom of Ulster, which was not conquered by the English until the 17th century. When the English withdrew in the 1920s, they had still not eradicated rural Donegal's Celtic inheritance. It thus shouldn't come as a surprise that County Donegal contains Ireland's largest Gaeltacht (Irish-speaking) area. Driving in this part of the country, you may either be frustrated or amused whenever you come to a crossroads. Signposts show only the Irish place-names, often so unlike the English versions as to be completely unrecognizable. All is not lost, however, as maps generally give both the Irish and the English names, and locals are usually more than happy to help out with directions (in English)—usually with a colorful yarn thrown in. So if you're in a hurry, first of all you're in the wrong place, and second, you should have started sooner.

Tucked into the folds of the hills, modest little market towns and unpretentious villages with muddy streets go about their business quietly. In the squelchy peat bogs, cutters working with long shovels pause in their labors to wave as you drive past. Remember to drive slowly along the country lanes, for around any corner you may find a whitewashed

Numbers in the text correspond to numbers in the margin and on the Yeats Country, Sligo Town, and the Northern Peninsulas maps.

If you have
2 days

Start in **Sligo Town** ❶–❼ ▸, and look at the Yeats memorabilia in the **Model Arts Centre and Niland Gallery** ❷. Take along a volume of W. B.'s poetry (or at the least his poem "The Lake Isle of Innisfree") as you follow the Yeats Trail around woody **Lough Gill** ❾. After the road north passes W. B.'s grave in **Drumcliff** ⓭ churchyard, head to Creevykeel, a tomb dating from 3000 BC. Drive through **Ballyshannon** ⓰ and on to ▸ **Donegal Town** ⓱. The next day head for the port of **Killybegs** ⓲, beyond which the views of Donegal Bay improve as the road twists and descends into Kilcar, a village known for its tweeds. The road then passes through moorland and reaches **Glencolumbkille** ⓴, a hamlet around the rocky harbor of Glen Bay. On the far side of the Glengesh Pass, the village of **Ardara** ㉑ is the center of the region's tweed heritage and also a good spot to hear traditional music. Return from here southward to Donegal Town and either to Dublin via Ballyshannon or to Galway via Sligo.

If you have
5 days

Stretch the first day of the itinerary above into two days. You may want to push on at the end of your second day to ▸ **Ardara** ㉑ and visit the tweed heritage center there rather than stopping at ▸ **Donegal Town** ⓱. On your third day, take the 30-odd mile drive northeast to thriving **Letterkenny** ㉒ and then head north into Plantation Country, where the English made their presence well known in the 17th century. Here you'll find **Ramelton** ㉓, a hilly town on the edge of Lough Swilly, one of the loveliest of Donegal's big fjordlike inlets but move on to a fitting overnight perch in ▸ **Rathmullan** ㉔, where a number of hotels are right on the shores of Lough Swilly. On your fourth day, head west to **Carrigart** ㉕, a village with old-fashioned pubs that gives access to a signposted Atlantic Drive around the Rosguill Peninsula. Forge on to **Creeslough** ㉖ to explore the mighty Doe Castle. Point yourself north to ▸ **Dunfanaghy** ㉘ to take in Horn Head, the grandest of County Donegal's Atlantic headlands. After an overnight there, head south on your fifth day to the region's Shangri-la, the **Glenveagh National Park** ㉚, presided over by Glenveagh's magical toy castle (Greta Garbo, art collectors, and millionaires loved coming here in the 1960s and 1970s). In the afternoon, continue on to the Glebe House and Gallery, on the northwest shore of **Gartan Lough** ㉛, which exhibits works by major Impressionists, Picasso, Jack B. Yeats, and Tory Islanders. As the fifth night rolls in, head back to the shining lights and welcoming hotels of Letterkenny.

---

thatched cottage with children playing outside its scarlet door, a shepherd leading his flock, a wayward sheep or two looking philosophical about having strayed from their field, or a farmer wobbling along in the middle of the road on his old faithful sit-up-and-beg bicycle.

The area is overwhelmingly rural and underpopulated. That's not to say there isn't a bit of action here. Sligo Town has gone through a major renaissance. On a typical weekday, the little winding streets are as busy as those of Galway, and, when it comes to stylish restaurants and trendy people, it seems to be giving Dublin's Temple Bar a run for its money—an amazing feat for a town of only 19,000 souls. Sligo Town pulses not only in the present but also with the charge of history, for it was the childhood home of W. B. and Jack B. Yeats, the place that, more than any other, gave rise to their particular geniuses—or, as Jack B. put it: "Sligo was my school and the sky above it." There are more bright lights in Letterkenny, which has to its credit the longest main street of any town in Ireland. Glenveagh National Park exemplifies the surprising alliance between nature and culture in northwest Ireland: here, perched on the edge of a glorious lake in the midst of 24,000 acres of thrilling wilderness, sits a fairy-tale castle. The castle reflects the life and times of the man who owned it for 50 years: Henry McIlhenny, the millionaire American philanthropist and art collector whose collection of Impressionist paintings now hangs in the Philadelphia Museum of Art.

Keep in mind, though, that the whole region—and County Donegal in particular—attracts droves of tourists during July and August; this is a favorite weekend vacation area for people who live in neighboring Northern Ireland. A few places, frankly, are quite spoiled by popularity with tourists, careless development, and uninspired architecture—particularly the ugly bungalows that have replaced thatched cottages and Georgian farmhouses as typical Irish rural homes. Bundoran, on the coast between Sligo Town and Donegal Town, a cheap and cheerful family beach resort full of so-called "Irish gift shops" and "amusement arcades," is one of the places to pass through rather than visit. On the whole, though, northwest Ireland is big enough, untamed enough, and grand enough to be able to absorb all of its summer (and weekend) tourists without too much harm.

Exploring the Northwest

This chapter outlines three autonomous routes through northwest Ireland. These routes can easily be linked if you want to poke around the area over five or so days. The first journey begins in Sligo Town and covers its immediate environs—all the major sights within a roughly 24-km (15-mi) radius, many of which have strong associations with the Yeatses. The second trip skirts the entirety of Donegal Bay, from Mullaghmore in the south to Glencolumbkille to the far north and west, before heading inland as far as Ardara. The last route begins at the other end of Donegal, in Letterkenny, and covers the far northwest corner of County Donegal before swinging you back toward the Inishowen Peninsula, the tip-top of Ireland, delicately balanced between the Republic and Northern Ireland. If you decide to explore this chapter from back to front (which makes sense if you're arriving from Northern Ireland), begin with the last itinerary in Letterkenny and pick up the middle tour from Gratan Lough.

About the Restaurants & Hotels

Although northwest Ireland has not been considered a great gastronomic center, in the last few years Sligo Town has established itself as a sort of last stop for food lovers, with a number of food-related shops worth

7

Féiles and Festivals

There is always something happening in the northwest, and the tradition of the *"féile"* (festival) is alive and well. Check on the Internet before you leave home, or with the Tourist Information Office when you arrive, and you may find yourself in luck. Each village tends to have its own celebration during the summer months and it is often worth making the effort to attend. Music festivals rule the roost, from the traditional Irish Sligo Feis Ceoil in mid-April to the Country and Western music extravaganza in Bundoran in June and the jazz and blues weekend fête in Gortahork, Donegal, in April. But being a Gaelic-speaking stronghold, the emphasis is on Irish traditional music. Every weekend during summer you are guaranteed a bit of *craic agus ceol,* or "fun and music," with lively sessions in most pubs—Sligo Town, Ardara, and Letterkenny are all hot spots. There are village festivals dedicated to hill-walking, fishing, poetry, art, and food; the Mullaghmore Lobster Festival in August always proves mighty tasty.

Seventh-Heaven Shopping

Hand-woven tweed, hand-knit Aran sweaters, fine parian china: The Northwest is seventh heaven for shoppers wanting to take home a piece of the shamrock. Just don't expect designer labels or trendy boutiques: Donegal Town and Sligo Town are both diminutive and there is nary a fashionista in this neck of the woods. There are a few familiar brand names lining the streets, but instead, head for the numerous small gift shops and traditional clothing stores offering something of tried-and-true Irish heritage. Worth visiting are specialist clothing stores who will run up a made-to-measure tweed suit. Sligo Crystal has a factory in Grange, County Sligo, and produces excellent hand-cut glasses and trinkets. Their craftsmen will also engrave family crests on mirrors and glassware. Deep in the Donegal Gaeltacht, there are ample craft villages and outlets producing and selling traditional arts and crafts. You can watch the masters at work while you browse their wares. The pretty villages of Ardara and Kilcar, in southern Donegal, are renowned for quality tweed and hand-made knitwear. Examples are on sale in shops in the villages. Donegal parian china, produced around Ballyshannon on the border with Northern Ireland, is famed for its delicate beauty, and a small souvenir can be picked up relatively cheaply.

The Great Outdoors

Along the rugged coasts of Sligo and Donegal, beaches come in all shapes and sizes. Chief among them is Strandhill, a few miles outside Sligo Town; it's a particularly delightful stretch of fine sand and rolling waves, perfect for surfers. Donegal's seaside resorts, like the family-oriented Bundoran on the west coast and Buncrana in northern Donegal, can get very crowded in the summer, and are packed full of amusement arcades. But there are quieter alternatives, like Rossnowlagh (meaning "heavenly cove"), in Donegal Bay, with its pristine shoreline. Water sports from wind-surfing to sailing are rife in both counties, and fishing enthusiasts will be in their element, with excellent fishing for salmon, sea, brown, and rainbow trouts in countless lakes, rivers and streams. The Atlantic coast offers unrestricted shore angling. The numerous headlands of the north Donegal coast are perfect settings for invigorating walks, with the fresh Atlantic sea air sure to blow away the cobwebs. See if you can get as far as Malin Head, the most northerly tip of Ireland. The Slieve League cliffs are the highest sea cliffs in Europe, and the view from the top will set your heart racing. Inland, the Blue Stack Mountains in Donegal offer wonderful views of the surrounding area, looming above Sligo Town, with the serene mass of Benbulben seeming to glow in the sunset. Both counties are justly famous for their loughs (lakes), from beautiful, gentle Lough Gill, with its tiny island of Innisfree, immortalized in a poem by W. B. Yeats, to the pilgrims' favorite Lough Derg, with its shrines to St Patrick.

---

visiting. Newcomers are serving up well-above-average food in memorable settings, though the majority of restaurants serve plain and simple fare, such as traditional Irish lamb stew or bacon and cabbage served with generous helpings of potatoes (often prepared in at least two ways on the same plate), washed down with creamy, lip-smacking pints of Guinness. You're likely to find the finest food at the higher-quality country houses, where chefs elegantly prepare local meat, fish, and produce in a hybrid Irish-French haute cuisine. Another trend: several of the area's more successful restaurants have added accommodations, making them good overnight destinations. Generally, restaurants in towns stay open all year round, as they do not have to rely solely on the tourist trade. But eateries in remote villages will often close for an extended period during the winter months, usually from November to mid-March. It does tend to vary, but check with the tourist office to avoid disappointment.

True, it's the farthest-flung corner of Ireland, but northwest Ireland has a steady stream of arrivals—especially in July and August. Thanks to the area's popularity, good bed-and-breakfasts and small hotels are prevalent. In the two major towns—Sligo Town and Donegal Town—and the small coastal resorts in between, many traditional provincial hotels have been modernized (albeit not always elegantly). Yet most manage to retain some of the charm that comes with older buildings and personalized service. Away from these areas, your best overnight choice is usually a modest guest house that includes bed, breakfast, and an evening meal, though you can also find first-class country-house hotels with a gracious professionalism comparable to properties elsewhere in Ireland. Consider staying in an Irish-speaking home to get to know members of the area's Gaeltacht population; the local Tourist Information Office (TIO) can be helpful in making a booking with an Irish-speaking family. On the chart below, hotel prices are listed for room rates that include no meals (EP, European Plan) or, if indicated, CP (with Continental breakfast) or BP (Breakfast Plan, with full breakfast). Higher prices prevail for board plans such as MAP (Modified American Plan, with breakfast and dinner); inquire when booking. Assume that all hotel rooms have air-conditioning, in-room phones and TVs, and private bathrooms unless otherless noted.

WHAT IT COSTS In euros					
	$$$$	**$$$**	**$$**	**$**	**¢**
RESTAURANTS	over €29	€22–€29	€15–€22	€8–€15	under €8
HOTELS	over €230	€180–€230	€130–€180	€80–€130	under €80

Restaurant prices are per person for a main course at dinner; note that if a restaurant offers only prix-fixe meals, it has been given the price category that reflects the full set-price. Hotel prices are for two people in a standard double room in high season, including V.A.T. and a service charge (often applied in larger hotels).

Timing

While July and August—when the weather may be warm enough for hardy folk to swim in the sea—sees fully-booked hotels, between November and February the area is empty of tourists, and with good reason—gales bring cold rain lashing in from the Atlantic, shrouding the wild, lonely scenery that is northwest Ireland's greatest asset. Because so many of the area's hotels are seasonal, choices in the winter months are limited. The best months to visit are April through June, September, and October.

YEATS COUNTRY: FROM SLIGO TO DRUMCLIFF

Just as James Joyce made Dublin his own through his novels and stories, Sligo and environs are bound to the work of W. B. Yeats (1865–1939), Ireland's first of four Nobel laureates, and, no less, his brother Jack B. (1871–1957), one of Ireland's most important 20th-century painters, whose expressionistic landscapes and portraits are as emotionally fraught as his brother's poems are lyrical and plangent. The brothers intimately knew and eloquently celebrated in their art not only Sligo Town itself but the surrounding countryside with its lakes, farms, woodland, and dramatic mountains that rise up not far from the center of town. Often on this route, you have glimpses of Ben Bulben Mountain, which looms over the western end of the Dartry range. The areas covered here are the most accessible parts of northwest Ireland, easily reached from Galway.

Sligo Town

★ *60 km (37 mi) northeast of Ballina, 138 km (86 mi) northeast of Galway, 217 km (135 mi) northwest of Dublin.*

Sligo (population 19,000), the only sizable town in the whole of northwest Ireland, is the best place to begin a tour of Yeats Country. It retains all the charm of smaller, sleepier villages, even though it's in the throes of an economic boom. Europe's largest videotape factory is just outside of town, it's the center of Ireland's plastics industry, and for the past three years the streets have been ringing with the bite of buzz saws, as apartments, shopping malls, and cinema complexes have been tastefully erected behind traditional facades. By day Sligo is as lively and crowded as Galway, its considerably larger neighbor to the southwest, with locals, students from the town's college, and tourists bustling past its historic buildings and along its narrow sidewalks and winding streets, and crowding its one-of-a-kind shops, restaurants, and traditional pubs.

Yeats Country

Glenties

N56 R250 · N253

Kilrean

Ardara 21

BLUE STACK MOUNTAINS

Glengesh Pass

N56

DONEGAL

R262

20 **Glencolumbkille (Gleann Cholm Cille)**

Malin More

An Charraig (Carrick)

SLIEVE LEAGUE MOUNTAINS

R263

TO LOUGH ESKE

Donegal Town 17 N15

N56

Teelin

Kilcar

Killybegs 19

Bruckless 18

Dunkineely

Mac Swyne's Bay

Inver Bay

Laghy R232

TO LOUGH DERG

Ballintra

St. John's Point

Rossnowlagh

Donegal Bay

NORTHERN IRELAND

IRELAND

Ballyshannon 16

TO LOUGH ERNE

Bundoran 15

Belleek

NORTHERN IRELAND

Mullaghmore 14

Kinlough

Lough Melvin

Cliffony

N15

Glenade

Garrison

R282

Creevykeel ◆

Grange

BEN BULBEN

Sligo Bay

Carney

Drumcliff 13

Drumcliff Bay

Rathcormack

◆ **Glencar Lough**

N16

Manorhamilton 11

R280

Rosses Point 12

Cregg R291

Sligo Town
1 – 7
see detail map

Strandhill

R292

Parke's Castle ◆

LEITRIM

8 **Knocknarea**

Templeboy N59

TO BALLINA

Carrowmore

Carrowmore

Beltra

Lough Gill 9

R286

10 ◆ **Creevelea Abbey**

Killarga

Lake Isle of Innisfree

Dromahair

R280

Ballygawley R290

R287

Collooney

R284

Drumkeeran

Ropefield N17

SLIGO

Riverstown

0 ——— 6 miles
0 ——— 9 km

TO GALWAY

Drumfin

N4

Ballymote ◆

Lough Arrow

TO CARRICK-ON-SHANNON

KEY

► *Start of itinerary*

More than any other town in northwest Ireland, Sligo has an energy that would surprise anyone who hasn't been there in the last few years.

Squeezed onto a patch of land between Sligo Bay and Lough Gill, Sligo is clustered on the south shore between two bridges that span the River Garavogue, just east of where the river opens into the bay. Thanks to the pedestrian zone conveniently located along the south shore of the river (between the two bridges), you can enjoy vistas of the river while right in the center of town. Along High Street and Church and Charles streets, Sligo has churches of all denominations. Presbyterians, Methodists, and even Plymouth Brethren are represented, as well as Anglicans (Church of Ireland) and, of course, Roman Catholics. According to the Irish writer Sean O'Faolain, "The best Protestant stock in all Ireland is in Sligo." The Yeats family was part of that stock.

Sligo was often a battleground in its earlier days. It was attacked by Viking invaders in 807 and, later, by a succession of rival Irish and Anglo-Norman conquerors. In 1642, the British soldiers of Sir Frederick Hamilton fell upon Sligo, killing every visible inhabitant, burning the town, and destroying the interior of the beautiful medieval abbey. Between 1845 and 1849, more than a million inhabitants of Sligo county died in the potato famine or fled to escape it—an event poignantly captured in a letter written by a local father, Owen Larkin, to his son in America in 1850, its words inscribed on a brass plaque down by the river: "I am now I may say alone in the world all my brothers and sisters are dead and children but yourself. We are all ejected out of Lord Ardilaun's ground, the times was so bad and all Ireland in such a state of poverty that no person could pay rent. My only hope now rests with you, as I am without one shilling and I must either beg or go to the poorhouse." Stand there a moment by the river, then turn again to the bustling heart of Sligo, and marvel at humanity's capacity to reinvent itself.

❶ The Sligo Art Gallery in the **Yeats Memorial Building** shows rotating exhibits of contemporary art; call to see if there's an exhibition during your visit. The Yeats International Summer School is conducted here every August. Across the street is Rohan Gillespie's innovative sculpture of the poet, draped in a flowing coat overlaid with excerpts from his work. It was unveiled in 1989 by Michael Yeats, W. B.'s son, in commemoration of the 50th anniversary of his father's death. ⊠ *Hyde Bridge* ☎ *071/914–5847 gallery, 074/914–2693 summer school* 🖶 *071/914– 7426* ⊕ *www.sligoartgallery.com* 🎫 *Free* ☉ *Mon.–Sat. 10–5:30.*

❷ The **Model Arts Centre and Niland Gallery,** beautifully housed in a 19th-century school, has one of Ireland's largest collections of works by 20th-century artists from Ireland and abroad. The gallery displays works by Jack B. Yeats, who said, "I never did a painting without putting a thought of Sligo in it." (Beckett wrote that Yeats painted "desperately immediate images"). Paintings by John Yeats (father of Jack B. and W. B.), who had a considerable reputation as a portraitist, also hang here, as do portraits by Sean Keating and Paul Henry. The center has performance and workshop spaces and hosts literature, music, and film programs. There's also The Atrium café. ⊠ *The Mall* ☎ *071/914–*

1405 ⊕ *www.modelart.ie* ✉ *Free* ☉ *Tues.–Sat. 10–5:30, Sun. 11–4, and during performances.*

❸ Maurice FitzGerald built the **Sligo Abbey,** the town's only existing relic of the Middle Ages, for the Dominicans in 1253. After a fire in 1414, it was extensively rebuilt, only to be destroyed again by Cromwell's Puritans under the command of Sir Frederick Hamilton in 1642. Today the abbey consists of a ruined nave, aisle, transept, and tower. Some fine stonework remains, especially in the 15th-century cloisters. The visitor center is the base for guided tours, which are included with admission. The site is accessible to the disabled, though some parts of the grounds are quite rocky. ✉ *Abbey St.* ☎ *071/914–6406* ⊕ *www.heritageireland. ie* ✉ *€2* ☉ *Apr.–Oct., daily 10–6; Nov.–Jan., Fri.–Sun. 9:30–4:30.*

❹ The **Courthouse,** built in 1878 in the Victorian Gothic style, has a flamboyant, turreted sandstone exterior. Unfortunately the structure is not open to tourists. After it was built, it became a symbol of English power. The Courthouse takes its inspiration from the much larger Law Courts in London. Just north of the Courthouse on the east side of Teeling Street, look for the window designating the law firm Argue and Phibbs, one of Sligo's most popular photo-ops. ✉ *Teeling St.* ☎ *No phone* ☉ *Closed to public.*

⑤ Designed in 1730 by Richard Castle, who designed Powerscourt and Russborough houses in County Wicklow, little **St. John's Cathedral** (Church of Ireland) has a handsome square tower and fortifications. In the north transept is a memorial to Susan Mary Yeats, mother of W. B. and Jack B. Next door is the larger and newer Roman Catholic Cathedral of the Immaculate Conception (with an entrance on Temple Street), consecrated in 1874. ⊠ *John St.* ☎ *No phone.*

⑥ Sligo's most famous pub, **Hargadon's,** is a dark, old-style public house with cozy, private, wood-paneled snugs (cubicles); stone and wood floors; rust-red interior walls; and a handsome golden-oak and green-painted facade. The pub has been operated by the Hargadon family since 1908; before that it was owned by a local member of the British parliament, who was more interested in debating with his peers in London than pulling pints in Sligo. As a "talking" pub, music is taboo here, so settle in for some good conversation (no wonder regulars like Nobel prize–winning poet Seamus Heaney keep coming back). It's also justly famous for its bowls of stew and creamy Guinness. ⊠ *4 O'Connell St.* ☎ *071/917–0933.*

⑦ The main items of interest at the **Sligo County Museum** are first editions by W. B. Yeats and memorabilia such as the author's personal letters and the Irish tricolor (flag) that draped his coffin when he was buried at nearby Drumcliff. The museum also has small sections on local society, history, and archaeology. Some artwork by Jack B. Yeats is hung in the adjoining church. ⊠ *Stephen St.* ☎ *071/914–2212* 🖼 *Free* 🕐 *June–Sept., Tues.–Sat. 10–5; Oct.–May, Tues.–Sat. 2–4:50.*

Where to Stay & Eat

$–$$ ✕ **Bistro Bianconi.** With blond-wood furniture and white-tile floors, Bianconi lives up to its name in the dining room's design, but it serves Italian food full of color. Peruse the long list of fancy pizzas baked in a wood-burning oven. Cannelloni and ravioli are also popular. ⊠ *44 O'-Connell St.* ☎ *071/914–1744* ▤ *MC, V* 🕐 *Closed Sun.*

$$$$ ✕🖼 **Cromleach Lodge.** Comfort is paramount at this small hotel with fantastic views out over Lough Arrow. Spacious country bedrooms are decorated in pastel shades. The restaurant ($$–$$$; reservations required) is notable; all tables have panoramic views. Two typical—and delicious—entrées are fillet of turbot on a julienne of fennel with Pernod cream, and warm salad of marinated lamb fillet with organic lentils. Staff members lead walks ranging from 20 minutes to two hours long. ⊹ *27 km (17 mi) east of Sligo, 8 km (5 mi) east of Ballymote* ⊠ *Off N4 at Castlebaldwin, Lough Arrow, Co. Sligo* ☎ *071/916–5155* 🖷 *071/916–5455* ⊕ *www.cromleach.com* ⇨ *11 rooms* ♿ *Restaurant, golf privileges, hiking, bar, Internet, meeting room; no a/c* ▤ *AE, DC, MC, V* ⏏ *BP, MAP* 🕐 *Closed Nov.–Jan.*

FodorśChoice ★

$$$ ✕🖼 **Markree Castle.** One of the most awe-inspiring fortress fronts in Ireland greets you on arrival at Markree, Sligo's oldest inhabited castle and the home of the Cooper family for 350 years. Today, Charles and Mary Cooper preside over this lush and lavish 1,000-acre estate. Renovated in 1802, the castle was given the full storybook treatment, with a vast and oak-paneled entry hall and skylit atrium. Atop the grand staircase is a glorious stained-glass window depicting the Cooper family tree (their roots are essentially English—having arrived with the bloody troops of Cromwell—but they were also related to the great Irish clan of the O'Briens). Upstairs, guest bedrooms are super-spacious, many adorned with cozy-sumptuous pieces of 19th century–style furniture; bathrooms are modern. Chandeliered and gilt, the restaurant dining room has ornate Louis XIV plasterwork—ask about the three-course table d'hôte menu (€38) that's occasionally served—and serves food good enough to pack in families for Sunday brunch. ⊹ *11 km (7 mi) south of Sligo Town* ⊠ *Off N4, Collooney, Co. Sligo* ☏ *071/916–7800* 🖷 *071/916–7840* ⊕ *www.markreecastle.ie* ➵ *30 rooms* ⚹ *Restaurant, horseback riding, bar; no a/c* ▭ *AE, MC, V* ⏐⊙⏐ *BP, MAP.*

★ $ ╳⊞ **Glebe House.** Dorothy and Jeremy Bird run a Georgian guest house and a restaurant ($$$$) with an emphasis on local produce. You might choose from roast rack of Sligo lamb in an herb crust or wild Owenmore salmon with an herb hollandaise on the prix-fixe menu. Indulge in pink grapefruit and gin sorbet or chocolate and Amaretto mousse for dessert. It's a relaxed place, with simple but pleasant guest rooms. ⊹ *12 km (7 mi) south of Sligo Town* ⊠ *Coolaney Rd., off N4 at second roundabout, Collooney, Co. Sligo* ☏ *071/916–7787* ⊕ *www.glebehousesligo. com* ➵ *4 rooms, 1 with bath* ⚹ *Restaurant, fishing, hiking, meeting rooms; no a/c, no room TVs* ▭ *MC, V* ⏐⊙⏐ *BP, MAP.*

$ ╳⊞ **Temple House.** Off the beaten path on more than 1,000 acres, this vast Georgian mansion and working organic farm has been in owners Sandy and Deb Perceval's family since 1665. Their son Roderick has recently taken over the management of the estate. Georgian and Victorian furniture—mahogany tables and original rugs—adorn the bedrooms. Outside, formal terraced gardens and a lake beckon. Deb prepares the prix-fixe evening meal ($$$$; book by noon) using the farm produce. Typical entrées include herbed leg of lamb with roast potatoes and tomato fondue with glazed carrots. High tea is served for children at 6:30 PM; they are not allowed at dinner. ⊹ *19 km (12 mi) south of Sligo* ⊠ *Off N17, Ballymote, Co. Sligo* ☏ *071/918–3329* 🖷 *071/918–3808* ⊕ *www.templehouse.ie* ➵ *6 rooms* ⚹ *Restaurant, boating, fishing; no a/c, no room phones, no room TVs* ▭ *AE, MC, V* ⏐⊙⏐ *BP* ⊙ *Closed Dec.–Mar.*

★ $–$$ ⊞ **Coopershill.** Seven generations of the O'Hara family have lived in this three-story Georgian farmhouse since it was built in 1774. Beyond the elegant, symmetrical stone facade, with its central Palladian window, an appealing mix of antique and modern furniture fills the large public spaces. Spacious, beautifully furnished guest rooms have floral wallpaper, and most have four-poster or canopy beds. Dine by candlelight on meals made with fresh Irish ingredients, accompanied by a wide choice of wines, served from a grand sideboard set with family silver and crystal. Non-guests are invited to dine only when the lodging is not full. ⊠ *Off N4, 17 km (11 mi) southeast of Sligo, Riverstown, Co. Sligo* ☏ *071/ 916–5108* 🖷 *071/916–5466* ⊕ *www.coopershill.com* ➵ *8 rooms* ⚹ *Dining room, tennis court, fishing, billiards; no a/c, no room TVs* ▭ *AE, DC, MC, V* ⏐⊙⏐ *BP* ⊙ *Closed Nov.–Mar.*

Nightlife & the Arts

PUBS A few miles south of town, a popular spot with the locals, the **Thatch pub** (✉ Thatch, Ballysodare ☎ 071/916–7288) has traditional music sessions from Thursday to Sunday. A sizable dance floor at **Toffs** (✉ Kennedy Parade ☎ 071/916–1250) teems with Sligo's younger set moving to a mix of contemporary dance music and older favorites. It stays open later than most places.

THEATER **Hawk's Well Theatre** hosts amateur and professional companies from all over Ireland (and occasionally from Britain) in an eclectic mix of shows. ✉ *Temple St.* ☎ *071/916–1526* 🎫 *€8–€15* ⊙ *Box office weekdays 10–6, Sat. 2–6.*

Sports & the Outdoors

For riding in the countryside around Sligo, contact the **Sligo Riding Centre** (✉ 3 km [2 mi] from Sligo Town, Carramore ☎ 087/0230–4828 🖨 071/916–2028 ⊕ www.irelandonhorseback.com).

Shopping

Sligo Town has northwest Ireland's most thriving shopping scene, with lots of food-related, craft, and hand-knits shops. In addition to stylish sweaters, **Carraig Donn** (✉ 41 O'Connell St. ☎ 071/914–4158 ⊕ www.carraigdonn.com) carries pottery, glassware, linens, and Aran knits for children. The **Cat & the Moon** (✉ 4 Castle St. ☎ 071/914–3686 ⊕ www.thecatandthemoon.com) specializes in eclectic and stylish Irish-made crafts, jewelry, pottery, ironwork, and scarves. The upscale deli **Cosgrove and Son** (✉ 32 Market St. ☎ 071/914–2809) sells everything from Parma ham to carrageen moss boiled in milk (a local cure for upset stomachs). Stock up here for a picnic. **Cross Sections** (✉ 2 Grattan St. ☎ 071/914–2265) sells lovely tableware, glassware, and kitchenware. **Tír na nóg** (✉ Grattan St. ☎ 071/916–2752), Irish for "Land of the Ever-young," sells organic foods, including local cheeses and honeys, and other health-oriented items. A sister store across the street sells cards and posters.

Knocknarea

❽ *8 km (5 mi) southwest of Sligo Town on R292 (Strandhill Rd.).*

Knocknarea—the "cairn-heaped grassy hill," as W. B. Yeats called it—rises 1,083-feet-high several miles southwest of Sligo Town on a promontory that juts into Sligo Bay. The mountain is also memorably depicted in brother Jack B.'s painting *Knocknarea and the Flowing Tide.* A car park on R292 gives pedestrian access (a 45-minute walk) to the summit, where there's a tremendous view of the mountains of counties Donegal and Sligo. At the summit, and visible from a distance, sits a huge cairn—a heaped-stone monument—made with 40,000 tons of rock. The cairn is traditionally associated with Maeve, the 1st-century AD Celtic queen of Connaught who went to war with the men of Ulster in a bid to win the mighty Bull of Cuailgne, and who was subsequently killed while bathing in a lake. The story is told in the *Táin,* the greatest of all the Irish heroic legends. Romantics like to think that Maeve is buried in this massive cairn, although archaeologists suspect that it more likely covers a 3,000-year-old grave. Either way, it's a pleasant climb on a summer day, and nature has installed a handy stream for washing off your boots as you take the lane back down.

Strandhill, a seaside resort with a touch of charm, is 3 km (2 mi) north-west of Knocknarea, off R292. It has a fine, sandy beach and rolling waves favored by surfers. The **Perfect Day Surf Club** (⊠ Esplanade, Strandhill ☎ 071/916–8464) caters to surfing novices and aficionados alike and is approved by the European Surf Federation and Irish Surfing Association. Two hours of instruction plus equipment is €25. **Celtic Seaweed Baths** (⊠ Esplanade, Strandhill ☎ 071/916–8686 ⊕ www.celticseaweedbaths.com) has a one-hour steam-and-seaweed bath treatment for €16.

Carrowmore, the largest group of megalithic tombs in the British Isles, is a short drive southeast of Knocknarea (on the minor road back to Sligo Town). The oldest of the 60 tombs, dolmens, and other ruins here predate those at Newgrange by roughly 700 years; most are communal tombs dating from 4800 BC. Unfortunately more than 100 have been badly damaged, leaving around 40. A restored cottage houses a small exhibition about the tombs. ⊠ *Carrowmore, Co. Sligo* ☎ *071/916–1534* 🖾 *€2* ☉ *May–Oct., daily 10–6.*

Lough Gill

★ ❾ *17½ km (11 mi) east of Knocknarea, 1½ km (1 mi) east of Sligo Town on R286.*

Beautiful, gentle Lough Gill means simply "Lake Beauty" in Irish. When the soldiers of Sir Frederick Hamilton sacked Sligo in 1642, legend has it that they flung the silver bell of the abbey into the depths of Lough Gill; today it is said that only the "pure" can hear it ring. In fine weather the river-fed lough and its surroundings are serenity itself: sunlight on the meadows all around, loughside cottages, the gentle sound of water, salmon leaping, a yacht sailing by. To get to the Lough from Sligo Town, take Stephen Street, which turns into N16 (signposted to Manorhamilton and Enniskillen). Turn right almost at once onto R286. Within minutes you can see gorgeous views of the lake so adored by the young W. B. Yeats.

An English Planter (a Protestant colonist settling on Irish lands confiscated from Catholic owners) built the fortified house, **Parke's Castle,** in the 17th century on the eastern shore of Lough Gill. He needed the strong fortifications to defend himself against a hostile populace. His relations with the people were made worse by the fact that he obtained his building materials mainly by dismantling a historic fortress on the site that had belonged to the clan leaders the O'Rourkes of Breffni (once the name of the district). The entrance fee includes a short video show on the castle and local history and a guided tour. In summer, boat tours of the lough leave from here. There's also a snack bar. ⊠ *R288, Fivemile Bourne, Co. Leitrim* ☎ *071/916–4149, 087/270–4032 for appointment* 🖾 *€3* ☉ *Apr.–Oct., 10–6 (last admission at 5:15); Nov.–Apr., by appointment.*

A few minutes' walk along a footpath south of Parke's Castle lie the handsome ruins of **Creevelea Abbey.** In fact not an abbey but a friary, Creevelea was founded for the Franciscans in 1508 by a later generation of O'Rourkes. It was the last Franciscan community to be founded before the suppression of the monasteries by England's King Henry VIII. Like many other decrepit abbeys, the place still holds religious significance for the locals, who revere it. One curiosity here is the especially large south transept; notice, too, its endearing little cloisters, with well-executed carvings on the pillars of St. Francis of Assisi. ✉ *R288, Dromahair, Co. Leitrim.*

Where to Stay & Eat

¢ ✕⌧ **Stanford Village Inn.** This stone-front inn is one of the few stops for sustenance near Lough Gill. A hearty meal of traditional, homey food ($–$$), an open fire, and, if your timing is good, an impromptu session of traditional Irish music await you. It has six newly refurbished country rooms. ⊹ *7 km (5 mi) from Parke's Castle, 19 km (12 mi) from Sligo Town* ✉ *Off R288, Dromahair, Co. Leitrim* ☎ *071/916–4140* 🖷 *071/916–4770* 🛏 *6 rooms* ⚘ *Restaurant, bar; no a/c* ▭ *MC, V* ⌯❘ *BP.*

Lake Isle of Innisfree

🔟 *15 km (9 mi) south of Sligo Town via Dromahair on N4 and R287.*

In 1890 W. B. Yeats was walking through the West End of London when, seeing in a shop window a ball dancing on a jet of water, he was suddenly overcome with nostalgia for the lakes of his Sligo home. It was the moment, and the feeling, that shaped itself into his most famous poem, "The Lake Isle of Innisfree":

I will arise and go now, and go to Innisfree,
And a small cabin build there, of clay and wattles made:
Nine bean-rows will I have there, a hive for the honey-bee,
And live alone in the bee-loud glade.

Though there is nothing visually exceptional about Innisfree (pronounced *innish*-free), the "Lake Isle" is a must-see if you're a W. B. Yeats fan. To reach Innisfree from Dromahair, take R287, the minor road that heads back along the south side of Lough Gill, toward Sligo Town. Turn right at a small crossroads, after 4 or 5 km (2 or 3 mi), where signposts point to Innisfree. A little road leads another couple of miles down to the lakeside, where you can see the island just offshore.

Manorhamilton

🔟🔟 *16 km (10 mi) northeast of Dromahair on R280, 25 km (15 mi) east of Sligo Town on N16.*

The small rural town of Manorhamilton was built in the 17th century for the Scottish planter Sir Frederick Hamilton, who had been given the local manor house by Charles I of England (hence the town's name). The manor itself is now an ivy-covered ruin, and there's not much to see here. The surrounding scenery, however, is spectacular.

en route

On your way to Manorhamilton, stop at **Glencar Lough** (⊠ N16, 9 km [5 mi] east of Sligo Town), where there are several waterfalls; a footpath veering off from a parking lot leads to one of the highest. The lake is fed by the River Drumcliff and streams at the foot of the Dartry Mountains: "Where the wandering water gushes/From the hills above Glencar/In pools among the rushes/That scarce could bathe a star," as W. B. Yeats put it in his poem "The Stolen Child."

Rosses Point

⑫ *38½ km (24 mi) west of Manorhamilton, 8 km (5 mi) northwest of Sligo Town on R291.*

It's obvious why W. B. and Jack B. Yeats often stayed at Rosses Point during their summer vacations: glorious pink-and-gold summer sunsets over a seemingly endless stretch of sandy beach. Coney Island lies just off Rosses Point. Local lore has it that the captain of the ship *Arathusa* christened Brooklyn's Coney Island after this island, but there's probably more legend than truth to this, as it's widely agreed that New York's Coney Island was named after the Dutch word *konijn* (wild rabbits); they abounded there during the 17th century.

The popular **County Sligo Golf Club** (⊠ Rosses Point ☎ 071/917–7186 ⊕ www.countysligogolfclub.ie) is one of Ireland's grand old venues; it's more than a century old, and has hosted most of the country's major championships. It has magnificent views of the sea and Ben Bulben. The **Sligo Yacht Club** (⊠ Rosses Point ☎ 071/917–7168 ⊕ www.rossespoint. com/sligoyc), with a fleet of some 25 boats, has sailing and social programs, and regularly hosts races.

Drumcliff

⑬ *15 km (9 mi) northeast of Rosses Point, 7 km (4½ mi) north of Sligo Town on N15.*

W. B. Yeats lies buried with his wife, Georgie, in an unpretentious grave in the cemetery of Drumcliff's simple Protestant church, where his grandfather was rector for many years. W. B. died on the French Riviera in 1939; it took almost a decade for his body to be brought back here—to the place that more than any other might be called his soulland. In the poem "Under Ben Bulben," he spelled out not only where he was to be buried but also what should be written on the tombstone: "Cast a cold eye/On life, on death./Horseman, pass by!" It is easy to see why the majestic Ben Bulben (1,730 feet), with its sawed-off peak (not unlike Yosemite's Half-Dome), made such an impression on the poet: the mountain gazes calmly down upon the small church, as it does on all of the surrounding landscape—and at the same time stands as a sentinel facing the mighty Atlantic.

Drumcliff is where St. Columba, a recluse and missionary who established Christian churches and religious communities in northwest Ireland, is thought to have founded a monastic settlement around AD 575. The monastery that he founded before sailing off to the Scottish isle of

Iona flourished for many centuries, but all that is left of it now is the base of a round tower and a carved high cross (both across N15 from the church) dating from around AD 1000, with scenes from the Old and New Testaments, including Adam and Eve with the serpent, and Cain slaying Abel.

Drumcliff Visitors' Centre is a good place to buy local crafts, books of W. B. Yeats's poetry, and books about the poet's life. You can also get a snack here. ⊠ *Next to the Protestant church, Co. Sligo* ☎ *071/914– 4956* ⏰ *Mon.–Sat. 9–6, Sun. 1–6.*

AROUND DONEGAL BAY

As you drive north to Donegal Town, the glens of the Dartry Mountains (to which Ben Bulben belongs) gloriously roll by to the east. Look across coastal fields for views of the waters of Donegal Bay to the west. In the distant horizon the Donegal hills beckon. This stretch, dotted with numerous prehistoric sites, has become northwest Ireland's most popular vacation area. There are a few small and unremarkable seashore resorts, and in some places you may find examples of haphazard and fairly tasteless construction that detracts from the scenery. In between these minor resort developments, wide-open spaces are free of traffic. The most intriguing area lies on the north side of the bay—all that rocky indented coastline due west of Donegal Town. Here you enter the heart of away-from-it-all: County Donegal.

Mullaghmore

🄮 *20 km (13 mi) northeast of Lissadell House, 37 km (24 mi) north of Sligo Town off N15.*

In July and August, the picturesque, sleepy fishing village of Mullaghmore gets congested with tourists. Its main attractions: a 3-km-long (2-mi-long) sandy beach; and the turreted, fairy-tale Classie Bawn—the late Lord Louis Mountbatten's home (he, his grandson, and a local boy were killed when the IRA blew up his boat in the bay in 1979). A short drive along the headland is punctuated by unobstructed views beyond the rocky coastline out over Donegal Bay. When the weather is fair, you can see all the way across to St. John's Point and Drumanoo Head in Donegal.

Creevykeel is one of Ireland's best megalithic court-tombs. There's a burial area and an enclosed open-air court where rituals were performed around 3000 BC. Bronze artifacts found here are now in the National Museum in Dublin. The site (signposted from N15) lies off the road, just beyond the edge of the village of Cliffony. ✛ *3 km (2 mi) southeast of Mullaghmore off N15.*

Where to Stay & Eat

$ ✕▥ **Beach Hotel.** If there's a chill in the air, you can warm up at the roaring fires in the restaurant ($–$$$) and residents' lounge of this large harborside Victorian hotel. The dramatic red building is decorated in a nautical theme to tout the history of the bay (it seems three galleons of the Spanish Armada went aground here in September 1588). Enjoy wonderful views of the pier and the bay from the hotel bars, or tuck into the de'Cuellar Restaurant's acclaimed seafood menu. Try the favorites: hot crab claws, lobster, and the house seafood platter. Save room for the home-made apple-and-rhubarb crumble. ⊠ *The Harbour, Co. Sligo* ☎ *071/ 916–6103* 🖷 *071/916–6448* ⊕ *www.beachhotelmullaghmore.com* ⇆ *29 rooms* ⚫ *Restaurant, indoor pool, gym, hair salon, hot tub, sauna, steam room, 2 bars; no a/c* ☰ *AE, MC, V* ⭕ *BP, MAP.*

Bundoran

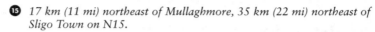 🅖 *17 km (11 mi) northeast of Mullaghmore, 35 km (22 mi) northeast of Sligo Town on N15.*

Resting on the south coast of County Donegal, Bundoran is one of Ire-land's most popular seaside resorts, a favorite haunt of the Irish from both the north and the south. To avoid souvenir shops and amusement arcades, head north of the center to the handsome beach at **Tullan Strand,** washed by good surfing waves. Between the main beach and Tul-lan, the Atlantic has sculpted cliff-side rock formations that the locals have christened with whimsical names such as the Fairy Bridges, the Wish-ing Chair, and the Puffing Hole (which blows wind and water from the waves pounding below).

Sports & the Outdoors

Good fishing is 6 km (4 mi) from Bundoran at **Lough Melvin.** Ask at **Pat Barrett's Tackle Shop** (⊠ Main St. ☎ 071/984–2266) for bait, tackle, and local information.

Bundoran Golf Club (⊠ Headland ☎ 071/984–1302) is an 18-hole, par-70 course on the cliffs above Bundoran Beach.

Ballyshannon

🅗 *6 km (4 mi) north of Bundoran, 42 km (26 mi) northeast of Sligo Town on N15.*

The former garrison town of Ballyshannon rises gently from the banks of the River Erne and has good views of Donegal Bay and the surrounding mountains. Come in early August, when this quiet village springs to life with a grand festival of folk and traditional music. The town is a hodge-podge of shops, arcades, and hotels. Its triangular central area has sev-eral bars and places to grab a snack. The town was also the birthplace of the prolific poet William Allingham.

A few kilometers down the road are several factories where eggshell-thin Irish porcelainware has been made by master craftsmen for gener-ations. It's said that if a newlywed couple receives a piece of this china, their marriage will be blessed with everlasting happiness. The name Belleek has become synonymous with much of Ireland's delicate ivory porce-lain figurines and woven baskets (sometimes painted with shamrocks); **Belleek Pottery Ltd.** is the best known of the producers, in operation since 1857. Their main factories are just down the road from Ballyshannon in Northern Ireland (which is why their prices are quoted in pounds sterling, not euros). Watch the introductory film, take the 30-minute tour, stop by for refreshment in the tearoom, or just head to the on-site shop. A cup-and-saucer set starts at UK£16 a typical basket UK£69, and prices head skyward from there. The factory-museum-store is near the border with Northern Ireland. Company products can also be found in the shops of Donegal and Sligo. ⊠ *6 km (4 mi) east of Ballyshannon, Belleek, Northern Ireland* ☎ *028/6865–8501 in Northern Ireland* ⊕ *www.belleek.ie* ☒ *UK£4* ☉ *Apr.–June, Sept., and Oct., weekdays 9–5:30, Sat. 10–5:30, Sun. 2–6; July and Aug., weekdays 9–8, Sat. 10–6, Sun. 11–6; Nov.–Mar., weekdays 10–5:30.*

The fourth generation (since 1866) of the Daly family handcrafts and paints the elaborate floral and basket-weave designs at **Celtic Weave China.** Because it's a small, personal operation, they can make a single piece of china to your specifications. Prices start at €7, and most pieces cost less than €125. ⊹ *5 km (3 mi) east of Ballyshanon* ⊠ *R230, Cloghore, Co. Donegal* ☎ *071/985–1844* ⊕ *www.celticweavechina.ie* ☒ *Free* ☉ *Mon.–Sat. 9–6.*

Donegal Irish Parian China Factory is the Republic's largest manufacturer of Parian china (so named because it resembles the clear white marble statuary from the Greek island of Paros)—the cream-color pottery crafted by traditional methods, to a large degree by hand. There's a 15-minute tour, a 10-minute video, a showroom, a shop, and a tearoom. The factory sells its wares at lower prices here than in retail stores. The least expensive items (spoons or thimbles) cost around €8. A full tea set starts at about €250. ⊠ *N15 just south of town, Co. Donegal* ☎ *071/985–1826* ⊕ *www.donegalchina.ie* ☒ *Free* ☉ *June–Aug., daily 9–5:30; Sept.–May, weekdays 9–5:30.*

off the beaten path

LOUGH DERG – From Whitsunday to the Feast of the Assumption (June to mid-August), tens of thousands beat a path to this lake, ringed by heather-clad slopes. In the center of the lough, Station Island—known as St. Patrick's Purgatory—is one of Ireland's most popular pilgrimage sites. It's also the most rigorous and austere of such sites in the country. Pilgrims stay on the island for three days without sleeping, and ingest only black tea and dry toast. They walk barefoot around the island, on its flinty stones, to pray at a succession of shrines. The pilgrimage has been followed since time immemorial; during the Middle Ages, devotees from foreign lands flocked here. Non-pilgrims may not visit the island from June to mid-August. To find out how to become a pilgrim, write to the Reverend Prior. To reach the shores of Lough Derg, turn off the main N15 Sligo–Donegal road in the village of Laghy onto the minor R232 Pettigo road, which hauls itself over the Black Gap and descends sharply into the border village of Pettigo, about 21 km (13 mi) from N15. From here, take the Lough Derg access road for 8 km (5 mi). ⊠ *Station Island, Lough Derg, Pettigo, Co. Donegal.*

Where to Stay & Eat

$$$$ ✕🏠 **Sandhouse Hotel.** Behind the mock manor-house exterior of this 19th-century former fishing lodge lies a large modern hotel. On Donegal Bay, this makes a peaceful, well-positioned base for sightseeing along the coast. The hotel has access to 3 km (2 mi) of beach. Renovated, well-kept bedrooms are decorated with antiques and overlook either the sea or the Donegal hills. Fresh seafood, including Donegal Bay oysters and mussels, is the specialty of the restaurant, which caters to hearty appetites. *⊹ 8 km (5 mi) northwest of Ballyshannon ⊠ Off R231, Rossnowlagh, Co. Donegal ☎ 071/985–1777 ☎ 071/985–2100 ⊕ www.sandhouse-hotel.ie ⏎ 64 rooms ⌂ Restaurant, golf privileges, tennis court, spa, fishing, horseback riding, bar, Internet, meeting rooms, helipad; no a/c ⊟ AE, DC, MC, V ◯ BP, MAP ⊘ Closed Dec. and Jan.*

Nightlife

The biggest and most popular pub, **Seán Óg's** (⊠ Market St. ☎ 071/985–8964), has live music on Friday, Saturday, and Sunday evenings.

Donegal Town

⑰ *21 km (13 mi) north of Ballyshannon, 66 km (41 mi) northeast of Sligo Town on N15.*

The town of Donegal was previously known in Irish as Dun na nGall, "Fort of the Foreigners." The foreigners were Vikings, who set up camp here in the 9th century to facilitate their pillaging and looting. They were driven out by the powerful O'Donnell clan (originally Cinel Conaill), who made it the capital of Tyrconail, their extensive Ulster territories. Donegal was rebuilt in the early 17th century, during the Plantation period, when Protestant colonists were planted on Irish property confiscated from its Catholic owners. The **Diamond,** like that of many other Irish villages, dates from this period. Once a marketplace, it has a 20-foot-tall obelisk monument to the Four Masters.

With a population of about 3,000, Donegal is northwest Ireland's largest small village—marking the entry into the back-of-the-beyond of the wilds of County Donegal. The town is centered on the triangular Diamond, where three roads converge (N56 to the west, N15 to the south and the northeast) and the mouth of the River Eske pours gently into Donegal Bay. You should have your bearings in five minutes, and seeing the historical sights takes less than an hour; if you stick around any longer, it'll probably be to do some shopping—arguably Donegal's top attraction.

Donegal Castle was built by clan leader Hugh O'Donnell in the 1470s. More than a century later, this structure was the home of his descendant Hugh Roe O'Donnell, who faced the might of the invading English and was the last clan chief of Tyrconail. In 1602 he died on a trip to Spain while trying to rally reinforcements from his allies. In 1610, its new English owner, Sir Basil Brooke, reconstructed the little castle, adding the fine Jacobean fortified mansion with towers and turrets that can still be seen (he was responsible for the town's Diamond road crossway as well). Inside, there are only a few rooms to see, including the garderobe (the restroom) and a great hall with an exceptional vaulted wood-beam roof. The small enclosed grounds are pleasant. ✉ *Tir-chonaill St., near north corner of the Diamond* ☎ *074/972–2405* 🖾 *€4* ⊙ *Easter–Oct., daily 10–5:30.*

The ruins of the **Franciscan Abbey,** founded in 1474 by Hugh O'Don-nell, are a 5-minute walk south of town at a spectacular site perched above the Eske River, where it begins to open up into Donegal Bay. The complex was burned to the ground in 1593, razed by the English in 1601, and ransacked again in 1607; the ruins include the choir, south transept, and two sides of the cloisters, between which lie hundreds of graves dat-ing to the 18th century. The abbey was probably where the *Annals of the Four Masters,* which chronicles the whole of Celtic history and mythology of Ireland from earliest times up to the year 1618, was writ-ten from 1632 to 1636. The Four Masters were monks who believed (correctly, as it turned out) that Celtic culture was doomed by the En-glish conquest, and they wanted to preserve as much of it as they could. At the National Library in Dublin, you can see copies of the monks' work; the original is kept under lock and key. ✉ *Off N15, behind Hyland Cen-tral Hotel* 🖾 *Free* ⊙ *Freely accessible.*

Where to Stay & Eat

★ ¢ ✕ **Blueberry Tea Room.** Proprietors Brian and Ruperta Gallagher serve breakfast, lunch, afternoon tea, and a light evening meal—always using home-grown herbs. Daily specials—Irish lamb stew, pasta dishes, and quiche—are served from 8 AM to 8 PM. Soups, sandwiches, salads, and fruit are on the regular menu, along with homemade desserts, breads, scones, and jams. Upstairs is an Internet café. It's across the street from Donegal Castle. ✉ *Castle St.* ☎ *074/972–2933* 🚭 *V* ⊙ *Closed Sun.*

$$$$ ✕🖾 **St. Ernan's House.** A most sweetly situated country house, St. Ernan's FodorśChoice sits on its own wooded tidal island in Donegal Bay. Fitted out with a ★ lordly verandah, white stone trim, and a facade that glows in lilac hues, the two-story house was built by a nephew of the duke of Wellington in 1826. Today this forgetaway remains a relaxed, serene lodging, thanks to owner–managers Brian and Carmel O'Dowd. Guest rooms are neatly refurbished; most of the furnishings are standard-issue an-tique or traditional chair or sofa stylishly done up in plaid ticking. All fades into insignificance when you drink in the bay views. Dinner, from a light meal to a leisurely five-course event, is served in the intimate din-ing room ($$$). Menu choices are based on fresh local foodstuffs: homemade tagliatelle with smoked salmon is a typical starter; crispy breast of duckling or wild salmon might follow. ✛ *3 km (2 mi) south of Done-gal Town* ✉ *Off R267, St. Ernan's, Co. Donegal* ☎ *074/972–1065* 🖷 *074/972–2098* ⊕ *www.sainternans.com* 🖙 *10 rooms, 2 suites* ♿ *Restaurant; no a/c* 🚭 *MC, V* ⊙❘ *BP* ⊙ *Closed Nov.–mid-Apr.*

$$$ ✕🖾 **Harvey's Point.** Complimentary decanters of brandy and sherry await you in spacious, crisp-white rooms with cherrywood beds. The Swiss-owned hotel has spirit-lifting views of Lough Eske at the foot of the Blue Stack Mountains. The dining room ($$$$), facing the lake, serves a four-course dinner with a choice of roast Donegal lamb with crispy sweetbreads, monkfish, hake, and other fresh Irish fare served with a French twist. ✛ *6 km (4 mi) northwest of Donegal Town* ✉ *Off N15,*

Lough Eske, Co. Donegal ☎ *074/972–2208* 🖷 *074/972–2352* ⊕ *www. harveyspoint.com* ✑ *33 rooms* ⚷ *Restaurant, bicycles, bar, meeting rooms; no a/c* ▱ *AE, DC, MC, V* ⫯◯⫯ *MAP.*

$ 🖽 **Central Hotel.** This family-run hotel on Donegal's central square is affiliated with Best Western. Huge picture windows in the back reveal lovely views of Donegal Bay. The efficient staff serves good, filling food in the large dining room. ✉ *The Diamond, Co. Donegal* ☎ *074/972–1027* 🖷 *074/972–2295* ⊕ *www.bestwestern.com* ✑ *212 rooms* ⚷ *Restaurant, in-room data ports, cable TV, indoor pool, health club, bar, no-smoking rooms; no a/c* ▱ *AE, DC, MC, V* ⫯◯⫯ *BP, MAP.*

Nightlife

The **Abbey Hotel** (✉ The Diamond ☎ 074/972–1014 ⊕ www.whites-hotelsireland.com) has music every night in July and August and a disco every Saturday and Sunday night throughout the year. During summer, people pack **McGroarty's Bar** (✉ The Diamond ☎ 074/972–1049) to hear traditional music Thursday nights and contemporary music on weekends. It's also a good place to stop for a casual bite to eat.

Sports & the Outdoors

Donegal Golf Club (✛ 8 km [5 mi] from Donegal Town ✉ Murvagh, Laghy, Co. Donegal ☎ 074/973–4054 ⊕ www.donegalgolfclub.ie) is one of Ireland's great 18-hole championship courses. The daily fees are €50 for Monday to Thursday and €55 for Friday to Sunday.

Shopping

Long the principal marketplace for the region's wool products, Donegal Town has several smaller shops with local hand weaving, knits, and crafts. **Browse a While** (✉ Main St. ☎ 074/912–2783) is a good place to stop off if you're in the mood for some light reading. The shop is stocked with tons of magazines and a small selection of pulp fiction. Explore **Donegal Craft Village** (✉ N15, 1½ km [1 mi] south of town ☎ No phone), a complex of workshops where you can buy pottery, handwoven goods, and ceramics from local young craftspeople. You can even watch the items being made Monday to Saturday 9–6, and Sunday 11–6.

The main hand-weaving store in town, **Magee's** (✉ The Diamond ☎ 074/972–2660 ⊕ www.mageeshop.com) carries renowned private-label tweeds for both men and women (jackets, hats, scarves, suits, and more), as well as pottery, linen, and crystal. **Simple Simon's** (✉ The Diamond ☎ 074/972–2687), the only fresh food shop here, sells organic vegetables, essential oils, and other whole-earth items, as well as breads and cakes from the kitchen on the premises. They also stock a lot of local Irish cheeses.

en route As you travel west on N56, which runs slightly inland from a magnificent shoreline of rocky inlets with great sea views, it's worthwhile turning off the road from time to time to catch a better view of the coast. About 6 km (4 mi) out of Donegal Town, N56 skirts Mountcharles, a bleak hillside village that looks back across the bay.

Bruckless

18 *19 km (12 mi) west of Donegal Town on N56.*

Don't be fooled by the round tower in the churchyard at Bruckless—it's 19th-century, not medieval. Soon after Bruckless, N56 turns inland across the bogs toward Ardara. The road now becomes R263, which runs through attractive heathland and wooded hills down to Killybegs.

Where to Stay & Eat

★ $ ✕⊞ **Castle Murray House Hotel.** Panoramas of distant mountains, the sapphire-blue waters of MacSwyne's Bay, and the long, narrow peninsula, punctuated at its tip by a lighthouse, await you at this hotel 1½ km (1 mi) out on the 10-km-long (6-mi-long) St. John's Point Peninsula. The original house has been extended and modernized; rooms are basic and contemporary, with individual color schemes. Natives trek here for the white-tablecloth restaurant overlooking the bay ($$$$). Prix-fixe selections might include glazed duck breast with confit of sweet ginger or steamed black sole with brandy cream. Lobster is a specialty. ⊹ *3 km (2 mi) southeast of Bruckless, 1½ km (1 mi) from Dunkineely* ⊠ *Off N56, Dunkineely, Co. Donegal* ☎ *074/973–7022* 🖷 *074/973–7330* ⊕ *www.castlemurray.com* ➟ *10 rooms* ⼎ *Restaurant, bar; no a/c* ⊟ *MC, V* ⫮⃝⊢ *BP* ☉ *Hotel closed mid-Jan.–mid-Feb.; restaurant closed Mon. and Tues., Jan.–Mar.*

$ ⊞ **Bruckless House.** A two-story, 18th-century farmhouse on the north side of Donegal Bay, this B&B occupies 19 acres, including woods, gardens, and a meadow where Irish draft horses and Connemara ponies roam. Public rooms in the main building have a fine view of Bruckless Bay. The Asian-inspired interior reflects the years the owners, Clive and Joan Evans, spent in Hong Kong. Upstairs, bedrooms are conventional but comfortable. A separate two-bedroom self-catering gate cottage, the former servants quarters, is at the entrance to the estate. Wholesome breakfasts are prepared with fruit from the Evanses' garden and freshly laid eggs from their hens. ⊠ *N56, Co. Donegal* ☎ *074/973–7071* 🖷 *074/973–7070* ➟ *4 rooms, 2 with bath; 1 cottage* ⼎ *Dining room, Internet; no a/c, no room phones, no room TVs* ⊟ *MC* ⫮⃝⊢ *BP* ☉ *Closed Oct.–Mar.*

Killybegs

19 *6 km (4 mi) west of Bruckless on R263, 28 km (17 mi) west of Donegal Town.*

Trawlers from Spain and France are moored in the harbor at Killybegs, one of Ireland's busiest fishing ports. Though it's one of the most industrialized places along this coast, it's not without some charm, thanks to its waterfront location. Killybegs once served as a center for the manufacture of Donegal hand-tufted carpets, examples of which are in the White House and the Vatican. **Killbegs Carpets** (⊠ Kilcar Rd. ☎ 074/973–1688) has a factory on the outskirts of the village, and produces high-quality hand-knotted and hand-tufted carpets to order: a square meter costs around €2,000. Visitors are welcome to commission a piece, but examples of the carpets are not sold off the peg.

en route

The narrows, climbs, and twists of R263 afford terrific views of Donegal Bay before descending into pretty Kilcar, a traditional center of tweed making. Signposted by its Irish name, the next village, An Charraig (Carrick), clings to the foot of the **Slieve League Mountains,** whose dramatic, color-streaked ocean cliffs are, at 2,000 feet, the highest in Ireland and among the most spectacular. Slieve League (Sliah Liec, or Mountain of the Pillars) is a ragged, razor-backed rise bordered by the River Glen. To see the cliffs, take the little road to the Irish-speaking village of Teelin, 1½ km (1 mi) south from Carrick. Then take the narrow lane (signposted to the Bunglass Cliffs) that climbs steeply to the top of the cliffs. The mountain looks deceptively climable from the back (the inaccessible part borders the Atlantic), but once the fog rolls in, the footing can be perilous. If you want to take in this thrilling perspective—presuming you're hardy and careful—walk along the difficult coastal path from Teelin.

Where to Stay & Eat

$ ✕⊡ **Bay View Hotel.** Across from Killybegs's harbor, the Bay View is the town's most bustling spot. The hotel lobby, in light wood, offers a modern take on classic designs, and the functional bedrooms are decorated in pale colors. The Irish table d'hôte menu changes daily, with Bruckless mussels in a white wine and garlic sauce and braised young duckling served with market vegetables and an orange and cherry coulis as potential options ($$$$). The hotel is well placed for seeing the glorious north shore of Donegal Bay. Special rates include golf greens fees for Portnoo (outside Ardara) and Murvagh (outside Donegal). ✉ *Main St., Co. Donegal* ☎ *074/973–1950* 🖷 *074/973–1856* ⊕ *www.bayviewhotel.ie* ↩*40 rooms with bath* ☖ *Restaurant, indoor pool, health club, bar; no a/c* ⊟ *AE, MC, V* ⧀ *BP, MAP.*

Shopping

The **Harbour Store** (✉ Main St. ☎ 074/973–2122), right on the wharf, has plenty to make both fisherfolk and landlubbers happy, including boots and rain gear, competitively priced sweaters, and unusual bright-yellow or -orange fiberglass-covered gloves (made in Taiwan).

Glencolumbkille

㉑ *27 km (17 mi) west of Killybegs on R263, 54 km (27 mi) west of Donegal Town.*

At the far end of a stretch of barren moorland, the tiny hamlet of Glencolumbkille (pronounced glen-colm-*kill*) clings dramatically to the rockbound harbor of Glen Bay. Known alternatively as Gleann Ghom Cille, it remains the heart of County Donegal's shrinking Gaeltacht region and retains a strong rural Irish flavor, as do its pubs and brightly painted row houses. The name means St. Columba's Glen; the legend goes that St. Columba, the Christian missionary, lived here during the 6th century with a group of followers. Some 40 prehistoric cairns, scattered around the village, have become connected locally with the St. Columba myths. The **House of St. Columba,** on the cliff top rising north of the village, is a small oratory said to have been used by the saint himself. In-

DREAM-WEAVERS

MOST OF THE ARAN SWEATERS YOU'LL SEE *throughout Ireland are made in County Donegal, the area most associated with* high-quality, handwoven tweeds and hand-knit items. Made of plain, undyed wool and knit with distinctive crisscross patterns, Aran sweaters are durable, soft, often weatherproof, and can be astonishingly warm. They once provided essential protection against the wild, stormy Atlantic Ocean. Indeed, these Arans can hold 30 percent of their weight in water before they even start to feel wet. Not so long ago, these pullovers were worn by every County Donegal fisherman, usually made to a design belonging exclusively to his own family. It is said that a native can tell which family the knitter belongs to from the patterns used in a genuine Aran sweater. Produced for centuries in the fishing communities of north and west Ireland, they are painstakingly knitted by hand, a

process which can take weeks. As a result, prices are not cheap, and if you think you've found a bargain, check the label before buying—it's more likely a factory copy. When it comes to Donengal tweed, weavers—inspired by the soft greens, red rusts, and dove grays of the famed Donegal landscape—have been producing it for centuries. In long-gone days, crofters' wifes concocted the dyes to give Donegal tweed its distinctive flecks, and then their husbands wove the cloth into tweed. Traditional Donegal tweed was a salt-and-pepper mix, but gradually weavers began adding dyes distilled from yellow gorse, purple blackberries, orange lichen, and green moss. Today most tweed comes from factories. However, there are still about 25 local craftsmen working from their cottages. Chic fashion designers like Armani, Ralph Lauren, and Burberry all use handwoven Donegal tweed—obviously, more fashionable than ever.

side, stone constructions are thought to have been his bed and chair. Every year on June 9, starting at midnight, local people make a 3-km (2-mi) barefoot procession called "An Turas" (the journey) around 15 medieval crosses and ancient cairns, collectively called the stations of the cross.

Walk through the **Folk Village Museum** to explore rural life. The complex, which was built after local priest Father McDyer started a cooperative to help combat rural depopulation, includes an interpretive center, 1881 schoolhouse, nature walk, tea shop, and crafts shop selling local handmade products, including, intriguingly, wines made from fuchsias and bluebells. Three small cottages, with bare-earth floors, represent the very basic living conditions of the 1720s, 1820s, and 1920s. ⚓ *Near the beach* ☎ *074/973–0017* ✉ *€3* ☉ *Easter–Sept., Mon.–Sat. 10–6, Sun. noon–6.*

Ardara

★ ㉑ *28 km (17 mi) northeast of Glencolumbkille, 40 km (25 mi) northwest of Donegal Town on N56.*

At the head of a lovely ocean inlet, the unpretentious, old-fashioned hamlet of Ardara is built around the L-shape intersection of its two main

432 <   **The Northwest**

streets. (If you come from Glencolumbkille, expect a scenic drive full of hairpin curves and steep hills as you cross over Glengesh Pass.) For centuries, great cloth fairs were held on the first of every month; cottage workers in the surrounding countryside still provide Ardara (and County Donegal) with high-quality, handwoven cloths and hand knits. Aran sweaters—an area specialty—are durable, soft, and often weatherproof, made of undyed wool knit in distinct crisscross patterns. Ardara has several stores to choose from.

Where to Stay & Eat

★ **$–$$$** ✕ **L'Atlantique Restaurant.** French couple Laure and Cyrille Troesch cook up excellent seafood in this relaxed little restaurant. Lobster, their specialty, drives the top price of main courses up, but the three-course prix-fixe menu (€18) is an excellent value. At this writing, the Troeschs were opening a pizzeria around the corner, which may well be worth a look. ⊠ *Main St.* ☎ *074/954–1707* ▤ *MC, V* ⊙ *Closed Tues. and Wed. Nov.–Jan. No dinner Sun.*

★ **$** ✕▭ **Woodhill House.** The cream-color exterior of John and Nancy Yates's spacious manor house is Victorian, but parts of the interior and the coach house date from the 17th century; there's even a small agricultural museum. High ceilings, marble fireplaces, and stained glass are part of the public spaces. Bedrooms have superb views of the Donegal highlands. The 40-seat restaurant ($$$$) uses local ingredients in dishes on its French-Irish table d'hôte menus: roast duckling with cherry and orange sauce, rack of lamb with herbs picked from the 18th-century walled garden, elaborate homemade desserts. Frequent Irish folk music sessions take place in the bar. ⊹ *Just outside Ardara* ⊠ *Donegal Rd., Co. Donegal* ☎ *074/954–1112* 🖷 *074/954–1516* ⊕ *www.woodhillhouse.com* ⇨ *9 rooms* ⊲ *Restaurant, fishing, horseback riding, bar; no a/c* ▤ *AE, DC, MC, V* ⓄⓈ *BP* ⊙ *Closed Christmas wk.*

¢ ▭ **Green Gate.** For an alternative to country estates and village hotels, **Fodor'sChoice** try Frenchman Paul Chatenoud's remote cottage B&B overlooking Ardara, the Atlantic, and spectacular Donegal scenery—it's one of Ireland's most beautiful little guest houses. The four spare rooms are in a converted stone outbuilding with a thatched roof. Chatenoud, as charming as his hideaway, eagerly directs you to Donegal's best-kept secrets. To reach the hotel from Ardara, follow the sign for Donegal and turn right after 200 yards. ⊠ *Ardvally, Co. Donegal* ☎ *074/954–1546* ⇨ *4 rooms* ⊲ *No a/c, no room phones, no room TVs* ▤ *No credit cards* ⓄⓈ *BP.*

Nightlife

For a small, old-fashioned village, Ardara has a surprising number of pubs, many of which have traditional music in the evenings. The **Central Bar** (⊠ Main St. ☎ 074/954–1311) has music almost every night in July and August and on weekends the rest of the year. One of the smallest bars in the Republic, **Nancy's Pub** (⊠ Front St. ☎ 074/954–1187) makes you wonder if you've wandered into the owner's sitting room, but it occasionally finds space for a folk group. The long-established **Nesbitt Arms** (⊠ Main St. ☎ 074/954–1103) is a good place for a reasonably priced drink and snack. It can get very crowded during July and August.

Shopping

Many handwoven and locally made knitwear items are on sale in Ardara; some stores commission goods directly from knitters, and prices are about as low as anywhere. Handsome, chunky Aran hand-knit sweaters (€76–€127), cardigans (similar prices), and scarves (€20) are all widely available. Stores such as **Campbells Tweed Shop** (⊠ Front St. ☎ 074/954–1128) carry ready-to-wear tweeds—sports jackets can run up to €100. **C. Bonner & Son** (⊠ Front St. ☎ 074/954–1303) stocks factory knitwear from €29 to €100, as well as pottery, tweeds, jewelry, and gifts. There is also a good selection of hand-knit Aran sweaters and cardigans available. **E. Doherty (Ardara) Ltd** (⊠ Front St. ☎ 074/954–1304) sells handwoven tweeds, from scarves for €25 to capes for €189, as well as traditional Irish products, such as glassware and linen, from Ardara and other parts of the country. At **John Molloy** (⊠ Main St. ☎ 074/954–1133) you will find a factory shop offering high-quality, hand-woven Donegal tweed, and hand-knit Aran sweaters.

NORTHERN DONEGAL

Traveling on northern County Donegal's country roads, you've escaped at last from the world's hurry and hassle. There's almost nothing up here but scenery, and plenty of it: broad, island-studded loughs of deep, dark tranquility; unkempt, windswept, sheep-grazed grasses on mountain slopes; ribbons of luminous greenery following sparkling streams; and the mellow hues of wide bog lands, all under shifting and changing cloudscapes. This trip could take anywhere from one day to a week, depending on how low a gear you slip into after a few breaths of Donegal air. It begins in Letterkenny, the largest town in the county (population 6,500), but if you want to pick up the journey from Ardara, follow the itinerary in reverse. If you choose to abbreviate the trip, try at least to catch the rewarding Fanad and Rosguill peninsulas and the drive around Sheephaven Bay. Connoisseurs of stately homes will make a beeline to the Irish Xanadu of Henry P. McIlhenny's Glenveagh Castle. Just one word of warning—don't be surprised if you find a sheep standing in the middle of a mountain road looking as though you, rather than it, are in the wrong place.

Letterkenny

㉒ *55 km (34 mi) northeast of Ardara, 51 km (32 mi) northeast of Donegal Town, 35 km (21 mi) west of Derry.*

One of the fastest-growing towns in all of Ireland, Letterkenny, like Donegal to the south, is at the gateway to the far northwest; you're likely to come through here if you're driving west out of Northern Ireland. Letterkenny's claim to fame has been that it has the longest main street in the whole country. None of Letterkenny's shops or pubs are particularly special, but lots of locals bustling around make it an interesting place to get a feel for what it's like to live in a modest-size Irish town. The 212-foot-high spire of **St Eunan's Cathedral** (⊠ Convent Rd. ☎ No phone) dominates the town, especially when illuminated at night. This striking, ornate neo-Gothic structure was finally finished in 1901, and is the only cathedral in the county. Designed by William Hague of Dublin and built of white Donegal sandstone, the exterior of the building is said to be in perfect classical-rule proportion. Inside, the intricate decorative ceilings and ceramic floor mosaics are the work of an Italian artist, Signor Amici of Rome. The main and side altars are carved from the finest Italian marble, while the great nave arch depicts the lives of St. Eunan and St. Columba in meticulous detail.

Where to Stay & Eat

$$ ✕⊡ **Mount Errigal Hotel.** One of County Donegal's smartest and most modern hotels, although not at all posh, Mount Errigal Hotel appeals to both business and family travelers. Service is friendly and professional. The clean and comfortable bedrooms are efficiently arranged with light-colored wood furnishings. The Glengesh, the hotel's popular and softly-lit restaurant serves contemporary Irish food ($$), while its Renaissance Bar's steel chandeliers, moderne seating, and wood paneled accents will light up any design aficionado's eyes. The bar buzzes with locals seeking a relaxed night out, and folk music, jazz, and dancing are frequently scheduled on weekends. ✉ *Ballyraine, Co. Donegal* ☎ *074/912–2700* 🖷 *074/912–5085* ⊕ *www.mounterrigal.com* ➶ *140 rooms, 2 suites* ⚵ *Restaurant, indoor pool, gym, health club, 2 bars, Internet, meeting rooms; no a/c* ⊟ *AE, DC, MC, V* ⦿ *BP, MAP.*

Ramelton

㉓ *13 km (8 mi) northeast of Letterkenny on R245.*

A small, handsome former Plantation town built by the prosperous Stewart family, Ramelton (or Rathmelton, though the pronunciation is the same) climbs uphill from a river harbor close to Lough Swilly, one of the loveliest of Donegal's big, fjordlike ocean inlets. The village was the birthplace of Francis Makemie (1658–1708), who preached here before emigrating and founding the American Presbyterian Church. In the 18th century it was an important port that exported salmon, butter, grain, linen, and iodine (made from the local seaweed). Houses of wealthy merchants lined the Mall, but the coming of the railway to nearby Letterkenny heralded the end of Ramelton's prosperity. However, Lough Swilly continued to play its part in history, sheltering vast fleets of British ships during the First World War, when Ireland was still part of the Empire. Heading north to Rathmullan, take the waterside road (the R247), which runs beside Lough Swilly.

Nightlife

The **Bridge Bar** (✉ Bridge End ☎ 074/915–1119), consistently named among the top 100 pubs in Ireland, has long been favored by locals and summertime visitors as a place to meet for a drink. Enjoy a good hearty meal (dinners are served upstairs, away from the bar), and take in the bands that regularly pack the place at night.

Rathmullan

㉔ *11 km (7 mi) northeast of Ramelton on R247.*

An ancient harbor village set among green fields, Rathmullan (Rath Maoláin, its Irish name, means "ring fort of Maoláin") looks across the

broad expanse of Lough Swilly to the Inishowen hills on the eastern shore. Holiday homes have sprung up near Lough Swilly's sandy shores, bringing with them vacationers who swell the town's ordinarily tiny population and make for a livelier summer scene. Rathmullan's modest harbor was where English naval officers, posing as ordinary merchant seamen, captured Red Hugh O'Donnell in 1587. They invited him aboard to taste some of their "cargo of foreign wines," and the sociable clan leader fell for it. Once on board, he was shipped to imprisonment in Dublin Castle. After six years he escaped and returned to Donegal with added determination to defend his homeland—but to no avail. In 1607, Rathmullan's harbor was the scene of the Flight of the Earls, the great exodus of Ulster nobility, which brought to an end the 13-year war with the English.

The **Flight of the Earls Heritage Centre** commemorates when the million-acre Ulster territories became part of the English domain. Two years later the Plantation era began: English and Scots Protestant colonists were "planted" here, and with them were sown the seeds of the Troubles that still dominate the affairs of Northern Ireland. ☎ *074/915–8178* ⊕ *www. flightoftheearls.com* ✉ *€3* ☉ *Limited hours vary.*

Where to Stay & Eat

★ **$$$–$$$$** ✕▦ **Rathmullan House.** Behind the rambling three-bay signature facade of this two-story, cream-color mansion awaits a place that's graceful *and* relaxed. Fine antiques and oil paintings fill the public rooms, including the bright-yellow drawing room. Bedrooms vary from old-fashioned-basic to grand, but all have antiques, elegant wallpaper, and lovely fabrics, and succeed in being elegant-but-not-stuffy. Those in the front overlook Lough Swilly and its deserted beach, separated from the house only by a ribbon of trees and the award-winning gardens. There's a speedboat available for a spin, and deep-sea angling. In a pavilion with a tented ceiling and floor-to-ceiling windows, the dining room ($$$$) has views of the gardens and the lake and a delicious prix-fixe menu, on which fish and Donegal lamb are favored choices. Breakfast is a feast. ⊠ *Lough Swilly, Rathmullan, Co. Donegal* ☎ *074/915–8188* 🖷 *074/915–8200* ⊕ *www.rathmullanhouse.com* ⤴ *32 rooms* ⌂ *Restaurant, 2 tennis courts, indoor pool, massage, spa, steam room, beach, boating, fishing, croquet, bar, lounge, library, Internet, meeting rooms; no a/c* ▱ *AE, DC, MC, V* ❘◯❘ *BP, MAP* ☉ *Closed Nov.–mid-Feb.*

★ **$$** ▦ **Fort Royal Hotel.** Tim Fletcher's spacious hotel attracts a regular clientele that enjoys its relaxed professionalism and marvelous location on 18 acres of verdant grounds beside the waters of Lough Swilly. Once an aristocratic private home, Fort Royal has two lounges—one a shimmering Wedgwood blue, the other in rosy peach—that are among the sweetest and comfiest around. Patterned wallpapers—pinstripes and florals—and gilt frames set the traditional tone for the guest rooms. Children under 10 dine at 6, not with the adults at the prix-fixe evening meal. ⊠ *Lough Swilly, Rathmullan, Co. Donegal* ☎ *074/915–8100* 🖷 *074/ 915–8103* ⊕ *www.fortroyalhotel.com* ⤴ *15 rooms* ⌂ *Restaurant, 9-hole golf course, tennis court, beach, bar; no a/c* ▱ *AE, DC, MC, V* ❘◯❘ *BP, MAP* ☉ *Closed Nov.–Mar.*

en route Extending north from Rathmullan is the barren and rock-strewn Fanad Peninsula. The signposted Fanad Scenic Drive takes you 27 km (17 mi) up the west shore of Lough Swilly to low-lying Fanad Head at its northern tip, then down again through the tiny resort village of Kerrykeel, with views of long, narrow Mulroy Bay to your right. If you want to cut the journey short, you can take the back road directly from Rathmullan to Kerrykeel for 10 km (6 mi).

Carrigart

㉕ *14 km (9 mi) north of Ramelton on R245.*

A small village with a lot of charm and many old-fashioned pubs, Carrigart (or Carraig Airt in Irish) is at the base of a slender isthmus. This is the neck of the extremely beautiful Rosguill Peninsula, which has a rocky heart and a fringe of sand dunes and beaches and is encircled by the signposted 15-km (9-mi) Atlantic Drive. It's not as far off the beaten track as you might think; there are several RV sites and housekeeping cottages, popular with people from Northern Ireland. The little resort town of **Downings** (Na Dúnaibh), near Carrigart, has a long, sandy beach and good fishing. Tweeds can be bought from **McNutts of Downings** (✉ Downings ☎ 074/915–5314).

Creeslough

㉖ *16 km (10 mi) southwest of Carraig Airt on N56.*

To the southwest of the Rosguill Peninsula and across Sheephaven Bay lies this small town at the foot of Muckish Mountain. On the southern end of Sheephaven Bay stands **Doe Castle,** protected on three sides by the sea and by a moat on its fourth side. The tall, weather-beaten tower is at the center of a complex structure enclosed within sturdy defenses. Described by attacking English forces in 1587 as "the strongest fortress in all the province," the edifice dates from at least 1440, when it became the home of MacSweeney Doe, one of the "gallowglasses" (from the Irish *gall o glach*)—foreign mercenaries employed by the O'Donnell clan. Despite the castle's poor condition, it was occupied by his descendants until 1890. MacSweeney Doe's curiously carved tombstone is fixed to the southwest tower of the outer wall. It's usually open; if the tower area is locked, inquire at the caretaker's cottage on the approach path. ⊹ *5 km (3 mi) northeast of Creeslough* ✉ *Off N56* ☎ *No phone* 🅰 *Free* ⊙ *Freely accessible.*

Ards Forest Park

㉗ *8 km (5 mi) north of Creeslough on N56.*

Clinging to Sheephaven Bay's southwest shore, the 1,188-acre Ards Forest Park (reached by passing through adjacent Creeslough [pronounced *creesh*-la]) is the former wooded estate of a Capuchin friary. The friary itself is still occupied by the Capuchins. Four prehistoric, fortified sites and one dolmen lie within the grounds, which have some of the most varied landscape of any of Ireland's national forest parks, including rivers, loughs, salt marshes, valleys, and, of course, the bay. If the weather is fine, the park's forest trails and picnic sites are great places to enjoy the scrubbed sea air. ☎ 074/912–1139 ☒ *Free* ☉ *Apr.–Sept., daily 10–9; Oct.–Mar., daily 10–4:30.*

Dunfanaghy

㉘ *8 km (5 mi) northwest of Ards Forest Park on N56.*

On the edge of Sheephaven Bay, Dunfanaghy (Dun Fionnachaid) is a tidy, former Plantation village, the kind of place you might enjoy settling into a hotel lunch of decent, unpretentious local grub. The town's main attraction is **The Workhouse,** whose exhibits illustrate the harsh life of a workhouse, where people turned when the famine forced them to accept hard labor for a roof and food. Follow the story of "Wee Hannah" from her farmhouse upbringing through famine to an eventual peaceful old age. The center has a café and an Irish handicrafts shop. ☒ *N56, just west of town* ☎ *074/913–6540* ⊕ *www.theirishfamine.com* ☒ *€4* ☉ *Mar.–Oct., daily 10–5.*

The town environs offer a bouquet of natural treasures. When the tide goes out, the vast sand flats of **Killyhoey Beach** are uncovered, but as it rises again, the sands are submerged in double-quick time. On the west side of Dunfanaghy, the signpost to **McSwyne's Gun** (McSwyne is the old spelling of MacSweeney) leads to a huge natural blowhole that gives out a deafening bang when the tide rushes in during rough weather. A little back road runs from Dunfanaghy up to **Horn Head,** the most spectacular of County Donegal's Atlantic headlands. From its sheer 600-foot cliffs, the views along the coast to the other headlands ranged one behind the other are inimitable. Bird-watchers should note that the cliffs are packed with hundreds of seabirds, including puffins and guillemots.

Where to Stay & Eat

$–$$ ✕▦ **Arnold's Hotel.** This friendly hotel has been run by three generations of the Arnold family and is a favorite with Irish vacationers. Rooms are unassuming, with floral bedspreads, curtains, and wallpaper. Ask for one overlooking the landscaped garden. You can eat generous, traditional Irish meals in the dining room or in the more casual Gallery Bistro ($$–$$$). Special-interest classes, such as photography, bridge, and painting, are sometimes available on weekends. As the hotel's web site puts it, "The area is awash with color and texture—from Muckish Mountain brushed with wind and weather, to the three local brown trout fishing lakes of Purt, Sessiagh, and New Lake, the natural habitat of swans, duck, and other wild fowl that frequent the lakes during the year." Budding Audubons, you know where to head. ☒ *Main St. Co. Donegal* ☎ *074/ 913–6208* ☐ *074/913–6352* ⊕ *www.arnoldshotel.com* ⇆ *30 rooms* ⚘ *Restaurant, café, tennis court, horseback riding, bar, baby-sitting; no a/c* ⊟ *AE, DC, MC, V* ⟦◎⟧ *BP, MAP* ☉ *Closed Nov.–mid-Mar.*

⌐ **en route** ⌐ West of Dunfanaghy the terrain is rougher, wilder, and rockier; you're also likely to hear the Irish language being spoken. The N56 reaches round 11 km (7 mi) to Fal Carrach (Falcarragh), the site of an Irish-language college. Another 13 km (8 mi) around the rugged seashore, you can catch a ferry—in good weather—from Meenlaragh (near Gortahork) to Tory Island.

Tory Island

㉙ *15 km (9 mi) offshore from Meenlaragh.*

Harsh weather and difficult currents make Tory Island fairly inaccessible. (The boat trip lasts more than an hour on seas that are rough even on the best days. Be prepared to get soaked.) Despite being rocky, ocean-battered, and barren (not even a single tree), the island has been inhabited since prehistoric times. Islanders speak their own dialect and refer to the mainland as "Ireland." Prehistoric and medieval relics are scattered about the landscape. Poised on the cliffs is the partly ruined, pink-granite **round tower,** with its conical cap still intact. At Tory Island's eastern end, the prehistoric ruin **Balor's Fort** was purportedly the residence of Balor, the terrifying, one-eyed Celtic god of night and darkness. At the island's northeastern tip, the **Wishing Stone** has the power, it is said, to destroy enemies. Still talked about is the time (1884) when the stone's powers were invoked against the British gunboat *Wasp,* whose passengers (mainly policemen) had come to collect taxes—something the islanders were unaccustomed to paying. The ship sank, and all but six of the crew were lost.

Most of the islanders live the simple life of fisherfolk, though quite a few have unexpected sidelines as artists. In 1968, the well-known Irish painter Derek Hill met islander James Dixon, who believed that he could do a better job of painting than Hill. Many other Tory Island residents thought they could, too, and today the Tory Island artists, depicting their own life and landscape in naive style using nothing more than standard house paints, are widely acclaimed and have exhibited elsewhere in Ireland, including Glebe House and Gallery in Gartan Lough and abroad. James Dixon's outpost, **Dixon's Gallery** (⊠ Beside the hotel ☎ No phone) sells the work of the Tory Islanders; prices range from €63 to €254. The owner of the Tory Island Hotel watches over the gallery.

Where to Stay & Eat

$ ✕▦ **Tory Island Hotel (Ostan Thoraig).** After living and working in England for 10 years, native islander Pat Doohan returned with his wife, Berney, to build and run the Tory Island Hotel. (He also watches over the nearby Dixon's Gallery.) The comfortable guest rooms are large and sunny, decorated in a peach, blue, and green palette, with matching curtains and bedspreads. A fireplace warms the Peoples Bar, which is a popular local hangout. Traditional music sessions and *ceilí* (traditional dancing) regularly liven things up. The Lobster Room restaurant ($–$$) both overlooks the sea and showcases its fishy denizens on its menu. ⊠ *Main St., Co. Donegal* ☎ *074/91–35920* 🖷 *074/91–35613* ⊕ *www.toryhotel.com* 🛏 *12 rooms* ⚘ *Restaurant, bar; no a/c* ⊟ *AE, MC, V* ⊚ *BP, MAP* ⊗ *Closed Nov.–Mar.*

Glenveagh National Park

30 *32 km (18 mi) southeast of Tory Island on R251.*

Fodor'sChoice
★

Bordered by the Derryveagh Mountains (Derryveagh means "forest of oak and birch"), Glenveagh National Park encompasses 24,000 acres of wilderness—mountain, moorland, lakes, and woods—that has been called the largest and most dramatic tract in the wildest part of Donegal. Within its borders, a thick carpet of russet-color heath and dense woodland rolls down the Derryveagh slopes into the broad open valley of the River Veagh (or Owenbeagh), which opens out into Glenveagh's spine: long and narrow, dark and clear Lough Beagh.

The lands of Glenveagh (pronounced glen-*vay*) have long been recognized as a remote and beautiful region. Between 1857 and 1859, John George Adair, a ruthless gentleman farmer, assembled the estate that now makes up the park. In 1861, he evicted the estate's hundreds of poor tenants without compensation and destroyed their cottages. Nine years later, Adair began to build **Glenveagh Castle** on the eastern shore of Lough Veagh, but he soon departed for Texas. He died in 1885 without returning to Ireland, but his widow, Cornelia, moved back to make Glenveagh her home. She created four gardens, covering 27 acres; planted luxuriant rhododendrons; and began the job of making this turret-and-battlement laden 19th-century folly livable. At the end of a dramatic 2-mi-long entryway, perched over the lake waters, this is a true fairytale castle. Like a doll-house Balmoral, its castellated, rectangular keep, battlemented ramparts, and a Round Tower enchantingly conjure up all the Victorian fantasies of a medieval redoubt.

The gardens and castle as they appear today are almost entirely an American invention, the product of the loving attentions of Glenveagh's last owners, Mr. Kingsley Porter, a venerated professor of medieval art history at Harvard. He, then, passed the property over to U.S. millionaire Henry P. McIlhenny, who bought the estate in 1937 and, beginning in 1947, lived here for part of every year for almost 40 years. An avid art collector and philanthropist (his collection of Degas, Toulouse-Lautrec, and Ingres masterworks now resides at the Philadelphia Museum of Art), McIlhenny decorated every inch of the house himself in faux-baronial fashion and entertained the beau monde (Greta Garbo once slept in the Pink Room) lavishly. The house has been maintained just as it was on his last occupancy in 1983; later that year, he made a gift of the house to the nation. He had sold the government the surrounding land in 1975, which it opened to the public in 1984 as Ireland's third national park.

Beyond the castle, footpaths lead into more remote sections of the park, including the **Derrylahan Nature Trail,** a 1½-km (1-mi) signposted trail where you may suddenly catch sight of a soaring falcon or chance upon a shy red deer. The park is the home of one of Ireland's two largest herds; the other is at Killarney. Guided walks are held from May through October. The visitor center at the park's entrance has a permanent exhibition on the local way of life and on the influence of climate on the park's flora and fauna. Skip the sleep-inducing audiovisual and instead have a bite to eat in the cafeteria. A bus runs from the visitor center to the castle. ✉ *R251, Church Hill* ☎ *074/913–7090* ⊕ *www. heritageireland.ie* 🚌 *Bus €2 round-trip, castle tour and gardens €3* ⊙ *Mid-Mar.–Oct., daily 10–6:30.*

Gartan Lough

❸ *13 km (8 mi) southeast of Glenveagh National Park on R251.*

Gartan Lough and the surrounding mountainous country are astonishingly beautiful. St. Columba was supposedly born here in AD 521, and the legendary event is marked by a huge cross at the beginning of a footpath into Glenveagh National Park. (Close to Church Hill village, Gartan Lough is technically within the national park and is administered partly by the park authorities.) Nearby are other dubious "relics" of the saint, which are popularly believed to possess magical powers: the Natal Stone, where the saint is thought to have first opened his eyes, and the Stone of Loneliness, where he is said to have slept. The superstitions do rub off—the soil of Gartan was carried by soldiers from the area to the trenches of the First World War as a protective relic.

On the northwest shore of Gartan Lough just off R251 is **Glebe House and Gallery,** a sweetly elegant redbrick Regency manor with 25 acres of gardens. For 30 years, Glebe House was the home of the distinguished landscape and portrait artist Derek Hill, who furnished the house in a mix of styles with art from around the world; in 1981 he gave the house and its contents, including his outstanding art collection, to the nation. Highlights include paintings by Renoir and Bonnard, lithographs by Kokoschka, ceramics and etchings by Picasso, and the paintings *Whippet Racing* and *The Ferry, Early Morning* by Jack B. Yeats, as well as Donegal folk art produced by the Tory Islanders. The decoration and furnishings of the house, including original William Morris wallpaper, are also worth a look. ✉ *Church Hill* ☎ *074/913–7071* 🚌 *€3* ⊙ *Sat.–Thurs. 11–6:30.*

At the **Colmcille Heritage Centre** you can learn more about St. Columba and his times. The exhibition and interpretation center has medieval manuscripts, stained glass, and displays tracing the decline of the Celtic religion and the rise of Irish Christianity. Audiovisual displays and interactive computer presentations enhance the historical journey. The staff can show you walks in the area. ✉ *R254, Church Hill* ☎ *074/913–7306* 🚌 *€2* ⊙ *Mid-Apr.–Sept., Mon.–Sat. 10:30–6:30, Sun. 1–6:30.*

Grianan Fort

★ **❸** *29 km (18 mi) northeast of Letterkenny on N13.*

A circular stone Celtic fort, the Grianan Fort (Grianan Ailigh) definitely merits a visit, although it is, like the vast and verdant Inishowen Peninsula to the north, northeast of Letterkenny and thus closer to Northern Ireland than the majority of Donegal sites covered here. The fortress crowns an 810-foot-high hill. On a fine day, the panorama of the rolling Donegal and Derry landscape is breathtaking. To the north lies the

River Swilly, flowing around Inch Island into Lough Swilly. On either side rise the hills of the Fanad and Inishowen peninsulas, though they're often partly veiled by mists. The fort is a 76-foot-diameter circular stone enclosure, which you can enter through a gate. Inside, earth ramparts and concentric defenses punctured by passages surround a sturdy central structure. No one knows when Grianan Fort was built, but it was probably an Iron Age fortress. Its position was accurately recorded in the 2nd century AD by Ptolemy of Alexandria. In the 5th century it became the seat of Ulster's O'Neill chieftains and remained so until the 12th century, despite serious attempts by their enemies to destroy it, especially in the year 674 and again in 1101. The present-day fortress, however, owes a good deal to overzealous "restoration" in the 1870s by Dr. Walter Bernard, a Derry historian; before that, it was in ruins. If you're traveling north on N13, look for signs to Buncrana, because the easy-to-miss sign for the fort is opposite. Instead of turning to Buncrana, take the narrow lane that climbs and turns for more than 2 km (1 mi) to the top of the hill. The fort is freely accessible.

Inishowen Peninsula

㉝ *6 km (4 mi) north of Grianan Ailigh on R238.*

The most northerly point in all of Ireland, the huge Inishowen Peninsula is a grandly green, wild piece of land with a solid, mountainous interior. It's flanked by Lough Swilly on one side and Lough Foyle on the other, and the battering Atlantic thrashes to the north. Despite a string of small and untempting coastal resorts, the peninsula remains unspoiled and less traveled than most parts of the country. If you decide to make the Inishowen circuit from Fahan to Muff via Malin Head (known as the "Inishowen 100," for its length in miles) plus the 64-km (40-mi) round-trip to reach it from Letterkenny, you'll need to allow at least one whole day, though it's possible to make an abbreviated visit in less time.

Just off R238, as you head toward Buncrana, is **Fahan** (pronounced fawn), which has monastic ruins that include the early Christian St. Mura cross slab. A popular, downscale beach resort favored by Derry denizens, **Buncrana** has a 14th-century O'Doherty tower that gradually became part of an 18th-century mansion. Shortly after you pass Buncrana, turn left at the fork in the road away from R238 onto the coast road, which takes you past the 19th-century fort on Dunree Head, up and over the spectacular viewpoint of the **Gap of Mamore**, where the 1,250-foot Croaghcarragh rises up on one side and the 1,361-foot-high Mamore Hill echoes it on the other. The road heads north toward Dunaff Head, where Lough Swilly opens into the ocean. Rejoin R238 at Clonmany and take it through Ballyliffin, a small resort town with an O'Doherty tower on the beach, and a convenient place for a snack or meal.

By the junction of R238 and R240 is a church with a curious remnant of early Christianity against one wall—the decorated, 7th-century **Donagh Cross**, accompanied by a couple of pillar stones. The strange carvings on the stones clearly date from a pre-Christian period. Around the corner from the Donagh Cross, **Carndonagh**, the area's main market town, has several other medieval monastic remains. Slieve Snaght, Inishowen's highest peak at 2,019 feet, lies just southwest of town. As Slieve Snaght runs up beside Trawbreaga Bay, R238 turns into R242 shortly before the picturesque village of **Malin**; it's another 16 km (10 mi) up to Malin Head, the most northerly point in Ireland and an important spot for birds migrating south in autumn. Although it has good views, Malin Head is not as dramatic a spot as some of the other headlands.

From Malin Head, take the signposted route across Inishowen peninsula to Moville, a sleepy waterside resort on the Lough Foyle side. From here, it's 8 km (5 mi) to **Inishowen Head,** the peninsula's rocky eastern tip. On the way to the head, at Greencastle, you can see the fortifications of foreigners who tried to control the nine counties of Ulster: a 14th-century Anglo-Norman fortress and an English fort built five centuries later to defend against French support for the Irish. The drive along the lough shore toward Derry, though attractive, is punctuated by small, uninteresting villages whose modernized pubs cater to visitors from Derry. If you want to turn away from Derry toward Letterkenny before reaching the border, take R239 from Muff to **Bridge End,** where there's one of the most attractive of Ireland's many new Catholic churches.

Where to Stay & Eat

$-$$ ✕ **Corncrake Restaurant.** Bríd McCartney and Noreen Lynch gave up the Dublin rat race to open the most stylish restaurant between Derry and New York. They grow all their own herbs and specialize in seafood and lamb. Try the cod, prawn, and fennel chowder followed, perhaps, by the sea bass fillet drizzled with lemon sauce and served with spinach. The two also run excellent weekend cooking courses during November and March for €330, which includes all meals, instruction, and accommodation at the nearby Rossaor House. ⊠ *Mill Brae, Carndonagh* ☎ *074/937–4534* ⊟ *No credit cards.*

FodorsChoice ★

★ **$-$$$** ✕🏠 **St. John's Country House and Restaurant.** Intimate rooms graced with Victorian- and Georgian-era furnishings characterize this small lakeside country house. The experience here is enhanced by the exceptional hospitality of host Reggie Ryan. Homemade bread is baked daily—to serve with the fresh garden soups and pâtés. The five-course table d'hôte menu changes monthly ($$$$). Appetizers may include seafood salad or roast peppers with balsamic dressing. Cardamom and lime crepes stuffed with vegetables, and Irish beef sirloin with mushroom and Armagnach sauce are typical main courses. Desserts include homemade ice creams and carrageen moss with fruit coulis. ⊠ *Off R238, Fahan, Co. Donegal* ☎ *074/936–0289* 🖨 *074/936–0612* ⊕ *homepage.tinet. ie/~stjohnscountryhouse/* 🛏 *4 rooms with bath, 1 suite* � *No a/c* ⊟ *AE, DC, MC, V* ◯ *BP* ⊘ *Closed mid-Feb.–mid-Mar.*

$ 🏠 **Rossaor House.** A comfortable, warm guesthouse overlooking the majestic Pollen Bay (and only a short drive to Malin Head, the most northerly tip of Ireland), this 11-acre retreat will make you feel right at home because this *is* home to proprietors Brian and Anne Harkin. Mornings are a welcoming affair, thanks to the kitchen-made scones, jam, and even honey. Golfers will be in their element, with the challenging Ballyliffen golf course just 1 mi away. Decor is traditional and rooms are spotless; six cottages (with kitchens) are also available. ⊠ *Off R238, Ballyliffen Co. Donegal* ☎ *074/937–6498* 🖨 *074/937–6888.*

Shopping

National Knitting Centre and Cranaknits Sweater Shop (⊠ St. Oran's Rd., Buncrana ☎ 074/936–2355) sells hand-knit goods and gives classes in traditional Irish knitting.

THE NORTHWEST A TO Z

To research prices, get advice from other travelers, and book travel arrangements, visit www.fodors.com.

AIR TRAVEL

CARRIERS   Aer Arann has direct flights between Dublin and Knock International, Donegal, and Sligo Airports. British Airways City Express flies to Eglinton (Derry) Airport from Manchester and Glasgow. Ryanair has flights to Knock Airport from London Stansted daily.

🛫 **Airlines & Contacts Aer Arann** ☎ 081/821-0210 or 0800/587-2324 ⊕ www.aerarann. ie. **British Airways City Express** ☎ 0870/850-9850 ⊕ www.britishairways.com. **Ryanair** ☎ 0818/830-3030 ⊕ www.ryanair.com.

AIRPORTS

The principal international air-arrival point to northwest Ireland is the tiny airport at Charlestown, Knock International Airport, 55 km (34 mi) south of Sligo Town. City of Derry Airport, a few miles over the border, receives flights from Manchester and Glasgow. City of Derry (also called Eglinton) is a particularly convenient airport for reaching northern County Donegal. Donegal Airport, in Carrickfinn, is not far from Dungloe and typically receives flights from Dublin. Sligo Airport at Strandhill, 8 km (5 mi) west of Sligo Town, is the other area airport.

🛫 **Airport Information City of Derry Airport** ☎ 028/7181-0784. **Donegal Airport** ☎ 074/954-8232. **Knock International Airport** ☎ 094/936-7222. **Sligo Airport** ☎ 071/916-8280 or 071/916-8318.

TRANSFERS   If you aren't driving, Knock Airport becomes less attractive; there are no easy public transportation links, except the once-a-day (in season) local bus to Charlestown, 11 km (7 mi) away. Nor can you rely on catching a bus at the smaller airports, except at Sligo Airport, where buses run from Sligo Town to meet all flights.

You can get taxis—both cars and minibuses—right outside Knock Airport. The average rate is €1.27 per mile. If you're not flying into Knock, you may have to phone a taxi company. Phone numbers of taxi companies are available from airport information desks and are also displayed beside pay phones inside the airport terminals.

🚕 **Taxi Companies Castle Cabs** ☎ 087/638-8588. **OK Cabs** ☎ 087/639-6666. **Tom Cronnolly** ☎ 087/244-0597.

BUS TRAVEL

Bus Éireann can get you from Dublin to Sligo Town in four hours for €14 one-way, €23 round-trip. Four buses a day from Dublin are available. Another bus route, five times a day from Dublin (six on Friday), goes to Letterkenny, in the heart of County Donegal, in 4¼ hours, via a short trip across the Northern Ireland border; it's €15 one-way, €23 round-trip. Other Bus Éireann services connect Sligo Town to towns all over Ireland. Bus Éireann also operates out of Sligo Town and Letterkenny to destinations all over the region, as well as to other parts of Ireland. From Sligo Town, you can reach almost any point in the region for less than €15. McGeehans is one of several local bus companies linking towns and villages in northwest Ireland.

🚌 Bus Information **Bus Éireann** ☎ 01/836–6111 in Dublin, 071/916–0066 in Sligo Town, 074/21309 in Letterkenny. **McGeehans** ☎ 074/954–6150.

CAR RENTAL

You can rent a car in Sligo Town from Euro Mobil. Murray's Europcar rents cars from Knock Airport. A medium-size four-door costs around €65 per day with unlimited mileage (inclusive of insurance and taxes) or around €300 per week. If you're planning to tour mostly northern County Donegal, you may find it more convenient to rent a car in Derry from Ford. If you're planning to drive a rental car across the border to Northern Ireland, inform the company in advance and check the insurance policy.

🚗 Agencies **Avis** ☎ 071/916–8280 operates out of Sligo Airport. **Euro Mobil** ☎ 071/916–7291. **Ford** ☎ 028/7181–2222. **Murray's Europcar** ☎ 094/936–7221 at Knock Airport, 01/614–2800 for reservations.

CAR TRAVEL

Sligo, the largest town in northwest Ireland, is relatively accessible on the main routes. The N4 travels the 224 km (140 mi) directly from Dublin to Sligo. Allow at least four hours for this journey. The N15 continues from Sligo Town to Donegal Town and proceeds from Donegal Town to Derry City, just over the border in Northern Ireland. The fastest approach for anyone driving up from the west and the southwest is on N17, connecting Sligo to Galway, though the landscape is undistinguished.

ROAD CONDITIONS Roads are not congested, but in some places they are in a poor state of repair (French bus drivers refused to take their buses into County Donegal some summers back, as a gesture of protest about the state of the roads). In the Irish-speaking areas, signposts are written only in the Irish (Gaelic) language, which can be confusing. Make sure that your map lists both English and Irish place names.

EMERGENCIES

🚑 **Ambulance, fire, police** ☎ 999. **Letterkenny General Hospital** ⊠ High Rd., Letterkenny, Co. Donegal ☎ 074/912–5888. **Sligo General Hospital** ⊠ The Mall, Sligo Town, Co. Sligo ☎ 071/917–1111.

INTERNET

Most hotels will allow guests to use their Internet facilities, but cyber cafés are thin on the ground in this part of rural Ireland. There is one in Sligo Town, called the **Cygo Internet Café** (⊠ 19 O'Connell St. ☎ 071/914–0082) and its hook-up costs about €5 for one hour.

MAIL & SHIPPING

Mail service in the northwest of Ireland is reliable and efficient. The two main post offices in Donegal Town and Sligo Town are open weekdays

9 AM to 5:30 PM, Saturday 9 AM to 1 PM, and closed Sundays and public holidays. Look for the green signs that say "An Post." In rural villages, the opening hours are generally the same but most post offices will close for lunch from 1 to 2.

🖪 Post offices **Donegal Town post office** ✉ Tirconaill St ☎ 074/972-1024. **Sligo Town post office** ✉ Lower Knox St. ☎ 071/915-9273.

TOURS

Bus Éireann has budget-priced, guided, one-day bus tours of the Donegal Highlands and to Glenveagh National Park; they start from Bundoran, Sligo Town, Ballyshannon, and Donegal Town. For a friendly, relaxed minibus tour of the area in July and August, call John Houze. He's a knowledgeable guide who leads popular tours (€14 each) to the Lake Isle of Innisfree, the Holy Well, and Parke's Castle; and north of Sligo Town to W. B. Yeats's grave and Glencar Lake and waterfall.

Walking tours of Sligo Town may be arranged in advance for groups, and last about 1½ hours. Depending on the number of people, the charge is approximately €4.

🖪 Bus Tours **Bus Éireann** ☎ 01/836-6111 ⊕ www.buseireann.ie. **John Houze** ☎ 071/914-2747 or 086/193-5045.

🖪 Walking Tours **Sligo Path Guided Walking Tours** ☎ 071/915-0920.

TRAIN TRAVEL

Sligo Town is the northernmost direct rail link to Dublin. From Dublin, three trains a day make the three hour and 20 minute journey for €18 one-way, €27 round-trip. If you want to get to Sligo Town by rail from other provincial towns, you're forced to make some inconvenient connections and take roundabout routes. The rest of the region has no railway services.

🖪 Train Information **Irish Rail** ☎ 01/836-6222 ⊕ www.irishrail.ie.

VISITOR INFORMATION

The Tourist Information Office (TIO) in Sligo Town provides a walking map of Sligo, information about bus tours of Yeats Country, and details of boat tours of Lough Gill. It's also the main visitor information center for northwest Ireland. Open hours are September to mid-March, weekdays 9–5; mid-March to August, weekdays 9–6, Saturday 10–2, and Sunday 11–3. If you are traveling in County Donegal in the north, try the TIO at Letterkenny, about 1½ km (1 mi) south of town. It's open September to May, weekdays 9–5; June to August, Monday–Saturday 9–6 and Sunday 12–3. The offices at Bundoran and Dungloe are open only during the summer months (usually the first week in June to the second week in September).

🖪 Tourist Information **Bundoran TIO** ✉ Main St., Bundoran, Co. Donegal ☎ 071/984-1350. **Co. Donegal TIO** ✉ N13, Derry Rd., Letterkenny, Co. Donegal ☎ 074/912-1160. **Co. Sligo TIO** ✉ Temple and Charles Sts., Sligo Town, Co. Donegal ☎ 071/916-1201. **Donegal Town TIO** ✉ Quay St., Donegal Town, Co. Donegal ☎ 074/972-1148. **Dungloe TIO** ✉ Village Center, Dungloe, Co. Donegal ☎ 074/952-1297.

NORTHERN IRELAND

8

Updated by
Catherine
Morrison

LEGEND HAS IT THAT A MILLENNIUM ago a seafaring chieftain caught sight of the green shores of Northern Ireland, and offered the land to whichever of his two sons would be first to lay a hand upon it. As the two rivals rowed toward shore in separate boats, one began to draw ahead—whereupon the other drew his sword, cut off his own hand, and hurled it onto the beach—and so, by blood and sacrifice, gained the province. To this day the coat of arms of Northern Ireland bears the severed limb: the celebrated "Red Hand of Ulster."

From this ancient bardic tale to the time of the recent Troubles, from 1969 to 1994, Northern Ireland has had a long and often ferocious history. But all such thoughts vanish in the face of the country's outstanding natural beauty; its magnificent, stately houses; and the genuinely warm hospitality of its inhabitants. The Six Counties, or Ulster (as Northern Ireland is often called), cover less than 14,245 square km (5,500 square mi). Within these boundaries is some of the most unspoiled scenery you could hope to find—the granite Mountains of Mourne; the Giant's Causeway, made of extraordinary volcanic rock; more than 320 km (200 mi) of coastline beaches and hidden coves; and rivers and leaf-sheltered lakes that provide fabled fishing grounds, including the largest freshwater lake in Europe, Lough Neagh. Ancient castles and Palladian-perfect 18th-century houses are as numerous here as almost anywhere else in Europe, and each has its own tale of heroic feats, dastardly deeds, and lovelorn ghosts. Northern Ireland not only houses this heritage in its native stone, but has given the world the even greater legacy of a roster of celebrated descendants. Nearly one in six of the more than 4½ million Irish who made the fateful journey across the Atlantic to seek their fortune in the New World came from Ulster, and of this group (and from their family stock), more than a few left their mark in America: Davy Crockett, President Andrew Jackson, General Ulysses S. Grant, President Woodrow Wilson, General Stonewall Jackson, financier Thomas Mellon, merchant J. Paul Getty, writers Edgar Allan Poe and Mark Twain, and astronaut Neil Armstrong.

Present-day Northern Ireland, a province under the rule of the United Kingdom, includes six of the old Ulster's nine counties and retains its sense of separation, both in the vernacular of the landscape and (some say) in the character of the people. The hardheaded and industrious Scots-Presbyterians, imported to make Ulster a bulwark against Ireland's Catholicism, have had a profound and ineradicable effect on the place. The north has more factories, neater-looking farms, better roads, and—in its cities—more of the two-story redbrick houses typical of Great Britain than are found in the Republic. For all that, the border between north and south is of little consequence if you're just here to see the country.

Ireland's ancient history truly began in the north, when settlers came to the banks of the River Bann 9,000 years ago. Five thousand years later Bronze Age settlers built the great stone circles idiomatic to Counties Down and Tyrone, and later the Iron Age brought the Celts. St. Patrick, the son of a Roman official who was forced into slavery in County Antrim, returned to spread Christianity in the 5th century. But, starting with the first Norman incursions in the 12th century, the English made greater

Numbers in the text correspond to numbers in the margin and on the Northern Ireland and Belfast maps.

If you have 2 days

The first day, tour the bustling Victorian industrial metropolis and environs of **Belfast** ①–⑱ ⌐. The next morning, go north through the breathtaking **Glens of Antrim** ⑳ to the remarkable natural formations of the **Giant's Causeway** ㉒ and the teetering cliff-top remains of **Dunluce Castle** ㉔. Spend the night in 🚗 **Coleraine** ㉕, 🚗 Ballymena, or if you wish to return the way you came, you could stay in one of the coastal towns before Belfast.

8

If you have 4 days

Follow the two-day itinerary but continue on to spend the second night in the dramatically rejuvenated city of 🚗 **Derry** ㉘–㉟. In the morning, drive south to the tranquil beauty of **Lower Lough Erne** ㊲. You may want to go on a boat ride, take a pottery tour in **Belleek** ㊳, visit the historic town of **Enniskillen** ㊵, or view the exquisite Neoclassic 18th-century beauty of two of Northern Ireland's stateliest homes, **Florence Court** ㊵ and **Castle Coole** ㊶. On Day 3, follow the road through leafy **Armagh** ㊷, Ireland's ecclesiastical capital, then go southeast on B133 to the magnificent **Mountains of Mourne** ㊸. Spend the night in one of the towns in or near the mountains and work your way up the coast the next day past Strongford Lough to pay a call on the magical **Castle Ward** ㊻ in Strangford on your way back to Belfast.

If you have 7 days

Spend two nights in **Belfast** ①–⑮, including a country excursion to visit the fabled house of **Mount Stewart** ⑰; then head north on A2 on the morn of Day 3. Take your time exploring the **Glens of Antrim** ⑳ with a look at the characteristic twin towns of rugged Cushendall and pretty Cushendun, and **Ballycastle** ㉑. Stop along the coast for the night and after breakfast on Day 4 drive to **Giant's Causeway** ㉒. Continue with a tour and a sip of whiskey at **Bushmills** ㉓ before visiting **Dunluce Castle** ㉔. Continue on that evening to 🚗 **Derry** ㉘–㉟, where you spend that night. On Day 5 drive south and visit **Ulster-American Folk Park** ㊱ before continuing on to **Lower Lough Erne** ㊲. The famous pottery-making town of **Belleek** ㊳ is at the east end of the lake. At the west end is the historic town of **Enniskillen** ㊴, which is near **Florence Court** ㊵ and **Castle Coole** ㊶: take your pick. Day 6, it's on to the **Mountains of Mourne** ㊸, with their trails and overlooks. You can choose among several towns in which to spend the night from Kilkeel to Newcastle. On your last day, enjoy a visit to the grand **Castle Ward** ㊻, overlooking the water in Strangford, and then take in the Irish Linen Centre and Lisburn Museum in **Lisburn** ㊻ before returning to Belfast.

and greater inroads into Ireland, endeavoring to subdue what they believed was a potential enemy. Ulster proved the hardest to conquer, but in 1607 Ulster's beaten-down Irish nobility fled their homeland forever, many settling in France and Spain, in the great exodus known as the Flight of the Earls. Their abandoned lands were distributed by the English to "the Planters"—staunch Protestants from England and Scotland.

After three centuries of smoldering tensions and religious strife, 1916 saw the Easter Uprising and then, in the parliamentary elections of 1918, an overwhelming Nationalist vote across Ireland for Sinn Féin ("Ourselves Alone"), the party that believed in independence for all of Ireland. In the five northeastern counties of Ulster, however, only seven seats went to the Nationalists, and 22 to the Unionists, whose objective was to remain an integral part of the United Kingdom. At 2:10 AM on December 6, 1921, in the British prime minister's residence at 10 Downing Street, Michael Collins—the Republican leader and controversial hero—signed the Anglo-Irish Treaty. This designated a six-county North to remain in British hands in exchange for complete independence for Ireland's 26 counties as the Irish Free State.

Fast-forward to 1968, when, in the spirit of student uprisings occurring in Paris and Washington, and after 40 years of living with an apparently permanent and sectarian Unionist majority, students in Belfast's Queen's University launched a civil rights protest, claiming equal rights in jobs, housing, and opportunity. The brutality with which these marches were suppressed led to worldwide revulsion, riots, and counter-riots. The Irish Republican Army (IRA), which had been dormant for decades, took over what was left of the shattered civil rights movement, which once had a smattering of Protestant students among its ranks. Armed British troops who had at first been welcomed in the Catholic ghettos as protectors from Protestant paramilitaries now found themselves shunned by both sides. Britain imposed Direct Rule. No one was happy, and the decades of guerrilla conflict that ensued between the IRA, the UDA/UVF (Protestant/Loyalist paramilitaries), and the British government continued in a mix of lulls and terrors—apart from the IRA's annual Christmas "truce"—until the summer of 1994, when the "Provos," as they are colloquially known, called for an ongoing cease-fire, confirmed in July 1997.

After two years of intensive and complex talks, an agreement was finally reached between Northern Ireland's political parties in April 1998. The Good Friday Agreement (so called because it was secured on the Friday before Easter Sunday), also known as the Belfast Agreement, gave the province limited powers and its own parliament. Put to the people of both the north and south of Ireland in separate referenda, it was endorsed by an overwhelming majority and elections to the parliament were held in June 1998. But a mere two months later, the province's fragile peace was shattered when a massive car-bomb exploded in the quiet market town of Omagh, County Tyrone. On August 15, dissident Republicans—a minority within the movement who were, and still are, opposed to the Good Friday Agreement—succeeded in killing 31 people, including unborn twins. It was the single worst atrocity in the history of the Troubles. Despite this appalling act, the peace process continued and Unionists eventually entered government with Sinn Fein at the end of 1999. Since then, the assembly—the first democratically elected in the history of Northern Ireland—has been suspended three times. Political parties are divided into pro-agreement and anti-agreement camps and when fresh elections to the assembly were held in November 2003, it

8

Through the Keyhole

Ulster's stately homes are either proud reminders of a shared history with Britain or symbols of an oppressive colonial past—it depends on who you're talking to. But there is no denying the magnificence of these country estates and lavish mansions, erected by the Anglo-Irish Protestant Ascendancy in the 17th, 18th, and 19th centuries. In 1607, Ulster's nobility, beaten in battle by the English and fearing persecution, fled to the European continent. They left a vacuum of power, soon filled by aristocratic English and Scottish families fiercely loyal to the British crown. The native Irish were driven off almost 500,000 acres of the most fertile land in the province and staunch Protestant settlers were then "planted" into vast estates dotted throughout the province. The wealthy settlers constructed fabulous, ornate homes in various architectural styles, with Palladian designs very popular in the first half of the 18th century before the Neoclassical and neo-Gothic influences took over. Lord and Lady Bangor, of Castle Ward estate in County Down, could not—legend has it—agree on which style their home should be built in. So one facade of the house is strictly classical in design and the other—favored by Lady Bangor—is Gothic. The vast majority of houses, like Florence Court in County Fermanagh and Mount Stewart in County Down, are managed, if not owned, by the National Trust. For a minimal entrance fee, you can spend an entire day wandering about endless corridors in a perfectly preserved mansion, like Castle Coole outside Enniskillen, with its original Regency furniture still in place.

The Sounds of Music

Northern Ireland has a rich musical culture similar to that of the south of Ireland, with its strong folk roots and an added Scottish influence. Traditional Irish music, originally played at weddings and wakes, can be heard in most country pubs, and in a cluster of bars in the central district of Belfast. Old-style songs—popularly known as *séan nós,* a sort of storytelling with music—are still very popular in the border counties. "Sessions" have become the stuff of legend, and are best described as spontaneous gatherings of musicians, which anyone can join if they have an instrument. They usually feature the *bódhran* (a kind of drum), the tin whistle, the fiddle, and the *uillean* pipes—a fiendishly difficult instrument to master, much like the bagpipes. Unfortunately, today's visitors are more likely to hear a hired band playing traditional music than an authentic session, but the spirit remains. If you are a classical music buff, check out the world-class Ulster Orchestra, based in Belfast's Ulster Hall but also appearing in Derry, Armagh, and Enniskillen. If you love opera, don't miss Castle Ward Opera Festival—set in the spectacular surroundings of Castle Ward estate in Strangford, County Down, the annual event takes place in June. Meanwhile, Belfast's nightclubs groove on all frequencies, from pop hits to techno to hip-hop. Visitors should make like the locals and consult *The Big List,* a free and detailed guide to what's on in every pub and club in the city (which can be picked up at most bars and restaurants).

Enjoy Those Tipples

Going to the pub, short for "public house," is Northern Ireland's favorite national pastime and every village, no matter how small, has at least one, and usually several. In fact, rural pubs are often indistinguishable from the house next door, so it pays to check with the locals for the best place for a pint and a bit of "craic." In Belfast and Derry, ornate Victorian inns sit side by side with new, brash bars playing loud music. In the last five years, dozens of ultra-modern bars and nightclubs full of hip, fashionable young things have sprung up, particularly around the university area of Belfast. When it comes to the tipples, northerners are as fanatical as their southern counterparts and virtually every bar stocks a mind-boggling array of locally brewed and imported lagers, ales, stouts, and ciders. Guinness, of course, is the perennial favorite, but don't be surprised when the bartender asks you if you would prefer "normal" or "cold-flow." The latter was introduced in the mid-1990s and serves up a colder pint. Older drinkers, however, remain true to the original "porter" and simply ask for a pint "of the black stuff." Local lagers, like Harp, are popular and, at about £2.20 a pint, are often a good deal cheaper than imported beer. Smooth and creamy Caffrey's ale is delicious, but be warned: it packs quite a punch. Beer comes in two sizes—a "pint" and a "glass" (a half-pint). Then, of course, there's Bushmills whiskey, which makes a great Irish coffee (hot coffee with a shot of whiskey dropped in it, topped with a thick layer of double cream). Closing times vary: quieter pubs tend to shut at 11:30 PM but bars with music remain open until 1 AM. As a general rule, kids are welcome until 6 PM, as long as they are accompanied by an adult.

The Great Outdoors

With its unspoiled beaches, mountains, forest parks, lakes, and rivers, Northern Ireland has more than enough to satisfy the outdoor explorer. If you are after deserted beaches, try the north coast—five of Europe's blue-flag (top-rated) beaches can be found there, including Benone Strand, in County Derry, a seven-mile stretch of fine sand backed by dunes and dramatic 750-foot-high cliffs. In County Antrim, Ballycastle Beach offers magnificent views of Fairhead and Rathlin Island, and rarely gets crowded even in summer months. The rugged Antrim Coast is a surfer's paradise, with the Atlantic Ocean hammering against secluded coves. Wet suits are essential, even in summer, as the water temperature rarely rises above single figures Centigrade. Even on freezing cold winter days, the sandy beaches of Portballintrae, Portrush, and Portstewart, with its two-mi-long strand, are spectacular. The Mourne Mountains in County Down and the Sperrins in Derry are perfect for a gentle climb; or if you are looking for a good walk, the glacier-carved Glens of Antrim or the volcanic columns of the Giant's Causeway are just the ticket. Inland lies Lough Neagh, the largest lake in the British Isles—bring a fishing rod and catch your dinner. There are many miles of cruising waters on Fermanagh's Lough Erne. Hiring a boat is easy but can be expensive, at around £100 a day. The lake lands are stunning though, sprinkled with tiny islands, wooded parks, and monastic ruins.

---

was the anti-agreement Democratic Unionist Party that profited. Despite numerous setbacks, Northern Ireland is today enjoying the longest period of peace and stability in its history.

Exploring Northern Ireland

The city of Belfast is Northern Ireland's main gateway. A naturally lively, friendly city, Belfast has plenty of distinguished hotels and restaurants, fascinating museums, Victorian architecture, and strong maritime connections. It is testimony to the spirit of Belfast that the long years of sectarian violence have not dimmed its vivacity. Northern Ireland's second city, Derry, is also looking to the future and has an appealing personality all its own. Rows of beautiful Georgian houses are being restored and museums and crafts shops have opened in the small city center, still enclosed by its medieval walls and one of Europe's best-preserved examples of a fortified town.

Along the shores of Northern Ireland's coasts and lakes, green, gentle slopes descend majestically into hazy, dark-blue water against a background of more slopes, more water, and huge, cloud-scattered skies. The Antrim Coast is among the most scenic in all of Ireland: Dunluce Castle, the Giant's Causeway, and the small towns along the east coast give the traveler a choice of stops along excellent roads. Enniskillen, in County Fermanagh, is bright and bustling, and the surrounding Lough Erne has magnificent lake views, as well as one of Ireland's round towers, on Devenish Island. On the other side of Enniskillen stand Castle Coole and Florence Court, two exquisitely graceful mansions built for members of the 18th-century Anglo-Irish nobility.

About the Restaurants & Hotels

Belfast has witnessed an influx of international influences with restaurants, bistros, wine bars, and—as in Dublin—European-style café-bars, where you can get good food *and* linger over a drink. By and large, though, hearty, unpretentious cooking predominates, with fresh local fish and good-quality meat simply prepared. You're virtually guaranteed to find certain traditional dishes on menus here, such as Guinness and beef pie; champ (creamy, buttery mashed potatoes with scallions); oysters from Strangford Lough; Ardglass herring; mussels from Dundrum; and smoked salmon from Glenarm. The delights of ethnic restaurants, including Chinese, Japanese, Indian, Persian, and Thai, are available in Belfast, and even beyond. Casual dress is acceptable at most establishments, though jeans are discouraged. As for the cost of a meal here, by the standards of the Republic or the United States, or even the rest of the United Kingdom, restaurant prices are surprisingly moderate. A service charge of 10% may be indicated on the bill; it's customary to pay this, unless the service was unsatisfactory.

Major hotel chains based both in the Republic and abroad have invested in Northern Ireland's cities. In Belfast's environs you can also choose from the humblest terraced town houses or farm cottages to the grandest country houses. Dining rooms of country-house lodgings frequently match the standard of top-quality restaurants. All accommodations in the province are inspected and categorized by the Northern Ireland Tourist Board Information Centre, which publishes hostelry names, addresses, and ratings in the free guidebooks *Hotel and Guest House Guide* and *Bed & Breakfast Guide,* also available online. Hundreds of excellent-value specials—single nights to weekend deals, the most intimate bed-and-breakfasts to Belfast's finest hotels—become available in the low season, October to March. On the chart below, hotel prices are listed for room rates that include no meals (EP, European Plan) or, if indicated, CP (with Continental breakfast) or BP (Breakfast Plan, with full

Northern Ireland

Malin Head

Tory Island

Malin · Culdaff

Carndonagh

Inishowen Head

Cau Dunluc Castl

Moville

Port

25 C

Creeslough

Rathmullan

Carrowkeel

Lough Foyle

Blackhill
Aghadowey

Milford

Muff

27
Limavady

B66

Ramelton

Derry
28 - **35**
See detail map

Campsie

A2

Gar

K

Letterkenny

Dungiven

Claudy

A6

B190

Lifford

B48

MOUNTAINS

DERRY

Tobermore

Be

Stranorlar · Castlefin

Strabane
Sion Mills

SPERRIN

BLUE STACK MOUNTAINS

Ballybofey

A5

Newtownstewart

A505 · Cookstown

Ulster-American Folk Park **36**

Donegal Town

Omagh

Pomeroy

TYRONE

A29

A32

B46

Lower
Lough
Erne **37**

A47

B4

White Island

A32

Dromore

Fintona

Dungannon

A4

Linen Gree

38
Belleek

A46

Castle Archdale
Country Park

B122

Ballygawley

Lough Melvin

FERMANAGH

Devenish
Island

Ballinamallard

Irvingstown

Clogher

Augher

A28

Aughnacloy

Fivemiletown

Enniskillen

39 **41** **Castle Coole**

Lisbellaw
A4

Lisnaskea

Ke

Florence
Court **40**

Upper Lough Erne

Lisnaskea

Rosslea

Newtown Butler

KEY

▶ *Start of itinerary*

Rathlin
◆Island

nt's
vay
22

Carrick
-a-Rede
A2 B15
Fair Head

To Campbeltown, Scotland

23
Bushmills 21 Ballycastle

art

raine

Armoy

Cushendun

Ballymoney

Cushendall Red Bay

Glenariff

Glens of
20 Antrim

North Channel

A2

Carnlough Bay

Carnlough

A26

ANTRIM

A42

NORTHERN
IRELAND

IRELAND

Upperlands

hera Ballymena

TO CAIRNRYAN, SCOTLAND

Ballygally

hy ◆ Bellaghy
wn

A36

Larne

TO STRANRAER

Toome Randalstown

Ballyclare

A8

Magherafelt Antrim

Newtownabbey

Whitehead

TO HEYSHAM

Eden

TO ISLE OF MAN

19 Carrickfergus TO LIVERPOOL

Lough
Neagh

A52

Belfast Lough Bangor Donaghadee

Belfast
Castle 16

Crawfordsborn

Ulster Folk and
18 Transport Museum

Ardboe

Crumlin

Holywood Newtownards

artstown

Belfast
1 - 15
See detail map

Mount Stewart

A20

17

Greyabbey

Lisburn

Comber

Cragavon

Lurgan

Ards
Peninsula

46 Lisburn

A22 Strangford
Lough

A20

rtadown

A3

Hillsborough

Saintfield

Killyleagh

A1

Portaferry

magh

kethill

Ballynahinch

A24

Castle Ward 45

Car Ferry

Strangford

Banbridge

DOWN

A25

44 Downpatrick

Bessbrook

Castlewellan

Dundrum

Ardglass

Camlough Newry

R. Bann

A25

A2

Dundrum Bay

B133

Newcastle

Slieve Donard
Mountain

RMACH

Warrenpoint

43 The Mountains
of Mourne

Carlingford Lough

A2

Kilkeel

0   10 miles

0   15 km

breakfast). Higher prices prevail for board plans such as MAP (Modified American Plan, with breakfast and dinner); inquire when booking. Assume that all hotel rooms have air-conditioning, in-room phones and TVs, and private bathrooms unless otherwise indicated.

WHAT IT COSTS in pounds sterling					
	$$$$	**$$$**	**$$**	**$**	**¢**
RESTAURANTS	over £22	£18–£22	£13–£18	£7–£13	under £7
HOTELS	over £160	£115–£160	£80–£115	£50–£80	under £50

Restaurant prices are per person for a main course at dinner; note that if a restaurant offers only prix-fixe meals, it has been given the price category that reflects the full set-price. Hotel prices are for two people in a standard double room in high season, including VAT and a service charge (often applied in larger hotels).

Timing

The best time to visit the area is from May to September, when the weather is mild and a little friendlier to travelers, especially in coastal and lake areas. Apart from holiday weekends there should be no trouble getting accommodation anywhere, except for Belfast. If heading for Belfast, book in advance. Most of the city's cultural events—except early August's lively West Belfast Festival—take place in autumn.

BELFAST

Belfast was a great Victorian success story, an industrial boomtown whose prosperity was built on trade—especially linen and shipbuilding. Famously (or infamously), the *Titanic* was built here, giving Belfast, for a while, the nickname "Titanic Town." The key word here, of course, is *was*—linen is no longer a major industry, and shipbuilding is greatly diminished. For two decades, news about Belfast meant news about the Troubles—until the 1994 cease-fire. Since then, Northern Ireland's capital city has benefited from major hotel investment, gentrified quaysides (or strands), a heralded performing arts center, and strenuous efforts on the part of the tourist board to claim a share of the visitors pouring into the Emerald Isle. Although the 1996 bombing of offices at the Canary Wharf in London disrupted the 1994 peace agreement, cease-fire was officially reestablished on July 20, 1997, and this embattled city began its quest for a newfound identity. Magnificent Victorian structures still line the streets of the city center, but instead of housing linen mills or cigarette factories, they are home to chic new hotels and fashionable bars. Smart restaurants abound, and the people of Belfast, who for years would not venture out of their districts, appear to be making up for lost time. Each area of the city has changed considerably in the new peaceful era, but perhaps none more than the docklands around the Harland and Wolff shipyards, whose historic and enormous cranes, known to the locals as Sampson and Goliath, still dominate the city's skyline. New developments are springing up all around the now-deserted shipyards, from luxury hotels to modern office blocks. In the west of the city, the physical scars of the Troubles are still evident, from the *peace line* that divides

Catholic and Protestant West Belfast to the murals on every gable wall. Visitors are discovering that it is safe to venture beyond the city center; indeed, backpackers are becoming a regular sight on the Falls Road, and taxi tours of these once troubled areas are more popular than ever. As ever, Belfast remains a fascinating place. Emerging from the throes of a major historical transition, the city is home to some of the warmest, wryest people in all of Ireland—all with a palpable will to move forward.

Before English and Scottish settlers arrived in the 1600s, Belfast was a tiny village called Béal Feirste ("sandbank ford") belonging to Ulster's ancient O'Neill clan. With the advent of the Plantation period (when settlers arrived in the 1600s), Sir Arthur Chichester, from Devon in southwest England, received the city from the English crown, and his son was made Earl of Donegall. Huguenots fleeing persecution from France settled near here, bringing their valuable linen-work skills. In the 18th century, Belfast underwent a phenomenal expansion—its population doubled in size every 10 years, despite an ever-present sectarian divide. Although the Anglican gentry despised the Presbyterian artisans—who, in turn, distrusted the native Catholics—Belfast's growth continued at a dizzying speed. Having laid the foundation stone of the city's university in 1845, Queen Victoria returned to Belfast in 1849 (she is recalled in the names of buildings, streets, bars, monuments, and other places around the city), and in the same year, the university opened and took the name Queen's College. Nearly 40 years later, in 1888, Victoria granted Belfast its city charter. Today its population is 300,000—one-quarter of Northern Ireland's citizens.

Belfast is a fairly compact city, 167 km (104 mi) north of Dublin. The city center is made up of three roughly contiguous areas that are easy to navigate on foot; from the south end to the north it is about an hour's leisurely walk.

Golden Mile

This arrowhead-shape area extending from Howard Street in the north to Shaftesbury Square at the southern tip, bordered on the west by Great Victoria Street and on the east by Bedford Street and Dublin Road, is a great area from which to begin an exploration of Belfast. Although it doesn't quite glow the way the name suggests, bustling Golden Mile and its immediate environs harbor some of Belfast's most noteworthy historic buildings. In addition, the area is filled with hotels, major civic and office buildings, as well as some restaurants, cafés, and shops. Even if you don't end up staying here, you're likely to pass through it often.

a good walk

Begin your stroll at the central **Europa Hotel** ❶ ▶ and the Victorian-era showpiece, the **Grand Opera House** ❷ next door. Even if you're just starting out, at least poke your head in the glorious **Crown Liquor Saloon** ❸, a restored Victorian gin palace across the street from the Europa. From the Crown, turn right along Great Victoria Street and then right again onto Howard Street to reach Donegall Square, dominated by the columned and domed **City Hall** ❹. Walk away from Donegall Square and up May Street, taking an almost immediate right onto Alfred Street.

When you come to the junction with Clarence Street, the Tudor-Gothic **St. Malachy's Church ❺** is on the left. Stop in to gaze awhile at the beautiful fan-vault ceiling. From here, walk to the end of Clarence Street, and turn right onto Bedford Street into the Golden Mile proper, where you will come upon famed 19th-century **Ulster Hall ❻**.

TIMING You need about 1½ hours to enjoy this route—you can extend this time depending on how long you would like to spend soaking up the atmosphere of places like the Crown Liquor Saloon on your way.

What to See

★ ❹ **City Hall.** Massive, exuberant, Renaissance Revival City Hall dominates Donegall Square. Built between 1898 and 1906 and modeled on St. Paul's Cathedral in London, it was designed by Brumwell Thomas, who was knighted but had to sue to get his fee. Before you enter, take a stroll around Donegall Square, to see statues of Queen Victoria; a monument commemorating the *Titanic,* which was built in Belfast; and a column honoring the U.S. Expeditionary Force, which landed in the city on January 26, 1942—the first contingent of the U.S. Army to land in Europe in World War II. Enter under the porte cochere at the front of the building. From the entrance hall (the base of which is a whispering gallery), the view up to the heights of the 173-foot-high Great Dome is a feast for the eyes. With its complicated series of arches and openings, stained-glass windows, Italian-marble inlays, decorative plasterwork, and paintings, this is Belfast's most ornate public space—homage to the might of the British empire. The guided tour gives access to the Council Chamber, Great Hall, and Reception Room, all upstairs. ⊠ *Donegall Sq., Central District* ☎028/9032–0202 ⊕*www.belfastcity.gov.uk* ☜*Free* ☉*Mon.–Thurs. 9–5, Fri. 9–4.30; guided tours June–Sept., weekdays at 11, 2, and 3, Sat. at 2:30; Oct.–May, weekdays at 11 and 2:30, Sat. at 2:30.*

❸ **Crown Liquor Saloon.** Opposite the Europa Hotel on Great Victoria
Fodor'sChoice Street and now owned by the National Trust (the United Kingdom's of-
★ ficial conservation organization), the Crown is one of Belfast's glories. Built in 1894, the bar has richly carved woodwork around cozy snugs (cubicles), leather seats, colored tile work, and an abundance of mirrors. It has been kept immaculate and is still lit by gas. Most importantly it's a perfect place for a pint of Guinness and a plateful of oysters. When you settle in your snug, note the little gunmetal plates used by the Victorians for lighting their matches. ⊠ *46 Great Victoria St., Golden Mile* ☎028/9027–9901 ☉*Mon.–Sat. 11:30 AM–midnight, Sun. 11:30–10.*

▶ ❶ **Europa Hotel.** A landmark in Belfast, the Europa is a monument to the resilience of the city in the face of the Troubles. The most bombed hotel in western Europe, it was targeted 11 times by the IRA since the early 1970s and was refurbished every time, and today shows no signs of its explosive history. It is owned by affable Ulster millionaire and hotel magnate Billy Hastings. ⊠ *Great Victoria St. at Glengall St., Golden Mile* ☎ *028/9027–1066* ⊕ *www.hastingshotels.com.*

★ ❷ **Grand Opera House.** The Grand Opera House exemplifies the Victorians' fascination with ornamentation, opulent gilt moldings, and intricate plasterwork. The renowned theater architect Frank Matcham beautifully designed the building in 1894, and restoration was completed in the 1970s. Contemporary Irish artist Cherith McKinstry's exquisite angel-and-cherub-laden fresco floats over the ceiling. You can take a tour of the opera house, but by far the best way to see and enjoy the place is to attend a show. The theater regularly hosts musicals, operas, plays, and concerts. ⊠ *Great Victoria St., Central District* ☎ *028/9024–1919* ⊕ *www.goh.co.uk/menu.htm* ⊠ *£3* ⊗ *Tours Sat., hrs vary.*

❺ **St. Malachy's Church.** Just inside the doors to St. Malachy's Cathedral is a memorial to its chief benefactor, Captain Thomas Griffiths. The church, designed by Thomas Jackson, was built in 1844, and its interior is well worth a viewing. Pay particular attention to its fan-vaulted ceiling. Although many of the original fixtures and fittings have succumbed to the ravages of time, this swirling masterpiece of plasterwork survives intact. Inspiration for the design was taken from the chapel of Henry VII at Westminster Abbey in London. Note the 150-year-old church organ. ⊠ *Alfred St., Golden Mile* ☎ *028/9032–1713* ⊠ *Free.*

❻ **Ulster Hall.** The home of the Ulster Orchestra, and host to occasional rock concerts (one of the most famous was marked by Led Zeppelin's stage debut of the song "Stairway to Heaven" in March 1971), Ulster Hall was built as a ballroom in 1862. The hall was the venue for the political rallying of Nationalist politicians, among them Charles Stewart Parnell (1846–91) and Patrick Henry Pearse (1879–1916), before the Irish Republic was formed in 1921. There's also a splendid Mulholland Organ, a Victorian instrument of considerable size. There's no charge for looking around when shows are not going on. ⊠ *Bedford St., Golden Mile* ☎ *028/9032–3900* ⊕ *www.ulsterhall.co.uk.*

Central District

Belfast's Central District, immediately north of the Golden Mile, extends from Donegall Square north to St. Anne's Cathedral. It's not geographically the center of the city, but it's the old heart of Belfast. Shoppers note: it also has the highest concentration of retail outlets in town. It's a frenetic place—the equivalent of Dublin's Grafton and Henry streets in one—where both locals *and* visitors shop. Cafés, pubs, offices, and stores of all kinds, from department stores to the Gap and Waterstone's (there's even a Disney store), occupy the redbrick and white-Portland-stone and modern buildings that line its narrow streets. Many of the streets are pedestrian-only, so it's a good place to take a leisurely stroll, browse, and see some sights to boot.

a good walk

Begin at the **Linen Hall Library** ❼ ⌐, the gray building on Donegall Square's northwest corner. North on Donegall Place, Belfast's main shopping street, is the Northern Ireland Tourist Board Information Centre. Continue down Donegall Place as it becomes Royal Avenue, and turn right onto Church Street, at the end of which is **St. Anne's Cathedral** ❽. Take Donegall Street to North Street and go east down **High Street** to busy Victoria Street and the leaning **Albert Memorial Clock Tower** ❾. From here, walk up Queen's Square to the river and Donegall Quay. You can see parts of Belfast's historic shipyards and, on Queen's Island, two of the

CloseUp

BELFAST'S WALL MURALS

I N NORTHERN IRELAND *they say the Protestants make the money and the Catholics make the art, and as with all clichés, there is some truth in it.*

It is a truth that will become clear as you look up at the gable walls of blue-collar areas of Belfast on which the two communities—Catholic and Protestant—have expressed themselves in colorful murals that have given rise to one of the more quirky tours of the city.

Although the wildly romantic Catholic murals often aspire to the levels of Sistine Chapel–lite, those in Protestant areas (like the tough, no-nonsense Shankill and the Newtownards Road) are more workmanlike efforts that sometimes resemble war comics without the humor. It was not always this way.

In Protestant areas, murals were once painted by skilled coachbuilders to mark the 12th of July celebrations of the defeat of the Catholic king James by King William at the Battle of the Boyne. As such, they typically depicted William resplendent in freshly laundered scarlet tunic and plumed cap, sitting on a white stallion that has mastered the art of walking on water. On the banks of the Boyne sits a mildly disheveled James, the expression on his face making him look as if he has just eaten an overdose of anchovies.

Other popular themes in Protestant areas are the Red Hand of Ulster, symbolizing the founding of the province, and, on Carnmore Street, the 13 Protestant apprentice boys shutting the gates of Derry against King James in 1688, leading to the famous siege.

More recently, though, Protestant murals have taken on a grimmer air, and typical subjects include wall-eyed paramilitaries perpetually standing firm against increasing liberalism, nationalism, and all

the other isms that Protestants see eroding their stern, Bible-driven way of life.

Nationalist murals, on the other hand, first sprang up in areas like the Falls Road in 1981, when IRA inmates of the Maze prison began a hunger strike in an unsuccessful bid to be recognized by the British government as political prisoners rather than common criminals. Ten died, and the face of the most famous, Bobby Sands, looks down now from a gable wall on the Falls Road alongside the words: "Our revenge will be the laughter of our children."

Since then, themes of freedom from oppression and a rising Nationalist confidence have expressed themselves in murals that romantically and surreally mix and match images from the Book of Kells, the Celtic Mist mock-heroic posters of Irish artist Jim Fitzpatrick, assorted phoenixes rising from ashes, and revolutionaries clad in splendidly idiosyncratic sombreros and bandannas from ideological battlegrounds in Mexico and South America.

Gaelic words and phrases that you will see springing up regularly include the much-used slogan "Tiocfaidh ár lá" (pronounced chucky or law and meaning "Our day will come") and the simple cry "Saoirse" (pronounced seer-she), meaning "Freedom".

The murals in both Protestant and Catholic areas are safe to view in daylight and outside the sensitive week of the 12th of July marches by Protestant Orangemen. However, the most sensible way to view them would be to take a guided tour with Citybus.

world's largest cranes in the Harland and Wolff shipyard, where the *Titanic* was built. Veer left at the river to the **Lagan Lookout Visitor Centre** ⑩. Perched on the river, the center is opposite the back of the Victorian **Custom House** ⑪. Walk south along Oxford Street to Waterfront Hall, on the river at the end of the street. From here, you can return to the city center via busy Chichester Street. Or instead wander north behind St. Anne's to the Cathedral Quarter, a maze of cobbled streets that the city fathers plan to transform over the next few years into a funky combination of Temple Bar in Dublin and the Left Bank in Paris.

TIMING   It's easy to get waylaid shopping and investigating sights along the river when taking this walk, so give yourself at least two hours to cover the area comfortably.

What to See

❾ Albert Memorial Clock Tower. Tilting a little to one side, not unlike Pisa's more notorious leaning landmark, is the clock tower that was named for Queen Victoria's husband, Prince Albert. The dilapidated square on which it stands has undergone a face-lift. The tower itself is not open to the public. ⊠ *Victoria Sq., Central District.*

⑪ Custom House. The 19th-century architect Charles Lanyon designed the Custom House. This building, along with many others in Belfast, including the main building of Queen's University and the unusual Sinclair Seaman's Church, bear the hallmarks of his skill. It is not open to the public, but it's worth circling the house to view the lofty pediment of Brittania, Mercury, and Neptune on the front, carved by acclaimed stonemason Thomas Fitzpatrick. ⊠ *Donegall Quay, Central District.*

★ High Street. Off High Street, especially down to Ann Street (parallel to the south), run narrow lanes and alleyways called entries. Though mostly cleaned up and turned into chic shopping lanes, they still hang on to something of their raffish character, and have distinctive pubs with little-altered Victorian interiors. Among the most notable are the Morning Star (Pottinger's Entry off High Street), with its large windows and fine curving bar; White's Tavern (entry off High Street), Belfast's oldest pub, founded in 1630, which, although considerably updated, is still warm and comfortable, with plush seats and a big, open fire; Magennis's Whiskey Café (on May Street), in splendid counterpoint to the Waterfront Hall's space-age style; and McHugh's (in Queen's Square), in what is reckoned to be the city's oldest extant building, dating from 1710.

Lagan Boat Company. Take a guided 75-minute river tour that departs from the dock by the Lagan Lookout Visitor Centre and travels down to Stranmillis and back, with commentary on the history of the city. A one-hour Titanic tour takes in the shipyard where the famous liner was built and harbor sights related to the ship. Each tour costs £5. ⊠ *48 St. John's Close, at Laganbank Rd., Central District* ☎ *028/9033–0844* ⊕ *www.laganboatcompany.com.*

Ⓒ ⑩ Lagan Lookout Visitor Centre. At the edge of Lagan Weir, the center delves into the history of the River Lagan and the weir by means of interactive exhibits. It's a good way for children to learn about the river's his-

Belfast

tory and surroundings. At night, the exterior of the building is flooded with blue light, adding to the feel that the riverside developments in Belfast have been inspired by the Southbank in London. The famous shipyard cranes, Samson and Goliath, are visible beyond. ⊠ *Lagan Weir, Donegall Quay, Central District* 🕾 *028/9031–5444* ⊕ *www.laganside.com* 🖾 *£2* ⊘ *Apr.–Sept., weekdays 11–5, Sat. noon–5, Sun. 2–5; Oct.–Mar., Tues.–Fri. 11–3:30, Sat. 1–4:30, Sun. 2–4:30.*

➤ ❼ **Linen Hall Library.** This gray building on Donegall Square's northwest corner is in fact a comfortable private library, founded in 1788 and designed by Charles Lanyon. The library has an unparalleled collection of 80,000 documents relating to the Troubles. One early librarian, Thomas Russell, was hanged in 1803 for supporting an Irish uprising. On the walls are paintings and prints depicting Belfast views and landmarks. Much of this artwork is for sale. It's an ideal hideaway for relaxing with a newspaper and enjoying the library's café. ⊠ *17 Donegall Sq. N, Central District* 🕾 *028/9032–1707* ⊕ *www.linenhall.com* 🖾 *Free* ⊘ *Weekdays 9:30–5:30, Sat. 9:30–4.*

❽ **St. Anne's Cathedral.** A somber heaviness—a hallmark of the Irish neo-Romanesque style—marks this large edifice, which is basilican in plan and was built at the turn of the 20th century. Lord Carson (1854–1935), who was largely responsible for keeping the six counties inside the United Kingdom, is buried here beneath a suitably austere gray slab. New landscaping around the Anglican cathedral provides a perch to rest your legs in good weather. The guides on duty show you around for no charge. ⊠ *Donegall St., Central District* 🕾 *028/9032–8332* ⊕ *www.belfastcathedral.com* 🖾 *Free* ⊘ *Daily 10–4.*

need a break?

At the start of Royal Avenue, turn left onto Bank Street to find **Kelly's Cellars** (⊠ 30–32 Bank St., Central District 🕾 028/9024–2628), a circa-1720 pub with loads of character. Try the two specialties: Ulster fry or champ and sausages. Two centuries ago, Kelly's Cellars was the regular meeting place of a militant Nationalist group, the Society of United Irishmen, whose leader, Wolfe Tone (who was a Protestant), is remembered as the founder of Irish Republicanism.

🕓 **W5: Whowhatwherewhywhen.** Part of the Odyssey complex in Belfast's docks, this science discovery center takes a high-tech, hands-on approach to interpreting science, engineering, and technology for adults and children. Video displays and flashing lights provide a modernistic feel, and you can do everything from explore the weather to build bridges and robots. ⊠ *2 Queen's Quay, Central District* 🕾 *028/9046–7700* ⊕ *www.w5online.co.uk* 🖾 *£6* ⊘ *Mon.–Sat. 10–6, Sun. noon–6; last admission at 5.*

University Area

At Belfast's southern end, the part of the city around Queen's University is dotted with parks, botanical gardens, and leafy streets with fine, intact, two- and three-story 19th-century buildings. The area evokes an older, more leisurely pace of life. The many pubs and excellent restaurants make this area the hub of the city's nightlife.

a good walk

From the southern tip of Shaftesbury Square, head south down Botanic Avenue and watch the cityscape quickly transform into a peaceful and residential university area. Take note of the Lower Crescent, with its bars and restaurants, on your right. Continue, crossing University Street, and you come to the 19th-century **Union Theological College** ⑫ ☛ on your left. To your right is the Tudor Revival–style **Queen's University** ⑬. Walk around the campus via University Square and University Road to Stranmillis Road. To the left are the historic **Botanic Gardens** ⑭, and next to the gardens is the **Ulster Museum** ⑮.

TIMING   Allow a leisurely morning or afternoon to visit the sights, taking your time at the Botanic Gardens and Ulster Museum.

What to See

★ ⑭ **Botanic Gardens.** In the Victorian heyday, it was not unusual to find 10,000 of Belfast's citizens strolling about on a Saturday afternoon. These gardens are a glorious haven of grass, trees, flowers, curving walks, and wrought-iron benches laid out in 1827 on land that slopes down to the River Lagan. The curved-iron and glass Palm House is a conservatory marvel designed, in 1839, by Charles Lanyon. The Tropical Ravine House, though not architecturally distinguished, has an outstanding collection of tropical flora, in addition to some indigenous plants (it was famously said that it once held more Killarney ferns than could be found in Killarney itself). Once known as "the Glen," the Ravine House is unusually and exotically built over a faux-ravine that you walk around. ✉ *Stranmillis Rd., University Area* ☎ *028/9032–4902* ✍ *Free* ☉ *Gardens daily dawn–dusk; Palm House and Tropical Ravine House Apr.–Aug., weekdays 10–5, weekends 1–5; Sept.–Mar., weekdays 10–4, weekends 2–4.*

⑬ **Queen's University.** Dominating University Road is Queen's University itself. The main buildings, modeled on Oxford's Magdalen College and designed by the ubiquitous Charles Lanyon, were built in 1849 in the Tudor Revival style. The long, handsome redbrick-and-sandstone facade of the main building features large lead-glass windows, and is topped with three square towers and crenellations galore. University Square, really a terrace, is from the same era. The Seamus Heaney Library is named after the Ulster-born 1997 Nobel prize–winning poet. The visitor center displays university artifacts and hosts exhibitions, and there's a small shop where you can buy gifts and university souvenirs. ✉ *University Rd., University Area* ☎ *028/9033–5252* ⊕ *www.qub.ac.uk* ☉ *May–Sept., Mon.–Sat. 10–4; Oct.–Apr., weekdays 10–4.*

Stranmillis. Once its own village, Stranmillis is now an off-campus quarter—an appealing neighborhood with tree-lined residential streets and a wide choice of ethnic eateries. You can get here via Stranmillis Road (near the Ulster Museum). The "Little Paris" stretch of shops and cafés extends down to the riverside towpath along the Lagan. Malone Road joins the river farther south, close to the out-of-town Giant's Ring (off Ballyleeson Road), a large, Neolithic earthwork focused on a dolmen.

CHURCHES AROUND THE CITY

BELFAST HAS SO MANY CHURCHES you could visit a different one nearly every day of the year and still not make it to all of them. The oldest house of worship is the Church of Ireland **Knockbreda Parish Church** (✉ Church Rd. off A24, South Belfast ☎ 028/9064–5372). This dark, sturdy, and atmospheric structure was built in 1737 by Richard Cassels, who designed many of Ireland's finest mansions. It quickly became the place to be buried—witness the vast 18th-century tombs in the churchyard. Closer to the city center, the **First Presbyterian Church** (✉ Rosemary St., Central District) dates from 1783 and has an interesting elliptical interior. It also hosts lunchtime concerts. The Church of Ireland's **St. George's** (✉ High St., Central District ☎ 028/9023–1275), built in 1816, has a tremendous Georgian portico and pretty box pews. By the riverfront is one of the most appealing churches, Presbyterian

Sinclair Seamen's Church (✉ Corporation Sq. off Donegall Quay, Central District ☎ 028/9082–5278). It was designed by Charles Lanyon, the architect of Queen's University, and has served the seafaring community since 1857. A maritime theme pervades the building: the pulpit is shaped like a ship's prow; the bell is from HMS Hood, sunk in 1916; and even the collection plates are shaped like lifeboats. The elegant neo-Gothic towers of **Saint Peter's Cathedral** (✉ St. Peters Square, West Belfast ☎ 028/9032–7573), dubbed the "twin spires" by locals, dominates the skyline of West Belfast. Finding this Roman Catholic cathedral, hidden among the terraced houses of the Lower Falls Road, is difficult, but worth the effort. Built in 1866, when the Catholic population was rapidly increasing, St. Peter's acted as a focal point for the community and hundreds would pack the chapel for mass every Sunday.

To get this far, unless you're a vigorous walker (it's possible to come all the way on the Lagan towpath), you may be happier driving or taking a bus. Ulsterbus 13 passes close to the site, and on the return journey it will take you back to Donegall Square.

15 **Ulster Museum.** Pick up a free guidebook at the reception desk to help you explore the history and prehistory of Ireland, in particular Northern Ireland, at the three-story Ulster Museum. The most imaginative, user-friendly sections are on the first floor: one exhibit colorfully traces the rise of Belfast's crafts, trade, and industry; another tells the story of the Nationalist movement and explains the separation of the north from the rest of the country. In the natural history section, a large skeleton of the extinct Irish giant deer is a highlight. Another major holding is the trove of jewelry and gold ornaments—as well as a cannon and other armaments—recovered from the Spanish Armada vessel *Girona* and two sister galleons sunk off the Antrim coast in 1588. There is also a considerable collection of 19th- and 20th-century art and a small café on level three. The museum is at the southwest corner of the Botanic Gardens. ✉ *Stranmillis Rd., University Area* ☎ *028/9038–3000* ⊕ *www. ulstermuseum.org.uk* ✉ *Free* ☉ *Weekdays 10–5, Sat. 1–5, Sun. 2–5.*

▶ ⑫ **Union Theological College.** Like Queen's University on the opposite side of the street, the Union Theological College, with its colonnaded, Doric facade, owes the charm of its appearance to architect Charles Lanyon. The building's other claim to fame is that, before the completion of the parliament buildings at Stormont, Northern Ireland's House of Commons was convened in its library, and the college's chapel played host to the Senate. At this writing, the college is finishing a renovation; upon reopening, it will offer tours to visitors. ⊠ *108 Botanic Ave., University Area* ☎ *028/9020–5080* ⊕ *www.union.ac.uk* ⊠ *Free.*

Belfast Environs

The three sights below are closer to Belfast than others covered in this chapter. However, none of the sites along the Ards Peninsula and the north coast are more than a few hours' drive from Belfast—perfect for day trips.

What to See

⑯ **Belfast Castle.** In 1934 the castle, built for the Marquis of Donegall in 1865, was passed to Belfast Corporation. Although the castle functions primarily as a restaurant, it also houses the Cave Hill Heritage Centre, which provides information about the castle's history and its natural surroundings in Cave Hill Country Park. The best reason to visit is to take a stroll in the lovely ornamental gardens and then make the ascent to McArt's Fort. This promontory, at the top of sheer cliffs 1,200 feet above the city, affords an excellent view across Belfast. Take the path uphill from the parking lot, turn right at the next intersection of pathways, and then keep left as you journey up the sometimes steep hill to the fort. ⊠ *4 km (2½ mi) north of Belfast on Antrim Rd.* ☎ *028/9077–6925* ⊠ *Free* ⊗ *Visitor center daily 9–6.*

ℂ **Belfast Zoo.** The zoo has a children's farm and underwater views of the resident penguins and sea lions. It's near Belfast Castle, and city buses 45 and 51 will bring you to both. ⊠ *Antrim Rd.* ☎ *028/9077–6277* ⊠ *£6* ⊗ *Apr.–Sept., daily 10–5; Oct.–Mar., daily 10–2:30.*

★ ⑰ **Mount Stewart.** The grandest stately house near Belfast, this was the country seat of the Marquesses of Londonderry, whose fame, or infamy, became known round the world thanks to the historical role played by the 2nd Marquess—known as Castlereagh, this Secretary of Ireland put down the Rising of 1798, helped forge the Act of Union, and killed himself by cutting his own throat. Mount Stewart was constructed in two stages where an earlier house stood: George Dance designed the west facade (1804–05), and William Vitruvius Morrison designed the Neoclassic main part of the building (1845–49), complete with awe-inspiring Grecian portico facade. When the 7th Marquess was appointed to a political post in Belfast in the 1920s, his fashion-plate wife, Edith, decided to transform the dank estate into a showplace with gardens that took advantage of the unique microclimate of the Ards Peninsula. In short order, a Sunk Garden, Shamrock Garden, Italian Garden, and Dodo Garden (ornamented with stone figures that honored her closed circle of friends—-the "Warlock" is Winston Churchill, for instance) were seeded. Today, they are among the finest gardens in the British Isles. Edith also managed to wave her wand over the interior—after a fashion: Chinese vases, Louis-Philippe tables, and Spanish oak chair do their worst to clutter up the rooms here. Still, the house does have some noted 18th-century interiors, including the Central Hall and the grand staircase hung with one of George Stubbs's most famous portraits, that of the celebrated racehorse Hambletonian, after he won one of the most prominent contests of the 18th century—this is perhaps the greatest in-situ setting for a painting in Ireland. On the grounds, don't miss the octagonal Temple of the Winds—a copy of a similar structure in Athens—and there's a remarkable bathhouse and pool at the end of the wooded peninsula just before the entrance to the grounds. ⊠ *Portaferry Rd., Newtownards, Co. Down* ☎ *028/4278–8387* ⊕ *www.nationaltrust.org.uk* ⊡ *£5* ⊙ *Gardens Apr., daily 10–6; May–Sept., daily 10–8; Oct., daily 10–6; Nov.–Mar., daily 10–4; house by guided tour Mar. and Apr., weekends 12–6; May and June, Mon., Wed.–Fri. 1–6, weekends 12–6; July and Aug., daily 12–6; Sept., Wed.–Mon. 12–6; Oct., weekends 12–6.*

need a break?

Reputed to be the oldest pub in Ireland, **Grace Neill's** (⊠ 33 High St. (22 km/13 mi from Mt. Stewart), Donaghadee ☎ 028/9188–4595) served its first pint in 1611 and has hosted such luminaries as Peter the Great, Franz Liszt, and John Keats. Behind the original pub, a cubby under the stairs with bar stools, is a larger bar where you can try a simple peppered beef sandwich with a pint of Guinness. Saturday sees jazz, and on Sunday afternoons, there's music.

★ ⑱ **Ulster Folk and Transport Museum.** Devoted to the province's social history, the excellent Ulster Folk and Transport Museum vividly brings Northern Ireland's past to life with a score of reconstructed buildings moved here from around the region. These structures represent different facets of northern life—a traditional weaver's dwelling, terraces of Victorian town houses, an 18th-century country church, a village flax mill, a farmhouse, and a rural school. Inside each, an appropriately dressed attendant explains what it was like to live in these regional edifices back when. You start your visit with the Folk Gallery, which explains the background of each building. Across the main road (by footbridge) is the beautifully designed Transport Museum, where exhibits include locally built airplanes and motorcycles; the iconoclastic car produced by former General Motors whiz kid John De Lorean in his Belfast factory in 1982; and a moving section on the *Titanic,* the Belfast-built luxury liner that sank on her first voyage, in 1912, killing 1,500 of the passengers and crew. A miniature railway runs on Saturday in July and August. The museum is on the 70 acres of Cultra Manor, encircled by a larger park and recreation area. ⊠ *16 km (10 mi) northeast of Belfast on A2, Cultra* ☎ *028/9042–8428* ⊕ *www.nidex.com/uftm* ⊡ *£5* ⊙ *Mar.–June, weekdays 10–5, Sat. 10–6, Sun. 11–6; July–Sept., Mon.–Sat. 10–6, Sun. 11–6; Oct.–Feb., weekdays 10–4, Sat. 10–5, Sun. 11–5.*

Where to Eat

The food scene in Belfast is experiencing the same renaissance as the city itself. Two or three of Belfast's best kitchens are a match for anything else in Ireland. The best chefs—Michael Deane, the Rankins, and Robbie Millar—have brought back to Ireland, from their work abroad, a sophisticated, internationalist approach to cooking. Beyond the top-tier places, there are plenty of restaurants with fresh local fish and delectable meat dishes prepared simply but with style.

$$$

Fodor'sChoice

★

✕ **Shanks.** Like many of Ireland's best young chefs, Robbie Millar studied under the noted Paul Rankin (now at Cayenne), and he spares nothing to produce wonderful fish and game dishes. How demanding is he? A scuba diver hand-picks his scallops from the Irish Sea (they are more tender than those dredged by trawler). Start with grilled tuna and eggplant chutney, then indulge in a standout main course—peppered loin of venison with red cabbage. A three-course set menu is £38. The restaurant is on a 3,000-acre golf estate; to get here you can take a train from Belfast to Bangor and then a taxi. ⊹ *Right on Crawfordsburn Rd., 19 km (12 mi) from Belfast* ✉ *Blackwood Golf Centre, Bangor* ☎ *028/ 9185–3313* ⌂ *Reservations essential* ▤ *AE, MC, V* ⊘ *Closed 3 wks in July, Sun. and Mon. No lunch Sat.*

$$$

✕ **Zen.** Entrepreneur Eddie Fong has miraculously transformed a red-brick 19th-century Belfast mill into an Asian oasis housing the city's finest Japanese restaurant. Upstairs, you traverse a 30-ft-long mirrored catwalk with glass walkway to get to the seating area. Choose between wooden booths, or, if you're prepared to sit on the floor, opt for the traditional Japanese dining area. Downstairs, hand-pick your meal at the sushi bar, or for a more comfortable option, choose a discreet table for two under the serene gaze of (reputedly) Ireland's largest Buddha. Zen—meaning "higher place"—opened in 2003 and quickly garnered a reputation for authentic, fresh sushi, and sashimi. Purists may be bemused at the deep-fried prawns but everyone declares them delicious. ⊹ *Behind the city hall* ✉ *55–59 Adelaide St., Central District* ☎ *028/ 9023–2244* ▤ *AE, MC, V* ⊘ *No lunch Sat.*

★ **$-$$$**

✕ **Aldens.** East Belfast was a gastronomic wilderness until this cool modernist restaurant opened with chef Cath Gradwell at the helm. Now city-center folk regularly make the pilgrimage to take advantage of an opulent menu and wine list at comparably reasonable prices. The set dinner menus Monday to Thursday are particularly good value—£16 for three courses. Dublin Bay prawns make for a standout starter. Try grilled quails with wild cranberry compote and baked polenta, and beef sausages with red wine sauce and mashed potatoes as entrées. The mood here is relaxed, and the staff perpetually friendly. ✉ *229 Upper Newtownards Rd., East Belfast* ☎ *028/9065–0079* ▤ *AE, DC, MC, V* ⊘ *No lunch weekends, no dinner Sun.*

★ **$$**

✕ **Cayenne.** One of Belfast's most exciting restaurants, Cayenne explodes with culinary fireworks. To wit, the duck and shitake pot stickers with sesame ginger sauce or the salt ëní chilli squid with chilli jam and aioli—and let's not forget the hot banana strudel. These are just a few of the creations of celebrity TV chefs Paul and Jeanne Rankin. They travel widely, have several other restaurants, but happily mastermind this Golden Mile spot. The cutting-edge fusion cuisine, always with that Asian twist, comes up winners with such other dishes as coconut-crusted cod, breast of duck with wild rice pancakes, and Donegal wild salmon with hazelnut beurre blanc. Cayenne takes orders until 11:15 on Friday and Saturday evenings, so it's a welcoming place if you want a meal after a concert in Waterfront Hall. ⊠ *Shaftesbury Sq., at Great Victoria St., Golden Mile* ☎ *028/9033–1532* ▭ *AE, DC, MC, V* ✆ *No lunch Sat.*

$–$$ ✕ **Deane's.** Chef Michael Deane has long been a chef-celebrity in the
Fodor'sChoice   Belfast area. His tastes are eclectic—he has worked in Bangkok, and the
★   influence of Thai cooking is revealed in his especially subtle way with spices. Squab is a specialty, served as a kedgeree with cucumber and quail eggs for a starter. As a main dish he serves French squab with local rabbit, roast potato, and parsnip with Madeira. Ravioli of lobster is excellent as well. A nine-course menu is £55, and a two-course option £31. The brasserie is downstairs, and the more formal restaurant above. ⊠ *34–40 Howard St., Golden Mile* ☎ *028/9033–1134 restaurant, 028/9056–0000 brasserie* ▭ *AE, MC, V* ✆ *Restaurant closed Sun.–Tues., brasserie closed Sun.*

$–$$ ✕ **Nick's Warehouse.** Nick Price has created one of Belfast's most relaxing watering holes in this cool, cozy wine bar with adjacent restaurant. At the busy bar you can get warm salads with a choice of nut oils and tasty casseroles. In the slightly more formal restaurant, top bets include duck with red cabbage and apple compote, and halibut with langoustine and sweet peppers. Finish off your meal with a sampling of the cheese selection. The wine and imported beer lists are impressive. Nick's is on a narrow cobbled street in an increasingly fashionable area. Reservations are essential for the restaurant. ⊠ *35 Hill St., Central District* ☎ *028/9043–9690* ▭ *AE, MC, V* ✆ *Closed Sun. No lunch Sat. No dinner Mon.*

¢–$ ✕ **The Morning Star.** Halfway down a narrow lane is the 19th-century Morning Star, one of the city's most historic pubs, first built as a coaching stop for the Belfast to Dublin post. There's a traditional bar downstairs and a cozy velvet and wood-panel restaurant upstairs. Head chef Seamus McAlister, far from resting on the pub's laurels, is constantly experimenting—he's known for his quirky takes on fresh local ingredients. You might find venison and game in winter, lamb in spring, and in summer grilled haddock with dark rum or roast Antrim pork. Also notable is the steak menu; you'd be hard-pressed to find a larger assortment of aged beef cuts. Sizzling steaks arrive at the table on red-hot cast-iron skillets and are served with a flourish by the friendly staff. ⊠ *17–19 Pottingers Entry, Central District* ☎ *028/9023–5986* ▭ *MC, V* ✆ *Closed Sun.*

¢–$ ✕ **The Northern Whig.** The latest addition to Belfast entrepreneur Jas Mooney's stable of designer pubs, The Northern Whig is housed in an elegant former newspaper building. Three 30-foot-high statues of Soviet heroes that once topped Communist Party headquarters in Prague dominate the spacious and stylish wood-and-leather interior. In the evenings, one wall slides away so you can watch classic movies, a jazz band, or a DJ playing laid-back blues, soul, or retro. The food is brasserie-style—good, not astonishing. It's the environment, the thoughtful wine list, and the cocktail bar, which specializes in rare vodkas, that are the main draw. ⊠ *2 Bridge St., Central District* ☎ *028/9050–9888* ▭ *MC, V.*

¢–$ ✕ **Raj Put.** You won't leave this Indian restaurant feeling as if you've been kissing a flame-thrower: in even the hottest dishes, nuanced flavors shine through. Aromatic spices, nuts, and herbs mingle in the piquant chicken masala. For side dishes, favorites include a tasty *saag aloo* (spicy potatoes and spinach). Wash it all down with cold Indian lager. ⊠ *461 Lisburn Rd., University Area* ☎ *028/9066–2168* ⊟ *AE, MC, V.*

★ ¢ ✕ **Café Paul Rankin.** This city-center bakery-café is a good choice if you want to enjoy the culinary delights of chefs Paul and Jeanne Rankin (of Cayenne fame) without the Golden Mile mindset. This spot has a Parisian sensibility to it, especially if the weather is fine and you're sitting outside. Try the walnut bread, sun-dried tomato bread, focaccia, and the delicious soups and desserts. Before you leave, take a look at the take-out section, where the shelves groan with homemade goodies, such as savory celery and black pepper shortbread and a superb apple chutney. ⊠ *27–29 Fountain St., Central District* ☎ *028/9031–5090* ⊟ *AE, MC, V* ☽ *Closed Sun.*

★ ¢ ✕ **Long's.** Long's has been serving fish-and-chips in its tiny, completely basic Athol Street premises for more than 80 years. Garbage collectors, millionaires, and every sector in between flocks here for the secret-batter-recipe fish, served with chips, bread, butter, and a mug of tea. ⊠ *39 Athol St., Golden Mile* ☎ *028/9032–1848* ⊟ *No credit cards* ☽ *Closed Sun.*

Central District

★ $$$ ▥ **McCausland Hotel.** The renaissance of Belfast's industrial Langanside district was spearheaded in part by the spiffy renovation of this historic structure, comprised of two 1867 grain warehouses. While the original cast-iron pillars and beams were retained, many areas have been opened up and the resultant feeling of light and space creates a sumptuous minimalism, gorgeously tempered by a luxe array of Victorian and Edwardian chairs, couches, antiques, and potted palms. The well-equipped bedrooms, with entertainment centers that include VCRs and CD players, are tastefully color-coordinated. Dining, orchestrated by the inspired chef Alexander Plumb, takes place in the Marco Polo bar-bistro or the more formal Merchants Brasserie. On the edge of the blossoming Laganside area, the hotel is a 5-minute walk from the heart of the city center. ⊠ *34–38 Victoria St., Central District BT1 3GH* ☎ *028/ 9022–0200* 🖷 *028/9022–0220* ⊕ *www.slh.com* ⬎ *61 rooms with bath, 15 suites* ♿ *Restaurant, bar, meeting rooms; no a/c* ⊟ *AE, DC, MC, V* ⦿ *BP, MAP.*

$–$$$ ▥ **Belfast Hilton.** This riverside hotel should be able to cater to your every whim with its excellent business and leisure facilities. Earthy colors and bold stripes decorate the beds and windows. Ask for a suite or room with a view of the river. The restaurant serves contemporary cuisine and it has good views of the river and the city. The hotel is beside Waterfront Hall, in an area undergoing urban renewal. ⊠ *4 Lanyon Pl., Central District BT1 3LP* ☎ *028/9027–7000* 🖷 *028/9027–7277* ⊕ *www. hilton.com* ⬎ *181 rooms with bath, 14 suites* ♿ *Restaurant, in-room data ports, minibars, cable TV, indoor pool, hair salon, sauna, bar, business services, meeting rooms, no-smoking floors* ⊟ *AE, DC, MC, V* ⦿ *BP.*

Golden Mile

★ $$$ ▥ **TENsq.** You don't get much more downtown or contemporary than this fashionable boutique hotel right behind City Hall. The neoclassical facade of this former post office hides a serene interior that also houses Red, a popular and fashionable urban bar; the cool yet cozy Wine Café; and the Restaurant Porcelain, where European dishes are given a Japanese touch. The bedrooms are minimalist-Asian in style—with big, low-lying beds topped with white duvets, soft armchairs to sink into, and fresh flowers brought daily. There are ISDN lines for computers in all rooms, and a common DVD and CD library. ⊠ *10 Donegall Sq. S, Golden Mile BT1 5JD* ☎ *028/9024–1001* 🖨 *028/9024–3210* ⊕ *www.ten-sq. com* 🖙 *23 rooms with bath* ⟁ *Restaurant, café, in-room data ports, 2 bars, concierge, free parking* ☰ *AE, MC, V* ⟩⊙⟨ *BP, MAP.*

$$–$$$ 🏨 **Holiday Inn Belfast.** Expect outstanding facilities at a reasonable price. Furnishings are modernist blond wood and leather, and rooms are best described as Japan-meets-Sweden: strong, simple colors and sliding wooden screens (a lovely touch) instead of curtains. Superbly located, with only a 10-minute walk to the city center and five minutes to the Golden Mile. ⊠ *22 Ormeau Ave., Golden Mile BT2 8HS* ☎ *870/ 0400–9005* 🖨 *028/9062–6546* ⊕ *www.holiday-inn.co.uk* 🖙 *170 rooms with bath* ⟁ *Restaurant, indoor pool, health club, hot tub, massage, sauna, steam room, bar; no a/c* ☰ *AE, DC, MC, V* ⟩⊙⟨ *BP, MAP.*

$ 🏨 **Benedict's of Belfast.** Friendly, lively, and convenient, Benedict's stands out on Shaftsbury Square. Rooms on the second floor are bright and colorful, and have wooden floors; rooms on the third floor are darker, with an Asian influence—dark wood and light walls, simple but comfortable. If you don't feel like straying too far from home for some nightlife, Benedict's has a buzzing bar and restaurant serving finely done Continental food. ⊠ *7–21 Bradbury Pl., Golden Mile BT7 1RQ* ☎ *028/ 9059–1999* 🖨 *028/9059–1990* ⊕ *www.benedictshotel.co.uk* 🖙 *32 rooms with bath* ⟁ *Restaurant, in-room data ports, cable TV, bar; no a/c* ☰ *AE, MC, V* ⟩⊙⟨ *BP.*

$ 🏨 **Jurys Inn Belfast.** The first Jurys north of the border brings the chain's flat-rate formula—one price for up to three adults or two adults and two children—to the Golden Mile. Once you get past the forbidding warehouselike exterior, a spacious, marble-tile foyer with warm green and salmon hues awaits. Room decor is pretty standard. Some rooms overlook College Square, the cricket lawn of the 1814 Royal Belfast Academical Institution. The Arches restaurant serves well-prepared hotel food. Tartan fabrics and dark wood decorate the Inn Pub, which serves pub-grub all day. ⊠ *Fisherwick Pl. at Great Victoria St., Golden Mile BT2 7AP* ☎ *028/9053–3500* 🖨 *028/9053–3511* ⊕ *www.jurysdoyle.com* 🖙 *190 rooms with bath* ⟁ *Restaurant, in-room data ports, bar, meeting rooms, no-smoking floors; no a/c* ☰ *AE, DC, MC, V* ⟩⊙⟨ *CP.*

Outside the City Center

★ $$$$ ✕🏨 **Culloden Hotel.** Built in 1876 by the very rich William Robinson and christened in honor of his wife's famed family, this imposingly grand vision in Belfast stone presides over the forested slopes of the Holywood hills and the busy waters of Belfast Lough. Topped off with a storybook turret and crenellated tower, the Scottish Baronial mansion was greatly enlarged in the early 20th century when it was given as a residence to the Bishops of Down, then transformed in the 1960s into a hotel (today, the flagship of the luxe Hastings chain). Inside, Neoclassical salons warmed by lime green walls, gilded coiffered ceilings, 19th-century paintings, stained-glass accents, and overstuffed Louis XV-style chairs make you feel like you're one of the Robinson family. Antiques and silk and velvet fabrics grace guest rooms both in the original section and in a newer wing; all rooms have fine views. At mealtime choose from the posh Mitre restaurant—transformed from the former refectory and now a pleasant room of paneled walls, green-fabric booths, and presided over by a statue of St. Pat—and the Cultra Inn, which serves snacks and full meals. The hotel is close to both the village of Holywood (temptingly filled with boutiques) and the Ulster Folk and Transport Museum. Chances are, however, that you won't want to leave Culloden's lovely 12 acres of grounds. Even those tempted by a quick walk to the nearby Royal Belfast Golf Club may not be able to forgo another afternoon spent at the hotel's Elysium Spa, a glamorous Beverly-Hills type affair. ✢ *8 km (5 mi) east of Belfast on A2* ✉ *142 Bangor Rd., Holywood, Co. Down BT18 0EX* ☎ *028/9042–1066* 🖷 *028/9042–6777* ⊕ *www.devereonline.co.uk* ⮒ *79 rooms, 10 suites* ♻ *2 restaurants, tennis court, indoor pool, hair salon, sauna, spa, croquet, squash, bar, laundry service, Internet, meeting rooms, no-smoking rooms; no a/c* ⊟ *AE, DC, MC, V* ⑩ *BP, MAP.*

★ **$–$$** ✕▦ **The Old Inn.** Set in the village of Crawfordsburn, this 1614 coach inn, reputedly Ireland's oldest, looks the part: it's pure 17th-century England, with a sculpted thatched roof, half doors, and leaded-glass windows. As it was near one of the leading cross-channel ports linking Ireland and England, the coach always stopped here, often bearing visitors with names like Swift, Tennyson, Thackery, Dickens, and Trollope. More recently, C. S. Lewis and his wife, Joy, "booked" the inn to enjoy a belated honeymoon. You can see why: Some of the finest bedrooms have 17th-century style woodwork, sitting rooms, and faux-Jacobean beds while, downstairs, public salons offer beamed ceilings, roaring log fires, and lots of Ulster "craic" (chat). Repair to the grand 1614 restaurant to tuck into a Finnebrogue venison with sweet potato pureé, red onion marmalade and thyme beurre blanc and also savor the delicious setting of flocked curtains, English wood panels, sculpted portrait medallions, and a soaring coved ceiling. "Pub Fayre" is offered at the Churn Bistro, where you'll find the menu is solidly Irish, the staff jovial, and the locals inquisitive. Over the centuries, large portions of the inn were rebuilt and the East Wing is a completely modern take on Irish Georgian style. But if you're lucky enough to stay in the oldest parts, you still may be able to uncover a secret hiding place for contraband, as smugglers, like the famous highwayman Dick Turpin, made this one of their favored homes-away-from-home. ✢ *16 km (10 mi) east of Belfast on A2* ✉ *15 Main St., Crawfordsburn, Co. Down BT19 1JH* ☎ *028/9185–3255* 🖷 *028/9185–2775* ⊕ *www.theoldinn.com* ⮒ *32 rooms* ♻ *Restaurant, 2 bars, Internet; no a/c* ⊟ *AE, MC, V* ⑩ *BP.*

$–$$ ▦ **Rayanne House.** Famous both for its food and for its hospitality, this country house run by the devoted Bernadette McClelland is in leafy Holywood, 10 km (6 mi) from Belfast city center. Rooms are airy, each with individual country furnishings and garden views. Breakfast includes an Irish grill and such specialties as prune soufflé on a purée of green figs, and hot Rayanne baked cereal (laced with spices, fruit, whiskey, honey, and cream). The meal is served in an intimate dining room, among family antiques, paintings, and candelabra. Lunch and dinner are available by request 24 hours in advance. ✛ *8 km (5 mi) east of Belfast on A2* ✉ *60 Demesne Rd., Holywood, Co. Down BT18 9EX* 🏠 *028/ 9042–5859* ⊕ *www.rayanne-house.activehotels.com* ⟋ *9 suites* ⌂ *Dining room, meeting rooms; no a/c* ▤ *MC, V* ⊚ *BP, MAP.*

¢–$ ⬚ **Roseleigh House.** This charming Victorian guesthouse on a tree-filled avenue in residential south Belfast is a friendly option. Light-filled, spacious rooms decorated in calming blues with traditional floral bedspreads have modern comforts. Fresh flowers and daily newspapers adorn the coffee table in the residents' drawing room. Although Roseleigh is much renovated, stained-glass windows, elaborate fireplaces, and period cornicing on the ceilings point to the late Victorian date of the house. Evening meals can be requested with 24 hours' notice and breakfasts are healthy and robust. ✛ *6 km (4 mi) south of Belfast on the Ormeau Road* ✉ *16 Rosetta Park, Belfast BT6 ODL* 🏠 *029/9064–4414* ⊕ *www.roseleighhouse.co. uk* ⟋ *9 rooms* ⌂ *Dining room, lounge; no a/c* ▤ *MC, V* ⊚ *BP, MAP.*

University Area

$$$ ⬚ **Wellington Park Hotel.** Formerly a private residence and currently run by the Mooney family, this modern establishment is among the best in the University Area. The quiet, contemporary bedrooms are well designed, with built-in wood furniture; some have sleeping lofts. There is traditional European food in both the bar and restaurant—though the menu in the restaurant is slightly more expansive and expensive than in the bar. There's live music at the bar Friday and Saturday nights (soul, jazz, and Irish). ✉ *21 Malone Rd., University Area BT9 6RU* 🏠 *028/ 9038–1111* 🏠 *028/9066–5410* ⊕ *www.mooneyhotelgroup.com* ⟋ *75 rooms* ⌂ *Restaurant, bar, laundry service, meeting rooms; no a/c* ▤ *DC, MC, V* ⊚ *BP.*

★ $–$$ ⬚ **Ash-Rowan Guest House.** Thomas Andrews, designer of the ill-fated *Titanic,* brought his bride to live in this spacious Victorian home after their wedding, then went off to work 14-hour days at the Harland and Wolff shipyard. Former restaurateurs Sam and Evelyn Hazlett now own, run, and cook for this outstanding B&B on a tranquil residential avenue. Every bedroom has its own style, all with Victorian overtones. Feel free to take advantage of the reading lounge, as well as the books around the house, and the conservatory. Breakfasts and dinners are firstrate. ✉ *12 Windsor Ave., University Area BT9 6EE* 🏠 *028/9066–1758* 🏠 *028/9066–3227* ⊕ *www.a1tourism.com/uk/ashrowan.html* ⟋ *5 rooms* ⌂ *Dining room, lounge; no a/c, no smoking* ▤ *MC, V* ⊚ *BP, MAP* ⊘ *Closed Christmas wk.*

$ ⬚ **Dukes Hotel.** Although this distinguished redbrick Victorian building has only 20 rooms, it has big-hotel amenities, including a spacious lobby, extensive exercise facilities, and a restaurant that serves healthy, local cuisine (traditionalists won't be disappointed, however, as fried food can be had). The hotel's color scheme is a distinguished, executive-style gray, enlivened with plenty of greenery, and a waterfall splashes down parallel to the stairway. Although not exceptional, the rooms are modern and comfortable, decorated in neutral shades. The lively bar is popular with staff and students from nearby Queen's University. ⊠ *65–67 University St., University Area BT7 1HL* ☎ *028/9023–6666* ≞ *028/ 9023–7177* ⊕ *www.dukeshotelbelfast.com* ⟿ *20 rooms* ♧ *Restaurant, gym, sauna, bar, meeting rooms; no a/c* ⊟ *AE, DC, MC, V* ¶◯ *BP.*

$ 🖻 **Madison's.** Another gracious hotel run by the Mooney family, Madison's is in one of Belfast's liveliest spots—surrounded by shops and cafés on the lovely, tree-lined Botanic Avenue. The facade and public areas are decorated in a modish Barcelona-inspired take on Art Nouveau. Modern rooms—in primary yellows, reds, and rich blues—are stylish if sparsely furnished. The downstairs houses a restaurant that serves tasty contemporary cuisine at reasonable prices, and hip Club 33 fills the basement. Staying here you have discounted access to the extensive fitness facilities of Queen's University, including a pool. ⊠ *59 Botanic Ave., University Area BT7 1JL* ☎ *028/9050–9800* ≞ *028/9050–9808* ⊕ *www. madisonshotel.com* ⟿ *35 rooms* ♧ *Restaurant, bar, business services; no a/c* ⊟ *AE, MC, V* ¶◯ *BP.*

$ 🖻 **Old Rectory.** Mary and Jerry Callan's well-appointed house was built in 1896 as a rectory. Rooms are decorated in pastels and have good views of the mountains. Enjoy complimentary whiskey each evening in the parlor. Breakfast is hearty but healthy, a rarity in Ulster B&Bs: there's smoked salmon, scrambled eggs, fresh fruit salad, vegetarian sausages, homemade low-sugar jams, wheat bread, and freshly squeezed blended juices. ⊠ *148 Malone Rd., University Area BT9 5LH* ☎ *028/9066–7882* ≞ *028/9068–3759* ✍ *info@anoldrectory.co.uk* ⟿ *6 rooms* ♧ *No a/c* ⊟ *No credit cards* ¶◯ *BP, MAP.*

¢ 🖻 **All Seasons.** Enjoying a superb location on the fashionable Lisburn Road in the south of the city, this spot has some of the city's most stylish boutiques and trendiest bars on its doorstep. Friendly owner Theodore McLaughlin has created a cozy home with a comfortable lounge, spacious dining room, and spotlessly clean rooms. Cranmore Park, a popular venue during the summer for sunbathers, is two minutes away on foot. ⊠ *356 Lisburn Rd., University Area BT9 6GJ* ☎ *028/9068–2814* ⊕ *www.allseasonsbelfast.com* ⟿ *5 rooms* ♧ *No a/c* ⊟ *MC, V* ¶◯ *BP.*

Nightlife & the Arts

Nightlife

Belfast has dozens of pubs packed with relics of the Victorian and Edwardian periods. Although pubs typically close around 11:30 PM, many city-center/Golden Mile nightclubs stay open until 1 AM.

CENTRAL DISTRICT The **Apartment** (⊠ 2 Donegall Sq. W, Central District ☎ 028/9050–9777), beside City Hall, is the city center's trendiest bar, serving drinks and brasserie-style pub grub to Belfast's cool young things. Extensive but inexpensive wine and cocktail lists attracts a good crowd. **Bittles Bar** (⊠ 70 Upper Church La., Central District ☎ 028/9031–1088), on Victoria Square, serves pub grub. Gilded shamrocks bedeck this interesting triangular-shaped Victorian pub on the fringes of the Cathedral Quarter. Paintings of literary characters and local landmarks adorn the walls, while a high, wood-paneled ceiling gives an illusion of space. **Kelly's Cellars** (⊠ 30–32 Bank St., Central District ☎ 028/9024–2628), open since 1720, has blues bands on Saturday night. **Madden's Bar** (✉ Berry St., behind Castle Court, Central District ☎ 028/9024–4114) is a popular pub with traditional tunefests on occasion. At **Magennis' Bar and Whiskey Café** (✉ 83 May St., Central District ☎ 028/9023–0295) you get two pubs for the price of one: the quiet, 100-year-old bar frequented by older regulars, and the hip café, crowded with younger clientele. The free tapas on Friday evenings pull in the after-work crowd, who pop in for a quick pint and end up staying all night. Live folk music on Sunday afternoons is a great finish to the weekend. Regulars prop up the horseshoe-shaped bar in the Victorian showpiece, the **Morning Star** (✉ 17–19 Pottinger's Entry, Central District ☎ 028/9023–5968), from noon til night. Strike up a conversation with some of the locals and you're guaranteed a bit of craic.

McHugh's (✉ 29–30 Queen's Sq., Central District ☎ 028/9050–9990), in Belfast's oldest building, dating from 1711, has three floors of bars and restaurants, and live music on weekends. **Pat's Bar** (✉ 19–22 Prince's Dock St., Central District ☎ 028/9074–4524) has first-rate sessions of traditional music on Saturday nights. The **Rotterdam** (✉ 54 Pilot St., Central District ☎ 028/9074–6021), which housed convicts bound for Australia until it became a pub in 1820, is filled with fascinating old junk. It hosts traditional Irish music on Mondays and Thursdays, jazz on Tuesdays, and rock on Fridays and Saturdays. Dating from 1630, **White's Tavern** (✉ 2–12 Winecellar Entry, Central District ☎ 028/9024–3080) claims to be the oldest public house in Belfast. In winter, a roaring fire greets you as soon as you enter the bar. Upstairs, the restaurant serves good pub grub and is justifiably famous for its "champ," a creamy, buttery, cholesterol-laden concoction of mashed potatoes and spring onions. Enjoy the live jazz on Friday nights.

GOLDEN MILE AREA   The glorious Crown Liquor Saloon is far from being the only old pub in the Golden Mile area—most of Belfast's evening life takes place in bars and restaurants here. There are a number of replicated Victorian bars where more locals and fewer visitors gather.

The **Beaten Docket** (✉ 48 Great Victoria St., Golden Mile ☎ 028/9024–2986), named after a losing betting slip, is a noisy, modern pub that attracts a young crowd. Here they play up-to-the-minute music, but it can get a bit boisterous, so some may prefer a quiet snug (booth) across the road in the famed Crown Liquor Saloon. **Benedict's** (✉ 7–21 Bradbury Pl., Golden Mile ☎ 028/9059–1999) is a bar, music venue, disco, 150-seat restaurant, and hotel. One of the city's newest additions to the Golden Mile, the faux-Gothic exterior of the hotel belies its modern origins. Straying from the model of the Victorian-style public house, the **Limelight** (✉ 17 Ormeau Ave., Golden Mile ☎ 028/9032–5968) is a disco-nightclub with cabaret on Tuesday, Friday, and Saturday, and recorded music on other nights. It is extremely popular with students, and books musicians as well as DJs.

The **M-Club** (✉ 23 Bradbury Pl., University Area ☎ 028/9023–3131) is Belfast's hottest place for dedicated clubbers, with soap-opera celebrities flown in weekly to mix with the local nighthawks. **Morrisons** (✉ 21 Bedford St., Golden Mile ☎ 028/9032–0030) is a haunt of media types.

It has a music lounge upstairs, and hosts discussions for film buffs arranged by local directors in conjunction with the Northern Ireland Film Council. **Robinson's** (⊠ 38–40 Great Victoria St., Golden Mile ☎ 028/9024–7447), two doors from the Crown, is a popular pub that draws a young crowd with folk music in its Fibber Magee's bar on Sunday and funk in the trendy BT1 wine and cocktail bar on weekends.

UNIVERSITY AREA The stylish and modern **Bar Twelve** (⊠ Crescent Town House, 13 Lower Crescent, University Area ☎ 028/9032–3349) is an excellent venue for some stylish wine-sipping. On weekend nights, DJs spin 1960s and '70s soul and funk tunes. Settle into the comfortable leather armchairs for a long chat while you work your way through the impressive wine list. The **Botanic Inn** (⊠ 23–27 Malone Rd., University Area ☎ 028/9050–9740), known as "the Bot" to its student clientele, is a big, popular disco-pub. The **Chelsea Wine Bar** (⊠ 346 Lisburn Rd., University Area ☎ 028/9068–7177) is packed with affluent professionals determined to prove that 30 is where life begins. The contemporary cuisine is reasonably priced. **Cutter's Wharf** (⊠ 4 Lockview Rd., University Area ☎ 028/9066–3388), down by the river south of the university, is at its best on summer evenings and during music performances on Sundays after 6. Spacious and light inside, it rarely gets too packed; if seating is limited, try the picnic tables and chairs on the wooden deck outside.

The **Eglantine Inn** (⊠ 32–40 Malone Rd., University Area ☎ 028/9038–1994), known as "the Egg," faces the Bot across Malone Road. The **Empire Music Hall** (⊠ 42 Botanic Ave., University Area ☎ 028/9032–8110), a deconsecrated church, is the city's leading music venue. Stand-up comedy nights are usually on Tuesday. The **Fly Bar** (⊠ 5–6 Lower Crescent, University Area ☎ 028/9050–9750), with its over-the-top interior playing on the fly theme, is a lively spot for a cocktail in the evening.

Lavery's Gin Palace (⊠ 12 Bradbury Pl., University Area ☎ 028/9087–1106) mixes old-fashioned beer-drinking downstairs with dancing upstairs. On the increasingly fashionable Lisburn Road, **TaTu** (⊠ 701 Lisburn Rd., University Area ☎ 028/9038–0818) is a spacious homage to industrial chic filled with a cool, under-30 crowd. It serves good casual food.

The Arts

The **Northern Ireland Arts Council** (☎ 028/9038–5200 ⊕ www.artscouncil-ni.org) produces the bimonthly *Artslink* poster-brochure listing happenings throughout Belfast and the North. It's widely available throughout the city. The **Belfast Festival at Queen's University** (Festival office ⊠ 25 College Gardens, University Area ☎ 028/9066–6321 ⊕ www.belfastfestival.com), which lasts for three weeks each November, is the city's major arts festival. The **Promenade Concerts** (☎ 028/9066–8798 ⊕ www.ulster-orchestra.or.uk) are performed in June by the Ulster Orchestra in conjunction with the BBC.

ART GALLERIES **Bell Gallery.** This gallery in Nelson Bell's Victorian home shows many of Ireland's more traditional and representational painters from the 18th to the 21st century. ⊠ *13 Adelaide Park, at Malone Rd., South University* ☎ *028/9066–2998* ⊕ *www.bellgallery.com* ⊙ *Mon.–Thurs. 9–5, Fri. 9–3.*

Fenderesky Gallery. Under the same roof as the Crescent Arts Centre, Iranian philosopher Jamshid Mirfenderesky's gallery is one of the few in Ireland with a stable of modern Irish artists known throughout Europe. ⊠ *Crescent Arts Centre, 2 University Rd., University Area* ☎ *028/9023–5245* ☉ *Tues.–Sat. 11:30–5.*

Ormeau Baths Gallery. Works of major contemporary international and Irish artists now hang in the white, airy spaces of this former municipal bathhouse. ⊠ *18A Ormeau Ave., Golden Mile* ☎ *028/9032–1402* ☉ *Tues.–Sat. 10–6.*

FILM **Queen's Film Theatre** (⊠ 20 University Sq., University Area ☎ 028/9024–4857), Belfast's main art cinema, shows domestic and foreign movies on its two screens. **UGC Cinemas** (⊠ 14 Dublin Rd., Golden Mile ☎ 028/9024–5700) has 10 screens of major British and American box-office favorites.

MAJOR VENUES **Crescent Arts Centre.** Watch experimental dance and theater, witness provocative art in the Fenderesky Gallery, and listen to lively jazz concerts: it's all part of the Crescent. You can also take classes in this huge, rambling stone building, a former girls' high school off the campus end of Bradbury Place. ⊠ *2–4 University Rd., University Area* ☎ *028/9024–2338* ⊕ *www.crescentarts.org.*

Grand Opera House. Shows from all over the British Isles—and sometimes farther afield—play at this beautifully restored Victorian theater. Though it has no company of its own, there's a constant stream of West End musicals and plays of widely differing kinds, plus occasional operas and ballets. It's worth going to a show if only to enjoy the opera house itself. ⊠ *2 Great Victoria St., Golden Mile* ☎ *028/9024–1919* ⊕ *www.goh.co.uk.*

King's Hall. Pop and rock concerts take center stage at this venue that also serves as a conference center. ⊠ *484 Lisburn Rd., South University* ☎ *028/9066–5225* ⊕ *www.kingshall.co.uk.*

Lyric Theatre. Traditional and contemporary Irish culture inspires the thoughtful dramas staged here. In the south of Belfast, it's located at King's Bridge on the banks of the Lagan. ⊠ *55 Ridgeway St., South University* ☎ *028/9038–1081.*

The Odyssey. This multipurpose megacomplex was built as a millennium project. On-site is a 10,000-seat arena, an IMAX cinema, an interactive science center, bistros, bars, and theme restaurants. In addition to major concerts, it also hosts Belfast's first professional ice hockey team, the Giants. ⊠ *Queen's Quay, East Belfast* ☎ *028/9045–1055* ⊕ *www. theodyssey.co.uk.*

Old Museum Arts Centre (OMAC). A powerhouse of challenging, avant-garde theater and modern dance, OMAC also has a risk-taking art gallery. ⊠ *7 College Sq. N, Central District* ☎ *028/9023–3332* ⊕ *www. oldmuseumartscentre.org.*

Ulster Hall. This, the main home to the Ulster Orchestra, has excellent acoustics and a splendid Victorian organ. The classical music season runs from

September through March; most concerts are on Friday. ⊠ *Bedford St., Golden Mile* ☎ *028/9032–3900* ⊕ *www.ulster-orchestra.org.uk.*

Waterfront Hall. Everyone in Belfast sings the praises of this striking civic structure. From the looks of it, the hall is an odd marriage of *Close Encounters* modern and Castel Sant'Angelo antique. It houses a major 2,235-seat concert hall (for ballet and classical, rock, and Irish music) and a 500-seat studio space (for modern dance, jazz, and experimental theater). The Terrace Café restaurant and two bars make the hall a convenient place to eat, have a pint, and enjoy the river views before or after your culture fix. ⊠ *Lanyon Pl., Central District* ☎ *028/9033–4455* ⊕ *www.waterfront.co.uk.*

Shopping

Belfast's main shopping streets include High Street, Royal Avenue, and several of the smaller streets connecting them. The area is mostly traffic-free (except for buses and delivery vehicles). The long thoroughfare of Donegall Pass, running from Shaftesbury Square at the point of the Golden Mile east to Ormeau Road, is a unique mix of biker shops and antiques arcades.

Market & Mall
Castle Court (⊠ 10 Royal Ave., Central District ☎ 028/9023–4591) is the city's largest and most varied upscale shopping mall. **Debenhams** (☎ 028/9043–9777) department store call fill many of your shopping needs, from cosmetics to kitchenware. Trendy stores like **Gap** (☎ 028/9023–6444) can be found under Castle Court's glass roof, alongside British clothing chains like **Miss Selfridge** (☎ 028/9023–5008) and **Warehouse** (☎ 02890/43–9606). Boys who like their toys will be in their element in **The Gadget Shop** (☎ 0800/7838343). Plenty of parking makes shopping easy in the mall. If you've an interest in bric-a-brac, visit the enormous, renovated **St. George's Market** (⊠ May St., Central District ☎ 028/9043–5704), an indoor flea market that takes place Friday and Saturday morning. Get there early on Saturday for an award-winning farmers' market, featuring organically grown fruit and vegetables, as well as treats such as homemade cakes and bread.

Specialty Shops
Clark and Dawe (⊠ 485 Lisburn Rd., University Area ☎ 028/9066–8228) makes and sells men's and women's suits and shirts. **Craftworks** (⊠ Bedford House, 16–22 Bedford St., Golden Mile ☎ 028/9024–4465) stocks crafts by local designers. **Natural Interior** (⊠ 51 Dublin Rd., Golden Mile ☎ 028/9024–2656) has Irish-linen throws, trimmed in velvet, by the designer Larissa Watson-Regan. It also stocks her vividly colored wall panels and cushions.

Buy 12-inch-high puppets of Northern Ireland politicians at **Open Window Productions** (⊠ 1–3 Exchange Pl., Central District ☎ 028/9032–9669). For £175, you can have a puppet made to order of a favorite celebrity, or even of yourself. **Smyth and Gibson** (⊠ Bedford House, Bedford St., Golden Mile ☎ 028/9023–0388) makes and sells beautiful, luxurious linen and cotton shirts and accessories. Looking for linen souvenirs?

Smyth's Irish Linens (✉ 65 Royal Ave., Central District ☎ 028/9024–2232) carries a large selection of handkerchiefs, tablecloths, napkins, and other traditional goods. It's opposite Castle Court Mall. **The Steensons** (✉ Bedford House, Bedford St., Golden Mile ☎ 028/9024–8269) sells superb, locally designed jewelry.

THE GIANT'S CAUSEWAY COAST

Starting in Belfast, stretching for 80 km (50 mi) along Northern Ireland's Atlantic shore, the Causeway Coast holds many of the province's "don't miss" attractions. The man-made brilliance of the castle at Dunluce, the endless string of whitewashed fishing villages along the sea, and the world-famous natural wonder that is the Giant's Causeway are just some of the delights to be discovered here. Past some fair-size towns, your car—or mountain bike (this is ideal for the Causeway's flat terrain)—is soon in open country driving through splendid natural scenery in the Glens area—one of the more "gentle" (an Irish turn-of-phrase for supernatural) places in all Ireland. Here, ageless villages—still inhabited by descendants of the ancient Irish and the Hebridean Scots who hailed from across the narrow Sea of Moyle—are set in peaceful, old-growth forests that have become synonymous with Irishness. But once past the Giant's Causeway you'll find more cosmopolitan pleasures, including Bushmills—the oldest licensed distillery in the world—and the old walled city of Derry.

Carrickfergus

🔞 *16 km (10 mi) northeast of Belfast on A2.*

Carrickfergus, on the shore of Belfast Lough, grew up around its ancient castle. When the town was enclosed by ramparts at the start of the 17th century, it was the only English-speaking town in Northern Ireland. Not surprisingly, this was the loyal port where William of Orange chose to land on his way to fight the Catholic forces at the Battle of the Boyne in 1690. However, the English did have one or two small setbacks, including the improbable victory in 1778 of John Paul Jones, the American naval hero, over the British warship *HMS Drake*. While a long way from home, this stands as the first naval victory of America's fledgling navy fleet. After this battle, which was waged in Belfast Lough, the inhabitants of Carrickfergus stood on the waterfront and cheered Jones when his ship passed the town castle, demonstrating their support for the American Revolution.

Carrickfergus Castle, one of the first and one of the largest of Irish castles, is still in good shape. It was built atop a rock ledge in 1180 by John de Courcy, provincial Ulster's first Anglo-Norman invader. Apart from being captured briefly by the French in 1760, the castle stood as a bastion of British rule right up until 1928, at which time it still functioned as an English garrison. Walk through the castle's 13th-century gatehouse into the Outer Ward. Continue into the Inner Ward, the heart of the fortress, where the five-story keep stands, a massive, sturdy building with walls almost 8 feet thick. Inside the keep is the Cavalry Regimental Museum, with historic weapons and the vaulted Great Hall. These days Carrickfergus Castle hosts entertaining medieval banquets (inquire at Carrickfergus tourist information office or the Northern Ireland Tourist Board Information Centre). If you're here at the beginning of August, you can enjoy the annual Lughnasa festival, a lively medieval-costume entertainment. ⊠ *Off A2* ☎ *028/9335–1273* ⊕ *www.ehsni.gov.uk* ⊠ *£3* ⊙ *May–Sept., Mon.–Sat. 10–6, Sun. 2–6; Oct.–Apr., Mon.–Sat. 10–4, Sun. 2–4.*

Old buildings that remain from Carrickfergus's past include St. Nicholas's Church, built by John de Courcy in 1205 (remodeled in 1614) and the handsomely restored North Gate in the town's medieval walls. Dobbins Inn on High Street, which has been a hotel for more than three centuries, is a watering hole that's popular with locals.

The **Andrew Jackson Centre** tells the tale of the U.S. president whose parents emigrated from here in 1765. This thatched cottage just outside of town is a reconstruction of an 18th-century structure thought to resemble their home. ⊠ *2 km (1 mi) northeast of Carrickfergus, Larne Rd., Boneybefore* ☎ *028/9336–6455* ⊕ *www.carrickfergus.org* ⊠ *£1* ⊙ *Apr., May, and Oct., weekdays 10–1 and 2–4, weekends 2–4; June–Sept., weekdays 10–1 and 2–6, weekends 2–6.*

Glens of Antrim

★ ❷⓿ *Beginning 24 km (15 mi) north of Carrickfergus at Larne.*

Soon after Larne, the coast of County Antrim becomes spectacular— wave upon wave of high green hills that curve down to the hazy sea are dotted with lush glens, or valleys, first carved out by glaciers at the end of the last ice age. Nine wooded river valleys occupy the 86 km (54 mi) between Larne and Ballycastle. A narrow, winding, two-lane road (A2, which splits from the coastal at Cushendall) hugs the slim strip of land between the hills and the sea, bringing you to the magnificent Glens of Antrim running down from the escarpment of the Antrim Plateau to the eastern shore. Until the building of this road in 1834, the Glens were home to isolated farming communities—people who adhered to the romantic, mystical Celtic legends and the everyday use of the Gaelic language. Steeped in Irish mythology, the Glens were first inhabited by small bands of Irish monks as early as AD 700. Some residents proudly note that Ossian, the greatest of the Celtic poets, is supposedly buried near Glenaan. Given the original remoteness of the area, a great tradition of storytelling still exists. Locals will often talk of "the wee folk," who are said to reside in and around Lurigethan Mountain and Tiveragh Hill. The fairies inhabiting these places are mostly mischievous creations who mind ther own business but are said to take devastating revenge on anyone rash enough to cut down a fairy thorn.

The Glens are worth several days of serious exploration. Even narrower B-roads curl west off A2, up each of the beautiful glens where trails await hikers. You'll need a full week and a rainproof tent to complete the nine-glen circuit (working from south to north, Glenarm, Glencloy, Glenariff, Glenballyeamon, Glenaan, Glencorp, Glendun, Glenshesk, and Glentasie—Taisie was a princess of Rathlin Island); or you could just head for Glenariff Park, the most accessible of Antrim's glens. Tourist offices in the area, such as the one in Cushendall, sell a *Guide to the Glens*.

A little resort made of white limestone, **Carnlough** overlooks a charming harbor that's surrounded by stone walls. The harbor can be reached by crossing over the limestone bridge from Main Street, built especially for the Marquis of Londonderry. The small harbor, once a port of call for fishermen, now shelters pleasure yachts. Carnlough is surrounded on three sides by hills that rise 1,000 feet from the sea. There's a small tourist office inside the post office, which is useful if you need information on exploring the scenic Glens of Antrim and the coast road. ⊠ *24 km (15 mi) north of Larne on A2.*

★ In **Glenariff Forest Park** you can explore the most beautiful and unsettled of Antrim's glens. Glenariff was christened "Little Switzerland" by Thackeray for its spectacular combination of rugged hills and lush vales. The main valley opens onto Red Bay at the village of Glenariff (also known as Waterfoot). Inside the park are picnic facilities and dozens of good hikes. The 5½-km (3½-mi) Waterfall Trail, marked with blue arrows, passes outstanding views of Glenariff River, its waterfalls, and small but swimmable loughs. Escape from the summer crowds by taking the longest trails, such as the Scenic Hike. Pick up a detailed trail map at the park visitor center, which also has a small cafeteria. ⊹ *7 km (5 mi) north of Carnlough off A2* ⊠ *98 Glenariff Rd., Glenariff* ☎ *028/ 2175–8232* 🚗 *Vehicles £3, pedestrians £2* ☉ *Daily 10–dusk.*

Turnley's Tower—a curious, fortified square tower of red stone, built in 1820 as a curfew tower and jail for "idlers and rioters"—stands in **Cushendall**, at a crossroads in the middle of the village. Another village of the picture-postcard variety, Cushendall is called the capital of the Glens due to having a few more streets than the other villages hereabouts. The road from Waterfoot to Cushendall is barely a mile long and worth the walk or cycle to see the coastal caves (one of whose residents was called the Nun Marry) that line the route. ⊠ *3 km (2 mi) north of Glenariff on A2.*

★ Off the main A2 route, the road between Cushendall and Cushendun turns into one of a Tour-de-France hilliness, so cyclists beware. Your reward, however, will be the tiny jewel of a village, **Cushendun**, which was designed by Clough Williams-Ellis, who also designed the famous Italianate village of Portmeirion in Wales. From this part of the coast you can see the Mull of Kintyre on the Scottish mainland. ⊠ *2 km (1½ mi) north of Cushendall on Coast Rd.*

en route The narrow and precipitous Antrim Coast Road cuts off from A2 and heads north from Cushendun past dramatically beautiful Murlough Bay to Fair Head and on to Ballycastle. In this area is Drumnakill, a renowned pagan site; Torr Head, a jutting peninsula; and three state parks that allow for some fabulous hikes, fine hill-walking, and great views of Scotland from Fair Head. Or you can rejoin A2 at Cushendun via B92 (a left turn). After a few miles the road descends—passing ruins of the Franciscans' 16th-century Bonamargy Friary—into Ballycastle.

Where to Stay & Eat

$$$ ✕🏨 **Galgorm Manor.** The manor house itself is photogenic, and the estate grounds—where you may go riding, practice archery, and shoot clay pigeons—cinematic. Full privileges at an 18-hole, par-72 golf course five minutes from the hotel is an added treat. The River Maine (good for brown trout) flows within view of many of the large rooms, which have wood beams hanging on the ceilings above substantial dark wood beds. Gillies bar is decidedly Irish; the restaurant serves hearty portions of traditional Irish food ($–$$). Galgorm is off A42, 3 km (2 mi) west of Ballymena, 32 km (20 mi) inland of Larne, 40 km (25 mi) north of Belfast. ✛ *40 km (25 mi) east of Larne on A36* ✉ *136 Fenaghy Rd., Ballymena, Co. Antrim BT42 1EA* ☎ *028/2588–1001* 🖷 *028/2588–0080* ⊕ *www. galgorm.com* ↘ *24 rooms* ⚳ *Restaurant, golf privileges, fishing, archery, horseback riding, bar, meeting rooms; no a/c* ☱ *AE, MC, V* ☉ *BP, MAP.*

★ **$$** ✕🏨 **Londonderry Arms Hotel.** What awaits at Londonderry Arms are lovely seaside gardens, ivy-clad walls, gorgeous antiques, regional paintings and maps, and lots of fresh flowers. This ivy-covered traditional inn on Carnlough Harbor was built as a coach stop in 1848. In 1921 Sir Winston Churchill inherited it; since 1947 it has been owned and run by the hospitable O'Neill family. Both the original and the newer rooms have Georgian furnishings and luxurious fabrics, and are immaculately kept. The restaurant serves substantial, traditional Irish meals that emphasize fresh, local seafood, simply prepared ($–$$). The hotel has an elevator and is wheelchair accessible. ✉ *20 Harbour Rd., Carnlough, Co. Antrim BT44 0EU* ☎ *028/2888–5255* 🖷 *028/2888–5263* ⊕ *www.glensofantrim. com* ↘ *35 rooms* ⚳ *Restaurant, bar, meeting rooms; no a/c* ☱ *AE, DC, MC, V* ☉ *BP, MAP.*

$$ 🏨 **Ballygally Castle.** A baronial castle, built by a Scottish lord in 1625, rises dramatically beside Ballygally Bay. Attached to it is a modern extension that provides room for facilities but clashes a bit with the original. Bedrooms in the castle have retained beamed ceilings despite comfortable-if-bland furnishings throughout. Ask for a room in a turret—one comes complete with milady's ghost. On Saturday in the dining room, a decent table d'hôte evening meal is served to musical accompaniment; a Sunday bistro meal is available. ✉ *274 Coast Rd., Ballygally, Co. Antrim BT40 2QZ* ☎ *028/2858–1066* 🖷 *028/2858–3681* ⊕ *www.hastingshotels.com* ↘ *44 rooms* ⚳ *Dining room, bar, babysitting; no a/c* ☱ *AE, DC, MC, V* ☉ *BP.*

Ballycastle

㉑ *86 km (54 mi) northeast of Larne, 37½ km (23 mi) north of Carnlough.*

Ballycastle is the main resort at the northern end of the Glens of Antrim. People from the province flock here in the summer. The town is shaped like an hourglass—with its strand and dock on one end, its pubs and chippers on the other, and the 1-km (½-mi) Quay Road in between. Beautifully aged shops and pubs line its Castle, Diamond, and Main streets. Every year since 1606, on the last Monday and Tuesday in August, Ballycastle has hosted the **Oul' Lammas Fair,** a modern version of the ancient Celtic harvest festival of Lughnasa (Irish for "August"). Ireland's oldest fair, this is a very popular two-day event at which sheep and wool are still sold alongside the wares of more modern shopping stalls. Treat yourself to the fair's traditional snacks, "dulse" (sun-dried seaweed), and "yellow man" (rock-hard yellow toffee).

From Ballycastle town you have a view of L-shape **Rathlin Island,** where in 1306 the Scottish king Robert the Bruce took shelter in a cave (under the east lighthouse) and, according to the popular legend, was inspired to continue his armed struggle against the English by watching a spider patiently spinning its web. It was on Rathlin in 1898 that Guglielmo Marconi set up the world's first cross-water radio link, from the island's lighthouse to Ballycastle. Bird-watching and hiking are the island's main activities. Unless the sea is extremely rough, a ferryboat makes twice-daily journeys for £9. The trip can take up to 45 minutes; be mindful of the weather to ensure that you can return the same day. ⊠ *9½ km (6 mi) from Ballycastle.*

Off the Ballycastle coast you can see the **Carrick-a-Rede** rope bridge, which spans a 60-foot gap between the mainland and Carrick-a-Rede Island. The island's name means "rock in the road" and refers to how it stands in the path of the salmon who follow the coast as they migrate to their home rivers to spawn. For the past 150 years salmon fishermen have set up the rope bridge in spring, taking it down again after the salmon season ends. The bridge is open to the public and has some heart-stopping views of the crashing waves below. If you summon up the nerve to cross it once, of course you then have to do it again to get back to the mainland. ⊠ *8 km (5 mi) west of Ballycastle on B15* 🎫 *Free* ☾ *Mid-Mar.–June and Sept., daily 10–6; July and Aug., daily 9:30–7:30.*

Where to Eat

★ ¢–$$ ✕ **Wysner's.** Head chef Jackie Wysner has won several awards for both this small family restaurant and the eponymous butcher shop next door. Menus vary daily, though the cooking emphasizes fresh local ingredients—from the hills and the sea. Specialties of the upstairs restaurant include North Atlantic salmon (caught nearby at Carrick-a-Rede), fillet of halibut with langoustine, and filet of beef with mustard-seed cream sauce. A daytime menu is served downstairs in the informal café. ⊠ *16–18 Ann St.* ☎ *028/2076–2372* ▤ *MC, V* ☾ *Closed Sun.*

Giant's Causeway

② *19⅓ km (12 mi) west of Ballycastle.*

Fodor'sChoice
★

"When the world was moulded and fashioned out of formless chaos, this must have been a bit over—a remnant of chaos," said the great Thackeray about Northern Ireland's premier tourist draw, the Giant's Causeway. Imagine a mass of 37,000 mostly hexagonal pillars of volcanic basalt, clustered like a giant honeycomb and extending hundreds of yards into the sea. Legend has it this "causeway" was created 60 million years ago, when boiling lava, erupting from an underground fissure that stretched from Northern Ireland to the Scottish coast, crystallized as it burst into the sea, and formed according to the same natural principle that structures a honeycomb. As all Ulster folk know, though, the scientific truth is that the columns were created as stepping-stones by the giant Finn McCool in a bid to reach a giantess he'd fallen in love with on the Scottish island of Staffa (where the causeway resurfaces). Unfortunately, the giantess's boyfriend found out, and in the ensuing battle Finn pulled out a huge chunk of earth and flung it toward Scotland. The resulting hole became Lough Neagh, and the sod landed to create the Isle of Man.

To reach the causeway, you can either walk 1½ km (1 mi) down a long, scenic hill or take a minibus from the visitor center. West of the causeway, Port-na-Spania is the spot where the 16th-century Spanish Armada galleon *Girona* went down on the rocks. The ship was carrying an astonishing cargo of gold and jewelry, some of which was recovered in 1967 and is now on display in the Ulster Museum in Belfast. Beyond this, Chimney Point is the name given to one of the causeway structures on which the Spanish fired, thinking that it was Dunluce Castle, which is 8 km (5 mi) west.

Arriving by car at the Giant's Causeway, you first reach a cliff-top parking lot beside the modern visitor center, which houses displays about the area and a superb audiovisual exhibition explaining the formation of the causeway coast. Check with the staffers here about the fine hikes along the pristine coastline that stretches from here toward the ruin of Dunseverick Castle, 5 km (3 mi) away. ✉ *44 Causeway Rd., Bushmills* ☎ *028/2073–1855* ⊕ *www.nationaltrust.org.uk.* ✎ *Visitor center movie £1, guided tours £2, parking £5* ⊘ *Visitor center Mar.–May, daily 10–5; June, daily 10–6; July and Aug., daily 10–7; Sept. and Oct., daily 10–5; Nov.–Feb., daily 10–3.*

Bushmills

㉓ *3 km (2 mi) west of Giant's Causeway.*

The oldest licensed distillery in the world, Bushmills was first granted a charter by King James I in 1608, though historical records refer to a distillery here as early as 1276. Bushmills produces the most famous of Irish whiskeys—its namesake—and what is widely regarded as the best, the rarer black-label version known to aficionados as Black Bush. One-hour tours begin in the mashing and fermentation room, proceed to the maturing and bottling warehouse, and end with a complimentary shot of *uisce beatha,* the "water of life," in the visitor center gift shop. ✉ *Off A2* ☎ *028/2073–1521* ⊕ *www.whiskeytours.ie* ✎ *£4* ⊘ *Tours Apr.–Oct., Mon.–Sat. 9:30–5:30, Sun. noon–5:30; Nov.–Mar., 5 tours a day weekdays 10:30–3:30, 3 tours weekends 1:30–3:30.*

Where to Stay

$$$–$$$$ ▦ **Bushmills Inn.** Owner Roy Bolton oversees this cozy old coach inn. Stripped pine, peat fires, and gas lights warm the public rooms. Some of the bedrooms are quite small, so look before you decide. The livery stables now house the informal restaurant, which serves fresh and hearty food, and the bar. The staff can provide a baby-listening service—you leave the tot in the room with a phone that records any noise, and they alert you to cries. The distillery is a stroll away from the main square and the inn, as is the salmon-filled River Bush. ✉ *9 Dunluce Rd., Bush-*

mills, Co. Antrim BT57 8QG ☎ 028/2073–3000 🖷 028/2073–2048 ⊕ www.bushmills-inn.com ↩ 32 rooms with bath ⚹ Restaurant, bar, Internet, meeting rooms; no a/c ⊟ AE, MC, V ⦿ BP.

Dunluce Castle

★ ㉔ *3 km (2 mi) west of Bushmills.*

Halfway between Portrush and the Giant's Causeway, dramatically perched on a cliff at land's end, Dunluce Castle is one of the North's most evocative ruins. Originally a 13th-century Norman fortress, it was captured in the 16th century by the local MacDonnell clan chiefs—the so-called "Lords of the Isles." They enlarged the castle, paying for some of the work with their profits from salvaging the Spanish galleon *Girona,* and made it an important base for ruling northeastern Ulster. Perhaps they expanded the castle a little too much, for in 1639 faulty construction caused the kitchens (with the cooks) to plummet into the sea during a storm. ⊠ *Coastal Rd., Portrush* ☎ *028/2073–1938* ⊕ *www. northantrim.com/dunlucecastle.htm* 🖾 *£2* ⊙ *Apr.–Sept., Mon.–Sat. 10–6, Sun. 2–6; Oct.–Mar., Tues.–Sat. 10–4, Sun. 2–4.*

Dunluce Center is an entertainment complex with three floors of interactive play zones, shops, and a café near Dunluce Castle. ⊠ *10 Sandhill Dr., Portrush* ☎ *028/7082–4444* ⊕ *www.dunlucecentre.co.uk* 🖾 *£5 plus rides* ⊙ *Easter week, daily 10:30–7; Apr. and May, weekends 12–7; June, weekdays 10–5, weekends 12–7; July and Aug., daily 10:30–7; Sept.–Mar., weekends 12–5.*

Where to Eat

★ ¢–$$ ✕ **Ramore Wine Bar.** On Portrush's picturesque harbor, this spot has panoramic views, with daily offerings posted on a blackboard. ⊠ *The Harbor, Portrush* ☎ *028/7082–4313* 🖷 *028/7082–3194* ⊟ MC, V.

Sports & the Outdoors

The **Royal Portrush Golf Club** (⊠ Dunluce Rd., Portrush ☎ 028/7082–2311 ⊕ www.royalportrushgolfclub.com) has more than one course. The championship Dunluce is a sea of sand hills and curving fairways (£85). The valley course is a less-exposed, tamer track (£30). Both are open to visitors on weekdays. **Portstewart Strand** (⊠ Coastal Rd., Portrush) has some of Ireland's best surfing. It's signposted as "The Strand" on all major junctions in town.

Coleraine

㉕ *13 km (8 mi) southwest of Dunluce Castle.*

The 5th-century BC town of Coleraine became the home of the University of Ulster in 1968. The River Bann flows through the town, dividing the county of Antrim from that of Derry. As well as being a fishing town, Coleraine has an important linen industry. Some of Ireland's oldest relics, dating from the first inhabitants of this island (about 7000 BC), were found on Mountsandel, just south of Coleraine. One of the many dolmens in this region is called Slaghtaverty—after an evil dwarf who used his magical harp to mesmerize women. He was buried alive and upside down by the great Finn McCool (maker of the Giant's Causeway), so the sounds of his harp would not escape from the ground.

Where to Stay

$ 🏠 **Greenhill House.** A great base for exploring the Antrim coast, this charming Georgian country house is a peaceful retreat run by Elizabeth and James Hegarty. Floral fabrics and antique, carved furnishings decorate pleasant rooms. Breakfasts are substantial. The excellent dinners—of locally caught fish, Ulster beef, and homemade bread and cakes—must be booked by noon. ✥ *13 km (8 mi) south of Coleraine on A29* ⌂ *24 Greenhill Rd., Aghadowey, Co. Derry BT51 4EU* ☎ *028/7086–8241* 🖶 *028/7086–8365* ⊕ *www.greenhill.house.btinternet.co.uk* ➫ *6 rooms* ⏦ *Dining room, Internet; no a/c* ▤ *MC, V* ⑂ *BP, MAP* ⊙ *Closed Nov.–Feb.*

Upperlands

➋➏ *32 km (20 mi) south of Coleraine, 56 km (35 mi) northwest of Belfast.*

The River Bann—rich in eels for roasting and smoking and in salmon for poaching—flows out of Lough Neagh. On its left bank are the towns and fortifications of the 17th-century Planters, built by London's Livery Companies, whose descendants developed the linen industry. Today, virtually all of that rural industrial heritage is gone, with the notable exception of the village of Upperlands. Make sure you tour **William Clark and Sons,** a working linen mill where age-old wooden machinery still beetles (polishes by pounding with hammers) threads for the linen linings of suits for England's Royals. There's also a small linen museum here. ⌂ *A29, Upperlands* ☎ *028/7954–7200* ➫ *Free* ⊙ *By appointment Mon.–Thurs. 10–4.*

Where to Stay & Eat

$$$ ✕🏠 **Ardtara House.** A 19th-century Victorian home, Ardtara was built
Fodor'sChoice by a descendant of the founder of the town's first linen mill. Eight large
★ bedrooms are furnished with antiques, and each has a fireplace—as do some of the marble bathrooms. The terra-cotta-and-pink drawing room, with plaster moldings and a marble fireplace, looks out on the wide front lawn and tennis court. The hotel's restaurant ($$) is in the former snooker room, with dark panels and a wallpapered hunting scene. The terrine of duck appetizer is popular, as is the stellar poached fillet of lamb with buttered Savoy cabbage. ⌂ *8 Gorteade Rd., Co. Derry BT46 5SA* ☎ *028/7964–4490* 🖶 *028/7964–5080* ➫ *8 rooms* ⏦ *Restaurant, tennis court, meeting room; no a/c* ▤ *AE, MC, V* ⑂ *BP.*

Limavady

➋➐ *21 km (13 mi) west of Coleraine, 27 km (17 mi) east of Derry.*

In 1851, at No. 51 on Limavady's Georgian main street, Jane Ross wrote down the tune played by a traveling fiddler and called it "Londonderry Air," better known now as "Danny Boy." While staying at an inn on Ballyclose Street, William Thackeray (1811–63) wrote his rather lustful poem "Peg of Limavaddy" about a barmaid. Among the many

Americans descended from Ulster emigrants was President James Monroe, whose relatives came from the Limavady area.

Where to Stay & Eat

$$$ ✕⊡ **Radisson Roe Park Hotel & Golf Resort.** A country estate serves as the model for the deluxe modern resort amid 155 acres on the banks of the River Roe. Regular guest rooms have simple, clean-line beds in woods and rich earth tones. Suite furnishings move a bit up the ornate scale: canopy beds and velvet armchairs. Green's restaurant is formal and international ($–$$$); the Coach House brasserie is a relaxed place where golfers congregate; and O'Cahan's bar takes its name from a local chieftain besieged on a riverside promontory, whose Irish wolfhound leaped an impossible chasm to bring relief—doubtless an inspiration to golfers flagging at the ninth. ⊠ *Roe Park, Co. Derry BT49 9LB* ☎ *028/7772–2222* 🖨 *028/7772–2313* ⊕ *www.radissonsas.com* ⤳ *118 rooms, 6 suites* ⚌ *2 restaurants, 18-hole golf course, indoor pool, fitness classes, gym, hair salon, massage, sauna, steam room, fishing, horseback riding, 2 bars, baby-sitting, Internet, meeting rooms; no a/c* ⊟ *AE, DC, MC, V* ⫦⊙⫦ *BP, MAP.*

Derry

27 km (17 mi) southwest of Limavady on A2, 109 km (68 mi) north of Belfast, 53 km (33 mi) north of Omagh.

If Belfast were the Beethoven of Northern Ireland, Derry would be the Mozart—fey, witty, and a touch surreal. Every Halloween, for example, the entire populace of Derry—the second biggest city in Northern Ireland—turns out in wild homemade costumes, and pubs have been known to refuse a drink to anyone who hasn't made the effort to dress up. Despite the derelict factories along the banks of the River Foyle and a reputation marred by Troubles-related violence, the city has worked hard to move forward. Such efforts show in the quaint, bustling town center, encircled by 20-foot-tall 17th-century walls. The city's winding streets slope down to the Foyle, radiating from the Diamond—Derry's historic center—where St. Columba founded his first monastery in 546. Fine Georgian and Victorian buildings sit side by side with gaily painted Victorian-front shops, cafés, and pubs.

Derry's name is a shadow of its history. Those in favor of British rule call the city Londonderry, its old Plantation-period name: the "London" part was tacked on in 1613 after the Flight of the Earls, and the city and county were handed over to the Corporation of London, which represented London's merchants. The corporation brought in a large population of English and Scottish Protestant settlers, built towns for them, and reconstructed Derry within the city walls, which survive almost unchanged to this day. Both before then and after, Derry's sturdy ramparts withstood many fierce attacks—they have never been breached, which explains the city's coy sobriquet, "The Maiden City." The most famous attack was the siege of 1688–89, begun after 13 apprentice boys slammed the city gates in the face of the Catholic king, James II. Inhabitants, who held out for 105 days and were reduced to eating dogs, cats, and laun-

Derry

dry starch, nevertheless helped to secure the British throne for the Protestant king, William III. Whatever you choose to call it, Derry is one of Northern Ireland's most underrated towns.

Derry, incidentally, has links to Boston that date as far back as the 17th and 18th centuries, when many Derry residents escaped their hardships at home by emigrating to that U.S. city and beyond. Aviation fans, take note: Derry is where Amelia Earhart touched down on May 21, 1932, after her historic solo flight across the Atlantic. Local lore has it that the first man to reach her airplane greeted her in typically unfazed Derry fashion: "Aye, and what do you want, then?"

28 To really experience Derry's history, stroll along the parapet walkway atop the ramparts of the **city walls**, built between 1614 and 1618 and one of the few intact sets of city walls in Europe. Pierced by eight gates (originally four) and as much as 30 feet thick, the gray-stone ramparts are only 1½ km (1 mi) all around. Today most of the life of the town takes place outside of them. You can join one of the guided tours given by the information center, or follow the sites below in a counterclockwise direction.

Walking tours of the city walls leave from the **Tourist Information Centre** and last just under two hours. They depart at 2:30 weekdays year-round, as well as at 11:15 and 3:15 in July and August. ✉ *44 Foyle St., West Bank* ☎ *028/7126–7284 or 028/7137–7577* 📠 *028/7137–7992* ⊕ *www.derryvisitor.com* 🖂 *Center free, tour £4* ☉ *Mar. 15–June and Oct., weekdays 9–5, Sat. 10–5; July–Sept., weekdays 9–7, Sat. 10–6, Sun. 10–5; Nov.–Mar. 15, weekdays 9–5.*

29 Derry city council meets monthly at **Guildhall,** an ornate Victorian stone and sandstone building dating from 1890. The large stained-glass windows were shattered by two IRA bombs in June 1977 and rebuilt by the Campbell's firm in Belfast, which had installed the original windows in 1890 and still had the plans (now *that's* a filing system). The Guildhall also hosts occasional musical recitals. ✉ *Guildhall Sq., West Bank* ☎ *028/7137–7335* 🖂 *Free* ☉ *Weekdays 8:30–5.*

★ **30** Tall, brooding, medieval, and magical, a reconstructed granite-stone O'-Dohertys Tower contains the **Tower Museum,** which chronicles the history of Derry. The building was constructed in 1615 by the O'Dohertys for their overlords, the O'Donnells, in lieu of tax payments. Highlights of the museum include a small section on the eccentric Bishop Frederick Augustus Hervey (1763–1803), who conducted a lifelong affair with the mistress of Frederick William II of Prussia, built the now derelict Downhill Castle above the cliffs outside the city, and allegedly had his curates stage naked sprints along the beach while he horsewhipped them. The winners were awarded the most lucrative parishes in the district. There's excellent information celebrating the life and legacy of St. Columba. The vivid "Story of Derry" exhibition covers the city's history, from its origins as a monastic settlement in an oak grove up to the Troubles, beginning in 1969 after years of institutionalized discrimination in jobs and public housing. (A well-known Derry joke is that the skeleton in the city's coat of arms was actually a Catholic waiting for a house.) ✉ *Union Hall*

A POLITICAL ABC

DUP. Right-wing Democratic Unionist Party, founded by firebrand preacher Reverend Ian Paisley in 1971. Now increasingly sidelined.

IRA. Irish Republican Army. Largest group of Republican paramilitaries, responsible for thousands of murders and bombings.

Loyalist. Extreme Unionist.

Nationalist. Anyone supporting a united Ireland.

Northern Ireland Assembly. Regional government, sitting at Stormont.

Orange Order. Protestant organization whose annual 12th of July marches celebrate the 1690 victory of Protestant King William of Orange over Catholic King James.

Republican. Extreme Nationalist.

SDLP. Social, Democratic, and Labour Party. Largest and most moderate Nationalist party.

Sinn Féin. Literally "Ourselves Alone," political counterpart of IRA, although now firmly installed in democratic Northern Ireland Assembly.

The Troubles. The 1969–97 campaign by Republican and Loyalist terrorists in which 3,636 people were killed.

UDA. Ulster Defence Association. Largest Loyalist paramilitary group, involved in hundreds of murders.

UFF and UVF. Ulster Freedom Fighters and Ulster Volunteer Force, breakaway Loyalist paramilitary groups.

Ulster. Historic name for northern province of Ireland. Now generally used, especially by Protestants, to describe Northern Ireland.

Ulster Unionist Party. Largest and most moderate Unionist party.

Unionist. Anyone supporting continuing union with Great Britain.

Pl., West Bank ☎ 028/7137–2411 ☜ £4 ☉ Sept.–June, Tues.–Sat. 10–5; July and Aug., Mon.–Sat. 10–5, Sun. 2–5.

③① **Calgach Centre** provides a high-tech tour of the city's history, including its importance in creating the Irish diaspora of 17 million people. Sit in a comfortable armchair for a virtual-reality time-trip through the coming of the Vikings and the Normans, the flight of the Irish nobility from English persecution in 1601, and the famine of 1845–49, when 1½ million emigrated to the United States and a million died of starvation. At this writing the center was under repair, with reopening date uncertain. ⌧ 4–22 Butcher St., West Bank ☎ 028/7137–3177.

③② Imposing in its Scottish Baronial fortified grandeur, **Apprentice Boys' Memorial Hall** is a meeting place for the exclusively Protestant organization set up in 1715 to honor 13 apprentice boys who slammed the city gate in the face of the Catholic King James in 1688 and sparked the Siege of Derry, which has been a symbol of Protestant stubbornness ever since. Inside, there's an initiation room in which 20,000 have pledged to uphold Protestant values, and a magnificently chaotic museum filled to the brim with furniture, firearms, books, bombs, swords, and sculpture. It's a fascinating glimpse into a mostly closed world. An upstairs bar and dance hall—now used for meetings, initiations, and social events, organized by the Apprentice Boys—has walls lined with 12 banners representing the lost tribes of Israel. (Some Protestants believe the lost tribes of Israel ended up in Northern Ireland and are their forebears.) ⊠ *Society St., West Bank* ☎ *028/7134–6677* ⊠ *Donations accepted* ☉ *Tours by appointment; open to public second week of Aug.*

Walker Memorial, a statue of the governor of Derry during the siege, is a symbol of Derry's divided nature. It was blown up by the IRA in 1973, and the story goes that the statue's head rolled down the hill into the Catholic Bogside, where it was captured by a local youth. He ransomed it back to the Protestants for a small fortune, and today it sits on the shoulders of a replica of the original statue beside the Apprentice Boys' Memorial Hall. ⊠ *Apprentice Boys' Memorial Hall, Society St., West Bank.*

㉝ At **Free Derry Corner** is the white gable wall where Catholics defiantly painted the slogan "You are now entering Free Derry" as a declaration of a zone from which police and the British Army were banned until 1972, when the army broke down the barricades. That year, 13 civil rights marchers were shot and killed by British soldiers in an event that rankles Catholics to this day. "Bloody Sunday," as it became known, is commemorated by the mural of a civil rights march. ⊠ *Fahan and Rossville Sts., West Bank.*

㉞ **St. Columb's Cathedral** was the first Protestant cathedral built in the United Kingdom after the Reformation, and contains the oldest and largest bells in Ireland (dating from the 1620s). It's a treasure house of Derry Protestant emblems, memorials, and relics from the siege of 1688–89. The church was built in 1633 in simple Planter's Gothic style, with an intricate corbeled roof and austere spire. In the vestibule is the 270-pound mortar ball that during the Siege of Derry was fired over the wall with an invitation to surrender sent by King James. Legend has it that when it was read, every man, woman, and child in the city rushed to the walls and shouted, "No surrender!"—a Protestant battle cry to this day. The attached Chapter House Museum has the oldest surviving map of Derry (from 1600) and the Bible owned by Governor George Walker during the siege. Knowledgeable tour guides are on hand. ⊠ *London St., off Bishop St., West Bank* ☎ *028/7126–7313* ⊕ *www.stcolumbscathedral. org* ⊠ *£1* ☉ *Apr.–Oct., daily 9–5; Nov.–Mar., daily 9–4.*

need a break? Derry is packed with agreeable pubs, but **Badgers** (⊠ 16 Orchard St., West Bank ☎ 028/7136–0763) has the best choice of wholesome food. It's also the watering hole for local media types, artists, writers, and musicians.

㉟ Across the River Foyle from the city walls, the **Workhouse Museum** was built in 1832 as an institution to alleviate poverty but became the end of the road for people who had tried in vain to make their lives better. During the famine years (1845–49), the city was the main emigration port for Northern Ireland, and many families came to Derry hoping to get on a boat. Instead, unable to afford the trip, they ended up applying for aid at the Workhouse, where hard labor earned a bed and food.

Many families were separated once inside, and this was often the last time children saw their parents alive. From the beginning to the end of the famine, 1½ million people left Ireland and 1 million died. The museum details life in the workhouse and has some thoughtful exhibits about famine in general.

Many of the descendants of those who left came back during the Second World War: thousands of U.S. servicemen arrived in the city in 1942 to turn it into a base for the Battle of the Atlantic. Exhibits on the top two floors of the Workhouse chronicle the story of that battle, from the Yanks' arrival in the January rain (which prompted one of them to ask if the city's barrage balloons were actually there to stop the place from sinking) through the end of the war, when 64 U-boats lined up in the harbor to surrender. By 1946 the city's biggest export was G.I. brides. There is a space for traveling exhibitions that change regularly; call for details. ⊠ *23 Glendermott Rd., East Bank* ☎ *028/7131–8328* ☜ *Free* ☉ *Sept.–June, Mon.–Thurs. and Sat. 10–4:30; July and Aug., Mon.–Sat. 10:30–4:30.*

en route   For a delightfully rustic alternative to driving back to Belfast on A6, drive along the minor road B48, which skirts the foot of the Sperrin Mountains and reaches all the way to Omagh. Or, you may want to head north from Derry to explore the Inishowen Peninsula, the northernmost point of Ireland.

Where to Stay & Eat

$$ ✕ **The Exchange.** Overdressed twentysomethings lounge by the circular and ultra-modern bar in this chic new restaurant-cum-wine bar. It's *the* place to be seen in Derry, so weekend evenings can be extremely busy. Unfortunately, reservations are not taken so be prepared to wait at the bar—but with a chilled glass of sauvignon blanc from the excellent wine list, it is no hardship. Locally-caught seafood is delicious and stand-outs include the halibut in shrimp sauce and the *Hua Hin* crab cakes flecked with coconut. Service is super-efficient but can feel a touch brisk. ⊠ *Exchange House, Queen's Quay Central District* ☎ *028/7127–3990* 🖶 *028/7127–3991* ▭ *AE, MC, V.*

$ ✕ **Spice.** It's worth the walk up the hill from town to this cozy restaurant with food that draws heavily on Pan-Asian influences. Main course highlights include crab claws and red Thai curry, served with plain or fried rice or noodles. ⊠ *162–164 Spencer Rd., East Bank* ☎ *028/ 7134–4875* ▭ *MC, V.*

¢ ✕ **Fitzroy's.** This popular city center brasserie gives "quare packin' " (Derry-speak for good value for money), with belt-busting portions of old favorites like burgers, steaks, and Caesar salads in the evening. Lunchtimes are busy, with weary shoppers and office staff stopping by for a turkey-stuffing-and-cranberry *panini* sandwiches or a big bowl of homemade leek-and-potato soup. The fully licensed bar stocks a good range of bottled beers and wines. ⊠ *2–4 Bridge St. Central District* ☎ *028/ 7126–6211* ⊕ *www.fitzroys.net* ▭ *MC, V.*

$$ 🏠 **Beech Hill.** Journey past a fairy-tale gatehouse among clumps of beech trees, past streams and a duck pond on the grounds at Beech Hill. This grand 1729 country home is very much attuned to the present with a number of conveniences to satisfy the demanding traveler (a trouser press, and tea and coffeemakers in-room). The vast honeymoon suite, with a four-poster bed, overlooks the gardens. Rooms in the old building are decorated in Georgian style; 10 rooms in a modern extension are larger and contemporary. A small museum celebrates the fact that Beech Hill housed a contingent of U.S. Marines during World War II. ✛ *3 km (2 mi) southeast of town off A6* ✉ *32 Ardmore Rd., Beech Hill, BT47 3QP* ☎ *028/7134–9279* 🖷 *028/7134–5366* ⊕ *www.beech-hill.com* 🛏 *28 rooms with bath, 5 suites* △ *Restaurant, tennis court, gym, hot tub, massage, sauna, bar, Internet, meeting rooms; no a/c* ⊟ *AE, MC, V* ¡Ol *BP, MAP.*

$–$$ 🏨 **The Tower Hotel.** The only hotel within Derry city's historic walls, this modern and comfortable hotel has more to offer than its unequalled location. Rooms are decorated in vibrant shades of red and blue, with pine furnishings and well-stocked bathrooms. The sleek oak-wood bar, with its low-hanging lights, is a favorite watering hole with locals as well as visiting guests. The hotel opened in 2002, and the bistro-style restaurant has already won awards. But the location is prima—just check out the view of the Bogside and the "Free Derry" corner from the upper bedrooms and the fourth-floor gym. ✉ *Butcher St., Central District BT48 6HL* ☎ *028/7137–1000* 🖷 *028/7137–1234* ⊕ *www.towerhotelderry. com* 🛏 *90 rooms with bath, 3 suites* △ *Restaurant, bar, gym, sauna, Internet, meeting rooms; no a/c* ⊟ *AE, DC, MC, V* ¡Ol *BP, MAP.*

★ ¢ 🏨 **The Merchant's House.** No. 16 Queen Street was originally a Victorian merchant's family town home built to Georgian proportions, then a rectory and bank, before Joan Pyne turned it into the city's grandest B&B. Garnet-color walls, elaborate plasterwork, and a fireplace make the parlor warm and welcoming. Little wonder the guestbook features some prominent names, including the late Hurd Hatfield, star of the movie *The Picture of Dorian Gray.* Joan also owns a similar but smaller building three minutes' walk away called the Saddler's House. Charming and cozy, this Victorian jewel of a home (who can resist its faintingly pink living room parlor?) has been lovingly restored and is packed with interesting antiques and family portraits, and is another excellent value for the money. Incidentally, many architecturally interesting homes occupy the neighborhood. ✉ *16 Queen St., West Bank BT48 7EQ* ☎ *028/ 7126–4223* 🖷 *028/7126–6913* ⊕ *www.thesaddlershouse.com* 🛏 *6 rooms without bath* ⊟ *MC, V* ¡Ol *BP.*

Nightlife & the Arts

ART GALLERIES   The **Context Gallery** (✉ 5–7 Artillery St., West Bank ☎ 028/7137–3538) shows works by up-and-coming Irish and international artists. The **McGilloway Gallery** (✉ 6 Shipquay St., West Bank ☎ 028/7136–6011) stocks a broad selection of representational modern Irish art. Owner Ken McGilloway serves wine on Friday evenings until 9 PM during selected exhibitions. The **Orchard Gallery** (✉ Orchard St., West Bank ☎ 028/ 7126–9675) is known across Europe for its political and conceptual art.

PUBS & CLUBS   The **Gweedore Bar** (✉ 59–63 Waterloo St., West Bank ☎ 028/7126–3513) is a favorite for hip-hop and house music. Listen to traditional Irish music at **Peadar O'Donnell's** (✉ 63 Waterloo St., West Bank ☎ 028/7137–2318). **Sugar Nightclub** (✉ 33 Shipquay St., West Bank ☎ 028/7126–6017) is the place for disco.

THEATER &
OPERA The **Playhouse** (✉ 5–7 Artillery St., West Bank ☎ 028/7126–8027) stages traditional and contemporary plays and also holds contemporary music concerts. The newest edition to the theater scene is the catch-all **Millennium Forum Theatre and Conference Centre** (✉ Newmarket St., West Bank ☎ 028/7126–4455 ⊕ www.millenniumforum.co.uk), where everything and anything—from comedians to musicians to plays—goes on stage. The **Verbal Arts Centre** (✉ Bishop St., Stable La. and Mall Wall, West Bank ☎ 028/7126–6946 ⊕ www.verbalartscentre.co.uk) celebrates literature through performances and classes. It recreates the great old Irish tradition of fireside tales at regular storytelling events.

Shopping

Shopping in town is generally low-key and unpretentious, but there are some upscale gems of Irish craftsmanship. Stroll up Shipquay Street to find small arts and crafts stores and an indoor shopping center. **Bookworm** (✉ 18–20 Bishop St., West Bank ☎ 028/7128–2727) is the best bookshop in Ireland, according to writer Nuala O'Faoláin. **Occasions** (✉ 48 Spencer Rd., East Bank ☎ 028/7132–9595) sells Irish crafts and gifts. Stop at the gift shop **Pauline's Patch** (✉ 32 Shipquay St., West Bank ☎ 028/7127–9794) for knickknacks. Off Shipquay Street, the **Trip** (✉ 29 Ferryquay St., West Bank ☎ 028/7137–2382) is a teenage-clothing shop that specializes in knitwear. **Thomas the Goldsmith** (✉ 7 Pump St., West Bank ☎ 028/7137–4549) stocks exquisite work by international jewelry designers.

THE BORDER COUNTIES

While blissfully off the beaten track, these counties contain some dazzling sights: the Ulster-American Folk Park; the great stately houses of Castle Coole and Florence Court; the pottery town of Belleek; the ancient, ecclesiastical city of Armagh; and the wild Mountains of Mourne, one of Ireland's best-known and scenic ranges. During the worst of the Troubles, these counties of Tyrone, Fermanagh, Armagh, and Down, which border the Republic, were known as "bandit country," but now you can enjoy a worry-free trip through the calm countryside and stop in at some very "Ulster" towns, delightfully distinct from the rest of Ireland.

Omagh

55 km (34 mi) south of Derry on A5.

Omagh, the county town of Tyrone, lies close to the Sperrin Mountains, with the River Strule to the north. Playwright Brian Friel was born here. Sadly, it is more recently known as the scene of the worst atrocity of the Troubles, when an IRA bomb killed 29 people in August 1998. The town has two places of worship—a Church of Ireland church and a Catholic double-spire church. North of Omagh the country is pretty and rustic, with small farm villages. Several miles north of Omagh is the big ★ ③ attraction of the region: the excellent **Ulster-American Folk Park** re-creates a Tyrone village of two centuries ago, a log-built American settlement of the same period, and the docks and ships that the emigrants to America would have used. The centerpiece of the park is an old whitewashed cottage, now a museum, which is the ancestral home of Thomas

Mellon (1855–1937), the U.S. banker and philanthropist. Another thatched cottage is a reconstruction of the boyhood home of Archbishop John Hughes, founder of New York's St. Patrick's Cathedral. There are also full-scale replicas of Irish peasant cottages, Pennsylvania farmhouses, a New York tenement room, immigrant transport ship holders, plus a 19th-century Ulster village, complete with staff dressed in 19th-century costumes. Other exhibitions trace the contribution of the Northern Irish people to American history. The park also has a crafts shop and café. Last admission is 1½ hours before closing. ⊠ *Mellon Rd., 10 km (6 mi) north of town on A5, Castletown, Omagh, Co. Tyrone* ☎ *028/8224–3292* ⊕ *www.folkpark.com* ⊠ *£4* ⊙ *Apr.–Sept., Mon.–Sat. 10:30–6, Sun. 11–6:30; Oct.–Mar., weekdays 10:30–5.*

Take A5 north to **Strabane**, the birthplace of the surrealist novelist Brian O'Nolan, alias Flann O'Brien. James Wilson, grandfather of U.S. President Woodrow Wilson, emigrated from here. **Grays Printers Museum** (⊠ 49 Main St., Strabane ☎ 028/7188–4094) is in an 18th-century print shop with original 19th-century presses. John Dunlap (1746–1812), who apprenticed here before emigrating to Philadelphia, founded America's first daily newspaper, the *Philadelphia Packet,* in 1771 and was also the man who printed and distributed the American Declaration of Independence. ⊠ *31 km (19 mi) north of Omagh on A5.*

> **en route**
>
> Head east on A505 from Omagh into the pensive landscape of moist heath and peat bog. Left of A505, a few kilometers before Cookstown, Beaghmore is a Bronze Age ceremonial site preserved for millennia beneath a blanket of peat. It has seven stone circles and 12 cairns. A little beyond Wellbrook you come to Cookstown, a Plantation village with a broad main street. From here, head down the back lanes to Lough Neagh, the largest lake in the British Isles, noted for an abundance of eels. On its shore at Ardboe stands a remarkable 10th-century high cross, more than 18 feet tall and carved with intricate biblical scenes.
>
> **Wellbrook Beetling Mill** is where locally made linen was first "beetled"—pounded with noisy, water-driven hammers to give it a smooth finish. The National Trust keeps the mill in working order. ⊠ *20 Wellbrook Rd., Cookstown, Co. Tyrone* ☎ *028/8674–8210* ⊕ *www.nationaltrust.org.uk* ⊠ *£3* ⊙ *Mar.–June and Sept., weekends noon–6; July and Aug., daily noon–6.*

Lower Lough Erne

㊲ *38 km (23 mi) southwest of Omagh off A32.*

If you're driving in the vicinity of Lough Erne, don't rush—take your time and enjoy the panoramas of green wooded hills stretching down to the still waters. **Castle Archdale Country Park,** on the northeast side of Lough Erne, has a lakeside marina and a museum containing a World War II exhibition on the Battle of the Atlantic. ⊹ *Down a narrow road about 6½ km (4 mi) from Kesh* ⊠ *Off B82, Co. Fermanagh* ☎ *028/6862–1588* ⊠ *Free* ⊙ *Daily 9–dusk.*

BEAUTIFUL BELLEEK

THE ORIGINS OF BELLEEK *china are every bit as romantic as the Belleek blessing plates traditionally given to brides and grooms on their wedding day—that is, if you believe the legends. The story goes that in the mid 1800s, John Caldwell Bloomfield, the man behind the world-famous porcelain, accidentally discovered the raw ingredients necessary to produce china. After inheriting his father's estate in the Fermanagh Lakelands on the shore of the Erne River, he whitewashed his cottage using a flaky white powder dug up in his backyard. A passerby, struck by the luminescent sheen of the freshly-painted cottage, commented on the unusual brightness of the walls to the lord of the manor. Bloomfield promptly ordered a survey of the land, which duly uncovered all the minerals needed to make porcelain. The venture was complete when Bloomfield met his business partners— London architect Robert Armstrong and the wealthy Dublin merchant David McBirney. They decided to first produce earthenware, and then porcelain. And the rest, as they say, is history. The delicate, flawless porcelain (Bloomfield declared that any piece with even the slightest blemish should be destroyed) soon attracted the attention of Queen Victoria and many other aristos. Other companies tried to mimic the china's delicate beauty, but genuine Belleek porcelain is recognizable by its seashell designs, basket weaves, and marine themes. The company is now owned by an Irish-born American businessman, Dr. George Moore, and continues to flourish. It has become a favored tradition in Ireland to give a piece of Belleek china at weddings, giving rise to a saying: "If a newly married couple receives a piece of Belleek, their marriage will be blessed with lasting happiness."*

From Castle Archdale, a ferry (£3) runs from June through September, Tuesday through Sunday, taking passengers to see the carved Celtic figures on **White Island.** After you drive 13 km (8 mi) south from Castle Archdale Park to where the B82 joins the A32, a small sign shows the way to catch the little boat that goes to Devenish Island. The boat runs weekends-only April through September; you can also make a reservation with at least 24 hours' notice. On **Devenish Island** you can see Ireland's best example of a round tower, which stands 82 feet tall, and the extensive but ruined 12th-century monastery with a richly carved high cross.

Sports & the Outdoors

Inland cruising on the Erne waterway—777 square km (300 square mi) of lakes and rivers—is a major treat. Upper and Lower Lough Erne are enclosed by some of Ireland's finest scenery and are studded with more than 100 little islands. Out on the lakes and the River Erne, which links them, you have all the solitude you want, but you can find company at waterside hostelries. To hire a boat, contact **Erne Charter Boat Association** (✉ Belleek Charter Cruising, Erne Gateway Centre, Corry, Co. Fermanagh ☎ 028/6865–8027). Expect to pay at least £400 to hire a four-berth cruiser for two or three nights, available May to September.

Belleek

❸❽ *3 km (2 mi) west of Lower Lough Erne on A47.*

World-famous Belleek Pottery is made in the old town of Belleek on the northwestern edge of Lower Lough Erne, at the border with northwest Ireland. Other porcelainware makers are a few kilometers across the border. On the riverbank stands the visitor center of **Belleek Pottery Ltd.**, producers of Parian china, a fine, eggshell-thin, ivory porcelain shaped into dishes, figurines, vases, and baskets. There's a factory, showroom, exhibition, museum, and café. On tours of the factory you can get up close and talk to craftsmen—there's hardly any noise coming from machinery in the workshops. Everything here is made by hand in the same method used in 1857. The showroom is filled with beautiful but pricey gifts: a cup-and-saucer set costs about £16, and a bowl in a basket-weave style (typical of Belleek) runs £69 and up. For a history of the legend and beauty of this coveted porcelain, see the Close-Up box, "Blessed with Lasting Happiness: Belleek China." ☎ *028/6865–8501 ⊕ www.belleek. ie ☑ £4 ⊙ Apr.–June, Sept., and Oct., weekdays 9–5:30, Sat. 10–5:30, Sun. 2–6; July and Aug., weekdays 9–8, Sat. 10–6, Sun. 11–6; Nov.–Mar., weekdays 10–5:30.*

Enniskillen

❸❾ *5 km (3 mi) south of Devenish Island, Lower Lough Erne, on A32.*

Enniskillen is the pleasant, smart-looking capital of County Fermanagh and the only place of any size in the county. The town center is, strikingly, on an island in the River Erne between Lower and Upper Lough Erne. The principal thoroughfares, Townhall and High Streets, are crowded with old-style pubs and rows of redbrick Georgian flats. The tall, dark spires of the 19th-century St. Michael's and St. MacArtin's cathedrals, both on Church Street, tower over the leafy town center. Among the several relaxed and welcoming old pubs in Enniskillen's town center, the one with the most appeal is **Blake's of the Hollow** on the main street, a place hardly altered since it opened in 1887. Its name derives from the fact that the heart of the town lies in a slight hollow and the pub's landlord is named William Blake (don't ask, he's not related to the English poet, painter, and engraver). ⊠ *6 Church St., Co. Fermanagh* ☎ *028/6632–2143.*

Enniskillen's main sight is the waterfront **Enniskillen Castle,** one of the best-preserved monuments in the North. Built by the Maguire clan in 1670, this stronghold houses the local history collection of the Fermanagh County Museum and the polished paraphernalia of the Royal Inniskilling Fusiliers Regimental Museum. A Heritage Centre also stands within the curtilage of the castle. ⊠ *Castlebarracks, Co. Fermanagh* ☎ *028/6632–5000 ⊕ www.enniskillencastle.co.uk ☑ £2 ⊙ Jan.–Apr. and Oct.–late Dec., Mon. 2–5, Tues.–Fri. 10–5; May, June, and Sept., Mon. and Sat. 2–5, Tues.–Fri. 10–5; July and Aug., Mon. and weekends 2–5, Tues.–Fri. 10–5.*

At the Erne riverside, the 16th-century **Water Gate,** between two handsome turrets, protected the town from invading armies. Beyond the West

Bridge is **Portora Royal School,** established in 1608 by King James I. On the grounds are some ruins of Portora Castle. Among writers educated here are Samuel Beckett and Oscar Wilde, the pride of the school (until his trial for homosexuality).

Where to Stay & Eat

$$ 🏨 **The Manor House Hotel.** On the shores of Lower Lough Erne, this stately 19th-century manor harks back to a more tranquil age. Romantic canopied four-poster beds and traditional floral patterns await guests in the hotel's bedrooms, but be sure to ask for a room at the back so you can savor stunning views of the lakelands. Heavy linen napkins and silver cutlery add the finishing touches to the very good, if slightly formal, manor restaurant, presided over by the ambitious chef Jean-Michel Maquet. Why not take advantage of the excellent golf and fishing facilities and ask the friendly staff to book you a seat on the hotel's boat, the grandly-named Lady of the Lake for a cruise of Lough Erne? The idyllic location contributes to the hotel's laid-back relaxing air: sip a cocktail (or two) in the Belleek bar before dinner and you won't fail toun-wind. ⊠ *7 mi north-west of Enniskillen, Killadeas, County Fermanagh* ☎ *028/6862–2200* 🖷 *028/6862–1545* ⊕ *www.manor-house-hotel.com* ⤴ *81 rooms* ⌂ *Restaurant, 9-hole golf course, tennis court, indoor pool, health club, hot tub, sauna, fishing, boating, 2 bars, Internet; no a/c* ▭ *AE, MC, V* 🍴 *BP, MAP.*

Florence Court

★ ⑳   *11 km (7 mi) south of Enniskillen on A4 and A32.*

When it comes to Early Irish Georgian houses, there are few as magical as Florence Court. Less known than some showier estates, this three-story Anglo-Irish mansion was built around 1730 for John Cole, father of the first earl of Enniskillen. Topped off about 1760 with its distinctive two flanking colonnaded wings, the central house is adorably adorned with a positive surfeit of Palladian windows, keystones, and balustrades thanks to, as one architectural historian put it, "the vaingloriousness of a provincial hand." Even more impressive is its bucolically baroque setting, as the Cuilcagh Mountains form a wonderful contrast to the shimmering white stone facade. Up to five years ago, the house—victim of a disastrous fire in the 1950s—was barely furnished, but a magnificent National Trust restoration as well as a 1988 legacy left by the last countess of Enniskillen have now returned many family heirlooms to these interiors. Showstoppers in terms of decor are the Rococo plasterwork ceilings in the dining room; the Venetian Room; and the famous staircase, all ascribed to Robert West, one of Dublin's most famous stuccadores (plaster workers). For a peek at the "downstairs" world, check of the restored kitchen and other service quarters. Outside, the ancestral park is one of Northern Ireland's glories—dotted with noted heirloom trees (including the Florence Court weeping beech), it also has nooks and dells where, legend has it, you can hear the "song of the little people." ⊠ *11 km (7 mi) south of Enniskillen on A4 and A32, Co. Fermanagh* ☎ *028/6634–8249* ⊕ *www.nationaltrust.org.uk* 🎟 *£4* ⊙ *Grounds Oct.–Apr., daily 10–4; May–Sept., daily 10–8; man-*

sion Mar.–May and Sept., weekends 12–6; June, weekdays 1–6, weekends 12–6; July and Aug., daily 12–6.

Castle Coole

★ ㊶ *3 km (2 mi) east of Enniskillen on A4.*

In the 18th century and through most of the 19th, the Loughs of Erne and their environs were remote places far from Ireland's bustling cities. But it was just this isolated green and watery countryside that attracted the Anglo-Irish gentry, who built grand houses. This "uncommonly perfect" mansion (to quote the eminent architectural historian Desmond Guinness) is on its own landscaped oak woods and gardens at the end of a long tree-lined driveway. Although the Irish architect Richard Johnston made the original drawings in the 1790s, and was responsible for the foundation, the castle was, for all intents and purposes, the work of James Wyatt, commissioned by the first Earl of Belmore (whose family was related to the Counts of Enniskillen, who built Florence Court). One of the best-known architects of his time, Wyatt was based in London but only visited Ireland once, so Alexander Stewart was drafted as the resident builder-architect who oversaw much of the construction. The designer wasn't the only imported element; in fact, much of Castle Coole came from England, including the main facade, which is clad in Portland stone shipped from Dorset to Ballyshannon and then hauled here by horse and cart. And what a facade it is—in perfect symmetry, white colonnaded wings extend from either side of the mansion's three-story, nine-bay center block, with a Palladian central portico and pediment. It is perhaps the apotheosis of the 18th century's reverence for the Greeks.

Inside, the house is remarkably preserved; most of the lavish plasterwork and original furnishings are in place. On its completion in September 1798, the construction had cost £70,000 and the furnishings another £22,000, compared to the £6 million cost of a restoration in 1995–96, during which anything not in keeping with the original design was removed. The saloon is one of the finest rooms in the house, with a vast expanse of oak flooring, gilded Regency furniture, and gray scagliola pilasters with Corinthian capitals. The present earl of Belmore still lives on the estate and uses one wing of the house. He often attends the public concerts that are held here during the summer months. ✉ *Dublin Rd. (A4), Co. Fermanagh* ☎ *028/6632–2690* ⊕ *www.nationaltrust. org.uk* 🖼 *Grounds free, mansion £4* ☉ *Grounds Oct.–Apr., daily 10–4; May–Sept. daily 10–8; mansion Mar.–May and Sept., weekends 12–6; June, Wed.–Mon. 12–6; July–Aug., daily 12–6.*

Armagh

㊷ *74 km (42 mi) east of Castle Coole.*

The spiritual capital of Ireland for 5,000 years, and the seat of both Protestant and Catholic archbishops, Armagh is the most venerated of Irish cities. St. Patrick called it "my sweet hill" and built his stone church on the hill where the Anglican cathedral now stands. On the opposite hill, the twin-spired Catholic cathedral is flanked by two large marble statues of archbishops who look across the land. Despite the pleasing Georgian terraces around the elegant Mall east of the town center, Armagh can seem drab. Having suffered as a trouble spot in the sectarian conflict, though, it's now the scene of some spirited and sympathetic renovation.

The **Astronomy Centre and Planetarium** is undergoing a major one- to three-year refurbishment. It contains models of spacecraft, video shows of the sky, and hands-on computer displays. The Earthorium explores the world from three levels—its interior, surface, and atmosphere. The outdoor 30-acre AstroPark has a model solar system. At press time, the 16-inch telescope as well as the Robinson Dome, also known as "the 10-inch dome" for the 1875 Grub telescope it houses, were both closed until further notice. ⊠ *College Hill, Co. Armagh* ☎ *028/3752–3689* ⊕ *www.armaghplanet.com* ⊠ *AstroPark and Robinson Dome free; Earthorium £1; special shows and other exhibitions £3* ☉ *Weekdays 2–4:45; check for new schedule after facility reopens.*

The pale limestone, Gothic **St. Patrick's Roman Catholic Cathedral,** the seat of a Roman Catholic archdiocese, rises above a hill to dominate the north end of Armagh. Inside, the rather gloomy interior is enlivened by a magnificent organ whose potential is fully realized at services. Construction of the twin-spired Cathedral started in 1840 in the neo-Gothic style, but the Great Famine brought work to a halt until 1854. It was finally completed in 1873. An arcade of statues over the main doorway on the exterior is one of the cathedral's most interesting features. The altar is solid Irish granite and the woodwork is Austrian oak. ⊠ *Hilltop, Co. Armagh* ☎ *028/3752–3142* ⊕ *www.armagharchdiocese.org.*

Near the town center, a squat, battlement tower identifies **St. Patrick's Anglican Cathedral,** in simple, early-19th-century, low-Gothic style. It stands on the site of much older churches and contains several relics of Armagh's long history, including sculpted, pre-Christian idols. Brian Boru, the High King (king of all Ireland) who visited Armagh in 1004—and was received with great ceremony—is buried here. In 1014, at the Battle of Clontarf, he drove the Vikings out of Ireland—but was killed after the battle was won. Inside are memorials and tombs by important 18th-century sculptors such as Roubilliac and Rysbrack. ⊠ *Abbey St., Co. Armagh* ⊕ *www. stpatricks-cathedral.org* ⊠ *Free* ☉ *Tours June–Aug., Mon.–Sat. 11:30 and 2:30.*

Past the 13th-century Franciscan friary ruins, in the stables of the former archbishop's demesne, the **Palace Stables Heritage Centre** presents a diorama of everyday life—upstairs and downstairs—in the 18th-century days of the extremely wealthy Richard Robinson. Baron Rokeby was this man's ancestral title but he was best known as the region's archbishop of the Church of Ireland. He commissioned local architect Francis Johnston, who had designed much of Georgian Dublin, to create a new Armagh out of the slums into which it had degenerated. The archbishop gave the city a clean water supply and a sewer system, then turned the city's racecourse into an elegant mall. He paved and lit the streets; financed improvements to the Bishop's Palace and the Protestant cathedral; and endowed the public library, the observatory, the Royal School, and the county infirmary. ☒ *Palace Demesne, Friary Rd., Co. Armagh* ☏ *028/3752–9629* ☐ *£4* ☉ *Apr.–Aug., Mon.–Sat. 10–5, Sun. 1–6; Sept.–Mar., Mon.–Sat. 10–5, Sun. 2–5.*

Just outside Armagh, **Navan Fort** is Ulster's Camelot—the region's ancient capital. Excavations date evidence of activity going back to 700 BC. The fort has strong associations with figures of Irish history. Legend has it that thousands of years ago this was the site of the palace of Queen Macha; subsequent tales call it the barracks of the legendary Ulster warrior Cuchulainn and his Red Branch Knights. Remains dating from 94 BC are particularly intriguing: a great conical structure, 120 feet in diameter, was formed from five concentric circles made of 275 wooden posts, with a 276th, about 12 yards high, situated in the center. In a ritual whose meaning is not known, it was filled with brushwood and set on fire. ☒ *3 km (2 mi) west of Armagh on A28, Co. Armagh* ☐ *Free.*

off the beaten path

LINEN GREEN – Looking for a bargain? Venture north to Linen Green, an outlet mall where you can purchase clothing, lingerie, shoes, gifts, and furniture. You can buy woven items from well-known producers—such as Paul Costelloe, Ulster Weavers, Foxford, and Anne Storey—at a discount. ☒ *20 km (12 mi) north of Armagh off A29, Moygashel, Co. Armagh* ☏ *028/8775–3761* ⊕ *www. linengreen.com* ☉ *Mon.–Sat. 10–5.*

The Mountains of Mourne

43 *52½ km (32½ mi) southeast of Armagh on A28, 51 km (32 mi) south of Belfast.*

Subjects of a song that is sung on every Irish occasion from baptism to funerals, the Mountains of Mourne must surely qualify as one of Ireland's best-known ranges. According to those lyrics by Percy French, the Mountains of Mourne "sweep down to the sea," from 2,000-foot summits. East of the unprepossessing border town of Newry, this area was long considered ungovernable, its hardy inhabitants living from smuggling contraband into the numerous rocky coves on the seashore. Much of the Mourne range is still inaccessible except on foot. The countryside is gorgeous: high, windswept pasture and moorland threaded with bright streams, bound by a tracery of drystone walls, and dotted with sheep and whitewashed farmhouses snuggled in stands of sycamore. It's the perfect landscape for away-from-it-all walkers, cyclists, and serious climbers. Climbers should inform their hotel when and where they're going before setting off.

en route

Driving from Armagh to the Mountains of Mourne, take a detour off A2 and follow B133, on the right, south of Markethill. This will lead you through a rustic, drumlin landscape of vivid green pastures. The appearance of villages changes as you return toward the River Bann; houses and farms begin to resemble those of Britain rather than those in the Republic.

The road to the **Silent Valley** reservoir park leads to mountain views and excellent photo-ops. ✉ *6 km (4 mi) north of Kilkeel off B27, right turn, Co. Down* ☎ *028/9074–6581* 🖃 *Vehicles £3, pedestrians £2* ⊙ *June–Aug., daily 10–6:30; Sept.–May, daily 10–4.*

Newcastle, a bracing Victorian cold-water bathing station, is the main center for visitors to the hills. Looming above Newcastle is **Slieve Donard,** its panoramic, 2,805-foot-high summit grandly claiming views into England, Wales, and Scotland "when it's clear enough"—in other words, "rarely," say the pessimists. It is not possible to drive up the mountain so leave your car in Donard car park. It should take roughly three hours to climb to the summit of the mountain and no longer than two hours to descend. Experienced hikers should not find it difficult but if you prefer an easier trek, follow the trails signposted in Tollymore Forest Park. Hiking boots are essential and, as the weather can be unpredictable, it is advisable to take an extra layer of clothing, even in summer. Covering 1,200 acres and entered through picturesque Gothic gateways, **Tollymore Forest Park** extends up the valley of the River Shimna. Many pretty stone bridges cross over the sparkling waters here. ✉ *Tullybrannigan Rd., Newcastle, Co. Down* ☎ *028/4372–2428* ⊕ *www.forestserviceni.gov.uk* 🖃 *Vehicles £4, pedestrians £2* ⊙ *Daily 10–dusk.*

A huge maze, grown to symbolize the convoluted path to peace, is the latest addition to **Castlewellan Forest Park,** which comprises 1,150 acres of forested hills running between the Mourne Mountains and Slieve Croob. With the maze, lake, secluded arbors, and arboretum, the park makes an excellent introduction to the area. ✉ *Castlewellan, Co. Down* ☎ *028/4377–8664* ⊕ *www.forestserviceni.gov.uk* 🖃 *Vehicles £4, pedestrians £2* ⊙ *Daily 10–dusk.*

Where to Stay

$$$$ 🏨 **Slieve Donard Hotel.** A lavish redbrick monument to Victoriana, this turreted hotel stands like a palace on green lawns at one end of Newcastle's 6½-km (4-mi) sandy beach. The traditional furnishings may make you feel as if you're stepping back to the town's turn-of-the-20th-century heyday as an elegant seaside resort (though the rooms have modern comforts). Ask for a room overlooking the water. At the entrance to the grounds, the Percy French gatehouse restaurant serves adequate seafood dishes; there's music Friday and Saturday night. The Royal County Down Golf Club is next door, and the hotel has two exercise rooms. ✉ *Downs Rd., Newcastle, Co. Down BT33 0AH* ☎ *028/4372–1066* 🖶 *028/4372–1166* ⊕ *www.hastingshotels.com* 🛏 *124 rooms* ♨ *2 restaurants, indoor pool, 2 gyms, hair salon, hot tub, spa, steam room, bar, helipad; no a/c* 🖃 *AE, DC, MC, V* ⦿ *BP, MAP.*

$$–$$$ 🏨 **Burrendale Hotel & Country Club.** Thanks to the hotel's owners, the Small family, this low-slung modern building, shaded by clumps of beech, is one of the most relaxing establishments on the north's east coast. Staff members are cheery, and bedrooms are decorated in quiet tones. Chefs at the Cottage Kitchen and Vine restaurants are competent (the former is casual, the latter more formal) and clearly aim to please the locals, who like their plates overflowing. ✉ *51 Castlewellan Rd., Newcastle, Co. Down BT33 0JY* ☎ *028/4372–2599* 🖶 *028/4372–2328*

⊕ *www.burrendale.com* ↩ *69 rooms* ♿ *2 restaurants, indoor pool, gym, hot tub, sauna, steam room, 2 bars, Internet, meeting rooms; no a/c* ▭ *AE, DC, MC, V* ¶ *BP, MAP.*

$$–$$$ 🏨 **Glassdrumman Lodge.** For those who wish to be pampered as well as immersed in the ancient Kingdom of Mourne, Graeme and Joan Hall's eclectically simple and stylish lodge is the place. The outside of the house is less than spectacular, but the busy estate has more than enough drama to compensate, for the family grows their own crops, raises their own farm animals, churns their own butter, and bakes their own bread. Rooms are decorated in bright colors and have large windows with glorious views. ✉ *Mill Rd., Annalong, Co. Down BT34 4RH* ☎ *028/ 4376–8451* 🖷 *028/4376–7041* ↩ *10 rooms, 2 suites* ♿ *Restaurant, laundry service, business services; no a/c* ▭ *AE, DC, MC, V* ¶ *BP.*

Sports & the Outdoors

Tollymore Mountain Centre (✉ Bryansford, Newcastle, Co. Down ☎ 028/ 4372–2158) provides advice on mountain climbing and trails. The **Royal County Down** (✉ Off A2, Newcastle, Co. Down ☎ 028/4372–3314 ⊕ www.royalcountydown.org) is considered by many golfers to be one of the finest courses in the world. Between April and October, a game on the Championship Links can run up to £105; the Annesley Links top at £28.

Downpatrick

④④ *21 km (18 mi) east of Newcastle on A2 and A25.*

Downpatrick once was called "Plain and Simple Down" but had its name changed by John de Courcy, a Norman knight who moved to the town in 1176. De Courcy set about promoting St. Patrick, the 5th-century Briton who was captured by the Irish and served as a slave in the Down area before he escaped to France, where he learned about Christianity and bravely returned to try to convert the local chiefs. Although it is not true that Patrick brought a new faith to Ireland—there was already a bishop of Ireland before Patrick got here—he must have been a better missionary than most because he did indeed win influential converts. The clan chief of the Down area gave him land at the village of Saul, near Downpatrick, to build a monastery.

Down Cathedral is one of the disputed burial places of St. Patrick. In the churchyard, a somber slab inscribed "Patric" is supposedly the saint's tomb, but no one knows where he is actually buried. It might be here, at Saul, or, some scholars argue, more likely at Armagh. The church, which lay ruined from 1538 to 1790 (it reopened in 1818), preserves parts of some of the earlier churches and monasteries that have stood on this site, the oldest of which dates back to the 6th century. Even by then, the cathedral site had long been an important fortified settlement: Down takes its name from the Celtic word "dun," or fort. ✉ *Hilltop, Co. Down* ⊕ *www.cathedraldown.anglican.org* 🎟 *Free.*

For some hard facts concerning the patron saint of Ireland, visit the interactive exhibits of **St. Patrick Centre** next to the cathedral; It's housed, together with the Down Museum, inside a former 18th-century jail. The ancient myths and stories of early Christian Ireland are brought to life in this information center. Using cutting-edge exhibition technology, you can explore how St. Patrick's legacy developed in early Christian times and examine the art and metalwork which was produced during this "Golden Age." Younger children will love the puppet shows detailing the life of the saint and can even paint their own Book of Kells, with quills. The Grove art gallery exhibits jewelry, textiles, and paintings by local artists and craftsmen. If the weather is fine, have lunch on the terrace of the Cathedral Garden restaurant, with its dramatic views of Down Cathedral and the Mountains of Mourne. ⊠ *The Mall, Co. Down* ☎ *028/4461–9000* ⊕ *www.saintpatrickcentre.com* ⊠ *£5* ☉ *Oct.–Mar., Mon.–Sat. 10–5; Apr., May, and Sept., Mon.–Sat. 9:30–5:30, Sun. 1–5:30; June–Aug., Mon.–Sat. 9:30–7, Sun. 10–6.*

Where to Stay & Eat

★ $ ✕▥ **Dufferin Arms Coaching Inn.** Stewart and Morris Crawford preside over this 1803 inn next to Killyleagh Castle. Rooms in the bright-red Georgian building are luxurious, with four-poster beds. Downstairs, the original stables have been converted into the Kitchen Restaurant ($–$$), which sometimes hosts medieval feasts. It specializes in Irish cooking—the poached salmon and the roast duck in cherry sauce are two best bets. One of the bars has snugs, another an open fire. Diversions such as pub quizzes and Cajun and jazz music keep things lively. ⊹ *10 km (6 mi) north of Downpatrick* ⊠ *31–33 High St., Killyleagh, Co. Down BT30 9QF* ☎ *028/4482–8229* 🖷 *028/4482–8755* ⊕ *www.dufferincoachinginn. co.uk* ⮂ *6 rooms with bath* ⌂ *Restaurant, 3 bars, Internet, meeting rooms; no a/c* ▤ *AE, MC, V* ⊺◎⊦ *BP.*

Castle Ward

★ ㊺   *11 km (7 mi) northeast of Downpatrick, 3 km (2 mi) west of Strangford village on A25, on southern shore of Strangford Lough, entrance by Ballyculter Lodge*

They really had the life, those old aristos. With a 500-acre park, an artificial lake, a Neoclassical tempietto, and a vast house in Bath stone magically set on the slopes running down to the "Narrows" of the southern shore of Strangford Lough, Castle Ward must have been some place to call home. About two miles from the village of Strangford, off the road to Downpatrick, this regal stately home was designed around 1760 in, rather famously, two differing styles. Bernard Ward, 1st Viscount Bangor, could rarely see eye to eye (gossip had it) with his wife, Lady Anne, and the result was that he decided to make the entrance front and salons elegant exercises in Palladian Neoclassism, while milady transformed the garden facade and her own rooms using the most fashionable style of the day, Strawberry Hill Gothick. His white and beige Music Room is picked out in exquisite plasterwork (note how craftsmen decided to save a little money by taking objects, such as a tricorn hat and basket, and simply covering them in plaster), while her Boudoir has an undulating fan-vaulted ceiling that conjures up the "gothick" medievalisms of King Henry VII's chapel at Westminster. In point of fact, the couple's contre-temps were dinner-table hearsay and they actually got along famously. In point of fact, the Gothic style was used to beef up the ancestral image of a "Castle" Ward. After the estate fell into ruin (one Ward descendant resorted to selling bread at the estate gate), the Victorian era ushered in new wealth and the house today sparkles, no more so than during the summer evenings when it becomes Ireland's Glyndebourne and hosts opera performances in its small private theater. Be sure to walk through the park (which has its own Wildlife Center) to enjoy the wonderful vistas overlooking the waters to the town of Portaferry and the Ards Peninsula. ⊠ *1 mile west of Strangford on the Downpatrick Rd. (A25)* ☎ *028/4488–1204* ⊕ *www. nationaltrust.org.uk/main* 🎫 *£4.70* ☉ *July–Aug., daily 12–6; Sept.–June, Sat.–Sun. 12–6.*

Lisburn

 38 km (22 mi) northwest of Downpatrick, 9 km (6 mi) southwest of Belfast.

In the 18th, 19th, and early 20th centuries, linen, a natural fabric woven from the fibers of the flax plant, was the basis of Ulster's most important industry—and thus of much of its folk history and song. A century ago, 240,000 acres were given over to flax, whose pretty blue flowers sparkle for just a week in early July. Four hundred acres were designated as "bleach greens," where the woven fabric whitened in the summer sun. Eventually, American cotton and Egyptian flax killed off the mass-production linen trade, which had been centered on Lisburn, in mills powered by the River Lagan. What now survives of the linen industry does so by producing high-quality designer fabrics, plus traditional expensive damask. Today at the **Irish Linen Centre and Lisburn Museum,** a series of rooms traces this history. Weaving is demonstrated on a turn-of-the-20th-century hand loom (although the attached shop has a disappointing choice of linen goods). ⊠ *12 km (8 mi) southwest of Belfast, Market Sq.* ☎ *028/9266–3377* 🎫 *Free* ☉ *Mon.–Sat. 9:30–5.*

NORTHERN IRELAND A TO Z

To research prices, get advice from other travelers, and book travel arrangements, visit www.fodors.com.

AIR TRAVEL
Scheduled services from the United States and Canada are mostly routed through Dublin, Glasgow, London, or Manchester.

Frequent services to Belfast's two airports are scheduled throughout the day from London Heathrow, London Gatwick, and Luton (all of which have fast coordinated subway or rail connections to central London) and from 17 other U.K. airports. Flights from London take about one hour. Aer Arann flies twice daily from Dublin to Belfast on weekdays. British Airways flies to Belfast and Derry from Manchester, Glasgow, and Dublin. British Midland Airways flies from Belfast International and Belfast City to London Heathrow. British European Airways flies from Belfast City to Gatwick and London City Airport. EasyJet flies from Belfast

International to Amsterdam, Bristol, Edinburgh, Glasgow, Liverpool, Luton, and Stansted.

🚹 Carriers **Aer Arann** ☎ 081/821-0210 or 0800/587-2324 ⊕ www.aerarann.ie. **Aer Lingus** ☎ 0845/084-4444 ⊕ www.aerlingus.com. **British Airways** ☎ 0845/773-3377 ⊕ www.britishairways.com. **British European Airways** ☎ 0870/567-6676 or 089/092-5532 ⊕ www.flybe.com. **British Midland Airways** ☎ 0870/607-0555 ⊕ www.flybmi.com. **EasyJet** ☎ 0870/600-0000 ⊕ www.easyjet.com.

AIRPORTS

Belfast International Airport at Aldergove is the north's principal air-rival point, 30½ km (19 mi) north of town. Belfast City Airport is the secondary airport, 6½ km (4 mi) east of the city. It receives flights from U.K. provincial airports, from London's Gatwick and Heathrow, and from Stanstead and Luton (both near London). City of Derry Airport is 8 km (5 mi) from Derry and receives flights from Dublin, Glasgow, and Manchester.

🚹 Airport Information **Belfast City Airport** ☎ 028/9093-9093 ⊕ www.belfastcityairport.com. **Belfast International Airport at Aldergove** ☎ 028/9448-4848 ⊕ www.bial.co.uk. **City of Derry Airport** ☎ 028/7181-0784 ⊕ www.cityofderryairport.com.

TRANSFERS Ulsterbus operates a bus every half hour (one-way £6, round-trip £9) between Belfast International Airport and Belfast city center, as well as between Belfast City Airport and the city center (one-way £2). Contact Translink for information on all buses. From Belfast City Airport, you can also travel into Belfast by train from Sydenham Halt to Central Station or catch a taxi from the airport to your hotel. If you arrive at the City of Derry Airport, you may need to call a taxi to get to your destination.

🚹 **Eglinton Taxis** ☎ 028/7181-1231. **Delta Cabs** ☎ 028/7127-9999. **Foyle Taxis** ☎ 028/7126-3905. **Translink** ☎ 028/9066-6630 ⊕ www.translink.co.uk.

BOAT & FERRY TRAVEL

Norse Merchant Ferries has 11-hour daytime or overnight car ferries that connect Belfast with the English west-coast port of Liverpool every day. P&O European Ferries has a one-hour sailing to Larne from Cairnryan, Scotland; infrequent trains take passengers on to Belfast. The *Sea-Cat* high-speed catamaran sails between Belfast and Troon in Scotland, between Belfast and Glasgow, and between the Isle of Man and Belfast. The *StenaLine HSS* fast catamaran sails between Belfast and Stranraer, Scotland in 1½ hours.

🚹 Boat & Ferry Information **Norse Merchant Ferries** ✉ Victoria Terminal 2, West Bank Rd., Belfast ☎ 028/9077-9090 ⊕ www.norsemerchant.com. **P&O European Ferries** ☎ 0870/242-4777 ⊕ www.poirishsea.com. **SeaCat and Steam Packet Company Services** ☎ 0870/552-3523 ⊕ www.seacat.co.uk. *StenaLine HSS* ☎ 028/9074-7747 ⊕ www.stenaline.com.

BUS TRAVEL

Northern Ireland's main bus company, Ulsterbus, runs direct service between Dublin and Belfast. Queries about Ulsterbus service, or any other bus and rail transportation in Northern Ireland, can be answered by the national central reservation center, Translink. The Republic's Bus Éireann runs direct services to Belfast from Dublin. Buses arrive at and depart from Belfast's Europa Buscentre; the ride takes three hours. Buses to Belfast also run from London and from Birmingham, making the Stranraer ferry crossing.

You can take advantage of frequent and inexpensive Ulsterbus links between all Northern Ireland towns. In Belfast, the Europa Buscentre is just behind the Europa Hotel. The Laganside Buscentre is around the corner from Belfast's Albert Clock Tower and about 1 km (½ mi) from Central Station. Within Belfast the city bus service is comprehensive. All routes start from Donegall Square, where there's a kiosk with timetables.

🚌 Bus Depot **Europa Central Buscentre** ✉ Great Victoria St., Golden Mile, Belfast ☎ 028/9066-6630. **Laganside Buscentre** ✉ Oxford St., Central District Belfast ☎ 028/ 9066-663.

🚌 Bus Lines **Bus Éireann** ☎ 01/836-6111 in Dublin ⊕ www.buseireann.ie. **Translink** ☎ 028/9066-6630 ⊕ www.translink.co.uk.

FARES If you want to tour the north by bus, contact Translink: a Freedom of Northern Ireland Ticket allows unlimited travel on bus or train (£12 per day, £30 for three days, and £45 per week). An Irish Rover bus ticket from Ulsterbus covers Ireland, north and south, and costs £42 for 3 days, £93 for 8, and £145 for 15. An Emerald Card (bus and rail) costs £124 for 8 days and £214 for 15 days.

CAR RENTAL

You can choose among several rental companies, but renting a car won't be cheap. A compact car costs £150–£250 per week (including taxes, insurance, and unlimited mileage). If you're planning to take a rental car across the border into the Republic, inform the company and check its insurance procedures. Main rental offices include Avis, Dan Dooley, Europcar, Ford, and Hertz. A £300 security deposit is required at the Ford agency in Derry, and a £500 to £750 security deposit is required by Hertz.

🚗 Agencies **Avis** ✉ Belfast International Airport, Belfast ☎ 028/9442-2333 or 0870/ 606-0100 ✉ Belfast City Airport, Belfast ☎ 0870/606-0100 ✉ Great Victoria St., Belfast ☎ 028/9024-0404. **Dan Dooley** ✉ Belfast International Airport, Belfast ☎ 028/ 9445-2522 ⊕ www.dandooley.com. **Europcar** ✉ Belfast International Airport, Belfast ☎ 028/9442-3444 or 0800/068-0303 ✉ Belfast City Airport, Belfast ☎ 028/9045-0904 or 0800/068-0303 ⊕ www.europcar.ie. **Ford** ✉ Desmond Motors, City of Derry Airport, Derry ☎ 028/7181-2222. **Hertz** ✉ Belfast International Airport, Belfast ☎ 028/ 9442-2533 ✉ Belfast City Airport, Belfast ☎ 020/9073-2451.

CAR TRAVEL

Many roads from the Irish Republic into Northern Ireland were once closed for security reasons, but all are now reinstated, leaving you with a choice of legitimate crossing points. Army checkpoints at approved frontier posts are rare, and few customs formalities are observed. The fast N1/A1 road connects Belfast to Dublin in 160 km (100 mi) with an average driving time of just over two hours. In general, roads here are in much better shape and signposted more clearly than in the Irish Republic.

PARKING Belfast has many parking garages, as well as street meter-ticket parking. Before parking on the street, check the posted regulations: during rush hours many spots become no-parking.

TRAFFIC Bad rush-hour delays can occur on the West Link in Belfast joining M1 (heading south or west) and M2 (heading east or north). But on the whole, driving is quicker and easier in the north than in areas south of the border.

CONSULATES

🏴 Canada **Canadian Consulate** ⊠ 35 The Hill, Groomsport, Co. Down BT19 6JS ☎ 028/9127-2060.

🏴 New Zealand **New Zealand Consulate** ⊠ New Balance House, 118A Lisburn Rd., Glenavy, Co. Antrim BT29 4NY ☎ 028/9264-8098.

🏴 United States **United States Consulate** ⊠ Danesfort House, 223 Stranmillis Rd., University area, Belfast ☎ 028/9038-6100 ⊕ www.usembassy.org.uk.

EMERGENCIES

The general emergency number is 999. Belfast City Hospital and the Royal Victoria Hospital are the two Belfast hospitals with emergency rooms. Altnagelvin Hospital in Derry has an emergency room.

🏴 **Altnagelvin Hospital** ⊠ Glenshana Rd., On the outskirts of East Derry ☎ 028/7134-5171. **Ambulance, coast guard, fire, police** ⊠ 999. **Belfast City Hospital** ⊠ Lisburn Rd., University Area, Belfast ☎ 028/9032-9241. **Belfast's main police station** ⊠ 6-10 N. Queen St., Central District, Belfast ☎ 028/9065-0222. **Royal Victoria Hospital** ⊠ Grosvenor Rd., West Belfast ☎ 028/9024-0503.

MONEY MATTERS

The north uses British currency. Euros are rarely accepted. You may sometimes be given bank notes, drawn on Ulster banks. Be sure not to get stuck with a lot of these when you leave, because they are accepted with reluctance, if at all, in the rest of the United Kingdom and will be difficult to change at banks back home.

Main banks are open weekdays 9:30–4:30, smaller branches weekdays 10:30–3:30. Changing money outside banking hours is possible at Thomas Cook branches. The branch at Belfast Airport is open daily 6:45 AM–8 PM; the branch at Donegall Place is open from Monday through Wednesday, Friday, and Saturday 9–5:30, Thursday 10–5:30. You can also change bills at Travelex Worldwide Money.

🏴 Currency Exchange **Thomas Cook** ⊠ 11 Donegall Pl., Central District, Belfast ☎ 028/9088-3900 ⊕ www.thomascook.com. **Travelex Worldwide Money** ⊠ Belfast International Airport, Belfast ☎ 028/9444-7500 ⊕ www.travelex.co.uk.

TOURS

BIKE TOURS Irish Cycle Tours gives tours of Belfast (£12 singles, £20 couples) Saturday to Thursday at 6:30 PM and Sunday at 10 AM. They also organize 4- and 8-day tours of the Mournes, Glens of Antrim, and Causeway Coasts, and the Sperrin Mountains and Donegal.

🏴 Bike Touring **Irish Cycle Tours** ☎ 028/9064-2222 ⊕ www.irishcycletours.com.

BIRD-WATCHING Murphy's Wildlife Tours leads tours in all seasons, though if you're an TOURS advanced birder, you may want to concentrate on wintering wildfowl and waders that have migrated all the way from North America to the shores of Loughs Foyle, Neagh, and Strangford. Northern Ireland Tourist Information Offices and the Royal Society for the Protection of Birds can provide birding information.

🏠**Murphy's Wildlife Tours** ✉ Belvoir Park, 12 Belvoir Close, East Belfast, Belfast ☎ 028/9069-3232. **Royal Society for the Protection of Birds** ✉ Belvoir Park Forest, East Belfast, Belfast ☎ 028/9049-1547.

BOAT TOURS On the Lower Lough Erne, Erne Tours operates an approximately two-hour-long trip (£7) aboard the *Kestrel,* a 63-seat water bus, which leaves Round O Pier at Enniskillen daily May and June at 2:30, and daily July and August at 10:30, 2:15, and 4:15. Weekdays the boat stops for a half hour at Devenish Island. In September, tours leave Tuesday, Saturday, and Sunday at 2:30. Mid-May to mid-September, the company also has a Saturday evening dinner cruise departing at 6:30.

🏠**Erne Tours** ✉ Round O Pier, Enniskillen ☎ 028/6632-2882, 028/6632-4822 for dinner cruise.

BUS TOURS Citybus (contact via Translink) in Belfast has three tours. The Belfast City Tour (£9) covers the Harland and Wolff shipyard, City Hall, Queen's University, the Ulster Museum, Botanic Gardens, and the Grand Opera House. Tours leave Castle Place Monday and Friday at 11 AM and take 1½ hours. The Living History Tour (£5) passes Loyalist and Nationalist political wall murals, City Hall, the Odyssey complex, and the Waterfront Hall. It leaves Castle Place Monday to Saturday at 2:30. The Titanic Tour (£5) is both a walking and bus tour that leaves Wednesday at 11 AM and Sundays at 2:30, also from Castle Place.

Ulsterbus operates half-day or full-day trips June through September from Belfast to the Glens of Antrim, the Giant's Causeway, the Fermanagh lakes, Lough Neagh, the Mountains of Mourne, and the Ards Peninsula. Ulsterbus has also teamed up with the Old Bushmills Distillery to run the Bushmills Bus: an open-top tour bus running from Coleraine (via Bushmills to observe whiskey-making) to the Giant's Causeway and the coastal resorts. Contact Ulsterbus through Translink.

MiniCoach operates day tours of Belfast (£8–£12), and to the Giant's Causeway, Bushmills Distillery, and Carrickfergus.

🏠**MiniCoach** ✉ 22 Donegall Rd., Central District, Belfast ☎ 028/9032-4733 ⊕ www.minicoachni.co.uk. **Translink** ☎ 028/9066-6630 ⊕ www.translink.co.uk.

TAXI TOURS Belfast Cab Tours does 90-minute tours in a London-style black taxi of either Loyalist or Nationalist sights. The cost is £7 each for four or more, or £25 per taxi if three or less. Black Taxi Tours provide a similar itinerary at £8 per person for three or more, and £20 per taxi for one or two people. The Loyalist tours leave from North Street or Bridge Street; the Nationalist Tours pick you up at your hotel.

🏠**Belfast Cab Tours** ☎ 078/1003-3831 ⊕ www.belfastcabtours.com. **Black Taxi Tours** ☎ 078/6012-7207 ⊕ www.belfasttours.com. **Nationalist Tours** ☎ 028/9031-5777.

WALKING TOURS Historical Pub Tours of Belfast walking tours of the city's pubs leave on Tuesday at 7 PM and Saturday at 4 PM. The cost is £5. In Derry, walking tours (£4) are organized through the city's Tourist Information Centre.

Derry Tourist Information Centre ✉ 44 Foyle St., West Bank, Derry ☎ 028/
7126-7284 or 028/7137-7577 ⊕ www.derryvisitor.com. **Historical Pub Tours of Belfast**
✉ Depart from the Crown Liquor Saloon, 46 Great Victoria St., Golden Mile, Belfast
☎ 028/9268-3665.

TRAIN TRAVEL

The Dublin–Belfast Express train, run jointly by Northern Ireland Railways and Iarnród Éireann, travels between the two cities in about two hours. Eight trains (check timetables, as some trains are much slower) run daily in each direction (three on Sunday) between Dublin and Belfast's misnamed Central Station—it's not, in fact, that central. A free shuttle bus service from Belfast Central Station will drop you off at City Hall or Ulsterbus's city-center Europa Buscentre. You can change trains at Central Station for the city-center Great Victoria Street Station, which is adjacent to the Europa Buscentre and the Europa Hotel.

Northern Ireland Railways runs only four rail routes from Belfast's Central Station: northwest to Derry via Coleraine and the Causeway Coast; east to Bangor along the shore of Belfast Lough; northeast to Larne (for the P&O European ferry to Scotland; and south to Dublin. There are frequent connections to Central Station from the city-center Great Victoria Street Station and from Botanic Station in the university area. A Freedom of Northern Ireland Ticket allows unlimited travel on trains (£12 per day, £30 for three days, and £45 per week). An Irish Rover train ticket provides five days of rail travel for £90.

🚂 Train Lines **Iarnród Éireann** ☎ 850/366222 for timetables ⊕ www.irishrail.ie.
Northern Ireland Railways ✉ 28 Wellington Pl., Central District, Belfast ☎ 02/
9066-6630 Translink ⊕ www.translink.co.uk.
🚂 Train Stations **Botanic Station** ✉ Botanic Ave., University Area, Belfast ☎ 028/
9089-9411. **Central Station** ✉ E. Bridge St., Golden Mile, Belfast ☎ 028/9089-9411.

VISITOR INFORMATION

The Northern Ireland Tourist Board (NTIB) Information Centre in Belfast is the main tourist information center for the whole of the north. The office incorporates the plush, comprehensive Belfast Welcome Centre—the main tourist office for Belfast city, run by the Belfast Visitor and Convention Bureau. It's open October to May, Monday 9:30–5:30, Tuesday to Saturday 9–5:30; and June to September, Monday 9:30–5:30, Tuesday to Saturday 9–5:30, Sunday noon–5. Year-round Tourist Information Offices (TIOs) are listed below by town. June to August many more towns and villages open TIOs.

🚂 NTIB **Northern Ireland Tourist Board Information Centre** ✉ 47 Donegall Pl., Central District, Belfast BT1 5AU ☎ 028/9024-6609 ⊕ www.discovernorthernireland.com.
🚂 Regional Tourist Information **Armagh** ✉ 40 English St., Co. Armagh BT6 17BA ☎ 028/
3752-1800. **Ballycastle** ✉ 7 Mary St., Co. Antrim BT54 6QH ☎ 028/2076-2024. **Bangor** ✉ Quay St., Co. Down BT20 5ED ☎ 028/9127-0069. **Carrickfergus** ✉ Heritage
Plaza, Co. Antrim BT38 7DG ☎ 028/9336-6455. **Coleraine** ✉ Railway Rd., Co. Derry
BT52 1PE ☎ 028/7034-4723. **Derry** ✉ Foyle St., Co. Derry BT48 6AT ☎ 028/7126-7284
or 028/7137-7577. **Downpatrick** ✉ 53A Market St., Co. Down BT30 6L2 ☎ 028/4461-2233.
Enniskillen ✉ Lakeland Visitor Centre, Shore Rd., Co. Fermanagh BT74 7EF ☎ 028/
6632-3110. **Giant's Causeway** ✉ Visitor Centre, Co. Antrim BT57 8SU ☎ 028/2073-1855.

Killymaddy ⊠ Ballygally Rd., Co. Derry BT70 ITF ☎ 028/8776-7259. **Larne** ⊠ Narrow Gauge Rd., Co. Antrim BT40 1XB ☎ 028/2826-0088. **Limavady** ⊠ Connell St., Co. Derry BT49 OHA ☎ 028/7772-2226. **Lisburn** ⊠ 53 Lisburn Sq., Co. Antrim BT28 IAG ☎ 028/9266-0038. **Newcastle** ⊠ Central Promenade, Co. Down BT33 OAA ☎ 028/4372-2222. **Newtownards** ⊠ Regent St., Co. Down BT23 4AD ☎ 028/9182-6846. **Newry** ⊠ Town Hall, Bank Parade, Co. Armagh BT35 6HR ☎ 028/3026-8877.

Updated by
Tom Swift

ASK MOST GOLFERS WHERE TO FIND the golf vacation of a lifetime—breathtaking and diverse courses, lovely settings, history seeping into every shot—and they'll probably say Scotland. Unless, of course, they've been to Ireland. The nation's oldest course dates from 1881, and the Golfing Union of Ireland is the oldest such establishment in the world. It started in 1891: all nine original clubs were in Ulster. Now the number of affiliated golf clubs is 4,002, with over 200,000 members, and there are still more clubs that haven't joined.

Ireland is one of those remarkable places where mountains and sea often meet. Scraggly coastline and rolling hills of heather dominate the courses here, not the other way around. Real golfers are challenged, rather than deterred, by the vagaries of the elements—the wind, rain, and mist—and the lack of golf carts on courses in rougher terrain. Ireland's ever-beguiling (and often frustrating) courses attract players from around the globe. Tom Watson, winner of five British Opens, lists Ballybunion as his favorite course; so does the legendary writer Herbert Warren Wind—who, from an American viewpoint, put Irish golf on the map when he wrote, "To put it simply, Ballybunion revealed itself to be nothing less than the finest seaside course I have ever seen." And although Ballybunion is generally considered the Emerald Isle's prize jewel, many courses now rival it—from such classics as Portmarnock and Waterville to newer courses such as Mount Juliet, the K Club, and the Old Head of Kinsale.

There's more to Irish golf than its great links courses, though. Druids Glen features prominently alongside the likes of the K Club, Mount Juliet, Carlow, and Fota Island in every debate on the great inland golf courses. And although it's purely a matter of opinion—and, perhaps, your last scorecard—as to which is best, Druids Glen hosted the Irish Open Golf Championship for three years, was voted European Golf Course of the Year at the prestigious Hertz International Travel Awards for 2000, and is considered one of the top twenty courses in Ireland by *Golf Digest* magazine.

The wonderfully alive, challenging natural terrain is one of the things that makes Irish golf so remarkable. Of the estimated 150 top-quality links courses in the world, 39 of them are in Ireland. Most of these leading courses were designed by celebrated golf architects, such as Tom Morris, James Braid, Harry Colt, and Alister MacKenzie, who capitalized on spectacular landscapes. Others—such as Severiano Ballesteros, with his new course at Killenard in County Laois—will continue in their steps.

- **The Weather Factor.** You see all kinds of weather in Ireland—driving winds, rain, sleet, and sunshine—and you may see it all in one round. There are no rain-checks here. You play unless there's lightning, so pack your sweaters and rain gear, especially if you're planning your trip between fall and spring.

- **The Sunday Bag Factor.** If you don't have a golf bag that's light enough for you to carry for 18 holes, invest in one before your trip. Electric carts are generally available only at the leading venues, so you usually have the option of using a caddy or caddy car (pull cart) or of carrying your own bag. Many courses have caddies but don't guarantee their availability because they're not employed by the course—so you may have to tote your bag yourself. Be prepared with a carryall or a Sunday bag.

- **The Private Club Factor.** Unlike those in America, most private golf clubs in Ireland are happy to let visitors play their courses and use their facilities. It's important to remember, however, that such clubs place members first; guests come second. In some, you'll need a letter of introduction from your club in America to secure your playing privilege. There are often preferred days for visitors; call in advance to be sure that a club can make time for you.

- **The Northern Ireland Factor.** Some of the best and most beautiful courses are in Northern Ireland, where the leading venues—like Royal County Down and Royal Portrush—are less remote than in the Republic. Remember that this part of the island is under British rule, so all currency is in U.K. pounds, although many clubs and business will accept the euro. There are no restrictions when traveling from one part of the country to the other.

North of Dublin

County Louth Golf Club. Like many other Irish courses, County Louth is better known by the name of its hometown, Baltray, a village sandwiched by the Boyne Estuary to the west and the Irish Sea to the east. Long hitters will love the atypical layout, a par-73 that features five par-5s, but beware the well-protected, undulating greens. ⌂ *Baltray, Drogheda, Co. Louth* ☎ *041/988–1530* ⊕ *www.countylouthgolfclub.com* ⅃ *18 holes. Yardage: 6,936. Par 73. Practice area, caddies (reserve in advance), caddy carts, club rental, catering* ▭ *Fees: weekdays, €100; weekends, €120* ☉ *Visitors: Mon. and Wed.–Sun.*

Island Golf Club. Talk about exclusive—until 1960, the only way to reach this club was by boat. It was about as remote as you could get and still be only 24 km (15 mi) from Dublin. But things have changed. The Island has opened its doors to reveal a fine links course that rolls in and around sand hills, with small, challenging greens. ⌂ *Corballis, Donabate, Co. Dublin* ☎ *01/843–6205* ⊕ *www.theislandgolfclub.com* ⅃ *18 holes. Yardage: 6,800. Par 71. Practice area, caddies, caddy carts, catering* ▭ *Fees: €110* ☉ *Visitors: daily.*

Fodor'sChoice **Portmarnock Golf Club.** Across an estuary from Ireland's easternmost point,
★ Portmarnock is perhaps the most famous of Ireland's "Big Four" (Ballybunion, Royal County Down, and Royal Portrush are the others). Largely because of its proximity to Dublin, this links course has hosted numerous major championships. Known for its flat fairways and greens, it provides a fair test for any golfer who can keep it out of the heavy rough. ⌂ *Portmarnock, Co. Dublin* ☎ *01/846–2968* ⊕ *www. portmarnockgolfclub.com* ⅃ *27 holes. Yardage: 7,300, 3,449. Par 72, 37. Practice area, driving range, caddies (reserve in advance), caddy carts, catering* ▭ *Fees: weekdays, €165; weekends, €190* ☉ *Visitors: Mon., Tues., and Thurs.–Sun.*

Royal Dublin Golf Club. Links courses are usually in remote, even desolate areas, but this captivating one is only 6 km (4 mi) from the center of Dublin. On Bull Island, a bird sanctuary, Royal Dublin is Ireland's third-oldest club and is routed in the old tradition of seaside links—the front 9 goes out in a line (wind helping), and the back 9 comes back in a line (wind against). Don't expect to make a comeback on the way home if you've struggled going out. ⊠ *Dollymount, Dublin 3* ☎ *01/833–6346* ⊕ *www.theroyaldublingolfclub.com* ↖ *18 holes. Yardage: 6,963. Par 72. Practice area, caddies, caddy carts, club rental, catering* ▭ *Fees: €120* ☯ *Visitors: daily.*

St. Margaret's Golf and Country Club. Not all of the worthwhile golf in Ireland is played on century-old links courses. St. Margaret's, a parkland (inland) course, receives high praise from Ireland's golfing inner circle. If, after getting blown around on the seaside links, you long for a taste of Western golf, this is your haven. ⊠ *St. Margaret's, Co. Dublin* ☎ *01/ 864–0400* ⊕ *www.stmargaretsgolf.com* ↖ *18 holes. Yardage: 6,929. Par 73. Practice area, driving range, caddy carts, club rental, shoe rental, catering* ▭ *Fees: weekdays €75; weekends €90* ☯ *Visitors: daily.*

Carton House Golf Club. Though it only opened its doors in 2002, this just-outside-of-Dublin estate is being dubbed the rising star of Ireland's golfing destinations. It's in a majestic 1,100 acre park which was the ancestral home of the earls of Kildare, presided over by an enormous and very grand 18th-century stately house. Two of the biggest names in golf designed the championship courses here. The parkland Mark O'Meara course makes use of the estate's rolling hills, specimen trees, and the River Rye. Scottish golfing legend Colin Montgomerie designed the second 18 holes. He's created an inland links-style course which is flatter and virtually treeless. There is a good mix of long par-fours backed up with tricky short ones. Recessed pot bunkers lie in wait to pick up off-line shots. ⊠ *Maynooth, Co. Kildare* ☎ *01/628–6271* ⊕ *www.carton.ie* ↖ *36 holes. Yardage: 7,006. Par 72 (O'Meara); 7,310. Par 72. Practice area, caddies, caddy carts, buggies, catering* ▭ *Fees: Mon.–Thurs., €110; Fri.–Sun., €125* ☯ *Visitors: daily.*

South of Dublin

Druids Glen Golf Club. Owner Hugo Flinn presented designers Pat Ruddy and Tom Craddock with the brief "Build me the finest parkland course in Ireland, whatever the cost." After an outlay of more than $16 million their handiwork was opened to the public. It has been chosen four times as the venue for the Murphy's Irish Open. Ruddy unashamedly admits to having copied some key elements of Augusta National—particularly the extensive use of water—in the layout. The course, about 40 km (25 mi) south of Dublin in County Wicklow, is beautiful, particularly around the glen from which its name derives. It's essentially an American-style target course incorporating some delightful changes in elevation, and its forbidding, par-3 17th has an island green, like the corresponding hole at TPC Sawgrass. ⊠ *Newtownmountkennedy, Co. Wicklow* ☎ *01/287–3600* ⊕ *www.druidsglen.ie* ↖ *18 holes. Yardage: 7,046. Par 71. Practice area, caddies, caddy carts, buggies, catering* ▭ *Fees: €150* ☯ *Visitors: daily.*

Fodor'sChoice ★ **The K Club.** This is Ireland's premier luxury golf resort. It boasts two championship parkland courses. The north course was designed by Arnold

Palmer and offers a round of golf in lush, wooded surroundings bordered by the River Liffey. The generous fairways and immaculate greens are offset by formidable length, which makes it one of the most demanding courses in the Dublin vicinity. Additional stress is presented by negotiating the numerous doglegs, water obstacles, and sand bunkers. The new south course has been described as an "inland links" course. The signature 7th hole wows visitors with its water cascades and man-made rock-quarry feature. The on-site facilities are terrific and include a 95-room resort with three restaurants, a health club, tennis and squash courts, a pool, and massage and other spa treatments. ⊠ *Kildare Country Club, Straffan, Co. Kildare* ☎ *01/627–3333* ⊕ *www.kclub.ie* ⅂ *36 holes. Yardage: 7,337 (North), 7,277 (South). North Par 72, South Par 72. Practice area, driving range, caddies, caddy carts, club rental, shoe rental, catering* ⊟ *Fees: €185–€265* ⊗ *Visitors: daily.*

Mount Juliet Golf Course. Attached to a magisterial country-house hotel, this Jack Nicklaus–designed championship parkland course, 19 km (11 mi) from Kilkenny Town, includes practice greens, a driving range, and, for those who feel a little rusty, a David Leadbetter golf academy. The heavily forested course has 8 holes that play over water, including the three signature par-3s. The back 9 presents a series of difficult bunker shots. A sporting day out comes to a welcome end in the Hunter's Yard or Rose Garden lodge, which cater to both the thirsty and the hungry. Greens fees are above average, and although visitors are always welcome a weekday round is best, since it's often crowded with members on weekends. ⊠ *Mount Juliet Estate, Thomastown, Co. Kilkenny* ☎ *056/73000* ⊕ *www.mountjuliet.com* ⅂ *18 holes. Yardage: 7,112. Par 74. Practice area, driving range, caddies, caddy carts, club rental, lessons, catering* ⊟ *Fees: weekdays, €140; weekends, €155* ⊗ *Visitors: daily.*

Powerscourt Golf Club. Set on the most spectacular estate in Ireland (once presided over by the Slazenger family), these two recently built courses are nestled in the foothills of the Wicklow Mountains on the ancient Powerscourt lands, home to a legendary 18th-century stately home and garden. Panoramic views to the sea and Sugarloaf Mountain—and all those 200-year-old trees—give the impression that the course has been here for years. The older East course is a largely parkland course, but some holes have certain links characteristics. The course's tiered greens will test even the best golfers. The more recently built West course is even more challenging and is designed with top-class tournament golf in mind. ⊠ *Enniskerry, Co. Wicklow* ☎ *01/204–6033* ⊕ *www. powerscourt.ie* ⅂ *36 holes. Yardage: (East Course) 6421; (West course) 6390 Par 72. Practice area, driving range, caddies, caddy carts, catering* ⊟ *Fees: €110* ⊗ *Visitors: daily.*

Tulfarris Golf Club. Less than a year after being officially opened, the $20 million development at Tulfarris was chosen as the venue for the 2003 Irish Senior Professional Open. Designed by Patrick Merrigan, it spans a 200-acre site beside Poulaphouca Lake, 50 km (31 mi) from Dublin, in an area of outstanding natural beauty. It's classic parkland and has the potential to be among the country's leading venues. ⊠ *Blessington,*

Co. Wicklow ☎ *045/867–609* ⊕ *www.tulfarris.com* ⅃. *18 holes. Yardage: 7,116. Par 72. Practice area, caddies, caddy carts, catering* ☒ *Fees: weekdays, €80; weekends, €100* ☺ *Visitors: daily.*

Southwest

Adare Manor Golf Course. This parkland stretch is on the ancestral estate of the Earl of Dunraven. Its immediate success was virtually guaranteed by the international profile of its designer, Robert Trent Jones Sr. The grand old man of golf-course architects seemed far more comfortable with the wooded terrain than he was when designing the second links at Ballybunion. As a result, he delivered a course with the potential to host events of the highest caliber. The front 9 is dominated by an artificial 14-acre lake with a $500,000 polyethylene base. It is in play at the 3rd, 5th, 6th, and 7th holes. The dominant hazards on the homeward journey are the River Mague and the majestic trees, which combine to make the par-5 18th one of the most challenging finishing holes imaginable. ☒ *Adare, Co. Limerick* ☎ *061/395–044* ⊕ *www. adaremanor.com* ⅃. *18 holes. Yardage: 7,138. Par 72. Practice area, caddies, caddy carts, catering* ☒ *Fees: €120* ☺ *Visitors: daily.*

Fodor'sChoice
★
Ballybunion Golf Club. The Old Course was a virtual unknown until Herbert Warren Wind sang its praises in 1968, and today Ballybunion is universally regarded as one of golf's holiest grounds. On the shore of the Atlantic next to the southern entrance of the Shannon, it has the huge dunes of Lahinch without the blind shots. It's no pushover, but every hole is pleasurable. Watch out for "Mrs. Simpson," a double fairway bunker on the 1st hole, named after the wife of Tom Simpson, the architect who remodeled the course in 1937 (Tom Watson did the same in 1995). The Cashen Course, which opened in 1985, was designed by Robert Trent Jones Sr. ☒ *Sandhill Rd., Ballybunion, Co. Kerry* ☎ *068/ 27611* ⊕ *www.ballybuniongolfclub.ie* ⅃. *36 holes. Yardage: 6,593 (Old), 6,216 (New). Par 71, 72. Practice area, driving range, caddies, catering* ☒ *Fees: €125 (Old), €85 (Cashen), €160 (both on same day)* ☺ *Visitors: weekdays.*

Cork Golf Club. If you know golf-course architecture, you're familiar with the name Alister MacKenzie, who designed Cypress Point in California and Augusta National in Georgia. One of his few designs in Ireland is Cork, better known as Little Island. There's water on this parkland course, but it's not the temperamental ocean; instead, Little Island is in Cork Harbor, a gentle bay of the Irish Sea. The course is little known, but it's one of the Emerald Isle's best. ☒ *Little Island, Co. Cork* ☎ *021/435– 3451* ⊕ *www.corkgolfclub.ie* ⅃. *18 holes. Yardage: 6,119. Par 72. Practice area, caddies, caddy carts, club rental, catering* ☒ *Fees: weekdays, €80; weekends, €90* ☺ *Visitors: daily.*

Dooks Golf Club. On the second tier of courses in Ireland's southwest, Dooks doesn't quite measure up to the world-class tracks. It is, nonetheless, a completely worthwhile day of golf if you're touring the area. Built in the old tradition of seaside links, it's shorter and a bit gentler, although the greens are small and tricky. It's an excellent way to take a breather.

✉ *Dooks, Glenbeigh, Co. Kerry* ☎ *066/976–8205* ⊕ *www.dooks.com* ⅄. *18 holes. Yardage: 6,010. Par 68. Caddy carts, catering* ☱ *Fees: €48* ☉ *Visitors: weekdays.*

Heritage Golf and Country Club. The newest of Ireland's clubs is an 18-hole championship course, the only course in the country designed by Seve Ballesteros. The course has a mix of challenging doglegs and water traps, including five on course lakes. Add four demanding par-5s to the mix and the result is a truly world-class parkland course. The development of luxury on-site accommodation has also increased the club's attractiveness to the visiting golfer. ✉ *Killenard, Co. Loais* ☎ *0502/45040* ⅄. *18 holes. Yardage: 7,345. Par 70. Caddy carts, driving range, practice area, catering* ☱ *Fees: weekdays, €80; weekends, €100* ☉ *Visitors: daily.*

Killarney Golf and Fishing Club. Freshwater fishing is the sport here, for this club is among a stunning mixture of mountains, lakes, and forests. There are three golf courses: the Killeen Course; Mahony's Point, along the shores of Lough Leane; and the Lackabane, on the far side of the road from the main entrance. Killeen and Lackabane are longer; Mahony's places a premium on accuracy. Despite the abundance of seaside links, many well-traveled golfers name Killarney their favorite place to play in Ireland. ✉ *Mahony's Point, Killarney, Co. Kerry* ☎ *064/31034* ⊕ *www.killarney-golf.com* ⅄. *54 holes. Yardage: 6,474 (Killeen), 6,164 (Mahony's), 6,410 (Lackabane). All courses: par 72. Practice area, caddies, caddy carts, catering* ☱ *Fees: €85 (Killeen), €80 (Mahony's Point), €50 (Lackabane)* ☉ *Visitors: Mon.–Sat.*

Old Head Golf Links. On a celebrated 215-acre County Cork peninsula, which juts out into the wild Atlantic nearly 300 feet below, you'll find an awe-inspiring spectacle that defies comparison. The only golfing stretches that could be likened to it are the 16th and 17th holes at Cypress Point and small, Pacific sections of Pebble Beach, from the 7th to the 10th and the long 18th. Even if your golf is moderate, expect your pulse to race at the stunning views and wildlife. ✉ *Kinsale, Co. Cork* ☎ *021/477–8444* ⊕ *www.oldheadgolflinks.com* ⅄. *18 holes. Yardage: 7,215. Par 72. Practice area, caddies (reserve in advance), caddy carts, catering* ☱ *Fees: €250* ☉ *Visitors: daily.*

Tralee Golf Club. Tralee is what all modern-golf-course architects *wish* they could do in the States: find unspoiled, seaside links and route a course on it that's designed for the modern game. This is an Arnold Palmer–Ed Seay design that opened in 1984, and the location is fantastic—cliffs, craters, dunes, and the gale-blowing ocean. Don't let the flat front 9 lull you to sleep—the back 9 can be a ferocious wake-up call. ✉ *West Barrow, Ardfert, Co. Kerry* ☎ *066/713–6379* ⊕ *www.traleegolfclub.com* ⅄. *18 holes. Yardage: 6,840. Par 71. Practice area, caddies, catering* ☱ *Fees: €150* ☉ *Visitors: Mon., Tues., and Thurs.–Sat.*

Waterville Golf Links. Here's what you should know about Waterville before you play: the 1st hole of this course is aptly named "Last Easy." At 7,184 yards from the tips, Waterville is the longest course in Ireland or Britain, and it's generally regarded as their toughest test. Now the good news—the scenery is so majestic you may not care that your score

HELI-GOLFING, ANYONE?

IRELAND'S RUGGED and often unpredictable golf courses are famous the world over—and so are its rugged and unpredictable roads. That's why many visiting golfers with little time and lots of money are taking to the air. A growing number of companies are offering heli-golf packages where groups of avid golfers are ferried from course to course. On the time front, the math is hard to argue with. On a good day it will take you six and a half hours to drive from the Old Head Golf Links in Kinsale, County Cork to Royal County Down at the foothills of the Mourne Mountains. By helicopter, you can lift off from the 18th in Kinsale and land at the 1st tee in Down in under 2 hours.

Another obvious advantage is that you get a unique view of the Irish countryside. And you may also get an aerial insight into how you're going to tackle the tricky tenth as your chopper makes the approach to

your next golfing stopover. Too good to be true? Yes, you knew there was a catch—the price. Heli golf is expensive. Trips are charged relative to the time you spend in the air, with the average rate hovering around €1,600 per hour. However, if you're prepared to fork out the cash and can share the cost with a group of like-minded golfing enthusiasts, then it can make for the experience of a sporting lifetime. Here are some of the main outfitters. Links Helicopters (☎ 061/472–146 ☐ 061/472-145) is Shannon-based. Heligolf Ltd (☎ 066/713–6437 ☐ 066/713-6402) is Kerry-based. Irish Helicopters (☎ 066/713–6437 ☐ 066/713-6402) is Dublin-based. Executive Helicopters (☎ 091/792111 ☐ 091/792077) is Galway-based.

---

is approaching the yardage. Six holes run along the cliffs by the sea, surrounding the other 12, which have a tranquil, if not soft, feel to them. ⌧ *Waterville, Co. Kerry* ☎ *066/947–4545* 🏌 *18 holes. Yardage: 7,184. Par 74. Practice area, caddies, caddy carts, buggies, catering* 🍴 *Fees: €105–€150* ☉ *Visitors: daily.*

West

Carne Golf Links. This Eddie Hackett–designed links course takes advantage of its location, far to the west on the shores of Blacksod Bay. From the elevated tees and greens you can see a string of Atlantic islands: Inishkea, Inishglora, and Achill. But don't be distracted by the amazing views—you'll need all your wits about you to beat the constant challenge of the high winds that whip in off what's locally described as "the wild Atlantic." ⌧ *Carn, Belmullet, Co. Mayo* ☎ *097/82292* ⊕ *www. carnegolflinks.com* 🏌 *18 holes. Yardage: 6,608. Par 72. Practice area, caddies, caddy carts, catering* 🍴 *Fees: weekdays, €45; weekends, €50* ☉ *Visitors: daily.*

Connemara Golf Club. The local club for the town of Clifden, Connemara is a links course where you can get carried away not only by the golf but by the scenery. Immediately to the west you'll see the Atlantic and Ballyconneely Bay, and to the east you'll see the Twelve Bens Mountains. The course starts flat, then rises into the hills for the final, challenging 6 holes. The 14th and 15th pose a real test, with their elevated greens perched on the side of a hill. ⊠ *Ballyconneely, Clifden, Co. Galway* ☎ *095/23502* ⅃ *27 holes. Yardage: 6,339. Par 72. Practice area, caddies, caddy carts, catering* ⌂ *Fees: weekdays, €50; weekends, €55* ◔ *Visitors: daily.*

Lahinch Golf Club. The original course at Lahinch was designed by old Tom Morris, who, upon the unveiling in 1892, called it "as fine a natural course as it has ever been my good fortune to play over." That was when blind shots (those taken when you can't see your target) were in vogue; there are many here, as towering sand hills dominate every hole. Only a course with as much charm as this one could get away with that in today's game. The Castle Course is less of a challenge to the experienced player but it has its moments: awkwardly placed bunkers and water hazards lie in wait. ⊠ *Lahinch, Co. Clare* ☎ *065/708–1003* ⊕ *www. lahinchgolf.com* ⅃ *36 holes. Yardage: 6,220 (Old Course), 5,594 (Castle Course). Par 72, 70. Practice area, caddies, caddy carts, catering* ⌂ *Fees: €125 (Old Course), €50 (Castle)* ◔ *Visitors: daily.*

Westport Golf Club. Twice this inland course hosted the Irish Amateur Championship. It lies in the shadows of religious history: rising 2,500 feet above Clew Bay, with its hundreds of islands, is Croagh Patrick, a mountain that legend connects with St. Patrick. The mountain is considered sacred, and it attracts multitudes of worshippers to its summit every year. All the prayers might pay off at the 15th, where your drive has to carry the ball over 200 yards of ocean. ⊠ *Westport, Co. Mayo* ☎ *098/28262* ⊕ *www.golfwestport.com* ⅃ *18 holes. Yardage: 6,667. Par 73. Practice area, driving range, caddies, caddy carts, catering* ⌂ *Fees: €50* ◔ *Visitors: Sun.–Fri.*

Northwest

County Sligo Golf Club. More than a century old, the course at Sligo is one of the grand old venues of Ireland, having hosted most of the country's major championships. At 6,565 yards this links course isn't particularly long, but it still manages to have seven par-4s of 400 yards or more. A hidden jewel, Rosses Point clings to cliffs above the Atlantic. The third tee offers views of the ocean, the hills, and the unusual mountain Ben Bulben. ⊠ *Rosses Point, Co. Sligo* ☎ *071/917–7186* ⊕ *www. countysligogolfclub.ie* ⅃ *27 holes. Yardage: 6,043. Par 71. Practice area, caddies (summer only), caddy carts, club rental, catering* ⌂ *Fees: weekdays, €65* ◔ *Visitors: Mon., Tues., Thurs., and Fri.*

Donegal Golf Club. On the shores of Donegal Bay and approached through a forest, the windswept links are shadowed by the Blue Stack Mountains, with the Atlantic as a backdrop. The greens are large, but the rough is deep and penal, and there's a constant battle against erosion by the sea. Legendary golf writer Peter Dobereiner called it "hauntingly beautiful," perhaps recalling his experience on the par-3 5th, fittingly called "The Valley of Tears." ✉ *Murvagh, Laghey, Co. Donegal* ☎ *074/973–4054* ⊕ *www.donegalgolfclub.com* 🏌 *18 holes. Yardage: 7,153. Par 73. Practice area, caddies, caddy carts, catering* 🍴 *Fees: weekdays, €50; weekends, €65* ⊙ *Visitors: daily.*

Enniscrone Golf Club. Enniscrone's setting is a natural for good golf—it's a combination of flatlands, foothills, and the Atlantic. The course is not overly long on the scorecard, but the persistent winds can add yards to almost every hole. An extra nine holes have recently been added by reviving some old holes that had been abandoned and expanding into adjoining lands. It's among the small number of clubs in Ireland with electric caddy carts. ✉ *Enniscrone, Co. Sligo* ☎ *096/36297* 🏌 *27 holes. Yardage: 6,775. Par 73. Practice area, caddies (weekends and holidays), caddy carts, buggies, club rental* 🍴 *Fees: weekdays, €50; weekends, €63* ⊙ *Visitors: weekdays; weekends by appointment.*

Northern Ireland

Ballycastle Golf Club. Pleasure comes first here, with challenge as an afterthought. It's beautiful (five holes wind around the remains of a 13th-century friary), short (less than 6,000 yards), and right next to Bushmills, the world's oldest distillery—at nearly 400 years. ✉ *2 Cushendall Rd., Ballycastle BT54 6QP, Co. Antrim* ☎ *048/2076–2536* 🏌 *18 holes. Yardage: 5,927. Par 71. Practice area, caddy cars, catering* 🍴 *Fees: weekdays, £20; weekends, £30* ⊙ *Visitors: daily.*

Castlerock Golf Club. Where else in the world can you play a hole called "Leg o' Mutton"? It's a 200-yard par-3 with railway tracks to the right and a burn to the left—just one of several unusual holes at this course, which claims to have the best greens in Ireland. The finish is spectacular: from the elevated 17th tee, where you can see the shores of Scotland, to the majestic 18th, which plays uphill to a plateau green. The club also boasts the equally scenic 9-hole Bann course. ✉ *65 Circular Rd., Castlerock, Co. Derry* ☎ *048/7084–8314* 🏌 *27 holes. Yardage: 6,747; 4,892. Par 73, 67. Practice area, caddies (reserve in advance), caddy cars, catering* 🍴 *Fees: weekdays, £35 weekends, £90* ⊙ *Visitors: Mon.–Thurs.*

Malone Golf Club. Fisherfolk may find the 22-acre lake at the center of this parkland layout distracting because it's filled with trout. The golf, however, is just as well-stocked—with large trees and well-manicured, undulating greens, this is one of the most challenging inland tests in Ireland. Bring your power game—there are only three par-5s, but they're all more than 520 yards. However, for many, the feature hole is the par-3 15th. Water lies to the front and back of the small green and there are bunkers to the right, pinpoint accuracy is a must. ✉ *240 Upper Malone Rd., Dunmurry, Belfast* ☎ *048/9061–2695* ⊕ *www.malonegolfclub.co.uk* 🏌 *27 holes. Yardage: 6,599, 3,138. Par 71, 36. Practice area, catering* 🍴 *Fees: weekdays, £35* ⊙ *Visitors: Mon., Thurs., and Fri.*

Portstewart Golf Club. Over a century old, Portstewart may scare you with its opening hole, generally regarded as the toughest starter in Ireland. Picture a 425-yard par-4 that descends from an elevated tee to a small green tucked between the dunes. The greens are known for uniformity and speed, and seven of the holes have been redesigned to toughen the course. If you want a break from the grand scale of championship links, there's the Old Course 18 and the Riverside 9, 27 holes of downsize, executive-style golf. ⊠ *117 Strand Rd., Portstewart, Co. Derry* ☎ *048/ 7083–2015* ⊕ *www.portstewartgc.co.uk* ⅃ *45 holes. Yardage: 6,779 (Championship), 4,730 (Old Course), 2,662 (Riverside). Par 72, 64, 32. Practice area, caddies, caddy cars, buggies, catering* ▭ *Fees: weekdays, £65 (Championship), £10 (Old Course), £12 (Riverside); weekends, £85 (Championship), £14 (Old Course), £17 (Riverside)* ☉ *Visitors: Mon., Tues., and Fri.*

FodorsChoice
★
Royal County Down. Catch it on the right day at the right time and you may think you're on the moon; Royal County Down is a links course with a sea of craterlike bunkers and small dunes. And for better players, every day is the right one. Harry Vardon labeled it the toughest course on the Emerald Isle, and if you can't hit your drive long and straight, you might find it the toughest course in the world. ⊠ *Golf Links Rd., Newcastle, Co. Down* ☎ *048/4372–2419* ⊕ *www.royalcountydown. org* ⅃ *36 holes. Yardage: 7,065 (Championship), 4,708 (Annesley). Par 71, 65. Practice area, caddies, caddy cars, catering* ▭ *Fees: weekdays, £110 (Championship), £19 (Annesley); weekends, £125 (Championship), £30 (Annesley)* ☉ *Visitors: Sun.–Tues., Thurs., and Fri.*

FodorsChoice
★
Royal Portrush. The only club outside Scotland and England to have hosted a British Open, Portrush is perhaps the most understated of Ireland's "Big Four." The championship Dunluce course is named for the ruins of a nearby castle and is a sea of sand hills and curving fairways. The Valley course is a less-exposed, tamer track. Both are conspicuous for their lack of bunkers. In a poll of Irish golf legends, Dunluce was voted the best in Ireland. ⊠ *Dunluce Rd., Portrush, Co. Antrim* ☎ *048/ 7082–2311* ⊕ *www.royalportrushgolfclub.com* ⅃ *36 holes. Yardage: 6,845 (Dunluce), 6,304 (Valley). Par 72, 70. Practice area, caddies, caddy carts, buggies, catering* ▭ *Fees: weekdays, £90 (Dunluce), £32.50 (Valley)* ☉ *Visitors: weekdays.*

UNDERSTANDING
IRELAND

ÉIRE APPARENT

F YOU FLY INTO IRELAND your descent will probably be shrouded by gray clouds. As your plane breaks through the mists, you'll see the land for which the Emerald Isle was named: a lovely patchwork of rolling green fields speckled with farmhouses, cows, and sheep. Shimmering lakes, meandering rivers, narrow roads, and stone walls add to the impression that rolled out before you is a luxurious welcome carpet, one knit of the legendary "forty shades of green." (If you're lucky you may even see a rainbow—something you'll see again and again if you travel the countryside.) This age-old view of misty Ireland may be exactly what you imagined. Travelers still arrive expecting Eire to be the land of leprechauns, shillelaghs, shamrocks, and mist. Be warned, however—the only known specimens of leprechauns or shillelaghs are those in souvenir shop windows; shamrock only blooms on St. Patrick's Day or around the borders of Irish linen handkerchiefs and tablecloths; and the mists—in reality a soft, apologetic rain—can envelop the entire country, in a matter of minutes.

The Celtic Tiger

The real Ireland is two-faced, like the Janus stones and sheela-na-gigs of its pre-Christian past. It's a complex place where the mystic lyricism of Yeats, the hard Rabelaisian passions of Joyce, and the spare, aloof dissections of Beckett grew not only from a rich and ancient culture but also from 20th-century upheavals, few of which have been as dramatic as the transformation that has been changing Ireland for the past decade. Consider the evidence: more than 150 years since the apocalyptic Great Famine, Ireland's economy—christened the "Celtic Tiger"—is now one of the fastest-growing in the industrialized world. The country is the second-largest exporter of computer software in the world, after the United States.

Unemployment, which was 11.5% in 1996, fell to 4.2% in 2003, and 41% of Ireland's populace is under the age of 25, with 24% under 15, making it one of Europe's youngest nations. Most telling, however, is the fact that, in a profound demographic shift, Ireland's net emigration has reversed. There has been major *immigration* in each of the last three years—beginning in 2001 with 15,000—and that trend shows every sign of continuing. The young who once left for London and New York are now staying, more college graduates are returning than are leaving, and thousands of immigrants are arriving from other countries.

The foreign capital that has flowed into the country since it joined the Common Market (now the European Union) in 1973 has been crucial to this regeneration. But money alone doesn't guarantee culture, and Irish culture is thriving. Take just a few examples from literature: In 2003, after winning Ireland's fourth Nobel prize for literature (in 1995), Seamus Heaney won the prominent Truman Capote Award for his *Selected Prose. Angela's Ashes* and *'Tis,* Frank McCourt's memoirs of his early life in Limerick, found millions of readers and won every major American literary prize. Dublin-born hell-raiser Colin Farrell, star of *Tigerland* and *Minority Report,* is Hollywood's new chosen one. You name it—food, music, movies, literature, poetry, theater, art, fashion—and something innovative is afoot among the Irish at home and abroad. If you've been moved by seeing *Riverdance* or *Lord of the Dance* or hearing the Corrs, Enya, Van Morrison, U2, the Irish Tenors, or any of the hundreds of other prominent Irish musicians, you're likely to feel the spirit that touched you more palpably in Ireland itself as you meet its people and witness them imagining—and creating—the Irish spirit anew.

A Friendly People

Liam Neeson, Kenneth Branagh, Daniel Day-Lewis, Neil Jordan, and the Cranberries are just a few of the envoys extraordinaire for Irish culture around the world. To find the real Ireland, however, you must venture down its back roads. You'll quickly discover that hospitality is counted among the greatest of Irish virtues, a legacy from Celtic times, when anyone not offering the traveler food and drink was shamed. "You are welcome," people say in greeting the moment you cross the threshold of the smallest cottage, while total strangers will take you home for tea or supper and strike up conversations with ease and curiosity, entertaining you perhaps with an account of their second cousin's memorable fortnight in America (a fortnight's worth of stories if you have the time).

Time, in fact, is one of the greatest luxuries in Ireland—outside fast-forward Dublin, that is. On a fine day, along a lushly green country lane, you may pass a bicycle abandoned against a tree; looking for its owner, you'll find him reclining in the feathery hedgerows or on the long grass, contemplating fast-moving clouds like some philosopher-king. "Oh the dreaming, the dreaming, the heart-scalding bitter, maddening dreaming," cried the playwright George Bernard Shaw, but to knowing travelers in the stressed and industrialized world, this haven of dreamers is a pearl of great price, sought after and kept secret. Forget America's car culture—Ireland has cow culture. You'll find the moo-cows own the country lanes, staring haughtily and curiously at interloping motorists, lazily drooping timothy from their soft maws. In the end, with persuasion from harried livery, equipped with frisky dogs and long-knobbed sticks, they'll share the road—but on *their* schedule.

This may explain why Ireland is what some anthropologists call a "lived" culture, one that doesn't put all its stock in the outward monuments of achievement; where the most potent history is oral, where storytelling is an art, and where people will travel for miles for the *craic,* the Irish term for a rousing good time. Ireland teaches you patience, reminds you of the rhythms of the natural world, and convinces you, reassuringly, of the essential well-being of humanity.

This is nowhere more the case than in the local pub, the center of social life in Ireland. Even a small town such as Dingle in County Kerry (population 1,400) has 52 watering holes, open day and night. Protocol dictates that you enter and greet everyone, taking a seat alone until invited (as you inevitably are) to join a table. Then the ancient custom of rounds begins, with the newcomer offering to buy the first set of drinks, and when the pints are barely half full, another imbiber stands the round, and so on, in turn. Dark village pubs, with their scratched wooden counters, dusty tiled floors, and yeasty smell of Guinness, exude a feeling of sanctity and remove from worldly cares. Sit awhile and enjoy your stout, but know that wit also flows untapped. Nuance and irony are the law—anything less would be considered flat-footed. Irish expertise in doublethink and the witty tongue makes for a universally acknowledged aptitude for legal affairs, a gift for words of imagination and persuasiveness that you can find in the crossroads *shebeen* (pub) much as in Dublin's Leinster House, where the Irish Dáil (legislature) sits.

DESPITE IRELAND'S ACCESSIBILITY, you may feel a sense of otherness, attributable not only to the ever-green climate and leisurely pace but also to the layering of history and legend dug deep under the country's rich grassy surface. Standing stones and court graves, mottes and dolmens, holy wells and mass stones, round towers and Celtic crosses, churches and country houses—the artifacts of Ireland's long, turbulent history are everywhere, from the barren limestone Burren in County Clare to the Neolithic tombs and defenses of Newgrange in County Meath. Even an island off the main island—Inishmore, one of the Aran Islands far out in Galway Bay—claims its antiquity: Dún Aengus, which is 5,000 years older than the pyramids of Giza. Given how tempestuous the fortunes of this small island have been, you may be surprised by just how many of these sights remain.

Iron Age Celts from Central Europe settled in Ireland in the 4th century BC and left a legacy of an agrarian society based on a democratic kingship, a justice system known as the Brehon laws, and an artisan caste proficient in working gold and precious metals. (The National Museum in Dublin displays heaps of this Bronze Age gold jewelry.) Christianity arrived in Ireland in 432 with St. Patrick (or, perhaps, as some scholars suggest, with two and possibly more missionaries whose work became conflated into the Patrician story). By the 8th century, Ireland was in its golden age. In general, the country's proliferating religious orders received protection from God-fearing Irish kings. Monks labored for decades to produce the *Book of Kells* (now on display at Trinity College in Dublin). Having set up monasteries throughout Ireland, Irish monks set out for Europe, where they continued their expansion of monastic

communities from England to northern Italy. According to the Thomas Cahill best-seller *How the Irish Saved Civilization*, the medieval Irish monks who copied and standardized the masterpieces of Virgil and Horace helped to prevent the loss of classical Latin, the written language of Rome, to the vernacular Romance tongues of Italy, Spain, and France.

In about AD800, Viking longboats scourged the island's coasts. The Norsemen established settlements in Wexford, Cork, and Dublin (and left the mark of bright-red hair behind on their Irish descendants). Brian Boru, last of the High Kings to sit at Tara, won the Battle of Clontarf, defeating a troop of Viking raiders off the coast near Dublin in 1014. But Boru's subsequent murder marked the end of an era. Without his leadership, the power of the Irish kings dissipated, and in 1155, English-born pope Adrian IV boldly granted dominion over Ireland to his fellow Englishman King Henry II. Fourteen years later Norman Strongbow arrived in Ireland, opening the door to more than 800 years of strife between the English and the Irish.

By 1609, the last of the Irish chieftains had lost their land to the British and sailed for exile, making way for the Plantation period. During this era 200,000 Scottish Lowlanders were "planted" on native Irish lands. Oliver Cromwell, "the Avenger," arrived with his troops in 1649, intent on making Ireland a Protestant country. He conducted a ruthless campaign of persecution against the already bitter Irish Catholics—a campaign that included beheading thousands of men, women, and children.

The Famine & Its Aftermath

Throughout the early 19th century, poverty was endemic and disease was a simple fact of life. Irish peasants worked for absentee British landlords and either paid exorbitant rents for land that had probably belonged to their parents or grandparents, or simply starved. The system was unjust, but somehow the bulk of Ireland survived the lean years prior to 1845. Within a year, however, potato blight ruined crops throughout the country. In a decade, the population was decimated, reduced from 8 to 6 million inhabitants. Starvation was largely to blame for the decline, but this period also marks the beginning of the large-scale emigration—to America, Canada, and Australia—that continued, albeit at a slower pace, until the mid-1990s. More than 70 million of Ireland's descendants are scattered abroad in the Irish diaspora—including 44 million in the United States.

The mid-19th century also saw the rise of an Irish nationalist movement. Various groups, including the Fenians and the Irish Republican Brotherhood, agitated for equal rights for Catholics, land reform, the revival of Ireland's Gaelic heritage, and the expulsion of the British from Ireland. The movement exploded—literally—on Easter Sunday 1916, when Nationalists proclaimed a republic. England's merciless vengeance on the patriots—it shot 15 of the uprising's leaders—galvanized the country to the bitter War of Independence, which ended in 1920 with the partitioning of Ireland into 26 counties in the south, constituting the Irish Free State, and 6 in the north, making up the British-ruled province of Northern Ireland. The defining event of modern Irish history, the severing of north from south eventually spawned more than 30 years of Troubles in the north (though the roots of the Troubles date back 800 years) and cast a dark shadow over the country.

The Irish Ascendant

There's a place in an ancient Irish myth called Tír na nóg ("the land of the ever young"). Ancient though it may be, it's a surprisingly relevant image for Ireland today. The fact that the country is, for the first time in more than 150 years, holding on to many of its young speaks volumes—it is the era of the ascendant Irish. While past history is still treasured,

there's a growing feeling among the young to look ahead, not back. "Get over it!" was the headline cover about Boston's young Irish population and their increasing focus on the years ahead, not on time-stained stories about the Great Famine in the Old Sod across the Atlantic. There's a growing body of evidence for this newfound Irish assuredness—both within Ireland's shores and among the Irish abroad.

Together the north and south of Ireland welcome more visitors annually (5.2 million) than they have residents (5 million). Not surprisingly, Dublin, the booming capital of the republic, is the best place to take the nation's pulse. One-third of the republic's 3.6 million residents live in the capital. Dublin is the Celtic Tiger's beating heart, a far cry from Joyce's "dear, dirty Dublin." Dozens of cranes hover over new office buildings and hotels, and Georgian terrace houses are being brought back to glorious life. Visitors—especially weekenders from the Continent—fill Dublin's buzzing cafés, pubs, restaurants, and hotels, and pour out onto busy Grafton Street and the narrow cobblestone alleys of Temple Bar. Outside Dublin, the country's quickening pulse is also palpable. New golf courses, housing developments, and blue-signed divided highways indicate the changes afoot.

Less conspicuously, in villages throughout the country, heritage and genealogical centers have sprung up to accommodate the surge of interest among the Irish diaspora for information about their roots. This relationship between the past and the present, between those who left and those who stayed, is an elemental part of Ireland's identity. Today, throughout the Irish diaspora, there's a boundless yearning for all that Ireland embodies: indomitable strength against all odds, the romance of an ancient place, the longing for a lost world, the solace and transcendent possibility of art. It's likely that a trip to Ireland will put you in touch with the sources—historical and concrete, ineffable and mysterious—of this longing.

RITUAL DRINK

VEN IF YOU ORDER only a Bally-gowan, the Irish Evian, a visit to an Irish pub (or two or three) is a must. The Irish love to talk and there's no better forum than the pub for this sort of activity. Conversation will roam from the local GAA games (Gaelic Athletic Association football and hurling games) to the Ryder Cup, the state of the nation, the latest political scandal—even the price of the pint. Any one of life's events provides reasons to head for the she-been. It's not so much the drink that's the attraction, but the craic.

The Pint

There's a ritual involved with every pint that's pulled. The barman first fills the glass three-quarters of the way, lets the brew settle, then tops the glass off and brings it over to the bar. You should then wait again until the top-up has settled, at which point the brew turns a deep black. The mark of a perfect pint? As you drink the glass down, the brew will leave thin rings to mark each mouthful.

It's said that of the 10 million pints of Guinness produced daily, some 6 million are consumed in Ireland—not bad for a country whose population is 5 million. You'd start to believe infants must be drinking it in their bottles. When it was first concocted by Arthur Guinness in 1759, it wasn't known as a "stout" but rather as a "porter," a name derived from a heavy, cheaply made drink popular with working-class porters in London. Over the years, the name "stout" has stuck, and it aptly describes the formidable hearti-ness of this thick black brew (and its ef-fects on the human physique). But if you ask for a "stout," you'll get the more bit-ter bottled brew, so request "Guinness" if you want the smoother draught. Every Dublin drinker has heard the myths about exactly what goes on at night in the Guin-ness brewery, and God only knows what they cast into the huge turning vats to make the stuff taste so good.

The Etiquette

Even if you're a veteran barfly who's been booted out of gin mills and clip joints from Bombay to Baton Rouge, there may be aspects of Irish public house behavior that will perplex you. Many of these complexities come down to lan-guage and the way the locals use it. The word "whore," for instance, has many in-terpretations—in much the same way that the Eskimos have 84 different words for snow. For starters, it's gender-flexi-ble but is usually applied by males to other males. Go figure. For instance, "He's a cute whore" signifies that the so-described person is a canny man to seal a business deal; it's a phrase much heard in towns where cattle are bought and sold. Likewise, all the other swear words that are seldom heard in polite society in other developed countries find liberal employ here. The Irish have always been experts at giving a sentence even greater poetry with the inclusion of one of these epithets—they have no intention of giv-ing offense, it's simply another tool used to spin a good yarn.

Clear a path for the locals when the clock strikes half-past 12 and the owner flicks the lights to signify last call. Were Mari-lyn Monroe herself to offer all her charms to a sheep farmer from the Connemara Highlands, at 12:30 he'd put her on hold to get up there for that last pint. Maybe Ireland's pubs close too early, or maybe that final pint sipped amid the publican's plaintive cry, "Have ye no homes to go to?" is the sweetest of them all.

The round system is also, unfortunately, a mystery to many visitors. If you get into conversation with them, locals will auto-matically include you in the round—it's good manners as far as they're concerned, and the strongest means they have of saying "Good to meet you." Having accepted, woe betide you if the compliment isn't returned. The Irish won't care who you are or where you came from, but an absence of the required etiquette will not go down well.

Finally, a word to the ladies—know that most Irishmen under the age of 85 flirt outrageously with strangers. You'll hear poetry (Yeats continues to be the best aphrodisiac known on the island) and sonnets, and, as once witnessed at midnight on a rain-drenched street in Corofin, a man of 70 might just perform his version of a Fred Astaire tap dance for you. Don't be astonished. Consider it a form of theater, and take it as good fun. After all, that's what Irish women have been doing for generations.

BOOKS & MOVIES

Autobiography

Angela's Ashes (1996), Frank McCourt's enormously affecting memoir of growing up desperately poor in Limerick, has garnered every major American literary accolade, including the National Book Critics Circle Award. The memoir and its sequel, *'Tis* (1999), should definitely be on your must-read list. In *An Only Child* and *My Father's Son* (1969), Frank O'Connor, known primarily for his fiction and short stories, recounts his years as an Irish revolutionary and later as an intellectual in Dublin during the 1920s. Christy Brown's *My Left Foot* is the autobiographical account of a Dublin artist stricken with cerebral palsy. *On Another Man's Wound: A Personal History of Ireland's War of Independence* was republished in 2002. Originally published more than 60 years ago, it's the classic account of the years 1916–1921. Author Ernie O'Malley was only 23 years old when he joined the Irish Republican Army and reported directly to its controversial and heroic founder, Michael Collins. Irish journalist Nuala O'Faolain's unsentimental and wrenching memoir, *Are You Somebody? The Accidental Memoir of a Dublin Woman* (1999), an account of her Dublin childhood and the plight of Irish women, stayed on the Irish best-seller list for 20 weeks.

Travel Literature

Peter Somerville-Large's *Dublin* is filled with anecdotes relating to the city. *Georgian Dublin,* by Desmond Guinness, the founder of the Irish Georgian Society, explores the city's architecture, with photographs and plans of Dublin's most admirable buildings. An excellent work on the Aran Islands is Tim Robinson's award-winning *The Stones of Aran: Pilgrimage.* Robinson has also written a long introduction to the Penguin edition of J. M. Synge's 1907 classic, *The Aran Islands.* Tomas Ó Crohán's *The Islandman* provides a good background on Dingle and the Blasket Islands.

In *Round Ireland in Low Gear* (1988), British travel writer Eric Newby breezily pens the story of his bicycle journey with his wife around the wet Emerald Isle. Fifty years older but no less fresh is H. V. Morton's *In Search of Ireland* (1938). Rebecca Solnit uses Ireland as a sounding board for her meditations on travel in *A Book of Migrations: Some Passages in Ireland* (1997). *See It Ireland,* published by Fodor's, is a full-color guide packed with photographs; it is an excellent companion guide to this edition.

History & Current Affairs

For intriguing studies of Irish culture and history, consult Constantine FitzGibbon's *The Irish in Ireland* and Sean O'Faolain's *The Irish: A Character Study,* which traces the history of Ireland from Celtic times. J. C. Beckett's *The Making of Modern Ireland,* a concise introduction to Irish history, covers the years between 1603 and 1923. *Modern Ireland,* by R. F. Foster, spans the years between 1600 and 1972. Thomas Cahill's *How the Irish Saved Civilization* is a lively look at how Irish scholars kept the written word and culture alive in the so-called Dark Ages. Cecil Woodham-Smith's *The Great Hunger* (1962) details the history of the Irish potato famine of the 1840s. For an acclaimed history of Irish nationalism, try Robert Kee's *The Green Flag.* Peter De Rosa's *Rebels: The Irish Rising of 1916* is a popular, novelistic take on the defining event of modern Irish history. John Ardagh's *Ireland and the Irish: Portrait of a Changing Society* (1997) is one of the best sociological and economic analyses of modern Ireland. *"We Wrecked the Place": Contemplating an End to the Northern Irish Troubles* (1996) by Belfast-based journalist Jonathan Stevenson gives an insightful take on the subject. John Conroy's *Belfast Diary: War as a Way of Life* (1995) was reissued with a new afterword on the cease-fire. *The Lost Lives* (1999) is a heart-wrenching collection of biographies about many who have died during the Troubles. Paddy Logue's *The Border: Personal Reflections from Ireland—North and South* (2000) presents impressions of activists, artists, athletes, and community workers on national ramifications and the significance of the border between north and south on their lives. Marie de Paor's book *Patrick: The Pilgrim Apostle of Ireland* (2002) is a very modern interpretation of St. Patrick and his role as the patron saint of Ireland. Senan Molony's book *The Irish Aboard the Titanic* (2002) explores class structure and ethnic racism among the Irish and against them, from the building of the *Titanic* in Belfast to the moment the last Irish citizens boarded the lifeboats that fateful day. Every aspect of Irish involvement with the vessel is investigated here.

Literature

Ulysses (1922) is the linguistically innovative masterpiece by James Joyce, one of the titans of 20th-century literature. Emulating the structure of *The Odyssey,* and using an unprecedented stream-of-consciousness technique, Joyce follows Leopold and Molly Bloom and Stephen Daedalus through the course of a single day—June 16, 1904—around Dublin. More accessible introductions to Joyce's writing include *A Portrait of the Artist as a Young Man* (1916) and *Dubliners* (1914), a collection of short stories. (Its most accomplished story, "The Dead," was made into a movie starring Angelica Huston in 1988.) Joyce aficionados may want to tackle his final, gigantic work, *Finnegan's Wake* (1939), which takes the linguistic experimentation of *Ulysses* to an almost incomprehensible level. Arguably the greatest literary challenge of the 20th century, its pages include wordplay and phonetic metaphors in more than 100 languages. To prepare for reading Joyce, you might seek out audio recordings in which he reads in his inimitable lilting tenor voice.

Samuel Beckett fills his story collection *More Pricks than Kicks* (1934) with Dublin characters; if you enjoy literary gamesmanship, you may also want to try Beckett's 1950s trilogy—*Molloy, Malone Dies,* and *The Unnameable.*

If you're drawn to tales of unrequited love, turn to Elizabeth Bowen's stories and her novel *The Last September* (1929), set in Ireland during the Irish Civil War. If you prefer reading more magical novels, take a look at James Stephens's *A Crock of Gold* (1912), a charming and wise fairy tale written for adults, and Flann O'Brien's *At Swim-Two-Birds* (1939), a surrealistic tale full of Irish folklore.

One of Ireland's foremost fiction writers working today, Edna O'Brien began her career with the comic novel *The Country Girls* (1960) and continued with *House of Splendid Isolation* (1994) and *Down by the River* (1997). She is a superb short-story writer; her collection *A Fanatic Heart* (1985) is one of her best.

Thomas Flanagan's *The Year of the French* (1979) is a historical novel about the people of County Mayo, who revolted in 1798 with the help of French revolutionaries. *A Nest of Simple Folk,* by Sean O'Faolain, follows three generations of an Irish family between 1854 and 1916. Leon Uris's *Trinity* covers the years 1840–1916, as seen through the eyes of British, Irish Catholic, and Ulster Protestant families. In *No Country for Young Men,* Julia O'Faolain writes of two Irish families struggling to overcome the effects of the Irish Civil War. In John McGahern's prizewinning novel *Amongst Women,* modern-day Ireland attempts to reconcile itself to the upheavals of the early years of the 20th century. For a more contemporary look at life in urban Ireland, try the phenomenally successful Roddy Doyle. All three works from his "Barrytown Trilogy"—*The Snapper, The Commitments,* and *The Van*—have been made into films; *Paddy Clarke Ha Ha Ha* has followed suit as another success. John Banville's *The Book of Evidence* and *Ghosts* deal with contemporary Ireland's ruling classes with great insight and seriousness.

Movies

A fetching array of movies have been made in or about Ireland, and the number of Irish characters on screen is legion (the most numerous being priests, drunks, New York cops, and Old Mother Riley). Alfred Hitchcock's *Juno and the Paycock* (known in the United States as *The Shame of Mary Boyle* (1930) and *The Plough and the Stars* (1936), about the months leading up to the Easter Uprising, are early screen adaptations of Sean O'Casey's theatrical masterpieces. John Ford's superb *The Informer* (1935) is a full-blooded and highly stylized tale of an IRA leader's betrayal during the struggle for independence by a simpleminded hanger-on who wants to emigrate to the United States. Ford's boisterous comedy *The Quiet Man* (1952) is an Irish-village version of *The Taming of the Shrew,* with John Wayne playing a boxer who returns to his ancestor's village in the west of Ireland to claim local beauty Maureen O'Hara. David Lean's epic *Ryan's Daughter* (1970) is a four-hour pastoral melodrama of a village schoolmaster's wife falling for a British officer in the troubled Ireland of 1916; the film was a critical and commercial disaster for Lean, who didn't make another film for 14 years.

Daniel Day-Lewis and Brenda Fricker give Oscar-winning performances in Jim Sheridan's *My Left Foot* (1989), a biography of Christy Brown, the Irish writer and painter crippled from birth by cerebral palsy. *The Field* (1990), Ireland's first Oscar-nominated film, is a marker of just how far things have progressed in the Irish film business. Richard Harris and John Hurt played out the drama by John B. Keane around the village of Leenane in Connemara. Alan Parker's *The Commitments* (1991), from Roddy Doyle's bestseller, humorously recounts the efforts of

a group of young, working-class Northside Dubliners trying to make it as a soul band. *Into the West* (1992) has been embraced by moviegoers worldwide because of its fairy-tale plot. It follows two Irish traveler boys (gypsies) from Dublin projects to the west of Ireland in search of their beautiful horse Tír na nóg ("Land of Eternal Youth"), which was confiscated by an evil police officer. The film stars Gabriel Byrne.

In *A Man of No Importance* (1994), Albert Finney plays a sexually repressed bus conductor whose passion for poetry leads him to stage Wilde's *Salomé*. John Sayles hooked up with acclaimed cinematographer Haskell Wexler to make *The Secret of Roan Inish* (1996), a magical realist fable about a Selkie—a creature from Celtic folklore who is a seal in the water and a woman on land—and the fisherman's family whose lives she changes. *Waking Ned Devine* (1998) is a sidesplitting comedy about a small Irish village thrown into turmoil by a dead man's lottery winnings. *The Butcher Boy* (1997) is a dark comedy about a young boy who goes insane as his family splits up. Interestingly, it stars musician Sinead O'Connor as the Virgin Mary. *This is the Sea* (1997), a contemporary love story set in Northern Ireland after the 1994 cease-fire, was directed by Mary McGuickian. The film version of Frank McCourt's memoir *Angela's Ashes* (1999) has left an impact on some people as strong as the book itself. Gerry Stembridge's *About Adam* (2002), starring Kate Hudson, is one of the first movies to take a close, humorous look at modern, urban Irish life.

Some of the best movies made in Ireland deal with the Troubles that have afflicted Northern Ireland. *Four Days in July* (1984), directed by Mike Leigh in classic cinema verité style, is a poignant and compelling portrayal of the sectarian divide in working-class Belfast. Helen Mirren stars as the widow of an executed Protestant policeman in *Cal* (1984), based on Bernard MacLaverty's masterful novel about the Troubles. Daniel Day-Lewis was nominated for an Academy Award for his portrayal of Gerry Conlon, the wrongfully imprisoned Irish youth, in Jim Sheridan's *In the Name of the Father* (1993). Neil Jordan's *Michael Collins* (1996), with Liam Neeson and Julia Roberts, depicts the turbulent life of the heroic commander in chief of the Irish Republican Army from the Easter Uprising in 1916, when Collins was 25, until his assassination in West Cork six years later. Day-Lewis appears again in *The Boxer* (1997), the story of an ex-boxer and former IRA man who tries to put his life back together in contemporary, sectarian Belfast.

Poetry

The poems of William Butler Yeats, Ireland's most celebrated poet, often describe the Irish landscape, including the Sligo and Coole countryside. Go for the formidably large but marvelous *Collected Poems: 1909 to 1962* (1996 2nd rev. ed.), edited by Richard J. Finneran. A favorite poet among the Irish is Patrick Kavanagh, who wrote soberly—and exceptionally—about landscape, poverty, and rural farming life. His best-known and most controversial (long) poem, *The Great Hunger* (1942), caused some uproar when it was published, and won him a bit of notoriety. But now, finally, Kavanagh is seen as a tremendously important Irish poet. Born in Belfast in 1907 (his parents were from Connemara), Louis MacNeice is something of an anomaly. He is considered to be an Irish poet, though he spent much of his life in England. He worked as a writer and producer for BBC, for which he wrote some of his radio dramas. But MacNeice was mainly a poet, known for his long and marvelous poem *Autumn Journal*, which beautifully explores politics, history, and personal drama in alternating rhyming couplets. His poems are intimate, clever, and lyrical. MacNeice died in 1963.

For contemporary poetry, read Derek Mahon—the *Selected Poems* (1992) is a good start. Northern Ireland serves as the setting for many of Nobel Laureate Seamus Heaney's poems. *Opened Ground: Selected Poems 1966–1996* (1999) is a good overview of his lyrical, highly crafted style—like Yeats, Heaney is an intensely aural poet, a master of rhythm and sound. (He is also, thanks to his farmer father, obsessed with soil.) Diehard fans prefer his earlier, more rustic work. Take a look at his debut collection, *Death of a Naturalist* (1995 reprint), *The Haw Lantern* (1989), or *The Spirit Level* (1996) if you want to savor Heaney's more intimate voice. Paul Muldoon, from Belfast, is another major Irish poet. His *Selected Poems: 1968–1986* (1987) and *The Annals of Chile* (1994) are both good selections. Eavan Boland is widely regarded as among the top tier of Irish poets and the best-known woman poet in Ireland today. Two of her popular books are *Object Lessons: The Life of the Woman and the Poet in Our Time* (1995) and *An Origin Like Water: Collected Poems 1957–1987* (1996). One of Ireland's leading poets, Brendan Kennelly, selects and introduces his choices of the best Irish poetry in his book *Between Innocence and Peace: Favorite Poems of Ireland* (2002). He chooses from the works of Seamus Heaney, Eavan Boland, Michael Longley, Paul Durcan, and the grand masters—Yeats, Synge, and MacNeice.

Theater

Ireland's playwrights are as distinguished as its novelists and short-story writers. Samuel Beckett, who moved from Ireland to Paris and began writing in French, is the author of the comic modernist masterpiece *Waiting for Godot* (1952), among many plays. Oscar Wilde's finest plays, *The Importance of Being Earnest* and *An Ideal Husband* (both 1895), were playing to packed audiences in London when he was charged by his lover's father as a sodomite, setting in motion the trials that led to his downfall. Among the many plays of George Bernard Shaw, who grew up in Dublin, are *Arms and the Man* (1894), *Major Barbara* (1905), *Pygmalion* (1913), and *Saint Joan* (1923).

The history of Irish theater includes a number of controversial plays, such as J. M. Synge's *The Playboy of the Western World*, which was considered morally outrageous at the time of its opening in 1907 ("Playboy riots" took place in Dublin when the play was produced at the Abbey Theatre) but is appreciated today for its poetic language. Sean O'-Casey wrote passionately about social injustice and working-class characters around the time of the Irish Civil War in such plays as *The Plough and the Stars* (1926) and *Juno and the Paycock* (1924).

The Quare Fellow (1956), by Brendan Behan, challenged accepted mores of the 1950s and at the time could only be produced in London. Behan is also well known for his play *The Hostage* (1958) and for *Borstal Boy* (1958), his memoirs. Hugh Leonard (*Da* [1974] and *A Life* [1980]) and Brian Friel (*Philadelphia, Here I Come!* [1964], *The Faith Healer* [1979], and *Dancing at Lughnasa* [1990]) write works that often illuminate Irish small-town life. A group of young, brash Irish playwrights has taken London and Broadway by storm. It includes Martin McDonagh, whose most famous play is *The Beauty Queen of Linnane* (1996), and Conor McPherson, whose *The Weir* (1997) has won awards on both sides of the Atlantic.

CHRONOLOGY

ca. 3500 BC Neolithic (new Stone Age) settlers (origins uncertain) bring agriculture, pottery, and weaving. They also build massive megaliths—stone monuments with counterparts in England (Stonehenge), Brittany (Carnac), and elsewhere in Europe.

ca. 700 BC Celtic tribes begin to arrive via Britain and France; they divide Ireland into "fifths," or provinces, including Ulster, Leinster, Connaught, Meath, and Munster.

ca. AD 100 Ireland becomes the center of Celtic culture and trade without being settled by the Romans.

432 Traditional date for the arrival of St. Patrick and Christianity; in fact, Irish conversion to Christianity began at least a century earlier.

ca. 500–800 Golden age of Irish monasticism; as many as 3,000 study at Clonard (Meath). Irish missionaries carry the faith to barbarian Europe; art (exemplified by the *Book of Kells,* ca. 8th or 9th century) and Gaelic poetry flourish.

795 First Scandinavian Viking invasion; raids continue for the next 200 years. Viking towns founded include Dublin, Waterford, Wexford, Cork, and Limerick.

1014 Vikings decisively defeated at Clontarf by Irish troops under King Brian Boru of Munster. His murder cuts short hopes of a unified Ireland.

1172 Pope Alexander III confirms Henry II, king of England, as feudal lord of Ireland. Over the next two centuries, Anglo-Norman nobles establish estates, intermarry with the native population, and act in a manner similar to that of the neighboring Celtic chieftains. Actual control by the English crown is confined to a small area known as "the land of peace," or "the Pale," around Dublin.

1366 Statutes of Kilkenny attempt belatedly to enforce ethnic divisions by prohibiting the expression of Irish language and culture and intermarriage between the Irish and English, but Gaelic culture prevails and the Pale continues to contract. Constant warfare among the great landowners keeps Ireland poor, divided, and isolated from the rest of Europe.

1534–40 Henry VIII's break with the Catholic Church leads to insurrection in Ireland, led by Garret Mor's grandson Lord Offaly ("Silken Thomas"). He is executed with five of his brothers.

1558–1603 Reign of Queen Elizabeth I; her fear of Irish intrigue with Catholic enemies of England leads to expansion of English power.

1580–88 Edmund Spenser, an administrator for the Crown in Ireland, writes *The Faerie Queene.*

1591 Trinity College, Dublin, is founded.

1607 The Flight of the Earls and the beginning of the end of Gaelic Ireland. The earl of Tyrone and his ally Tyrconnell flee to Rome; their lands in Ulster are confiscated and opened to Protestant settlers, mostly Scots.

1641 Charles I's policies provoke insurrection in Ulster and, soon after, civil war in England.

1649 August: British leader Oliver Cromwell, having defeated Charles and witnessed his execution, invades Ireland, determined to crush Catholic opposition. Massacres at Drogheda and Wexford.

1652 Act of Settlement—lands of Cromwell's opponents are confiscated, and owners are forced across the Shannon to Connaught. Never fully carried out, this policy nonetheless establishes Protestant ascendancy.

1690 Battle of the Boyne—William of Orange lands in England and Catholic James II flees to Ireland to rally opposition. William pursues him with a large army and defeats him on the banks of the River Boyne in County Meath.

1775 American War of Independence begins, precipitating Irish unrest. Henry Grattan (1746–1820), a Protestant barrister, enters the Irish Parliament.

1782 Grattan's Parliament—Grattan asserts independence of Irish Parliament from Britain. Britain agrees, but independence is easier to declare than to sustain.

1823 Daniel O'Connell (1775–1847), "the Liberator," founds the Catholic Association to campaign for Catholic Emancipation.

1828 O'Connell's election to Parliament (illegal, because he was a Catholic) leads to passage of Catholic Emancipation Act in 1829; later, he works unsuccessfully for repeal of the Union.

1845–49 Failure of potato crop leads to famine; more than 1 million die, others migrate.

1856 Birth of George Bernard Shaw, playwright (d. 1950).

1858 Fenian Brotherhood founded in New York by Irish immigrants with the aim of overthrowing British rule. A revolt in 1867 fails, but it compels Gladstone, the British prime minister, to disestablish the Anglican Church (1869) and reform landholding (1870) in Ireland.

1865 Birth of William Butler Yeats, the great Irish poet (d. 1939).

1871 Isaac Butts founds parliamentary Home Rule Party, soon dominated by Charles Stewart Parnell (1846–91), descendant of English Protestants, who tries to force the issue by obstructing parliamentary business.

1890 Parnell is named corespondent in the divorce case of Kitty O'Shea; his career is ruined.

1893 Second Home Rule Bill passes Commons but is defeated by Lords. Subsequent policy is to "kill Home Rule with kindness" with land reform, but cultural nationalism revives with founding of Gaelic

League to promote Irish language. Yeats, John Synge (1871–1909), and other writers find inspiration in Gaelic past.

1898   On the anniversary of Wolfe Tone's rebellion, Arthur Griffith (1872–1922) founds the Dublin newspaper the *United Irishman,* preaching *sinn féin* ("we ourselves")—secession from Britain; Sinn Féin party founded 1905. Socialist James Connolly (executed 1916) founds the *Workers' Republic.*

1904   William Butler Yeats and Lady Gregory found the Abbey Theatre in Dublin.

1914   Despite fierce opposition the Third Home Rule Bill passes the Commons and the Lords but is suspended due to the outbreak of World War I.

1916   Easter Uprising—Irish Republican Brotherhood (IRB) stages insurrection in Dublin and declares independence; the uprising fails, but the execution of 15 leaders by the British turns public opinion in favor of the insurgents. Yeats writes "a terrible beauty is born."

1919   January: Irish Parliamentarians meet as the Dáil Éireann (Irish Assembly) and declare independence. September: Dáil suppressed; Sinn Féin made illegal.

1920–21   War breaks out between Britain and Ireland: the "Black and Tans" versus the Irish Republican Army (IRA). Government of Ireland Act declares separate parliaments for north and south and continued ties to Britain. Elections follow, but the Sinn Féin majority in the south again declare themselves the Dáil Éireann under Eamon de Valera (1882–1975), rejecting British authority. December 1921: Anglo-Irish Treaty grants the south dominion status as the Irish Free State, allowing the north to remain under Britain.

1922   De Valera and his Republican followers reject the treaty; civil war results. The Irish Free State adopts a constitution; William T. Cosgrave becomes president. Michael Collins, chairman of the Irish Free State and commander in chief of the army, is shot dead in County Cork, not far from where he was born. In Paris, James Joyce's *Ulysses* is published.

1923   De Valera is arrested and the civil war ends, but Republican agitation and terrorism continue. William Butler Yeats is the first Irish writer to be awarded the Nobel prize in literature; he also takes a seat in the first Irish Parliament.

1938   New constitution creates Republic of Ireland with no ties to Britain.

1939–45   Despite strong pressure from Britain and the United States, Ireland remains neutral throughout World War II.

1959   Eamon de Valera resigns as Taoiseach (prime minister) and is later elected president.

1963   John F. Kennedy, the first Irish-Catholic president of the United States, visits Ireland.

1972 Republic of Ireland admitted to European Economic Community. Troubles continue in the north. In Derry on January 30, British troops shoot 13 unarmed demonstrators on "Bloody Sunday." Stormont (the Northern Parliament) is suspended and direct rule from London is imposed. Acts of terrorism on both sides lead to draconian law enforcement by the British. "The Troubles," as the conflict is dubbed, will last 26 years and claim more than 3,000 lives.

1991 Mary Robinson becomes the first female president of the Republic of Ireland. Peace talks begin between the British and Irish governments and the main political parties of the north, excepting Sinn Féin.

1992 Ireland approves European Union. Sixty-two percent of the Irish vote "yes" in a referendum on whether to allow pregnant women to seek an abortion abroad.

1994 The IRA, in response to advances made by the Irish, British, and U.S. governments, announces a complete cessation of activities. Protestant paramilitary groups follow suit one month later. Gerry Adams, the leader of Sinn Féin, speaks on British TV and radio.

1996 Frustrated by the slow progress of the peace talks, the IRA explodes bombs on the British mainland, throwing the whole peace process into doubt. But violence did not return to the province, even though all parties continued to say they were committed to peace.

1997 The Republic of Ireland legalizes divorce. Newly elected British prime minister Tony Blair apologizes for the British government's policies during Ireland's Great Famine, acknowledging that his predecessors' policies prolonged "a massive human tragedy." The IRA reestablishes its cease-fire.

1998 On Good Friday 1998, all sides in the conflict agree on an arrangement for sharing power that guarantees the rights of the Catholic minority. Referenda in the north and the republic show overwhelming support. A splinter IRA group opposed to the agreement explodes a bomb in Omagh, killing more than 20 people. Catholic leader John Hume and Protestant David Trimble share the Nobel peace prize.

1999 Despite sporadic violence by splinter loyalist groups, an executive branch of government, the Northern Ireland Assembly, is formed at Stormont in Belfast on November 27. Northern Ireland is no longer governed directly from Westminster.

2000 Proposals are made to reform the RUC (Royal Ulster Constabulary) by making it half Catholic and half Protestant and renaming it the "Northern Irish Police Force." Tensions remain high over the decommissioning of weapons.

2001 President Bill Clinton visits Dundalk and Belfast during the final weeks of his presidency to encourage continued implementation of the Good Friday Agreement. Due to a rise in pipe-bomb attacks, British troops are put back on patrol in certain neighborhoods in Belfast and Derry.

2002 The IRA begins to decommission weapons in the wake of the September 11 attacks on the United States. The euro is phased in as the Republic of Ireland's national currency.

2003 Direct rule in the north reintroduced as power-sharing talks come to a halt. New efforts to resolve the impasse are undertaken by governments in Dublin and London. Irish economy starts to slow, but growth remains well above the European average.

2004 After several years of economic slowdown, the Celtic Tiger roars again and Ireland's economy picks up new speed, making headlines as it continues to create many new jobs in the computer sector.

IRISH FAMILY NAMES

Antrim
Lynch
McDonnell
McNeill
O'Hara
O'Neill
Quinn

Armagh
Hanlon
McCann

Carlow
Kinsella
Nolan
O'Neill

Cavan
Boylan
Lynch
McCabe
McGovern
McGowan
McNally
O'Reilly
Sheridan

Clare
Aherne
Boland
Clancy
Daly
Lynch
McGrath
McInerney
McMahon
McNamara
Molon(e)y
O'Brien
O'Dea
O'Grady
O'Halloran
O'Loughlin

Cork
Barry
Callaghan
Cullinane
Donovan
Driscoll
Flynn
Hennessey
Hogan
Lynch
McCarthy
McSweeney
Murphy
Nugent
O'Casey
O'Cullane
(Collins)

O'Keefe
O'Leary
O'Mahony
O'Riordan
Roche
Scanlon
Sheridan

Derry
Cahan
Hegarty
Kelly
McLaughlin

Donegal
Boyle
Clery
Doherty
Friel
Gallagher
Gormley
McGrath
McLoughlin
McSweeney
Mooney
O'Donnell

Down
Lynch
McGuinness
O'Neil
White

Dublin
Hennessey
O'Casey
Plunkett

Fermanagh
Cassidy
Connolly
Corrigan
Flanagan
Maguire
McManus

Galway
Blake
Burke
Clery
Fah(e)y
French
Jennings
Joyce
Kelly
Kenny
Kirwan
Lynch
Madden
Moran
O'Flaherty
O'Halloran

Kerry
Connor
Fitzgerald
Galvin
McCarthy
Moriarty
O'Connell
O'Donoghue
O'Shea
O'Sullivan

Kildare
Cullen
Fitzgerald
O'Byrne
White

Kilkenny
Butler
Fitzpatrick
O'Carroll
Tobin

Laois
Dempsey
Doran
Dunn(e)
Kelly
Moore

Leitrim
Clancy
O'Rourke

Limerick
Fitzgerald
Fitzgibbon
McKeough
O'Brien
O'Cullane
(Collins)
O'Grady
Woulfe

Longford
O'Farrell
Quinn

Louth
O'Carroll
Plunkett

Mayo
Burke
Costello
Dugan
Gormley
Horan
Jennings
Jordan
Kelly
Madden
O'Malley

Meath
Coffey
Connolly
Cusack
Dillon
Hayes
Hennessey
Plunkett
Quinlan

Monaghan
Boylan
Connolly
Hanratty
McKenna
McMahon
McNally

Offaly
Coghlan
Dempsey
Fallon
(Maher)
Malone
Meagher
Molloy
O'Carroll
Sheridan

Roscommon
Fallon
Flanagan
Flynn
Hanley
McDermot
McKeogh
McManus
Molloy
Murphy

Sligo
Boland
Higgins
McDonagh
O'Dowd
O'Hara
Rafferty

Tipperary
Butler
Fogarty
Kennedy
Lynch
Meagher
(Maher)
O'Carroll
O'Dwyer
O'Meara
Purcell
Ryan

Tyrone
Cahan
Donnelly
Gormley
Hagan
Murphy
O'Neill
Quinn

Waterford
Keane
McGrath
O'Brien
Phelan
Power

Westmeath
Coffey
Dalton
Daly
Dillon
Sheridan

Wexford
Doran
Doyle
Hartley
Kavanagh
Keating
Kinsella
McKeogh
Redmond
Walsh

Wicklow
Cullen
Kelly
McKeogh
O'Byrne
O'Toole

IRELAND AT A GLANCE

Fast Facts

Name in local language: Éire
Capital: Dublin
National anthem: *Amhrán Na bhFiann (Soldiers Song)*
Type of government: Republic
Administrative divisions: 26 counties
Independence: December 6, 1921 (from U.K.)
Constitution: December 29, 1937
Legal system: Based on English common law, substantially modified by indigenous concepts; judicial review of legislative acts in Supreme Court (judges appointed by the president on the advice of the prime minister and cabinet)
Suffrage: 18 years of age; universal
Legislature: Bicameral Parliament consists of the Senate or (60 seats: 49 elected by the universities and from candidates put forward by five vocational panels, 11 nominated by the prime minister; members serve five-year terms) and the House of Representatives (166 seats; members are elected by popular vote on the basis of proportional representation to serve five-year terms)
Population: 3.9 million

Population density: 148 people per square mi
Median age: Female 34, male 32.2
Life expectancy: Female 80.3, male 74.6
Infant mortality rate: 5.3 deaths per 1,000 live births
Literacy: 98%
Language: English, Irish (Gaelic), both official
Ethnic groups: Celtic, English
Religion: Roman Catholic 91.6%; other 5.9%; Church of Ireland 2.5%
Discoveries & Inventions: Boyle's Law (1662), heat-exchange for distilling (1830), self exacting dynamo (1838), hypodermic syringe (1844), spinning-cup anemometer (1846), guided missile (1875), Gregg shorthand (1888), steam turbine (1894), splitting the atom (1932), ejector seat (1945)

Ireland sober is Ireland stiff.

— James Joyce

It is often said that in Ireland there is an excess of genius unsustained by talent; but there is talent in the tongues.

— V.S. Pritchett

Geography & Environment

Land area: 68,890 square km (26,599 square mi), slightly larger than West Virginia
Coastline: 1,448 km (900 miles) along North Atlantic Ocean, Irish Sea
Terrain: Mostly level to rolling interior plain surrounded by rugged hills and low mountains; sea cliffs on west coast; highest point: Carrauntoohil 1,041 meters (3,415 ft)
Islands: Aran Islands, Blasket Islands, Achill, and Clare Island

Natural resources: Barite, copper, dolomite, gypsum, lead, limestone, natural gas, peat, silver, zinc
Environmental issues: Water pollution, especially of lakes, from agricultural runoff. Ireland exceeded international limits for greenhouse gas emissions by more than 10% in 2001.

Ireland's ruins are historic emotions surrendered to time.

— Horace Sutton

Economy

Currency: Euro
Exchange rate: € .85 = $1
GDP: € 96.6 billion ($113.7 billion)
Per capita income: € 21,278 ($25,500)
Inflation: 3.8%
Unemployment: 4.7%
Work force: 1.8 million, services 64%; industry 29%; agriculture 8%
Debt: $11 billion
Major industries: Brewing, chemicals, clothing, food products, glass and crystal, machinery, pharmaceuticals, textiles, transportation equipment, software
Agricultural products: Barley, beef, dairy products, potatoes, sugar beets, turnips, wheat

Exports: $86.6 billion
Major export products: Animal products, chemicals, computers, live animals, machinery and equipment, pharmaceuticals
Export partners: U.K. 23.3%; U.S. 16.7%; Belgium 14.6%; Germany 7.3%; France 5%
Imports: $48.6 billion
Major import products: Chemicals, clothing, data processing equipment, other machinery and equipment, petroleum and petroleum products, textiles
Import partners: UK 41.1%; US 15.3%; Germany 6.8%

Political Climate

The Good Friday Accord and the North-South Ministerial Council both established an uncommon peace in the late 1990s between the republic and Northern Ireland that held through the turn of the millennium. At the same time, England ended direct rule of Northern Ireland and the republic gave up territorial claims, but the moderate politicians who brokered much of that peace saw their support flee to hard-liners in Northern Ireland in the November 2003 elections. A coalition government of the Fianna Fáil and the Progressive Democrat parties won a solid majority in the 2002 general election in the republic. Family issues have spawned hot political debate. A referendum legalizing divorce passed by a narrow margin in 1995 and the government's strong anti-abortion stance has been vigorously protested.

One American said that the most interesting thing about Holy Ireland was that its people hate each other in the name of Jesus Christ. And they do!

— Bernadette Devlin, Irish politician

Did You Know?

• Long a land dominated by one religion, Ireland is slowly diversifying: The Muslim population quadrupled in the 1990s while the Roman Catholic population fell by more than three percent.

• The Irish have long had a reputation as lovers of alcohol, but recent studies show they are drinking even more: Consumption per person rose by 41% in the late 1990s, the highest increase in the European Union. New government programs have been put into place to combat alcoholism and its fallout in hospital expenses and in traffic accidents.

• Makes sense that the Emerald Isle would by home to the world's largest hedge. It is 11 meters (36 ft) high, at least 300 years old, and can be found at Birr Castle, County Offaly. The castle is also the home to the "Great Telescope," the largest of its kind when buit in the latter half of the 19th century.

• The hard-working George Bernard Shaw was the world's oldest practicing playwright when he died at the age of 93. Shaw wrote 57 plays including *Mrs. Warren's Profession, Man and Superman, Saint Joan, Candida* and *Pygmalion*. He won the Nobel Prize for Literature in 1925, 24 years before he would write his last play.

• In 2001, the Irish had the lowest life expectancy among any EU nation. Respiratory disease may have something to do with it: in 2000, Ireland had 204 deaths from respiratory ailments per 100,000 residents, the highest in the world.

• Some places in Ireland get 275 days of rain each year. The driest place in all of Ireland is Dublin, but the Irish are known for pointing out that "it doesn't rain in the pub!"

• About one-sixth of Ireland is covered by bogs, the accumulations of organic matter and water that eventually yield peat, a soil material that can be used as fertilizer or fuel.

• 1.57 million people can speak Irish (Gaelic), according to the 2002 census. Most live in rural areas, especially in the west.

• One Irish-style bar opens every day around the world, on average.

INDEX

FODOR'S KEY TO THE GUIDES

America's guidebook leader publishes guides for every kind of traveler.
Check out our many series and find your perfect match.

FODOR'S GOLD GUIDES
America's favorite travel-guide series
offers the most detailed insider reviews
of hotels, restaurants, and attractions in
all price ranges, plus great background
information, smart tips, and useful maps.

COMPASS AMERICAN GUIDES
Stunning guides from top local writers
and photographers, with gorgeous
photos, literary excerpts, and colorful
anecdotes. A must-have for culture
mavens, history buffs, and new residents.

FODOR'S CITYPACKS
Concise city coverage in a guide plus a
foldout map. The right choice for urban
travelers who want everything under
one cover.

FODOR'S EXPLORING GUIDES
Hundreds of color photos bring your
destination to life. Lively stories lend
insight into the culture, history, and
people.

FODOR'S TRAVEL HISTORIC AMERICA
For travelers who want to experience
history firsthand, this series gives in-
depth coverage of historic sights, plus
nearby restaurants and hotels. Themes
include the Thirteen Colonies, the Old
West, and the Lewis and Clark Trail.

FODOR'S POCKET GUIDES
For travelers who need only the
essentials. The best of Fodor's in pocket-
size packages for just $9.95.

FODOR'S FLASHMAPS
Every resident's map guide, with dozens
of easy-to-follow maps of
public transit, restaurants, shopping,
museums, and more.

FODOR'S CITYGUIDES
Sourcebooks for living in the city:
thousands of in-the-know listings for
restaurants, shops, sports, nightlife,
and other city resources.

FODOR'S AROUND THE CITY WITH KIDS
Up to 68 great ideas for family days,
recommended by resident parents.
Perfect for exploring in your own
backyard or on the road.

FODOR'S HOW TO GUIDES
Get tips from the pros on planning the
perfect trip. Learn how to pack, fly
hassle-free, plan a honeymoon or cruise,
stay healthy on the road, and travel with
your baby.

FODOR'S LANGUAGES FOR TRAVELERS
Practice the local language before you
hit the road. Available in phrase books,
cassette sets, and CD sets.

KAREN BROWN'S GUIDES
Engaging guides—many with easy-to-
follow inn-to-inn itineraries—to the
most charming inns and B&Bs in the
U.S.A. and Europe.

SEE IT GUIDES
Illustrated guidebooks that include the
practical information travelers need,
in gorgeous full color. Thousands of
photos, hundreds of restaurant and
hotel reviews, prices, and ratings for
attractions all in one indispensable
package. Perfect for travelers who want
the best value packed in a fresh, easy-
to-use, colorful layout.

OTHER GREAT TITLES FROM FODOR'S
Baseball Vacations, The Complete
Guide to the National Parks, Family
Vacations, Golf Digest's Places to Play,
Great American Drives of the East,
Great American Drives of the West,
Great American Vacations, Healthy
Escapes, National Parks of the West,
Skiing USA.

At bookstores everywhere.   www.fodors.com/books